FUNDAMENTALS OF A

402/

FUNDAMENTALS OF ACCOUNTING

[For Professional Education Examination I of Institute of Chartered Accountants of India]

Eighth Revised and Enlarged Edition

DR S N MAHESHWARI

DIRECTOR

DELHI INSTITUTE OF ADVANCED STUDIES, ROHINI, DELHI-110085

(Formerly, Principal, Hindu College, University of Delhi)

&

(Professor & Dean, Faculty of Commerce & Business Management, Goa University)

DR S K MAHESHWARI

ASSOCIATE PROFESSOR

DIVISION OF ACCOUNTANCY AND LEGAL ENVIRONMENT

MARSHALL UNIVERSITY,

HUNTINGTON (W.V.), USA

VIKAS PUBLISHING HOUSE PVT LTD

VIKAS PUBLISHING HOUSE PVT LTD
576, Masjid Road, Jangpura, **New Delhi**-110 014
Phones: 24314605, 24315313 • Fax: 24310879
E-mail: ***helpline@vikaspublishing.com***

First Floor, N.S. Bhawan, 4th Cross, 4th Main,
Gandhi Nagar, **Bangalore**-560 009 • Phone: 22353675
Damodhar Centre, New No. 62, Old No. 59, Nelson Manickam Road,
Aminjikarai, **Chennai**-600 029 • Phone: 23744547, 23746090
35, Palm Avenue, **Kolkata**-700 019 • Phone: 22872575
F-20, Nand Dham Industrial Estate, Marol,
Andheri (East), **Mumbai**-400 059 • Phone: 28502333, 28502324

Distributors:

UBS PUBLISHERS' DISTRIBUTORS PVT LTD
5, Ansari Road, **New Delhi**-110 002
Ph. 23273601, 23266646 • Fax: 23276593, 23274261
E-mail: ubspd@ubspd.com • Internet: www.gobookshopping.com
• 10, First Main Road, Gandhi Nagar, **Bangalore**-560 009 • Ph. 2253903
• 143, M P Nagar, Zone-1, **Bhopal**-462 011 • Ph. 5203183, 5203193
• 60, Nelson Manickam Road, Aminjikarai, **Chennai**-600 029 • Ph. 23746222
• 40/7940, Convent Road, **Ernakulam**-682 035 • Ph. 2353901, 2363905
• NVK Towers, 3-6-272 Himayat Nagar, 2nd floor,
  Adjacent to old Hyderabad Stock Exchange, **Hyderabad**-500 029
• 8/1-B, Chowringhee Lane, **Kolkata**-700 016 • Ph. 22521821, 22522910
• 1st Floor, Halwasiya Court Annexe, 11-MG Marg, Hazratganj,
  Lucknow-226 001 • Ph. 2294134
• 2nd Floor, Apeejay Chambers, 5 Wallace Street, Fort, **Mumbai**-400 001 • Ph. 56376922
• 5-A, Rajendra Nagar, **Patna**-800 016 • Ph. 2672856, 2673973
• 680 Budhwar Peth, 2nd Floor, Appa Balwant Chowk, **Pune**-411 002 • Ph. 56028921

ISBN: 81-259-1863-9

Eight Revised & Enlarged Edition 2005
Reprint 2005

Copyright © S N Maheshwari & S K Maheshwari, 1993, 2005

Information contained in this book has been published by VIKAS Publishing House Pvt. Ltd. and has
been obtained by its authors from sources believed to be reliable and are correct to the best of their
knowledge. However, the publisher and its authors shall in no event be liable for any errors, omissions
or damages arising out of use of this information and specifically disclaim any implied warranties or
merchantability or fitness for any particular use.

Printed at Hindustan Offset Printers, Delhi - 110 032

Dedicated to
my Parents
Late Shri Bridhi Chand Maheshwari
and
Smt. Sugan Devi Maheshwari

I have suceeded in whatever I have undertaken because I have willed it. I have never hesitated which has given me an advantage over the rest of mankind.

—NAPOLEON

PREFACE TO THE EIGHTH EDITION

We are pleased to place before the esteemed readers the Eighth Revised and Enlarged Edition of our book *Fundamentals of Accounting*. The heartwarming response given by the readers to each new edition of the book is really a matter of great satisfaction to us.

The new edition, besides maintaining the *PLUS* features of the Seventh Edition, *viz.*, simplicity of style, exhaustive text with plenty of illustrative material, questions and problems for self-study, has certain additional welcome features. These include the following:

❑ The book now meets all the more exhaustively the course requirements of the students preparing for Professional Education Examination-I (PEE-I) of the Institute of Chartered Accountants of India (ICAI) and similar courses.

❑ Since the publication of the seventh edition, two important developments have taken place in the accounting and legal world. These include:
- Issue of 29 Accounting Standards in all laying standards for recording, presenting and disclosure of accounting information.
- Enactment of the Negotiable Instruments (Amendment and Miscellaneous Provisions) Act, 2002.
- Issue of Preface to the Statements of Accounting Standards (Revised 2004) by the Council of the Institute of Chartered Accountants of India.

All these developments have been incorporated at appropriate places in the book.

❑ The implications of Accounting Standard 26: Intangible Assets and Accounting Standard 10: Accounting for Fixed Assets, which are now mandatory for all enterprises, have been incorporated respectively, in chapters Capital and Revenue (Section I) and Reconstitution of a Partnership Firm — I & II (Section III) of the book.

❑ Section IV, *Suggested Answers* has been updated by incorporating question set upto May 2004 of PEE-I of ICAI.

❑ The text-matter in several chapters has been considerably strengthened and simplified.

❑ The examination-oriented approach of the book has been further sharpened and enhanced.

❑ The book does not presuppose the knowledge of accountancy to the readers and hence is bound to make learning of accountancy a painless exercise for the beginners.

We hope with all these additions, adaptations and modifications, the readers will find the revised edition of the book all the more helpful and rewarding.

Constructive and helpful suggestions for improvement in the book will be gratefully acknowledged.

A-2/156, Paschim Vihar,   **Dr. S.N. Maheshwari**
Delhi 110 063   **Dr. S.K. Maheshwari**

PREFACE

TO THE FIRST EDITION

The Institute of Chartered Accountants of India has introduced a One-year Foundation Course as a pre-professional course with effect from 24th April, 1992. The first Foundation Examination will be held in June, 1993. The basic objective of introducing the Foundation Course is to enable the young students having aptitude for accounting education to make an early entry to the accounting profession. Students who have passed Senior Secondary (10 + 2) or equivalent examination are eligible for registration for the Foundation Course.

'Fundamentals of Accounting' is one of the four papers of the Foundation Examination. The course contents of the paper have been framed in a manner to ensure acquisition of theoretical knowledge sufficient to provide a foundation for the professional examination. The present book "FUNDAMENTALS OF ACCOUNTING" has been primarily written keeping in view the above requirements of the students. The book has several distinctive features:

* Comprehensively covers the course contents requirements of the students appearing at the CA Foundation Examination.

* Written in simple and straight style.

* Gives a lucid explanation of the basic concepts of accounting with plenty of illustrative material.

* The subject matter has been presented in a manner that even a student who has not studied Accountancy at 10 + 2 level can easily understand and have a grasp over the subject.

* Incorporates at the end of each chapter:

  - objective type questions with short answers to enable the students to test their understanding.
  - essay type questions for review, discussion and practice.
  - practical problems with short answers for practice to develop a sense of confidence amongst the students.

* Provides Learning Objectives at the begining of each chapter to tell the student what he will learn after studying the chapter.

* Defines Key Terms at the end of each chapter for recapitulation and better grasp over the subject.

I am confident that with all these PLUS features the readers will find the book extremely useful and rewarding for them. Their constructive suggestions for improvement in the book will be gratefully acknowledged.

A-2/156, Paschim Vihar
New Delhi - 110 063

Dr. S.N. Maheshwari

Professional Education Examination I
(One Paper of Three Hours Carrying 100 Marks)
Fundamentals of Accounting

Level of Knowledge : Basic Knowledge

Objectives

a.   To develop conceptual understanding of the fundamentals of financial accounting system which processes transactions and other events through a book-keeping mechanism to prepare financial statements.

b.   To impart skills in accounting kinds of business transactions.

S. No.	Contents	Section of the book	Chapter(s) of the book
1.	Accounting as a measurement discipline, accounting concepts, relationship of accounting with economics and statistics, role of an accountant in society.	1	1 & 2
2.	Accounting process: journals and ledgers leading to the preparation of trial balance including rectification of errors, and preparation of final accounts for non-corporate entities.	1	3 to 5 (excluding 8 to 12 chapter)
3.	Concept of accounting standards, standard-setting process.	1	2
4.	Accounting policies and their disclosure.	1	2
5.	Depreciation accounting including methods thereof.	1	13
6.	Inventory valuation.	1	4
7.	Accounting for special transactions:		
	a. Consignments	2	1
	b. Joint ventures	2	2
	c. Bills of exchange and promissory notes	1	6
	d. Insurance claims	2	5
	e. Goods on sale or return	2	6
8.	Bank reconciliation statement.	1	7
9.	Average due date, account current, self-balancing ledgers.	2	3 to 14
10.	Simple problems in partnership accounts.	3	1 to 4
11.	Receipts and Payments Account and Income and Expenditure Account and Balance Sheet including accounts of professional concerns.	1	15

CONTENTS

SECTION II: SPECIAL ACCOUNTING PROBLEMS

SECTION IV: SUGGESTED ANSWERS

SECTION I

Accounting Principles & Processes

Chapter 1

MEANING AND SCOPE OF ACCOUNTING

> **LEARNING OBJECTIVES**
>
> After studying this Chapter you should be able to:
>
> ☐ appreciate the need for accounting;
>
> ☐ perceive the development of accounting;
>
> ☐ explain the meaning of accounting;
>
> ☐ name the persons interested in accounting disclosures;
>
> ☐ identify the objectives of accounting;
>
> ☐ explain the relationship of accounting with economics and statistics;
>
> ☐ appreciate the role of accountant in the society; and
>
> ☐ explain the meaning of certain key terms.

NEED FOR ACCOUNTING

Accounting has rightly been termed as the language of the business. The basic function of a language is to serve as a means of communication. Accounting also serves this function. It communicates the results of business operations to various parties who have some stake in the business *viz.*, the proprietor, creditors, investors, Government and other agencies. Though accounting is generally associated with business but it is not only business which makes use of accounting. Persons like housewives, Government and other individuals also make use of accounting. For example, a housewife has to keep a record of the money received and spent by her during a particular period. She can record her receipts of money on one page of her "household diary", while payments for different items such as milk, food, clothing, house, education etc. on some other page or pages of her diary in a chronological order. Such a record will help her in knowing about:

(*i*) The sources from which she received cash and the purposes for which it was utilised.

(*ii*) Whether her receipts are more than her payments or vice-versa?

(*iii*) The balance of cash in hand or deficit, if any at the end of a period.

In case the housewife records her transactions regularly, she can collect valuable information about the nature of her receipts and payments. For example, she can find out the total amount spent by her during a period (say a year) on different items, say milk, food, education, entertainment, etc. Similarly she can find the sources of her receipts such as salary of her husband, rent from property, cash gifts from her near relations, etc. Thus, at the end of a period (say a year) she can see for herself about her financial position *i.e.* what she owns and what she owes. This will help her in planning her future income and expenses (or making out a budget) to a great extent.

The need for accounting is all the more greater for a person who is running a business. He must know: (*i*) What he owns? (*ii*) What he owes? (*iii*) Whether he has earned a profit or suffered a loss on account of running a business? (*iv*) What is his financial position *i.e.* whether he will be in a position to meet all his commitments in the near future or he is in the process of becoming a bankrupt.

DEVELOPMENT OF ACCOUNTING

Accounting is as old as money itself. In India, Chanakya in his *Arthashastra* has emphasized the existence and need of proper accounting and auditing. However, the modern system of accounting owes its origin to Pacoili who lived in Italy in the 18th Century. In those early days the business organisations and transactions were not so complex due to their being small and easily manageable by the proprietor himself. Things have changed fastly during the last fifty years. The advent of industrial revolution has resulted in large scale production, cut-throat competition and widening of the market. This has also reduced the effectiveness of personal supervision resulting in the decentralisation of authority and responsibility. Today there is a greater need for co-ordination and control. Old technique of management by intuition is no longer considered dependable in the situation in which the modern firm operates. Accounting today, therefore, cannot be the same as it used to be about half a century back. It has also grown in importance and change in its structure with the evolution of complex and giant industrial organisations. In the early stages accounting developed as a result of the needs of the business firms to keep track of their relationship with outsiders, listing of their assets and liabilities. In recent years changes in technology have also brought a remarkable change in the field of accounting. The whole concept of accounting has changed. "It has come to be recognized as a tool for mastering the various economic problems which a business organisation may have to face. It systematically writes the economic history of the organisation. It provides information that can be drawn upon by those responsible for decisions affecting the organisation's future. This history is written mostly in quantitative terms. It consists partly of files of data, partly of reports summarising various portions of these data, and partly of the plans established by management to guide its operations."[1]

DEFINITION AND FUNCTIONS OF ACCOUNTING

From the above discussion it is clear that over a period of time the concept of accounting and the role of accountant has undergone a revolutionary change. The change is particularly noticable during the last fifty years.

Earlier accounting was considered simply as a process of recording business transactions and the role of accountant as that of record-keeper. However, accounting is now considered to be a tool of management providing vital information concerning the organisation's future. Accounting today is thus more of an information system rather than a mere recording system.

---

[1] Mryon J. Gordon Shillinglaw, *"Accounting a Management Approach"*, p. 3, 4th edition.

It will be useful here to give in a chronological order the definitions given by some of the well established accounting bodies which show how the concept of accounting has undergone a change over a period of time.

In 1941, the American Institute of Certified Public Accountant (*AICPA*) defined accounting as follows:

"Accounting is the art of recording, classifying and summarising in significant manner and in terms of money, transactions and events which are, in part, at least of a financial character and interpreting the results thereof".

In 1966, the American Accounting Association (*AAA*) defined accounting as follows:

"Accounting is the process of identifying, measuring and communicating economic information to permit informed judgements and decisions by users of the information".

In 1970, the Accounting Principles Board (*APB*) of American Institute of Certified Public Accountants (*AICPA*) enumerated the functions of accounting as follows:

"The function of accounting is to provide quantitative information, primarily of financial nature, about economic entities, that is needed to be useful in making economic decisions".

Thus, accounting may be defined as the process of recording, classifying, summarising, analysing and interpreting the financial transactions and communicating the results thereof to the persons interested in such information.

An analysis of the definition brings out the following functions of accounting:

1. **Recording.** This is the basic function of accounting. It is essentially concerned with not only ensuring that all business transactions of financial character are in fact recorded but also that they are recorded in an orderly manner. Recording is done in the book "Journal". This book may be further sub-divided into various subsidiary book such as Cash Journal (for recording cash transactions), Purchases Journal (for recording credit purchase of goods), Sales Journal (for recording credit sales of goods), etc. The number of subsidiary books to be maintained will be according to the nature and size of the business.

2. **Classifying.** Classification is concerned with the systematic analysis of the recorded data, with a view to group transactions or entries of one nature at one place. The work of classification is done in the book termed as "Ledger". This book contains on different pages individual account heads under which all financial transactions of similar nature are collected. For example, there may be separate account heads for Travelling Expenses, Printing and Stationery, Advertising etc. All expenses under these heads after being recorded in the Journal will be classified under separate heads in the Ledger. This will help in finding out the total expenditure incurred under each of the above heads.

3. **Summarising.** This involves presenting the classified data in a manner which is understandable and useful to the internal as well as external end-users of accounting statements. This process leads to the preparation of the following statements:

(*i*) Trial Balance, (*ii*) Income Statement and (*iii*) Balance Sheet.

4. **Dealing with financial transactions.** Accounting records only those transactions and events in terms of money which are of a financial character. Transactions which are not of a financial character are not recorded in the books of account. For example, if a company has got a team of dedicated and trusted employees, it is of great use to the business but since it is not of a financial character and capable of being expressed in terms of money, it will not be recorded in the books of business.

5. **Analysing and Interpreting.** This is the final function of accounting. The recorded financial data is analysed and interpreted in a manner that the end-users can make a meaningful judgement about the financial condition and profitability of the business operations. The data is also used for preparing the future plan and framing of policies for executing such plans.

A distinction here can be made between the two terms—'Analysis' and 'Interpretation'. The term 'Analysis' means methodical classification of the data given in the financial statements. The figures given in the financial statements will not help one unless they are put in a simplified form. For example, at items relating to 'Current Assets' are put at one place while all items relating to 'Current Liabilities' are put at another place. The term 'Interpretation' means 'explaining the meaning and significance of the data so simplified.

However both 'Analysis' and 'Interpretation' are complementary to each other. Interpretation requires Analysis, while Analysis is useless without Interpretation.

6. **Communicating.** The accounting information after being meaningfully analysed and interpreted has to be communicated in a proper form and manner to the proper person. This is done through preparation and distribution of accounting reports, which include besides the usual income statement and the balance sheet, additional information in the form of accounting rations, graphs, diagrams, funds flow statements etc. The initiative, imagination and innovative ability of the accountant are put to test in this process.

BOOK-KEEPING AND ACCOUNTING

Some people take book-keeping and accounting as synonymous terms, but they are different from each other. Book-keeping is mainly concerned with recording of financial data relating to the business operations in a significant and orderly manner. A book-keeper may be responsible for keeping all the records of a business or only of a minor segment, such as a position of the Customers' accounts in a departmental store. A substantial portion of the book-keeper's work is of a clerical nature and is increasingly being accomplished through the use of mechanical and electronical devices.

Accounting is primarily concerned with designing the systems for recording, classifying and summarising the recorded data and interpreting them for internal and external endusers. Accountants often direct and review the work of the book-keepers. The larger the firm, the greater is the responsibility of the accountant. The work of an accountant in the beginning may include some book-keeping An accountant is required to have a much higher level of knowledge, conceptual understanding and analytical skill than what is required for a book-keeper.

The difference between book-keeping and accounting can be well understood with the help of the following example:

If A sells goods to B on credit, the only fundamental principle involved is of "dual aspect" and to give a true picture of the transaction, both the aspects must be considered. On the one hand, A has lost one assets $i.e.$ goods and on the other hand, he has obtained another asset $i.e.$ a "debt due from B". The book-keeper should debit B's account in A's books and credit the sales account. However, if at the end of a year, A has got some stock of goods with him, they should be properly valued in order to ascertain the true profit of the business. The principle to be followed in valuing the stock and many adjustment that will have to be made before the books of accounts can be closed and true profit or loss can be ascertained, are all matters of accounting. Thus, book-keeping is more of a routine work and a book-keeper, if instructed properly, can record the routine transactions quite efficiently even if he does not know much of accounting principles.

IS ACCOUNTING SCIENCE OR ART

Any organised knowledge based on certain basic principles is a 'science'. Accounting is also a science. It is an organised knowledge based on scientific principles which have been developed as result of study and experience. Of course, accounting cannot be termed as a "perfect science" like Physics or Chemistry where experiments can be carried and perfect conclusions can be drawn. It is a social science depending much on human behaviour and other social and economic factors. Thus, perfect conclusions cannot be drawn. Some people therefore, though not very correctly, do not take accounting as a science.

Art is the technique which helps us in achieving our desired objective. Accounting is definitely an art. The American Institute of Certified Public Accountants also defines accounting as "the art of recording, classifying and summarising the financial transactions". Accounting helps in achieving our desired objective of maintaining proper accounts *i.e.* to know the profitability and the financial position of the business, by maintaining proper accounts.

END USERS OF ACCOUNTING INFORMATION

Accounting is of primary importance to the proprietors and the managers. However, other persons such as creditors, prospective investors, employees, etc. are also interested in the accounting information.

1. **Proprietors.** A business is done with the objective of making profit. Its profitability and financial soundness are, therefore, matters of prime importance to the proprietors who have invested their money in the business.

2. **Managers.** In a sole proprietary business, usually the proprietor is the manager. In case of a partnership business either some or all the partners participate in the management of the business. They, therefore, act both as managers as well as owners. In case of joint stock companies, the relationship between ownership and management becomes all the more remote. In most cases the shareholders act merely as reinters of capital and the management of the company passes into the hands of professional managers. The accounting disclosures greatly help them in knowing about what has happened and what should be done to improve the profitability and financial position of the enterprise in the period to come.

3. **Creditors.** Creditors are the persons who have extended credit to the company. They are also interested in the financial statements because they will help them in ascertaining whether the enterprise will be in a position to meet its commitment towards them both regarding payment of interest and principal.

4. **Prospective Investors.** A persons who is contemplating an investment in a business will like to known about its profitability and financial position. A study of the financial statements will help him in this respect.

5. **Government.** The Government is interested in the financial statements of business enterprise on account of taxation, labour and corporate laws. If necessary, the Government may ask its officials to examine the accounting records of a business.

6. **Employees.** The employees are interested in the financial statements on account of various profit sharing and bonus schemes. Their interest may further increase in case they purchase shares of the companies in which they are employed.

7. Citizen. An ordinary citizen may be interested in the accounting records of the institutions with which he comes in contact in his daily life *e.g.* bank, temple, public utilities such as gas, transport and electricity companies. In a broader sense, he is also interested in the accounts of a Government Company, a public utility concern etc., as a voter and a tax payer.

ACCOUNTING AND OTHER DISCIPLINES

Accounting is closely related with other disciplines. It is therefore, necessary for the accountant to have a working knowledge of these disciplines for effective performance of his job. The relationship between accounting and some of the other disciplines is being discussed in the following pages:

Accounting and Economics

Economic is concerned with rational decision making regarding efficient use of scarce resources for satisfying human wants. The efficient utilisation of resources, particularly when they are scarce, is important both from the view point of a business firm and of the country as a whole.

Accounting is considered to be a system which provides appropriate information to the Management for taking rational decisions. Of course, some non-accounting information is also useful for decision making. However, accounting provides a major and dependable data base for decision making. The basic objective of management of a business organisation is to maximise the wealth of its owners. This is also the objective of economics. Efficient use of scarce resources results in maximising the wealth of the nation. Thus, accounting and economics both have a similarity in the sense that both seek of optimum utilisation resources of the firm or the nation, as the case may be. Moreover, the accountants have got the ideas such as value of assets, income, capital maintenance, etc. from economists. Of course, accountants have suitably adapted these ideas keeping in view their own requirements and limitations. For instance, according to economists the value of an asset is the present value of all future earnings that can be derived from the asset. However, it is a real difficult or almost impossible task for one to estimate correctly the future earnings particularly when an asset has a very long life—say 50 years or more. Accountants have therefore adopted a realistic basis for valuation of asset—the cost or the price paid for the acquisition of the asset. Similarly, the accountant's concept of marginal cost is different from the economist's concept of marginal cost. According to the accountants the marginal cost represents the variable cost *i.e.* the cost which varies in direct proportion of output. Such cost remains fixed per unit of output. However, according to the economists the marginal cost refers to the cost of the producing one additional unit. Such cost per unit may increase or decrease depending upon the law of returns. For example in case of law of increasing returns, the cost per unit would decrease while in case of law of decreasing returns, the cost per unit would increase.

Accounting and Statistics

Statistics is the science of numbers. It is concerned with numerical data as well as various statistical techniques which are used for collection, classification, analysis and interpretation of such data. The statistical techniques are now increasingly used for managerial decision making.

Accounting is an important information tool. It provides significant information about the working of a business firm to the outsiders *viz.* shareholders, creditors, financial institutions, etc. and the insiders *i.e.* the management.

Accounting has a close relationship with statistics. A number of statistical techniques are used in collection, analysis and interpretation of the accounting data. For instance, computation accounting ratios is based on statistical methods particularly averaging. Similarly the technique of regression is being increasingly used for forecasting, budgeting and cost control. The techniques of standard deviation, co-efficient of variation are used for capital budgeting decisions. The technique of index numbers is used for computation of present value of an asset in case of accounting for price level changes.

Accounting and Mathematics

Accounting bears a close relationship with mathematics too. As a matter of fact the dual aspect concept which is the basic concept of accounting is expressed in the form of a mathematical equation. It is popularly termed as "accounting equation". The knowledge of mathematics is now considered to be a pre-requisite for accounting computations and measurements. For example, computation of depreciation, ascertaining the cash price in case of hire purchase and instalment systems, determination of the loan instalment, settling of lease rentals—all require use of mathematical techniques.

The introduction of computer in accounting has further increased the importance of mathematics for the accountants. The accountants are now increasingly making the use of statistics and econometric models for decision making. The use of the technique of operation research has made accounting all the more mathematical. In view of these developments, it would not be incorrect to say that a good accountant has to be a good mathematician too.

Accounting and Law

A business entity operates within a legal frame work. An accountant records, classifies, summarises and presents the various transactions. Naturally these transactions have to be in accordance with the rules and regulations applicable to such business entity. There are laws which are applicable in general to all business transactions, *e.g*, the Indian Contract Act, the Sales of Goods Act, the Negotiable Instruments Act, etc. There are laws governing specific business entities, *e.g.*, the Companies Act is applicable to joint stock companies, the Banking Regulation Act is applicable to banking companies, the Insurance Act is applicable to insurance companies etc. While preparing the accounts of different business entities, the accountant has to be keep in mind the specific provisions given by the specific Acts applicable to the specific business entities. Similarly, there are a number of industrial laws such as the Factories Act, the Payment of Wages Act, the Minimum Wages Act, the Employees Provident Fund and Misc. Provisions Act, etc. governing payment of wages, salaries or other benefits to employees. The accountant has to abide by the provisions of these Acts and prepare and maintain appropriate records keeping in mind their provisions.

ROLE OF ACCOUNTANT

Accountants are the persons who practice the art of accounting. The Accounting System and the Accountants who maintain it, provide useful services to the society. Accountants can broadly be classified into two categories.

1. Accountants in Public Practice
2. Accountants in Employment.

Accountants in Public Practice

Accountants in public practice offer their services for conducting financial audit, cost audit, designing of accounting system and rendering other professional services for a fee. Such accountants are usually members of professional bodies. In our country there are two recognised professional bodies for this purpose. They are (i) the Institute of Chartered Accountants of India and (ii) the Institute of Cost and Works Accountants of India.

The accountants in public practice are also known as professional accountants. Such accountants are the members of the professional accounting bodies. These accounting bodies usually require from their members the following:

(i) Getting themselves trained in the prescribed manner over a prescribed period.

(ii) Pass the examination conducted by the professional bodies.

(iii) Undertake to observe the generally accepted accounting principles enunciated by the professional bodies concerned.

(iv) Observe the Code of Ethics laid down by the concerned accounting body.

(v) Subject themselves to disciplinary proceedings whenever it is alleged that the member has violated the Code of Ethics laid down by the concerned body.

Accountants in Employment

These are accountants who are employed in non-business entities or business entities. Non-business entities are a diverse set of organisations including Educational Institutions, Government, Churches, Museums, Hospitals, etc. Their object is not to earn profit. The accountants employed by business entities are frequently called Management Accountants since they report to, and are the part of, the entity's Management. These accountants provide information for the tax returns of the business, budgeting, routine operating decisions, investment decision, performance evaluation and external financial reporting. Most of these accountants are also members of a professional Accounting Body. Of course it is not necessary.

Accountants' Services

The services rendered by the accountants to the society can be summarised as follows:

1. **Maintenance of Books of Accounts.** An accountant keeps a systematic record of the transactions entered by a business firm or an institution in the normal course of its operations. This helps the organisation in ascertaining the profit or loss made for a particular period and also the financial position of the organisation as on a particular date.

The advantages derived through maintenance of a systematic record of all transactions can be summarised as follows:

(a) *Help to Management.* Accounting is an important managerial tool since it provides the management adequate information for its effective functioning. The basic functions of the management are planing, controlling, co-ordinating, motivating and communicating.

Accounting helps the management in planning by making available the relevant data after pruning and analysing suitably for effective planning and decision making.

Controlling involves evaluation of performance keeping in view that the actual performance coincides with the planned one and remedial measures are taken in the event of variation between the two. The techniques of budgeting control, standard of costing and departmental operating statements greatly help in performing these functions.

Co-ordinating involves inter-linking different divisions of the business enterprise in a way so as to achieve the objectives of the organisation as a whole, Thus, perfect co-ordination is required among production, purchase, finance, personnel and sales departments.

Effective co-ordination is achieved through departmental budgets and reports which form the nucleus of Management Accounting.

Motivating involves maintenance of high degree of morale in the organisation. Conditions should be such that each person gives his best to realise the goals of the enterprise. The superior should be in a position to find out whom to promote or demote or to reward or penalise. Periodical departmental profit and loss accounts, budgets and reports go a long way in achieving these objectives.

Communicating involves transmission of data results etc., both to the insiders as well as the outsiders. Accounting provides information both to the insiders *i.e.* management and the outsiders that is the creditors, prospective investors, shareholders, etc.

(*b*) *Replacement of memory.* A person cannot remember everything about his business transactions since human memory has its own limitations. It is, therefore, necessary that the transactions are recorded in the books of accounts at the earliest. This considerably relieves strain of one's memory.

(*c*) *Comparative study.* A system of recording the business transactions will help a business entity to make a comparative study and evaluation of its performance.

(*d*) *Acceptance by tax authorities.* Properly maintained accounting records are accepted by Income-tax or Sales Tax authorities.

(*e*) *Evidence in Court.* Properly maintained accounting records are often taken as good evidence by the court of law.

(*f*) *Sale of Business.* Properly maintained accounting records will help a business entity to fetch a proper price in the event of sale of the business.

2. Auditing of Accounts. The function of auditing is also performed by the accountants. Auditing is concerned with verification of accounting data for determining the accuracy and reliability of accounting statements and reports. It may be classified into two categories:

    (*i*) Statutory Audit, and

    (*ii*) Internal Audit.

Statutory Audit. Statutory Audit is required to be done because of the provisions of law. For example, under the Companies Act every company has to get its accounts audited by a qualified Chartered Accountant. The Statutory Auditor has to report whether in his opinion the profit & loss account shows the true profit or loss for the year and the balance sheet shows a true and fair view of the state of affairs of the business on the balance sheet date.

Internal Audit. Internal audit is a review of various operations of the company and of its records by the staff specially appointed for this purpose. Many large organisations have a system of internal audit within the organisation as an integral part of internal control. They have a separate internal audit department for this purpose. Generally the internal audit department is also headed by a professionally qualified accountant.

3. Taxation. Accountants also handles taxation matters of a person or a business organisation. Since an accountant has a comprehensive knowledge about the different accounting matters, he is in a position to present the case of his client before the Tax Authorities in the proper perspective. He also assists his client/organisation in reducing tax burden and making proper tax planning.

4. Financial Services. An accountant being well familiar with legal, accounting and taxation matters, can properly advise individual firms with regard to managing their financial affairs. For instance, he can assist his clients in selecting the most appropriate investment or insurance policy. Professional accountants have also these days started management consultancy services. Such services include designing of Management Information System, Corporate Planning, Conducting of Feasibility Studies, Executive Selection Services, etc.

In conclusion it can be said that the accountant is almost a caretaker of the society's resources. He sees that not only proper accounting is kept of the society's resources, but they are also used in the optimum manner. As a matter of fact, accountants will be presented with many opportunities for innovative actions in the global economic environment. In addition to their role of recording business transactions, providing accurate timely and relevant information, they will also be accepted to participate as business consultants and partners with management in the strategic planning process. Thus, there are tremendous possibilities for the accountants to shine as a professional group in the years to come. To fit in this role it is necessary that the accountants develops effective communication abilities, adopt a structured approach, a flexible accommodation and keep themselves aware with the latest evolving technologies in the profession.

BRANCHES OF ACCOUNTING

In order to satisfy needs of different people interested in the accounting information, different branches of accounting have developed. They can broadly be classified into two categories.

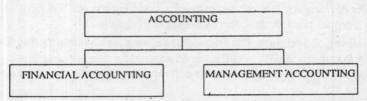

(*i*) **Financial Accounting.** It is the original form of accounting. It is mainly confined to the preparation of financial statements for the use of outsiders like shareholders, debenture holders, creditors, banks and financial institutions. The financial statements *i.e.* the Profit and Loss Account and the Balance Sheet, show them the manner in which operations of the business have been conducted during a specified period.

(*ii*) **Management Accounting.** It is accounting for the management *i.e.* accounting which provides necessary information to the management for discharging its functions. According to the Chartered Institute of Management Accountants, London, "management accounting is the application of professional information in such a way as to assist the management in the formation of policies and in the planning and control of the operations of the undertaking." It covers all arrangements and combinations or adjustments of the orthodox information to provide the Chief Executive with the information from which he can control the business *e.g.* information about funds, costs, profits, etc.

Management accounting covers various areas such as cost accounting, budgetary control, inventory control, statistical methods, internal auditing etc.

DIFFERENCE BETWEEN MANAGEMENT ACCOUNTING AND FINANCIAL ACCOUNTING

Financial accounting and management accounting are closely inter-related since management accounting is to a large extent rearrangement of the data provided by financial accounting. Moreover, all accounting is financial in the sense that all accounting systems are in monetary terms and management is responsible for the contents of the financial accounting statements. In spite of such a close relationship between the two, there are certain fundamental differences. These differences can be laid down as follows:

1. **Objectives.** Financial accounting is designed to supply information in the form of Profit and Loss Account and Balance Sheet to external parties like shareholders, creditors, banks, investors and Government. Information is supplied periodically and usually such in which management is not much interested. Management accounting is designed principally for internal use by the management.

2. **Analysing performance.** Financial accounting portrays the position of business as a whole. The financial statements like income statement and balance sheet report on overall performance or status of the business. On the other hand management accounting directs its attention to the various divisions, departments of the business and reports about the profitability, performance etc., of each of them. Financial accounting deals with the aggregates and therefore cannot reveal what part of the management action is going wrong and why. Management accounting provides detailed analytical data for these purposes.

3. **Data used.** Financial accounting is concerned with the monetary record of past events. It is a post-mortem analysis of past activity and therefore out of date for management action. Management accounting is an accounting for future and, therefore, it supplies data both for present and future duly analysed and in detail in the "management language" so that it becomes basis for management action.

4. **Monetary measurement.** In financial accounting only such economic events find a place which can be described in money. However the management is equally interested in non-monetary economic events *viz.* technical innovations, personnel in the organisation, changes in the value of money etc. These events affect management's decision and therefore management accounting cannot afford to ignore them. For example, change in the value of money may not find a place in financial accounting on account of "going concern concept", but, while effecting an insurance policy on an asset or providing for replacement of an asset, the management will have to take into account this factor.

5. **Periodicity of reporting.** The period of reporting in much longer in financial accounting as compared to management accounting. The Income Statement and the Balance Sheet are usually prepared yearly or in some cases half-yearly. Management requires information at frequent intervals and, therefore, financial accounting fails to cater to the needs of the management. In management accounting there is more emphasis on furnishing information quickly and at comparatively short intervals as per the requirements of the management.

6. **Precision.** There is less emphasis on precision in case of management accounting as compared to financial accounting since the information is meant for internal consumption.

7. **Nature.** Financial accounting is more objective while management accounting is more subjective. This is because management accounting is fundamentally based on judgement rather than on measurement.

8. **Legal compulsion.** Financial accounting has more or less become compulsory for every business on account of the legal provisions of one or the other Act. However, a business is free to install or not to install, a system of management accounting.

The above points of difference between financial accounting and management accounting prove that management accounting has a flexible approach as compared to rigid approach in case of financial accounting. In brief, financial accounting simply shows how the business has moved in the past while management accounting shows how the business has to move in the future.

OBJECTIVES OF ACCOUNTING

The following are the main objectives of accounting:

1. **To keep systematic records.** Accounting is done to keep a systematic record of financial transactions. In the absence of accounting there would have been terrific burden on human memory which in most cases would have been impossible to bear.

2. **To protect business properties.** Accounting provides protection to business properties from unjustified and unwarranted use. This is possible on account of accounting supplying the following information to the manager or the proprietor:

   (*i*) The amount of the proprietor's funds invested in the business.

   (*ii*) How much the business has to pay to others?

   (*iii*) How much the business has to recover from others?

   (*iv*) How much the business has in the form of (*a*) fixed assets, (*b*) cash in hand, (*c*) cash at bank, (*d*) stock of raw materials, work-in-progress and finished goods?

Information about the above matters helps the proprietor in assuring that the funds of the business are not unnecessarily kept idle or under-utilised.

3. **To ascertain the operational profit or loss.** Accounting helps in ascertaining the net profit earned or loss suffered on account of carrying the business. This is done by keeping a proper record of revenues and expenses of a particular period. The Profit and Loss Account is prepared at the end of a period and if the amount of revenue for the period is more than the expenditure incurred in earning that revenue, there is said to be a profit. In case the expenditure exceeds the revenue, there is said to be a loss.

Profit and Loss Account will help the management, investors, creditors, etc. in knowing whether running of the business has proved to be remunerative or not. In case it has not proved to be remunerative or profitable, the cause of such a state of affairs will be investigated and necessary remedial steps will be taken.

4. **To ascertain the financial position of business.** The Profit and Loss Account gives the amount of profit or loss made by the business during a particular period. However, it is not enough. The businessman must know about his financial position *i.e.* where he stands: what he owes and what he owns? This objectives is served by the Balance Sheet or Position Statement. The Balance Sheet is a statement of assets and liabilities of the business on a particular date. It serves as barometer for ascertaining the financial health of the business.

5. **To facilitate rational decision making.** Accounting these days has taken upon itself the task of collection, analysis and reporting of information at the required points of time to the required levels of authority in order to facilitate rational decision making. The American Accounting Association has also stressed this point while defining the term 'accounting' when it says that accounting is, "the process of identifying, measuring and communicating economic information to permit informed judgements and decisions by users of the information." Of course, this is by non means an easy task. However, the accounting bodies all over the world and particularly the International Accounting Standards Committee, have been trying to grapple with this problem and have achieved success in laying down some basic postulates on the basis of which the accounting statements have to be prepared. These postulates have been explained in the next chapter.

KEY TERMS

☐ **Accounting**: The process of identifying, measuring and communicating economic information to permit informed judgements and decisions by the users of information.

☐ **Financial Accounting**: The art of recording, classifying and summarising in a significant manner and in terms of money, transactions and events which are at least in part of a financial character and interpreting the results.

☐ **Management Accounting**: The presenting of accounting information in such a way as to assist management in the creation of the policy and in the day to day operation of the undertaking.

TEST QUESTIONS

Objective type | TEST YOUR UNDERSTANDING

1. State whether each of the following statement is 'True or 'False'
   (a) Accounting is the language of the business.
   (b) Accounting can be useful only for recording business transactions.
   (c) Accounting records only transactions which are of a financial character.
   (d) Book-keeping and Accounting are synonymous terms.
   (e) Accounting is as old as money itself.

   [**Ans.** (a) True, (b) False, (c) True, (d) False, (e) True.]

2. Indicate the best answer for each of the following questions:
   (i) The prime function of accounting is to:
      (a) record economic data.
      (b) provide the informational basis for action.
      (c) classifying and recording business transactions.
      (d) attain non-economic goals.
   (ii) The basic function of financial accounting is to:
      (a) record all business transactions.
      (b) interpret the financial data.
      (c) assist the management in performing functions effectively.
   (iii) Management Accounting provides invaluable services to management in performing:
      (a) all management functions.
      (b) co-ordinating management functions.
      (c) controlling functions.
   (iv) Book-keeping is mainly concerned with:
      (a) recording of financial data relating to business operations.
      (b) designing the systems in recording, class `ying, summarising the recorded data.
      (c) interpreting the data for internal and external end users.

   [**Ans.** (i) (c), (ii) (a), (iii) (a), (iv) (a)].

Essay type | FOR REVIEW, DISCUSSION AND PRACTICE

1. Define Accounting. State its functions. How does it differ from Book-keeping?
2. State the persons who should be interested in accounting information.
3. Explain the Role of Accountant in the present day economy.

Chapter 2

ACCOUNTING PRINCIPLES

LEARNING OBJECTIVES

After studying this chapter you should be able to:

- ☐ explain the meaning of accounting principles;
- ☐ differentiate between accounting concepts and conventions;
- ☐ appreciate the importance of different accounting concepts and conventions;
- ☐ name the accounting standards issued by the Institute of Chartered Accountants of India;
- ☐ describe the different systems of accounting; and
- ☐ explain the meaning of certain key terms.

MEANING OF ACCOUNTING PRINCIPLES

It has already been stated in the 1st Chapter that accounting is the language of business through which normally a business house communicates with the outside world. In order to make this language intelligible and commonly understood by all, it is necessary that it should be based on certain uniform scientifically laid down standards. These standards are termed as accounting principles.

Accounting principles[1] may be defined as those rules of action or conduct which are adopted by the accountants universally while recording accounting transaction. "They are a body of doctrines commonly associated with the theory and procedures of accounting, serving as an explanation of current practices and as a guide for selection of conventions or procedures where alternatives exist". These principles can be classified into two categories:

(*i*) Accounting Concepts.[2]

(*ii*) Accounting Conventions.

Accounting Concepts

The term 'concepts' includes those basic assumptions or conditions upon which the science of accounting is based. The following are the important accounting concepts:

(*i*) Separate Entity Concept.

---

[1] also termed as 'Accounting Standards'

[2] also termed as 'Accounting Postulates'.

(*ii*) Going Concern Concept.

(*iii*) Money Measurement Concept.

(*iv*) Cost Concept.

(*v*) Dual Aspect Concept.

(*vi*) Accounting Period Concept.

(*vii*) Periodic Matching of Cost and Revenue Concept.

(*viii*) Realisation Concept.

Accounting Conventions

The term 'conventions' includes those customs or traditions which guide the accountant while preparing the accounting statements. The following are the important accounting conventions:

(*i*) Convention of Conservatism.

(*ii*) Convention of Full Disclosure.

(*iii*) Convention of Consistency.

(*iv*) Convention of Materiality.

The preceding concepts and conventions can be put in the form of the following chart:

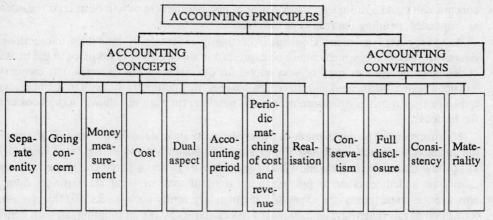

Each of the above concepts and conventions are being explained below.

ACCOUNTING CONCEPTS

1. Separate Entity Concept. In accounting business is considered to be a separate entity from the proprietor(s). It may appear to be ludicrous that one person can sell goods to himself but this concept is extremely helpful in keeping business affairs strictly free from the effect of private affairs of the proprietor(s). Thus, when one person invests Rs 10,000 into business, it will be deemed that the proprietor has given that much of money to the business which will be shown as a 'liability' in the books of the business. In case the proprietor withdraws Rs 2,000 from the business, it will be charged to him and the net amount payable by the business will be shown only as Rs 8,000.

The concept of separate entity is applicable to all forms of business organisations. For example, in case of a partnership business or sole proprietorship business, though the partners or sole proprietor are not considered as separate entities in the eyes of law, but for accounting purposes they will be considered as separate entities.

2. **Going Concern Concept.** According to this concept it is assumed that the business will continue for a fairly long time to come. There is neither the intention nor the necessity to liquidate the particular business venture in the foreseeable future. On account of this concept, the accountant while valuing the asset does not take into account forced sale value of assets. Moreover, he charges depreciation on fixed assets on the basis of their expected lives rather than on their market values.

It should be noted that the 'going concern concept' does not imply permanent continuance of the enterprise. It rather presumes that the enterprise will continue in operation long enough to charge against income, the cost of fixed assets over their useful lives, to amortize over appropriate period other costs which have been deferred under the accrual or matching concept, to pay liabilities when they become due and to meet the contractual commitments. Moreover, the concept applies to the business as a whole. When an enterprise liquidates a branch or one segment of its operations, the ability of the enterprise to continue as a going concern is not impaired normally.

The enterprise will not be considered as a going concern when it has gone into liquidation or it has become insolvent. Of course, the receiver or the liquidator may endeavour to carry on business operations for some period pending arrangement with the creditors or final buyer for the sale of the business as a going concern, the going concern status of the concern will stand terminated from the date of his appointment or will be at least regarded as suspended, pending the results of his efforts.

3. **Money Measurement Concept.** Accounting records only monetary transactions. Events or transactions which cannot be expressed in money do not find place in the books of accounts though they may be very useful for the business. For example, if a business has got a team of dedicated and trusted employees, it is definitely an asset to the business but since their monetary measurement is not possible, they are not shown in the books of the business.

Measurement of business event in money helps in understanding the state of affairs of the business in a much better way. For example if a business owns Rs 10,000 of cash, 600 kg. of raw materials, two trucks, 1,000 square feet of building space etc. these amounts cannot be added together to produce a meaningful total of what the business owns. However, if these items are expressed in monetary terms such as Rs 10,000 of cash, Rs 12,000 of raw materials. Rs 2,00,000 of trucks and Rs 50,000 of building, all such items can be added and much more intelligible and precise estimate about the assets of the business will be available.

4. **Cost Concept.** The concept is closely related to going concern concept. According to this concept:

    (a) an asset is ordinarily entered in the accounting records at the price paid to acquire it, and

    (b) this cost is the basis for all subsequent accounting for the assets.

If a business buys a plot of land for Rs 50,000, the asset would be recorded in the books at Rs 50,000 even if its market value at that time happens to be Rs 60,000. In case a year later the market value of this assets comes down to Rs 40,000, it will ordinarily continues to be shown at Rs 50,000 and not at Rs 40,000.

The cost concept does not mean that the asset will always be shown at cost. It has also been stated above that cost becomes the basis for all future accounting for the asset. It means that asset is recorded at cost at the time of its purchase but it may systematically be reduced in its value by charging depreciation.

Cost concept has the advantage of bringing objectivity in the preparation and presentation of financial statements. In the absence of this concept the figures shown in the accounting records would have depended on the subjective views of a person. However, on account of continued inflationary tendencies the preparation of financial statements on the basis of historical costs, has become largely irrelevant for judging the financial position of the business. This is the reason for the growing importance of inflation accounting.

5. **Dual Aspect Concept.** This is the basic concept of accounting. According to this concept every business transaction has a dual effect. For example, if A starts a business with a capital of Rs 10,000. There are two aspects of the transaction. On the one hand the business has asset of Rs 10,000 while on the other hand the business has to pay to the proprietor a sum of Rs 10,000 which is taken as proprietor's capital. This expression can be shown in the form of following equation:

$$\text{Capital (Equities)} = \text{Cash (Assets)}$$
$$10,000 = 10,000$$

The term 'assets denotes the resources owned by a business while the term "Equities" denotes the claims of various parties against the assets, Equities are of two types. They are owners' equity and outsiders' equity. Owners' equity (or capital) is the claim of owners against the assets of the business while outsiders' equity (or liabilities) is the claim of outside parties such as creditors, debenture-holders against the assets of the business. Since all assets of the business are claimed by someone (either owners or outsiders), the total of assets will be equal to total of liabilities, Thus:

$$\text{Equities} = \text{Assets}$$
or
$$\text{Liabilities} + \text{Capital} = \text{Assets}$$

In the example given above, if the business purchases furniture worth Rs 5,000 out of the money provided by A, the situation will be as follows:

$$\text{Equities} = \text{Assets}$$
$$\text{Capital Rs } 10,000 = \text{Cash Rs } 5,000 + \text{Furniture Rs } 5,000$$

Subsequently if the business borrows Rs 30,000 from a bank, the new position would be as follows:

$$\text{Equities} = \text{Assets}$$
$$\text{Capital Rs } 10,000 + \text{Bank Loan Rs } 30,000 = \text{Cash } 35,000 + \text{Furniture Rs } 5,000.$$

The term 'accounting equation' is also used to denote the relationship of equities to assets. The equation can be technically stated as "for very debit, there is an equivalent credit". As a matter of fact the entire system of double entry book-keeping is based on this concept. This has been explained in detail later in the chapter.

6. **Accounting Period Concept.** According to this concept, the life of the business is divided into appropriate segments for studying the results shown by the business after each segment. This is because though the life of the business is considered to be indefinite (according to going concern concept), the measurement of income and studying the financial position of the business after a very long period would not be helpful in taking proper corrective steps at the appropriate time. It is therefore, absolutely necessary that after each segment or time interval the businessman must 'stop and 'see back', how things are going. In accounting such a segment or time interval is called 'accounting period'. It is usually of a year.

At the end of each accounting period an Income Statement and a Balance Sheet are prepared. The Income Statement discloses the profit or loss made by the business during the accounting period while the Balance Sheet depicts the financial position of the business as on the last day of the accounting period. While preparing these statements a proper distinction has to be made between capital and revenue expenditures.

7. Periodic Matching of Costs and Revenues Concept. This is based on the accounting period concept. The paramount objective of running a business is to earn profit. In order to ascertain the profit made by the business during a period, it is necessary that 'revenues' of the period should be matched with the costs (expenses) of the period. The term 'matching, means appropriate association of related revenues and expenses. In other words, income made by the business during a period can be measured only when the revenue earned during a period is compared with the expenditure incurred for earning that revenue. The question when the payment was received or made is 'irrelevant'. For example, if a salesman is paid commission in January, 1989, for sales made by him in December, 1988, the commission paid to the salesman in January, 1989 should be taken as the cost for sales made by him in December, 1988. This means that revenues of December, 1988 (*i.e.* sales) should be matched with the costs incurred for earning that revenue (*i.e.* salesman's commission) in December 1988 (though paid in January, 1989). On account of this concept, adjustments are made for all outstanding expenses, accrued incomes, prepaid expenses and unearned incomes, etc., while preparing the final accounts at the end of the accounting period.

8. Realisation Concept. According to this concept revenue is recognised when a sale is made. Sale is considered to be made at the point when the property in goods passes to the buyer and he becomes legally liable to pay. This can be well understood with the help of following example:

A places an order with B for supply of certain goods yet to be manufactured. On receipt of order, B purchases raw materials, employs workers, produces the goods and delivers them to A. A makes payment on receipt of goods. In this case the sale will be presumed to have been made not at the time of receipt of the order for the goods but at the time when goods are delivered to A.

However, there are certain exceptions to this concept:

(*i*) In case of hire purchase to ownership of the goods passes to the buyer only when the last instalment is paid, but sales are presumed to have been made to the extent of instalment received and instalments outstanding (*i.e.* instalment due but not received.)

(*ii*) In case of contracts accounts, though the contractor is liable to pay only when the whole contract is completed as per terms of the contract, the profit is calculated on the basis of work certified year after year as per certain accepted accounting norms.

ACCOUNTING CONVENTIONS

1. Conservatism. In the initial stages of accounting certain anticipated profits which were recorded, did not materialise. This resulted in less acceptability of accounting figures by the end-users. On account of this reason, the accountants follows the rule 'anticipate no profit but provide for all possible losses' while recording business transactions. In order words, the accountant follows the policy of "playing safe". On account of this convention, the inventory is valued 'at cost or market price whichever is less'. Similarly a provision is made for possible bad and doubtful debts out of current year's profits. This concept affects principally the category of current assets.

The convention of conservatism has become target of serious criticism these days especially on the ground that it goes against the convention of full disclosure. It encourages the accountant to create secrete reserves (*e.g.* by creating excess provision for bad and doubtful debts, depreciation etc.), and the financial statements do not depict a true and fair view of state of affairs of the business. The Income Statement shows a lower net income, the Balance Sheet understates assets and overstates liabilities.

The research studies conducted by the American Institute of Certified Public Accountants have indicated that conservatism concept needs to be applied with much more caution and care if the results reported are not to be distorted.

2. Full Disclosure. According to this convention accounting reports should disclose fully and fairly the information they purport to represent. They should be honestly prepared and sufficiently disclose information which is of material interest to proprietors, present and potential creditors and investors. The convention is gaining more importance because most of big businesses are run by joint stock companies where ownership is divorced from management. The Companies Act, 1956, not only requires that Income Statement and Balance Sheet of a company must give a true and fair view of the state of affairs of the company but it also gives the prescribed forms in which these statements are to be prepared! 1 The practice of appending notes to the accounting statements (such as about contingent liabilities or market value of investments) is in pursuant to the convention of full disclosure.

3. Consistency. According to this convention accounting practices should remain unchanged from one period to another. For example, if stock is valued at "cost or market price whichever is less", this principle should be followed year after year. Similarly if depreciation is charged on fixed assets according to diminishing balance method, it should be done year after year. This is necessary for the purposes of comparison. However, consistency does not mean inflexibility. It does not forbid introduction of improved accounting techniques. However, if adoption of such a technique results in inflating or deflating the figures of profit as compared to the previous period, a note to that effect should be given in the financial statements.

4. Materiality. According to this convention the accountant should attach importance to material details and ignore insignificant details. This is because otherwise accounting will be unnecessarily overburdened with minute details. The question what constitutes a material details is left to the discretion of the accountant. Moreover, an item may be material for one purpose while immaterial for another. For example, while sending each debtor "a statement of his account", complete details up to paise have to be given. However, when a statement of outstanding debtors is prepared for sending to top management, figures may be rounded to the nearest ten or hundred. The Companies Act also permits ignoring of 'paise' while preparing financial statements. Similarly for tax purposes, the income has to be rounded to nearest ten.

Thus, the term 'materiality' is a subjective term. The accountant should regard an item as material if there is reason to believe that knowledge of it would influence the decision of the informed investor. According to Kohler "materiality means the characteristic attaching to a statement, fact or item whereby its disclosure or method of giving it expression would be likely to influence the judgement of a reasonable person."

It should be noted that accounting is a man-made art designed to help man in achieving certain objectives. "The accounting principles, therefore, cannot be derived from or proven

---

1 Sec. 211 of the Companies Act, 1956.

by laws of nature. They are rather in the category of conventions or rules developed by man from experience to fulfill the essential and useful needs and proposes in establishing reliable financial and operating information control for business entities. In this respect, they are similar to principles of commercial laws and other social disciplines."

ACCOUNTING PRINCIPLES AND THE INSTITUTE OF CHARTERED ACCOUNTANTS OF INDIA

In order to bring uniformity in terminology, approach and presentation of accounting results, the Institute of Chartered Accountants of India established on 21st April, 1977, an Accounting Standards Board (*ASB*). The main function of the *ASB* is to formulate accounting standards so that such standards will be established by the Council of the Institute of Chartered Accountants. While formulating the accounting standards, the *ASB* will give due consideration to the International Accounting Standards and try to integrate them to the extent possible. It will also take into consideration the applicable laws, customs, usages and the business environments prevailing in India.

PREFACE TO THE STATEMENTS OF ACCOUNTING STANDARDS[1]
(REVISED 2004)

The following are the specific features of the Preface to the Statements of Accounting Standards (Revised 2004), issued by the Council of the Institute of Chartered Accountants of India. With the issuance of this revised Preface, the Preface to the Statements of Accounting Standards, issued in January, 1979, stands superseded.

1. Formation of the Accounting Standards Board

    (1)   The Institute of Chartered Accountants of India (*ICAI*), recognising the need to harmonise the diverse accounting policies and practices in use in India, constituted the Accounting Standards Board (*ASB*) on 21st April, 1977.

    (2)   The composition of the *ASB* is fairly broad-based and ensures participation of all interest-groups in the standard-setting process. Apart from the elected members of the Council of the *ICAI* nominated on the *ASB*, the following are represented on the *ASB*:

        (*i*) Nominee of the Central Government representing the Department of Company Affairs on the Council of the *ICAI*.

       (*ii*) Nominee of the Central Government representing the Office of the Comptroller and Auditor General of India on the Council of the *ICAI*.

      (*iii*) Nominee of the Central Government representing the Central Board of Direct Taxes on the Council of the *ICAI*.

       (*iv*) Representative of the Institute of Cost and Works Accountants of India.

        (*v*) Representative of the Institute of Company Secretaries of India.

       (*vi*) Representatives of Industry Associations (1 from Associated Chambers of Commerce and Industry (*ASSOCHAM*), 1 from Confederation of Indian Industry (*CII*) and 1 from Federation of Indian Chambers of Commerce and Industry (*FICCI*).

---

[1] *The Chartered Accountant*, p. 972, March 2004.

(*vii*) Representative of Reserve Bank of India.

(*viii*) Representative of Securities and Exchange Board of India.

(*ix*) Representative of Controller General of Accounts.

(*x*) Representative of Central Board of Excise and Customs.

(*xi*) Representatives of Academic Institutions (1 from Universities and 1 from Indian Institutes of Management).

(*xii*) Representative of Financial Institutions.

(*xiii*) Eminent professionals co-opted by the *ICAI* (they may be in practice or in industry, government, education, etc.).

(*xiv*) Chairman of the Research Committee and the Chairman of the Expert Advisory Committee of the *ICAI*, if they are not otherwise members of the Accounting Standards Board.

(*xv*) Representative(s) of any other body, as considered appropriate by the *ICAI*.

2. Objectives and Functions of the Accounting Standards Board

The following are the objectives of the Accounting Standards Board:

(*i*) To conceive of and suggest areas in which Accounting Standards need to be developed.

(*ii*) To formulate Accounting Standards with a view to assisting the Council of the *ICAI* in evolving and establishing Accounting Standards in India.

(*iii*) To examine how far the relevant International Accounting Standard/International Financial Reporting Standard can be adapted while formulating the Accounting Standard and to adapt the same.

(*iv*) To review, at regular intervals, the Accounting Standards from the point of view of acceptance or changed conditions, and, if necessary, revise the same.

(*v*) To provide, from time to time, interpretations and guidance on Accounting Standards.

(*vi*) To carry such other functions relating to Accounting Standards.

The Accounting Standards are issued under the authority of the Council of the *ICAI*. The *ASB* has also been entrusted with the responsibility of propagating the Accounting Standards and of persuading the concerned parties to adopt them in the preparation and presentation of financial statements. The *ASB* will provide interpretations and guidance on issues arising from Accounting Standards. The *ASB* will also review the Accounting Standards at periodical intervals and, if necessary, revise the same.

3. General Purpose Financial Statements

(1) For discharging its functions, the *ASB* will keep in view the purposes and limitations of financial statements and the attest function of the auditors. The *ASB* will enumerate and describe the basic concept to which accounting principles should be oriented and state the accounting principles to which the practices and procedures should conform.

(2) The *ASB* will clarify the terms commonly used in financial statements and suggest improvements in the terminology wherever necessary. The *ASB* will examine the various current alternative practices in vogue and endeavour to eliminate or reduce alternatives within the bounds of rationality.

(3) Accounting Standards are designed to apply to the general purpose financial statements and other financial reporting, which are subject to the attest function of the members of the *ICAI*. Accounting Standards apply in respect of any enterprise (whether organised in corporate, co-operative or other forms) engaged in commercial, industrial or business activities, irrespective of whether it is profit oriented or it is established for charitable or religious purposes. Accounting Standards will not, however, apply to enterprises only carrying on the activities which are not of commercial, industrial or business nature, (e.g., an activity of collecting donations and giving them to flood affected people). Exclusion of an enterprise from the applicability of the Accounting Standards would be permissible only if no part of the activity of such enterprise is commercial, industrial or business in nature. Even if a very small proportion of the activities of an enterprise is considered to be commercial, industrial or business in nature, the Accounting Standards would apply to all its activities including those which are not commercial, industrial or business in nature.

(4) The term 'General Purpose Financial Statements' includes balance sheet, statement of profit and loss, a cash flow statement (wherever applicable) and statements and explanatory notes which form part thereof, issued for the use of various stakeholders, Governments and their agencies and the public. References to financial statements in the Preface and in the standards issued from time to time will be construed to refer to General Purpose Financial Statements.

(5) Responsibility for the preparation of financial statements and for adequate disclosure is that of the management of the enterprise. The auditor's responsibility is to form his opinion and report on such financial statements.

4. Scope of Accounting Standards

(1) Efforts will be made to issue Accounting Standards which are in conformity with the provisions of the applicable laws, customs, usages and business environment in India. However, if a particular Accounting Standard is found to be not in conformity with law, the provisions of the said law will prevail and the financial statements should be prepared in conformity with such law.

(2) The Accounting Standards by their very nature cannot and do not override the local regulations which govern the preparation and and presentation of financial statements in the country. However, the *ICAI* will determine the extent of disclosure to be made in financial statements and the auditor's report thereon. Such disclosure may be by way of appropriate note explaining the treatment of particular items. Such explanatory notes will be only in the nature of clarification and therefore need be treated as adverse comments on the related financial statements.

(3) The Accounting Standards are intended to apply only to items which are material. Any limitations with regard to the applicability of a specific Accounting Standard will be made clear by the *ICAI* from time to time. The date from which a particular Standard will come into effect, as well as the class of enterprises to which it will apply, will also be specified by the *ICAI*. However, no standard will have retroactive application, unless otherwise stated.

5. Procedure for Issuing an Accounting Standard

Broadly, the following procedure is adopted for formulating Accounting Standards:

(1) The *ASB* determines the broad areas in which Accounting Standards need to be formulated and the priority in regard to the selection thereof.

(2) In the preparation of Accounting Standards, the *ASB* will be assisted by Study Groups constituted to consider specific subjects. In the formation of Study Groups, provision will be made for wide participation by the members of the Institute and others.

(3) The draft of the proposed standard will normally include the following:

   (*a*) Objective of the Standard,

   (*b*) Scope of the Standard,

   (*c*) Definitions of the terms used in the Standard,

   (*d*) Recognition and measurement principles, wherever applicable,

   (*e*) Presentation and disclosure requirements.

(4) The *ASB* will consider the preliminary draft prepared by the Study Group and if any revision of the draft is required on the basis of deliberations, the *ASB* will make the same or refer the same to the Study Group.

(5) The *ASB* will circulate the draft of the Accounting Standard to the Council members of the *ICAI* and the following specified bodies for their comments:

   (*i*) Department of Company Affairs (*DCA*).

   (*ii*) Comptroller and Auditor General of India (*C & AG*).

   (*iii*) Central Board of Direct Taxes (*CBDT*).

   (*iv*) The Institute of Cost and Works Accountants of India (*ICWAI*).

   (*v*) The Institute of Company Secretaries of India (*ICSI*).

   (*vi*) Associated Chambers of Commerce and Industry (*ASSOCHAM*), Confederation of Indian Industry (*CII*) and Federation of Indian Chambers of Commerce and Industry (*FICCI*).

   (*vii*) Reserve Bank of India (*RBI*).

   (*viii*) Securities and Exchange Board of India (*SEBI*).

   (*ix*) Standing Conference of Public Enterprises (*SCOPE*).

   (*x*) Indian Banks' Association (*IBA*).

   (*xi*) Any other body considered relevant by the *ASB* keeping in view the nature of the Accounting Standard.

(6) The *ASB* will hold a meeting with the representatives of specified bodies to ascertain their views on the draft of the proposed Accounting Standard. On the basis of comments received and discussion with the representatives of specified bodies, the *ASB* will finalise the Exposure Draft of the proposed Accounting Standard.

(7) The Exposure Draft of the proposed Standard will be issued for comments by the members of the Institute and the public. The Exposure Draft will specifically be sent to specified bodies (as listed above), stock exchanges, and other interest groups, as appropriate.

(8) After taking into consideration the comments received, the draft of the proposed Standard will be finalised by the *ASB* and submitted to the Council of the *ICAI*.

(9) The Council of the *ICAI* will consider the final draft of the proposed Standard, and if found necessary, modify the same in consultation with the *ASB*. The Accounting Standard on the relevant subject will then be issued by the *ICAI*.

(10) For a substantive revision of an Accounting Standard, the procedure followed for formulation of a new Accounting Standard, as detailed above, will be followed.

(11) Subsequent to issuance of an Accounting Standard, some aspect(s) may require revision which are not substantive in nature. For this purpose, the *ICAI* may make limited revision to an Accounting Standard. The procedure followed for the limited revision will substantially be the same as that to be followed for formulation of an Accounting Standard, ensuring that sufficient opportunity is given to various interest groups and general public to react to the proposal for limited revision.

6. Compliance with the Accounting Standards

(1) The Accounting Standards will be mandatory from the respective date(s) mentioned in the Accounting Standards(s). The mandatory status of an Accounting Standard implies that while discharging their attest functions, it will be the duty of the members of the Institute to examine whether the Accounting Standard is complied with in the presentation of financial statements covered by their audit. In the event of any deviation from the Accounting Standard, it will be their duty to make adequate disclosures in their audit reports so that the users of financial statements may be aware of such deviation.

(2) Ensuring compliance with the Accounting Standards while preparing the financial statements is the responsibility of the management of the enterprise. Statutes governing certain enterprises require of the enterprises that the financial statements should be prepared in compliance with the Accounting Standards, e.g., the Companies Act, 1956 (section 211), and the Insurance Regulatory and Development Authority (Preparation of Financial Statements and Auditor's Report of Insurance Companies) Regulations, 2000.

(3) Financial Statements cannot be described as complying with the Accounting Standards unless they comply with all the requirements of each applicable Standard.

Issue of Accounting Standards: The *ASB* has so far issued twenty-nine definitive standards. These standards are as under:

No.		Title	Mandatory from accounting period beginning on or after
AS 1		Disclosure of Accounting Policies	1.4.1991
AS 2		Valuation of Inventories	1.4.1999
AS 3	(Revised)	Cash Flow Statements	1.4.2001
AS 4	(Revised)	Contingencies and Events occurring after Balance Sheet Date	1.4.1995
AS 5	(Revised)	Prior Period and Extraordinary Items and Changes in Accounting Policies	1.4.1996
AS 6	(Revised)	Depreciation Accounting	1.4.1995
AS 7		Accounting for Construction Contracts	1.4.2003
AS 8		Accounting for Research and Developments	1.4.1991
AS 9		Revenue Recognition	1.4.1991
AS 10		Accounting for Fixed Assets	1.4.1991
AS 11	(Revised 2003)	Accounting for the Effects of Changes in Foreign Exchange Rates	1.4.2004
AS 12		Accounting for Government Grants	1.4.1995

(Contd...)

No.	Title	Mandatory from accounting period beginning on or after
AS 13	Accounting for Investments	1.4.1995
AS 14	Accounting for Amalgamations	1.4.1994
AS 15	Accounting for Retirement Benefits in Employer's Financial Statements	1.4.1995
AS 16	Borrowing Costs	1.4.2000
AS 17	Segment Reporting	1.4.2001
AS 18	Related Party Disclosures	1.4.2001
AS 19	Leases	1.4.2001
AS 20	Earnings per share	1.4.2001
AS 21	Consolidated Financial Statements	1.4.2001
AS 22	Accounting for Taxes on Income	1.4.2001
AS 23	Accounting for Investments in Consolidated Financial Statements	1.4.2002
AS 24	Discontinuing Operations	1.4.2004
AS 25	Interim Financial Reporting	1.4.2002
AS 26	Intangible Assets	1.4.2003
AS 27	Financial Reporting of Interest in Joint Ventures	1.4.2002
AS 28	Impairment of Assets	1.4.2004
AS 29	Provisions, Contingent Liabilities & Contingent Assets	1 4.2004

Besides the above twenty-nine Accounting Standards, the *ASB* has issued the "Accounting Terminology" and also prepared a "Framework for the Preparation and Presentation of Financial Statements". It has also specified, in consultation with the *RBI*, modifications with which the Accounting Standards will be applicable to banks and other financial institutions.

ASB also carries out the task of revising the Accounting Standards, issue of clarifications and guidance notes. In March 2004, *ASB* issued clarifications interpreting applicability of AS 9, AS 17, AS 18, AS 21, AS 23 and AS 25. An exposure draft to revise AS 15 "Employee Benefits" has been issued in September 2004 on which the comments are to be received by October 30, 2004. A Guidance Note on *ESOP* is also to be issued shortly.

ASB is thus on the move. Its efforts are directed at establishing accounting standards which will be adopted by managements of different enterprises and will definitely result in the improvement of quality of presentation of financial statements in our country.

AS: 1 Disclosure of Accounting Policies

The main features of the Standard AS: 1 announced by the *ASB*, regarding Disclosure of Accounting Policies, are as follows:

(1) Fundamental Accounting Assumptions

(*i*) Certain fundamental accounting assumptions underlie the preparation and presentation of financial statements. They are usually not specifically stated because their acceptance and use are assumed.

(*ii*) Fundamental accounting assumptions are:

(*a*) Going concern; (*b*) Consistency; and (*c*) Accrual (They have already been explained earlier). If any fundamental accounting assumption is not followed, the fact should be disclosed.

(2) Accounting Policies

(*i*) Accounting polices refer to the specific accounting principles and the methods of applying those principles adopted by enterprises in the preparation and presentation of financial statements. There is no single list of accounting policies which are applicable to all circumstances. The different circumstances in which the enterprises operate in a situation of diverse and complex economic activity make alternative accounting principles and methods of applying those principles acceptable. The choice of appropriate accounting principles in the specific circumstances of each enterprise calls for considerable judgement by the management of the enterprise.

(*ii*) The following are the examples of the areas in which different accounting policies may be adopted by different enterprises:

(*a*) Methods of depreciation, depletion and amortisation. (*b*) Treatment of expenditure during the construction. (*c*) Conversion or translation of foreign currency items. (*d*) Valuation of inventories. (*e*) Treatment of goodwill. (*f*) Valuation of investments. (*g*) Treatment of retirement benefits. (*h*) Recognition of profit on long-term contracts. (*i*) Valuation of fixed assets. (*j*) Treatment of contingent liabilities.

The above list of examples is not intended to be exhaustive.

(*iii*) The primary consideration in the selection of accounting policies by an enterprise is that the financial statements prepared and presented on the basis of such accounting policy, should represent a true and fair view of the state of affairs of the enterprise, as at the balance sheet date and of the profit or loss for the period ended on that date. For this purpose, the major considerations governing the selection of and application of accounting policies are: (*a*) Prudence; (*b*) Substance over form; (*c*) Materiality.

(These have already been explained earlier).

(*iv*) To ensure proper understanding of financial statements, all significant accounting policies adopted in the preparation should be disclosed.

(*v*) The disclosure of the significant accounting policies as such should form a part of the financial statements and the significant accounting policies should normally be disclosed at one place.

(*vi*) Any change in the accounting policy which has a material effect in the current period or which is reasonably expected to have a material effect in the later periods should be disclosed. In the case of a change in the accounting policy which has a material effect in the current period, the amount by which an item, in the financial statement is affected by such a change, should also be disclosed, to the extent ascertainable. Where such an amount is not ascertainable wholly or in part, the fact should be indicated.

ASB is thus on the move. Its efforts to establish accounting standards and their adoption by management of different enterprises will definitely result in improvement in the quality of presentation of financial statements in our country.

SYSTEMS OF BOOK KEEPING

Book-keeping, as explained earlier, is the art of recording pecuniary or business transactions in a regular and systematic manner. This recording of transactions may be done according to any of the following two systems:

1. Single Entry System. An incomplete double entry can be termed as a single entry system. According to Kohler, "it is a system of book-keeping in which as a rule only records of cash and personal accounts are maintained, it is always incomplete double entry, varying with circumstances". This system has been developed by some business houses, who for their convenience, keep only some essential records. Since all records are not kept, the system is not reliable and can be used only by small business firms. The working of his system has been discussed in detail later in a separate chapter.

2. Double Entry System. The system of 'double entry' book-keeping which is believed to have originated with the venetian merchants of the fifteenth century, is the only system of recording the two-fold aspect of the transaction. This has been, to some extent, explained while discussing the 'dual aspect concept' earlier in this chapter. The system recognizes that every transaction have a two-fold effect If some one receives something than either some other person must have given it, or the first mentioned person must have lost something, or some service etc. must have been rendered by him.

Accounting Equation

The system of double entry system of book-keeping can very well be explained by the "accounting equation" given below:

$$Assets = Equities$$

The properties owned by business are called 'assets'. The rights to the properties are called 'Equities'. Equities may be sub-divided into two principal types: the rights of the creditors and the rights of the owners. The equity of creditors represents debts of the business and are called liabilities. The equity of the owners is called capital, or proprietorship or owner's equity. Thus:

$$Assets = Liabilities + Capital$$

or
$$Assets - Liabilities = Capital$$

The Accounting Equation can be understood with the help of the following transactions:

Transaction 1. *A* Starts business with a capital of Rs 10,000.

There are two aspects of the transaction. The business has received cash of Rs 10,000. It is its asset but on the other hand it has to pay a sum of Rs 10,000 to *A*, the proprietor. Thus:

Capital and Liabilities	Rs	Assets	Rs
Capital	10,000	Cash	10,000

Transaction 2. *A* purchases furniture for cash worth Rs 2,000. The position of his business will be as follows:

Capital and Liabilities	Rs	Assets	Rs
Capital	10,000	Cash	8,000
		Furniture	2,000
	10,000		10,000

Transaction 3. *A* purchases cotton bales from *B* Rs 5,000 on credit. He sells for cash cotton bales costing Rs 3,000 for Rs 4,000 and Rs 1,000 for Rs 1,500 on credit to *P*.

As a result of these transactions the business makes a profit of Rs. 1,500 (*i.e.* Rs. 5,500-Rs. 4,000) this will increase *A*'s Capital from Rs. 10,000 to Rs. 11,5000. The business will have a liability of Rs. 5,000 to *B* and two more assets in the form of a debtor *P* for Rs. 1,5000 and stock of cotton bales of Rs. 1,000. The position of his business will now be as follows:

Capital and Liabilities	Rs	Assets	Rs
Creditor (*B*)	5,000	Cash (Rs 8,000 + 4,000)	12,000
Capital	11,500	Stock of Cotton Bales	1,000
		Debtor (*P*)	1,500
		Furniture	2,000
	16,500		16,500

Transaction 4. *A* withdraws cash of Rs. 1,000 and cotton bales of Rs 200 for his personal use. The amount and the goods withdrawn will decrease relevant assets and *A*'s capital. The position will be now as follows:

Capital and Liabilities	Rs	Assets	Rs
Creditor (*B*)	5,000	Cash (Rs 12,000 - Rs 1,000)	11,000
Capital		Stock of Cotton Bales	800
(Rs 11,500 - Rs 1,200)	10,300	Debtor (*P*)	1,500
		Furniture	2,000
	15,300		15,300

The above type of statement showing the financial position of a business on a certain date is termed as balance sheet.

The result of applying the system of double entry system may be summarised in the form of following rule:

"For every debit there must be equivalent credit and *vice versa.*"

The rules, of *Debit* and *Credit* have been explained in the succeeding Chapter.

Illustration 2.1 Anil had the following transactions. Use accounting equation to show their effect on his assets, liabilities and capital:

	Rs
1. Started business with cash	5,000
2. Purchased goods on credit	400
3. Purchased goods for cash	100
4. Purchased Furniture	50
5. Withdrew for personal use	70
6. Paid rent	20
7. Received Interest	10
8. Sold goods costing Rs 50 on credit for	70
9. Paid to creditors	40
10. Paid for salaries	20
11. Further capital invested	1,000
12. Borrowed from P	1,000

Solution:

Accounting equation: Assets = Liabilities + Capital

No.	Transaction	Assets = Liabilities + Capital				
		Rs		Rs		Rs
1.	Anil started business with cash Rs 5,000	5,000	=	0	+	5,000
2.	Purchased goods on credit for Rs 400	400	=	400	+	0
	New Equation	5,400	=	400	+	5,000
3.	Purchase goods for cash Rs 100	+100				
		−100	=	0	+	0
	New Equation	5,400	=	400	+	5,000
4.	Purchased furniture Rs 50	+50				
		−50	=	0	+	0
	New Equation	5,400	=	400	+	5,000
5.	Withdrew for personal use Rs 70	−70	=	0	−	70
	New Equation	5,330	=	400	+	4930
6.	Paid rent	−20	=	0	+	−20
	New Equation	5,310	=	400	+	4,910
7.	Received interest Rs 10	+10	=	0	+	10
	New Equation	5,320	=	400	+	4,920
8.	Sold goods consisting Rs 50 on credit for Rs 70	+70				
		−50	=	0	+	20
	New Equation	5,340	=	400	+	4,940
9.	Paid to creditors Rs 40	−40	=	−40	+	0
	New Equation	5,300	=	360	+	4,940
10.	Paid for salaries Rs 20	−20	=	0	−	20
	New Equation	5,280	=	360	+	4,920
11.	Further Capital Invested	1,000	=	0	+	1,000
	New Equation	6,280	=	360	+	5,920
12.	Borrowed from P Rs 1,000	1,000	=	1,000	+	0
	New Equation	7,280	=	1,360	+	5,920

SYSTEMS OF ACCOUNTING

There are basically two systems of accounting:

(i) **Cash system of accounting.** It is a system in which accounting entries are made only when cash is received or paid. No entry is made when a payment or receipts is merely due. Government system of accounting is mostly on the cash system. Certain professional people record their income on cash basis, but while recording expenses they take into account the outstanding expenses also. In such a case, the financial statement prepared by them for determination of their income is termed as Receipts and Expenditure Account.

(ii) **Mercantile or accrual system of accounting.** It is a system in which accounting entries are made on the basis of amounts having become due for payment or receipt. This system recognises the fact that if a transaction or an event has occured; its consequences cannot be avoided and therefore should be brought into books in order to present a meaningful picture of profit earned or loss suffered and also of the financial position of the firm concerned.

The difference between "cash and mercantile systems" of accounting will be clear with the help of the following example:

A firm close its books on 31st December each year. A sum of Rs 500 has become due for payment on account of rent for the year 1990. The amount has, however, been paid in January, 1991.

In this case, if the firm is following cash system of accounting, no entry will be made for the rent having become due in the books of accounts of the firm in 1990. The entry will be made only in January 1991 when the rent is actually paid. However, if the firm is following mercantile system of accounting, two entries will made: (*i*) on 31st December 1990, rent account will be debited while the landlord's account will be credited by the amount of outstanding rent; (*ii*) In January, 1991 landlord's account will be debited while the cash account will be credited with the amount of the rent actually paid. (This has been discussed in detail later while dealing with adjustment relating to final accounts).

The 'mercantile system' is considered to be better since it takes into account the effects of all transactions already entered into. This system is followed by most of the industrial and commercial firms.

KEY TERMS

☐ **Accounting Principles**: Rules of action or conduct adopted by the accountants universally while recording accounting transactions.

☐ **Accounting Concepts**: Basic assumptions or conditions upon which the science of accounting is based.

☐ **Accounting Conventions**: Customs and traditions which guide the accountants while preparing the accounting statements.

☐ **Cash System of Accounting**: A system in which accounting entries are made only when cash is received or paid.

☐ **Mercantile System of Accounting**: A system in which accounting entries are made on the basis of amounts having become due for payment or receipt. It is also termed as Accrual System of Accounting.

TEST QUESTIONS

Objective type | TEST YOUR UNDERSTANDING |

1. State whether each of the following statement is 'True' or 'False'.

   (*a*) Accounting principles are rules of action or conduct which are adopted by the accountants universally while recording accounting transactions.

   (*b*) It is on the basis of going concern concept that the assets are always valued at market price.

   (*c*) The convention of disclosure implies that all material information should be disclosed in the accounts.

   (*d*) The convention of conservatism takes into account all prospective profits but leaves all prospective losses.

   (*e*) Since the life of the business is assumed to be indefinite, the financial statements of the business should be prepared only when it goes into liquidation.

   (*f*) In accounting all business transactions are recorded as having a dual aspect.

   [**Ans.** (*a*) True, (*b*), False, (*c*) True, (*d*), False, (*e*) False, (*f*) True]

2. Choose the correct answer:

   (*i*) Accounting principles are generally based on

      (*a*) practicability.

      (*b*) subjectivity.

(c) convenience in recording.

(ii) The system of recording transactions based on dual aspect concept is called
- (a) double account system.
- (b) double entry system.
- (c) single entry system.

(iii) The practice of appending notes regarding contingent liabilities in accounting statements is in pursuant to:
- (a) convention of consistency.
- (b) money measurement concept.
- (c) convention of conservatism.
- (d) convention of disclosure.

(iv) According to money measurement concept, the following will be recorded in the books of accounts of the business:
- (a) health of the Managing Director of the company.
- (b) quality of company's goods.
- (c) value of plant and machinery.

(v) The convention of conservatism is applicable
- (a) in providing for discount on creditors.
- (b) in making provision for bad and doubtful debts.
- (c) providing for depreciation.

(vi) The convention of conservatism, when applied to the balance sheet, results in
- (a) understatement of assets
- (b) understatement of liabilities
- (c) overstatement of capital.

[Ans. (i) (a), (ii) (b), (iii) (d), (iv) (c), (v) (b), (vi) (a).]

Essay type   FOR REVIEW, DISCUSSION AND PRACTICE

1. Discuss briefly the basic accounting concepts and fundamental accounting assumptions.
2. What are the accounting concepts and conventions? Name them and explain any two accounting concepts in detail.
3. Explain any three of the following accounting concepts:
   - (a) Money measurement concept
   - (b) Business entity concept
   - (c) Going concern concept
   - (d) Realisation concept
   - (e) Cost concept.
4. According to the principles of 'Double entry system', 'Every debit has a corresponding credit.' Explain clearly. Discuss the merits of double entry system also.
5. Differentiate between Cash and Mercantile Systems of Accounting.
6. Explain the Realisation Concept and Going Concern Concept.
7. Write short notes on
   - (a) Money Measurement Concept.
   - (b) Dual Aspect Concept.
   - (c) Periodic Matching of Cost and Revenue Concept.

PRACTICAL PROBLEMS

1. Show the effect of the following transactions on the assets, liabilities and capital of Mr. Abhay Kumar through the accounting equation:
   1. He started business with cash of Rs 20,000.

2. He purchased goods for cash for Rs 10,000.
3. Purchased goods on credit from Mr. Mohan Lal for Rs 8,000.
4. Sold goods for cash costing Rs 8,000 for Rs 10,000.
5. Withdrew Rs 1,000 from business in cash to pay for his private expenses.
6. Electricity bills paid for Rs 100.
7. He sold goods on credit costing Rs 5,000 to Mr. Surendra for Rs 6,000.
8. Rent outstanding Rs 400.
9. He borrowed Rs 5,000 from Mr. Lalit.
10. Purchased goods for cash Rs 2,000.

2. From the following transactions relating to Mr. Anil Kumar, show the effect on his assets, liabilities and capital by using the accounting equation:
1. Started business with cash Rs 10,000
2. Purchased goods on credit Rs 8,000.
3. Plant purchased for cash Rs 2,000.
4. Sold goods costing Rs 1,000 for Rs 2,000 for cash.
5. Sold goods on credit to Mahendra costing Rs 800 for Rs 1,500.
6. Drew for personal use Rs 500.
7. Paid for salaries Rs 300.
8. Received cash from Mahendra Rs 700.

3. Show accounting equation on the basis of the following transactions:
1. Laxman started business with cash of Rs 20,000.
2. He purchased goods on credit Rs 8,000
3. He sold goods for cash Rs 2,500 for Rs 3,000.
4. He purchased furniture for cash Rs 2,000.
5. He sold goods to Hari costing Rs 400 for Rs 800 on credit.
6. He received cash from Hari Rs 500 towards payment of the price of the goods.
7. He received dividend on securities Rs 200.
8. He paid life insurance premium on his life policy Rs 400.
9. He purchased goods from Mukesh for cash Rs 300.

Chapter 3

JOURNALISING TRANSACTIONS

LEARNING OBJECTIVES

After studying this chapter you should be able to:

- ☐ identify the stages of the accounting cycle;
- ☐ appreciate the role of Journal in recording business transactions;
- ☐ understand the rules of debit and credit applicable to different types of business transactions;
- ☐ describe the various categories of accounts;
- ☐ pass appropriate entries for recording transactions in the Journal; and
- ☐ explain the meaning of certain key terms.

It has been explained in Chapter 1, that Accounting is the art of recording, classifying and summarising the financial transactions and interpreting the results therefore. Thus, accounting cycle involves the following stages:

1. **Recording of transactions.** This is done is the book termed as 'Journal'.

2. **Classifying the transactions.** This is done in the book termed as 'Ledger'.

3. **Summarising the transactions.** This includes preparation of the trial balance, profit and loss account and balance sheet of the business.

4. **Interpreting the results.** This involves computation of various accounting ratios, etc., to know about the liquidity, solvency and profitability of business.

The recording of transactions in the Journal is being explained in this chapter.

JOURNAL

The Journal records all daily transactions of a business into the order in which they occur. A Journal may therefore be defined as a book containing a chronological record of transactions. It is the book in which the transactions are recorded first of all under the double entry system. Thus, Journal is the books, of original record. A Journal does not replace but precedes the Ledger. The process of recording transaction in a Journal, is termed as 'Journalising. A proforma of journal is given below:

JOURNAL

Date	Particulars	L.F.	Debit Rs	Credit Rs
(1)	(2)	(3)	(4)	(5)

1. **Date.** The date on which the transaction was entered is recorded here.

2. **Particulars.** The two aspects of transaction are recorded in this column, *i.e.*, the details regarding accounts which have to be debited and credited.

3. **L.F.** It means Ledger Folio. The transactions entered in the Journal are later on posted to the ledger. Procedure regarding posting the transactions in the Ledger has been explained in the succeeding chapter.

4. **Debit.** In this column, the amount to be debited is entered.

5. **Credit.** In this column, the amount to be credited is shown.

RULES OF DEBIT AND CREDIT

The transactions in the Journal are recorded on the basis of the rules of debit and credit. For this purpose business transactions have been classified into three categories:

(*i*) Transactions relating to persons.

(*ii*) Transactions relating to properties and assets.

(*iii*) Transactions relating to incomes and expenses.

On this basis, it becomes necessary for the business to keep an account of:

(*i*) Each person with whom it deals.

(*ii*) Each property or asset which the business owns.

(*iii*) Each item of income or expense.

The accounts falling under the first heading are called as 'Personal Accounts'. The accounts falling under the second heading are termed as 'Real Accounts'. The accounts falling under the third heading are termed as 'Nominal Accounts'. The classifications of the accounts, as explained above, can be put in the form of the following chart:

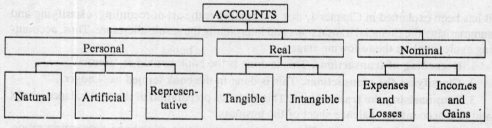

Each of the above categories of accounts and the relevant rule for 'debit and credit' have been explained in detail in the following pages:

Personal Accounts. Personal accounts include the accounts of persons with whom the business deals. These accounts can be classified into the three categories.

1. *Natural Personal Accounts.* The term 'Natural Persons' means persons who are creation of God. For example, Mohan's Account, Sohan's Account, Abha's Account etc.

2. *Artificial Personal Accounts.* These accounts include account of corporate bodies or institutions which are recognised as persons in business dealings. For example, the account of a Limited Company, the account of a Co-operative Society, the account of a Club, the account of Government, the account of an Insurance Company etc.

3. *Representative Personal Accounts.* These are accounts which represent a certain person or group of persons. For example, if the rent is due to the landlord, an outstanding rent account will be opened in the books. Similarly, for salaries due to the employees (not paid), an outstanding salaries account will be opened. The outstanding rent account represents the account of the landlord to whom the rent is to be paid while the outstanding

salaries account represents the accounts of the persons to whom the salaries have to be paid. All such accounts are therefore termed as 'Representative Personal Accounts'.

The rule is:

```
DEBIT THE RECEIVER
CREDIT THE GIVER
```

For example, if cash has been paid to Ram, the account of Ram will have to be debited. Similarly. if cash has been received from Keshav, the account of Keshav will have to be credited.

Real Accounts. Real accounts may be of the following types:

1. *Tangible Real Accounts*. Tangible Real Accounts are those which relate to such things which can be touched, felt, measured etc. Examples of such accounts are cash account, building account, furniture account, stock account, etc. It should be noted that bank account is a personal account; since it represents the account of the banking company—an artificial person.

2. *Intangible Real Accounts*. These accounts represent such things which cannot be touched. Of course, they can be measured in terms of money. For example, patent's account, goodwill account, etc.

The rule is:

```
DEBIT WHAT COMES IN
CREDIT WHAT GOES OUT
```

For example, if building has been purchased for cash, building account should be debited (since it is coming in the business) while cash account should be credited since cash is going out the business. Similarly when furniture in purchased for cash, furniture account should be debited while the cash account should be credited.

Nominal Accounts. These accounts are opened in the books to simply explain the nature of the transactions. They do not really exist. For example, in a business, salary is paid to the manager, rent is paid to the landlord, commission is paid to the salesmen, cash goes out of the business and its is something real; while salary, rent or commission as such do not exist. The accounts of these items are opened simply to explain how the cash has been spent. In the absence of such information, it may difficult for the person concerned to explain how the cash at his disposal was utilised.

Nominal Accounts include accounts of all expenses, losses, incomes and gains. The examples of such accounts are rent, rates lighting, insurance, dividends, loss by fire, etc.

The rule is:

```
DEBIT ALL EXPENSES AND LOSSES
CREDIT ALL GAINS AND INCOMES
```

Tutorial Note. The student should note that when some prefix or suffix is added to a Nominal Account, it becomes a Personal Account. A table is being given to explain the above rule:

Nominal Account	Personal Account
1. Rent account	Rent pre-paid account, Outstanding rent account.
2. Interest account	Outstanding interest account, Interest received in advance account, Prepaid interest account.

Contd....

Nominal Account	Personal Account
3. Salary account	Outstanding salaries account, Prepaid salaries account.
4. Insurance account	Outstanding insurance account, Prepaid insurance account.
5. Commission account	Outstanding commission account, Prepaid commission account

Illustration 3.1. From the following transactions find out the nature of account and also state which account should be debited and which account should be credited.

(a) Rent paid.
(b) Salaries paid.
(c) Interest received.
(d) Dividends received.
(e) Furniture purchased for cash.
(f) Machinery sold.

(g) Outstanding for salaries.
(h) Telephone charges paid.
(i) Paid to Suresh.
(j) Received from Mohan (the proprietor).
(k) Lighting

Solution:

	Transaction	Accounts involved	Nature of Accounts	Debit/Credit
(a)	Rend paid	Rent A/c	Nominal A/c	Debit
		Cash A/c	Real A/c	Credit
(b)	Salaries paid	Salaries A/c	Nominal A/c	Debit
		Cash A/c	Real A/c	Credit
(c)	Interest received	Cash A/c	Real A/c	Debit
		Interest A/c	Nominal A/c	Credit
(d)	Dividends received	Cash A/c	Real A/c	Debit
		Dividends A/c	Nominal A/c	Credit
(e)	Furniture purchased	Furniture A/c	Real A/c	Debit
		Cash A/c	Real A/c	Credit
(f)	Machinery sold	Cash A/c	Real A/c	Debit
		Machinery A/c	Real A/c	Credit
(g)	Outstanding for salaries	Salaries A/c	Nominal A/c	Debit
		Outstanding salaries A/c	Personal A/c	Credit
(h)	Telephone charges paid	Telephone charges A/c	Nominal A/c	Debit
		Cash A/c	Real A/c	Credit
(i)	Paid to Suresh	Suresh	Personal A/c	Debit
		Cash A/c	Real A/c	Credit
(j)	Received from Mohan (the proprietor)	Cash A/c	Real A/c	Debit
		Capital A/c	Personal A/c	Credit
(k)	Lighting	Lighting A/c	Nominal A/c	Debit
		Cash A/c	Real A/c	Credit

The journalising of the various transactions is explained now with the help of the following illustration:

Illustration 3.2. Ram starts a business with capital of Rs 20,000 on January 1, 1990.

In this case there are two accounts involved. They are:

(i) The account of Ram.
(ii) Cash Account.

Ram is natural person and, therefore, his account is a Personal Account. Cash Account is a tangible asset and, therefore, it is a Real Account. As per the rules of Debit and Credit, applicable to Personal Accounts, Ram is the giver and, therefore, his account, *i.e.*, Capital Account should be credited. Cash is coming in the business and, therefore, as per the rules applicable to Real Accounts, it should be debited. The transaction will now be entered in the Journal as follows:

JOURNAL

Date	Particulars	L.F.	Debit Rs	Credit Rs
1990 Jan.1	Cash Account Dr. To Capital Account (Being commencement of business)		20,000	20,000

The words put within brackets "Being commencement of business" constitute the narration for the entry passed, since, they narrate the transaction.

2. He purchased furniture for cash for Rs 5,000 on January 5, 1990.

The two accounts involved in this transaction are the Furniture Account and the Cash Account. Both are Real Accounts. Furniture is coming in and, therefore, it should be debited while cash is going out and, therefore, it should be credited. The Journal entry will, therefore, be as follows:

JOURNAL

Date	Particulars	L.F.	Rs	Rs
1990 Jan.5	Furniture Account Dr. To Cash Account (Being purchase of furniture)		5,000	5,000

3. He paid rent for business premises Rs 2,000 on January 10, 1990.

In this transaction, two accounts involved are the Rent Account and the Cash Account. Rent Account is a nominal Account. It is an expense and, therefore, it should be debited. Cash Account is a Real Account. It is going out of the business and, therefore, it should be credited. The journal entry will, therefore, be as follows:

JOURNAL

Date	Particulars	L.F.	Rs	Rs
1990 Jan.10	Rent Account Dr. To Cash Account (Being payment of rent)		2,000	2,000

4. He purchased goods on credit of Rs 2,000 from Suresh on January 20, 1990.

The two accounts involved in the transaction are those of Suresh and Goods. The account of Suresh is a Personal Account while that of Goods is a Real Account. Suresh is the giver of goods and, therefore, his account should be credited while Goods are coming in the business and, therefore, Goods Account should be debited.

JOURNAL

Date	Particulars	L.F.	Rs	Rs
1990 Jan.20	Goods Account Dr. To Suresh (Being purchase of goods on credit)		2,000	2,000

Classification of Goods Account. The term goods include articles purchased by the business for resale. Goods purchased by the business may be returned back to the supplier. Similarly, goods sold by the business to its customers can also be returned by the customers back to the business due to certain reasons. In business, it is desired that a separate record be kept of all sale, purchase and return of goods. Hence, Goods Account can be classified into the following categories:

(*i*) *Purchases Account.* The account is meant for recording all purchases of goods. Goods "come in" on purchasing of goods and, therefore, the Purchases Account is debited on purchase of goods.

(*ii*) *Sales Account.* The account is meant for recording of selling of goods. The goods "go out" on selling of goods, and therefore, on sale of goods, the Sales Account is credited.

(*iii*) *Purchases Returns Account.* The account is meant for recording return of goods purchased. The goods "go out" on returning of goods to the suppliers and, therefore, the account should be credited on returning goods purchased.

(*iv*) *Sales Returns Account.* The account is meant for recording return of goods sold, by the customers. The goods "come in" and, therefore, the Sales Returns Account should be debited on return of goods.

The above classification of Goods Account can be shown in the form of the following chart:

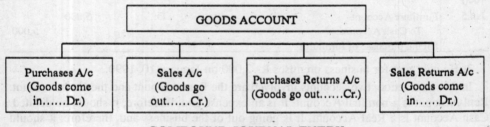

COMPOUND JOURNAL ENTRY

Sometimes there are a number of transactions on the same date relating to one particular account or of the one particular nature. Such transactions may be recorded by means of a single journal entry instead of passing several journal entries. Such entry regarding recording a number of transactions is termed as a "Compound Journal Entry". It may be recorded in any of the following three ways:

(*i*) One particular account may be debited while several other accounts may be credited.

(*ii*) One particular account may be credited while several other accounts may be debited.

(*iii*) Several accounts may be debited and several other accounts may also be credited.

This has been explained in the following illustration.

Illustration 3.3. Pass a compound journal entry in each of the following cases:

1. Payment made to Ram Rs 1,000. He allowed a cash discount of Rs 50.

2. Cash received from Suresh Rs 800 and allowed him Rs 50 as discount.

3. A running business was purchased by Mohan with following assets and liabilities:
   Cash Rs 2,000, Land Rs 4,000, Furniture Rs 1,000, Stock Rs 2,000, Creditors Rs 1,000, Bank Overdraft Rs 2,000.

Solution:

JOURNAL

Sl. No.	Particulars		L.F.	Debit Rs	Credit Rs
1.	Ram	Dr.		1,050	
	To Cash A/c				1,000
	To Discount				50
	(Being payment made to Ram Rs 1,000, and he allowed Rs 50 as discount)				
2.	Cash A/c	Dr.		800	
	Discount A/c	Dr.		50	
	To Suresh				850
	(Being cash received from Suresh Rs 800, and discount allowed Rs 50)				
3.	Cash A/c	Dr.		2,000	
	Land A/c	Dr.		4,000	
	Furniture A/c	Dr.		1,000	
	Stock A/c	Dr.		2,000	
	To Creditors				1,000
	To Bank Overdraft				2,000
	To Capital A/c				6,000
	(Being commencement of business by Mohan by taking over a running business)				

Notes:

1. The total of payment due to Ram was Rs 1,050. A payment of Rs 1,000 has been made to him and he allowed a discount of Rs 50. This means by paying Rs 1,000, a full credit for Rs 1,050 has been obtained. The account of Ram is a Personal Account, and therefore, it has been debited as he is the receiver. The cash has gone out of the business and, therefore, Cash Account being a Real Account, has been credited. Discount Account is a Nominal Account, getting discount is a gain to the business and, therefore, it has been credited.

2. Suresh was to pay sum of Rs 850. He paid Rs 800 and he was allowed a discount of Rs 50. It means by paying Rs 800 only, Suresh could get a full credit of Rs 850. The Cash Account is a Real Account and, therefore, it has been debited since cash is coming in. Discount Account is a Nominal Account, it has been debited since it is a loss to the business. Suresh is the giver. His account being a Personal Account, it has been credited by Rs 850.

3. It is not necessary that a person should start business only with cash. He may bring the assets into the business or he may purchase a running business. Mohan in the present case has purchased the assets of some other business. The net assets (i.e. assets—liabilities taken over) will be the capital of Mohan. The business is getting various assets and, therefore, the assets accounts have been debited. The business creates certain liabilities in the form of creditors, bank overdraft, and, therefore, these accounts have been credited. Mohan's Account i.e., his Capital Account has been credited by the balance since it represents the capital brought in by him.

Illustration 3.4. Journalise the following transactions. Also state the nature of each account involved in the Journal entry.

1. Dec. 1, 1990, Ajit started business with Cash Rs 40,000.
2. Dec. 3, he paid into the Bank Rs 2,000.
3. Dec. 5, he purchased goods for cash Rs 15,000.
4. Dec. 8, he sold goods for cash Rs 6,000
5. Dec. 10, he purchased furniture and paid by cheque Rs 5,000.
6. Dec. 12, he sold goods to Arvind Rs 4,000.
7. Dec. 14, he purchased goods from Amrit Rs 10,000.
8. Dec. 15, he returned goods to Amrit Rs 5,000.
9. Dec. 16, he received from Arvind Rs 3,960 in full settlement.
10. Dec. 18, he withdrew goods for personal use Rs 1,000.
11. Dec. 20, he withdrew cash from business for personal use Rs 2,000.
12. Dec. 24, he paid telephone charges Rs 1,000.
13. Dec. 26, cash paid to Amrit in full settlement Rs 4,900.
14. Dec. 31, paid for stationery Rs 200, rent Rs 500 and salaries to staff Rs 2,000.
15. Dec. 31, goods distributed by way of free samples Rs 1,000.

Solution:

JOURNAL

Sl. No.	Date	Particulars		Nature of Account	L.F.	Debit Rs	Credit Rs
1.	Dec. 1	Cash A/c	Dr.	Real A/c		40,000	
		To Capital A/c		Personal A/c			40,000
		(Being commencement of business)					
2.	Dec. 3	Bank A/c	Dr.	Personal A/c		20,000	
		To Cash A/c		Real A/c			20,000
		(Being cash deposited in the Bank)					
3.	Dec. 5	Purchases A/c	Dr.	Real A/c		15,000	
		To Cash A/c		Real A/c			15,000
		(Being purchase of goods for cash)					
4.	Dec. 8	Cash A/c	Dr.	Real A/c		6,000	
		To Sales A/c		Real A/c			6,000
		(Being goods sold for cash)					
5.	Dec. 10	Furniture A/c	Dr.	Real A/c		5,000	
		To Bank A/c		Personal A/c			5,000
		(Being purchase of furniture, paid by cheque)					
6.	Dec. 12	Arvind	Dr.	Personal A/c		4,000	
		To Sales A/c		Real A/c			4,000
		(Being sale of goods)					
7.	Dec. 14	Purchases A/c	Dr.	Real A/c		10,000	
		To Amrit		Personal A/c			10,000
		(Being purchase of goods from Amrit)					
8.	Dec. 15	Amrit	Dr.	Personal A/c		5,000	
		To Purchases Returns A/c		Real A/c			5,000
		(Being goods returned to Amrit)					
9.	Dec. 16	Cash A/c	Dr.	Real A/c		3,960	
		Discount A/c	Dr.	Nominal A/c		40	
		To Arvind		Personal A/c			4,000

Contd....

Sl. No.	Date	Particulars	Nature of Account	L.F.	Debit Rs	Credit Rs
		(Being cash received from Arvind in full settlement and allowed him Rs 40 as discount)				
10.	Dec. 18	Drawings A/c Dr.	Personal A/c		1,000	
		To Purchases A/c	Real A/c			1,000
		(Being withdrawal of goods for personal use)				
11.	Dec. 20	Drawings A/c Dr.	Personal A/c		2,000	
		To Cash A/c	Real A/c			2,000
		(Being cash withdrawal from the business for personal use)				
12.	Dec. 24	Telephone Expenses A/c Dr.	Nominal A/c		1,000	
		To Cash A/c	Real A/c			1,000
		(Being telephone expenses paid)				
13.	Dec. 26	Amrit Dr.	Personal A/c		5,000	
		To Cash A/c	Real A/c			4,900
		To Discount A/c	Nominal A/c			100
		(Being cash paid to Amrit and he allowed Rs 100 as discount)				
14.	Dec. 31	Stationery Expenses Dr.	Nominal A/c		200	
		Rent A/c Dr.	Nominal A/c		500	
		Salaries A/c Dr.	Nominal A/c		2,000	
		To Cash A/c	Real A/c			2,700
		(Being expenses paid)				
15.	Dec. 31	Advertisement Expenses A/c Dr.	Nominal A/c		1,000	
		To Purchases A/c	Real A/c			1,000
		Being distribution of goods by way (of free samples)				
		Total			1,21,700	1,21,700

Notes:

Transactions 9. Ajit was to receive Rs 4,000 from Arvind. He accepts only Rs 3,960 in full settlement. It means, he allows Rs 40 as discount to him. The journal entries will be:

(i)	Cash A/c	Dr.	3,960	
	To Arvind			3,960
(ii)	Discount A/c	Dr.	40	
	To Arvind			40

A single entry may be passed in place of two entries stated above Cash is a Real Account and, therefore, it should be debited. Discount is a Nominal Account and, therefore, it should also be debited. The account of Arvind is a Personal Account and he is entitled to get a full credit of Rs 4,000 by paying only Rs 3,960. His account should, therefore, be credited by Rs 4,000.

It may be remembered that cash or bank account and discount account go together. It means if cash is debited, the discount account should also be debited. In case the cash is credited, the discount account should also be credited. This is because when cash is received, discount is allowed to debtors. Cash Account is a Real Account and, therefore, it should be debited by the amount of cash actually received. The discount account is a Nominal Account and, therefore, on receipt of cash when discount is allowed, this is a loss which should be debited. Similarly, when cash is paid, discount is earned from the creditors. On payment of cash, therefore, Cash Account should be credited (since cash is a Real Account and it is going out of the business) and Discount Account should be credited (since Discount Account is a Nominal Account and discount received is a gain to the business).

Transaction 10. When goods are withdrawn by the proprietor of the business for his personal use, he is to be charged for them since business and the proprietor are two different persons as per separate entity concept. The problem is at what price should he be charged? He cannot be charged at the selling price for the goods. It will not be fair. He has to be charged with only the cost price of the goods withdrawn by him. It will be, therefore, appropriate to reduce the purchases of the business by the amount of goods withdrawn by the proprietor for his personal use as if the goods were purchased partly for the business and partly for him.

The same rule applies in those cases, where the goods purchased by the business are used for the purpose of business itself. For example in case of a stationery business, some stationery may be used for the business itself. In such case, the following journal entry will be passed:

Stationery Expenses Account	Dr.
To Purchases Account	

The same rule has been followed in case of the last entry given in the illustration.

Transaction 13. In case of this transaction two entries could have been passed as under:

(i)	Amrit		Dr.	4,900
	To Cash A/c			4,900
(ii)	Amrit		Dr.	100
	To Discount A/c			100

In place of passing the above two entries a single compound entry has been passed.

Transaction 14. Three entries could have been based as follows:

(i)	Stationery Expenses A/c		Dr.	200
	To Cash A/c			200
(ii)	Rent A/c		Dr.	500
	To Cash A/c			500
(iii)	Salaries A/c		Dr.	2,000
	To Cash A/c			2,000

In place of these three entries, a single compound entry has been passed.

OPENING ENTRY

In case of a running business, the assets and liabilities appearing in the previous year's balance sheet will have to be brought forward to the current year. This is done by means of a journal entry which is termed as "Opening Entry". All Assets Accounts are debited while all Liabilities Accounts are credited. The excess of assets over liabilities is the proprietor's capital and is credited to his Capital Account. This will be clear with the help of the following illustration:

Illustration 3.5. Pass the Opening Entry on January 1, 1990 on the basis of the following information taken from the business Mr. Sunil:

		Rs
(i)	Cash in Hand	2,000
(ii)	Sundry Debtors	6,000
(iii)	Stock of Goods	4,000
(iv)	Plant	5,000
(v)	Land and Buildings	10,000
(vi)	Sundry Creditors	10,000

Solution:

JOURNAL

Date	Particulars		L.F.	Rs	Rs
1990					
Jan.1	Cash A/c	Dr.		2,000	
	Sundry Debtors A/c	Dr.		6,000	
	Stock A/c	Dr.		4,000	
	Plant A/c	Dr.		5,000	
	Land & Buildings A/c	Dr.		10,000	
	To Sundry Creditors				10,000
	To Capital A/c (balancing figure)				17,000
	(Being balances brought forward from the last year)				
				27,000	27,000

Illustration 3.6. Journalise the following transactions in the books of a trader.

Debit Balance on Jan. 1, 1989:

Cash in hand Rs 8,000, Cash at Bank Rs 25,000 Stock of Goods Rs 20,000, Furniture Rs 2,000, Building Rs 10,000. Sundry Debtors: Vijay Rs 2,000, Anil Rs 1,000, and Madhu Rs 2,000.

Credit Balance on Jan. 1, 1989:

Sundry Creditors: Anand Rs 5,000, Loan from Bablu Rs 10,000.

Following were further transactions in the month of January, 1989:

2. Jan. 1, Purchased goods worth Rs 5,000 for cash less 20% trade discount and 5% cash discount.
3. Jan. 4, Received Rs 1,980 from Vijay and allowed him Rs 20 as discount.
4. Jan. 6, Purchased goods from Bharat Rs 5,000.
5. Jan. 8, Purchased plant from Mukesh for Rs 5,000 and paid Rs 100 as cartage for bringing the plant to the factory and another Rs 200 as installation charges.
6. Jan. 12, Sold goods to Rahim on credit Rs 600.
7. Jan. 15, Rahim became an insolvent and could pay only 50 paise in a rupee.
8. Jan. 18, Sold goods to Ram for cash Rs 1,000.
9. Jan. 20, Paid salary to Ratan Rs 2,000.
10. Jan. 21, Paid Anand Rs 4,800 in full settlement.
11. Jan. 26, Interest received from Madhu Rs 200.
12. Jan. 28, Paid to Bablu interest on loan Rs 500.
13. Jan. 31, Sold Goods for cash Rs 500.
14. Jan. 31, Withdrew goods from business for personal use Rs 200.

Solution:

JOURNAL

Sl. No.	Date	Particulars		L.F.	Debit Rs	Credit Rs
	1989					
1.	Jan. 1	Cash A/c	Dr.		8,000	
		Bank A/c	Dr.		25,000	
		Stock A/c	Dr.		20,000	
		Furniture A/c	Dr.		2,000	
		Buildings A/c	Dr.		10,000	
		Vijay	Dr.		2,000	
		Anil	Dr.		1,000	
		Madhu	Dr.		2,000	
		To Anand				5,000
		To Bablu's Loan A/c				10,000
		To Capital A/c				55,000
		(Being balances brought forward from last year)				
2.	Jan. 1	Purchases A/c	Dr.		4,000	
		To Cash A/c				3,800
		To Discount A/c				200
		(Being purchase of goods for cash worth Rs 5,000, allowed 20% trade discount and 5% cash discount on Rs 4,000)				
3.	Jan. 4	Cash A/c	Dr.		1,980	
		Discount A/c	Dr.		20	
		To Vijay				2,000
		(Being cash received from Vijay, allowed Rs 20 as cash discount)				
4.	Jan. 6	Purchases A/c	Dr.		5,000	
		To Bharat				5,000
		(Being purchases of goods from Bharat)				
5.	Jan. 8	Plant A/c	Dr.		5,300	
		To Mukesh				5,000
		To Cash				300
		(Being purchase of plant for Rs 5,000 and payment of Rs 100 as cartage and Rs 200 as installation charges)				
6.	Jan. 12	Rahim	Dr.		600	
		To Sales A/c				600
		(Being sale of goods to Rahim)				
7.	Jan. 15	Cash A/c	Dr.		300	
		Bad Debts A/c	Dr.		300	
		To Rahim				600
		(Being cash received from Rahim after his being declared as an insolvent. 50% of the amount due has been received and the rest has been taken as a bad debt)				
8.	Jan. 18	Cash A/c	Dr.		1,000	
		To Sales A/c				1,000
		(Being cash sales)				

Contd....

Sl. No.	Date	Particulars	L.F.	Debit Rs	Credit Rs
9.	Jan. 20	Salary A/c .... Dr. To Cash (Being salary paid)		2,000	2,000
10.	Jan. 21	Anand .... Dr. To Cash To Discount (Being cash paid to Anand and he allowed Rs 200 as discount)		5,000	4,800 200
11.	Jan. 26	Cash A/c .... Dr. To Interest (Being receipt of interest)		200	200
12.	Jan. 28	Interest on Loan .... Dr. To Cash (Being payment of interest on loan)		500	500
13.	Jan. 31	Cash A/c .... Dr. To Sales A/c (Being goods sold for cash)		500	500
14.	Jan. 31	Drawings A/c .... Dr. To Purchases A/c (Being goods withdrawn for personal use)		200	200
		Total		96,900	96,900

Illustration 3.7. Journalise the following transactions:

(1) Purchased goods from Mukesh & Co. on credit Rs 10,000.

(2) On obtaining delivery of goods, it was found that the goods have been damaged to the extent of Rs 1,000.

(3) Mukesh & Co. admitted the claim for breakage to the extent of Rs 800.

Solution:

JOURNAL

Sl. No.	Particulars	L.F.	Rs	Rs
1.	Purchases A/c .... Dr. To Mukesh & Co. (Being goods purchased from Mukesh & Co.)		10,000	10,000
2.	Loss in Transit A/c .... Dr. To Purchases A/c (Being damage to the goods purchased in transit)		1,000	1,000
3.	Mukesh & Co. .... Dr. To Loss in Transit (Being claim admitted for loss in transit by Mukesh & Co.)		800	800

Notes:

The entries show that against a loss of Rs 1,000, Mukesh & Co. has admitted a claim of only Rs 800. The loss of Rs 200 will have to be suffered by the proprietor of the business. He will transfer this loss to the Profit & Loss Account at the end of the accounting year:

1.48

	KEY TERMS
☐	**Journal**: A book containing a chronological record of business transactions. It is the book of original records.
☐	**Compound Journal Entry**: A journal entry recording more than one business transaction.
☐	**Nominal Accounts**: These are accounts opened in the books simply to explains the nature of the transaction. They include accounts of all incomes/gains and expenses/losses.
☐	**Opening Journal Entry**: A journal entry passed for bringing forward balances of assets and liabilities of the previous period to the current period.
☐	**Journalising**: The process of recording transactions in the journal.
☐	**Personal Accounts**: These are accounts of persons with whom the business deals.
☐	**Real Accounts**: These are accounts of tangible objects or intangible rights owned by an enterprise and carrying probable future benefits.

TEST QUESTIONS

Objective type   TEST YOUR UNDERSTANDING

1. State under what heading (Personal, Real or Nominal) would you classify each of the following accounts:
   (i) Salary Prepaid Account.
   (ii) Salary Outstanding Account.
   (iii) Rent Account.
   (iv) Bank Account.
   (v) Insurance Unexpired.
   (vi) Proprietor's Account.
   (vii) Bad Debts Account.
   (viii) Furniture Account.
   (ix) Goodwill Account.
   (x) Patents Account.

   [**Ans.** (i) Personal, (ii) Personal, (iii) Nominal, (iv) Personal, (v) Personal, (vi), Personal, (vii) Nominal, (viii) Real, (ix) Real, (x) Real].

2. Select the most appropriate answer:
   (i) The amount brought in by the proprietor in the business should be credited to
      (a) Cash Account.
      (b) Capital Account.
      (c) Drawing Account.
   (ii) The amount of salary paid to Suresh should be debited to
      (a) The account of Suresh.
      (b) Salaries Account.
      (c) Cash Account.
   (iii) The return of goods by a customer should be debited to

    (a) Customer's Account.
    (b) Sales Returns Account.
    (c) Goods Account.
(iv) Sales made to Mahesh for cash should be debited to
    (a) Cash Account.
    (b) Mahesh.
    (c) Sales Account.
 (v) The rent paid to the landlord be credited to
    (a) Landlord's Account.
    (b) Rent Account.
    (c) Cash Account.
(vi) The Cash Discount allowed to a debtor should be credited to
    (a) Discount Account.
    (b) Customer's Account.
    (c) Sales Account.
(vii) In case of a debt becoming bad, the amount should be credited to
    (a) Debtor's Account.
    (b) Bad Debts Account.
    (c) Sales Account.

[**Ans.** (i) (b), (ii) (b), (iii) (b), (iv) (a), (v) (c), (vi) (b), (vii) (a)]

Essay type   FOR REVIEW, DISCUSSION AND PRACTICE

1. Explain the different categories in which the accounting transactions can be classified. Also state the rules of 'debit and credit' in this connection.
2. Explain the meaning of term "Journal" and state its significance.
3. Explain the different rules for journalising the transaction with appropriate illustrations.

PRACTICAL PROBLEMS

1. Enter the following transactions in the journal of Arun for the month of December, 1990.

		Rs
1	Arun commenced his business with a capital of	10,000
1	Bought machinery	300
2	Bought goods for cash from Ram	500
2	Sold goods for cash to Hari	4,000
3	Purchased goods from Jai on credit	2,200
4	Cash sales to Hari	2,000
5	Bought goods from Sunder on credit	1,920
5	Credit sales to Hari	3,200
6	Bought goods from Jai on credit	2,300
8	Bought office furniture for cash from A Ltd.	3,050
12	Paid cartage to Golden Transport Co.	70
15	Paid carriage-outward to Hanuman	20
17	Paid trade expenses	10
18	Paid advertisement expenses to Sunil Agencies	200
19	Received interest from Anil	50
20	Deposited cash into bank	1,000
22	Paid rent	150
27	Paid insurance premium	30
29	Paid salary to Nagendra, a clerk	325

2. Journalise the following transactions:

			Rs
1990			
Jan.	1	Girdhari commenced business with cash	7,500
Jan.	3	Goods purchased for cash	1,000
Jan.	4	Bought of Hari	250
Jan.	8	Furniture purchased from Murari for cash	50
Jan.	9	Furniture purchased from Murari	250
Jan.	12	Cash paid to Hari in full settlement of his account	240
Jan.	15	Goods purchased from Anil and he allowed us 10% trade discount	350
Jan.	20	Cash paid to Anil in full satisfaction	300
Jan.	21	Prince Behari bought from us	115
Jan.	22	Cash paid by Prince Behari	15
Jan.	25	Prince Behari became insolvent, a final composition of 50 P. in the rupee received from his official receiver out of a debt of Rs 100	50
Jan.	26	Paid for Miscellaneous Expenses	25
Jan.	28	Withdrawn by Girdhari for his personal use	100

3. Surendra Commenced business on 1st January, 1987. His transactions for the month are given below. Journalise them.

			Rs
1987			
Jan.	1	Commenced business with a cash capital	20,000
Jan.	2	Paid into Bank	10,000
Jan.	3	Bought goods from Ramesh & Co.	5,000
Jan.	3	Sold goods to Rajesh	4,000
Jan.	7	Bought goods of Ram Chand	6,000
Jan.	8	Paid wages in cash	200
		Sold goods to Mahesh Chand	5,000
Jan.	10	Received cheque from Rajesh (discount allowed Rs 200)	3,800
Jan.	10	Paid into bank	4,000
Jan.	11	Paid to Ramesh & Co. (discount received Rs 200)	4,000
Jan.	12	Paid rent for three months to March	400
Jan.	13	Bought goods from C. Khare	7,400
Jan.	15	Wages paid in cash	80
Jan.	15	Paid office expenses in cash	70
Jan.	16	Sold Goods to Jagdish	3,200
Jan.	17	Sold goods to Rajesh	1,600
Jan.	21	Sold good to Mahesh Chand	2,500
Jan.	21	Payment received by cheque from Jagdish	3,200
Jan.	22	Paid wages in cash	80
Jan.	22	Paid office expenses in cash	50
Jan.	25	Paid Ram Chand by cheque (discount Rs 200)	5,800
Jan.	26	Received cheque from Mahesh (Chand (Discount Rs 200)	4,800
Jan.	27	Mahesh Chand returned goods not up to the sample	200
Jan.	29	Paid wages in cash	80
Jan.	31	Paid office expenses in cash	40
Jan.	31	Paid salaries for the month	300
Jan.	31	Cash used at home	400

4. From the following transactions of M/s Read and Write, write up the Journal in proper form:

1990

Jan. 1 *Assets:* Cash in hand Rs 2,000 Cash at bank Rs 68,000, Stock of goods Rs 40,000, Machinery Rs 1,00,000, Furniture Rs 10,000, M/s Surya Bros. owe Rs 15,000, M/s Balu Bros. owe Rs 25,000.
Liabilities: Loan Rs 50,000, Sum owing to Jain Ltd. Rs 20,000.

			Rs
Jan.	2	Bought goods on credit from Samuel & Co.	10,000
Jan.	3	Sold goods for cash to Dhiraj & Co.	4,000
Jan.	4	Sold goods to Surya Bros. on credit	10,000
Jan.	5	Received from Surya Bros. in full settlement of amount due on Jan. 1	14,500
Jan.	6	Payment made to Jain Bros. Ltd. by cheque	9,750
		they allowed discount	250
Jan.	9	Old furniture sold for cash	1,000
Jan.	10	Bought goods for cash	7,500
Jan.	11	Balu Bros. pay be cheque; Cheque deposited in Bank	25,000
		Paid for repairs to machinery	1,000
Jan.	13	Bought goods of Jain Bros. Ltd.	10,000
		Paid carriage on these goods	500
Jan.	16	Received cheque from Surya Bros., cheque deposited in bank	9,500
		Discount allowed to them	500
Jan.	17	Paid cheque to Jain Bros. Ltd.	10,000
Jan.	18	Bank intimates that cheque of Surya Bros. has been returned unpaid	
Jan.	19	Sold good for cash to Kay Bros.	6,000
Jan.	21	Cash deposited in bank	5,000
Jan.	24	Paid Municipal Taxes in cash	1,000
Jan.	25	Borrowed from Maheshwari Investment Co. Ltd for constructing own premises. Money deposited with bank for the time being	10,000
Jan.	26	Old newspapers sold	200
Jan.	28	Paid for advertisements	1,000
Jan.	31	Paid rent by cheque	1,500
		Paid salaries for the month	3,000
		Drew out of bank for private use	2,500
		Surya Bros. becomes insolvent, a dividend of 50 P. in the rupee is received	
		An old amount, written off as bad debt in 1987 is recovered	1,500

5. The following entries have been passed by a student. You have to state whether these entries are correctly passed. If not so, pass the correct journal entries.

(i)	Cash Account	Dr.	7,000	
	To Interest Account			7,000
	(Being interest paid)			
(ii)	Mohan	Dr.	10,000	
	To Purchases Account			10,000
	(Being purchase of goods from Mohan)			
(iii)	Hari	Dr.	5,000	
	To Sales Account			5,000
	(Being credit sales of goods to Hari)			
(iv)	Mukesh	Dr.	1,000	
	To Bank Account			1,000
	(Being salary paid to Mukesh)			

Contd....

(v)	Freight Account	Dr.	1,000	
	To Cash Account			1,000
	(Being freight paid)			
(vi)	Repairs Account	Dr.	1,000	
	To Cash Account			1,000
	(Being charges paid for overhauling an old machine purchased)			
(vii)	Cash Account	Dr.	200	
	To Rakesh			200
	(Being an amount of debt which was written off as bad debt last year, is received during the year)			
(viii)	Purchases Account	Dr.	1,000	
	To Hari			1,000
	(Being goods Sold to Hari earlier, now returned by him)			

[**Ans.** (*i*) Wrong, reverse should have been done, (*ii*) Wrong, reverse should have been done, (*iii*) Correct, (*iv*) Wrong, Salary Account should have been debited in place of Mukesh, (*v*) Correct, (*vi*) Wrong, Machine Account should have been debited in place of Repairs Account, (*vii*) Wrong, the amount should have been credited to Bad Debts recovered account in place of Rakesh, (*viii*) Wrong, the amount should have been debited to Sales Returns account in place of Purchases Account].

Chapter 4

LEDGER POSTING AND TRIAL BALANCE

LEARNING OBJECTIVES

After stydying this chapter you should be able to:

- ☐ appreicate the role of Ledger in recordinng business transactions;
- ☐ understand the meaning and rules regarding posting;
- ☐ describe the meaning and the objects of preparing a trial balance;
- ☐ make posting and prepare a trial balance; and
- ☐ explain the meaning of certain key terms.

It has already been explained in an earlier chapter that accounting involves recording, classifying and summarising the financial transactions. Recording is done in the Journal. This has already been explained in the preceding chapter. Classifying of the recorded transaction is done in the Ledger. This is being explained in the present chapter.

LEDGER

Ledger is a book which contains various accounts. In other words, Ledger is a set of accounts. It contains all accounts of the business enterprise whether Real, Nominal or Personal. It may be kept in any of the following two forms:

(*i*) Bound Ledger, and (*ii*) Loose Leaf Ledger.

It is common to keep the Ledger in the form of loose-leaf cards these days. This helps in posting transactions particularly when mechanised system of accounting is used.

POSTING

The term "Posting" means transferring the debit and credit items from the Journal to their respective accounts in the Ledger. It should be noted that the éxact names of accounts used in the Journal should be carried to the Ledger. For example, if in the Journal, Expenses Account has been debited, it would not be correct to debit the Office Expenses Account in the Ledger. Though, in the Journal, it might have been indicated clearly in the narration that it is an item of office expenses. The correct course would have been to record the amount to the Office Expenses Account in the Journal as well as in the Ledger.

Posting may be done at any time. However, it should be completed before the financial statements are prepared. It is advisable to keep the more active accounts posted to date. The examples of such accounts are the cash account, personal accounts of various parties ~tc.

The posting may be done by the book-keeper from the Journal to the Ledger by any of the following methods:

- (*i*) He may take a particular side first. For example, he may take the debits first and make the complete postings of all debits from the Journal to the Ledger.
- (*ii*) He may take a particular account and post all debits and credits relating to that account appearing on one particular page of the Journal. He may then take some other accounts and follow the same procedure.
- (*iii*) He may complete postings of each journal entry before proceeding to the next journal entry.

It is advisable to follow the last method. One should post each debit and credit item as it appears in the Journal.

The Ledger Folio (L.F.) column in the Journal is used at the time when debits and credits are posted to the Ledger. The page number of the Ledger on which the posting has been done is mentioned in the L.F. column of the Journal. Similarly a folio column in the Ledger can also be kept where the page from which posting has been done from the Journal may be mentioned. Thus, there are cross references in both the Journal and the Ledger.

A proper index should be maintained in the Ledger giving the names of the accounts and the page numbers.

RELATIONSHIP BETWEEN JOURNAL AND LEDGER

Both Journal and Ledger are the most important books used under Double Entry System of book-keeping. Their relationship can be expressed as follows:

- (*i*) The transactions are recorded first of all in the Journal and then they are posted to the Ledger. Thus, the Journal is the book of first or original entry, while the Ledger is the book of second entry.
- (*ii*) Journal records transactions in a chronological order, while the Ledger records transactions in an analytical order.
- (*iii*) Journal is more reliable as compared to the Ledger since it is the book in which the entry is passed first of all.
- (*iv*) The process of recording transactions is termed as "Journalising" while the process of recording transactions in the Ledger is called as "Posting."

RULES REGARDING POSTING

The following rules should be observed while posting transactions in the Ledger from the Journal:

- (*i*) Separate accounts should be opened in the Ledger for posting transactions relating to different accounts recorded in the Journal. For example, separate accounts may be opened for sales, purchases, sales returns, purchases returns, salaries, rent, cash, etc.
- (*ii*) The concerned account which has been debited in the Journal should also be debited in the Ledger. However, a reference should be made of the other account which has been credited in the Journal. For example, for salaries paid, the salaries account should be debited in the Ledger, but reference should be given of the Cash Account which has been credited in the Journal.
- (*iii*) The concerned account, which has been credited in the Journal should also be credited in the Ledger, but reference should be given of the account, which has

been debited in the Journal. For example, for salaries paid, Cash Account has been credited in the Journal. It will be credited in the Ledger also, but reference will be given of the Salaries Account in the Ledger.

Thus, it may be concluded that while making posting in the Ledger, the concerned account which has been debited or credited in the Journal should also be debited or credited in the Ledger, but reference has to be given of the other account which has been credited or debited in the Journal, as the case may be. This will be clear with the following example:

Suppose salaries of Rs 10,000 have been paid in cash, the following entry will be passed in the Journal:

Salaries Account	(i)		Dr.	10,000
To Cash Account	(ii)			10,000

In the Ledger two accounts will be opened (i) Salaries Account, and (ii) Cash Account. Since Salaries Accounts has been debited in the Journal, it will also be debited in the Ledger. Similarly Cash Account has been credited in the Journal and, therefore, it will also be credited in the Ledger, but reference will be given of the other account involved. Thus, the accounts will appear as follows in the Ledger:

Dr.   SALARIES ACCOUNT   Cr.

	Rs	Particulars	
Cash A/c (ii)	10,000		

Dr.   CASH ACCOUNT   Cr.

Particulars	Rs	Particulars	Rs
		Salaries A/c (i)	10,000

Use of the words "To" and "By"

It is customary to use words 'To and 'By' while making posting in the Ledger. The word 'To' is used with the accounts which appear on the debit side of a Ledger Account. For example in the Salaries Account, instead of writing only "Cash" as shown above, the words "To Cash" will appear on the debit side of the account. Similarly, the word "By" is used with accounts which appear on the credit side of a Ledger Account. For example in the above case, the words "By Salaries A/c" will appear on the credit side of the Cash Account instead of only "Salaries A/c". The words 'To' and 'By' do not have any specific meanings. Modern accountants are, therefore, ignoring the use of these words.

The procedure of posting from the Journal to the Ledger will be clear with the help of the illustrations given in the following pages.

Illustration 4.1. Journalise the following transactions and post them into the Ledger:

1. Ram started business with a capital of Rs 10,000.
2. He purchased furniture for cash Rs 4,000.
3. He purchased goods from Mohan on credit Rs 2,000.
4. He paid cash to Mohan Rs 1,000.

Solution:

JOURNAL

Date	Particulars		L.F.	Debit Rs	Credit Rs
1	Cash Account	Dr.		10,000	
	To Capital Account				10,000 ← 5
2	Furniture Account	Dr.		4,000	
	To Cash Account				4,000 ← 6
3	Purchases Account	Dr.		2,000	
	To Mohan				2,000 ← 7
4	Mohan	Dr.		1,000	
	To Cash Account				1,000 ← 8

Ledger

CASH ACCOUNT

1	To Capital A/c	10,000	By Furniture A/c	4,000 ← 6
			By Mohan	1,000 ← 8

CAPITAL ACCOUNT

			By Cash A/c	10,000 ← 5

FURNITURE ACCOUNT

2	To Cash A/c	4,000		

PURCHASES ACCOUNT

3	To Mohan	2,000		

MOHAN

4	To Cash A/c	1,000	By Purchases A/c	2,000 ← 7

Balancing of an Account

In business, there may be several transactions relating to one particular account. In Journal, these transactions appear on different pages in a chronological order while they appear in a classified form under that particular account in the Ledger. At the end of a period (say a month, a quarter or a year), the businessman will be interested in knowing the position of a particular account. This means, he should total the debits and credits of the account separately and find out the net balance. This technique of finding out the net balance of an account, after considering the totals of both debits and credits appearing in the account is known as 'Balancing the Account'. The balance is put on the side of the account which is smaller and a reference is given that it has been carried forward or carried down (c/f or c/d) to the next period. On the other hand, in the next period a reference is given that the opening balance has been brought the forward or brought down (b/f or b/d) from the previous period. This will be clear with the help of the following illustration.

Illustration 4.2. Journalise the following transactions, post them in the Ledger and balance the accounts on 31st January.

1. Ram started business with a capital of Rs 10,000.
2. He purchased goods from Mohan on credit Rs 2,000.
3. He Paid cash to Mohan Rs 1,000.

4. He sold goods to Suresh Rs 2,000.
5. He received cash from Suresh Rs 3,000.
6. He further purchased goods from Mohan Rs 2,000.
7. He paid cash to Mohan Rs 1,000.
8. He further sold goods to Suresh Rs 2,000.
9. He received cash from Suresh Rs 1,000.

Solution:

JOURNAL

Particulars		L.F.	Debit Amount Rs	Credit Amount Rs
Cash Account	Dr.		10,000	
To Capital Account				10,000
(Being commencement of business)				
Purchases Account	Dr.		2,000	
To Mohan				2,000
(Being purchase of goods on credit)				
Mohan	Dr.		1,000	
To Cash				1,000
(Being payment of cash to Mohan)				
Suresh	Dr.		2,000	
To Sales				2,000
(Being goods sold to Suresh)				
Cash Account	Dr.		3,000	
To Suresh				3,000
(Being cash received from Suresh)				
Purchases Account	Dr.		2,000	
To Mohan				2,000
(Being purchase of goods from Mohan				
Mohan	Dr.		1,000	
To Cash Account				1,000
(Being payment of cash to Mohan)				
Suresh	Dr.		2,000	
To Sales Account				2,000
(Being goods sold to Suresh)				
Cash Account	Dr.		1,000	
To Suresh				1,000
(Being cash received from Suresh)				
Total			24,000	24,000

Ledger

Dr. CASH ACCOUNT **Cr.**

Date	Particulars	Amount Rs	Date	Particulars	Amount Rs
	To Capital A/c	10,000		By Mohan	1,000
	To Suresh	3,000		By Mohan	1,000
	To Suresh	1,000	Jan. 31	By Balance c/d	12,000
		14,000			14,000
Feb. 1	To Balance b/d	12,000			

Dr.		CAPITAL ACCOUNT					Cr.
Date	Particulars	Amount Rs	Date	Particulars			Amount Rs
Jan. 31	To Balance c/d	10,000		By Cash A/c			10,000
		10,000					10,000
			Feb. 1	By Balance b/d			10,000

PURCHASES ACCOUNT

Date	Particulars	Rs	Date	Particulars	Rs
	To Mohan	2,000	Jan.31	By Balance c/d	4,000
	To Mohan	2,000			
		4,000			4,000
Feb.1	To Balance b/d	4,000			

MOHAN

Date	Particulars	Rs	Date	Particulars	Rs
	To Cash	1,000		By Purchases	2,000
	To Cash	1,000		By Purchases	2,000
	To Balance c/d	2,000			
		4,000			4,000
			Feb.1	By Balance b/d	2,000

SURESH

Date	Particulars	Rs	Date	Particulars	Rs
	To Sales	2,000		By Cash A/c	3,000
	To Sales	2,000		By Cash A/c	1,000
		4,000			4,000

SALES ACCOUNT

Date	Particulars	Rs	Date	Particulars	Rs
Jan.31	To Balance c/d	4,000		By Suresh	2,000
				By Suresh	2,000
		4,000			4,000
			Feb.1	By Balance b/d	4,000

It is to be noted the balance of an account is always known by the side which is greater. For example, in the above illustration, the debit side of the Cash Account is greater than the credit side by Rs 12,000. It will be therefore said that Cash Account is showing a debit balance of Rs 12,000. Similarly, the credit side of the Capital Account is greater than debit side by Rs 10,000. It will be, therefore, said that the Capital Account is showing a credit balance of Rs 10,000.

TRIAL BALANCE

In case, the various debit balances and the credit balances of the different accounts are taken down in a statement, the statement so prepared is termed as a 'Trial Balance. In other words, Trial Balance is a statement containing the various ledger balances on a particular date. For example, with the balances of the ledger accounts prepared in Illustration 4.2, the Trial Balance can be prepared as follows:

TRIAL BALANCE

as on 31st January

Particulars	Debit Rs	Credit Rs
Cash Account	12,000	
Capital Account		10,000
Purchases Account	4,000	
Mohan		2,000
Sales Account		4,000
	16,000	16,000

Thus, the two sides of the Trial Balance tally. It means the books of accounts are arithmetically accurate.

Objects of preparing a Trial Balance

1. *Checking of the arithmetical accuracy of the accounting entries.* As indicated above, Trial Balance, helps in knowing the arithmetical accuracy of the accounting entries. This is because according to the dual aspect concept for every debit, there must be an equivalent credit. Trial Balance represents a summary of all ledger balances and, therefore, if the two sides of the Trial Balance tally, it is an indication of this fact that the books of accounts are arithmetically accurate. Of course, there may be certain errors in the books of accounts in spite of an agreed Trial Balance. For example, if a transaction has been completely omitted from the books of accounts, the two sides of the Trial Balance will tally, in spite of the books of accounts being wrong. This has been discussed in detail later in a separate chapter.

2. *Basis for financial statements.* Trial Balance forms the basis for preparing financial statements such as the Income Statement and the Balance Sheet. The Trial Balance represents all transactions relating to different accounts in a summarised form for a particular period. In case, the Trial Balance is not prepared, it will be almost impossible to prepare the financial statements as stated above to know the profit or loss made by the business during a particular period or its financial position on a particular date.

3. *Summarised ledger.* It has already been stated that a Trial Balance contains the ledger balances on a particular date. Thus, the entire ledger is summarised in the form of a Trial Balance. The position of a particular account can be judged simply by looking at the Trial Balance. The Ledger may be seen only when details regarding the accounts are required.

Illustration 4.3. Prepare the Ledger Accounts and the Trial Balance on the basis of transactions given in Illustration 3.6.

Solution:

Dr.   CASH ACCOUNT   Cr.

Date	Particulars	L.F.	Amount Rs	Date	Particulars	L.F.	Amount Rs
1989				1989			
Jan.1	To Balance b/d		8,000	Jan.1	By Purchases A/c		3,800
Jan.4	To Vijay		1,980	Jan.8	By Plant A/c		300
Jan.15	To Rahim		300	Jan.20	By Salary A/c		2,000
Jan.18	To Sales A/c		1,000	Jan.21	By Anand		4,800

Contd....

Date	Particulars	L.F.	Amount Rs	Date	Particulars	L.F.	Amount Rs
Jan.26	To Interest A/c		200	Jan.28	By Interest on Loan A/c		500
Jan.31	To Sales A/c		500	Jan.31	By Balance c/d		580
			11,980				11,980
Feb.1	To Balance b/d		580				

Dr.   INTEREST ACCOUNT   **Cr.**

Date	Particulars	Amount Rs	Date	Particulars	Amount Rs
Jan.31	To Balance c/d	200	Jan.26	By Cash A/c	200
		200			200
			Feb.1	By Balance b/d	200

BANK ACCOUNT

Date	Particulars	Amount Rs	Date	Particulars	Amount Rs
Jan.1	To Balance b/d	25,000	Jan.31	By Balance c/d	25,000
		25,000			25,000
Feb.1	To Balance b/d	25,000			

STOCK ACCOUNT

Date	Particulars	Amount Rs	Date	Particulars	Amount Rs
Jan.1	To Balance b/d	20,000	Jan.31	By Balance c/d	20,000
		20,000			20,000
Feb.1	To Balance b/d	20,000			

FURNITURE ACCOUNT

Date	Particulars	Amount Rs	Date	Particulars	Amount Rs
Jan.1	To Balance b/d	2,000	Jan.31	By Balance c/d	2,000
		2,000			2,000
Feb.1	To Balance b/d	2,000			

BUILDING ACCOUNT

Date	Particulars	Amount Rs	Date	Particulars	Amount Rs
Jan.1	To Balance b/d	10,000	Jan.31	By Balance c/d	10,000
		10,000			10,000
Feb.1	To Balance b/d	10,000			

VIJAY

Date	Particulars	Amount Rs	Date	Particulars	Amount Rs
Jan.1	To Balance b/d	2,000	Jan.4	By Cash A/c	1,980
				By Discount A/c	20
		2,000			2,000

Dr.　　　　　　　　　　　　　　　　　　　　**ANIL**　　　　　　　　　　　　　　　　　　　　**Cr.**

Date	Particulars	Amount Rs	Date	Particulars	Amount Rs
Jan.1	To Balance b/d	1,000	Jan.31	By Balance c/d	1,000
		1,000			1,000
Feb.1	To Balance b/d	1,000			

MADHU

Date	Particulars	Amount Rs	Date	Particulars	Amount Rs
Jan.1	To Balance b/d	2,000	Jan.31	By Balance c/d	2,000
		2,000			2,000
Feb.1	To Balance b/d	2,000			

ANAND

Date	Particulars	Amount Rs	Date	Particulars	Amount Rs
Jan.21	To Cash A/c	4,800	Jan.1	By Balance b/d	5,000
Jan.21	To Discount A/c	200			
		5,000			5,000

CAPITAL ACCOUNT

Date	Particulars	Amount Rs	Date	Particulars	Amount Rs
Jan.31	To Balance c/d	55,000	Jan.1	By Balance b/d	55,000
		55,000			55,000
			Feb.1	By Balance b/d	55,000

BABU'S LOAN ACCOUNT

Date	Particulars	Amount Rs	Date	Particulars	Amount Rs
Jan.31	To Balance c/d	10,000	Jan.1	By Balance b/d	10,000
		10,000			10,000
			Feb.1	By Balance b/d	10,000

PURCHASES ACCOUNT

Date	Particulars	Amount Rs	Date	Particulars	Amount Rs
Jan.1	To Cash A/c	3,800	Jan.31	By Drawings A/c	200
Jan.1	To Discount A/c	200	Jan.31	By Balance c/d	8,800
Jan.6	To Bharat	5,000			
		9,000			9,000
Feb.1	To Balance b/d	8,800			

Dr.   DISCOUNT ACCOUNT   **Dr.**

Date	Particulars	Amount Rs	Date	Particulars	Amount Rs
Jan.4	To Vijay	20	Jan.1	By Purchases A/c	200
Jan.31	To Balance c/d	380	Jan.21	By Anand	200
		400			400
			Feb.1	By Balance b/d	380

BHARAT

Date	Particulars	Amount Rs	Date	Particulars	Amount Rs
Jan.31	To Balance c/d	5,000	Jan.6	By Purchases A/c	5,000
		5,000			5,000
			Feb.1	By Balance b/d	5,000

PLANT ACCOUNT

Date	Particulars	Amount Rs	Date	Particulars	Amount Rs
Jan.8	To Mukesh	5,000	Jan.31	By Balance c/d	5,300
Jan.8	To Cash A/c	300			
		5,300			5,300
Feb.1	To Balance b/d	5,300			

INTEREST ON LOAN ACCOUNT

Date	Particulars	Amount Rs	Date	Particulars	Amount Rs
Jan.28	To Cash A/c	500	Jan.31	By Balance c/d	500
		500			500
Feb.1	To Balance b/d	500			

MUKESH

Date	Particulars	Amount Rs	Date	Particulars	Amount Rs
Jan.31	To Balance c/d	5,000	Jan.8	By Plant A/c	5,000
		5,000			5,000
			Feb.1	By Balance b/d	5,000

SALES ACCOUNT

Date	Particulars	Amount Rs	Date	Particulars	Amount Rs
Jan.31	To Balance c/d	2,100	Jan.21	By Rahim	600
			Jan.18	By Cash A/c	1,000
			Jan.31	By Cash A/c	500
		2,100			2,100
			Feb.1	By Balance b/d	2,100

Dr.   RAHIM   Cr.

Date	Particulars	Amount Rs	Date	Particulars	Amount Rs
Jan.12	To Sales A/c	600	Jan.15	By Cash A/c	300
			Jan.15	By Bad Debts A/c	300
		600			600

BAD DEBTS ACCOUNT

Date	Particulars	Amount Rs	Date	Particulars	Amount Rs
Jan.15	To Rahim	300	Jan.31	By Balance c/d	300
		300			300
Feb.1	To Balance b/d	300			

SALARY ACCOUNT

Date	Particulars	Amount Rs	Date	Particulars	Amount Rs
Jan.20	To Cash A/c	2,000	Jan.31	By Balance b/d	2,000
		2,000			2,000
Feb.1	To Balance b/d	2,000			

DRAWINGS ACCOUNT

Date	Particulars	Amount Rs	Date	Particulars	Amount Rs
Jan.31	To Purchases A/c	200	Jan.31	By Balance c/d	200
		200			200
Feb.1	To Balance b/d	200			

TRIAL BALANCE
(as on 31st January, 1989)

Particulars	Debit Rs	Credit Rs
Cash Account	580	
Interest		200
Bank Account	25,000	
Stock Account	20,000	
Furniture Account	2,000	
Building Account	10,000	
Anil	1,000	
Madhu	2,000	
Capital Account		55,000
Babu's Loan Account		10,000
Purchases Account	8,800	
Discount Account		380
Bharat		5,000
Plant Account	5,300	
Interest on Loan Account	500	
Mukesh		5,000

Contd....

Particulars	Debit Rs	Credit Rs
Sales Account		2,100
Bad Debts Account	300	
Salary Account	2,000	
Drawing Account	200	
	77,680	77,680

VOUCHER SYSTEM

In a small organisation, it is possible for the proprietor to supervise personally all important matters. However, in case of large organisations, delegation of authority is required and therefore, it is necessary to have a proper internal check system for prevention of errors and frauds in recording the transactions and receiving or making final cash payments. The chances of frauds in case of cash payments are all the more. It is almost impossible for the disbursing official to have all information regarding the goods and services in respect of which he is required to make payments. This is because even in case of organisations of moderate size, the responsibility for issuing purchase orders, inspecting commodities received, verifying contractual and arithmetical details of invoices is divided among the employees of the various departments. The disbursing official should have, therefore, assurance of all concerned officials before making payments that the terms of the contract have been complied with and he is paying the exact amount of obligation. This is possible only when all the activities mentioned above are properly coordinated and linked with ultimate issuance of cheques to the creditors. One of the most effective system employed for this purpose is termed as Voucher System.

Voucher System may therefore be defined as "a plan and method of procedure for the verification, recording and payment of all items (other than items to be paid from petty cash) which require the disbursement of cash." As a matter of fact, it is mainly a plan of internal check for all cash disbursement items. There are three basic requirements of Voucher System:

(a) A Voucher is to be prepared for each item of expenditure.

(b) No payment shall be made without a properly verified and authorised voucher.

(c) Development of a proper and efficient system for determining the amount to be paid on each day. This helps the disbursing official in determining the amount to be paid and the management in conveniently and continuously forecasting the amount of the cash required to meet maturing obligations.

The following documents are used in the Voucher System:

1. Vouchers. In general terms, a Voucher means a documentary evidence in support a business transaction. It is a documentary evidence by which the accuracy of an entry made in the books of account can be substantiated. It may be a receipt, a counterfoil of a receipt book, an invoice or even correspondence with the concerned parties. The term Voucher has a narrower meaning when applied to the Voucher System. It is a special form on which is recorded pertinent data about a liability and the particulars of its payments.

Vouchers are generally prepared by the accounting department on the basis of invoices or returns that serves as the evidence of expenditure. This is done after the following comparisons and verifications have been completed and noted on the invoices:

(i) Comparison with the copy of Purchase Order to verify the quantities prices and terms.

(ii) Comparison with the Goods Received Returns to determine the receipt of items recorded in the invoices.

(iii) Verification of the arithmetical accuracy of the Invoices.

After making the above verifications and comparisons, the invoices or other supporting evidence is attached to the voucher and is presented to the concerned official for his final approval.

2. Voucher Register. The Voucher Register is a columnar journal giving the details about the Voucher Nos., and different items of expenses in respect of which payments have to be made. A Proforma of a Voucher Register is given later.

The Vouchers are recorded in a numerical sequence. The credit is given to the accounts payable while debit is given to the account or accounts to be charged for expenditure. On making payment, the date of payment and the no. of cheques are inserted in the appropriate columns in the Voucher Register. The objective of such a recording is to provide ready information about determining the amount of individual unpaid vouchers. The total outstanding liability on account of vouchers unpaid at a particular date can be found out by adding up the individual amount of the unpaid vouchers as shown in the Voucher Register.

3. Unpaid Voucher File. After the Vouchers have been prepared and recorded in the Voucher Register, they are filed in an Unpaid Voucher File. They remain there till they are paid. The amount due on each voucher represents the credit balance of an account payable. Each Voucher in itself is comparable to an individual account in a Creditors' Ledger. Hence, no separate Creditors Ledger is necessary.

4. Cheque Register. The payment of a Voucher is recorded in Cheque Register, the proforma of which is given below:

VOUCHER REGISTER

Date	Payee	Voucher No.	Paid		Credit	Debit					
			Date	Cheque No.	Voucher Payable	Purchases	Wages	Salaries	Office Expenses	Selling Expenses	Sundries
1995					Rs	Rs	Rs	Rs	Rs	Rs	Rs
May 1	Mohan	501	May 5	430	250	250					
May 8	Kishan	502	–	–	300	300					
May 15	David	503	May 20	431	500	–	500				
					1,050	550	500				

CHEQUE REGISTER

Date	Cheque No.	Payee	Voucher No.	Accounts Payable Dr.	Discount Cr.	Bank Cr.
May 5	430	Mohan	501	250	10	240
May 15	431	David	503	500	5	465
				700	15	735

The Cheque Register is a modified form of Cash Payment Journal and it is so called because it is a complete record of all cheques issued. It is customary to record all cheques in a Cheque Register in the order of their sequence to avoid mistake in their recording.

When a Voucher is to be paid, it is removed from the Unpaid Voucher File. On issue of a cheque, the date, the number of cheque and amount are listed on the back of the Voucher. This helps in recording the payments in the Cheque Register. The paid vouchers and the supporting documents are cancelled through a cancelling stamp to prevent their accidental or intentional reuse.

5. Paid Voucher File: After payments, vouchers are generally filed in numerical sequence in Paid Voucher File. They are then readily available for examination by employees or independent auditors who may require information about a specific expenditure. The paid vouchers are finally destroyed in accordance with the firm's policy concerning the retention of records.

6. Vouchers Payable Account: Vouchers Payable Account is similar to Total Creditors Account. It is credited with the total amount payable on account of different vouchers and is debited with the amount of payments made. The balance of the Vouchers Payable account should agree with the total of the Unpaid Vouchers File and also with the sum of unpaid vouchers as shown in the Voucher Register. A proforma of a Vouchers Payable Account is given below:

VOUCHERS PAYABLE ACCOUNT

Date	Particulars	Amount Rs	Date	Particulars	Amount Rs
1986			1986		
May 31	To Cheque Register	735	May 31	By Voucher Register	1,050
	To Discount	15			
	To Balance c/d	300			
		1,050			1,050

Advantages of the Voucher System

The Voucher System offers the following advantages:

(*i*) *Safeguards cash disbursements:* Voucher System provides for a Systematic plan for the verification and approval of all invoices, bills and other items requiring disbursement of cash. Thus, it safeguards all cash disbursements.

(*ii*) *Reduces book-keeping work:* Voucher System considerably reduces the book-keeping work. The voucher itself works as an account of the creditor and total amount due to the creditors can be found out with the help of the Unpaid Vouchers File.

(*iii*) *Recording of all current liabilities:* The Voucher System provides for the immediate recording of all current liabilities. It is generally found in case of firms which do not use Voucher System they fail to record bills for items such services and expenses till such time they are actually paid. As a matter of fact, it is desirable to show all liabilities in the books of the business from the time they are incurred.

(*iv*) *Strengthening of internal check system.* The placing of responsibilities for verification and approvals strengthens the system of internal check.

(*v*) *Planning future cash requirements.* Voucher System provides continuous information for planning the future cash requirements. This enables the management to make maximum use of cash resources. Invoices in respect of which cash discounts are allowed can be paid within the discount period. Other invoices can be paid in accordance with the credit items. This helps in minimising cost and maintaining a favourable credit standard. Moreover, seasonal borrowings for working capital can also be planned more effectively resulting in saving in interest cost.

Limitations of the Voucher System

Voucher System has the following limitations:

(*i*) *Unsuitable for small concerns.* Voucher System is neither suitable nor necessary for small business enterprises particularly those with high degree of proprietary supervision and control.

(*ii*) *Proper personnel and finances required.* Voucher System requires sufficient personnel as well as finances for its successful operation. It will be a cumbersome exercise especially for an enterprise which is not well organised. If an enterprise which uses voucher system does not have sufficient cash and is not in a position to pay the approved vouchers according to schedule, it may develop an unwieldy file of approved unpaid vouchers.

(*iii*) *Fails to provide overall creditor's account position.* The system does not provide for giving an overall position of a creditor's account.

(*iv*) *Difficulties in case of partial payments, returns etc.* The system proves as a hinderance rather than as a help in case of concerns which have many returns of goods and other corrections after approving and recording of purchase invoices. Such concerns have to make many partial payments of approved vouchers. In some cases, they have to defer payments also.

From the above, it may be concluded that Voucher System is suitable only for an enterprise which is well equipped both in respect of personnel and finances. It is not suitable for small concerns. Moreover, suitable modifications may have also to be made in the operation of the system as to meet the specific needs of a particular enterprise.

KEY TERMS

☐ **Ledger:** A book containing different accounts of an entity.

☐ **Posting:** Transferring the debit and credit items from the Journal to the respective accounts in the Ledger.

☐ **Trial Balance:** A statement containing the various ledger balances on particular date.

☐ **Voucher System:** A plan and method of procedure for the verifications, recording and payment of all items (other than items to be paid from petty cash) which require disbursement of cash.

TEST QUESTIONS

Objective type

TEST YOUR UNDERSTANDING

1. State whether each of the following statements is True or False.
- (*a*) The "Posting" is done in the Journal.
- (*b*) Ledger is a set of accounts.
- (*c*) Transactions are recorded first of all in the Ledger.
- (*d*) Journal records transactions in a chronological order.
- (*e*) Ledger records transactions in an analytical order.
- (*f*) While posting transactions in the ledger, if the account is debited in the Journal, it will be credited in the Ledger.
- (*g*) The word "To" is used with the accounts which appear on the Debit side of a ledger account.
- (*h*) Trial Balance helps in knowing the arithmetical accuracy of the accounting entries.

[**Ans.** (*a*) False, (*b*) True, (*c*) False, (*d*) True, (*e*) True, (*f*) False, (*g*) True, (*h*) True].

2. Fill in the blanks:
- (*a*) The process of transferring the debit and credit items from a Journal to their respective accounts in the Ledger is termed as.........
- (*b*) Journal is the book of.........entry, while Ledger is the book of.........entry.
- (*c*) The word "By" is used with an account while making posting on the.........side of an account.
- (*d*) The technique of finding the net balance of an account after considering the totals of both debits and credits appearing in the account is known as.........
- (*e*) The statement containing various ledger balances on a particular date is known as.........
- (*f*) If the two sides of the trial balance tally, it is an indication of the fact that the books of accounts are.........accurate. [**Ans.** (*a*) posting, (*b*) first, second, (*c*) credit, (*d*) balancing of an account, (*e*) trial balance, (*f*) arithmetically].

Essay type   FOR REVIEW, DISCUSSION AND PRACTICE

1. Explain the rules regarding posting of transactions into the Ledger.
2. What is a trial balance? Explain its objectives.

PRACTICAL PROBLEMS

1. Journalise the following transaction and post them into the Ledger.

1990			Rs
Jan.	1	Surendra started business with cash	5,000
Jan.	2	Goods purchased from Prasad on credit	200
Jan.	3	Goods sold to Prem	500
Jan.	4	Good purchased from Sohan for cash	400
Jan.	5	Paid for wages	50
Jan.	15	Goods purchased from Prem	100
Jan.	17	Goods sold to Om	50
Jan.	21	Good purchased from Charanjit	300
Jan.	23	Paid for interest	15
Jan.	24	Goods purchased from Om	200
Jan.	28	Cash received from Prem	100
Jan.	31	Cash paid to Charanjit	300
Jan.	31	Paid for Rent	10

2. Give journal entries of the following posting in the ledger accounts.

(a)   DIVIDENDS

		By Cash	1,500

(b)   INSURANCE

To A	2,000		

(c)   DISCOUNT

To Bank	20		

(d)   RENT

To Cash	1,200		

(e)   PLANT

To Cash	20,000		
To Manohar	40,000		

(f)   SALES

		By Cash	54,000
		By Naresh	37,000

3. Journalise the following transactions and post them into Ledger.

1989

September   1   Started business with Rs 50,000, out of which paid into Bank Rs 20,000.
September   2   Bought furniture for Rs 5,000 and machinery for Rs 10,000.
September   3   Purchased goods for Rs 14,000.
September   6   Sold goods for Rs 8,000.
September   8   Purchased goods from Malhotra & Co. Rs 11,000.

September 10 Paid telephone rent for the year by cheque Rs 500.

September 11 Bought one typewriter for Rs 2,100 from Universal Typewriter Co. on credit.

September 15 Sold goods to Keshav Ram for Rs 12,000.

September 17 Sold goods to Rajesh Kumar for Rs 2,000 for cash.

September 19 Amount withdrawn from bank for personal use Rs 1,500.

September 21 Received cash from Keshav Ram 11,900, discount allowed Rs 100.

September 22 Paid into bank Rs 5,800.

September 23 Bought 50 shares in X Y & Co. Ltd at Rs 60 per share, brokerage paid Rs 20.

September 25 Goods worth Rs 1,000 found defective were returned to Malhotra & Co. and the balance of the amount due to them settled by issuing a cheque in their favour.

September 28 Sold 20 shares of X Y & Co. Ltd at Rs 65 per share, brokerage paid Rs 20.

September 28 Bought goods worth Rs 2,100 from Ramesh and supplied them to Suresh at Rs 3,000.

September 30 Suresh returned goods worth Rs 100, which in turn were sent to Ramesh.

September 30 Issued a cheque for Rs 1,000 in favour of the landlord for rent for September.

September 30 Paid salaries to staff Rs 1,500 and received from travelling salesman Rs 2,000 for goods sold by him, after deducting the travelling expenses Rs 100.

September 30 Paid for: Charity   Rs 101
                        Stationery   Rs 450
                        Postage   Rs 249

4. On 1st January, 1991, the following were the ledger balances of Rajan & Co.:

Cash in hand Rs 900; Cash at bank Rs 21,000; Soni (Cr.) Rs 3,000; Zahir (Dr.) Rs 2,400; Stock Rs 12,000; Prasad (Cr.) Rs 6,000, Sharma (Dr.) Rs 4,500; Lall (Cr.) Rs 2,700; Ascertain Capital.

Transactions during the month were:

			Rs
1989			
Jan.	2	Bought goods of Prasad	2,700
Jan.	3	Sold to Sharma	3,000
Jan.	5	Bought goods of Lall for cash, paid by cheque	3,600
Jan.	7	Took goods for personal use	200
Jan.	13	Received from Zahir in full settlement	2,350
Jan.	17	Paid to Soni in full settlement	2,920
Jan.	22	Paid cash for stationery	50
Jan.	29	Paid to Prasad by cheque	2,650
		Discount allowed by him	50
Jan.	30	Provided interest on capital	100
		Rent due to landlord	200

Journalise the above transactions and post to the ledger and prepare a Trial Balance.

5. Journalise the following transactions, post them in the ledger and prepare a Trial Balance:

January 1, 1990.

Assets: Furniture Rs 5,000; Machinery Rs 10,000; Stock Rs 4,000; Cash in hand Rs 550; Cash at bank Rs 7450; Amount due from Ramesh & Co. Rs 1,000 and amount due from Suresh Rs 2,000.

Liabilities: Amount due to Rama Rs 4,500; Amount due to Ranjeet Rs 2,000; and amount due to Shyam Rs 1,500.

1.70

1990			Rs
Jan.	1	Purchased goods from Ajay	4,500
Jan.	3	Sold goods for cash	1,500
Jan.	5	Paid to Himanshu by cheque	5,500
Jan.	10	Deposited in bank	2,800
Jan.	13	Sold goods on credit to Mukesh	1,700
Jan.	15	Paid for postage	100
Jan.	16	Received cash from Rakesh	2,200
Jan.	17	Paid telephone charges	250
Jan.	18	Cash sales	1,500
Jan.	20	Purchased Govt. Securities	500
Jan.	22	Purchased goods worth Rs 1,600 *less* 20% trade discount and 5% cash discount from Mahesh and Co. for cash and supplied them to Ramesh and Co. at list price *less* 10% trade discount[1]	
Jan.	25	Cash purchases	16,500
Jan.	27	Goods worth Rs 500 were damaged in transit; a claim was made on the railway authorities for the same.[2]	
Jan.	28	Suresh is declared insolvent and a dividend of 50 paise in the rupee is received from him in full settlement	
Jan.	28	Bought a horse for Rs 2,600 and a carriage for Rs 1,200 for delivering goods to customers. Paid by cheque	
Jan.	30	The horse bought on Jan. 29 dies, and the carriage was sold for Rs 1,000	
Jan.	31	Allowed interest on capital @10% p.a. for one month	
Jan.	31	Paid for: Salaries Rs 150, Rent Rs 60	

[Hints

1. Sales price: Rs 1,600 *less* 10% trade discount.

2. *Debit* Loss in Transit Account and *Credit* Purchases Account. One receipt of money from the Railways *Debit* Bank Account *Credit* Loss in Transit Account. Transfer any difference to *P*. and *L*. Account].

Chapter 5

SUB-DIVISION OF JOURNAL

LEARNING OBJECTIVES

After studying this chapter you should be able to

☐ appreciate the importance of sub-division of Journal;

☐ name the different types of Journals;

☐ record transactions in different Journals; and

☐ explain the meaning of certain key terms.

It has already been explained in an earlier chapter that Journal is the book of prime entry. It means all business transactions are to be first recorded in the Journal. However, in a big business recording of all transactions in one Journal will not only be inconvenient but also cause delay in collecting information required. The Journal is, therefore, sub-divided into many subsidiary books. This sub-division results in the following advantages:

(*i*) **Convenience.** As stated above maintenance of one Journal only, will make it quite bulky and difficult to handle. Sub-division or Journal will result in reducing, the size of Journal and making it convenient to handle.

(*ii*) **Division of labour.** Sub-division of Journal helps in division of labour since different persons can write different Journals.

(*iii*) **Classified information.** Each Journal provides information relating to a particular aspect of the business. For example, a Purchases Journal gives information about the total credit purchases may by the business. Similarly a Sales Journal gives information about the total credit sales made by the business. Thus, the business-man gets the information relating to different aspects of the business in a classified form in the shortest possible time.

SUB-DIVISION OF JOURNAL

The sub-division of Journal can be explained with the help of the following chart:

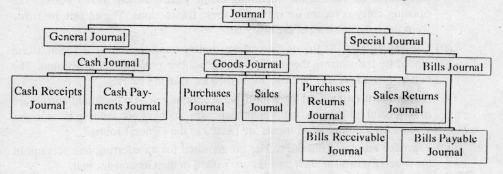

Each of the above types of Journals have been explained in the following pages:

1. **Special Journal.** The term 'Special Journal' means a Journal which is meant for a special purpose. The following are the various types of Special Journals.

   (*i*) **Cash Journal.** Cash Journal is meant for recording all cash transactions. It may be further classified into Cash Receipts Journal and Cash Payments Journal. Cash Receipts Journal records all cash receipts while Cash Payments Journal records all cash payments.

   (*ii*) **Goods Journal.** The Journal is meant for recording all transactions relating to goods. It may, further, be classified into following categories:

   (*a*) *Purchases Journal.* The Journal is meant for recording all credit purchases of goods. Cash purchases are to be recorded in the Cash Journal. Moreover, only purchases of goods is to be recorded in this Journal. The term "goods" means articles purchased for resale.

   (*b*) *Sale Journal.* The Journal is meant for recording all credit sales of goods. Cash sales of the goods are to be recorded in the Cash Journal.

   (*c*) *Purchases Returns Journal.* It is meant for recording all returns of goods purchased on credit. It is also known as Returns Outward Journal.

   (*d*) *Sales Returns Journal.* It is meant for recording all return of goods sold on credit. It is also known as Returns Inward Journal.

   (*iii*) **Bills Journal.** The Journal is meant for recording all bills of exchange or promissory notes received or issued by the business. It can be classified into two categories:

   (*a*) *Bills Payable Journal.* It is meant for recording all bills of exchange or promissory notes received by the business from its debtors.

   (*b*) *Bills Payable Journal.* It is meant for recording all bills of exchange or promissory notes issued by the business in favour of its creditors.

Transactions relating to bills of exchange and promissory notes have been explained later in a separate chapter.

2. **General Journal.** It is also known as Journal Proper. It is meant for recording all such transactions for which no special journal has been kept by the business. As a matter of fact, it is meant for recording such transactions which do not occur frequently in the business and, therefore, do not warrant setting up of special journals. Examples of such transactions are as follows:

   (*i*) **Opening entries.** When a new set of books is started, the old accounts have to be brought forward in the beginning of the year from last year's books. The opening entry is meant for recording these transactions. The entries are made from the balance sheet of the last year.

   (*ii*) **Closing entries.** At the of the end accounting year, the nominal accounts are closed by transferring them to trading account or profit and loss account. The entries passed for this purpose are termed as 'Closing Entries'.

   (*iii*) **Adjustment entries.** At the end of the accounting year, adjustment entries are to be passed for outstanding/prepaid expenses, accrued/outstanding income etc. Entries for all these adjustments are passed in the General Journal.

   (*iv*) **Transfer entries.** Transfer entries are required for transferring one account to the other. Entries for such transfer are passed in the General Journal.

(v) **Rectification entries.** Rectification entries are passed for rectifying the errors which might have been committed in the books of accounts. For example, the account of Mohan might have been debited in place of the account of Sohan. The necessary rectifying entry will be passed in the General Journal.

(vi) **Purchase of fixed assets.** The entries for purchases of fixed assets such as plant, machinery, furniture, etc., on credit are also passed in this Journal.

In the following pages, we are explaining the method of recording business transactions in each Journal and their posting into the ledger.

CASH JOURNAL

Cash Journal or Cash book is meant for recording all cash transactions. It is a very important Journal of business on account of the following reasons:

(i) The number of cash transactions is quite large in every business. The business has to pay for salaries, rent, lighting, insurance, purchase of goods and it has to receive cash for sales of goods and capital assets.

(ii) The chances of fraud being committed regarding cash are higher as compared to other assets. A strict control is, therefore, required. A properly maintained cash book helps in achieving this objective.

(iii) Cash is the nerve centre of the business. Timely payments to its creditors increases the reputation of the business. Similarly timely payments from its debtors improves the financial position of the business.

The cash book can be any of the following types:

(i) Simple Cash book

(ii) Two Columnar Cash Book

(iii) Three Columnar Cash Book

(iv) Multi Columnar Cash Book

(v) Cash Receipts Book

(vi) Cash Payments Book

(i) **Simple (Single Column) Cash Book.** Simple Cash Book is like an ordinary cash account. Its proforma is given below:

Dr.   SIMPLE CASH BOOK   Cr.

Date	Particulars	L.F.	Amount	Date	Particulars	L.F.	Amount

The recording of the transactions in the simple Cash Book and their posting in the Ledger can be understood with the help of the following illustration:

Illustration 5.1. Record the following transactions in the Cash Book and post them in the ledger:

Jan.	1	Opening Cash balance Rs 5,000.
Jan.	4	Rent paid Rs 2,000.
Jan.	6	Interest received Rs 3,000.
Jan.	15	Cash purchases Rs 4,000.
Jan.	25	Cash sales Rs 8,000.
Jan.	31	Salaries paid Rs 2,000.

Solution:

Dr.   CASH BOOK   Cr.

Date	Receipts	L.F.	Amount Rs	Date	Particulars	L.F	Amount Rs
Jan. 1	To Balance b/d		5,000	Jan. 4	By Rents		2,000 ← 1
Jan. 2	To interest ←		3,000	Jan. 15	By Purchases A/c		4,000 ← 2
Jan. 25	To sales ←		8,000	Jan. 31	By Salaries A/c		2,000 ← 3
				Jan. 31	By Balance c/d		8,000
			16,000				16,000
	To Balance b/d		8,000				

Ledger

Dr.   INTEREST ACCOUNT   Cr.

		By Cash A/c	3,000

SALES ACCOUNT

		By Cash A/c	8,000

RENT ACCOUNT

To Cash A/c	2,000	1 ←	

PURCHASES ACCOUNT

To Cash A/c	4,000	2 ←	

SALARIES ACCOUNT

To Cash A/c	2,000	3 ←	

It should be noted that in the ledger no separate cash account will be opened. The Cash Book functions both as a book as well as an account as shown in the illustration above.

(*ii*) **Two (Double) Columnar Book.** Such a Cash Book has two columns: (*i*) Cash Column, and (*ii*) Discount Column. Cash column is meant for recording cash receipts and payments while discount column is meant for recording discount received and the discount allowed. The discount column on the debit side represents the discount allowed while discount column on the credit side represents the discount received.

It should be noted that while the cash column of the cash book serves both the functions of a book as Sell as an account but discount column does not serve the function of a discount account. A separate discount account has to be opened in the ledger in which total debits and credits from the Cash Book are posted. Sometimes, two separate discount accounts are kept in the ledger—one for discount allowed and the other for discount received.

Trade Discount and Cash Discount

The following are the points of distinction between trade discount and cash discount:

(*i*) Trade discount is a deduction granted by a supplier from the list price of the goods due to large quantity of sales or business tradition. While cash discount is allowed by the creditor to the debtor for either buying in cash or for making payment before the stipulated period.

(*ii*) Trade discount is allowed on sale of goods while cash discount is allowed on payment of money.

(*iii*) Trade discount is not recorded in the books of account. The goods are recorded on the net price. While cash discount is shown in the books of account.

(*iv*) Trade discount may vary with the quantity of goods purchased while cash discount may vary with the time period.

The recording of transactions in a two columnar cash book will be clear with the help of the following illustration:

Illustration 5.2. Record the following transactions in the Cash Book and post them in the ledger:

1. Jan. 1 Cash Balance Rs 5,000
2. Jan. 6 sold goods to Mahesh Rs 4,000.
3. Jan 8 Purchased goods from Mukesh Rs 3,000.
4. Jan 15 Cash received from Mahesh Rs 3,900 in full satisfaction.
5. Jan 20 Paid to Mukesh Rs 2,830 in full satisfaction.
6. Jan 25 Sold goods to Suresh Rs 3,000.
7. Jan · 31 Received cash from Suresh Rs 2,900 in full satisfaction.

Solution:

Dr.   CASH BOOK   Cr.

Date	Particulars	L.F.	Discount Rs	Cash Rs	Date	Particulars	L.F.	Discount Rs	Cash Rs
Jan. 1	To Balanced b/d			5,000	Jan. 20	By Mukesh		150	2,800
Jan. 25	To Mahesh		100	3,900	Jan. 31	By Balance c/d			8,950
Jan. 31	To Suresh		100	2,900					
			200	11,800				150	11,800

Ledger

MAHESH

Date	Particulars	Amount Rs	Date	Particulars	Amount Rs
Jan. 6	To Sales A/c	4,000	Jan. 31	By Cash	3,900
			Jan. 15	By Discount A/c	100

SURESH

Date	Particulars	Amount Rs	Date	Particulars	Amount Rs
Jan. 25	To Sales A/c	3,000	Jan. 31	By Cash	2,900
			Jan. 31	By Discount	100

MUKESH

Date	Particulars	Rs	Date	Particulars	Rs
Jan. 6	To Sundries	4,850 150	Jan. 8	By Purchases A/c	3,000

DISCOUNT ALLOWED ACCOUNT

Date	Particulars	Rs	Date	Particulars	
Jan. 6	To Sundries	200	Jan. 8	By Purchases A/c	

DISCOUNT ALLOWED ACCOUNT

Date	Particulars	Rs	Date	Particulars	Rs
			Jan. 31	By Sundries	150

Notes:

1. Transactions 2 and 6 relate to credit sales of goods and, therefore, they have not been recorded in the cash book. They will be recorded in the Sales Book and the posting will be done in the personal accounts of Mahesh and Suresh from there as shown in the Ledger.

2. Transactions 3 relates to credit purchase of goods. It has, therefore, not been recorded in the Cash Book. It will be recorded in the Purchases Book from where posting will be done in the personal account of Mukesh as shown in the Ledger.

3. The total of the debit side of the discount column has been taken to the 'Discount Allowed Account' in the ledger. The word 'sundries' has been put in the 'particulars' column. Any person who is interested in knowing the person to whom the discount has been allowed can find it out from the Cash Book.

4. The total of the discount column appearing on the credit side of the cash book has been taken to 'Discount Received Account' in the ledger. The word 'sundries' has been put in the 'particulars' column. Any person who is interested in knowing the names of the persons from whom the discount has been received can find it out from the cash book.

(iii) **Three Columnar Cash Book.** This type of cash book contains the following three columns on each side:

(i) Cash column for cash received and cash paid.

(ii) Discount column for discount received and discount allowed.

(iii) Bank column for money deposited and money withdrawn from the bank.

The proforma of such a Cash Book is as follows:

Dt.	Particulars	L.F.	Discount	Cash	Bank	Dt.	Particulars	L.F.	Discount	Cash	Bank

The recording of transactions in three-columnar cash book will be clear with the help of the following Illustration.

Illustration 5.3.

Jan.	1	Opening Balance: Cash Rs 3,000.
		Bank Rs 4,000
Jan.	4	Rent paid by cheque Rs 2,000.
Jan.	6	Received on account of cash sales Rs 3,000.
Jan.	8	Paid to Mehta Bros. by cheque Rs 2,000 and earned Rs 200 as cash discount.
Jan.	10	Received from Suresh by cheque Rs 2,000 and allowed him Rs 100 as cash discount.
Jan.	12	Cash sales Rs 20,000.
Jan.	20	Cash purchases Rs 15,000.
Jan.	31	Salaries paid Rs 5,000.

Solution:

CASH BOOK

Dt.	Particulars	L.F.	Dis. Rs	Cash Rs	Bank Rs	Dt.	Particulars	L.F.	Dis. Rs	Cash Rs	Bank Rs
Jan.						Jan.					
1	To Balance b/d			3,000	4,000	6	By Rent A/c				2,000
6	To Sales A/c			3,000		8	By Mehta Bros.		200		2,000
10	To Suresh		100		2,000	20	By Purch. A/c			15,000	
12	To Sales A/c			20,000		31	By Salaries A/c			5,000	
						31	By Balance c/d			6,000	2,000
			100	26,000	6,000				200	26,000	6,000
	To Balance b/d			6,000	2,000						

Ledger

Dr.   SALES ACCOUNT   Cr.

Date	Particular	Amount Rs	Date	Particulars	Amount Rs
		—	Jan. 1	By Cash A/c	3,000
			Jan. 10	By Cash A/c	20,000

SURESH

Date	Particular	Amount Rs	Date	Particulars	Amount Rs
			Jan. 10	By Bank A/c	2,000
				By Discount A/c	100

RENT ACCOUNT

Date	Particular	Amount Rs	Date	Particulars	Amount Rs
Jan. 4	To Bank A/c	2,000			

MEHTA BROS

Date	Particulars	Amount Rs	Date	Particulars	Amount
Jan. 8	To Bank A/c	2,000			
Jan. 8	To Discount A/c	100			

PURCHASES ACCOUNT

Dated	Particulars	Rs	Date	Particulars	Rs
Jan. 20	To Cash A/c	15,000			

SALARIES ACCOUNT

Date	Particulars	Rs	Date	Particulars	Rs
Jan. 31	To Cash A/c	5,000			

DISCOUNT ALLOWED ACCOUNT

Date	Particulars	Rs	Date	Particulars	Rs
Jan. 31	To Sundries A/c	100			

DISCOUNT RECEIVED ACCOUNT

Date	Particulars	Rs	Date	Particulars	Rs
			Jan. 31	By Sundries	200

Contra Entry

As explained above, a three columnar cash book contains columns both for cash and bank transactions. An accounting transaction involves two accounts and there may be a transaction where both Cash Account and Bank Account are involved. Since in the ledger, there are no separate Cash Account and Bank Account, therefore, no posting will be done from the Cash Book to the Ledger in case of such a transaction. The transaction will be recorded on both sides of the Cash Book. For example, if cash is withdrawn from the bank, the two accounts involved are the Cash Account and the Bank, Account. In the Cash Book, on the debit side, the amount will be put in cash column against the words 'To Bank' while on the credit side of the Cash Book, the amount will be written in the bank column against the words By Cash. Such an accounting entry which is recorded on both the debit and credit side of the cash book is known as a Contra Entry. In order to give a hint to the ledger-keeper, that no posting is required for such an entry, the word 'C' is put in the ledger folio column on both the sides of the Cash Book.

Special points regarding cheques. A business may receive cheques from its customers or it can issue cheques in favour of its customers or other creditors. Following are some special points which should be kept in view while making accounting entries in the Cash Book regarding such cheques received or issued.

1. *Receipt of cheques.* There can be two situations:

(a) A cheque may be received by the business and sent to the Bank the same day for collection. In such a case, it will be better to put the cheque received in the debit side of the bank column as soon as it is received. For example, if on January 10, a cheque is received from A for Rs 10,000 and is sent to the Bank for collection on the same day, the entry for receipt of the cheque will appear in the Cash Book as follows:

CASH BOOK (RECEIPTS SIDE)

Date	Particulars	Discount	Cash Rs	Bank Rs
Jan. 10	To A			10,000

(b) In case, a cheque received from a party is sent to the Bank at a later date, it will be better to take the cheque as receipt of cash when it is received and deposit of cash in the bank when the cheque is sent for collection to the Bank. For example, if on January 10, a cheque is received from A for Rs 10,000 and is sent to the Bank for collection on January 14, the entries in the Cash Book will appear as follows:

Dr.   CASH BOOK (CASH AND BANK COLUMNS)   Cr.

Date	Particulars	L.F.	Cash Rs	Bank Rs	Date	Particulars	L.F.	Cash Rs	Bank Rs
Jan. 10	To A		10,000		Jan. 14	By Bank	C	10,000	
Jan. 14	To Cash	C		10,000					

Tutorial Note. In the absence of any specific instructions in the question, the students should presume that the cheque received from a party was sent to the Bank the same day for collection.

2. *Endorsement of cheques received.* A cheque received by the business may not be sent by it to the Bank for collection, but may be endorsed by the business in favour of a creditor of the business. In such a case, the cheque received will be taken as a receipt of cash. Similarly, the cheque endorsed, will be taken as payment of cash. For example if on January 10, a cheque was received from A for Rs 10,000 and it was endorsed on January 14 in favour of B, a creditor of the business, the entries in the Cash Book will appear as follows:

CASH BOOK (CASH COLUMN ONLY)

Date	Particulars	L.F.	Amount Rs	Date	Particulars	L.F.	Amount Rs
Jan. 10	To A		10,000	Jan. 14	By B		10,000

3. *Dishonour of cheques.* The term 'dishonour of cheque' means non-payment of the cheque by the drawee Bank on its being presented for payment. There can be two different situations:

(i) A cheque received by a business and sent to the Bank for collection may be dishonoured on presentation for payment. In such a case, the party from whom the cheque was received should be debited while the account of the Bank should be credited. For example, if a cheque received from 'A' for Rs 10,000 on January 10, is dishonoured by his bankers on presentation for payment on January 14, entries in the Cash Book will appear as follows:

Dr.   CASH BOOK (BANK COLUMN)   Cr.

Date	Particulars	L.F.	Amount Rs	Date	Particulars	L.F.	Amount Rs
Jan. 10	To A		10,000	Jan. 14	By A		10,000

Similarly when a cheque received from a customer and endorsed in favour of a creditor is dishonoured, the entries to be passed in the Cash Book can be well understood on the basis of the following journal entries:

(a) On receipt of cheque
     Cash A/c   Dr.
        To Customer
(b) On endorsement of cheque
     Creditor   Dr.
        To Cash
(c) On dishonour of the cheque
     Customer   Dr.
        To Creditor

Thus, it is clear that no entries will be passed in the Cash Book in the event of dishonour of a cheque received from a customer and endorsed in favour of a creditor. Entries (a) and (b) will be passed through the Cash Book while entry (c) will be passed through the Journal Proper.

(ii) Cheques issued by the business in favour of third parties may be dishonoured by the Bank. In such a case, the entry to be passed in the Cash Book can be understood by passing the following journal entries:

(a) On issue of a cheque in favour of a creditor
     Creditor   Dr.
        To Bank
(b) On dishonour of the cheque issued by the Bank
     Bank   Dr.
        To Creditor

Thus, when the cheque is issued in favour of a creditor, the creditor is debited and the Bank Account, is credited. The entry will appear in the Cash Book on the credit side in the Bank column. On return of the cheque by the creditor on account of its non payment, the Creditor's Account which was previously debited would now be credited while the Bank Account, which was previously credited would now be debited. The entry for dishonour will therefore, appear on the debit side of the Cash Book in the Bank column.

The recording of transactions in a three-columnar cash book and from there posting into the ledger will be clear with the help of the following illustration.

Illustration 5.4. Enter the following transactions in the appropriate type of cash books, and post the same to the relevant ledger accounts:

1990

July 1 Started business with an investment of Rs 9,000.

July 2 Deposited in Bank of India, Rs 7,000.

July 4 Acquired a building by issuing a cheque of Rs 5,000.

July 10 Paid the bill of the furniture by cheque Rs 1,000.

July 15 Purchased Rs 800 of merchandise by cheque.

July 18 Withdrew Rs 100 from the bank.

July 20 Sold merchandise for Rs 1,200.

July 22 Deposited Rs 2,000 into the bank.

July 25 Bought Rs 1,000 merchandise.

July 26 Sold Rs 1,500 merchandise by crossed cheque.

July 27 Paid Rs 100 by cheque as the premium for insuring building against fire.

July 28 Paid freight Rs 50.

July 30 Withdrew from bank for personal use Rs 500.

July 31 Cleared electricity bill Rs 90.

July 31 Paid to Manesh Rs 1,080 in full satisfaction by cheque. We owed to Mahesh Rs 1,100 for goods purchased.

31 Received from Suresh a cheque for Rs 1,480, in full satisfaction of the debt of Rs 1,510.

Solution:

Dr.   CASH BOOK   Cr.

Date	Particulars	L.F.	Dis. Rs	Bank Rs	Cash Rs	Date	Particulars	L.F.	Dis. Rs	Bank Rs	Cash Rs
1990						1990					
Jul. 1	To Capital				9,000	Jul. 2	By Bank	C			7,000
Jul. 2	To Cash	C		7,000		Jul. 4	By Building			5,000	
Jul. 18	To Bank	C			100	Jul. 10	By Furniture			1,000	
Jul. 20	To Sales				1,200	Jul. 15	By Purchases			800	
Jul. 22	To Cash	C		2,000		Jul. 18	By Cash	C		100	
Jul. 26	To Sales			1,500		Jul. 22	By Bank	C			2,000
Jul. 31	To Suresh		30	1,480		Jul. 25	By Purchases				1,000
						Jul. 27	By Insurance Premium			100	
						Jul. 28	By Freight				50
						Jul. 30	By Drawings			500	
						Jul. 31	By Electricity				90
						Jul. 31	By Mahesh		20	1,080	
						Jul. 31	By Bal. c/d			3,400	160
			30	11,980	10,300				20	11,980	10,300
Aug. 1	To Bal. b/d			3,400	160						

Ledger

Dr.   CAPITAL ACCOUNT   Cr.

Date	Particulars	Amount Rs	Date	Particulars	Amount Rs
			July 1	By Cash	9,000

Dr.		BUILDING ACCOUNT				Cr.
July 4	To Bank	5,000				

PURCHASES ACCOUNT

July 15	To Bank	800				
July 25	To Cash	1,000				

FREIGHT ACCOUNT

July 28	To Cash	50				

ELECTRICITY ACCOUNT

July 31	To Cash	90				

SALES ACCOUNT

			July 20	By Cash	1,200
			July 26	By Bank	1,500

FURNITURE ACCOUNT

July 10	To Bank	1,000				

INSURANCE PREMIUM ACCOUNT

July 27	To Bank	100				

DRAWINGS ACCOUNT

July 30	To Bank	500				

DISCOUNT ACCOUNT

July 31	To Sundries	35	July 31	By Sundries	20

Notes:

(*i*) Cash and Bank columns in the cash book serve the purpose of prime as well as final entries. Hence, in the ledger no Cash and Bank Accounts have been opened.

(*ii*) Cash Account never shows a credit balance, since, a person cannot spend more then what he has. While, the Bank Account may show a credit balance, since a bank may permit a customer to overdraw his account (*i.e.*, withdraw more money than what he has in his account). In such a case, it will be said that the customer has an over-draft with the Bank.

(*iii*) Postings to the discount Account is done at the end of the period with Total Discount Received and Total Discount Allowed.

Cash Receipts and Payments Journal. If is common practice these days to keep separate Cash Books for receipts and payments. Thus, the business maintains two Cash Journals:—(*i*) Cash Receipts Journal, and (*ii*) Cash Payments Journal.

Cash Receipts Journal. The Journal is meant for recording all cash receipts. The posting is done daily from the Cash Receipts Book to the Journal. The concerned accounts are all credited with amount mentioned in the Cash Receipts Journal. The total cash received as shown by the Cash Receipts Journal is debited to the Cash Account at the end of a period usually at the end of a week.

Cash Payments Journal. The book is meant for recording all cash payments. The posting is done daily from this book to the ledger and the concerned accounts are debited. At the end of a period (usually at the end of the week), cash account is credited with the total cash paid during the period.

PETTY CASH BOOK

Petty Cash Book is maintained by the business to record petty cash expenses of the business, such as postage, cartage, stationery, cleaning charges etc. In every business, there are many payments like the above which are of small amounts. In case all these transactions are recorded in the Main Cash Book, their recording will not only be inconvenient but also consume a lot of valuable time of the Cashier and the posting clerk. A Petty Cashier is appointed by the business to make payments of all such petty expenses. He works under the supervision of the Chief Cashier, who advances money in the beginning of every month/quarter to meet petty expenses. At the end of the month/quarter, the Petty Cashier submits a statement of account of the expenses incurred by him during the month/quarter and gets a fresh advance.

The Petty Cash Book is usually maintained on the basis of Imprest System. According to this system, a fixed amount is advanced to the Petty Cashier at the beginning of the period by the Chief Cashier. He submits his accounts at the end of the period and the Chief Cashier after examining his accounts gives him a fresh advance equivalent to the amount spent by him, during the period. Thus, in the beginning of the each period (month or quarter as the case may be), the Petty Cashier has a fixed balance. The amount so advanced to him is termed as "Imprest" or "Float".

The recording of transactions in a Petty Cash Book will be clear with the help of the following Illustration.

Illustration 5.5. Enter the following transactions in the Petty Cash Book (maintained on Imprest system) for the months of January, 1990:

Jan. 1 Cash Received from the Chief Cashier Rs 200.
Jan. 3 Typing paper Rs 8
Jan. 6 Office cleaning Rs 4.
Jan. 8 Postage Rs 2
Jan. 10 Cartage Rs 2.
Jan. 15 Postage Rs 6.
Jan. 18 Ink Rs 3, Typing paper Rs 10.
Jan. 20 Typewriter ribbon Rs 10.
Jan. 22 Telephone charges Rs 7.
Jan. 24 Office cleaning Rs 2.
Jan. 25 Nails' polish Rs 27.
Jan. 27 Telegrams Rs 25.
Jan. 29 Typing paper Rs 30.

(For Solution please see page 1.83.)

Postings from the Petty Cash Book. Postings in the Ledger from the Petty Cash Book is done at the end of the period, *i.e.*, month or quarter as the case may be. There are two alternative ways of making postings from the Petty Cash Book.

   1. *Petty Cash Book maintained as a Memorandum Book only.* In such a case, the total of the various expenses from the Petty Cash Book is debited, to the concerned accounts at the end of the period and credit is given to the Cash Account with the

(Contd. on page 1.84.)

Solution:

PETTY CASH BOOK

Receipts				Date	Particulars	Voucher Nos.	Stationery Rs	Postal charges etc. Rs	Cartage Rs	Cleaning	Miscellaneous Rs	Total Rs
Date	Particulars	Cash Book Folio	Total Rs									
1990 Jan.1	To Cash from Chief Cashier		200	3	Typing paper, postage	1, 2	8	4				12
				6	Office cleaning	3				4		4
				8	Postage, office cleaning	4, 5		2		2		4
				10	Cartage	6			2			2
				15	Postage	7		6				6
				18	Ink, typing paper	8, 9	13					13
				20	Typewriter ribbon	10	10					10
				22	Telephone charges	11		7				7
				24	Cleaning	12				2		2
				25	Nails Polish	13					27	27
				27	Telegrams	14		25				25
				29	Typing paper	15	30					30
			200				61	44	2	8	27	142
Feb.1	To Balance b/d		58		Balance c/d		2	3	4	5	6	58
Feb.1	To Cash from Chief Cashier		142									200

Note: Voucher nos., Ledger Folio nos. are imaginary.

actual expenditure incurred. The amount advanced by the Chief Cashier to the Petty Cashier is recorded by him as a memorandum by way of a note in the Cash Book itself. This method is usually not followed.

2. *Where Petty Cash Book is taken as a part of the Double Entry System.* This method is quite popular. The recording is done regarding the petty cash transactions on the basis of the following entries:

(*i*) When money is advanced to the Petty Cashier:

Petty Cash Account   Dr.
    To Cash Account
(The Petty Cash Account is debited with the actual
amount of money advanced).

(*ii*) On submission of accounts by the Petty Cashier:

Expenses Accounts   Dr.
    To Petty Cash Account
(Each expense is to be debited separately with the
expenditure incurred during the period as shown by the
Petty Cash Book).

Thus, in the Ledger, there is a Petty Cash Account as well as separate Expenses Accounts for each of the expenses.

Taking the figures as given in the preceding illustration, the various ledger accounts according to the second method will appear as follows:

Dr.   PETTY CASH ACCOUNT   Cr.

Date	Particulars	Amount	Date	Particulars	Amount
Jan.1	To Cash	200	Jan.3	By Stationery	61
				By Postal Charges	44
				By Cartage	2
				By Cleaning	8
				By Miscellaneous	27
				By Balance c/d	58
		200			200
Feb.1	To Balance b/d	58			

STATIONERY ACCOUNT

Jan.31	To Petty Cash A/c	61			

POSTAL CHARGES ACCOUNT

Jan.31	To Petty Cash A/c	71			

CARTAGE ACCOUNT

Jan.31	To Petty Cash A/c	2			

CLEANING ACCOUNT

Jan.31	To Petty Cash A/c	8			

MISCELLANEOUS ACCOUNT

Jan.31	To Petty Cash A/c	27			

PURCHASES JOURNAL

The Purchases Journal is meant for recording credit purchases of goods. It is also known as the Purchases or Bought Day Book. It has columns for date of purchase, invoice number, name of the party, ledger folio and the amount of purchases. It should be noted that the book records only purchase of good on credit. Purchases of items other than goods on credit is recorded in the General Journal. Similarly, cash purchases are recorded in the cash book.

Posting. The posting is done in the the Personal Accounts daily from the Purchases Book. At the end of a week/month, the total of the Purchases Book is debited to the Purchases Account in the ledger.

The following illustration will make clear the recording of transactions in the Purchases Journal and their subsequent posting in the ledger.

Illustration 5.6. Record following transactions in the Purchases Journal and post them in the Ledger.

```
1992
Jan.    1  Purchased from Ram & Co. on credit:
              38 Immersion Heaters  @ Rs 10.
              20 Philips Tubelights  @ Rs 20.
Jan.    4  Purchased from Shyam & Co. on credit:
              40 Immerson Heaters  @ Rs 10.
              20 E.C.E. Tubelights  @ Rs 15.
Jan.    8  Purchased from Bajaj & Co. on credit:
              20 Electric Irons      @ Rs 40.
              3 Electric Mixers      @ Rs 100.
Jan.   24  Purchased from K.C. & Co. on credit:
              30 Electric Kettles    @ Rs 20.
              40 Table Fans          @ Rs 200.
```

Solution:

PURCHASES JOURNAL

Date	Invoice No.	Particulars	L.F.	Amount Rs	Amount Rs
1992					
Jan. 1	50	Ram & Co.:	4		
		30 Immersion Heater @ Rs 10		300	
		20 Phillips Tubelights @ Rs 20		400	700
Jan. 4	55	Shyam & Co.:	8		
		40 Immersion Heater @ Rs 10		400	
		20 E.C.E., Tubelights @ Rs 15		300	700
Jan. 8	62	Bajaj & Co.:	12		
		20 Electric Irons @ Rs 40		800	
		3 Electric Mixers @ Rs 100		300	1,100
Jan. 24	65	K.C. & Co.:	13		
		30 Electric Kettles @ Rs 20		600	
		40 Table Fans @ Rs 200		8,000	8,600
Jan. 31		Purchases Account Dr.	14		11,100

Ledger

RAM & CO. *(Folio 4)*

Date	Particulars	Amount	Date	Particulars	Amount
			Jan.1	By Purchases	700

SHYAM & CO. *(Folio 8)*

			Jan.4	By Purchases	700

BAJAJ & CO. *(Folio 12)*

			Jan.8	By Purchases	1,100

K.C. & CO. *(Folio 13)*

			Jan.24	By Purchases	8,000

PURCHASES ACCOUNT *(Folio 14)*

Jan.31	To Sundries	11,100			

Notes:

(*i*) Folio Nos. are all imaginary.

(*ii*) Purchases Account has been debited with the total purchases made during the month. This has been done at the end of the month. A firm may make the posting in the Purchase Account weekly also.

(*iii*) Posting is done in the Personal Accounts daily.

SALES JOURNAL

The Journal is meant for recording all sales of goods on credit. This is also known as Sales of Sold Day Book. It should be noted that Cash Sales are recorded in the Cash Book while sales of articles other than goods on credit is to be recorded in the General Journal.

Posting is done is the Personal Accounts daily from the Sales Book. They are debited with individual amounts. The Sales Account is credited with the total sales made during the period (*i.e.* a week or month) at the end of the period.

The recording of the transactions in the Sales Book and their posting in the Ledger will be clear with the help of the following illustration.

Illustration 5.7. Record the following transactions in the Sales Day Book and post them into the Ledger.

```
1992
Jan.    1  Sold to Mukesh & Co:
              10 Electric Heaters        @          Rs  20.
              10 Table Lamps             @          Rs  30.
Jan.   10  Sold to Suresh & Brothers:
              10 Table Fans              @          Rs 250.
              20 Philips Tubelights      @          Rs  30.
Jan.   25  Sold to Ramesh & Co.:
              10 Electric Kettles        @          Rs  50.
              20 E.C.E. Tubelights       @          Rs  30.
```

Solution:

SALES JOURNAL

Date	Invoice No.	Particulars	L.F.	Amount Rs	Amount Rs
1992					
Jan. 1	101	Mukesh & Co.:	4		
		10 Electric Heaters @ Rs 20		200	
		10 Table Lamps @ Rs 30		300	500
Jan. 10	102	Suresh & Brothers:	6		
		10 Table Fans @ Rs 250		2,500	
		20 Philips Tubelights @ Rs 30		600	3,100
Jan. 25	103	Ramesh & Co.:	8		
		10 Electric Kettles @ Rs 50		500	
		20 E.C.E. Tubelights @ Rs 30		600	1,100
		Sales A/c Cr.	10		4,700

Ledger

MUKESH & CO. *(Folio 4)*

Date	Particulars	Amount Rs	Date	Particulars	Amount Rs
Jan.1	To Sales	500			

SURESH & BROTHERS *(Folio 6)*

Date	Particulars	Amount Rs	Date	Particulars	Amount Rs
Jan.10	To Sales	3,100			

RAMESH & CO. *(Folio 8)*

Date	Particulars	Amount Rs	Date	Particulars	Amount Rs
Jan.25	To Sales	1,100			

SALES ACCOUNT *(Folio 10)*

Date	Particulars	Amount	Date	Particulars	Amount Rs
			Jan.31	By Sundries	4,700

Notes:

(*i*) Folio Nos., Invoice Nos. are all imaginary.

(*ii*) Posting is done is the Personal Accounts daily. The total sales are posted at the end of the month (or week) on the credit side of the Sales Account, against the word 'Sundries'. Any person interested in finding out the names of the parties to whom the sales have been made can do so by looking to the Sales Book.

SALES RETURNS JOURNAL

The Journal is meant for recording return of goods sold on credit. The goods which are sold for cash, if returned, are either exchanged for new goods or the parties are paid in respect of them depending upon the circumstances. In case the goods returned are not immediately exchanged for the other goods or not paid for in cash, they are recorded in a memorandum book only. Thus, goods sold for cash and returned do not find a place in the Sales Returns Journal. They are recorded in the Cash Book in the case cash is paid for them or no entry will be passed in case they have been recorded in a memorandum book only. A proforma of Sales Returns Journal is as under:

SALES RETURNS JOURNAL

Date	Credit Note No.	Particulars	L.F.	Amount Rs	Amount Rs
Jan. 10	202	Ram & Co.			
		5 Electric Heaters @ Rs 20		100	
		3 Philips Tubelights @ Rs 30.		90	190
		Sales Returns A/c Dr.			190

The posting from the Sales Returns Journal will be done daily in the personal accounts. For example, in the above case, the account of Ram & Co. will be credited with a sum of Rs 190 on Jan. 10. The total of the Sales Returns Journal will be posted to the debit of Sales Returns Account at the end of the period say a week or month.

Credit Note. The customer who returns the goods, gets credit for the value of the goods returned. A Credit Note is sent to him intimating that his account has been credited with the value of the goods returned. The Note is prepared in duplicate. Its Proforma is as under:

MAHESHWARI BROTHERS
3, Strand Road, CALCUTTA
No. 202   Date Jan. 10, 1992
To
  Ram & Co.,
  21, Shri Ram Road, Delhi.
  We have credited your account in respect of the following goods returned by you:
                                                                          Rs   Rs
  (i) 5 Electric Heaters @Rs 20   100
  (ii) 3 Philips Tubelights @ Rs 30   90   190
                                                           For Maheshwari Brothers
                                                                              Sunil
                                                                            Manager

PURCHASES RETURNS JOURNAL

The book is meant for recording return of goods purchased on credit. The goods purchased for cash and returned are not recorded in this book. They are recorded in a memorandum book only. On receipt of cash in respect of the goods returned, the entry will be passed through cash book. In case, the goods are exchanged for other goods of the same value, no entry will be required. The entry in the memorandum book will be cancelled on getting cash or goods for goods returned. A proforma of the Purchases Returns Journal is given below:

PURCHASES RETURNS JOURNAL

Date	Debit Note No.	Particulars	L.F.	Amount Rs	Amount Rs
Jan. 12	301	Shyam & Co.			
		3 Electric Irons @ Rs 40			120
Jan. 21	302	Bajaj & Co.			
		3 Electric Mixers @ Rs 300			900
		Purchases Returns A/c Cr.			1,020

Note. The entries in the Personal Accounts are done daily from the Purchases Returns Book. They are debited with the respective amounts. The total of the Purchases Returns Book is posted to the credit of Purchases Returns Account at the end of the period say a week or a month as the case may be.

Debit Note. When the goods are returned to the supplier, a debit note is sent to him indicating that his account has been debited with the amount mentioned in the Debit Note. Its proforma is given as under:

MAHESHWARI BROTHERS
3, Strand Road CALCUTTA

No. 301   Date Jan. 12, 1992

To

   Shyam & Co.

   3, Clive Road, Calcutta.

Dear Sir,

   We have debited your account for the goods returned by us as under:

   4 Electric Irons @Rs 30   Rs 120

For Maheshwari Brothers
Sunil
Manager

Thus, in case of purchases returns or sales returns of goods, the flow of *Debit Note or Credit Note* can be put as follows:

(*i*) The **Debit Note** is sent by the Purchaser of goods to the Seller of goods on return of goods by the Purchaser to the Seller.

(*ii*) The **Credit Note** is sent by the Seller of goods to the Purchaser of goods on return of goods to the Seller by the Purchaser.

A comprehensive illustration is given below for explaining the recording of transactions in the various Journals, their posting into the Ledger and finally preparation of the Trial Balance.

Illustration 5.8. Record the following transactions in various subsidiary books and post them into Ledger and prepare a Trial Balance:

1990

June	1	Cash in hand, Rs 15,700, Cash at bank Rs 25,400 and Capital Account Rs 41,100.
June	3	Bought goods for cash Rs 4,100.
June	4	Purchased goods from Mahesh & Co. For Rs 5,800 *less* 10% trade discount.
June	7	Sold goods to Bindia & Co. for Rs 8,900 less 20% trade discount.
June	9	Withdrew Rs 500 from bank for private use.
June	12	Sold goods to Amjad for Rs 6,400.
June	15	Rs 5,000 paid to Mahesh & Co. in full settlement of their account.
June	18	Goods worth Rs 400 returned by Amjad.
June	20	Received Rs 4,000 from Amjad.
June	21	Purchased goods from Shiv & Co. for Rs 8,700.
June	23	Rs 6,000 paid to Shiv & Co. by cheque; discount allowed Rs 300.
June	24	Purchased furniture for Rs 800 from Surjeet Furniture House on credit.
June	26	Paid into bank Rs 2,200.
June	28	Amjad declared insolvent; a first and final dividend of 50 paise in a rupee is received from him.
June	29	Goods worth Rs 600 returned to Shiv & Co.
June	30	Interest on capital provided Rs 411.

June 30 Goods worth Rs 400 taken by the proprietor for his personal use.
June 30 Paid Rs 500 for advertisement by cheque.
June 30 Paid salaries to staff, Rs 1,800.
June 30 Cash sales Rs 21,800.
June 30 Paid into bank Rs 20,000.
June 30 Bought 100 shares in Hind Mills Ltd. at Rs 11 per share brokerage paid Rs 25.
June 30 Received Rs 5,900 from Bindia & Co.; discount allowed Rs 100.

Solution:

JOURNAL PROPER

Date	Particulars	L.F.	Debit Amount Rs	Credit Amount Rs
1990 June 24	Furniture Account Dr. To Surjeet Furniture House (Being furniture purchased on credit)		800	800
June 28	Bad Debts Account Dr. To Amjad (Being 50% amount due written off as bad debt on Amjad becoming insolvent)		1,000	1,000
June 30	Interest on Capital Account Dr. To Capital Account (Being interest on capital provided)		411	411
June 30	Drawings Account Dr. To Purchases Account (Being goods taken for personal use of the proprietor)		400	400
June 30	Capital Account Dr. To Drawings Account (Being transfer of balance of Drawings Account)		900	900
			3,511	3,511

SALES BOOK

Date	Particulars	L.F.	Amount Rs	Amount Rs
1990 June 7	Bindia and Co.: Goods sold Less: 20% Trade Discount		8,900 1,780	7,120
June 12	Amjad			6,400
June 30	Sales Account Cr.			13,520

PURCHASES BOOK

Date	Particulars	L.F.	Amount Rs	Amount Rs
1990 June 4	Mahesh & Co.: Goods Purchased Less: 10% Trade Discount		5,800 580	5,220
June 21	Shiv and C.			8,700
June 30	Purchases Account Dr.			13,920

SALES RETURNS BOOK

Date	Particulars	L.F.	Amount Rs	Amount Rs
1990 June 28	Amjad			400
June 30	Sales Returns Account Dr.			400

PURCHASES RETURNS BOOK

Date	Particulars	L.F.	Rs	Rs
1990 June 29	Shiv and Co.			600
June 30	Purchases Returns Account Cr.			600

Ledger

Dr.   CAPITAL ACCOUNT   Cr.

Date	Particulars	Rs	Date	Particulars	Rs
1990 June 30	To Drawings A/c	900	June 1	By Balance b/d	41,100
June 30	To Balance c/d	40,611	June 30	By Interest on Capital	411
		41,511			41,511
			July 1	By Balance c/d	40,611

FURNITURE ACCOUNT

Date	Particulars	Rs	Date	Particulars	Rs
June 24	To Surjeet Furniture House	800	June 30	By Balance c/d	800
		800			800
July 1.	To Balance b/d	800			

SURJEET FURNITURE HOUSE

Date	Particulars	Rs	Date	Particulars	Rs
June 30	To Balance c/d	800	June 24	By Furniture A/c	800
		800			800
			July 1	By Balance b/d	800

BAD DEBTS ACCOUNTS

Date	Particulars	Rs	Date	Particulars	Rs
June 28	To Amjad	1,000	June 30	By Balance c/d	1,000
		1,000			1,000
July 1	To Balance b/d	1,000			

AMJAD

Date	Particulars	Rs	Date	Particulars	Rs
June 12	To Sales A/c	6,400	June 18	By Sales Returns A/c	400
			June 20	By Cash A/c	4,000
			June 28	By Cash A/c	1,000
			June 28	By Bad Debts	1,000
		6,400			6,400

THREE COLUMNAR CASH BOOK

Dr.								Cr.				
Date	Particulars	L.F	Discount Rs	Cash Rs	Bank Rs		Date	Particulars	L.F.	Discount Rs	Cash Rs	Bank Rs
1990							1990					
June 1	To Balance b/d			15,700	25,400		June 3	By Purchases A/c			4,100	
June 20	To Amjad	C		4,000			June 9	By Drawings A/c				500
June 26	To Cash	C			2,200		June 15	By Mahesh & Co.		220	5,000	
June 28	To Amjad			1,000			June 23	By Shiv & Co.		300		6,000
June 30	To Sales A/c			21,800			June 26	By Bank	C		2,200	
June 30	To Cash	C			20,000		June 30	By Advertisement A/c				500
June 30	To Bindia and Co.		100	5,900			June 30	By Salaries A/c	C		1,800	
							June 30	By Bank			20,000	
							June 30	By Investment in Shares A/c			1,125	
							June 30	By Balance c/d			14,175	40,600
			100	48,400	47,500					520	48,400	47,600
July 1	To Balance b/d			14,175	40,600							

Dr. INTEREST ON CAPITAL ACCOUNT **Cr.**

Date	Particulars	Rs	Date	Particulars	Rs
June 3	To Capital A/c	411	June 30	By Balance c/d	411
		411			411
July 1	To Balance b/d	411			

DRAWING ACCOUNT

Date	Particulars	Rs	Date	Particulars	Rs
June 9	To Bank A/c	500	June 30	By Capital A/c	900
June 30	To Purchases A/c	400			
		900			900

PURCHASES ACCOUNT

		Rs			Rs
June 4	To Cash A/c	4,100	June 30	By Drawings	400
June 30	To Sundries (as per		June 30	By Balance c/d	17,620
	Purchases Book)	13,920			
		18,020			18,020
July 1	To Balance b/d	17,620			

BINDIA & CO.

Date	Particulars	Rs	Date	Particulars	Rs
June 7	To Sales A/c	7,120	June 30	By Cash A/c	5,900
			June 30	By Discount A/c	100
			June 30	By Balance c/d	1,120
		7,120			7,120
July 1	To Balance b/d	1,120			

SALES ACCOUNT

Date	Particulars	Rs	Date	Particulars	Rs
June 30	To Balance c/d	35,320	June 30	By Sundries (amount as per Sales Book)	13,520
			June 30	By Cash A/c	21,800
		35,320			35,320
			July 1	By Balance c/d	35,320

MAHESH & CO.

Date	Particulars	Rs	Date	Particulars	Rs
June 15	To Cash A/c	5,000	June 1	By Purchases A/c	5,220
June 15	To Discount A/c	220			
		5,220			5,220

SHIV & CO.

Date	Particulars	Rs	Date	Particulars	Rs
June 23	To Bank A/c	6,000	June 21	By Purchases A/c	8,700
June 23	To Discount A/c	300			

Contd....

Date	Particulars	Rs	Date	Particulars	Rs
June 29	To Purchases Returns A/c	600			
June 30	To Balance c/d	1,800			
		8,700			8,700
			July 1	By Balance b/d	1,800

Dr. **SALES RETURNS ACCOUNT** **Cr.**

Date	Particulars	Rs	Date	Particulars	Rs
June 30	To Sundries (amount as per Returns Book)	400	June 30	By Balance c/d	400
		400			400
July 1	To Balance b/d	400			

PURCHASES RETURNS ACCOUNT

Date	Particulars	Rs	Date	Particulars	Rs
June 30	To Balance c/d	600	June 30	By Sundries (amount as per Purchases Returns Book)	600
		600			600
			July 1	By Balance b/d	600

ADVERTISEMENT ACCOUNT

Date	Particulars	Rs	Date	Particulars	Rs
June 30	To Bank A/c	500	June 30	By Balance c/d	500
		500			500
July 1	To Balance b/d	500			

SALARIES ACCOUNT

Date	Particulars	Rs	Date	Particulars	Rs
June 30	To Cash A/c	1,800	June 30	By Balance c/d	1,800
		1,800			1,800
July 1	To Balance b/d	1,800			

INVESTMENT IN SHARES ACCOUNT

Date	Particulars	Rs	Date	Particulars	Rs
June 30	To Cash A/c	1,125	June 30	By Balance c/d	1,125
		1,125			1,125
July 1	To Balance b/d	1,125			

DISCOUNT ACCOUNT

Date	Particulars	Rs	Date	Particulars	Rs
June 30	To Sundries (Amount as per Cash Book)	100	June 30	By Sundries (Amount as per Cash Book)	520
June 30	To Balance c/d	420			
		520			520
			July 1	By Balance b/d	420

TRIAL BALANCE
as at June 30, 1990

Sl. No.	Name of the Account	L.F.	Debit Balance	Credit Balance
1.	Capital Account			40,611
2.	Furniture Account		800	
3.	Surjeet Furniture House			800
4.	Bad Debts Account		1,000	
5.	Interest on Capital Account		411	
6.	Purchases Account		17,620	
7.	Bindia and Co.		1,120	
8.	Sales Account			35,320
9.	Shiv and Co.			1,800
10.	Sales Returns Account		400	
11.	Purchases Returns Account			600
12.	Advertisement Account		500	
13.	Salaries Account		1,800	
14.	Investment in Shares Account		1,125	
15.	Discount Account			420
16.	Cash in hand (as per Cash Book)		14,175	
17.	Cash at Bank (as per Cash Book)		40,600	
			79,551	79,551

KEY TERMS

☐ **Cash Journal**: A journal meant for recording all cash transactions.

☐ **Contra Entry**: An accounting entry which is recorded on both the debit and credit sides of the Cash Book.

☐ **Bills Journal**: A journal meant for recording all transactions relating to bills of exchange or Promissory Notes received or issued by the business.

☐ **General Journal**: A journal meant for recording all such transactions for which no special journal has been kept by the business.

☐ **Goods Journal**: A journal meant for recording all credit transactions relating to goods.

☐ **Imprest**: The amount advanced to the petty cashier in the beginning of a period. It is also termed as float.

☐ **Petty Cash Book**: A book meant for recording all petty cash expenses of the business.

☐ **Special Journal**: A journal meant for recording transactions of a specific type.

TEST QUESTIONS

Objective type ┌─ TEST YOUR UNDERSTANDING ─┐

1. State whether each of the following statements is 'True' or 'False'.
   (a) Purchase Journal is meant for recording all purchases of goods.
   (b) Posting is done in the personal accounts from the Purchases Book daily.
   (c) Sales Journal is meant for recording all cash sales of goods.
   (d) Sales Returns Journal is also known as Returns Inward Journal.
   (e) Purchases Returns Journal is meant for recording all returns of goods purchased.
   (f) Credit Note is sent to a customer when goods sold are returned by him.
   (g) Debit Note is sent to the supplier of the goods when the goods are returned.
   (h) Office equipment purchased on credit will be recorded in the Purchases Book.

   [**Ans.** (a) False, (b) True, (c) False, (d) True, (e) False, (f) True, (g) True, (h) False.]

2. Fill in the blanks:
   (a) Purchases Journal records only.........purchase of goods.
   (b) Sales Journal records all.........sales of goods.
   (c) A.........is sent to a customer when he returns the goods.
   (d) When the goods are returned to the supplier a.........is sent to him.
   (e) .... give item-wise information about the goods purchased, sold or returned during a particular period.
   (f) Total purchases are posted to the.........at the end of a week or a month.
   (g) Goods Outward Journal is meant for recording all returns of goods.........on credit.

   [**Ans.** (a) credit, (b) credit, (c) credit note, (d) debit note, (e) Columnar journals, (f) purchases account, (g) purchased.]

Essay type ┌─ FOR REVIEW, DISCUSSION AND PRACTICE ─┐

1. What is a special purpose subsidiary book. Give a specimen of such a book showing atleast five entries.
2. Explain the Imprest System of Petty Cash Book.
3. Explain the different types of Goods Journals with suitable examples.
4. What do you understand by subsidiary books. Describe the objectives of preparing them.
5. What do you mean by sub-division of Journal.

PRACTICAL PROBLEMS

Single Column Cash Book

1. Prepare a Cash Book (with cash column only) from the following transactions:

1988			Rs
March	1	Mr. Ganesh Lal commenced business with cash	65,000
March	3	Bought goods for cash	6,850
March	4	Paid Sharad cash	950
March	5	Discount allowed	60
March	6	Deposited in Bank	40,000
		Paid for office furniture in cash	4,650
March	9	Sold goods for cash	30,000
March	12	Paid wages in cash	1,200
March	13	Paid for stationery	400
March	15	Sold goods for cash	25,000
March	16	Paid for miscellaneous expenses	450

March	19	Received cash from Mr. Trilok Chand	4,850
		Allowed him discount	150
	21	Purchased a radio set	2,500
March	22	Paid salary	4,000
March	25	Paid rent	900
March	28	Paid electricity bill	350
March	29	Paid advertising	400
March	30	Paid into bank	25,000

[**Ans.** Cash Balance Rs 37,200]

Two-columnar Cash Book

2. Prepare a two-columnar Cash Book from the following transactions of Shri R.K. Gupta:

1988			*Rs*
Jan.	1	Cash in hand	2,000
Jan.	6	Cash purchases	2,000
Jan.	10	Wages paid	40
Jan.	11	Cash sales	6,000
Jan.	12	Cash received from Suresh	1,980
		and discount allowed	20
Jan.	19	Cash paid to Munna	2,470
		and discount received	30
Jan.	27	Cash paid to Radhey	400
Jan.	28	Purchased goods for cash	2,070

Find out the total discount allowed and received.

[**Ans.** Cash Balance (closing) Rs 5,000, Discount Total Dr. Rs 20, Cr. Rs 30].

Three-columnar Cash Book

3. From the following particulars, write out a Cash Book, with Cash, Bank and Discount columns of M/s. Ramji and Co., Calcutta, for the month of January, 1988 and balance the Cash Book.

1988

Jan. 1 Balance of cash on hand Rs 2,000 and overdraft with State Bank of India Rs 10,000.

Jan. 5 Received cash from Chetty & Co. Rs 2,000 and allowed him discount Rs 60.

Jan. 7 Paid into Bank Rs 3,500.

Jan. 15 Paid to Govind by cheque Rs 520 in full settlement of his account for Rs 550.

Jan. 20 Received for cash sales: cash Rs 175 and cheque Rs 100.

Jan. 22 Paid Ram & Co. by cheque Rs 1,200, discount allowed Rs 45..

Jan. 25 Paid by cheque to Shanti Kumar Stores, for private use of the proprietor Rs 525..

Jan. 28 Drew for office use Rs 500.

Jan. 31 Harish paid directly into our Bank Account Rs 600.

[**Ans.** Cash in hand Rs 1,175; Bank overdrawn Rs 8,545; Discount: (Dr.) Rs 60; (Cr.) Rs 75]

4. Record the following transactions in the Three Columnar Cash Book:

1990

Jan. 1 Balances: Cash Rs 500, and Bank (Cr.) Rs 12,000

Jan. 2 Investment additional capital of Rs 12,000.

Jan. 5 Deposited Rs 8,000 in the bank.

Jan. 8 Received from Roy Rs 890, allowed him discount Rs 5

Jan. 12 Paid Rs 1,200 to Ghose who allowed us discount of Rs 30.

Jan. 15 Bought merchandise for cash Rs 700.

Jan. 17 Sold merchandise for cash Rs 1,000.

Jan. 18 Purchased furniture by cheque Rs 1,500.

Jan. 19 Received a crossed cheque of Rs 230 from Sundram in full settlement of the debt of Rs 240.

Jan. 22 Paid commission Rs 150 by cheque.

Jan. 25 Withdrew for personal use of Rs 300.

Jan. 26 Paid to Krishanan Rs 700 by cheque; discount received Rs 20.

Jan. 27 Withdrew for personal use Rs 300.

Jan. 29 Received dividend by an order cheque Rs 30, deposited in the bank on the same day.

Jan. 30 Cleared telephone bill Rs 50.

Jan. 31 Paid manager's salary Rs 350, rent Rs 200, and wages Rs 150.

[**Ans.** Discount: (Dr.) Rs 15, (Cr.) Rs 50, Cash Balance Rs 5,140, Bank Balance Rs 3,910.]

5. Mr. Sadanand operates two Bank Accounts both of which are maintained in the Columnar Cash Book itself. You are required to draw up a pro-forma of the Cash Book and show how the following transactions relating to 29th February, 1992 will appear therein and close the Cash Book for the day:

(1) Opening Balances:

	Rs
Cash	150
National Bank	11,240 (O/D)
Overseas Bank	35,460

(2) Received cheque for Rs 1,250 in respect of sales for realising which the National Bank charged Rs 1.50 and credited the balance.

(3) Purchased goods for Rs 13,210 and a cheque issued on the Overseas Bank. The Bank charged Rs 3 for collection of the cheque to the concerned party.

(4) Paid office expenses: Rs 45 and Rs 15.50 for stationery.

(5) Out of Cash sales of Rs 13,265 a sum of Rs 10,000 was, deposited in the National Bank.

(6) Credit purchases of Rs 15,000 were made from Mr. Smith who sent the documents relating to the goods though the Overseas Bank for 90 per cent of their value. The bank charged Rs 115 for releasing the documents.

(7) Deposited Rs 5,000 in National Bank.

(8) A "Bill Receivable" for Rs 10,000 was discounted with the Overseas Bank, which charges 1 per cent towards discounting.

(9) Withdrew Rs 5,000 from the Overseas Bank.

(10) A demand draft was purchased for Rs 3,000 from a bank after paying Rs 2 towards their charges and paid to the Electricity Department as a deposit.

(11) Interest of Rs 122 and Rs 50 were credited and debited respectively by the Overseas Bank and National Bank.

(12) An amount of Rs 1,500 was withdrawn from the Overseas Bank and Salaries paid to that extent.

(13) Manager's Salary of Rs 1,000 was paid by cheque drawn on the National Bank.

(14) Overseas Bank collected dividends of Rs 1,250 and sent a credit note.

(15) An amount of Rs 1,500 was transferred from the Overseas Bank to the National Bank.

[**Ans.** Closing Balances: National Bank Rs 5,458.50; Overseas Bank Rs 11,907.00; and Cash Rs 352.50]

Petty Cash Book

6. Shri Ramaswamy maintains a Columnar Petty Cash book on the Imprest system. The imprest amount is Rs 500 . From the following information, show how his Petty Cash Book would appear for the week ended 12th September, 1990.

Date	Particulars	Rs
7–9–1990	Balance in hand	134.90
	Received cash re-imbursement to make up the imprest	
	Postage	12.30
	Stationery	32.10
	Entertainment	5.40
8–9–1990	Travelling and Conveyance	12.60
	Miscellaneous Expenses	1.10
	Entertainment	7.20
9–9–1990	Repairs	156.70
10–9–1990	Postage	17.40
	Entertainment	12.70
	Travelling	38.40
11–9–1990	Stationery	67.30
	Entertainment	4.10
12–9–1980	Miscellaneous Expenses	1.20
	Postage	5.10
	Repairs	48.30

[**Ans.** Balance on Sept. 14: Rs 78.10]

Goods Journals

7. Enter the following transactions in proper Subsidiary Books of Ram:

1990		Rs
Jan.	1 Sold goods to Ramesh	525
Jan.	1 Bought of Hari Ram	780
Jan.	2 .Ramesh returned goods	75
Jan.	2 Sold to Dina Nath	550
Jan.	2 Purchased goods from Mangal	700
Jan.	4 Returned goods to Mangal	100
Jan.	4 Bought of Devi Dayal	325
Jan.	4 Sold to Zakir Husain	350
Jan.	5 Zakir Husain returned goods	45
Jan.	6 Sold to Ram Saran	500
Jan.	6 Sold to Ghanshyam	300
Jan.	7 Ram Saran returned goods	50
Jan.	7 Bought of Devi Dayal	700
Jan.	8 Returned goods to Devi Dayal	75
Jan.	9 Purchased goods from Raghunath subject to a trade discount of 10%	1,000
Jan.	10 Sold to Raja Ram goods subject to trade discount of 5%	500

[**Ans.** Total of Purchases Book, Rs 3,405; Sales Book, Rs 2,700; Purchases Returns Book, Rs 175; Sales Returns Book, Rs 170.]

Comprehensive Problems

8. The following were the balances of account appearing in the book of Shyam Mohan, Iron and Steel Merchant on the 31st December, 1990:

Debit Balances: Stock in Warehouse, Rs 21,000; Fixtures and Fittings, Rs 6,300; Motor Lorries, Rs 35,000; Harish Rs 9,600; Ramesh Rs 3,200; Sohan Rs 8,900; Cash in hand Rs 2,500; Cash at bank Rs 17,300.

Credit Balances: Suresh Rs 17,900: Gyan Rs 9,900.

Enter the above and the following transactions into proper books of account, post them into ledger and prepare a Trial Balance.

1990			Rs
Jan.	1	Sold to Sohan, 3 tonnes of steel angles per tonne	5,000
Jan.	2	Paid Suresh by cheque on account	10,000
Jan.	3	Received cheque from Ramesh in settlement of his account owing on 31st December, 1990 *less* 5% discount	
Jan.	5	Bought of Hari 5 tonnes of J.C. Tube—per tone	1,500
Jan.	6	Allowed discount to Sohan on 3 tonnes angles invoiced 1st January, these having been cut to wrong length—per tonne	200
Jan.	8	Sundry Cash Sales	1,600
Jan.	11	Drew and cashed cheque for office purposes	2,000
Jan.	12	Paid cash for carriage charges	250
Jan.	14	Sold to Ramesh 5 tonnes Steel Rounds—per tonne	1,900
Jan.	16	Received cheque on account from Sohan	8,500
		Paid Gyan his account by cheque less discount	450
Jan.	18	Received from Harish cheque on account	8,000
Jan.	19	Bought of Suresh 6 tonnes steel frame—per tonne	1,800
		Sent debit note to Ramesh for under charge on 5 tonnes Bar supplied to him on 14th January per tonne	100
Jan.	21	Sold to Tara Chand 4 tonnes I.C. Tubes—per tonne	2,000
Jan.	22	Paid rent by cheque	2,500
		Paid wages in cash	2,150
Jan.	23	Received information that Harish had wound up the business and gone abroad. Wrote off balance of his account as a bad debt	
Jan.	25	Paid Suresh By cheque less 2% discount	
Jan.	26	Paid cash for cleaning warehouse windows	70
Jan.	29	Shyam Mohan withdrew cash for his own use	2,500

9. Enter the following transactions in the proper books of the Golden Tobacco Co. for January 1991.

1991			Rs
Jan.	1	*Assets*: Leasehold Premises, Rs 18,000; Machinery Rs 27,600; Stock of Raw tobacco Rs 51,900; Cash at Bank Rs 7,620; Cash in Hand Rs 860; due from Mohan and Co. Rs 1,460; due from Cavendish and Co. Rs 1,260; Furniture Rs 1,500.	
		Liabilities: Loan @ 6% Rs 20,000; due to Wilson and Grey Rs 6,000	
Jan.	3	Drawn from Bank (for wages to be paid the following day)	1,500
Jan.	4	Wages paid	1,435
Jan.	7	Bought of Wilson and Grey: 896 kg. Borneo Leaf @ Rs 4.00 per Kg.; 672 kg. West Indian Leaf Rs 3.40 per kg.; charges Rs 47	
Jan.	9	Returned 128 kg. of West Indian Leaf as not being upto quality.	
Jan.	12	Paid customs duty by cheque	6,860

Jan.	17	Sold to Mohan and Co. 75 kg. Royal Mixture @ Rs 20.00 per kg; 20,000 Aromatic Cigarettes @ Rs 50.00 per 1,000; 40 kg. Five Flakes @ Rs 80.00 per kg.	

Jan. 17 Sold to Mohan and Co. 75 kg. Royal Mixture @ Rs 20.00 per kg; 20,000 Aromatic Cigarettes @ Rs 50.00 per 1,000; 40 kg. Five Flakes @ Rs 80.00 per kg.

Jan. 18 Paid Wilson and Grey by cheque in full settlement of amount due on January, 1   5,850

Jan. 18 Received from Cavendish and Co. by cheque in full settlement   1,235

Jan. 19 Bought of Sharp Bros and Co. advertising posters   1,100

Jan. 24 Northern Engine Co. Ltd charges for repairing machinery, paid cash   250

Jan. 24 Sold to Cavendish and Co. 10,000 Aromatic Cigarettes Rs 50 per 1,000

Jan. 25 Bought of Johan Barnes and Co. Indian Leaf 1,120 kg. @ Rs 3.00 per kg.

Jan. 26 Received from Mohan and Co. on account, cheque   2,000

Jan. 27 Bank notifies that Cavendish and Co.'s cheque is dishonoured.

Jan. 28 Bought of Dale and Sons; Borneo Leaf 882 kg. @ Rs 4.00 per kg. and Indian Leaf 560 kg. @ Rs 3.00 per kg., charges Rs 7.

Jan. 29 Paid for advertisements   230

Jan. 31 Paid for repairs to furniture   30

Jan. 31 Paid Ground Rent   300

Jan. 31 Drawn from Bank for private use   400

Jan. 31 Bank charged interest for the month   35

Jan. 31 Received intimation that Cavendish and Co. are insolvent, no possibility of recovering anything.

Jan. 31 Allowed interest on capital @ 5% per annum.

Jan. 31 Cigarettes taken for private use   10

Jan. 31 Sold to Blunt & Co. 50 kg. Five Flakes @ Rs 80.00; 10,000 Aromatic Cigarettes @Rs 52.00 per 1,000. Packing charges Rs 30.

[**Ans.** Cash Book: Cash Balance Rs 115: Bank Overdraft Rs 5,025; Purchases Book total Rs 14,558; Sales Book Total Rs 10,750; Returns Outward Book Total Rs 448.]

Chapter 6

NEGOTIABLE INSTRUMENTS

LEARNING OBJECTIVES

After studying this chapter you should be able to:

☐ understand the concept of negotiable instrument ;

☐ explain the different types of negotiable instruments;

☐ record the transactions relating to negotiable instruments in an appropriate manner; and

☐ explain the meaning of certain key terms.

There are certain documents which are freely used in commercial transactions and monetary dealings. They are transferable by delivery and confer a good title to any one who takes them *bona fide* and for value. Such documents are termed as Negotiable Instruments. Bills of Exchange, Promissory Notes and Cheques are all Negotiable Instruments. These Instruments can be made "payable to order" or "payable to bearer." In the former case, they are known as "order" instruments" while in the latter case they are known as "bearer instruments." In case of an order instrument the payment is to be made either to the person named in the instrument or according to his order. In case of a bearer instrument, the payment is to be made to the person who is its bearer. The provisions of the Negotiable Instruments Act, 1881 apply to them. We shall be discussing here only those legal provisions of the Act which shall enable the students to have a clear understanding of the accounting aspect of these instruments.[1]

PROMISSORY NOTE

Definition. Section 4 of the Negotiable Instruments Act defines a Promissory Notes as "an instrument in writing (*not being a bank note and a currency note*) containing an unconditional undertaking singed by the maker, to pay a certain sum of money only to, or to the order of a certain person or to the bearer of the instrument."

Essentials. The following are essential features of a Promissory Note:

1. *There are two parties.* The Promissor is termed as the Maker and the Promissee is called as the Payee. The former is the "Debtor" while the latter is the "Creditor"

2. *It is an instrument in writing.* More verbal promise will not amount to a Promissory Note.

---

[1] For a detailed study of legal provision please refer to Sec IV: "Principles of Mercantile Law, *A Manual of Business Laws* " (2nd edition) by S.N. Maheshwari & S.K Maheshwari.

3. *The promise to pay should be unconditional i.e.*, without any condition attached to it, for example, a promise to pay sum of money on the marriage of a particular person will not amount to Promissory Note.

4. *The promise should be to pay money to another person.* If a person promises to supply goods, it shall not be a Promissory Note.

5. *The amount should be certain.* If interest is also to be paid, the rate of interest should be given.

6. The payee must also be certain, either by name or by designation.

7. A Promissory Note can be made payable to the bearer. However, a bearer Promissory Note cannot be drawn by private individuals. It can be drawn only by the Reserve Bank of India, as per the provisions of Section 31 of the Reserve Bank of India Act. The objective is to protect Government's monopoly of issuing currency notes.

8. Bank notes and currency notes, though are similar to promissory notes in every respect, have been expressly excluded. They are considered as money and not merely securities for money. A currency note is a note issued by the Government containing a promise to pay to the bearer a certain sum of money on demand. A 'bank note' is a promissory note issued by a bank for payment of money to the bearer on demand. The banks now cannot issue such notes which are payable to the bearer on demand on account of section 31 of the Reserve Bank of India Act. Only the Reserve Bank of India is now authorised to issue such notes.

SPECIMEN OF A PROMISSORY NOTE

Rs 500

Delhi
Jan. 4, 1990

On demand[1], I promise to pay Kaushal or order the sum of Five hundred rupees, value received.

(Stamp)
sd/-
Ramesh

Ramesh is the Maker and Kaushal is the Payee.

BILL OF EXCHANGE

Definition. Section 5 of the Negotiable Instruments Act defines a Bill of Exchange as "an instrument in writing containing an unconditional order, signed by the maker, directing a certain person, to pay a certain sum of money only to, or to the order of a certain person or to the bearer of the instrument".

Essentials. The essentials of a Bill of Exchange are similar to those of a Promissory Note except that:

1. In case of a Bill of Exchange, there are three parties, the "Maker" is termed as the "Drawer". He is the creditor. The person liable to pay the money is called as the "Drawee". The person entitled to get the money is termed as the "Payee". It should

---

[1] In case of time promissory notes, the words 'on demand' will be instituted by words "......months or......days after date or after sight."

be noted that drawer himself can also be the payee. There are only two parties in case of a Promissory Note.

2. In case of a Bill of Exchange, the drawer being the creditor, orders the drawee to pay a certain sum of money; while in case of a Promissory Note, the drawer, being the debtor, himself, he promises to pay a certain sum of money.

3. A Time Bill of Exchange (i.e. a B/E payable after some time) can be made payable to the bearer, while the Promissory Note cannot be made payable to the bearer by person other than the Reserve Bank of India or the Central Government.

Classification of Bills of Exchange

Bills of Exchange can be classified as follows:

1. *Time and demand bills.* When payment of a Bill of Exchange is to be made after a particular period of time, the bill is termed as a 'Time Bill.' In such a case, date of maturity is always calculated by adding three days of grace. Such bills requires the "Acceptance" of the drawee. It is generally given by writing across the face of the instrument as shown above:

In case of 'Demand Bill', payment is to be made on demand. Neither the acceptance of the drawee is necessary nor any days of grace are allowed in this case.

2. *Trade and accommodation Bills.* Where a Bill of Exchange has been drawn and accepted for a genuine trade transaction, it is termed as a 'Trade Bill.' For example, *A* sells goods worth Rs 10,000 to *B*. He draws a Bill of Exchange on *B* for the said amount and the same is accepted by *B*. This is a Trade Bill. Where a Bill of Exchange is drawn and accepted for providing funds to a friend in need, it is termed as an Accommodation Bill. For example *C* may be in want of money. He may approach his friends *A* and *B*, who instead of lending the money directly to him, propose to draw an "Accommodation Bill" for Rs 10,000 payable three months after, in his favour. *C* promises to reimburse *B* (the acceptor before the period of three months is up). *C* can get this bill discounted from his bankers. Thus, his needs of funds will be met.

3. *Inland and foreign bills.* A Bill is termed as an Inland Bill, if
   (*a*) it is drawn in India on a person residing in India whether payable in or outside India, or
   (*b*) it is drawn in India on a person residing outside India but payable in India.

A Bill which is not an Inland Bill is a Foreign Bill.

A Foreign Bill is generally drawn up in triplicate and each copy is sent by separate post, so that at least one copy reaches the concerned party. Of course, when payment is made on one copy, the other two copies become inoperative.

CHEQUE

Definition. Section 6 defines a cheque as 'A bill of exchange drawn on a specified banker and not expressed to be payable otherwise than on demand and it includes the electronic image of a truncated cheque and a cheque in the electronic forrm'.

Essentials. A cheque is similar to a bill of exchange with three additional qualifications:

1. It is always drawn on a specified banker.

2. It is always payable on demand.

3. It includes the electronic image of a truncated cheque and also a cheque in the electronic form. The two terms: 'A truncated cheque' and 'A cheque in the electronic form' having been defined under the Act as under:

   (*i*) 'A truncated cheque' means a cheque which is truncated during the course of a clearing cycle, either by the clearing house or by the bank whether paying or receiving payment, immediately on generation of an electronic image for transmission, substituting the further physical movement of the cheque in writing.

(*ii*) 'A cheque in the electronic form' means a cheque which contains the exact mirror image of a paper cheque, and is generated, written and signed in a secure system ensuring the minimum safety standards with the use of digital signature (with or without biometrics signature) and asymmetric crypto system.

Thus, all cheques are bills of exchange but all bills of exchange are not cheques.

SOME IMPORTANT TERMS

1. Maker or Drawer. The person who draws or makes a Promissory Note, Cheque or Bill of Exchange is called the Maker or the Drawer.

2. Drawee or Acceptor. The person on whom the Bill of Exchange or Cheque is drawn and who is directed to pay is called the "Drawee." In case of a Bill of Exchange, the Drawee becomes the acceptor, when he accepts the bill.

3. Payee. The person named in the Bill/Promissory Note or Cheque, to whom or to whose order the money in the instrument is directed to be paid, is called the "Payee."

4. Holder. The person who is entitled to the possession of the Bill, Promissory Note or Cheque, in his own name and who has a right to receive or recover the amount due on the instrument, is called the 'Holder.' A person who obtains the possession of the instrument by illegal means is not a Holder. For example, a person who has stolen a cheque cannot be its holder.

5. Holder in due course. A Holder in due course, is a holder who obtains a negotiable instrument:

    (*i*) for valuable consideration,

    (*ii*) in good faith, and,

    (*iii*) before maturity.

A holder in due course will have a valid title over the instrument (*i.e.*, he can get its payment) though the title of the transferor may be defective. For example, if *A* gets a cheque for Rs 10,000 signed by *B*, by threatening him, and later on endorses it to *C, C* will be a holder in due course if he accepts the cheque in good faith (*i.e.*, without knowing that force was used by *A*), for consideration (*i.e.*, by giving something in return for the cheque). In case of a Bill of Exchange, he must also get the instrument before the date of maturity. A cheque is payable on demand and hence the condition of maturity is not applicable.

6. Acceptance of Bill. The process of consenting to the order by the drawee of a Bill of Exchange is known as acceptance of a Bill of Exchange.

7. Endorsement. The payee of a negotiable instrument may not himself keep the instrument with him. He may transfer the ownership of the instrument in favour of another person. Such a person can get the payment of the instrument from the drawee. The process of transferring of ownership of the instrument is termed as "endorsement" of the instrument. According to the Negotiable Instruments Act, "when the maker or holder of a negotiable instrument signs his name otherwise than as such maker, for the purpose of negotiation, on the back or face thereof, or on a slip of paper annexed thereto, or so signs for the same purpose a stamped paper intended to be completed as a negotiable instrument, he is said to endorse the instrument. The person endorsing the instrument is called the 'Endorser.' The person to whom the instrument is endorsed, is called the 'Endorsee.'

8. Drawee in case of need. Sometimes the drawer or endorser of a Bill of Exchange may instruct the holder to present the bill to a second party in case the drawee or acceptor dishonours the bill. Such a second party is called "Drawee in case of need."

9. Maturity of Bill. A Bill of Exchange or Promissory Note matures on the date on which it falls due. If the instrument is payable on demand, it becomes due immediately on presentation for payment. If it is payable after the expiry of a particular period of time, the date of maturity will be calculated after adding three days of grace.

The word 'punctually' after the date fixed for payment cannot deprive the maker of the days of grace to which he is legally entitled to and payment made till the expiry of the third day of grace shall be valid. These days of grace, however, are not available in case of negotiable instruments payable on demand, at sight or on presentment such as a cheque or a demand bill.

Examples

(*i*) A bill dated 30th November is made payable three months after date. It falls due on 3rd March.

(*ii*) A bill of exchange dated 1st January is payable "one month after sight", It is presented for acceptance on 3rd January. The bill will fall due for payment on 6th February.

(*iii*) A hundi payable on 28th January will fall due on 31st January.

If an instrument is payable by instalments, it must be presented for payment on the third day after the day fixed for the payment of each instalment. Days of grace are allowed on each instalment.

10. **Dishonour.** Non-payment of the amount of a Promissory Note, Cheque or Bill of Exchange on the date of maturity is called dishonour of the instrument. In case of Bill of Exchange, it will also said to be dishonoured if the drawee refuses to accept the Bill.

11. **Noting.** Noting is the authentic and official proof of presentment and dishonour of a negotiable instrument. It is a memorandum of a minute recorded by a notary public upon the dishonoured instrument or upon a paper attached thereto or partly upon each. Its need arises in the case of the dishonour of a Bill of Exchange or a Promissory Note. However, noting is not compulsory. It specifies the date of dishonour and reasons, if any, assigned for dishonour and the noting charges. It should be made within a reasonable time after dishonour.

12. **Protesting.** Protest is a formal certificate of dishonour issued by the notary public to the holder of a bill or note on his demand. It contains the following particulars:

(*i*) The instrument itself or an exact copy thereof.

(*ii*) The name of the person for and against whom the instrument is protested.

(*iii*) A statement that payment or acceptance for better security, as the case may be, was demanded by notary public from the person concerned and he refused to give it or did not answer or that he could not be found.

(*iv*) The fact of dishonour, time and place of dishonour.

(*v*) The signature of the notary public.

It is to be noted that foreign bills of exchange must be protested for dishonour when such protest is required by the law of the place, where they are drawn.

13. **Retiring of a Bill.** If all parties agree, a bill may be withdrawn before maturity either because the acceptor desires its withdrawal to avoid its dishonour or because he is desirous of paying the amount without waiting till its due date. In the former case, it is same as dishonour except noting and protesting will not be required. In the latter case, usually some rebate is allowed to the acceptor for pre-payment.

14. **Renewal of Bill.** When the original bill has been dishonoured or retired (where the drawee is not in a position to pay), if the parties agree, a new bill in place of the original bill may be accepted by the drawee. This is termed as Renewal of Bill. The new bill may be for the full amount *i.e.*, of the old bill and noting charges, if any, plus interest.

ACCOUNTING ENTRIES

Regarding Cheques

Accounting entries regarding receipts and issue of cheques have already been explained in Chapter 5, while explaining recording of cash transactions.

Regarding Bills of Exchange and Promissory Notes

Bills of Exchange and Promissory Notes, being Negotiable Instruments, are freely transferable. The transfer is made by endorsement and delivery in case of order instrument, in case of non-payment of the bill, or promissory note can recover the money from all previous endorsers or the payee or the maker of the instrument. Moreover, the title of a holder-in due course remains goods though the title of the transferrer may be defective. On account of these two important reasons. *i.e.*, negotiability and liability of the endorsers, a bill of exchange or a promissory note is considered to be an excellent security by the bankers. They are generally willing to advance money to a holder of bill of exchange or promissory note at commercial rate of discount. Thus, a person who receives a bill of exchange or promissory not has the following alternatives with him:

(i) He can keep the bill of exchange or promissory note with himself till the date of maturity.

(ii) He can pass it to one of his creditors.

(iii) He can get it doscounted from his bank.

In the following pages, we are explaining the accounting to be made in the books of the receiver of a bill of Exchange or a Promissory Note (*i.e.*, the Creditor or the Drawer or the Promisee in case or a Promissory Note) and the Acceptor (*i.e.* the Debtor, or the Drawee or the Maker in case of a Promissory Note). For the former it is a Bill Receivable (the term is also used for a promissory note received) and for the latter, it is a Bill Payable (the term is also used for a promissory note given).

When a Bill of Exchange is kept till the Date of Maturity

In case, the receiver of a bill of exchange keeps the Bill of Exchange till the date of maturity with him, the following accounting entries will be passed in the books of the receiver of the Bill of Exchange (*i.e.*, the Drawer) and the Drawee of the Bill of Exchange.

In the Books of the Drawer

(i) On Selling on goods on credit to the Drawee

    Drawee   Dr.

        To Sales A/c

(ii) On receipt of Bill of Exchange duly accepted by the Drawee

    Bill Receivable A/c   Dr

        To Drawee

(iii) On receiving payment on maturity of the Bill

    Cash A/c   Dr.

        To Bills Receivable Account

In the Books of the Drawee

(i) On purchasing goods on credit from the Drawer

    Purchases A/c   Dr.

        To Drawer

    (*ii*) On acceptance of the Bill of Exchange in favour of Drawer

        Drawer   Dr.
            To Bills Payable Account

    (*iii*) On payment of the Bill on maturity

        Bill Payable Account   Dr.
            To Cash

When the Bill of Exchange is endorsed in favour of a Creditor

In case the drawer of the Bill of Exchange endorses the Bill of Exchange received in favour of a creditor and the Bill is met on maturity, the following journal entries will be passed in the books of the Drawer as well as the Drawee of the Bill of Exchange.

Books of the Drawer

The entries regarding selling of goods and receiving of the Bills of Exchange will be the same, as explained before. However, the following entry will be passed when the Bill of Exchange is endorsed in favour of a Creditor.

        Creditor A/c   Dr.
            To Bills Receivable A/c

On the date of maturity when the Bill is met, no entry is required in the books of the Drawer. This is because in his books, the Bills Receivable Account has already been closed and he has no liability, if the bill is met on maturity.

Books of the Drawee

The Drawee is not at all concerned with the endorsement of the Bill by the Drawer to a third-party. Accounting entries in his books will therefore be the same as explained before.

When Bill of Exchange is discounted with a Bank

The Drawer of a Bill of Exchange may get the Bill of Exchange discounted from his bankers. In such a case, the following journal entries will be passed in the books of the Drawer and the Drawee.

Books of the Drawer

The entries regarding selling of goods and receipt of Bill of Exchange will be the same as explained before. However, the following entry will be passed in the books of the drawer when he gets the Bill of Exchange discounted from his bankers.

        Bank Account   Dr.
        Discount Account   Dr.
            To Bills Receivable Account

Books of the Drawee

The entries in the books of the Drawee will remain the same as explained before. He is not at all concerned whether he keeps the Bill with him or he gets it discounted from his bankers.

Dishonour of a Bill of Exchange

A Bill of Exchange is to be presented on maturity for payment. In case, the acceptor of the Bill refuses to make payment of the Bill on the date of maturity, it is said that the Bill of Exchange has been dishonoured. In order to get an authenticate proof of this fact that the Bill of Exchange was really presented for payment and was dishonoured, the Drawer (or holder) may get the Bill of Exchange noted and protested. The Notary Officer appointed by the Government for this purpose issues a certificate to this effect. He charges some fee for this work which is termed as "Noting Charges".

The entries for dishonour of the bill in the books of the Drawer (or holder) and the acceptor will be as follows.

Books of the Drawer

(*i*) If the bill is kept by the Drawer (or the holder) with himself till the date of maturity:

On dishonour of the Bill:

Drawee/Acceptor	Dr.
To Bills Receivable A/c	
To Cash A/c	

(The account of the drawee or acceptor will be debited with the amount of the bill plus noting charges. The Bills Receivable Account will be credited with the amount of the Bill while Cash Account will be credited with the amount of the noting charges incurred).

(*ii*) If the Bill is discounted with the bankers and is dishonoured:

On Dishonour of the Bill:

Drawee/Acceptor	Dr.
To Bank	

(The account of the acceptor will be debited not only with the amount of the Bill but also with the amount of Nothing Charges which the Bank might have paid. The account of the Bank will be credited with the total amount).

(*iii*) If the Bill is endorsed by the Drawer in favour of a Creditor and it is dishonoured:

On dishonour:

Drawee/Acceptor	Dr.
To Creditor's A/c	

(The account of the drawee will be debited with the amount of the Bill as well as the amount of Noting Charges which the creditor might have incurred. The creditor will be given credit with the total amount).

Books of the Acceptor

The acceptor will pass the following entry irrespective of the fact whether the Bill of Exchange is with the Drawer himself or it has been endorsed or discounted by him. He is concerned only with the Drawer and therefore, he is going to give him credit with the amount of the Bill plus any noting charges that might have been incurred either by him or by any other person who happens to be holder of the Bill of Exchange.

Bills Payable A/c	Dr.
Noting Charges	Dr.
To Drawer	

Renewal of a Bill

The acceptor of the Bill may not be in a position to meet the Bill on the date of maturity. However, he may accept to meet the bill in case, he is given some time by the drawer for making payment of the Bill. He may, therefore, request the Drawer to cancel the old Bill and draw a new Bill on him. The Drawer may charge some interest for the delayed payment at mutually agreed rate of interest. The amount of interest may be paid in cash or it may be included in the amount of the new Bill. The following journal entries will be passed in the books of the Drawer and the Drawee on renewal of a Bill of Exchange.

Books of the Drawer

(i) Cancellation of the old Bill

Drawee's Personal A/c   Dr.
   To Bills Receivable A/c

(The entry is the same as for dishonour of a Bill of Exchange, except there will be no need for getting the Bill noted and protested since the Drawee himself has requested for cancellation of the Bill).

(ii) On receipt of amount of Interest in cash

Cash A/c   Dr.
   To Interest

(The interest will be charged for the delay in payment *i.e.*, the date by which the payment would be made as per the new Bill and the date by which payment should have been made as per the old Bill of Exchange).

(iii) In case, the interest is not payable in cash

Drawee's Personal A/c   Dr.
   To Interest A/c

(iv) for receipt of the new Bill

Bills Receivable A/c   Dr.
   To Drawee's Personal A/c

(The amount will include the amount of interest also if it is not paid in cash).

Books of the Drawee

(i) On cancellation of the old Bill

Bills Payable A/c   Dr.
   To Drawer's Personal A/c

(The entry is similar to dishonour of the bill except that there will be no necessity for getting the bill noted and protested and therefore, there will be no charge for Noting Charges).

(ii) When Interest is paid in cash

Interest A/c   Dr.
   To Cash A/c

(iii) In case the interest is not paid in cash

Interest A/c   Dr.
   To Drawer's Personal A/c

(iv) On acceptance of the new Bill

Drawer's Personal A/c   Dr.
   To Bills Payable A/c

(The amount may include the amount of interest if it has not been paid in cash).

Retiring of a Bill under rebate

The acceptor of a Bill may be in a position to meet the Bill before maturity. He may, therefore, approach the acceptor to make the payment of the Bill before the due date of the Bill. In such a case, usually, the Drawer gives some rebate to the Drawer for early payment of the Bill. The following are the journal entries to be passed in the books of the Drawer as well as the acceptor.

Retiring of a Bill of Exchange which is with the Drawer

Books of the Drawer

On receipt of payment of the Bill

Cash A/c	Dr.
Rebate A/c	Dr.
To Bill Receivable A/c	

(Rebate is a loss to the Drawer and, therefore, it is debited)

Books of the Drawee

Bills Payable A/c	Dr.
To Cash A/c	
To Rebate A/c	

(Rebate is a gain to Drawee and, therefore, it has been credited).

Retiring of Bill of a Exchange discounted or endorsed by the Drawer

In case the acceptor requests the drawer to accept retirement of a bill which has been endorsed or discounted by the drawer, the drawer will have to request the bank or the creditor (endorsee) to return the bill back to him. He will then get the payment from the drawee and allow him rebate for pre-payment. Similarly, the bank or the creditor may also allow some rebate to the drawer on account of his making pre-payment to the bank or the creditor, as the case may be. The accounting entries will be as follows:

In the Books of the Drawer

On return of the bill from the bank/creditor

Bills Receivable A/c	Dr.
To Bank/Creditor	

On receiving payment from the drawee:

Cash A/c	Dr.
Rebate Allowed A/c	Dr.
To Bills Receivable A/c	

On making payment to the Bank/Creditor:

Bank/Creditor A/c	Dr.
To Cash A/c	
To Rebate A/c	

In the Books of the Drawee

The Drawee is concerned only with the Drawer. Hence on payment of the bill under rebate the entry will be the same as if the bill was with the Drawer *i.e.*,

Bills Payable A/c	Dr.
To Cash A/c	
To Rebate A/c	

1.112

The journal entries given in the preceding pages both in the Book of the Drawer of the Bill as well as the Acceptor of the Bill can be summarised as follows:

BOOKS OF THE DRAWER OF THE BILL

Sl. No.	Transaction	Debit	Credit
1.	On Selling of goods	Purchaser's A/c	Sales A/c
2.	On receipt of the bill from the purchaser	Bill Receivable A/c	Purchaser's A/c
3.	Disposal of the Bill:		
	(a) When the bill is kept by the receiver till the date of maturity	No entry	No entry
	(b) When the bill is discounted with a banker	Bank A/c Discount A/c	Bill Receivable A/c
	(c) When the bill is endorsed in favour of a creditor	Creditor's A/c	Bills Receivable A/c
4.	On maturity, if the bill is honoured		
	(a) If the bill is kept by the receiver till the date of maturity	Cash A/c	Bills Receivable A/c
	(b) If the bill was discounted with the banker by the receiver	No entry	No entry
	(c) If the Bill was endorsed in favour of a creditor	No entry	No entry
5.	On maturity of the bill, if dishonoured		
	(a) If it is with the Drawer and he incurs Noting Charges	Drawee's/Purchasers' A/c (Amount of the Bill + Noting Charges)	Bills Receivable A/c (amount of the Bill) Cash A/c (Noting Charges)
	(b) If the bills was discounted and thereafter is now in the hands of the banker and noting charges are incurred.	Drawee's A/c (with the amount of the bill and noting charges)	Bank A/c (with the amount of the Bill and Noting Charges)
	(c) If the bill was transferred to a Creditor and thereafter it is now in his hands and he incurs noting charges.	Drawee's A/c (with the amount of Bill and noting changes)	Creditor's A/c (with the amount of the Bill and noting charges)
6.	Renewal of the Bill		
	(i) The entries will be similar to dishonour of the Bill except that there will be no expense by way of noting charges.		
	(ii) For interest paid in cash	Cash A/c	Interest A/c
	(iii) If interest not paid in cash	Drawee's A/c	Interest A/c
	(iv) For receipts of new bill	Bills Receivable A/c	Drawee's A/c
7.	Retirement of the Bill		
	(i) When the Bill is with the Drawer	Cash A/c, Rebate A/c	Bills Receivable A/c
	(ii) In case the Bill is with the Bank or with a creditor.		
	(a) On return of Bill from bank/creditor	Bills Receivable A/c	Bank/Creditor's A/c
	(b) On receiving payment from the drawee	Cash A/c Rebate Allowed A/c	Bills Receivable A/c
	(c) On making payment to bank/creditor	Bank/Creditor A/c	Cash A/c Rebate Received A/c

ENTRIES IN THE BOOKS OF THE DRAWEE OR ACCEPTOR OF THE BILL

Sl No.	Transaction	Debit	Credit
1.	On purchases of goods.	Purchases A/c	Seller's or the Drawer's A/c
2.	On acceptance of the bill	Drawer's A/c	Bills Payable A/c
3.	On payment of the bill	Bills Payable A/c	Cash A/c
4.	On dishonor of Bill and he has to bear the noting charges	Bills Payable A/c Noting Charges A/c	Drawer's A/c (amount of bill plus noting charges)
5.	Renewal of the Bill		
	(i) Entry will be similar to dishonour of a bill except there will be no noting charges	Bills Payable A/c	Drawer's A/c
	(ii) (a) For interest paid in cash	Interest A/c	Cash A/c
	(b) For interest not aid in cash	Interest A/c	Drawer's A/c
	(c) For accepting new Bill	Drawer A/c	Bills Payable A/c
6.	On retirement of Bill	Bills Payable A/c	Cash A/c, Rebate A/c

Notes:

1. No entry is passed in the Acceptor's books for discounting or endorsing of bill of exchange by the Drawer/Receiver of the bill.

2. If the Drawee has transferred or got discounted the bill of exchange, and the Bill is dishonoured, the Drawee will credit the account of the Drawer only and no other account.

The comprehensive illustration given in the following pages will make clear to the readers the entries to be passed in he books of the Drawer as well as the Drawee of a bill of exchange.

Illustration 6.1. A sold goods to B for Rs 5,000. B accepted two bills of Rs 2,500 each for 2 months. A endorsed one bill to C for Rs 2,600. on due date both the bills were met.

Pass journal entries in the books of A and B.

Solution:

BOOKS OF A

Date	Particulars		L.F.	Dr. Rs	Cr. Rs
	B	Dr.		5,000	
	To Sales A/c				5,000
	(Being sale of goods to B)				
	Bills Receivable A/c	Dr.		5,000	
	To B				5,000
	(Being two Bills Receivable of Rs 2,500 each received from B)				
	C	Dr.		2,600	
	To Bills Receivable A/c				2,500
	To Discount A/c				100
	(Being one Bill Receivable endorsed to C).				
	Bank A/c	Dr.		2,500	
	To Bills Receivable A/c				2,500
	(Being payment received of another Bill Receivable)				

1.114

Date	Particulars		L.F.	Dr. Rs	Cr. Rs
	Purchase A/c	Dr.		5,000	
	To A				5,000
	(Being goods purchased from A)				
	A	Dr.		5,000	
	To Bills Payable A/c				5,000
	(Being two acceptances of Rs 2,500 each given to A)				
	Bills Payable A/c	Dr.		5,000	
	To Bank				5,000
	(Being acceptance met on maturity)				

Illustration 6.2. A owes to B Rs 1,000. On 1st January, 1988, A accepts a three months' bill for Rs 975 in full settlement. At the due date the Bill is dishonoured. Make journal entries in the books of both A and B.

Solution:

Books of A

JOURNAL

Date	Particulars		Dr. Amount Rs	Cr. Amount Rs
1988				
Jan. 1	B	Dr.	1,000	
	To Bills Payable A/c			975
	To Discount A/c			25
	(Bill Payable accepted in full settlement)			
April 14	Bills Payable A/c	Dr.	975	
	Discount A/c[1]	Dr.	25	
	To B			1,000
	(Bill Payable dishonoured)			

Books of B

JOURNAL

Date	Particulars		Dr. Amount Rs	Cr. Amount Rs
Jan. 1	Bills Receivable A/c	Dr.	975	
	Discount A/c	Dr.	25	
	To A			1,000
	(Bill Receivable received in full settlement)			
April 4	A	Dr.	1,000	
	To Bill Receivable A/c			975
	To Discount A/c[1]			25
	(Bill Receivable dishonoured)			

Illustration 6.3. Give necessary entries as would appear in A's Books:

1988

May 5 A drew three bills on B for Rs 500, Rs 400 and Rs 300 payable at 4, 3 and 2 months respectively.

---

[1] Please note that discount previously allowed has been disallowed.

May 12 He endorsed the first bill in favour of his customer *C* at Rs 475.
May 19 He Discounted the second bill with his banker for Rs 380.
May 26 He was paid the proceeds of the third bill at a rebate of 5% on the total amount of the bill.

On due dates the first and second bills were dishonoured but the third one was paid.

Solution:

JOURNAL

Date	Particulars		Dr. Amount Rs	Cr. Amount Rs
1988				
May 5	Bills Receivable A/c	Dr.	1,200	
	To B			1,200
	(Three Bills for Rs 500, Rs 400 and Rs 300 were received from B)			
May 12	C	Dr.	475	
	Discount A/c	Dr.	25	
	To Bills Receivable A/c			500
	(The first bill for Rs 500 was endorsed in favour of C for Rs 475)			
May 19	Bank A/c	Dr.	380	
	Discount A/c	Dr.	20	
	To Bills Receivable A/c			400
	(The second bill for Rs 400 was discounted with Bank)			
May 26	Bank A/c	Dr.	285	
	Rebate allowed A/c	Dr.	15	
	To Bills Receivable A/c			300
	(The third bill was retired at a rebate of 5% on the amount of the bill)			
Aug. 8	B	Dr.	400	
	To Bank A/c			400
	(The second bill dishonoured on maturity)			
Sept. 8	B	Dr.	500	
	To C			500
	(The first bill dishonoured on maturity)			

Note. The third bill has been paid before maturity and the entry for its payment has been passed on May 26.

Illustration 6.4. Sujesh owed money to Brijesh and hence accepted two bills each of Rs 5,000 at three months' duration drawn on him by the latter on January, 1, 1988. Brijesh discounted one of the bills with his bank for net proceeds of Rs 4,800 and endorsed the other in favour of Mukesh to whom he owed a like sum, on the same date.

Sujesh paid the bill held by Mukesh on the due date, but failed to meet the bill presented by the bank. The bank debited Brijesh's account on April 4, 1988 inclusive of bank charges of Rs 10. Sujesh paid the amount inclusive of charges to Brijesh on April 10, 1988.

Show the Journal entries in respect of the above in the books of Sujesh and Brijesh.

Solution:

JOURNAL OF SUJESH

Date	Particulars		Dr. Amount Rs	Cr. Amount Rs
1988				
Jan. 1	Brijesh	Dr.	10,000	
	To Bills Payable A/c			10,000
	(Being acceptance of two drafts of Rs 5,000 each for three months)			
April 4	Bills Payable A/c	Dr.	5,000	
	To Cash A/c			5,000
	(Being honour of own acceptance at maturity)			
April 4	Bills Payable A/c	Dr.	5,000	
	Sundry Charges A/c	Dr.	10	
	To Brijesh			5,010
	(Being dishonour of own acceptance at maturity and sundry charges of Rs 10 recoverable from us)			
April 10	Brijesh	Dr.	5,010	
	To Cash			5,010
	(Being discharge for the dishonoured acceptance)			

JOURNAL OF BRIJESH

Date	Particulars		Dr. Amount Rs	Cr. Amount Rs
1988				
Jan. 1	Bills Receivable A/c	Dr.	10,000	
	To Sujesh			10,000
	(Being receipt of two acceptances of Rs 5,000 each)			
Jan. 1	Bank A/c	Dr.	4,800	
	Discount A/c	Dr.	200	
	To Bills Receivable A/c			5,000
	(Being discounting of one B/R with the banker)			
Jan. 1	Mukesh	Dr.	5,000	
	To Bills Receivable A/c			5,000
	(Being endorsement of another bill receivable)			
April 4	Sujesh	Dr.	5,010	
	To Bank			5,010
	(Being dishonour of discounted B/R and the extra liability to bank for bank charges of Rs 10)			
April 4	Cash/Bank	Dr.	5,010	
	To Sujesh			5,010
	(Being receipt for the dishonoured acceptance)			

Illustration 6.5. Punit draws a bill of exchange of Rs 1,000 for three months on Sunil on 1st September, 1988 which is duly accepted by the latter. On October 1, one month after acceptance, Punit discounts the bill with his bankers at 6 per cent. On the date of maturity, Sunil, not being able to meet the bill, offers Punit Rs 450 and asks him to draw another bill for three months for the balance plus interest at 6 per cent. Punit agrees to this arrangement, but before the second bill becomes due Sunil becomes bankrupt. Sunil's estate pays fifty paise in a rupee.

Give Journal Entries in the books of Punit and Sunil.

Solution:

In the Books of Punit
JOURNAL ENTRIES

Date	Particulars	L.F.	Dr. Amount Rs	Cr. Amount Rs
1988 Sep. 1	Bills Receivable A/c Dr.		1,000.00	
	To Sunil			1,000.00
	(Being the bill received after acceptance)			
Oct. 1	Bank A/c Dr.		990.00	
	Discount A/c Dr.		10.00	
	To Bills Receivable A/c			1,000.00
	(Being the bill discounted @ 6%)			
Dec. 4	Sunil Dr.		1,000.00	
	To Bank A/c			1,000.00
	(Being the bill dishonoured)			
Dec. 4	Bank A/c Dr.		450.00	
	To Sunil			450.00
	(Being the amount received)			
Dec. 4	Sunil Dr.		8.25	
	To Interest A/c			8.25
	(Being the amount of interest due on the balance @ 6% p.a.)			
Dec. 4	Bills Receivable A/c Dr.		558.25	
	To Sunil			558.25
	(Being the new bill accepted)			
March 7	Sunil Dr.		558.25	
	To Bills Receivable A/c			558.25
	(Being the bill dishonoured)			
March 7	Bank A/c Dr.		279.13	
	Bad Debts A/c Dr.		279.12	
	To Sunil			558.25
	(Being the amount received from Sunil's estate @ 50 P. per rupee)			

In the Books of Sunil
JOURNAL ENTRIES

Date	Particulars	L.F.	Amount Rs	Amount Rs
1988 Sept. 1	Punit Dr.		1,000.00	
	To Bills Payable A/c			1,000.00
	(Being the acceptance given)			
Dec. 4	Bills Payable A/c Dr.		1,000.00	
	To Punit			1,000.00
	(Being the bill dishonoured)			
Dec. 4	Punit Dr.		450.00	
	To Bank A/c			450.00
	(Being the amount paid)			

Contd....

Date	Particulars		L.F.	Amount Rs.	Amount Rs.
Dec. 4	Interest A/c 　　To Punit (Being the amount of interest due on the balance @ 6% p.a.)	Dr.		8.25	8.25
Dec. 4	Punit 　　To Bills Payable A/c (Being the acceptance given to the new bill)	Dr.		558.25	558.25
Mar. 7	Bill Payable A/c 　　To Punit (Being the bill dishonoured)	Dr.		558.25	558.25
Mar. 7	Punit 　　To Bank A/c 　　To Deficiency A/c (Being the amount paid @ fifty paise per rupee)	Dr.		558.25	279.13 279.13

Working Notes:

The amount due by Sunil to Punit has been found out by preparing Sunil's Account in Punit's books.

SUNIL

Date	Particulars	Amount Rs	Date	Particulars	Amount Rs
1988			1988		
Sep. 1	To Balance b/d	1,000.00	Sep. 1	By Bills Receivable A/c	1,000.00
Dec. 4	To Bank A/c	1,000.00	Dec. 4	By Bank A/c	450.00
Dec. 4	To Interest A/c	8.25	Dec. 4	By Bills Receivable A/c	558.25
March 7	To Bills Receivable A/c	558.25	March 7	By Balance	558.25*
		2,566.50			2,566.50

*50% of the balance has been recovered. The rest has been taken as a bad debt.

Illustration 6.6 Bhaskar Brothers are customers of *ABC* Ltd. The following are the details of invoices in respect of sales made by the latter to the former during the month of July, 1988.

Date	Invoice No.	Values Rs
1.7.1988	00212	20,000
4.7.1988	00224	21,412
9.7.1988	00344	14,210
17.7.1988	00433	17.230
25.7.1988	01820	21,630

ABC Ltd. draw bills of exchange for every sale payable at 30 days sight, and discount the bills at discounting charges of 1.5% p.m. You are required to show:-

(a) the entries in the sales Day Book of *ABC* Ltd. for the above;

(b) the journal entries for drawing and discounting of bills on the respective days in the books of *ABC* Ltd.; and

(c) Bhaskar Brothers A/c in the ledger of *ABC* Ltd.

Solution:

SALES DAY BOOK OF ABC LTD.

Date	Particulars	Outward Invoice No.	L.F.	Amount Rs
1988				
July 1	Bhaskar Brothers	00212		20,000
July 4	Bhaskar Brothers	00224		21,412
July 9	Bhaskar Brothers	00344		14,210
July 17	Bhaskar Brothers	00433		17,230
July 25	Bhaskar Brothers	01820		21,630
				94,482

JOURNAL ENTRIES

Date	Particulars		Debit Rs	P	Credit Rs	P
1988						
July 1	Bills Receivable A/c	Dr.	20,000	00		
	To Bhaskar Brothers				20,000	00
	(Being receipts of bill of exchange No. 1 payable at 30 days' sight for invoice No. 00212)					
	Bank A/c	Dr.	19,700	00		
	Discount A/c	Dr.	300	00		
	To Bills Receivable A/c				20,000	00
	(Being discounting of B/R No. 1 with Bank at 1½% p.m.)					
July 4	Bill Receivable A/c	Dr.	21,412	00		
	To Bhaskar Brothers				21,412	00
	(Being receipt of bill of exchange No. 2 for invoice No. 00224 payable at 30 days' sight)					
	Bank A/c	Dr.	21,090	82		
	Discount A/c	Dr.	321	18		
	To Bill Receivable A/c				21,412	00
	(Being discounting of B/R No. 2 with Bank at 1½% p.m.)					
July 9	Bills Receivable A/c	Dr.	14,210	00		
	To Bhaskar Brothers				14,210	00
	(Being receipt of bill of exchange No. 3 payable at 30 days sight for invoice No. 00344)					
	Bank A/c	Dr.	13,996	85		
	Discount A/c	Dr.	213	15		
	To Bill Receivable A/c				14,210	00
	(Being discounting of B/R No. 3 with Bank at 1.5% p.m.)					
Jul. 17	Bill Receivable A/c	Dr.	17,230	00		
	To Bhaskar Brothers				17,230	00
	(Being receipt of bill of exchange No. 4 payable at 30 days sight for the invoice No. 00433)					
	Bank A/c	Dr.	16,971	55		
	Discount A/c	Dr.	258	45		
	To Bill Receivable A/c				17,230	00
	(Being discounting of Bills Receivable No. 4 with Bank at 1.5% p.m.)					

Contd....

Date	Particulars		Debit		Credit	
			Rs	P	Rs	P
Jul. 25	Bill Receivable A/c Dr.		21,630	00		
	To Bhaskar Brothers				21,630	00
	(Being receipt of bill of exchange No. 5 payable at 30 days' sight for the invoice No. 01820)					
	Bank A/c Dr.		21,305	55		
	Discount A/c Dr.		324	45		
	To Bill Receivable A/c				21,630	00
	(Being discounting of Bill Receivable No. 5 with Bank at 1.5% p.m.)					

BHASKAR BROTHERS

Date	Particulars	Amount Rs	Date	Particulars	Amount Rs
1988			1988		
July 1	To Sales	20,000	July 1	By Bill Receivable (No.1)	20,000
July 4	To Sales	21,412	July 4	By Bill Receivable (No.2)	21,412
July 9	To Sales	14,210	July 9	By Bill Receivable (No.3)	14,210
July 17	To Sales	17,230	July 17	By Bill Receivable (No.4)	17,230
July 25	To Sales	21,630	July 25	By Bill Receivable (No.5)	21,630
		94,482			94,482

Illustration 6.7. Ram accepted on 1st April, 1990 a bill for Rs 10,000 drawn by Shyam at 3 months. Shyam immediately discounted the bill with his banker at 7 per cent. Ram failed to meet the bill in due time and at his request Shyam renewed it for 3 months by adding 12 per cent interest to the amount on Ram's furnishing security. Ram endorsed two of his customers' bills for Rs 7,000 and Rs 5,400 due on 20the Augest, 1990 and 10th September, 1990 respectively. Shyam discounted all the three bills at 7% with the bankers; but on the due date the second customer's bill was dishonoured. Ram became bankrupt. Enter the transactions in Shyam's books.

Solution:

BOOKS OF SHYAM
JOURNAL

Date	Particulars		Rs Dr.	Rs Cr.
1990 April 1	Bill Receivable A/c Dr.		10,000	
	To Ram			10,000
	(Bill for Rs 10,000 payable 3 months received from Mr. Ram)			
April 1	Bank A/c Dr.		9,825	
	Discount A/c Dr.		175	
	To Bills Receivable A/c			10,000
	(The bill received from Ram discounted at 7% p.a.)			
July 4	Ram Dr.		10,000	
	To Bank			10,000
	(The bill receivable having been dishonoured credited to Bank and to the debit of Ram)			
July 4	Ram Dr.		300	
	To Interest Account			300
	(Interest charged to Ram on renewal of the bill for 3 months (assumed) @ 12%)			

Contd....

Date	Particulars		Dr. Rs	Cr. Rs.
July 4	Bills Receivable Account	Dr.	22,700	
	To Ram			22,700
	(Bill receivable for Rs 10,300 received from Ram on renewal of the previous bill alongwith bills for Rs. 12,400 as colateral security)			
July 4	Bank A/c	Dr.	22,376	
	Discount A/c	Dr.	324*	
	To Bills Receivable A/c			22,700
	(The three bills for Rs 10,300, Rs 7,000 and Rs 5,400 discounted at 7%)			
Sep 10	Ram	Dr.	5,400	
	To Bank A/c			5,400
	(The bill for Rs 5,400 received from Ram as collateral security dishonoured)			
Oct. 7	Ram	Dr.	10,300	
	To Bank A/c			10,300
	(Bills Receivable for Rs 10,300 received from Ram dishonoured, debited to Ram and credited to Bank)			

*Calculation of Discount:

	Rs
On 10,300 @ 7% for 3 months	180.25
On 7,000 @ 7% for 51 days	68.50
On 5,400 @ 7% for 72 days	75.60
Total	324.35 (rounded-of to Rs 324)

Ledger Accounts

Dr.   BILLS RECEIVABLE ACCOUNT   Cr.

Date	Particulars	Rs	Date	Particulars	Rs
1998			1998		
April 1	To Ram	10,000	April 1	By Sundries: Bank	9,825
				Discount	175
July	To Ram	22,700	July 4	By Sundries: Bank	22,376
				Discount	324
		32,700			32,700

RAM

Date	Particulars	Rs	Date	Particulars	Rs
1998			1998		
April 1	To Balance b/d (assumed)	10,000	April 1	By Bills Receivable A/c	10,000
July 4	To Bank (B/R dishonoured)	10,000	July 4	By Bills Receivable	22,700
	To Interest	300	Oct. 7	By Balance c/d	3,300
Oct. 7	To Bank (Bills dishonoured)	10,300			
Sep. 10	To Bank (Bills Dishonoured)	5,400			5,400
		36,000			36,000

BANK ACCOUNT

Date	Particulars	Rs	Date	Particulars	Rs
1998			1998		
April 1	To Bills Receivable A/c	9,825	July 4	By Ram	10,000
July 4	To Bills Receivable A/c	22,376	Oct. 7	By Ram	10,300
			Sep. 10	By Ram	5,400

INTEREST ACCOUNT

Date	Particulars	Rs	Date	Particulars	Rs
			July 4	By Ram	300

DISCOUNT ACCOUNT

Date	Particulars	Rs	Date	Particulars	Rs
April 1	To Bills Receivable A/c	175			
July 4	To Bills Receivable A/c	324			

Illustration 6.8. *A*, a small trader has a supplier, *B* and a customer, *C* with whom the following transactions took place:

1990 July 5 Bought goods on credit from *B* Rs 3,330
     July 7 Accepted bill from *B* at one month for Rs 1,000.
     July 9 Sold goods on credit to *C* Rs 1,200.
     July 11 Drew bill on *C* for this amount at two months and endorsed the bill to *B*
     July 14 Goods sold to *C* proved defective. Goods invoiced at Rs 150 were returned and an allowance of Rs 200 was made to him to cover claims on the remainder.
     July 26 Returned goods to *B* Rs 140.
     Aug. 3 Paid *B* Rs 500, withdrew his bill of July 7th and accepted another at two months for the opening balance on his account plus Rs 40 interest.
     Aug. 24 *C* being in financial difficulties, *A* agreed to accept cash for 80 per cent of his indebtedness in full settlement. This was duly paid on August 26th, 1990.
     Sep. 14 Met *C*'s bill on presentation by *B*.

Solution:

Books of *A*
JOURNAL

Date	Particulars		Dr. Rs	Cr. Rs
1990				
July 5	Purchases Account	Dr.	3,330	
	To *B*			3,330
	(Goods purchased from *B*)			
July 7	*B*	Dr.	1,000	
	To Bills Payable Account			1,000
	(Acceptance of *B*'s draft for Rs 1,000 at one month)			
July 9	*C*	Dr.	1,200	
	To Sales Account			1,200
	(Sales to *C*)			
July 11	Bills Receivable Account	Dr.	1,200	
	To *C*			1,200
	(Bills drawn on *C* for Rs 1,200 at two months)			

Contd....

Date	Particulars		Dr. Rs	Cr Rs
July 14	B	Dr.	1,200	
	To Bills Receivable Account			1,200
	(C's acceptance endorsed in favour of B)			
July 14	Sales Returns Account	Dr.	150	
	Sales Account	Dr.	200	
	To C			350
	(Goods returned by C and allowance made to him in respect of defective goods)			
July 26	B	Dr.	140	
	To Purchases Returns Account			140
	(Goods returned to B)			
Aug. 3	Bills Payable Account	Dr.	1,000	
	To B			1,000
	(The acceptance dated 7th July, 1998 withdrawn)			
Aug. 3	Interest Account	Dr.	40	
	To B			40
	(Interest payable to B as per settlement)			
Aug. 3	B	Dr.	2,030	
	To Cash			500
	To Bills Payable Account			1,530
	(Payment of cash Rs 500, and acceptance to the bill for the remaining balance in favour of B)			
Aug. 24	C	Dr.	1,200	
	To B's Suspense Account			1,200
	(C debited for his acceptance which will not be met on presentation-credit to B's Suspense Account because the date of maturity is on 14th September)			
Aug. 26	Cash	Dr.	680	
	Bad Debts Account	Dr.	170	
	To C			850
	(Cash received in full settlement-80% of Rs 850; balance written off)			
Sep. 14	B's Suspense Account	Dr.	1,200	
	To Cash			1,200
	(C's acceptance (held by B) on presentation see entry on August 24)			

BOOKS OF B

JOURNAL

Date	Particulars		Dr. Rs	Cr Rs
1990				
July 5	A	Dr.	3,330	
	To Sales Account			3,330
	(Sales were made to A)			

(Contd....)

Date	Particulars		Dr. Rs	Cr. Rs
July 7	Bills Receivable Account To A (A's acceptance for Rs 1,000 received at one month)	Dr.	1,000	1,000
July 11	Bills Receivable Account To A (C's acceptance for Rs 1,200 received from A at two months)	Dr.	1,200	1,200
July 26	Sales Returns Account To A (Goods received back from A)	Dr.	140	140
Aug. 3	A To Bills Receivable Account (Acceptance by A, as per settlement)		1,000	1,000
Aug. 3	Cash Bills Receivable Account To A (Receipt of cash, Rs 500 and acceptance for the remaining balance due from him)	Dr. Dr.	500 1,530	2,030
Sept. 14	Cash To Bills Receivable Account (Cash received from A against C's acceptance)	Dr.	1,200	1,200

Books of C
JOURNAL ENTRIES

Date	Particulars		Dr. Rs	Cr. Rs
1990 July 9	Purchases Account To A (Goods purchased from A)	Dr	1,200	1,200
July 11	A To Bills Payable Account (Acceptance of Rs 1,200 issued in favour of A)	Dr	1,200	1,200
July 14	A To Purchase Returns A/c To Purchases Account (Goods returned to A and allowance received from him in respect of defective units, as per his Credit Note No........................ Dated...........................)	Dr	350	150 200
Aug. 24	Bills Payable Account To A (There being no possibility of meeting the acceptance in favour of A, cancellation of the same)	Dr	1,200	1,200
Aug. 26	A To Cash To Deficiency Account (Payment to A 80% of the amount due to him)	Dr	850	680 170

BILLS SENT FOR COLLECTION

The holder of a bill may keep the bill of exchange with himself in place of getting it discounted with his bankers or endorsing it to a third-party. He may utilise the services of the bank for collecting the amount of the bill. In such a case the accounting entries will be as follows:

Entries in the Books of the Drawer (or Holder) of the Bill

  (*i*) When the Bill is sent for collection:

      Bills for Collection A/c   Dr.
        To Bills Receivable Account

  (*ii*) When the Bill is actually collected:

      Bank A/c   Dr.
        To Bills for Collection A/c

  (*iii*) When the Bill is dishonoured:

      Drawee A/c   Dr.
        To Bills for Collection A/c

Any balance in the Bills for Collection Account will appear as an asset in the Balance Sheet.

Entries in the Books of the Bank

  (*i*) When the Bill is received for collection:

      Bills Receivable being Bills for Collection A/c   Dr.
        To Bills for Collection being Bills Receivable A/c

  (*ii*) When the Bill is Collected:

    (*a*) Cash A/c   Dr.
        To Party's Account
        To Commission Account
      (The bank may charge some commission for collecting the bill)

    (*b*) Bills for Collection being Bills Receivable A/c   Dr.
        To Bills Receivable being Bills for Collection A/c
      (With the amount of bills collected)

  (*iii*) When the Bill is dishonoured:

    (*a*) Bills for Collection being Bills Receivable A/c   Dr.
        To Bills Receivable being Bills for Collection A/c
    (*b*) Party's A/c   Dr.
        To Commission A/c
      (The Bank may charge commission for presenting the bill for payment)

Illustration 6.9. Mr. Ram sold goods to Mr. Ahmed for Rs 10,000 on 13th June, 1990, for which the latter accepted 4 bills of Rs 2,500 each payable after 2 months, 4 months, 6 months and 8 months respectively, Mr. Ram retained the first bill. The second bills was sent to bank for collection. The third bill was endorsed in favour of Mr. *C.* The fourth bill was discounted with his bankers at 12% per annum.

The first bill was met on the due date. As regards the second bill, the drawee approached Mr. Ram on 23rd September, 1990 paid him Rs 1,500 and requested him to draw a fresh bill for the balance together with interest at 12% per annum. The term of this bill was 3 months and the bill was duly paid on maturity as had been the case with the third bill before it. Mr. Ahmed was declared insolvent on 31st December, 1990 and Mr. Ram's bankers accordingly debited Mr. Ram on that day in respect of the fourth bill. It was ascertained that only 50 paise in a rupee be recovered from Mr. Ahmed's estate. Make necessary journal entries in the Books of Mr. Ram and Mr. Ahmed.

Solution:

JOURNAL OF MR. RAM

Date	Particulars		Dr. Amount Rs	Cr. Amount Rs
1990 June 13	Ahmed	Dr.	10,000	
	To Sales Account			10,000
	(Goods sold for Rs 10,000)			
June	Bills Receivable Account	Dr.	10,000	
	To Ahmed			10,000
	(Four bills for Rs 2,500 each received from Ahmed payable 2, 4, 6 and 8 months after date)			
June	Bills for Collection Account	Dr.	2,500	
	To Bills Receivable Account			2,500
	(Ahmed's second bill, payable 4 months after date, sent to Bank for collection)			
June	C	Dr.	2,500	
	To Bills Receivable A/c			2,500
	(Ahmed's third bill endorsed to C)			
June	Bank Account	Dr.	2,300	
	Discount Account	Dr.	200	
	To Bills Receivable A/c			2,500
	(Ahmed's fourth bill for Rs 2,500 discounted @ 12% per annum)			
1990 Aug. 16	Bank Account	Dr.	2,500	
	To Bills Receivable A/c			2,500
	(Amount received for Ahmed's first bill)			
Sep. 23	Ahmed	Dr.	2,500	
	To Bills for Collection A/c			2,500
	(Ahmed's second bill sent for collection withdrawn before due date—Oct.16)			
Sep. 23	Ahmed	Dr.	30	
	To Interest Account			30
	(Interest due on Rs 1,000 @12% for 3 months for the new bill to be accepted)			
Sep. 23	Bank Account	Dr.	1,500	
	Bills Receivable Account	Dr.	1,030	
	To Ahmed			2,530
	(Receipt from Ahmed of Rs 1,500 in cash and a bill for Rs 1,030)			
Dec. 26	Bank Account	Dr.	1,030	
	To Bills Receivable Account			1,030
	(Amount received against Ahmed's fifth bill for Rs 1,030)			

Contd....

Date	Particulars		Dr. Amount Rs	Cr. Amount Rs
Dec. 31	Ahmed	Dr.	2,500	
	To Bank Account			2,500
	(Ahmed's fourth bill, discounted with the bank, to be treated dishonoured this day)			
Dec.	Bad Debts Account	Dr.	1,250	
	To Ahmed			1,250
	(50% of the amount due from Ahmed written off as bad as the balance expected to be received)			

JOURNAL OF MR. AHMED

Date	Particulars		Dr. Amount Rs	Cr. Amount Rs
1990 June 13	Purchases Account	Dr.	10,000	
	To Ram			10,000
	(Amount of credit purchases from Ram)			
June	Ram	Dr.	10,000	
	To Bills Payable Account			10,000
	(Four bills payable of Rs 2,500 each issued to Ram payable 2, 4, 6 and 8 months after date).			
Dec. 16	Bills Payable A/c	Dr.	2,500	
	To Bank Account			2,500
	(First bill payable met on the due date)			
Sep. 23	Bills Payable A/c	Dr.	2,500	
	To Ram			2,500
	(Second bill payable issued to Ram withdrawn for cancellation)			
	Ram	Dr.	2,500	
	Interest	Dr.	30	
	To Bank			1,500
	To Bills Payable A/c			1,030
	(Amount paid and fresh bill issued, with interest to Ram in lieu of the 2nd bill)			
Dec. 16	Bills Payable Amount	Dr.	2,500	
	To Bank Account			2,500
	(Third Bill for Rs 2,500 met on the due date)			
Dec. 26	Bills Payable Account	Dr.	1,030	
	To Bank			1,030
	(Fifth bill issued to Ahmed paid this day)			
Dec. 31	Bills Payable Account	Dr.	2,500	
	To Ram			2,500
	(The fourth bill treated cancelled on account of financial difficulties)			

ACCOMMODATION BILLS

Accounting entries regarding accommodation bills can be studied under two heads:

    (*i*) When a bill is drawn up for the accommodation of one of the parties.

    (*ii*) When a bill is drawn up for mutual accommodation.

When a bill is drawn up for the accommodation of one of the parties. Usually the accommodated party is the drawer of the bill. The bill is returned to the drawer by the drawee after accepting it. The drawer gets the bill discounted with his banker. On the due date he sends the amount due under the bill to the drawee to enable the drawee to meet the bill on maturity.

-**Illustration 6.10.** In order to accommodate B, A agrees to accept a bill of exchange for Rs 1,000. B discounts the bill for Rs 980 with his bankers. Before the due date, B sends a sum of Rs 1,000 to A. A meets the bill on maturity. Make necessary journal entries in the books of both A and B.

A's JOURNAL (DRAWEE)

Date	Particulars		Dr. Amount Rs	Cr. Amount Rs
	B	Dr.	1,000	
	To Bills Payable A/c			1,000
	(Being acceptance given)			
	Cash/Bank A/c	Dr.	1,000	
	To B			1,000
	(Being money reimbursed by B)			
	Bills Payable A/c	Dr.	1,000	
	To Cash or Bank A/c			1,000
	(Being bill met on maturity)			

B's JOURNAL (DRAWER)

Date	Particulars		Dr. Amount Rs	Cr. Amount Rs
	Bills Receivable A/c	Dr.	1,000	
	To B			1,000
	(Being A's acceptance received)			
	Bank A/c	Dr.	980	
	Discount A/c	Dr.	20	
	To Bills Receivable A/c			1,000
	(Being the bill discounted with bank)			
	A	Dr.	1,000	
	To Bills Receivable A/c			1,000
	(Being amount of the bill reimbursed to A)			

When a bill is drawn up for mutual accommodation. In this case there may be two different situations:

(*i*) Only one bill may be drawn.

(*ii*) Two bills may be drawn.

When only one bill is drawn. In this case the drawer and the drawee share the proceeds of the bill on being discounted with the bank, in the agreed ratio. The drawer sends the drawee's share soon after getting the bill discounted. The discount is borne by both the parties in the ratio in which they share the proceeds of the discounted bill. On the due date the drawer sends the remaining amount of the bill to enable the drawee to meet the bill on maturity.

Illustration 6.11. S. Sarkar draws on R. Shanker a bill for Rs 2,000 on 1st May 1990 for 3 months for mutual accommodation R. Shankar returns the bill duly accepted and S. Sarkar discounted the bill with the Punjab National Bank for Rs 1,990. He remits half the proceeds to R. Shankar. On the date of maturity he merits the balance and the bill is met on presentation.

Solution:

S. SARKAR'S JOURNAL

Date	Particulars		Dr. Amount Rs	Cr. Amount Rs
1990 May 1	Bills Receivable A/c To R. Shankar (Acceptance received from R. Shankar for mutual accommodation)	Dr.	2,000	2,000
	Bank A/c Discount A/c To Bills Receivable A/c (For bills discounted)	Dr. Dr.	1,980 20	2,000
	R. Shankar To Bank A/c To Discount A/c (For remittance of half the proceeds to R. Shankar)	Dr.	1,000	990 10
Aug. 4	R. Shankar To Bank A/c (For balance due remitted)	Dr.	1,000	1,000

R. SHANKAR'S JOURNAL

Date	Particulars		Dr. Amount Rs	Cr. Amount Rs
1990 May 1	S. Sarkar To Bills Payable A/c (For acceptance given)	Dr.	2,000	2,000
	Bank A/c Discount A/c To S. Sarkar (For half of the proceeds Received from S. Sarkar)	Dr. Dr.	990 10	1,000
	Bank A/c To S. Sarkar (For balance due recevied form S. Sarkar)	Dr.	1,000	1,000
	Bill Receivable A/c To Bank A/c (Being payment made for acceptance	Dr.	2,000	2,000

Illustration 6.12. Shri R.C. Tewarson and Shri M.C. Macmillan enter into an accommodation arrangement whereunder the proceeds are to be shared 2/3 and 1/3 respectively. Shri Tewarson draws a bill for Rs 9,000 on Shri Macmillan on 2nd January, 1990 for three

months. Shri Tewarson gets it discounted with Central Bank of India for Rs 8,820 and on 3rd January remits Shri Macmillan's share to him, which Shri Macmillan received on 5th January, 1990. On the due date, Shri Macmillan pays the bill, though Shri Tewarson fails to remit the amount due to the former. On 6th April, Shri Tewarson accepts a bill for Rs 12,600 drawn on him by Shri Macmillan for three months, which Shri Macmillan discounts on 7th April for Rs 12,330 and remit Rs 2,220 to Shri Tewarson the next day. Before the maturity of the second bill, Shri Tewarson becomes insolvent and only 50% was realised from his estate on 10th July, 1990.

Pass necessary journal entries in the books of Shri Macmillan.

Solution:

JOURNAL OF SHRI MACMILLAN

Date	Particulars		Dr. Amount Rs	Cr. Amount Rs
1990				
Jan. 2	R. C. Tewarson	Dr.	9,000	
	To Bills Payable A/c			9,000
	(Acceptance given to Shri Tewarson for Rs 9,000 payable 3 months after date, for mutual accommodation)			
Jan. 5	Bank Account	Dr.	2,940	
	Discount Account	Dr.	60	
	To R.C. Tewarson			3,000
	(1/3 of the proceeds received against own acceptance from shri R.C. Tewarson)			
April 5	Bills Payable A/c	Dr.	9,000	
	To Bank			9,000
	(Payment of Bills Payable given to Mr. Tewarson on 2nd Jan.			
April 6	Bills Receivable A/c	Dr.	12,600	
	To R.C. Tewarson			12,600
	(Acceptance received from R.C. Tewarson for mutual accommodation and in payment of Rs 6,000 due from him)			
April 7	Bank Account	Dr.	12,330	
	Discount Account	Dr.	270	
	To Bills Receivable A/c			12,600
	(Proceeds of discounting of the bills receivable received from R.C. Tewarson)			
April 8	R.C. Tewarson	Dr.	2,400	
	To Bank Account			2,220
	To Discount Account			180
	(Amount remitted to R.C. Tewarson, discount debited to him being $270 \times \dfrac{8,220}{12,330}$ or Rs 180)			
July 10	R.C. Tewarson	Dr.	12,600	
	To Bank			12,600
	(Bill Receivable received from R.C. Tewarson dishonoured on his being adjudged insolvent)			

Contd....

Date	Particulars		Dr. Amount Rs	Cr. Amount Rs
July 10	Bank Account	Dr.	4,200	
	Bad Debts Account	Dr.	4,200	
	To R.C. Tewarson			8,400
	(Received a dividend of 50% from the estate of R.C. Tewarson in full and final settlement)			

When two bills are drawn. In such a case each party draw one bill of exchange on the other. Thus, each party, becomes drawer as well as the drawee. Each party gets the bill discounted from its banks and uses the proceeds of the bill discounted for meeting its requirements. On the due date each party meets the bill for which it is the drawee. They also settle the account in between themselves.

Illustration 6.13. On 1st January, 1989 A drew and B accepted a bill at three months for Rs 1,000. On 4th January A Discounted the Bill for Rs 980 and remitted half the proceeds to B. On 1st February, B drew and A accepted a bill at three months for Rs 400. On 4th February B discounted the bill for Rs 390 and remitted half the proceeds to A. A and B agreed to share the discounts equally.

At maturity, A met his acceptance but B failed to meet, and recourse was had to A. A drew and B accepted a new bill at three months for the amount of the old bill and interest @ 5% p.a.

On July 1, B became a bankrupt. A first and final dividend of 50 paise in a rupee was declared by the official receiver on 31st Oct. B was discharged on 5th Dec., 1989, and he agreed to pay the unsatisfied balance of his account, this was paid on 10th Nov. 1990.

Make journal entries and write up B's Account in A's books of 1989 and state how would you advice A to treat the balance in B's account as on 31st December, 1989.

Solution:

A's JOURNAL

Date	Particulars		Dr. Amount Rs P	Cr. Amount Rs P
1989 Jan. 1	Bills Receivable A/c	Dr.	1,000	
	To B			1,000
	(For mutual accommodation bill accepted by B)			
Jan. 4	Bank A/c	Dr.	980	
	Discount A/c	Dr.	20	
	To Bills Receivable A/c			1,000
	(Bill Receivable discounted with the Bank)			
Jan. 4	B	Dr.	500	
	To Bank A/c			490
	To Discount A/c			10
	(Half of the proceeds sent to B)			
Feb. 1	B	Dr.	400	
	To Bills Payable A/c			400
	(Acceptance given to the mutual accommodation bill)			
Feb. 4	Bank A/c	Dr.	195	
	Discount A/c	Dr.	5	
	To B			200
	(Half of the proceeds of the bill payable discounted received from B)			

Contd....

Date	Particulars		Dr. Amount Rs	Cr. Amount Rs
April 4	B	Dr.	1,000	
	To Bank A/c			1,000
	(For bill dishonoured by B on due date)			
April 4	B	Dr.	12.50	
	To Interest A/c			12.50
	(Interest for 3 months of Rs 1,000 @ 5% p.a.)			
April 4	Bill Receivable A/c	Dr.	1,012.50	
	To B			1,012.50
	(New bill received from B)			
May 4	Bills Payable A/c	Dr.	400	
	To Bank A/c			400
	(Acceptance met on maturity)			
July 7	B	Dr.	1,012.50	
	To Bills Receivable A/c			1,012.50
	(Bill receivable dishonoured)			
Oct. 31	Bank A/c	Dr.	356.25	
	To B			356.25
	(A Dividend of 50 paise in a rupee was received from the estate of B)			

A's Ledger

B's ACCOUNT

Date	Particulars	Rs P	Date	Particulars	Rs P
1989			1989		
Jan.4	To Bank A/c (half proceeds of bill discounted)	490	Jan.1	By Bills Receivable A/c (due on 4th April, 1990)	1,000
	To Discount A/c (half charge of discount)	10	Feb.4	By Cash A/c (half proceeds of bill discounted)	195
Feb.1	To Bills Payable A/c (due on 4th May)	400		By Discount A/c	5
April 4	To Bank A/c (Bill due on 4th April dishonoured)	1,000	April 4	By Bills Receivable A/c (due on 7th July, 1990)	1,012.50
April 4	To Interest A/c (at 5% for 3 months)	12.50	Oct. 31	By Bank (first & final dividend)	356.25
July 7	To Bill Receivable A/c (dishonour)	1,012.50	Dec. 31	By Balance c/d[*]	356.25
		2,925.00			2,925.00

[*]**Note.** On October 31, when A receives a first and final dividend of 50 paise in a rupee, he can write off the balance of Rs 356.25 taking it as a bad debt. He may postpone making of this entry till 31st December. Alternatively, he should make provision for bad debts for Rs 356.25 since B has made no doubt a promise, but he is not bound to pay.

BILLS RECEIVABLE AND PAYABLE BOOKS

Where dealings in bills are numerous, to save time separate books are kept both for bills received and bills issued, with complete details. These books are—(i) Bills Receivable Book, and (ii) Bills Payable Book.

These books have two advantages: (i) they help in finding out details regarding each bill at a glance (ii) they reduce clerical work since there is no need of journalising each receipt of bill or issue of bill. Of course other transactions such as endorsement, dishonour or renewal of a bill will have to be journalised. When a bill is discounted, the entry will be made in the discount (for discount allowed) and bank (for cash received) columns of the Cash book. In case of bills payable, the total of the amount column will be credited to Bills Payable Account at the end of a period and debited to individual creditors accounts in the ledger daily. Similarly, the total of the amount column of Bills Receivable book will be debited to Bills Receivable Account at the end of a period, and credited individually to debtors account daily.

Illustration 6.12. Make entries in proper books of account on the basis of following particulars on 1st December, 1990.

Balances	Rs
Bank (Dr.)	1,500
Debtors	
A	500
B	800
C	1,350
D	1,400
Creditors	
E	500
F	1,200
G	600

Following transactions took place in the month of December, 1990:

Dec. 3 Drew on A (Bill No. 85) at two months after date for Rs 480 in full settlement A accepts the bill and returns on December 5.

Dec. 6 Bills No. 85 discounted for Rs 470.

Dec. 9 B sends a Promissory Note for Rs 800 payable three months after date.

Dec. 10 B's promissory note discounted with the bank for Rs 780.

Dec. 12 Accepted F's draft for Rs 1,200 payable two months after date (No. 100).

Dec. 20 D sends his promissory note for Rs 600 towards payment of a past loan, payable two months after date.

Dec. 21 D's promissory note transferred to G.

Dec. 25 Accepted E's draft for Rs 500 payable three months after date.

Dec. 31 C sends Rs 1,000 in cash and a promissory note for the balance payable three months after date in full settlement of his account.

Solution:

CASH BOOK

Date	Particulars	Discount	Bank	Date	Particulars	Discount	Bank
1990							
Dec. 1	To Balance b/d		1,500	Dec.31	By Balance c/d		3,750
Dec.6	To B/R	10	470				
Dec. 10	To B/R	20	780				
Dec. 31	To C	—	1,000				
		30	3,750			—	3,750

BILLS RECEIVABLE BOOK

Serial No.	Date	From whom received	Acceptor	Date of Bill	Term	Maturity	Amount Rs	L.F.	Disposal
	1990					1990			
85	Dec. 6	A	A	Dec. 6	2 months	Feb. 6	480		Discounted on Dec. 6, 1990
86	Dec. 9	B	B	Dec 9	3 months	Mar. 12	800		Discounted on Dec. 10, 1990
87	Dec. 20	D	D	Dec. 20	2 months	Feb. 23	600		endorsed to G on Dec. 21, 1990
88	Dec. 31	C	C	Dec. 31	3 months	April 3	350		
						Total Rs	2,230		

BILLS PAYABLE BOOK

Serial No.	Date	Drawn by	Payee	Term	Maturity	Amount Rs	L.F.	Payable at	Disposal
	1990				1990				
100	Dec. 12	F	F	2 months	Feb. 15	1,200	—	—	—
101	Dec. 25	E	E	3 months	March 28	500	—	—	—
					Total Rs	1,700			

JOURNAL.

Date	Particulars		Dr. Amount Rs	Cr. Amount Rs
Dec. 3	Discount A/c	Dr.	20	
	To A			20
	(For discount allowed to A on the bill received from him)			
Dec. 21	G	Dr.	600	
	To Bills Receivable A/c			600
	(Endorsement in favour of G of D's acceptance)			

Ledger Accounts

Dr.   A   Cr.

Date	Particulars	Amount Rs	Date	Particulars	Amount Rs
1990 Dec. 1	To Balance b/d	500	Dec. 3	By Bills Receivable A/c	480
				By Discount A/c	20
		500			500

B

Date	Particulars	Amount Rs	Date	Particulars	Amount Rs
Dec. 1	To Balance b/d	800		By Bills Receivable	800
		800			800

C

Date	Particulars	Amount Rs	Date	Particulars	Amount Rs
Dec. 1	To Balance b/d	1,350		By Bills Receivable	1,000
				By Bills Receivable	350
		1,350			1,350

D

Date	Particulars	Amount Rs	Date	Particulars	Amount Rs
Dec. 1	To Balance b/d	1,400	Dec. 20	By Bills Receivable	600
			Dec. 31	By Balance c/d	800
		1,400			1,400

E

Date	Particulars	Amount Rs	Date	Particulars	Amount Rs
Dec. 1	To Bill Payable A/c	500	Dec. 1	By Balance b/d	500
		500			500

F

Date	Particulars	Amount Rs	Date	Particulars	Amount Rs
Dec. 12	To Bills Payable A/c	1,200	Dec. 1	By Balance b/d	1,200
		1,200			1,200

Dr.   G   Cr.

Date	Particulars	Amount Rs	Date	Particulars	Amount Rs
Dec.31	To Bills Receivable A/c	600 600	Dec. 1	By Balance b/d	600 600

BILLS RECEIVABLE ACCOUNT

Date	Particulars	Amount Rs	Date	Particulars	Amount Rs
Dec. 31	To Sundries (total from B/R book)	2,230 2,230	Dec. 6 Dec. 10 Dec. 31	By Cash a/c By Cash A/c By Balance c/d	480 800 950 2,230
Jan. 1	To Balance b/d	950			

BILLS PAYABLE ACCOUNT

Date	Particulars	Amount Rs	Date	Particulars	Amount Rs
Dec. 31	To Balance c/d	1,700 1,700	Dec. 31	By Sundries (Total From B/P book)	1,700 1,700
			Jan.1	By Balance b/d	1,700

DISCOUNT ACCOUNT

Date	Particulars	Amount Rs	Date	Particulars	Amount Rs
Dec. 3 Dec. 2	To A To Sundries (total from cash book)	20 30 50	Dec. 31	By Balance c/d	50 50
Jan.1	To Balance b/d	50			

KEY TERMS

☐ **Accommodation Bill:** A bill drawn and accepted for providing funds to a friend in need.

☐ **Bill of Exchange:** An instrument in writing containing an unconditional order signed by the maker, directing the said person to pay a certain sum of money only to or to the order of a certain person or to the bearer of the instrument.

☐ **Cheque:** A bill of exchange drawn on a specified banker and payable on demand.

☐ **Demand Bill:** A bill of exchange payable on demand.

☐ **Promissory Note:** An instrument in writing, containing an unconditional undertaking, signed by the maker, to pay a certain sum of money only to or to the order of certain person or the bearer of the instrument.

☐ **Time Bill:** A bill of exchange payable after a particular period of time.

☐ **Trade Bill:** A bill drawn and accepted for a genuine trade transaction.

TEST QUESTIONS

Objective type | TEST YOUR UNDERSTANDING |

1. State whether each of the following statement is True or False:
   - (a) A Bill of Exchange contains a unconditional order to a certain person to pay a certain sum of money.
   - (b) There are only two parties in case of a Bill of Exchange.
   - (c) A Bill of Exchange payable otherwise than on demand can be made payable to the bearer.
   - (d) An Accommodation Bill is drawn and accepted for genuine trade transactions.
   - (e) A Bill drawn in India on a person residing outside India but payable in India is an Inland Bill.
   - (f) There is no difference between a holder and a holder in due course.
   - (g) Retiring of a Bill is different from dishonour of a bill.
   - (h) No accounting entry is passed in the books of the drawee when a bill receivable is either discounted from the bank or endorsed to some other party.
   - (i) The journal entries in respect of bills receivable discounted from the bank and of bills receivable sent to the bank for collection are the same.

     [**Ans.** (a) True, (b) False, (c) True, (d) False, (e) True, (f) False, (g) True, (h) True, (i) False].

2. Fill in the blanks:
   - (a) A Bill of Exchange payable after a certain period is known as a ......Bill.
   - (b) A Bill drawn and accepted for a genuine trade transaction is termed as a ......Bill.
   - (c) A Bill which is not an Inland Bill is a......Bill.
   - (d) A person who draws a Bill of Exchange is known as the......
   - (e) A person named in a negotiable instrument to whom or to whose order the money in the instrument is directed to be paid is called as the ......

(f) Noting charges are paid in the event of......of a Bill.

(g) In case of Accommodation Bills, if one party becomes insolvent than that party credits the short remittance to......

(h) At the time of the renewal of a bill, interest account is......in the books of the drawee.

(i) ......days of grace are allowed in case of Time Bills for calculating date of maturity.

[**Ans.** (a) Time, (b) Trade, (c) Foreign, (d) Drawer, (e) Payee, (f) dishonour, (g) Deficiency Account, (h) debited, (i) Three.

Essay type

FOR REVIEW, DISCUSSION AND PRACTICE

1. Differentiate between a Bill of Exchange and a Promissory Note.
2. Give a specimen with at least five entries of the following;
     (a)   A Bills Receivable Book;
     (b)   A Bills Payable Book,
   You are also required to make the posting of these entries in the ledger,
3. Differentiate between:
     (a)   A Trade Bill and an Accommodation Bill.
     (b)   Retiring of a Bill and Renewal of a Bill.
     (c)   A Time Bill and a Demand Bill.

PRACTICAL PROBLEMS

Payment of Bill on maturity

1. On 1st April, 1988, A sold goods to B for Rs 5,000. A bill of exchange for the said amount was drawn by A which was duly accepted by B payable three months after date. The bill was met on maturity. You are required to pass the necessary journal entries in the books of A and B.
2. X sold goods of Rs 5,000 to Y on 1st January 1990 and drew a bill for the above amount on Y payable two months after date. On the same date X purchased goods of Rs 5,000 from Z and endorsed the bill received from Y in favour of Z towards payment of the purchase price. The bill was met on maturity. You are required to pass necessary journal entries in the books of X, Y and Z.

Dishonour of the Bill

3. A bill for Rs 5,000 is drawn by B and accepted by C. Show what entries would be passed in the books of B in each of the following circumstances:
     (a)   If he retained the bill till the due date and then realised it on maturity.
     (b)   If he discounted it with his bank for Rs 4,800; and
     (c)   If he endorsed it over to his creditor M in settlement of a debt.
   State what further entries would be necessary in the books of B in each of the above circumstances, if the bill was dishonoured on the due date.
4. Sujesh owed money to Brijesh and hence accepted two bills each of Rs 5,000 at three months' duration drawn on him by the latter on January 1, 1987. Brijesh discounted one of the bills with his bank for net proceeds of Rs 4,800 and endorsed the other in favour of Mukesh to whom he owned a like sum, on the same date.

   Sujesh paid the bill held by Mukesh on the due date, but failed to meet the bill presented by the bank. The bank debited Brijesh's account on April 4, 1987 inclusive of bank charges of Rs 10. Sujesh paid the amount inclusive of charges to Brijesh on April 10, 1987.

   Show the Journal entries in respect of the above in the books of Sujesh and Brijesh.

Renewal of the Bill

5. Patel received from one of his customers a bill at three months for Rs 16,000. He discounted it on the same day at 10 per cent per annum with his bankers. On the date of maturity, the bill was dishonoured and the bank incurred noting charges of Rs 80. However, the customers paid him Rs 2,000 plus noting charges plus interest for three months amounting to Rs 420, in cash

and accepted a fresh bill at three months for Rs 14,000, being the balance amount due from him. Patel gave the second bill to Mr. Narayan, one of his creditors. The second bill was duly honoured on due date. Record these transactions in the Journal of Patel.

6. On 15th January, 1986 Sudarshan sold goods to Shashi for Rs 3,000. Shashi paid Rs 600 in cash and for balance accepts three bills—No. 1 for Rs 700 at one month, No. 2 for Rs 800 at two months, and No. 3 for Rs 900 at three months.

   Sudarshan endorses 1st bill to Nahar his creditor on 16th January in full settlement of Rs 710; discounted the 2nd bill at his bank for Rs 792 and retained the third bill till maturity.

   The first bill is met at maturity. The second bill is dishonoured and Rs 10 being paid as noting charges. Sudarshan charges Rs 15 for interest and draws on Shashi a fourth bill for the amount at three months. At maturity the third bill was renewed with interest of 5% p.a. for three months. The 5th was duly accepted by Shashi. The fourth and fifth bills were met on maturity.

   Give journal entries in the books of Sudarshan.

7. On 1st January, 1987 Julie supplied goods to Vikram of the value of Rs 9,000 and settled the account by means of three bills of Rs 3,000 each, due after two, three and four months respectively.

   A week later Julie discounted the first bill at a discount of Rs 60. The other two bills were held till maturity.

   The first two bills were duly met on maturity. On the maturity of the third bill, however, Vikram arranged to retire the bill paying Rs 1,000 in cash and giving Julie a fresh bill for four months to cover the balance together with 12% interest per annum. Julie discounted this bill for Rs 2,000. The bill was met on maturity.

   Pass the necessary Journal Entries in the Books of Julie and Vikram: (Narration to entries may not be given).

8. On 1st January, 1988 Bimal drew on Chetan three Bills of Exchange in full settlement of claim. The first for Rs 14,000 at one month. The second for Rs 16,000 at two months and the third for Rs 18,000 at three months. The bills were duly accepted by Chetan.

   The first bill was endorsed by Bimal to his creditor Tarun on 3rd January, 1988, the second bill was discounted on 15 January, 1989, for Rs 15,900 and the third bill was sent to Bank for collection on 4th February, 1989. All the bills were duly met on maturity expect the second bill which was dishonoured, noting charging being Rs 240. Bimal charged Chetan Rs 300 for interest and drew on him a fourth bill for two months for the amount due. The fourth bill was duly met on maturity.

   Pass the Journals entries (including narration) in the books of Bimal.

Bills for Collection

9. On 1st December 1990, B sold goods to the value of Rs 1,000 to C and Rs 1,000 to D. B draws on each of them a bill of exchange at three months. He received the bills duly accepted on 2nd December.

   B goes to his banker for getting them discounted on 1st January. The Bank discounts the first bill at 6% p.a. while declines to discount the bill accepted by D, but offers as an alternative a loan at 6% p.a. to the full extent of the bill until matured. The bill is endorsed and handed to the bank for collection. B agrees for it and the transaction is carried out on the same date.

   On 1st March, on the request of C, the bill is returned. B accepts Rs 990 in full satisfaction and the Bank allows a rebate of Rs 2 to B.D. meets the bill on maturity.

   Make necessary journal entries in the book of B.

Accommodation Bills

10. On January 1, 1987 A and B drew on each other a bill for Rs 1,000, payable three months after date for their mutual benefit. On 4th January, 1987 they discounted with their banks each other's bill at 15% per annum. On the due date, each meets his own acceptance. Record the above transactions in the Journals of A and B.

11. A and B were both in need of temporary accommodation. On 1st April, 1987, A accepted B's draft for Rs 2,000 for three months and B accepted A's draft for Rs 1,000 for 3 months. The two bills were discounted at the respective banks for Rs 1,970 and Rs 980. On the due date A met his acceptance but B could not arrange to send the required amount to A and accepted A's draft for Rs 1,500 for 2 months. This was discounted for Rs 1,460 and A remitted to B Rs 230. On September 6, 1987 B was declared insolvent and his estate paid only 30%.

Give Journal entries in the books of A

12. X, for mutual and temporary accommodation of himself and Y; draws upon the latter a bill of exchange at three months for Rs 1,800 dated 1st January 1990. Y accepts the bill and sends it to X. X discounts the bill immediately at his bank, the rate of discount being 6% per annum and hands over half the proceeds to Y. Y for a similar purpose and at the same time, draws a bill at three months on X for Rs 900. X accepts the bill. Y discounts the bill at 6% per annum and hands over half the proceeds to X. Y becomes insolvent on 31st March, 1990 as such fails to meet his acceptance on maturity. On 30th June, 1990, a first and final dividend of 25 paise in the rupee was paid out of his estate in settlement of his dues.

Write up the Journal entries in X's books and draw up Y's account in X's ledger, assuming that discounts were shared equally by X and Y.

13. On 1st May, 1990 A drew and B accepted a bill at three months for Rs 2,000. On 4th May, 1990 A discounted the bill at his bank for 6 per cent per annum and remitted half the proceed by cheque to B. On 1st June, 1990 B drew and A accepted a bill at three months for Rs 500. On 4th June, 1990 B discounted the bill with his bank at 6% p.a. and remitted half the proceeds to A. A and B agreed to share the discounts equally.

At maturity A met his acceptance but B failed to meet his and A therefore, had to pay it. A then drew and B accepted a new bill at three months for the amount of the original bill plus Rs 30 for interest.

On 1st November, 1990, B became insolvent and paid to his creditors 50 paise in a rupee in full satisfaction.

Write up B's account in A's ledger together with necessary journal entries.

14. Natha Singh of Nakodar and Prem Singh of Patiala agree to draw an accommodation bill. Natha Singh draws the bill of the value of Rs 20,000 payable three months after-date. The same is discounted by Natha Singh with the State Bank of India, Nakodar, his bankers, the rate of discount being 12% p.a. They share the proceeds equally. On due date, Prem Singh expresses his inability to contribute his share. Subsequently the bill is taken up by Natha Singh from his bankers. Natha Singh now draws a bill on Prem Singh payable two months after date along with interest @12% p.a. on the amount due. On due date, the bill is dishonoured and Natha Singh Pays noting charges Rs 50. In course of time a first and final dividend of 60% was received from Prem Singh. Prepare the necessary ledger accounts in the books of Natha Singh.

(Ans. Bad debts Rs 4,100)

Bills Receivable and Bills Payable Books

15. Enter the following transactions in the Bills Receivable Book of H. Bhagwan:

1989

Feb. 1. Drew on Gopikrishan at 30 days sight Rs 10,000 against sales.

2. Drew on Ramanlal at 45 days sight Rs 15,750, against sales.

3. Drew on Gopikrishan at 30 days sight Rs 14,200 against sales. Drew on Ramanlal at 45 days sight Rs 16,000 against sales.

On the 4th February all the above bills were discounted by H. Bhagwan with his bank, the discount rates being:

(a) Rs 15 per thousand in the case of 30 days bills; and

(b) Rs 22.50 per thousand in the case of 45 days bills.

Fractions of thousand are treated as a thousand for discount rate purposes.

Show also the entries in the Books of H. Bhagwan in:

(*i*)   The Bills Receivable A/c;

(*ii*) Gopikrishan's A/c; and

(*iii*) Ramanalal's A/c,

[Ans. Discount Total Rs 1,095]

16. Enter the following transactions in proper books of accounts:

Balances as on 31st December, 1989:

			Rs
Balance at Bank			Dr. 7,500
Debtors balances	X	:	:2,500
	Y	:	4,000
	Z	:	6,500
	P	:	7,000
Creditors balances	Q	:	2,500
	R	:	6,000
	S	:	3,000

Following transactions took place in the month of January, 1990.

Jan.	1	Drew on X (Bill no. 10) payable three months after date for Rs 2,400 in full settlement. Accepted bill and returned it on Jan. 4, 1990.
Jan.	10	Bill No. 10 discounted with the bankers for Rs 2,350.
Jan.	12	Y sends a Promissory Note for Rs 4,000 payable three months after date.
Jan.	15	Y's Promissory Note discounted with the Bank for Rs 3,900.
Jan.	20	Accepted R's draft for Rs 6,000 payable three months after date.
Jan.	22	Received a Promissory Note From Z for Rs 6,600 payable two months after date.
Jan.	30	Endorsed the Promissory Note from Z in favour of T.
Jan.	31	Accepted S's draft for Rs 3,000 payable two months after date.

Chapter 7

BANK RECONCILIATION STATEMENT

> **LEARNING OBJECTIVES**
>
> After studying this chapter you should be able to:
>
> ☐ appreciate the utility of keeping an account with a bank by a business firm;
>
> ☐ identify the causes of difference between the balance shown by the bank Pass Book and the firm's Cash Book;
>
> ☐ explain the meaning and objectives of preparing a Bank Reconciliation Statement;
>
> ☐ prepare a Bank Reconciliation Statement, and
>
> ☐ explain the meaning of certain key terms.

ADVANTAGES OF KEEPING BANK ACCOUNT

While explaining recording of cash transactions in an earlier chapter, it has already been stated that a firm may keep account (s) with one or more Banks. The advantages of keeping an account (s) with a Bank (s) are as follows:

1. Avoidance of risk. Keeping large cash balances in the office is risky. In case money is deposited from time to time in the Bank such risk can be avoided.

2. Prevention of fraud and misappropriation. Deposits of money into the Bank and disbursements of money through the Bank reduces the chances of misappropriation of funds and fraud being played by the employees of the firm. All receipts can immediately be deposited at the end of the day in the Bank. Similarly all payments may be made by means of cheques. Thus, the quantum of cash to be handled by the employees of the business is considerably reduced resulting into less chances of fraud and misappropriations.

3. Reduction in accounting work. Depositing of money into the Bank and making payments through a Bank considerably reduces the firm's accounting work. As a matter of fact in case of large business houses or institutions, the Banks open extension counters where all payments can be received and made. Thus, the accounting work at the firm's level is considerably reduced since the firm's cash accounting work is more or less done by the Bank.

When the money is deposited by the firm into a Bank, the firm debit the bank account since bank account is a personal account and as per accounting rule, the Bank being the receiver has to be debited. Similarly, when money is withdrawn from the Bank, the firm give credit to the bank account since Bank is the giver. On the other hand on receipt of money from the customer (*i.e.*, the firm), the Bank give credit to the customer since the customer's account is a personal account and he is the giver. Similarly on money being withdrawn by the customer, the Bank debits the account of the customer since he is the receiver. The above rules of accounting as regards bank transactions can be summarised as follows:

(i) On deposit of money by the Firm into the Bank account, the Firm debits the Bank account while the Bank credits the Firm's account.

(ii) On withdrawal of money by the Firm from the Bank, the Firm credits the Bank's account while the Bank debits the Firm's account.

Thus, the balance as shown by the firm's books in the bank account should tally with the balance shown by the bank's books in the account of the firm. Of course, if in the books of the firm the bank account shows a debit balance, in the books of the Bank, the firm's account will show a credit balance and *vice-versa*. However, the two balances rarely tally on account of the reasons given later in the chapter.

All transactions relating to the Bank *i.e.*, deposits or withdrawals of the money in or from the Bank are recorded by the firm in the bank column maintained on each side of the cash book. The deposit of the money into the business bank account is recorded on the debit side of the cash book in the bank column, while the withdrawal of money from the bank is recorded on the credit side in the bank column of the cash book. The bank also maintains the firm's account in its books. A copy of this account, it submits to the firm from time to time. The account so submitted by the bank to the customer is known as the Bank Pass Book or Bank Statement. A proforma of one page of Bank Pass Book is given below:

INDIAN OVERSEAS BANK
SAVINGS BANK ACCOUNT
.........Branch

Name of the Depositor(s)... A/c No................

Address...

Date	Cheque No.	Particulars	Debit Rs	Credit Rs	Balance Rs	Initials

The Pass Book or the Bank Statement is submitted by the bank to the customer for his information and verification. As already stated before, the balance shown by the bank column of the Cash Book and the Bank Pass Book normally do not tally on account of certain reasons. These reasons are being explained in the following pages.

CAUSES OF DIFFERENCE

The following are the causes of difference between the balance as shown by the Bank Pass Book and the balance as shown by the Firm's Cash Book.

(i) **Cheques issued but not presented for payment.** The firm issues cheques from time to time for making different payments. As soon as a cheque is issued the firm debits the party's account in whose favour the cheque is issued and credits the bank's account. However, the Bank comes to know of issue of such cheques only when they are presented for payment. The Bank, therefore, debits the firm's account only when the cheque is actually presented for payment. It may, therefore, be possible that on a particular date when the Bank is submitting the firm's statement of account, it may not include certain cheques which have been issued by the firm because they may not have yet been presented. Thus, the balance shown by the Bank's books in the firm's account will be higher than the balance shown by the Firm's books in the Bank account. For example, a firm issues a cheque in favour of a creditor on 28th December, 1990 for a sum of Rs 10,000. The cheque is presented by the creditor on 3rd January, 1991 for payment. In case, the Bank submits a statement of account to the firm upto 31st December, 1990, there will be a difference of Rs 10,000 between the balance as shown by the firm's books and the balance as shown by the Pass Book.

(*ii*) **Cheques sent for collection but not yet collected.** A firm receives from time to time cheques from its customers and it sends them to its bankers for collection and crediting the proceeds to its account. The firm debits the account of the Bank as soon as it sends the cheques to the Bank for collection. However, the Bank gives credit to the firm only when the cheques are actually collected. Thus, on a particular date it may be possible that certain cheques which were sent for collection by the firm to the Bank may not have been collected by the Bank and, therefore, not credited to the firm's account. The two balances, *i.e.*, the balance as shown by the Bank Pass Book and the firm's Cash Book will, therefore, be different. For example, if a firm sends a cheque of Rs 5,000 on 25th December, 1990 to the Bank for collection which is collected by the Bank on 5th January, 1991, in the statement of account which may be submitted by the Bank for the year ending 31st December, 1990, there will be no credit to the customer for the cheque which it has not yet collected. Thus, the balance shown by the firm's Cash Book will be different from the balance as shown by the Bank Pass Book.

(*iii*) **Bank charges.** The Bank charges its customers for the services it renders to its customers from time to time. The Bank may charge its customer for remitting funds at his instructions from one place to another. It may also charge for collecting the outstation cheques or bills of exchange of its customer. The Bank debits the customer's account as soon as it renders such a service. However, a customer will know of such charges only when he receives a statement of account from the Bank. Thus, on a particular date, the balance shown by the Bank Pass Book may be different from the balance shown by the Cash Book.

(*iv*) **Direct collections on behalf of customers.** A banker may receive amounts due to the customer directly from customer's debtors. For example, the banker may get dividends, rents, interest, etc, directly from the persons concerned on account of the standing instructions of the customer to such persons. The Bank gives credit to the customer for such collections as soon as it gets such payments. However, the customer comes to know of such collections only when he receives the statement of accounts from his Banker. Thus, the balance shown by the Bank Pass Book and the Firm's Cash Book may not be the same on account of this reason.

(*v*) **Errors.** There may be errors in the account maintained by the customer as well as the Bank. A wrong credit or debit may be given by the customer or the Bank. The two balances, therefore, may not tally.

MEANING AND OBJECTIVE OF BANK RECONCILIATION STATEMENT

A Bank Reconciliation Statement is a statement reconciling the balance as shown by the Bank Pass Book and the balance as shown by the Cash Book. The objective of preparing such a statement is to know the causes of difference between the two balances and pass necessary correcting or adjusting entries in the books of the firm. It should be noted that every reason of difference does not require an adjusting or correcting entry. Some reasons for difference are automatically adjusted. For example., if a cheque has been sent for collection, but it has not yet been collected, this is a cause of difference between the balance as shown by the Bank Pass Book and the balance as shown by the Cash Book, but no adjusting entry is required in the Cash Book for such a difference even after it has been found out. This is because the Bank will credit the firm's account as soon as the cheque is collected. This is only a question of time. However, if the cheque sent for collection to the Bank has been returned by the Bank on account of its being dishonoured, the firm should pass an adjusting entry for return of such cheque if it has not already been passed. Similarly, the firm has also to pass in its books, the entries for bank charges or direct payments received by the Bank on behalf of the firm.

IMPORTANCE OF BANK RECONCILIATION STATEMENT

The importance of Bank Reconciliation Statement can be judged on the basis of the following facts:

(i) It highlights the causes of difference between the bank balance as per cash book and the bank balance as per pass book. Necessary adjustments or corrections can therefore be carried out at the earliest.

(ii) It reduces the chances of fraud by the cash staff. It may be possible that the cashier may not deposit the money in the bank in time though he might have passed the entry in the bank column of the cash book. The Reconciliation Statement will point out to such discrepancies.

(iii) There is a moral check on the staff of the organisation to keep the cash records always up to date.

TECHNIQUE OF PREPARING BANK RECONCILIATION STATEMENT

A Bank Reconciliation statement is prepared usually at the end of a period, *i.e.*, a quarter, a half year or a year, as may be found convenient and necessary by the firm taking into account the number of transactions involved. The following are the step to be taken for preparing a Bank Reconciliation Statement:

(i) The Cash Book should be completed and the balance as per the Bank column on a particular date should be found out covering the period for which the Bank Reconciliation Statement has to be prepared.

(ii) The Bank should be requested to complete and send to the firm the Bank Pass Book upto the date mentioned in Point (i) above.

(iii) The balance as shown by any book (*i.e.*, the Cash Book or the Bank Pass Book) should be taken as the base. This is as a matter of fact the starting point for determining the balance as shown by the other book after making suitable adjustments taking into account the causes of difference.

(iv) The effect of the particular cause of difference should be studied on the balance shown by the other book.

(v) In case, the cause has resulted in a increase in the balance shown by the other book, the amount of such increase should be added to the balance as per the former book which has been taken as the base.

(vi) In case, the cause has resulted in decrease in balance shown by the other book, the amount of such decrease should be subtracted from the balance as per the former book which has been taken as the base.

1.146

In case. the books show an adverse balance (i.e., an overdraft) the amount of the overdraft should be put in the minus column. The Reconciliation Statement should then by prepared on the same pattern as if there is a favourable balance instead of their being an overdraft.

The above technique will be clear with the help of the illustration given in the following pages.

WHERE CAUSES OF DIFFERENCE ARE GIVEN

Illustration 7.1. From the following particulars prepare a Bank Reconciliation Statement as on 31st December, 1990.

(i) Balance as per Cash Book Rs 5,800.

(ii) Cheques issued but not presented for payment Rs 2,000.

(iii) Cheques sent for collection but not collected upto 31st December, 1990 Rs 1,500.

(iv) The Bank had wrongly debited the account of the firm by Rs 200 which was rectified by them after 31st December.

Balance as per Pass Book is Rs 6,100.

Solution:

There is a difference of Rs 300 between the balance as shown by the Cash Book and the balance as shown by the Bank Pass Book. A reconciliation statement can be prepared to reconcile on the following basis the balances shown by the two books;

(i) The balance as shown by the Cash Book will be taken as the starting point.

(ii) The cheques issued but not presented for payment have not been recorded in the Bank Pass Book. The balance as per Pass Book has to be found out. The Bank has not yet passed the entry for the payment of these cheques since they have not been prsented for payment. The balance. therefore, in the Pass Book should be more. The amount of Rs 2,000 should, therefore, be added to the balance as shown by the Cash Book.

(iii) Cheques sent for collection but not yet collected must have been entered in the Cash Book but must not have been credited by the Bank to the firm's account since they have not yet been collected. The balance in Pass Book should therefore, be less as compared to the Cash Book. The amount of Rs 1,500 should, therefore, be deducted out of the balance as shown by the Cash Book.

(iv) The Bank has wrongly debited the firm's account. This must have resulted in reducing balance as per the Bank Pass Book. The amount should, therefore, be deducted out of the balance shown as per the Cash Book.

The Bank Reconciliation Statement will now appear as follows:

BANK RECONCILIATION STATEMENT

	Particulars	+ Rs	− Rs
(i)	Balance as per Cash Book	5,800	
(ii)	Add: Cheques issued but not presented for payment	2,000	
(iii)	Less: Cheques sent for collection but not yet collected		1,500
(iv)	Less: Amount wrongly debited by the Bank		200
		7,800	1,700
	Balance as per Bank Pass Book	6,100	

Illustration 7.2. From the following particulars, prepare a Bank Reconciliation Statement showing the balance as per Cash Bank as on 31st December 1990.

(i) Out of cheques of Rs 9,000 paid on 29th December, Rs 4,000 appear to have been credited in the Pass Book under date 2nd January, 1991.

(ii) I had issued cheques in December, 1990 amounting in all to Rs 16,000 of which I find that Rs 7,000 worth have been cashed in the same month, a cheque of Rs 5,000 has been cashed on January 3, 1991 and the rest have not been presented at all.

(iii) My Bankers have given me a wrong credit in my Joint Account with wife in respect of a cheque of Rs 2,000 paid into my personal account.

(iv) Rs 1,000 for interest on overdraft charged in the Pass Book on 31st December have been entered in my Cash Book as on 4th January, 1991.

(v) My Pass Book shows a credit of Rs 1,200 to my account being interest on my securities collected by my Bankers.

(vi) The Bank Balance as per my Pass Book showed an overdraft of Rs 19,000.

Solution:

BANK RECONCILIATION STATEMENT
(as on 31st December, 1990)

	Particulars	+ Rs	− Rs
	Overdraft as per Pass Book		19,000
Add:	Cheques not yet credited	4,000	
Less:	Cheques not yet presented		9,000
Add:	Cheques not yet credited to my personal account	2,000	
Add:	Interest on overdraft charged in the Pass Book on 31st December, not entered in Cash Book	1,000	
Less:	Interest on securities collected by bankers not entered in Cash Book		1,200
		7,000	29,200
	Overdraft as per Cash Book		22,200

Illustration 7.3. Janardan and Co. have bank accounts with two banks, *viz.*, Dena Bank and Bank of India. On 31st December, 1988, his Cash Book (bank columns) shows balance of Rs 5,000 with Dena Bank and overdraft of Rs 2,250 with Bank of India. On further verification, the following facts were discovered:

(a) A deposit of Rs 1,500 made in Dena Bank on 20th December, 1988 has been entered in the column for Bank of India.

(b) A withdrawal of Rs 500 from Bank of India on 2nd November, 1988 has been entered in the column for Dena Bank.

(c) Two cheques of Rs 500 and Rs 750 deposited in Dena Bank on 1st December, 1988 (and entered in the Bank of Indian column) have been dishonoured by the Bankers. The entries for dishonour have been made in the Bank of India column.

(d) Cheques were issued on 29th December, 1988 on Dena Bank and Bank of India of Rs 10,000 and Rs 1,000 respectively. These have not been cashed till 31st December, 1988.

(e) Incidental charges of Rs 10 and Rs 25 charged by Dena Bank and Bank of India respectively have not been entered in the books.

(f) Dena Bank has credited an interest of Rs 50 and Bank of India has charged interest of Rs 275. These have not been recorded in the books.

(g) The deposits of Rs 5,000 and Rs 3,500 made into Dena Bank and Bank of India respectively have not yet been credited to by them till 31st December, 1988.

Draw up the two Bank Reconciliation Statements.

Solution:

M/s Janardan & Co.

RECONCILIATION STATEMENT WITH DENA BANK
(as on 31st December, 1988)

		Particulars	+ Rs	− Rs
		Balance as per Cash Book	5,000	
Add:	(a)	Deposit made on 20.12.1988 but wrongly debited to Bank of India	1,500	
	(b)	Withdrawal made on 2.11.1988 wrongly entered in the above account instead of Bank of India	500	
	(c)	These entries have no effect in either account	—	
	(d)	Cheque issued on 29.12.1988 but not yet encashed with the Bank	10,000	
Less:	(e)	Incidental charges not yet credited by us		10
Add:	(f)	Interest credited by Bank but not yet debited by us in our books	50	
Less:	(g)	Cheque deposited but the proceeds of the same not yet credited by Bank		5,000
			17,050	5,010
		Balance as per Bank Pass Book (favourable)	12,040	

RECONCILIATION STATEMENT WITH BANK OF INDIA
(as on 31st December, 1988)

		Particulars	+ Rs	− Rs
		Overdraft as per Cash Book		2,250
Less:	(a)	Deposit made into Dena Bank on 20.12.1988 but wrongly debited to the above account		1,500
	(b)	Withdrawal made on 21.1.1988, but wrongly entered in Dena Bank Account		500
	(c)	These entries have no effect in either Account		
Add:	(d)	Cheque issued on 29.12.1988 but not yet enacashed with the Bank	1,000	
Less:	(e)	Incidental charges not yet credited by us		25
	(f)	Interest charged by Bank but not yet recorded by us in the Books		275
	(g)	Cheques deposited, but the proceeds of the same not yet credited by Bank		3,500
			1,000	8,050
		Overdraft as per Bank Pass Book		7,050

WHERE CASH BOOK BALANCE HAS TO BE ADJUSTED

Illustration 7.4. The Cash Book of Mr Gadbadwala shows Rs 8,364 as the balance at Bank as on 31st December, 1990 but you find that this does not agree with the balance as per the Bank Pass Book. On scrutiny, you find the following discrepancies:

(i) On 15th December, 1990, the payments side of the Cash Book was undercast by Rs 100.

(ii) A cheque for Rs 131 issued on 25th December, 1990 was taken in the Cash column.

(iii) A deposit of Rs 150 was recorded in the Cash Book as if there is no Bank Column therein.

(iv) On 18th December, 1990, the debit balance of Rs 1,526 as on the previous day, was brought forward as credit balance.

(v) Of the total cheques amounting to Rs 11,514 drawn in the last week of December, 1990, cheques aggregating Rs 7,815 were encashed in December.

(vi) Dividends of Rs 250 collected by the Bank and subscription of Rs 100 paid by it were not recorded in the Cash Book.

(vii) One out-going cheque of Rs 350 was recorded twice in the Cash Book.

Prepare a Reconciliation Statement when:

(a) the books are not to be closed on 31st December.

(b) the books are to be closed on 31st December.

Solution:

If the books are not to be closed on 31st December, 1990.

BANK RECONCILIATION STATEMENT
(as on 31st December, 1990)

	Particulars	+ Rs	– Rs
	Balance as per Cash Book	8,364	
Add:	Mistake in bringing forward Rs 1,526 debit balance as credit balance as on 18.12.1990	3,052	
	Cheques issued but not presented:		
	Issued 11,514		
	Cashed 7,815	3,699	
	Dividends directly collected by bank but not yet entered in the Cash Book	250	
	Cheque recorded twice in the Cash Book	350	
	Deposit not recorded in the Bank column	150	
Less:	Wrong casting in the cash book on 15.12.90		100
	Cheques issued but not entered in the Bank column		131
	Subscription paid by the Bank directly not yet recorded in the Cash Book		100
		15,865	331
	Balance as per Pass Book	15,534	

If the books are to be closed on 31st December, 1990

In such a case necessary corrections for mistake committed will have to be made in the Cash Book and correct balance as per Cash Book will have to be found out. A Bank Reconciliation Statement will then be prepared.

ASCERTAINMENT OF CORRECT BALANCE

	Particulars	Rs	Rs
	Balance of Cash Book as given		8,364
Add:	Mistake in the bringing forward the balance on 18th December		3,052
	Dividends collected by the bank		250
	Cheque recorded twice in the Cash Book		350

Contd....

Particulars	Rs	Rs
Deposit not recorded in the Bank column		150
		12,166
Less: Wrong casting of the Cash Book on 15th December	100	
Cheques issued but not entered in the Bank column	131	
Subscription paid by the Bank directly not yet recorded in the Cash Book	100	331
Correct Balance as per Cash Book (for Balance Sheet purposes)		11,835

BANK RECONCILIATION STATEMENT
(as on 31st December, 1990)

	Rs
Balance as per Cash Book (corrected)	11,835
Add: Cheques issued but not yet presented	3,699
Balance as per Pass Book	15,534

WHERE ABSTRACTS FROM THE CASH BOOK AND THE PASS BOOK ARE GIVEN

In such a case there can be two situations:

(i) *When the abstracts relate to the same period.* In such a case such transactions should be found which are not common in both the abstracts. These constitute the causes of difference (*See Illustration 7.5*).

(ii) *When the pass book relates to the suceeding period.* In such a case compare those transactions which are common in both the abstracts. These constitute causes of difference (*See Illustration 7.6*).

Illustration 7.5. The following are the Cash Book and Bank Pass Book of Niranjan for the month of April, 1988:

CASH BOOK (BANK COLUMN)

Date	Particulars	Rs	Date	Particulars	Rs
1.4.1988	To Balance b/d	12,500	1.4.1988	By Salaries A/c (Ch.No. 183)	4,000
4.4.1988	To Sales A/c	8,000	6.4.1988	By Purchases A/c (Ch. No. 184)	3,200
8.4.1988	To Parimal A/c	1,500	11.4.1988	By Machinery A/c (Ch. No. 185)	6,000
13.4.1988	To Mahim A/c	3,400	15.4.1988	By Om Prakash A/c (Ch. No. 186)	1,000
18.4.1988	To Kamal A/c	4,600	19.4.1988	By Drawing A/c (Ch. No. 187)	800
21.4.1988	To Furniture A/c	1,200	23.4.1988	By Kishore A/c (Ch. No. 188)	2,000
25.4.1988	To Sales A/c	3,800	27.4.1988	By Suresh A/c (Ch. No. 189)	1,000
30.4.1988	To Firoz A/c	3,000	30.4.1988	By Printing A/c (Ch. No. 190)	500
			30.4.1988	By Balance c/d	19,500
		38,000			38,000

BANK PASS BOOK

Date	Particulars	Deposits	Withdrawal	Balance
1.4.1988	Balance			12,500
2.4.1988	Cheque 183		4,000	8,500
6.4.1988	Cash	8,000		16,500
6.4.1988	Cheque 184		3,200	13,300
10.4.1988	Cheque	1,500		14,800
16.4.1988	Cheque	3,400		18,200
17.4.1988	Cheque 187		800	17,400
20.4.1988	Cheque	4,600		22,000
24.4.1988	Cheque	3,800		25,800
28.4.1988	Cheque 185		6,000	19,800
28.4.1988	Cheque 189		1,000	18,800
30.4.1988	Interest	100		18,900
30.4.1988	Deposit (Firoz)	3,000		21,900
30.4.1988	Charges		10	21,890

You are required to prepare a Bank Reconciliation Statement as on 30th April, 1988.

Solution:

BANK RECONCILIATION STATEMENT OF NIRANJAN
(as on 30th April, 1988)

Particulars	+ Rs	– Rs
Balance as per Cash Book	19,500	
Less: Amount deposited but not credited		120
Add: Cheques drawn but not presented		
Cheque No. 186 1,000		
Cheque No. 188 2,000		
Cheque No. 190 500	3,500	
Add: Interest allowed by bank but not posted in Cash Book	100	
Less: Charges debited by bank but not posted in Cash Book		10
	23,100	1,210
Balance as per Pass Book	21,890	

Illustration 7.6. From the following entries in the Bank column of the Cash Book of Mr. A. Kartak and the corresponding Bank Pass Book, prepare Reconciliation Statement as on 31st March, 1989:

CASH BOOK (BANK COLUMN ONLY)

Date	Particulars	Rs	Date	Particulars	Rs
1989			1989		
March 1	To Balance b/d	3,400	March 7	By Drawings	1,500
March 10	To Madan & Sons	500	March 8	By Salary	2,200
March 13	To Jerbai	4,000	March 15	By Ardesar & Co.	3,000
March 18	To Cawasji & Co.	1,200	March 28	By Merwan Bros.	1,550
March 28	To Dinshwa & Co.	2,200	March 29	By Raj & Sons	800
March 29	To Dhanbura Co.	5,700	March 30	By Macmillon Radios	400
March 31	To Antony	3,425	March 31	By Chandu, H.	1,600
			March 31	By Balance c/d	9,375
		20,425			20,425

BANK PASS BOOK
(Mr. Kartak in Current Account with Central Bank)

Date	Particulars	Rs	Date	Particulars	Rs
1989			1989		
April 1	To Balance (Overdraft)	750	April 2	By Dividends	500
April 2	To Raj & Sons	800	April 2	By Dinshaw & Co.	2,200
April 4	To Macmillon Radios	400	April 2	By Hosang	200
April 8	To Salary	2,300	April 3	By Dhanbura Co.	5,700
April 10	To Drawings	500	April 3	By Antony	3,425
April 10	To Antony (Cheque dishonoured)	3,425	April 5	By Romy	170

Solution:

BANK RECONCILIATION STATEMENT OF MR. K. KARTAK
(as on 31st March, 1989)

Particulars		+ Rs	− Rs
Balance as per Cash Book		9,375	
Less: Cheques deposited but not credited:			
Dinshaw & Co.	2,200		
Dhanbura Co.	5,700		
Antony	3,425		11,325
Add: Cheques drawn but not presented:			
Raj & Sons	800		
Macmillon Radios	400	1,200	
		10,575	11,325
Overdraft as per Pass Book			Rs 750

KEY TERMS

☐ **Bank Reconciliation Statement:** A statement reconciling the balance as shown by the Bank Pass Book and the balance as shown by the Cash Book.

☐ **Pass Book:** It is a copy of the firm's account with a bank.

TEST QUESTIONS

Objective type | TEST YOUR UNDERSTANDING |

1. State whether each of the following statements is True or False:
   (a) Pass Book is the Statement of Account of the customer maintained by the Bank.
   (b) The balance as shown by the Bank Pass Book and the balance as shown by the Bank Column of the Cash Book are always equal.
   (c) Cheques issued but not presented for payment will reduce the balance as per the Pass Book.
   (d) Cheques sent for collection but not yet collected will result in increasing the balance of the Cash Book as compared to the Pass Book.
   (e) Direct collections received by the Bank on behalf of its customers will increase the balance as per the Bank Pass Book as compared to the balance as per the Cash Book.

(f) The Bank Reconciliation Statement is prepared to reconcile the balance as shown by the Cash Book and the balance as shown by the Pass Book.

(g) The debit balance of the bank account in the books of the business should be equal to the credit balance of the account of the business in the books of the Bank.

[**Ans.** (a) True, (b) False, (c) False, (d) True, (e)True, (f) True, (g) True].

2. Fill in the blanks:

(a) When money is withdrawn from the Bank, the Bank ....the account of the customer.

(b) In case the Pass Book shows a favourable balance and it is taken as the starting point for preparing a Bank Reconciliation Statement, cheques issued but not presented for payment should be........to find out cash balance.

(c) In case, the overdraft as per the Pass Book is taken as the starting point, it should be put in........column of the Bank Reconciliation Statement.

(d) Cheques sent for collection, but not yet collected should be added when favourable balance as per............... is taken as the starting point.

(e) Favourable balance as per Cash Book means........in the Bank Column of the Cash Book.

[**Ans.** (a) debits, (b) deducted, (c) minus, (d) Pass Book, (e) debit balance].

Essay type | FOR REVIEW, DISCUSSION AND PRACTICE |

1. What is a Bank Reconciliation Statement? How is it prepared? submit a proforma of a Bank Reconciliation Statement with imaginary figures.

2. "Balance as shown by the Bank Pass Book should tally with the balance as shown by the Cash Book of the business". Do you agree? If not, explain the reasons with suitable examples of difference between the two.

PRACTICAL PROBLEMS

Pass/Cash book Favourable Balance

1. From the following particulars prepare a bank reconciliation statement of Messrs Krishna & Co. showing the balance as per Bank Pass Book on March 31, 1990.

(i) On March 31, 1990, the bank balance as per cash book was Rs 9,800.

(ii) The following cheques were paid into the firm's bank current account in March 1990, but were credited by bank in April, 1990: Raman Rs 400; Chand Ram Rs 300; and Mohan Rs 200.

(iii) The following cheques were issued by the firm in March, 1990, but were not cashed in April, 1990: Gopalan Rs 500 and Krishnan Rs 250.

(iv) The pass book shows a credit of Rs 180 for interest and a debit of Rs 40 for bank charges.

(v) The pass book also contains an entry for Rs 240 being payment made by a customer direct into bank.

[**Ans.** Balance as per Pass Book Rs 10,030.]

2. From the following particulars prepare a Bank Reconciliation Statement as at 31st December, 1990 of M/s A. B. & Co. who had cash at bank as per cash book Rs 10,500.40 and as per pass book Rs 12,350.60:

(a) The following cheques were deposited on 30th and 31st December but were not collected by 31st December, 1990:

(i) Rs 300.25, (ii) Rs 500, (iii) Rs 200.15.

(b) The following cheques were issued but not cashed by 31st December 1990:

(i) Rs 600.25, (ii) Rs 200 (iii) Rs 489.25, (iv) Rs 50.

(c) The bank collected a bill of Rs 1,500 on the 31st December, 1990 but the intimation was received by the firm on 1st January, 1991.

(d) The bank allowed interest Rs 20.30 and a commission was charged Rs 9.20 on 31st December, 1990.

[**Ans.** Balance as per Pass Book Rs 12,350.60]

3. On 31st December, 1988, the Pass Book of a merchant shows a credit balance of Rs 3,357.

The cheques and draft sent to the bank but not collected and credited amounted to Rs 790 and three cheques drawn for Rs 300, Rs 150 and Rs 200 respectively were not presented for payment till 31st January next year.

Bank has paid a bill payable amounting to Rs 1,000 but it has bot been entered in the Cash Book and a bill receivable of Rs 500 which was discounted with the bank was dishonoured by the drawee on due date.

The bank has charged Rs 13 as its commission for collecting outstation cheques and has allowed interest Rs 10 on the trader's balance.

Prepare a bank Reconciliation Statement and show the balance as shown by the Cash Book.

[**Ans.** Balance a per Cash Book Rs 5,000]

Pass/Cash Book Overdraft

4. The bank pass book of Mr. X showed an overdraft of Rs 33,575 on 31st March, 1988. On going through the pass book, the accountant found the following:
   (i) A cheque of Rs 1,080 credited in the pass book on March 28 being dishonoured is debited again in the pass book on 1st April, 1988. There was no entry in the Cash Book about the dishonour of the cheque until 15th April.
   (ii) Bankers had credited his account with Rs 2,800 for interest collected by them on his behalf, but the same had not been entered in his Cash Book.
   (iii) Out of Rs 20,500 paid in by Mr. X in cash and by cheques on 31st March, cheques amounting to Rs 7,500 were collected on 7th April.
   (iv) Out of cheques amounting to Rs 7,800 drawn by him on 27th March, cheques for Rs 2,500 was encashed on 3rd April.

Prepare Bank Reconciliation Statement on March 31, 1989.

[**Ans.** Overdraft as per Cash Book Rs 31,375]

Pass/Cash Book Overdraft

5. Prepare a Bank Reconciliation statement on 31st December, 1990 from the following particulars:
   (a) A's overdraft as per Pass Book Rs 12,000 as at 31st December.
   (b) On 30th December, cheques had been issued for Rs 70,000 of which cheques worth Rs 3,000 only had been encashed upto 31st December.
   (c) Cheques amounting to Rs 3,500 had been paid into the bank for collection but of these only Rs 500 had been credited in the Pass Book.
   (d) The Bank has charged Rs 500 as interest on overdraft and the intimation of which has been received on 2nd January, 1991.
   (e) the Bank Pass Book shows credit for Rs 1,000 representing Rs 400 paid by debtor of A direct into the Bank and Rs 600 collected direct by Bank in respect on A's investments. A had no knowledge of these items.
   (f) A cheque for Rs 200 has been debited in bank column of Cash Book by A, but it was not sent to Bank at all.

[**Ans.** Overdraft as per Cash Book Rs 76,300]

6. From the following particulars taken on 31st December, 1990, you are required to prepare a bank reconciliation statement to reconcile the bank balance shown in the Cash Book with that shown in the Pass Book:
   (i) Balance as per Pass Book on 31st December, 1990, O/D Rs 1,027.
   (ii) Four cheques drawn on 31st December but not cleared till January following Rs 12; Rs 1,021; Rs 98; and Rs 113.

(iii) Interest on O/D not entered in cash book Rs 51.

(iv) Three cheques received on 30th December and entered in the Bank column of the cash book but not lodged in bank for collection till 3rd January next: Rs 1,160; Rs 2,100; and Rs. 2,080.

(v) Cost of cheque book, pass book, etc., Rs 1.50 entered twice erroneously in cash book in November.

(vi) A bill Receivable for Rs 250 due on 29th December, 1990 was passed to the bank for collection on 28th December, 1990 and was entered in cash book forthwith whereas the proceeds were credited in the pass book only in January following.

(vii) Chamber of Commerce subscription Rs 10 paid by bank on 1st December, 1990 had not been entered in the cash book.

(viii) Bank charges of Rs 5 had been debited in the pass book twice erroneously.

[Ans. Credit Balance as per Cash Book Rs 3,383.50]

Comprehensive Problems

7. Ram, a sole trader, maintains two Bank Accounts, No.1 Account is for his business, No.2 Account is his private Account.

On June 30,1987, there was a balance of Rs 890 standing to his credit in No.1 Account. It was discovered that:

(i) The receipt column of the Cash Book has been overcast by Rs 1,000.

(ii) Cheques amounting to Rs 3,760 entered in Cash Book as paid into the Bank have not been cleared.

(iii) Cheques issued amounting to Rs 5,230 have not been presented.

(iv) Discount allowed Rs 110 has been included through mistake in the Bank column of the Cash Book.

(v) A trader's credit note of Rs 290 was received in June 1987, but not recorded in the books.

(vi) A cheque for Rs 100 originally issued in 1986 was replaced when out of date and entered again in the Cash Book, it was still outstanding (and not out of date) on June 30, 1987. Both the cheques were included in the total of unpresented cheques Rs 5,230.

(vii) The Bank has charged the No. 2 Account with a cheque for Rs 2,000 in error. This should have been charged to No.1 Account.

(viii) Make the appropriate adjustment in the Cash Book Balance.

(ix) Prepare a Bank Reconciliation Statement to show the Bank Balance as per No. 1 Account.

[Ans. Adjusted Balance as per Cash Book Rs 170; Balance appearing in the Pass Book Rs 3,540].

8. On 31st December, 19..., the Cash Book of a merchant showed a debit balance of Rs 850. On comparing the Cash Book with the Bank Pass Book, the following discrepancies were noted:

(a) Cheques issued for Rs 600 were not presented at Bank by 31st December, 19...

(b) Cheques for Rs 800 were deposited in Bank but were not cleared.

(c) Rs 2,000 being the proceeds of a Bill Receivable collected appear in the Pass Book but not in the Cash Book.

(d) A cheque for Rs 100 received from X & Co. and deposited in Bank was dishonoured. No advice of non payment was received from Bank till the 1st of next January, 19...

(e) The Bank has paid a Bill Payable amounting to Rs 450 but it has not been entered in the Cash Book.

(f) A Bill Receivable for Rs 800 which was discounted with the Bank was due this month. It was dishonoured by the drawee on due date.

(g) A cheque for Rs 510 was paid into Bank but the Bank credited the account with Rs 501 by mistake.

(h) A cheque for Rs 50 was deposited into Bank but the same was credited to a wrong account.

(i) Rs 200 was deposited by a customer direct into the Bank.

(j) The Bank received interest on debentures on behalf of the trader the amount being Rs 250.

(k) A cheque for Rs 150 received from a customer deposited into bank but the same was not entered into the Cash Book.

(l) The Bank paid Rs 125 by way of Insurance Premium.

(m) The Bank charged Rs 9 as their commission for collecting outstation cheques and allowed interest of Rs 10 on the trader's balance.

(n) A cheques for Rs 25 entered into the Cash Book was omitted to be banked.

Prepare a Bank Reconciliation Statement and show the balance as per Pass Book.

[**Ans.** Balance as per Pass Book Rs 1,692].

9. Prepare a Bank Reconciliation Statement from the following particulars. You are required to ascertain the Bank balance as it would appear in Cash Book of Shri Gobind as at 31st December, 1989. Would the balance be different in case Shri Gobind closes his books on 31st December?

(a) The Bank Pass Book showed an overdraft of Rs 9,500 on 31st December, 1989.

(b) Interest on overdraft for six months ending 31st December, 1989 Rs 250 is debited in the Pass Book, but is not entered in the Bank column of Cash Book.

(c) Cheques issued but not cashed, prior to 31st December, 1989 amounted to Rs 1,500.

(d) Club bill directly debited to his bank account not yet reflected in the Cash Book Rs 2,700.

(e) Cheques paid into bank, but not cleared and credited before 31st December, 1989 Rs 2,500.

(f) Interest on Investments collected by the Bankers and credited in the Pass Book amounted to Rs 1,800.

(g) Shri Gobind issued a cheque of Rs 900 for his *LIC* Premium, which was returned as the amount in figure and words was not tallying. Shri Gobind,. therefore, paid premium by cash and this way not rectified in his books of accounts.

[**Ans.** Overdraft as per Cash Book Rs 8,250. In case books are closed on 31st December, the overdraft would be Rs 8,500].

10. The Cash Book of a trader showed an overdraft balance of Rs 32,750 on 31st December, 1992. On scrutiny of the Cash Book and Pass Book it was discovered that

(a) On 22nd December, sundry cheques totalling Rs 6,500 were sent to Bank for collection out of which a cheque for Rs 1,500 was wrongly recorded on the side of the Cash Book and cheques amounting to Rs 3,300 could not be collected by the Bank till 6th January next.

(b) A cheque for Rs 4,000 was issued to a supplier on 28th December. This cheque was not presented to Bank till 10th January.

(c) Bank had debited Rs 2,000 towards interest on overdraft and Rs 600 for Bank charges, but the bank advice was sent on 15th January.

(d) Credit side of the Bank Column of the Cash Book was undercast by Rs 100.

(e) Cheques for Rs 2,000 drawn for office expenses were not encashed till 2nd January.

(f) A cheque for Rs 1,000 was issued to a creditor on 27th December and was omitted to be entered in the Cash Book. It was, however, presented to Bank within 31st December.

(g) Dividends amounting to Rs 500 had been paid direct to the Bank and not entered in the Cash Book.

You are are required to make necessary corrections in the Cash Book and starting with the amended balance, prepare a Bank Reconciliation Statement as at 31st December, 1992.

[**Ans.** Cash book corrected balance (overdraft) Rs 32,950; Overdraft as per Pass Book Rs 30,250].

11. From the following details, prepare a Bank Reconciliation Statement on 30th June, 1990.

1.157

BANK PASS BOOK

Date	Particulars	Withdrawals Rs	Deposits	Dr. or Cr.	Balance Rs
1990					
June 1	By Balance b/d			Cr.	11,5000
June 4	By Mahesh Bansal's Cheques		750	Cr.	12,250
June 7	By Santosh Sood's Cheques		1,000	Cr.	13,250
June 10	To Ved Prakash	850		Cr.	12,400
June 15	To Cash	2,400		Cr.	10,000
June 20	By Vikas Kalra (Cash)		500	Cr.	10,500
June 23	To Vishal Tandon	700		Cr.	9,800
June 26	To Insurance Premium	500		Cr.	9,300
June 30	To Bank Charges	50			9,250
June 30	By Interest		110		9,360
June 30	By Interest on Investments		640		10,000

CASH BOOK (BANK COLUMN ONLY)

Date	Particulars	Amount Rs	Date	Particulars	Amount Rs
1990			1990		
June 1	To Balance b/d	11,500	June 10	By Ravi Raj	900
June 1	To Mahesh Bansal	750	June 12	By Ved Prakash	850
June 5	To Santosh Sood	1,000	June 15	By Cash	2,400
June 18	To Ramesh Kumar	600	June 18	by Vishal Tandon	700
June 26	To Vinay Kumar	400	June 25	By Sunil Gupta	440
			June 28	by Abhey Kumar	660
			June 30	By Balance c/d	8,300
		14,250			14,250
July 1	To Balance b/d	8,300			

12. From the following entries in the bank column of the Cash Book of Mr. *A* and corresponding bank pass book, prepare a Bank Reconciliations Statement as on 31st March, 1992.

CASH BOOK (BANK COLUMN)

Date	Particulars	Amount Rs	Date	Particulars	Cheque Number	Amount Rs
1992			1992			
Mar. 2	To Balance	3,400	Mr. 5	By Drawings	526	1,500
Mar. 10	To M. Dass—Cheque	500	Mar. 8	By Salaries	527	2,200
Mar. 13	To J. Day—Cash	4,000	Mar. 15	By Purchases	528	3,000
Mar. 18	To C. Lal—Cheque on Delhi	1,200	Mar. 20	By R. Bros.	529	1,550
Mar. 20	To A Boman—Cheque	2,200	Mar. 29	By House Rent	530	800
Mar. 29	To D. Bros—Cheque	5,700	Mar. 30	By K. Bros	531	400
Mar. 31	To A. Jeewan—Cheque	3,425	Mar. 31	By N Koomar	532	1,600
			Mar. 31	By Balance		9,375
		20,425				20,425

1.158

BANK PASS BOOK

Date	Particulars	Cheque Number	Amount Rs	Date	Particulars	Amount Rs
1992				1992		
Apr. 1	To Balance (Overdraft)		350	Apr. 1	By Divdend	750
Apr. 2	To C. Ramdas	530	800	Apr. 3	By A. Boman	2,200
Apr. 4	To K. Bros.	531	400	Apr. 4	By J. Jeewan	400
Apr. 8	To Self	534	2,200	Apr. 7	By D. Bose	5,700
Apr. 10	To Self	535	700	Apr. 9	By A. Jeewan	3,425
Apr. 12	N. Koomar	532	1,600	Apr. 11	By C. Lal Cheque on Delhi cleared less charges	1,198
Apr. 15	To Balance c/d		8,323	Apr. 15	Intt. on G.P. Note	700
			14,373			14,373

Chapter 8

MATCHING CONCEPT

> **LEARNING OBJECTIVES**
>
> After studying this chapter you should be able to:
>
> ☐ appreciate the importance of matching concept in computing the income or profit of a business;
>
> ☐ identify the problems in matching;
>
> ☐ explain the circumstances where an expense will be treated as the one incurred for earning revenue during a particular period;
>
> ☐ differentiate between traditional approach and replacement cost approach for determination of business income; and
>
> ☐ explain the meaning of certain key terms.

It has already been explained in an earlier chapter that one of the basic objectives of maintaining the books of accounts of a business is to ascertain the amount of profit or loss made or suffered during a particular period. This requires proper matching of expense with the revenue. However, it will be appropriate here to understand the meanings of the terms Revenue, Expense and Expenditure before proceeding further with the Matching Concept.

1. **Revenue.** The term "Revenue" means income of recurring nature from any source. Source may be sale of goods, performance of service for a customer, the rental of a property, etc.

2. **Expense.** The term "Expense" denotes the cost of services and things used for generating revenue.

3. **Expenditure.** The term "Expenditure" means payment or the incurring of a debt for an asset or an expense. If an asset is acquired or an expense is incurred, an expenditure is said to have been made whether or not the cash is paid immediately.

Thus, every expense is an expenditure, while each expenditure is not necessarily an expense. For example, the salaries paid to the employees of a firm is both an expenditure as well as an expense. But, the amount paid for the acquisition of the fixed asset for the business, *e.g.*, plant is an expenditure but not an expense. While calculating the income or the profit of a business, for a particular period, the revenue earned during the period is to be matched with expense incurred in earning that revenue.

PROBLEMS IN MATCHING

The following are the two basic problems which one has to face in matching expense with the revenue.

1. **When to match.** Profit determination requires matching of the expense with the revenue. However, to decide at what point of time the expense is to be matched with the revenue, is a problem in itself. There are two alternatives available:

(*i*) Expense may be matched with the revenue at the end of the life of the business. In case, this alternative is adopted, the income or profit made by the firm will be known only when the business is closed down. However, this practice cannot be adopted on account of the following reasons:

(*a*) The information regarding the profitability of a business, only on its liquidation, will not be of much use to the businessman since it will be an obsolete information and he will not be in a position to take any corrective measures in time.

(*b*) The outsiders, *i.e.*, the banks, creditors and financial institutions who are interested in the business will not be in a position to get the required information about the business in time.

(*c*) Taxation laws require determination of profit on year to year basis.

(*ii*) Expense may be matched with the revenue at the end of each year. This is usually done. A period of 12 months is considered as an ideal accounting period. At the end of that period, the expense is matched with the revenue earned during that period. This helps the businessman in knowing the profitability and financial position of his business from time to time and also take possible corrective measures.

2. **What to match.** Of course, 'expense' is to be matched with revenue for determination of business income but measurement of both correct amount of 'revenue' as well as 'expense' is a difficult problem. This has been discussed in detail below:

(*i*) **Measurement of revenue.** Following are the two basic points which should be kept in view while measuring revenue:

(*a*) Revenue is measured according to the Accrual Concept. This means revenue and cash are two different things. Earning of revenue does not mean receipt of cash and *vice-versa*. In other words, revenue earned in a particular year may be received in cash in the next year. Similarly, cash received in a year may be the revenue of the next year. For example, if the business receives interest in advance for the year 1991 in the year 1990, the cash has been received but it will be taken as revenue of the year 1991 and not of the year 1990. Similarly, if an income has become due, but it has not been received during the accounting year, it will be taken as revenue of the accounting year in which it has become due though it may be received next year. Adjustments regarding such outstanding revenues or revenues received in advance have been discussed in detail later in the chapter on Final Accounts.

(*b*) Revenue is considered to be earned on its being realised. This means while matching expense with the revenue only such items of revenue are considered which are being regarded as realised. Revenue is generally taken to have been realised in that period in which goods or services are furnished to the customers in exchange of cash or some other valuable consideration. For example, if a business manufactures the machine in December, ships and bills it to a customer in March and receives payment in May, the revenue from this transaction shall be deemed to be realised in the month of March in which the exchange has taken place and not in the month of December or May. Thus, revenue is recognised when the actual sales take place and the ownership in goods has been transferred to the customers.

However, there are certain exceptions to this general rule explained above:

(a) In case of industries where there are compelling reasons for the maintenance of large inventory for any purpose whatsoever, or where there is a ready market for the goods manufactured, revenue is deemed to have been realised at the time of completion of production. This is particularly true in case of certain mining industries such as gold and silver and extractive industries like oil, etc. In case of these industries the revenue is recognised in the accounting period in which the gold or silver is mined or oil has been extracted out.

(b) In case of long-term contracts, the realisation of the revenue is not postponed till the completion of the contract. This is because recognition of revenue on completion of contract may result in a huge profit and attracting a high rate of income-tax in the year in which the contract is completed. Moreover, shareholderds or the proprietors of the business may get disillusioned and discouraged on account of no profit shown by the books of accounts during the period in which the work of the contract was in progress. Therefore, in case of long-term contracts, a proportion of the amount of revenue representing part of the contract completed by the end of the year is treated as realised even before the completion of the contract.

(c) Revenue may not be recognised in the period in which the goods are delivered if there is a considerable doubt about the amount of cash which is going to be finally received from the customers to whom the goods have been sold. For example, in case of hire purchase or instatement sale transactions, revenue is considered to be realised only to the extent of the instalment which have been received in cash in cases where the seller has doubts about the uncertainty of realising the full amount of selling price from the buyer.

(ii) **Measurement of expense.** There are two problems regarding measurement of expense which is to be matched with the revenue for determination of income:

(a) The period in which the expense is to be recognised, and

(b) The basis on which the amount of the expense is to be determined.

PERIOD OF RECOGNITION

An expense will be recognised as an expense incurred for earning revenue during a particular period in each of the following cases:

(i) If the expense can be directly identified or associated with the revenue of the period. For example, when sale of goods is treated as revenue of a particular period, the cost incurred for manufacturing of such goods such as those of raw materials, wages and other direct charges will be recognised as an expenditure for earning that revenue.

(ii) If the expense can be indirectly associated with the revenue of the period. For example, salary of the manager, rent, insurance, advertisements incurred during a particular period can be charged against the revenue earned during that period. However, if some part of these indirect cost relate to the future revenue, such portion of the indirect cost will be deferred and shown in the Balance Sheet as an asset. The remaining portion of these costs will be matched against the revenue of the current year.

(*iii*) Losses which have no potential for producing the revenue in future will not be deferred but will be recognised as the expense of the period in which they have occurred. It should be noted that expenses are deferred only when there is an apparent probability of such expenses producing revenue in future. Since, losses are those costs which fail to produce revenue, no purpose will be served if they are carried forward to the next period. For example, damage to property on account of earthquakes, loss of plant, machinery, etc, due to fire should not be carried forward. They should, rather be met out of the revenue of the year in which they have occurred.

DETERMINATION OF AMOUNT OF EXPENSE

There are two approaches regarding determination of amount of expense to be matched with revenue for measurement of business income.

(*a*) **Traditional approach.** According to this approach, the actual cost incurred for the expense is to be matched with revenue for determination of the business income. For example, if the goods purchased last year @Rs 20 per kg are sold during the current year @Rs 30 per kg., the profit per kg., would be taken as Rs 10 irrespective of the purchase price of the goods in the current year. Similarly, according to this approach, depreciation is charged on the book value of the asset irrespective of their market value. For example, if a plant was purchased for a sum of Rs 20,000, 10 years back and has a book value of Rs 10,000 today, depreciation will be charged only on Rs 10,000 though its present market value may be Rs 40,000.

(*b*) **Replacement approach.** According to this approach, while comparing expense with the revenue, the replacement cost should be considered in place of original cost. For example, if the goods purchased last year @ Rs 20 per kg. are being sold during the current year at Rs 30 per kg. and the current market price for purchasing the goods is Rs 25 per kg., the profit according to this approach should be determined as follows:

	Rs
Sales	30
Less: Replacement cost of the goods sold	25
	5
Add: Profit realised from market fluctuations and price level changes	5
Total Profit	10

Of course, it will be seen that under both the approaches, the profit shown by the books is the same, *i.e.*, Rs 10. However, in case replacement cost approach is followed, it gives a better analysis of the profit earned by the business. This is why, Replacement Cost Approach is preferred to the Traditional Approach in spite of the Traditional Approach being simple to understand and easy to work out.

AS : 9 REVENUE RECOGNITION

The following are the salient features of AS : 9.

1. Revenue from sales or service transactions should be recognised when the requirements as to performance set out in paragraphs 2 and 3 are satisfied, provided that at the time of performance it is not unreasonable to expect ultimate collection. If at the time of

raising of any claim it is unreasonable to expect ultimate collection, revenue recognition should be postponed.

2. In a transaction involving the sale of goods, performance should be regarded as being achieved when the following conditions have been fulfilled:

(*i*) the seller of goods has transferred to the buyer the property in the goods for a price or all significant risks and rewards of ownership have been transferred to the buyer and the seller retains no effective control of the goods transferred to a degree usually associated with ownership; and

(*ii*) no significant uncertainty exists regarding the amount of the consideration that will be derived from the sale of the goods.

3. In a transaction involving the rendering of services, performance should be measured either under the completed service contract method of under the proportionate completion method, whichever relates the revenue to the work accomplished. Such performance should be regarded as being achieved when no significant uncertainty exists regarding the amount of the consideration that will be derived from rendering the service.

4. Revenue arising from the use by others of enterprise resources yielding interest, royalties and dividends should only be recognised when no significant uncertainty as to measurability exists. These revenues are recognised on the following bases:

(*i*) Interest: on a time proportion basis taking into account the amount outstanding and the rate applicable;

(*ii*) Royalties: on an accrual basis in accordance with the terms of the relevant agreement;

(*iii*) Dividends from investments in shares: when the owner's right to receive payment is established.

5. In addition to the disclosures required by Accounting Standard-1 on Disclosure of Accounting Policies (AS-1), an enterprise should also disclose the circumstances in which revenue recognition has been postponed pending the resolution of significant uncertainties.

The standard will be mandatory in respect of accounts for periods commencing on or after 1-4-1991.

KEY TERMS

☐ **Expense**: Cost of services and things used for generating revenue.

☐ **Expenditure**: Payment or incurring of a debt for an asset or an expense.

☐ **Replacement Cost Approach**: An approach which provides for consideration of replacement cost while comparing expense with the revenue for determination of business income.

☐ **Revenue**: Income of a recurring nature from any source.

☐ **Traditional Approach**: A technique which provides for matching of the actual cost incurred for an expense with revenue for determination of business income.

TEST QUESTIONS

1. State whether each of the following statements is True or False:
   (a) An income earned by a business during a particular period is determined by matching expense with revenue.
   (b) The terms "Expenditure" and "Expense" have synonymous meanings.
   (c) Matching of expense with revenue should be carried out at the end of the life of the business.
   (d) Revenue results in equivalent amount of cash.
   (e) In matching process, only such revenues are taken into account which are regarded as realised.
   (f) In case of manufacturing companies, the revenue is said to be realised when the goods are manufactured.
   (g) Losses are those costs which fail to produce revenue.

   [**Ans.** (a) True, (b) False, (c) False, (d) False, (e) True, (f) False, (g) True]

2. Select the most appropriate answer:
   (a) Revenue is said to be realised
      (i) when the sales are made.
      (ii) when the goods are manufactured.
      (iii) when cash is received.
   (b) The term "Expense" denotes
      (i) payment or the incurring of a debt for an asset.
      (ii) cost of services and things used for generating revenue.
      (iii) cost which fails to produce revenue.
   (c) In case of gold, revenue is recognised in the accounting period in which the gold
      (ii) is mined.
      (ii) is sold.
      (iii) is delivered.
   (d) In case of long-term contracts, revenue is generally recognised
      (i) only on full completion of the contract.
      (ii) only when the full cash is received.
      (iii) even when a part of the contract has been completed.
   (e) In case of Traditional Approach, the expense to be matched with revenue is based on
      (i) original cost.
      (ii) replacement cost.
      (iii) cash cost.

   [**Ans.** (a) (i), (b) (ii), (c) (i), (d) (iii), (e) (i)].

1. "Measurement of business income requires matching of cost with revenue". Explain.
2. "Revenue earned and cost of earning revenue should be properly identified for a period". Explain this statement.
3. Define 'revenue-expense' matching. What are the criteria for measurement of revenue and expenses for the matching process?
4. Would you prefer replacement cost approach as compared to traditional approach for measurement of expense. If so, why?
5. Explain the Accounting Concept of Income.

Chapter 9

CAPITAL AND REVENUE

LEARNING OBJECTIVES

After studying this chapter you should be able to:

☐ understand the meaning of capital income and revenue income;

☐ differentiate between capital expenditure and revenue expenditure;

☐ appreciate the importance of identifying the income or expenditure as capital or revenue;

☐ enumerate the circumstances where revenue expenditure may be taken as capital expenditure;

☐ differentiate between capital receipts and revenue receipts; and

☐ explain the meaning of certain key terms.

In the preceding chapter, we have explained that determination of the net profit or net income of a business requires matching of expense with the revenue. This means that first of all revenue is determined and then the expense incurred for earning that revenue is matched with that revenue for determination of net income or net profit. For example, if a sale of Rs 20,000 has been made during a particular period, the cost of goods sold will have to be matched with the revenue realised on account of sale. In case the cost of sale amounts to Rs 15,000, it will be said that a net profit or net income of Rs 5,000 has been made.

It should be noted that while matching cost with revenue, the fact payment has been received or made is not material. For example, a businessman might have purchased goods on credit or he might have not paid the salaries which have become due by a particular date. While determining the profit or loss made during a particular period, all incomes relating to that period (whether received or not) are to be compared with the expenditure relevant to such income (whether actually paid or not). However, one must understand clearly the nature of different types of income and expenditure, receipts and payments before matching revenue with expense for ascertaining the amount of profit or loss made during a particular period.

CLASSIFICATION OF INCOME

Income can be classified into two categories:

(*i*) **Capital income.** The term 'Capital Income' means an income which does not grow out of or pertain to the running of the business proper. It is synonymous to the term 'Capital Gain'. For example, if a building costing Rs 10,000 purchased by a business for its use is sold for Rs 15,000, Rs 5,000 will be taken as a capital profit.

However, it should be noted that only the profit realised over and above the cost of the fixed asset should be taken as a capital profit. The profit realised over and above book value of the asset till it does not exceed the original cost of the asset should be taken as a revenue profit though it does not strictly arise out of and in the course of regular business transactions. This is because, the depreciation against the fixed asset has already been charged to the Profit & Loss Account of the earlier years and any profit which is now made on the sale of a fixed asset (not exceeding the original cost of the fixed asset) is simply recovery of excess provision for depreciation made in the earlier years. This is also provided by the Income Tax Rules. For example, if a plant originally purchased for Rs 10,000 standing in the books at Rs 6,000 (on account of charging depreciation) is sold for Rs 12,000, there is a profit of Rs 6,000 on the sale of this plant. Out of this profit, Rs 2,000 (*i.e.*, the amount over and above cost of the asset) should be taken as a capital profit while the balance of Rs 4,000 should be taken as a revenue profit. Capital profit is transferred to the Capital Reserve and is shown in the Balance Sheet on the liabilities side while revenue profit is credited to the Profit & Loss Account.

(*ii*) **Revenue income.** Revenue Income means an income which arises out of and in the course of the regular business transactions of a concern. For example, in the course of running business, the profit is made on sale, of goods, income is received from letting out the business property, dividends are received on business investments etc. All such incomes are revenue incomes. It should be noted that the terms "Revenue profit' and Revenue Income' synonymous.

CLASSIFICATION OF EXPENDITURE

Expenditure can be classified into three categories:

1. Capital expenditure. It means an expenditure which has been incurred for the purpose of obtaining a long-term advantage for the business. Such expenditure is either incurred for acquisition of an asset (tangible or intangible) which can later be sold and converted into cash or which result in increasing the earning capacity of the business or which affords some other advantage to the business. In other words, such an expenditure does not grow out or pertain to the running of the business proper.

Following are some of the examples of Capital Expenditure:

(*i*) Expenditure incurred in increasing the quality of fixed assets, *e.g.*, purchase of additional furniture, plant, building for permanent use in the business.

(*ii*) Expenditure incurred in increasing the quantity of a fixed asset, *e.g.*, expenditure incurred for increasing the useful life or capacity or efficiency of a fixed asset.

(*iii*) Expenditure incurred for substitution of a new asset for an existing asset.

(*iv*) Expenditure incurred in connection with the purchase, receipt, erection of a fixed asset, *e.g.*, the cartage charges paid for bringing to the factory plant and machinery purchased, erection charges of a new plant.

(*v*) Expenditure incurred for acquiring the right of carrying on a business, *e.g.*, purchase of patent rights, copy rights, goodwill etc.

It should be noted that an expenditure connot be taken as a capital expenditure merely because the amount is large or the amount has been paid in lump sum or the amount has been paid out of the proceeds received on account of sale of a fixed asset or the receiver of the amount is going to use it for purchase of a fixed asset.

2. Revenue expenditure. An expenditure that arises out of and in the course of regular business transactions of concern is termed as a revenue expenditure. It may simply be termed as "Expense". Following are few examples of revenue expenditure:

(*i*) Expenditure incurred in the normal course of running the business, *e.g.*, expenses of administration, cost incurred in manufacturing and selling the products.

(*ii*) Expenditure incurred to maintain the business *e.g.*, money spent for repairs of existing fixed assets or cost of stores consumed, etc.

(*iii*) Cost of goods purchased for resale.

(*iv*) Depreciation on fixed assets, interest on loans for the business.

Distinction between Capital Expenditure and Revenue Expenditure

The following are the points of distinction between a Capital Expenditure and a Revenue Expenditure:

(*a*) Capital expenditure is incurred for acquisition of fixed assets for the business. While revenue expenditure is incurred for day-to-day operation of the business.

(*b*) Capital expenditure is incurred for increasing the earning capacity of the business while revenue expenditure is incurred for maintaining the earning capacity of the business.

(*c*) Capital expenditure is of non-recurring nature while revenue expenditure is of a recurring nature.

(*d*) The benefit of capital expenditure is received over a number of years and only a small part of it, as depreciation, is charged to the profit and loss account each year. The rest appears in the balance sheet as an asset. While the benefit of revenue expenditure expires in the year in which the expenditure is incurred and it is entirely charged to the profit and loss account of the relevant year.

3. Deferred revenue expenditure. It is that class of revenue expenditure which is incurred during an accounting period, but is applicable either wholly or in part to future periods. Picklets and Dunkerley have in their book *Accountancy* classified it into four distinct types as follows:

(*i*) Expenditure wholly paid for in advance, where no service has yet been rendered, necessitating its being carried forward *i.e.*, the showing of such outlay as an asset in the Balance Sheet as prepaid expenditure, *e.g.*, telephone rental, or office rent paid in advance, etc.

(*ii*) Expenditure partly paid in advance, where a portion of the benefit has been derived within the period under review, the balance being as yet "unused", and therefore shown in the Balance Sheet as an asset, *e.g.,* proportion of rates paid in advance or special advertising expenditure incurred in introducing a new line or developing a new market. Most items paid in advance will fall either under head (*i*) or (*ii*), according as the payment relates wholly or partly to future periods.

(*iii*) Expenditure in respect of service rendered which for any should reason is considered as an asset, or more properly, is not considered to be allocable to the period in question, *e.g.*, development costs in mines and plantations, discount on debentures in limited companies and cost of experiments.

The practice, which varies considerably in detail, is to write off the amount over a period of years. If the expenditure can be earmarked as being in respect of a specific object, the expenditure should be written off during the life of that object *e.g.*, in the case of debenture discount at the latest by the time the debentures are redeemed.

(*iv*) Amounts representing losses of an exceptional nature, *e.g.*, properly confiscated in a foreign country, heavy loss of non-insured assets through, say, fire.

As a rule an item falling under this heading is a fictitious asset, *i.e.*, although it is shown an the assets side of the Balance Sheet, it is not really an asset at all but a capital or abnormal loss which has not been written off.

Accounting Standard 26 "Intangible Assets" has almost eliminated the concept of deferred revenue expenditure. The Standard is now applicable to all enterprises *w.e.f.* 1.4.2004. According to this Standard an asset should be recognized as intangible asset when it is "identifiable non-monetary asset, without physical substance, held to use in the production or supply of goods or services, for rental to others, or for administrative purposes." Expenditure on an intangible item should be recognised as an expense when it does not meet the above criteria. As a result an expenditure on intangible item incurred after 1.4.2004 viz. preliminary expenses, heavy advertisement expenditure, training cost, compensation for voluntary retirement should be expensed when incurred since it does not meet the definition of an asset as per AS 26.

Revenue Expenditure becoming Capital Expenditure

Following are some of the circumstances under which an expenditure which usually of a revenue nature may be taken as an expenditure of a capital nature:

1. **Repairs.** The amount spent on repairs of plant, furniture, building, etc., is taken as a revenue expenditure. However, when some second-hand plant, motor car, etc., is purchased, the expenditure incurred for immediate repairs of such plant, motor car, etc., to make it fit for use will be taken as a capital expenditure.

2. **Wages.** The amount spent as wages is usually taken as a revenue expenses. However, amount of wages paid for erection of a new plant or machinery or wages paid to workmen engaged in construction of a fixed asset are taken as expenditure of a capital nature.

3. **Legal charges.** Legal charges are usually taken as expenditure of a revenue nature, but legal charges incurred in connection with purchase of fixed assets should be taken as a part of the cost of the fixed asset.

4. **Transport charges.** Transport Charges are generally of a revenue nature, but transport charges incurred for a new plant and machinery are taken as expenditure of a capital nature and are added to the cost of the asset.

5. **Interest on capital.** Interest on Capital paid during the construction of works or buildings or plant may be capitalised and thus added to the cost of the asset concerned.

6. **Raw materials and stores.** They are usually taken as of a revenue nature, but raw materials and stores consumed in construction of the fixed assets should be treated as capital expenditure and be taken as a part of the cost of such fixed asset.

7. **Development expenditure.** In case of some concerns such as tea, rubber plantations, horticulture a long period is required for development. They start earning only after expiry of a long period which can be termed as development period. The expenditure incurred during such periods is termed as Development Expenditure and may be treated as a Capital Expenditure. For example, in case of tea industry, it takes 4-5 years for a tea plant to mature. When a new tea garden is to be started, new tea plants have to be planted. They have to be cared and looked after at least for 5 years before any tea can be manufactured. All such expenditure during this period is development expenditure and, therefore, of a capital nature. However, once the tea plants begin to bear tea leaves, the expenditure incurred to maintain then will be revenue expenditure.

8. **Advertising.** Cost of advertising for the purpose of introducing a new product should be treated as capital expenditure, since, the benefit of such expenditure will be available only in future years.

9. **Preliminary expenses.** Expenses incurred in formation of a new company are termed as preliminary expenses and should be treated as capital expenditure.

Expenditures covered under paras 8 and 9 were generally used to be treated as Deferred Revenue Expenditure. They were written off over a period of 3-4 years. However as per AS 26, as discussed earlier, such an expenditure has to be expensed in the year it is incurred.

Revenue Loss

Revenue Losses are those losses which arise during the normal course of running the business because of fall in the value of the current assets of the business. The term 'Revenue Loss' is similar to the term 'Revenue Expenditure' in this respect that it is also charged to the Profit and Loss Account of the business like Revenue Expenditure. However, the term expenditure is different from the term loss. Expenditure is supposed to bring some benefit to the firm, whereas a loss brings no benefit to the firm. For example, loss on account of bad debts, loss on account of destruction of goods by fire, etc.

CLASSIFICATION OF RECEIPTS

Receipts can be classified into two categories: Capital Receipts, and Revenue Receipts.

(*i*) **Capital receipts.** Capital Receipts consist of additional payments made to the business either by shareholders of the company or by the proprietors of the business or receipts from sale of fixed assets of a business. For example, the amount raised by the company by way of share capital is a capital receipt. Similarly, if a firm sells its machinery for a sum of Rs 10,000, the receipt is a capital receipt.

It should be noted that a capital receipt is different from a capital profit. Receipt denotes receiving payment in cash. Moreover, the whole of it may or may not be a capital profit. There may be a capital loss too. For example, if a plant costing Rs 10,000 is sold for Rs 12,000, there is a capital receipt of Rs 12,000, but there will be a capital profit of only Rs 2,000. Similarly, if the same plant had been sold only for Rs 8,000, there is a capital receipt of Rs 8,000 but there is a capital loss of Rs 2,000.

(*ii*) **Revenue receipts.** Any receipt which is not a capital receipt is a revenue receipt. In business most of the receipts are revenue receipts. However, a revenue receipt is also different from revenue profit or revenue income. Receipt denotes receiving of payment in cash. Moreover, the entire amount of receipt may or may not be a revenue income. For example, if the goods costing Rs 20,000 are sold for Rs 25,000, there is a revenue receipt of Rs 25,000, but revenue profit or income is only of Rs 5,000.

The distinction between capital and revenue is important both for income determination and taxation purposes. Various tests have been laid down from time to time for distinguishing between these two. Some of these are based on economic considerations, some on accounting principles and some have been pronounced by the courts. However, difficulties still arise in making a clear cut distinction between these two. There have been cases which fall on the border line. In many cases, the policies of those incharge of the business will decide whether certain expenditure or income should be classified revenue or capital. However, the rules given in the preceding pages and the illustrations given in the following pages will to a great extent help a student in making a fairly reasonable distinction between capital and revenue.

Illustration 9.1. State whether the following items of expenditure are of capital or revenue nature:

(*a*) A second-hand car was purchased for a sum of Rs 20,000. A sum of Rs 5,000 was spent on its overhauling.

(b) Rs 1,000 were spent on painting the factory.

(c) Freight and cartage amounting to Rs 1,000 were paid on purchase of a new plant and a sum of Rs 200 were spent as erection charges of that plant.

(d) Furniture of the book value of Rs 1,500 was sold for a sum of Rs 1,000. New furniture of Rs 2,000 was purchased and sum of Rs 20 was spent by way of cartage.

Solution:

(a) The total expenditure of Rs 25,000 should be taken as Capital Expenditure. The sum of Rs 20,000 was spent on a capital asset while another Rs 5,000 was spent from making the capital asset fit for use.

(b) The painting charges are for maintenance of a capital asset, hence they are of a revenue nature.

(c) The expenditure incurred by was of freight and cartage amounting to Rs 1,000 and the erection charges Rs 200 are both of a capital nature. The former has been incurred in connection with the receipt of a capital asset while the later has been incurred for erecting it so that it may be used for business purposes.

(d) The loss suffered on sale of old furniture amounting to Rs 500 should be taken as a revenue loss. This is because the furniture was used for business purposes and loss on its sale show that proper depreciation was not charged. The amount spent on purchases of new furniture and the cartage charges should be taken as capital expenditure. The former represents the cot of acquisition of a capital asset while the later represents the cost incurred for receipt of such a capital asset, to make it available for use in the business.

Illustration 9.2. Classify the following between Capital Expenditure and Deferred Revenue Expenditure giving brief reasons in each case:

(i) Cost of Rs 30,000 for dismantling, removing and reinsatlling plant by a Sugar Mill incurred in connection with the removal of works to a more suitable locality.

(ii) A sum of Rs 10,000 spent for alternation of existing plant incorporating thereby ne devices which could affect substantial reduction in power consumption.

(iii) Imported goods worth Rs 20,000 confiscated by Customs Authorities for disclosure for material facts.

Solution:

(i) The expenditure of Rs 30,000 incurred on dismantling, removing and reinstalling the plant to a more suitable locality should strictly be treated as a deferred revenue expenditure. This is because the expenditure has not resulted in any tangible asset. Moreover, the increase in profit in view of the new locatio, is difficult to assess exactly. The expenditure be written, off over a period of 4 or 5 years/ The amount not yet written off should be shown in the Balance Sheet on the assets side.

It may not also be wrong to write off the entire expenditure of Rs 30,000 from the Profit and Loss account of the current year, since the expenditure of Rs 30,000 is quite small looking to the fact that the factory is manufacturing sugar which necessarily follows that it must be of a big size.

(ii) The expenditure of Rs 10,000 on alteration of existing plant so as to incorporate a new device leading to reduced consumption of power in future should be treated as a Capital Expenditure. This is because it will result in definite saving in the years to come. Deprecation may be charged on the increased value of the machine, on account of this expenditure being capitalised.

(*iii*) The confiscation of imported goods by the Customs Authorities is a loss. Of course, the loss has arisen on account of gross negligence and is of an abnormal nature. If will be better to write it off from the Profit and Loss Account as a revenue loss, with proper description. This course should be adopted only when the amount of loss is small in relation to the current year's profit. However, if the profits of the current year are inadequate, the loss by treated as a deferred revenue expenditure, to be written off over a period of 2 or 3 years.

KEY TERMS

□ **Capital Expenditure:** An expenditure which has been incurred for the purpose of obtaining a long term advantage for the business.

□ **Capital Income:** An income which does not grow out of or pertain to the running of the business proper.

□ **Capital Receipt:** A receipt from the owners of the business by was of additional capital or from sale of fixed assets of the business.

□ **Revenue Expenditure:** An expenditure which arises out of and in the course of regular business transactions of a firm.

□ **Revenue Income:** An income which arises out of and in the course of regular business transactions of a concern.

□ **Revenue Receipt:** A receipt by the business during the normal course of running the business operations.

TEST QUESTIONS

Objective type

TEST YOUR UNDERSTANDING

1. State whether the following are Capital or Revenue items:
   (*a*) Carriage paid on goods purchased.
   (*b*) Legal expense incurred for abuse of Trade Mark.
   (*c*) Money raised by issue of equity shares.
   (*d*) Expenditure incurred on issue of equity shares.
   (*e*) Cost of formation of a new company.
   (*f*) Payment of compensation to a discharge employee.
   (*g*) Legal expenses incurred in defending a suit for breach of contract to supply goods.

   [**Ans** (*a*) Revenue Expenditure, (*b*) Revenue Expenditure, (*c*) Capital Receipt, (*d*) Capital Expenditure, (*e*) Capital Expenditure, (*f*) Revenue Expenditure, (*g*) Revenue Expenditure].

2. Select the most appropriate answer.
   (*i*) Cost of goods purchased for resale is an example of
   (*a*) Deferred Revenue Expenditure.
   (*b*) Revenue Expenditure.
   (*c*) Capital Expenditure.
   (*ii*) Rs 5,000 spent on replacement of worn out part of the machine will be charged as
   (*a*) Capital Expenditure.
   (*b*) Revenue Expenditure.
   (*c*) Deferred Revenue Expenditure.
   (*iii*) Discount allowed on issues of shares is an example of
   (*a*) Capital Expenditure.

    (b) Revenue Expenditure.

    (c) Deferred Revenue Expenditure.

(iv) Preliminary Expenses are an example of

    (a) Revenue Expenditure.

    (b) Deferred Revenue Expenditure.

    (c) Capital Expenditure.

(v) An expenditure is treated as of capital nature, when

    (a) the receiver of the amount is going to use it for the purchase of fixed assets.

    (b) it increases the quantity of fixed assets.

    (c) it is paid for meeting the normal expenses of the business.

(vi) Depreciation of fixed assets is an example of

    (a) Revenue Expenditure.

    (b) Capital Expenditure.

    (c) Deferred Revenue Expenditure.

(vii) Repairs incurred before using a second hand car purchased recently is a

    (a) Capital Expenditure.

    (b) Revenue Expenditure.

    (c) Deferred Revenue Expenditure.

[**Ans.** (i) (b), (ii) (b), (iii) (c), (iv) (b), (v) (b), (vi) (a), (vii) (a)].

Essay type | FOR REVIEW, DISCUSSION AND PRACTICE

1. State the considerations which would guide you in deciding whether any particular item should be regarded as of a capital or of a revenue nature.

2. Why is the distinction between capital and revenue is of great importance in accounting? Give certain examples illustrating how a certain expenditure can be regarded as a capital expenditure as well as a revenue expenditure under different circumstances.

PRACTICAL PROBLEMS

1. State with reasons which of the following items should be taken as of a Capital and which of a Revenue nature:

    (a) Rs 2,000 spent on dismantling, removing and reinstalling plant and machinery to a more convenient site.

    (b) Rs 600 paid for removal of stock to a new site.

    (c) Rs 1,000 paid for erection of a new machine.

    (d) Rs 2,000 paid on repairing of the new factory.

    (e) A car engine, rings and pistons were changed at a cost of Rs 3,000. This resulted in improvement of petrol consumption to 30 kms per litre. It had fallen from 15 kms. to 8 kms.

    (f) A building constructed in 1960 was written down by 1990 to Rs 5,000. It was demolished and a new building was constructed at a cost of Rs 3 lakhs including Rs 10,000 for demolishing the old building.

[**Ans.** (a) Revenue Expenditure, (b) Revenue Expenditure, (c) Capital Expenditure, (d) Capital Expenditure presuming that it has been incurred on a second-hand factory purchased, (e) Revenue Expenditure, (f) Loss on account of scrapping of the building is a revenue loss. Cost of construction of a new building is a capital expenditure].

2. State with reasons whether the following should be taken as of Capital or Revenue nature.

    (a) A sum of Rs 20,000 was spent by a large factory in overhauling its entire plant which resulted in adding three years to its working life.

(b) Heavy legal expenditure incurred by a newspaper company to defend a legal suit.

(c) Cost of experimenting a new product which did not result in success.

(d) Cost of Rs 10,000 incurred in increasing the sitting accommodation and Rs 5,000 in repainting of a cinema house.

(e) Cost of Rs 10,000 incurred in dismantling, removing and reinstalling factory to more suitable premises.

[**Ans.** (a) Capital Expenditure; (b) Deferred Revenue Expenditure; (c) Deferred Revenue Expenditure; (d) Capital Expenditure; (e) Revenue Expenditure (may also be taken as Deferred Revenue Expenditure).]

3. Show, by giving reasons, whether the following items of expenditure are Capital or Revenue:

(a) Carriage paid on goods purchased.

(b) Wages of workmen employed for setting up new machinery.

(c) Replacement cost of a worn-out part of plant.

(d) Repairs to furniture purchased second hand.

(e) Damages paid on account of the breach of a contract to supply certain goods.

[**Ans.** (a Revenue; (b) Capital; (c) Revenue; (d) Capital; (e) Revenue]

4. Sugesan Industries removed their Works to a more suitable premises:

(a) A sum of Rs 4,750 was expended on dismantling, removing and re-installing Plant, Machinery and Fixtures.

(b) Plant and Machinery which stood in the books at Rs 7,500 included a machine at a book value of Rs 1,700. This being obsolete was sold off at Rs 450 and was replaced by a new machine which cost Rs 2,400.

(c) The freight and cartage on the new machine amounted to Rs 150 and the erection charges cost Rs 275.

(d) A sum of Rs 1,100 was spent on painting the new factory.

State which item of expenditure would be charged to Capital and which to Revenue. Give reasons.

[**Ans.** (a) Deferred Revenue, (b) Revenue loss Rs 1,250, Capital Expenditure Rs 2,400, (c) Capital, (d) Revenue.]

Chapter 10

FINAL ACCOUNTS

LEARNING OBJECTIVES

After studying this Chapter you should be able to:

- ☐ identify the objectives of preparing final accounts;
- ☐ list the various statements/accounts which comprise final accounts of a business entity;
- ☐ understand the treatment of different items in preparation of the final accounts;
- ☐ appreciate the meaning and importance of different adjustment entries;
- ☐ pass appropriate adjustment entries;
- ☐ appreciate the role of work sheet in preparing final accounts;
- ☐ prepare Trading, Profit & Loss Account and Balance Sheet; and
- ☐ explain the meaning of certain key terms.

It has been explained in a preceding Chapter that the accuracy of the books of accounts is determined by means of preparing a Trial Balance. Having determined the accuracy of the books of accounts every businessman is interested in knowing about two more facts. They are: (*i*) Whether he has earned a profit or suffered a loss during the period covered by the Trial Balance, (*ii*) Where does he stand now? In other words, what is his financial position?

The determination of the Profit or Loss is done by preparing a Trading and Profit and Loss Account (or an Income Statement). While the financial position is judged by means of preparing a Balance Sheet of the business. The two statements together (*i.e.*, Income Statement and the Balance Sheet) are termed as Final Accounts. As the term indicates, Final Accounts means accounts which are prepared at the final stage to give the financial position of the business.

Trading and Profit and Loss Account

The Trading and Profit and Loss Account is a final summary of such accounts which affect the profit or loss position of the business. In other words, the account contains the items of Incomes and Expenses relating to a particular period. The account is prepared in two parts (*i*) Trading Account, and (*ii*) Profit and Loss Account.

TRADING ACCOUNT

Trading Account gives the overall result of trading, *i.e.*, purchasing and selling of goods. In other words, it explains whether purchasing of goods and selling them has proved to be profitable for the business or not. It takes into account on the one hand the cost of goods sold and on the other the value for which they have been sold away. In case the sales value is higher than the cost of goods sold, there will be a profit, while in a reverse case, there will be a loss. The profit disclosed by the Trading Account is termed as Gross Profit. Similarly the loss disclosed by the Trading Account is termed as Gross Loss.

This will be clear with the help of the following illustration:

Illustration 10.1. Following figures have been taken from the Trial Balance of a trader:

	Rs
	Rs
Purchases	30,000
Purchases Returns	5,000
Sales	40,000
Sales Returns	5,000

Calculate the amount of profit or loss made by the trader.

Solution:

The profit or loss made by the trader can be found out by comparing the cost of goods sold with sales value. This has been done as follows:

Particulars	Amount Rs	Amount Rs
Sales	40,000	
Less Sales Returns	5,000	35,000
Purchases	30,000	
Less Purchases Returns	5,000	25,000
Gross Profit		10,000

Opening and Closing Stocks

In the Illustration 10.1, we have presumed that all goods purchased have been sold away by the trader. However, it does not normally happen. At the end of the accounting year, a trader may be left with certain unsold goods. Such stock of goods with a trader unsold at the end of the accounting period is termed as Closing Stock. Such a stock will become the Opening Stock for the next period. For example, if a trader has with himself goods amounting to Rs 5,000 unsold at the end of the year 1988, this stock of Rs 5,000 will be termed as his Closing Stock. For the year 1989, this stock of Rs 5,000 will be termed as his Opening Stock. While calculating the amount of profit or loss on account of trading, a trader will have to take such Opening and Closing Stocks into consideration. This will be clear with the help of the following illustration:

Illustration 10.2. Taking the figures given in Illustration 10.1, calculate the amount of Gross Profit if stock of Rs 5,000 is left at the end of the accounting period.

Solution:

In the case, all goods purchased have not been sold away. Goods of Rs 5,000 are still left with the trader. Stock of such goods is termed as Closing Stock. Thus, cost of goods sold will be calculated as follows:

> COST OF GOODS SOLD = NET PURCHASES – CLOSING STOCK

$$= 25,000 - 5,000$$
$$= 20,000$$

The Gross Profit now can be computed as follows:

Gross Profit	= Net Sales – Cost of goods sold
	$= 35,000 - 20,000$
	$= 15,000$

Illustration 10.3. From the following data calculate the profit made by a trader in 1988.

	Rs
Stock of goods on 1.1.1988	10,000
Purchases during the year	40,000
Purchases Returns during the year	3,000
Sales during the year	60,000
Sales returns during the year	10,000
Stock of goods on 31-12-1988	15,000

Solution:

Particulars	Amount Rs	Amount Rs
Sales	60,000	
Less: Sales Returns	10,000	50,000
Cost of goods sold:		
Opening Stock	10,000	
Add: Net Purchases (Rs 40,000–5,000)	35,000	
	45,000	
Less: Closing Stock	15,000	30,000
Gross Profit		20,000

Expenses on Purchases etc.

In the Illustrations given above, we have presumed that the trader has not incurred any expenses for purchase of goods and bringing them to his shop for sale. However, a trader has to incur various types of expenses for purchasing of goods as well as for bringing them to his shop for sale. Such expenses may include brokerage or commission paid to agents for purchase of goods, cartage or carriage charges for bringing the goods to the trader's shop, wages paid to coolies for transportation of goods etc. All such expenses increase the cost of the goods sold and hence they have also to be included in the cost of purchasing the goods. In other words, cost of goods sold will be calculated as of follows:

> COST OF GOODS SOLD = OP. STOCK + NET PURCHASES + EXPS ON
> PURCHASING OF GOODS – CL. STOCK

Cost of goods sold calculated as above will then be compared with the net sales to find out the amount of profit or loss made by the business. This will be clear with the following Illustrations.

Illustration 10.4. Calculate the amount of the profit made by the trader with the help of data given in Illustration 10.3, if the wages, carriage charges etc. incurred for bringing the goods to the trader's shop amount to Rs 5,000.

Solution:

Particulars	Amount Rs
Net Sales	50,000
Less: Cost of goods sold (30,000 + 5000)	35,000
Gross Profit	15000

The term 'merchandise' is also used for the term 'goods'.
Thus:

```
COST OF GOODS            = COST OF MERCHANDISE
COST OF GOODS PURCHASED  = COST OF MERCHANDISE
                           PURCHASED
COST OF GOODS SOLD       = COST OF MERCHANDISE SOLD
```

Illustration 10.5. Find out the cost of merchandise purchased, cost of merchandise sold, cost of merchandise unsold and Gross Profit from the following transactions:

	Rs
Purchases (3,000 articles)	25,000
Freight	1,000
Local Taxes	1,000
Salaries	2,500
Shop Rent	500
Godown Rent	500
Electrical Charges	600
Municipal Taxes	200
Stationery	250
Furniture (estimated life 5 years)	12,000
Sales (2,700 articles)	32,000

Solution:

Particulars	Amount Rs
Cost of Merchandise purchased	
This consists of:	
Purchases	25,000
Freight	1,000
Local Taxes	1,000
	27,000
Cost of Merchandise sold	
Cost of 3,000 units of merchandise purchased	27,000
Cost of one unit of merchandise	9
Cost of 2,700 units of merchandise sold	24,300
Gross Profit	
Sales of 2,700 units of merchandise	32,000
Less: Cost of merchandise sold	24,300
	7,700
Cost of Merchandise unsold,	
300 units @ Rs 9 per unit	2,700

All other expenses including annual depreciation of furniture (amounting in all to Rs 6,950) will be considered for computing the Net Profit of the business. The concept of Net Profit has been explained later in the chapter.

Equation for Preparing Trading Account

On the basis of the Illustrations given in the preceding pages, the following equation can be derived for preparing Trading Account:

Gross Profit = Sales − Cost of goods sold

Cost of goods sold = Opening Stock + Purchases + Direct Expenses − Closing Stock

Therefore, Gross Profit = Sales − (Opening Stock + Purchases + Direct Expenses − Closing stock)

Or Gross Profit = (Sales + Closing Stock) − (Opening Stock + Purchases + Direct Expense)

The term "Direct Expenses" include those expenses which have been incurred in purchasing the goods, bringing them to the business premises and making them fit for sale. Examples of such expenses are carriage charges, octroi, import duty, expenses for seasoning the goods, etc.

The Trading Account can be prepared in the following form on the basis of equation given above.

TRADING ACCOUNT

Dr. for the period[1] ending... Cr.

Particulars	Amount Rs	Particulars	Amount Rs
To Openeing Stock	......	By Sales *Less*: Returns	......
To Purchases *Less*:	......	By Closing Stock	......
Returns	......		
To Direct Expenses	......		......
	......		......

Illustration 10.6. Prepare the Trading Account of Mr. Ramesh for the year ending 31st December, 1988 from the data as follows:

	Rs		Rs
Purchases	10,000	Wages	4,000
Purchases Returns	2,000	Carriage Charges	2,000
Sales	20,000	Stock on 1.1.1988	4,000
Sales Returns	5,000	Stock on 31.12.1988	6,000

TRADING ACCOUNT
for the year ending 31-12-1988

Particulars		Amount Rs	Particulars		Amount Rs
To Opening Stock		4,000	By Sales	20,000	
To Purchases	10,000		*Less*: Sales		
Less: Returns	2,000	8,000	Returns	5,000	15,000
To Wages		4,000	By Closing Stock		

Contd.....

[1] Usually "half year" or "a year".

Particulars	Amount Rs	Particulars	Amount Rs
To Carriage Charges	2,000		
To Gross Profit	3,000		
	21,000		21,000

Important Points Regarding Trading Account

1. **Stock.** The term 'Stock' includes goods lying unsold on a particular date. The Stock may be of two types:

(i) Opening Stock

(ii) Closing Stock.

The term 'Opening Stock' means goods lying unsold with the businessman in the beginning of the accounting year. This is shown on the debit side of the Trading Account.

The term 'Closing Stock' includes goods lying unsold with the businessman at the end of the accounting year. It should be noted that stock at the end of the accounting year is taken after the books of accounts have been closed. The following journal entry is passed in the Journal Proper to record the amount of closing stock:

Closing Stock Account   Dr.
    To Trading Account

The amount of closing stock is shown on the credit side of the Trading Account and as an asset in the Balance Sheet. This has been explained later. The Closing Stock at the end of the accounting period will become the Opening Stock for the next year. The Opening Stock is, therefore, shown on the debit side of the Trial Balance.

Valuation of closing stock. The closing stock is valued on the basis of "cost or market price whichever is less" principle. It is, therefore, very necessary that the cost of the goods lying unsold should be carefully determined. The market value of such goods will also be found out on the Balance Sheet date. The closing stock will be valued at the lower of the two values. For example, if the goods lying unsold at the end of the accounting period is Rs 11,000, while their market price on the Balance Sheet date amounts to Rs 10,000, the closing stock will be valued at Rs 10,000. This valuation is done because of the accounting convention of conservatism, according to which expected losses are to be taken into account but not expected profits.

2. **Purchases.** The term "Purchases" includes both cash and credit purchases of goods. The term "goods", as already explained in an earlier chapter, means items purchased for resale. Assets purchased for permanent use in the business such as purchase of plant, furniture, etc., are not included in the purchase of goods. Similarly, purchase of articles such as stationery meant for using in the business will also not be included in the item of purchases. In case, a proprietor has himself used certain goods for his personal purposes, the value of such goods at cost will be deducted from the purchases and included in the drawings of the proprietor. The journal entry in such a case would be as follows:

Drawings Account   Dr.
    To Purchases Account

Similarly in case certain goods are given by way of free samples, etc., the value of such goods should be charged to advertisement account and deducted from purchases. The journal entry in scuh a case would be as follows:

Advertisement Account   Dr.
    To Purchases Account

The amount of purchases will be the net purchases made by the proprietor. The term 'net purchases' means total purchases of goods made by the businessman less the goods that he has returned back to the suppliers. In other words, purchases will be taken to the Trading Account after deducting purchases returns from the gross purchases made during the accounting period.

3. Sales. The term 'Sales' includes both cash and credit sales. Gross sales will be shown in the inner column of the Trading Account out of which "sales returns" will be deducted. The net sales will then be shown in the outer column of the Trading Account. Proper care should be taken in recording sale of those goods which have been sold at the end of the financial year but have not yet been delivered. The sales value of such goods should be included in the sales, but care should be taken that they are not included in the closing stock at the end of the accounting period.

Sales of assets like plant and machinery, land and building or such other assets which were purchased for using in the business, and not for sale, should not be included in the figure of 'sales' to be taken to the Trading Account.

4. Wages. The amount of wages is taken as a direct expense and, therefore, is debited to the Trading Account. Difficulty arises in those cases when the Trial Balance includes a single amount for "wages and salaries". In such a case, the amount is taken to the Trading Account. However, if the Trial Balance shows "salaries and wages", the amount is taken to the Profit and Loss Account. In actual practice such difficulties do not arise because the businessman knows for which purpose he has incurred the expenditure by way of wages or salaries. However, in an examination problem, it will be useful for the students to follow the principle given above *i.e.*, "wages and salaries" to be charged to Trading Account while "wages and salaries" to be charged to the Profit and Loss Account. Wages paid for purchase of an asset for long-term use in the business *e.g.* wages paid for plant and machinery or wages paid for construction of a building should not be charged to the Wages Account. They should be charged to the concerned Asset Account.

5. Customs and import duty. In case the goods have been imported from outside the country, customs and import duty may have to be paid. The amount of such duty should be charged to the Trading Account.

6. Freight, carriage and cartage. Freight, Carriage and Cartage are taken as direct expenses incurred on purchasing of the goods. They are therefore, taken to the debit side of the Trading Account. The terms "Freight In", "Cartage In" and "Carriage In" have also the same meaning. However, "Cartage Out", "Freight Out" and "Carriage Out" are taken to be the expenses incurred on selling the goods. They are, therefore, charged to the Profit and Loss Account. The term "Inward" is also used for the term "*IN*". Similarly, the term "Outward" is also used for the term "*OUT*". In other words, "Carriage" or "Carriage Inward" or "Carriage In" are used as synonymous terms. Similarly "Carriage Out" or "Carriage Outward" are also synonymous terms. The same is true for other expenses like Freight or Cartage.

7. Royalty. Royalty is the amount paid to the owner for using his rights. For example, the royalty is paid by a "Lessee" of a coalmine to its owner for taking out the coal from the coalmine. Similarly, royalty is paid to the owner of a patent for using his right. It is generally taken as a direct expense and, therefore, is charged to the Trading Account.

However, where royalty is based on sales, for example in case of the book publishing trade, it may be charged to the Profit and Loss Account.

8. Gas, electricity, water, fuel, etc. All these expenses are direct expenses and, therefore, they are charged to the Trading Account.

9. Packing materials. Packing Materials used for packing the goods purchased for bringing them to the shop or convert them into a saleable state are direct expenses and, therefore, they are charged to the Trading Account. However, packing expenses incurred for making the product look attractive or packing expenses incurred after the product has been sold away are charged to the Profit and Loss Account.

Closing Entries

Closing Entries are entries passed at the end of the accounting year to close different accounts. These entries are passed to close the accounts relating to incomes, expenses, gains and losses. In other words, these entries are passed to close the different accounts which pertain to Trading and Profit and Loss Account. The accounts relating to assets and liabilities are not closed but they are carried forward to the next year. Hence, no closing entries are to be passed regarding those accounts which relate to the Balance Sheet.

The principle of passing a closing entry is very simple. In case an account shows a debit balance, it has to be credited in order to close it. For example, if the Purchases Account is to be closed, the Purchases Account will have to be credited so that it may be closed because it has a debit balance. The Trading Account will have to be debited.

The closing entries are passed in the Journal Proper. The different closing entries to be passed by the accountant for preparing a Trading Account are being explained below:

(i) Trading Account		Dr.
To Stock Account (Opening)		
To Purchases Account		
To Sales Returns Account		
To Carriages Account		
To Customs Duty Account		
(ii) Sales Account		Dr.
Purchases Returns Account		Dr.
Stock Account (Closing)		Dr.
To Trading Account		

In case the total of the credit side of the Trading Account is greater than the total of the debit side of the Trading Account, the difference is known as Gross Profit. In a reverse case it will be a Gross Loss. Gross Profit or Gross Loss disclosed by the Trading Account is transferred to the Profit and Loss Account.

Importance of the Trading Account

Trading Account provides the following information to a businessman regarding his business:

1. Gross Profit disclosed by the Trading Account tells him the upper limit within which he should keep the operating expenses of the business besides saving something for himself. The cost of purchasing and the price at which he can sell the goods are governed largely by market factors over which he has no control. He can control only his operating expenses. For example, if the cost of purchasing an article is Rs 10 and it can be sold in the market at Rs 15 per unit, the gross margin available on each article is Rs 5. In case a businessman proposes to sell

1,000 units of that article in a year, his gross profit or gross margin will be Rs 5,000. His other expenses should therefore be less than Rs 5,000 so that he can also save something for himself.

2. He can calculate his Gross Profit Ratio[1] and compare his performance year after year. A fall in the Gross Profit Ratio means increase in the cost of purchasing the goods or decrease in the selling price of the goods or both. In order to maintain at least same figure of gross profit in absolute terms, he will have to push up the sales or make all out efforts to obtain goods at cheaper prices. Thus, he can prevent at least fall in the figure of his gross profit if can not bring any increase in it.

3. Comparison of stock figures of one period from another will help him in preventing unnecessary lock-up of funds in inventories.

4. In case of new products, the businessman can easily fix up the selling price of the products by adding to the cost of purchases, the percentage gross profit that he would like to maintain. For example, if the trader has been so far maintaining a rate of gross profit of 20% on sales and he introduces a new product in the market having a cost of Rs 100, he should fix the selling price at Rs 125 in order to maintain the same rate of gross profit (i.e., 20% on sales).

PROFIT AND LOSS ACCOUNT

The Trading Account simply tells about the gross profit or loss made by a businessman on purchasing and selling of goods. It does not take into account the other operating expenses incurred by him during the course of running the business. For example, he has to maintain an office for getting orders and executing them, taking policy decision and implementing them. All such expenses are charged to the Profit and Loss Account. Besides this, a businessman may have other sources of income. For example, he may receive rent from some of his business properties. He may have invested surplus funds of the business in some securities. He might be getting interest or dividends from such investments. In order to ascertain the true profit or loss which the business has made during a particular period, it is necessary that all such expenses and incomes should be considered. Profit and Loss Account considers all such expenses and incomes and gives the net profit made or loss suffered by a business during a particular period. It is generally prepared in the following form:

PROFIT AND LOSS ACCOUNT

Dr.		for the year ending......		Cr.
Particulars	Rs	Particulars		Rs
To Gross Loss b/d	......	By Gross Profit b/d		......
To Salaries	......	By Discount received		......
To Rent	......	By Net Loss transferred		
To Commission	......	to Capital A/c		......
To Advertisements	......			
To Bad Debts	......			
To Discount	......			
To Net Profit Transferred				
to Capital Account	......			
	......			......

---

[1] $\dfrac{\text{Gross Profit}}{\text{Sales}} \times 100$

Important points regarding Profit and Loss Account

1. Gross Profit or Gross Loss. The figure of gross profit or gross loss is brought down from the Tading Account. Of course, there will be only one figure, *i.e.*, either of gross profit or gross loss.

2. Salaries. Salaries payable to the employees for the services rendered by them in running the business being of indirect nature are charged to the Profit and Loss Account. In case of a partnership firm, salaries may be allowed to the partners. Such salaries will also be charged to the Profit and Loss Account.

3. Salaries less tax. In case of employees earning salaries beyond a certain limit, the employer has to deduct at source income tax from the salaries of such employees. In such a case, the amount of gross salaries should be charged to the Profit and Loss Account, while the tax deducted by the employer will be shown as a liability in the Balance Sheet of the business till it is deposited with the Tax Authorities. For example, if salaries paid are Rs 2,400 after deducting income-tax of Rs 600, the amount of salaries to be charged to the Profit and Loss Account will be a sum of Rs 3,000. The amount of tax-deducted at source by the employer, *i.e.*, Rs 600 will be shown as a liability in the Balance Sheet.

4. Salaries after deducting provident fund contribution etc. In order to provide for old age of the employees, employers contribute a certain percentage of salaries of the employees to the Provident Fund. The employee is also required generally to contribute an equivalent amount. The share of the employee's contribution to Provident Fund is deducted from the salary due to him and the net amount is paid to him. The amount of salaries to be charged to the Profit and Loss Account will be the gross salary payable to the employee, *i.e.*, including the employee's contribution to the Provident Fund. The contribution by the employer will also be charged as an expense to the Profit and Loss Account. Both employer's and employee's contributions to the Provident Fund will also be shown as liability in the Balance Sheet under the heading "Employees Provident Fund".

5. Interest. Interest on loans whether short-term or long-term is an expense of an indirect nature and, therefore, is charged to the Profit and Loss Account. However, interest on loans advanced by a firm to third-parties is an item of income and, therefore, will be credited to the Profit and Loss Account.

6. Commission. Commission may be both an item of income as well as an item of expense. Commission on business brought by agents is an item of expense while commission earned by the business for giving business to others is an item of income. Commission to agents is, therefore, debited to the Profit and Loss Account while commission received is credited to the Profit and Loss Account.

7. Trade expenses. Trade expenses are expenses of a miscellaneous nature. They are of small amounts and varied in nature and, therefore, it is not considered worthwhile to open separate accounts for each of such types of expenses. The term "Sundry Expenses", "Miscellaneous Expenses" or "Petty Expenses" have also the same meaning. They are charged to the Profit and Loss Account.

8. Printing and stationery. This item of expense includes expenses on printing of bills, invoices, registers, files, letter heads, ink, pencil, paper and other items of stationery, etc. It is of an indirect nature and, therefore, charged to the Profit and Loss Account.

9. Advertisements. Advertisement expenses are incurred for attracting the customers to the shop and, therefore, they are taken as selling expenses. They are debited to the Profit and Loss Account. However, advertisement expenses incurred for purchasing of goods should be charged to the Trading Account, while an advertisement expenses incurred for purchase of a capital asset (*e.g.*, cost of insertion in a newspaper for purchase of car) should be taken as a capital expenditure and debited to the concerned asset account. Similarly advertisement expenditure incurred for sale of a capital asset should be deducted out of the sale proceeds of the asset concerned.

10. **Bad debts.** Bad Debts denotes, the amount lost from debtors to whom the goods were sold on credit. It is a loss and therefore, should be debited to the Profit and Loss Account.

11. **Depreciation.** Depreciation dentoes decrease in the value of an asset due to wear and tear, lapse of time, obsolescence, exhaustion and accident. For example, a motor car purchased gets depreciated on account of its constant use. A property purchased on lease for Rs 12,000 for 12 years will depreciate at the rate of Rs 1,000 per year. On account of new inventions, old assets become obsolete and they have to be replaced. Mines etc. get exhausted after the minerals are completely taken out of them. An asset may meet an accident and may lose its value. It is necessary that depreciation on account of all these factors is charged to the Profit and Loss Account to ascertain the true profit or loss made by the business.

Accounting (Closing) Entries for preparing Profit and Loss Account

Following journal entries will be passed in the Journal Proper for preparing the Profit and Loss Account.

(*i*) For transfer of items of expenses, losses, etc., appearing on the debit side of the Trial Balance

Profit and Loss Account .... Dr.
 To Salaries
 To Rent
 To Commission
 To Advertisements
 To Bad Debts
 To Discount
 To Printing and Stationery

(*ii*) For transfer of items of incomes, gains, etc., appearing on the credit side of the Trial Balance

Interest Account .... Dr.
Dividends Account .... Dr.
Discount Account .... Dr.
 To Profit and Loss Account

(*iii*) For transfer of net profit or net loss:

In case the total of the credit side of the Profit and Loss Account is greater than the debit side of the Profit and Loss Account, the difference is termed as Net Profit. In a reverse case, it will be termed as Net Loss. The amount of Net Profit or Net Loss shown by the Profit and Loss Account will be transferred to Capital Account in case of sole–proprietary firm. In case of a partnership firm, the amount of net profit or net loss will be transferred to the Partners' Capital Accounts in the agreed ratio. In the absence of any agreement, the partners will share profits and losses equally.

   For transfer of Profit
   Profit and Loss Account .... Dr.
    To Capital Account(s)

For transfer of Net Loss

    Capital Account(s)   Dr.

    To Profit and Loss Account

Illustration 10.7. From the following balances, taken from the Trial Balance of Shri Suresh, prepare a Trading and Profit and Loss Account for the year ending 31st Dec., 1988:

Particulars	Dr. Rs	Cr. Rs
Stock on 1.1.1988	2,000	
Purchases and Sales	20,000	30,000
Returns	2,000	1,000
Carriage	1,000	
Cartage	1,000	
Rent	1,000	
Interest received		2,000
Salaries	2,000	
General Expenses	1,000	
Discount		500
Insurance	500	

The Closing Stock on 31st December, 1988 is Rs 5,000.

Solution:

TRADING AND PROFIT AND LOSS ACCOUNT
for the year ending 31st December, 1988

Dr.   Cr.

Particulars	Rs		Particulars	Rs	
To Opening Stock		2,000	By Sales	30,000	
To Purchases	20,000		*Less.* Returns	2,000	28,000
Less. Returns	1,000	19,000	By Closing stock		5,000
To Carriage		1,000			
To Cartage		1,000			
To Gross Profit c/d		10,000			
		33,000			33,000
To Rent		1,000	By Gross Profit b/d		10,000
To Salaries		2,000	By Interest		2,000
To General Expenses		1,000	By Discount		500
To Discount		1,000			
To Insurance		500			
To Net Profit taken to					
Capital Account		8,000			
		12,500			12,500

Importance of Profit and Loss Account

The Profit and Loss Account Provides information regarding the following matters:

(*i*) It provides information about the net profit or net loss earned or suffered by the business during a particular period. Thus, it is an index of the profitability or otherwise of the business.

(*ii*) The Profit figure disclosed by the Profit and Loss Account for a particular period can be compared with that of the other period. Thus, it helps in ascertaining whether the business is being run efficiently or not.

(*iii*) An analysis of the various expenses included in the Profit and Loss Account and their comparison with the expenses of the previous period or periods helps in taking steps for effective control of the various expenses.

(*iv*) Allocation of profit among the different periods or setting aside a part of the profit for future contingencies can be done. Moreover, on the basis of profit figures of the current and the previous period estimates about the profit in the year to come can be made. These projections will help the business in planning the future course of action.

MANUFACTURING ACCOUNT

In the preceding pages, we have explained the preparation of the Trading and Profit and Loss Account from the point of view of a trader, *i.e.*, a person who purchases and sells goods. However, a person may manufacture goods by himself for selling them at a profit. In case of such a person, *i.e.*, a manufacturer, it will be necessary to ascertain the cost of manufacturing the goods. In his case, therefore, the profit or loss made by him will be ascertained by preparing the following three accounts:

(*i*) **Manufacturing account.** This account gives the cost of the goods manufactured by a manufacturer during a particular period.

(*ii*) **Trading account.** This account gives information about the gross profit or loss made by a manufacturer in selling the manufactured goods. In case a manufacturer also functions as a trader, *i.e.*, besides manufacturing and selling goods of his own, he also purchases and sells goods of others, he will be a manufacturer-cum-trader. In such a case, his Trading Account will disclose not only the profit made by him on selling his manufactured goods, but also the profit made by him in selling the goods purchased by him from others.

(*iii*) **Profit and loss account.** This account gives the overall profit or loss made or suffered by the manufacturer or manufacturer–cum–trader during a particular period. The proforma of a Manufacturing Account is given below:

MANUFACTURING ACCOUNT

Dr.   *for the year endig......*   Cr.

Particulars		Rs	Particulars		Rs
To Work-in-process (Opening)		......	By Work-in-process (Closing)		......
To Raw Materials consumed:			By Sale of Scrap		......
Opening Stock	......		By Cost of Production of		
Add: Purchases of Raw			finished goods during the		
Materials	......		period transferred to the		......
Less: Closing Stock of			Trading Account		
Raw Materials	......	......			
To Direct or Productive wages		......			
To Factory Overheads:		......			
Power and Fuel		......			
Repairs of Plant		......			
Depreciation on Plant		......			
Factory Rent		......			
		......			......

The Trading Account in case of a manufacturer wil appear as follows:

TRADING ACCOUNT

Dr.   for the year ending......   Cr.

Particulars	Rs	Particulars	Rs
To Opening Stock of Finished Goods	......	By Sales less Returns	......
To Cost of Production of finished goods transferred form Manufacturing Account	......	By Closing Stock of Finished Goods	
		By Gross Loss c/d*	......
To Purchases of Finished Goods less: Returns	......		
To Carriage Charges on goods purchased	......		
To Gross Profit c/d*	......		
	......		......

*Only one figure of profit or loss will appear.

The Gross Profit or Loss shown by the Trading Account will be taken to the Profit and Loss Account which will be prepared in the usual way as explained in the preceding pages.

Important Points Regarding Manufacturing Account

1. **Stocks.** In case of a manufacturer, there can be stocks of three types:
   (i) **Stock of raw materials.** It includes stock of raw materials or finished components which might have been purchased by the manufacturer for using them in the products manufactured by him but still lying unsold.
   (ii) **Stock of work-in-process.** This is also termed as stock of work-in-progress. It includes goods in semi-finished form.
   (iii) **Stock of finished goods.** It includes stock of those goods which have been completely processed and are lying unsold at the end of a period with the manufacturer. It also includes stock of those finished goods which might have been purchased by a manufacturer-cum-trader from outside parties, but still lying unsold with him at the end of the accounting period.

2. **Raw materials consumed.** It is customary to show in the Manufacturing Account, the value of raw materials consumed for manufacturing goods during a particular period. This is computed as follows:

Opening Stock of Raw Materials	......
Add: Purchase of Raw Materials	......
	......
Less: Closing Stock of Raw Mateirals	......
	......

For example, if the opening stock of raw materials is Rs 5,000, purchases of raw materials is Rs 20,000 and closing stock of raw materials is Rs 8,000, the value of raw materials consumed will be calculated as follows:

	Rs	Rs
Opening Stock of Raw Materials	5,000	
Add: Purchase of Raw Materials	20,000	25,000
Less: Closing Stock of Raw Materials		8,000
Raw Materials Consumed		17,000

3. **Carriage inwards, etc.** The expenses incurred for bringing the raw materials to the factory or the octroi or customs duty paid by the manufacturer on the raw materials purchased or imported by him will also be charged to Manufacturing Account.

4. **Factory overheads.** The term "Overheads" includes indirect material, indirect labour and indirect expenses. The term "Factory Overheads", therefore, stands for all factory indirect material, indirect labour, and indirect expenses. For exampele, in case of a manufacturer of chairs, the cost of timber purchased will be taken as raw materials. However, the polishing material used by him will be taken as indirect material and will be taken as an item of factory overheads. Similarly, the wages paid to the carpenters who have been employed for making chairs will come as cost of direct labour since they are actively engaged in manufacturing the chairs. However, the salaries of the supervisor or the wages of the gate-keeper will be taken as indirect labour cost and come in the definition of factory overheads. Similarly, the carriage charges paid for bringing the raw materials to the factory are considered to be direct charges since they can directly be charged to the raw materials purchased. However, the rent for the factory, depreciation of the factory machines, insurance of the factroy are all taken as indirect factory expenses and, therefore, covered under the category of factory overheads.

5. **Cost of production.** The Manufacturing Account gives the cost of manufacturing the goods during a particular period. This is computed by deducting from the total of the dedit side of the Manufacturing Account, the total of the various items appearing on the credit side of the Manufacturing Account as shown in the proforma of the Manufacturing Account given earlier in the chapter.

6. **Sale of scrap.** In manufacturing operations, certain scrap is unavoidable. It may or may not have any sales value. In order to calculate the true cost of manufacturing the goods, it is necessary that the money realised on account of sale of scrap (or realisable value of the scrap in case it has not been sold) should be considered. The amount of scrap is, therefore, credited to the Manufacturing Account.

Illustration 10.8. From the following details, prepare a Manufacturing and a Trading Account for the year ending 31st December, 1988:

	Rs
Stock on 1.1.1988	
Raw Materials	10,000
Work–in–process	5,000
Finished goods	20,000
Stock on 31.12.1988	
Raw Materials	5,000
Work–in–Process	15,000
Finished goods	30,000
Purchase of Raw Materials	50,000
Direct Wages	10,000
Carriage Charges on purchase of raw materials	5,000
Factory Power	5,000
Depreciation on Factory Machines	5,000
Purchase of Finished Goods	30,000
Cartage paid on Finished Goods purchased	2,000

Solution:

MANUFACTURING ACCOUNT
for the year ending 31.12.1988

Particulars		Rs	Particulars	Rs
To Work-in-process as on 1.1.1988		5,000	By Work-in-process on 31.12.1988	15,000
To Raw Materials consumed			By Cost of Production transferred to Trading	
Stock on 1.1.1988	10,000		Account	70,000
Add: Purchases	50,000			
	60,000			
Less: Closing Stock	5,000	55,000		
To Direct Wages		10,000		
To Carriage Charges		5,000		
To Factory Power		5,000		
To Depreciation on Factory Machines		5,000		
		85,000		85,000

TRADING ACCOUNT
for the year ending 31.12.1988

Particulars	Rs	Particulars	Rs
To Stock of Finished Goods 1.1.1988	20,000	By Stock of Finished Goods on 31.12.1988	30,000
To Cost of Production of finished goods transferred from Manufacturning Account	70,000	By Sale of Finished Goods	1,00,000
To Purchases of Finished Goods	30,000		
To Cartage on Finished Goods purchased	2,000		
To Gross Profit transferred to Profit and Loss A/c	8,000		
	1,30,000		1,30,000

Tutorial Note. Following points may further be noted by students:

(i) It is customary to give a separate heading to the Manufacturing Account as shown above. However, the Trading and Profit and Loss Account are not given separate headings. There will be a common heading for both these accounts as shown below:

TRADING AND PROFIT AND LOSS ACCOUNT
for the year ending......

(ii) In case in an examination question, a Manufacturing Account is not separately asked, the examinees may show all items relating to the Manufacturing Account in the Trading Account itself. However, it will be advisable in such a case to prepare a Manufacturing Account, if possible.

(*iii*) In case of Joint Stock Companies, the heading given is only, "Profit and Loss Account for the year ending..." and not Trading and Profit and Loss Account. However, the amount of Gross Profit and Net Profit may be calculated separately.

BALANCE SHEET

Having prepared the Manufacturing. Trading and Profit and Loss Account, a businessman will like to know the financial position of his business. For this purpose, he prepares a statement of his assets and liabilities as on a particular date. Such a statement is termed as "Balance Sheet". Thus, Balance Sheet is not an account but only a statement containing the assets and liabilities of a business on a particular date. It is as a matter of fact a classified summary of the various remaining accounts after accounts relating to Incomes and Expenses have been closed by transfer to Manufacturing, Trading and Profit and Loss Account.

Balance Sheet has two sides. On the left hand side, the "liabilities" of the business are shown while on the right hand side the assets of the business appear. These two terms have been explained later in the chapter.

It will be useful here to quote definitions of the Balance Sheet given by some prominent writers. According to Palmer, "The Balance Sheet is a statement at a given date showing on one side the trader's property and possessions and on the other side his liabilities." According to Freeman, "A Balance Sheet is an itemised list of the assets, liabilities and proprietorship of the business of an individual at a certain date." The definition given by the American Institute of Certified Public Accountants makes the meaning of Balance Sheet more clear. According to it, Balance Sheet is "a list of balances of the asset and liability accounts. This list depicts the position of assets and liabilities of a specific business at a specific point of time."

Proforma of Balance Sheet

There is no prescribed form of Balance Sheet for a sole proprietary and partnerhip concern. However, the assets and liabilities may be shown in any of the following order.

1. Liquidity Order.
2. Permanency Order.

1. **Liquidity order.** In case a concern adopts liquidity order, the assets which are more readily convertible into cash come first and those which cannot be so readily converted come next and so on. Similarly those liabilities which are payable first come first, and those payable later, come next and so on. A proforma of Balance Sheet according to liquidity order is given below:

BALANCE SHEET
as on.....

Liabilities	Rs	Assets		Rs
Bank Overdraft	......	Cash in hand		......
Outstanding Expenses	......	Cash at Bank		......
Bills Payable	......	Prepaid Expenses		......
Sundry Creditors	......	Bills Receivable		......
Long-term Loans	......	Sundry Debtors		....
Capital	......	Closing Stock:		
		Raw Materials	......	
		Work-in-progress	......	
		Finished goods	....	......
		Furniture		.....

Contd....

Liabilities	Rs	Assets	Rs
		Plant and Machinery	......
		Building	......
		Land	......
		Goodwill	......
	︙		︙

2. **Permanency order.** In case of permanency order, assets which are more permanent come first, less permanent come next and so on. Similarly liabilities which are more permanent come first, less permanent come next and so on. In other words an asset which will be sold in the last or a liability which will be paid in the last come first and that order is followed both for all assets and liabilities. In case a balance sheet is to be prepared according to permanency order, arrangement of assets and liabilities will be reversed than what has been shown above in case of liquidity order.

Arrangement of assets according to any of these orders is also termed as "Marshalling of Assets and Liabilities".

Distinction between Profit and Loss Account and Balance Sheet

The points of distinction between Profit and Loss Account and Balance Sheet are:

(i) A profit and loss account shows the profit or loss made by the business during a particular period. While a balance sheet shows the financial position of the business on a particular date.

(ii) A profit and loss account incorporates those items which are of a revenue nature while a balance sheet incorporates those items which are of a capital nature.

(iii) Of course, both profit and loss account and the balance sheet are prepared from the Trial Balance. However, the accounts transferred to the profit and loss account are finally closed while the accounts transferred to the balance sheet represent those accounts whose balances are to be carried forward to the next year.

Important Points Regarding Balance Sheet

1. **Liabilities.** The term "Liabilities" denotes claims against the assets of a firm whether those of owners of the business or of the creditors. As a matter of fact, the term "Equity" is more appropriate than the term "Liabilities". This is supported by the definition given by American Accounting Association. According to this Association, Liabilities are "claims of the creditors against the enterprise arising out of past activities that are to be satisfied by the disbursement or utilisation of corporate resources". While the term "Equity" stands both for owners equity (owners claims) as well as the outsiders equity (outsiders claims). However, for the sake of convenience, we are using the term "Liabilities" for purposes of this book.

Liabilities can be classified into two categories:

(i) Current Liabilities, and   (ii) Long Term of Fixed Liabilities.

Current liabilities. The term "Current Liabilities" is used for such liabilities which are payable within a year form the date of the Balance Sheet either out of existing current assets or by creation of new current liabilities. The broad categories of current liabilities are as follows:

(a) Accounts Payable, i.e., bills payable and trade creditors.

(b) Outstanding Expenses, i.e., expenses for which services have been received by the business but for which payments have not been made.

(c) Bank Overdraft.

(d) Short-term Loans, i.e., loans from Bank which are payable within one year from the date of the Balance Sheet.

(e) Advance payments received by the business for the services to be rendered or goods to be supplied in future.

Fixed liabilities. All liabilities other than Current Liabilities come within this category. In other words, these are liabilities which do not become due for payment in one year and which do not require current assets for their payment.

2. Assets. The term "Assets" denotes the resources acquired by the business from the funds made available either by the owners of the business or others. It thus includes all rights or properties which a business owns. Cash, investments, bills receivable, debtors, stock of raw materials, work in progress and finished goods, land, building, machinery, trade marks, patent rights, etc., are some examples of assets.

Assets may be classified into the following categories:

(a) **Current assets.** Current Assets are those assets which are acquired with the intention of converting them into cash during the normal business operations of the enterprise. According to Grady, "the term Current Assets is used to designate cash and other assets or resources commonly identified as those which are reasonably expected to be realised in cash or sold during the normal operating cycle of the business".[1] Thus, the term " Current Asset" includes cash and bank balances, stocks of raw materials, work-in-progress and finished goods, debtors, bills receivable, short-term investments, prepaid expenses, etc.

(b) **Liquid assets.** Liquid Assets are those assets which are immediately convertible into cash without much loss. Liquid Assets are a part of current assets. In computing liquid assets, stock of raw materials, work-in-progress and finished goods and prepaid expense are excluded while all other current assets are taken.

(c) **Fixed assets.** Fixed assets are those which are acquired for relatively long periods for carrying on the business of the enterprise They are not meant for resale. Land and building, machinery, furniture are some of the examples of Fixed Assets. Sometimes, the term "Block Capital" is also used for them.

(d) **Intangible assets.** Intangible Assets are those assets which cannot be seen and touched. Goodwill, patents, trade marks, etc., are some examples of Intangible Assets.

(e) **Fictitious assets.** There are assets not represented by tangible possession or property. Examples of such assets are formation expenses incurred for establishing a business such as registration charge paid to the registrar of a joint stock company for getting a company incorporated, discount on issue of shares, debit balance in the Profit and Loss Account when shown on the assets side in case of a joint stock company etc.

Illustration 10.9. From the following balance extracted from the books of M/s Rajendra Kumar Gupta & Co., pass the neccessary closing entries, prepare a Trading and Profit and Loss Account and a Balance Sheet.

Particulars	Rs	Particulars	Rs
Opening Stock	1,250	Plant and Machinery	6,230
Sales	11,800	Returns Outwards	1,380
Depreciation	667	Cash in hand	895
Commission (Cr).	211	Salaries	750
Insurance	380	Debtors	1,905
Carriage Inwards	300	Discount (Dr).	328
Furniture	670	Bills Receivable	2,730
Printing Charges	481	Wages	1,589
Carriage Outwards	200	Returns Inwards	1,659
Capital	9,228	Bank Overdraft	4,000
Creditors	1,780	Purchases	8.679
Bills Payable	541	Petty Cash in hand	47
		Bad Debts	180

1 Paul Grady, "Inventory of Generally Accepted Accounting Principles for Business Enterprises" Page 234–35.

The value of stock on 31st December, 1990 was Rs 3,700.

Solution:

JOURNAL

Date	Particulars		Dr. Amount Rs	Cr. Amount Rs
	Trading A/c	Dr.	13,477	
	To Opening Stock A/c			1,250
	To Purchases A/c			8,679
	To Wages A/c			1,589
	To Returns Inward A/c			1,659
	To Carriage Inward A/c			300
	(For closing all accounts to be debited to Trading A/c)			
	Sales A/c	Dr.	11,800	
	Returns Outward A/c	Dr.	1,380	
	To Trading A/c			13,180
	(For closing all accounts to be credited to the Trading A/c)			
	Trading A/c	Dr.	3,403	
	To Profit and Loss A/c			3,403
	(For transfer of Gross Profit)			
	Profit and Loss A/c	Dr.	2,986	
	To Depreciation A/c			667
	To Insurance A/c			380
	To Printing Charges A/c			481
	To Carriage Outward A/c			200
	To Salaries A/c			750
	To Discount A/c			328
	To Bad Debts A/c			180
	(For closing all indirect and selling expenses accounts)			
	Commission A/c	Dr.	211	
	To Profit and Loss A/c			211
	(For closing commission account)			
	Protif and Loss A/c	Dr.	628	
	To Capital A/c			628
	(For tranferring Net Profit to Capital Account)			

TRADING AND PROFIT & LOSS ACCOUNT
for the year ending 31st Dec., 1990

Particulars		Amount Rs	Particulars		Amount Rs
To Opening Stock		1,250	By Sales	11,800	
To Purchases	8,679		*Less:* Returns		
Less: Returns Outward	1,380	7,299	Inwards	1,659	10,141
To Wages		1,589	Closing Stock		3,700
To Carriage Inward		300			
To Gross Profit c/d		3,403			
		13,841			13,841
To Depreciation		667	By Gross Profit b/d		3,403
To Insurance		380	By Commission		211
To Printing Charges		481			

Contd....

Particulars	Amount Rs	Particulars	Amount Rs
To Carriage Outwards	200		
To Salaries	750		
To Discount	328		
To Bad Debts	180		
To Net Profit	628		
	3,614		3,614

BALANCE SHEET
as on 31st December, 1990

Liabilities		Amount Rs	Assets	Amount Rs
Bills Payable		541	Cash	895
Creditors		1,780	Petty Cash	47
Bank Overdraft		4,000	Bills Payable	2,730
Capital	9,228		Debtors	1,905
Add: Net Profit	628	9,856	Closing Stock	3,700
			Plant and Machinery	6,230
			Furniture	670
		16,177		16,177

Illustration 10.10. From the following Trial Balance prepare the Manufacturing Account, the Trading and Profit and Loss Account for the year ending 31st March, 1991 and the Balance Sheet as on that date:

Particulars	Debit Rs	Credit Rs
Shri Banker's Captial Account		41,000
Shri Banker's Drawing Account	6,100	
Mrs Banker's Loan Account		4,000
Sundry Creditors		45,000
Cash in Hand	250	
Cash at Bank	4,000	
Sundry Debtors	40,500	
Patents	2,000	
Plant and Machinery	20,000	
Land and Buildings	26,000	
Purchases of Raw Materials	35,000	
Raw Material : 1.4.1990	3,500	
Work-in-process : 1.4.1990	2,000	
Finished Stock : 1.4.1990	18,000	
Carriage Inwards	1,100	
Wages	27,000	
Salary of Works Manager	5,600	
Factory Expenses	3,400	
Factory Rent and Taxes	2,500	
Royalties (paid on sales)	1,200	
Sales (less Returns)		1,23,400
Advertising	3,000	

Contd....

Particulars	Debit Rs	Credit Rs
Office Rent and Insurance	4,800	
Printing and Stationery	1,000	
Office Expenses	5,800	
Carriage Outwards	600	
Discounts	1,400	2,100
Bad Debts	750	
	2,15,500	2,15,500

The Stock on 31st March, 1991 was as follows:

Rs 4,000 Raw materials, Rs 4,500 Work-in-progress and Rs 28,000 Finished Goods.

Solution:

MANUFACTURING ACCOUNT
for the year ending March 31, 1991

Particulars		Amount Rs	Particulars	Amount Rs
To Opening Work-in-process		2,000	By Transfer to Trading Account	
To Raw Materials used:			(cost of finished goods produced)	71,600
Opening Stock	3,500		By Closing Work-in-process	4,500
Add: Purchases	35,000			
	38,500			
Less: Closing Stock	4,000	34,500		
To Carriage Inwards		1,100		
To Wages		27,000		
To Salary of Works Manager		5,600		
To Factory Expenses		3,400		
To Factory Rent and Taxes		2,500		
		76,100		76,100

TRADING AND PROFIT & LOSS ACCOUNT
for the year ending March 31, 1991

Particulars	Amount Rs	Particulars	Amount Rs
To Opening Stock of		By Sales	1,23,400
finished goods	18,000	By Closing Stock of	
To Manufacturing A/c	71,600	finished goods	28,000
(Cost of goods produced)			
To Gross Profit c/d	61,800		
	1,51,400		1,51,400
To Royalties	1,200	By Gross Profit b/d	61,800
To Advertising	3,000	By Discount received	2,100
To Office Rent and Insurance	4,800		
To Printing and Stationery	1,000		
To Office Expenses	5,800		
To Carriage Outwards	600		
To Bad Debts	750		
To Discount Allowed	1,400		
To Net Profit carried to			
Capital Account	45,350		
	63,900		63,900

BALANCE SHEET
as on 31st March, 1991

Liabilities		Amount Rs	Assets		Amount Rs
Sundry Creditors		45,000	Current Assets:		
Mrs. Banker's Loan		4,000	Cash in hand		250
Capital Account:			Cash at Bank		4,000
Balance on			Sundry Debtors		40,500
1.4.1990	41,000		Closing Stock:		
Profit	45,350		Raw Materials	4,000	
	86,350		Work-in-process	4,500	
Less: Drawings	6,100	80,250	Finished goods	28,000	36,500
			Fixed Assets:		
			Patents		2,000
			Plant and Machinery		20,000
			Land and Buildings		26,000
		1,29,250			1,29,250

ADJUSTMENT ENTRIES

In the preceding pages, we have explained the preparation of the Final Accounts, without any adjustments. We have presumed that the accountant has taken into consideration all important facts before closing the books of accounts and preparing the Final Accounts. However, it may not always happen. The accountant may come to know of certain adjustments to be made in the books of accounts to give a true picture of the state of affairs of the business after closing the books of accounts and preparing the Trial Balance. These adustments usually relate to the following:

1. Closing stock
2. Outstanding expenses
3. Prepaid expenses
4. Outstanding or accrued income
5. Income received in advance or unearned income
6. Depreciation
7. Bad debts
8. Provision for bad debts
9. Provision for discount on debtors
10. Reserve for discount on creditors
11. Interest on capital
12. Interest on drawings.

Each of these adjustments are being explained in detail in the following pages:

Closing Stock

We have already explained about the treatment of the stock at the end of the accounting year while explaining Final Accounts in the preceding pages. The following journal entry is passed for the unsold stock at the end of the accounting period:

     Closing Stock A/c   Dr.
          To Trading Account

The stock at the end appears in the Balance Sheet and its balance at the end of the accounting year is carried forward to the next year. It comes as opening stock in the Trial Balance of the next year from where it is transferred to the Trading Account on the debit side. The Trading Account is debited and the stock in the beginning of the accounting year (which was Closing Stock last year) is credited. Stock Account is thus closed.

Sometimes the value of the stock at the end of the accounting year, is given in the Trial Balance. In such a case, the Closing Stock will be shown only in the Balance Sheet. This is because it means that the Closing Stock has already been taken into account while computing the cost of goods sold. This will be clear with the help of the following example:

TRIAL BALANCE

Particulars	Dr. Amount Rs	Cr. Amount Rs
Opening Stock	10,000	
Purchases	30,000	
Sales		40,000

Stock at the end of the accounting year is Rs 15,000

In this case, the Closing Stock has been given outside the Trial Balance and, therefore, the different items will appear in the Final Accounts as follows:

Dr.		TRADING ACCOUNT		Cr.
Particulars	Amount Rs	Particulars		Amount Rs
To Opening Stock	10,000	By Sales		40,000
To Purchases	30,000	By Closing stock		15,000
To Gross Profit taken to				
Profit and Loss Account	15,000			
	55,000			55,000

BALANCE SHEET

Liabilities	Amount Rs	Assets	Amount Rs
		Closing Stock	15,000

The Opening and Closing Stock may both be adjusted with purchases and the cost of sales may be found out separately. In such a case, the items in the Trial Blance will appear as follows:

TRIAL BALANCE

Particulars	Dr. Amount Rs	Cr. Amount Rs
Adjusted Purchases or Cost of Sales	25,000	
Sales		40,000
Closing Stock	15,000	

The different items will now appear in the Final Accounts as follows:

Dr.	TRADING ACCOUNT			Cr.
Particulars	Amount Rs	Particulars		Amount Rs
To Adjusted Purchases	25,000	By Sales		30,000
To Gross Profit taken to Profit and Loss Account	15,000			
	40,000			40,000

BALANCE SHEET

Liabilities	Amount Rs	Assests	Amount Rs
		Closing Stock	40,000

Outstanding Expenses

Outstanding Expenses refer to those expenses which have become due during the accounting period for which the Final Accounts have been prepared but have not yet been paid. This happens particularly regarding those expenses which accrue from day to day business but which are recorded only when they are paid. Examples of such expenses are rent, salaries, interest, etc. Some of these expenses may have remained unpaid at the end of the accounting period and, therefore, no entry might have been passed in the books of accounts. For example, if the salary for the month of December has not been paid, no entry might have been passed in the books for the salary remaining outstanding on 31st December. However, in order to ascertain the true profit or loss made during the accounting year ending 31st December, it is necessary that such outstanding salaries are taken into account. The following journal entry will be passed in case of such outstanding expenses:

        Salaries A/c   Dr.
            To Outstanding Salaries A/c

Salaries Account is a nominal account and, therefore, it should be charged to the Profit and Loss Account, while the Outstanding Salaries Account is a personal account representing the persons to whom the salary has to be paid. It is, therefore, shown in the Balance Sheet on the liabilities side.

Illustration 10.11. Following are the extracts from the Trial Balance of a firm as on 31st December, 1990:

TRIAL BALANCE
as on 31st December, 1990

Particulars	Dr. Amount Rs	Cr. Amount Rs
Salaries A/c	10,000	
Rent A/c	5,000	

Additional Information:

(i) Salary for the month of December Rs 2,000 has not yet been paid.

(ii) Rent amounting to Rs 1,000 is still outstanding.

You are required to pass the necessary adjusting entries and show how the above items will appear in the Firm's Final Accounts:

Solution:

JOURNAL PROPER

Date	Particulars		Dr. Amount Rs	Cr. Amount Rs
	Salaries A/c	Dr.	2,000	
	To Outstanding Salaries A/c			2,000
	(Being salaries due but not paid)			
	Rent A/c	Dr.	1,000	
	To Outstanding Rent A/c			1,000
	(Being rent due but not paid)			

The items will appear in the Final Accounts as follows:

Dr. PROFIT AND LOSS ACCOUNT Cr.

Particulars		Amount Rs	Particulars	Amount Rs
To Salaries	10,000			
(as given in the				
Trial Balance)				
Add: Outstanding				
Salaries	2,000	12,000		
To Rent	5,000			
(as given in the				
Trial Balance)				
Add: Outstanding				
Rent	1,000	6,000		

BALANCE SHEET

Liabilities		Amount Rs	Assets	Amount Rs
Outstanding Expenses:				
Outstanding Salaries	2,000			
Outstanding Rent	1,000	3,000		

It should be noted that any item given outside the Trial Balance will be recorded at two places on account of Dual Aspect Concept. For example, in the above illustration, the amount of outstanding salaries has been shown in the Profit and Loss Account and also in the Balance Sheet.

However, if the accountant had come to know about these outstanding expenses before closing the books of accounts, the Salaries Account and Outstanding Salaries Account, Rent Account and Outstanding Rent Account would have appeared in the ledger as follows:

Dr. SALARIES ACCOUNT Cr.

Particulars	Amount Rs	Particulars	Amount Rs
To Bank	10,000	By Balance c/d	12,000
To Outstanding Salaries	2,000		
	12,000		12,000

Dr.   OUTSTANDING SALARIES ACCOUNT   Cr.

Particulars	Amount Rs	Particulars	Amount Rs
To Balance c/d	2,000	By Salaries	2,000
	2,000		2,000

RENT ACCOUNT

Particulars	Amount Rs	Particulars	Amount Rs
To Bank	5,000	By Balance c/d	6,000
To Outstanding Rent	1,000		
	6,000		6,000

OUTSTANDING RENT ACCOUNT

Particulars	Amount Rs	Particulars	Amount Rs
To Balance c/d	1,000	By Rent A/c	1,000
	1,000		1,000

The above balances would have appeared in the Trial Balance as follows:

TRIAL BALANCE
as on 31st December, 1990

Particulars	Dr. Amount Rs	Cr. Amount Rs
Salaries A/c	12,000	
Rent A/c	6,000	
Outstanding Salaries A/c		2,000
Outstanding Rent A/c		1,000

The above accounts would have appeared in the Final Accounts as follows:

PROFIT & LOSS ACCOUNT
for the year ending 31.12.1990

Particulars	Amount Rs	Particulars	Amount Rs
To Salaries	12,000		
To Rent	6,000		

BALANCE SHEET
as on 31.12.1990

Liabilities	Amount Rs	Assets	Amount Rs
Outstanding Salaries	2,000		
Outstanding Rent	1,000		

Thus, the position in both the cases is the same. The point to be noted is that any item appearing in the Trial Balance is recorded at only one place in the Final Accounts while any item outside the Trial Balance is recorded at two places in the Final Accounts.

Prepaid Expenses

Prepaid Expenses are those expenses which have been paid in advance. In other words, these are the expenses which have been paid during the accounting period for which the Final Accounts are being prepared but they relate to the next period. For example, during the accounting year ending on 31st December, 1990, insurance premium for the year ending 31st March, 1991 might have been paid. It means insurance for three months it has been paid in advance. In order to ascertain true profit or loss only expenses relating to the accounting period should be charged to the Profit and Loss Account. Any expenses paid in advance should be carried forward to the next year. The following journal entry is passed for an expense paid in advance:

Prepaid Expense A/c   Dr.
    To Expense A/c

Expense Account is a nominal account and, therefore, the amount should be credited to the Profit and Loss Account, preferably the amounts should be deducted from the relevant Expense Account is respect of which the payment has been made in advance. Prepaid Expense Account is a personal Account, it represents the account of the person to whom payment has been made in advance. It is, therefore, shown on the Balance Sheet on the assets side.

Illustration 10.12. Following are the extracts from the Trial Balance of a firm as on 31st December, 1990.

TRIAL BALANCE
as on 31st December, 1990

Particulars	Dr. Amount Rs	Cr. Amount Rs
Insurance	8,000	
Rent	4,000	

Additional Information:

(*i*) Insurance premium has been paid in advance amounting to Rs 1,000 for the next year.

(*ii*) Rent Rs 500 has been paid for the next year.

You are required to pass the necessary adjusting entries and show how the items will appear in the firm's Final Accounts.

Solution:

JOURNAL PROPER

Date	Particulars		Dr. Amount Rs	Cr. Amount Rs
	Prepaid Insurance A/c	Dr.	1,000	
	To Insurance A/c			1,000
	(Being Insurance premium paid in advance)			
	Prepaid Rent A/c	Dr.	500	
	To Rent A/c			500
	(Being rent paid in advance)			

PROFIT AND LOSS ACCOUNT
as on 31st December, 1990

Particulars		Amount Rs	Particulars	Amount Rs
To Insurance	8,000			
Less: Prepaid	1,000	7,000		
To Rent	4,000			
Less: Prepaid	500	3,500		

BALANCE SHEET
as on 31st December, 1990

Liabilities	Amount Rs	Assets	Amount Rs
		Prepaid Insurance	1,000
		Prepaid Rent	500

Outstanding Incomes

Outstanding Income means income which has become due during the accounting year but which has not so far been received by the firm. In order to ascertain the true profit or loss, adjustments for such income must be made in the Final Accounts of the business. The following journal entry will be passed:

Outstanding Income A/c   Dr.
     To Income A/c

Accrued Income. Accrued Income means income which has been earned by the business during the accounting year but which has not yet become due and, therefore, has not been received. Adjusting entry for such income is also on the pattern of outstanding income as shown below:

Accrued Income A/c   Dr.
     To Income A/c

A distinction has to be made between accrued income and outstanding income. Though, both the incomes have been earned by the business and not yet received but in case of accrued income, the income has not become due to the business while outstanding income is an income which has become due to the business. For example, if a loan of Rs 10,000 has been given @ 12% p.a. and interest is payable monthly, if interest for one month, *i.e.*, Rs 100 has not been received by the business, the income will be termed as an Outstanding Income since interest has become due but it has not yet been received by the business. However, in case of those securities where interest is payable on definite dates, interest may have been earned by the business, but it will become due not earlier than the definite date. For example, if a business has purchased 6% Government Securities of Rs 10,000 on which interest is payable on 31st March and 30th September, for the accounting year ending on 31st December interest for 3 months (*i.e.*, Rs 150 for October, November and December) will be taken as accrued interest and not an outstanding interest. This is because interest will become due after 30th September, only on 31st March and not earlier.

Illustration 10.13. Following are the extracts from the Trial Balance of a firm on 31st December, 1990.

Particulars	Dr. Amount Rs	Cr. Amount Rs
6% Loan	20,000	
Investments in 6% Debentures of 'B' Ltd.	30,000	
(Interest payable on 31st March and 30th Sept.)		
Interest on loan received upto 31st October, 1990		1,000
Interest on Investments		900

Solution:

In the above case, interest on loan for a period of two months is still outstanding. The amount of such interest is Rs 200. In case of debentures, interest for three months has been earned by the business but it has not become due. The amount of accrued interest, therefore, comes to Rs 450. The following adjusting entries will, therefore, be passed in the journal proper.

Date	Particulars		Dr. Amount Rs	Cr. Amount Rs
	Outstanding Interest A/c	Dr.	200	
	To Interest A/c			200
	(Being interest on loan due but not received)			
	Accrued Interest A/c		450	
	To Interest on Investments A/c			450
	(Being interest earned, not due and not received)			

Outstanding Interest Account and Interest Accrued Account are personal accounts. They represent the accounts of the persons from whom the interest has to be received. They will, therefore, be shown on the 'assets side' in the Balance Sheet. Interest Account is a nominal account, it has been credited. The amount of interest will, therefore, be added to the amount of interest already appearing in the Trial Balance.

The items will appear in the Final Accounts as follows:

PROFIT AND LOSS ACCOUNT
for the year ending 31st December, 1990

Particulars	Amount Rs	Particulars		Amount Rs
		By Interest on Loan	1,000	
		Add: Outstanding		
		Interest	200	1,200
		By Interest on Investments	900	
		Add: Accrued		
		Interest	450	1,350

BALANCE SHEET
as on 31st December, 1990

Liabilities	Amount Rs	Assets	Amount Rs
		Outstanding Interest A/c	200
		Accrued Interest A/c	450

Income Received in Advance

Income received in advance means income which has been received by the business before it being earned by the business. This includes certain pre-payments which the business may receive during the course of the accounting year. In order to ascertain the true profit or loss, it is necessary that such income is not taken into account while preparing the Profit and Loss Account for the year. The following adjustment entry is passed for such income:

Income A/c   Dr.
    To Income Received in Advance A/c

Illustration 10.14. Following are the extracts from the Trial Balance of a firm on 31st December, 1990. You are required to pass the necessary adjustment entries and show how the various will appear in the firm's Final Accounts.

TRIAL BALANCE
as on 31st December, 1990

Particulars	Dr. Amount Rs	Cr. Amount Rs
Rent received for 12 months ending 31st March, 1991		1,200
Interest on Loan		2,000

Additional Information. Interest on Loan has been received in advance to the extent of Rs 500.

Solution:

JOURNAL ENTRIES

Date	Particulars		Dr. Amount Rs	Cr. Amount Rs
	Rent A/c	Dr.	300	
	To Rent received in Advance A/c			300
	(Being rent received in advance for three months)			
	Interest A/c	Dr.	500	
	To Interest received in Advance A/c			500
	(Being interest received in advance)			

PROFIT AND LOSS ACCOUNT
for the year ending 31st December, 1990

Particulars	Amount Rs	Particulars		Amount Rs
		By Interest	2,000	
		Less: Received in advance	500	1,500
		By Rent	1,200	
		Less: Received in advance	300	900

BALANCE SHEET
as on 31st December, 1990

Liabilities	Amount Rs	Assets	Amount Rs
Rent received in advance	300		
Interest received in advance	500		

Depreciation

Depreciation denotes decrease in the value of an asset due to wear and tear, lapse of time, obsolescence, exhaustion and accident. In order to ascertain, the true profit for the business, it is necessary that depreciation is charged on the fixed assets of the business. The following entry will be passed for depreciation.

Depreciation A/c Dr.	
To Fixed Asset A/c	

Illustration 10.15. Following are the extracts from the Trial Balance of a firm.

TRIAL BALANCE
as on 31st December, 1990

Particulars	Dr. Amount Rs	Cr. Amount Rs
Plant	30,000	
Buildings	50,000	

Additional Information:

(*i*) Charge depreciation on plant @ 10% per annum,

(*ii*) Charge depreciation on buildings @ 5% per annum.

Solution:

JOURANL ENTRIES

Date	Particulars		Dr. Amount Rs	Cr. Amount Rs
	Depreciation A/c	Dr.	5,500	
	To Plant A/c			3,000
	To Buildings A/c			2,500
	(Being depreciation charged on Plant and Buildings)			

PROFIT AND LOSS ACCOUNT
for the year ending 31st December, 1990

Particulars	Amount Rs		Particulars	Amount Rs
To Depreciation:				
Plant	3,000			
Buildings	2,500	5,500		

BALANCE SHEET
as on 31st December, 1990

Liabilities	Amount Rs	Assets		Amount Rs
		Plant	30,000	
		Less: Depreciation	3,000	27,000
		Buildings	50,000	
		Less: Depreciation	2,500	47,500

Depreciation on Assets acquired during the course of the year

Sometimes fixed assets are acquired during the course of the year. In such a case, the problem arises whether depreciation should be charged for the full accounting year or it should be charged only for a part of the accounting year. In such a situation in the absence of any specific instructions in the question, it will be appropriate to charge depreciation for the full year even in respect of those assets which have been acquired during the course of the year. However, where depreciation rate has been given as per annum and the date of acquisition of the fixed assets has been given, it will be appropriate to charge depreciation only for the remaining part of the accounting year.

Illustration 10.16. Following are the extracts from the Trial Balance of a firm.

TRIAL BALANCE
as on 31st December, 1990

Particulars	Dr. Amount Rs	Cr. Amount Rs
Furnitures and Fixtures	10,000	
Plant and Machinery	40,000	

Additional Information:

   (*i*) Furniture of Rs 5,000 was purchased on 1st July, 1990. Charge depreciation @ 10% p.a.

   (*ii*) Plant of Rs 10,000 was acquired on 1st July 1990. Charge depreciation @ 20%.

Pass the necessary journal entries and show how the items will appear in the firm's Final Accounts:

Solution:

JOURNAL ENTRIES

Date	Particulars	Dr. Amount Rs	Cr. Amount Rs
	Depreciation A/c Dr.	8,750	
	To Furniture & Fixtures A/c		750
	To Plant and Machinery A/c		8,000
	(Being depreciation charged on furniture and fixtures and Plant and Machinery including additions)		

PROFIT AND LOSS ACCOUNT
for the year ending 31st December, 1990

Particulars	Amount Rs		Particulars	Amount Rs
To Depreciation:				
Furniture and Fixtures	750			
Plant and Machinery	8,000	8,750		

BALANCE SHEET
as on 31st December, 1990

Particulars	Amount Rs	Particulars		Amount Rs
		Furniture & Fixtures	10,000	
		Less: Depreciation	750	9,250
		Plant & Machinery	40,000	
		Less Depreciation	8,000	32,000

Notes:

   (*i*) Since depreciation has been given on furniture at 10% p.a., depreciation for only 6 months has been charged for furniture acquired on 1st July, 1990.

   (*ii*) In case of plant, the rate of depreciation has been given as 20%, hence, depreciation for the full year has been charged even on plant which has been acquired on 1st July, 1990.

Tutorial Note. The students should give note regarding their workings. In case, the question is silent regarding charging of depreciation on additions to fixed assets made during the year, the students can also presume that no depreciation is to be charged on additions. However, a specific note should be given to that effect.

Bad Debts

Credit sales have become a must these days and bad debts occur when there are credit sales. Bad Debt is a loss to the business and a gain to the debtor. The following journal entry should, therefore, be passed in the event of a debt becoming bad.

Bad Debts A/c	Dr.
To Debtor's Personal A/c	

Illustration 10.17. Following are the extracts from Trial Balance of a business.

TRIAL BALANCE
as on 31st December, 1990

Particulars	Dr. Amount Rs	Cr. Amount Rs
Sundry Debtors	50,000	
Bad Debts	5,000	

Additional information: Mahesh, one of the debtros became insolvent and it was learnt on 31st December, that out of the total debt of Rs 5,000 only Rs 2,500, will be recovered from him. No adjustment has so far been made.

You are required to pass necessary adjusting entries and show how the items will appear in the Final Accounts of the business.

Solution:

JOURNAL

Date	Particulars		Dr. Amount Rs	Cr. Amount Rs
	Bad Debts A/c	Dr.	2,500	
	To Mahesh			2,500
	(Being Rs 2,500 became irrecoverable)			

PROFIT AND LOSS ACCOUNT
for the year ending 31st December, 1990

Particulars	Amount Rs	Particulars	Amount Rs
To Bad Debts	5,000		
(as give in the Trial Balance)			
Add: Additional bad debts	2,500 7,500		

BALANCE SHEET
as on 31st December, 1990

Liabilities	Amount Rs	Assets		Amount Rs
		Sundry Debtors	50,000	
		Less: Bad Debts	2,500	47,500

Provision for Bad Debts

In an earlier chapter, we have already explained that in accounting we observe the "convention of conservatism" while recording business transactions. This means that we make provision for expected losses but we do not take credit for expected profits. A firm, therefore, makes provision at the end of the accounting year for likely bad debts which may happen during the course of the next year. This is for the simple reason that if out of credit sales made during a particular year some sales are likely to become bad in the course of the next year, the proper course would be to charge the same accounting year with such likely bad debts in which the sales have been made, since, the profit on such sales has been considered in the year in which the sales have been made.

The following journal entry is passed for creating a provision for bad debts.

    Profit & Loss A/c   Dr.
        To Provision for Bad Debts

The provision for bad debts is charged to the Profit & Loss Account and is deducted from debtors in the Balance Sheet.

Illustration 10.18. Following are the extracts from the Trial Balance of a firm.

TRIAL BALANCE
as on 31st December, 1990

Particulars	Rs	Rs
Sundry Debtors	30,000	
Bad Debts	5,000	

Additional Information:

(*i*) After preparing the Trial Balance, it is learnt that a debtor Ramesh has become insolvent and therefore, the entire amount of Rs 3,000 due from him was irrecoverable.

(*ii*) Create 10% provision for bad and doubtful debts.

You are required to pass necessary adjusting entries and show how the items will appear in the firm's Balance Sheet.

Solution:

ADJUSTING JOURNAL ENTRIES

Date	Particulars		Dr. Amount Rs	Cr. Amount Rs
	Bad Debts A/c	Dr.	3,000	
	To Ramesh			3,000
	(Being amount due from Ramesh proved to be bad)			
	Profit & Loss A/c	Dr.	2,700	
	To Provision for Bad and Doubtful Debts			2,700
	(Being bad debts provision created)			

PROFIT AND LOSS ACCOUNT
for the year ending 31st December, 1990

Particulars		Amount Rs	Particulars	Amount Rs
To Bad Debts (as given in the Trial Balance)	5,000			
Add: Additional bad debts	3,000			
Add: Provision for bad debts	2,700	10,700		

BALANCE SHEET
as on 31st December, 1990

Liabilities	Amount Rs	Particulars		Amount Rs
		Sundry Debtors	30,000	
		Less: Additional bad debts	3,000	
			27,000	
		Less: Provision for bad debts	2,700	24,300

The provision for bad debts created at the end of the accounting year is carried forward to the next year and the bad debts occuring during the course of the next year are met out of this provision. At the end of the next year, suitable adjusting entry is passed for keeping the provision for doubtful debts at an appropriate amount to be carried forward.

Illustration 10.19. Following are the extracts from the Trial Balance of a firm:

TRIAL BALANCE
as on 31st December, 1990

Particulars	Dr. Amount Rs	Cr. Amount Rs
Sundry Debtors	50,000	
Provision for Doubtful Debts		5,000
Bad Debts	3,000	

Additional Information:

(*i*) Additional bad debts Rs 3,000.

(*ii*) Keep the provision for bad debts @ 10% on debtors.

You are required to pass the necessary journal entries and prepare Provision for Doubtful Debts Account and show how the different items will appear in the firm's Final Accounts.

JOURNAL ENTRIES

Date	Particulars		Dr. Amount Rs	Cr. Amount Rs
	Bad Debts A/c	Dr.	3,000	
	To Sundry Debtors			3,000
	(Being additional bad debts of Rs 3,000)			

Contd....

Date	Particulars		Dr. Amount Rs	Cr. Amount Rs
	Provision for Bad Debts A/c	Dr.	6,000	
	To Bad Debts A/c			6,000
	(Being bad debts, Rs 3,000 appearing in the Trial Balance + Rs 3,000 additional bad debts, transferred to Provision for Bad Debts A/c)			
	Profit and Loss A/c	Dr.	5,700	
	To Provision for Bad Debts A/c			5,700
	(Being amount charged from P. & L. A/c to keep provision for bad debts @ 10% on debtors)			

PROVISION FOR BAD DEBTS ACCOUNT

Particulars	Amount Rs	Particulars	Amount Rs
To Bad Debts A/c	6,000	By Balance b/d	5,000
To Balance c/d	4,700	By Profit & Loss A/c	5,700
	10,700		10,700

PROFIT AND LOSS ACCOUNT
as on 31st December, 1990

Particulars		Amount Rs	Particulars	Amount Rs
To Bad Debts	3,000			
(as given in the Trial Balance)				
Add: Additional bad debts	3,000			
	6,000			
Add: New provision for bad debts	4,700			
	10,700			
Less: Old provision for bad debts	5,000	5,700		

BALANCE SHEET
as on 31st December, 1990

Particulars	Amount Rs	Particulars		Amount Rs
		Sundry Debtors	50,000	
		Less: Additional bad debts	3,000	
			47,000	
		Less: New provision for bad debts	4,700	42,300

Provision for Discount on Debtors

Discount may have to be allowed to the debtors on account of their making prompt payments. When discount is allowed, following journal entry is passed:

Discount A/c   Dr.
    To Debtor's Personal A/c

At the end of the accounting year, the firm also estimates the amount of discount which it may have to give to the debtors outstanding at the end of the accounting year in the course of the next year. This is done by creating a provision for discount on debtors. The following journal entry is passed:

Profit and Loss A/c   Dr.
    To Provision for Discount A/c

It shoule be noted that 'provision for discount' will be created only on good debtors. In other words, provision for discount should be made after deducting bad debts and provision for bad debts from the debtors' balances.

Illustration 10.20. Following are the extracts from the Trial Balance of a firm:

TRIAL BALANCE
as on 31st December, 1990

Particulars	Amount Rs	Amount Rs
Sundry Debtors	50,000	
Bad Debts	3,000	
Discount	2,000	

Additional Information:

(*i*) Create a provision for doubtful debts @ 10% on debtors.

(*ii*) Create a provision for discount on debtors @ 5% on debtors.

(*iii*) Additional discount given to the debtors Rs 1,000.

You are required to pass the necessary journal entries and show how the different items will appear in the Final Accounts.

Solution:

JOURNAL ENTRIES

Date	Particulars	Dr. Amount Rs	Cr. Amount Rs
	Discount A/c Dr.	1,000	
	To Sundry Debtors A/c		1,000
	(Being discount allowed to debtors)		
	Profit & Loss A/c Dr.	4,900	
	To Provision for Bad Debts A/c		4,900
	(Being provision for bad debts created at the rate of 10% on debtors of Rs 49,000)		
	Profit & Loss A/c Dr.	2,205	
	To Provision for Discount		2,205
	(Being provision for discount created @ 5% on debtors of Rs 44,100 (*i.e.*, Rs 49,000–Rs 4,900)		

PROFIT AND LOSS ACCOUNT
for the year ending 31st December, 1990

Particulars	Amount Rs	Particulars	Amount Rs
To Bad Debts	3,000		

Contd....

Particulars	Amount Rs		Particulars	Amount Rs
(as given in the Trial Balance) Add: Provision for bad debts	4,900	7,900		
To Discount (as given in the Trial Balance) Add: Additional discount Add: Provision for discount	2,000 1,000 2,205	5,205		

BALANCE SHEET
as on 31st December, 1990

Liabilities	Amount Rs	Assets		Amount Rs
		Debtors	50,000	
		Less: Additional discount	1,000	
			49,000	
		Less: Provision for bad debts	4,900	
			44,100	
		Less: Provision for discount	2,205	41,895

Illustration 10.21. Following are the extracts from the Trial Balance of a firm:

TRIAL BALANCE
as on 31st December, 1990

Particulars	Dr. Amount Rs	Cr. Amount Rs
Sundry Debtors	50,000	
Provision for Bad Debts		5,000
Provision for Discount		2,000
Bad Debts	3,000	
Discount	1,000	

Additional Information:

(i) Additional Bad Debts Rs 1,000.

(ii) Additional Discount Rs 500.

(iii) Create a provision for bad debts @ 10% on debtors.

(iv) Create a provision for discount @ 5% on debtors.

Pass the necessary journal entries, prepare Provision for Bad Debts Account and Provision for Discount on Debtors Account and show how the different items will appear in the Firm's Final Accounts.

Solution:

JOURNAL ENTRIES

Date	Particulars		Dr. Amount Rs	Cr. Amount Rs
	Bad Debts A/c	Dr.	1,000	
	Discount A/c	Dr.	500	
	To Sundry Debtors			1,500
	(Being additional bad debts and additional discount on debtors)			
	Provision for Bad Debts A/c	Dr.	4,000	
	To Bad Debts A/c			4,000
	(Being bad debts written off from Provison for Bad Debts A/c)			
	Provision for Discount on Debtors A/c	Dr.	1,500	
	To Discount A/c			1,500
	(Being discount allowed written off from Provision for Discount on Debtors A/c)			
	Profit and Loss A/c	Dr.	3,850	
	To Provision for Bad Debts A/c			3,850
	(Being amount charged from P & L A/c to maintain a provision of 10% for bad debts on debtors amounting to Rs 48,500)			
	Profit and Loss A/c	Dr.	1,682.50	
	To Provision for Discount A/c			1,682.50
	(Being amount charged from P & L A/c for keeping the provision for discount @ 5% on good debtors amounting to Rs 43,650)			

PROVISION FOR BAD DEBTS ACCOUNT

Particulars	Amount Rs	Particulars	Amount Rs
To Bad Debts A/c	4,000	By Balance b/d	5,000
To Balance c/d	4,850	By Profit & Loss A/c	3,850
	8,850		8,850

PROVISION FOR DISCOUNT ACCOUNT

Particulars	Amount Rs	Particulars	Amount Rs
To Discount A/c	1,500.00	By Balance b/d	2,000.00
To Balance c/d	2,182.50	By P. & L. A/c	1,682.50
	3,682.50		3,682.50

PROFIT AND LOSS ACCOUNT
for the year ending 31st December, 1990

Particulars		Amount Rs	Particulars	Amount Rs
To Bad Debts (as given in the Trial Balance)	3,000			
Add: Additional bad debts	1,000			
Add: New provision for bad debts	4,850			
	8,850			
Less: Old provision for bad debts	5,000	3,850		
To Discount (as given in the Trial Balance)	1,000			
Add: Additional discount	500			
Add: New provision for discount.	2,182.50			
	3,682.50			
Less: Old provision	2,000.00	1,682.50		

BALANCE SHEET
as on 31st December, 1990

Liabilities	Amount Rs	Assets		Amount Rs
		Sundry Debtors	50,000	
		Less: Additional bad debts and additional discount	1,500	
			48,500	
		Less: New provision for bad debts	4,850	
			43,650	
		Less: New provision for discount	2,182.50	41,467.50

Reserve for Discount on Creditors

A firm may like to create a reserve for discount on its creditors on a similar pattern on which a provision for discount on debtors is made. However, creating of such a reserve is against the fundamental convention of conservatism. Such a reserve, therefore, is usually not created. However, if this is done the accounting entries are passed on the same pattern on which the accounting entries are passed for provision for discount on debtors.

On receipt of additional discount from creditors:

      Sundry Creditors A/c   Dr.
          To Discount A/c

For creating a reserve for discount on creditors:

      Reserve for Discount on Creditors   Dr.
          To Profit and Loss A/c

Illustration 10.22. Following are the extracts from the Trial Balance of a firm.

TRIAL BALANCE
as on 31st December, 1990

Particulars	Amount Rs	Amount Rs
Sundry Creditors		30,000
Discount		1,000
Reserve for Discount on Creditors	2,000	

Additional information:

  (i) Additional discount received from creditors after closing the accounts Rs 1,500.
  (ii) Create a reserve for discount on creditors @ 10%.

You are required to pass the necessary journal entries, prepare Reserve for Discount Account and show how the various items will appear in the Firm's Final Accounts.

Solution:

JOURNAL ENTRIES

Date	Particulars	Dr. Amount Rs	Cr. Amount Rs
	Sundry Creditors A/c Dr.	1,500	
	To Discount A/c		1,500
	(Being additional discount received from Creditors)		
	Discount A/c Dr.	2,500	
	To Reserve for Discount on Creditors		2,500
	(Being discount received transferred to Reserve for Discount A/c)		
	Reserve for Discount A/c Dr.	3,350	
	To Profit and Loss A/c		3,350
	(Being amount credited to Profit and Loss Account for maintaining Reserve for Discount Account at 10% on creditors)		

Dr.	RESERVE FOR DISCOUNT ON CREDITORS ACCOUNT		Cr.
Particulars	Amount Rs	Particulars	Amount Rs
To Balance b/d	2,000	By Discount A/c	2,500
To Profit and Loss Account	3,350	By Balance c/d	2,850
	5,350		5,350

PROFIT AND LOSS ACCOUNT
for the year ending 31st December, 1990

Particulars	Amount Rs	Particulars	Amount Rs
		By Discount 1,000 (as given in the Trial Balance *Add:* Additional discount received 1,500 *Add:* New Reserve	

Contd....

Particulars	Amount Rs	Particulars		Amount Rs
		for discount	2,850	
			5,350	
		Less: Old Reserve for discount	2,000	3,350

Interest on Capital

Funds provided by the proprietor to run the business is termed as Capital. In order to determine the real profit made by the business, it is necessary that the profit should be determined after deducting interest on such funds, which the proprietor could have earned otherwise. The entry for interest on proprietor's funds (or capital) is passed as follows:

Interest on Capital A/c   Dr.
    To Capital A/c

In case of a partnership firm, interest will be allowed on the capital of each partner. The following journal entry will be passed:

Interest on Capital A/c   Dr.
    To Partner's Capital Account

Interest on capital is allowed on the balance in the Capital Account in the beginning of the accounting year. However, in case the proprietor has introduced further capital duing the course of the accounting year, interest on such capital will also be allowed from the date on which such further capital was introduced till the end of the accounting period.

Illustration 10.23. Following are the extracts from the Trial Balance of a firm:

TRIAL BALANCE
as on 31st December, 1990

Particulars	Dr. Amount Rs	Cr. Amount Rs
Capital Accounts:		
Ramesh		30,000
Suresh		20,000

Additional information:

(*i*) Interest on capital is to be allowed @ 10% p.a.

(*ii*) Suresh introduced additional capital amounting to Rs 5,000 on 1st July, 1990.

You are required to pass the necessary journal entries and show how the different items will appear in the Firm's Final Accounts.

Solution:

JOURNAL ENTRIES

Date	Particulars		Dr. Amount Rs	Cr. Amount Rs
	Interest on Capital A/c	Dr.	4,750	
	To Ramesh's Capital A/c			3,000
	To Suresh's Capital A/c			1,750
	(Being interest on capital allowed to Ramesh on Rs 30,000 for full year and to Suresh on Rs 15,000 for full year and on Rs 5,000 for 6 months)			

BALANCE SHEET
as on 31st December, 1990

Liabilities		Amount Rs	Assets	Amount Rs
Capital Accounts:				
Ramesh	30,000			
Add: Interest on capital	3,000	33,000		
Suresh	20,000			
Add: Interest on capital	1,750	21,750		

PROFIT AND LOSS ACCOUNT
for the year ending 31st December, 1990

Particulars		Amount Rs	Particulars	Amount Rs
To Interest on Capital:				
Ramesh	3,000			
Suresh	1,750	4,750		

Interest on Drawings

Drawings denote the money withdrawn by the proprietor from the business for his personal use. It is usual practice to charge interest on drawings in case interest is allowed to the proprietor on his capital. The following journal entry is passed for interest on drawings.

Capital A/c   Dr.
    To Interest on Drawings A/c

In case of a partnership firm, interest on drawings will be charged on the drawings made by each partner. The journal entry will be as follows:

Partners Capital/Current Accounts*   Dr.
    To Interest on Drawings A/c

Computation of Interest on Drawings

There is a difference between the method of computation of interest on capital and computation of interest on drawings. In most cases, interest on capital is charged on the opening balance in the Capital Account. However, in case of additional capital introduced during the year by the proprietor, interest may be charged from the date of introducing additional capital till the end of the accounting period. This does not create much problem. However, in case of drawings, the things are different. The proprietor does not usually make the entire amount of drawings on a particular date for the whole accounting year.

---

* Partners Capital Accounts can be maintained either on a Fixed or a Fluctuating Capital System. In case of a Fixed Capital System, two accounts are maintained for each partner: (i) Capital Account, and (ii) Current Account. Capital Account is credited with the amount of capital introduced by the partner or debited with the amount of capital withdrawn by the partner. While all adjustments regarding interest on capital, share of profit, drawings, etc., are made in the Current Accounts. Thus, balance in the Capital Account remains more or less fixed. This is the reason for calling it as a Fixed Capital System. In case of Fluctuating Capital System all adjustments regarding capital, drawings, interest, share or profit etc. are made only in the Capital Account. Thus, the balance of the Capital Account goes on fluctuating. This is the reason for calling this system as Fluctuating Capital System. This has been discussed in detail in Partnership Accounts explained in Section III of the book.

For example, if the proprietor has withdrawn Rs 12,000 from the business, it cannot reasonably be pressured that he must have withdrawn the entire amount in the beginning of the accounting year.

Since, the interest is to be charged on the amount withdrawn by the proprietor from the date on which he withdrew the amount from the business till the end of the accounting period, it requires computation of interest on each withdrawal made by the proprietor separately. In the absence of any specific information, it can reasonably be presumed that the drawing were made evenly throughout the year. Moreover, for computation of interest, any of the following three presumptions can reasonably be made;

(i) The proprietor withdrew the money on the 1st of each month. In such a case, interest should be charged for 6½ months on the total amount at the given rate of interest.

(ii) The proprietor withdrew the money on the 15th of each month. In such a case, interest should be charged on the total amount of drawings for six months.

(iii) The proprietor withdrew the money at the end of each month. In such a case, interest should be charged on the total amount for 5 ½ months.

Tutorial Note. The students may adopt the second presumption in the absence of any specific instructions in the question.

Illustration 10.24. Following are the extracts from the Trial Balance of a Firm.

TRIAL BALANCE
as on 31st December, 1990

Particulars	Dr. Amount Rs	Cr. Amount Rs
Capital Accounts:		
A's Capital		30,000
B's Capital		20,000
Drawings:		
A	6,000	
B	3,000	

Additional information:

(i) Interest on capital is to be allowed to the partners @ 10% p.a. on the opening balances standing to the credit of their Capital Accounts.

(ii) Interest on drawings is to be charged @ 12% p.a.

You are required to pass the necessary journal entries and show how the different items will appear in the Firm's Final Accounts. You may presume that the drawings were made evenly throughout the year on 15th of each month.

Solution:

JOURNAL ENTRIES

Date	Particulars		Dr. Amount Rs	Cr. Amount Rs
	Interest on Capital A/c	Dr.	5,000	
	To A's Capital A/c			3,000
	To B's Capital A/c			2,000
	(Being interest on capital @ 10% p.a.)			

Contd....

Date	Particulars		Dr. Amount Rs	Cr. Amount Rs
	A's Capital A/c	Dr.	360	
	B's Capital A/c	Dr.	180	
	To Interest on Drawings A/c			540
	(Being interest on drawings charged for 6 months @ 12% p.a. on the total amount)			

PROFIT AND LOSS ACCOUNT
for the year ending 31st December, 1990

Particulars	Amount Rs		Particulars	Amount Rs	
To Interest on Capital:			By Interest on Drawings:		
A	3,000		A	360	
B	2,000	5,000	B	180	540

BALANCE SHEET
as on 31st December, 1990

Liabilities		Amount Rs	Assets	Amount Rs
Capital Accounts:				
A's Capital	30,000			
Add: Interest on Capital	3,000			
	33,000			
Less: Drawings	6,000			
	27,000			
Less: Interest on Drawings	360	26,640		
B's Capital	20,000			
Add: Interest on Capital	2,000			
	22,000			
Less: Drawings	3,000			
	19,000			
Less: Interest on Drawings	180	18,820		

WORK SHEET

In the preceding pages, we have explained about the passing of the necessary adjusting entries in the books of accounts so that final accounts represent the true position of the business. As a result of these adjusting entries and their posting into the ledger, some new accounts are opened in the books while the balances of some of the existing accounts appearing in the Trial Balance also get changed. In order to prevent errors and facilitate the preparation of the final accounts, it is sometimes considered necessary to prepare a preliminary draft incorporating all balances of the Trial Balance, the necessary adjustments to be made therein and showing separately the items relating to Income Statement and the Balance Sheet. Such a preliminary draft is termed as a Work Sheet.

The Work Sheet contains the following information:

(i) The Trial Balance as originally prepared.

(ii) The necessary adjustments to be carried out on account of adjustment entries.

(iii) The new Trial Balance after making the necessary adjustments as required under point *(ii)* above. The new Trial Balance is termed as the 'Adjusted Trial Balance'.

(iv) Classification of the items appearing in the Trial Balance between those relating to Income Statement and those relating to Balance Sheet.

A Work Sheet may therefore be defined as a large columar statement specially designed to organise and arrange all accounting data required at the end of the accounting period.

The necessary closing entries are passed on the basis of Adjusted Trial Balance. The Final Accounts are then prepared on the basis of the classification of the items made in the Work Sheet as explained under point *(iv)* above.

It should be noted that Work Sheet is not a part of the accounting records. It is, therefore, not supplied to the bankers, creditors and share holders. It is, simply a working tool of the accountant prepared by him for his own convenience as an aid to preparing the financial statements at the end of the year. A Proforma of Work Sheet is given below:

PROFORMA OF WORK SHEET

Sl. No.	Name of Account	L.F.	Trial Balance		Adjustments		Adjusted Trial Balance		Income Statement		Balance Sheet	
			Dr.	Cr.	Dr.	Cr.	Dr.	Cr.	Dr.	Cr.	Dr.	Cr.

Advantages of Work Sheet

The Works Sheet offers following advantages:

(i) It brings together the Trial Balance and the adjusting data. Thus, it reduces the chances of errors and at the same time assists the location of errors which may be made in adjusting, closing and balancing accounts.

(ii) It classifies and summarises the information shown by the Trial Balance and the adjusting data. It thus, facilitates preparation of Final Accounts and passing of closing entries.

(iii) The net results of the business operations are known even before preparing formal Final Financial Statements. It makes possible the preparation of the statements during the financial period without the necessity of formal adjusting and closing entries.

Thus, Work Sheet is extremely useful for the management since it furnished a quick means of determining the business results.

Illustration 10.25. From the following Trial Balance and additional information, you are required to prepare a Work Sheet and Final Accounts.

TRIAL BALANCE
as on 31st December, 1990

Particulars	Dr. Amount Rs	Cr. Amount Rs
Capital		20,000
Sundry Debtors	5,400	
Drawings	1,800	
Machinery	7,000	
Sundry Creditors		2,800
Wages	10,000	

Contd....

Particulars	Dr. Amount Rs	Cr. Amount Rs
Purchases	19,000	
Opening Stock	4,000	
Bank Balance	3,000	
Carriage Charges	300	
Salaries	400	
Rent and Taxes	900	
Sales		29,000
	51,800	51,800

Additional Information:

(i) Closing Stock Rs 1,200.

(ii) Outstanding Rent and Taxes Rs 100.

(iii) Charge depreciation on machinery at 10%.

(iv) Wages prepaid Rs 400.

(For Solution please see page 1.222 and below).

TRADING AND PROFIT AND LOSS ACCOUNT
for the year ending 31st December, 1990

Particulars	Amount Rs	Particulars	Amount Rs
To Opening Stock	4,000	By Sales	29,000
To Adjusted Purchases	17,800	By Gross Loss c/d	2,700
To Wages	9,600		
To Carriage	300		
	31,700		31,700
To Gross Loss b/d	2,700	By Net Loss taken to Capital A/c	4,800
To Salaries	400		
To Rent and Taxes	1,000		
To Depreciation on Machinery	700		
	4,800		4,800

BALANCE SHEET
as on 31st December, 1990

Liabilities		Amount Rs	Assets	Amount Rs
Outstanding Rent		100	Cash at Bank	3,000
Creditors		2,800	Debtors	5,400
Capital	20,000		Closing Stock	1,200
Less: Net Loss	4,800		Prepaid Wages	400
	15,200		Machinery	6,300
Less: Drawings	1,800	13,400		
		16,300		16,300

Illustration 10.26. From the following figures extracted from the books of Shri Govind, you are required to prepare a Trading and Profit & Loss Account for the year ended 31st March, 1990 and a Balance Sheet as on that date after making the necessary adjustments:

Contd. on page 1.223

Solution (Illustration 10.25):

WORK SHEET

Sl No.	Name of the Account	L.F.	Trial Balance Dr.	Trial Balance Cr.	Adjustments Dr.	Adjustments Cr.	Adjusted Trial Balance Dr.	Adjusted Trial Balance Cr.	Income Statement Dr.	Income Statement Cr.	Balance Sheet Dr.	Balance Sheet Cr.
1.	Capital			20,000				20,000				20,000
2.	Sundry Debtors		5,400				5,400				5,400	
3.	Drawings		1,800				1,800				1,800	
4.	Machinery		7,000			700	6,300				6,300	
5.	Sundry Creditors			2,800				2,800				2,800
6.	Wages		10,000			400	9,600		9,600			
7.	Purchases/Adjusted Purchases		19,000			1,200	17,800		17,800			
8.	Opening Stock		4,000				4,000		4,000			
9.	Cash at Bank		3,000				3,000				3,000	
10.	Carriage		300				300		300			
11.	Salaries		400				400		400			
12.	Rent and Taxes		900		100		1,000		1,000			
13.	Sales			29,000				29,000		29,000		
14.	Closing Stock				1,200		1,200				1,200	
15.	Outstanding Rent					100		100				100
16.	Prepaid Wages				400		400				400	
17.	Depreciation on Machinery				700		700		700			
18.	Net Loss									4,800	4,800	
			51,800	51,800	2,400	2,400	51,900	51,900	33,800	33,800	22,900	22,900

Particulars	Amount Rs	Particulars	Amount Rs
Shri Govind's Capital	2,28,800	Stock 1.4.1989	38,500
Shri Govind's Drawings	13,200	Wages	35,200
Plant and Machinery	99,000	Sundry Creditors	44,000
Freehold Property	66,000	Postage and Telegrams	1,540
Purchases	1,10,000	Insurance	1,760
Returns Outwards	1,100	Gas and Fuel	2,970
Salaries	13,200	Bad Debts	660
Office Expenses	2,750	Office Rent	2,360
Office Furniture	5,500	Freight	9,900
Discounts A/c (Dr.)	1,320	Loose Tools	2,200
Sundry Debtors	29,260	Factory Lighting	1,100
Loan to Shri Krishna @		Provision for D/D	880
10% p.a.-balance on 1.4.89	44,000	Interest on loan to Shri Krishna	1,100
Cash at Bank	29,260	Cash on hand	2,640
Bills Payable	5,500	Sales	2,31,440

Adjustments:

1. Stock on 31st March 1990 was valued at Rs 72,600.
2. A new machine was installed during the year costing Rs 15,400, but it was not recorded in the books as no payment was made for it. Wages Rs 1,100 paid for its erection have been debited to wages account.
3. Depreciate:
   Plant and Machinery by 33 ⅓ %.
   Furniture by 10%
   Freehold Property by 5%
4. Loose tools were valued at Rs 1,760 on 31.3.1990.
5. Of the Sundry Debtors Rs 600 are bad and should be written off.
6. Maintain a provision of 5% on Sundry Debtors for doubtful debts.
7. The manager is entitled to a commission of 10% of the net profits after charging such commission. *(C.A. Entrance Nov., 1990)*

Solution:

Shri Govind

TRADING AND PROFIT & LOSS ACCOUNT
for the year ended 31.3.1990

Particulars		Amount	Particulars	Amount
To Stock (1.4.89)		38,500	By Sales	2,31,440
To Purchases	1,10,000		By Closing Stock	72,600
Less: Returns	1,100	1,08,900		
To Wages	35,200			
Less: Erection of machinery	1,100	34,100		
To Gas and Fuel		2,970		
To Freight		9,900		
To Factory Lighting		1,100		
To Gross Profit c/d		1,08,570		
		3,04,040		3,04,040

Contd....

1.224

Particulars		Amount	Particulars		Amount
To Salaries		13,200	By Gross Profit b/d		1,08,570
To Office Expenses		2,750	By Interest	1,100	
To Postage & Telegram		1,540	Add: Outstanding	3,300	4,400
To Insurance		1,760			
To Office Rent		2,860			
To Discounts		1,320			
To Bad Debts	660				
Add: Addl. Bad Debts	600				
Add: New Provision	1,430				
	2,690				
Less: Old Provision	880	1,870			
To Depreciation:					
Machinery	38,500				
Furniture	550				
Freehold Property	3,300				
Losse Tools	440	42,790			
To Commission to Manager		4,080			
To Net Profit taken to					
Balance Sheet		40,800			
		1,12,970			1,12,970

Shri Govind

BALANCE SHEET

as at 31.3.1990

Liabilities		Amount Rs	Assests		Amount Rs
Capital	2,28,800		Plant & Machinery	99,000	
Add: Net Profit	40,800		Add: New Machinery		
	2,69,600		(15,400 + 1,100)	16,500	
Less: Drawings	13,200	2,56,400		1,15,500	
Bills Payable		5,500	Less: Depreciation	38,500	77,000
Sundry Creditors		59,400	Freehold Property	66,000	
Manager's Commission			Less: Depreciation	3,300	62,700
Outstanding		4,080	Office Furniture	5,500	
			Less: Depreciation	550	4,950
			Loose Tools	2,200	
			Less: Depreciation	440	1,760
			Closing Stock		72,600
			Sundry Debtors	29,260	
			Less: Addl. bad debts	660	
				28,600	
			Less: Provision for		
			doubtful debts	1,430	27,170
			Loan to Sh. Krishna	44,000	
			Add: Interest accured		
			and oustanding	3,300	47,300
			Cash at Bank		29,260
			Cash in Hand		2,640
		3,25,380			3,25,380

Illustration 10.27. The following is the Trial Balance of Shri Om, as on 31st March, 1991. You are requested to prepare the Trading and Profit and Loss Account for the year ended 31st March, 1991 and Balance Sheet as on that date after making the necessary adjustments:

Particulars	Debit Rs	Credit Rs
Sundry Debtors	5,00,000	......
Sundry Creditors	......	2,00,000
Outstanding Liability for Expenses	55,000	......
Wages	1,00,000	......
Carriage Outwards	1,10,000	......
Carriage Inwards	50,000	......
General Expenses	70,000	......
Cash Discounts	20,000	......
Bad Debts	10,000	......
Motor Car	2,40,000	......
Printing and Stationery	15,000	......
Furniture and Fittings	1,10,000	......
Advertisement	85,000	......
Insurance	45,000	......
Salesmen's Commission	87,500	......
Postage and Telephone	57,500	......
Salaries	1,60,000	......
Rates and Taxes	25,000	......
Drawings	20,000	......
Capital Account	......	14,43,000
Purchases	15,50,000	......
Sales	......	19,87,500
Stock on 1.4.90	2,50,000	......
Cash at Bank	60,000	......
Cash in Bank	10,500	......
	36,30,500	36,30,500

The following adjustments are to be made:
(1) Stock on 31st March, 1991 was valued at Rs 7,25,000.
(2) A Provision for Bad and Doubtful Debts is to be created to the extent of 5 per cent on Sundry Debtors.
(3) Depreciate:
Furniture and Fittings by 10%
Motor Car by 20%
(4) Shri Om had withdrawn goods worth Rs 25,000 during the year.
(5) Sales include goods worth Rs 75,000 sent out to Shanti & Company on approval and remaining unsold on 31st March, 1991. The cost of the goods was Rs 50,000.
(6) The Salesmen are entitled to a Commission of 5% on total sales.
(7) Debtors include Rs 25,000 bad debts.
(8) Printing and Stationery expenses of Rs 55,000 relating to 1989–90 had not been provided in that year but was paid in this year by debiting outstanding liabilities.
(9) Purchases include purchase of Furniture worth Rs 50,000.

(C.A. Entrance Nov., 1991)

Solution:

Shri Om

TRADING AND PROFIT AND LOSS ACCOUNT

for the year ended 31st March, 1991

Particulars	Amount Rs		Particulars	Amount Rs	
To Opening Stock		2,50,000	By Sales	19,87,500	
To Purchases	15,50,000		Less: Goods sent on		
Less: Drawings	25,000		Approval	75,000	19,12,500
	15,25,000		By Closing stock	7,25,000	
Less: Furniture	50,000	14,75,000	Add: Stock on		
To Wages		1,00,000	approval (at cost)	50,000	7,75,000
To Carriage Inwards		50,000			
To Gross Profit c/d		8,12,500			
		26,87,500			26,87,500
To Salaries		1,60,000	By Gross Profit b/d		8,12,500
To Rates and Taxes		25,000			
To Postage and Telephone		57,500			
To Insurance		45,000			
To Printing and Stationery		15,000			
To General Expenses		70,000			
To Depreciation:					
Furniture (11,000 + 5,000)		16,000			
Motor Car		48,000			
To Salesmen's Commission		95,625			
(5% on Rs 19,12,500)					
To Advertisement		85,000			
To Carriage Outwards		1,10,000			
To Bad Debts	10,000				
Add: Addl. Bad Debts	25,000				
Add: Prov. for Bad Debts					
(5% on Rs 4,00,000:	20,000	55,000			
See WN 3)					
To Cash Discount		20,000			
To Net Profit		10,375			
		8,12,500			8,12,500

Shri Om

BALANCE SHEET

as on 31.3.1991

Liabilities	Amount Rs		Assets	Amount Rs	
Capital as on	Rs		Furniture &	Rs	
31.3.91	14,43,000		Fittings	1,10,000	
Add: Net Profit	10,375		Additions during the yr.	50,000	
	14,53,375			1,60,000	
Less: Drawings			Less: Depn.	16,000	1,44,000
(20,000 + 25,000)	45,000		Motor car	2,40,000	
	14,08,375		Less: Depn.	48,000	1,92,000

Contd....

Liabilities		Amount Rs	Assets		Amount Rs
Less: Printing & Stationery of last year	55,000	13,53,375	Closing Stock (7,25,000 + 50,000)		7,75,000
Sundry Creditors		2,00,000	Sundry Debtors	5,00,000	
Salesmen's Commission Outstanding (Rs 95,625 – Rs 87,530)		8,125	Less: Goods sent on approval	75,000	
				4,25,000	
			Less: Addl. Bad debts	25,000	
				4,00,000	
			Less: Provision for doubtful debts 5% on 4,00,000	20,000	3,80,000
			Cash at Bank		60,000
			Cash in Hand		10,500
		15,61,500			15,61,500

Working Notes:

1. Both Sales and Sundry Debtors have been reduced by Rs 75,000 representing invoice value of goods sent on approval. Rs 50,000 have been added to the closing stock being the cost of goods sent on approval.
2. Last year's short provision for Printing and Stationery has not been charged to the current year's Profit & Loss Accounts. It is preferable to charge it directly to in the Capital Account.
3. Sundry Debtors = Rs 5,00,000 – (Rs 75,000 Goods on Approval + Rs 25,000 Bad Debt) = Rs 4,00,000.

Illustration 10.28. From the undermentioned particulars of Mr. Philip, prepare the Manufacturing, Trading and Profit and Loss Account for the year ended 31.3.1990 and Balance Sheet as at that date after making the necessary adjustments:

	Rs
Capital as at 1.4.1989	25,000
Drawings Account	7,000
Sundry Creditors	8,000
Discount Received	702
Allahabad Bank (Cr.)	4,000
Reserve for Bad and Doubtful Debts	600
Purchase Returns	530
Sales	67,500
Sales Returns	86
Stock as at 1.4.1989	9,000
Plant and Machinery (including Machinery for Rs 5,000 purchased on 1.1.1990)	17,000
Furniture	1,500
Buildings	15,000
Purchases	30,230
Sundry Debtors	11,000
Manufacturing Wages	6,000
Manufacturing Expenses	5,000
Carriage Inwards	400
Carriage Outwards	420

Contd....

	Rs
Bad Debts	150
Salaries	2,800
Interest and Bank Charges (Dr.)	126
Discount allowed	150
Insurance (Dr.)	300
Bank of Bikaner (Dr.)	140
Cash on hand	30
Stock as at 31.3.1990	7,550

Adjustments

1. Provide for:

(a) Interest on capital at 10% p.a. (no interest is to be provided on drawings).

(b) Outstanding Expenses:

		Rs
(i)	Salaries	100
(ii)	Manufacturing Wages	50
(iii)	Interest on Bank Loan	100

(c) Depreciation on:

(i) Machinery at 10% p.a.

(ii) Furniture at 10% p.a.

(iii) Buildings at 2 ½% p.a.

(d) Pre-paid expenses:

		Rs
(i)	Insurance	100
(ii)	Salary	50

(e) Provision for Bad and Doubtful Debts at 10% of Debtors.

Furniture costing Rs 500 was sold for Rs 350 on 1.4.1989 and this amount was later credited to Furniture Account.

Solution:

Mr. Philip

MANUFACTURING TRADING AND PROFIT AND LOSS ACCOUNT

for the year ended 31st March, 1990

Particulars	Amount Rs	Particulars	Amount Rs
To Pruchase less Returns	29,700	By Trading A/c (transfer of	
To Carriage Inward	400	Cost of Goods produced)	42,475
To Manufacturing Wages	6,050		
To Manufacturing Expenses	5,000		
To Depreciation on			
Machinery	1,325		
	42,475		42,475
To Opening Stock	9,000	By Sales less Returns	67,414
To Manufacturing A/c	42,475	By Closing Stock	7,550
(Cost of goods produced)			
To Gross Profit c/d	23,489		
	74,964		74,964

Contd....

Particulars	Amount Rs		Particulars	Amount Rs
To Salaries	2,850		By Gross Profit b/d	23,489
To Interest and Bank Charges	226		By Discount	702
To Discount	150			
To Insurance	200			
To Carriage Outward	420			
To Provision for bad and doubtful debts *(See Note 1)*	650			
To Loss on Sale of Furniture	150			
To Depreciation:				
Building	375			
Furniture	135	510		
To Interest on Capital		2,500		
To Net Profit to Capital A/c		16,535		
		24,191		24,191

Mr. Philip
BALANCE SHEET
as on 31st March, 1990

Liabilities	Amount Rs		Assets	Amount Rs	
Capital Account:			Fixed Assets:		
Opening Balance	25,000		Buildings		
Add: Interest	2,500		Balance as on 1.4.89	15,000	
Add: Profit	16,535		*Less*: Depericiation		
	44,035		wiritten off	375	14,625
Less: Drawings	7,000	37,035	Plant & Machinery		
Liabilities:			Balance as on 1.4.89	12,000	
Bank Overdraft		4,000	Additions during the yr.	5,000	
Sundry Creditors		8,000		17,000	
Outstanding Expenses		250	*Less*: Dep. written off	1,325	15,675
			Furniture:		
			Balance as on 1.4.89	1,850	
			Less: Cost of furniture disposed of during the year	500	
				1,350	
			Less Depreciation written off	135	1,215
			Current Assets:		
			Stock-in-trade (assumed at cost)		7,550
			Debtors	11,000	
			Less: Provision for bad and doubtful debts	1,100	9,900
			Cash in Hand		30
			Cash in Bank		140
			Prepaid Expenses		150
		49,285			49,285

Notes:

1. Loss on sale of furniture has been deducted from the book value of furniture before calculating depreciation.

2. Provision of Bad and Doubtful Debts:

	Rs
Provision required	1,100
Add: Bad Debts	150
	1,250
Less: Opening balance	600
	650

Illustration 10.29. The Trial Balance of Jagfay Corporation, New Delhi, as on 30.9.1990 is as below:

Particulars	Amount Rs	Amount Rs
Capital Account (including Rs 5,000 introduced on 1.4.1990)		22,500
Stock as on 1.10.1989:		
Finished Goods	3,500	
Work-in-progress	7,000	
Raw Materials	3,000	13,500
Purchase of Raw Materials		70,500
Machinery		22,500
Sales		1,26,225
Carriage Inwards		750
Carriage Outwards		450
Rent (including Rs 450 for the factory premises)		1,350
Rebates and Discounts allowed		105
Fire Insurance (for machinery)		210
Sundry Debtors		18,900
Sundry Creditors		5,100
Reserve for Bad and Doubtful Debts		60
Printing and Stationery		180
Miscellaneous Expenses		840
Advertisement		4,500
Drawings of Proprietor		1,800
Office Salaries		5,400
Manufacturing Wages		6,000
Furniture and Fixtures		2,250
Factory Power and Fuel		300
Cash on hand		600
Balance with Bank of Bikaner Ltd., Delhi (Dr.)		3,750

Adjustments

(*i*) Provide for interest @ 10% per annum on Capital. (No interest on drawings need be provided).

(*ii*) A motor car purchased on 1.4.1990 for Rs 6,000 has been included in "Purchases"

(*iii*) Provide depreciation:

Machinery @ 10% p.a., Motor Car @ 20% p.a., Furniture and Fixtures @ 10% p.a.

(iv) Provision for unrealised rent is respect of a portion of the office sub-let at Rs 50 per month from 1.4.1990 has to be made.

(v) Sundry Debtors include bad debts of Rs 400 which must be written off.

(vi) Provision for Bad and Doubtful Debts as on 30.9.1990 should be maintained at 10% of the Debtors.

(vii) A sum of Rs 2,000 transferred from the Current Account with Bank of Bikaner Ltd., to Fixed Deposit Account on 1.2.1990 has not been passed through books. Make suitable adjustments and provide for accrued interest @ 6% p.a.

(viii) Stock as on 30.9.1990:

Finished goods Rs 5,000, Raw Materials Rs 1,000, Work-in-progress Rs 5,500.

Prepare the Manufacturing, Trading and Profit and Loss Account for the year ended 30.9.1990 and Balance Sheet as on that date after making the necessary adjustments (Journal entries are not required).

Solution:

Messers Jagfay Corporation, New Delhi

MANUFACTURING ACCOUNT
for the year ended 30.9.1990

Particulars		Amount Rs	Particulars	Amount Rs
To Work-in-progress		7,000	By Cost of Manufactured	
To Materials used:			goods transferred to	
Opening Stock	3,000		Trading Account	75,710
Purchases	64,500		By Work-in-progress at end	5,500
	67,500			
Less: Closing Stock	1,000	66,500		
To Carriage Inwards		750		
To Factory Power and Fuel		300		
To Manufacturing Wages		6,000		
To Factory Rent		450		
To Fire Insurance for Machinery		210		
		81,210		81,210

TRADING AND PROFIT AND LOSS ACCOUNT
for the year ended 30.9.1990

Particulars		Amount Rs	Particulars	Amount Rs
To Opening Stock:			By Sales	1,26,225
Finished Goods		3,500	By Closing Stock:	
To Cost of Goods transferred			Finished Goods	5,000
from Manufacturing A/c		75,710		
To Gross Profit c/d		52,015		
		1,31,225		1,31,225
To Office Salaries		5,400	By Gross Profit b/d	52,015
To Rent		900	By Rent Receivable	300
To Advertisement		4,500	By Interest receivable	
To Carriage Outwards		450	(on fixed deposit for Rs 2,000	
To Rebates and Discounts		105	for 8 months @ 6% p.a.)	80
To Bad Debts writtem off	400			

Contd....

Particulars	Amount Rs		Particulars	Amount Rs
Add: New provision				
for bad debts	1,850			
	2,250			
Less: Old provision				
for bad debts	60	2,190		
To Printing and Stationery		180		
To Miscellaneous Expenses		840		
To Depreciation written off		3,075		
To Interest on Capital		2,000		
To Net Profit transferred to				
Capital A/c		32,755		
		52,395		52,395

BALANCE SHEET
as on 30.9.1990

Liabilities	Amount Rs		Assets	Amount Rs	
Capital			Machinery:		
Account:			As per last		
Balance	22,500		Balance Sheet	22,500	
Add: Profit for the year	32,755		Less: Depreciation	2,250	20,250
Interest	2,000		Motor Car:		
	57,255		Cost	6,000	
Less: Drawings	1,800	55,455	Less: Depreciation	600	5,400
Sundry Creditors		5,100	Furniture & Fixtures:		
			as per last		
			Balance Sheet	2,250	
			Less: Depreciation	225	2,025
			Closing Stock:		
			Finished goods	5,000	
			Work-in-progress	5,500	
			Raw Materials	1,000	11,500
			Sundry Debtors	18,900	
			Less: Bad debts writter off	400	
				18,500	
			Less: Provision for bad		
			and doubtful debts	1,850	16,650
			Interest Accrued		80
			Rent Receivable		300
			Bank Balance:		
			Fixed Deposit with Bank		
			of Bikaner Ltd.		2,000
			Balance with Bank of		
			Bikaner Ltd.		1,750
			Cash in hand		600
		60,555			60,555

KEY TERMS

☐ **Assets:** Tangible objects or intangible rights owned by an enterprise and carrying probable future benefits.

☐ **Adjustment Entry:** A journal entry passed at the end of an accounting period to record the completed portion of an incomplete continuous event.

☐ **Balance Sheet:** A statement of financial position of an enterprise as at a given period.

☐ **Current Assets:** Cash and other assets that are expected to be converted into cash or consumed in the production of goods or rendering of services in the normal course of business.

☐ **Current Liabilities:** Liabilities payable within a year from the date of Balance Sheet either out of existing current assets or by creation of new current liabilities.

☐ **Fixed Assets:** Assets held for the purpose of providing or producing goods and services and not held for resale in the normal course of business.

☐ **Fictitious Assets:** Assets not represented by tangible possession or property.

☐ **Fixed Liabilities:** All liabilities other than current liabilities.

☐ **Liabilities:** The claims of outsiders (other than owners) against the firm's assets.

☐ **Liquid Assets:** Assets which are immediately convertible into cash without much loss.

☐ **Manufacturing Account:** An account giving the cost of goods manufactured by the manufacturer during a particular period.

☐ **Profit & Loss Account:** An account presenting the revenues and expenses of an enterprise for an accounting period and shows the excess of revenues over expenses and *vice-versa*. It is also known as Income Statement.

☐ **Trading Account:** An account giving the overall result of trading *i.e.*, purchasing and selling of goods.

TEST QUESTIONS

Objective type | TEST YOUR UNDERSTANDING |

1. State whether each of the following statements is True or False:
   (a) The 'Current Liabilities' is used to denote those laibilities which are payable after a year.
   (b) The term 'Current Assets' and 'Liquid Assets' have synonymous meanings.
   (c) All Intangible Assets are fictitious assets.
   (d) Creating reserve for discount on creditors is not strictly according to the principle of conservatism.
   (e) Stock at the end, if appears in the Trial Balance, is taken only to the Balance Sheet.

(*f*) Goods taken out by the proprietor from the business for his personal use are credited to Sales Account.

(*g*) 'Salary paid in advance' is not an expense because it neither reduces assets nor increases liabilities.

(*h*) The term "Accrued Income" and "Outstanding Income" have synonymous meanings.

(*i*) Premium paid on the life policy of the proprietor is debited to the Profit and Loss Account.

[**Ans.** (*a*) False, (*b*) False, (*c*) False, (*d*) True, (*e*) True, (*f*) False, (*g*) True, (*h*) False, (*i*) False]

2. Select the most appropriate answer:

(*i*) Sales are equal to
   (*a*) Cost of goods sold + Profit.
   (*b*) Cost of good sold – Gross Profit.
   (*c*) Gross Profit – Cost of goods sold.

(*ii*) Interest on Drawings is
   (*a*) Expenditure for the business.
   (*b*) Expense for the business.
   (*c*) Gain for the business.

(*iii*) Goods given as samples should be credited to
   (*a*) Advertisement Account.
   (*b*) Sales Account.
   (*c*) Purchases Account.

(*iv*) Oustanding Salaries are shown as
   (*a*) an expense.
   (*b*) a liability.
   (*c*) an asset.

(*v*) Income Tax paid by a sole proprietor on his business income should be
   (*a*) Debited to the Trading Account.
   (*b*) Debited to the Profit and Loss Account.
   (*c*) Deducted from the Capital Account in the Balance Sheet.

[**Ans.** (*i*) (*a*), (*ii*) (*c*), (*iii*) (*c*), (*iii*) (*c*), (*iv*) (*b*), (*v*) (*c*)]

Essay type | FOR REVIEW, DISCUSSION AND PRACTICE |

1. What are Final Accounts? What purpose do they serve?
2. What is meant by Marshalling of Assets and Liabilities?
3. Differentiate between:
   (*a*) Outstanding Expense and Prepaid Expense.
   (*b*) Outstanding Income and Accrued Income.
   (*c*) Interest on Capital and Interest on Drawings.
4. Why adjustment entries are required to be made at the time of preparing Final Accounts? Give illustrative examples of any four such adjustment entries.
5. Write short notes on:
   (*a*) Closing entries
   (*b*) Trading account
   (*c*) Work Sheet.
6. What do you understand by the terms 'Grouping' and 'Marshalling', used in connection with the Balance Sheet? Illustrate the different forms of Marshalling.
7. Distinguish between Trial Balance and Balance Sheet.

PRACTICAL PROBLEMS

Final Accounts without Adjustments

1. Prepare Manufacturing, Trading and Profit and Loss Account from the following figures relating for the year 1988:

	1.1.88 Rs	31.12.88 Rs
Stcok:		
Finished Goods	33,000	27,500
Raw Materials	16,000	18,300
Work-in-progress	11,100	9,400
Purchase of Materials		1,50,900
Carriage on Purchases		4,100
Wages		65,000
Factory Salaries		26,000
Office Salaries		18,000
Repair and Maintenance:		
Machinery		8,300
Office Equipment		1,700
Depreciation:		
Machinery		25,000
Office Equipment		8,100
Sundry Expenses:		
Factory		5,300
Office		17,800
Sales		3,60,000

It is the firm's practice to transfer goods from the Factory to Sales godown at cost plus 10%.
[**Ans.** Manufacturing Profit Rs 28,400; Gross Profit Rs 42,100; Net Loss Rs 3,500]

2. From the following particulars, prepare Manufacturing Account, Trading Account, and Profit and Loss Account:

	Rs
Purchases of Raw Materials	13,195
Return Inward	70
Stock on 31.12.1988:	
Raw Materials	1,210
Work-in-progress	1,000
Finished Goods	1,370
Productive Wages	2,000
Factory Expenses	1,840
General Office Expenses	300
Salaries	600
Distributing Expenses	100
Selling Expenses	700
Purchasing Expenses	600
Export Duty	300
Import Duty	200
Interest on Bank Loan	600

Contd....

	Rs
Stock on 1-1-1988:	
Raw Materials	400
Work-in-progress	300
Finished Goods	410
Sales	19,500
Returns Outward	85
Carriage Outward	105
Carriage Inward	100
Cash Discount (allowed)	10
Sale of scrap	20
Depreciation of Machinery	500
Repairs of Machinery	100
Depreciation of Office Furniture	40

[**Ans.** Gross Profit Rs 3,470; Net Profit Rs 7,150]

3. From the following Trial Balance, prepare a Trading, Manufacturing and Profit and Loss Account and Balance Sheet as on 31st December, 1990.

TRIAL BALANCE
as on 31st December, 1990

Particulars	Amount Rs	Amount Rs
Stock on 1.1.1990:		
Raw Materials	2,000	
Work-in-progress	5,000	
Finished Goods	10,000	
Manufacturing Wages	10,000	
Purchases of Raw Materials	30,000	
Factory Rent	5,000	
Carriage of Raw Materials	3,000	
Salary of the Works Manager	2,000	
Office Rent	2,000	
Printing and Stationery	1,000	
Bad Debts	1,000	
Sales		60,000
Land and Buildings	30,000	
Plant and Machinery	20,000	
Depreciation on Plant	2,000	
Sundry Debtors	5,000	
Sundry Creditors		30,000
Cash in hand	5,000	
Capital		43,000
	1,33,000	1,33,000

Closing Stocks on 31st December, 1990 were as follows:

	Rs
Raw Materials	5,000
Work-in-process	4,000
Finished Goods	10,000

[**Ans.** Cost of Production Rs 50,000, Gross Profit Rs 10,000, Net Profit Rs 6,000, Total of Balance Sheet Rs 79,000].

4. Prepare Manufacturing, Trading and Profit and Loss Account for the year ended 31st March, 1990 and Balance Sheet as at the end of the year from the following Trial Balance:

Particulars	Dr. Amount Rs	Cr. Amount Rs
Opening Stock of Raw Materials	30,000	
Opening Stock of Finished Goods	16,000	
Opening Stock of Work-in-progress	5,000	
Capital		72,000
Purchases of Raw Materials	2,50,000	
Sales		4,00,000
Purchases of Finished Goods	8,000	
Carriage Inwards	4,000	
Wages	50,000	
Salaries (75% Factory)	26,000	
Commission	3,000	
Bad Debt	2,000	
Insurance	4,000	
Rent, Rates and Taxes (50% Factory)	12,000	
Postage and Telegram	2,800	
Tea and Tiffin	1,600	
Travelling and Conveyance (25% Factory)	3,500	
Carriage Outwards	2,600	
Machinery	40,000	
Furniture	5,000	
Debtors	60,000	
Creditors		53,500
	5,25,500	5,25,500

The Closing Stocks are as follows:

	Rs
Raw Materials	40,000
Work-in-progress	12,000
Finished Goods	8,000

[Ans. Cost of Production Rs 3,13,375, Gross Profit Rs 70,625, Net Profit Rs 39,500, Balance Sheet Total Rs 1,65,000].

5. From the following balances draw up a Trading and Profit and Loss Account and Balance Sheet:

Particulars	Amount Rs
P. Parikh Capital	20,000
Bank Overdraft	5,000
Machinery	13,400
Cash in Hand	1,000
Fixtures & Fittings	5,500
Opening Stock	45,000
Bills Payable	7,000
Creditors	40,000
Debtors	63,000
Bills Receivable	5,000
Purchases	50,000

Contd....

Particulars	Amount Rs
Sales	1,29,000
Returns from Customers	1,000
Returns to Creditors	1,100
Salaries	9,000
Manufacturing Wages	4,000
Commission and T.A.	5,500
Trade Expenses	1,500
Discount (Cr.)	4,000
Rent	2,200

The Closing Stock amounted to Rs 52,000.

[**Ans.** Gross Profit Rs 82,100; Net Profit Rs 67,900 and Balance Sheet Total Rs 1,39,900].

6. From the under-stated Trial Balance of M/s Suneel Brothers prepare (a) Manufacturing Account; (b) Trading and Profit and Loss Account; and (c) Balance Sheet:

TRIAL BALANCE

as on 31st December, 1988

Debit Balances	Amount Rs	Credit Balances	Amount Rs
Wages	20,000	Sales	1,74,000
Stock (Raw Materials)		Profit and Loss	
1.1.1988	5,710	Balance 1.1.1988	12,000
Purchases	88,274	Capital	1,30,000
Carriage Inward	3,686		
Repairs	6,000		
Salaries (Factory)	2,100		
Salaries General	1,000		
Rates and Taxes	2,240		
Travelling Expenses	3,550		
Insurance (Factory)	700		
Insurance General	80		
Bad Debts	410		
General Expenses	2,942		
Carriage Outward	9,424		
Various Assets	1,13,884		
Stock 1.1.88 (finished goods)	56,000		
	3,16,000		3,16,000

Closing Stock: Raw Materials, Rs 5,272; Finished Goods, Rs 34,324.

[**Ans.** Cost of Production, Rs 1,21,198; Gross Profit Rs 31,126; Net Profit Rs 11,480; Balance Sheet Total Rs 1,53,480].

7. The following are the Trading and Profit & Loss Account and Balance Sheet of B as on December, 31, 1990. Redraw them in proper form, giving reasons for your correction.

TRADING AND PROFIT & LOSS ACCOUNT

for the year ended 31-12-1990

Particulars	Amount Rs	Particulars	Amount Rs
Pruchases	4,66,800	Sales	5,59,900
Stock	55,110	Profit on Consignment to A &	
Salaries	11,010	Co., Bombay	19,080

Contd....

Particulars	Amount Rs	Particulars	Amount Rs
B's Drawings	19,170	Interest on Capital	7,500
Wages	65,590	Stock (1st Jan.)	50,310
Rent	2,250	Commission received	27,990
General Expenses	17,470	Discount received	11,250
Interest on Loan	3,000		
Bad Debts	11,890		
Net Profit to B/S	23,740		
	6,76,030		6,76,030

BALANCE SHEET
as on 31-12-1990

Liabilities	Amount Rs	Assets	Amount Rs
Creditors	1,95,070	Debtors	2,61,580
Bills Receivable	1,30,140	Cash	960
Capital (1.1.1990)	1,50,000	Bank	52,210
Net Profit from P & L A/c	23,740	Loan from Bank	75,000
		Stock (31-12-1990)	55,110
		Bills Payable	54,090
	4,98,950		4,98,950

[**Ans.** Gross Profit Rs 32,310, Net Profit Rs 37,510 Balance Sheet Total Rs 5,00,000].

Final Accounts with Adjustments

8. State how the following must be dealt with in the final accounts of a firm for the year ended 31.12.1988 giving reasons in brief:

   (i) Advertisement expenditure of Rs 10,000 paid on 30.12.1988, the advertisement in respect of which has appeared in the magazines only in January, 1989.

   (ii) Cost of temporary pandal erected for an exhibition on 1.7.1988, the exhibition being expected to be over by June 1989: Rs 17,000

   (iii) Cost of a second-hand scooter purchased on 1.10.1988 for Rs 2,500, which was totally destroyed in an accident on 30.11.1988, the insurance company paying Rs 1,000 in full settlement in January, 1989.

   (iv) Petrol expenses of Rs 420 paid for the car of one of the partners for an official visit, the car not being an asset of the firm.

   (v) Hire charges of Rs 1,000 for a compressor, when the firm's own compressor was under break-down. *(C.A. Entrance, Nov. 1979, adapted)*

   [**Ans.** (i) Prepaid expense (ii) Chareg Rs 8,500 to P & L in 1988 and carry forward the balance to 1989 (iii) Write off Rs 1,500 from P & L (iv) Charge P. & L A/c as a travelling expense (v) Charge Manufacturing A/c (if prepared) or P & L A/c].

9. (a) On 1st January, 1988 the Provision for Doubtful Debts Account in the books of a firm which maintains it at 5% had a credit balance of Rs 1,100. During the year the Bad Debts amounted to Rs 800 and the debtors at the end of the year were Rs 20,000. Show Provision for Doubtful Debts Account and Bad Debts Account for the year 1988.

   (b) At the end of an accounting year, a trader finds that no entry has been passed in the books of accounts in respect of the following transactions:

   (i) Outstanding salary at the end of the year Rs 200.

(*ii*) Goods given as charity during the year Rs 300.

(*iii*) Stock-in-hand at the end of the year Rs 20,000. Journalise these transactions.

10. The following balances were taken from the records of a firm. For each account give the adjusting journal entry which may have resulted in the change in that account balance.

Particulars	Trial Balance	Adjusted Trial Balance
Advances from customers	20,000	16,000
Prepaid Insurance	8,000	6,000
Wages Payable	3,000	5,000
Interest (Credit Balance)	1,000	1,200
Accumulated Depreciation	15,000	20,000

Assume that the final accounts were prepared from the unadjusted balance. How would the Profit and Loss account and Balance Sheet be affected in each of the above cases?

11. The following items are found in the Trial Balance of John on 31st December, 1988:

	Rs
Debtors	16,000
Bad Debts	300
Bad and Doubtful Debts Provision 1.1.1988	700

You are to provide for the bad and doubtful debts @ 5%. Give the necessary journal entries and prepare the Bad Debts Account, Bad and Doubtful Debts Provision Account, Profit and Loss Account, Sundry Debtors Account in the ledger and a Balance Sheet appearing after the final adjustments.

12. A firm had the following Balances on 1st January, 1988:

		Rs
(*a*)	Provision for Bad and Doubtful Debts	2,500
(*b*)	Provision for Discount on Debtors	1,200
(*c*)	Provision for Discount on Creditors	1,000

During the year Bad Debts amounted to Rs 2,000, Discounts allowed were Rs 100 and Discounts received were Rs 200. During 1989 Bad Debts amounting to Rs 1,000 were written off while Discounts allowed and received were Rs 2,000 and Rs 500 respectively.

Total Debtors on December, 31, 1988 were Rs 48,000 before writing off Bad Debts, but after allowing Discounts. On December 31, 1988 the amount was Rs 19,000 after writing off the Bad Debts, but before allowing Discounts. Total Creditors on these two dates were Rs 20,000 and Rs 25,000 respectively.

It is the firm's policy to maintain a provision of 5% against Bad & Doubtful Debts and 2% for Discount on Debtors and a provision of 3% for Discount on Creditors.

Show the accounts relating to Provision on Debtors and Provision on Creditors for the year 1988 and 1989.

[**Ans.** Balances on 31.12.1989 Bad debts Provision Rs 850, Provision for Discount on Debtors Rs 323, and Provision for Discount on Creditors Rs 750].

13. Apear Ltd. makes provision for doubtful debts at the end of each year against specific debtors. On 30th June, 1989 the following debtors' balances were considered doubtful and provided for:

	Rs
Raman	1,500
Jalil	400
Nagpal	250
Sharma	500

Following are the particulars for the year ended 30th June, 1990.

(a) Bad Debts written off:

	Rs
Raman	1,200
Sharma	350
Gupta	300
Ramesh	200
Atmaram	150

(b) Amounts realised against debts written off in earlier years:

	Rs
Hossain	350
Kriparam	175
Dayaram	225

(c) Debts cosidered doubtful (after taking into account all realisations during the year) at the end of the year:

	Rs
Abraham	180
Ganesh	230
Gangasarn	375
Ramchandra	470

You are required to draw up:

(i) Bad Debts Account

(ii) Provision for Doubtful Debts Account and to show the relevant amounts in the Profit & Loss Account for the year ended 30th June, 1990.

[**Ans.** Amount charged from P & L A/c for Bad Debts Provision Rs 805, Bad Debts recovered Rs 750 Credited to P & L A/c].

14. The Accountant of M/s Kasturi Agencies extracted the following Trial Balance as on March, 31,1987:

Particulars	Dr. Amount Rs	Cr. Amount Rs
Capital		1,00,000
Drawings		18,000
Buildings	15,000	
Furniture & Fittings	7,500	
Motor Van	25,000	
Loan from Hari @ 12% interest	15,000	
Interest paid on above	450	
Sales		1,00,000
Purchases	75,000	
Stock as at 1.4.86	25,000	
Stock as at 31.3.87		32,000
Establishment Expenses	15,000	
Freight Inward	2,000	
Freight Outward		1,000
Commission received		7,500
Sundry Debtors	28,100	
Bank Balance	20,500	
Sundry Creditors		10,000
	2,28,550	2,68,500

The Accountant located the following errors but is unable to proceed any further:

(*a*) A totalling error in bank column of payment side of Cash Book whereby the column was under totalled by Rs 500.

(*b*) Interest on loan paid for the quarter ending December, 31, 1986, Rs 450 was omitted to be posted in the ledger. There was no further payment of interest.

You are required to set right the Trial Balance and to prepare the Trading and Profit and Loss Account for the year ended March 31, 1987 and the Balance Sheet as at the date after carrying out the following:

(*i*) Depreciation is to be provided on the assets as follows:

Buildings	2 ½% p.a.
Furniture & Fittings	10% p.a.
Motor Van	25% p.a.

(*ii*) Balance of interest due on the loan is also to be provided for.

[**Ans.** Correct Trial Balance Total Rs 2,32,500, Gross Profit Rs 30,000, Net Profit Rs 12,775 Balance Sheet Total Rs 1,20,225]

15. The following is the Schedule of balances as on 31.3.1988 extracted from the books of Shri Gavaskar, who carries on business under the name and style of Messrs Gavaskar Viswanath & Co., at Bombay:

Particulars	Dr. Amount Rs	Cr. Amount Rs
Cash in Hand	1,400	
Cash at Bank	2,600	
Sundry Debtors	86,000	
Stock as on 1.4.1987	62,000	
Furniture & Fixtures	21,400	
Office Equipment	16,000	
Buildings	60,000	
Motor Car	20,000	
Sundry Creditors		43,000
Loan from Viswanath		30,000
Reserve for Bad Debts		3,000
Purchases	1,40,000	
Purchase Returns		2,600
Sales		2,30,000
Sales Returns	4,200	
Salaries	11,000	
Rent for Godown	5,500	
Interest on loan from Viswanath	2,700	
Rates and taxes	2,100	
Discount allowed to Debtors	2,400	
Discount received from Creditors		1,600
Freight on Purchases	1,200	
Carriage Outwards	2,000	
Drawings	12,000	
Printing & Stationery	1,800	
Electric Charges	2,200	

Contd....

Particulars	Dr. Amount Rs	Cr. Amount Rs
Insurance Premium	5,500	
General Office Expenses	3,000	
Bad Debts	2,000	
Bank Charges	1,600	
Motor Car Expenses	3,600	
Capital Account		1,62,000
	4,72,200	4,72,200

Prepare Trading and Profit & Loss Account for the year ended 31st March, 1988 and the Balance Sheet as at that date after making provision for the following:

1. Depreciate—
   (a) Buildings used for business by 5%.
   (b) Furniture and Fixtures by 10%—one steel table purchased during the year for Rs 1,400 was sold for same price but the sale proceeds were wrongly credited to sales account.
   (c) Office Equipment by 15%—Purchases of a typewriter during the year for Rs 4,000 has been wrongly debited to purchases.
   (d) Motor car by 20%.
2. Value of stock at the close of the year was Rs 44,000
3. One months rent for godown is outstanding.
4. One months salary is outstanding.
5. Interest on Loan from Viswanath is payable at 12% p.a. This loan was taken on 1.5.1987.
6. Reserve for Bad debts is to be maintained at 5% of Sundry Debtors.
7. Insurance premium includes Rs 4,000 paid towards proprietor's Life Insurance Policy and the balance of the insurance charges cover the period from 1.4.1987 to 30.6.1988.
8. Half of the buildings are used for residential purposes of Shri Gavaskar.

(C.A. Entrance May, 1978, adapted)

[**Ans.** Gross Profit Rs 71,800, Net Profit Rs 18,400, Balance Sheet Total Rs 2,38,000].

16. From the following trial balance of Shri Goyal, prepare Trading and Profit & Loss Account for the year ending 31st Dec., 1986, and Balance Sheet as on that date after taking into consideration the adjustments given at the end of the trial balance:

TRIAL BALANCE
as on 31st December, 1986

Particulars	Dr. Amount Rs	Cr. Amount Rs
Sales	—	3,70,000
Purchases (adjusted)	3,49,600	
Wages	10,450	
Capital Account		34,250
National Insurance	150	
Carriage Inwards	200	
Carriage Outwards	250	
Lighting	300	
Rates and Insurance (including premium of Rs 150 p.a. up to 30th June, 1987)	200	
Stock at 31.12.1986	30,625	

Contd....

Particulars	Dr. Amount Rs	Cr. Amount Rs
Cash in Hand and at Bank	875	
Discount earned		300
Plant and Machinery	15,000	
Discount allowed	50	
Debtors and Creditors	3,000	10,000
Furniture	4,000	
Dividends received		150
	4,14,700	4,14,700

Adjustments:

(i) National Insurance also includes employees contribution of Rs 75. Wages are shown "Net" after deducting national insurance contribution borne by the employees.

(ii) Owing to the nature of employment, some employees are housed in the building of the business. The rental value of such portion is assessed at Rs 250 per annum. The benefit to the employee treated as wages and the rental as income for Shri Goyal.

(iii) Depreciate Plant & Machinery at 15% per annum and Furniture at 10% p.a.

(iv) Goods worth Rs 2,000 given by Shri Goyal to his son at cost.

(v) The Manager is entitled to a commission of 20% of the Net Profits after charging his commission. (Calculations may be made nearest to the multiple of a rupee).

(C.A. Entrance, Nov., 1987)

[**Ans.** Gross Profit Rs 11,350; Net Profit Rs 7,229, Balance Sheet Total Rs 50,925].

17. The following Trial Balance is extracted from the book of a merchant on 31st December, 1987:

Particulars	Amount Rs	Amount Rs
Furniture and Fittings	640	
Motor Vehicles	6,250	
Buildings	7,500	
Capital Account		12,500
Bad Debts	125	
Provision for Bad Debts		200
Sundry Debtors and Creditors	3,800	2,500
Stock on January 1, 1987	3,460	
Purchase and Sales	5,475	15,450
Bank Overdraft		2,850
Sales and Purchase Returns	200	125
Advertising	450	
Interest (on Bank Overdraft)	118	
Commission		375
Cash	650	
Taxes and Insurance	1,250	
General Expenses	782	
Salaries	3,300	
	34,000	34,000

The following adjustments are to be made:

(a) Stock in hand on 31st December, 1987 was Rs 3,250.

(b) Depreciate buildings at the rate of 5%, Furniture & Fittings @ 10% and Motor Vehicles @ 20%.

(c) Rs 85 is due for interest on bank overdraft.

(d) Salaries Rs 300 and Taxes Rs 120 are outstanding.

(e) Insurance amounting to Rs 100 is prepaid.

(f) One-third of the commission received is in respect of work to be done next year.

(g) Write off a further sum of Rs 100 as bad debts and provision for bad debts to be made equal to 10 per cent on sundry debtors. *(C.A. Entrance, Nov., 1988)*

[**Ans.** Gross Profit Rs 9,690; Net Profit Rs 1,551; Balance Sheet Total Rs 20,031].

18. From the following balances taken from the ledger of Shri Krishana on 31st March 1989, prepare the Trading and Profit & Loss Account for the year ended 31st March, 1989 and the Balance Sheet as at 31st March, 1989 of Shri Krishana:-

Particulars	Amount Rs	Particulars	Amount Rs
Sundry Creditors	19,000	Bad Debts	100
Building	15,000	Loan from Ram	2,500
Income-Tax	1,025	Sundry Debtors	9,500
Loose Tools	1,000	Investments	6,500
Cash at Bank	16,200	Bad Debts Reserve	1,600
Sundry Expenses	1,990	Rent and Rates	850
Bank Interest (Cr.)	75	Furniture	3,000
Purchases	1,57,000	Stock (1.4.1988)	27,350
Wages	10,000	Capital	47,390
Carriage Inwards	1,120	Discount allowed	630
Sales	1,85,000	Dividends received	535
Motor Van	12,500	Drawings	2,000
Cash in Hand	335	Bills payable	10,000

Adjustments to be taken into account:-

(a) Write off further Rs 300 as bad out of Sundry Debtors and create a Reserve for Bad Debts at 20% on Debtors.

(b) Dividends accrued and due on Investments is Rs 135. Rates paid in advance Rs 100 and wages owing Rs 450.

(c) On 31.3.1989 stock was valued at Rs 15,000 and Loose Tools were valued at Rs 800.

(d) Write off 5% for depreciation on Buildings and 40% on Motor Van.

(e) Provide for interest at 12% per annum due on loan taken on 1.6.88.

(f) Income-tax paid has to be treated as Drawings. *(C.A. Entrance, Nov., 1989)*

[**Ans.** Gross Profit Rs 4,080; Net Loss Rs 5,385; Balance Sheet Total Rs 71,180)

19. The following Trial Balance was extracted from the books of Mr. A as on 30th September 1988:

Particulars	Dr. Amount Rs	Cr. Amount Rs
Capital Account		1,00,000
Plant & Machinery	78,000	
Furniture	2,000	
Sales		1,27,000
Purchases	60,000	
Returns	1,000	750
Opening Stock	30,000	

Contd....

Particulars	Dr. Amount Rs	Cr. Amount Rs
Discount	425	800
Sundry Debtors	45,000	
Sundry Creditors		25,000
Salaries	7,550	
Manufacturing Wages	10,000	
Carriage Outward	1,200	
Provision for Bad Debts		525
Rent, Rates and Taxes	10,000	
Advertisement	2,000	
Cash	6,900	
	2,54,075	2,54,075

Prepare Trading and Profit & Loss Account for the year ended 30th September, 1988 and a Balance Sheet as on that date after taking into account the following adjustments:

1. Closing Stock was valued at Rs 34,220
2. Provision for Bad Debts is to be kept at Rs 500.
3. Allow Interest on Capital at 10% per annum.
4. Furniture was sold and the same was disposed off for Rs 760 in exchange of new furniture costing Rs 1,680. The net invoice of Rs 920 was passed through Purchase Register. (No depreciation need be charged on old and new furniture).
5. Depreciate Plant and Machinery by 10% per annum.
6. The proprietor Mr. A has taken goods worth Rs 5,000 for personal use, and distributed goods worth Rs 1,000 as samples. *(C.A. Entrance, May, 1989)*

[**Ans.** Gross Profit Rs 67,890; Net Profit Rs 27,500; Balance Sheet total Rs 1,57,500].

20. The following are the balances extracted from the ledger of Shri Popatlal for the year ended 31.12.1990:

	Rs
Capital Account	2,25,000
Sales	15,25,600
Purchases	10,00,650
Factory Salaries & Wages	1,35,680
Carriage Inward	10,200
Discounts received	4,560
Office Salaries (incl. Rs 6,000 to Shri Popatlal)	25,720
Sundry Creditors	23,840
Factory Insurance	2,600
Electricity	25,200
Office Rent	12,200
Discounts paid	1,520
Postage & Telegrams	2,050
General Reserve	2,20,000
Sundry Expenses	2,200
Printing & Stationery	2,600
Insurance	2,400
Sundry Debtors	35,500

Contd....

	Rs
Plant & Machinery	40,500
Furniture & Fixtures	10,500
Provision for Doubtful Debts	600
Investments (4% 1986-87 Loan)	20,000
Advertisements	1,02,250
Factory Buildings	1,45,000
Opening Stock:	
Raw Materials	2,13,800
Finished Goods	91,080
Cash Drawings	24,000
Interest received on Investments	400
Cash at Bank	7,250
Carriage Outwards	16,370
Cash at hand	70,730

From the above and the following information, prepare the Manufacturing Account, the Trading Account, Profit & Loss Account and the Balance Sheet:

(1) The closing stock comprise of Raw Materials Rs 1,80,300 and Finished Goods Rs 96,080.

(2) Sums aggregating Rs 2,000 have to be written off as Bad Debts and the Provision for Doubtful Debts has to kept at 5 per cent of the Sundry Debtors at close.

(3) The following items were utilised by Shri Popatlal for his personal use:

		Rs
(a)	Raw Materials	3,455
(b)	Finished Goods	5,000
(c)	Electricity	1,640
(d)	Rent	2,400
(e)	Printing & Stationery	380
(f)	Postage	580

(4) Depreciation has to be provided at the following rates per annum:

On Furniture   @ 10%
On Machinery & Plant @ 5%
On Buildings   @ 2½%

No Depreciation need to be provided in respect of assets sold during this year.

(5) Insurance Premia were found to have been paid upto 31st March, 1991. It was the first time that Insurance was taken out on 1.4.1990.

(6) Electricity includes Rs 19,800 towards Factory Power.

(7) General Reserve is to be raised to Rs 3 Lakhs.

(8) Make provision in respect of the following liabilities outstanding as at 31.12.1990:

	Rs
Office Salaries	2,500
Office Rent	1,100
Advertisement	900
Sundry Expenses	500

{**Ans.** Cost of Production Rs 12,03,975, Gross Profit Rs 3,31,625; Net Profit Rs 1,66,750; Balance Sheet Total Rs 5,97,135].

21. From the following balances and additional information you are required to parpare 'Work Sheet' and 'Adjusted Trial Balance':

Particulars	Rs	Rs
Cash	2,000	
Debtors	3,000	
Provision for Bad Debts		100
Purchases	10,500	
Prepaid Expenses	500	
Fixed Assets	5,000	
Capital		9,900
Salaries	2,000	
Sales		12,000
Creditors		1,000
	23,000	23,000

Adjusments:

(i) Closing Stock Rs 500

(ii) Depreciation on Fixed Assets 1%.

(iii) Rs 100 are to be adjusted to Rent Account out of Prepaid Expenses Account.

(iv) 1% of the sales of Rs 2,000 is to be considered doubtful.

[Ans. Gross Profit Rs 2,000, Net Loss Rs 170, Balance Sheet Total Rs 10,730].

[Hint. Out of Prepaid Expenses Rs 500, Rs 100 have to be charged as Rent for the current year. Increase Provision for doubtful debts by Rs 20].

Chapter 11

RECTIFICATION OF ERRORS

LEARNING OBJECTIVES

After studying this chapter you should be able to:

- [ ] understand the concept of the different types of errors;
- [ ] identify the procedure for locating errors;
- [ ] appreciate the meaning and importance of suspense account;
- [ ] rectify accounting errors by means of appropriate journal entries;
- [ ] understand the effect of different errors on computation of business profits; and
- [ ] explain the meaning of certain key terms.

In the preceding chapters we have explained about the preparation and presentation of Final Accounts. The basic information for this purpose is supplied by the Trial Balance. Thus, the accuracy of the Trial Balance determines to a great extent the accuracy or otherwise of the information provided by Final Accounts. However, the Trial Balance provides only proof of the arithmetical accuracy of the books of accounts. It simply assures that for every debit there is an equivalent credit entry. It means that in spite of an agreed Trial Balance, it is not necessary that there are no errors in the books of accounts. For example, if a transaction is not at all recorded in the books of accounts, the Trial Balance will tally, but the books of accounts cannot be termed as a accurate. In any case, if the two sides of the Trial Balance do not tally, it is a definite proof of this fact that there are certain errors in the books of accounts. Thus, errors may be there in recording, classifying and summarising the financial transactions whether the Trial Balance tallies or whether it does not tally.

CLASSIFICATION OF ERRORS

Errors can broadly be classified as shown in the following chart:

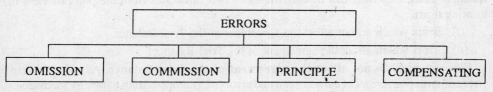

1. **Errors of omission.** These errors are incurred in those cases when a transaction is completely omitted from the books of accounts. It happen when a transaction is not

recorded in the books of the original entry (*i.e.*, various journals). For example, if a purchase of goods on credit from Shri Ram Lal has not at all been recorded in the books of accounts, such an error will be termed as an error of omission. Since, there has been neither a debit entry nor a credit entry, therefore, the two sides of the Trial Balance will not be at all affected on account of this error. Such errors, therefore, cannot be located out very easily. They come to the notice of the businessman when statement of accounts are received from or sent to creditors or debtors as the case might be.

2. Errors of commission. Such errors include errors on account of wrong balancing of an account, wrong posting, wrong carry forwards, wrong totalling, etc. For example, if a sum of Rs 50 received from Mukesh is credited to his account as Rs 500, this is an error of commission. Similarly, if the total of the debit side of an account is carried forward from one page to another and the mistake is committed in such carry forward (*e.g.* total of Rs 996 is carried forwards as Rs 699) such an error is an error of commission. Errors of commission affect the agreement of the Trial Balance and, therefore, their location is easier.

3. Errors of principle. Errors of principle are committed in those cases where a proper distinction between revenue and capital items is not made. *i.e.*, a capital expenditure is taken as a revenue expenditure or *vice-versa*. Similarly, a capital receipt may have been taken as a revenue receipt or *vice- versa*. For example, a sale of old furniture of Rs 500 should be credited to the furniture account, but if it is credited to the Sales Account, it will be termed as an error of principle. Sale of old furniture is a capital receipt. If it is credited to Sales Account, it has been taken as a revenue receipt. Such errors by themselves do not affect the agreement of the Trial Balance. Therefore, they also are difficult to be located.

4. Compensating errors. As the name indicates, compensating errors are those errors which compensate each other. For example, if a sale of Rs 500 to Ram is debited as only of Rs 50 to his account, while a sale of Rs 50 to Shyam is debited as of Rs 500 to his account, it is a compensating error. These errors also do not affect the agreement of the Trial Balance and, therefore, their location is also difficult.

Thus, errors of omission, errors of principle and compensating errors by themselves alone do not affect the agreement of the Trial Balance. In case these errors get combined with errors of commission, they may affect the agreement of the Trial Balance. For example, if a sale of old furniture of Rs 500 is credited to the Sales Account only as of Rs 50, the error combines in itself both an error of principle as well as error of commission. Thus, such an error will affect the agreement of the Trial Balance.

LOCATION OF ERRORS

Location of errors of principle, errors of compensating nature and errors of omission is slightly difficult because of the fact that such errors do not affect the agreement of the Trial Balance and, therefore, their location may be considerably delayed. However, location of errors of commission is comparatively easier because they affect the agreement of the Trial Balance. Thus, the errors can be classified into two categories from the point of view of locating them:

(*i*) Errors which do not affect the agreement of the Trial Balance.

(*ii*) Errors which affect the agreement of the Trial Balance.

Errors which do not affect the agreement of the Trial Balance. As stated before, errors of omission, errors of commission and errors of a compensating nature by themselves do not affect the agreement of the Trial Balance. Their location is therefore a difficult process. They are usually found out when statement of accounts are received by the business or sent to the customers or during the course of internal or external audit and sometimes by chance. For example, if a credit purchase of Rs 500 from Ram has not been recorded in the books of accounts, the error will not affect the agreement of the Trial Balance and, therefore, at the time of finalising the accounts it may not be traced out. However, this will be found out when a statement of account is sent to Ram showing the money due to him or when a statement of account is received from Ram showing the money recoverable by him.

Errors which affect the agreement of the Trial Balance. Such errors are easy to be located since they are caught at an early stage. As soon as the Trial Balance does not tally, the accountant can proceed to find out these errors. The procedure to be followed for location of such errors can be put as follows:

(i) The difference of the two sides of the Trial Balance should be found out. The amount should then be divided by two. The two sides of the Trial Balance should then be checked to find out if there is an amount equal to that figure. It is possible that the amount may have been placed to a wrong side resulting in difference in the totals of the Trial Balance. For example, if the total of the debit side of the Trial Balance is Rs 450 more than the credit side of the Trial Balance, Rs 450 should be divided by 2, thus giving a figure of 225. The debit side should then be checked to find out if there is an amount of Rs 225 appearing on that side. If it is so, it should be seen whether the amount has been correctly put to that side or it should have gone to the credit side.

(ii) If the mistake is not found out by taking step number (i), the difference should be divided by 9. If the difference is completely divisible, it can be an error of transposition of figures. For example, if the figure of 698 is written as 896, the difference is of Rs 198. This figure is completely divisible by 9. Thus it can be concluded that in such cases where the difference is divisible by 9, there can be a probability of this type of error.

(iii) In case, the difference is still not traceable, the following further possibilities should be checked:

(a) If the difference is in a round figure, there is a possibility of wrong casting or wrong carry forwards of the totals of a subsidiary books or there is an error in balancing the accounts.

(b) In case, the difference is not in a round figure, there is a possibility of error being committed in posting the transactions from the Journal to the Ledger.

(c) If the difference is of a substantial amount, it will be appropriate to compare the Trial Balance of the current year with the Trial Balance of the preceding year and see whether there is any abnormal difference between the balances of important accounts of the two Trial Balances.

(iv) Since, cash and bank account are not maintained usually in the Ledger, it will be also advisable to check whether the balances of the cash and bank accounts have been taken in the Trial Balance or not.

(v) The schedules of sundry debtors and sundry creditors should be checked to find out whether all balances of debtors and creditors have been included in these schedules or not.

(vi) The totals of the subsidiary books such as the Sales Book, Purchases Book should be checked and it should be seen whether posting has been done from these two books correctly to the Sales, Purchases or other accounts as the case might be.

(vii) If the error is still not traceable, check thoroughly the books of original entry and their posting into the Ledger and finally the balancing of different accounts.

(viii) A business may keep ledgers on sectional/self balancing system. In such a case, there are three ledgers: (a) Sales Ledger containing personal accounts of all trade debtors, (b) Purchases Ledger containing personal accounts of all trade creditors, and (c) General Ledger containing all other real, nominal and personal accounts except those of trade debtors and trade creditors. However, there will be two total accounts in this ledger: (i) Total Debtors Account, and (ii) Total Creditors Account. The balance of the Total Debtors Account should tally with the total of the Schedule of Debtors as prepared from the Sales Ledger. Similarly, the balance of the Total Creditors Account should tally with the total of the Schedule of Creditors as prepared from the Purchases Ledger. In case, the balance of Total Debtors Account does not tally with the total of the Schedule of Debtors, the personal accounts in the Sales Ledger should be checked and the other Ledger may not be touched. Same is true of the Total Creditors Account and the Schedule of Total Creditors.

SUSPENSE ACCOUNT

The accountant should take the above mentioned steps one after the other to locate the difference in the totals of the Trial Balance. In case, he is not in a position to locate the difference and he is in a hurry to close the books of accounts, he may transfer the difference to an account known as "Suspense Account". Thus, Suspense Account is an account to which the difference in the Trial Balance has been put temporarily. On locating the errors in the beginning or during the course of the next year, suitable accounting entries are passed (as explained later) and the Suspense Account is closed. However, it should be noted that Suspense Account should be opened by the accountant only when he has failed to locate the errors in spite of his best efforts. It should not be by way of a normal practice, because the very existence of the Suspense Account creates doubt about the authenticity of the books of accounts. The result shown by the books of accounts may not be trusted by the proprietors, tax officials and other government authorities in such a case. This may create complications for the business.

RECTIFYING ACCOUNTING ENTRIES

The errors committed in the books of accounts when located out, have to be corrected. However, corrections in the books of accounts should be done by passing proper rectifying entries and not by cutting or erasing figures. Such entries, as explained earlier, are passed in the General Journal or Journal Proper. The passing of proper rectifying entries is being explained below with suitable examples.

Example 1. The Sales Book overcast by Rs 50.

Over-casting of Sales Book will result in over-credit to Sales Account by Rs 50 since the total of the Sales Book is posted to the credit of the Sales Account at the end of a period. There can be two situation in such a case:

(i) The error might have been located out by the accountant before transferring the difference to the Suspense Account. In such a case, there is mistake only in one account, *i.e.*, the Sales Account. It has been credited more by Rs 50. The error can be rectified if the Sales Account is debited by Rs 50. Thus, the following will be the rectifying entry in the Journal Proper:

Particulars		Dr. Rs	Cr. Rs
Sales Account	Dr.	50	
(Being excess credit to sales account, now rectified)			

No account is to be credited since the error affects only one account.

(*ii*) The error might have been located out by the accountant after transferring the difference in the Trial Balance to a Suspense Account. In such a case two accounts are involved: (*a*) Sales Account, and (*b*) Suspense Account. Since Sales Account had been credited more by Rs 50 the credit side of the Trial Balance must have been more than the debit side of the Trial Balance. The Suspense Account should, therefore, have been put on the debit side of the Trial Balance in order to balance the two sides as shown below:

TRIAL BALANCE

Particulars	Dr. Rs	Cr. Rs
Excess Credit to Sales Account		50
Suspense Account	50	
	50	50

The Sales Account has been credited more by Rs 50. In order to rectify the error, the Sales Account should therefore be debited by Rs 50. Suspense Account has been debited because of this mistake which has now been found out. It should therefore, be closed by giving credit to it. The rectifying accounting entry should, therefore, be passed as follows:

Particulars		Dr. Rs	Cr. Rs
Sales Account	Dr.	50	
To Suspense Account			50

Example 2. A credit sale of Rs 100 to Ramesh has been entered in the Sales Book as a sale of Rs 1,000.

In order to pass a rectifying entry, it will be appropriate to find out the accounts involved. In this case, the error involves two accounts: (*i*) Sales Account, and (*ii*) the account of Ramesh. This is because the posting is done in the individual accounts from the Sales Book and therefore, if a transaction is wrongly recorded in the Sales Book (which is the book of original entry) not only the total of the Sales Book will be wrong, but also the entry in the personal account will be wrong as shown below:

SALES BOOK

Particulars		Rs
Sales to Ramesh (wrongly recorded in place of Rs 100)		1,000
Sales Account	Cr.	1,000

Ledger

Dr.   RAMESH   Cr.

Particulars			Particulars	Rs
To Sales A/c	1,000			

SALES ACCOUNT

Particulars	Rs		Particulars	Rs
			By Sundries (including sales to Ramesh)	1,000

The recording of the transactions as shown above shows that the Sales Account has been credited by Rs 1,000 in place of Rs 100. Similarly, the account of Ramesh has been debited by Rs 1,000 in place of Rs 100. Thus, Sales Account has been over-credited by Rs 900, while the account of Ramesh has been over-debited by Rs 900. In order to set the matters right, Sales Account should now be debited by Rs 900 and the account of Ramesh should be credited by Rs 900. The errors should not have affected the agreement of the Trial Balance because of the same amount being put to the debit as well as the credit sides. The Suspense Account is, therefore, not at all involved.

The rectifying accounting entry will, therefore, be as follows:

Particulars		Rs	Rs
Sales Account	Dr.	900	
To Ramesh			900

Example 3. A sale of Rs 50 to Suresh was posted to his account as a sale of Rs 5.

In this case, the account of Suresh has been debited by only Rs 5, in place of Rs 50. His account has, therefore, been under-debited by Rs 45. It means the credit side of the Trial Balance must have been more by Rs 45 on account of this error. In case, the Suspense Account has been opened, it should have been debited by Rs 45. The rectifying entry should, therefore, give debit of Rs 45 to Suresh, and give credit of Rs 45 to Suspense Account. The entry willl thus be as follows:

Particulars		Rs	Rs
Suresh	Dr.	45	
To Suspense Account			45

The Suspense Account which was showing the debit balance of Rs 45 would now be closed on account of passing of this rectifying entry.

Example 4. A sale of Rs 50 to Kamlesh was entered in the Sales Book as of Rs 500, from where he was debited by Rs 5,000.

This is a multiple type of error. It affects more than two accounts. The accounts involved are (i) Kamlesh, (ii) Sales Account, and (iii) Suspense Account.

The total of the Sales Book is posted to the Sales Account. The sale has been recorded as of Rs 500 in the Sales Book from where the posting must have been done to the Sales Account. Thus, the Sales Account has been credited by Rs 500 instead of Rs 50. It has been credited more by Rs 450. In order to rectify the error, it should, therefore, be debited by Rs 450. The account of Kamlesh should have been debited by Rs 50 only but it has been debited by Rs 5,000. It has, therefore been debited more by Rs 4,950. In order to rectify the matters, it should be credited by Rs 4,950. These two errors must have created difference in the Trial Balance which should have gone to the Suspense Account. Sales Account comes on the credit side of the Trial Balance. It has been credited by Rs 450 more and, therefore, the credit side of the Trial Balance will be more by this amount on account of this error. On the other hand, Kamlesh is a debtor, his account has been excess debited by Rs 4,950. The debit side of the Trial Balance should therefore, be more by this amount. The net effect is that the debit side of the Trial Balance must have been more by Rs 4,500 which must have been put to the Suspense Account by giving credit to it. The rectifying entry will therefore be as follows:

Particulars		Rs	Rs
Suspense A/c	Dr.	4,500	
Sales A/c	Dr.	450	
To Kamlesh			4,950

Thus, on the basis of the above examples, the following rules can be framed out;

  (*i*) Find out the accounts affected by the error.

  (*ii*) Find out what should have been done and what has been done.

  (*iii*) Credit or Debit the respective account in order to set the matters right.

  (*iv*) Put the difference to Suspense Account.

The above rules will be further clear by the following example.

Example 5. A sales of Rs 1,000 to Suresh was entered in the Purchases Book from where the account of Suresh was debited by Rs 100.

The above error affects the following accounts: (*i*) Sales Account, (*ii*) Purchases Account, and (*iii*) Account of Suresh.

Sales Account should have been credited by a sum of Rs 1,000. It has not been done since it has been recorded in the Purchases Book. Thus, Sales Account should be credited (*i.e.*, what should have been done).

Purchases Account has been debited since the transaction has been entered in the Purchases Book from where it must have been posted to the Purchases Account. It has been debited by a sum of Rs 1,000. unnecessarily. It should, therefore, be credited to rectify what has been done wrongly.

Account of Suresh should have been debited by Rs 1,000. In the normal course, since the transaction has been recorded in the Purchases Book, his account should have been credited. However, the accountant has debited his account by Rs 100 instead of Rs 1,000. His account should therefore be debited by Rs 900 more in order to give full debit to his account.

The difference if any should be transferred to the Suspense Account as given in rule (*iv*) explained above.

The rectifying journal entry will, therefore, be as follows:

Particulars		Dr. Rs	Cr. Rs
Suspense A/c	Dr.	1,100	
Suresh	Dr.	900	
To Purchases A/c			1,000
To Sales A/c			1,000

The comprehensive illustrations given in the following pages will further clarify the accounting entries required to be passed for rectification of different types of errors.

Illustration 11.1. The Trial Balance of Arun on 31st December, 1990, showed a difference of Rs 580 (excess debit). It was put to a Suspense Account and the books were closed. On going through the books in January, 1991, following errors were discovered. You are required to pass suitable rectifying journal entries and prepare the Suspense Account.

1. Rs 540 received from M. Mehta was posted to the debit of his account.
2. Rs 100 being Purchases Returns was posted to the debit of Purchases Account.
3. Discount Rs 200 received, entered in the cash book was not posted to the Ledger.
4. Rs 574 paid for repairs to motor-car was debited to the motor-car account as Rs 574.
5. A sale of Rs 350 to Sethi was entered in the Sales Book as of Rs 530.
6. While carrying forward total of one page in Kalra's Account, the amount of Rs 250 was written on the credit side instead of debit side.
7. The purchase of machinery on 1st January, 1990 for Rs 6,000 was entered in the Purchases Account.

Solution:

JOURNAL PROPER

Sl. No.	Particulars	L.F.	Dr. Rs	Cr. Rs
1.	Suspense A/c Dr.		1,080	
	To M. Mehta			1,080
	(Being Rs 540 received from M. Mehta debited to his account, the error now rectified)			
2.	Suspense A/c Dr.		200	
	To Purchases A/c			100
	To Purchase Returns A/c			100
	(Being purchases returns of Rs 100 posted to the debit of Purchases A/c, the error now rectified)			
3.	Suspense A/c Dr.		200	
	To Discount A/c			200
	(Being discount received not posted to Discount A/c, the error now rectified)			
4.	Repairs A/c Dr.		574	
	To Motor Car A/c			174
	To Suspense A/c			400
	(Being repairs to motor car, Rs 574, debited to Motor Car A/c as Rs 174 wrongly, the error now rectified)			
5.	Sales A/c Dr.		180	
	To Sethi			180
	(Being sales of Rs 350 to Sethi entered in the Sales Book as of Rs 530, the error now rectified)			
6.	Kalra		500	
	To Purchases A/c			500
	(Being Kalra's A/c credited by Rs 250 instead of being debited by Rs 250, the error now rectified)			
7.	Machinery A/c Dr.		6,000	
	To Purchases A/c			6,000
	(Being purchase of machinery debited to Purchases A/c instead of Machinery A/c, the error now rectified)			

Notes:

1. The amount of M. Mehta should have been credited by Rs 540. It has been debited. In order to set the matters right, it is necessary to credit his account by Rs 1,080 (*i.e.*, to cancel unnecessary debit of Rs 540 and to give him credit of Rs 540).

2. The Purchases Returns Account should have been credited by a sum of Rs 100 on account of return of the goods. It has not been at all credited. It has, therefore, been credited by Rs 100. The Purchases Account should not have been at all debited. It has, therefore, been credited by Rs 100. Suspense Account has been debited by Rs 200, since no other account is available and it must have been credited earlier on account of these errors.

3. The amount of discount received is credited to the Discount Account. It has not been done, Discount Account, has therefore, been credited now, Suspense Account has been debited because it must have been credited earlier on account of this error.

4. Repairs to motor-car is a revenue expenditure. It should has been debited to the Repairs Account. It has not been done. The Repairs Account has, therefore, been debited by Rs 574. Motor Car Account has been unnecessarily debited by Rs 174. It should, therefore, be credited by this amount. The difference has been put to the Suspense Account.

5. The sale to Sethi was only of Rs 350, but it has been recorded as a sale of Rs 530. It means the account of Sethi has been unnecessarily debited by Rs 180. It has, therefore, been credited by this amount. Sales Account has been credited by Rs 530, instead of Rs 350. It has, therefore, been debited by Rs 180, the excess credit.

6. The account of Kalra should have been debited by Rs 250. It has been credited by Rs 250. His account should, therefore, be debited by Rs 500 to cancel unnecessary credit of Rs 250 and to keep his account debited by Rs 250. Suspense Account has been credited by Rs 500 since no other account is involved.

7. Purchase of Machinery of Rs 6,000 should have been debited to the Machinery Account. It was not done. The Machinery Account has therefore been debited by Rs 6,000. Purchases Account was unnecessarily debited by Rs 6,000. It has, therefore, been credited by the above amount.

Tutorial Note. While passing the rectifying journal entries, the students should put the difference to the Suspense Account, in case it has been opened and no other account is available.

Dr.		SUSPENSE ACCOUNT		Cr.
Particulars	Rs	Particulars		Rs
To M. Mehta	1,080	By Balance b/d		580
To Purchases	100	By Repairs Account		400
To Purchases Returns A/c	100	By Kalra		500
To Discount A/c	200			
	1,480			1,480

Illustration 11.2. In taking out a Trial Balance, a Book-keeper finds that debit total exceeds the credit total by Rs 352. The amount is placed to the credit of a newly opened Suspense Account. Subsequently the following mistakes were discovered. You are required to pass the necessary entries for rectifying the mistakes, and show the Suspense Account:

(*a*) Sales Day Book was overcast by Rs 100.

(b) A sale of Rs 50 to Shri Ram was wrongly debited to Shri Krishna.

(c) General Expenses Rs 18 were posted as Rs 80.

(d) Cash received from Shri Govind was debited to his account Rs 150.

(e) While carrying forward the total of one page of the Purchases Book to the next, the amount of Rs 1,235 was entered as Rs 1,325.

(C.A. Entrance, Nov., 1990)

Solution:

Sl. No.	Particulars		Dr. Rs	Cr. Rs
(a)	Sales A/c	Dr.	100	
	To Suspense A/c			100
	(Being overcasting of Sales Day book rectified)			
(b)	Shri Ram	Dr.	50	
	To Shri Krishna			50
	(Being the wrong debit given to Shri Krishna rectified)			
(c)	Suspense A/c	Dr.	62	
	To General Expenses A/c			62
	(Being rectification of the wrong posting made in General Expenses Account)			
(d)	Suspense A/c	Dr.	300	
	To Shri Govind			300
	(Being rectification of the wrong debit given to Shri Govind)			
(e)	Suspense A/c	Dr.	90	
	To Purchases A/c			90
	(Being rectification of the wrong carry forward in the Purchases Book)			

SUSPENSE ACCOUNT

Particulars	Rs	Particulars	Rs
To General Expenses	62	By Balance b/d	352
To Govind	300	By Sales	100
To Purchases	90		
	452		452

Illustration 11.3. A trader has tallied the Trial Balance by putting the difference of Rs 310 to the debit of Suspense Account and has prepared a Trading and Profit & Loss Account and the Balance Sheet. On subsequent scrutiny the books disclosed several errors as detailed below. Rectify these errors and prepare Suspense Account:

(i) A sale of goods to X for Rs 350 has been credited to his account.

(ii) Goods purchased from Y amounting to Rs 750 were entered in the Purchases Day Book but were omitted from Y's Account in the Creditors' Ledger.

(iii) An Office Typewriter purchased for Rs 500 has been passed through the Purchases Account.

(iv) Goods returned to S. Sen, valued Rs 75 were debited to P. Sen's Account.

(v) Repairs to Office Car valued Rs 750 were debited to the Office Car Account.

(vi) Goods sold to R. Banerjee valued Rs 730 have been posted in his account as Rs 370.

(C.A. Entrance, Nov., 1988)

Solution:

Sl. No.	Particulars	Dr. Rs	Cr. Rs
(i)	X Dr.	700	
	To Suspense A/c		700
	(Being amount of sale of Rs 350 wrongly credited to Mr. X error now rectified)		
(ii)	Suspense A/c Dr.	750	
	To Y		750
	(Being amount of goods purchased from Mr. Y not credited to his account now recorded)		
(iii)	Office Equipment A/c Dr.	500	
	To Profit & Loss Adjustment A/c		500
	(Being cost of typewriter purchased wrongly debited to purchases account, error now rectified)		
(iv)	S. Sen Dr.	75	
	To P. Sen		75
	(Being amount of goods returned to S. Sen wrongly debited to P. Sen, now rectified)		
(v)	Profit & Loss Adjustment Account Dr.	750	
	To Office Car A/c		750
	(Being amount of repairs of office car wrongly capitalised, now rectified)		
	R. Banerjee Dr.	360	
	To Suspense A/c		360
	(Being goods sold to R. Banerjee for Rs 730 debited to him as Rs 370, now rectified)		
	Capital A/c Dr.	250	
	To Profit & Loss Adjustment A/c		250
	(Being balance of Profit & Loss Adjustment Account transferred)		

SUSPENSE ACCOUNT

Particulars	Rs	Particulars	Rs
To Balance b/d	310	By X	700
To Y	750	By R. Banerjee	360
	1,060		1,060

Illustration 11.4. The Trial Balance of Messrs. *A*, *B* and *C* did not agree. A Suspense Account was opened with the amount of the difference. The following errors were discovered on scrutiny.

(1) The addition of the Analysis Column of the Tabular Purchase Journal posted to Goods Purchased for Resale Account was found to be short by Rs 150 though the addition of the total column was correct.

(2) A dishonoured B/R for Rs 400 returned to the firm by bank had been credited to Bank Account for Collection of Bills and debited to B/R Account. A cheque was later received from the customer for Rs 400 and was dully paid into the firm's bank account.

(3) An amount of Rs 450 treated as paid in advance on account of Insurance in the previous year was not brought forward.

(4) Sales on approval amounting to Rs 2,000 were included in the Sales Account. Half of these were returned but no entries were passed in respect of these. However, the returned goods have been included in the closing stock at their cost price of Rs 500.

(5) Of the total amount of Rs 38,356 shown as sundry creditors, Rs 1,260 represent credits given to customers when the payments against sales invoices were received. However, these invoices themselves were not entered in the books. A discount of 10% is allowed on the selling price in all such invoices.

You are required to pass rectifying entries making use of the Suspense Account, wherever necessary.

Solution:

JOURNAL

M/s A, B, and C

Sl. No.	Particulars		Dr. Rs	Cr. Rs
1.	Purchases for Resale A/c	Dr.	150	
	To Suspense Account			150
	(Short debit to 'Purchases for Resale Account' on account of undercasting—now corrected)			
2.	Customer's A/c	Dr.	400	
	To Bills Receivable A/c			400
	(Amount of dishonoured bill receivable previously debited to Bills Receivable Account, error now rectified)			
3.	Insurance Account	Dr.	450	
	To Suspense Account			450
	(Prepaid insurance in the previous year not brought forward, now debited to the Insurance Account)			
4.	Sales Account	Dr.	1,000	
	To Customer's Account			1,000
	(Goods worth Rs 1,000 returned by a customer on sale or return basis, previously omitted to be recorded; error now rectified)			
5.	Discount Account	Dr.	140	
	Customer's Account	Dr.	1,260	
	To Sales Account*			1,400
	(Credit sales of Rs 1,400 previously omitted from the books error now rectified)			

*Payment being equal to 90%, the gross sales is Rs 1,400 (*i.e.*, 1,260 × 100/90), 1/10 of this amount in discount.

However, since the discount of 10% is allowed in all cases, it would be better to treat the sale to be Rs 1,260 and not Rs 1,400—the discount is trade discount for which no account is opened, the sales being recorded at the net amount.

EFFECT ON PROFIT

Errors committed in a year may affect the profit of that year. This happens when the errors relate to such accounts which are taken into account while computing gross or net profit of the business. In other words, if the errors relate to such accounts which find their place in the Trading Account or the Profit and Loss Account, the errors will affect the profit of the business. For example, errors involving Purchases Account, Sales Account, Expense Account, Income Account will all affect the profit of the business. In case on account of errors such accounts are either not debited or unnecessarily credited, this will result in increase in profit of the business. For example, if repairs of machinery amounting to Rs 500 has been debited to the Machinery Account by mistake, the net profit will increase by Rs 500. Similarly, if on account of such errors such accounts are unnecessarily debited or are not unnecessarily credited, the errors will reduce the net profit of the business. For example, if a sale of Rs 100 is recorded in the books as only a sale of Rs 10, it will result in reducing the net profit of the business by Rs 90. The following illustration will make this point more clear.

Illustration 11.5. Taking the illustration 11.1 as the basis, compute the effects:

(*i*) on profit for the year 1990 of the errors committed, and

(*ii*) on profit of 1991 of the errors being rectified.

Solution:

EFFECT OF ERRORS ON PROFIT OF 1990

Sl. No.	Particulars	Increase (+) Rs	Decrease (−) Rs
1.	No effect on profit since no account relates to Trading or Profit & Loss Account.		
2.	The net profit will decrease by Rs 200 because both the Purchases and Sales Account relate to Trading Account.		200
3.	The net profit will decrease by Rs 200, since the account not credited relates to Profit & Loss Account.		200
4.	The net profit will increase by Rs 574, since the account not debited relates to Profit & Loss Account.	574	
5.	The net profit will increase by Rs 180, since excess credit has been given to an account which relates to Trading Account.	180	
6.	No effect on profit since no account relates to Trading or Profit & Loss Account.		
7.	The net profit will decrease by Rs 6,000; since the account given unnecessarily debit relates to Trading Account.		6,000
		754	6,400

Thus, on the whole, the net profit of the business for the year would decrease by Rs 5,646.

EFFECT OF RECTIFICATION OF ERRORS ON PROFIT OF 1991

Sl. No.	Particulars	Increase (+) Rs	Decrease (−) Rs
1.	No effect on profit since no account relates to Trading or Profit & Loss Account.		
2.	The net profit would increase by Rs 200 since both the accounts credited relate to Trading Account.	200	

Contd....

Sl. No.	Particulars	Increase (+) Rs	Decrease (−) Rs
3.	The net profit will increase by Rs 200, since the account credited relates to Profit & Loss Account	200	
4.	The net profit will decrease by Rs 574, since the account debited relates to Profit & Loss Account.		574
5.	The net profit will decrease by Rs 180, since the account debited relates to Trading Account.		180
6.	No effect on profit since neither account relates to Trading or Profit & Loss Account.		
7.	The net profit will increase by Rs 6,000, since the account credited relates to Trading Account.	6,000	
		6,400	754

Thus, on account of rectification of errors, the net profit of 1991 will increase by Rs 5,646.

Tutorial Note. From the above, it is clear that if the net profit has decreased on account of committing of errors, it will increase on account of rectifying those errors or *vice-versa*. Thus, the effect on net profit can be found out simply by preparing one statement either showing the effect or errors on net profit or showing the effect of rectification of errors on net profit. If one effect is found out, the other will be just reverse of it.

Illustration 11.6. On going through the Trial Balance of Ball Bearings Co. Ltd., you find that the debit is in excess by Rs 150. This was credited to "Suspense Account". On a close scrutiny of the books, the following mistakes were noticed:

(1) The total of debit side of an Expense Account has been cast in excess by Rs 50.

(2) The Sales Account has been totalled short by Rs 100.

(3) One item of purchase of Rs 25 has been posted from the day book to ledger as Rs 250.

(4) The sale return of Rs 100 from a party has not been posted to that account, though the party's account has been credited.

(5) A cheque of Rs 500 issued to the Suppliers' Account (shown under Sundry Creditors) towards his dues has been wrongly debited to the purchases account.

(6) A credit sale of Rs 50 has been credited to the Sales and also to the Sundry Debtors' Account.

(*i*) Pass necessary journal entries for correcting the above;

(*ii*) Show how they affect the Profits; and

(*iii*) Prepare the "Suspense Account" as it would appear in the ledger.

Solution:

JOURNAL ENTRIES

Particulars	Dr. Rs	Cr. Rs
Suspense Account Dr.	50	
To Expense Account		50
(Being the mistake in totalling of a Expense Account rectified)		

Contd....

Particulars		Dr. Rs	Cr. Rs
Suspense Account	Dr.	100	
To Sales Account			100
(Being the mistake in totalling of Sales Account rectified)			
Supplier*	Dr.	225	
To Suspense Account			225
(Being wrong posting from the day book)			
Sales Returns Account	Dr.	100	
To Suspense Account			100
(Being the sales return from a party not posted to Sales Returns Account, now adjusted)			
Sundry Creditors	Dr.	500	
To Purchases Account			500
(Being the payment made to supplier wrongly posted to purchases account, now rectified)			
Sundry Debtors	Dr.	100	
To Suspense Account			100
(Being the sales wrongly credited to Customer's Account, now rectified)			

*It has been assumed that the day-book is the Purchase Day Book hence only the Supplier's Account has been posted wrongly (credit of Rs 250 instead of Rs 25). If, however, by day-book is meant a book in which all transactions are recorded and posted to the ledger therefrom it would mean that both Supplier's Account and Purchases Account are wrongly posted.

Dr.   SUSPENSE ACCOUNT   Cr.

Particulars	Rs	Particulars	Rs
To Expense Account	50	By Difference in Trial Balance	150
To Sales Account	100	By Sundry Creditors	225
To Balance c/d	425	By Sales Returns Account	100
		By Sundry Debtors	100
	575		575
		By Balance b/d	425

Since the Suspense Account does not balance, it is clear that all the errors have not been traced. As a result of the above corrections, the Net Profit will stand increased by Rs 550 as shown below:

Particulars	Increase Rs	Decrease Rs
Mistake in totalling in "Expenses"	50	
Mistake in totalling in "Sales"	100	
Mistake in posting from day book to Ledger under "Purchases"	500	
Omission in posting under "Sales Returns"		100
	650	100
Net Increase	550	

1.264

Rectification of Errors through Profit & Loss Adjustment Account

Illustration 11.5, given before indicates that on account of errors in the year 1990 and their subsequent rectification in the year 1991 according to the procedure which has been followed in the preceding pages, the figures of profits both for 1990 and 1991 are wrong. The profit of 1990 has been unnecessarily reduced by Rs 5,646 on account of these errors while the profit for 1991 has unnecessarily been increased by the same amount on account of the rectification of errors in that year. It is, therefore, considered advisable to find out separately the effect of rectification of these errors on the profit of the business. Such profit or loss can be added to or subtracted from the profit of the year in which the errors were committed. Thus, the true profits for both the years (i.e., for the year in which errors were committed and the year in which the errors are rectified) can be found out. This is done by opening a Profit & Loss Adjustment Account. The Profit & Loss Adjustment Account is debited or credited while passing rectifying accounting entries in place of those accounts which relate to Trading and Profit & Loss Account. This will be clear with the help of the following illustration.

Illustration 11.8. Taking Illustration 11.1 as the basis, pass the necessary rectifying journal entries (without narratives) if the rectification of errors has to be done through Profit and Loss Adjustment Account.

Solution:

Sl. No.	Particulars		Dr. Amount Rs	Cr. Amount Rs
1.	Suspense A/c	Dr.	1,080	
	To M. Mehta			1,080.
2.	Suspense A/c	Dr.	200	
	To Profit & Loss Adjustment A/c			200
3.	Suspense A/c	Dr.	200	
	To Profit & Loss Adjustment A/c			200
4.	Profit & Loss Adjustment A/c	Dr.	574	
	To Motor Car A/c			174
	To Suspense A/c			400
5.	Profit & Loss Adjustment A/c	Dr.	180	
	To Sethi			180
6.	Kalra	Dr.	500	
	To Suspense A/c			500
7.	Machinery A/c	Dr.	6,000	
	To Profit & Loss Adjustment A/c			6,000

The Profit & Loss Adjustment Account will now appear as follows:

Dr.　　　　　PROFIT & LOSS ADJUSTMENT ACCOUNT　　　　　Cr.

Particulars	Rs	Particulars	Rs
To Motor Car Ac	174	By Suspense A/c	200
To Suspense A/c	400	By Suspense A/c	200
To Sethi	180	By Machinery A/c	6,000
To Balance (being increase in profit)	5,646		
	6,400		6,400

The balance shown by the Profit & Loss Adjustment Account. Rs 5,646 (increase in profit) will either be added to the balance of profit brought forward in the accounts of 1991 from last year (in case of limited companies) or be transferred to the Capital Account (s) in all other cases.

Illustration 11.9. Mr. Roy was unable to agree the Trial Balance last year and wrote off the difference to the profit and loss account of that year. Next year, he appointed a Chartered Accountant who examined the old books and found the following mistakes:

(1) Purchase of a scooter was debited to conveyance account Rs 3,000.

(2) Purchase account was over-cast by Rs 10,000.

(3) A credit purchase of goods from Mr. *P*, for Rs 2,000 was entered as a sale.

(4) Receipt of cash from Mr. *A* was posted to the account of Mr. *B*., Rs 1,000.

(5) Receipt of cash from Mr. *C* was posted to the debit of his account Rs 500.

(6) Rs 500 due by Mr. *Q* was omitted to be taken to trial balance.

(7) Sales of goods to Mr. *R* for Rs 2,000 was omitted to be recorded.

(8) Payment of Rs 2,395 for purchase was wrongly posted as Rs 2,593.

(9) Mr. Roy used to charge 10% depreciation on vehicles.

Suggest the necessary rectification entries.

Solution:

JOURNAL OF MR. ROY

Sl. No.	Particulars		Dr. Rs	Cr. Rs
(1)	Motor Vehicles Account	Dr.	2,700	
	To Profit & Loss Adjustment Account			2,700
	(Purchase of scooter wrongly debited to conveyance account now rectified capitalisation of Rs 2,700 i.e., Rs 3,000 *less* 10% depreciation)			
(2)	Suspense Account	Dr.	10,000	
	To Profit and Loss Adjustment Account			10,000
	(Purchase Account overcast in the previous year, error now rectified)			
(3)	Profit & Loss Adjustment Account	Dr.	4,000	
	To P			4,000
	(Credit purchase from P, Rs 2,000 entered as sales last year, now rectified)			
(4)	B	Dr.	1,000	
	To A			1,000
	(Amount received from A wrongly posted to the account of B; now rectified)			
(5)	Suspense Account	Dr.	1,000	
	To C			1,000
	(Rs 500 received from C wrongly debited to his account; now rectified)			
(6)	Sundry Debtors (Q)	Dr.	500	
	To Suspense Account			500
	(Rs 500 due by Q not taken into trial balance, now rectified)			
(7)	R	Dr.	2,000	
	To Profit & Loss Adjustment A/c			2,000
	(Sales to R omitted last year, now adjusted)			

Contd....

Sl. No.	Particulars		Dr. Rs	Cr. Rs
(8)	Suspense Account	Dr.	198	
	To Profit & Loss Adjustment A/c			198
	(Excess posting to purchase account last year, Rs 2,953, instead of Rs 2,395, now adjusted)			
(9)	Profit & Loss Adjustment A/c	Dr.	10,898	
	To Roy's Capital A/c			10,898
	(Balance of Profit & Loss Adjustment Account transferred to Capital Account)			
(10)	Roy's Capital Account	Dr.	10,698	
	To Suspense Account			10,698
	(Balance of Suspense Account transferred to the Capital Account)			

PROFIT AND LOSS ADJUSTMENT ACCOUNT

Particulars	Rs	Particulars	Rs
To P	4,000	By Motor Vehicles A/c	2,700
To Roy's Capital (Transfer)	10,898	By Profit & Loss Adjust. A/c	10,000
		By R	2,000
		By Suspense A/c	198
	14,898		14,898

SUSPENSE ACCOUNT

Particulars	Rs	Particulars	Rs
To Profit & Loss Adjust. A/c	10,000	By Sundry Debtors (Q)	500
To C	1,000	By Roy's Capital A/c (transfer)	10,698
To Profit & Loss Adjust. A/c	198		
	11,198		11,198

Illustration 11.10. The Profit and Loss Account of a business for the year ended 30th June, 1985 and its Balance Sheet as at that date, were prepared after making the following adjustments:

(*i*) Depreciation, on time basis, was charged on Machinery and Furniture at 10% p.a. and on Motor-Car at 20% p.a.

(*ii*) A provision for bad debts was created at 2% on the outstanding debtors on the closing date.

(*iii*) The difference in Trial Balance was carried to the Balance Sheet as a Suspense Account.

In the subsequent year, the following errors were discovered:

(*a*) Wages included a sum of Rs 5,000 for the installation of a new machine on 1st October, 1984.

(*b*) A credit invoice of Rs 2,000 was omitted to be passed through the Sales Day Book. Subsequently, a cheque for Rs 1,000 was received from the party as a part payment, was credited to Creditors' Account.

(*c*) Certain items of old Furniture, whose book value on 1st July, 1984 was Rs 2,500 were disposed of for Rs 1,300 on 1st April, 1985. This sum of Rs 1,300 was credited, through the cash book, to Motor-car Account.

(d) Cash paid to creditors Rs 1,200 was posted to the credit of Creditors Account as Rs 200.

(e) Rent of office building paid in advance for Rs 1,500 was debited to Rent Account.

You are required to pass necessary rectification entries in respect of the above.

Solution:

JOURNAL

Particulars		Dr. Rs	Cr. Rs
Machinery Account	Dr.	4,625	
To Profit & Loss Adjustment A/c			4,625
(Being wrong debit to Wages A/c for installation of a new machinery on 1st October now rectified: Cost Rs 5,000 *less* Rs 375 depreciation for 9 months)			
Sundry Debtors A/c	Dr.	1,000	
Sundry Creditors A/c	Dr.	1,000	
To Profit & Loss Adj. A/c			1,980
To Provision or Bad Debts A/c			20
(Adjustment entries being made for omission to enter the credit invoice for Rs 2,000 in the Sales Day Book and wrong credit to Sundry Creditors A/c for part payment of the amount due and Provision for Bad Debts @ 2% on Rs 1,000)			
Motor Car A/c	Dr.	1,235	
Profit & Loss Adjustment A/c	Dr.	1,015	
To Furniture A/c			2,250
(Rectification of (*i*) Omission of credit to furniture on sale present book value Rs 2,500 *less* depreciation Rs 250 *i.e.*, Rs 2,250; (*ii*) Wrong credit to motor Car, necessitating lower depreciation charge of Rs 65 reducing the wrong credit to Rs 1,235)			
Sundry Creditors A/c	Dr.	1,400	
To Suspense A/c			1,400
(Wrong credit to Sundry Creditors A/c on payment to creditors now rectified)			
Rent paid in Advance A/c	Dr.	1,500	
To Profit & Loss Adjustment A/c			1,500
(Rent paid in advance, shown as Rent now adjusted)			
Profit & Loss Adjustment A/c	Dr.	7,090	
To Capital Account			7,090
(Profit on rectification transferred to Capital A/c)			

Rectification of Errors through Capital Account

Sometimes the difference in the Trial Balance is transferred to Capital Account in place of the Suspense Account. The Final Accounts are than prepared. In such a case, rectifying entries are passed on errors being found out in the usual way, as explained earlier. However, the balance of the Suspense Account, opened for rectifying the errors, is transferred to the Capital Account. Similarly the balance in the Profit & Loss Adjustment Account (if any) is also transferred to the Capital Account. This willl be clear with the help of the following illustration.

Illustration 11.10. A firm found that its Trial Balance on 31.12.1990 did not agree. The difference was transferred to the Capital Account. You are required to pass the necessary correcting entries (without narratives) to rectify the errors in a way not to affect the profit or loss of 1991, the year in which the errors have been discovered.

(a) While carrying forward the figure of Rs 459, in the account of Yusuf, a creditor, from one page to another, it was written as Rs 495 on debit side.

(b) Sale of office furniture Rs 760 was entered in the Sales Book as Rs 670, and was posted in the account of the Purchaser on the credit side.

(c) Cash received Rs 400 from M. Ray was debited to the account of N. Ray in the personal ledger.

(d) Customs Duty Rs 2,500 paid on plant and equipment was debited to the Customs Duty account as Rs 250.

Solution:

JOURNAL

Sl. No.	Particulars		L.F.	Dr. Rs	Cr. Rs
(a)	Suspense A/c	Dr.		954	
	To Yusuf				954
(b)	Profit & Loss Adjustment A/c	Dr.		670	
	Purchaser's A/c	Dr.		1,430	
	To Furniture A/c				760
	To Suspense A/c				1,340
(c)	Suspense A/c	Dr.		800	
	To M. Ray				400
	To N. Ray				400
(d)	Plant & Equipment A/c	Dr.		2,500	
	To Profit & Loss Adjustment A/c				250
	To Suspense A/c				2,250
(e)	Suspense A/c	Dr.		1,836	
	To Capital A/c				1,836
(f)	Capital A/c	Dr.		420	
	To Profit & Loss Adjustment A/c				420

Notes:

(a) The account of Yusuf was debited by Rs 495 instead of being credited by Rs 459. His account has, therefore, now been credited by Rs 954 (Rs 459 + Rs 495) in order to cancel wrong debit and give him the correct credit.

(b) This is a multiple error. The following accounts were affected by this error (i) Sales Account, (ii) Furniture Account, (iii) Purchaser's Account. Sale of office furniture should not have been entered in the Sales Book. It was done. The Sales Account was therefore credited by Rs 670. In order to rectify the error, the Sales Account should be debited by Rs 670. Since, the rectifying entry should not affect the current year's profit, the P. & L. Adjustment Account has been debited instead of

Sales Account. The Furniture Account should have been credited by Rs 760. It was not done. It has therefore been credited by Rs 760. The Purchaser's Account should have been debited by Rs 760, but it has been credited by Rs 670 from the Sales Book. His account has, therefore been debited by Rs 1,430 (Rs 670 + 760) in order to correct it.

(c) The two accounts involved are the account of M. Ray and N. Ray. The cash received should have been credited to the account of M. Ray. His account was not credited. It has, therefore, been credited now. On the other hand, the account of N. Ray was unnecessarily debited. It has also, therefore, been credited now.

(d) The customs duty paid on plant and equipment should have been debited, to the Plant and Equipment Account. It was not done. The Plant & Equipment Account has, therefore, been debited by Rs 2,500. Customs Duty Account was unnecessarily debited by Rs 250. It should therefore be credited by Rs 250. Since, the rectification of errors should not affect current year's profit; therefore, the Profit & Loss Adjustment Account has been credited by Rs 250 instead Customs Duty Account.

(e) The balance of the Suspense Accounts has been transferred to the Capital Account, since, the difference in the Trial Balance was also transferred earlier in the Capital Account. The balance of Rs 1,836 in the Suspense Account has been found out as follows:

Dr.   SUSPENSE ACCOUNT   Cr.

Particulars	Rs	Particulars	Rs
To Yusuf	954	By Sundries	1,340
To Sundries	800	By Plant and Equipment A/c	2,250
To Balance transferred to Capital A/c	1,836		
	3,590		3,590

(f) The balance shown by the Profit & Loss Adjustment Account has been transferred to the Capital Account. The balance of Rs 420 has been arrived at as follows:

PROFIT & LOSS ADJUSTMENT ACCOUNT

Particulars	Rs	Particulars	Rs
To Sundries	670	By Plant & Equipment A/c	250
		By Balance transferred to Capital A/c	420
	670		670

Alternative treatment. In illustration given above, the Suspense Account has been opened. Alternatively, the Suspense Account may not have been opened and the Capital Account could have been debited or credited in place of the Suspense Account, since the question says that the difference in the Trial Balance had been transferred to the Capital Account. This could have saved passing of one entry for transferring the balance of Suspense Account to the Capital Account. However, the method explained above is preferable since it also informs the accountant the extent to which the difference in the Trial Balance has been adjusted. The accountant can verify from last year's Trial Balance whether the whole of the difference as shown by the last year's Trial Balance has been adjusted or not or there are still some errors to be located out.

KEY TERMS

☐ **Compensating Errors:** Errors which compensate each other.

☐ **Errors of Omission:** Errors committed because of complete omission of a transaction from the books of accounts.

☐ **Errors of Commission:** Errors on account of wrong balancing of an account, wrong posting, wrong carry forward, wrong totalling, etc.

☐ **Errors of Principle:** Errors committed because of failure to make a proper distinction between revenue and capital items.

☐ **Suspense Account:** An account to which the difference in the trial balance has been put temporarily.

TEST QUESTIONS

Objective type | TEST YOUR UNDERSTANDING

1. State whether each of the following statements is 'True' or 'False':

    (a) Error of omission does not affect the agreement of the Trial Balance.

    (b) Errors of Principle affect the agreement of the Trial Balance.

    (c) If the two sides of the Trial Balance tally, the books of accounts can be taken as absolutely accurate.

    (d) Errors of Commission are committed in those cases where proper distinction between revenue and capital items is not made.

    (e) All errors affect the agreement of the Trial Balance.

    (f) In case the difference of the two sides of the Trial Balance is divisible by 9, it can be presumed that the amount has been put on the wrong side.

    (g) Profit and Loss Adjustment Account is used for rectifying errors when it is intended that rectification of errors should not affect the current year's profit.

    [**Ans.** (a) True, (b) False, (c) False, (d) False, (e) False, (f) False, (g) True].

2. Choose the most appropriate answer:

    (i) Sales to Ram Rs 336 posted to his account as Rs 363 would affect.

    (a) Sales Account, (b) Ram's Account, (c) Cash Account.

    (ii) Sales to Ram of Rs 500 not recorded in the books would affect:

    (a) Sales Account, (b) Ram's Account, (c) Sales Account and Ram's Account.

    (iii) Carriage charges paid for a new plant purchased if debited to carriage account would affect:

    (a) Plant Account, (b) Carriage Account, (c) Plant and Carriage Account.

    (iv) A sale of Rs 100 to A recorded in the Purchases Book would affect:

    (a) Sales Account, (b) Purchases Returns Account, (c) Sales Account, Purchases Account and A's Account.

    (v) A purchases returns of Rs 200 to P if entered in the Sales Book would affect:

    (a) P's Account, (b) Purchases Returns Account, (c) Sales Account, (d) Purchases Returns Account and Sales Account.

    (vi) An amount of Rs 200 received from P credited to Q would affect:

    (a) Account of P and Q, (b) Cash Account, (c) P's Account.

    (vii) A sum of Rs 200 written off as bad debt now received credited to the account of the debtor would:

(a) increase the net profit by Rs 200, (b) decrease the profit by Rs 200, (c) no effect on profit.

(viii) Goods purchased from A for Rs 2,000 passed through the Sales Book. The rectification of error will result in:

(a) increase of gross profit, (b) decrease of gross profit, (c) no effect on gross profit.

[**Ans.** (i) (b),(ii) (c), (iii) (c), (iv) (c), (v) (d), (vi) (a), (vii) (b), (viii) (b)].

Essay type | FOR REVIEW, DISCUSSION AND PRACTICE |

1. Explain the different types of errors with suitable examples and state how they affect the Trial Balance.
2. "A Trial Balance is only a *prima facie* evidence of the accuracy of the books of account". Comment.
3. In case of disagreement of the Trial Balance what steps would you take to locate the errors.

PRACTICAL PROBLEMS

1. Rectify the following errors:
   (i) Furniture purchased for Rs 250 was debited to Purchases Account.
   (ii) A sum of Rs 100 paid to Ram was debited to Shyam's Account.
   (iii) A Bill Receivable for Rs 500 received from Ram has been omitted to be entered.
   (iv) Goods worth Rs 200 taken away by the proprietor were debited to B.
   (v) An engine purchased for Rs 1,250 had been posted to Purchases Account.

2. Rectify the following errors:
   (i) Wages paid for the construction of office debited to wages account Rs 1,500.
   (ii) Cartage paid for the newly purchased furniture Rs 10, posted to Cartage Account.
   (iii) Furniture purchased on credit from Ram for Rs 300 posted as Rs 30.
   (iv) Sales to X Rs 400, posted to Y's account.
   (v) Wages paid Rs 2,550 were recorded in the cash book as Rs 2,505.
   (vi) Purchases from Y Rs 1,002 were omitted from the books.

3. Rectify the following errors:
   (i) While posting from the Sales Book, a personal account was credited by Rs 1,000 instead of being debited.
   (ii) Furniture purchased for Rs 4,000 was debited to Purchases Account.
   (iii) Atma Ram returned goods worth Rs 2,000. No entry was passed in the books to this effect.
   (iv) Rs 750 paid to Ram Prasad for salary for the months of January was debited to his personal account.
   (v) Goods sold to Babu Ram for Rs 1,350 were entered in the Sales Books as Rs 1,530.

4. On 31st March, 1989 while balancing the books of account of Shri Ramdass, they did not agree. The difference in Trial Balance amounting to Rs 783 was debited to Suspense Account. Later, the following errors were noticed. Give the Journal entries for rectification and prepare the Suspense Account:
   (a) The total of Purchases Book for March, 1989 has been undercast by Rs 30.
   (b) Rs 228 paid for repairing the Machinery has been debited to Machinery Account.
   (c) The Sales Book has been overcast by Rs 150.
   (d) A Sales of Rs 1,200 to Mr. David has been passed through the Purchases Book.
   (e) Cash Rs 117 received from Shri M. Das, though entered in the Cash Book has not been posted to Shri M. Das's account.
   (f) Goods returned by Mr. N. Navin Rs 225 have been entered in the Returns Outwards Book. However, Mr. N. Navin's account is correctly posted. (*C.A. Entrance, Nov., 1989*)

5. Write out the journal entries to rectify the following errors using a Suspense Account:

(1) The total of 'Discount Allowed" from the Cash Book for the month of December, 1992 amounting to Rs 350 was not posted.

(2) An amount of Rs 175 entered in the Sales Return Book has been posted to the debit of Mr. Roberts who returned the goods.

(3) Bad debts aggregating Rs 250 were written off during the year in the sales ledger but were not adjusted in the general ledger.

(4) Goods of the value of Rs 500 returned by Mr. Smith were entered in the Sales Day Book and posted therefrom to the credit of his account.

(5) A sales of Rs 800 made to Mr. Peter was correctly entered in the Sales Day Book but wrongly posted to the debit of Mr. Armstrong as Rs 80.

[**Ans.** Opening Balance Suspense Account (Dr.) Rs 1,720].

6. In 1990 Mr. Parekh found that his books for the year 1989 contained some errors in spite of an agreed Trial Balance The errors were:

(1) A invoice for Rs 50 for goods purchased from Mr. Balu was entered in Sales Returns, Book; in the ledger, this was debited to the account of Mr. Balu.

(2) Goods bought on credit from Mr. Kishan for Rs 150 were entered in the Sales Book as Rs 105. Mr. Kishan's account was credited with this amount of Rs 105.

(3) The Sales Book for the month of April, 1989 was overcast by Rs 150.

(4) A sale of Rs 257 to Mr. Dutt was entered in the Sales Book as Rs 527. Mr. Dutt was debited with Rs 752.

(5) Rs 79 paid for freight on machinery was debited to Freight Account as Rs 97.

Give journal entries to rectify the errors using a Suspense Account where necessary.

[**Ans.** Suspense Account shows a closing credit balance of Rs 17, showing that some errors are still to be traced].

7. Pass Journal Entries to rectify the following errors:

(1) A cheque of Rs 750 received for loss of stock by fire had been deposited in the proprietor's Private Bank Account.

(2) An item of purchase of Rs 151 was entered in the Purchase Book as Rs 15 and posted to the Supplier's A/c as Rs 51.

(3) A sale return of Rs 500 was not entered in the financial accounts though it was duly taken in the stock book.

(4) An amount of Rs 300 was received in full settlement from a customer after he was allowed a discount of Rs 50 but while writing the books, the amount received was entered in the Discount Column and the Discount allowed was entered in the Cash Column.

(5) Bill receivable from Mr. A of Rs 1,000 was posted to the credit of Bills Payable Account and also credited to the A/c of Mr. A.

[**Ans.** Opening balance in Suspense A/c Rs 2,036 (Dr.)].

8. State which of the following errors will affect the agreement of the Trial Balance and which will not. Give rectifying journal entries wherever relevant assuming the difference in trial Balance has been placed to Suspense Account.

(i) Purchase of a second-hand Motor Car for Rs 15,000 has been debited to Motor Car Maintenance Account.

(ii) A sale of Rs 5,000 to Shriram has been wrongly entered in the Sales Day Book as Rs 500.

(iii) An entry in the Purchases Returns Book of Rs 2,000 has been omitted to be posted in the Account of Shri Ramji, the Supplier.

(iv) An amount of Rs 2,000 received from Shrikant has been posted to the credit of Shriman as Rs 200.

(v) The total of the Sales Day Book for the month of July, Rs 1,50,000 has been omitted to be posted in the ledger.

> [**Ans.** Errors (iii), (iv) and (v) will affect the agreement of the Trial Balance. Remaining errors [viz, (i) and (ii)], however will not affect the agreement of the Trial Balance].

9. An accountant could not tally the Trial Balance. The difference was temporarily placed to Suspense Account for preparing the final accounts. The following errors were later discovered.
   (a) The Sales Book was undercast by Rs 50.
   (b) Entertainment expenses Rs 95, though entered in the Cash Book were omitted to be posted in the Ledger.
   (c) Discount column of the receipt side of the Cash Book was wrongly added as Rs 140 instead of Rs 120.
   (d) Commission of Rs 25 paid, was posted twice, once to discount account and once to commission account.
   (e) A Sale of Rs 139 to Ramanlal though correctly entered in sales book, was posted wrongly to his account as Rs 193.
   (f) A Purchase from Niranjan of Rs 92 though correctly entered in purchase book, was wrongly debited to his personal account.

   You are required to:
   (i) Pass the necessary rectifying entries,
   (ii) Prepare Suspense Account, and
   (iii) State the effect of each of the rectification on the profit.

   What would be the correct profit if the profit originally arrived at was Rs 10,000?

   > [**Ans.** Suspense Account, Opening Balance Rs 238 (Cr.). Correct Profit Rs 10,000)].

10. Messrs Modern Chemicals were unable to agree the Trial Balance on 30th June, 1989 and have raised a Suspense Account for the difference.

    Later the following errors were discovered and rectified and the Suspense Account was balanced.
    (a) The addition of the "Sundry Purchases" column in the Tabular Purchases Journal was short by Rs 150 and other totals were in order.
    (b) A Bill of Exchange (received from Gupta) for Rs 2,000 had been returned by the Bank as dishonoured and had been credited to the Bank and debited to Bills Receivable Account.
    (c) Goods of the value of Rs 105 returned by the customer, Thomas, had been posted to the debit to Thomas and also to the Sales Returns.
    (d) Sundry items of Furniture sold for Rs 3,000 had been entered in the Sales Day Book, the total of which had been posted to Sales Account.
    (e) An amount of Rs 600 due from Vaz, a customer, had been omitted from the Schedule of Sundry Debtors.
    (f) Discounts amounting to Rs 30 allowed to a customer had been duly posted in his account, but not posted to Discount Account.
    (g) Insurance premium of Rs 450 paid on 30th June, 1988 for the year ended 30th June 1989 had not been brought forward.
        (i) Pass Journal Entries to rectify the above mistakes.
        (ii) Draw up the Suspense Account after rectifying the above mistakes and explain how the above errors affect the book profit for the year ended 30th June, 1989.

    > [**Ans.** Suspense Account Opening Balance (Dr.) Rs 1,020; Profit for 1988–89 overstated by Rs 3,630].

11. The undermentioned errors were discovered in the books of Shri Ramnarayan after the Profit and Loss Account had been prepared for the year ended 31st March, 1986. The difference in

1.274

Trial Balance was carried to suspense account in the Balance Sheet. Shri Ramnarayan provided depreciation on Machinery at 10% p.a. and on Furniture at 5% p.a. A Reserve for Bad Debts was provided at 2% on outstanding debtors. Net profit for the year was transferred to Capital Account.

(a) A cheque received for Rs 8,000 from a customer was not posted to ledger. The corresponding Sales Invoice was for Rs 12,000 which had been wrongly passed through the Sales Day Book as Rs 2,000.

(b) A machinery purchased for Rs 20,000 on 1st April, 1985 was wrongly debited to Furniture Account.

(c) Sales included Rs 25,000 for goods sold for cash on behalf of Shri Chandrakant. Shri Ramnarayan was entitled to a Commission of 10% on sales plus expenses for which no adjustment was made. His trade expenses included Rs 1,500 as selling expenses in connection with the above sale.

(d) Some old furniture (book value on 1st April, 1985 Rs 6,000) was disposed of for Rs 3,000 on 30th Sept. 1985 but the proceeds had been wrongly credited to Sales Account.

(e) A Credit Sale for Rs 5,000 had been passed twice through the Sales Day Book.

[Ans. Capital Account debited by Rs 22,640 being debit balance in P & L Adj. A/c].

12. The annual accounts of Patel Chemical Works prepared on 31st December, disclosed a net profit of Rs 48,576 and the Balance Sheet total of Rs 1,35,427. These accounts were, however, prepared without any regard to the following matters which relate to the year in question:

(a) Goods valued at Rs 750 were purchased, received and taken into stock, but were not recorded in the books.

(b) Expenses outstanding: Wages Rs 950; Salaries Rs 450; Advertisement Rs 250; Law Charges Rs 100; Electricity Charges Rs 175.

(c) Interest accrued on investments Rs 375.

(d) Goods costing Rs 250 were taken away by the trader for his personal use, and goods costing Rs 500 were given away free to a hospital.

(e) Depreciation to be written off: Building Rs 2,500; Machinery Rs 12,500; Motor Vehicles Rs 3,500; Furniture Rs 300.

(f) A reserve of Rs 800 is to be created for bad and doubtful debts.

(g) Rs 650 cash stolen by an ex-employee stood debited to a Suspense Account.

Give journal entries to record these matter and show how the figure of net profit and the total of the Balance Sheet would be affected by them.

[Ans. Profit Rs 26,276; Total of Balance Sheet Rs 1,15,552].

Chapter 12

ACCOUNTING CONCEPT OF INCOME

LEARNING OBJECTIVES

After studying this chapter you should be able to:

- [ ] understand the concept of income;
- [ ] appreciate the effect of different accounting concepts on measurement of business income;
- [ ] explain the role of expired cost in income measurement;
- [ ] identify the different alternatives regarding recognition of the time when the income could be taken as realised;
- [ ] differentiate between Accountant's concept and Economist's concept of Capital and Income; and
- [ ] explain the meaning of certain key terms.

In a preceding Chapter, we have explained the preparation of the Income Statement (or Profit and Loss Account). The Income Statement measures the income of a business during a particular period of time. It is of greater importance than even the Balance Sheet since the main objective of running a business enterprise is to maximise business wealth and this depends to a great extent over the income which a business makes year after year. On account of this reason, management, workers, shareholders, government all have interest in proper preparation and presentation of the Income Statement. Since, income is the focal point of the Income Statement, it will be useful, for us to know correctly the meaning of the term Income and the problems in its determination. This is as a matter of fact the subject matter of this Chapter.

CONCEPT OF INCOME

In common parlance, the term Income means the reward or payment received in exchange for the production of goods and services. For example, the salary received by the clerk is his income, since it is the reward received by him for his services. Similarly, the rent received by the owner of a property is his income. It is the reward for the services rendered by him through his property. In case a craftsman earns some money by selling some of the articles made by him, the money so earned will be taken as the income of the craftsman.

Income may be of different types. *e.g.*, Personal Income, National Income, Business Income, Gross Income, Net Income, etc. The term Income, therefore, by itself cannot give any precise meaning unless it is used with some adjective.

In accounting, we are mainly concerned with Business Income, a term which is synonymous with the term Business Profit. It can be defined as the excess of the revenue over the expenditure incurred by the business over a period. According to Smith, "the Net Income for the period is the excess of revenues realised during the period by a specific accounting entity over the cost expired (including losses) during the same period".

The most accepted and authentic definition of Income is that which has been given by the American Accounting Association. It is being reproduced as follows:

"The Realised Net Income of an enterprise measures its effectiveness as an operative unit and is the change in its net assets arising out of (a) the excess or deficiency of revenue compared with related expired cost, and (b) other gains or losses to the enterprise from sales, exchange or other conversion of assets".

Thus, according to this definition, Income is the outcome of the following:

(i) Excess or deficiency of revenue over related expired cost, and

(ii) Gains or losses to the enterprise from sales, exchange or other conversion of assets.

Moreover, according to the American Accounting Association, the term Business Income includes realised net income and not income only. It means income will be considered to be business income only when it has been actually realised. Notional Income such as appreciation in the market value of the assets of the firm cannot be taken as business income unless the assets have really been disposed off.

The computation of income thus involves according to the definition given above, matching of the expired cost or expense with the revenue. This has already been explained in detail in a preceding Chapter. However, we propose to emphasise here the practical difficulties that are confronted by the accountant in measuring business income. These difficulties arise on account of two reasons:

(i) The measurement of accounting income is subject to several accounting concepts and conventions, and

(ii) Determination of the expired cost is a difficult exercise on account of complex series of business transactions of different multitudes.

ACCOUNTING CONCEPTS AND INCOME MEASUREMENT

Measurement of the accounting income is subject to a number of accounting concepts and conventions. These concepts and conventions have already been explained in detail in Chapter 2 of the book. We are giving below the impact of these concepts and conventions on measurement of the accounting income.

1. **Convention of conservatism.** According to the convention of conservatism the accountant always follows the policy of playing safe while determining business income. The conservatism principle thus seeks to ensure that the reported profit is not over-stated. However, it cannot be said that this principle ensure that the reported profit is not under-stated. The business income may be understated by providing excessive depreciation, excessive provision for doubtful debts, etc. Thus, the income as disclosed by the Financial Statements may not be the real income of the business.

2. **Consistency.** According to this concept, a business enterprise should be consistent in the accounting practice that it follows, in the treatment of its assets, liabilities, revenues and expenses. It may sometimes be difficult for the accountant to strictly follow the concept of consistency. Changes may be required in the treatment of different items on account of legal requirements or change in the accounting methods. For example, a concern may

change the method of valuation of its stock-in-trade or the method of charging depreciation from one year to another year. Such a change will result in determination of the accounting income on a different pattern than what has been done so far. Thus, the measurement of business income also depends to a great extent upon the basis which has been followed year after year regarding treatment of different items which form part of the Income Statement of the business. However, accounting profession and the corporate laws of most of the countries require that financial statement must be made out on the basis that figures stated are consistent with those of the preceding year. In case any changes in the accounting treatment are made, the resulting changes in profit or loss should be disclosed separately.

3. **Accounting period concept.** As a matter of fact, the income from a business enterprise can be precisely determined only at the end of its life, *i.e.*, when the business is finally closed down. However, in order to have an idea about the progress made by the business and to take remedial measures in time, business income is determined after the expiry of a reasonable period. Such a period is termed as 'accounting period'. The income disclosed by the Income Statement is the income made during the accounting period. However, this is only an interim report. The actual income earned by the business will be known only when the business is finally closed down. Thus, the measurement of accounting income is also subject to the Accounting Period Concept.

4. **Accrual concept.** The measurement of accounting income is also subject to the accrual concept. At the end of the accounting period, when the final accounts are prepared there may be many business activities at different stages of progress. Some of the goods might be lying unsold, some work may be still in progress, money may have still to be collected from the debtors etc. In accounting, the revenue is generally treated to be realised when the goods or services are furnished to the customers and not when cash or other valuable consideration has been received from them. It may be possible that some of the items for which the revenue has been treated as realised may not result in any revenue on account of subsequent non-payments. Thus, the income disclosed by the Income Statement may not be the real income of the business.

5. **Going concern concept.** The measurement of business income is also subject to the Going Concern Concept. According to this concept, it is assumed that the business will continue for a fairly long time. On account of this reason, the accountant charges depreciation on the fixed assets of the business not on the basis of their market values, but on the basis of their original cost. In case of inflationary economy charging of depreciation on the basis of original cost of the fixed assets while taking revenue on the basis of the current market prices may result in considerable overstatement of business income.

6. **Separate entity concept.** According to this concept, the business and the proprietor are taken as two different persons. Thus, income of the business cannot be taken as the income of the proprietor of the business. For example interest on capital, is income from the point of view of the proprietor of the business but it is an expense from the point of view of the business. Thus, one should not confuse "business income" with "personal income" of the proprietor of the business. Of course, ultimately the business income also becomes a part of the personal income of the proprietor.

EXPIRED COST AND INCOME MEASUREMENT

The definition of the business income as given by American Accounting Association states that the revenue has to be compared with the related expired cost (or expense) for the purpose or determination of business income. In other words, the expired cost or the expense has to be identified in some fashion or the other with one or more elements of revenue. In real life situations, it is extremely difficult and in many cases, it is almost impossible to achieve such identification. This is because in business there is not one transaction but there are a series of transactions of different varieties and magnitudes. Moreover, it is not always necessary that income during the accounting period is earned only on account of the cost or expenditure incurred during that accounting period. It may be a result of the efforts or expenditure which might have been made or incurred during the preceding few years. Similarly efforts or expenditure made or incurred during an accounting period may bring results in the years to come. It, therefore, becomes almost impossible to determine the actual cost incurred for a particular revenue which has been earned during the course of a particulars year. For example, goods purchased or manufactured during a particular period may not be sold in the year. They may be sold in the next year together with part or whole of the goods which have been manufactured or purchased during that year. Similarly, advertisement costs incurred during a particular period may bring benefit to the business only in the next few years. It is almost an impossible task in such cases to decide how much expenses have been incurred for the revenue which is being earned during the accounting period.

In order to give a better idea about the real problem faced by the accountant, in determining the real business income, we are explaining the problem on the basis of different types of costs which may be involved in the process of determination of business income.

For the purpose of cost analysis, we can divide the business concerns into two categories:

   (*i*) Trading Concerns, and

   (*ii*) Manufacturing concerns.

Trading concern purchase goods from outside sources and sell them at profitable prices Manufacturing concerns, on the other hand, purchase raw materials and convert them into finished goods through different manufacturing operations. The basic difference between trading concerns and manufacturing concerns lies in the kind of inventory they carry and the nature of the cost incurred. In case of trading concerns, the stock primarily consists of finished goods while in case of manufacturing concerns, stock may be of raw materials, work-in-progress or finished goods. In case of trading concerns, for the purposes of income determination, the cost of goods sold together with relevant other expenses such as administrative, selling and distribution expenses are to be compared with the revenue of the period, while in case of manufacturing concerns, the cost of goods manufactured and sold is to be compared with the revenue for the purpose of income determination. Thus, both in case of trading and manufacturing concerns, cost of goods sold has to be determined. While in case of trading concerns, the cost of goods sold depends upon the price at which the goods are purchased in case of manufacturing concerns, it depends upon the cost at which the goods have been manufactured. In both cases for determination of income made during a particular period, the operating expenses of the business have also to be considered. Besides, these costs, there are certain extraordinary expenses or losses such as losses due to natural calamities, development expenditure, etc., which are also to be considered for the purpose of determination of income. Thus, determination of business income requires determination of the expired cost or expense which may consist of the following types of costs; (*i*) Cost of goods sold which includes both direct and indirect costs, (*ii*) Inventory cost, (*iii*) Intangible cost, (*iv*) Imputed cost, (*v*) Extraordinary cost, etc. Determination of each of these costs is a complex and difficult affair. We are explaining below the problems faced by the accountant in determination of these costs.

(*i*) **Cost of goods sold/purchased.** Income determination requires in case of both manufacturing and trading concerns, the cost of goods sold. In case of trading concerns, the job is comparatively easy since the cost of goods sold can be easily found out be taking into account the cost at which the goods have been purchased. However, in case of manufacturing concerns, the cost of goods sold is to be found out taking into consideration the cost involved in their manufacture. Manufacturing costs can be both direct as well as indirect. Direct costs are those costs which can be directly, conveniently and wholly identified with specific products, jobs or manufacturing processes, *e.g.*, cost of raw materials used for manufacturing the products, cost of factory labour etc. Indirect manufacturing costs are those costs which cannot be directly be identified with specific jobs products or processes, *e.g.*, salary paid to the factory manager, rent, rates, lighting, depreciation of factory machines, etc. These cost are to be apportioned on different products on some reasonable basis *e.g.*, the salary paid to the factory manager may be charged to different products on the basis of direct wages for each product. Similarly, rent paid for the factory may be charged to different products on the basis of departmental area occupied by each of the production departments. Apportionment of the indirect costs so made cannot be fairly accurate and, therefore, the cost of the products so computed cannot also be very accurate. Moreover, some costs such as depreciation of plant and machinery or depreciation of factory buildings cannot themselves be determined accurately. Depreciation depends on the cost of the assets, its scrap value and the estimated life of the assets. It is very difficult to make a fair estimate about the scrap value and life of the asset. The amount of depreciation charged may not, therefore, be very correct. Thus, when estimation of the various elements which constitute cost cannot correctly by made, the measurement of income on the basis of such estimates cannot also be very accurate.

(*ii*) **Inventory cost.** The term Inventory includes (*i*) Stock of raw materials, (*ii*) Stock of work-in-progress, and (*iii*) Stock of finished Goods. The computation of the cost of inventory is also a tedious process. The valuation of the stock of raw materials will depend upon the method of pricing materials issues followed by the business. Materials may be issued to production according to First In First Out (*FIFO*) Method, Last In First Out (*LIFO*) Method, Weighted Average Price Method, etc. In each of these cases, the value of the inventory of raw materials may widely differ. This will be clear with the help of the following example.

A business buys raw materials in two different lots. In the first lot 1,000 units are purchased @ Rs 10 per unit. In the second lot, 2,000 units are purchased @ Rs 12 per unit. In case the stock of raw materials at the end of the accounting period is of 1,000 units, the value of the inventory according to each of the methods stated above will be as follows:

(*a*) **FIFO method:**

1,000 Units @ Rs 12 per unit = Rs 12,000
(Since materials first purchased will be taken to have been issued to production first of all, the inventory of raw material will, therefore, consist of latest purchases).

(*b*) **LIFO method:**

1,000 Units @ Rs 10 per unit = Rs 10,000
(Since materials purchased in the last will be taken to have been issued to

production first of all, the inventory will, therefore, consist of the earliest purchases).

(c) **Weighted Average Price Method:**

1,000 Units @ Rs 11.333 = Rs 11,333

(The total units purchased are 3,000 for a total cost of Rs 34,000. This gives a weighted average price Rs 11.333 per unit).

Whatever has been said about stock of raw materials, is also true for stock of work-in-progress and finished goods. In case of work-in-progress, it may be valued at the factory cost or the total cost of production. The stock of finished goods is based on the principle of cost or market price whichever is less. Thus, the value of inventory may have no relevance with the actual costs incurred for purchasing or manufacturing the items involved in inventory valuation.

Further problems arise when the goods are sold. According to the matching concept, the costs are to be identified with the revenue earned. This is again a tedious task. It may be almost impossible to identify the cost of goods sold with the volume of sales made during a particular period because the cost of goods sold will again depend upon *FIFO*, *LIFO* or Average Method which may have been followed by a firm. Thus, determination of exact income made during a particular period is almost impossible.

(*iii*) **Intangible cost.** The determination of the cost of intangible assets such as patents, goodwill, trade marks, etc., used in earning revenue poses another problem in determination of the income made by a business during a particular period. In case of some of these assets, such as patents, trade marks copy rights, licenses, etc., which have a definite legal life, the determination of the cost is not difficult. However, difficulty arises in case of assets like goodwill, heavy advertisement expenditure, preliminary expenses, whose utility life cannot be exactly determined. The cost incurred for acquisition of these assets or in respect of these assets is written off from the Profit and Loss Accounts of several years on some arbitrary basis. This brings inexactness in determination of the business income.

(*iv*) **Imputed costs.** In determining business income, some imputed cost such as interest on capital, salary for the proprietor, rent of the building owned by the proprietor and used for the business purposes, are considered. These costs are only notional costs and are taken into account only for managerial decision-making. For example, when a person intends to start a business with an investment of Rs 1,00,000, he should take into account, before deciding whether to start business or not, the interest that he could have earned on his investment (in the business) and the salary that he could have earned otherwise. However, the charge for interest or the charge for salary is made on a notional basis. Their amounts cannot be exactly determined Thus, the income computed after taking into account these notional charges cannot be taken as the real income of the business.

(*v*) **Extraordinary costs.** In business, certain extraordinary costs or some extraordinary losses, may also be incurred. Extraordinary expenditure might be incurred because of change in business policy or strategy in response to external events, *e.g.*, when certain production facilities are abandoned or new lines of production are taken up due to reasons beyond management's control, factory premises may have to be shifted from one place to another on account of legal requirements, etc. There may be some extraordinary losses due to natural calamities or accidents, *e.g.*, losses due to floods, fire, etc. Identification of these costs or losses with the revenue cannot be made. Abnormal losses such as those on account of fire, etc., are usually not carried forward. They are charged against the revenue of the period in which they are incurred while unusual costs such as those resulting on account of shifting of factory or office premises may be spreaded over a period of 2–3 years in case they are heavy in amount. This is not exactly according to the Matching Cost Principle.

REALISATION PRINCIPLE AND INCOME MEASUREMENT

It has already been stated that the American Accounting Association has laid emphasis on the realisation aspect of income while defining the term Income. It is, therefore, very important to decide at what time the income or the revenue should be taken as realised. While explaining matching of cost with the revenue with the preceeding Chapter, we have dealt with this aspect in brief. However, here we are discussing this aspect in detail.

There are four distinct alternatives regarding recognition of the time when the revenue/income could be taken as realised.

(i) Recognition at the time of sale.

(ii) Recognition at the time of when sales value is collected.

(iii) Recognition when production is completed.

(iv) Recognition proportionately over the performance of the contract.

All these alternatives are being explained in the following pages.

(i) **Recognition at the time of sale.** This is the most common basis of revenue recognition. The objective of manufacturing or purchasing goods is achieved in the business when the goods are sold away. Thus, income is deemed to be realised when a sale in the ordinary course of business is effected unless the circumstances are such that collection of the sales price is not reasonably assured. From the legal point of view, the sale is taken to be completed when the ownership in goods is transferred from the seller to the buyer. It should be noted that transfer of ownership does not depend on delivery of goods or payment of the price. Both of these obligations may be performed in future also. What is necessary is that the buyer should be responsible to take delivery of the goods or make payment of the price for them. Whether, he takes delivery of goods or makes payment of the price now or later is immaterial. Difficulties arise in recognising revenue in case of those businesses which are engaged in providing services rather than selling of goods, e.g., public utility concerns such as Electricity Companies, Water Works, Railways, etc. In case of such businesses, the revenue should be taken to be realised when the invoicing or billing is done for furnishing of services. In other words, accrual basis is the most appropriate basis for recognition of revenue in such cases.

(ii) **Recognition at the time when sales value is collected.** Many concerns use the cash basis for recognising revenue rather than the accrual basis. In case of accrual basis, as explained above, revenue is taken to be realised when the payment for goods or services becomes due to the business. For example, in case of trading business, revenue will be taken to have been realised when the goods have been sold though the payment might be received later on. This is because as the goods have been sold away, the business becomes entitled to receive payment for them. In case, cash basis is followed, the revenue will be taken to have been realised only when payment for goods or services has been actually received. This basis for recognising revenue is generally followed in case of sale of goods on instalment system (*i.e.*, a system where sales value is to be collected in agreed number of instalments). The basis is not very satisfactory because it fails to match cost with the revenue in those case cases where there is a considerable time lag between sale of goods or rendering of services and receiving payment for them.

(*iii*) **Recognition when the production is completed.** It is generally recognised that income accrues only at the time of sale and gain should not be anticipated by reflecting assets at their current market prices. However, in case of certain industries where products have an immediate marketability at more or less fixed prices, the revenue may be recognised as soon as the production is completed. The amount of income earned is the excess of the estimated sale prices of the products completed over the costs of their production or extraction. However, any expenditure incurred in the disposal of these products should be charged to such income and should be disclosed fully in the financial statements. This is particularly true in case of precious metals such as gold and silver and extractive industries (*e.g.* oil) and agriculture. In case of these industries, the inventories are stated at sales prices.

(*iv*) **Recognition proportionately over the performance of the contract.** According to this basis, revenue is recognised even in those cases where the work has not been completed in all respects. This is particularly true in case of long-term contracts which may take few years to complete. In case of such contracts, revenue is recognised on the basis of the work which has been completed and approved by the contractee (technically known as work certified). This is done on the basis of certain accepted norms which are given below:

   (*i*) When less than one-fourth of the contract is completed, no profit should be taken to the Profit and Loss Account.

  (*ii*) When one-fourth or more but less than one-half of the contract is completed, one-third of the profit made to date should be taken to the Profit and Loss Account. This may, further, be reduced on the basis of cash received by the contractor from the contractee. This is technically known as reducing profit on cash basis.

 (*iii*) If half or more of the contract has been completed, two-third of the profit as reduced on cash basis may be taken to the Profit and Loss account.

The degree of completion of the contract is computed by comparing the work certified with the contract price. The norms given above will be clear with the help of the following example.

Contract Price: Rs 30,000. The contract is likely to take three years to complete. In the First year Rs 10,000 have been spent and the work has been certified by the contractee for Rs 15,000. The contractee pays cash to the extent of 80% of the work certified.

The profit to be taken to the Profit and Loss Account (*i.e.*, the extent to which the income will be taken to have been realised) will be computed as follows:

	Rs
Value of work certified	15,000
Costs incurred so far	10,000
Profit made during the accounting year	5,000

The contract price is Rs 30,000, while the value of the work certified is Rs 15,000. Hence, one-half of the contract has been completed. The amount to be taken to the Profit and Loss Account for the current year will be computed as follows:

$$= \text{Rs } 5,000 \times \frac{2}{3} \times \frac{80}{100}$$

$$= \text{Rs } 2,666.$$

Thus, according to the basis of recognition of revenue proportionately over performance of the contract, revenue/income has been recognised to the extent of Rs 2,666.

On the basis of whatever has been stated in the preceding pages, the factors to be taken into account by the accountant for measurement of business income can be summarised as follows:

(*i*) Accounting concepts and conventions.

(*ii*) Correct computation of expired cost.

(*iii*) Correct recognition of revenue.

Each of these factors is affected by and dependent on a number of others factors as explained in the preceding pages. On account of this reason, the computation of business income is not only the most important but also the most difficult job of the accountant these days.

ACCOUNTANT'S AND ECONOMIST'S CONCEPTS OF CAPITAL AND INCOME

The Economist's concepts of capital and income are different from those of the Accountant. According to the Economists the term 'capital' refers to such assets which are used for producing goods and services. It comprises of both tangible assets *viz.* building, land, plant and machinery, furniture, equipment and intangible assets *viz.* human skills, technology, etc.

According to Accountants the term 'capital' or 'capital employed' refers to all tangible and intangible assets owned and employed in the business for earning revenue. They include both fixed as well as current assets. Assets taken on lease are not included in the capital employed. Similarly assets like human skills are also not included while computing the capital employed. As a matter of fact the salaries paid for utilising human resources is taken as a revenue expenditure and hence written off from profits.

According to the Economists the term 'income' means "the current flow of goods and services over a period of time". For example if the Economists says that the national income of India during 1990–91 was Rs 80,000 crores, he means that Rs 80,000 crores worth of goods and services were produced during 1990–91. An Economist is mainly concerned with individual (per capita) or national income.

Moreover, while determining income, an Economist considers both monetary and non-monetary aspects. For example, if a factory is started in a particular area, it creates more employment opportunities for the people of that area. They stand to gain monetarily. However, pollution of the environment on account of poisonous gases coming out of the factory chimnies create a health hazard and in that respect, the people of the area have also to suffer. An Economist while determining the impact of the starting of the factory on the income of the people will consider both the aspects. Thus, he takes both monetary as well as non-monetary (imputed or social) benefits and costs for income determination. In other words while determining the income of an individual or a society, the Economist considers the real income which, of course, is subject to high degree of subjectivity of value. On the other hand, the Accountant is mainly concerned with the monetary income, *i.e.*, income earned by a business capable of being expressed in monetary terms. Thus, an Accountant is more exact in the computation of income as compared to an Economist.

The Economist's concept of the term profit is also different from that of an Accountant. According to the Accountant, the terms profit and income are synonymous. Profit or Income is computed by deduction from the total revenue, the expenditure incurred for earning that revenue. However, an Economist regards profit as a factor return like wages, interest and rent. If wages is the reward for the labour, profit is return to the entrepreneur for his entrepreneuring ability. The term entrepreneuring ability includes ability to bear the risk and to take the initiative. In other words, profit is the reward to the entrepreneur both for uncertainty bearing and innovations. The return for the routine management matters (*i.e.*, for his ordinary services) will be taken as wages and not profit.

An Accountant does not make such a distinction. According to him, the residue left after meeting all business expenses will be taken as the profit of the business. It includes remuneration both for entrepreneurial skill as well as routine management services.

Economists concepts of capital and income are closely related to each other. According to Irving Fisher[1] the term capital refers to "stock of wealth existing at a given period of time while the times" while the term income refers to "a flow of benefits from wealth through a given period of time". For instance, agricultural land is capital; but the benefit flowing from it in the form of agricultural produce is income. Thus income is derived from capital. On the other hand the value of capital is also based on the value of income. It can be further elaborated by saying that according to the Economists the value of an asset is the present value of all future benefits which the asset can provide. This can be understood with the following illustration:

Illustration 12.1. A purchased a machinery for a sum of Rs 1,50,000 on January 1, 1990. He expects an annual cash flow of Rs 50,000 at the end of each year for 5 years. The cost of capital is 15% and the present value of an annuity of Re 1 [annual payment of Re 1 for 5 years (in all Rs 5)] at 15% discount factor per annum is 3.3522. You are required to calculate the value of machinery on January 1, 1990, both according to the Accountant's and the Economist's concepts.

Solution:

According to the Accountant the value of machinery on January 1, 1990 would be Rs 1,50,000. This is based on the "cost concept".

According to the Economist the machinery will be valued on January 1, 1990 at the present value of future benefit. It has been given in the question that Re 1 paid annually for 5 years (*i.e.*, Rs 5 in all) have a present value of Rs 3.3522 at 15% discount factor. In other words Rs 50,000 received annually over a period of 5 years have a present value of Rs 1,67,610 (Rs 50,000 × 3.3522).

Illustration 12.2. Compute the amount of income according to the Economist's concept for the year 1990 on the basis of data given in Illustration 12.1.

Solution:

In order to compute to income for the year 1990 we will have to calculate the value of machinery (or capital) at the end of the year 1990.

At the end of the year 1990 Rs 50,000 has been actually realised while there is an expectation of Rs 50,000 getting every year for the next 4 years. From the annuity table we can find out the present value of an annuity of Re 1 for 4 years at 15% discount factor. The value given in the annuity table is 2.8550.

[1] Fisher Irving, *Elementary Economics*, p. 38.

The value of capital at the end of 1990 (symbolically $C_1 t_1$) can be computed as follows:
$$C_1 t_1 = \text{Rs } 50,000 + (\text{Rs } 50,000 \times 2.8550) = \text{Rs } 1,92,750.$$

The income earned by the business for the year 1990 is the excess of the "value of capital at the end of 1990 (symbolically $C_1 t_1$) over that value in the beginning of 1990" (symbolically $C_0 t_0$).

The income earned by the business for the year 1990 can be computed by comparing the value of capital at the following two periods—in the beginning of 1990 and at the end of 1990. This can be symbolically presented as follows:
$$I = C_1 t_1 - C_0 \, t_0$$

where I = Income

$C_1 t_1$ = Value capital at the end of period 1

$C_0 t_0$ = Value capital at the beginning of period 0.

On putting the figures in the above equation income for 1990
$$= \text{Rs } 1,92,750 - \text{Rs } 1,67,610 = \text{Rs } 25,140.$$

Ex-ante Income

In the illustration given above the income of the business for the period t_1 (for the year 1990) has been computed on the basis of the present value of the cash flows estimated in the beginning of the period t_0 (*i.e.*, January 1, 1990). Of course the expectation about the cash flows at t_1 (*i.e.*, end of 1990) may not be the same as expected at t_0 *i.e.*, in the beginning of 1990). The income computed on the basis of the present value of expected cash flows at 't_0' period is known "*ex-ante* income."

Ex-post Income

As stated above the expected cash flows from the asset concerned may be different after the expiry of a period for the balance of the life of the asset. In such a case the revised cash flows from the asset will have to be calculated. The income computed on the basis of the difference between the present value of the revised cash flow (*i.e.*, taking t_1 as the base) and the present values of the original cash flows (*i.e.*, taking t_0 as the base) is termed as '*ex-post* income'.

Illustration 12.3. On the basis of the data given in illustration 12.1 compute the ex-post income if the revised cash flows at the end of the year 1990 for the next 4 yeas are as follows:

End of the Year:	Revised Cash Flows (Rs)	Present Value Factor at 15%:
1991	60,000	0.756
1992	70,000	0.658
1993	80,000	0.572
1994	50,000	0.497

Solution:

COMPUTATION OF EX-POST INCOME FOR 1990

	At the end of the year	Cash Flows Rs	Present Value Factor at 15%	Present Value Rs
1	1990	50,000	1.000	50,000
2	(1991)	60,000	0.756	45,360
3	(1992)	70,000	0.658	46,060
4	(1993)	80,000	0.572	45,760

Contd....

At the end of the year	Cash Flows Rs	Present Value Factor at 15%	Present Value Rs
5 (1994)	50,000	0.497	24,850
		Revised C_1t_1	2,12,030

Ex-post Income:= Revised $C_1t_1 - C_0t_0$ = Rs 2,12,030 − 1,67,610 = 44,420.

It may be noted that if there is no change in the expected cash flows at the end of period 1 (t_1), the *ex-ante* income and the *ex-post* income will be identical.

KEY TERMS

☐ **Ex-ante Income:** The excess of value of the capital for the current period over that of the base period (termed as '0' period) with reference to the present value of the future expected returns on base period basis.

☐ **Ex-post Income:** The excess of the value of the capital for the current period over that of the base period with reference to future expected returns on current period basis.

☐ **Income:** The excess of revenue realised during a period by a specific accounting entity over the expired cost (including losses) during the same period.

TEST QUESTIONS

Objective type | TEST YOUR UNDERSTANDING |

1. State whether each of the following statements is True or False.
   (i) Economists and Accountants have got different concepts of the term 'Income'.
   (ii) An Economist is more exact in computation of income than an Accountant.
   (iii) Notional Incomes should also be taken into account in computation of business income.
   (iv) The Conservatism Concept ensures that the reported income is not under-stated.
   (v) The actual income earned by business can be known only when the business is finally closed down.
   (vi) In case of inflationary conditions, charging of depreciation on original cost of the fixed assets will result in over-statement of business income.
   (vii) The business income also includes the personal income of the proprietor of the business.
   (viii) Revenue is recognised generally at the time when the sale of goods takes place.

   [**Ans.** (i) True, (ii) False, (iii) False, (iv) False, (v) True, (vi) True, (vii) False, (viii) True].

2. Fill in the blanks, with the most appropriate words.
   (i) Income is the outcome of excess or deficiency of revenue over related………
   (ii) The term Business Income includes………net income.
   (iii) The concept of conservatism ensures that the reported profit is not………stated.
   (iv) In accounting, the revenue is generally treated to be realised when the goods or services are………to the customers.
   (v) According to *FIFO* Method, the inventory of raw materials will consist of………purchases.
   (vi) According to *LIFO* Method, material purchased in the last are taken to be issued………

(vii) The basis for recognition of revenue, at the time the production is completed, is generally followed in case of.........industries.

(viii) The principle of recognising revenue proportionately on the basis of work actually done is generally followed in case of.........contracts.

[Ans. (i) expired cost, (ii) realised, (iii) over, (iv) furnished, (v) latest, (vi) first, (vii) extractive, (viii) long- term].

Essay type | FOR REVIEW, DISCUSSION AND PRACTICE |

1. What do you understand by Accountant's Concept of Income?
2. When is business revenue considered as accrued? What are the exceptions to this rule?
3. Differentiate between Accountant's Concept of Income and Economist's Concept of Income.

PRACTICAL PROBLEMS

1. A machine is purchased for Rs 50,000 on 1st Jan. 1992. Its working life is expected to be of 10 years with an annual cash inflow of Rs 8,000 every year.

   Compute the value of the machinery on 1st Jan, 1992 according (i) the accountant and (ii) the economist. The cost of capital is taken as 10%. The present value of an annuity of Re 1 for 10 years at 10% is 6.145.

   [Ans. (i) 50,000 (ii) 8,000 × 6.145 = Rs 49,160]

2. The capital employed in a business was Rs 1,00,000 at '0' time period. For the next five years the cash inflows were expected at Rs 40,000 every year. However at the end of year 1, due to change of circumstances. The expected cash flows for next four years were revised as follows:

Year end	Cash Flows Rs
2	50,000
3	60,000
4	50,000
5	40,000

   The cost of capital is taken as 10%. The present value of an annuity of Re 1 for 5 years and 4 years at 10% discount rate is taken cash 3.605 and 3.037 respectively while the present value of Re 1 at the end of each year at 10% discount is as follows:

Year	Present value of Re 1 at 10%
1	0.909
2	0.826
3	0.751
4	0.683
5	0.621

   You are required to compute (i) ex-ante and (ii) ex-post income.

   [Ans. (i) Rs 17,280 {i.e., (40,000 + 40,000 × 3.037) – (40,000 × 3.605)}
   (ii) Rs 41,150 {i.e. (40,000 + 50,000 × .826 + 60,000 × .751 + 50,000 × .683 + 40,000 × .621) – (40,000 × 3.605)}]

Chapter 13

DEPRECIATION ACCOUNTING

LEARNING OBJECTIVES

After studying this chapter you should be able to:-

- [ ] understand the concept of depreciation;
- [ ] identify the causes of depreciation;
- [ ] differentiate depreciation from depletion, amortization and dilapidation;
- [ ] explain the meaning of depreciation accounting;
- [ ] compute depreciation according to different methods of providing depreciation;
- [ ] make critical evaluation of providing depreciation on replacement cost;
- [ ] appreciate the role of a proper depreciation policy;
- [ ] decribe the salient features of Accounting Standard: 6 regarding Depreciation Accounting; and
- [ ] explain the meaning of certain key terms.

CONCEPT OF DEPRECIATION

The concept of depreciation is closely linked to the concept of business income. In the revenue generating process the use of long-term assets tend to consume their economic potential. At some point of time these assets becomes useless and are disposed of and possibly replaced. The economic potential so consumed represents the expired cost of these assets and must be recovered from the revenue of the business in order to determine the income earned by the business. Depreciation may, therefore, be defined as that portion of the cost of the assets that is deducted from revenue for assets' services used in the operation of a business.

In order to have a clear understanding about the concept of depreciation, it will be useful to quote definitions given by some prominent writers.

According to Pickles, "Depreciation is the permanent and continuing diminution in the quality, quantity or value of an asset".

The Institute of Chartered Accountants of England and Wales defines depreciation as "that part of the cost of a fixed asset to its owner which is not recoverable wthen the asset is finally put out of use by him. Provision against this loss of capital is an integral cost of conducting the business during the effective commercial life of the asset and is not dependent upon the amount of profit earned".

According to Spicer and Pegler, depreciation may be defined as, "the measure of the exhaustion of the effective life of an asset from any cause during a given period".

From the above definitions, it can be concluded that depreciation is a gradual decrease in the value of an asset from any cause.

CAUSES OF DEPRECIATION

The causes of depreciation are as follows:

1. **Wear and tear.** Assets get worn or torn out on account of constant use as is the case with plant and machinery, furniture and fixtures used in a factory.

2. **Exhaustion.** An asset may get exhausted through working. This is the case with mineral mines, oil wells etc. On account of continuous extraction of minerals or oil, a stage comes when the mine or well gets completely exhausted and nothing is left.

3. **Obsolescence.** Some assets are discarded before they are worn out because of changed conditions. For example, an old machine which is still workable may have to be replaced by a new machine because of the latter being more efficient and economical. Such a loss on account of new inventions or changed fashions is termed as loss on account of obsolescence.

4. **Efflux of time.** Certain assets get decreased in their value with the passage of time. This is true in case of assets like leasehold properties, patents or copy rights.

5. **Accidents.** An asset may meet an accident and, therefore, it may get depreciated in its value.

On the basis of the above causes, it can be said that depreciation is the decrease or depletion in the value of an asset due to wear and tear, lapse of time, obsolescence, exhaustion and accidents.

BASIC FEATURES OF DEPRECIATION

1. The term depreciation is used only in respect of fixed assets. Of course, the current assets may also lose their value. Loss on account of fall in their value is taken care of by valuing them for Balance Sheet purposes "at cost or market price whichever is less".

2. Depreciation is a charge against profits. This means that true profit of the business cannot be ascertained without charging depreciation.

3. Depreciation is different from maintenance. Maintenance expenses are incurred for keeping the machine in a state of efficiency. However, any degree of mainte-nance cannot assure that the asset will never reach a state of scrap. Of course, good maintenance delays this stage but it cannot absolutely prevent it.

4. All fixed assets, with certain possible exceptions e.g., land, and antiques etc., suffer depreciation although the process may be invisible or gradual.

DEPRECIATION, DEPLETION, AMORTIZATION AND DILAPIDATIONS

The term 'depreciation' is to be distinguished from other terms such as depletions, amorti-zation etc. though they are used often interchangeably.

Depletion. Depletion implies removal of an available but irreplaceable resource such as extracting coal from a coal mine or oil out of an oil well.

Amortization. The process of writing off intangible assets is termed as amortization. Some intangible assets like patents, copyrights, leaseholds have a limited useful life. Hence, their cost must be written off over such period.

The American Institute of Certified Public Accountants (AICPA) has put the difference between depreciation, depletion, and amortization in the following words.

"Depreciation can be distinguished from other terms with specialised meanings used by accountants to describe assets cost allocation procedures. Depreciation is concerned with charging the cost of man made fixed assets to operations (and not with determination of asset value for the balance sheet). Depletion refers to cost allocations for natural resources such as oil and mineral deposits. Amortization relates to cost allocation for intangible assets such as patent and leaseholds. The use of the term depreciation should also be avoided in connection with the valuation procedures for securities and investments".

Dilapidations. The term dilapidation refers to damage done to a building or other property during tenancy. When a property is taken on lease, is returned to the landlord he may ask the lessee as per agreement to put it in as good condition as it was at the time it was leased out. In order to meet cost of such dilapidation, a provision may be created by debiting the property account with the estimated amount of dilapidation and crediting the provision for dilapidations account. Depreciation may then be charged on the total cost of the asset so arrived at. Any payment made later on dilapidation may be debited to the provision for dilapidation account. The balance, if any, may be transferred to profit and loss account.

MEANING OF DEPRECIATION ACCOUNTING

Depreciation Accounting is mainly concerned with a rational and systematic distribution of cost over the estimated useful life of the asset. According to the American Institute of Certified Public Accountants, Depreciation Accounting is 'a system of accounting which aims to distribute the cost or other basic values of the tangible capital assets less salvage (if any) over the estimated useful life of the unit (which may be a group of assets) in a systematic and rational manner. It is the process of allocation and not of valuation".

The objective of Depreciation Accounting is to absorb the cost of using the assets to different accounting periods in a way so as to give the true figure of profit or loss made by the business.

OBJECTIVES OF PROVIDING DEPRECIATION

The following are objectives of providing depreciation:

1. **Ascertainment of true profits.** When an asset is purchased, it is nothing more than a payment in advance for an expense. For example, if a building is purchased for Rs 10,000 for business, the effect of such a purchase will be saving in the cost of rent in the future. But, after a certain number of years, the building will become useless. The cost of the building is, therefore, nothing except paying rent in advance for a period of years. If the rent had been paid, it would have been charged as an expense for determination of the true profits, made by the business during a particular period. The amount paid for the purchase of building should, therefore, be charged over a period of time for which the asset would be serviceable.

2. Presentation of true financial position. The assets get depreciated in their value over a period of time on account of various factors, as explained before. In order to present a true state of affairs of the business, the assets should be shown in the Balance Sheet, at their proper values.

3. Replacement of assets. Assets used in the business need replacement after the expiry of their service life. By providing depreciation a part of the profits of the business is kept in the business which can be used for purchase of new assets on the old fixed assets becoming useless.

FIXATION OF DEPRECIATION AMOUNT

Following are the three important factors which should be considered for determining the amount of depreciation to be charged to the Profit and Loss Account in respect of a particular asset.

1. Cost of the asset. The cost of the asset includes the invoice price of the asset, less any trade discount plus all costs essential to bring the asset to a useable condition. It should be noted that financial charges, such as interest on money borrowed for the purchase of the asset, should not be included in the cost of the asset.

2. Estimated scrap value. The term scrap value means the residual or the salvage value which is estimated to be realised on account of the sale of the asset at the end of its useful life. In determining the scrap value, the cost to be incurred in the disposal or removing of the asset should be deducted out of the total realisable value.

3. Estimated useful life. This is also termed as economic life of the asset. This may be calculated in terms of years, months, hours, units of output of other operating measures such as kilometers in case of a taxi or a truck.

METHODS OF RECORDING DEPRECIATION

Depreciation can be recorded in the books of account by two different methods:

1. When a provision for depreciation account is maintained. In case of this method, the amount of depreciation to be charged in a particular year is credited to Provision for Depreciation Account and debited to Profit and Loss Account. The Asset Account appears in the books at original cost. In case the asset is sold, the Provision for Depreciation Account is transferred to the Asset Account. Any amount realised on account of sale of the asset is also credited to the Asset Account. The balance, if any, in the Asset Account is transferred to the Profit and Loss Account.

The following journals enteries are passed in case this method is followed:

(*i*) For providing depreciation:

Depreciation Account   Dr.
     To Provision for Depreciation Account

(*ii*) For transfer of depreciation to Profit and Loss Account:

Profit and Loss Account   Dr.
     To Depreciation Account

(*iii*) On sale of asset:

   (*a*) Provision for Depreciation Account   Dr.
       To Asset Account

   (*b*) In case of profit or loss on sale of an asset:
      If Profit: Asset Account   Dr.
         To Profit and Loss Account

If Loss: Profit and Loss Account   Dr.
      To Asset Account

Alternatively, on sale of an asset, an 'asset disposal account' may be opened. The following entries will be passed in such a case on sale of an asset:

Asset Disposal Account   Dr.
      To Asset Account
(with original cost of the asset)
Bank Account   Dr.
      To Asset Disposal Account
(with the actual sale proceeds on account of sale of asset)
Provision for Depreciation Account   Dr.
      To Asset Disposal Account
(with the accumulated depreciation on the asset sold)
Profit & Loss Account   Dr.
      To Asset Disposal Account
(for transfer of loss on sale of the asset).

In case of profit, the above entry would be reversed.

2. When a provision for depreciation account is not maintained. In case a Provision for Depreciation Account is not maintained, the amount of depreciation is debited to the Depreciation Account and credited to the Asset Account. The Asset Account thus appears in the books at a written down value (*i.e.,* the value remaining after deducting depreciation). The Depreciation Account is transferred to the Profit and Loss Account like any other item of expense.

The following journal entries are passed in case depreciation is provided according to this method:

(*i*) For providing depreciation:

Depreciation Account   Dr.
      To Asset Account

(*ii*) For transfer of depreciation to the Profit and Loss Account:

Profit and Loss Account   Dr.
      To Depreciation Account

In case the asset is sold, the amount realised is credited to the Asset Account. Any profit or loss on the sale of the asset is transferred to the Profit and Loss Account.

METHODS FOR PROVIDING DEPRECIATION

The following are various methods for providing depreciation:
1. Uniform charge methods
   (*a*) Fixed instalment method
   (*b*) Depletion method
   (*c*) Machine hour rate method
2. Declining charge or accelerated depreciation methods:
   (*a*) Diminishing balance method
   (*b*) Sum of years digits method
   (*c*) Double declining method

3. Other methods:

    (a) Group depreciation method

    (b) Inventory system of depreciation

    (c) Annuity method

    (d) Depreciation fund method

    (e) Insurance policy method.

1. Uniform Charge Methods

In case of these methods depreciation is charged on uniform basis year after year. Such methods are considered appropriate only for such assets which are uniformly productive. Following three methods fall in this category.

    (a) **Fixed instalment method.** This is also termed as Straight Line Method (*SLM*). According to this method, depreciation is charged evenly every year throughout the effective life of the asset. The amount of depreciation is calculated as follows.

$$\text{Depreciation} = \frac{\text{Original Cost of the Fixed Asset} - \text{Estimated Scrap Value}}{\text{Life of the Asset in Number of Accounting Periods}}$$

or $$D = \frac{C - S}{N}$$

The depreciation to be charged each year can also be expressed as a percentage of cost. This percentage can be calculated as follows:

or $$R = \frac{D}{C} \times 100$$

For example, if an asset has been purchased for Rs 10,000 and it will have a scrap value of Rs 1,000 at the end of its useful life of 10 years, the amount of depreciation to be charged every year over the effective life of the asset will be computed as follows:

$$\text{Depreciation} = \frac{10,000 - 1,000}{10 \text{ years}}$$

$$= \text{Rs 900 each year or 9\%}$$

Merits. (i) The method is simple to understand and easy to apply.

(ii) The value of the asset can be reduced to zero (or its scrap value) under this method.

(iii) The method is very suitable particularly in case of those assets which get depreciated more on account of expiry of period *e.g.*, lease-hold properties, patents, etc.

Demerits. (i) The method does not take into account the effective utilisation of the asset. The same amount of depreciation is charged from year to year irrespective of the use of the asset.

(ii) The total charge for use of the asset (*i.e.*, depreciation and repairs) goes on increasing from year to year though the asset might have been used uniformly from year to year. For example, in the initial years, the amount spent on repairs is quite normal. It goes on increasing in the latter years. The amount of depreciation remains the same for each year. Thus, each subsequent year is burdened with greater charge for the use of asset on account of increasing cost on repairs.

(iii) The method tends to report an increasing rate of return on investment in the asset on account of the fact that net balance of the asset account is taken. For example, if the cost of an asset is Rs 10,000, life 10 years, net revenue before charging depreciation Rs 2,000, the earnings for the first three years will be calculated as follows:

	Year 1	Year 2	Year 3
	Rs	Rs	Rs
Revenue	2,000	2,000	2,000
Less: Depreciation	1,000	1,000	1,000
Profit	1,000	1,000	1,000
Book value of the asset (capital employed)	10,000	9,000	8,000
Rate of Return	10%	11.1%	12.5%

The idea of an increasing rate of return as an asset approaches retirement does not seem to be justifiable. Reason suggests that the rate of return either remains constant or actually decreases somewhat as the asset ages.

Illustration 13.1. A firm purchases a plant for a sum of Rs 10,000 on 1st January, 1990. Installation charges are Rs 2,000. Plant is estimated to have a scrap value of Rs 1,000 at the end of its useful life of five years. You are required to prepare Plant Account for five years charging depreciation according to Straight Line Method.

Solution:

PLANT ACCOUNT

Date	Particulars	Amount Rs	Date	Particulars	Amount Rs
1990			1990		
Jan. 1.	To Bank	12,000	Dec. 31	By Depreciation A/c	2,200
			Dec. 31	By Balance c/d	9,800
		12,000			12,000
1991			1991		
Jan. 1.	To Balance b/d	9,800	Dec. 31	By Depreciation A/c	2,200
			Dec. 31	By Balance c/d	7,600
		9,800			9,800
1992			1992		
Jan. 1.	To Balance b/d	7,600	Dec. 31	By Depreciation A/c	2,200
			Dec. 31	By Balance c/d	5,400
		7,600			7,600
1993			1993		
Jan. 1.	To Balance b/d	5,400	Dec. 31	By Depreciation A/c	2,200
			Dec. 31	By Balance c/d	3,200
		5,400			5,400
1994			1994		
Jan. 1.	To Balance b/d	3,200	Dec. 31	By Depreciation A/c	2,200
			Dec. 31	By Balance c/d	1,000
		3,200			3,200

(b) **Depletion method.** This is also known as productive output method. According to this method the charge for depreciation in respect of the use of an asset will be based on the following factors:

(i) Total amount paid.

(ii) Total estimated quantities of the output available.

(iii) The actual quantity taken out during the accounting year.

The method is suitable in case of mines, queries, etc., where it is possible to make an estimate of the total output likely to be available. Depreciation is calculated per unit of output. The amount of depreciation to be charged in a particular year is computed by multiplying the units of output with the rate of depreciation per unit of output. For example, if a mine is purchased for Rs 20,000 and it is estimated that the total quantity of mineral in the mine in 40,000 tonnes, the rate of depreciation per tonne would amount to 50 paise per tonne (Rs 20,000/40,000 tonnes). In case output in a year amounts to 10,000 tonnes, the amount of depreciation to be charged to the Profit and Loss Account would Rs 5,000 (*i.e.*, 10,000 tonnes × Re 0.50).

The method has the advantage of correlating the amount of depreciation with the productive use of the asset. However, it requires making of a reasonably correct estimate of the output likely to be there. In the absence of correct estimate, the amount charged by way of depreciation will not be correct.

(*c*) **Machine hour rate method.** This is also known as Service Hours Method. This method takes into account the running time of the asset for the purpose of calculating depreciation. The method is particularly suitable for charging depreciation on plant and machinery, air-crafts, etc. The amount of depreciation is calculated as follows:

$$\frac{\text{Original Cost of the Asset} - \text{Scrap Value}}{\text{Life of the Asset in hours}}$$

For example, if a machine (having a scrap value of Rs 1,000) is purchased for Rs 20,000 and it has an effective life of 10 years of 1,000 hours each, the amount of depreciation per hour will be computed as follows:

$$\text{Depreciation} = \frac{\text{Original Cost} - \text{Scrap Value}}{\text{Life of the Asset in hours}}$$

$$= \frac{\text{Rs } 10,000 - \text{Rs } 1,000}{10,000 \text{ hours}}$$

$$= \text{Re } 0.90.$$

This means that, there will be a depreciation of 90 paise in case machine runs for an hour. If in a particular year, the machine runs for 600 hours, the amount of depreciation will be Rs 540 (*i.e.*, Re .90 × 600).

The method has the advantage of correlating the charge for depreciation, to the actual working time of the machine. However, this method can be used only in case of those assets whose life can be measured in terms of working time.

2. Declining Charge Depreciation Methods

In case of these methods the amount charged for depreciation declines over the asset's expected life. These methods are suitable in those case where (*a*) the receipts are expected to decline as the asset gets older and (*b*) it is believed that the allocation of depreciation should be related to the pattern of asset's expected receipts.

Following methods fall in this category.

(*a*) **Diminishing balance method.** According to this method, depreciation is charged on the book value of the asset each year. Thus, the amount of depreciation goes on decreasing every year. For example, if the cost of an asset is Rs 20,000, and the rate of depreciation is 10%, the amount of depriciation to be charged in the first year will be a sum of Rs 2,000. In the second year, depreciation will be charged at 10% on the book value of the asset, *i.e.*, Rs 18,000 (*i.e.*, Rs 20,000– Rs 2,000) and so on.

The formula for calculating the rate of depreciation under diminishing balance method (where 'n' = years of economic life of the asset) is as follows:

$$\text{Depreciation rate} = 1 - n \sqrt{\frac{\text{Net Residual Value}}{\text{Acquisition Cost}}}$$

For example, if the cost of an asset is Rs 10,000, residual value Rs 1,296, economic life 4 years, the rate of depreciation would be 40%, calculated as follows:

$$\text{Depreciation rate} = 1 - 4\sqrt{\frac{1,296}{10,000}}$$
$$= 1 - 6/10$$
$$= 40\%$$

Merits. (*i*) The method puts an equal burden for use of the asset on each subsequent year. The amount of depreciation goes on decreasing for each subsequent year while the charge for repairs goes on increasing for each subsequent year. Thus, increase in the cost of repairs for each subsequent year is compensated by decrease in the amount of depreciation for each subsequent year.

(*ii*) The method is simple to understand and easy to follow.

Demerits. (*i*) The value of the asset cannot be brought down to zero under this method.

(*ii*) The determination of a suitable rate of depreciation is also difficult under this method as compared to the Fixed Instalment Method.

Illustration 13.2. A firm purchases plant and machinery on 1st January, 1980 for Rs 10,000. Prepare the Plant Account for three years charging depreciation @ 10% p.a. according to the Diminishing Balance Method.

Solution:

PLANT AND MACHINERY ACCOUNT

Date	Particulars	Amount	Date	Particulars	Amount
1990 Jan. 1	To Bank	10,000	1990 Dec. 31	By Depreciation	1,000
			Dec. 31	By Balance c/d	9,000
		10,000			10,000
1991 Jan. 1	To Balance b/d	9,000	1991 Dec. 31	By Depreciation	900
			Dec. 31	By Balance c/d	8,100
		9,000			9,000
1992 Jan. 1	To Balance b/d	8,100	1992 Dec. 31	By Depreciation	810
			Dec. 31	By Balance c/d	7,290
		8,100			8,100

(*b*) **Sum of years digits (or SYD) method.** This method is on the pattern of Diminishing Balance Method. The amount of depreciation to be charged to the Profit and Loss Account under this method goes on decreasing every year. The depreciation is calculated according to the following formula:

$$\frac{\text{Remaining Life of the Asset (including the current year)}}{\text{Sum of all the digits of the life of the asset in years}} \times \text{Original Cost}$$

For example, if the cost of an asset is Rs 10,000 and it has an effective life of 5 years, the amount of depreciation to be written off each year will be computed as follows:

1st year $= \dfrac{5}{1+2+3+4+5} \times 10{,}000$

$= \dfrac{5}{15} \times 10{,}000$

$= \dfrac{10{,}000}{3} = \text{Rs } 3{,}333$

2nd year $= \dfrac{4}{15} \times 10{,}000 = \text{Rs } 2{,}666$

3rd year $= \dfrac{3}{15} \times 10{,}000 = \text{Rs } 2{,}000$

4th year $= \dfrac{2}{15} \times 10{,}000 = \text{Rs } 1{,}333$

5th year $= \dfrac{1}{15} \times 10{,}000 = \text{Rs } 667$

(c) **Double declining balance method.** This method is similar to reducing or declining balance method explained above except that the rate of depreciation is charged at the rate which is twice the straight line rate. While computing this rate two things have been kept in mind;

(a) No allowance is to be made for the scrap value of the asset.

(b) The total cost should not be reduced by charging the depreciation to an amount lower than the estimated scrap value of the asset.

The method is prevalent in *USA* and is permitted under the federal tax laws.

Illustration 13.3. A plant having a scrap value of Rs 1,000 and life of 5 years was purchased for Rs 10,000 in January, 1990. You are required to calculate the amount depreciation for each of the years according to Double Declining Method.

Solution:

According to the Fixed Installment Method (without considering the salvage value) the depreciation would amount to Rs 2,000 (*i.e.*, Rs 10,000, 5 years) each year. The rate of depreciation therefore comes to 20%. In case of Double Declining Method the rate of depreciation would be the twice of this rate *i.e.*, 40%. The amount of depreciation for each year would therefore be as follows:

Year	Book value in the beginning of the year	Amount of Depreciation
1	10,000	4,000
2	6,000	2,400
3	3,600	1,440
4	2,160	860
5	1,300	300*

*The depreciation at 40% come to Rs 520. However, since the value of the asset has not to be reduced below the scrap value of the asset (*i.e.*, Rs 1,000), only a sum of Rs 300 will be charged by way of depreciation.

The declining charge methods of depreciation are preferred over uniform charge methods of depreciation on account of the following reasons:

(i) The total cost for use of the asset is evenly spreaded over the useful life of the asset. Such cost of the use of the asset includes both depreciation and repairs. With the asset growing order, the repairs cost goes on increasing while the amount of the depreciation goes on decreasing. Thus, increase in repairs cost is compensated by decrease in depreciation cost.

(ii) The rate of depreciation in case of declining charge methods of depreciation is higher as compared to the rates in case of uniform charge methods of depreciation. Thus, the charge for depreciation in the initial years will be more and this will result in a considerable tax advantage to the business in these years when the demand for funds is also more. Higher depreciation in the initial years is also beneficial because a rupee saved to day in much more important than a rupee saved in future. Thus, accelerated depreciation creates a shield that enables the business to retain more resources in the early years than it can be under straight line method. These resources can be reinvested for more profits.

3. Other Methods

Following are some of the other methods of providing depreciation.

(a) **Group depreciation method.** Under this method all homogenous assets, generally having similar average life expectancy are grouped together in a single asset category. One summary account is established for each group and original cost of all assets in the group is charged to this account, Depreciation is charged for the group in total and not item by item. The essential features this method are as follows:

(i) A summary account is established for each category of homogenous assets e.g. 10 motor vehicles owned by a Company may be put in one account while 15 typewriters owned by the company may be but in another account.

(ii) Depreciation is charged for the group in total at a rate based on expected average service life and scrap values of the assets of the group.

(iii) On purchase of an asset the group asset account is debited with cost.

(iv) The amount of depreciation is calculated on the balance in the group asset account, It is debited to Depreciation Account (or *P. & L.* Account) and credited to Accumulated Depreciation Account.

(v) In case an asset is sold the amount received on account of sale of the asset is credited to group asset account. The difference between the cost of the asset and the sales value is transferred to Accumulated Depreciation Account.

It should be noted that no single item of the group can be considered to have a book value. Hence, no gain or loss is recorded on disposal of any item of the group in the normal course of events.

Illustration 13.44. A company purchased 10 identical machines on January 1st at a cost of Rs 11,000 each. Each having a zero scrap value and an average life of 5 years. At the end of the 2nd year the company sold one machine for Rs 6,000 and purchased another for Rs 14,000 in the beginning of the 3rd year.

Journalise the above transaction in the books of the Company for the 1st three years.

Solution:

COMPUTATION OF DEPRECIATION RATE

Cost of 10 Machines (10 × 11,000)	Rs 1,10,000
Less. Scrap value	Nil
Depreciation to be written off over 5 years	1,10,000
Yearly Depreciation	22,000
Rate of Depreciation 20%	

JOURNAL

Date	Particulars		Dr. Amount Rs	Cr. Amount Rs
1st Year				
	Machines A/c	Dr.	1,10,000	
	To Bank			1,10,000
	(For machines purchased)			
	Depreciation A/c	Dr.	22,000	
	To Accumulated Depreciation A/c			22,000
	(For depreciation @ 20% on Rs 1,10,000			
2nd Year				
	Depreciation A/c	Dr.	22,000	
	To Accumulated Depreciation A/c			22,000
	(For depreciation on Rs 1,10,000)			
	Bank A/c	Dr.	6,000	
	Accumulated Depreciation A/c	Dr.	5,000	
	To Machines A/c			11,000
	(Being sale of Machines)			
3rd Year			14,000	
	Machines A/c	Dr.	14,000	
	(Being purchase of Machine)			
	Depreciation A/c	Dr.	22,600	
	To Accumulated Depreciation A/c			22,600
	(Being depreciation of Machines on Rs 1,13,000 @ 20%)			

(b) **Inventory system of depreciation.** The method is followed in case of those assets which are of small values such as loose tools or where the life of the asset cannot be ascertained with certainty *e.g.*, live stock etc. In case of these assets the depreciation is charged on the following basis:

Cost of the assets in working condition at the beginning of the accounting year. ......

Add: Cost of the assets purchased during the accounting year. ......

......

Less: Cost of the assets in working condition at the end of the accounting year. ......
Depreciation to be charged ......

For example, a firm has loose tools in working condition costing Rs 2,000 on 1.1.1985 and purchases during 1985 loose tools of Rs 3,000. The cost of the loose tools in working condition on 31.1.1985 is Rs 2,000. The amount of depreciation to be charged to the Profit & Loss Account comes to Rs 3,000 (*i.e.*, Rs 2,000 + Rs 3,000 – Rs 2,000).

The following journal entry is passed for recording the amount of depreciation:

Depreciation A/c   Dr.
To Asset Account

(c) **Annuity method.** The Fixed Instalment Method and the Reducing Balance Method of charging depreciation ignore the interest factor. The Annuity Method takes care of this factor. Under this method, the depreciation is charged on the basis that besides losing the original cost of the asset, the business also loses interest on the amount used for buying the asset. The term "Interest" here means the interest which the business could have earned otherwise if the money used in purchasing the asset would have been invested in some other form of investment. Thus, according to this method, such an amount is charged by way of depreciation which takes into account not only the cost of the asset but also interest thereon at an accepted rate. The amount of interest is calculated on the book value asset, in the beginning of each year. The amount of depreciation is uniform and is determined on the basis of annuity table.

An extract from such a table has been given as an *Appendix* at the end of this book.

The following journal entries are passed in case depreciation is charged according to this method.

   (i) *On purchase of asset:*

      Asset Account   Dr.
         To Bank

   (ii) *For charging interest:*

      Asset Account   Dr.
         To Interest Account

   (iii) *For charging depreciation:*

      Depreciation Account   Dr.
         To Asset Account

Illustration 13.5. A firm purchases a lease-hold property for a period of five years for Rs 10,000 on 1.1.1985. It decides to write off the lease by Annuity Method presuming the rate interest at 5% p.a. The Annuity Table shows that the annual amount necessary to write off Re 1 at 5% p.a. is Re 0.230976. You are required to prepare the Lease Hold Property Account for five years and show the net amount to be charged to the Profit & Loss Account for these five years.

Solution:

Dr.   LEASEHOLD PROPERTY ACCOUNT   Cr.

Date	Particulars	Amount Rs	Date	Particulars	Amount Rs
1985			1985		
Jan. 1	To Bank	10,000.00	Dec. 31	By Depreciation	2,309.76
Dec. 31	To Interest	500.00	Dec. 31	By Balance c/d	8,190.24
		10,500.00			10,500,00
1986			1986		
Jan. 1	To Balance b/d	8,190.24	Dec. 31	By Depreciation A/c	2,309.76
Jan. 31	To Interest	409.52	Dec. 31	By Balance c/d	6,290.00
		8,599.76			8,599.76
1987			1987		
Jan. 1	To Balance b/d	6,290.00	Dec. 31	By Depreciation A/c	2,309.76
Dec. 31	To Interest	314.50	Dec. 31	By Balance c/d	4,294.74
		6,604.50			6,604.50
1988			1988		
Jan. 1	To Balance b/d	4,294.74	Dec. 31	By Depreciation A/c	2,309.76
Dec. 31	To Interest	214.74	Dec. 31	By Balance c/d	2,199.72
		4,509.48			4,509.48

Contd....

Date	Particulars	Amount Rs	Date	Particulars	Amount Rs
1989			1989		
Jan. 1	To Balance b/d	2,199.72	Dec. 31	By Depreciation A/c	2,309.76
Dec. 31	To Interest	110.04			
		2,309.76			2,309.76

STATEMENT SHOWING THE AMOUNT CHARGEABLE TO THE PROFIT & LOSS ACCOUNT

Year	Depreciation (debited)	Interest (credited)	Net Charge against profits
1985	2,309.76	500.00	1,809.76
1986	2,309.76	409.52	1,900.24
1987	2,309.76	314.50	1,995.26
1988	2,309.76	214.74	2,095.02
1989	2,309.76	110.04	2,199.72
	11,548.80	1,548.80	10,000.00

(*d*) **Depreciation (or sinking) fund method.** One of the objectives of providing for depreciation (as explained earlier) is to provide for replacement of the asset at the end of its useful life. In case of the three methods discussed earlier, the amount of depreciation charged from the Profit & Loss Account continues to remain in the business. However, this amount may get invested in the course or running the business is some other assets. It may, therefore, not be possible for the business to have sufficient liquid resources to purchase a new asset at the time when it needs funds for replacement. Depreciation Fund Method takes care of such a contingency. According to this method, the amount charged by way of depreciation is invested in certain securities carrying a particular rate of interest. The amount received on account of interest from these securities is also invested from time to time together with the annual amount charged by way of depreciation. At the end of the useful life of the asset, when replacement is required, the securities are sold away and money realised on account the sale of the securities is used for purchase of a new asset. The method has the advantage of providing a separate sum for replacement of the asset. However, the method has a disadvantage. It puts an increasing burden on the profit and loss of each year on account of a fixed charge for depreciation but increasing charge for repairs.

The accounting entries are as follows:

(*a*) *At the end of the 1st accounting year*

(*i*) On setting aside the amount for depreciation:

Depreciation Account (or Profit & Loss Account) Dr.
  To Depreciation Fund Account

(The amount to be charged by way of depreciation is determined on the basis of Sinking Fund Table given an Appendix at the end of this book.)

(*ii*) For investing the money charged by way of depreciation:

Depreciation Fund Investment A/c Dr.
  To Bank

(b) At the end of each subsequent accounting year

(iii) For receipt of interest

Bank A/c   Dr.
    To Depreciation Fund A/c
(Interest will be received at the specified rate on
balance of Depreciation Fund Investment outstanding
in the beginning of each year)

(iv) For setting aside the amount of depreciation:

Profit and Loss A/c   Dr.
    To Depreciation Fund A/c

(v) For investing the money:

Depreciation Fund Investment A/c   Dr.
    To Bank
(Annual instalment plus interest received)

(c) At the end of the last year

(vi) For receipt of interest:

Bank A/c   Dr.
    To Depreciation Fund A/c

(vii) For setting aside the amount for depreciation:

Profit and Loss A/c   Dr.
    To Depreciation Fund A/c
(No investment will be made at the end of the last year,
since the asset is due for replacement and no purpose
will be served by simply investing the money and then
selling the investment either on the same day or on the
subsequent day.)

(viii) For the sale of investments:

Bank A/c   Dr.
    To Depreciation Fund Investment A/c

(ix) The profit of loss on sale of Depreciation Fund Investments will be transferred to the Depreciation Fund Account.

(x) For sale of the old asset:

Bank A/c   Dr.
    To Asset Account

(xi) The balance in the Depreciation Fund represents accumulated depreciation. It will be transferred to the Old Asset Account.

(xii) The balance in the Old Asset Account represents profit or loss. It will be transferred to the Profit and Loss Account.

(xiii) The proceeds realised on account of sale of the asset and investment will be utilised for purchase of new asset.

New Asset A/c   Dr.
    To Bank

Illustration 13.6. Suresh bought a plant on 1.1.1985 for a sum of Rs 1,00,000 having a useful life of 5 years. It is estimated that the plant will have a scrap value of Rs 16,000 at the end of its useful life. Suresh decides to charge depreciation according to depreciation fund method. The depreciation fund investments are expected to earn interest @ 5% p.a. Sinking Fund table shows that Re 0.180975 if invested yearly at 5% p.a. produces Re 1 at the end of 5 years. The investments are sold at the end of 5th year for a sum of Rs 65,000. A new plant is purchased for Rs 1,20,000 on 1.1.1980. The scrap of the old plant realises Rs 17,000.

You are required to prepare the necessary accounts in the books of Suresh.

Solution:

PLANT ACCOUNT

Date	Particulars	Amount Rs	Date	Particulars	Amount Rs
1985			1985		
Jan. 1	To Bank	1,00,000	Dec. 31	By Balance b/d	1,00,000
1986			1986		
Jan. 1	To Balance b/d	1,00,000	Dec. 31	By Balance c/d	1,00,000
1987			1987		
Jan. 1	To Balance b/d	1,00,000	Dec. 31	By Balance c/d	1,00,000
1988			1988		
Jan. 1	To Balance b/d	1,00,000	Dec. 31	By Balance c/d	1,00,000
1989			1989		
Jan. 1	To Balance b/d	1,00,000	Dec. 31	By Depreciation Fund A/c	83,478
Dec. 31	To P. & L. A/c (Profit)	478	Dec.31	By Bank (Scrap sold)	17,000
		1,00,478			1,00,478

NEW PLANT ACCOUNT

Date	Particulars	Amount Rs	Date	Particulars	Amount Rs
1990					
Jan. 1	To Bank A/c	1,20,000			

DEPRECIATION FUND ACCOUNT

Date	Particulars	Amount Rs	Date	Particulars	Amount Rs
1985			1985		
Dec. 31	To Balance c/d	15,202	Dec. 31	By P. & L. A/c	15,202
1986			1986		
Dec. 31	To Balance c/d	31,164	Jan. 1	By Balance b/d	15,202
			Dec. 31	By Bank (Interest)	760
			Dec. 31	By P. & L. A/c	15,202
		31,164			31,164
1987			1987		
Dec. 31	To Balance c/d	47,924	Jan. 1	By Balance b/d	31,164
			Dec. 31	By Bank (Interest)	1,558
			Dec. 31	By P. & L. A/c	15,202
		47,924			47,924

Contd....

Date	Particulars	Amount Rs	Date	Particulars	Amount Rs
1988 Dec. 31	To Balance c/d	65,522	1988 Jan. 1	By Balance b/d	47,924
			Dec. 31	By Bank (Interest)	2,396
			Dec. 31	By P. & L. A/c	15,202
		65,522			65,522
1989 Dec. 31	To Depreciation Fund Investment A/c (loss on sale of investment)	522	1989 Jan. 1	By Balance b/d	65,522
			Dec. 31	By Bank (Interest)	3,276
Dec. 31	To Plant A/c (accumulated depreciation)	83,478	Dec. 31	By P. & L. A/c	15,202
		84,000			84,000

DEPRECIATION FUND INVESTMENT ACCOUNT

Date	Particulars	Amount Rs	Date	Particulars	Amount Rs
1985 Dec. 31	To Bank	15,202	1985 Dec. 31	By Balance c/d	15,202
		15,202			15,202
1986 Jan. 1	To Balance b/d	15,202	1986 Dec. 31	By Balance c/d	31,164
Dec. 31	To Bank (15,202 + 760)	15,962			
		31,164			31,164
1987 Jan. 1	To Balance b/d	31,164	1987 Dec. 31	By Balance c/d	47,924
Dec. 31	To Bank (15,202 + 1,558)	16,760			
		47,924			47,924
1988 Jan. 1	To Balance b/d	47,924	1988 Dec. 31	By Balance c/d	65,522
Dec. 31	To Bank (15,202 + 2,396)	17,598			
		65,522			65,522
1989 Jan. 1	To Balance b/d	65,522	1989 Dec. 31	By Bank	65,000
				By Depreciation Fund A/c (loss on sale of investment)	522
		65,522			65,522

Note: The amount to be charged to the Profit and Loss Account has been arrived as follows:

Original Cost of the Plant	1,00,000
Less: Estimated scrap value	16,000
Depreciation on the plant for its whole life	84,000

The amount to be charged to the Profit and Loss Account $= Rs\ 84,000 \times 0.180975$

$$= Rs\ 15,201.90$$
$$= or\ Rs\ 15,202$$

(*e*) **Insurance Policy Method.** The method is similar to the Depreciation Fund Method as explained above. However, instead of investing the money in securities an insurance policy for the required amount is taken. A fixed amount as premium is paid every year. However, this amount will have to be paid in the beginning of each year. At the end of the specified period, the insurance company pays the agreed amount with which the new asset can be purchased.

The accounting entries can be put as follows:

(*a*) *First and subsequent years*

In the beginning of the year for insurance premium paid:

    Depreciation Insurance Policy A/c   Dr.
       To Bank

At the end of the year for providing depreciation:

    Profit and Loss A/c   Dr.
       To Depreciation Provision A/c
    (with the amount of premium paid)

(*b*) *At the end of the last year*

On realisation of money from the insurance company:

    Bank A/c   Dr.
       To Depreciation Policy A/c

For transfer of profit on insurance policy:

    Depreciation Insurance Policy A/c   Dr.
       To Depreciation Provision A/c

For transfer of accumulated depreciation to the Asset Account:

    Depreciation Provision A/c   Dr.
       To Asset A/c

On purchase of new asset:

    New Asset A/c   Dr.
       To Bank

Illustration 13.7. A firm purchases a lease for 3 years for Rs 30,000 on 1.1.1987. It decided to provide for its replacement by means of Insurance Policy for Rs 30,000. The annual premium is Rs 9,500.

On 1.1.1990, the lease is renewed for a further period of 3 years for Rs 30,000. You are required to show the necessary Ledger Accounts.

Solution:

LEASE ACCOUNT

Date	Particulars	Amount Rs	Date	Particulars	Amount Rs
1987			1987		
Jan. 1	To Bank	30,000	Dec. 31	By Balance c/d	30,000
1988			1988		
Jan. 1	To Balance b/d	30,000	Dec. 31	By Balance c/d	30,000
1989			1989		
Jan. 1	To Balance b/d	30,000	Dec. 31	By Dep. Provision A/c	30,000

1.306

DEPRECIATION PROVISION ACCOUNT

Date	Particulars	Amount Rs	Date	Particulars	Amount Rs
1987			1987		
Dec. 31	To Balance c/d	9,500	Dec. 31	By P. and L. A/c	9,500
1988			1988		
Dec. 31	To Balance c/d	19,000	Jan. 1	By Balance b/d	9,500
			Dec. 31	By P. and L. A/c	9,500
		19,000			19,000
1989			1989		
Dec. 31	To Lease Account	30,000	Jan. 1	By Balance b/d	19,000
			Dec. 31	By P. and L. A/c	9,500
			Dec. 31	By Depreciation Insurance Policy A/c	1,500
		30,000			30,000

DEPRECIATION INSURANCE POLICY ACCOUNT

Date	Particulars	Amount Rs	Date	Particulars	Amount Rs
1987			1987		
Jan. 1	To Bank—Premium	9,500	Dec. 31	By Balance c/d	9,500
1988			1988		
Jan. 1	To Balance b/d	9,500	Dec. 31	By Balance c/d	19,000
Jan. 1	To Bank—Premium	9,500			
		19,000			19,000
1989			1989		
Jan. 1	To Balance b/d	19,000	Dec. 31	By Bank	30,000
Jan. 1	To Bank—Premium	9,500			
Dec. 31	To Profit—Transferred to Depreciation Provision A/c	1,500			
		30,000			30,000

LEASE (NEW) ACCOUNT

Date	Particulars	Amount Rs	Date	Particulars	Amount Rs
1990					
Jan. 1	To Bank	30,000			

Depreciation on an asset purchased in the course of a year. There are two alternatives available regarding charging of depreciation on an asset which has been purchased during the course of an accounting year.

(a) Depreciation may be charged for the full year irrespective of the date of purchase at the given rate.

(b) Depreciation may be charged only for the part of the year for which the asset could have been made available for use on account of its being purchased during the course of the year. For example, if the asset has been purchased on 1st July, 1990 and the accounting year ends on 31st December, depreciation may be charged only for a period of six months.

Tutorial Note. The students are advised to give the assumption made by them in the absence of any instruction in the question. However, if the rate of depreciation has been given as a certain percentage per annum and the date of the purchase of the asset has been given, it would be advisable to charge depreciation only for the part of the accounting year for which the asset has been made available for use.

Sale of an asset during the year. In case an asset is sold during the course of the year, the amount realised should be credited to the Asset Account. Depreciation for the period for which the asset has been used should be written off in the usual manner. Any balance in the Asset Account representing profit or loss on sale of the asset should be transferred to the Profit and Loss Account.

Illustration 13.8. A firm purchases a truck for a sum of Rs 1,00,000 on 1st January, 1989. It charges 20% depreciation per annum according to the Diminishing Balance Method. The truck was sold on 1st July, 1990 for a sum of Rs 80,000. You are required to prepare the Truck Account for 1989 and 1990.

Solution:

TRUCK ACCOUNT

Date	Particulars	Amount Rs	Date	Particulars	Amount Rs
1989 Jan. 1	To Bank	1,00,000	1989 Dec. 31 Dec. 31	By Depreciation By Balance c/d	20,000 80,000
		1,00,000			1,00,000
1990 Jan. 1 Dec. 31	To Balance b/d To P. & L. A/c (profit on sale)	80,000 8,000	1990 July 1	By Depreciation (depreciation for 6 months) By Bank (Sale Proceeds)	8,000 80,000
		88,000			88,000

In case it is desired to prepare separately Provision for Depreciation Account, Truck Disposal Account etc., the solution of the question will be as follows:

TRUCK ACCOUNT

Date	Particulars	Amount Rs	Date	Particulars	Amount Rs
1989 Jan. 1	To Bank A/c	1,00,000	1989 Dec. 31	By Balance c/d	1,00,000
		1,00,000			1,00,000
1990 Jan. 1	To Balance b/d	1,00,000	1990 July 1	By Asset Disposal A/c	1,00,000
		1,00,000			1,00,000

PROVISION FOR DEPRECIATION ACCOUNT

Date	Particulars	Amount Rs	Date	Particulars	Amount Rs
1989			1989		
Dec. 31	To Balance c/d	20,000	Dec. 31	By Depreciation A/c (or P. & L. a/c)	20,000
		20,000			20,000
1990			1990		
July 1	To Truck Disposal A/c	28,000	Jan. 1	By Balance b/d	20,000
			July 1	By Depreciation A/c (Dep. for 6 months)	8,000
		28,000			28,000

TRUCK DISPOSAL ACCOUNT

Date	Particulars	Amount Rs	Date	Particulars	Amount Rs
1990			1990		
July 1	To Truck A/c	1,00,000	July 1	By Provision for Dep. A/c	28,000
Dec. 31	To P. & L. A/c (profit on sale)	8,000	July 1	By Bank (sale proceeds)	80,000
		1,08,000			1,08,000

Change in the Method of Depreciation

Sometimes a change in the method of depreciation may be required. For example, a firm may change the method of depreciation from Fixed Instalment Method to Reducing Balance Method or *vice versa*. In such a case, there can be two different situations:

(i) Change in the method of depreciation may be desired from the current year onwards. In such a case, depreciation will be charged according to the new method from the current year (*See Illustrations 13.9 and 13.12*).

(ii) Change in the method of depreciation may be desired from a back date. This will require necessary adjustments to be made in the current year for any extra or less depreciation charged in earlier years. In such a case, the best course would be to compute the amount of depreciation which has already been charged according to the old method and the amount of depreciation that is to be charged according to the new method. The difference if any should be credited (or debited) to the Asset Account in the current year and should be shown as a separate charge (or income) in the Profit and Loss Account of the current year of the firm. (*See Illustrations 13.10 and 13.11*).

Illustration 13.9. On 1st July, 1987, a company purchased a Plant for Rs 20,000. Depreciation was provided at 10% per annum on straight line method on 31st December every year. With effect from 1.1.89, the company decided to change the method of depreciation to Diminishing Balance Method @ 15% p.a. On 1.7.1990, the plant was sold for Rs 12,000. Prepare Plant Account from 1987 to 1990.

Solution:

PLANT ACCOUNT

Date	Particulars	Amount Rs	Date	Particulars	Amount Rs
1987			1987		
July 1	To Cash	20,000	Dec. 31	By Depreciation	1,000
			Dec. 31	By Balance c/d	19,000
		20,000			20,000
1988			1988		
Jan. 1	To Balance b/d	19,000	Dec. 31	By Depreciation	2,000
			Dec. 31	By Balance c/d	17,000
		19,000			19,000
1989			1989		
Jan. 1	To Balance b/d	17,000	Dec. 31	By Depreciation	2,550
				By Balance c/d	14,450
		17,000			17,000
1990			1990		
Jan. 1	To Balance b/d	14,450	June 31	By Dep. (for 6 months)	1,084
			July 1	By Cash	12,000
			July 1	By P. and L. A/c	1,366
		14,450			14,450

Illustration 13.10. On the basis of the information given in Illustration 13.9, prepare Plant Account from 1987 to 1990, if the firm decides on 1.1.1989 to charge depreciation according to Diminishing Balance Method *w.e.f.* 1.7.1987 and to make adjustments for arrears of depreciation in the year 1989.

Solution:

PLANT ACCOUNT

Date	Particulars	Amount Rs	Date	Particulars	Amount Rs
1987			1987		
July 1	To Cash	20,000	Dec. 31	By Depreciation	1,000
			Dec. 31	By Balance c/d	19,000
		20,000			20,000
1988			1988		
Jan. 1	To Balance b/d	19,000	Dec. 31	By Depreciation	2,000
			Dec. 31	By Balance c/d	17,000
		19,000			19,000
1989			1989		
Jan. 1	To Balance b/d	17,000	Dec. 31	By Balance of Dep. for 1987 & 1988	1,275
			Dec. 31	By Depreciation for 1989	2,359
			Dec. 31	By Balance c/d	13,366
		17,000			17,000

Contd....

Date	Particulars	Amount Rs	Date	Particulars	Amount Rs
1990 Jan. 1	To Balance b/d	13,434	1990 June 30	By Dep. (for 6 months)	1,002
			July 1	By Bank (Sale)	12,000
			July 1	By P. and L. A/c (loss on sale)	364
		13,366			13,366

Working Notes.

1. Adjustment for arrears of depreciation in 1989

Year	Fixed Instalment Method	Diminishing Balance Method
1987 (for half year)	1,000	1,500
1988	2,000	2,775
	3,000	4,275

Extra depreciation to be charged in 1989 is Rs 1,275 on account of change in the method of depreciation.

2. Depreciation for 1989 on Rs 15,725 at 15% comes to Rs 2,359.

Illustration 13.11. A firm purchased a plant for Rs 10,000 on 1.1.1985. It was charging depreciation at 10% p.a. according to the fixed instalment method. At the end of 1988, the firm decided to change the method of depreciation from the Fixed Instalment Method to the Diminishing Balance Method *w.e.f.* 1.1.1985. The rate of depreciation was to be at 12% p.a. You are required to prepare the Plant Account for the three years ending 31st December, 1988 and also show how the depreciation item would appear in the Profit and Loss Account of the year 1988.

Solution:

COMPUTATION OF DEPRECIATION

	Fixed Instalment Method			Diminishing Balance Method	
Year	Book value of the asset	Depreciation	Year	Book value of the asset	Depreciation
1985	10,000	1,000	1985	10,000	1,200
1986	9,000	1,000	1986	8,800	1,056
1987	8,000	1,000	1987	7,744	929
		3,000			3,185

From the above figures, it is clear that on account of change in the method of depreciation Rs 185 will have to be charged as extra depreciation for the last 3 years in the year 1988 besides the usual depreciation for the year. In 1988, the depreciation will be charged according to the Diminishing Balance Method which comes to Rs 818 on the book value of Rs 6,815. (*i.e.*, Rs 7,744 – Rs 929). The Plant Account can now be prepared as follows.

PLANT ACCOUNT

Date	Particulars	Amount Rs	Date	Particulars	Amount Rs
1985 Jan. 1	To Bank	10,000	1985 Dec. 31	By Depreciation	1,000
				By Balance c/d	9,000
		10,000			10,000

Contd....

Date	Particulars	Amount Rs	Date	Particulars	Amount Rs
1986 Jan. 1	To Balance b/d	9,000	1986 Dec. 31	By Depreciation By Balance c/d	1,000 8,000
		9,000			9,000
1987 Jan. 1	To Balance b/d	8,000	1987 Dec. 31	By Depreciation (extra for 1985–1987) By Depreciation for 1988 (according to the Diminishing Balance Method) By Balance c/d	185 818 6,997
		8,000			8,000

PROFIT AND LOSS ACCOUNT

Dr.   *for the year ending 31.12.1988*   Cr.

Particulars	Amount Rs	Particulars	Amount Rs
To Depreciation for 1988	818		
Add: Additional depreciation for 1985 to 1987 on account of change to Diminishing Balance Method from Fixed Instalment Method	185	1,003	

Illustration 13.12. A firm purchased on 1st January, 1984 certain Machinery for Rs 58,200 and spent Rs 1,800 on its erection. On 1st July, 1984 additional machinery costing Rs 20,000 was purchased. On 1st July, 1986 the machinery purchased on 1st January, 1984 having become obsolete was auctioned for Rs 28,600 and on the same date fresh machinery was purchased at a cost of Rs 40,000.

Depreciation was provided for annually on 31st December at the rate of 10 per cent on written down value. In 1987, however, the firm changed this method of providing depreciation on the original cost of the machinery.

Give the Machinery Account as it would stand at the end of each year from 1984 to 1987.

Solution:

MACHINERY ACCOUNT

Date	Particulars	Amount Rs	Date	Particulars	Amount Rs
1984 Jan. 1 July 1	To Cash (58,200 + 1,800) To Cash	60,000 20,000	1984 Dec. 31	By Depreciation (6,000 + 1,000) By Balance c/d	7,000 73,000
		80,000			80,000

Contd....

Date	Particulars	Amount Rs	Date	Particulars	Amount Rs
1985 Jan. 1	To Balance b\d	73,000	1985 Dec. 31	By Depreciation	7,300
				By Balance c/d	65,700
		73,000			73,000
1986 Jan. 1	To Balance b/d	65,700	1986 July 1	By Cash (sale price)	28,600
July 1	To Cash	40,000		By Depreciation on Machine soled	2,430
				By P. & L. A/c	17,570
				By Depreciation (1,710 + 2,000)	3,710
				By Balance c/d	53,390
		1,05,700			1,05,700
1987 Jan. 1	To Balance b/d	53,390	1987 Dec. 31	By Depreciation @ 5% on original cost of machines (Rs 20,000 + Rs 40,000)	3,000
				By Balance c/d	50,390
		53,390			53,390

Note. Loss on sale of machinery purchased on Jan. 1, 1984.

	Rs
Cost Price	60,000
Less: Depreciation for 1984	6,000
	54,400
Less: Depreciation for 1985	5,400
	48,600
Less: Depreciation for 1986 (6 months)	2,430
Book value on July 1, 1986	46,170
Less: Sales value	28,600
Loss on sale	17,570

Illustration 13.13. On 1st April, 1988 a new plant was purchased for Rs 40,000 and a further sum of Rs 2,000 was spent on its installation.

On 1st October, 1990 another plant was acquired for Rs 25,000.

Due to an accident on 3rd January, 1991 the first plant was totally destroyed and the remnants were sold for Rs 1,000 only.

On 21st January, 1992 a second hand plant was purchased for Rs 30,000 and a further sum of Rs 5,000 was spent for bringing the same to use on and from 15th March, 1992.

Depreciation has been provided at 10 per cent on straight line basis. It was a practice to provide depreciation for full year on all acquisition made at any time during any year and to ignore depreciation on any item sold or disposed of during the year. None of the assets were insured. The accounts are closed annually to 31st March.

It is now decided to follow the rate of 15 per cent on diminishing balance method with retrospective effect in respect of the existing items of plant and to make the necessary adjustment entry on 1st April, 1992.

Show the journal entries to be passed for the purpose and the Plant Account and the Depreciation Provision Account for all the years.

Solution:

PLANT ACCOUNT

Date	Particulars	Amount Rs	Date	Particulars	Amount Rs
1988			1989		
April 1	To Bank (Cost & instal.)	42,000	March 31	By Balance c/d	42,000
1989			1990		
April 1	To Balance b/d	42,000	March 31	By Balance c/d	42,000
1990			1991		
April 1	To Balance b/d	42,000	Jan. 3	By Bank	1,000
Oct. 1	To Bank	25,000	March 31	By Dep. Provision A/c	8,400
				By Profit & Loss A/c	32,600
				By Balance c/d	25,000
		67,000			67,000
1991			1992		
April 1	To Balance b/d	25,000	March 31	By Balance c/d	60,000
1992					
Jan. 21	To Bank	30,000			
	To Bank	5,000			
		60,000			60,000

PROVISION FOR DEPRECIATION ACCOUNT

Date	Particulars	Amount	Date	Particulars	Amount
1989			1989		
Mar. 31	To Balance c/d	4,200	Mar. 31	By Depreciation	
				(10% on 42,000)	4,200
1990			1989		
Mar. 31	To Balance c/d	8,400	April 1	By Balance b/d	4,200
			1990		
			Mar. 31	By Depreciation	4,200
		8,400			8,400
1991			1990		
Jan. 3	To Plant A/c	8,400	April 1	By Balance b/d	8,400
Mar. 31	To Balance c/d	2,500	1991		
			Mar. 31	By Depreciation A/c	2,500
		10,900			10,900
1992			1991		
Mar. 31	To Balance c/d	8,500	April 1	By Balance b/d	2,500
			Mar. 12	By Depreciation A/c	6,000
		8,500			8,500
			1992		
			April 1	By Balance b/d	8,500
				By Depreciation	
				(additional)	3,687

JOURNAL

Date	Particulars	L.F.	Dr. Amount Rs	Cr. Amount Rs
1992 April 1	Depreciation A/c Dr. To Provision for Depreciation A/c (Being the provision made for the additional amount of depreciation required due to the change in the basis of depreciation to 15% on reducing balance method with retrospective effect).		3,687	3,687

Working Note.

Depreciation @ 15% on *w.d.v.* basis:

			Depreciation		
			90–91	91–92	Total
		Rs	Rs	Rs	Rs
Plant Purchased in:	1990–91	25,000	3,750	3,187	6,937
	1991–92	35,000	—	5,250	5,250
			3,750	8,437	12,187
Provision already existing					8,500
Additional Provision required					3,687

Illustration 13.14. Giri Raj Enterprises purchased some second-hand machinery on 1st April, 1987 for Rs 3,70,000 and installed at a cost of Rs 30,000. On 1st October, 1988, it purchased another machine for Rs 1,00,000 and on 1st October, 1989, it sold off the first machine purchased in 1987, for Rs 2,80,000.

On the same date it purchased a machinery for Rs 2,50,000. On 1st October, 1990, the second machinery purchased for Rs 1,00,000 was sold off for Rs 20,000.

In the beginning depreciation was provided on machinery at the rate of 10% p.a. on the original cost each year on 31st March. From the year 1988–89, however, the trader changed the method of providing depreciation and adopted the written down value method, the rate of depreciation being 15% p.a.

Give the Machinery Account for the period 1987 to 1991.

(C.A. Entrance, Nov., 1991)

Solution:

In the books of Giri Raj Enterprises
MACHINERY ACCOUNT

Date	Particulars	Amount Rs	Date	Particulars	Amount Rs
1987 April 1	To Bank A/c To Bank (Exp.)	3,70,000 30,000 4,00,000	1988 Mar. 31	By Depreciation A/c (10% on Rs 4,00,000) By Balance c/d	40,000 3,60,000 4,00,000

Contd....

Date	Particulars	Amount Rs	Date	Particulars	Amount Rs
1988 April 1 Oct. 1	To Balance b/d To Bank	3,60,000 1,00,000	1989 Mar. 31	By Depreciation A/c (15% on Rs 3,60,000 & 15% on Rs 1,00,000 for 6 months) By Balance c/d (Rs 3,06,000 + 92,500)	54,000 ⎤ 7,500 ⎦ 3,98,500
		4,60,000			4,60,000
1989 April 1 Oct. 1	To Balance b/d (Rs 3,06,000 + 92,500) To Bank A/c	3,98,500 2,50,000	1989 Oct. 1 1990 Mar. 31	By Bank A/c By Depreciation A/c (15% on Rs 3,06,000 for 6 months) By P & L A/c (Loss on Sale) By Depreciation A/c (15% on Rs 92,500 & 15% on Rs 2,50,000 for 6 months) By Balance c/d (Rs 78,625 + Rs 2,31,250)	2,80,000 22,950 3,050 13,875 ⎤ 18,750 ⎦ 3,09,875
		6,48,500			6,48,500
1990 April 1	To Balance b/d (Rs 78,625 + Rs 2,31,250)	3,09,875	1990 Oct. 1 1991 Mar. 31	By Bank A/c By Depreciation A/c (15% on Rs 78,625 for 6 months) By P. & L. A/c (Loss on Sale) By Depreciation A/c (15% on Rs 2,31,250) By Balance c/d	20,000 5,896.88 52,728.12 34,687.50 1,96,562.50
		3,09,875.00			3,09,875.00

Working Notes:

(1) *Loss on sale of machine on 1.10.1989*

	Rs	Rs
Written down value on 1.4.1989		3,06,000
Less: Depreciation for 6 months	22,950	
Sale price	2,80,000	3,02,950
Loss on sale		3,050

(2) *Loss on sale of machine on 1.10.1990*

	Rs	Rs
Written down value on 1.4.1990		78,625.00
Less: Depreciation for 6 months	5,896.88	
Sale price	20,00,000	25,896.88
Loss on sale		52,728.12

DEPRECIATION OF DIFFERENT ASSETS

The following observations can be made regarding charging of depreciation on different assets:

1. **Goodwill.** Depreciation does not arise in the value of the goodwill of the business unless the profits of the firm are declining. Since, goodwill is an intangible asset, it will be advisable to write off the value of the goodwill over a reasonable period. The amount written off should be shown separately in the Profit and Loss Account.

2. **Free-hold land.** No depreciation need be charged in case of such properties.

3. **Free-hold buildings, plants, machinery, ship, etc.** Fixed Instalment Method or Diminishing Balance Method may be used for charging depreciation on these assets. The endeavour should be to write off the asset during its effective life. In case of Plant and Machinery, the Machine Hour Rate method can also be profitably used.

4. **Lease-hold land and buildings.** The Fixed Instalment Method should generally be used for writting off depreciation in respect of such assets.

However, Depreciation Fund Method or Insurance Policy Method can also be used profitably for assets coming in the 3rd and 4th category discussed above.

5. **Loose tools, jigs, live stock, etc.** Revalution Method is the most appropriate method for charging depreciation on these assets.

6. **Patents, trade marks, etc.** These assets have a maximum legal life. However, their commercial life may be much shorter. Such assets should, therefore, be depreciated according to the Fixed Instalment Method in a way so that they are written off within the legal or commercial life, whichever is shorter.

7. **Mines, oil wells, quarries, etc.** Depreciation should be charged according to the Depletion Method in case of these assets.

It should be noted that the method of charging depreciation in respect of assets should be consistent year after year. In case the method of depreciation is changed, such fact together with the effect on profit on account of change in the method of depreciation has to be disclosed by way of a note in the final accounts of the business. Similarly, if it has not been possible to charge depreciation on assets on account of inadequacy of profits in any year, such fact should also be disclosed in the Final Accounts of the business for that particular year.

DEPRECIATION ON REPLACEMENT COST

In recent years, there has been a lot of controversy regarding charging of depreciation on historical *vs.* replacement cost of the asset. It is being argued by the protagonists of 'replacement cost' that since one of the major objectives of providing depreciation is to provide enough funds for the replacement of an asset at the end of its useful life, it will be appropriate to provide for depreciation on the replacement cost of the asset rather than its historical cost. This is particularly true in the context of present inflationary conditions. If depreciation is charged on the basis of historical cost, there will not be enough funds to replace the asset at the end of its useful life on account of substantial increase in the price of the new asset to be purchased for replacing the old asset. Thus, they argue that the very purpose of providing depreciation is completely defeated if the depreciation is charged on the basis of historical cost of the asset.

There is considerable strength in the arguments put forward by the protagonists of charging depreciation on the replacement cost. However, the following are the practical difficulties in adopting this approach.

1. It is difficult to estimate the replacement cost well in advance. The cost can be correctly known only when the asset is replaced.

2. The new asset purchased for replacing the old asset is always of a better type in respect of its quality as well as efficiency. Of course, one has to pay more for the new asset, but the profitability of the business also increases on account of new and better quality of the asset. In case depreciation is charged on replacement cost, depreciation is charged for the improved asset even when such asset has not been used for generating revenue during those years.

3. Income Tax Authorities do not give recognition to the concept of charging depreciation on replacement cost.

4. Under the Companies Act, depreciation is to be charged only on original cost of the asset. Any profit or loss made on scrapping the asset over its book value should be credited or debited to the Profit and Loss Account of the year in which the asset is scrapped.

5. Businessmen favour charging of depreciation on replacement cost under inflationary conditions. It is doubtful whether they would favour charging depreciation on the replacement cost of the asset in periods when the prices are falling.

On account of the above practical difficulties, it will be advisable to charge depreciation on the historical cost of the asset. However, in case it is desired to provide enough funds for replacement of the asset at the end of its useful life, the following steps may be taken.

1. A replacement reserve may be created in the books of accounts of the business. The additional amount required for replacing the asset over and above the original cost of the asset may be estimated. Every year, an appropriate amount may be transferred from the P. & L. Account besides usual depreciation on the asset to provide for additional amount required for replacement of the asset over and above the original cost of the asset. It may be debited to the Profit and Loss Appropriation Account and credited to the Replacement Reserve Account.

2. The Replacement Reserve Account should be credited every year with interest at the current rate on the accumulated balance standing to the credit of this account.

In case, the above procedure is followed, the business will have sufficient funds to replace the old asset by a new one as and when the necessity arises.

DEPRECIATION POLICY

The management has to adopt a suitable depreciation policy keeping in view the following objectives:

(i) Recovery of the original investment, i.e. the acquisition cost of the asset, before the expiry of the economic life of the asset.

(ii) Ensuring a uniform rate of return on investments.

(*iii*) Generating sufficient funds for the replacement of the asset after the expiry of its economic life.

(*iv*) Deriving maximum tax benefit.

(*v*) Ascertainment of correct profit or loss.

The above objectives can be considerably achieved if the management takes care of the following aspects in framing its depreciation policy.

(*i*) **Selection of an appropriate method.** The management should select an appropriate method keeping in view the nature of the asset and the prime objective of the management.

(*ii*) **Periodic review of provision.** The choice of the method determines the amount of the depreciation and the mode of its recording. However, the management must review periodically whether the provision for depreciation which is being made is proper or not. Any under or over provision in the context of changed circumstances should properly be adjusted in the books of accounts.

(*iii*) **Evaluation and disclosure of depreciation policy.** The depreciation policy being followed by the business should be evaluated in the context of tax, independence of price level changes, Governments regulations etc. The effect of any change in the depreciation policy in an accounting period should be quantified and disclosed in the financial statements of the business.

ACCOUNTING STANDARD 6 (REVISED)
DEPRECIATION ACCOUNTING

The following are the salient features of the Revised Accounting Standard on Depreciation Accounting issued by the Institute of Chartered Accountants of India in September, 1994.[1]

1. The standard applies to all depreciable assets except the following items to which special considerations apply:

(*a*) forests, plantations and similar regenerative natural resources;

(*b*) wasting assets including expenditure on the exploration for the extraction of minerals oils, natural gas and similar non/regenerative resources;

(*c*) expenditure on research and development;

(*d*) goodwill;

(*e*) livestock;

(*f*) land unless it has a limited useful life for the enterprise.

2. The depreciable amount of a depreciable asset should be allocated on a systematic basis to each accounting period during the useful life of the asset.

3. The depreciation method selected should be applied consistently from period to period. A change from one method of providing depreciation to another should be made only if the adoption of the new method is required by statute or for compliance with an accounting standard or if it is considered that the change would result in a more appropriate preparation or presentation of the financial statements of the enterprise. When such a change in the method of depreciation is made, depreciation should be recalculated in accordance with the new method from the date of the asset coming into use. The deficiency or surplus arising from retrospective recomputation of depreciation in accordance with

---

[1] Chartered Accountant, Sept. 1994 P. 77.

the new method should be adjusted in the accounts in the year in which the method of depreciation is changed. In case the change in the method results in deficiency in depreciation in respect of past years, the deficiency should be charged in the statement of profit and loss. In case the change in the method result in surplus, the surplus, should be credited to the statement of profit and loss. Such a change should be treated as a change in accounting policy and its effect should be quantified and disclosed.

4. The useful life of a depreciable asset should be estimated after considering the following factors:

(*i*) expected physical wear and tear;

(*ii*) obsolescence;

(*iii*) legal or other limits on the use of the asset.

5. The useful lives of major depreciable assets or classes of depreciable assets may be reviewed periodically. Where there is a revision of the estimated useful life of an asset, the unamortised depreciable amount should be charged over the revised remaining useful life.

6. Any addition or extension which becomes an integral part of the existing asset should be depreciated over the remaining useful life of that asset. The depreciation on such addition or extension may also be provided at the rate applied to the existing asset. Where an addition or extension retains a separate identity and is capable of being used after the existing asset is disposed of, depreciation should be provided independently on the basis of an estimate of its own useful life.

7. Where the historical cost of a depreciable asset has undergone a change due to increase or decrease in long-term liability on account of exchange fluctuations, price adjustments, changes in duties or similar factors, the depreciation on the revised unamortised depreciable amount should be provided prospectively over the residual useful life of the asset.

8. Where the depreciable assets are revalued, the provision for depreciation should be based on the revalued amount and on the estimate of the remaining useful lives of such assets. In case the revaluation has a material effect on the amount of depreciation, the same should be disclosed separately in the year in which revaluation is carried out.

9. If any depreciable asset is disposed of, discarded, demolished or destroyed, the net surplus or deficiency, if material, should be disposed separately.

10. The following information should be disclosed in the financial statements:

(*i*) the historical cost or other amount substituted for historical cost of each class of depreciable assets;

(*ii*) total depreciation for the period for each class of assets; and

(*iii*) the related accumulated depreciation.

11. The following information should also be disclosed in the financial statements along with the disclosure of other accounting policies:

(*i*) depreciation methods used; and

(*ii*) depreciation rates or the useful lives of the assets, if they are different from the principal rates specified in the statute governing the enterprise.

The standard has become mandatory in respect of accounting periods beginning on or after 1st April, 1995.

KEY TERMS

☐ **Amortization**: The process of writing off the intangible assets.

☐ **Depletion**: The portion of the cost of the natural resources recognised as an expense for each period.

☐ **Dilapidation**: Damage done to a building or other property during the tenancy.

☐ **Depreciation**: The portion of the cost of tangible operating assets (other than land) recognised as an expense for each period.

☐ **Depreciation Accounting**: A system of accounting which aims to distribute the cost or other basic values of tangible capital assets (less salvage, if any) over the estimated useful life of the asset in a systematic and rational manner.

TEST QUESTIONS

Objective type | TEST YOUR UNDERSTANDING |

1. State whether each of the following statements is True or False:
   (a) The objective of charging Profit and Loss Account with the amount of depreciation is to spread the cost of an asset over its useful life for the purpose of income determination.
   (b) The amount of depreciation is credited to Depreciation Fund Account in case of Annuity Method.
   (c) The charge for use of the asset remains uniform each year in case of straight line method.
   (d) Depreciation is charged on the book value of the asset each year in case of Diminishing Balance Method.
   (e) Depletion Method is suitable for charging depreciation in case of live stock or loose tools.
   (f) Net charge to the Profit and Loss Account is the same under both Annuity Method and Depreciation Fund Method.
   (g) The amount of depreciation is credited to the Depreciation Fund Account in the Depreciation Fund Method.
   (h) The asset appears always at original cost in case depreciation is credited to Provision for Depreciation Account.
   (i) In case of Insurance Policy Method, the depreciation is credited to the Asset Account.

   [**Ans.** (a) True, (b) False, (c) False, (d) True, (e) False, (f) True, (g) True,
   (h) True, (i) False].

2. Choose the most appropriate answer:
   (i) Depreciation is the process of
      (a) apportionment of the cost of the asset over its useful life.
      (b) valuation of assets.
      (c) maintenance of asset in a state of efficiency
   (ii) Machine Hour Rate Method of charging depreciation is useful when
      (a) output can be effectively measured.
      (b) use of the asset can be measured in terms of time.
      (c) utility of the asset can be directly related to its productive use.
   (iii) Profit and Loss on depreciation fund investment is transferred to:
      (a) Profit and Loss Account.
      (b) the Asset Account.

      (c)   Depreciation Fund Account.

(iv) The profit on depreciation policy is transferred to:

      (a)   Depreciation Reserve Account.

      (b)   Profit and Loss Account

      (c)   Asset Account.

(v) In case of Annuity Method, the amount of depreciation is

      (a)   increasing every year.

      (b)   fixed for all the years.

      (c)   decreasing every year.

(vi) For providing depreciation on leasehold property, the appropriate method of depreciation is

      (a)   Replacement Method.

      (b)   Revaluation Method.

      (c)   Fixed Instalment Method.

(vii) Depletion method of depreciation is used in

      (a)   cattle, loose tools etc.

      (b)   mines, quarries etc.

      (c)   machinery, building, furniture etc.

(viii) The interest lost on the acquisition of an asset is taken into account in calculating depreciation in

      (a)   Depletion Method

      (b)   Annuity Method

      (c)   Diminishing Balance Method.

(ix) In this method depreciation is charged by allocating depreciable cost in proportion of the annual output to the probable life-time output:

      (a)   Working Hours Method

      (b)   Production Units Method

      (c)   Revaluation Method.

[**Ans.** (i) (a), (ii) (b), (iii) (c), (iv) (a), (v) (b), (vi) (c), (vii) (b), (viii) (b), (ix) (b)].

Essay type   FOR REVIEW, DISCUSSION AND PRACTICE

1. Explain the need and significance of depreciation? What factors should be considered for determining amount of depreciation?

2. Distinguish between "straight line method" and "diminishing balance method" of providing depreciation. Which one of the above two methods would you recommed to provide depreciation on Plant and Machinery?

3. Explain the circumstances under which different methods of depreciation can be employed.

4. Write short notes on:

    (a)   Group Depreciation Method;

    (b)   Double Declining Balance Method; and

    (c)   Accounting Standard 6: Depreciation Accounting.

5. What is Depreciation? Discuss the merits and demerits of Sinking Fund Method of depreciation.

PRACTICAL PROBLEMS

Straight-line Method

1. On 1st January, 1988, a merchant purchased some furniture costing Rs 55,000. It is estimated that its working life is 10 years at the end of which it will fetch Rs 5,000. Additions are made on 1st January, 1989 and 1st July, 1991 to the value of Rs 9,500 and Rs 8,400 (residual values

Rs 500 and Rs 400 respectively). Show the Furniture Account for the first four years, if depreciation is written off according to the straight- line method.

[**Ans.** Balance of Furniture Account on 1st Jan., 1992 Rs 49,800].

2. A company provides depreciation under the straight line method at the rate of 10% p.a. The balance standing in the Plant and Machinery Account on 31st Dec., 1985, after writing off depreciation for the year, was Rs 1,95,150 (total cost price of the plant was Rs 3,58,000).

During January 1986 new plant was purchased at a cost of Rs 29,500 and one machine which had cost Rs 5,500 in 1974 was sold as scrap for Rs 400.

During January 1987, there were additions costing Rs 18,000 and a machine which had cost Rs 7,000 in 1982 was sold for Rs 3,500.

Write up Plant and Machinery Account for 1986 and 1987.

[**Ans.** Balance as on Dec. 31, 1986 Rs 1,85,900, Dec. 31, 1987, Rs 1,60,550]

[**Hint.** Profit of Rs 400 on machinery sold as scrap will be taken direct to P. & L. Account.]

3. The following balances appear in the books of Mahajan Brothers:

		Rs
Jan. 1, 1990	Machinery Account	40,000
Jan. 1, 1990	Provision for Depreciation	18,000

On 1st January, 1990 they decided to sell a machinery for Rs 4,350. This machine was purchased for Rs 8,000 in January, 1986.

You are required to prepare Machinery Account and Provision for Depreciation Account on 31st Dec. 1990, assuming the firm has been charging depreciation at 10% p.a. on straight line method.

[**Ans.** Balances: Machinery Account Rs 32,000; Provision for Depreciation Account Rs 18,000]

Diminishing Balance Method

3. A plant is purchased for Rs 20,000. It is depreciated at 5% per annum on reducing balance for five years when it becomes obsolete due to new method of production and is scrapped. The scrap produces Rs 5,385. Show the plant account in the ledger.

[**Ans.** Loss on sale Rs 10,091; Depreciation 1st year Rs 1,000; 2nd year Rs 950; 3rd year Rs 902; 4th year Rs 857; 5th year Rs 815].

4. On 1st January, 1982 Bhola Nath Dutt & Sons purchased a machine costing Rs 1,00,000. Its working life is 10 years. It has been decided to depreciate it at the rate of 12 ½% on the Diminishing Balance Method. Show the Machinery Account for first three years.

5. If an asset was purchased for Rs 50,000 on 1st January, 1988, what would be its book value three years after if it was depreciated according to the following methods: (i) Straight Line Method, and (ii) Written Down Value Method. The rate of depreciation is 10% per annum. Show your answer by a tabular ledger account.

[**Ans.** Straight Line Method Rs 35,000; Written Down Value Method Rs 36,450]

Depreciation Fund Method

6. A company purchased a four years' lease on January 1, 1985 for Rs 20,150. It is decided to provide for the replacement at the end of four years by setting up a Depreciation Fund. It is expected that investments will fetch interest at 4 per cent. Sinking Fund tables show that to provide the requisite sum at 4 per cent at the end of four years, an investment of Rs 4,745.02 is required. Investments are made to the nearest rupee.

On December 31, 1988, the investments are sold for Rs 14,830. On 1st January, 1989, the same lease is renewed for a further period of 4 years by payment of Rs 22,000.

Show journal entries and give the important ledger accounts to record the above.

[**Ans.** Amount credited to the Profit and Loss Account at the end of December, 1988 Rs 17.56].

Insurance Policy Method

7. Chilies Ltd. acquired a long-term lease of property on payment of Rs 60,000. A Lease-hold Redemption Policy was taken out on which an annual premium of Rs 1,440 was payable. The surrender value of the policy on 31st March, 1987 was Rs 12,896 to which amount the policy account stood adjusted. Next premium was paid on 20th December, 1987 and the surrender value on 31st March, 1988 was Rs 14,444.

   (i) Show the Redemption Fund Account and the Policy Account for the year ended 31st March, 1988.

   (ii) Assuming that on maturity, a sum of Rs 60,100 was received and the balance in Policy Account then stood at Rs 59,920 give the ledger accounts showing the entries necessary to close the accounts concerned.

   [Ans. (i) Balance at the end of 1988 Fund A/c & Policy A/c Rs 14,444 each,
   (ii) Transfer to P & L A/c: profit on maturity Rs 100].

Depletion Method

8. Burdwan Collieries Ltd. acquired the lease right for 20 years of a mine on January 1, 1979 on a lump payment of Rs 5,00,000 to the landlord. It was estimated by the expert that the coal deposit of the mine was Rs 20,00,000 tonnes, 75 per cent, of which could be raised within the time period. The company decided to write off the Lease Account under straight line method of depreciation. The Lease Account was shown accordingly for the first five years. On 31st October, 1984, the Board of Directors decided to depreciate the Lease on "Depletion" method with retrospective effect from January 1, 1979. The annual raisings were:

1979	20,000 tonnes
1980	30,000 tonnes
1981	1,00,000 tonnes
1982	2,00,000 tonnes
1983	2,00,000 tonnes
1984	2,00,000 tonnes

You are required to show the Lease A/c from 1st January, 1979 to 31st December, 1984 showing clearly your calculations.

   [Ans. Arrears of depreciation in 1984 Rs 58,333, Balance in the Lease Account
   at the end of 1984 Rs 2,50,000].

Group Depreciation Method

9. The valuation of a group of assets (Plant and Machinery), on 1st January, 1984 was Rs 32,000 and the estimated life was 8 years. The following purchases and sales took place upto 31st December, 1986:

Purchases: March 31, 1984 Cost Rs 15,000, estimated life 10 years.

   Sept. 30, 1985 Cost Rs 12,000, estimated life 6 years.

   April 31, 1986 Cost Rs 20,000 estimated life 8 years.

Sales: Out of initial group of assets, a machine (whose valuation on 1st January, 1984 was Rs 5,000) sold for Rs 4,700 on 30th June, 1986.

Assuming the break-up value of each asset to be 10 per cent of the initial valuation or original cost, prepare the Asset Account for the 1st three years.

   [Ans. Balance on 31st December, 1986, Rs 57,424].

Change and Disposal

10. A company purchased a second-hand machine on January 1, 1984 for Rs 37,000 and immediately spent Rs 2,000 on its repairs and Rs 1,000 on its erection. On July 1, 1985 it purchased another machine for Rs 10,000 and on July 1, 1986 it sold off the first machine for Rs 28,000 bought another for Rs 25,000. On July 1, 1987, the second machine was also sold off for Rs 2,000.

Depreciation was provided on machinery at 10% on the original cost annually on December 31. In 1985, however, the company changed the method of providing depreciation and adopted the written down value method, the rate of depreciation being 15% per annum.

Give the Machinery Account for four years commencing from the acquisition of machine. Amounts to be calculated to nearest ten rupees.

[**Ans.** Balance in the Machinery Account on 31.12.1987 Rs 19,650, Loss on sale of machine in 1985 Rs 300, in 1987 Rs 5,270].

11. A second-hand machinery was purchased on 1st January, 1985 for Rs 30,000 and Rs 6,000 and Rs 4,000 were spent on its repairs and erection immediately. On 1st July, 1986, another machinery was purchased for Rs 26,000 and on 1st July, 1987, the first machinery having become obsolete was auctioned for Rs 30,000. On the same date another machine was purchased for Rs 25,000. On 1st July, 1988 the second machinery was also sold off and it fetched Rs 23,000.

Depreciation was provided on machinery at the rate of 10% on the original cost annually on 31st December. In 1987, the method of providing depreciation was changed to the written down (diminishing value) method, the rate of depreciation being 15%.

You are required to prepare machinery account for all the calendar years mentioned above.

[**Ans.** No Profit or Loss on machinery sold in 1987. Profit on sale of Machinery in 1988 Rs 3,580, Balance in the Machinery account Rs 19,656].

12. A firm purchased on 1st January, 1984 certain Machinery for Rs 58,200 and spent Rs 1,800 on its erection. On 1st July, 1984 additional machinery costing Rs 20,000 was purchased. On 1st July, 1986 the machinery purchased on 1st January, 1984 having become obsolete was auctioned for Rs 28,600 and on the same date fresh machinery was purchased at a cost of Rs 40,000.

Depreciation was provided for annually on 31st December at the rate of 10 per cent on written down value. In 1987, however the firm changed this method of providing depreciation and adopted the method of providing 5 per cent per annum depreciation on the original cost of the machinery.

Give the Machinery Account as it would stand at the end of each year from 1984 to 1987.

(C.A. Entrance, May, 1978, adapted)

[**Ans.** Balance on Jan. 1, 1988 Rs 53,500].

13. Messrs. Mill and Wright commended business on 1st January, 1980 when they purchased plant and equipment for Rs 7,00,000. They adopted a policy of (*i*) charging depreciation at 15% per annum on diminishing balance basis and (*ii*) charging full year's depreciation on additions.

Over the years, their purchases of plant have been:

Date	Amount Rs
1.8.1981	1,50,000
30.9.1984	2,00,000

On 1.1.1984 it was decided to change the method and rate of depreciation to 10% on straight line basis with retrospective effect from 1.1.1980, the adjustment being made in the accounts for the year ending 31st December, 1984.

Calculate the difference in depreciation to be adjusted in the Plant and Equipment Account on 1.1.1984 and show the ledger account for the year 1984.

(C.A. Entrance, May, 1979, adapted)

[**Ans.** Balance on Jan. 1, 1985 Rs 6,20,000].

14. ABC & Co. close their account on 31st March every year. On 1.7.1986 machineries costing Rs 60,000 were purchased. Further on 1.1.1987 a machinery costing Rs 60,000 was purchased and another machine costing Rs 10,000 on 1.10.1987.

Out of the machineries which were purchased on 1.7.1986, one machine costing Rs 20,000 became obsolete and was sold for Rs 6,000 on 1.4.1988.

On 1.1.1989 a new machine was purchased for Rs 30,000.

Show how the Machinery account would appear for all the three years in the books of *ABC* & Co. after charging depreciation at 33 ⅓% on written down value method. While preparing the machinery account you are required to observe the following notes:

(*i*) Calculate the amount of depreciation to the nearest rupee.

(*ii*) Provide depreciation for the full year even if the machinery has been used for a part of the year.

[**Ans.** Depreciation 1986 Rs 40,000; 1987 Rs 30,000; 1988 Rs 27,037].

Chapter 14

SECTIONAL AND SELF-BALANCING SYSTEMS

LEARNING OBJECTIVES

After studying this chapter you should be able to:

- ☐ understand the concept of sectional and self balancing;
- ☐ appreciate the role of sectional and sale balancing systems in recording business transactions;
- ☐ record business transactions according to sectional and self-balancing systems; and
- ☐ explain the meaning of certain key terms.

In a preceding chapter, we have explained that transactions, after being recorded in the Journal, are classified in the ledger. A small business can do with only one ledger. However, in case of a big business, the number of personal accounts may be quite large and, therefore, it may not be convenient to keep all the accounts into one ledger. The ledger is, therefore, sub-divided into the following three ledgers:

(i) Debtors or Sales Ledger;

(ii) Creditors or Purchases Ledger; and

(iii) General Ledger

Having sub-divided the ledger into the above categories the business may record the transactions either according to the Sectional or Self-balancing System.

SECTIONAL BALANCING

The following are the main features of this system:

(i) The Debtors Ledger contains the personal accounts of each of the firm's trade debtors. Similarly, the Creditors Ledger contains the personal accounts of each of the firm's trade creditors.

(ii) The General Ledger contains all accounts real, personal and nominal except those of trade debtors and trade creditors. It, however, contains two total accounts for trade debtors and trade creditors: (a) Total Debtors Account and (b) Total Creditors Account.

(iv) The accounts of individual trade debtors and trade creditors are posted without completing the double entry. The double entry is completed only in General Ledger in respect of total debtors account, total creditors account and other relevant accounts.

(v) The balance of the total debtors account in the general ledger at the end of a period should tally with the total of individual balances in the debtors ledger. Similarly the balance of the total creditors account, in the general ledger should tally with the total of individual balance in the creditors ledger. Thus, the accuracy of the entries made in the debtors and creditors ledger can be checked and errors located at an early stage.

(vi) Since double entry is completed only in respect of general ledger and not in respect of the debtors and creditors ledgers, a trial balance of only the general ledger can be prepared and not of the debtors and creditors ledgers.

Thus, only one section of the ledger can be balanced. Sectional balancing is, therefore, self-balancing of a section of group ledgers.

Working of the System

The working of the system can be understood with the help of the following example.

DETAILS OF TRANSACTIONS OF A FIRM IN JULY, 1991

Debtors	Credit Sales	Cash Received	Discount allowed
A	1,000	500	50
B	2,000	1,000	100
C	3,000	1,000	100
Total	6,000	2,500	250

The following entries will be made in the books of accounts in case of Sectional Balancing System:

In the Debtors Ledger

(i) *For credit sales*: Accounts of A, B & C will be debited with Rs 1,000, Rs 2,000 and Rs 3,000 respectively.

(ii) *For cash received:* The accounts of A, B & C will be credited with Rs 500, Rs 1,000 and Rs 1,000 respectively.

(iii) *For discount allowed:* The accounts of A, B & C will be credited with Rs 50, Rs 100 and Rs 100 respectively.

It may be noted that there will be no double entry in the debtors ledger for the above transactions. Moreover, the above entries are to be made in the personal accounts of the debtors as and when the transactions take place.

In General Ledger

(i) *For credit sales*

Total Debtors Account	Dr.	6,000	
To Sales Account			6,000

(ii) *For cash received*

Cash Account	Dr.	2,500	
To Total Debtors Account			2,500

(iii) *For discount allowed*

Discount Account	Dr.	250	
To Total Debtors Account			250

The entries in the General Ledger are made at the end of a period, a week, a month or a quarter as the case may be.

The various accounts will appear as follows:

Debtors Ledger

A

Particulars	Amount Rs	Particulars	Amount Rs
To Sales Account	1,000	By Cash	500
		By Discount	50
		By Balance c/d	450
	1,000		1,000

B

Particulars	Amount Rs	Particulars	Amount Rs
To Sales Account	2,000	By Cash Account	1,000
		By Discount Account	100
		By Balance c/d	900
	2,000		2,000

C

Particulars	Amount Rs	Particulars	Amount Rs
To Sales Account	3,000	By Cash Account	1,000
		By Discount Account	100
		By Balance c/d	1,900
	3,000		3,000

A Schedule of Debtors from Debtors Ledger can be prepared as follows:

A	450
B	900
C	1,900
	3,250

General Ledger

TOTAL DEBTORS ACCOUNT

Particulars	Amount Rs	Particulars	Amount Rs
To Sales Account	6,000	By Cash Account	2,500
		By Discount Account	250
		By Balance Account	3,250
	6,000		6,000

DISCOUNT ACCOUNT

Particulars	Amount Rs	Particulars	Amount Rs
To Total Debtors Account	250	By Balance c/d	250
	250		250

CASH ACCOUNT

Particulars	Amount Rs	Particulars	Amount Rs
To Total Debtors A/c	2,500	By Balance c/d	2,500
	2,500		2,500

SALES ACCOUNT

Particulars	Amount Rs	Particulars	Amount Rs
To Balance c/d	6,000	By Total Debtors A/c	6,000
	6,000		6,000

Trial Balance of the General Ledger will appear as follows:

Particulars	Dr Rs	Cr Rs
Total Debtors Account	3,250	
Discount Account	250	
Cash Account	2,500	
Sales Account		6,000
	6,000	6,000

The balance in the Total Debtors Account in General Ledger Rs 3,250 tallys with the balance as shown by the Schedule of Debtors prepared from the Debtors Ledger. It proves the accuracy of the entries made in Debtors Ledger.

Transactions relating to creditors viz., credit purchases, discount received, cash paid etc. are recorded in the Creditors Ledger on the same pattern as explained above. At the end of the period, a Schedule of Creditors is prepared from the Creditors Ledger and tallied with the balance in the Total Creditors Account, in order to check the accuracy of the postings made in the Creditors Ledger.

Sub-division of Debtors and Creditors Ledgers

In case of a business where the number of personal accounts of the trade debtors and trade creditors is quite large, the debtors ledger and the creditors ledger may, further, be sub-divided according to areas, cities and alphabets etc. With such classification, the number of control or total accounts will also increase. For example, if the ledgers are classified according to alphabets into two categories (i) A-M and (ii) N-Z, the following control accounts will have to be kept in the general ledger:

(i)   Total Debtors Account (A to M)

(ii) Total Debtors Account (N to Z)

(iii) Total Creditors Account (A to M)

(iv) Total Creditors Account (N to Z)

At the end of a period (week, month or quarter, as the case may be), the balance in the respective total accounts will have to be compared with the total of the schedule of debtors or creditors prepared from the respective ledgers. Such a comparison will help in determining the accuracy or otherwise of the postings made into the debtors or creditors ledgers.

Transfer from one ledger to another

Transfer entries will have to be passed because of the same person being trade debtor as well as trade creditor of the business. For example, the business may have purchased

1.330

goods of Rs 100 from A as well as sold goods of Rs 150 to A. In such a case A's account will appear in the debtors ledger as well as in the creditors ledger. As a matter of fact he is debtor of the business only to the extent of Rs 50 net. At the end of the accounting period, the following entries will have to be passed to adjust the account of A:

A (in the Creditors Ledger)	Dr.	100	
To A (in the Debtors Ledger)			100
Total Creditors Account	Dr.	100	
To Total Debtors Account			100

Debtors and Creditors Ledgers having both debit and credit balances

Generally accounts in the Debtors Ledger have debit balances while the accounts in the Creditors Ledger have credit balances. However, the debtors ledger may have credit balance in some of its accounts. This happens when a business has received from its debtors more than what was due from them. For example, the business sells goods of Rs 1,000 to A. He remits Rs 800 and later on returns goods of Rs 400 on account of their being of poor quality. In this case the account of A will show a credit balance of Rs 200. Similarly in case some excess payment has been made to a creditor, his account will show a debit balances. Separate schedule of such debtors and creditors should be prepared and their balances should be shown separately in the total debtors and total creditors accounts. However, in the Balance Sheet, total debtors or total creditors should be shown only at the net figure. The credit balances in the debtors ledger should be adjusted against the debit balances in that ledger. Similarly the debit balances in the creditors ledger should be adjusted against credit balances in that ledger.

Illustration 14.1. A trading concern divides its Sales Ledger into two sections, Delhi and Aligarh each being self balancing. The following were the material figures obtained from the books in connection with the monthly balancing at the end of March, 1989:

		Delhi	Aligarh
Ledger Balance: 28th February	Dr.	3,175	1,942
Ledger Balance: 28th February	Cr.	28	6
Ledger Balance: 31st March	Dr.	4,327	1,709
Ledger Balance: 31st March	Cr.	47	17
Sales for month	...	2,260	682
Returns	...	65	22
Cash Received	...	897	974
Discount Allowed	...	13	5
Bad debts written off	...	8	2
Bills Receivable	...	67	...

Draw up the Total Accounts and suggest any inference which you consider may be drawn from the results.

Solution:

General Ledger

DELHI LEDGER TOTAL DEBTORS ACCOUNT

Date	Particulars	Amount Rs	Date	Particulars	Amount Rs
1989			1989		
March 1	To Balance b/d	3,175	March 1	By Balance b/d	28
Mar. 31	To Sales	2,260	Mar. 31	By Sales Returns	65

Contd....

Date	Particulars	Amount Rs	Date	Particulars	Amount Rs
	To Balance c/d	47		By Cash	897
				By Discount	13
				By Bad Debts	8
				By Bill Receivable	67
				By Balance c/d	4,327
		5,482			5,405
1989					
April 1	To Balance b/d	4,327		By Balance b/d	47

ALIGARH LEDGER TOTAL DEBTORS ACCOUNT

Date	Particulars	Amount Rs	Date	Particulars	Amount Rs
1989			1989		
March 1	To Balance b/d	1,942	March 1	By Balance b/d	6
	To Sales	682		By Returns	22
	To Balance c/d	17		By Cash	974
				By Discount	5
				By Bad Debts	2
				By Balance c/d	1,709
		2,641			2,718
1989			1989		
April 1	To Balance b/d	1,709	April 1	By Balance b/d	17

Conclusion. There is a difference of Rs 77 in the Dr. and Cr. totals of the Delhi and Aligarh accounts. The difference may be due to wrong posting of cash received. Cash received from Delhi debtors seems to have been posted to the Aligarh Total Debtors Account.

Illustration 14.2. Mr. X keeps his books according to Sectional Balancing System. From the following details, you are required to prepare the Total Creditors Account for the month of January, 1991:

	Rs
Credit balances in Creditors' Accounts as on 1.1.1991	10,000
Debit balances in Creditors Accounts as on 1.1.1991	2,000
Cash purchases	5,000
Credit purchases	10,000
Bill payable accepted	5,000
Bill payable paid	3,000
Purchases returns	1,000
Cash paid to creditors	3,000
Discounted allowed by them	200
Transfers to Debtors Ledger	1,000
Debit Balances in Creditors Account	500
Bills payable dishonoured	2,000

Solution:

TOTAL CREDITORS ACCOUNT

Particulars	Amount (Rs)	Particulars	Amount (Rs)
To Balance b/d	2,000	By Balance b/d	10,000
To Bills Payable A/c	5,000	By Purchases A/c	10,000
To Purchases Returns A/c	1,000	By Bills Payable dishonoured	2,000
To Cash A/c	3,000	By Balance c/d	500
To Discount A/c	200		
To Transfer to Debtors' Ledger	1,000		
To Balance c/d	10,300		
	22,500		22,500

SELF-BALANCING SYSTEM

It has already been explained in the preceeding pages that in the case of sectional balancing system, only general ledger can be balanced. This means that trial balance cannot be prepared of the debtors and the creditors ledgers. This drawback is removed under self-balancing system where the trial balance of each of the ledgers can be prepared. Thus, it is a system where each ledger is self balancing. The essential features of the systems are as follows:

(*i*) In the Debtors Ledger, besides personal accounts of trade debtors, a General Ledger Adjustment Account is opened. The account is just reverse of 'Sales Ledger Adjustment Account' (explained later), in the General Ledger.

(*ii*) In the Creditors Ledger, besides the personal accounts of the trade creditors, a General Ledger Adjustment Account is opened. The account is just reverse of Purchases Ledger Adjustment Account (explained later), in the General Ledger.

(*iii*) In the General Ledger, two control accounts are opened for trade debtors and trade creditors. The control account for trade debtors is termed as "Sales Ledger Adjustment Account" and that for trade creditors is termed as "Purchases Ledger Adjustment Account". These two control accounts are in fact 'Total Debtors Accounts' and 'Total Creditors Account' as in the case of Sectional Balancing.

(*iv*) Besides, passing the usual accounting entries, additional entries are passed at the end of period for the control accounts. The subsidiary books are suitably ruled in a manner that they readily show the periodic (generally monthly) total of transactions to be posted in the various ledgers according to the self balancing system.

(*v*) Since there is a complete double entry of each of the ledgers, the trial balance of each one of them can be prepared and the accuracy of postings made therein can be checked.

Difference between Self-balancing System and Sectional Balancing System

The following are the points of distinction between self-balancing ledgers and sectional balancing system:

(*i*) In self-balancing system, adjustment accounts are prepared in each ledger while in sectional balancing system, only control accounts are prepared in the general ledger.

(*ii*) In self-balancing, a separate trial balance of each of the ledgers can be prepared. While in sectional balancing only the trial balance of the general ledger can be prepared.

(*iii*) In self-balancing, double entry is completed in respect of each ledger while in sectional balancing system, double entry is completed only in respect of general ledger. Personal accounts of debtors and creditors are maintained on single entry basis only.

Working of the System

The working of the system can be understood with the help of the following example:

Debtors	Credit Sales	Cash Recd.	Discount allowed	Creditors	Credit Purchases	Cash paid	Discount received
A	5,000	1,000	100	X	4,000	1,000	100
B	4,000	2,000	200	Y	2,000	1,000	100
C	4,000	2,000	200	Z	1,000	500	50
	13,000	5,000	500		7,000	2,500	250

Date	Particulars		Dr. Amount Rs	Cr. Amount Rs
	For Credit Sales			
	A	Dr.	5,000	
	B	Dr.	4,000	
	C	Dr.	4,000	
	To Sales Account			13,000
	(as and when sales in made)			
	Sales Ledger Adjustment Account	Dr.	13,000	
	(in General Ledger)			
	To General Ledger Adjustment Account			
	(at the end of the period)			
	For Cash Received			
	Cash Account	Dr.	5,000	
	To A			1,000
	To B			2,000
	To C			2,000
	(as and when cash is received)			
	General Ledger Adj. A/c (in General Ledger)	Dr.	5,000	
	To Sales Ledger Adj. A/c. (at the end of the period)			5,000
	For Discount Allowed			
	Discount Account	Dr.	500	
	To A			100
	To B			200
	To C			200
	(as and when discount is allowed)			
	General Ledger Adjustment Account	Dr.	500	
	(in Sales Ledger)			
	To Sales Ledger Adj. A/c (in General Ledger)			
	For Credit Purchases			
	Purchases Account	Dr.	7,000	
	To X			4,000
	To Y			2,000
	To Z			1,000
	(as and when purchases are made)			
	General Ledger Adj. A/c (in Purchases Ledger)	Dr.	7,000	
	To Purchase Ledger Adj. A/c (in General Ledger)			7,000
	(as the end of the period)			
	For Cash Paid			
	X	Dr.	1,000	
	Y	Dr.	1,000	
	Z	Dr.	500	
	To Cash Account			2,500
	(as and when cash is paid)			

Contd...

Date	Particulars		Dr. Amount Rs	Cr. Amount Rs
	Purchase Ledger Adj. A/c (in General Ledger)	Dr.	2,500	
	To General Ledger Adj. A/c (in Purchases Ledger)			2,500
	For Discount Received			
	X	Dr.	100	
	Y	Dr.	100	
	Z	Dr.	50	
	To Discount A/c			250
	(as and when discount is received)			
	Purchases Ledger Adj. A/c. (in General Ledger)	Dr.	250	
	To General Ledger Adj. A/c (in Purchases Ledger)			250
	(at the end of the period)			

Sales Ledger

A

Particulars	Amount Rs	Particulars	Amount Rs
To Sales A/c	5,000	By Cash A/c	1,000
		By Discount A/c	100
		By Balance c/d	3,900
	5,000		5,000

B

Particulars	Amount Rs	Partiulars	Amount Rs
To Sales A/c	4,000	By Cash A/c	2,000
		By Discount A/c	200
		By Balance c/d	1,800
	4,000		4,000

C

Particulars	Amount Rs	Particulars	Amount Rs
To Sales A/c	4,000	By Cash A/c	2,000
		By Discount A/c	200
		By Balance c/d	1,800
	4,000		4,000

GENERAL LEDGER ADJUSTMENT ACCOUNT[1]

Particulars	Amount Rs	Particulars	Amount Rs
To Sales Ledger Adj. A/c: Cash recd.	5,000	By Sales Ledger Adj. A/c: Credit Sales	13,000

Contd....

[1] Reverse of Sales Ledger Adj. Account in General Ledger.

Particulars	Amount Rs	Particulars	Amount Rs
Discount	500		
To Balance c/d	7,500		
	13,000		13,000

TRIAL BALANCE OF SALES LEDGER

Particulars	Dr. Amount Rs	Cr. Amount Rs
Trade Debtors:		
A	3,900	
B	1,800	
C	1,800	
General Ledger Adj. A/c		7,500
	7,500	7,500

Purchases Ledger

X

Particulars	Amount Rs	Particulars	Amount Rs
To Cash A/c	1,000	By Purchases A/c	4,000
To Discount A/c	100		
To Balance c/d	2,900		
	4,000		4,000

Y

Particulars	Amount Rs	Particulars	Amount Rs
To Cash A/c	1,000	By Purchases A/c	2,000
To Discount A/c	100		
To Balance c/d	900		
	2,000		2,000

Z

Particulars	Amount Rs	Particulars	Amount Rs
To Cash A/c	500	By Purchases A/c	1,000
To Discount A/c	50		
To Balance c/d	450		
	1,000		1,000

GENERAL LEDGER ADJUSTMENT ACCOUNT

Particulars	Amount Rs	Particulars	Amount Rs
To Purchases Ledger Adj. A/c:		By Purchases Ledger Adj. A/c:	
Credit Purchases	7,000	Cash received	2,500
		Discount	250
		By Balance c/d	4,250
	7,000		7,000

TRIAL BALANCE OF PURCHASES LEDGER

Particulars	Dr. Amount Rs	Cr. Amount Rs
Creditors:		
X		2,900
Y		900
Z		450
General Ledger Adj. A/c	4,250	
	4,250	4,250

General Ledger

SALES ACCOUNT*

Particulars	Amount Rs	Particulars	Amount Rs
To Balance c/d	13,000	By A	5,000
		B	4,000
		C	4,000
	13,000		13,000

PURCHASES ACCOUNT*

Particulars	Amount Rs	Particulars	Amount Rs
To X	4,000	By Balance c/d	7,000
Y	2,000		
Z	1,000		
	7,000		7,000

CASH ACCOUNT

Particulars	Amount Rs	Particulars	Amount R
To A	4,000	By X	1,000
B	2,000	By Y	1,000
C	2,000	By Z	500
		By Balance c/d	2,500
	5,000		5,000

DISCOUNT ALLOWED ACCOUNT*

Particulars	Amount	Particulars	Amount
To A	100	By Balance c/d	500
B	200		
C	200		
	500		500

DISCOUNT RECEIVED ACCOUNT*

Particulars	Amount Rs	Particulars	Amount Rs
To Balance c/d	250	By X	100
		By Y	100
		By Z	50
	250		250

Contd....

*In case postings are made from Sales Book, Purchases Book, Cash Book, the words "To Sundries" or "By Sundries" will be used in place of names of the individuals and entry will be made with total amount at the end of a period.

SALES LEDGER ADJUSTMENT ACCOUNT*

Particulars	Amount Rs	Particulars	Amount RS
To General Ledger Adj. A/c:		By General Ledger Adj. A/c:	
Credit Sales	13,000	Cash	5,000
		Discount	500
		By Balance c/d	7,500
	13,000		13,000

*Similar to Total Debtors Account.

PURCHASES LEDGER ADJUSTMENT ACCOUNT*

Particulars	Amount Rs	Particulars	Amount Rs
To General Ledger Adj. A/c:		By General Ledger Adj. A/c:	
Cash	2,500	Credit Purchases	7,000
Discount	250		
To Balance c/d	4,250		
	7,000		7,000

*Similar to Total Creditors Account.

TRIAL BALANCE OF GENERAL LEDGER

Particulars	Dr. Amount Rs	Cr. Amount Rs
Sales A/c		13,000
Purchase A/c	7,000	
Cash A/c	2,500	
Discount Allowed A/c	500	
Discount Received A/c		250
Sales Ledger Adj. A/c	7,500	
Purchases Ledger Adj. A/c		4,250
	17,500	17,500

Transfer from one Ledger to another

Whenever a balance is transferred from one account to another e.g., from Purchases Ledger to Sales Ledger, six different accounts are affected. Thus, three Journal entries will have to be passed. For example, if A is a debtor by Rs 1,000 and also a creditor by Rs 1,200, the following entries will have to be passed for transferring balance of A's account in the Debtors' Ledger to A's account in the Creditors' Ledger

(i)	A (in the Creditors Ledger)	Dr.	1,000	
	To A (in the Debtors Ledger)			1,000
(ii)	General Ledger Adj. A/c (in Sales Ledger)	Dr.	1,000	
	To Sales Ledger Adj. A/c (in General Ledger)			1,000
(iii)	Purchases Ledger Adj. A/c (in General Ledger)	Dr.	1,000	
	To General Ledger Adj. A/c (in Purchases Ledger)			1,000

Illustration 14.3. Below are given particulars from the Sales ledger of Shri Ramlal, a trader, for the month of March, 1990:

Date	Particulars	Rs
March 1, 1990	Opening Balance	31,000
March 31, 1990	Total Sales for the month	91,000
	Sales return	1,500
	Cash received from debtors	41,500
	Bills receivable	16,000
	Bills dishonoured	2,500
	Discount allowed to debtors	1,400
	Bad debts	1,350
	Transfer from another ledger	1,750
	Bills receivable endorsed to suppliers	2,200

You are required to prepare the relative 'Sales Ledger' and 'General Ledge' adjustment accounts. *(C.A. Entrance, Nov., 1990)*

Solution:

Books of Ramlal
SALES LEDGER ADJUSTMENT ACCOUNT IN GENERAL LEDGER

Date	Particulars	Amount Rs	Date	Particulars	Amount Rs
1990			1990		
March 1	To Opening Balance b/d	31,000	Mar. 31	By Gen. Ledger Adj. A/c:	
Mar. 31	To Gen. Ledger Adj. A/c			Sales Return	1,500
	Sales	91,000		Cash (received from	
	Bills Receivable			debtors)	41,000
	(dishonoured)	2,500		Bills Receivable	16,000
				Discount	1,400
				Bad debts	1,350
				Transfer from another	
				Ledger	1,750
				By Balance c/d	61,500
		1,24,500			1,24,500

GENERAL LEDGER ADJUSTMENT ACCOUNT IN SALES LEDGER

Date	Particulars	Amount Rs	Date	Particulars	Amount Rs
1990			1990		
Mar. 31	To Sales Ledger		March 1	By Balance b/d	31,000
	Adjustment Account:		March 31	By Sales Ledger	
	Sales Return	1,500		Adjustment Account:	
	Cash (received from			Sales	91,000
	debtors)	41,000		Bills Receivable	
	Bills Receivable	16,000		dishonoured	2.5000
	Discount	1,400			
	Bad Debts	1,350			
	Transfer from another				
	Ledger	1,750			
	To Balance c/d	61,500			
		1,24,500			1,24,500

Note:

Bills Receivable endorsed to suppliers will not affect the above accounts. The transaction will affect Creditors Ledger Adjustment Account (in the General Ledger) and General Ledger Adjustment Account (in the Creditors' Ledger).

Illustration 14.4. From the following particulars write up necessary Adjustment Accounts as they would appear in the General Ledger:

	Rs	
Debtors' in Ledger Adjustment Account Balance	49,850	(Debit)
Creditors' in Ledger Adjustment Account Balance	28,010	(Credit)
Credit Sales	40,400	
Cash Sales	18,080	
Cash Purchases	15,930	
Credit Purchases	27,600	
Creditors paid off	26,500	
Received from Debtors	44,100	
Discount allowed to the business	1,450	
Discount allowed by the business	1,540	
Return Inwards	1,795	
Return Outwards	2,240	
Bill Payable accepted	5,300	
Bill Receivable received	3,500	
Bill Receivable dishonoured	325	
Interest charge for dishonoured Bill	20	
Allowances	1,605	
Bad debts	1,495	
Transfer from Debtors Ledger to Creditors Ledger	400	

Solution:

In the General Ledger

DEBTORS' LEDGER ADJUSTMENT ACCOUNT

Particulars	Amount Rs	Particulars	Amount Rs
To Balance b/d	49,850	By General Ledger Adjustment A/c	
To General Ledger		(In Debtor's Ledger):	
Adjustment A/c		Cash Receipts	44,100
(In Debtors' Ledger)		Discount Allowed	1,540
Credit Sales	40,400	Returns Inward	1,795
Bill Receivable	325	Bills Receivable Received	3,500
dishonoured		Allowances	1,605
Interest charged	20	Bad Debts	1,495
		Transfer	400
		By Balance c/d	36,160
	90,595		90,595
To Balance b/d	36,160		

CREDITORS' LEDGER ADJUSTMENT ACCOUNT

Particulars	Amount Rs	Particulars	Amount Rs
To General Ledger		By Balance b/d	28,010
Adjustment A/c		By General Ledger	
(in Creditors Ledger):		Adjustment A/c	
Payments made	26,500	(in Creditors' Ledger):	
Discount Received	1,450	Credit Purchases	27,600
Returns Outwards	2,240		
Bills Payable	5,300		
Transfer	400		
To Balance c/d	19,720		
	55,610		55,610
		By Balance b/d	19,720

Note:

Cash Sales and Cash Purchases are not posted to any individual Debtor's Account and Creditor's Account and hence will not be entered in the Total Accounts.

Illustration 14.5. Prepare (i) the Creditors' Ledger Adjustment Account; and (ii) the Debtors's Ledger Adjustment Account as would appear in the General Ledger of M/s Hindustan Traders for the year ended 31st October, 1989 from the following information:

	Rs
Opening Balances (1-1-1988):	
Creditors' Ledger (Dr.)	2,610
(Cr.)	35,820
Debtors' Ledger (Dr.)	43,860
(Cr.)	720
Transactions during the year 1988-89:	
Purchases	1,98,540
Purchases Returns	7,680
Sales	2,62,470
Sales Returns	3,510
Cash Received from Debtors	2,28,630
Discount allowed	8,460
Cash paid to Creditors	1,75,290
Discount Received	4,980
Cash refunded to Debtors	520
Bill Receivable Received	12,360
Bill Payable issued	6,750
Bills Receivable dishonoured	750
Closing Balances (31-10-1989):	
Creditors' Ledger (Dr.)	2,310
Debtors' Ledger (Cr.)	1,360

Solution:

General Ledger of Hindustan Traders Ltd.
CREDITORS' LEDGER ADJUSTMENT ACCOUNT

Date	Particulars	Amount Rs	Date	Particulars	Amount Rs
1988			1988		
Nov. 1	To Balance b/d	2,610	Nov. 1	By Balance b/d	35,820
1989			1989		
Oct. 31	To General Ledger Adjustment Account:		Oct. 31	By General Ledger Adjustment Account:	
	Purchases Returns	7,680		Purchases	1,98,540
	Cash	1,75,290		By Balance c/d	2,310
	Discount	4,980			
	Bills Payable	6,750			
	To Balance c/d	39,360			
		2,36,670			2,36,670
Nov. 1	To Balance b/d	2,310	Nov. 1	By Balance b/d	39,360

DEBTORS' LEDGER ADJUSTMENT ACCOUNT

Date	Particulars	Amount Rs	Date	Particulars	Amount Rs
1988			1988		
Nov. 1	To Balance b/d	43,860	Nov. 1	By Balance b/d	720
1989			1989		
Oct. 31	To General Ledger Adjustment Account:		Oct. 31	By General Ledger Adjustment Account:	
	Sales	2,62,470		Sales Returns	3,510
	Cash	520		Cash	2,28,630
	Bills Receivable dishonoured	750		Discount	8,460
	To Balance c/d	1,360		Bills Receivable	12,360
				By Balance c/d	55,280
		3,08,960			3,08,960
Nov. 1	To Balance b/d	55,280	Nov. 1	By Balance b/d	1,360

Advantages of Self-balancing System

The following are the advantages of the accounts maintained under self-balancing system:

(*i*) The system localises the errors and facilitates in their quick detection with minimum effort.

(*ii*) It facilitates division of work among different employees of the organisation.

(*iii*) Responsibility for committing errors can be fixed. Thus, the system serves as a deterrent on careless work by employees,

(*iv*) Different ledgers are kept by different employees, hence the possibility of collusion among them to defraud is minimized.

Disadvantages of Self-balancing System.

The following are the disadvantages of maintaining self-balancing system:

(*i*) It involves a lot of clerical work since additional columns have to be maintained in subsidiary books.

(*ii*) The maintenance of system is costly due to additional work. Hence, it is not suitable for small firms.

RECTIFICATION OF ERRORS

The technique of rectification of errors as explained in Chapter 11, can also be safely applied to rectification of errors when accounts are maintained under Sectional or Self-balancing System. However, the following points should be kept in view while passing rectifying entries:

(1) In case of Sectional Balancing System, there is no double entry in respect of Debtors Ledger and in the Creditors Ledger. Any error in these ledgers should, therefore, be rectified by means of a single entry. For example, if *A*, a debtor has been wrongly debited in place of being credited by Rs 200, only *A*'s account is wrong. The error should, therefore, be rectified by simply crediting his account by Rs 400.

However, if an error affects the total accounts also, a rectifying entry will also have to be passed for rectifying the total accounts too.

For example, if good of Rs 500 are returned to *B*, a creditor, have not been recorded in the books, the following rectifying entries will be required in case of Sectional Balancing System:

(*i*) Debit *B* with Rs 500

(*ii*) Total Creditors A/c	Dr.	500
To Purchases Returns A/c		500

(2) In case of self-balancing system, besides passing usual rectifying entry, additional entry or entries will be required for rectifying error(s) in the Total Accounts also.

For example, if purchases returns of Rs 500 to *B* have not been recorded in the books, the following rectifying entries will have to be passed:

(*i*) *Usual Rectifying Entry*		
B	Dr.	500
To Purchases Returns Account		500
(*ii*) *For Correcting the Total Accounts*		
Purchases Ledger Adj. A/c (in General Ledger)	Dr.	500
To General Ledger Adj. A/c (in Purchases Ledger)		500

Illustration 14.6. Write out the journal entries using a Suspense Account presuming— (*a*) when the system of self-balancing is not in use and (*b*) when the system of self-balancing is in use.

(1) Goods of the value of Rs 100 returned by Mr. Sharma were entered in the Sales Day Book and posted therefrom to the credit of his account.

(2) An amount of Rs 150, entered in the Sales Returns Book, has been posted to the debit of Mr. Philip, who returned the goods.

(3) A sale of Rs 200 made to Mr. Ghanshyam was correctly entered in the Sales Day Book but wrongly posted to the debit of Mr. Radhesham as Rs 20.

(4) Bad Debts aggregating Rs 450 were written off during the year in the Sales Ledger but were not adjusted in General Ledger.

(5) The total of "Discount Allowed" column in the Cash Book for the month of September, 1990, amounting to Rs 250 was not posted.

Solution:

(a) When the System of Self-balancing is not in use

JOURNAL

	Particulars		Dr. Amount Rs	Cr. Amount Rs
(1)	Sales Account	Dr.	100	
	Sales Returns Account	Dr.	100	
	To Suspense Account			200
	(The value of goods returned by Mr. Sharma wrongly posted to Sales and omission of debit to Sales Returns Account, now retified).			
(2)	Suspense Account	Dr.	300	
	To Mr. Philip			300
	(Wrong debit to Mr. Philip for goods, returned by him, now rectified)			
(3)	Mr. Ghanshyam	Dr.	200	
	To Mr. Radhesham			20
	To Suspense Account			180
	(Omission of debit to Mr. Ghanshyam and wrong credit to Mr. Radhesham for sale of Rs 200, now rectified).			
(4)	Bad Debts Account	Dr.	450	
	To Suspense Account			450
	(The amount of Bad Debts written off not adjusted in General Ledger, now rectified).			
(5)	Discount Account	Dr.	250	
	To Suspense Account			250
	(The total of Discount allowed during September, 1990, not posted from the Cash Book; error now rectified).			

(b) When the System of Self-balancing is in use

		Particulars		Dr. Amount Rs	Cr. Amount Rs
(1)	(i)	Sales Account	Dr.	100	
		Sales Returns Account	Dr.	100	
		To Suspense Account (In Sales Ledger)			200
	(ii)	General Ledger Adjustment Account	Dr.	200	
		(In Sales Ledger)			
		To Sales Ledger Adjustment Account			200
		(In General Ledger)			
(2)		Mr. Philip	Dr.	300	
		To Suspense Account			300
		(In Sales Ledger)			
(3)		Mr. Ghanshyam	Dr.	200	
		To Mr. Radhesham			20
		To Suspense Account			180
		(In Sales Ledger)			
(4)	(i)	Bad Debts Account	Dr.	450	
		To Suspense Account			450
		(In Sales Ledger)			

	Particulars		Dr. Amount Rs	Cr. Amount Rs
(ii)	General Ledger Adjustment Account (In Sales Ledger) To Sales Ledger Adjustment Account (In General Ledger)	Dr.	450	450
(5) (i)	Discount Account To Suspense Account	Dr.	250	250
(ii)	General Ledger Adjustment Account (In Sales Ledger) To Sales Ledger Adjustment Account (In General Ledger)	Dr.	250	250

Note: In case of entries 4 and 5, it has been assumed that entries have been completely omitted from the General Ledger.

Illustration 14.7. The following balances extracted from the subsidiary ledgers of Nation Slide Bank did not tally with their respective balances in the General Ledger as on 31st December, 1990. The difference was placed to Suspense Account for the time being:

		Rs
1.	Loan Ledger	18,65,750
2.	Fixed Deposit Ledger	35,07,320
3.	Savings Account Ledger	1,39,85,692
4.	Current Account Ledger No. 11	94,34,281
5.	Current Account Ledger No. 17	32,71,009

On a close scrutiny of these ledgers the following mistakes were found:

1. A sum of Rs 2,00,000 granted as loan to a borrower and debited to his account in the Loan Ledger was not passed through General Ledger.

2. Rs 7,500 debited to a constituent's account in Loan Ledger for interest was credited to the Loan Ledger Account in General Ledger.

3. Rs 50,000 received from a Savings Account holder was credited to customer's account in Fixed Deposit Ledger.

4. Rs 11,575 received from an account holder in Current Account Ledger No 17 was credited in the General Ledger to Current Account Ledger No. 11.

5. Fixed Deposit receipt for Rs 10 lakhs paid by transfer to the credit of the depositor's account in Current Account Ledger No. 11 was ommitted to be debited to the account holder's account in Fixed Deposit Ledger.

Pass the necessary Journal Entries rectifying foregoing mistakes.

Solution:

National Slide Bank
JOURNAL

	Particulars		Dr. Amount Rs	Cr. Amount Rs
(1)	Loan Ledger Account To Suspense A/c (Being the amount of loan granted not previously debited to Loan Ledger A/c, now rectified)	Dr.	2,00,000	2,00,000

Contd....

	Particulars		Dr. Amount Rs	Cr. Amount Rs
(2)	Loan Ledger Account	Dr.	15,000	
	To Suspense Account			15,000
	(Being the item of debit of Rs 7,500 wrongly entered previously as a credit in the Loan Ledger A/c, now adjusted)			
(3)	Customer's Account (in Fixed Deposit Ledger)	Dr.	50,000	
	To Customer's A/c (in Savings Account Ledger)			50,000
	(Being the amount of a savings deposit wrongly passed previously through Fixed Deposit Ledger (in the A/c, of M/s.........); error now rectified).			
(4)	Current Account Ledger No. 11	Dr.	11,575	
	(The wrong credit in Current A/c Ledger No. 11 instead of No. 17 now rectified)			
(5)	Debit Customer's Account in the Fixed Deposit Ledger			
	(Being the entry to rectify the omission of debit in F.D.. Ledger)		10,00,000	

Notes:

(*i*) It is assumed that the Suspense Account was raised only in the General Ledger in respect of own trial balance and that subsidiary ledgers are only sectional.

(*ii*) It is also assumed that the control accounts in the General Ledger in respect of (3) and (5) were correctly posted.

(*iii*) In respect of no (5) which is a one sided error, no double entry will be completed.

KEY TERMS

☐ **Sectional Balancing:** A system where only one section or a group of Ledger can be balanceu.

☐ **Self Balancing:** A system where each group of Ledger can be balanced.

☐ **Transfer Entry:** An entry required for transferring an account from one ledger to another.

TEST QUESTIONS

Objective type   TEST YOUR UNDERSTANDING

1. State whether each of the following statements is True or False:

   (*i*) Sectional Balancing and Self Balancing are synonymous terms.

   (*ii*) Separate Trial Balance for each of the Ledgers can be prepared under Sectional Balancing System.

   (*iii*) The General Ledger contains all accounts except the personal accounts of trade debtors and trade creditors.

   (*iv*) The Debtors Ledger contains all personal accounts.

   (*v*) Self-balancing system can be introduced even in a small business where there is only one ledger.

   (*vi*) The Sales Ledger Adjustment Account in the General is just reverse of General Ledger Adjustment Account in the Sales Ledger.

(vii) In case of transfer from one ledger to another, three entries will have to be made in case of self-balancing system.

[**Ans.** (i) False; (ii) False; (iii) True; (iv) False; (v) False; (vi) True; (vii) True].

2. Select the most appropriate answer:

(i) Provision for doubtful debts account is opened in:

(a) Debtors Ledger

(b) Creditors Ledger

(c) General Ledger.

(ii) General Ledger Adjustment Account(s) is/(are) opened in:

(a) Debtors Ledger

(b) Creditors Ledger

(c) in both Debtors and Creditors Ledgers.

(iii) Bad Debts previously written off now recovered will be recorded in:

(a) General Ledger Adjustment Account in the Sales Ledger,

(b) General Ledger Adjustment Account in the Purchases Ledger,

(c) None of the above two accounts.

(iv) Under Sectional Balancing System, the ledger which usually made to balance is:

(a) the Debtors Ledger,

(b) the Creditors Ledger,

(c) the General Ledger.

[**Ans.** (i) c; (ii) c; (iii) c; (iv) c].

Essay type | FOR REVIEW, DISCUSSION AND PRACTICE

1. What is Sectional Balancing? Briefly explain how the system works with examples.
2. Differentiate between Sectional and Self-balancing Systems. What are the advantages of maintaining ledgers under self-balancing system?

PRACTICAL PROBLEMS

Sectional Balancing

1. From the following particulars prepare the Total Debtors and Total Creditors Accounts:

Date	Particulars	Rs
Jan. 1, 1989	Balance of Sundry Debtors	16,000
	Balance of Sundry Creditors	18,500
Jan. 31, 1989	Credit Purchases	4,500
	Credit Sales	9,800
	Cash Sales	1,500
	Paid to Creditors	9,875
	Discount allowed by them	325
	Cash received from debtors	7,800
	Allowed them discount	200
	Bills payable accepted	1,500
	Bills receivable received	3,000
	Returns Inwards	875
	Returns Outwards	600
	Rebates allowed to Debtors	275
	Rebates allowed by Creditors	150
	Provision for doubtful debts	320
	Bad debts	450
	Bills receivable dishonoured	375

[**Ans.** Balance Total Debtors Account Rs 13,575. Total Creditors Account Rs 10,550].

Self-Balancing System

2. Total Accounts are employed in the business of X in relation to the Sales Ledger. The following are the materials for the year 1989:

Particulars		Rs
Opening Balances:	Debit	12,500
	Credit	300
Sales		31,200
Sales returns		3,120
Cash received from Customers		20,050
Discount allowed to Customers		1,300
Bad Debits written off		350
Provision for Bad Debts		3,000
Bad Debts previously written off, now received		560
Allowances to customers		400
Bills receivable received		1,300
Bills receivable dishonoured		500
Closing Balance: Credit		700

You are required to prepare the Sales Ledger Adjustment Account as would appear at the end in the Nominal Ledger.

[Ans. Dr. Balance Rs 18,080].

3. From the following details in Bought Ledger and Sold Ledger write General Adjustment Accounts as on 31st December, 1989.

Particulars	Rs
Debtors (1st January, 1989) Dr.	18,000
Debtors (1st January, 1989) Cr.	400
Creditors (1st January, 1989) Cr.	27,000
Creditors (1st January, 1989) Dr.	250
Purchases (Credit)	50,000
Sales (Credit)	78,000
Cash paid to Creditors	21,000
Bills received from debtors	9,000
Bills dishonoured	300
Bills accepted for creditors	7,500
Discount allowed to debtors	250
Discount allowed to debtors but later on disallowed	50
Cash received from debtors	8,900
Discount allowed by creditors	450
Cash paid to debtors	25
Transfer from debtors to creditors ledger	1,200
Cash purchases	4,500
Cash sales	7,500
Bad debts written off	250

(C.A. Entrance, May, 1980, adapted)

[Ans. General Ledger Adjustment A/c in Sales Ledger Rs 76,375 (Cr.), General Ledger Adjustment A/c in Bought Ledger Rs 46,600 (Dr.)].

4. The undermentioned particulars have been obtained from the books of Mr. Ram who keeps only one Sales Ledger under the Self-Balancing System. Prepare the relative Sales Ledger Adjustment Account and General Ledger Adjustment Account as on 31st December, 1986:

	Rs
30th June 1986:	
Debtors Balances	21,300
Transactions during the Half Year ended 31st Dec. 1986:	
Total Sales amount to Rs 77,000 of which cash sales amount to	33,200
Returns from Debtors	525
Cash Received from Debtors	30,975
Discount allowed to Debtors	1,125
Acceptances received from Debtors	3,150
Acceptances returned dishonoured	450
Bad Debts, written off	675
Sundry charges debited to Debtors	22
Bad Debts recovered	51
Reserve for Bad Debts	200

(C.A. Entrance, May, 1987)

(Ans. Sales Ledger Adjustment Account Closing Balance (Debit) - Rs 29,122, General Ledger Adjustment Account Closing Balance (Credit) Rs 29,122).

5. The undermentioned particulars have been obtained from the books of Mr. P. who keeps only Sales Ledger. Prepare the relative Sales Ledger Adjustment Account and General Adjustment Account as on December 31, 1987:-

	Rs
June 30, 1987	
Debtors' Balances	28,400
December 31, 1987	
Transaction for the half year to date	
Sales to Debtors	58,400
Returns from Debtors	700
Cash received from Debtors	41,300
Discount allowed to Debtors	1,500
Acceptance received from Debtors	4,200
Acceptance returned dishonoured	600
Bad Debts written off	900
Sundry charges debited to Debtors	29

(C.A. Entrance, May, 1988)

(Ans. Closing Balance of Sales Ledger Adjustment Account (Debit) - Rs 38,829)

6. From the following particulars prepare the relevant adjustment account as should appear in the General Ledger of Mr. Vasu for the month of 1987:

Date	Particulars
1.	Purchased from Mr. *X* Rs 2,000
2.	Paid Rs 1,600 after adjusting the initial advance in full to Mr. *X*.
13.	Paid Rs 1,000 to Mr. *R* towards the purchases made in February in full.
13.	Paid advance to Mr. *Y* Rs 3,000.
14.	Purchased goods from Mr *A* Rs 4,000.
25.	Returned goods worth Rs 500 to Mr. *A*.
26.	Settled the balance due to *A* at a discount of 10 per cent.
27.	Goods purchased from Mr. *Y* Rs 2,500 against the advance paid on 13th.

Date	Particulars
28.	Received back the advance from Mr. *P* paid on 28th February 1987, Rs 2,000
30.	Purchases from *B* Rs 2,000.
31.	Goods returned to *Q* Rs 750. The goods were originally purchased for cash in February.

[**Ans.** Closing Balance (Dr.) Rs 1,250; (Cr.) Rs 2,000].

7. The following opening balances and transactions are extracted from the records of Nagesh & Co. (P) Ltd.:

		R.
Opening Balances:		
Bought Ledger	Credit balances	2,70,900
	Debit balances	29,000
Sales Ledger	Debit balances	3,27,000
	Credit balances	—
Transactions:		
Purchases returns		2,700
Cheques issued in favour of Creditors		8,32,800
Acceptance of Bills Payable		1,00,000
Credit Sales		18,27,000
Credit Purchases		9,27,600
Discount received		22,500
Receipts from Debtors		13,42,000
Bills Receivable drawn		6,00,000
Discounts allowed		7,500

You are required to prepare:
(i) Bought Ledger Adjustment Account in General Ledger,
(ii) Sales Ledger Adjustment Account in General Ledger, and
(iii) General Ledger Adjustment Account in Sales Ledger.

[**Ans.** Balance (i) Rs 2,11,500 (Cr.), (ii) Rs 2,04,500 (Dr.), (iii) Rs 2,04,500 (Cr.)].

8. From the following details extracted from the books of *Y* Ltd., for the year ended 31st March, 1991, prepare a Sales Ledger Adjustment Account as it would appear in the General Ledger.

		Rs
Opening balance on 1.4.1990:		
Sales Ledger	Dr.	45,256
	Cr.	156
Provision for bad and doubtful debts		5,000
Sales during period:	Cash	15,200
	Credit	1,25,656
Amount received from customers		1,56,215
Bills accepted by the customers		1,250
Cheques dishonoured		1,270
Bad debts written off		256
Interest on overdue accounts		82
Cash discounts allowed		1,527
Bad debts previously written off recovered		465
Returns from customers		726

1.350

Goods of the sales value of Rs 150 were returned by a customer for which fresh goods were issued. Though a credit note was issued for the return of goods, the sales invoice was inadvertently not prepared for the issue of fresh goods.

[**Ans.** Dr. Balance Rs 12, 284].

(**Hint.** Provision for Bad Debts, Cash Sales, Bad Debts recovered do not concern the Sales Ledger Adjustment Account).

Transfer Entries

9. A firm has two sales ledgers: East and West. Mr. Abraham who owed Rs 3,000 to the firm shifted to Gauhati from Kanpur. His account was therefore transferred from East to the West ledger. Give journal entries to record the above transactions presuming that:
   (i) the system of sectional balancing is in use,
   (ii) the system of self-balancing is in use.

10. A is debtor of the firm by Rs 1,000. His account is also in the creditors ledger because of his having supplied goods to the firm for Rs 800. You are required to pass the necessary transfer entries if the firm is following:
    (i) Sectional balancing System;
    (ii) Self-balancing System.

Rectification of Errors

11. Give rectifying Journal Entries in each of the following cases:
    (i) When the system of self-balancing is in use,
    (ii) When system of self-balancing is in use,
    (iii) When neither self-balancing nor sectional balancing system is in use.
      (a) The Sales Book was found undercast by Rs 1,000.
      (b) Discount allowed to K. Krishnamurti correctly entered in the Cash Book but was not posted to his account.
      (c) Credit balance of 310 in Rao's account in the Purchases Ledger was to be transferred to his account in the Sales Ledger.

12. Messrs. Pioneer & Co. are maintaining accounts on self-balancing system. On 31-12-1986, the General Ledger discloses the following balance:

		Rs
Sales Ledger Adjustment Account	Dr.	35,235
Purchase Ledger Adjustment Account	Cr.	15,530

On scrutinising the Ledgers, the following mistakes were noticed:
   (i) A credit purchase of Rs 4,350 has been credited to the Sales Ledger Adjustment Account though the payment has been debited to the Purchase Ledger Adjustment Account, However, in the subsidiary books, these two entries have been entered only in the Purchase Ledger.
   (ii) Rs 1,000 paid to Mr. Boldger for goods purchased has been debited to the Sales Ledger Adjustment Account. In the subsidiary books, the party's account shows a debit balance in the Sales Ledger and a credit balance in the Purchases Ledger.
   (iii) Rs 4,750 was due from Mr. Albert in the Sales Ledger as against Rs 7,740 due to him for purchases made and entered in the Purchases Ledger.
   (iv) The Sales Ledger Balances disclose that sums aggregating Rs 740 have to be written off as Bad Debts and Discounts.

Prepare the necessary journal entries in the General Ledger and other Subsidiary Books

Chapter 15

ACCOUNTS OF NON-PROFIT MAKING ORGANISATIONS

LEARNING OBJECTIVES

After stydying this chapter you should be able to:

- [ ] identify non-profit making organisations;

- [ ] get familiar with the statements or accounts which form final accounts of a non-profit making organisation;

- [ ] understand the meaning and preparation of Receipts & Payments account and income and Expenditure Account;

- [ ] identify and understand the accounting treatment of items which are peculiar to a non-profit making organisation;

- [ ] appreciate the meaning and preparation of Receipts and Expenditure Account; and

- [ ] explain the meaning of certain key terms.

In the preceding chapters we have explained the preparation of final accounts in case of profit making organisations or institutions *i.e.*, those whose objective is to earn profit through business operations. However, there are organisations or institutions whose main objective is not to earn profit; but to provide service to the society. These institutions can broadly be divided into three categories.

(i) Institutions which work for the general welfare of their members *e.g.* clubs, staff associations, residents associations etc.

(ii) Charitable institutions *viz.* educational institutions, hospitals, etc.

(iii) Professional firms *viz.* Chartered Accountants, Advocates, Tax Consultants, Doctors, etc.

The non-profit making organisations or institutions are different from profit making institutions in several respects. They have not to purchase or sale goods or receive bills of exchange nor do have to make credit transactions. Most of their transactions are cash transactions and therefore they need not maintain detailed books of accounts like profit making concerns. However, they do maintain Cash Book and minimum number of such other books which may be required for their purposes. For example a Register of Members and a Minute Book are maintained in case of a club or society, a Student Fee Register is maintained in case of a school or college, a summary record of outstanding fees may be kept by an Advocate or a Chartered Accountant. At the end of the accounting period, a non-profit making institution also prepares its final accounts which include the following:

(i) Receipts and Payments Account

(ii) Income and Expenditure Account

(iii) Balance Sheet

In the present chapter we are first explaining the preparation of final accounts which are applicable to all non-profit making organisations in general. However, some specific aspects relating to educational institutions and professionals are being discussed later in the chapter.

RECEIPTS AND PAYMENTS ACCOUNT

Receipts and Payments Account is merely a summary of the cash transactions under proper heads which have taken place during the accounting period. It is prepared at the end of the accounting period from the cash book. The Cash Book contains a record of cash receipts and cash payments in a chronological order while receipts and payments account is a summary of total cash receipts and total cash payments received and made under different heads during a particular period. For example, if a club receives subscriptions from its members on different dates of the accounting year, they will be recorded on these dates separately in the Cash Book. However, Receipts and Payments Account will contain the total subscription received during the accounting year. Similarly Cash Book contains payment of salaries made on different dates of the month on different pages. The Receipts and Payments Account will show the total salaries paid during the accounting period.

The main features of the Receipts and Payments Account can be summarised as follows:

(i) It is an abbreviated copy of the cash book. The cash and bank items are usually merged in one column. Thus, contra entries between cash and bank are eliminated.

(ii) It is a Real Account.

(iii) All cash receipts are recorded on the debit side while all cash payments are recorded on the credit side.

(iv) It records all cash receipts and payments irrespective of the fact whether they are of capital or revenue nature or whether they relate to the current year or not. Similarly, it records all cash payments whether they are of capital or revenue nature or whether they relate to the current year or the next year. What is necessary is the receipts and payments should have been received or made during the period to which the Receipts and Payments Account relates.

(v) It starts with the balance in the beginning of the accounting year and ends with the balance at the end of the accounting year.

Illustration 15.1. From the following particulars taken from the Cash Book of a Club, prepare a Receipts and Payments Account.

	Rs
Opening Balance:	
Cash in Hand	100
Cash at Bank	500
Receipts:	
Subscriptions	3,300
Donations	260
Payments:	
Investment Purchased	1,000
Rent-paid	400
General Expenses	210
Postage and Stationery	70
Sundry Expenses	30
Closing Cash Balance	20

Solution:

RECEIPTS AND PAYMENTS ACCOUNT
for the year ended....

Receipts		Amount (Rs)	Payments		Amount (Rs)
To Balance b/d:			By Investments		1,000
Cash in Hand	100		By Rent		400
Cash at Bank	500	600	By General Expenses		210
			By Postage & Stationery		70
To Subscriptions		3,300	By Sundry Expenses		30
To Donations		260	By Balance c/d:		
			Cash in Hand	20	
			Cash at Bank		
			(balancing figure)	2,430	2,450
		4,160			4.160

INCOME AND EXPENDITURE ACCOUNT

This may be described as equivalent of the Profit and Loss Account. It performs the same functions and is compiled and constructed on precisely the same principles. Its essential features can be put as follows:

(*i*) It is a Nominal Account.

(*ii*) It records all losses and expenses on its debit side while all incomes and gains on its credit side.

(*iii*) The balance of this account represents either the excess of income over the expenditure (if the total of the credit side is more than that of the debit side) or excess of expenditure over income (if the total of the debit side of the account is more than that of its credit side).

Distinction between Receipts and Payments Account and Income and Expenditure Account

The following are the points of distinction between a Receipts and Payments Account and an Income and Expenditure Account:

(*i*) Receipts and payments account is like a consolidated cash account showing total cash receipts and total cash payments of during a particular period. While income and expenditure account is on the pattern of a profit and loss account showing incomes and expenses during a particular period.

(*ii*) Receipts and payments account starts with an opening balance representing cash or bank balance in hand while an income and expenditure starts with no such opening balance.

(*iii*) Receipts and payments account records all cash receipts and cash payments whether of a capital or a revenue nature. While income and expenditure account records only income and expenses of a revenue nature.

(*iv*) A receipts and payments account records all receipts and payments made during a particular period whether they relate to the current year, next year or previous year. While an income and expenditure account records only income and expenses relating to that particular period.

(*v*) The excess of receipts over payments show the cash balance at the end of a period. In case the cash payments exceed the cash receipts, it represents a bank overdraft. While in case of income and expenditure account, the excess of income over expenditure shows the net income made by the organization. Similarly, the excess of expenditure over income shows the net loss suffered by the organization.

Illustration 15.2. From the information given in Illustration 15.1, prepare an Income and Expenditure Account.

INCOME AND EXPENDITURE ACCOUNT
for the year ending on...

Expenditure	Amount (Rs)	Income	Amount (Rs)
To Rent	400	By Subscriptions	3,300
To General Expenses	210	By Donations	260
To Postage and Stationery	70		
To Sundry Expenses	30		
To Excess of Income over			
Expenditure	2,850		
	3,560		3,560

BALANCE SHEET

Balance Sheet in case of a non-trading concern is prepared in the usual way and contains particulars of all assets and liabilities of the concern/institution on the date on which it is prepared. The excess of assets over liabilities is termed as Capital Fund. The Capital Fund is made up of excess of income over expenditure and other incomes or surplus which might have been capitalised by the institution from time to time. Sometimes two Balance Sheets may have to be prepared—(i) Balance Sheet in the beginning of the accounting year to ascertain the amount of Capital Fund in the beginning of the accounting year, and (ii) Balance Sheet at the end of the accounting year to show the financial position of the Institution as on that date.

ITEMS PECULIAR TO NON-TRADING CONCERNS

The technique of preparing the Final Accounting of a non-trading concern is similar to that used for preparing the Final Accounts of a trading concern. However, there are certain peculiar items in case of a non-trading concern. The treatment of these items and their presentation in the Final Accounts is being explained below:

1. **Subscriptions.** In case of trading concerns, subscriptions are usually given, e.g., subscriptions for trade journals, subscriptions for membership of a club, etc. In case of a non-trading concern, subscriptions are usually received. For example, a club receives subscriptions from its members and this may be a major source of the club. The Receipts and Payments Account records the amount of actual subscriptions received while the Income and Expenditure Account records only the subscriptions which relate to the accounting period; whether received or not. Adjustments may, therefore, be required to find out the actual amount of income from subscriptions. The following illustrations are being given to clarify this point:

Illustration 15.3. From the following extracts of the Receipts and Payments Account and the additional information, you are required to compute the income from subscription for the year ending 31st December, 1990 and show the subscriptions item in the Final Accounts of the Club.

RECEIPTS AND PAYMENTS ACCOUNT
for the year ending 31st December, 1990

Receipts	Amount Rs	Payments	Amount Rs
Subscriptions	10,000		

Additional Information
- (i) Subscriptions outstanding on 31.12.1989, Rs 2,000.
- (ii) Subscriptions outstanding on 31.12.1990, Rs 4,000.
- (iii) Subscriptions received in advance as on 31.12.1989, Rs 3,000.
- (iv) Subscriptions received in advance as on 31.12.1990, Rs 2,000.

Solution:

INCOME AND EXPENDITURE ACCOUNT
for the year ending 31st December, 1990

Expenditure	Amount (Rs)	Income		Amount (Rs)
		By Subscriptions	10,000	
		Add: Subscriptions		
		outstanding		
		on 31.12.90	4,000	
		Add: Subscriptions		
		recd in advance		
		on 31.12.1989	3,000	
			17,000	
		Less: Subscriptions		
		outstanding		
		on 31.12.89	2,000	
			15,000	
		Less: Subscriptions		
		recd in advance		
		on 31.12.1990	2,000	13,000

BALANCE SHEET
as on 31st December, 1990

Liabilities	Amount (Rs)	Assets	Amount (Rs)
Subscriptions received in advance (as on 31.12.1990)	2000	Outstanding Subscriptions (as on 31.12.1990)	4,000

Illustration 15.4. From the following extracts of the Receipts and Payments Account and the additional information, you are required to compute the income from subscriptions for the year ending 31.12.1990 and show the subscription item, in the Final Accounts of the club.

Receipts	Amount (Rs)	Payments	Amount (Rs)
To Subscriptions:			
1989	1,800		
1990	10,000		
1991	4,000		

Additional Information

    (*i*) Subscriptions outstanding as on 31.12.1989:   Rs 2,000.
    (*ii*) Subscriptions outstanding as on 31.12.1990:   Rs 3,000.
    (*iii*) Subscriptions received in advance as on 31.12.1989: Rs 2,000.

Solution:

Expenditure	Amount (Rs)	Income		Amount (Rs)
		By Subscriptions	10,000	
		Add: Subscriptions		
		outstanding for		
		32.12.1990		
		(Rs 3,000 – 200)	2,800	

Contd...

Expenditure	Amount Rs	Income		Amount Rs
		Add: Subscriptions received in advance as on 31.12.1989	2,000	14,800

BALANCE SHEET
as on 31st December, 1990

Liabilities	Amount Rs	Assets		Amount Rs
Subscriptions received in advance as on 31.12.1990	4,000	Subscriptions outstanding as on 31.12.1990:		
		for 1989	200	
		for 1990	2,800	3,000

Notes:

 (*i*) Subscriptions received for the year 1990 have been given separately in the Receipts and Payments Account. The amount does not include any subscriptions which has been received on account of the last year or the next year as was the case in the previous illustration.

 (*ii*) Subscriptions outstanding as on 31.12.1990 amounts to Rs 3,000. It, therefore, includes subscriptions outstanding for the year 1989 amounting Rs 200. The subscriptions outstanding for the year 1990, therefore, amounts to only Rs 2,800.

In case the question had stated—'Subscriptions outstanding for 1990 are Rs 3,000', this would have meant that subscriptions amounting Rs 3,000 are outstanding only for the year 1990. In the Income and Expenditure Account the subscriptions outstanding would have been taken as Rs 3,000, and not as Rs 2,800 as has been done in the present illustration. In the Balance Sheet, the total amount of subscriptions outstanding would have been shown at Rs 3,200, *i.e.*, Rs 3,000 for 1990 and Rs 200 for 1989.

 2. **Donations.** A charitable institution may receive donations from time to time. The amount of donations may be taken as income or capitalised and taken to Balance Sheet depending upon whether it is a specific donation or a general donations.

 (*a*) **Specific donation.** In case a donation has been received for a specific purpose, the donation is termed as a specific donation. For example, an institution may receive donation for construction of building or for giving prizes to the best sportsman. The amount of such donation cannot, therefore, be used for any other purpose. It should be taken to the Balance Sheet on the liabilities side and be used only for the purpose for which it is meant, irrespective of the amount.

 (*b*) **General donation.** A donation not received for a specific purpose is termed as a General Donation. Its treatment depends upon the amount received. In case, the donation is of a substantial amount, it can be fairly taken for granted that such donation is of a non-recurring nature and, therefore, should be taken to the Balance Sheet on the liabilities side. However, if the donation is of a small amount and not meant for a specific purpose, it can be safely taken to the Income and Expenditure Account.

The size and nature of the institution will to a great extent decide about the amount of donation being small or big. For example, in case of a hospital of a moderate size, a sum of Rs 10,000 can be taken as a small donation, but for a badminton club, the amount of

Rs 10,000 is quite substantial and, therefore, it will be proper to take the amount of such donation received to the Balance Sheet.

Illustration 15.5. Following are the extracts from the Receipts and Payments Account of a sports club. You are required to show the different items in the Income and Expenditure Account and Balance Sheet of the club after taking into account the additional information given.

RECEIPTS AND PAYMENTS ACCOUNT
for the year ending 31st December, 1990

Receipts	Amount Rs	Payments	Amount Rs
To Donations for Pavilion	5,000		
To Subscriptions for			
Governor's Party	2,000		
To Donations	100		

Additional Information

   (*i*) Amount spent on Pavilion Rs 1,000.

  (*ii*) Outstanding subscriptions for Governor's Party Rs 500.

Solution:

INCOME AND EXPENDITURE ACCOUNT
for the year ending 31st December, 1990

Expenditure	Amount Rs	Income	Amount Rs
		By Donations	100

BALANCE SHEET
as on 31st December, 1990

Liabilities	Amount Rs	Assets	Amount Rs
Fund for Pavilion		Outstanding Subscriptions for	
(donations received)	5,000	Governor's Party	500
Subscriptions for Governor's Party		Pavilion (cost incurred)	1,000
(including outstanding)	2,500		

Notes:

   (*i*) The amount of donations received for Pavilion is a specific donation and, therefore, has been taken to the Balance Sheet on the liabilities side.

  (*ii*) The subscriptions received for Governor's Party is also for a specific purpose, and, therefore, has been taken to the Balance sheet. The amount of outstanding subscription has also been added to this amount and has been shown on both sides of the Balance Sheet.

 (*iii*) The expenditure of Rs 1,000 incurred on construction of Pavilion has been shown as an asset in the Balance Sheet. It is not to be subtracted from the Pavilion Fund. As a matter of fact, the Pavilion Fund was previously represented by cash, now it is partly represented by cash and partly by the cost incurred on the construction of Pavilion so far.

3. Special funds. An institution may keep special funds for some special purposes. For example, a sports club may keep a special fund for meeting sports expenses or for awarding of sports prizes. In case such special funds are maintained, any income relating to such special funds should be added to these funds in the Balance Sheet on the liabilities side. Similarly, all expenses on account of these funds should be deducted out of these funds. In case of a deficit, the amount should be met out from the Income and Expenditure Account. In case of a surplus, it will be better on account of convention of conservatism, to keep it in the Balance Sheet or merge it with the Capital Fund.

However, whatever has been stated above is not applicable to any income which an institution may receive on account of General Fund. Income on account of General Fund investments can very well be taken to Income and Expenditure Account.

Illustration 15.6. Following is the information given in respect of certain items of a sports club. You are required to show them in the Income and Expenditure Account and the Balance Sheet of the Club.

	Rs
Sports Fund as on 1.1.1990	10,000
Sports Fund Investments	10,000
Interest on Sports Fund Investments	1,000
Donation for Sports Fund	4,000
Sports Prizes awarded	3,000
Expenses on Sports Events	1,000
General Fund	20,000
General Fund Investments	20,000
Interest on General Fund Investments	2,000

Solution:

INCOME AND EXPENDITURE ACCOUNT
for the year ending 31st December, 1990

Expenditure	Amount Rs	Income	Amount Rs
		By Interest on General Fund Investments	2,000

BALANCE SHEET
as on 31st December, 1990

Liabilities		Amount Rs	Assets	Amount Rs
Sports Fund	10,000		Sports Fund Investments	10,000
Add Interest on Sports			General Fund Investments	20,000
Fund Investment	1,000			
Sports Fund Donations	4,000			
	15,000			
Less Sports Prizes				
awarded	3,000			
	12,000			
Less Expenses on				
Sports Events	1,000	11,000		
General Fund		20,000		

4. **Legacy.** Legacy refers to the amount which one gets on account of a will. The amount received on account of a legacy is as good as donation and should generally be taken to.

the Balance Sheet on the liabilities side since it is generally of a non-recurring nature. However, small amounts received on account of legacy may be taken to the Income and Expenditure Account.

5. **Entrance fee.** Entrance Fee or Admission Fee is usually charged by a club or a society or an educational institution from the new entrants. It is usually taken as an item of income. However, in case of clubs and similar institutions some people favour capitalising the entrance fee on the ground that it is of a non-recurring nature and being charged by the club as a premium from the new members towards the capital cost involved in establishing and maintaining the club by older members. This argument, of course, is not applicable in case of educational institutions or hospitals where admission fee is charged from students or patients. In the absence of any specific instructions in the question, the students should generally take it as an item of income.

6. **Fee for life membership.** Certain institutions charge fee for making persons as life members. Such members have to pay fee only once in their life-time. Of course they continue to enjoy the benefits from the institution throughout their life.

The amount received as life membership fee can be dealt in the accounts of the institution by any of the following methods:-

(i) The amount received may be taken as a capital receipt and therefore be taken to the Balance Sheet on the liabilities under the head "Life Membership Fee".

(ii) The amount received as life membership fee may be credited to a separate account viz. "Life Membership Fee Account". The normal annual subscriptions may be transferred from the "Life Membership Fee Account" to the Income and Expenditure Account and the balance may be carried forward till it is exhausted. In case of death of a member, the balance if any, in the "Life Membership Fee Account" may be transferred to "Capital Fund Account".

(iii) The amount received may be credited to "Life Membership Fee Account". The amount computed according to the average life of a member may annually be transferred from this account to "Income and Expenditure Account".

Tutorial Note: The students are advised to adopt the first method in the absence of any specific instructions in an examination problem.

7. **Sale of old newspapers.** The amount received on account of sale of old newspapers is of a recurring nature and should, therefore, be taken as income in the Income and Expenditure Account.

8. **Miscellaneous.** Adjustments may have to be made in respect of certain items such as sports material, printing and stationery material, etc. to find out the actual materials used during a particular period for the concerned expenditure. This will be clear with the help of the following illustration.

Illustration 15.7. From the following information, compute the amount to be debited or credited to the Income and Expenditure Account in respect of the following items:

		Rs
(i)	Sports Material:	
	Opening Stock as on 1.1.1990	2,000
	Purchases of Sports Material during 1990	8,000
	Stock of Sports Material on 31.12.1990	3,000
	Sale of Sports Material scrapped	50
(ii)	Printing and Stationary Material:	
	Opening Stock on 1.1.1990	3,000

Contd....

	Rs
Purchases of Printing and Stationery	5,000
Stock of Printing and Stationery on 31.12.1990	2,000
(iii) Tinned Provisions:	
Stock as on 1.1.1990	2,000
Purchases during the year	10,000
Stock as on 31.12.1990	3,000
Sale of tinned provisions	15,000

Solution:

INCOME AND EXPENDITURE ACCOUNT
for the year ended on 31st December, 1990

Expenditure		Amount Rs	Income	Amount Rs
To Sports Material used:			By Sale of Sports Material	50
Opening Stock	2,000		By Sale of Tinned Provisions	15,000
Add Purchases	8,000			
	10,000			
Less Closing Stock	3,000	7,000		
To Printing & Stationery Material used:				
Opening Stock	3,000			
Add Purchases	5,000			
	8,000			
Less Closing Stock	2,000	6,000		
To Cost of Tinned Provisions sold:				
Opening Stock	2,000			
Add: Purchases	10,000			
	12,000			
Less: Closing Stock	3,000	9,000		

In the following pages, we are giving comprehensive illustrations to cover the four different types of problems which are generally asked in the examinations.

These types are:

(i) Preparation of the Income and Expenditure Account and the Balance Sheet from the Receipts and Payments Account and additional information.

(ii) Preparation of Receipts and Payments Account from the Income and Expenditure Account with additional information.

(iii) Preparation of Balance Sheet from the Receipts and Payments Account and Income and Expenditure Account.

(iv) Preparation of correct statements/accounts from wrong statements/accounts.

Preparation of Income and Expenditure Account and Balance Sheet from Receipts and Payments Account etc.

Illustration 15.8. Given below is the Receipts and Payments Account of the National Club for the year ended 31st March, 1990 :

Receipts	Rs	Payments	Rs
To Balance b/d	1,025	By Salaries	600
To Subscriptions:		By General Expenses	80
1988–89	40	By Entertainment Programme	
1989–90	2,050	Expenses	430
1990–91	60	By Newspapers	150
To Donations	540	By Municipal Taxes	50
To Proceeds of Entertainment		By Charity	350
Programme	950	By Investment (Govt. Bonds)	2,000
To Sale of Waste Paper	45	By Electricity Charges	140
		By Balance c/d	890
	4,710		4,710

Prepare the Club's Income and Expenditure Account for the year ended 31st March, 1990 and the Balance Sheet as on that date, after taking the following information into account :

(a) There are 500 members each paying an annual subscription of Rs 5 and Rs 50 is still in arrear for 1988–89.

(b) Municipal taxes amounting to Rs 40 per annum have been paid upto 30th June 1990, and Rs 50 for salaries is outstanding.

(c) Buildings stand in the books at Rs 5,000 and it is required to write off depreciation @ 5% per annum.

(d) Six per cent per annum interest is accrued on Government Bonds for 5 months.

(C.A. Entrance, Nov., 1990)

Solution:

National Club
INCOME & EXPENDITURE ACCOUNT
for the year ended 31.3.1990

Expenditure		Rs	Income		Rs
To Salaries	600		By Subscriptions	2,050	
Add: Outstanding	50	650	Add: Outstanding	450	2,500
To General Expenses		80	By Donations		540
To News Papers		150	By Proceeds of Entertainment		
To Municipal Taxes	50		Programme	950	
Less: Pre-paid	10	40	Less: Expenses	450	500
To Charity		350	By Sale of Waste Paper		45
To Electricity Charges		140	By Interest on Govt. Bonds		50
To Excess of Income					
over Expenditure		1,975			
		3,635			3,635

National Club
BALANCE SHEET
as on 31.3.1990

Liabilities		Amount Rs	Assets		Amount Rs
Opening Capital Fund:	6,115		Building:	5,000	
Add: Excess of Income			Less: Depreciation	250	4,750
over Expenditure	1,975	8,090			

Contd....

Liabilities	Amount Rs	Assets		Amount Rs
Subscriptions received in advance (1990-91)	60	Investments in Govt. Bonds		2,000
Outstanding Expenses	50	Interest Receivable		50
		Subscriptions		
		Outstanding 1989-90	450	
		1988-89	50	500
		Prepaid Taxes		10
		Cash in Hand		890
	8,200			8,200

Working Notes:

1.

National Club
BALANCE SHEET
as on 1.4.1989

Liabilities	Amount Rs	Assets	Amount Rs
Capital Fund (balancing figure)	6,115	Cash in Hand	1,025
		Buildings	5,000
		Subscriptions receivable for 1988-89 (Rs 40 + Rs 50)	90
	6,115		6,115

2. Donation has been presumed to be general donation. In case it is treated as a special donation, the amount will be taken to Balance Sheet on the liabilities side.

Illustration 15.9. The Receipts and Payments Account of Navkar Football Club for the year ended 31st March, 1991 was as under.

Receipts	Amount Rs	Payments	Amount Rs
To Balance b/d 1.4.90	48,000	By Purchase of Balls	80,000
To Subscriptions received	2,46,000	By Tournament Fees	10,000
To Interest	2,000	By Affiliation Fees	2,000
To Sale of Furniture	10,000	By Rent of play-ground	5,000
To Donations for Club Building	60,000	By Refreshment Expenses	4,000
		By Travelling Expenses	30,000
		By Investments Purchased at face value	1,00,000
		By Salary	12,000
		By Miscellaneous Expenses	8,000
		By Balance c/d 31.3.91	1,15,000
	3,66,000		3,66,000

Prepare the Club's Income and Expenditure Account for the year ended 31 March, 1991 and the Balance Sheet as on that date, after taking the following information into account:

(1) The subscriptions received include Rs. 10,000 outstanding subscriptions of the year 1990-1991 amounting to Rs 16,000 is still outstanding from members, Some members have paid subscription for the year 1991-1992 amounting to Rs. 8,000 which is included in the subscription received.

(2) Interest accrued but not received Rs 500

(3) The book-value of the furniture sold was Rs 14,000.

(4) The rent of play-ground Rs 6,000 and salary Rs 5,000 of the year 1990–91 are still outstanding and rent of play-ground of the year 1989–90 Rs 1,000 has been paid during this year.

(5) There is a stock of balls with the club Rs 4,000 on 31st March, 1991.

(C.A. Entrance, Nov., 1991)

Solution:

Navkar Football Club

INCOME AND EXPENDITURE ACCOUNT

for the year ended 31st March, 1991

Particulars		Amount Rs	Particulars		Amount Rs
To Balls consumed	80,000		By Subscriptions	2,46,000	
Less: Closing stock	4,000	76,000	Add: Outstanding for		
To Tournament Fees		10,000	the current year	16,000	
To Affiliation Fees		2,000		2,62,000	
To Rent of Play-ground	5,000		Less: Outstanding for		
Add: Outstanding for			last year	10,000	
the current year	6,000			2,52,000	
	11,000		Less: Received in		
Less: Rent outstanding			advance for next year	8,000	2,44,000
for last year	1,000	10,000	By Interest	2,000	
To Refreshment of			Add: Interest due but		
Players		4,000	not received	500	2,500
To Player's Travelling Expenses		30,000			
To Salary	12,000				
Add: Outstanding for					
the current year	5,000	17,000			
To Office Expenses		8,000			
To Loss on Sale of Furniture					
(14,000–10,000)		4,000			
To Excess of Income					
over Expenditure		85,500			
		2,46,500			2,46,500

Navkar Football Club

BALANCE SHEET

as on 31st March, 1991

Liabilities		Amount Rs	Assets	Amount Rs
Subscriptions received			Cash	1,15,000
in advance		8,000	Investments	1,00,000
Outstanding Expenses:			Accrued Interest	500
Salary	5,000		Outstanding Subscriptions	16,000
Rent	6,000	11,000	Stock of Balls	4,000
Building Fund		60,000		

Contd....

Liabilities		Amount Rs	Assets	Amount Rs
Capital Fund as on 1.4.90	71,000			
Add: Excess of Income over Expenditure	85,000	1,56,500		
		2,35,500		2,35,500
		2,35,500		2,35,500

Working Note:

Navkar Football Club

BALANCE SHEET
as on 1st April, 1990

Liabilities	Amount Rs	Assets	Amount Rs
Outstanding rent for 1989–90	1,000	Cash	48,000
Capital Fund (balancing figure)	71,000	Subscriptions Outstanding	10,000
		Furniture	14,000
	72,000		72,000

Illustration 15.10. The following is the Receipts and Payments Account of the Madras Sports Club for the year ended 31st December, 1985:

Receipts	Rs	Payments	Rs
To Balance 1.1.85	2,400	By Secretary's Salary	3,600
To Entrance Fees	500	By Upkeep of Grounds	2,100 (c)
To Subscriptions	8,700 (a)	By Wages of Groundsmen	2,400 (d)
To Proceeds of Concerts	1,500	By Ground Rent	150
To Interest on Investments	500 (b)	By Printing and Postage	200
		By Sundry Repairs	175
		By Balance 31.12.85	4,975
	13,600		13,600

(a) This item includes subscriptions outstanding brought over from previous year Rs 500. (b) This amount includes Rs 100 in respect of interest accrued in the preceding period. (c) This item includes Rs 300 applicable to the previous year. (d) This item includes Rs 150 applicable to the previous year.

Other ledger balances at the commencement of the financial period were: Capital Fund Rs 40,100; Income and Expenditure Account credit balance brought forward Rs 8,900; Club Premises and Grounds (as per valuation) Rs 30,000; Investments Rs 10,000; Sports Materials Rs 2,450; Furniture and Fixtures Rs 4,000.

From the above particulars, prepare a Balance Sheet at the commencement of the period, and Income and Expenditure Account for the period and a Balance Sheet at the close of the period.

Entrances Fees are to be capitalised. The outstanding liabilities on 31st December, 1985 were: Wages Rs 200 and Printing Rs 100. Interest accrued and outstanding on investments was Rs 120. Depreciate Club Premises by 2%, Furniture by 5% and Sports Equipment by 33 1/3%.

Solution:

BALANCE SHEET
as at 1st January, 1985

Liabilities	Amount Rs	Assets	Amount Rs
Income and Expenditure Account:		Cash	2,400
Credit balance brought		Premises	30,000
forward	8,900	Investments	10,000
Outstandings Expenses	450	Furniture and Fixtures	4,000
Capital Fund (balancing figure)	40,100	Outstanding Interest	100
		Outstanding Subscriptions	500
		Sports Equipment	2,450
	49,450		49,450

INCOME AND EXPENDITURE ACCOUNT
for the year ending 31.12.1985

Liabilities	Amount Rs	Assets	Amount Rs
To Secretary's Salary	3,600.00	By Subscriptions	8,200.00
To Wages of Groundsman	2,450.00	By Proceeds of Concerts	1,500.00
To Upkeep of Grounds	1,800.00	By Interest on Investments	520.00
To Printing and Postage	300.00		
To Sundry Repairs	175.00		
To Ground Rent	150.00		
To Depreciation:			
Sports Equipment	816.67		
Premises	600.00		
Furniture	200.00		
To Excess of Income over			
Expenditure	128.33		
	10,220.00		10,220.00

BALANCE SHEET
as on December 31, 1985

Liabilities		Amount Rs	Assets	Amount Rs
Capital Fund	40,100.00		Premises less depreciation	29,400.00
Add: Entrance fees	500.00	40,600.00	Furniture less depreciation	3,800.00
*Income and Expenditure A/c			Sports Equipment less	
Balance b/d	8,900.00		depreciation	1,633.33
Add: Income of			Investments	10,000.00
current year	128.33	9,028.33	Interest Outstanding	120.00
Outstanding Expenses		300.00	Cash Balance	4,975.00
		49,928.33		49,928.33

*Alternatively the amount could have been added to Capital Fund.

Illustration 15.11. On 1st January, 1985, the following were the assets and liabilities of the Delhi Club:

Land and Buildings Rs 60,000; Furniture and Fittings Rs 6,000; General Fund Investments Rs 1,20,000; Sports Fund Investments Rs 10,000; Stock of Cutlery and Crockery Rs 1,000; Stock of tinned provisions Rs 1,000; Outstanding subscriptions Rs 900; Balance at Bank Rs 3,400; Cash in hand Rs 700; Income and Expenditure Account, Credit Balance Rs 9,200; Sports Fund Rs 10,000; Subscriptions received in advance Rs 800; Outstanding for salaries Rs 800; and Printing and Stationery Bill Rs 200.

The receipts during the year were Entrance Fees Rs 6,000 (half of which is to be credited to the General Fund); Subscriptions Rs 10,000; Donations to Sports Fund Rs 2,000. This amount was placed with the Bank on Fixed Deposit. Interest on General Fund Investments Rs 6,000; Interest on Sports Fund Investments Rs 500, Receipts from Catering Rs 12,000. The payments were: Salaries Rs 9,600; Printing and Stationery bills for 1985 Rs 1,200; Expenses on Sports events Rs 400; Repairs to Buildings Rs 4,000; Catering expenses Rs 8,000; Purchase of tinned provisions Rs 3,000; Sundry expenses Rs 800. The balance at Bank on 31st December, 1985 was Rs 10,600.

You are told that subscriptions for 1985 Rs 700 were outstanding and Rs 600 salaries were not paid; Rs 600 were received as subscriptions for 1986. The unused stock of tinned provisions was valued at Rs 1,400.

From the above details you are required to prepare an Income and Expenditure Account for the year ended 31st December, 1985 and a Balance Sheet as at that date after providing for depreciation on Land and Buildings at 2 per cent and Furniture and Fittings at 5 per cent and writing off half the value of Cutlery and Crockery.

Solution:

Delhi Club

INCOME AND EXPENDITURE ACCOUNT
for the year ending 31.12.1985

Expenditure		Rs	Income		Rs
To Salaries	9,600		By Entrance Fees	6,000	
Add: Outstanding	600		Less: Credited to		
	10,200		General Fund	3,000	3,000
Less: Relating to 1984	800	9,400	By Subscriptions	10,000	
To Printing and Stationery		1,200	Less: Relating to 1984	900	
To Repairs to Buildings		4,000		9,100	
To Sundry Expenses		800	Add: Recd. in '84 for '85	800	
To Depreciation on:				9,900	
Land and Buildings	1,200		Add: Outstanding	700	
Furniture and Fixtures	300			10,600	
Cutlery and Crockery	500	2,000	Less: Relating to 1976	600	10,000
To Excess of Income			By Interest on General		
over Expenditure		3,000	Fund Investments		6,000
			By Catering Receipts	12,000	
			Less: Expenses	8,000	
			Tinned provision		
			used	2,600	10,600	1,400
		20,400			20,400

Delhi Club

BALANCE SHEET
as on 31.12.1985

Liabilities	Amount Rs		Assets		Amount Rs
Subscriptions received			Land & Buildings	60,000	
in advance		600	Less: Depreciation	1,200	58,800
Printing & Stationery outstanding		200	Furniture & Fittings	6,000	
Salaries outstanding		600	Less: Depreciation	300	5,700
Sports Fund		12,100	General Fund		
General Fund	1,20,000		Investments		1,20,000
Add: Entrance Fee	3,000	1,23,000	Sports Fund Investments		10,000
Capital Fund	62,000		Stock of Cutlery and Crokery		500
Add: Excess of Income over			Stock of Tinned		
Expenditure for 1984	9,200		Provisions		1,400
	71,200		Subscriptions due		700
Add: Excess of Income			Cash at Bank		10,600
over Expenditure for			Fixed Deposit with Bank		2,000
1985	3,000	74,200	Cash in hand		1,000
		2,10,700			2,10,700

Working Notes:

Delhi Club

(1)

BALANCE SHEET
as on 31.12.1984

Liabilities	Rs	Assets	Rs
Sports Fund	10,000	Land & Buildings	60,000
General Fund	1,20,000	Furniture & Fittings	6,000
Subscriptions recd. in advance	800	General Fund Investments	1,20,000
Salaries outstanding	800	Sport Fund Investments	10,000
Printing and Stationery		Stock of Cutlery and Crockery	1,000
outstanding	200	Stock of Tinned Provisions	1,000
Excess of Income over	9,200	Subscriptions due	900
Expenditure for 1984		Cash at Bank	3,400
Capital Fund (Bal. figure)	62,000	Cash in Hand	700
	2,03,000		2,03,000

(2) TINNED PROVISIONS CONSUMED:

	Rs	
Opening stock	1,000	
Add: Purchases	3,000	
	4,000	
Less: Closing stock	1,400	2,600

(3) RECEIPTS AND PAYMENTS ACCOUNT

Receipts	Rs	Payments	Rs
To Balance at Bank	3,400	By Fixed Deposit with Bank	2,000
To Cash in Hand	700	By Salaries	9,600
To Entrance Fees	6,000	By Printings and Stationery	1,200
To Subscriptions	10,000	By Sports Events	400

Contd....

Receipts	Rs	Payments	Rs
To Donations to Sports Fund	2,000	By Repairs to Buildings	4,000
To Interest on General Fund		By Catering Expenses	8,000
Investments	6,000	By Tinned Provisions	3,000
To Catering	12,000	By Sundry Expenses	800
To Interest on Sports Fund	500	By Balance:	
		Cash at Bank	10,600
		Cash in hand (bal. fig.)	1,000
	40,600		40,600

Illustration 15.12. The cashier of a charitable trust furnishes you with the following information to enable you to prepare the final accounts of the Trust:

	Dr. Amount Rs	Cr. Amount Rs
Interest		30,000
Rent		12,000
Donations for Clinic Fund		6,000
Sundry Collections from parties		3,000
Salaries	6,000	
Medicines and Surgical Expenses	14,000	
Clinical Equipments purchased	5,000	
Educational Scholarships	10,000	
Printing, Stationery and Postage	800	
Travelling Expenses of Trustees	1,000	
Conveyance Allowance to Staff	200	
Furniture purchased	4,000	
Investments (purchased on the last day of the year)	10,000	
Cash and Bank Balances:		
Cash	1,600	1,000
Bank	13,400	14,000
	66,000	66,000

Trust fund originally consisted of Buildings valued at Rs 1,50,000, 9% Government securities of the face value of Rs 3,50,000 (cost of Rs 3,20,000) and the Bank Balance of Rs 10,000.

Bank interest collectable at the end of the year was Rs 2,500. Interest accrued on investments at the beginning of the year was Rs 3,500, and at the end of the year Rs 5,000. The Trust owed suppliers of medicines Rs 1,200 and Rs 800 respectively at the beginning and the end of the year. Furniture at the beginning of the year was valued at Rs 3,000.

You have to provide depreciation on the book values of buildings at 2 ½% and on other assets at 20%.

Solution:

Charitable Trust

OPENING BALANCE SHEET

Liabilities	Rs	Assets	Rs
Trust Fund		Building	1,50,000
(1,50,000 + 3,20,000 + 10,000)	4,80,000	Investments	3,20,000

Contd....

Liabilities	Rs	Assets	Rs
Creditors for supplies	1,200	Furniture	3,000
Revenue Fund (bal. fig.)	10,300	Bank	14,000
		Cash	1,000
		Accrued Interest	3,500
	4,91,500		4,91,500

RECEIPTS AND PAYMENTS ACCOUNT

Receipts		Rs	Payments		Rs
To Opening balance b/d:			By Capital Payments:		
Cash	1,000		Investments	10,000	
Bank	14,000	15,000	Furniture	4,000	
To Capital Fund:			Clinical Equipment	5,000	19,000
Donations for Clinic Fund		6,000	By Revenue Payments:		
To Revenue Receipts:			Salaries	6,000	
Interest	30,000		Medicines	14,000	
Rent	12,000		Scholarships	10,000	
Sundries	3,000	45,000	Printing etc.	800	
			Travelling	1,000	
			Conveyance	2,000	32,000
			By Balance c/d		
			Cash	1,600	
			Bank	13,400	15,000
		66,000			66,000

INCOME & EXPENDITURE ACCOUNT

Expenditure		Amount Rs	Income	Amount Rs
To Salaries		6,000	By Interest	
To Medical and Surgical expenses			(30,000 + 5,000 - 3,500)	31,500
(14,000 + 800 - 1,200)		13,600	By Rent	12,000
To Educational Scholarships		10,000	By Sundry Contributions	3,000
To Printing, Postage &			By Interest accrued	
Stationery		800	on Bank Deposits	2,500
To Travelling Expenses				
of Trustees		1,000		
To Conveyance Allowance				
to Staff		200		
To Depreciation on assets:				
Building at 2 1/2%	3,750			
Furniture 20%	1,400			
Elec. Equips. at 20%	1,000	6,150		
To Excess of Income				
over Expenditure				
transferred to				
Revenue Fund		11,250		
		49,000		49,000

BALANCE SHEET

at the end of the year

Liabilities	Amount Rs		Assets	Amount Rs
Trust Capital Fund as per			Fixed Assets:	
Opening Balance Sheet		4,80,000	Building *less* depreciation	1,46,250
Add: Donations for clinic		6,000	Furniture *less* depreciation	5,600
		4,86,000	Surgical equips. *less* dep.	4,000
Revenue Fund as per			Investments at cost	
Balance Sheet	10,300		(F.V. Rs 3,60,000)	3,30,000
Add: Surplus	11,250	21,550	Current Assets:	
Creditors for Supplies		800	Accrued Interest	7,500
			(on bank and Investments)	
			Cash	1,600	
			Bank	13,400	22,500
		5,08,350		5,08,350

Illustration 15.13. Punya Trust runs a charitable hospital and a dispensary and for the year ended 31st March, 1991, the following balances were extracted from its books:

	Rs	Dr. Rs	Cr. Rs
Capital fund			18,00,000
Donations received in the year			12,00,000
Fees received from patients			6,00,000
Recovery for amenities—rent etc.			5,50,000
Recovery for food supplies			2,80,000
Surgical equipments		9,10,000	
Buildings, theaters etc.		6,40,000	
Consumption of:			
Medicines	2,40,000		
Foodstuffs	1,80,000		
Chemicals etc.	60,000	4,80,000	
Closing stock of:			
Medicines etc.	40,000		
Foodstuffs	8,000		
Chemicals etc.	2,000	50,000	
Sales of medicines (dispensary)			6,20,000
Opening stock of medicines (dispensary)		1,10,000	
Purchases of medicines (dispensary)		6,00,000	
Salaries:			
Administrative staff	60,000		
Doctors, Nurses, orderlies etc.	3,00,000		
Assistants at dispensary	30,000	3,90,000	
Electricity and power charges:			
Hospital	2,10,000		
Dispensary	4,000	2,14,000	
Furniture, fittings and equipments		1,60,000	
Ambulance		60,000	
Postage, telephone charges etc. *less* recovery		52,000	
Subscriptions to medical journals		42,000	
Ambulance maintenance charges *less* recoveries			1,600
Consumption of linen, bedsheets etc.		1,80,000	

Contd....

	Rs	Dr. Rs	Cr. Rs
Fixed deposites (made on 10–8–1989 for three years at interest of 11% p.a.)		10,00,000	
Cash in hand		12,100	
Cash at bank		70,500	
Sundry debtors (dispensary)		1,21,000	
Sundry creditors (dispensary)			82,000
Remuneration to trustees, trust office expenses etc.		42,000	

Additional information:

(i) The dispensary supplies medicines to hospitals on requisitions and delivery notes; for which no adjustment has been made in the books. Cost of such supplies in the year was Rs 1,20,000;

(ii) Stock of medicines at close at dispensary was Rs 80,000;

(iii) Stock of medicines on 31st March, 1991 at he hospital included Rs 8,000 worth of medicines belonging to patients; this has not been considered in arriving at the figure of consumption of medicines;

(iv) Donations were received towards the corpus of the trust;

(v) One of the well-wishers donated surgery equipment, whose market value was Rs 80,000, on 15th August, 1990;

(vi) The hospital is to receive a grant of 25% of the amount spent on treatment of poor patients, from the local branch of the Red Cross Society. Such expenditure in the year was Rs 1 lakh;

(vii) Out of the fees recovered from the patients, 10% is to be given to specialists as retained;

(viii) Depreciation on assets, on closing balances is to be provided on:

Surgical equipments	20%
Buildings	5%
Furniture and fittings	10%
Ambulance	30%

Prepare the Income and Expenditure Statements of the Dispensary, Trust and the Hospital for the year ended 31st March, 1991 and Statement of Affairs of the trust as at that date.

Solution:

Punya Trust

INCOME & EXPENDITURE STATEMENT

for the year ended 31st March 1991

Particulars	Rs
Dispensary:	
Sales of Medicines	6,20,000
Medicines issued to Hospital	1,20,000
	7,40,000
Less: Cost of Medicines sold/issued:	
Opening stock	1,10,000
Add: Purchases	6,00,000
	7,10,000
Less: Closing Stock	80,000 6,30,000
Gross Income	1,10,000

Contd....

Particulars		Rs
Less: Operating Expenses:		
Salaries of Assistants	30,000	
Electricity and Power charges	4,000	34,000
Net Income transferred to General Trust Account		76,000

Hospital
Incomes:

		Rs
Fees Recovered from patients		6,00,000
Recovery for room rent etc.		5,50,000
Recovery for food supplied		2,80,000
Ambulance receipts (net)		1,600
Grant receivable from Red Cross Society		25,000
		14,56,600
Less: Expenses:		
Consumption of Medicines		
(2,40,000 + 8,000 + 1,20,000)	3,86,000	
Food Stuffs	1,80,000	
Chemicals etc.	60,000	6,08,000
Salaries:		
Doctors, Nurses etc.	3,00,000	
Administrative staff	60,000	3,60,000
Returns due to specialists		60,000
Electricity & Power charges		2,10,000
Subscriptions to medical journals		42,000
Consumption of linen, bedsheets etc.		1,80,000
Depreciation:		
Surgical Equipment (20% on 9,10,000 + 80,000)	1,98,000	
Buildings @ 5%	32,000	
Furniture, Fittings etc. @ 10%	16,000	
Ambulance @ 30%	18,000	2,64,000
		17,24,000
Excess of Expenditure over Income transferred to General Trust Account		2,67,400

GENERAL TRUST ACCOUNT

		Rs
Net Income from Dispensary		76,000
Interest due on fixed deposits		1,10,000
Net Income		1,86,000
Less: Excess of Expenditure over Income from Hospital	2,67,400	
Postage, Telephone charges etc.	52,000	
Trustee's Remuneration, expenses etc.	42,000	3,61,400
Net Excess of Expenditure over Income (or Deficit)		1,75,400

Punya Trust
STATEMENT OF AFFAIRS
as on 31st March, 1991

Liabilities	Amount Rs	Assets	Amount Rs
Capital Fund:		Cash in Hand	12,100
As on 1st Apr. '90 18,00,000		Cash at Bank:	
Add: Donations		Current Account	70,500

Contd....

Liabilities		Amount Rs	Assets		Amount Rs
received	12,00,000		Fixed Deposit	10,00,000	10,70,500
Market value of			Interest accrued on		
gift equip..	80,000		Fixed Deposit		1,10,000
	30,80,000		Sundry Debtors		1,21,000
Less: Deficit for			Grant Due from		
the year	1,75,400	29,04,600	Red Cross Society		25,000
Sundry Creditors:			Stocks of Goods:		
Medicines	82,000		Medicines: (Dispensary)	80,000	
Retainer fees due			Hospital:		
to specialists	60,000	1,42,000	Medicines	32,000	
			Food	8,000	
			Chemicals	2,000	42,000	1,22,000
			Surgical Equipments:		
			as on 1–4–90	9,10,000	
			Add: Gift Received	80,000	
				9,90,000	
			Less: Depreciation	1,98,000	7,92,000
			Buildings Theatre etc.		
			as on 1.4.90	6,40,000	
			Less: Depreciation	32,000	6,08,000
			Furniture Fittings etc.		
			as on 1.4.90	1,60,000	
			Less: Depreciation	16,000	1,44,000
			Ambulance:		
			as on 1.4.90	60,000	
			Less: Depreciation	18,000	42,000
		30,46,600			30,46,600

Illustration 15.14. The following is the Receipts and Payments Account of the Three Hundred Club for the year ending 30th September, 1984:

Receipts	Rs	Rs	Payments	Rs
Opening Balance:			Honoraria to Secretary & Treasurer	4,800
Cash in Hand	150		Rates & Taxes etc.	1,260
Balance as per Bank			Printing & Stationery	470
Pass Book	8,230	8,380	Other Misc. Exp.	1,530
Subscriptions		10,710	Groundman's Wages	840
Receipts from Fetes		2,400	Expenditure on Fetes	2,390
Net proceeds of variety			Payment for Bar	
Entertainment		4,270	Purchases	5,770
Bank Interest		230	Repairs etc.	320
Bar takings		7,450	New Car (less sale	
Cash overspent		20	proceeds of	12,600
			old car Rs 3,000)	
			Closing balance as per	
			Bank Pass Book	3,480
		33,460		33,460

You are given the following additional information:

	1.10.83 Rs	30.9.84 Rs
(1) Subscriptions Due	1,200	980
(2) Unpresented cheques being payment on printing	90	30
(3) Club premises at cost	29,000	......
(4) Depreciation on Club premises	18,800	......
(5) Car at cost—(BRM 2016)	12,190	......
(6) Depreciation on car	10,290	......
(7) Value of Bar Stock	710	870
(8) Amount due for Bar Purchases	590	430

(9) Cash overspent represents amount of honorarium to the treasurer not drawn due to shortage of funds. But the total salary payable to him for the year was already included in Rs 4,800.

(10) Depreciation is to be provided @ 5% p.a. on the written down value of the Club Premises and @ 15% p.a. on Car for the whole year.

You are required to adjust Bank Balance according to Cash Book and prepare:

(1) An Income and Expenditure Account of the Club as at 30th September, 1984; and

(2) A Balance Sheet as at 30th September 1984.

Solution:

Three Hundred Club

INCOME & EXPENDITURE ACCOUNT

for the year ending 30th September, 1984

Expenditure		Rs	Income	Rs
To Honoraria Secretary and			By Subscriptions	10,490
Treasurer		4,800	By Bar Takings	7,450
To Rates & Taxes etc.		1,260	By Receipts from Fetes	2,400
To Printing & Stationery		410	By Net Proceeds of Variety	
To Groundman's Wages		840	Entertainment	4,270
To Repairs etc.		320	By Bank Interest	230
To Bar Expenses Stock on			By Profit on sale of Motor Car	1,100
1.10.83	710			
Purchases	5,610			
	6,320			
Less: Stock on 30.9.84	870	5,450		
To Expenditure on Fetes		2,390		
To Other Mesc. Expenses		1,530		
To Depreciation:				
Premises	510			
Motor Car	2,340	2,850		
To Excess of Income over Expen.				
transferred to Capital Fund		6,090		
		25,940		25,940

Three Hundred Club

BALANCE SHEET
as at 30th September, 1984

Liabilities		Rs	Assets			Rs
Capital Fund:			Club Premises:			
As at 1.10.1983	21,710		Cost as at 1.10.83		29,000	
Add: Excess of Income			Less: Depreciation:			
over Expenditure			As at 1.10.83	18,800		
for the year	6,090	27,800	For the year	510	19,310	9,690
Outstanding liabilities:			Motor Car:			
For Purchases	430		Cost as at 1.10.83		12,190	
For Expenses	20	450	Additions during the year		15,600	
					27,790	
			Less: Cost of Car sold		12,190	
					15,600	
			Less: Depreciation		2,340	13,260
			Bar Stock			870
			Outstanding Subscriptions			980
			Cash & Bank Balances:			
			On Hand		Nil	
			At Bank		3,450	3,450
		28,250				28,250

Working Notes:

1. Adjusted Bank Balance

Balance as per Pass Book	3,480
Less: Cheques issued but not presented	30
Balance as per Cash Book	3,450

2. Adjusted Cash Balance

Amount overspent	20
Less: Honorarium to Secretary & Treasurer not drawn	20
Cash Balance on Hand	Nil

3. Depreciation on Premises and Car and Profit on sale of car

		Rs Premises		Rs Car	Rs
Cost on 1.10.1983		29,000		12,190	
Depreciation on 1st October, 1983		18,800		10,290	
		10,200		1,900	
Sale proceeds				3,000	
Profit on sale				1,100	
Cost of new car				15,600	
Depreciation	@ 5%	510	@ 15%	2,340	

4. Capital Fund as on 1.10.1983

Club Premises		29,000
Less: Depreciation		18,800	10,200

Contd....

	Rs	Rs	Rs
Car		12,190	
Less: Depreciation		10,290	1,900
Bar Stock			710
Outstanding Subscriptions			1,200
Cash on Hand			150
Cash at Bank:			
As per Pass Book		8,230	
Less: Cheques not presented		90	8,140
			22,300
Less: Outstanding Liability for Bar Purchases			590
			21,710

5. **Printing & Stationery**

	Rs
Amount as per Receipts & Payments Account	470
Add: Cheque issued but not yet account for	30
	500
Less: Cheque for 1982–83 included this year	90
Printing & Stationery for 1983–84	410

6. **Bar Purchases**

	Rs
Amount as per Receipts & Payments Account	5,770
Add: Amount still due	430
	6,200
Less: Amount due on 30.9.83	590
	5,610

Subscriptions:

	Rs
Received	10,710
Add: Outstanding on 30.9.84	980
	11,690
Less: Outstanding on 30.9.83	1,200
	10,490

Preparation of Receipts and Payments Account from Income and Expenditure Account and the Balance Sheet:

This requires finding out of Cash receipts and Cash payments received or made during the accounting year. This can be done by simply putting the things in the reverse gear, *i.e.*, items which are added while preparing an Income and Expenditure Account from a Receipts and Payments Account should now be subtracted and *vice-versa*.

Illustration 15.15. From the following details calculate the amount of subscriptions received and rent paid during the year 1988.

INCOME AND EXPENDITURE ACCOUNT
for the year ending 31st December, 1988

Expenditure	Rs	Income	Rs
To Rent	5,000	By Subscriptions	10,000

Additional information:

	Rs
Subscriptions outstanding as on 1.1.1988	2,000
Subscriptions outstanding as on 31.12.1988	3,000

	Rs
Subscriptions received in advance as on 1.1.1988	3,000
Subscriptions received in advance as on 31.12.1988	2,000
Rent outstanding as on 1.1.1988	2,000
Rent outstanding as on 31.12.1988	3,000

Solution:

Subscriptions received during 1988

Subscriptions as per Income and Expenditure Account		10,000
Add: Subscriptions outstanding as on 1.1.1988 (since they must have been received during the year)		2,000
		12,000
Less: Subscriptions outstanding as on 31.12.1988 (not received)		3,000
		9,000
Less: Subscriptions received in advance as on 1.1.1988 (not received during the year but included in the total subscriptions income)		3,000
		6,000
Add: Subscriptions received in advance as on 31.12.1988		2,000
		8,000

Rent paid during 1988

Rent as per Income and Expenditure Account	5,000
Add: Outstanding rent as on 1.1.1988 (should have been paid during the year)	2,000
	7,000
Less: Rent outstanding as on 31.12.1988 (not paid though taken as an expense)	3,000
Rent Paid	4,000

Illustration 15.16. The Income and Expenditure of the Delhi Club for the year 1988 is as follows:

INCOME AND EXPENDITURE ACCOUNT
for the year ended 31.12.1988

Expenditure	Rs	Income	Rs
To Salaries	4,750	By Subscriptions	7,500
To General Expenses	500	By Entrance Fees	250
To Audit Fees	250	By Contribution for Annual Dinner	1,000
To Secretary's Honorarium	1,000	By Profit on Annual Sports	750
To Printing & Stationery	450		
To Annual Dinner Expenses	1,500		
To Insurance and Bank Charges	150		
To Depreciation	300		
To Surplus	600		
	9,500		9,500

This account has been prepared after the following adjustments:

	Rs 600
Subscriptions outstanding at the end of 1987	Rs 600
Subscriptions received in advance on 31.12.1987	450
Subscriptions received in advance on 31.12.1988	270
Subscriptions outstanding on 31.12.1988	750

The salaries outstanding at the beginning and at the end of 1988 were respectively Rs 400 and Rs 450. General expenses include insurance prepaid to the extent of Rs 60. Audit fees for 1988 are as yet unpaid. During 1988, audit fees for 1987 were paid amounting Rs 200.

The club owned a freehold lease of grounds valued at Rs 10,000. The club had sports equipments on 1.1.1988 valued at Rs 2,600. At the end of the year, after depreciation, the equipment amounted to Rs 2,700. In 1987, the club had raised a bank loan of Rs 2,000. This was outstanding throughout 1988. On 31st December, 1988 cash in hand amounted Rs 1,600.

Prepare a Receipts and Payments Account for 1988 and Balance Sheet at the end of the year.

Solution:

Delhi Club
RECEIPTS AND PAYMENTS ACCOUNT
for the year ending 31.12.1988

Receipts		Rs	Payments		Rs
To Balance b/d (balancing figure)		1,390	By Salaries	4,750	
To Subscriptions	7,500		Less: Outstanding at the end of 1987	450	
Add: Outstanding 1987	600			4,300	
	8,100		Add: Outstanding in the beginning of 1987	400	4,700
Less: Received in advance 1987	450		By General Expenses	500	
	7,650		Add: Prepaid	60	560
Add: Received in advance 1988	270		By Audit Fee for 1987		200
	7,920		By Secretary's Honorarium		1,000
Less: Outstanding 1988	750	7,170	By Printing & Stationery		450
To Entrance Fee		250	By Annual Dinner Expenses		1,500
To Contribution to Annual Dinner		1,000	By Insurance and Bank Charges		150
To Profit on Annual Sports		750	By Sports Equipment purchased		400
			By Balance: Cash in hand		1,600
		10,560			10,560

SPORTS EQUIPMENT

Particulars	Rs	Particulars	Rs
To Balance b/d	2,600	By Depreciation	300
To Cash (Purchases)	400	By Balance c/d	2,700
	3,000		3,000

Delhi Club
BALANCE SHEET
as on 31st December, 1988

Liabilities	Rs	Assets	Rs
Subscription received in advance	270	Cash in Hand	1,600
Salaries Outstanding	450	Subscriptions Outstanding	750

Contd....

Liabilities		Rs	Assets	Rs
Audit Fee Outstanding		250	Sports Equipments	2,700
Bank Loan		2,000	Freehold Grounds	10,000
Capital Fund:				
as on 1.3.1988	11,540			
Add: Surplus	600	12,140		
		15,110		15,110

Working Notes:

Delhi Club
BALANCE SHEET
as on 31st December, 1987

	Rs		Rs
Subscription Received in Advance	450	Cash in Hand	1,390
Salaries Outstanding	400	Subscriptions Outstanding	600
Audit Fee Outstanding	200	Sports Equipments	2,600
Bank Loan	2,000	Freehold Grounds	10,000
Capital Fund	11,540		
	14,590		14,590

Illustration 15.17. Chail Cricket Club gives you the following information:

INCOME & EXPENDITURE ACCOUNT
for the year ended 31.12.89

Expenditure	Rs	Income		Rs
To Remuneration to Coach	18,000	By Donations & Subscriptions		1,02,000
To Salaries & Wages	24,000	By Bar Room:		
To Rent	12,000	Receipts	24,000	
To Repairs	11,000	Expenses	20,000	4,000
To Miscellaneous Expenses	7,000	By Bank Interest		2,000
To Honorarium to Secretary	18,000	By Hire-Club Hall		12,000
To Depreciation on Equipment	5,000			
To Surplus	25,000			
	1,20,000			1,20,000

BALANCE SHEET
as at 31.12.89

1988 Rs	Liabilities	1989 Rs	1988 Rs	Assets	1989 Rs
	Capital Fund as on	.	25,000	Equipment	20,000
48,000	31 December	48,000		Outstanding	
—	Entrance Fees	10,000	6,000	Subscriptions	8,000
—	Surplus	25,000	5,000	Cash in Hand	4,000
48,000		83,000	2,500	Cash at Bank	10,000
4,000	Subscriptions in Advance	3,000	20,000	Fixed Deposit	50,000
	Outstanding Liabilities:				
	Miscellaneous Expenses				
1,500	Expenses	1,000			
2,000	Salary & Wages	3,000			
3,000	Honorarium to Secretary	2,000			
58,500		92,000	58,500		92,000

Prepare the Receipts and Payments Account of the Club for the year ended 31st December, 1989.

Solution:

Chail Cricket Club

RECEIPTS AND PAYMENTS ACCOUNT

for the year ending 31 December, 1989

Receipts	Rs	Payments	Rs
To Balance b/d		By Remuneration to Coach	18,000
Cash in hand	5,000	By Rent	12,000
Cash at Bank	2,500	By Repairs	11,000
To Donations & Subscriptions	99,000	By Misc. Expenses	7,500
To Entrance Fee	10,000	By Salaries & Wages	23,000
To Bar Receipts	24,000	By Honorarium to Secretary	19,000
To Bank Interest	2,000	By Fixed Deposit	30,000
To Hire of Club Hall	12,000	By Bar Expenses	20,000
		By Balance c/d	
		Cash in Hand	4,000
		Cash in Bank	10,000
	1,54,500		1,54,500

Working Notes:

	Rs	Rs
(i) Donations & Subscriptions received:		
As per Income & Expenditure A/c		1,02,000
Add: received for 1990		3,000
received for 1988		6,000
		1,11,000
Less: Outstanding for 1989	8,000	
received in 1988 for 1989	4,000	12,000
		99,000
(ii) Salaries and Wages paid:		
Salaries & Wages as per Income & Expenditure A/c		24,000
Add: Paid for 1988		2,000
		26,000
Less: Outstanding for 1989		3,000
		23,000
(iii) Honorarium paid to Secretary:		
as per Income & Expenditure A/c		18,000
Less: Outstanding for 1989		2,000
		16,000
Add: Paid for 1988		3,000
		19,000
(iv) Misc. Expenses paid:		
As per Income & Expenditure Account		7,000
Less: Outstanding for 1989		1,000
		6,000
Add: Paid for 1988		1,500
		7,500

Preparation of Balance Sheet from Receipts and Payments Account and Income and Expenditure Account:

This requires the following steps:

1. Ascertain the amount of Capital Fund in the beginning of the accounting year by preparing an Opening Balance Sheet.

2. Compare each item of Income and Expenditure Account with each item of Receipts and Payments Account. This will help in ascertaining the amount of outstanding or prepaid expenses or incomes. For example, if the Income and Expenditure Account shows the amount of salary as Rs 10,000 while the Receipts and Payments Account shows payment of only Rs 8,000, it means salary of Rs 2,000 is outstanding.

3. The fixed assets shown in the Opening Balance Sheet should be taken in the Closing Balance Sheet after charging depreciation as per the Income Expenditure Account.

4. Sale or Purchase of any asset should be ascertained from the Receipts and Payments Account.

5. The amount of cash in hand as well as cash at bank, at the end of the accounting year, should be ascertained from the Receipts and Payments Account.

Illustration 15.18. The following particulars relate to the Ajmer Club:

INCOME AND EXPENDITURE ACCOUNT
for the year ended 31.12.1990

Expenditure	Rs	Income	Rs
To Salaries	1,500	By Entrance Fees	10,500
To Printing & Stationery	2,200	By Subscriptions	15,600
To Advertising	1,600	By Rents	4,000
To Audit Fees	500		
To Fire Insurance	1,000		
To Depreciation on Sports Equip.	9,000		
To Excess of Income over Expend.	14,300		
	30,100		30,100

RECEIPTS AND PAYMENTS ACCOUNT
for the year ended 31.12.1990

Reciepts	Rs	Payments	Rs
To Balance b/d	4,200	By Salaries	1,000
To Entrance Fees	10,500	By Printing & Stationery	2,600
To Subscriptions:		By Advertising	1,600
1989	600	By Fire Insurance	1,200
1990	15,000	By Investments	20,000
1991	400	By Balance c/d	7,800
To Rents Received	3,500		
	34,200		34,200

The Assets on 1.1.1990 included Club Grounds and Pavilion Rs 44,000; Sports Equipments Rs 25,000 and Furniture and Fixtures Rs 4,000. Subscriptions in arrears on that date were Rs 800.

Prepare the Balance Sheet as at 31.12.1990.

Solution:

BALANCE SHEET
as on 31st December, 1990

Liabilities	Rs	Assets	Rs
Subscriptions received in advance	400	Club Ground and Pavilion	44,000
Salaries Outstanding	500	Sports Equipments	16,000
Audit Fees Outstanding	500	Furniture & Fixtures	4,000

Contd....

Liabilities		Rs	Assets	Rs
Capital Fund	78,000		Subscription Outstanding	800
Add: Excess of Income			Cash in Hand	7,800
over Expenditure	14,300	92,300	Rent Receivable	
			Outstanding	500
			Fire Insurance Prepaid	200
			Printing & Stationery	
			Prepaid	400
			Investments	20,000
		93,700		93,700

Working Note:

BALANCE SHEET
as on 31.12.1989

Liabilities	Rs	Assets	Rs
Capital Fund (balancing figure)	78,000	Club Grounds and Pavilion	44,000
		Sports Equipments	25,000
		Furniture & Fixtures	4,000
		Subscriptions Outstanding	800
		Cash in Hand	4,200
	78,000		78,000

Note. Rs 400 for Printing and Stationary is assumed to have been paid in advance. Rs 200 in respect of Insurance is assumed for the next year.

Preparation of Correct Accounts from Wrong Accounts given

Illustration 15.19. The account set out below has been submitted to you for audit. If you do not approve of it, criticise and amend it. Also prepare the Balance Sheet of the Club.

Able Checkers Society

INCOME AND EXPENDITURE ACCOUNT
31st Dec., 1991

Expenditure		Rs	Income	Rs
To Entrance Fees (21 @ 10)		210	By Salaries & Wages	675
To Fees for Life Membership			By Secretary's Salary	350
(5 @ Rs 52)		260	By Rent, Rates etc.	1,265
To Annual Subscriptions	1,565		By Printing & Postage	37
Annual Subscriptions			By Repairs to Premises	124
paid in advance	65	1,630	By Interest on Bank Loan	57
To Interest on G.P. Notes		70	By Balance carried down	960
To Sundry Receipts		60		
To Bal. from last year		1,238		
		3,468		3,468

Treasurer's Note. The subscriptions in arrears amount to Rs 120. Sundry Tradesmen's bills Rs 42 were outstanding on 31st December, but have since been paid. The Secretary's salary although sanctioned by resolution of the Committee, has not yet been paid. The 3 1/2% G.P. Notes of the face value of Rs 2,000 were purchased at Rs 90. The lease of the club premises cost Rs 2,124. The balance of the Bank Loan now outstanding is Rs 1,000 secured by mortgage on the leasehold premises.

Solution:

Able Checkers Society

INCOME AND EXPENDITURE ACCOUNT
for the year ending 31st December, 1991

Expenditure	Rs	Income	Rs
To Salaries & Wages	675	By Entrance Fees	210
To Secretary's Salary: Outstanding	350	By Annual Subscription 1,630	
To Rent Rates etc.	1,265	Less: Received in Adv. 65	1,565
To Printing & Postage	37	By Interest on G.P. Notes	70
To Repairs to Premises	124	By Sundry Receipts	60
To Interest to Bank Loan	57	By Excess of Expenditure over	
To Sundry Expenses: Outstanding	42	Income	645
	2,550		2,550

Able Checkers Society

BALANCE SHEET
as on 31.12.91

Liabilities	Rs		Assets	Rs
Subscriptions recd. in advance		65	Cash in hand	1,190
Outstanding Secretary's salary		350	G.P. Notes	1,800
Outstanding Sundry Expenses		42	Outstanding Subscriptions	120
Bank Loan		1,000	Leasehold Club Premises	2,124
Fee for Life Membership		260		
Capital Fund	4,162			
Less: Excess of				
Expenditure over				
Income	645	3,517		
		5,234		5,234

Working Notes:

RECEIPTS & PAYMENTS ACCOUNT

Receipts	Rs	Payments	Rs
To Balance b/d	1,238	By Salaries & Wages	675
To Entrance Fees	210	By Rent, Rates etc.	1,265
To Fees for Life Membership	260	By Printing & Postage	37
To Subscriptions Received		By Repairs to Premises	124
(1,565–120+65)	1,510	By Interest on Bank Loan	57
To Sundry Receipts	60	By Balance c/d	1,190
	3,348		3,348

BALANCE SHEET
as on 1st January, 1991

Liabilities	Rs	Assets	Rs
Bank Loan	1,000	Cash in hand	1,238
Capital Fund	4,162	G.P. Notes	1,800
		Leasehold Club Premises	2,124
	5,162		5,162

ACCOUNTING FOR EDUCATIONAL INSTITUTIONS

Educational Institutions like schools, colleges, institutes also prepare their final accounts on the pattern explained in the previous pages. In other words they also prepare Receipts and Payments Account and Income and Expenditure Account and the Balance Sheet. However, certain special features relating to an educational institutions are explained in the following pages:

1. *Organisational pattern*: Most of the educational institutions in India are functioning as Societies registered under Indian Societies Act, 1860. However, some of the States have enacted Public Trust Acts requiring the societies to also get themselves registered under such Acts.

The societies function as autonomous bodies. The office bearers consist of President, Secretary, Treasurer and Executive Committee Members. In case of societies/trusts running a number of schools or colleges, etc., there is a governing body for each school or college. The head of the school or the college, the Headmaster or the Principal as the case may be, is also a member of the Governing Body.

The University Acts of different universities have made formation of Governing Body for each college as a statutory requirement. The Principal of the college is ex-officio Secretary of the Governing Body.

2. *Sources of Finance*: The following are the main sources of finance of an educational institution:

    (i) *Grants from Government*. This is a major source of finance for most of the educational institutions. Grants are generally of four kinds (a) maintenance grant, (b) equipment grant, (c) building grant and (d) other grants.

Maintenance grant is of a recurring nature while equipment grant and building grant are of non-recurring nature. Other grants include grants which may be sanctioned by the Government under special circumstances from time to time.

It may be noted that only grants of a recurring nature are to be taken to Income & Expenditure Account. Specific grants, are to be utilised only for the specific purposes for which they have been given. Any unutilised amount of such grant will have to be returned back to the Government.

    (ii) *Donations from Public*. Donations may be of recurring or non-recurring nature. They may be in the form of cash or kind. Donations in kind *e.g.* land, building, shares, securities, utensils, furnitures and fixtures are of a non-recurring nature. It may be noted that only donations of recurring nature are to be taken to the Income and Expenditure Account. Others are to be taken to the Balance Sheet.

    (iii) *Capitation Fee*. This fee is collected in a lumpsum from the students seeking admission in a school or a college. This amount is quite heavy and is meant for development of educational institution or incurring some capital expenditure. The amount of capitation fee should therefore be taken to the Balance Sheet either as a separate item or added to the capital fund of the institution. Charging of such fee has come under severe criticism these days.

    (iv) *Admission Fee*. Such fees are also collected from the students seeking admission in an educational institution. The amount is not very heavy and not meant for specific purpose. Such fees are therefore taken as income and credited to Income and Expenditure Account.

(v) *Laboratory & Library Deposits*. Laboratory deposits are collected from science students while library deposits are collected from all students of the college for using library facilities. They are of the nature of security deposits to be refunded to the students on their leaving the college or the University, as the case may be. Such deposits should therefore be taken to the Balance Sheet on the liabilities side.

Illustration 15.20. Cosmopolitan School is having three Sections: Primary, Matriculation and Professional. The Receipts and Payments for the year ending 31.12.1986 are as below:

Particulars	Primary Amount Rs	Matriculation Amount Rs	Professional Amount Rs
(1) Balance with Bankers on 1.1.86	2,525	5,230	255
(2) Grants received from Government	10,000	20,000	15,000
(3) Fees Collected	45,239	52,540	50,258
(4) Fines & Special Fees Collected	2,250	3,155	2,100
(5) Sale of Handicraft Articles			1,215
(6) Staff Salaries	35,288	50,257	40,520
(7) Printing & Stationery	1,529	2,550	1,720
(8) Prizes and Scholarships to Students	1,560	5,250	3,780
(9) Repairs to Furniture	738	529	359
(10) Travelling & Conveyance	1,252	3,525	2,522
(11) Miscellaneous Expenses	5,239	2,325	2,525
(12) Balance with Bankers on 31.12.86	14,408	16,489	17,402

Prepare the Income & Expenditure Statement for each Section in a columnar form for the year ending 31.12.1986 after taking into account the following:

(1) Fees collected include the following sums due for the year ended 31.12.85

	Rs
Primary	4,139
Matriculation	5,240
Professional	4,228

(2) Fees Receivable on 31.12.86 are as below:

	Rs
Primary	5,230
Matriculation	6,260
Professional	4,250

(3) The fee collection of Rs 6,250 relating to the Matriculation Section has been included in the Primary Section.

(4) Provide for the following:

	Primary Rs	Matriculation Rs	Professional Rs
Salaries	2,400	4,200	5,400
Depreciation	520	1,400	1,270
Misc. Expenses	480	650	540

(5) The Salaries payable on 31.12.1985:

Primary	1,888
Matriculation	2,227
Professional	2,400

Contd. on page 1.387

Solution:

Cosmopolitan School
INCOME AND EXPENDITURE STATEMENT
for the year ending 31.12.1986

Expenditure	Primary Rs	Matriculation Rs	Professional Rs	Income	Primary Rs	Matriculation Rs	Professional Rs
To Salaries	35,800	52,230	43,520	By Fees Collections	40,800	59,810	50,280
To Printing & Stationery	1,529	2,550	1,720	By Grants received	10,000	20,000	15,000
To Prizes & Scholarships	1,560	5,250	3,780	By Fines & Special Fees	2,250	3,155	2,100
To Repairs to Furniture	738	529	359	Sale of Handicrafts	—	—	1,215
To Travelling & Conveyance	1,252	3,525	2,522				
To Miscellaneous Expenses	5,719	2,975	3,065				
To Depreciation	520	1,400	1,270				
To Excess of Income over Expenditure	5,212	14,506	12,359				
	52,330	82,965	68,595		52,330	82,965	68,595

Working Notes:

Particulars	Primary Rs	Matriculation Rs	Professional Rs
(i) **Fee Collections:**			
Receipts	45,239	52,540	50,258
Add: Outstanding on 31.12.86	5,230	6,260	4,250
	50,469	58,800	54,508
Less: Outstanding on 1.1.1986	4,139	5,240	4,228
	46,330	53,560	50,280
Matriculation Fees wrongly shown in Primary Section	(−)6,250	(+)6,250	—
	40,080	59,810	50,280
(ii) Salaries Expenses: Paid	35,288	50,257	40,520
Add: Outstanding on 31.12.1986	2,400	4,200	5,400
	37,688	54,457	45,920
Less: Outstanding on 31.12.1985	1,888	2,227	2,400
	35,800	52,230	43,520
(iii) Miscellaneous Expenses:			
Expenses paid	5,239	2,325	2,525
Unpaid	480	650	540
	5,719	2,975	3,065

ACCOUNTING FOR PROFESSIONALS

Professionals like Chartered Accountants, Doctors, Tax Consultants, etc. generally prefer to prepare their final accounts as explained in the preceding pages. In other words they also prepare a Receipts and Payments Account and Income and Expenditure Account and a Balance Sheet. The preparation of final accounts in their case is therefore also done in the usual manner as explained in the preceding pages. Of course items like donations, legacies, subscriptions, life membership fee, etc. do not appear as incomes. Rather they may appear as expenses in their books.

The following two special features of accounting records kept by professionals:

1. **Clients Disbursements Account:** Professionals have to make payments to different authorities on behalf of their clients. These disbursements may be dealt in their books in any of the following manner:

(a) The amount paid on behalf of the client may be charged to the clients account by means of following journal entry:

Client's Account   Dr.
    To Bank/Cash

(b) A separate account termed as Clients Disbursement Account may be opened in the books. On making payment on behalf of a client, the following journal entry may be made:

Clients' Disbursement Account   Dr.
    To Bank/Cash

On raising a Bill against the client, the following entry may be passed:

Client's Account   Dr.
    To Clients' Disbursement Account

The balance in the Clients' Disbursement Account represents amount spent; but not charged to the customer. This would be shown as an asset in the Balance Sheet.

It may be noted that the Client's Account has to be debited in the normal course with the fee due by the client. The following journal entry is passed:

Client's Account   Dr.
     To Fee Receivable Account

On receipt of fee the Client's Account would be credited by means of the following journal entry:

Bank/Cash Account   Dr.
     To Client's Account

The debit balance in the client's account represents the outstanding fee from the client which will be shown as an asset in the Balance Sheet. In case the client's account shows a credit balance, it may represent the fee received in advance from the client which will appear as a liability in the Balance Sheet.

In the Clients' Ledger a separate account for each client is kept. It has separate columns for fees, disbursements and the total.

2. Receipts and Expenditure Account: Some professionals prepare Receipts & Expenditure Account in place of Income and Expenditure Account to determine the income earned by them during a particular period. While preparing the Receipts and Expenditure Account these persons follow cash system for recording income; but mercantile system for recording their expenditure. This means that they do take into account outstanding expenses but not such incomes which have not been received. This is because of the reason that they generally do not file a suit for the recovery of their dues.

In order to prepare a Receipts and Expenditure Account, the following steps should be taken:

(*i*) The Income and Expenditure Account should be prepared in the usual way after taking into account all fees and charges in respect of which bills have been submitted and also any work-in-progress. This is necessary to ascertain the true income for the year.

(*ii*) A full provision should be made in respect of fees and charges that are outstanding as well as for the value of work-in-progress for which credit may have been taken. Thus, the effect of giving credit for the fees outstanding or value of work-in-progress is nullified.

The account so prepared is termed as Receipts & Expenditure Account. In the Balance Sheet the amount of fees outstanding and the value of work-in-progress are shown as the full value but the amount of provisions created against them are deducted therefrom.

Illustration 15.20. Dr. Gupta commenced practice on 1st January, 1990. He gives the following Receipts & Payments Account for 1990:

RECEIPTS & PAYMENTS ACCOUNT

Receipts	Rs	Payments	Rs
To Capital Introduced	5,000	By Furniture	2,000
To Visits	16,000	By Equipment	2,500
To Receipts from Dispensing	10,000	By Purchase of Drugs	3,000
To Miscellaneous Receipts	100	By Salary of Assistant	2,000
		By Rent	1,500
		By Conveyance	1,000
		By Stationery	100
		By Lighting	150
		By Journals	250
		By Drawings	12,000
		By Balance c/d	6,600
	31,100		31,100

Amounts still receivable on account of visits and dispensing are Rs 1,000 and Rs 600 respectively. Salary of Assistant still payable is Rs 200. 40% of conveyance is for domestic purpose. Stock of drugs still on hand is Rs 300; amount still payable for their purchase is Rs 200. Furniture & Equipment are both subject to depreciation at 10%.

Prepare the Receipts and Expenditure Account of Dr. Gupta for 1990 and his balance sheet at its end.

Solution:

Dr. Gupta
RECEIPTS & EXPENDITURE ACCOUNT
for the year ending 31st December, 1990

Receipts	Rs	Rs	Expenditure	Rs	Rs
To Conveyance	1,000		By Visits	16,000	
Less: Drawings	400	600	*Add*: Outstanding	1,000	17,000
To Salary of Assistant	2,000		By Dispensings	10,000	
Add: Outstanding	200	2,200	*Add*: Outstandings	600	10,600
To Rent		1,500	By Miscellaneous Receipts		100
To Stationery		100	By Stock of Drugs		800
To Lighting		150			
To Journals		250			
To Drugs	3,000				
Add: Outstanding	200	3,200			
To Depreciation on:					
Furniture	200				
Equipment	250	450			
To Provision for					
Outstandings					
(1,000 + 600)		1,600			
To Excess of Income over					
Expenditure		18,450			
		28,500			28,500

Dr. Gupta
BALANCE SHEET
as on 31st December, 1990

Liabilities	Rs	Rs	Assets		Rs
Salary Outstanding		200	Furniture	2,000	
Drugs Outstanding		200	*Less*: Depreciation	200	1,800
Capital:	5,000		Equipment	2,500	
Add: Excess of Income			*Less*: Depreciation	250	2,250
over Expenditure	18,450		Outstandings	1,600	
	23,450		*Less*: Provision	1,600	
Less: Drawings	12,400	11,050	Cash in Hand		6,600
			Stock of Drugs		800
		11,450			11,450

Illustration 15.21. From the following details prepare the Income and Expenditure Account and Balance Sheet of *A, B* & Co., Chartered Accountants for the year ending 31st December, 1991.

BALANCE SHEET
as on 31st December, 1991

Liabilities		Rs	Assets		Rs
Capital Accounts			Motor Car		10,000
A	13,000		Office Equipments		1,500
B	9,000	22,000	Furniture		4,000
Outstanding Expenses		250	Outstanding audit fees		
Provisions against Outstanding Fee		4,500	A's Clients	2,000	
Advance Audit Fee recd:			B's Clients	2,500	4,500
A's Clients		500	Cash at Bank		6,250
Clients' Account		1,000	Cash in Hand		750
			Library Books		1,250
		28,250			28,250

The following summary has been prepared from the Firm's Cash Book for the year ended 31st December, 1992:

Receipts		Rs	Payments		Rs
Opening Balance			Establishment Charges		12,000
Cash in hand	750		Motor Car Expenses		5,000
Cash at Bank	6,250	7,000	Printing & Stationery		350
Audit Fees			Postage & Telegram		150
A's Clients	45,000		Subscription for Journals		300
B's Clients	25,000	70,000	Library Books		750
Fees for other services			Office Equipments		3,750
A's Clients	20,000		Travelling & Conveyance		1,250
B's Clients	10,000	30,000	Membership Fee		200
Miscellaneous Income		250	Drawings–A	25,000	
			Drawings–B	20,000	45,000
			Disbursement on Clients' A/c		750
			Closing Balance		
			Cash in hand	1,250	
			Cash at Bank	36,500	37,750
		1,07,250			1,07,250

Additional Information:

1. Provide depreciation at the following rates:

Motor Cars	20% per annum
Office Equipment	15% per annum
Library books	10% per annum
Furniture	10% per annum

2. Outstanding audit fees as on 31st December, 1992.

A's Clients	Rs 3,000
B's Clients	Rs 1,000

3. Establishment Charges are outstanding to the extent of Rs 500 as on 31st December, 1992.

4. The partnership agreement provides that 40% of the audit fee and 20% of fees for other services should be transferred to Income and Expenditure Account. The balance has to be directly credited to the capital accounts of the partners. The profits are to be shared by the partners in the ratio of 2:1.

5. You are required to prepare an Income and Expenditure Account for the year ending 31st December, 1992 and the Balance Sheet as on the date.

Solution:

Basic calculations for preparing Income and Expenditure Account:

1. **Income from Audit Fees:** The Balance Sheet for the year ending 31st December, 1991 shows outstanding audit fees of Rs 4,500 on the assets side while equivalent provision for outstanding audit fees on the liability side. It can, therefore, be inferred that it is the practice of the firm not to take credit for the outstanding audit fees. Hence, the income from audit fees for the purpose of Income and Expenditure Account has been computed on receipts basis as shown below.

Particulars	A Rs	B Rs
Fees collected	45,000	25,000
Add: Outstanding audit fees at the end of the year	3,000	1,000
Received in advance last year	500	—
	48,500	26,000
Less: Provision required for outstanding audit fees	3,000	1,000
Fees received for the year	45,500	25,000
Transferred to:		
Income & Expenditure Account (40%)	18,200	10,000
Capital Accounts (60%)	27,300	15,000
	45,500	25,000

It may be noted that no adjustment is necessary for the outstanding audit fees in the begining of the accounting year since it is completely offset by an equivalent provision.

2. **Fees for other services:** These fees have been distributed as follows:

Particulars	A Rs	B Rs
Total Collections	20,000	10,000
Transferred to:		
Income & Expenditure Account (20%)	4,000	2,000
Capital Accounts (80%)	16,000	8,000
	20,000	10,000

The Income and Expenditure Account can now be prepared as follows:

AB & Co., Chartered Accountants

INCOME AND EXPENDITURE ACCOUNT
for the year ended 31st December, 1992

Particulars	Amount Rs	Particulars	Amount Rs
To Establishment charges	12,250	By Audit Fee	28,200
To Motor Car Expenses	5,000	By Fee for Other Services	6,000
To Printing & Stationery	350	By Miscellaneous Receipts	250
To Postage & Telegrams	150		
To Subscriptions for Journals	300		
To Travelling & Conveyance	1,250		
To Membership Fees	200		
To Depreciation			
Motor Car	2,000		

Contd....

Particulars		Amount Rs	Particulars	Amount Rs
Office Equipment*	788			
Library Books*	200			
Furniture*	400	3,388		
To Profit: Excess of Income over Expenditure				
A's capital A/c	7,708			
B's capital A/c	3,854	11,562		
		34,450		34,450

*Including additions

Note: The Income and Expenditure Account given above is in reality a Receipts and Expenditure Account since it has considered all expenditure whether paid or outstanding and all incomes which have been received. Outstanding incomes have not been considered while preparing the above account.

Basic calculations for preparing the Balance Sheet.

The preparation of Balance Sheet requires the computation of the balances in the Partners' Capital Accounts. This has been done as follows:

CAPITAL ACCOUNTS OF PARTNERS

Particuxlars	A Rs	B Rs	Particulars	A Rs	B Rs
To Drawings	25,000	20,000	By Balance b/d	13,000	9,000
To Balance c/d	39,008	15,845	By Audit Fees	27,300	15,000
			By Other Services	16,000	8,000
			By Share of Profit	7,708	3,854
	64,008	35,854		64,008	35,854

AB & Co.

BALANCE SHEET
as on 31st December, 1992

Liabilities		Rs	Assets		Rs
Outstanding Expenses		500	Cash in Hand		1,250
Clients Account:			Cash at Bank		36,500
Opening Balance	1,000		Outstanding Audit Fees		
Less: Disbursement			A's Clients	3,000	
made on their behalf	750	250	B's Clients	1,000	4,000
Provision against			Library Books:		
Outstanding:			Opening Balance	1,250	
Audit Fees		4,000	Add: Purchases	750	
Capital Accounts				2,000	
A	39,000		Less: Depreciation	200	1,800
B	15,854	54,862	Office Equipment:		
			Opening Balance	1,500	
			Add: Purchases	3,750	
				5,250	
			Less: Depreciation	788	4,462
			Furniture	4,000	
			Less: Depreciation	400	3,600

Contd....

Liabilities	Rs	Assets		Rs
		Motor Car	10,000	
		Less: Depreciation	2,000	8,000
	59,612			59,612

KEY TERMS

☐ **Donations:** These are amounts given by members or by outsiders for the general functioning of a non-profit organisation or for a particular purpose, not in anticipation of any return; but simply as a token of appreciation of the organisation's services to the society.

☐ **Entrance Fees:** This is synonymous with admission fees. It is the amount which a club or association may require its members to pay at the time of seeking admission.

☐ **Legacies:** They are similar in nature to donations except that they are given to a non-profit organisation as per a Will on the death of the contributor(s).

☐ **Income and Expenditure Account:** A final statement often prepared by non-profit making institutions, to present their revenues and expenses for an accounting period and show the excess of revenues over expenses (or *vice-versa*) for that period.

☐ **Receipts & Expenditure Account:** An account often prepared by professionals presenting their revenues on cash basis and expenses on mercantile basis for an accounting period to show the excess of receipts over expenditure (or *vice-versa*) for that period.

☐ **Receipts and Payments Account:** A summary of cash transactions, often prepared by a non-profit making organisation, presenting receipts and payments for an accounting period and showing the excess of receipts over payments or (*vice-versa*) for that period.

☐ **Subscriptions:** They are amounts received/receivable from the members of a non-profit making organisation for being entitled to the service rendered by it. It is a major source of income of the organisation.

TEST QUESTIONS

Objective type | TEST YOUR UNDERSTANDING |

1. State whether each of the following statements is True or False.
   - (*i*) Receipts and Payments Account is a nominal account.
   - (*ii*) Income and Expenditure Account is a real account.
   - (*iii*) Receipts and Payments Account starts with an opening balance.
   - (*iv*) Income and Expenditure Account records all incomes and expenses received or paid during the year in cash.

(v) The Income and Expenditure Account does not make difference between capital and revenue receipts or payments.

(vi) A heavy cash balance in the Receipts and Payments Account at the end of the accounting period does not necessarily mean that the institution has made a heavy income.

[**Ans.** (i) False, (ii) False, (iii) True, (iv) False, (v) False, (vi) True].

2. Choose the most appropriate answer.

(i) Donations received for a special purpose will be taken to
 (a) Income and Expenditure Account.
 (b) Assets side of the Balance Sheet.
 (c) Liabilities side of the Balance Sheet.

(ii) Receipts and Payments Account records receipts and payments of
 (a) Capital nature only.
 (b) Revenue nature only.
 (c) Both capital and revenue nature.

(iii) Income and Expenditure Account is
 (a) a real account.
 (b) a nominal account.
 (c) a personal account.

(iv) Legacies are generally
 (a) capitalised and taken to Balance Sheet.
 (b) treated as income.
 (c) treated as expenditure.

(v) In case a Sports Fund is kept, expenses on account of sports events should be
 (a) charged to the Sports Fund.
 (b) charged to the Income and Expenditure Account.
 (c) taken to the Balance Sheet on the Assets side.

[**Ans.** (i) (c), (ii) (c), (iii) (b), (iv) (a), (v) (a)].

Essay type | FOR REVIEW, DISCUSSION AND PRACTICE

1. State the difference between Receipts and Payments Account and Income and Expenditure Account

2. Explain the meaning of the following terms and show how will you deal with them while preparing Final Accounts of a club. Your answer should be supported by proper examples:.

(a) Subscriptions, (b) Entrance Fee, (c) Life Membership Fee, (d) Donations, (e) Receipts for a Sports Fund.

PRACTICAL PROBLEMS

Preliminary:

1. How will you deal the following items while preparing the Income and Expenditure Account and Balance Sheet of a club for the year ended 31st December, 1988.

	Rs
Subscriptions outstanding on 31.12.1987	200
Subscriptions received in 1987:	
For 1988	300
For 1989	100
Total Subscriptions received during the year 1988	5,800
Subscriptions outstanding on 31.12.1988	
For the year 1987	50
For the year 1988	250

Contd....

Subscriptions received in advance during the year 1988:

For 1989	Rs 350
For 1990	150

[**Ans.** Income from subscriptions for 1988 Rs 5,650]

2. Calculate what amount will be posted to Income and Expenditure Account for the year ending 31st December, 1988:

Stock of stationery on 1st January, 1988:	Rs 300
Creditors for stationery on 1st January, 1988:	200
Advances paid for stationery carried forward from 1987:	20
Total amount paid for stationery during the year 1988:	1,080
Stock of stationery on 31st December, 1988:	50
Creditors for stationery on 31st December, 1988:	130
Advance paid for stationery on 31st December, 1988:	30

[**Ans.** Stationery purchased during 1988 Rs 1,000;
Stationery consumend during 1988 Rs 1,250]

Preparation of Income and Expenditure Account

3. Convert the following Receipts and Payments Account of the Delhi Nursing Society for the year ended 30th June, 1988, into an Income and Expenditure Account:

Receipts	Amount Rs	Payments	Amount Rs
Balance at Bank 1.7.1987	2,010	Salaries of Nurses	656
Subscriptions	1,115	Board, Laundry and	
Fees from Non-members	270	Domestic help	380
Municipal Grant	1,000	Rents, Rates and Taxes	200
Donations for Building		Cost of Car	840
Fund	1,560	Expenses of Car	840
Interest	38	Drugs and Incidental Expenses	670
		Balance c/d	1,247
	5,993		5,993

A donation of Rs 100 received for Building Fund was wrongly included in Subscriptions Account. A bill of medicines purchased during the year amounting to Rs 128 was outstanding.

[**Ans.** Excess of Expenditure over Income Rs 551].

4. The following Receipts and Payments Account has been prepared from the Cash Book of the Saraswati Club, Allahabad:

Receipts	Rs	Payments	Rs
Balance on 1.1.88	255	Rent and Rates	1,680
Member Entrance Fees	231	Printing and Advertising	800
Subscriptions of Playing		Postage and Stationery	278
Members		Wages and Umpire's Fees	1,200
1987	63	Players Travelling Expenses	500
1988	600	Repairs to Pavilion	209
Subscriptions of Honorary		Extensions of Pavilion	1,956
Members		Wicket Matting	221
1987	260	Bats, Balls etc.	455
1988	4,725	Balance on 31.12.88	216
1989	120		
Public Matches	1,120		
Interest on Fixed Deposit	141		
	7,515		7,515

An examination of invoices, vehicles and other records disclosed the following information:

Rent at Rs 100 per month has been paid only upto 30th September, 1988 and Rates have been paid in advance to the extent of Rs 120. There is Rs 180 owing for wages and umpires fees and a bill for Rs 55 for bats, balls etc. is still outstanding. Playing members subscriptions are Rs 40 in arrear for the year and the amount still owing by honorary members is Rs 425.

Make out the Income and Expenditure Account for the year ended 31st December, 1988.

[**Ans.** Excess of Income over Expenditure Rs 1,524].

(**Hint.** Wicket matting, bats balls etc., have been charged to the Income and Expenditure Account).

5. Given below is the Receipts and Payments Accounts of a Club for the year ending 31st December, 1986.

RECEIPTS AND PAYMENTS ACCOUNT FOR 1986

Receipts	Rs	Payments	Rs
To Balance	1,025	By Salaries	600
To Subscriptions		By Expenses	75
19.	40	By Drama Expenses	450
198	2,050	By Newspapers	150
198	60	By Municipal Taxes	40
To Donations	540	By Charity	350
To Sale of Drama tickets	950	By Investments	2,000
To Sale of Waste Paper	45	By Electric Charges	145
		By Balance	900
	4,710		4,710

Prepare the Club's Income and Expenditure Account for the year ended 31st December and its Balance Sheet as on that date after taking the following information into account.

(*i*) There are 500 members each paying an annual subscriptions of Rs 5, Rs 50 being in arrears for 1985.

(*ii*) Municipal Taxes amounting Rs 40 per annum have been paid upto 31st March, 1987 and Rs 50 for salaries is outstanding.

(*iii*) Buildings stand in the books at Rs 5,000.

(*iv*) 6% interest has accrued on investments for five months.

(*B. Com. Hons., Delhi 1977, adapted*)

[**Ans.** Excess of Income over Expenditure Rs 2,235 and Total of Balance Sheet Rs 8,420].

The following is the Receipt and Account of Silver Streek Cricket Club for the year ended 31.12.1983. You are required to prepare the Income & Expenditure Account for 1983 and Balance Sheet as at 31.12.1983 of the Club:-

Receipts		Rs.	Payments		Rs.
Opening Balance:	Cash	290	New Building constructed		75,000
	Bank	3,710	Souvenir		2,000
Subscriptions		12,000	Salaries		6,000
Donations		13,000	Postage		500
Activities Collection		6,900	Telephone		500
Sale of Old Newspapers		300	Electricity		600
Souvenir Advertisement		5,800	Maintenance Expenses		12,000
Endowment Income		3,000	Newspapers		500
Sale proceeds of Old Building			Closing Balance:	Cash	300
at book value		60,000		Bank	11,600
Income from Investments @ 10%		4,000			
		1,09,000			1,09,000

Subscriptions:

	Rs
For 1982 (due as at 31.12.82 Rs 1,500) Received.	1,000
For 1984 Advance	1,200
Due for 1983	800

Expenses Outstanding

Salary	1,200
Electricity	100
Telephone	100
Postage	100

Provide Depreciation of Building @ 5%.

[**Ans.** Excess of Income over Expenditure Rs 16,250; Opening Capital Fund
Rs 1,05,500; Total Balance Sheet Rs 1,24,450].

7. The following is the Receipts and Payments Account of Delhi Football Association for the first
year ending 31st December, 1987:-

Dr.   RECEIPTS AND PAYMENTS ACCOUNT   Cr.

Receipts	Amount Rs.	Payments	Amount Rs.
To Donation	50,000	By Pavilion Offices (constructed)	40,000
To Reserve Fund		By Expenses in connection	
(Life membership		with matches	900
and entrance fees recd.)	4,000	By Furniture	2,100
To Receipts from football matches	8,000	By Investments at cost	16,000
To Revenue Receipts:		By Revenue Payments:	
Subscriptions	5,200	Salaries	1,800
Locker Rents	50	Wages	600
Interest on Securities	240	Insurance	350
Sundries	350	Telephone	250
		Electricity	110
		Sundry Expenses	210
		By Balance in Hand	5,520
	67,840		67,840

(i) Subscriptions outstanding for 1987 are Rs 250.

(ii) Salaries unpaid for 1987 are Rs 170.

(iii) Wages unpaid for 1987 are Rs 90.

(iv) Outstanding Bills for Sundry Expenses are Rs 40.

(v) Donations received have to be capitalized.

Prepare from the details given above, an Income and Expenditure Account for the year ended
31.12.1987 arid the Balance Sheet of the Association as on 31st December, 1987.

[**Ans.** Excess of Income over Expenditure Rs 2,470; Total of Balance Sheet
Rs 63,870).

8. The following is a Receipts and Payments Account drawn from the Cash Book of the Bharat
Cricket Club for the year ended December 31st, 1984:

1984	Receipts	Amount Rs	1984	Payments	Amount Rs
Jan. 1	Cash in Hand	1,000	Dec. 31	Remuneration to	
	Balance at Bank as per			Cricket Coach	4,500
	Bank Pass Books:			Groundman's Pay	3,000

Contd....

1984	Receipts	Amount Rs	1984	Payments	Amount Rs
	Savings Account	20,300		Purchase of equipments	
	Current Account	6,000		& Mowing Machines	15,000
Dec. 31	Bank Interest	300		Bar Room Expenses	2,500
	Entrance Fees	2,000		Ground Rent	2,500
	Donations and			Club Night Expenses	4,000
	Subscriptions	26,000		Printing & Stationery	2,800
	Bar Room Receipts	3,000		Repairs to Equipments &	
	Contribution to			Machinery	5,000
	Club Night	1,000		Honorariam to Secretary	
	Sales of Equipment	800		for the year 1983	4,000
	Net Proceeds of			Balance at Bank as per	
	Club Night	7,800		Bank Pass Books	
				Savings Account	20,900
				Current Account	1,500
				Cash on hand	2,500
	Total	68,200		Total	68,200

You are given the following information:

		On January 1st, 1984 Rs	On December 31st, 1984 Rs
(1)	Subscriptions due from members	1,500	1,000
(2)	Sums due for Printing & Stationery	1,000	800
(3)	Unpresented cheques on Current Account, being payments for repairs	3,000	2,500
(4)	Interest on Savings Bank Account not entered in Pass Book	—	200
(5)	Estimated value of Machinery & Equipments	8,000	17,500
(6)	For the year ended December 31st, 1984, the honoraria to the Secretary to be increased by a total of Rs 2,000 and the groundman to receive a bonus of Rs 2,000		

You are required to prepare:

(a) an Income & Expenditure Account for the year ended December 31st, 1984; and

(b) a Balance Sheet as on that date.

[Ans. Excess of Income over Expenditure Rs 3,500; Balance Sheet Total Rs 42,100 and Opening Capital Fund as 28,800].

Preparation of Receipts and Payments Account

9. From the following Income & Expenditure Account of the Calcutta City Club for the year ended 31st March, 1989 and the Balance Sheet as on the date, you are required to prepare Receipts and Payments Account for the year ended 31st March, 1989:-

Expenditure	Amount Rs	Income	Amount Rs
To Salaries	4,200	By Subscriptions	5,500
To Stationery	680	By Surplus on Sports-Meet	2,400
To Rates	1,240	By Dividends	2,700
To Telephone	270		
To Sundry Expenses	1,710		

Contd....

Expenditure	Amount Rs	Income	Amount Rs
To Depreciation on Building	1,000		
To Excess of Income over Expenditure	1,500		
	10,600		10,600

BALANCE SHEET
as on 31st March 1989

Liabilities		Amount Rs	Assets		Amount Rs
Capital Fund	61,440		Building:		
Add: Income	1,500	62,940	1.4.1988	20,000	
Subscriptions in advance		630	Less: Depreciation	1,000	19,000
Telephone Bill-Outstanding		70	Investments: 1.4.1988	40,000	
			Add: Additions		
			during the year	2,500	42,500
			Stock of Stationery		180
			Rates prepaid		300
			Subscriptions outstanding		300
			Cash in hand		1,360
		63,640			63,640

Additional Information:

(a) Subscription of Rs 100 was in arrear on 1.4.88.

(b) On 1.4.88 Stock of Stationery was worth Rs 100.

(c) On 1.4.88 Sundry Expenses outstanding were Rs 190.

(d) On 1.4.88 Rates prepaid were Rs 300.

[Ans. Receipts & Payments Account Opening Balance Rs 1,130].

10. The Income and Expenditure Account of Jollymen's Club for the year 1988 is as follows:

INCOME AND EXPENDITURE ACCOUNT
for the year ended 31st Dec., 1988

Particulars		Amount	Particulars		Amount
To Salaries and Wages		9,500	By Subscriptions		15,000
To Miscellaneous Expenses (including insurance)		1,000	By Entrance Fees received		500
To Audit Fees		500	By Profit on Annual		
To Chief Executive's Honorarium		2,000	Sports Meet Receipts	3,000	
To Printing & Stationery		900	Expenses	1,500	1,500
To Annual Day Celebration Expenses	3,000				
Less: Donations Collected	2,000	1,000			
To Interest on Bank Loan		300			
To Depreciation on Sports Equipment		600			
To Excess of Income over Expenditure		1,200			
		17,000			17,000

Prepare (i) Receipts and Payments Account for the year, 1988, and (ii) Balance Sheet as at the end of 1988, from the following information:

			Rs
(1)	Subscriptions:	Outstanding as on 31.12.87	1,2000
		Received in advance as at 31.12.1987	900
		Received in advance as at 31.12.88	540
		Outstanding as at 31.12.88	1,500
(2)	Salaries:	Outstanding as at 31.12.1987	800
		Outstanding as at 31.12.1988	900

(3) Audit Fees: The fees for 1988 were outstanding on 31.12.88. But during 1988, Audit Fees for 1987 amounting to Rs 400 were paid.

(4) Prepaid Insurance as at 31.12.1988 was Rs 120.

(5) The Club had owned grounds having a book value of Rs 20,000. The Sports Equipment as on 31.12.1987 and as on 31.12.1988 after depreciation, amounted to Rs 5,200 and Rs 5,400 respectively.

(6) In 1987 the Club and raised a Bank Loan of Rs 4,000 which was outstanding throughout 1988.

(7) On 31st December, 1988, cash in hand amounted to Rs 3,200.

[Ans. Opening Cash Balance Rs 14,340; Total of Balance Sheet Rs 30,220; Opening Capital Fund Rs 23,080].

Preparation of Balance Sheet

11. The following particulars related to Fast Sports Club.

INCOME & EXPENDITURE ACCOUNT
for the year ended 31-12-1989

Expenditure	Amount Rs	Income	Amount Rs
To Salaries	6,000	By Admission fees	15,000
To Printing & Stationery	2,500	By Subscriptions	25,000
To Advertising	1,000	By Rent Receivable	4,800
To Insurance Charges	900		
To Electricity Charges	500		
To Dep. on Sports Equipment	12,000		
To Excess of Income over			
Expenditure	21,900		
	44,800		44,800

RECEIPTS & PAYMENTS ACCOUNT
for the year ended 31-12-1989

Receipts		Amount Rs	Payments	Amount Rs
To Balance b/d		5,000	By Salary (incl. Advance)	7,500
To Admission Fees:			By Printing & Stationery	2,500
1988	2,500		By Advertising	1,000
1989	13,500	16,000	By Insurance charges	
			(partly for the next year)	1,200
To Subscriptions: 1988	1,000		By Electricity	500
1989	23,000		By Purchases of Fixed Assets	20,000
1990	2,000	26,000	By Balance	17,900
To Rent		3,600		
		50,600		50,600

On 1st January, 1989 the club had the following assets:

	Rs
Land & Buildings	60,000
Sports Equipment	30,000
Furniture	4,500

Prepare opening and closing Balance Sheets.

(C.A. Entrance, May, 1980)

[Ans. Opening Balance Sheet Total Rs 1,03,000, Closing Balance Sheet Total Rs 1,26,900**]**.

12. The following are the items of Receipts and Payments of the All India Club as summarised from the Books of Accounts maintained by the Secretary:

Receipts	Amount Rs	Payments	Amount Rs
Opening balance: 1.1.85	4,200	Manager's Salary	1,000
Entrance fees (1984)	1,000	Printing & Stationery	2,600
(1985)	10,000	Advertising	1,800
Subscriptions (1984)	600	Fire Insurance	1,200
(1985)	15,000	Investment purchased	20,000
Interest received on Investments	3,000	Closing Balance: 31-12-1985	7,600
Subscriptions (1986)	400		
	34,200		34,200

It was ascertained from enquiry that the following represented a fair picture of the Income & Expenditure of the Club for the year 1985 for audit purposes:

Expenditure		Amount Rs	Income	Amount Rs
Manager's salary		1,500	Entrance Fees	10,500
Printing & Stationery	2,000		Subscriptions	15,600
Add: accrued	400	2,400	Interest on Investments receivable	4,000
Advertising (accrued Nil)		1,600		
Audit Fees		500		
Fire Insurance		1,000		
Depreciation		4,940		
Excess of Income over Expenditure		18,160		
		30,100		30,100

You are required to prepare the Balance Sheets of the Club as on 31.12.1984 and 31.12.1985 so as to give a fair picture of the assets, outstandings and liabilities. It being given that the book values of the fixed assets as on 31.12.84 were, Building Rs 44,000, Cricket Equipment Rs 25,000 and Furniture Rs 4,000. The rates of depreciation are: Buildings 5%, Cricket Equipment 10%, Furniture 6%. You are entitled to make assumptions as may be justified.

[Ans. Opening Capital Fund Rs 78,000, Total of Closing Balance Sheet Rs 97,960**]**.

Wrong Statements

13. The following so-called Balance Sheet is submitted to you by the Secretary of the Alpha Social Club of which you are the President. You ascertained that the money of the club was not kept separate by the Secretary, but presumably mixed up with his own private cash. Draft the

accounts in the form in which you would like to present them before the members of the club who will not be satisfied with merely a cash account.

Alpha Social Club

BALANCE SHEET

for the year ending 31st December, 1990

Receipts	Amount Rs	Expenditure	Amount Rs
Opening balance	75	Rent and Expenses	204
Arrears of subscription	11	Salary of clerk	25
Subscription (current year)	164	Cost of charity show	15
Charity show tickets sold	21	Club day collection cost	10
Club day collections	14	Owing for charity show ticket	5
Refreshment sold	235	Owing for donations for building	7
Receipt from games	17	Refreshment bought	170
Donations for building	19	Stock of refreshment	15
		Subscriptions owing	8
		Cost of Furniture	35
		Closing balance	62
	556		556

[Ans. Cash balance Rs 97; Excess of Income over Expenditure Rs 55; Balance Sheet Total Rs 167; Capital Fund in the beginning Rs 86].

Accounting for Educational Institutions

14. Excellent Library Society showed the following position on 31st December 1985:

BALANCE SHEET

as at 31.12.1985

Liabilities	Amount Rs	Assets	Amount Rs
Capital Fund	79,300	Electrical Fittings	15,000
Expenses Due	700	Furniture	5,000
		Books	40,000
		Investments in Securities	15,000
		Cash at Bank	2,500
		Cash in Hand	2,500
	80,000		80,000

The Receipts Payments and Account for the year ending on 31st December, 1986, is given below:

Receipts		Amount Rs	Payments	Amount Rs
To Balance b/d			By Electric Charges	720
Cash at Bank	2,500		By Postage	500
Cash in Hand	2,500	5,000	By Telephone and Stationery	500
To Entrance Fees		3,000	By Books purchased (on 1.1.86)	6,000
To Membership Subscription		20,000	By Rent Account	8,800
To Sale proceeds of old papers		150	By Outstanding Expenses paid	700
To Hire of Lecture Hall		2,000	By Investment in Securities	4,000
To Interest on Securities		800	By Salaries Account	6,600
			By Balance c/d	
			Cash in Bank	2,000
			Cash in Hand	1,130
		30,950		30,950

You are required to prepare an Income and Expenditure Account for the year ending 31.12.1986 and a Balance Sheet as on that date after making the following adjustments:

1. Membership subscriptions included Rs 1,000 received in advance.
2. Provide for Outstanding Rent Rs 400 and Salaries Rs 300.
3. Books to be depreciated @10% including additions. Electrical Fittings and Furniture are also to be depreciated at the same rate.
4. 75% of the Entrance fees is to be capitalised.
5. Interest on Securities is to be calculated @ 5% p.a. including purchase of investment made on 1.7.86 for Rs 4,000.

(Ans. Excess of Expenditure over Income - Rs 1,670; Total of Balance Sheet Rs 81,580).

15. The Balance Sheet as on 30.6.1986 and the Receipts and Payments Account for the year ended 30.6.1987 of Mathura Literary Society, Mathura are as below:

BALANCE SHEET
as on 30.6.1986

Liabilities		Amount Rs	Assets	Amount Rs
Capital Fund:			Buildings	25,000
As per last Balance			Furniture & Fixtures	2,000
Sheet	58,500		Books	1,150
Add: Excess of			Sports Equipments	2,000
Income over Exp.	3,000	61,500	Fixed Deposit with	
Subscriptions recd. in advance		400	Bank of India Ltd.	30,000
			Interest accrued on Investments	200
			Subscriptions Receivable	1,000
			Cash in Hand	150
			Cash with Bank	400
		61,900		61,900

RECEIPTS AND PAYMENTS ACCOUNT
for the year ended 30.6.1987

Receipts	Amount Rs	Payments	Amount Rs
Opening Balance (1.7.86)		By Salaries	2,560
Cash in Hand	150	By Printing & Stationery	220
Cash with Bank	400	By Taxes & Insurance	180
Subscriptions received	6,080	By Subscriptions to Newspapers	550
Hall rent received	1,750	By Repairs & Renewals	650
Interest received	1,200	By Sports Equipments Purchased	
Sales of Old Newspapers etc.	160	(1.1.87)	1,000
Donations received	3,200	By Fixed Deposit with Central	
		Bank of India Ltd. (1.4.87)	5,000
		By Closing Balance (30.6.87):	
		Cash in Hand	150
		By Balance with Central Bank of	
		India Ltd.	2,630
	12,940		12,940

The following information is supplied to you:

(1) Subscription for the year 1987–88 received during the year Rs 500.

(2) The Society consists of 500, Members. the Annual Subscription payable by each Member being Rs 12.

(3) The rent for the Society's Hall is Rs 250 per day and Hall was let out on hire 8 days in the year.

(4) Interest accrued on Fixed Deposit with the Bank has to be provided @ 6% per annum.

(5) Depreciation on Buildings and other assets @ 10% per annum has to be provided.

(6) Donations have been collected for constructing a Building and, therefore, have to be shown under the Building Fund Account.

Prepare the Income and Expenditure Account for the year ended 30.6.87 and Balance Sheet as on 30.6.1987.

(**Ans.** Excess of Income over Expenditure Rs 2,810; Balance Sheet Total Rs 68,010).

Accounting for Professionals

16. Dr. Kabra commenced practice as a Dentist, investing Rs 50,000 in equipment, on 1st January, 1991. The Receipts and Payments Account for the year was follows:

Receipts	Amount Rs	Payments	Amount Rs
To Fees	1,00,000	By Rent	6,000
To Miscellaneous Receipts	200	By Salaries to Assistants	15,000
To Equipment sold	4,000	By Journals	2,000
		By Library Books	6,000
		By Equipment purchased	8,000
		By Drawings	24,000
		By Balance:	
		At Bank	43,000
		In hand	200
	1,04,200		1,04,200

Rs 3,000 of the fees were still outstanding. Equipment sold and purchased was on 1st October, 1991, the cost of the equipment sold being Rs 6,000. Depreciation on equipment is 20% and on Library Books 5%. Salaries to Assistants still payable is Rs 2,000. Prepare the Receipts and Expenditure Account and the Balance Sheet relating to 1991.

[**Ans.** Surplus Rs 63,700; Balance Sheet Total Rs 91,700].

17. A, B and C are three doctors who are running a Polyclinic, D, E, F and G were then taken in on payment of Rs 10,000 by each of them as Goodwill and also Rs 40,000 to be brought in by each of them as capital. Goodwill is shared by the existing partners equally. Each of the original partners also contributed Rs 40,000 by way of capital. The terms of sharing profits or losses were as follows:

(i) 60% of the visiting fee is to go to the specialist concerned.

(ii) 40% of the chamber fee will be payable to the individual specialist.

(iii) 50% of operation fees and fees for pathological reports, X-ray and ECG will accrue in favour of the doctor concerned.

(iv) Balance of profit or loss is shared equally.

(v) The proportion of fees and charges accruing in favour of individual doctors are to be withdrawn then and there.

(vi) The receipts for the year after the admission of new partners are:

Particulars	Visiting fees Rs	Chamber fees Rs	Fees for reports operation etc Rs
General Practitioner	60,000	80,000	–
Gynaecologist	10,000	70,000	40,000
Cardiologist	–	40,000	30,000
Child Specialist	40,000	60,000	–
Pathologist	–	–	40,000
Radiologist	–	16,000	80,000
Dentist	–	10,000	60,000

(vii) Expenses for the year are as follows:

		Rs
Rent		31,000
Light		5,000
Nurses Salary		12,000
Attendants' Wages		6,000
Telephones		8,200
Printing and Stationery		2,000
Medicines, band aids, injections etc.		4,000
Depreciation:		
Furniture	2,000	
X-Ray Machine	10,000	
ECG Equipments	4,000	
Dentist Chairs	2,000	
Surgical Equipments	2,000	20,000

Prepare the Profit and Loss Account of the Polyclinic, also showing the final distribution of Profit or Loss among the partners. All workings should form part of your answers.

[**Ans.** Net Fees earned (*less* share of specialist and expenses) = Rs 2,46,400;
Share of each specialist in general pool = Rs 35,200;
Net Surplus — Profit & Loss Account = Rs 5,47,800;
Share of Net Profit transferred to General Practitioner = Rs 1,03,200;
Gynaecologist = Rs 89,200;
Cardiologist = Rs 66,200;
Child Specialist = Rs 83,200;
Pathologist = Rs 55,200;
Radiologist = Rs 81,600;
Dentist = Rs 69,200]

Section II

Special Accounting Problems

Chapter 1

CONSIGNMENT ACCOUNTS

LEARNING OBJECTIVES

After studying this chapter you should be able to:

- ☐ Understand the concept of consignment;
- ☐ get familiar with the special items concerning consignment transactions;
- ☐ prepare consignment accounts; and
- ☐ explain the meaning of certain key terms.

MEANING OF CONSIGNMENT

The increasing size of the market is making more and more difficult for the manufacturer or wholeseller to come in direct contact with customers living at far off distances. This has made imperative for him to enter into an agreement with a reliable local trader who can sell goods on his behalf and at his (Principal) risk for an agreed amount of commission. Such a despatch of goods from one person to another person at a different place for the purpose of warehousing and ultimate sale is termed as consignment. Goods so sent are termed as 'Goods sent on Consignment', the sender is called "Consignor" and the receipient 'Consignee.'

For example if *A* of Bombay sends 100 radio sets to *B* of Delhi to sell on his (*A*'s) behalf and at his (*A*'s) risk, the transaction between *A* and *B* is a consignment transaction. *A* is the consignor and *B* is the consignee.

It should be noted that in the above example, *A* continues to be the owner of the goods. *B* is simply an agent of *A*. He has not purchased the goods. He has agreed to sell the goods of *A* to the best of his ability and capacity. He will, therefore, be responsible to *A* for payment only when he has sold away the goods. Of course, he will be reimbursed by *A* for any expenses incurred by him in obtaining and selling the goods besides remuneration for selling the goods as per the agreed terms.

The main features of a consignment transaction can now therefore be put follows:

 (*i*) Consignment of goods is not a sale. It is mere transfer of possession of goods.

 (*ii*) The consignee sells goods at the risk of the consignor. He is not responsible for any loss or destruction of goods.

 (*iii*) The sale proceeds belong to the consignor and the consignee merely gets commission and expenses that he might have incurred.

 (*iv*) The relationship between consignor and consignee is that of a Principal and an Agent.

IMPORTANT TERMS

1. Proforma invoice. It is a statement prepared by the consignor stating quantity, quality and price of goods. It is sent with goods depatched to consignee.

A proforma invoice is different from Invoice.

Invoice implies that a sale has taken place. It is statement describing the goods despatched to the buyer and showing the total amount due by him to the seller. A proforma invoice is simply a statement of information in the form of invoice to apprise the party, who has not bought the goods but shall be having their possession, or dealing with them, of certain essential particulars of the goods. Such an invoice is sent by the intending seller to his agent or the intending buyer before the sale actually takes place. It does not show that the person to whom it is sent is indebted to the sender.

2. Account sales. It is a periodical statement rendered by the Consignee to the Consignor containing details of goods received, sales made, expenses incurred, commission charged, remittances made and balance due by him to the consignor. The following is a specimen of an Account Sales.

Account Sales of 50 radiograms ex S.S. San Pedro received and sold on account of Robbins & Sons, Chicago by:

M/s Chiman Lal Desai & Co. Bombay

Particulars		Rs	Rs
40 radiograms at Rs 1,200 per radiogram		48,000.00	
10 radiograms at Rs 1,100 per radiogram		11,000.00	59,000.00
Less: Charges:			
Dock Dues	700		
Customs Duty	2,000		
Freight	1,300		
Godown Rent	500	4,500.00	
Less: Commission at 5 per cent		2,950.00	7,450.00
			51,550.00
Less: Draft accepted			20,000.00
Balance due, Bank draft enclosed			31,550.00

E. & O.E.   For Messrs Chiman Lal Desai & Co.

                                      (sd) Ashoka Kumar

Bombay, the 15th Jan. 90   Manager

3. Commission. It is the remuneration payable to the consignee for sale made by him. This can be simple, over-riding and del-credere.

Simple commission is calculated as per terms laid down by the consignor. Usually this is a fixed percentage on total sales.

In order to give further incentive, sometimes an extra commission termed as over-riding commission is allowed to consignee, in case the sales exceed a specified amount. It is also calculated on total sales.

Where the consignee agrees to meet any loss which the consignor may suffer by reason of bad debts, one more extra commission known as del-credere commission is given to consignee. This is also normally calculated on total sales.

Illustration 1.1. Gopi Cycles (P) Ltd. Hyderabad, sent 2,000 dynamos costing Rs 50 each for sale on consignment basis to Ramoo of Vijaywada, subject to the following terms:

(*i*) Normal selling price per dynamo Rs 60.

(*ii*) Consignee's commission to be calculated as under:

    (*a*) 5 per cent on normal selling price;

    (*b*) 1 per cent additional commission if selling price is more than normal price; and

    (*c*) ½ per cent del-credere commission on total sales for guaranteeing collection of credit sales.

Ramoo reported sales as follows:

	Rs
Cash Sales:	
500 dynamos at Rs 60 each	30,000
200 dynamos at Rs 75 each	15,000
Credit Sales:	
400 dynamos at Rs 75 each	30,000
400 dynamos at Rs 80 each	32,000
Total	1,07,000

Ascertain the commission due to consignee.

Solution:

STATEMENT OF COMMISSION DUE TO CONSIGNEE

	Rs
Normal (or Simple) Commission:	
$1,500 \times 60 \times 5/100$	4,500
Additional (or Over-riding) Commission:	
$77,000 \times 1/100$	770
Del credere commission:	
$1,07,000 \times ½/100$	535
	5,805

4. Direct expenses. These are expenses which are incurred for placing the goods in a saleable condition. All expenses till the goods reach the godown of the consignee come in this category. These expenses are of a non-recurring nature and increase the value of goods. Examples of such expenses are freight, carriage, insurance, loading and unloading charges etc.

5. Indirect expenses. These are expenses incurred after the goods reach the consignee's godown. They are of a recurring nature and do not increase the value of goods. Examples of such expenses are godown rent, storage charges, advertisement expenses, salaries of salesmen, etc.

The distinction between direct and indirect expenses is of special importance at the time of the valuation of the unsold stock. Direct expenses form a part of the cost and, therefore, a proportion of such expenses is included in the cost of stock, while the indirect expenses do not form part of the cost and, therefore, excluded while valuing the unsold stock. This has been explained in detail later.

6. Advance. The consignor may ask the consignee to deposit some money with him to be kept by him as security in respect of the goods sent by him on consignment. It is usually a certain percentage of the value of goods sent on consignment. For example; if the value of goods sent on consignment is to be Rs 50,000, and the consignee is asked to deposit (say) 10 per cent of the value of the goods to be sent, the amount of advance will be Rs 5,000. This covers to certain extent the risk of the consignor. The amount is adjusted against the amount due from consignee when the accounts are finally settled. However, the consignor may like to keep with himself a certain percentage of value of the goods lying with the consignee. In such a case advance will be adjusted only to the extent of the proportionate goods sold.

Example. Goods of Rs 50,000 are sent on consignment to A who sells away 50 per cent of the goods for Rs 40,000, consignor required that 10 per cent of the value of the goods should be kept as an advance with him. A's expenses and commission amount to Rs 5,000. The amount to be sent by A will be calculated as follows:

	Rs	Rs
Sales value of the goods		40,000
Commission and Expenses	5,000	
Advance deposited 10 per cent of Rs 25,000	2,500	7,500
Amount to be sent by A		32,500

Thus, 10 per cent of the value stock lying with the consignee *i.e.*, Rs 2,500 will still remain as advance with the consignor till these goods are finally sold.

ACCOUNTING RECORDS

A proper record of all transactions relating to a particular consignment is necessary for ascertaining Net Profit or Net Loss on each separate consignment. To attain this objective the consignor usually maintains three accounts:

(1) Consignment Account.

(2) Consignee's Account.

(3) Goods Sent On Consignment Account.

Consignment Account is a Nominal Account. It is in fact a special Trading and Profit & Loss Account and, therefore, its balance shows the Profit or Loss made on a particular consignment.

Consignee's Account is a Personal Account and, therefore, in case the Consignee has not remitted the balance due by him in full, he will be a debtor, whereas it he has remitted more than the balance due by him, he will be a creditor.

Goods sent on Consignment Account is a Real Account. It is closed up by transferring its balance to Purchases Account (sometimes it is also transferred to the credit side of Trading Account).

The above accounts are maintained in respect of each of the consignments. For example, if goods have been sent on Consignment to Bombay, Calcutta and Madras, Consignment Account, Consignee's Account and Goods sent on Consignment Account will be maintained in respect of each of these consignments.

Pricing of Goods Sent on Consignment

Goods can be consigned to the consignee either (*i*) at cost or (*ii*) at invoice price.

At cost. In case of this method the goods are charged to the consignment at cost price to the consignor. The proforma invoice is also prepared at this price. For example if the goods costing Rs 10,000 are purchased by A and 80 per cent of such goods are sent by him on consignment to Bombay, proforma invoice will show the value of goods as Rs 8,000 and the Consignment to Bombay account will also be charged with this price. The consignee may be given the direction regarding the price at which he should sell the goods (*see* Illustration 1.2.).

At invoice price. In case of this method the goods are charged to the consignment at a price higher than cost. The proforma invoice also shows the value of goods at such higher price. The excess of invoice price over the actual cost, represents the profit which the consignor intends to make on the goods consigned. For example, if in the above case the goods are consigned at a profit of 25 per cent on cost (or 20 per cent on invoice price), the consignment account will be charged with Rs 10,000 (*i.e.*, Rs 8,000 + Rs 2,000) for the value of goods sent on consignment. However, in order to find out the profit, at the end of the accounting period, the consignment account will be given credit with the excess price so charged. In this case, the credit to the consignment account will be of Rs 2,000. Thus, in fact, consignment account has been charged only with the cost (*i.e.*, Rs 10,000 – Rs 2,000) of the goods sent on consignment as has been done in the first case. Suitable adjustment for profit element included in the stock with the consignee has also to be made (*see* Illustration 1.4).

The following are the advantages of invoicing goods to consignee at a price higher than the cost:

(*i*) The consignor can keep secret from the consignee the profit that he is making on the goods sold, thus reducing the possibility of bringing more competition in the field.

(*ii*) The consignee can be directed to sell the goods at the invoice price only. Thus, he is prevented from charging different prices from different customers.

(*iii*) Control over stock with the consignee becomes slightly easier. The value of stock with the consignee at any time will be the difference between the value of goods sent on consignment and the sales made by him.

The accounting entries to be recorded in the books of the consignor in both the cases are being explained in the following pages.

Book of Consignor
JOURNAL ENTRIES

	Transaction	Debit	Credit
(1)	When Security is asked	Bank or Cash or B/E.	Consignee's A/c.
(2)	When goods are sent:	Consignment A/c.	Goods sent on
	(*a*) at cost.		Consignment A/c. (with cost price).
	(*b*) at Invoice Price.	(*i*) Consignment A/c.	Goods sent on Consignment A/c. (at invoice price)
	In order to bring down the goods sent on consignment to cost, an adjustment entry will be necessary	(*ii*) Goods sent on Consignment A/c. (with the difference between invoice price and cost price)	Consignement A/c.
(3)	For expenses incurred by the consignor.	Consignment A/c.	Cash A/c.
(4)	When goods are received by the consignee.	No entry	
(5)	When Account Sales is received from the consignee		
	(*a*) for sales made by Consignee	Consignee's A/c.	Consignment A/c.
	(*b*) for expenses incurred by Consignee.	Consignment A/c.	Consignee's A/c.
	(*c*) for commission.	Consignment A/c.	Consignee's A/c.
(6)	If bad debts incur and consignee is a delcredere agent.	No entry	
(7)	When bad debts take place and consignee is not a del-credere agent.	Consignment A/c.	Consignee's A/c. (because he was debited with total sales).

Contd....

	Transaction	Debit	Credit
(8)	For stock in the hands of the consignee	Stock on	Consignment A/c.
	(a) If the goods were sent at cost.	Consignment A/c.	
		(with cost price)	
	(b) If the goods were sent at invoice price.	(i) Stock on	Consignment A/c.
		Consignment A/c.	
		(with invoice price)	
	In order to write off the unrealised profit on stock an adjusting entry will be necessary.	(ii) Consignment A/c.	Stock Reserve A/c.
		(with the difference between invoice price of stock and cost price)	
	The balance of Stock Reserve A/c will be carried to the B/S and will be deducted from the value of stock on consignment.	(with the difference between invoice price of stock and cost price)	
	In the following period, the consignment stock of last period will be transferred to the debit side of the consignment account. The stock reserve on such stock will be transferred to the credit side of that account.		
(9)	For settlement of accounts with the consignee		
	(i) If the consignee owes money he will pay it in cash or send B/E etc.	Bank/Cash or B/E.	Consignee's A/c.
	(ii) If the consignor owes money to the consignee, he will pay him in cash or send B/E.	Consignee's A/c.	Cash or B/E A/c.
	(in case accounts are not settled the balance of Consignee's Account will be carried forward).		
(10)	If the B/E received from the consignee is discounted.	Bank A/c. Discount A/c.	B/E A/c.
(11)	The discount A/c is closed by transferring it to P & L A/c.	P & L A/c.	Discount A/c.
(12)	The consignment account will be closed by transferring the balance (i.e., Profit or Loss) to P & L A/c		
	(a) In case of profit.	Consignment A/c.	P & L A/c.
	(b) In case of a large number of consignment accounts, a separate 'Profit & Loss on Consignment A/c' can be opened. Profit or Loss on each individual Consignment A/c will be transferred to this account and ultimately the balance of this account will be transferred to P & L A/c.	For loss a reverse entry will be passed	
(13)	Goods sent on Consignment A/c will be closed by transferring its balance to Purchases or Trading A/c.	Goods sent on Consignment A/c.	Purchases A/c. or Trading A/c.
(14)	"Consignment Stock A/c" will appear as an asset in the Balance Sheet.		

Illustration 1.2. On 1st April 1989, Aditya Mills Ltd., Delhi, consigns 500 pieces of shirting costing Rs 5,000 to Birla Stores, Bombay. The consignee is entitled to 5% selling commission and 1% del-credere commission.

Following expenses were incurred by the consignor:

	Rs
Carriage	200
Insurance	100
Freight	150

Aditya Mills Ltd. draws a Bill of Exchange for Rs 2,000 on Birla Stores, Bombay, which was duly accepted by them. It is discounted for Rs 1,950.

On 31st May 1989, Birla Stores send the Account Sales which shows that they have sold goods for Rs 7,500 and paid expenses amounting to Rs 150. Stock in Consignee's hands on 31st May, 1989 is valued at Rs 1,500.

Birla Stores enclose a sight draft with the Account Sales, for the net amount due to Aditya Mills Ltd. Give journal entries and ledger accounts in the books of the consignor.

Solution:

JOURNAL

Date	Particulars		Dr. Amount Rs	Cr. Amount Rs
1989 April	Consignment to Bombay A/c	Dr.	5,000.000	
	To Goods Sent on Consignment A/c			5,000.00
	(500 pieces of shirting consigned to Birla Sores, Bombay)			
	Consignment to Bombay A/c	Dr.	450.00	
	To Cash A/c			450.00
	(Expenses incurred: Carriage Rs 200, Insurance Rs 100, and Freight Rs 150)			
	Bills Receivable A/c	Dr.	2,000.00	
	To Birla Stores, Bombay			2,000.00
	(Bill of exchange recd from Birla Stores, Bombay)			
	Bank A/c	Dr.	1,950.00	
	Discount A/c	Dr.	50.00	
	To Bills receivable A/c			2,000.00
	(Bills Receivable discounted for 1,950)			
	Consignment to Bombay A/c	Dr.	150.00	
	To Birla Stores			150.00
	(Expenses incurred by the consignee in connection with consignment) .			
	Consignment to Bombay	Dr.	450.00	
	To Birla Stores, Bombay			450.00
	(Commission due to Birla Stores, Bombay being ordinary @ 5% and del credere @ 1% on Rs 7,500)			
	Birla Stores Ltd.	Dr.	7,500.00	
	To Consignment to Bombay A/c			7,500.00
	(Being sales made)			
	Stock on Consignment A/c	Dr.	1,500.00	
	To Consignment to Bombay A/c			1,500.00
	(Stock with consignee)			

Contd....

Date	Particulars		Dr. Amount Rs	Cr. Amount Rs
Dec.31	Goods Sent on Consignment A/c	Dr.	5,000.00	
	To Trading A/c			5,000.00
	(Being transfer of goods sent on consignment to Trading A/c)			
	Bills Receivable A/c	Dr.	4,900.00	
	To Birla Stores Ltd.			4,900.000
	(B/R received for net balance due)			
	Consignment to Bombay A/c	Dr.	2,950.00	
	To P & L A/c			2,950.00
	(Transfer of the profit on consignment)			
Dec.31	P & L A/c	Dr.		
	To Discount A/c		·50.00	
	(Discount written off)			50.00

Ledger Accounts

CONSIGNMENT TO BOMBAY ACCOUNT

Date	Particulars	Amount Rs	Date	Particulars	Amount Rs
1989					
April	To Goods sent on Consignment	5,000.00	May 31	By Birla Stores, Bombay	7,500.00
				By Stock on Consignment	1,500.00
	To Cash (Expenses)	450.00			
	To Birla Stores, Bombay (Expenses)	150.00			
May 31	To Birla Stores, Bombay (Commission)	450.00			
	To P & L A/c (transfer of Profit)	2,950.00			
		9,000.00			9,000.00

BIRLA STORES, BOMBAY

Date 1989	Particulars	Amount Rs	Date 1989	Particulars	Amount Rs
	To Consignment A/c (Sale proceeds)	7,500.00	April	By Bills Receivable A/c	2,000.00
				By Consignment A/c (Expenses)	150.00
				By Consignment A/c (Commission)	450.00
				By B/R	4,900.00
		7,500.00			7,500.00

GOODS SENT ON CONSIGNMENT ACCOUNT

Date	Particulars	Amount Rs	Date	Particulars	Amount Rs
1989			1989	By Consignment A/c	5,000.00
Dec. 31	To Trading A/c	5,000.00	April		

VALUATION OF UNSOLD STOCK

Where all the goods have not been sold, it becomes necessary to value the unsold goods. Such goods are similar to closing stock in case of a Trading Account. This stock should be valued at a price which will include:

(i) proportionate cost price and

(ii) proportionate direct expenses, i.e., proportionate expenses incurred both by the consignor and the consignee till the goods reach the godown of the consignee.

It should be noted that direct expenses will include all expenses incurred by the consignor while only such expenses of the consignee which are incurred by him till goods reach his godown. Examples of such expenses are: carriage charges, freight, octroi, import duty etc., paid by the consignee. Expenses like godown rent, selling expenses, insurance of the godown etc. paid by the consignee, should be excluded.

Moreover, the fundamental principle of accounting regarding valuation of stock should also be taken into consideration i.e., stock should be valued at cost or market price whichever is less. Cost price stands for cost + proportionate direct expenses.

Tutorial Note. In case in an examination question, the details regarding expenses incurred by the consignee have not been given (e.g. the question states "expenses incurred by the consignee are Rs 2,000" or "the consignee paid Rs 2,000 as cartage, godown rent, insurance etc."), the student are advised to consider only proportionate expenses incurred by the Consignor, while valuing the unsold stock).

Illustration 1.3. G. Mehta consigns 100 radiograms to H. Singh. Each radiogram costs Rs 800. G. Mehta pays the following expenses:

	Rs
Freight	1,000
Insurance	400
Carriage	500
H. Singh pays the following expenses:	
Customs duty	2,000
Dock dues	500
Godown rent	500
Salary to salesman	500
Goods reach the godown of the consignee.	

At the end of the year 25 radiograms required with H. Singh. The market value of each radiograms is Rs 850. You are required to calculate value of stock lying with H. Singh.

Solution:

STATEMENTS SHOWING VALUE OF STOCK

Particulars	Rs	Rs
Cost of 25 radiograms @ Rs 800 per radiogram		20,000.00
¼ of Direct Expense (i.e., 25/100)		
Freight	250.00	
Insurance	100.00	
Carriage	125.00	
Customs Duty	500.00	
Dock dues	125.00	1,100.00
		21,100.00

Market value of stock is Rs $25 \times 850 =$ Rs 21,250.

Cost being less and therefore

25 radiograms should be valued at Rs 21,100.00.

LOSS OF STOCK

In the course of consignment transactions some loss of stock may occur. It may be in the course of transit before or after taking delivery of the goods by the consignee or it may occur at the godown of the consignee. Such loss of stock may be normal or abnormal. Normal Loss is due to inherent characteristics of goods, e.g., loss due to evaporation, sublimation, drying up of goods etc. If loss occurs on account of reasons which are only accidental or which rarely happen the loss is termed as Abnormal. The examples of such losses are—theft of goods or destruction of goods by fire.

Normal loss. It is not shown in the consignment account. This is included in the value of goods sold and closing stock by inflating the rate per unit. The value of closing stock will, therefore, be that proportion of total value of goods sent which number of units in hand bear to total number of units as diminished by loss (i.e., the units actually received by the consignee). *In short cost of goods sent becomes cost of goods received.*

This can be put in the form of the following formula:

$$\text{Value of Closing Stock} = \frac{\text{Total value of goods sent} \times \text{Units of Closing Stock}}{\text{Units actually received by the consignee}}$$

Illustration 1.4. A consigned 2,000 tonnes of coal @ Rs 50 per tonne to B of Delhi. He paid Rs 20,000 as freight. Due to normal wastage only 1,950 tonnes were received by B. He also paid Rs 5,000 as unloading and cartage charges. The goods unsold amount to 650 tonnes. You are required to calculate the value of closing stock.

Solution:

	Rs
Cost price of 2,000 tonnes of coal @ Rs 50 per tonne	1,00,000.00
Freight paid by the consignor	20,000.00
Unloading and cartage charges paid by Consignee	5,000.00
Cost of 1,950 tonnes	1,25,000.00

Cost of 650 tonnes $\dfrac{650}{1,950} \times 1,25,000 =$ Rs 41,667

Abnormal loss. This loss should be debited to Abnormal Loss Account and credited to Consignment Account. Abnormal Loss Account may be closed by transferring to P & L Account.

The credit to the consignment account with the value of Abnormal Loss is given because it will make possible for the management to judge properly the profitability or otherwise of the consignment.

The valuation of stock destroyed on account of abnormal reasons will be done on the same basis as valuation of Stock on Consignment i.e., proportionate cost price plus proportionate direct expenses incurred up to the date of loss.

While valuing abnormal loss, care should be taken of the stage where abnormal loss took place since only such expenses have to be included in the valuation of such abnormal loss which have been incurred upto that stage. This will be clear with the help of the following illustration.

Illustration 1.5. A consigned to B 100 cases of tea costing Rs 100 per case. He paid Rs 1,000 as freight and cartage. B could take deliver of only 90 cases since 10 cases were lost in transit. He paid Rs 2,000 as unloading and carriage charges. At the end of the year he reported that he has sold away 80 cases at Rs 150 per case. You are required to calculate. (i) the value of abnormal loss and (ii) the value of closing stock.

Solution:

(i)
VALUE OF ABNORMAL LOSS

	Rs
Cost of 100 case @ Rs 100 per case	10,000
Direct Expenses incurred by the Consignor	1,000
Total Cost of 100 cases	11,000

$$\text{Value of Abnormal Loss} = \frac{\text{Total cost} \times \text{Units of Abnormal Loss}}{\text{Total Units to be received by the Consignee}}$$

$$= \frac{\text{Rs } 11,000}{100} \times 10 = \text{Rs } 1,100$$

(ii)
VALUE OF CLOSING STOCK

	Rs
Total Cost of 100 cases calculated as above: Rs 11,000	
Cost of 10 cases (i.e., units of closing stock)	1,100
Add: Proportionate Expenses incurred by the Consignee	
$\dfrac{\text{Rs } 2,000 \times 10}{90}$	222
	1,322

Illustration 1.6. Calculate the (i) value of abnormal loss and (ii) value of stock on the basis of the data give in Illustration 1.5, given above, if the abnormal loss of 10 cases happens at the godown of the consignee in place of in transit from A to B.

Solution:

(i)
VALUE OF ABNORMAL LOSS

	Rs
Cost of 100 cases @ Rs 100 per case	10,000
Expenses incurred by the Consignor	1,000
Direct Expenses incurred by the Consignee	2,000
Total Cost of 100 cases	13,000

$$\text{Value of Abnormal Loss} = \frac{\text{Total Cost} \times \text{Units of Abnormal Loss}}{\text{Total Units to be received by the Consignee}}$$

$$= \frac{\text{Rs } 13,000 \times 10}{100} = \text{Rs } 1,300$$

(ii)
VALUE OF CLOSING STOCK

	Rs
Total Cost of 100 cases calculated as above	13,000
Value of Closing Stock (10 units): $\dfrac{\text{Rs } 13,000 \times 10}{100} = \text{Rs } 1,300$	

Abnormal loss and insurance. An insurance policy may be obtained in respect of the goods sent or received on consignment by the consignor or the consignee. Such a policy is obtained only in respect of abnormal loss which may be caused to the goods. The following accounting entries will be passed in the books of the consignor in such a case:

(i) On payment of insurance premium

Consignment A/c   Dr.
    To Bank (or Consignee, if he has paid the premium)
    (with the premium paid)

(ii) On happening of Abnormal Loss.

Abnormal Loss A/c   Dr.
    To Consignment A/c
    (with the value of abnormal loss)

(iii) On admission of claim by Insurance Company

Insurance Company A/c   Dr.
    To Abnormal Loss A/c
    (with the amount of claim admitted)

(iv) On receipt of claim from Insurance Company

Bank A/c   Dr.
    To Insurance Company
    (with the amount received)

(v) The balance, if any, in the Abnormal Loss Account represents Profit or Loss which will be transferred to Profit and Loss Account.

If Profit:
Abnormal Loss Account   Dr.
    To Profit & Loss Account

If Loss:
Profit & Loss Account   Dr.
    To Abnormal Loss Account.

Illustration 1.7. A & Co. of Calcutta sent on consignment account goods to B & Co. of Bombay at an invoice price of Rs 29,675 and paid for freight Rs 762, cartage Rs 232 and insurance Rs 700. Half the goods were sold by agents for Rs 17,500, subject to the agent's commission of Rs 875, storage expenses of Rs 200 and other selling expenses of Rs 350. One-fourth of the consignment was lost by fire and a claim of Rs 5,000 was recovered. Draw up the necessary accounts in the books of A & Co. and ascertain the profit or loss made on consignment. The consignor received a two months bill of exchange from the agents in satisfaction of the dues.

Solution:

CONSIGNMENT OF BOMBAY ACCOUNT

Particulars		Rs	Particulars	Rs
To Goods sent on Consignment		29,675.00	By B & Co. Ltd. (sale proceeds)	17,500.00
To Cash:			By Abnormal Loss A/c	7,843.00
Freight	762		By Consignment Stock A/c	7,843.00
Cartage	232			
Insurance	700	1,694.00		

Contd....

Particulars		Rs	Particulars	Rs
To B & Co:				
Commission	875			
Storage Exp.	200			
Other Selling Exp.	350	1,425.00		
To Net Profit (transferred to				
P. & L. A/c)		392.00		
		33,186.00		33,186.00

B & CO., BOMBAY

Particulars	Rs	Particulars	Rs
To Consignment to Bombay		By Consignment to Bombay	
(sale proceeds)	17,500.00	(expenses and commission)	1,425.00
		By Bills Receivable A/c	16,075.00
	17,500.00		17,500.00

ABNORMAL LOSS ACCOUNT

Particulars	Rs	Particulars	Rs
To Consignment A/c	7,843.00	By Bank	
		(received from Insurance Co.)	5,000.00
		By P. and L. A/c	2,843.00
	7,843.00		7,843.00

Working Notes:

Calculation of Abnormal Loss:

	Rs
¼ of Invoice Price of goods	7,419 (approx.)
Add: ¼ of Freight, Cartage and Insurance	424 (approx.)
Total Abnormal loss	7,843
Less: Recovered from Insurance Co.	5,000
Net Abnormal Loss	2,843

The value of closing stock has also been calculated on the same basis.

Illustration 1.8. P of Ranchi consigned goods of the invoice price of Rs 2,00,000 which is 25% above cost, to D of Delhi, on the following conditions:

(i) Consignee to get a commission of 5% on all sales.

(ii) Any goods taken by the consignee himself or lost through consignee's negligence shall be valued at cost plus 12 ½% and no commission would be allowed on them.

The expenses incurred by consignor were Carriage and Freight Rs 6,720 and Insurance Rs 3,440.

The consignor received Rs 50,000 as advance against the consignment.

Account Sale together with a draft for the balance due was received by the consignor showing the following position:

Goods of the invoice price of Rs 1,60,000 were sold for Rs 2,48,000. Goods of the invoice prices of Rs 10,000 and Rs 5,000 were taken by D and lost through his negligence, respectively. Amounts of Rs 1,720 on advertisement and Rs 1,080 on selling expenses were incurred by D.

Prepare Consignment Account and Consignee's Account in the books of the Consignor.

Solution:

CONSIGNMENT TO DELHI ACCOUNT

Particulars	Rs	Particulars	Rs
To Goods Sent on Consignment	2,00,000	By D (Sales)	2,48,000
To Bank (Carriage & Freight)	6,720	By D (*See Working Note 1*)	13,500
To Bank (Insurance)	3,440	By Goods Sent on Consignment	40,000
To D (Expenses)	2,800	By Consignment Stock	26,270
To D (Commission)	12,400		
To Consignment Stock Reserve	5,000		
To Profit and Loss A/c	97,410		
	3,27,770		3,27,770

D's (CONSIGNEE'S ACCOUNT)

Particulars	Rs	Particulars	Rs
To Consignment A/c	2,48,000	By Bank	50,000
To Consignment A/c	13,500	By Consignment A/c (Expenses)	2,800
		By Consignment A/c (Commission)	12,400
		By Balance c/d	1,96,300
	2,61,500		2,61,500

Working Notes:

1. *Amount to be charged to D*

	Rs
1. Goods lost (invoice value)	10,000
Goods taken by consignee (invoice value)	5,000
	15,000
Less: Profit margin (⅕)	3,000
Cost of the goods	12,000
Add: 12 ½% extra	1,500
	13,500

2. *Valuation of Consignment Stock*

	Rs	Rs
Stock at Invoice Price		25,000
Add: Proportionate Expenses:		
Freight	6,720	
Insurance	3,440	
Total Expenses	10,160	
Stock left is only ⅛ of total goods sent hence expenses to be added are:		1,270
		26,270

Illustration 1.9. Sri Mehta of Bombay consigns 1,000 cases goods costing Rs 100 each to Shri Sundaram of Madras.

Sri Mehta pays the following expenses in connection with the consignment.

	Rs
Carriage	1,000
Freight	3,000
Loadings Charges	1,000

Sri Sundaram sells 700 cases at Rs 140 per case and incurs the following expenses.

	Rs
Clearing Charges	850
Warehousing and Storage	1,700
Packing and Selling Expenses	600

It is found that 50 cases have been lost in transit and 100 cases are still in transit.

Sri Sundaram is entitled to a Commission of 10 per cent on gross sales. Draw up the Consignment Account and Sundaram's Account in the books of Sri Mehta.

Solution:

Sri Mehta

CONSIGNMENT TO MADRAS ACCOUNT

Particulars	Rs	Particulars	Rs
To Goods sent on Consignment	1,00,000	By Sundaram (sales)	98,000
To Bank (Expenses)	5,000	By Abnormal Loss	
To Sundaram (Expenses)	3,150	(Loss in transit)	
To Sundaram (Commission)	9,800	50 cases @ Rs 105 each	5,250
To Profit on consignment transfd.		By Consignment Stock A/c	
to Profit & Loss A/c	11,700	in hand	
		150 @ Rs 106 each 15,900	
		in transit	
		100 @ Rs 105 each 10,500	26,400
	1,29,650		1,29,650

SUNDARAM'S ACCOUNT

Particulars	Rs	Particulars	Rs
To Consignment to Madras A/c	98,000	By Consignment A/c (Expenses)	3,150
		By Consignment A/c	
		(Commission)	9,800
		By Balance c/d	85,050
	98,000		98,000

Working Notes:

(i) Consignor's expenses on 1,000 cases are Rs 5,000. It comes to Rs 5 per case. The cost of cases lost will therefore be computed at Rs 105 (i.e., Rs 100 + Rs 5) per case.

(ii) Sundaram has incurred Rs 850 on clearing 850 cases i.e., Re 1 per case. The Consignment Stock in hand has therefore been valued at Rs 106 (i.e., Rs 105 + Re 1) each.

Illustration 1.10. On 1st September, 1986 goods of the value of Rs 2,64,000 were consigned by Shri Shyamlal of Bangalore to his agent Shri Mahesh of Cochin at proforma invoice price of 20% profit on cost price. Shri Shyamlal paid insurance and other forwarding charges on consignment amounting to Rs 10,000. Shri Mahesh was allowed Rs 2,000 being establishment cost. He was entitled to 5% commission on gross sales and an additional 3% Delcredere Commission on credit sales only. Shri Mahesh made an expense of Rs 2,040 as landing charges.

Three fourth of the goods were sold at 33 1/3% profit on cost, half of which were credit sales. One half of the balance of goods were destroyed by fire and a claim lodged for

Rs 28,000 was settled at a discount of 10%. The balance of goods were is stock. Show the Consignment Account and the Stock Loss on Consignment Account as on 31.12.1986 in the books of Shri Shyamlal. *(C.A. Entrance, Nov., 1987)*

Solution:

Books of Shri Shyamlal
CONSIGNMENT TO COCHIN ACCOUNT

Date	Particulars	Amount Rs	Date	Particulars	Amount Rs
1986			1986		
Sep. 1	To Goods sent on Consignment	3,16,800	Dec. 31	By Sh. Mahesh: Cash Sales 1,32,000 Credit Sales 1,32,000	2,64,000
	To Bank (insurance and forwarding charges)	10,000		By Stock lost on Consignment A/c (WN 1)	34,505
Dec. 31	To Sh. Mahesh: Establishment 2,000 Landing Charges 2,040 Comm. @ 5% 13,200 Delcredere Commission @ 3% 3,960	21,200		By Stock on Consignment (WN 2) By Goods sent on Consignment (loading)	41,105 52,800
	To Stock Reserve Account	6,600			
	To Net Profit transferred to Profit & Loss A/c	37,810			
		3,92,410			3,92,410

STOCK LOST ON CONSIGNMENT ACCOUNT

Particulars	Rs	Particulars	Rs
To Consignment A/c	34,505	By Insurance Claim (28,000–2,800) By Profit & Loss A/c	25,200 9,305
	34,505		34,505

Working Notes:
1. STOCK LOST ON CONSIGNMENT

	Rs
Invoice Price of stock lost on consignment (3,16,800 × ⅛)	39,600
Add: Proportionate Charges (12,040 × ⅛)	1,505
	41,105
Less: Loading (39,600 × 20/120)	6,600
	34,505

2. CLOSING STOCK ON CONSIGNMENT

	Rs
Invoice Price of unsold stock (⅛)	39,600
Add: Proportionate Expenses	1,505
	41,105

3.   CASH SALES AND CREDIT SALES

	Rs
Cost Price of 3/4th of the goods *i.e..*, Rs 2,64,000 × ¾	1,98,000
Sold at a profit of 33 ⅓% on cost (1,98,000 × 400/300)	2,64,000

Out of total sales of Rs 2,64,000 half is cash sales = Rs 1,32,000.

The balance of Rs 1,32,000 is therefore credit sales.

Illustration 1.11. Goods are invoiced by Shri Amar, consignor, to his agent Shri Ashok at selling price. The agent reports sales made and collection of book-debts by him by monthly advice. He received 5% commission on cash collected plus an allowance of expenses at the rate of Rs 400 per month.

During the half year ended 30.9.1989 goods were invoiced to the agent at a value of Rs 80,600. Such goods cost Shri Amar Rs 59,000 plus freight and packing charges thereon Rs 3,740. During the same period, sales were made by the agent amounting to Rs 68,400. Debts collected were Rs 57,600 and discounts were allowed amounting to Rs 400. The agent remitted to Shri Amar Rs 56,000.

Some of the goods consigned to Shri Ashok were damaged in transit and a claim on the insurance company was settled for Rs 1,240.

On 30.9.1989, the stock in the hands of the agent and unsold represented a cost to Shri Amar Rs 8,200.

Prepare the Consignment Account and the account of Shri Ashok in the books of Shri Amar, for the half-year ended 30.9.1989.   (*C.A. Entrance, Nov., 1990*)

Solution:

Books of Shri Amar
CONSIGNMENT TO SHRI ASHOK ACCOUNT

Particulars	Rs	Particulars	Rs
To Goods sent on		By Ashok (Sales)	68,400
Consignment	59,000	By Loss in transit (*WN* 1)	776
To Cash (Freight and		By Stock with consignee:	
Packing Charges)	3,740	Cost (*WN* 2)	8,720
To Ashok (Discount)	400		
To Ashok (Allowance for			
expenses for ½ year)	200		
To Ashok (Commission)	2,880		
To Profit transferred to			
Trading Account	11,676		
	77,896		77,896

ACCOUNT OF SH. ASHOK

Particulars	Rs	Particulars	Rs
To Consignment A/c	68,400	By Consignment A/c:	
		Discount	400
		Allowances	200
		Commission	2,880
		By Bank	56,000
		By Balance c/d	8,920
	68,400		68,400

Working Notes:

		Rs
1.	Loss in transit:	
	Cost of goods sent	59,000
	Less: Cost of goods sold (68,400 × 59,000)/80,600	50,070
	Expected stock with consignee	8,930
	Less: Actual stock with consignee	8,200
	Cost of goods damaged	730
	Add: Proportionate Expenses (3,740 × 730)/59,000	46
	Total Cost of goods lost in transit	776

The claim for stock damaged has been admitted at Rs 1,240. However, consignment account will be credited only with Rs 776. The profit made should be transferred to Profit & Loss Account.

		Rs
2.	Stock with Consignee:	
	Cost of Stock	8,200
	Add: Proportionate Expenses (8,200 × 3,740)/59,000	520
	Stock at cost with consignee	8,720

Illustration 1.12. 2,000 Shirts were consigned by Bhagwan & Company of Delhi to Shreyans of Tokyo at a cost of Rs 150 each. Bhagwan & Company paid freight Rs 20,000 and insurance Rs 3,000.

During the transit 200 shirts were totally damaged by fire. Shreyans took delivery of the remaining shirts and paid Rs 28,800 as customs duty.

Shreyans has sent a bank draft to Bhagwan & Company for Rs 1,00,000 as advance payment. 1,600 Shirts were sold by him at Rs 200 each. Expenses incurred by Shreyans on godown rent and advertisement, etc. amounted to Rs 4,000. He is entitled to a commission of 5 per cent.

One to the customers to whom the goods were sold on credit could not pay the cost of 10 Shirts.

Prepare the Consignment Account and the account of Mr. Shreyans in the books of Bhagwan & Company. Shreyans settled his account immediately. Nothing was recovered from the insurers for the damaged goods.

(C.A. Entrance, Nov., 1991)

Solution:

In the Books of Bhagwan & Co.

CONSIGNMENT TO TOKYO ACCOUNT

Particulars	Rs	Rs	Particulars	Rs	Rs
To Goods sent on			By Shreyans (Sales)		
Consignment A/c		3,00,000	(1,600 × Rs 200)		3,20,000
To Bank A/c:			By Stock on Consignment		
Freight	20,000		A/c *(Working Note 2)*		35,500
Insurance	3,000	23,000	By Abnormal Loss		
To Shreyans:			*(Working Note 1)*		32,300
Customs Duty		28,800			

Contd....

Particulars	Rs	Rs	Particulars	Rs	Rs
To Shreyans:					
Expenses	4,000				
Commission	16,000				
(5% on Rs 3,20,000)					
Bad debts					
((10 × Rs 200)	2,000	22,000			
To Profit & Loss A/c		14,000			
		3,87,800			3,87,800

SHREYANS ACCOUNT

Particulars	Rs	Particlulars	Rs
To Consignment A/c (Sales)		By Consignment A/c:	
(1,600 × Rs 200)	3,20,000	Customs Duty	28,800
		By Consignment A/c:	
		Expenses	4,000
		Commission	16,000
		Bad Debts	2,000
		By Bank	1,00,000
		By Bank	1,69,200
	3,20,000		3,20,000

Working Notes:

		Rs
(1)	**Amount of Abnormal Loss**	
	200 shirts at Rs 150 each	30,000
	Add: Freight & Insurance	
	$\left[\dfrac{200}{2,000} \times Rs\ 23,000\right]$	2,300
		32,300
(2)	**Value of Closing Stock**	Rs
	200 Shirts at Rs 150 each	30,000
	Add: Freight & Insurance	
	(23,000 × 20/2000)	2,300
	Customs Duty	
	(28,800 × 200/1,800)	3,200
		35,500

Illustration 1.13. A Co. Ltd., manufactures and deals in edible oil, consigned to their Bangalore agent, 1,000 crates of oil (each crate containing 12 one-kilo sachets) in March, 1991. The consignment was sent at 20% over the cost price of Rs 30 per kilo. A bill was drawn on the agent for 80% of the value of the consignment which was met on presentation. Expenses incurred by the company by way of freight and insurance came to Rs 12,000,

The agent received the consignment by lorry and sold in March, 1991, 900 crates at a profit margin of 25% on his cost (excluding consignor's expenses). He found that 500 sachets had got damaged in transit—the manufacturer accepted this as a normal loss—and these were sold to consumers at Rs 20 per sachet. The insurance company settled the loss claim for Rs 2,500.

Agent incurred expenses of Rs 5,000 on his own account (unconnected with the liability under the agreement) and Rs 3,000 on consignor's account. He is entitled to a commission of 5% on sales effected. By 15th April, 1991, the agent remitted the balance due by him to the company.

Draw the accounts in the books of A Co. Ltd., to record the above transactions.

(C.A. Inter, Nov., 1991)

Solution:

A Company Limited

CONSIGNMENT TO BANGALORE ACCOUNT

Date	Particulars	Amount Rs	Date	Particulars	Amount Rs
1991			1991		
March 1	To Goods sent on Consignment A/c	4,32,000	Mar. 31	By Bangalore Agent A/c (Sales)	
	To Bank (Expenses)	12,000		(900 × 12 × 45)	4,86,000
Mar. 31	To Stock Reserve (loading on closing stock of sachets @ Rs 6 on 700 sachets)	4,200	Mar. 31	By Loss in Transit A/c (500 Sachets @ Rs 37)	18,500
			Mar. 31	By Goods sent on Consignment A/c:	
Mar. 31	To Bangalore Agent A/c:			(Loading on transfer)	72,000
	Expenses 3,000		Mar. 31	By Balance c/d:	
	Commission			Closing stock of 700	
	@ 5% on (4,86,000			sachets @ Rs 37	25,900
	+ 10,000) 24,800	27,800			
Mar. 31	To Balance being profit transfd. to P & L A/c	1,26,400			
		6,02,400			6,02,400

LOSS IN TRANSIT ACCOUNT

Date	Particulars	Amount Rs	Date	Particulars	Amount Rs
Mar. 31	To Consignment to Bangalore A/c	18,500	Mar. 31	By Bangalore Agent A/c (500 × 20)	10,000
			Mar. 31	By Bank (Insurance Claim)	2,500
			Mar. 31	By Profit & Loss A/c (Transfer)	6,000
		18,500			18,500

GOODS ON CONSIGNMENT ACCOUNT

Date	Particulars	Amount Rs	Date	Particulars	Amount Rs
Mar. 31	To Consignment to Bangalore A/c	72,000	March 1	By Consignment to Bangalore A/c	4,32,000
	To Trading A/c (Transfer)	3,60,000			
		4,32,000			4,32,000

BANGALORE AGENT ACCOUNT

Date	Particulars	Amount Rs	Date	Particulars	Amount Rs
Mar. 31	To Consignment to Bangalore A/c	4,86,000	Mar. 3	By Bank-remittance	3,45,600
Mar. 31	To Loss in Transit A/c	10,000	Mar. 31	By Consignment to Bangalore A/c: Exp. & Commission	27,800
			April 15	By Bank (remittance)	1,22,600
		4,96,000			4,96,000

Working Notes:

		Rs
(1)	Goods sent on Consignment:	
	1,000 crates × 12 one–kilo sachets × Rs 30	3,60,000
	Add: Loading-20% on cost	72,000
	Invoice Price	4,32,000

		Rs
(2)	Consignment Sale Price:	
	Invoice Price per Kg.	36
	Add: Profit @ 25%	9
		45

Books of Consignee

The consignee does not purchase the goods. He obtains delivery of goods only for the purpose of selling them on behalf of and at the risk of the consignor for an agreed commission. Thus, only such entries will be made which directly affect him.

Entries to be made in the books of the Consignee

(1) When he gives security

    Consignor's A/c   Dr.
        To Bank or B/P
    (With the amount of security given).

(2) When goods are received by him, no entry will be passed except a record of this fact will be made in his Stock Register.

(3) When he incurs expenses for goods received on consignment

    Consignor's A/c   Dr.
        To Bank or Creditor's A/c
    (With the amount of expenses incurred).

(4) For Sales made

    Bank or Debtors A/c   Dr.
        To Consignor's A/c
    (With the amount of sales).

(5) For Commission earned by him

    (i) Consignor's A/c   Dr.
         To Commission A/c
      (With the amount of commission)

    (ii) In case 'del credere commission' is payable to him this will be credited to a special account i.e., del credere commission account. Any bad debts incurred will be debited to this account. The balance will be transferred to Consignee's P. & L. A/c.

(6) For stock in hand with the consignee

No entry will be passed.

Note. It will not make any difference for the consignee whether the goods are sent to him at cost price or at invoice price (*i.e.*, a price higher than cost price).

Illustration 1.14. On the basis of data given in Illustration 1.7, pass the Journal entries and prepare the necessary accounts in the books of the Consignee.

Solution:

JOURNAL

Particulars		Rs	Rs
A & Co., Calcutta	Dr.	550	
To Bank A/c			550
(Expenses incurred in connection with receipt of Consignment from A & Co.)			
Bank A/c	Dr.	17,500	
To A & Co.			17,500
(A & Co, credited for sales proceeds)			
A & Co., Calcutta	Dr.	875	
To Commission A/c			875
(For commission earned.)			
A & Co., Calcutta	Dr.	16,075	
To Bills Payable A/c			16,075
(Bills payable accepted in settlement of account)			
Bills Payable A/c	Dr.	16,075	
To Bank A/c			16,075
(Payment made on maturity)			

Dr.   A & CO., CALCUTTA   Cr.

Particulars	Rs	Particulars	Rs
To Bank (expenses)	550	By Bank	17,500
To Commission	875		
To Bills Payable A/c	16,075		
	17,500		17,500

BILLS PAYABLE ACCOUNT

Particulars	Rs	Particulars	Rs
To Bank	16,075	By A & Co, Calcutta	16,075

COMMISSION ACCOUNT

Particulars	Rs	Particulars	Rs
To P. & L. A/c	875.00	By A & Co., Calcutta	875.00

BANK ACCOUNT

Particulars	Rs	Particulars	Rs
To A. & Co., Calcutta	17,500	By A. & Co., Calcutta A/c	550
		By Bills Payable	16,075
		By Balance c/d	875
	17,500		17,500

KEY TERMS

☐ **Account Sale:** A periodical statement rendered by the consignor to the consignee containing details of the goods sold by the consignee together with balance finally due by him to the consignor.

☐ **Consignment:** A despatch of goods from one person to another person at a different place for the purpose of sale on behalf and at the risk of the sender.

☐ **Consignor:** The person sending goods on consignment.

☐ **Consignee:** The recipient of the goods sent on consignment.

☐ **Delcredere Commission:** Commission allowed to consignee for his agreeing to meet any loss which the consignor may suffer on account of bad debts.

☐ **Overriding Commission:** Commission allowed to the consignee in case the sales exceed a specific amount.

☐ **Proforma Invoice:** A statement of information in the form of invoice prepared by the consignor to apprise the consignee about certain essential particulars of the goods.

TEST QUESTIONS

Objective type | TEST YOUR UNDERSTANDING

1. State whether each of the following statements is 'True' or 'False'.
   (a) Despatch of goods on consignment amounts to sale of goods by the consignor.
   (b) A consignee is paid over-riding commission for bearing the risk of bad debts on account of credit sales made by him.
   (c) Sales Account and Account Sales are synonymous terms.
   (d) The consignee passes no entry in his books for unsold stock of the consignor, lying with him.
   (e) Discount on bills discounted is debited to Profit and Loss Account and not to the Consignment account on account of it being treated as a financial expense.
   (f) Abnormal loss of stock arises on account of natural and inherent characteristics of goods.

   {Ans. (a) False; (b) False; (c) False; (d) True; (e) True; (f) False].

2. Choose the most appropriate answer:
   (i) Consignment account is of the nature of a:
      (a) Real Account,
      (b) Nominal Account,
      (c) Personal Account.
   (ii) Goods sent on Consignment Account is a:
      (a) Real Account,
      (b) Personal Account,
      (c) Nominal Account.
   (iii) Del credere commission is allowed to the consignee to bear:
      (a) Normal Loss,
      (b) Abnormal Loss,

      (c) Loss on account of bad debts.

   (iv) The Abnormal Loss on Consignment is credited to:
- (a) Profit & Loss Account.
- (b) Consignee's Account.
- (c) Consignment Account.

   (v) Over-riding commission is calculated on:
- (a) Total Sales.
- (b) Credit Sales.
- (c) Cash Sales.

   (vi) On sales being made by the consignee of the goods received by him on consignment, the amount is credited by him to:
- (a) Sales Account.
- (b) Consignee's Account.
- (c) Purchases Account.

[**Ans.** (i) (b); (ii) (a); (iii) (c); (iv) (c); (v) (a); (vi) (b)].

Essay type | FOR REVIEW, DISCUSSION AND PRACTICE

1. Define Consignment? Distinguish it from a sale.
2. What is an "account sales"? How does it differ from an invoice?
3. How will you treat the bad debts when:
   - (a) Consignee gets *del credere* commission.
   - (b) Consignee does not get *del credere* commission.
4. Write two lines about each of the following:
   - (a) Pro-forma invoice.
   - (b) Abnormal loss.
   - (c) Valuation of consignment stock.

PRACTICAL PROBLEMS

1. Motiram of Bombay sent 4,000 transistors each costing Rs 150 to Reddi of Hyderabad for sale on consignment:

   The important terms of the arrangement were:
   - (a) The minimum selling price per piece was to be Rs 200.
   - (b) Commission payable to Reddi was to be on the following basis:
     - (i) For the Sales in first month: 5% on minimum price; additional 2% on price in excess of minimum price.
     - (ii) For sales in subsequent months: The above rates are subject to a deduction of ½% on both for each subsequent month.
   - (c) Reddi to remit the proceeds at the completion of each month.

   On arrival of the consignment Reddi paid Rs 1,000 as freight and clearing charges which were to be reimbursed by the consignor. He reported sales as follows and sent his remittances for each month on the due dates.

Month	Quantity	Price (Rs)
June	1,500	200
June	200	230
July	1,200	250
July	50	225
July	50	220
August	500	220
August	500	200

Prepare a statement showing the amount Reddi would have sent at the end of each month.

(C.A. Entrance, Nov., 1977)

[**Ans.** Commission; June Rs 17,420; July Rs 15,435; August Rs 8,500, Amount to be remitted; June Rs 3,27,580; July Rs 3,06,815; August Rs 2,01,500].

2. Hari sold goods on behalf of Kailash Agencies on consignment basis. On April 1, 1985, he had with him a stock of Rs 20,000 on consignment.

Hari had instructions to sell the goods at cost plus 25% and was entitled to a commission of 4% on sales. He was also entitled to 1% del credere commission on total sales for guaranteeing collection of all sale proceeds.

During the half-year ended September 30, 1985, cash sales were Rs 1,20,000, credit sales were Rs 1,05,000. Hari's expenses relating to the consignment were, Rs 3,000, being salaries and insurance. Bad debts were Rs 3,000, Goods sent on Consignment were Rs 2,00,000. Prepare Consignment account in the books of Kailash Agencies showing the profit or loss for the half-year.

[**Ans.** Closing Stock Rs 40,000; Profit Rs 30,750].

3. A of Ahmedabad consigned goods to B of Bombay for sale at *pro forma* invoice price or over. B is entitled to a commission on sale at 5 per cent on *pro forma* invoice price and 25 per cent of any surplus price realised.

Goods consigned by A to B during the year ended 31st March, 1988, cost A Rs 20,900 and invoiced at Rs 28,400. A paid Rs 1,045 as freight and received Rs 15,000 as advance from B. 80 per cent of the goods were sold by B for Rs 26,000. B remitted the balance of proceeds after deducting his commission.

Prepare necessary ledger accounts in the books of A.

[**Ans.** Profit Rs 6,488; Amount received from consignee after adjusting full advance Rs 9,044]

[**Hint.** Commission has been calculated as follows:

(i) Commission of 5% on invoice price = 5% on 80% of

Rs 28,400, *i.e.*, $\frac{5}{100} \times$ Rs 22,720 = Rs 1,136

(ii) Commission of 25% on surplus = 25% of (Rs 26,000 – Rs 22,720) = Rs 820
Total Commission is therefore = 1,136 + 820 = Rs 1,956].

4. Ram & Co. of Delhi sent on consignment to their agent in Calcutta goods invoiced at Rs 45,000, this being selling price of the consignment obtained by adding 30% to the cost price to cover expenses, profit and selling commission.

At the end of six months the agent remitted the sum of Rs 12,000 made as under:

	Rs	Rs
Proceeds of goods sold		13,000
Less: 5% Commission	650	
Expenses	350	1,000
Net proceeds		12,000

The agent reported that the goods of the invoice value of Rs 600 have been damaged in transit, and he sent a list of stock still held amounting to Rs 31,400.

Give the Journal entries necessary to record these details in the books of consignor.

[**Ans.** Profit Rs 2,000; Loading in invoice price of goods sent Rs 10,384.62; Consignment Stock Reserve A/c Rs 7,246.15; Abnormal Loss Rs 461.54].

5. From the following particulars, prepare the necessary ledger accounts in the books of the consignors and those of the consignees.

(i) The firm of Dilwali Traders of Delhi consigned to Premier & Co. of Rangoon 50 cases of piece goods valued at Rs 350 each.

(*ii*) The consignors paid freight and insurance thereon Rs 1,800.

(*iii*) They received as an advance from Premier & Co. Rs 8,000.

(*iv*) Received an Account Sales from Premier & Co. giving particulars as under:

Gross proceeds Rs 28,000, expenses of ware housing, carriage, dock dues, etc. incurred by them amounted to Rs 900, and their commission amounted to Rs 1,000.

(*v*) Received a bank demand draft of the balance due by them on the consignment.

[**Ans.** Profit Rs 6,800, Amount of bank draft Rs 18,100].

6. Chhotamul Ltd. of Calcutta shipped in November, 1988 to their agents Badamul Ltd. of Rangoon, 140 cases of goods, costing to Chhotamul Ltd. Rs 1,29,000. Badamul Ltd. were to sell the goods an account of their consignors and were to receive a commission of 5% on the gross proceeds with a further 2% as *del credere* commission.

Chhotamul Ltd. incurred the following charges in connection with the consignment:

Carriage Rs 280, Loading charges Rs 210, Insurance and freight Rs 3,290, Cables and expenses Rs 40.

Badamul Ltd. sold 120 cases for an average of Rs 1,500 per case incurring bad debts of Rs 4,310 and paid the following expenses.

Landing charges of 470, Warehouse and insurance Rs 1,800, Packing and selling expenses Rs 1,580. Raise the necessary accounts in the books of Chhotamul Ltd. to record the above transactions.

[**Ans.** Value of Stock Rs 19,041, Profit on consignment Rs 49,771].

7. On January 15, 1988 Prem sends a consignment of goods costing Rs 24,000 to Sunder invoiced at Rs 30,000 to be sold at a commission of 4% on sale price. He was also allowed an overiding commission of 1% on sale. By March 1988, 80% of the goods are sold for Rs 32,000.

Prem and Sunder have respectively incurred the following expense on the consignment.

	Rs	Rs
Prem:		
Freight	350	
Cartage	400	
Insurance	250	1,000
Sunder :		
Customs duty	960	
Cartage	360	
Sales Expenses	120	
Warehouse Expense	120	1,560

Prem decides to adopt the invoice amount for entering in the consignment account and also to take customs duty paid by Sunder as part of the cost of the closing stock in addition to expenses incurred by him.

Write up the relevant accounts in the books of Prem and Sunder, the money due to Prem as on March 31, 1988 being paid by means of cheque.

[**Ans.** Profit Rs 9,104, Stock at the end at invoice price Rs 6,464, amount remitted by consignee Rs 28,840]

8. On 1st January, 1990, 'X' of Delhi consigned to 'Y' of Bombay goods for sale at invoice price. Y is entitled to commission of 4% on invoice price and 20% of any surplus price realised. Goods costing Rs 12,000 were consigned to Bombay at the invoice price of Rs 14,400. The expenses of the consignment amounted to Rs 1,000. On 31st March, 1990, an Account Sales was received from 'Y' showing that he had effected sales of Rs 12,000 in respect of ¾th of the quantity of goods consigned to him. His actual out of pocket expense amounted to Rs 600. 'Y' accepted a bill drawn by 'X' for Rs 5,000 and remitted the balance due from him in cash.

Give Consignment Account and Y's account in the books of X.

(B.Com. Pass, Delhi, 1981)

[**Ans.** Profit on Consignment Rs 978].

9. Miss Rakhi consigned 1,000 radio sets costing Rs 900 each to Miss Geeta, her agent on 1st July 1987. Miss Rakhi incurred the following expenditure on sending the consignment.

	Rs
Carriage	650
Freight	7,000
Insurance	3,250

Miss Geeta received the delivery of 950 radio sets. An Account Sale dated 30th November, 1989 showed that 750 sets were sold for Rs 9,00,000 and Miss Geeta incurred 3,000 for carriage and Rs 7,500 for the customs duty at the time of taking the delivery. Miss Geeta was entitled to a commission @ 6% on the sales affected by her. She incurred expenses amounting to Rs 2,500 for repairing the damaged radio sets remaining in the stock.

Miss Rakhi lodged a claim with the insurance company which was admitted at Rs 35,000. Show the Consignment Account and Miss Geeta's Account in the books of Miss Rakhi.

(C.A. Entrance, May, 1980, adapted)

[Ans. Gross Abnormal Loss Rs 45,545; Consignment Stock Rs 1,84,391; Profit Rs 1,52,036].

10. Dinesh of Bombay consigned medicines to Rao of Madras costing Rs 1,00,000. The invoice was made proforma so as to show a profit of 25 per cent on cost. Dinesh paid freight, insurance Rs 2,000.

Rao sold part of consignment for Rs 88,000 at uniform price of 10 per cent over invoice price and spent Rs 3,000 as warehousing charges, Rs 1,000 as selling expenses.

Sri Rao is entitled to a commission of 5 per cent on sales and 20 per cent of the net profit after charging such commission on sales. Sri Rao paid the amount due by bank draft.

Draw up the consignment account and Rao's Account in the books of Dinesh.

(C.A. Inter, May, 1982)

[Ans. Profit Rs 11,456, Rao remits Rs 76,736].

11. Vikram Milk Foods Co. Ltd. of Vikrampur sent to Sunder Stores, Sonepuri, 5,000 kgs. of baby food packed in 2,000 tins of net weight 1 kg and 6,000 packets of net weight ½ kg. for sale on consignment basis. The consignee's commission was fixed at 5% of sale proceeds.

The cost price and selling price of the product were as under.

	1 Kg. tin Rs	1/2 kg. packet Rs
Cost Price	10	6
Selling Price	15	7

The consignment was booked on freight "To Pay" basis and freight charges came to 2% of selling value. One case containing 50 1-kg. tins was lost in transit and the transport carrier admitted a claim of Rs 450.

At the end of the first half year, the following information is gathered from the "Account Sales" sent by the consignee:

(i) Sale proceeds: 1,500   1-kg tins
                    4,000   ½ kg packets

(ii) Store rent and insurance charges Rs 600.

Find out the value of closing stock on consignment.

Show the Consignment A/c and the Consignee's A/c in the books of Vikram Milk Food Co. Ltd., assuming that the consignees has paid the amount due from them.

(C.A. Entrance, May, 1979)

[Ans. Profit Rs 7,365, Amt. received from consignee Rs 45,935; Value of Closing Stock Rs 16,915].

12. A consigned to B on 1st January, 1986 500 bales of cotton costing Rs 100 per bale. Freight charges incurred on the consignment were Rs 5,000. A drew a bill on B for Rs 50,000 payable

on 30th June, 1986 which B accepted. The bill was discounted by A with his bankers on 31st January 1986 at 12 per cent p.a.

B rendered account to A on 31st March, 1986 showing sales of 300 bales for Rs 80,000 and selling expenses of Rs 5,000. B's commission was 10 per cent. On this date B remitted to A the net amount due to him.

On 31st May, 1986 B sold the balance stock for Rs 30,000 after incurring expenses of Rs 4,000. He remitted Rs 20,000 to A, the balance being treated as commission earned by him. On 30th June 1986 the bill accepted by B was dishonoured by him and the amount due to the bank was paid off by a A along with incidental charges of Rs 200.

Pass journal entries in the books of A (including bank transactions).

(C.A. Inter NS, Nov., 1976, adapted)

[Ans. Profit Rs 32,000].

13. Ali of Calcutta sent a consignment of ready made clothes to Rahim of Karachi at an invoice price of Rs 1,000 which was made up by adding 25% to the cost. Ali incurred the following expenses:

Packing Rs 24, Carriage Rs 16, Insurance Rs 12 and Other expenses Rs 26.

After three months an account sales was received intimating that half the consignment was sold at Rs 600. Consignee incurred the following expenses:

Freight Rs 30, Fire insurance Rs 18 and Other Expenses Rs 10. He was entitled to a commission of 6% on sales and *del credere* 1 1/2%.

No sale could be made of the remainder. It was brought back after another 9 months at a further cost of Rs 60. The goods were damaged and valued at 20% below cost. Find the profit on consignment assuming interest at 5% p.a. on cost.

[Ans. Value of stock Rs 320, Interest Rs 25.27, Consignee sends Rs 497, Loss Rs 146.27].

[Hint. (i) When goods are returned back to consignor all expenses incurred should be excluded in the valuation of stock returned.] (ii) Interest has been calculated as follows:

5% on Rs 878 (i.e., Rs 800 + Rs 78) for three months = Rs 10.98; 5% on Rs 381 (i.e., Rs 878– Rs 497) for 9 months = Rs 14.29).]

14. Niresh consigns 1,000 bats costing Rs 500 each to Swaroop for sales and incurs Rs 4,000 towards freight and Rs 1,000 for insurance. Swaroop was able to take delivery of 900 bats only and 100 bats were destroyed in transit. Insurance Co. admitted the claim and paid the same. Swaroop will be entitled to a commission of 5% on sales, 2% del credere commission on credit sales only. He will be entitled for additional commission of 25% of the excess if the sale price exceeds the cost price by more than 20%. Swaroop has spent Rs 2,000 towards sales expenses. The sale account is as under:

500 bats at Rs 600 per bat for cash.
200 bats at Rs 700 per bat for credit.

Consignment debtors paid their dues except one customer to whom 4 bats sold for Rs 2,800, could pay only Rs 800.

Show consignment account, consignment debtors account. Swaroop's Account and commission calculation.

(C.A. Entrance, Dec., 1985)

(Ans. Consignment Profit–Rs 54,700; Commission total Rs 29,800 Cash received from Swaroop in final settlement–Rs 2,70,200).

15. On 1st September, 1985 Faquirchand of Kanpur consigned to Akbar of Aizawal 100 bales of cloth invoiced at Rs 60 each. The invoice price was made up to 20% above cost. The freight and other charges amount to Rs 310. Faquirchand also drew a bill on Akbar for Rs 3,000 and discounted the same with the bank for Rs 2,980. Akbar duly met the bill on the due date.

On 25th December, 1985 Akbar sent Account Sales together with the necessary remittance showing that 40 bales had realised Rs 60 each and 30 bales at Rs 70 each and that 30 bales remained unsold, out of these 20 bales were damaged due to faulty packing and that he estimated the selling price of damaged goods to be Rs 20 per bale.

Akbar was entitled to a selling commission of 5%.

Show the Consignment Account in the Books of Faquirchand. Also ascertain the final remittance made by Akbar.

(**Ans.** Profit Rs 7,193; Amount received from consignee on final settlement Rs 1,275).

16. On 1st January 1987, Lila and Co. of Calcutta consigned 100 cases of Milk powder of Shila & Co. of Bombay. The goods were charged at a proforma invoice value of Rs 10,000 including a profit of 25% on invoice price. On the same date consignors paid Rs 600 for Freight and Insurance. On 1st July, the consignees paid Import Duty Rs 1,000, Dock Dues Rs 200 and sent to the consignors a Bank Draft of Rs 4,000 as advance. On 1st August, they sold 80 cases for Rs 10,500 and sent a remittance for the balance due to the consignors after deducting commission at the rate of 5% on gross sale proceeds. Show the Consignment Account and Shila & Co.'s Account in the books of Lila & Co.

(*C.A. Entrance, Nov., 1988*)

(**Ans.** Consignment Stock (at invoice price) Rs 2,360; Profit Rs 2,535).

17. On 1st July, 1986, Mantu of Madras consigned goods of the value of Rs 50,000 to Pandey of Patna. This was made by adding 25% on the cost. Mantu paid thereon Rs 2,500 for freight and Rs 1,500 for insurance. During transit one-tenth of the goods was totally destroyed by fire and a sum of Rs 2,400 was realised from the Insurance Company.

On arrival of the goods, Pandey paid Rs 1,800 as carriage to godown. During the year ended 30th June 1987, Pandey paid Rs 3,000 for godown rent and Rs 1,900 for selling expenses.

One-ninth of the remaining goods was again destroyed by fire in godown and nothing was recovered from the Insurance company.

On 1st June 1987, Pandey sold half the original goods for Rs 30,000 and charged a commission of 5% on sale. On 30th June, 1987, Pandey sent a Bank Draft to Mantu for the amount so far due from him.

You are requested to prepare the following ledger accounts in the books of Mantu of Madras for the year ended 30th June, 1987:

(*a*) Consignment to Patna Account

(*b*) Goods destroyed by Fire Account and

(*c*) Personal Account of Pandey. (*I.C.W.A. Inter, Dec., 1987*)

(**Ans.** Closing Consignment Stock at Invoice price–16,000; Goods destroyed by fire at invoice price–Rs 11,000; No Profit or loss on consignment; Amount received from Pandey in final settlement Rs 21,200).

18. On 1.1.1989 Mr. John of Bombay consigned to Mr. Raj of Madras goods for sale at invoice price. Mr. Raj is entitled to a commission of 5% on sales at invoice price and 20% of any surplus price realised. Goods costing Rs 1.00 lac were consigned to Madras at the Invoice price of Rs 1,50,000. The direct expenses of the consignment amounted to Rs 10,000. On 31.3.1989 an account sales was received by Mr. John from Mr. Raj showing that he had effected sales of Rs 1,20,000 in respect of 4/5th of the quantity of goods consigned to him. His actual expenses were Rs 3,000. Mr. Raj accepted a bill drawn by Mr. John for Rs 1,00,000 and remitted the balance due in cash.

Show the Consignment Account and the account of Mr. Raj in the Books of Mr. John.

(*C.A. Entrance, Nov., 1989*)

(**Ans.** Profit Rs 23,000; Cash received from Mr. Raj Rs 11,000).

Chapter 2

JOINT VENTURE ACCOUNTS

LEARNING OBJECTIVES

After studying this chapter you should be able to:

☐ explain the meaning of joint venture;

☐ differentiate between joint venture and partnership;

☐ get familiar with different methods of maintaining joint venture records;

☐ prepare different accounts relating to joint venture; and

☐ explain the meaning of certain key terms.

MEANING OF JOINT VENTURE

A joint venture is an association of two or more than two persons who have combined for the execution of a specific transaction and divide the profit or loss thereof in the agreed ratio. For example if *A* and *B* undertake the job of construction of a school building for a sum of Rs 1,00,000 their coming together for this specific job will be termed as a joint venture and each one of them will be termed as a co-venturer. The venture will be over as soon as this transaction is over *i.e.*, the school building is completed. Joint venture agreements can be made for similar other transactions, *e.g.* joint consignment of goods, underwriting of the shares or debentures issued by a particular company, purchasing and selling of a specific property etc.

The essential features of a joint venture agreement can be put as follows:

(*i*) There is an agreement between two or more than two persons.

(*ii*) The agreement is made for the execution of a specific venture.

(*iii*) The profit or loss on account of the venture is shared by the venturers in the agreed ratio. However, in the absence of any agreement between the venturers, the profits and losses are to be shared equally.

(*iv*) The agreement regarding the venture is automatically over as soon as the transaction is completed.

JOINT VENTURE AND PARTNERSHIP

According to the Indian Partnership Act. "Partnership is the relations between persons who have agreed to share the profits of a business carried on by all or any of them acting for all." Thus, both in joint venture and partnership there is some business activity whose profit (or loss) is agreed to be shared by two or more than two persons. As a matter of fact in law, a joint venture is treated as a partnership. Of course, a partnership covers or is meant to cover a long period whereas a joint venture is only for a limited purpose sought to be achieved in a short period. On account of this reason, joint venture is also sometimes termed as a 'temporary partnership' or 'partnership for a specific venture' or 'particular partnership'.

JOINT VENTURE AND CONSIGNMENT

The following are the points of distinction between joint venture and consignment:

(*i*) **Relationship:** In case of a consignment transaction, the relationship between the consignor and the consignee is that of a principal and an agent. While in case of joint venture, the relationship amongst various venturers is that of partners, i.e., mutual agency. Each venturer is a principal as well as an agent for the other venturer.

(*ii*) **Sharing of profits:** In case of consignment, the consignee gets only a commission on the goods sold by him on behalf of the consignor while in case of joint venture each venturer gets a share in the profits of the venture.

(*iii*) **Transfer of risk:** In case of consignment, till the goods are sold the risk continues to be of consignor while a joint venture is a temporary partnership hence the risk continues of all venturers.

ACCOUNTING RECORDS

There are three ways in which Joint Venture Accounts can be kept. They are as follows:

1. When *Separate Set of Books* for the venture are maintained. This will be necessary when venture is of a large magnitude.

2. When *One Venturer* keeps the accounts. In this case entire work is entrusted to one of the venturers and the rest simply contribute their share of investment and place it at the disposal of the working venturer.

3. When *All Venturers* keep accounts. Where venture is not of such magnitude as to warrant a distinct set of books being kept, each venturer will record only such transactions as directly concern him.

In the following pages each of these methods, has been discussed in detail.

WHEN SEPARATE SET OF BOOKS ARE MAINTAINED

Where a complete set of books are maintained for the Joint Venture, following accounts are opened: (*i*) Joint Bank Account (*ii*) Joint Venture Account (*iii*) Personal accounts of each Venturer.

In this method parties first pay their contribution to joint funds in the Joint Bank Account and their payments on joint account are made out of Joint Bank Account.

Joint Venture Account is of the nature of an ordinary Trading and Profit & Loss Account. It is debited with goods purchased, and expenses incurred, while credited with the sales made. It's balance shows the profit or loss incurred on the joint venture.

Personal account of each venturer is also opened. It is credited with the amount of contribution made by him to the joint funds and his share of profit (and debited in case of loss).

JOURNAL ENTRIES

Date	Transaction	Debit	Credit
1.	When venturers contribute cash to the joint funds	Joint Bank A/c (with total amt.)	Venturer's A/c (with individual contribution separately)
2.	When amount is spent on account of expenses, or for purchasing goods for the venture.	Joint Venture A/c	Joint Bank A/c

Contd...

Date	Transaction	Debit	Credit
3.	If any expenses are paid by the venturers.	Joint Venture A/c	Venturer's A/c
4.	For Sales:		
	(i) Cash	Joint Bank A/c	Joint Venture A/c
	(ii) Credit	Sundry Drs. A/c	Joint Venture A/c
5.	If Stock is taken by a venturer	Venturer's A/c	Joint Venture A/c
6.	If any stock remains unsold.	Joint Venture Stock A/c	Joint Venture A/c
7.	Balance of the Joint Venture A/c will be either profit or loss.		
	(i) if profit	Joint Venture A/c	Venturer's A/c
	(ii) if loss.	Venture's	Joint Venture A/c
8.	Joint Bank account and personal accounts of venturers' will be automatically closed by introduction or withdrawal of cash.		

Illustration 2.1. Banerjee and Mukherjee agree to import Russian timber into India. On 1st July, 1984 the opened a joint bank account with Rs 25,000 towards which Banerjee contributed Rs 15,000 and Mukherjee contributed Rs 10,000. They agree to share profits and losses in proportion to their cash contributions.

They remitted to their agent in Russia Rs 20,000 to pay for timber purchased, and later Rs 2,100 in settlement of his account. Freight, insurance and dock charges amounted to Rs 3,900. On Dec. 31, 1984 the sales amounted to Rs 28,740 which enabled them to repay themselves with cost originally advanced, (no account to be taken of interest). They then decided to close the venture and Mukherjee agreed to take over the timber unsold for Rs 1,260, which is to be deducted from his share of profit.

Prepare the necessary accounts showing the amount of each available for division by way of profits and how the same is divisible between Banerjee and Mukherjee.

Solution:

JOINT VENTURE ACCOUNT

Particulars	Amount Rs	Particular	Amount Rs
To Joint Bank A/c	20,000	By Joint Bank A/c (Sales)	28,740
To Joint Bank A/c		By Mukherjee	1,260
(commission of agent)	2,100		
To Joint Bank A/c			
(freight and insurance)	3,900		
To Profit transferred to:			
Banerjee 3/5	2,400		
Mukherjee 2/5	1,600		
	30,000		30,000

JOINT VENTURE ACCOUNT

Particulars	Amount Rs	Particular	Amount Rs
To Banerjee	15,000	By Joint Venture A/c	20,000
To Mukherjee	10,000	By Joint Venture A/c	2,100
To Joint Venture A/c	28,740	By Joint Venture A/c	3,900
		By Banerjee	17,400
		By Mukherjee	10,340
	53,740		53,740

BANERJEE

Particulars	Amount Rs	Particulars	Amount Rs
To Joint Bank A/c	17,400	By Joint Bank A/c	15,000
		By Joint Venture A/c	2,400
	17,400		17,400

MUKHERJEE

Particulars	Amount Rs	Particulars	Amount Rs
To Joint Venture A/c	1,260	By Joint Bank A/c	10,600
To Joint Bank A/c	10,340	By Joint Venture A/c	1,600
	11,600		11,600

Illustration 2.2. Prakash and Suresh doing business separately as building contractors, undertake jointly to construct a building for a newly started Joint Stock Company for a contract price of Rs 1,00,000 payable as to Rs 80,000 by instalment in cash and Rs 20,000 in fully paid shares of the Company. A Bank account is opened in their joint names, Prakash paying in Rs 50,000 and Suresh Rs 25,000. They are to share profit or loss in the proportion of 2/3 and 1/3 respectively. Their transactions were as follows:

	Rs
Paid wages	30,000
Bought materials	40,000
Material supplied by Prakash from his stock	5,000
Material supplied by Suresh from his stock	4,000
Architect's fees paid by Prakash	2,000

The contract was completed and price duly received. The Joint Venture was closed by Prakash taking up all the shares of the Company at an agreed valuation of Rs 16,000.

Prepare the Joint Venture Account, showing profit or loss, and the accounts of Prakash and Suresh showing the final distribution.

Solution:

JOINT VENTURE ACCOUNT

Particulars		Amount Rs	Particulars	Amount Rs
To Joint Bank A/c (wages)		30,000	By Joint Bank A/c	80,000
To Joint Bank A/c (materials)		40,000	By Prakash (shares)	16,000
To Prakash (materials)		5,000		
To Suresh (materials)		4,000		
To Prakash (architect's fees)		2,000		
To Profit:				
Prakash	10,000			
Suresh	5,000	15,000		
		96,000		96,000

JOINT BANK ACCOUNT

Particulars	Amount Rs	Particulars	Amount Rs
To Prakash	50,000	By Joint Venture A/c	30,000
To Suresh	25,000	By Joint Venture A/c	40,000
To Joint Venture A/c	80,000	By Prakash	51,000
		By Suresh	34,000
	1,55,000		1,55,000

PRAKASH

Particulars	Amount Rs	Particulars	Amount Rs
To Joint Venture A/c (shares)	16,000	By Joint Bank A/c	50,000
To Joint Bank A/c	51,000	By Joint Venture A/c (materials)	5,000
		By joint Venture A/c (architect's fees)	2,000
		By Joint Venture A/c (profit)	10,000
	67,000		67,000

SURESH

Particulars	Amount Rs	Particulars	Amount Rs
To Joint Bank A/c	34,000	By Joint Bank A/c	25,000
		By Joint Venture A/c	4,000
		By Joint Venture A/c (profit)	5,000
	34,000		34,000

Illustration 2.3. Wadekar and Pataudi enter into a joint venture to develop some building sites and sell them on the understanding that the result of the venture would be shared in the ratio of 4 : 5 between them. It is also agreed that any cash investment they make in the venture would be entitle to interest at 10% p.a.

They chose a five acre agricultural plot and purchased it for Rs 60,000. They approached a nationalised bank which agreed to finance them to the extent of 80% of the cost at 16% interest per annum. The buying arrangements were finalised on 1st July 1987 and the vendors paid off on the same day. Balance of purchase consideration and also the registration expenses which came to 8% were met by Wadekar from out of own his resources.

Pataudi met the cost of preparation of the layout, advertisement etc. which were as under:

(a)	Levelling and engineering costs paid to architects and town planners on 1.8.1987	At Rs 250 per ground
(b)	Municipal fees on 1.9.1987	At Rs 400 per ground
(c)	Advertisement expenses on 1.10.1987	Rs 17,500 per ground
(d)	Entertainment expenses on 31.12.1987	Rs 1,120 per ground

Plots were advertised for sale in newspapers on 15.9.1987 and on the basis of response, the entire are was dealt with as under.

(i) 15% of the total are was to be left for roads, market place, police station and park.

(ii) 10 plots each of 3, 2 1/2 and 1 1/2 grounds were made.

(iii) The balance area was taken equally by Wadekar and Pataudi at cost.

(*iv*) 1 1/2 ground plots carried a premium of 50%, 2 1/2 ground plots a premium of 40% and 3 ground plots a premium of 25% over cost.

(*v*) Pataudi to receive 8% of the sale proceeds as management fee for his efforts.

The entire transactions were put through by 31st December, 1987. Show the joint venture account and the statement of account settlement between the venturers. (1 acre is equal to 18 grounds of 2,400 sq. feet each).   (*C.A. Inter, May, 1979, adapted*)

Solution:

M/s Wadekar & Pataudi
JOINT VENTURE ACCOUNT

Particulars		Amount Rs	Particulars	Amount Rs
To Joint Venture Bank A/c			By Joint Venture Bank A/c	
(cost of land)		48,000	(sale proceeds of the plots)	1,61,500
To Wadekar (part cost of land &			By Pataudi	
registration charges)		16,800	(cost of plots taken over)	5,525
To Pataudi			By Wadekar	
Levelling	22,500		(cost of plots taken over)	5,525
Municipal fees	36,000			
Advt. charges	17,500			
Ent. charges	1,120	77,120		
To Joint Venture Bank A/c		3,840		
To Interest to Wadekar		840		
To Interest to Pataudi		2,575		
To Management fee to				
Pataudi @ 8%		12,920		
To Profit transferred to				
Wadekar		4,647		
Pataudi		5,808		
		1,72,550		1,72,550

WADEKAR'S ACCOUNT

Particulars	Amount Rs	Particulars	Amount Rs
To Joint Venture Account		By Joint Venture Account:	
(cost of plots)	5,525	Expenses	16,800
To Joint Venture Bank A/c	16,762	Interest	840
		Profit	4,647
	22,287		22,287

PATAUDI'S ACCOUNT

Particulars	Amount Rs	Particulars	Amount Rs
To Joint Venture Account		By Joint Venture Account:	
(cost of plots taken over)	5,525	Sundry Expenses	77,120
To Joint Venture Bank A/c	92,898	Management Fee	12,920
		Interest	2,575
		Profit	5,808
	98,423		98,423

JOINT VENTURE BANK ACCOUNT

Particulars	Amount Rs	Particulars	Amount Rs
To Joint Venture Account (sale proceeds)	1,61,500	By Joint Venture A/c (cost of land)	48,000
		By Joint Venture A/c (interest)	3,840
		By Wadekar	16,762
		By Pataudi	92,898
	1,61,500		1,61,500

Working Notes:

1. Number of Grounds:

	Grounds
Area 5 acres	90.0
Area for road, market place, police station and park 15%	13.5
Balance	76.5
Plots for sale 10 × (3 + 2.5 + 1.5)	70.0
Plots for co-ventures	6.5

2. Cost of Land:

	Rs
Registration Charges @ 8%	60,000
Levelling and Engineering Cost @ Rs 250 per ground	4,800
Municipal Fee @ Rs 400 per ground	22,500
Interest due on Bank Loan on Rs 48,000 @ 16% p.a. for six months	36,000
Interest on Wadekar on Rs 16,800 @ 10% p.a. for six months	3,840
Interest on Pataudi:	840
on Rs 22,500 @ 10% for 5 months	937.50
on Rs 36,000 @ 10% for 4 months	1,200.00
Cost of 76.5 grounds	1,30,117.50
Cost per ground	Rs 1,700 (approx)

3.

SALE PROCEEDS

Particulars	Sale price per ground Rs	Total sale proceeds Rs
Selling price per plot of		
1 1/2 ground plots: 2,550+50%	3,825	38,250
2 1/2 ground plots: 4,250+40%	5,950	59,500
3 ground plots: 5,100+25%	6,375	63,750
		1,61,500

WHEN ONE VENTURER KEEPS ACCOUNTS

Where work for recording joint venture transactions is entrusted to one of the co-venturers, he is usually allowed an extra remuneration out of the profit for his services. Following main accounts are maintained by him:

(i) Joint Venture Account which shows the amount of Profit or Loss made on the venture.

(ii) Personal accounts of all other co-venturers.

JOURNAL ENTRIES

Sl	Transaction	Debit	Credit
1.	When the working partner receives from other co-venturers their share of investment	Cash/Bank	Venturer's A/c

Contd....

Sl	Transaction	Debit	Credit
2.	When goods are purchased.	Joint Venture A/c	Cash or Crs. A/c
3.	When expenses for the venture are incurred.	Joint Venture A/c	Cash A/c
4.	When goods are sold.	Cash or Drs. A/c	Joint Venture A/c
5.	When he is allowed an extra commission for his services.	Joint Venture A/c	Commission A/c (later on transferred to his P. & L. A/c)
6.	The balance of Joint Venture Account will show either a profit or loss.		
	(i) His own share of profit will be transferred to his P. & L. A/c.	Joint Venture A/c	P. & L. A/c
	(ii) The shares of co-venturers will be transferred to their respective personal accounts.	Joint Venture A/c	Individual A/cs of the co-venturers.
	(iii) The venturers accounts will then show what is due to them in respect of their investments and their share of profit or loss.		

Illustration 2.4. A and B entered into a joint venture agreement to share the profit and losses in the ratio of 2 : 1. A supplied goods worth Rs 60,000 to B incurring expenses amounting to Rs 2,000 for freight and insurance. During transit goods costing Rs 5,000 became damaged and a sum of Rs 3,000 was recovered from the insurance company. B reported that 90% of the remaining goods were sold at a profit of 30% of their original cost. Towards the end of the venture, a fire occurred and as a result the balance stock lying unsold with B was damaged. The goods were not insured and B agreed to compensate A by paying in cash 80% of the aggregate of the original cost of such goods plus proportionate expenses incurred by A. Apart from the joint venture share of profit, B was also entitled under the agreement to a commission of 5% of net profits of joint venture after charging such commission. Selling expenses incurred by B totalled Rs 1,000. B had earlier remitted an advance of Rs 10,000. B duly paid the balance due to A by draft.

You are required to prepare in A's books:

(i) Joint Venture Account.

(ii) B's account.

Solution:

Books of A

JOINT VENTURE ACCOUNT

Particulars	Amount Rs	Particulars	Amount Rs
To Purchases (Cost of goods suppld.)	60,000	By Bank (Insurance Claim)	3,000
To Bank (Expenses)	2,000	By B (Sales)	64,350
To B (Expenses)	1,000	By B (agreed value for damaged goods)	4,546
To B (Commission—1/21 of 8,896)	424		
To Profit transferred to:			
P. & L. A/c	5,648		
B	2,824		
	71,896		71,896

B'S ACCOUNT

Particulars	Amount Rs	Particulars	Amount Rs
To Joint Venture A/c (Sales)	64,350	By Bank (Advance)	10,000
To Joint Venture A/c (Claim portion)	4,546	By Joint Venture A/c (Expenses)	1,000
		By Joint Venture A/c (Commission)	424
		By Joint Venture A/c (Share of profit)	2,824
		By Bank (Balance received)	54,648
	68,896		68,896

Working Notes:

1. It has been assumed that the goods damaged in-transit have no residual value.

2. Computation of Sales

	Rs
Cost of goods sent	60,000
Less: Cost of damaged goods	5,000
	55,000
Cost of goods remaining unsold	5,500
Cost of goods sold	49,500
Profit @ 30%	14,850
Sales	64,350

3. Claim for loss of fire admitted by B

	Rs
Cost of goods	5,500
Add: Proportionate expenses (2,000 × 5,500)/60,000	183
	5,683
Less: 20%	1,137
Amount of claim	4,546

WHEN ALL VENTURERS KEEP ACCOUNTS

There are two methods of keeping books:

(i) When each party informs the other party regarding transactions made by him on account of joint venture at regular intervals.

(ii) When such information is furnished at the completion of the venture. This is popularly known as 'memorandum method'.

1. *When each Venturer gets complete information from other Venturer(s).* In this case each party maintains the following accounts:

(a) *Joint Venture Account.* It is similar to an ordinary P. & L. A/c. It is debited with total purchases and total expenses incurred and credited with the amount of sales and stock in hand. The balance of this account is either a profit or a loss.

(b) *Personal Account or Accounts of the Co-venturers.* This personal account is written as "Joint Venture with... Account" The words "Joint Venture with..." are added before the name of the Venturer, only to distinguish it from other personal accounts of the main business. It is a record of transactions made by the co-venturer on account of joint venture. The account is closed by settling the balance.

The Journal entries to be passed in case of this method are given below:

JOURNAL ENTRIES

	Transaction	Debit	Credit
(1)	When goods are brought or money is spent on Joint Venture.	Joint Venture A/c	Seller's A/c or Bank A/c
(2)	When he receives a report that his co-venturer has bought goods or spent money on the Joint Venture.	Joint Venture A/c	Co-venturer's Personal A/c
(3)	When he sells goods bought on Joint Venture A/c	Cash A/c or Purchaser's A/c	Joint Venture A/c
(4)	When he receives a report that his co-venturer has sold goods bought on Joint Venture A/c.	Co-venturer's A/c	Joint Venture
(5)	The balance of Joint Venture A/c will be either Profit or Loss.		
	(i) For his share of profit.	Joint Venture A/c	P. & L. A/c
	(ii) For his co-venturer's share of profit. In case of loss entries will be reversed.	Joint Venture A/c	Co-venturer's A/c
(6)	The personal account of the co-venturer when balanced will show what is due from him or what is due to him.		

Illustration 2.5. X and Y entered into a joint-venture of underwriting the subscription at par of the entire share capital of Copper Mines Limited consisting of 10,000 shares of Rs 10 each and to pay all expenses up to allotment. They were to share profits in the ratio of 3 : 2 respectively. The consideration in return for the guarantee was 1,200 other shares of Rs 10 each fully paid to be issued to them.

X provided the funds for registration fees Rs 1,200; advertising Rs 1,100 and printing and stationery Rs 950. Y contributed towards payment of office rent Rs 300; legal charges Rs 1,550 and staff salaries Rs 900.

The prospectus was issued and the applications fell short of the full issue by 1,500 shares. X took these over on joint account and paid for the same in full. They received the 1,200 fully paid shares as underwriting commission. They sold their entire holding at Rs 12 per share. The proceeds were received by X for 1,500 shares and by Y for 1,200 shares.

Write up the necessary accounts in the books of both the parties showing the final adjustment.

Solution:

In the Books of X

JOINT VENTURE ACCOUNT

Particulars	Rs	Particulars	Rs
To Bank (Registration Fee)	1,200	By Y (Sales)	14,400
To Bank (Advertising)	1,100	By Bank (Sales)	18,000
To Bank (Printing and Stationery)	950		
To Y (Office Rent)	300		
To Y (Legal Charges)	1,550		
To Y (Staff Salaries)	900		
To Bank (Shares)	15,000		
To Profit:			
P. & L. A/c	6,840		
Y	4,560		
	32,400		32,400

Y's ACCOUNT

Particulars	Rs	Particulars	Rs
To Joint Venture A/c	14,400	By Joint Venture A/c	300
		By Joint Venture A/c	1,550
		By Joint Venture A/c	900
		(Profit)	4,560
		By Bank	7,090
	14,400		14,400

In the Books of Y

JOINT VENTURE ACCOUNT

Particulars	Rs	Particulars	Rs
To X	1,200	By Bank	14,400
To X	1,100	By X	18,000
To X	950		
To Bank	300		
To Bank	1,550		
To Bank	900		
To X	15,000		
To Profit:			
P. & L. A/c	4,500		
X	6,840		
	32,400		32,400

X'S ACCOUNT

Particulars	Rs	Particulars	Rs
To Joint Venture A/c	18,000	By Joint Venture A/c	1,200
To Bank A/c	7,090	By Joint Venture A/c	1,100
		By Joint Venture A/c	950
		By Joint Venture A/c	15,000
		By Joint Venture A/c	6,840
	25,090		25,090

Illustration 2.6. A and B entered into a joint venture contract for sharing the profits and losses in the ratio of 60 per cent and 40 per cent. A purchased goods worth Rs 3,00,000 and despatched to B. A paid Rs 24,000 in the process. B reported after some time that he had sold the goods for Rs 3,20,000 and the remaining were not being sold. Later on A and B decided to despatch the goods on consignment basis to M/s C & Co., who agreed to sell the goods on their behalf. C was to be paid all the expenses plus 5 per cent commission. After few days C sent an Account Sales alongwith a cheque for Rs 35,000 to B (after deducting expenses Rs 5,000 and commission). The unsold (remaining) goods were returned to B. B purchased the goods for Rs 20,000.

B prepared a statement of account to A and informed that he spent Rs 14,500 on this joint venture. They agreed to settle their accounts. Prepare the necessary ledger accounts in the books of A and B showing the final settlement of accounts.

Solution:

Books of A

JOINT VENTURE ACCOUNT

Particulars	Rs	Particulars	Rs
To Bank A/c (Goods purchased)	3,00,000	By B	3,20,000
To Bank A/c (Exp.)	24,000	By B	35,000
To B (Exp.)	14,500	By B (Stock)	20,000
To Profit & Loss A/c	21,900		
To B	14,600		
	3,15,000		3,75,000

B'S ACCOUNT

Particulars	Rs	Particulars	Rs
To Joint Venture A/c (Sales)	3,20,000	By Joint Venture A/c (Exp.)	14,500
To Joint Venture A/c		By Joint Venture A/c (Profit)	14,600
(Sales through Agent)	35,000	By Bank A/c	3,45,900
To Joint Venture A/c (Stock taken)	20,000		
	3,75,000		3,75,000

Books of B

JOINT VENTURE ACCOUNT

Particulars	Rs	Particulars	Rs
To A (Good supplied)	3,00,000	By Cash (Sales)	3,20,000
To A (Expenses)	24,000	By Cash (Sales through Agent)	35,000
To Cash (Expenses)	14,500	By Purchases (Stock)	20,000
To Profit & Loss A/c	14,600		
To A	21,900		
	3,75,000		3,75,000

A'S ACCOUNT

Particulars	Rs	Particulars	Rs
To Bank A/c	3,45,900	By Joint Venture A/c (Goods)	3,00,000
		By Joint Venture A/c (Expenses)	24,000
		By Joint Venture (Profit)	21,900
	3,45,900		3,45,900

2. *Memorandum Joint Venture Method or Memorandum Method.* The following are the salient features of this method:

   (i) Each party will maintain only ONE account in his books. This account will be personal account of other parties. It may be very carefully noted that even if there are more than two venturers only one personal account is to be opened in each party's books. For example, if A, B, C, have entered into a joint venture. A will open one personal account of B and C in his books and not separate accounts. Similarly B will open joint personal account of A and C and C will maintain joint account of A and B.

   (ii) Each party will record only such transactions as entered by him on joint venture account e.g. if goods are purchased by A, it will be recorded in A's books and not in the books of B and C.

(*iii*) In order to find out profit or loss made on the venture a 'Memorandum Joint Venture Account' will be opened. It is merely a combination of personal accounts, *i.e.*, debit side of personal accounts is posted on the debit side of Memorandum Joint Venture Account and credit side of personal accounts is posted on the credit side of Memorandum Joint Venture Account. However, such transactions which will not affect profit or loss on the venture *e.g.* receiving or sending of cash by one venturer from or to another will not be entered in his account.

Illustration 2.7. *A* and *B* entered into a joint venture as dealers in land with effect from 1st July, 1985. On the same day *A* advanced Rs 90,000 and a plot of land measuring 9,000 square yards, was purchased with this money. It was decided to sell the land in smaller plots and a plan was got prepared at a cost of Rs 1,000 paid by *B*. In the said plan 1/3 of the total area of the land was left over for public roads and the remaining land was divided into 6 plots of equal size. On 1st October 1985, two of the plots were sold at Rs 30 per square yard, the buyer deducting Rs 1,000 per plot for stamp duty and registration expenses agreed to be borne by the sellers. The remaining plots were sold at a net price of Rs 25 per square yard on 1st December 1985. The sale proceeds of all the plots were received by *A*. After charging interest at 6% p.a. on the investments of *A* (allowing for money received by him) and allowing 1% on the net sale proceeds of plots as commission to *B*, the net profit of the joint venture is to be shared in proportion of 3/4 to *A* and 1/4 to *B*.

Draw up the Memorandum Joint Venture and personal accounts in the books of *A* and *B* showing the balance payable by one to the other.

Assume joint venture was completed on December 1.

Solution:

A's Books

Dr.   JOINT VENTURE WITH *B* ACCOUNT   Cr.

Particulars	Rs	Particulars		Rs
To Bank (Advance)	90,000.00	By Bank (Sale)		
To Interest (See Working Notes)	1,670.00	$2,000 \times 30 =$	60,000	
To P. & L. A/c (Share of Profit)	47,812.50	Less @ Rs 1,000		
To Bank (Final Settlement)	18,517.50	per plot	2,000	58,000.00
		By Bank (Sales) $4,000 \times 25$		1,00,000.00
	1,58,000.00			1,58,000.00

B's Books

JOINT VENTURE WITH *A* ACCOUNT

Particulars	Rs	Particulars	Rs
To Bank (Expense)	1,000.00	By Bank (Final Settlement)	18,517.50
To (Commission)	1,580.00		
To P. & L. A/c (Share of Profit)	15,937.50		
	18,517.50		18,517.50

MEMORANDUM JOINT VENTURE ACCOUNT

Particulars	Rs	Particulars	Rs
To Purchases (A)	90,000	By Sales	1,58,000
To Interest (A)	1,670		

Contd....

Particulars		Rs	Particulars	Rs
To Expenses (B)		1,000		
To Commission (B)		1,580		
To Profit				
A	47,812.50			
B	15,937.50	63,750		
		1,53,000		1,58,000

Working Notes:

Interest receivable by A:
July 1, 1985 to Dec. 1, 1985.

Rs $90,000 \times \dfrac{6}{100} \times \dfrac{5}{12}$ = Rs 2,250

Interest payable by A:
1st October, 1985 to Dec. 1, 1985.

Rs $58,000 \times \dfrac{6}{100} \times \dfrac{2}{12}$ = Rs 580

Net interest receivable by A 1,670

Illustration 2.8. A and B enter into a joint venture sharing profit and losses equally. A purchased goods for Rs 5,000 and B spent Rs 1,000 for freight on 1st January, 1986. On the same day B bought goods worth Rs 10,000 on credit. Further expenses were incurred as follows:

on 1.2.1986 Rs 1,500 by B
on 1.3.1986 Rs   500 by A

Sales were made against each as follows:

15.1.1986 Rs 3,000 by A
31.1.1986 Rs 6,000 by B
15.2.1986 Rs 3,000 by A
1.3.1986   Rs 4,000 by B

Creditors for goods were paid as follows:

1.2.1986 Rs 5,000 by A
1.3.1986 Rs 5,000 by B

On 31st March, 1986 the balance stock was taken over by B at Rs 9,000. The accounts between the ventures were settled by cash payment on this date. The venturers are entitled to interest of 12% per annum.

Prepare necessary ledger accounts in the books of the venturers.

(C.A. Inter NS, May, 1976, adapted)

Solution:

MEMORANDUM JOINT VENTURE ACCOUNT

Particulars	Rs	Particulars	Rs
To Cost of Goods: A	5,000	By Sales: A	6,000
B	10,000	B	10,000
To Freight-B	1,000	By Interest-B	50
To Expenses-A	500	By Stock-B	9,000
To Expense-B	1,500		
To Interest-A	135		

Contd....

Particulars	Rs	Particulars	Rs
To Profit:			
A	3,457		
B	3,458		
	25,050		25,050

Calculation of Interest

PAYMENTS BY A

Date	Amount Rs	Month	Int. till 31-3-86 @ 1% p.m. Rs	Rs
1.1.86	5,000	3	150	
1.3.86	500	1	5	
1.2.86	5,000	2	100	255

AMOUNTS RECEIVED BY A

15.1.86	3,000	2 1/2	75	
15.2.86	3,000	1 1/2	45	120
Net Interest due to A				135

PAYMENTS BY B

1.1.86	1,000	3	30	
1.2.86	1,500	2	30	
1.3.86	5,000	1	50	110

AMOUNT RECEIVED BY B

31.1.86	6,000	2	120	
1.3.86	4,000	1	40	160
Net Interest due to B				50

A's Ledger

JOINT VENTURE WITH B ACCOUNT

1986	Particulars	Rs	1986	Particulars	Rs
Jan. 1	To Bank (Purchase)	5,000	Jan. 15	By Bank (Sale proceeds)	3,000
Feb. 1	To Bank (Purchase)	5,000	Feb. 15	By Bank (Sale proceeds)	3,000
Mar. 1	To Bank (Expenses)	500	Mar. 31	By Bank (amount	
Mar. 31	To Interest A/c	135		received in settlement)	8,092
	To Profit & Loss A/c				
	(Share of Profit)	3,457			
		14,092			14,092

B's Ledger

JOINT VENTURE WITH A ACCOUNT

1986	Particulars	Rs	1986	Particulars	Rs
Jan. 1	To Bank (Freight)	1,000		By Bank (Sales)	6,000
	To Creditors (goods		Mar. 1	By B (Creditors paid)	5,000*
	bought on credit)	10,000*		By Bank (Sales)	4,000
Feb. 1	To Bank (Exp.)	1,500	Mar. 1	By Purchases A/c (stock	
Mar. 31	To Profit & Loss A/c			taken over)	9,000

Contd....

1986	Particulars	Rs	1986	Particulars	Rs
	(share of profit)	3,458	Mar. 31	By Interest A/c	50
	To Bank (amount paid to				
	A in settlement)	8,092			
		24,050			24,092

*Alternatively only Rs 5,000 be debited to Joint Venture Account in B's Ledger.

KEY TERMS

☐ **Joint Venture:** An association of two or more persons who have combined for the execution of a specific transaction and divide the profit or loss thereof in the agreed ratio.

☐ **Joint Venturer:** A person who has joined a joint venture.

TEST QUESTIONS

Objective type TEST YOUR UNDERSTANDING

1. State whether each of the following statements is 'True' or 'False':
   (i) Joint Venture and Partnership are synonymous terms.
   (ii) A Joint Venture business has an indefinite life.
   (iii) Persons agreeing to participate in a joint venture business are termed as co-venturers.
   (iv) A co-venturer works on commission basis.
   (v) Principle of 'mutual agency' is applicable in case of joint venture.
   (vi) No accounting entry is passed when the goods are transferred from one venturer to the other.

   [Ans. (i) False; (ii) False; (iii) True; (iv) False; (v) True; (vi) True].

2. Select the most appropriate answer:
   (i) Joint Venture Account is: (a) a Nominal Account. (b) a Personal Account. (c) A Real Account.
   (ii) Joint Bank Account is opened: (a) When no separate books for the venture are maintained. (b) When separate books for the venture are maintained. (c) Under no circumstances.
   (iii) When goods are purchased for the Joint Venture, the amount is debited to: (a) Purchases Account; (b) Joint Venture Account (c) Venturer's Capital Account.
   (iv) In case of Memorandum Method when there are three co-venturers, each co-venturer opens in its books for the Venture; (a) One account; (b) Two accounts; (c) Three accounts.
   (v) When a Venturer recording the transactions brings goods to the joint venture from his own stock, the amount is credited to: (a) Joint Venture Account; (b) Purchases Account; (c) Capital Account.

   [Ans. (i) (a); (ii) (b); (iii) (b); (iv) (a); (v) (b)].

Essay type FOR REVIEW, DISCUSSION AND PRACTICE

1. Define Joint Venture. Distinguish it from partnership.
2. Describe briefly in two lines each the different methods of recording transactions of joint venture.

PRACTICAL PROBLEMS

When Separate Set of Books are maintained for the Joint Venture.

1. X and Y of Bombay agreed to import cotton into India on joint venture. On Jan. 1, 1988 they opened a bank account, X contributing Rs 1,40,000 and Y Rs 1,00,000 and agreed to divide profits and losses according to their cash contributions.

   They remitted Rs 1,80,000 to their agent in Egypt to pay for the cotton purchased there and later on a further Rs 10,000 in settlement of his account.

   The freight, insurance and dock charges were all paid in Bombay and amounted to Rs 10,000.

   On July 31, 1988 the various sales realised Rs 2,40,000 net which enabled them to repay themselves (taking no account of interest) the cash respectively advanced by them on Jan. 1. The venture is then closed by X taking over the balance of cotton unsold for Rs 38,000 for which he paid a cheque into the bank account.

   You are required to write up necessary accounts dealing with these transactions and to finally close them.

   [**Ans.** Profit on Join Venture Rs 78,000; X Share Rs 45,500 and Y's Share Rs 32,500].

2. Rajiv and Shyam enter into a joint venture to import silk. On 1st January, 1988, they opened a Joint Bank Account with the Syndicate Bank, Rajiv contributing Rs 20,000 and Shyam Rs 10,000. They agreed to share profits in the ratio of the capitals introduced by them. On 15th February, 1988, they remitted to a manufacturer in Japan Rs 25,000 for the goods received and incurred an expense of Rs 800 for freight, insurance, etc. The goods were sold for Rs 33,000 for which the selling expenses were as follows:

   Godown rent Rs 200; Commission payable to Shyam on the gross amount of sales 10%; and Misc. expenses 300.

   Give Journal entries and the necessary ledger accounts showing the final distribution of cash among the co-venturers.

   [**Ans.** Profit on Joint Venture Rs 3,400, Rajiv gets Rs 22,267 and Shyam gets Rs 14,433 in final settlement].

3. Gavaskar and Biswanath jointly underwrite and place on the market 50,000 shares of Bombay Machineries Ltd. of Rs 10 each. It was agreed with the company that they would be allotted 2,000 shares as fully paid towards their remuneration.

   Their profit sharing ratio is 3:2.

   Applications were received from the public only for 45,000 shares.

   Gavaskar paid Rs 4,000 for postage and advertisement in addition to 60% of the amount required to take up the short subscription.

   Biswanath financed the balance amount. These are accounted for through Joint Bank Account. All the shares including those allotted for remuneration were sold. Gavaskar sold 3,000 shares for Rs 35,000 and Biswanath sold the balance shares for Rs 48,000. Biswanath incurred expenses of Rs 2,000. Sale proceeds were retained individually.

   Show necessary accounts in the books of the Venturers which were separately started for this purpose.

   The interest account was settled through the Joint Bank Account.

   (C.A. Inter NS, May, 1980)

   [**Ans.** Net Profit Rs 27,000, Gavaskar brings Rs 15,200 and Biswanath is paid Rs 15,200].

4. Mr. S and Mr. R carrying on a business separately as contractors, jointly take up the work of constructing a building at an agreed price of Rs 3,50,000 payable in cash Rs 2,40,000 and in fully paid shares of a company for the balance of Rs 1,10,000. A Bank account is opened in

which Mr. S and Mr. R paid Rs 75,000 and Rs 50,000 respectively. The following costs were incurred in completing the construction and the contract price was duly realised:

(i) Wages paid Rs 90,000;

(ii) Materials purchased for cash Rs 2,10,000;

(iii) Materials supplied by R from his stock Rs 27,000;

(iv) Consulting Engineer's fees paid by Mr. S Rs 6,000.

The accounts were closed, Mr. S taking up all the shares of the company at an agreed valuation of Rs 48,000, treating loss on shares as Joint Venture Loss and Mr. R taking the remaining stock of materials at Rs 9,000.

Prepare and close the Joint Venture Account and the Personal Accounts of Mr. S and Mr. R assuming that separate set of books are opened for this purpose and that the net result of the venture is shared by Mr. S and Mr. R in the ratio of 2:1.

(C.A. Entrance, May, 1987)

[Ans. Joint Venture Loss - Rs 36,000; Amounts paid out of Joint Bank Account: S - Rs 9,000 & R - Rs 56,000].

5. X and Y enter into a Joint Venture to build a multi-storeyed building. They agree to share the profits and losses equally upto Rs 50,000 from the venture. Thereafter the profits and losses are to be shared in the following proportion:

$X = 3/5$

$Y = 2/5$

X contributes plant and machinery worth Rs 40,000 and meets registration expenses worth Rs 10,000.

Y contributes the plot on which the building is to be built, valued of Rs 1,00,000.

Other expenses incurred are:

	Rs
Fuel and Electricity	40,000
Raw Materials	1,60,000
Labour Charges	75,000
Advertisement Expenses	5,000

All the expenses were met from the Bank Account opened for the Joint Venture. At the end of the venture X agreed to take the Plant and Machinery valued at Rs 10,000.

Y sold off the multi-storeyed building for a total of Rs 7,20,000 and collected all dues from the buyers except for one flat, valued at Rs 1,80,000 which he kept for himself in lieu of his expected share of profit.

The venturers who had agreed to maintain Venture accounts in separate sets of books, asks you to prepare the Joint Venture Account, Joint Bank Account and Venturers' Capital Accounts.

(I.C.W.A. Inter, June, 1988)

[Ans. Profit on Venture-Rs 4,80,000; Y brings Rs 6,03,000 and X is paid Rs 3,23,000 on final settlement].

When all Venturers keep Accounts

6. Ram and Laxman were participants in a Joint Venture, sharing profits and losses in the proportion of 2/3 and 1/3 respectively. Each party maintain a complete record in his own books. Ram supplies goods to the value of Rs 15,000 and incurs an expenditure of Rs 600 on them, and Laxman supplies goods to the extent of Rs 12,000 and his expenses amount to Rs 900. Ram sells all the goods for Rs 36,000 for which he is entitled to receive a commission at 5%. Accounts are settled by bank draft. Give the necessary journal entries and the ledger accounts in the books of Ram to record the above transactions.

[Ans. Profits on the venture Rs 5,700 Amount paid to Laxman in settlement of his account Rs 14,800].

7. Shanker of Calcutta enter into a joint venture with Wadekar of Bombay to ship jute bales to Samuel of Singapore. Shanker consigns jute of the value of Rs 50,000 and pays insurance and freight charges of Rs 2,500 and customs duty etc. of Rs 1,200. Wadekar sends goods valued Rs 40,000, pays freight Rs 1,800, dock dues Rs 300, customs duty Rs 900 and other expenses Rs 400. Shanker advanced to Wadekar Rs 25,000 and account of the venture. Shanker received account sales and remittance of net proceeds from Samuel in Singapore amounting to Rs 1,22,000.

Show how these transactions would appear in the ledgers of both parties assuming that they have agreed to share the net profit or loss of the venture in the ratios of Shanker 2: Wadekar 1.

[Ans. Profit on venture Rs 24,900; Shanker pays to Wadekar Rs 26,700].

8. A and B enter into a Joint Venture to take a building contract for Rs 2,40,000. They provide the following information regarding the expenditure incurred by them.

	A (Rs)	B (Rs)
Materials	68,000	50,000
Cement	13,000	17,000
Wages	—	27,000
Architect's Fee	10,000	—
Licence Fee	—	5,000
Plant		20,000

Plant was valued at Rs 10,000 at the end of the contract and B agreed to take it at that value. Contract amount of Rs 2,40,000 was received by A.

Show:

(i) Joint Venture Account and B's Account in the books of A; and

(ii) Joint Venture Account and A's Account in the books of B.

(C.A. Entrance, May, 1988)

[Ans. Net Profit Rs 40,000, A pays B Rs 1,29,000 on final settlement].

Memorandum Method

9. Bharat and Sharad joined together as co-venturers for equal share in profits through sale of television cabinets. On March 1, 1986, Bharat purchased 2,000 cabinets at Rs 250 each for cash and sent 1,500 of these to Sharad for sale, the selling price of each being Rs 300. All the cabinets were sold by April 30, 1986 by both and the proceeds collected.

Each venturer recorded in his books only those transactions concluded by him, final profit/loss being ascertained through a Memorandum Joint Venture Account.

The expenses met by the venturers were:

				Rs
Bharat	...	Freight and Insurance	...	9,000
		Selling Expenses	... ...	4,500
Sharad	...	Coolie and Clearing Charges	...	900
		Selling Expenses	...	13,500

Final settlement between the venturers took place on May 31, 1986. You are required to show:

(a) Joint Venture A/c with Sharad in the books of Bharat;

(b) Joint Venture A/c with Bharat in the books of Sharad, and

(c) Memorandum Joint Venture A/c.

[Ans. Profit on Joint Venture Rs 72,100, Bharat gets from Sharad Rs 3,99,550, in final settlement].

10. Sakti and Sadhan agree to enter into a joint venture to buy and sell television sets. Profits and Losses were to be shared equally.

On 5th May, 1990 Sakti purchased three television sets for Rs 3,000, Rs 3,500 and Rs 4,000 respectively. He bought a special cabinet costing Rs 750 which he fixed for one of the sets. On

31st May, 1990 he sold two of the sets for Rs 4,000 each, paying the proceeds into his private bank account.

On 15th June, 1990 he sold the other set for Rs 4,500 which amount he paid over to Sadhan who paid it into his Bank account.

On 6th May, 1990 Sadhan purchased at TV set for Rs 3,000 having incurred expenditure of Rs 200 on repairing, sold it on 14th May, 1990 for Rs 3,800 paying the proceeds into his own bank account. This set developed mechanical trouble and on 26th May, 1990 Sadhan agreed to take the set back at a price of Rs 2,800 which he paid cut of his Bank Account. The set was still unsold at 30th June, 1990 and it was agreed that Sadhan should take it over for his personal use at a valuation of Rs 2,600.

Sakti incurred Rs 300 as showroom charges and Sadhan incurred Rs 225 as travelling and postage.

You are required to prepare (a) the account of Joint Venture with Sakti as it would appear in the books of Sadhan and (b) Memorandum Joint venture Account showing the net profit.

(I.C.W.A. Inter, Dec., 1980, adapted)

[Ans. Joint Venture Profit Rs 1,125, Amount paid to Sakti Rs 4,112.50].

11. Adarsh of Delhi and Laxman of Bangalore entered into a joint venture for purchase and sale of one lot of mopeds. The cost of each moped was Rs 3,600 and the fixed retail selling price was Rs 4,500. The following were the recorded transactions during 1990:

Jan. 1.   Adarsh purchased 100 mopeds paying 72,000 in cash on account. Adarsh raised a loan from A. Bank for Rs 50,000 at 18% p.a. interest, repayable with interest on 1.3.1990.

Adarsh forwarded 80 mopeds to Laxman incurring Rs 2,880 as forwarding and insurance charges.

Jan. 7.   Laxman received the consignment and paid Rs 720 as clearing charges.

Feb. 1.   Adarsh sold 5 mopeds for cash.

Laxman sold 20 mopeds for cash.

Laxman raised a loan of Rs 1,50,000 from B. Bank, repayable with interest at 18% p.a. on 1.3.90.

Laxman telegraphically transferred Rs 1,50,000 to Adarsh incurring charges Rs 50.

Adarsh paid balance due for the mopeds.

Feb. 26.   Adarsh sold the balance mopeds for cash.

Laxman sold balance mopeds for cash

Adarsh paid selling expenses 5,000.

Laxman paid selling expenses Rs 20,000.

Mar. 1.   Accounts settled between the venturers and loans repaid, profit being appropriated equally.

You are required to show:

1. The Memorandum Joint Venture A/c.
2. Joint Venture with Laxman Account in Adarsh's books; and
3. Joint Venture with Adarsh Account in Laxman's books.

You are to assume that each venturer recorded only such transaction as concluded by him.

(C.A. Entrance, June, 1981, adapted)

[Ans. Profit Rs 57,600 Adarsh gets Rs 1,58,180 in final settlement].

12. Hari, an architect and Ram, a real estate dealer enter into an agreement for the purpose of purchasing a large land and converting it into plots. The purchase price (Rs 1,60,000) and the legal expenses (Rs 11,100) are paid by Hari, who borrowed the money from the bank.

Ram provides the materials costing Rs 58,000 for the levelling of land and the development of plots. 10 plots of 200 sq. mts each and 5 plots of 400 sq mts. each are sold respectively @ Rs 75 per sq. mt. and @ Rs 70 per sq. mt. The sales proceeds are 5 plots of 200 sq. mts. each are received by Ram. The balance is received by Hari, who paid Rs 15,000 for sales expenses. Hari repaid the loan and interest thereon amounting to Rs 9,600.

The agreement provides that after crediting Hari with the interest charged on the borrowed money and allowing 15 per cent on the cost of the levelling to cover overhead expenses, Hari is to receive two-third of the profit and Ram one-third.

Each party's ledger contains records of his own receipts and payments on the Joint Account. You are required to prepare (a) a statement showing the result of the Venture, and (b) the account of the venture in each party's ledger as it will finally appear

(C.A. Entrance, Dec., 1984)

[**Ans.** Joint Venture Profit Rs 27,600; Amount due by Hari to Ram Rs 900].

13. Bhim and Arjun entered into a Joint Venture for buying and selling plastic goods and agreed to share profits and losses in the ratio of 3:2.

On October 1, 1988, Bhim purchased goods at a cost of Rs 60,000 and half of the goods were handed over to Arjun. On October 15, he again purchased goods worth Rs 20,000. He incurred expenses Rs 2,000.

On October 15, Arjun also made a purchase of Rs 37,500 and on the same day he sent to Bhim goods worth Rs 15,000. He incurred expenses of Rs 900.

On October 20, Bhim in order to help Arjun sent Rs 16,000 to him.

Both the parties sold goods at a profit of 25% on sale.

On March 31, 1989, Bhim had unsold stock of goods of Rs 12,500, of these goods costing Rs 5,000 were taken away by him and the remainder sold for Rs 8,000. Arjun was able to sell away complete goods excepting goods costing Rs 2,500 which were badly damaged and were treated as unsaleable. Rs 3,000 owing to Bhim was unrecoverable and treated as joint loss.

On March 31, 1989 parties decided to close the books.

You are required to prepare:

    (a) Joint Venture Account as it would appear in the books of Bhim recording his own transactions, and

    (b) Memorandum Joint Venture Account, showing the profits of the business.

(I.C.W.A. Inter, Dec., 1989)

[**Ans.** Joint Venture Profit Rs 26,267).

14. M and N entered into a Joint Venture for the purchase and sales of second-hand motor cars and to share profits and losses in the ratio 3:2.

On January 15, 1987 M bought 5 cars for Rs 43,000 and on January 20, 1987, he paid tax and insurance amounting to Rs 1,600. On January 31, 1987 he sold these cars for Rs 58,000 out of which he remitted Rs 11,000 to N paying the balance into his own bank account.

On January 20, 1987 N bought 3 cars for Rs 36,000 and on January 25, 1987 he paid tax and insurance Rs 1,400 and repair charges amounting to Rs 2,000. He sold one car on February 2, 1987 for Rs 14,000 which he paid into his own bank account. M then took over other cars at a valuation of Rs 26,000 and the venture was closed on February 10, 1987.

Prepare the Memorandum Joint Venture Account and the Account of the Joint Venture with N in the books of M.

(C.A. Entrance, May, 1988)

[**Ans.** Joint Venture Profit - Rs 14,000: Amount paid to N on February 10-Rs 20,000).

Chapter 3

ACCOUNT CURRENT AND AVERAGE DUE DATE

ACCOUNT CURRENT

In case there are several transactions between two parties, it will be necessary to take into account the question of interest besides ensuring the correctness of amount due by one party to the other. It will be appropriate in such a case that each party should send a statement of account to the other party instead of settling each transaction individually. Such a statement when rendered in the form of an account by one party to another, duly setting out in chronological order the details of the transactions together with interest, is termed as an *Account Current*. The main heading of the account is preceded by the name of the party to whom it is rendered and is succeeded by the name of the party sending the statement. For example, if *A* sends an account current to *B*, the heading of the account current will be:

B in account current with *A*

In case the account current is being sent by *B* to *A*, the heading of the account current. will be:

A in account current with *B*

Account current is sent by one person to another in case of following types of relationship:

(*a*) Principal and Agent, (*b*) Consignor and Consignee, (*c*) Supplier of goods and Customer, (*d*) Co-venturers.

Computation of Interest

Interest is usually calculated on the basis of number of days. Thus, computation of interest involves.

(1) Calculation of days.

(2) Calculation of the amount of interest.

(1) **Calculation of days.** Following points should be kept in mind while calculating the number of days.

(*i*) There are three methods for calculating the number of days:

(*a*) **Forward method.** The method is most common. The number of days are calculated from the due date of the transaction to the date of settlement.

(*b*) **Backward or epoque method.** In case of this method the number of days are counted from the opening date (*i.e.*, the date of commencement of the account current) of the account current to the due date of the transaction.

(*c*) **Daily balance method.** The method is used by banks. Days are calculated from the due date of a transaction to the due date of the next transaction.

(*ii*) The effective date of the transaction should be considered for calculating the number of days irrespective of the method followed. For example if as per terms of trade, some credit period is allowed, interest is to be charged only with effect from the date after the expiry of such a period. Similarly when bills of exchange are received or issued, the due date of the bill (including 3 days of grace) will be the effective date for this purpose.

(*iii*) The date of the transaction should be excluded for calculating the number of days. For example if days are to be calculated from 5th January, 1989 (the date of transaction) to 31st January 1989 (settlement date) the number of days will be taken as 26, the day of 5th January will be excluded.

(*iv*) In case, some balance has been brought forward from the previous period, the first day of the new period will also be considered. For example if the opening balance is on 1st March and the settlement date is 30th June, the number of days will be counted as follows:

March 31 + April 30 + May 31 + June 30 = 122

However, if a new transaction takes place on 1st March, the day of 1st March will not be counted for calculating the number of days.

(2) **Calculation of amount of Interest.** There are three methods for charging interest:

(*i*) **Calculating interest on each item**

In case of this method interest is calculated on each item separately. The days are calculated from the date of the transaction to the settlement date and interest is charged for the number of days so calculated at agreed rate of interest.

Illustration 3.1. The following are a series of transactions between *A* and *B* for the three months ending on 31st March 1989. Calculate the amount of interest to be payable by one party to the other @ 10% p.a.

Books of *A*

		Rs
Jan. 1	Opening balance (Dr)	5,000
Jan. 10	Sold goods to *B*	10,000
Jan. 15	Cash recd. from *B*	10,000
Feb. 15	Sold goods to *B*	10,000
March 1	Cash received from *B*	5,000

Solution:

B IN ACCOUNT CURRENT WITH A

Date	Particulars	Amount Rs	Date	Particulars	Amount Rs
Jan. 1	To Balance b/d	5,000	Jan. 15	By Cash	10,000
Jan. 10	To Sales	10,000	March 1	By Cash	5,000
Feb. 15	To Sales	10,000	March 31	By Balance c/d	10,217
March 31	To Interest	217			
	(see Working Note)				
		25,217			25,217

Working Note:

COMPUTATION OF INTEREST

	Debit Items	Rs		Credit Items	Rs
(i)	$5,000 \times \dfrac{90}{365} \times \dfrac{10}{100}$	= 123	(i)	$\dfrac{10,000 \times 75 \times 10}{365 \times 100}$	= 206
(ii)	$10,000 \times \dfrac{80 \times 10}{365 \times 100}$	= 220	(ii)	$\dfrac{5,000 \times 30 \times 10}{365 \times 100}$	= 41
(iii)	$\dfrac{10,000 \times 44 \times 10}{365 \times 100}$	= 121			

Total Interest to be charged to B = (123 + 220 + 121) − (206 + 41) = Rs 217

(ii) Product Method

This is a modification of the first method. In place of making separate calculations, the amount involved in each transaction is multiplied by the number of days (or months) from its date to the date of settlement. Interest is calculated on the balance of the products for one day (or month) and is put on the side the sum of the products is more. However, if the rates of interest are different for debits and credits, interest for debits and credits will have to be calculated separately.

Illustration 3.2. With the figures given in the Illustration 3.1, calculate the amount of interest according to the Product Method.

(For Solution please see page 2.56)

Red Ink Interest

Some times the due date of a transaction falls after the closing date of the account current. For example, an account current is prepared for the quarter ending 31st March, 1989. A receives a bill or exchange from B for Rs 10,000 on 15th March due one month after date. The due date of the transaction is therefore 18th April, 1989 i.e., 18 days after the closing date of the account current. A on 31st March is entitled to get interest from B for 18 days instead of allowing interest to him for this transaction. In the statement to be rendered by A to B the product of 1,80,000 will be subtracted from the total of the products of other items. In order to differentiate it from other products, the product of such an amount is entered in **red ink**. This is the reason why such a product is known as "red ink interest" product.

Illustration 3.3. From the following transactions in the books of X, prepare an account current to be sent by X to Y for the quarter ending 31st March, charging and allowing interest at 12% p.a.

Solution (Illustration 3.2.):

B IN ACCOUNT CURRENT WITH A

Date	Particulars	Amount Rs	Days	Product	Date	Particulars	Amount Rs	Days	Product
Jan. 1	To Balance b/d	5,000	90	4,50,000	Jan. 15	By Cash	10,000	75	7,50,000
Jan. 10	To Sales	10,000	80	8,00,000	Mar. 1	By Cash	5,000	30	1,50,000
Feb. 15	To Sales	10,000	44	4,40,000	Mar. 31	By Balance of Products			7,90,000
Mar. 31	To Int. on balance of products for one day $\frac{7,90,000 \times 10}{100 \times 365}$	217			Mar. 31	By Balance c/d	10,217		
		25,217		16,90,000			25,217		16,90,000

Solution (Illustration 3.3.):

Books of A

Y IN ACCOUNT CURRENT WITH X

Date	Particulars	Amount Rs	Days	Product	Date	Particulars	Amount Rs	Days	Product
Jan. 1	To Balance b/d	3,000	90	2,70,000	Feb. 11	By Bank	4,000	48	1,92,000
Jan. 14	To Sales	5,000	76	3,80,000	Feb. 19*	By B/R due on April 22	5,000	22	(1,10,000)
Feb. 17	To Sales	3,000	42	1,26,000	Mar. 31	By Balance of Products			6,84,000
Mar. 31	To Interest $\frac{6,84,000 \times 12}{100 \times 365}$	225			Mar. 31	By Balance c/d	2,225		
		11,225		7,76,000			11,225		7,76,000

*To be in red ink.

Illustration 3.3. From the following transactions in the books of X, prepare an account current to be sent by X to Y for the quarter ending 31st March, charging and allowing interest at 12% p.a.

		Rs
Jan. 1	Balance in Y's account (Dr)	3,000
Jan. 14	Sold goods to Y	5,000
Feb. 11	Cash received from Y	4,000
Feb. 17	Sold goods to Y	3,000
Feb. 19	Received a bill of exchange from Y due two months after date	5,000

(For Solution please see page 2.56)

(iii) Epoque Method

This method is the reverse of the first two methods. Interest is computed from opening date of the account current to the date of each transaction. Thus, no interest is charged on the opening balance while interest for the whole period will be charged on the closing balance.

Interest is calculated at the agreed rate on the balance of the products for one day (or month) and entered on the side which has smaller product. In case rates of interest are different for debits and credits, interest for each side will have to be calculated separately.

Illustration 3.4. With the figures given in the Illustration 3.1, calculate the amount of interest according to Epoque method.

(For Solution please see page 2.58)

(iv) Periodical Balance Method

The method is usually followed in banks. The balance is struck after each transaction and is multiplied by the number of days up to the next transaction. Interest is charged for one day on the difference of the products. In case the rates of interest are different for debits and credits interest will be calculated for the debits of the products and the credits of the products separately. The difference of the two amounts will be the amount of interest chargeable to or receivable from the party concerned.

Illustration 3.5. Suneel opened a current account with New Bank of India on 1st January 1989. The details of the transactions for the quarter ending 31st March, 1989 are as follows:

		Rs
Jan. 1	Deposited	10,000
Jan. 15	Deposited	5,000
Feb. 12	Deposited	10,000
Feb. 15	Withdrew	30,000
Mar. 10	Withdrew	5,000

The bank allow interest on credit balance at 2% p.a., while it charges on debit balances at 10% p.a.

Prepare Suneel's account in the Bank's ledger.

(For Solution please see page 2.58)

Solution (Illustration 3.4):

B IN ACCOUNT CURRENT WITH A

Date	Particulars	Amount Rs	Days	Product	Date	Particulars	Amount Rs	Days	Product
Jan. 1	To Balance b/d	5,000	—	—	Jan. 15	By Cash	10,000	15	1,50,000
Jan. 10	To Sales	10,000	10	1,00,000	Mar. 1	By Cash	5,000	60	3,00,000
Feb. 15	To Sales	10,000	46	4,60,000	Mar. 31	By Balance (excluding Int.)	10,000	90	9,00,000
Mar. 31	To Balance of Products			7,90,000	Mar. 31	By Balance (including Int.)	10,217		
Mar. 31	To Interest $\frac{7,90,000 \times 10}{100 \times 365}$	217							
		25,217		13,50,000			25,217		13,50,000

Solution (Illustration 3.5):

SUNEEL IN ACCOUNT CURRENT WITH NEW BANK OF INDIA

Date	Particulars	Dr	Cr	Dr or Cr	Balance	Days	Dr Product	Cr Product
1989								
Jan. 1	By Cash		10,000	Cr	10,000	14		1,40,000
Jan. 15	By Cash		5,000	Cr	15,000	28		4,20,000
Feb. 12	By Cash		10,000	Cr	25,000	3		75,000
Feb. 15	To Self	30,000		Dr	5,000	23	1,15,000	
Mar. 10	To Self	5,000		Dr	10,000	21	2,10,000	
Mar. 31	To Interest	54		Dr	10,054			
		35,054	25,000			54	3,25,000	6,35,000
April 1	To Balance b/d			Dr	10,054			

Note. Rs 10,000 was deposited on January, 1, 1989. The next deposit was on January 15. Thus, interest on Rs 10,000 should be allowed for 14 days. Similarly on 15th there was another deposit of Rs 5,000. The next deposit was on February 12. Thus, interest for 28 days should be allowed on Rs 15,000. The total of credit column of the product is 6,35,000. While that of debit is 3,25,000. Interest to be charged is Rs 89 $\left(i.e., \frac{3,25,000 \times 2 \times 1}{100 \times 365} \right)$, while interest to be allowed is Rs 35 $\left(i.e., \frac{6,35,000 \times 2 \times 1}{100 \times 365} \right)$. Thus, the net interest to be charged is a sum of Rs 54.

AVERAGE DUE DATE

Average Due Date may be defined as the mean or equated date on which one payment may be made in lieu of several payments due on different dates without loss of interest to either party. For example, *A*, a businessman may have a series of transactions involving receipts and payments of money due on different dates with *B*, another businessman. They may decide to settle their accounts on a particular date, after taking into account the amount of interest which may have become due by one party to another. There are two alternatives available in such a case:

(*a*) Interest may be calculated separately for each transaction; or

(*b*) A mean date may be determined and the interest may be calculated from such mean date to the date of actual settlement on the total amount due by one party to another.

Alternative (*b*) is preferable since it will reduce a lot of clerical work. The mean date so calculated is termed as the Average Due Date.

Utility of Average Due Date

Average due date is useful in the following types of accounting problems:

1. Problems relating to settlement of accounts involving a series of bills of exchange due on different dates.
2. Problems relating to calculation of interest of partners' drawings made on different dates.
3. Problems involving piece-meal realisation of assets during the partnership dissolution.
4. Problems involving settlement of accounts where money advanced is to be received in a number of installments due on different dates.

Types of Problems

Broadly the problems relating to computation of the Average Due Date, can be put into two categories:

(*i*) Calculation of Average Due Date when the amount is lent in a number of instalments and repayment is made in one instalment; and

(*ii*) Calculation of Average Due Date when the amount is lent in one instalment and repayment is made in a number of instalments.

Each of these types of problems have been exhaustively explained in the following pages.

(*i*) Where the amount is lent in a number of instalments

The calculation of the Average Due Date in this case can be done by taking the following steps:

1. A certain convenient basic date (or zero date) is taken as a starting point. This is usually the date of one of the transactions and preferably the due date of the first transaction.
2. In respect of each transaction, the number of days (or months) filling in between the basic date and date of the transaction are ascertained.
3. The amount of the transaction is multiplied by the number of days (or months) ascertained by step 2 above.
4. Both the products as ascertained by step 3 above as well as the amounts are added up.
5. The total of the products is divided by the sum total of the amount.

6. The result is the number of days (or months) by which the Average Due Date is distant from the chosen date. In other words the basic date + number of days (or months), calculated in this way will give Average Due Date.

In case some amounts have been paid out and some have been received, the products for the two should be added up separately. The difference between the two totals of the products should then be divided by the difference in the sum total of the amounts of Debit and Credit. However, it should be noted that the basic date for both group of transactions should be the same.

Calculation of Interest

The computation of the Average Due Date simplifies interest calculations. The amount of interest can be calculated from the Average Due Date to the date of settlement instead of making separate calculation for interest for each transaction. This will be clear with the following illustration:

Illustration 3.6. Sunil is a partner in a firm Sunil, Sharad & Co. His drawings from the business during the year 1990 are as follows:

Month	Rs	Month	Rs
Jan. 31	150	Jul. 31	250
Feb. 28	100	Aug. 31	150
Mar. 31	160	Sep. 30	120
Apr. 30	200	Oct. 31	100
May 31	140	Nov. 30	180
June 30	70	Dec. 31	300

You are required to calculate the Average Due Date and the amount of interest @ 10% p.a. payable by Sunil for his transactions:

(a) taking Jan. 1 as the basic date.

(b) taking Dec. 31 as the basic date.

Solution:

Month	Amount Rs	Dec. 31 being used as basic date — Months before 31st Dec.	Product	Jan. 1 being used as basic date — Months after 1st Jan.	Product
1990					
Jan. 31	150	11	1,650	1	150
Feb. 28	100	10	1,000	2	200
Mar. 31	160	9	1,440	3	480
Apr. 30	200	8	1,600	4	800
May 31	140	7	980	5	700
June 31	70	6	420	6	420
July 31	250	5	1,250	7	1,750
Aug. 31	150	4	600	8	1,200
Sep. 30	120	3	360	9	1,080
Oct. 31	100	2	200	10	1,000
Nov. 30	180	1	180	11	1,980
Dec. 31	300	0	0	12	3,600
	1,920		9,680		13,360

Average Due Date when December 31st is taken as the basic date = 9,680/1,920 = 5 Months (approx) prior to 31st December

Hence, the Average Due Date is 31st July.

Average Due Date when January 1st is taken as the basic date = 13,360/1,920 = 7 months (approx.) subsequent to January 1st.

Hence, the Average Due Date is 31st July.

In case Sunil had paid the amount of Rs 1,920 to the firm on the Average Due Date *i.e.*, 31st July, there would have been no loss of interest to either party. Since the accounts are being settled not on 31st July but on 31st December, Sunil is liable to pay to the firm interest for 5 months. The amount comes to: $1,920 \times \dfrac{10}{100} \times \dfrac{5}{12} = $ Rs 80.

(*ii*) Where the amount is lent in a single instalment

In this case where the amount is lent in one single instalment while repayment is made in a number of equal instalments, the average due date can be calculated by taking the following steps:

1. The numbers of days (months or years) from the date of lending money to the date of each repayment should be calculated.
2. The total of such days (months or years) should be found out.
3. The total calculated as per step 2 above should be divided by the number of instalments payable for repayment of the amount.
4. The result as per step 3 above will be the number of days (months or years) by which the Average Due Date is away from the date on which the loan was given.

The above steps for calculation of the Average Due Date can be put in the form of the following formula:

$$ADD = D + \frac{SDP}{N}$$

Where *ADD* = Average Due Date

D = Date of lending

SDP = Sum of Days (months or years) from the date of lending to the date of repayment of each instalment.

N = Number of instalments.

Illustration 3.7. Rs 10,000 lent on 1st January, 1987 is repayable in 5 equal annual instalments commencing from 1st January, 1988. Find the Average Due Date.

Solution:

$$ADD = D + \frac{SDP}{N}$$

Where *ADD* = Average Due Date

D = Date of lending *i.e.*, 1st January, 1987

SDP = Sum number of years from 1st Jan. 87 to the repayment of each instalment

N = Number of instalments

$$= \text{1st Jan. 87} + \frac{(1+2+3+4+5)}{5} \text{ years}$$

= 1st January, 1987 + 3 yrs

= 1st January, 1990

Illustration 3.8. Mr *X* lends Rs 1,000 to Kumar Bros. On 1st January, 1985. The amount is repayable in 5 half-yearly equal instalments commencing from 1st January, 1986.

Calculate the Average Due Date and interest at 10% p.a.

Solution:

In order to calculate the Average Due Date, the sum of period from the date of lending to the date of each transaction will have to be calculated.

1st payment is made after 12 months from the date of lending.
2nd payment is made after 18 months from the date of lending.
3rd payment is made after 24 months from the date of lending.
4th payment is made after 30 months from the date of lending.
5th payment is made after 36 months from the date of lending.

Total $\overline{120}$

$$ADD = D + \frac{SDP}{N}$$

$$= \text{1st Jan. 1985} + \frac{120}{5} \text{ months}$$

$$= \text{1st Jan. 1985} + 24 \text{ months}$$

$$= \text{1st Jan. 1987.}$$

If Mr X had lent the money on 1st January, 1987 and Kumar Bros. had paid the money as per the above schedule, there would have been no loss of interest to either party. Since X lent money to Kumar Bros not on 1st January, 1987 but 1st January, 1985 *i.e.*, 2 years earlier he is entitled to get interest for this period of two years from Kumar Bros.

The amount of interest has been calculated as follows:

$$\frac{1,000 \times 10 \times 2}{100} = \text{Rs 200}$$

Illustration 3.9. Ramkumar having accepted the following bills drawn by his creditor Prakash Chand due on different dates approached his creditor to cancel them all and allow him to accept a single bill for the payment of his entire liability on the average due date. You are requested to ascertain the total amount of the bill and its due date.

Bill No.	Date of Drawing	Date of Acceptance	Amount of the Bill (Rs)	Tenor
1.	16.2.90	20.2.90	8,000	90 days after sight
2.	6.3.90	7.3.90	6,000	2 months after date
3.	24.5.90	31.5.90	2,000	4 months after sight
4.	1.6.90	4.6.90	9,000	1 month after date

(I.C.W.A. Inter, June, 1981, adapted)

Solution:

COMPUTATION OF AVERAGE DUE DATE

Starting date = 23.5.90 (The date when the first bill is due for payment)

Bill No.	Due date	Amount	No of days from the starting date (i.e., 23.5.90)	Product
	1	*2*	*3*	*4 = (2 × 3)*
1.	23.5.90	8,000	0	0
2.	9.5.90	6,000	(−) 14	(−) 84,000
3.	3.10.90	2,000	133	2,66,000
4.	4.7.90	9,000	42	3,78,000
	Total	25,000		5,60,000

Average Due Date$= 23.5.80 + \dfrac{5,60,000}{25,000} = 23.5.80 + 22$ days (approx) $= 14.6.90.$

Thus, if payment is to be effected on the basis of average due date, the total amount of the single bill shall be Rs 25,000 due on 14.6.90.

Notes: (*i*) Starting date is also known as 'basic date' or 'zero date'. This is usually taken on basis of the due date of the first transaction. There is, however, no harm, if some other day is chosen for the purpose.

(*ii*) Due dates of the individual bills are calculated after taking 3 days of grace into consideration.

KEY TERMS

☐ **Account Current:** An account rendered by one party to another duly setting out in chronological order the details of the transactions together with interest and the ultimate balance due by one party to another.

☐ **Average Due Date:** A mean or equated date on which one payment may be made in lieu of several payments due on different dates, without loss of interest to either party.

☐ **Zero Date:** A certain convenient basic date which is taken as the starting point for computing the average due date.

TEST QUESTIONS

Objective type | TEST YOUR UNDERSTANDING |

1. State whether each of the following statements is 'True' or 'False.'
   (*i*) Account Current and Current Account are synonymous terms.
   (*ii*) In case of *Epoque Method* the number of days are counted from the opening date to the date of the transaction.
   (*iii*) The problem of *red ink interest* arises when the due date of a transaction falls after closing date of the account current.
   (*iv*) *Average Due Date* is the date on which accounts are actually settled by the parties.
   (*v*) While calculating *Average Due Date*, only the due date of the first transaction should be taken as the basic date.

   [Ans. (*i*) F; (*ii*) T; (*iii*) T; (*iv*) F; (*v*) F].

2. Select the most appropriate answer :
   (*i*) The account maintained by a businessman with his bankers is known as
      (*a*) Current Account.
      (*b*) Account Current.
      (*c*) Savings Bank Account.
   (*ii*) Payment on average due date results in loss of interest to
      (*a*) the debtor.
      (*b*) the creditor.
      (*c*) neither party.
   (*iii*) The number of days are calculated from the date of the transaction to the date of settlement in case of
      (*a*) Forward Method

2.64

(b) Epoque Method
(c) Daily Balance Method

[Ans. (i) (a); (ii) (c); (iii) (a)].

Essay type   FOR REVIEW, DISCUSSION AND PRACTICE

1. Define an Account Current. Explain the different methods for computing interest.
2. What is an Average Due Date ? Explain the various steps that are to be taken for computation of an Average Due Date.
3. Differentiate between
   (a) Forward Method and Backward Method in Account Current.
   (b) Account Current and Current Account.
   (c) Average Due Date and the Date of Settlement.

PRACTICAL PROBLEMS

Account Current

1. From the following particulars prepare the Account Current to be rendered by Mr Singh to Mr Paul as on 31.8.1987. Interest must be calculated @ 10% per annum:

		Rs
11.6.87	Goods sent to Mr Paul	1,020
15.6.87	Cash received from Mr Paul	500
20.6.87	Goods sent to Mr Paul	650
7.7.87	Goods sent to Mr Paul	700
8.8.87	Cash received from Mr Paul	1,000

[Ans. Interest (Dr.) Rs 29, Balance (Dr.) 899].

2. Mehra owed Rs 3,000 on 1st January, 1988 to Mr Somesh. The following are the transactions that took place between them during1987. It is agreed between the parties that interest @ 6% per annum is to be calculated on all transactions.

1988		Rs
January, 16	Mr Somesh sold goods to Mr Mehra	2,000
January, 29	Mr Somesh purchased goods from Mr Mehra	1,500
February, 10	Mr Somesh pays cash	1,500
March, 10	Mr Mehra accepts a bill drawn by Mr Somesh for one month	2,000

They desire to settle their accounts by one single payment on 15th March, 1988. Ascertain the amount to be paid to the nearest rupee. Ignore days of grace.

[Ans. Interest Rs 62, Total Amount Rs 3,062].

3. From the following particulars make up an Account Current to be rendered by S. Dasgupta to A. Halder at 31st December reckoning interest at 5 per cent per annum.

1989		Rs
June 31	Balance owing by A. Halder	520
July 17	Goods sold to A. Halder	40
August 1	Cash received from A. Halder	500
August 19	Goods sold to A. Halder	720
August 30	Goods sold to A. Halder	50
September 1	Cash received from A. Halder	400
September 1	Halder accepted Dasgupta's Draft at 3 months' date	300
October 22	Goods bought from A. Halder	20
November 12	Goods sold to A. Halder	14
December 14	Cash received from A. Halder	50

(I.C.W.A. Inter, Dec., 1979, adapted)
[Ans. Interest (Dr.) Rs 9.72, Balance (Dr.) Rs 83.72].

4. Following transactions took place between *X* and *Y* during the month of April 1985.

1985		Rs
April 1	Amount payable by *X* to *Y*	10,000
April 7	Received acceptance of *X* to *Y* for 2 months	5,000
April 10	Bills Receivable (accepted by *Y*) on 7.2.85 is honoured on this due date	10,000
April 10	*X* sold goods to *Y* (invoice dated 10.5.85)	15,000
April 12	*X* received cheque from *Y* dated 15.5.85	7,500
April 15	*Y* sold goods to *X* (Invoice dated 15.5.85)	6,000
April 20	*X* returned goods sold by *Y* on 15.4.85	1,000
April 20	Bill accepted *Y* is dishonoured on this due date	5,000

You are required to make out an account current by products method to be rendered by *X* to *Y* as on 30.4.1985, taking interest into account at the rate to 10% per annum.

(I.C.W.A. Inter, June, 1985)

(Ans. Interest (credit) Rs 114.38; Balance on April 30 Rs 2,385.62 (Dr)).

Average Due Date

5. *A* owes *B* Rs 890 on 1st January, 1986. From January to March, the following further transactions take place between *A* and *B*:

		Rs
January, 16	*A* buys goods	910
February, 2	*A* receives cash loan	750
March, 5	*A* buys goods	810

A pays whole amount on 31st March 1986 together with interest at 5% per annum. Calculate the interest by the average due date method.

(C.A. Inter OS, May, 1976, adapted)

[Ans. Rs 28.93].

6. Anand sold goods to Balwant as detailed below:

Date of Invoice	Value of goods sold (Rs)
5.5.87	3,000
12.5.87	1,500
19.5.87	3,500
26.5.87	2,250
1.6.87	2,000
3.6.87	1,000

The payments were agreed to be made by bills payable 90 days from the respective dates of the invoice. However, Balwant wanted to arrange for payment of all the bills to be made on a single date.

Calculate the date on which such a payment could be made without loss of interest to either party.

[Ans. 20th August, 1987].

7. Radheshyam purchased goods from Hariram, the due dates for payment in cash being as follows:

	Rs	
March 15	400	Due 18th April
April 21	300	Due 24th May
April 27	200	Due 30th June
May 15	250	Due 18th July

Hariram agreed to draw a Bill for the total amount due on the average due date. Ascertain that date.

[Ans. 30th May].

8. A trader having accepted the following several bills falling due on different dates, now desires to have these bills cancelled and to accept a new bill for the whole amount payable on the average due date.

Serial No.	Date of Bill	Amount Rs	Usance of the bill
1.	1st March, 1984	400.00	2 months
2.	10th March, 1984	300.00	3 months
3.	5th April, 1984	200.00	2 months
4.	20th April, 1984	375.00	1 month
5.	10th May, 1984	500.00	2 months

You are required to find the said average due date.

(C.A. Inter OS, Nov., 1974)
[**Ans.** June 7, 1984].

9. Strong lent to Weak Rs 6,000 on 1st January 1990. The loan is repayable in three equal instalments at an interval of two years commencing from 30th June, 1991. Calculate the Average Due Date.

[**Ans.** June 30, 1994].

10. Mohan Ram accepted the following Bills drawn by Sumanth.

On	8th	March, 1984	Rs 4,000 for 4 months.
On	6th	March, 1984	Rs 5,000 for 3 months.
On	7th	April, 1984	Rs 6,000 for 5 months.
On	17th	May, 1984	Rs 5,000 for 3 months.

He wants to pay all the bills on a single day. Find out this date.

Interest is charged @ 18% p.a. and Mohan Ram wants to save Rs 150 by way of interest. Find out the date on which he has to effect the payment to save interest of Rs 150.

(C.A. Entrance, June, 1985)
(**Ans.** July 19, 1984)

11. A drew upon B several bills of exchange due for payment on different due dates as under:

Date	Amount Rs	Tenure
2.10.1989	600	3 months
20.10.1989	800	2 months
10.11.1989	1,000	3 months
27.11.1989	750	3 months
8.12.1989	900	1 months
16.12.1989	1,200	2 months

Find out the Average Due Date on which payment may be made in one single amount.

(I.C.W.A. Inter, Dec., 1989)
(**Ans.** 30th Jan., 1989)

Chapter 4

INVENTORY VALUATION

LEARNING OBJECTIVES

After studying this chapter you should be able to:

- ☐ define the term inventory;
- ☐ appreciate the objectives of inventory valuation;
- ☐ explain different inventory systems;
- ☐ enumerate different methods of inventory valuation;
- ☐ prepare inventory records according to different inventory systems/methods;
- ☐ value inventory for balance sheet purposes;
- ☐ list the essential requirements of Accounting Standard: 2 regarding valuation of inventories, and
- ☐ explain the meaning of certain key terms.

MEANING OF INVENTORY

Inventories are unconsumed or unsold goods purchased or manufactured. According to the International Accounting Standard: 2 (IAS: 2), inventories are tangible property.

(a) held for sale in the ordinary course of business,

(b) in the process of production for such sale, or

(c) to be consumed in the production of goods or services for sale.

Thus, the term inventory includes stock of (i) finished goods, (ii) work in-progress and (iii) raw materials and components. In case of a trading concern inventory primarily consists of finished goods while in case of a manufacturing concern, inventory consists of raw materials, components, stores, work-in-process and finished goods.

OBJECTIVES OF INVENTORY VALUATION

Inventory has to be properly valued because of the following reasons:

(i) **Determination of income.** The valuation of inventory is necessary for determining the true income earned by a business during a particular period. Gross profit is the excess of sales over cost of goods sold. Cost of goods sold is ascertained by adding opening inventory to and deducting closing inventory from purchases.

(*ii*) **Determination of financial position.** The inventory at the end of a period is to be shown as a current asset in the balance sheet of the business. In case the inventory is not properly valued, the balance sheet will not disclose the correct financial position of the business.

INVENTORY SYSTEMS

Records pertaining to quantity and value of inventory-in-hand can be maintained according to any of the following two systems:

(*i*) Periodic Inventory system.

(*ii*) Perpetual Inventory system.

Periodic Inventory System

In case of this system the quantity and value of inventory is found out only at the end of the accounting period after having a physical verification of the units in hand. The system does not provide the information regarding the quantity and value of materials in hand on a continuous basis. The cost of materials used is obtained by adding the total value of inventory purchased during the period to the value of inventory in hand in the beginning of the period and subtracting the value of inventory at the end of the period. For example, if the inventory in the beginning was 1,000 units of Rs 10,000, purchases during the period were of 5,000 units of Rs 50,000 and the closing inventory 1,500 units of Rs 15,000, the cost of materials used will be taken as Rs 45,000 (*i.e.*, Rs 10,000 + Rs 50,000 − Rs 15,000). It is, thus, assumed that materials not in stock have been used. No accounting is done for shrinkage, losses, theft and wastage.

Perpetual Inventory System

It is also known an Automatic Inventory System.

According to the Chartered Institute of Management Accountants London, it is "a system of records maintained by the controlling department, which reflects the physical movement of stocks and their current balance." The definition given by Wheldon is more exhaustive and explanatory. According to him, it is "a method of recording inventory balances after every receipt and issue, to facilitate regular checking and to obviate closing down for stocktaking".[1] In case of this system the stores ledger gives balance of raw materials, work-in-progress ledger gives the balance of work-in-progress and finished goods ledger gives the balance of finished goods in hand on a continuing basis. The basic objective of this system is to make available details about the quantity and value of stock of each item at all times. The system, thus, provides a rigid control over stock of materials as physical stock can regularly be verified with the stock records kept in the stores and the cost office.

METHODS OF VALUATION OF INVENTORIES

According to International Accounting Standard: 2 (IAS: 2), the inventories should be valued at the lower of "historical cost" and "net realisable value".

Historical Cost

Historical cost of inventories is the aggregate of costs of purchase, costs of conversion and other costs incurred in bringing the inventories to their present location and condition.[2]

---

[1] "Cost Accounting & Costing Methods", 13th edition, p.60.
[2] International Accounting Standard: 2.

Thus Historical cost includes not only the price paid for acquisition of inventories but also all costs incurred for bringing and making them fit for use in production or for sale *e.g.* transportation costs, duties paid, insurance-in-transit, manufacturing expenses, wages paid or manufacturing expenses incurred for converting raw materials into finished products etc. Selling expenses such an advertisement expenses or storage costs should not be included.

A major objective of accounting for inventories is the proper determination of income through the process of matching appropriate costs against revenues. It requires assigning of proper costs to inventory as well as goods sold.

However, it should be noted that assigning of such costs need not conform to the physical flow of goods.

The various methods for assigning historical costs to inventory and goods sold are being explained below.

1. Specific Identification Method

According to this method each item of inventory is identified with its cost. The total of the various costs so identified constitute the value of inventory. This method is generally used when the materials or goods have been purchased for a specific job or customer. Such materials or goods when received are earmarked for the job or customer for whom they are purchased and are issued or sold to the particular job or customer whenever demanded.

This technique of inventory valuation can be adopted only by a company which is handling a small number of items. In case of a manufacturing company having a number of inventory items, it is almost impossible to identify the cost of each individual item of inventory. Thus, this method is inappropriate in most cases on account of practical considerations. Moreover, the method opens door to income manipulation when like items are purchased at different prices. For example, a company purchases 10,000 units of an item in equal lots of 2,500 each at costs of Rs 2.50, Rs 3, Rs 3.50 and Rs 4 per unit. It sells 7,500 units at Rs 4 per unit. In case the management follows this method for valuation of inventory, it can determine the income reported for the period by selecting that lot of units which will produce the desired objective. If it is assumed that the inventory consists of the last lot purchased, the value of the inventory would be a sum of Rs 10,000 as compared to the presumption that the inventory consists of units purchased in the first lot in which case the value of inventory would be Rs 6,250. The working of the system can be understood with the help of the following illustration.

Illustration 4.1. The following is the record of receipts of certain materials during the month of February, 1988:

Feb. 1   Received 400 units for Job No. 12 @ Rs 10 per unit.
Feb. 4   Received 300 units for Job No. 13 @ Rs 11 per unit.
Feb. 16   Received 200 units for Job No. 14 @ Rs 12 per unit,
Feb. 25   Received 400 units for Job No. 15 @ Rs 13 per unit.
During February 1988 following issue of materials are made.
Feb. 10   Issued 200 units to Job No. 12.
Feb. 15   Issued 100 units to Job No. 13.
Feb. 17   Issued 200 units to Job No. 12.
Feb. 20   Issued 200 units to Job No. 14.
Feb. 26   Issued 100 units to Job No. 13.
Feb. 28   Issued 200 units to Job No. 15.

Show how these transactions will appear in the Stores Ledger and state the amount of inventory of Feb. 28, 1988.

Solution:

Stores Ledger

Date	Receipts				Issues						Balance	
	Job No.	Qty.	Rate Rs	Amt. Rs	Date	Job No.	Qty.	Due	Rate Rs	Amt. Rs	Qty.	Amt. Rs
1988					1988							
Feb. 1	12	400	10	4,000	Feb.	...	...	...	...	...	400	4,000
Feb. 4	13	300	11	3,300	...	...	...	...	...	...	700	7,300
					10	12	200	200	10	2,000	500	5,300
					15	13	100	200	11	1,100	400	4,200
Feb. 16	16	200	12	2,400	...	...	...	...	...	...	600	6,600
					17	12	200	...	10	2,000	400	4,600
					20	14	200	...	12	2,400	200	2,200
Feb. 25	15	400	13	5,200	...	...	...	...	...	...	600	7,400
					26	13	100	100	11	1,100	500	6,300
					28	15	200	200	13	2,600	300	3,700
Total		1,300		14,900			1,000			11,200	300	3,700*

*This consists of:

	Rs
100 units for Job No. 13 @ Rs 11 per unit	1,100
200 units for Job No. 15 @ Rs 13 per unit	2,600
300 units	3,700

2. First In First Out Method (FIFO)

Under this method, it is assumed that the materials/goods first received are the first to be issued/sold. Thus, according to this method, the inventory on a particular date is presumed to be composed of the items which have been acquired most recently. The working of this method can be understood with the following illustration.

Illustration 4.2. The following are the details regarding purchases of a certain item during the month of January.

January 1	Purchases	200 units	@ Rs 7	Rs 1,400
January 8	Purchases	900 units	@ Rs 8	Rs 7,200
January 25	Purchases	300 units	@ Rs 9	Rs 2,700
January 30	Purchases	400 units	@ Rs 10	Rs 4,000
				Rs 15,300

A physical inventory of the items taken on January 31 shows that there are 700 units in hand. You are required to calculate the value of the inventory according FIFO method.

Solution:

In case of FIFO method, the inventory is presumed to be consisting of items purchased most recently. Accordingly the value of the inventory on 31st January will be as follows:

January 31	Purchases	400 units	@ Rs 10	Rs 4,000
January 25	Purchases	300 units	@ Rs 9	Rs 2,700
				Rs 6,700

In the above case, the valuation of inventory has been done on the presumption that the concern follows "periodic inventory system". Of course, in case of *FIFO* method, the value of inventory would remain the same even if the perpetual inventory system is followed. For example, if out of 1,100 units issued, 150 units were issued of January 4, while 950 units were issued on January 10, the valuation of inventory using perpetual inventory system will be calculated as follows:

Stock Ledger

Date	Receipts			Issues			Balance	
	Qty.	Rate	Amount	Qty.	Rate	Amount	Qty.	Amount
January 1	200	7	1,400	—	—	—	200	1,400
January 4	—	—	—	150	7	1,050	50	350
January 8	900	8	7,200	—	—	—	950	7,550
January 10	—	—	—	50	7	350	—	—
				900	8	7,200		
January 25	300	9	2,700	—	—	—	300	2,700
January 30	400	10	4,000	—	—	—	700	6,700

It is clear from the above that the value of the inventory in case of periodic inventory system as well as perpetual system is the same *i.e.*, Rs 6,700, if the *FIFO* method is followed. The cost of goods sold in both the cases, therefore, also amounts to Rs 8,600 (*i.e.*, Rs 15,300 – Rs 6,700).

Advantages. The *FIFO* method has the following advantages:

1. It values stock nearer to current market prices since stock is presumed to be consisting of the most recent purchases.
2. It is based on cost and, therefore, no unrealised profit enters into the financial accounts of the company.
3. The method is realistic since it takes into account the normal procedure of utilising/selling those materials/goods which have been longest in stock.

Disadvantages. The method suffers from the following disadvantages:

1. It involves complicated calculations and hence increases the possibility of clerical errors.
2. Comparison between different jobs using the same type of material becomes some times difficult. A job commenced a few minutes after another job may have to bear an entirely different charge for materials because the first job completely exhausted the supply of materials of the particular lot.

The *FIFO* method of valuation of inventories is particularly suitable in the following circumstances:

(i) The materials/goods are of a perishable nature.
(ii) The frequency of purchases is not large.
(iii) There are only moderate fluctuations in the prices of materials/goods purchased.
(iv) Materials are easily identifiable as belonging to a particular purchase lot.

3. Last In First Out Method (LIFO)

This method is based on the assumption that last item of materials/goods purchased are the first to be issued/sold. Thus, according to this method, inventory consists of items purchased at the earliest cost.

Illustration 4.3. Calculate the value of the inventory of January 31 from the following data using (i) periodic inventory system and (ii) perpetual inventory system.

Receipts				Rs
January 1	Inventory in hand	200 units	@ Rs 7	1,400
January 8	Purchases	1,100 units	@ Rs 8	8,800
January 25	Purchases	300 units	@ Rs 9	2,700
January 31	Purchases	400 units	@ Rs 10	4,000

Issued for sale			
January 6	100 units	January 15	400 units
January 9	200 units	January 27	600 units

Solution:

(i) Valuation of inventory under periodic inventory system:

				Rs
January 1	Opening inventory	200 units	@ Rs 7	1,400
January 8	Purchases	500 units	@ Rs 8	4,,000
	Total	700 units		5,400

(ii) Valuation of inventory under perpetual inventory system:

STOCK LEDGER

Date	Receipts			Issues			Balance	
	Qty.	Rate	Amount	Qty.	Rate	Amount	Qty.	Amount
January 1	—	—	—	--	--	—	200	1,400
January 6	—	—	—	100	7	700	100	700
January 8	1,100	8	8,800	—	—	—	1,200	9,500
January 9	—	—	—	200	8	1,600	1,000	7,900
January 15	—	—	—	400	8	3,200	600	~4,700
January 25	300	9	2,700	—	—	—	900	7,400
January 27	—	—	—	300	9	2,700	300	2,300
				300	8	2,400		
January 31	400	10	4,000	—	—	—	700	6,300*

*The value of inventory on Jan. 31.

Advantages: The method has the following advantages:

1. It takes into account the current market conditions while valuing materials issued to different jobs or calculating the cost of goods sold.
2. The method is based on cost and, therefore, no unrealised profit or loss is made on account of use of this method.

The method is most suitable for materials which are of a bulky and non-perishable type.

FIFO and LIFO Methods and Markets Fluctuations

Both *FIFO* and *LIFO* methods of pricing inventories are based on actual cost and hence both value the products manufactured at true costs. However, both have conflicting results in periods rising and falling prices.

In periods of rising prices. In periods of rising prices *FIFO* method will result in production being relatively undercharged since replenishment of stock will be at higher prices than the prices of issue of materials. On the same pattern the cost of goods sold will also be relatively deflated. Thus, profits will be inflated and there will be more liability for payment of taxes. The situation will be just the reverse if *LIFO* method is followed—the production will be relatively overcharged resulting in lower profitability, deflating profits and reducing income tax liability.

In periods of falling prices. In periods of falling prices *FIFO* method will result in production being relatively overcharged, resulting in deflating the profits and reducing the income tax liability. The reverse will be the case if *LIFO* method is followed. Production will be charged at the most recent prices of purchase of materials or goods, resulting in inflating of profits and increasing the tax liability.

In periods of rising prices the inventory will be valued in *FIFO* method at a price higher than that in case of *LIFO* method. The reverse will be the case in case of periods of falling prices. Thus, it may be concluded that in periods of rising price *LIFO* method tends to give a more meaningful income statement but a less realistic balance sheet, whereas *FIFO* method gives a more meaningful balance sheet but a less realistic income statement. The reverse will be the situation in periods of falling prices.

It may also be noted that no sweeping generalisation can be made regarding superiority of *LIFO* over *FIFO* or *vice versa*. Each method has its own merits and demerits depending upon the circumstances prevailing at a particular moment of time.

4. Highest in First Out Method (HIFO)

According to this method, the inventory of materials or goods should be valued at the lowest possible prices. Materials or goods purchased at the highest prices are treated as being first issued/sold irrespective of the date of purchase. This method is very suitable when the market is constantly fluctuating because cost of heavily priced materials or goods is recovered from the production or sales at the earliest. However, the method involves too many calculations as is the case of *FIFO* or *LIFO* method. The method has therefore, not been adopted widely.

5. Base Stock Method

The method is based on the contention that each enterprise maintains at all times a minimum quantity of materials or finished goods in its stock. This quantity is termed as base stock. The base stock is deemed to have been created out of the first lot purchased and, therefore, it is always valued at this price and is carried forward as a fixed asset. Any quantity over and above the base stock is valued in accordance with any other appropriate method. As this method aims at matching current costs to current sales, the *LIFO* method will be most suitable for valuing stock of materials or finished goods other than the base stock. The base stock method has the advantage of charging out materials/goods at actual cost. Its other merits or demerits will depend on the method which is used for valuing materials other than the base stock.

6. Next if First out Method (NIFO)

The method attempts to value materials issues or goods sold at an actual price which is as near as possible to the market price. Under this method the issues are made or cost of goods sold is taken at the next price, *i.e.*, the price of materials or goods which has been ordered but not yet received. In other words, issues of goods for further processing or sale are at the latest price at which the company has been committed even though materials/goods have not yet been physically received. This method is better than marked price method under which every time when materials or goods are issued or sold, their market price will have to be ascertained. In case of this method materials or goods will be issued at the price at which a new order nas been placed and this price will hold good for all future issues till a next order is placed. For example, 100 units of material *A* purchased @ Re 1 per unit are lying in the store and an order for another 100 units @ Rs 1.25 has already been placed. If a requisition of 50 units from a department is made, they will be issued to the department at Rs 1.25 per unit (*i.e.*, the price at which the materials are yet to be received).

The value of inventory on a particular date is ascertained by deducting the cost of materials issued or goods sold from the total value of materials or goods purchased.

Calculations of issue prices are complicated in this method and therefore the method is not widely used.

7. Weighted Average Price Method

This method is based on the presumption that once the materials are put into a common bin, they lose their separate identity. Hence, the inventory consists of no specific batch of goods. The inventory is thus priced on the basis of average prices paid for the goods, weighted according to the quantity purchased at each price.

Illustration 4.4. From the following details, calculate value of inventory on January 31 according to the weighted Average Price Method when the firm follows: (*i*) Periodic Inventory System and (*ii*) Perpetual Inventory System.

Jan. 1	Purchases	100 units	@ Rs 4 per unit
Jan. 8	Purchases	200 units	@ Rs 5 per unit
Jan. 20	Sales	100 units	
Jan. 25	Purchases	200 units	@ Rs 6 per unit
Jan. 31	Sales	200 units	

Solution:

(*i*) VALUATION OF INVENTORY UNDER PERIODIC INVENTORY SYSTEM

Jan. 1	Purchases	@ Rs 4	100 units	Rs 400
Jan. 8	Purchases	@ Rs 5	200 units	1,000
Jan. 24	Purchases	@ Rs 6	200 units	1,200
	Total		500	2,600

Weighted Average Price Rs 2,600/500 = Rs 5.2
Value of Inventory on Jan. 31: 200 units @ Rs 5.20 = Rs 1,040.

(*ii*) VALUATION OF INVENTORY UNDER PERPETUAL INVENTORY SYSTEM

Date	Receipts			Issues/Sales			Balance		
Jan.	Qty.	Rate	Amt.	Qty.	Rate	Amt.	Qty.	Rate	Amt.
1	100	4	400	—	—	—	100	4	400
8	200	5	1,000	—	—	—	300	4.67	1,400
20				100	4.67	467	200	4.67	933
25	200	6	1,200	—	—	—	400	5.33	2,133
31	—	—	—	200	5.33	1,066	200	5.33	1,067*

*Value of Inventory on January 31.

Weighted Average Price Method is very popular on account of its being based on the total quantity and value of materials purchased besides reducing number of calculations. As a matter of fact the new average price is to be calculated only when a fresh purchase of materials is made in place of calculating it every now and then as is the case with the FIFO, LIFO, NIFO or HIFO methods. However, in case of this method different prices of materials are charged from production particularly when the frequency of purchases and issues/sales is quite large and the concern is following perpetual inventory system.

The following comprehensive illustrations will further help the students in understanding the working of different methods.

Illustration 4.5. M/s Swadeshi Cotton Mills Ltd. take a periodic inventory of their stocks on chemical y at the end of each month. The physical inventory taken on June 30 shows a balance of 1,000 litres of chemical y in hand @ Rs 2.28 per litre.

The following purchases were made during July.

July 1	14,000 liters @ Rs 2.30 per litre.
July 7	10,000 litres @ Rs 2.32 per litre.
July 9	20,000 litres @ Rs 2.33 per litre.
July 25	5,000 litres @ Rs 2.35 per litre.

A physical inventory on July 31 discloses that there is a stock of 10,000 litres.

You are required to compute the inventory value on July 31, by each of the following methods:

(i) First in First out; (ii) Last in First out; (iii) Average Cost Method.

Solution:

(i) *First in First Out Method*

			Rs
July 25	5,000 litres @ Rs 2.35	=	11,750
July 9	5,000 litres @ Rs 2.33	=	11,650
Closing inventory on July 31: 10,000 litres of			23,400

(ii) *Last in First Out Method*

			Rs
June 30	1,000 litres @ Rs 2.28	=	2,280
July 1	9,000 liters @ Rs 2.30	=	20,700
Closing inventory on July 31; 10,000 litres of			22,980

(iii) *Average Cost Method*

			Rs
June 30	1,000 litres @ Rs 2.28	=	2,280
July 1	14,000 litres @ Rs 2.30	=	32,200
July 7	10,000 litres @ Rs 2.32	=	23,200
July 9	20,000 litres @ Rs 2.33	=	46,600
July 25	5,000 liters @ Rs 2.35	=	11,750
Total 50,000 litres of			1,16,030

$$\text{Average cost per litre} = \frac{1,16,030}{50,000} = 2.3206$$

Total value of Inventory on July 31 = 10,000 × 2.3206
= Rs 23,206.

Illustration 4.6. Following are the details regarding the receipts and issues of material X in respect of a firm.

Receipts: Jan. 1 Balance 50 units @ Rs 4 per unit
Jan. 5 Purchase Order No. 10, 40 units @ Rs 3 per unit
Jan. 8 Purchase Order No. 12, 30 units @ Rs 4 per unit
Jan. 15 Purchase Order No. 11, 20 units @ Rs 5 per unit
Jan. 26 Purchase Order No. 13, 40 units @ Rs 3 per unit

Issues Jan. 10 Material Requisition No. 4, 70 units
Jan. 12 Material Requisition No. 5, 10 units
Jan. 20 Material Requisition No. 6, 20 units
Jan. 24 Material Requisition No. 7, 10 units
Jan. 31 Shortage 5 units

The firm follows the perpetual inventory system for maintaining its stores records. You are required to calculate the value of inventory on Jan., 31 according to: (*i*) FIFO; (*ii*) LIFO; (*iii*) HIFO and (*iv*) Weighted Average Prices Methods.

Solution:

(*i*)

STORES LEDGER CARD (FIFO)
MATERIAL X

Date	Receipts				Issues				Balance	
Jan.	Ref.	Qty.	Rate Rs	Amt. Rs	Ref.	Qty. Rs	Rate Rs	Amt. Rs	Qty. Rs	Amt. Rs
1	Balance	50	4	200	...	...	...	...	50	200
5	P.O. No. 10	40	3	120	...	...	...	...	90	320
8	P.O. No. 12	30	4	120	...	...	...	...	120	440
10	...	...	...	...	M.R. No. 4	50	4	200	50	180
						20	3	60		
12	...	...	...	...	M.R. No. 5	10	3	30	40	150
15	P.O. No. 11	20	5	100	...	...	...	...	60	250
20	...				M.R. No. 6	10	3	30	40	180
24	...					10	4	40		
26					M.R. No. 7	10	4	40	30	140
	P.O. No. 13	40	3	120	...	...	...	...	70	260
31	...	...	...	...	Shortage	5	4	20	65	240*

*The stock consists of:

40 units	purchased on Jan. 26 @ Rs 3 per unit	=	Rs 120
20 units	purchased on Jan. 15 @ Rs 5 per unit	=	100
5 units	purchased on Jan. 9 @ Rs 4 per unit	=	20
		Total	240

(*ii*)

STORES LEDGER CARD (LIFO)
MATERIAL X

Date	Receipts				Issues				Balance	
Jan.	Ref.	Qty.	Rate Rs	Amt. Rs	Ref.	Qty. Rs	Rate Rs	Amt. Rs	Qty. Rs	Amt. Rs
1	Balance	50	4	200	...	...	...	...	50	200
5	P.O. No. 10	40	3	120	...	...	...	...	90	320
8	P.O. No. 12	30	4	120	...	...	...	...	120	440
10	...	...	...	...	M.R. No. 4	30	4	120	50	200
						40	3	120		
12	...	...	...	...	M.R. No. 5	10	4	40	40	160
15	P.O. No. 11	20	5	100	...	...	...	...	60	260
20	...	...	...	...	M.R. No. 6	20	5	100	40	160
24	...	.	...	...	M.R. No. 7	10	4	40	30	120
26	P.O. No. 13	40	3	120	...	...	...	...	70	240
31	...	...	...	...	Shortage	5	3	15	65	225*

*The stock consists of:

			Rs
30 units of the balance on Jan. 1 @ 4		=	120
35 units of the balance on Jan. 26 @ 3		=	105
			225

(iii)

STORES LEDGER CARD (HIFO)
MATERIAL X

Receipts					Issues					Balance	
Date	Reference	Qty.	Rate Rs	Amt. Rs	Date	Reference	Qty. Rs	Rate Rs	Amt. Rs	Qty. Rs	Amt. Rs
Jan. 1	Balance	50	4	200	...	...	...	...	...	50	200
Jan. 5	P.O. 10	40	3	120	...	...	...	...	...	90	320*
Jan. 8	P.O. 12	30	4	120	...	...	...	...	...	120	440
					Jan. 10	M.R. 4	70	4	280	50	160
					Jan. 12	M.R. 5	10	4	40	40	120
Jan. 15	P.O. 11	20	5	100	...	...	...	...	...	60	220
					Jan. 20	M.R. 6	20	5	100	40	120
					Jan. 24	M.R. 7	10	3	30	30	90
Jan. 26	P.O. 13	40	3	120	...	...	...	...	...	70	210
					Jan. 27	Shortage	5	3	15	65	195*

*This consists of units purchased on Jan. 5 and Jan. 26. This stock has been valued at the lowest price.

(iv)

STORES LEDGER CARD (WEIGHTED AVERAGE PRICE)
MATERIAL X

Date	Receipts				Issues				Balance		
	Reference	Qty.	Rate Rs	Amount Rs	Reference	Qty.	Rate Rs	Amount Rs	Qty. Rs	Amount Rs	Weighted Average Price
Jan.											
1	Balance	50	4	200		...			50	200	4
5	P.O. 10	40	3	120		...			90	320	3.56
8	P.O. 12	30	4	120		...			120	440	3.67
10					M.R. 4	70	3.67	256.90	50	183.10	...
12	...	...	...	...	M.R. 5	10	3.67	36.70	40	146.40	...
15	P.O. 11	20	5	100					60	246.40	4.16
20	...	...	...	...	M.R. 6	20	4.16	83.20	40	163.20	...
24	P.O.13	40	3	120	M.R. 7	10	4.16	41.60	30	121.20	...
26	...	...	...	...					70	241.60	3.45
31					Shortage	5	3.45	17.25	65	224.35	...

Net Realisable Value

According to International Accounting Standard: 2 (IAS: 2), the net realisable value means, "the estimated selling price in the ordinary course of business less costs of completion and less costs necessarily to be incurred in order to make the sale". Thus, net realisable value is to be calculated after taking into consideration all expenses which might have to be incurred for making sales. For example, if the seller will have to pay a commission of 20% on sales, the net realisable value of an article having a selling price of Rs 10 should be taken as only Rs 8.

Inventories are to be valued at cost or net realisable value, whichever is less. The ascertainment of net realisable value of different items and its comparison with the historical costs can be done by any of the following methods:

1. **Aggregate or total inventory method.** According to this method, the total cost prices of the different items of inventories are calculated and the total so calculated is compared with the total of net realisable value of the different items of inventory. Inventory is valued at a price which is lower of the two.

2. **Group method.** According to this method, groups are formed of homogenious items of inventory. The cost and the net realisable value of each group so formed are found out. The lower of the cost or net realisable value of each group of items is taken for valuation of inventory.

3. **Item by item method.** According to this method, the cost and net realisable prices of each item of inventory are found out. Each item is valued at a price which is lower of the cost or net realisable value.

IAS: 2 has recommended the use of "group" or "item by item" method for valuation of inventory. The "aggregate or total inventory" method has not found favour with the International Accounting Standards Committee.

The following illustration will explain the difference between all the three methods.

Illustration 4.7. Following are the details regarding inventories of a manufacturing concern as on 31st December, 1991:

Inventory categories	Cost(Rs)	Market Price (Rs)
Category 1: A	6,000	9,000
B	10,000	9,500
Category 2: C	15,000	17,000
D	20,000	14,000
Total	51,000	49,500

You are required to determine inventory value using "lower of cost or market value basis", according to each of the following methods:

(i) Aggregate or total inventory method, (ii) Group method, (iii) Item by item method.

Solution:

DETERMINATION OF VALUE OF INVENTORY
at 31st December, 1991

Items	Cost Rs	Market Price Rs	Aggregate inventory	Group method Rs	Item by Item method Rs
Category 1: A	6,000	9,000			6,000
B	10,000	9,500			9,500

Contd....

Items		Cost Rs	Market Price Rs	Aggregate inventory	Group method Rs	Item by Item method Rs
	(i)	16,000	18,500		16,000	
Category 2: C		15,000	17,000			15,000
D		20,000	14,000			14,000
	(ii)	35,000	31,000		31,000	
Total inventory (i) + (ii)		51,000	49,500	49,500		
Inventory valuation (at lower of cost or market price)				49,500	47,000	44,500

Anticipated Price Declines

The principle that inventory should be valued at 'lower of cost or net realisable value' is applicable only to price declines which have actually occurred, and not to possible future declines in prices. This has also been clarified by the American Institute of Certified Public Accountants as follows:

'It has been argued with respect to inventories that losses which will have to be taken in periods of receding price levels have their origins in periods of rising prices, and that therefore reserves to provide for future price declines should be created in periods of rising prices by charges against operations of those periods. Reserves of this kind involve assumptions as to what future price levels will be, what inventory quantities will be on hand if and when a major decline takes place, and finally whether loss to the business will be measured by the amount of the decline in prices. The bases for such assumptions are so uncertain that any conclusions drawn from them would generally seem to be speculative guesses rather than informed judgments.'[1]

VALUATION OF INVENTORY FOR BALANCE SHEET PURPOSES

In the preceding pages, we have explained that inventory is to be valued at cost or market price, whichever is less. We have also explained the various methods for calculation of the cost as well as the market price. However, in certain cases, it will not be possible for the business to take inventory on the date of the balance sheet. The inventory might have been taken on a date earlier or later than the date of the balance sheet. In such a case the value of inventory on the date of the balance sheet can be found out by making suitable adjustments in the value of the inventory as taken on a particular date. Some of the important adjustments and their treatment are explained below:

(i) **If inventory is taken on a date after the balance sheet date.** For example, if the balance sheet is to be prepared as on 31st December, 1991 and the inventory has been taken as on 31st January, 1992, the following adjustments will generally be required:

Inventory as on 31st January, 1992
Less: Purchases made between 1st January, 1992 to 31st January, 1992 ......
Less: Sales returns (at cost price between Jan. 1, 1992 to 31st Jan. 1992) ......
Add: Sales (at cost price between 1 Jan. 1992 to 31st Jan. 1992) ......
Add: Purchases returns between 1 January, 1992 to 31st January, 1992 ......
Value of Inventory as on 31st Dec., 1991

[1] Accounting Research and Terminology Bulletin, Final Edition Ch. 6, p. 42.

(*ii*) **If inventory is taken on a date before the balance sheet date.** In case the inventory is taken, 'say' on 30th November, 1992 and the balance sheet is to be prepared as on 31st December, 1992, the above adjustment will be done in a reverse order taking inventory as on 30th November, 1991 as the base. In other words, items which have been added above will be subtracted and items which have been subtracted will be added to find out the inventory as on 31st December, 1992.

Particular care has to be taken of the items which have been sold at a rate of gross profit lower or higher than the normal rate of gross profit.

The following illustrations will help the students in understanding the various adjustments required for valuation of inventories.

Illustration 4.8. Mr. Vijay's financial year ends on 30th June 1987, but actual stock is not taken until the following 8th July, 1987, when it is ascertained at Rs 7,425.

You find that :

(1) Sales are entered in the sales book on the same day as despatched and returns inward in the return inward book the day the goods are received back.

(2) Purchases are entered in the Purchases day book as the invoices are received.

(3) Sales between 30th June 1987 and 8th July 1987 as per the sales day book and cash book are Rs 8,600.

(4) Purchases between 30th June 1987 and 8th July 1987 as per the Purchases day book are Rs 660 but, of these goods amounting to Rs 60 are not received until after the stock was taken.

(5) Goods invoiced during the June (before 30th June) but not received until after 30th June amounted to Rs 500 of which Rs 350 worth are received between 30th June 1987 and 8th July 1987.

(6) Rate of Gross Profit is 33 ⅓% on cost.

Ascertain the value of Stock on 30th June, 1987. *(C.A. Entrance, Nov., 1987)*

Solution:

COMPUTATION OF STOCK
as on 30th June 1987

Particulars		Rs
Stock as on 8th July, 1987		7,425
Add: Cost of goods sold:		
Sales	8,600	
Less: Gross Profit 25% on Sales	2,150	6,450
		13,875
Less: Purchases entered (between 30th June to 8th July)	660	
Less: Received after 8th July 1987	60	600
		13,275
Add: Purchases invoiced before 30th June, 1987 not received upto 8th July 1987 (500 – 350)		150
Stock on 30th June, 1987 ...		13,425

Illustration 4.9. The financial year of Mr. Philip ends on 31st March, 1989 but the stock on hand was physically verified only on 7th April, 1989. You are required to determine the value of Closing Stock (at cost) as on 31st March, 1989 from the following information:

(i) The stock (valued at cost) as verified on 7th April, 1989 was Rs 15,400.

(ii) Sales have been entered in the Sales Day Book only after the despatch of goods and Sales Returns only on receipt of the goods.

(iii) Purchases have been entered in the Purchase Day Book on receipt of purchase invoice irrespective of the date of receipt of goods.

(iv) Sales as per the Sales Day Book for the period 1st April, 1989 to 7th April, 1989 (before the actual verification) amounted to Rs 6,880 of which goods of a sale value of Rs 1,200 had not been delivered at the time of verification.

(v) Purchases as per the Purchased Day Book for the period 1st April, 1989 to 7th April, 1989 (before the actual verification) amounted to Rs 5,800 of which goods for purchases of Rs 1,500 had not been received at the date of verification and goods for purchases of Rs 2,000 had been received prior to 31st March, 1989.

(vi) In respect of goods costing Rs 5,000 received prior to 31st March, 1989, invoices had not been received upto the date of verification of stocks.

(vii) The gross profit is 25% on sales.

Solution:

STATEMENT SHOWING VALUE OF STOCK
as on March 31, 1989

Particulars	Rs	Rs
Stock as verified on April 7, 1989		15,400
Add: Cost of goods sold:		
Sales for the period April 1, 1989 to April 7, 1989	6,880	
Less: Goods not yet delivered	1,200	
	5,680	
Less: Gross Profit @ 25%	1,420	4,260
		19,660
Less: Purchases for the period April 1, 1987 to April 7, 1989	5,800	
Less: Goods not received upto April 7, 1989	1,500	
Purchases for which goods were received prior to Mar. 31, '89	2,000	3,500	2,300
		17,360
Less: Goods received before March 31, 1989 but in respect of which invoices have not been received yet*		5,000
Stock as on 31st March, 1989 at cost		12,360

*These have been excluded since purchase invoices are entered in the Purchases Day Book on their receipt, the date of the receipt of the goods being ignored.

Alternatively, the value of the stock may be considered to be Rs 19,360 provided an entry is passed Debiting the Purchases Account and Crediting Sundry Creditors by Rs 7,000, the cost of goods actually received prior to March 31, 1989 but in respect of which invoices have been received only afterwards.

Illustration 4.10. A firm has to take complete stock on 21st June, 1987 because of a deal for sale of business which fell through only at the last stage. As a consequence, it decided not to carry out stock taking on 30th June, 1987 when accounts were closed for the year. The stock on 21st June, 1987 was Rs 67,460. The following information is supplied to you regarding transactions in stock between 21st June, 1987 and 30th June, 1987.

1. Goods purchased from 21.6.87 to 30.6.87 amounted to Rs 4,820 out of which goods worth Rs 1,900 were received on 2.7.87.

2. Sales during the period from 21.6.87 to 30.6.87 amounted to Rs 16,800 including Rs 3,600 for goods sent of approval, half of which were still returnable on 30.6.87. The firm sells goods at cost plus 25% but there was one lot of goods which had cost Rs 2,800 but had to be sold for Rs 1,200 due to damage. The stock as on 21st June, 1987 included these goods at cost.

3. Unsold goods in the hands of a consignee on 30th June 1987 were revalued at Rs 3,200.

Prepare a statement showing the actual value of stocks as on 30th June, 1987.

Solution:

STATEMENT OF ACTUAL VALUE OF STOCK
as 30 June, 1987

Particulars	Rs	Rs
Stock as on 21st June, 1987		67,460
Add: Goods purchased between 21.6.87 and 30.6.87	4,820	
Less: Goods not yet received	1,900	2,920
Goods in hands of consignee		3,200
		73,580
Less: Cost of goods sold		
Sales	16,800	
Less: Goods still returnable by customers	1,800	
	15,000	
Less. "Special" Sale	1,200	
	13,800	
Gross Profit @ 25/125	2,760	11,046
		52,540
Less: Cost of goods included in stock on 21.6.87, since sold		2,800
Stock on 30th June, 1987		59,740

Note. If a separate Consignment Account has been opened, Rs 3,200 (for goods in hands of the consignee) may be excluded from the value of stock on 30th June, 1987. It is assumed the goods in the hands of the consignee were despatched to him before 21st June 1987.

ACCOUNTING STANDARD: 2(REVISED): VALUATION OF INVENTORIES

The following is the text of the Revised Accounting Standard (AS2 : Revised), 'Valuation of Inventories', issued by the Council of the Institute of Chartered Accountants of India. The revised Standard supersedes Accounting Standard (AS) 2, Valuation of Inventories, issued in June, 1981. The revised standard comes into effect in respect of accounting periods commencing on or after April 1, 1999 and is mandatory in nature.

1. Objective. A primary issue in accounting for inventories is the determination of the value at which inventories are carried in the financial statements until the related revenues are recognised. This statement deals with the determination of such value, including the ascertainment of cost of inventories and any written down thereof to net realisable value.

2. Scope. This Statement should be applied in accounting for inventories other than:

(a) work in progress arising under construction contracts, including directly related service contracts;

(b) work in progress arising in the ordinary course of business of service providers;

(c) shares, debentures and other financial instruments held as stock-in-trade; and

(d) producers' inventories of livestock, agricultural and forest products, and mineral oils, ores and gases to the extent that they are measured at net realisable value in accordance with well established practice in those industries.

---

1. Chartered Secretary, July, 1999

3. Definitions. The following terms are used in this Statement the meaning specified:

(i) *Inventories* are assets:

(a) held for sale in the ordinary course of business;

(b) in the process of production for such sale; or

(c) in the form of materials or supplies to be consumed in the production or in the rendering of services.

(ii) *Net realisable value* is the estimated selling price in the ordinary course of business *less* the estimated cost of completion and the estimated cost necessary to make the sale.

Inventories encompass goods purchased and held for resale, or land and other property held for resale. Inventories also encompass finished goods produced, or work in progress being produced, by the enterprise and include materials, maintenance supplies, consumables and loose tools awaiting use in the production process. Inventories do not include machinery spares which can be used only in connection with an item of fixed asset and whose use is expected to be irregular, such machinery spares are accounted for in accordance with Accounting Standard (AS) 10, Accounting For Fixed Assets.

4. Measurement of Inventories. Inventories should be valued at the lower of cost and net realisable value.

5. Cost of Inventories. The cost of inventories should comprise all costs of purchase, costs of conversion and other cost incurred in bringing the inventories to their present location and condition.

6. Costs of Purchase. The costs of purchase consist of the purchase price including duties and taxes (other than those subsequently recoverable by the enterprises from the taxing authorities) freight inwards, other expenditure directly attributable to the acquisition. Trade discounts, rebates, duty drawbacks and other similar items are deducted in determining the costs of purchase.

7. Costs of Conversion. The costs of conversion of inventories include costs directly related to the units of production, such as direct labour. They also include a systematic allocation of fixed and variable production overheads that are incurred in converting materials into finished goods.

8. Other Costs. Other costs are included in the cost of inventories only to the extent that they are incurred in bringing the inventories to their present location and condition. For example, it may be appropriate to include overheads other than production overheads or the costs of designing products for specific customers in the cost of inventories.

9. Cost Formulas. The cost of inventories of items that are not ordinarily interchangeable and goods or services produced and segregated for specific projects should be assigned by specific identification of their individual costs.

The cost of inventories, other than those dealt with in paragraph 9, should be assigned by using first-in first-out (FIFO), or weighted average cost formula. The formula used should reflect the fairest possible approximation to the cost incurred in bringing the items of inventory to their present location and condition.

10. Net Realisable Value. Inventories are usually written down to net realiable value on an item-by-item basis.

However, materials and other supplies held for use in the production of inventories are not written draw below cost if the finished products in which they will be incorporated are expected to be sold at or above cost.

11. Disclosure. The financial statements should disclose:

(a) the accounting policies adopted in measuring inventories, including the cost formula used; and

(b) the total carrying amount of inventories and its classification appropriate to the enterprise.

KEY TERMS

☐ **Historical Cost of Inventories:** It is the aggregate of cost of purchase, cost of conversion and other costs incurred in bringing the inventories to their present locations and conditions.

☐ **Inventory:** Tangible property to be consumed in production of goods or services or held for sale in the ordinary course of business.

☐ **Net Realisable Value:** The estimated selling price in the ordinary course of business less cost necessarily to be incurred to make the sale.

☐ **Periodic Inventory System:** A system of inventory accounting where the quantity/value of inventory is found out only at the end of the accounting period after having a physical verification of the units in hand.

☐ **Perpetual Inventory System:** A method of recording inventory balances after every receipt and issue to facilitate regular checking and to obviate closing down for stock taking.

TEST QUESTIONS

Objective type | TEST YOUR UNDERSTANDING |

1. State whether each of the following statements is 'True' or 'False'.
   (i) The valuation of inventory only affects the income statement.
   (ii) Periodic inventory gives a continuous balance of stock in hand.
   (iii) *FIFO* method correlates the current costs with the current market prices.
   (iv) Inventory should be valued at the lower of historical cost and current replacement cost.
   (v) *LIFO* method is suitable for items which are of a non-perishable and bulky type.
   (vi) Changes in the accounting policies relating to stock valuation are explained only to statutory auditors and not disclosed in the financial statements.

   [Ans. (i) False, (ii) False, (iii) False, (iv) False, (v) True, (vi) False].

2. Indicate the correct answer:
   (i) The test of objectivity and verifiablity is satisfied by valuing inventory at:
      (a) Historical Cost.
      (b) Current Replacement price.
      (c) Net Realisable Value.
   (ii) Inventory is valued at lower of the cost or net realisable value on account of the accounting principle of:
      (a) Consistency.
      (b) Conservatism.
      (c) Realisation.
   (iii) The system which gives a continuous information regarding quantum and value of inventory is known as:
      (a) Continuous Stock-taking.
      (b) Periodic Inventory.
      (c) Perpetual Inventory.
   (iv) The value of inventory will be the least in case of:

(a) Aggregate or Total Inventory Method.
(b) Item by Item Method.
(c) Group or Category Method.

[**Ans.** (*i*) *a*, (*ii*) *b*, (*iii*) c, (*iv*) *b*].

Essay type | FOR REVIEW, DISCUSSION AND PRACTICE |

1. Define "Inventory". Why proper valuation of inventory is important?
2. Discuss the different methods of inventory valuation with suitable examples.
3. Compare LIFO with FIFO as methods of inventory valuation.
4. Write a note on inventory valuation through "NIFO" method.
5. State the salient features of AS: 2 regarding inventory valuation.

PRACTICAL PROBLEMS

1. From the following data calculate the value of inventory on 31st Jan. 1990, by (*i*) *LIFO* and (*ii*) *FIFO* methods:

   1990

1st Jan.	Opening Stock	200 pieces @ Rs 2 each
4th Jan.	Purchases	100 pieces @ Rs 2.20 each
10th Jan.	Purchases	150 pieces @ Rs 2.40 each
20th Jan.	Purchases	180 pieces @ Rs 2.50 each
2nd Jan.	Issues	150 pieces
7th Jan.	Issues	100 pieces
12th Jan.	Issues	200 pieces

   [**Ans.** Stock *LIFO* 80 units of Rs 172 and *FIFO* 80 units of Rs 200]

2. Calculate the value of inventory using
   (a) Weighted Average Method.
   (b) the *LIFO* Method, or pricing issues, in connection with the following transactions:

April		Units	Value
1.	Balance in hand b/f	300	600
2.	Purchased	200	440
4.	Issued	150	
6.	Purchased	200	460
11.	Issued	150	
19.	Issued	200	
22.	Purchased	200	480
27.	Issued	250	

   In a period of rising prices such as above, what are the effects of each method.

   (I.C.W.A. Inter NS, Dec., 1977, adapted)

   [**Ans.** (*a*) 150 units of Rs 342, (*b*) 50 units of Rs 300]

3. Purchases of a certain product during March, 1992 are set out below:

   March 1 100 units @ Rs 10
   12 100 units @ Rs 9.80
   15 50 units @ Rs 9.60
   20 100 units @ Rs 9.40

   Units sold during the month were as follows:

   March 10 80 units
   14 100 units
   30 90 units

   No opening inventories.

You are required to determine the cost of goods sold for March under the different valuation methods, viz., FIFO, LIFO and Weighted Average.Cost.

[**Ans.** FIFO 270 units of Rs 2,648, LIFO 270 units of Rs 2,626, Weighted Average 270 units of Rs 2,639]

4. Oil India is a bulk distributor of high octane petrol. A periodic inventory of petrol on hand is taken when the books are closed at the end of each month. The following summary of information in available for the month of June, 1987:

Sales	...	...	Rs 9,45,000
General Administration Cost	...	...	Rs 25,000
Opening Stock: 1,00,000 litres @ Rs 3 per litre			Rs 3,00,000

Purchases (including freight in)

June 1	2,00,000 litres @ Rs 2.85 per litre	
June 30	1,00,000 litres @ Rs 3.03 per litre	
Closing Stock June 30	1,30,000 litres.	

Compute the following data by the first in first out, weighted average and last in first out method of inventory costing:

(a) Value of inventory of June 30.

(b) Amount of the cost of goods sold for June.

(c) Profit or loss for June.   (C.A. Inter NS, Nov., 1977, adapted)

[**Ans.**

Method	Value of Inventory Rs	Cost of goods sold Rs	Profit or loss Rs
FIFO	3,88,500	7,84,500	1,35,500
Weighted Average	3,90,000	7,83,000	1,37,000
LIFO	3,93,000	7,80,000	1,50,000]

[**Hint.** Administrative costs have not been included in the cost of goods sold]

5. The following details relate to the value of inventories of different items as on 31st December, 1991. You are required to calculate the value of inventory for balance sheet purposes on the basis of cost or net realisable value, whichever is less, by the following methods:

(i) Aggregate Method, (ii) Group Method, (iii) Item by Item Method

Articles	Group	Number of items	Cost per item (Rs)	Net realisable value per item (Rs)
A	X	5	10	12
B	X	4	14	12
C	Y	6	10	8
D	Y	10	15	20
E	Y	5	20	15
F	Z	4	15	10
G	Z	5	20	16
H	P	4	6	4
I	P	3	4	5
J	P	3	3	2

[**Ans.** (i) Rs 588, (ii) Rs 573, (iii) Rs 525]

6. FY Ltd. conducts physical stock taking every year at the end of the accounting year. Due to certain difficulties, it was not possible for it to conduct physical stock taking at the end of the accounting year ending 30th June, 1984. Physical stock taking was taken on 8th July 184 when it was valued at Rs 34,500.

The following transactions took place during 1st July to 8th July 1984:

(1) Net sales during the period were Rs 9,340. These goods were sold at the usual rate of gross profit of 25% on cost except goods which realised Rs 840 on the basis of 20% profit on cost.

(2) Purchases during the period were Rs 7,500 of which Rs 800 worth of goods were delivered to the company only on 10th July, 1984.

(3) Sales return during the period were Rs 1,500 of which 50% were out of the sales at 20% gross profit mentioned above.

(4) On 5th July, 1984, goods worth Rs 4,000 were received, which were to be sold on consignment basis.

You are required to prepare a statement showing clearly the value of the stock, to be taken into account in FY Ltd's final accounts for the year ended 30th June, 1984.

(C.A. Entrance, Dec., 1984)

(Ans. Value of stock on 30th June Rs 30,075).

7. On account of unavoidable circumstances M/s Mahesh Electricals could not do stock-taking on 31.12.1984. However the stock was taken on Jan 10, 1985.

The following are details of transactions from January 1st to 10th on which day inventory was taken:

		Rs
1.	Purchases in January upto 10th	45,000
	Goods received after 10th	5,000
	Purchase returns	3,000
2.	Purchases include special items for	11,000
3.	Sales	80,000
	Sales returns	2,000
	Sales of goods invoiced but delivered after 10th	8,000
4.	Sales include half the quantity of special items purchased for	6,600
	Balance left in stock	
5.	Gross Profit Ratio 25%. Inventory taken on 10th Jan.	1,75,000

Find out the value of stock as on 31.12.1984.

(C.A. Entrance, Dec., 1985)

(Ans. Value of Stock on 31.12.1984 Rs 1,91,050).

8. A trader prepares his accounts to 31st March, each year. Due to some unavoidable reasons, no stock taking could be possible till 15th April 1986 on which date the total cost of goods in his godown came to Rs 60,500. The following facts were established in between 31st March and 15th April:

(a) Sales—Rs 45,590 (including cash sales Rs 10,120)

(b) Purchases—Rs 16,710 (including cash purchases Rs 5,990)

(c) Sales Returns Rs 1,200

(d) Collections from Debtors—Rs 14,600

(e) Payment to Creditors—Rs 7,816

(f) On 15th March, 1986 goods of the sale value of Rs 6,800 were sent on sale or return basis to a customer, the period of approval being four weeks. He returned 40% of the goods on 10th April, 1986, approving the rest; the customer was billed on 16th April.

(g) The trader had received goods costing Rs 8,000 in March, 1986 for sale on consignment basis; 20% of the goods had been sold by 31st March, 1986 and another 40% by 15th April, 1986.

These sales are not included in (a) above.

Goods are sold by the trader at a profit of 20% on sales. You are required to ascertain the value of stock on hand on 31st March, 1986.

(C.A. Inter OS, Nov., 1976, adapted)

[**Ans.** Value of Stock Rs 79,366]

9. The Profit and Loss Account of Cardamom for the year ended 31st December, 1991 showed a net profit of Rs 1,400 after taking into account the closing stock of Rs 2,360.

On a scrutiny of the books the following information could be obtained.

(1) Cardamom has taken goods valued Rs 750 for his personal use without making entry in the books.

(2) Purchases of the year included Rs 300 spent on acquisition of a ceiling fan for his shop.

(3) Invoices for goods amounting to Rs 2,000 have been entered on 29th December, 1991 but such goods were not included in stock.

(4) Rs 250 have been included in closing stock in respect of goods purchased and invoiced on 28th December, 1991 but included in purchases for January, 1992.

(5) Sale of goods amounting to Rs 305 sold and delivered in December, has been entered in January, 1992 sales.

You are required to ascertain the correct amount of closing stock as on 31st December, 1991 and the adjusted net profit for the year ended on that date.

(C.A. Inter OS, May, 1972, adapted)

[Ans. Correct Closing Stock Rs 4,360; Correct Net Profit Rs 4,505]

10. A company closes its accounts on 31st December each year. It could not complete the physical verification of stock on 31st December, 1988; which continued upto 7th January, 1989. The stock is disclosed by the books was Rs 1,80,250. The following facts came to notice during physical verification.

(*i*) Goods received on consignment amounting to Rs 6,600 was included in stock.

(*ii*) Sales from 1st January, to 7th January, 1989 amounted to Rs 21,500 and included the following:

(*a*) Goods sent on consignment Rs 12,500 at invoice price, which is made up of cost plus 25%.

(*b*) Goods sent to branch at invoice price Rs 4,200. Invoice price is made at a profit of ⅙th of the sale.

(*c*) Goods sold for Rs 800 at a loss of 20% of cost.

(*d*) Other sales are at a profit of ⅓rd of cost.

(*iii*) Goods amounting to Rs 2,000 has been received in the stores but has not been passed through the books before 31.12.1988.

(*iv*) Invoices were issued for Rs 2,800 on 31.12.1988, but goods had not been delivered on that day.

Determine the value of stock to be taken for the purpose of preparing the final accounts of the company for the year ended 31st Dec., 1988.

(I.C.W.A. Final, Dec., 1979, adapted)

[Ans. Value of Stock Rs 1,91,050]

Chapter 5

INSURANCE CLAIMS

LEARNING OBJECTIVES

After studying this chapter, you should be able to:

☐ identify the major risks to which a business is exposed

☐ compute the amount of loss recoverable from the insurance company against a policy for loss of stock or consequential loss

☐ make necessary accounting entries and

☐ explain the meaning of certain key terms.

In the course of running the business, a businessman is exposed to a number of risks such as fire, burglary, accidents, etc. Out of all these risks, the fire risk is the most dangerous. In case it goes out of control, it may involve loss both in terms of property as well as human lives. A prudent businessman secures himself against such losses by taking a proper insurance policy. Such policy is usually taken for two types of losses: (i) loss to the property such as stock, plant, buildings, etc. and (ii) loss of profits on account of dislocation of the business.

 'n the present chapter, we are mainly concerned with estimating the amount of loss of stock and profits as a result of fire.

LOSS OF STOCK

A fire insurance policy can be taken for indemnification against loss of stock on account of fire. The policy is usually for a year. The insurance company agrees to compensate the insured for any loss that he may suffer on account of loss of stock on account of fire, in consideration of a certain amount being paid as premium.

The value of stock lost on account of fire can be ascertained by finding out the value of stock on the date of fire *less* the value of the salvaged stock. The value of stock on the date of fire can be ascertained as follows:

Computation of Loss of Stock

Stock in the beginning of the accounting year	. . .
Add: Purchases from the beginning of the accounting year to the date of fire	. . .
Less: Cost of goods sold (from the beginning of the accounting year to the date of fire)	. . .
Value of stock on the date of fire	. . .
Less: Stock of salvaged	. . .
Value of stock lost on account of fire	. . .

The value of stock can also be ascertained by preparing a Memorandum Trading Account. All figures relating to the opening stock, purchases, wages, sales, gross profit, etc. will be entered in the Memorandum Trading Account. The balancing figure will be the value of stock on the date of fire.

The amount of claim for loss of stock to be filed with the insurance company depends on two important factors:

1. Rate of gross profit. As explained above, for determination of the loss of stock, the information regarding cost of sales is necessary. This can be ascertained by deducting the amount of "gross profit" from the "sales" made by the business. The rate of gross profit can be ascertained on the basis of the performance of the business during the preceding 3–4 years. While calculating such rate of gross profit, any abnormal factor affecting the rate of gross profit should be ignored. For example, if certain damaged goods had to be sold away at a price lower than the cost of sale of such goods, they need not be considered for the purpose of determination of the rate of gross profit. Moreover, if the gross profit percentage is showing a definite trend (for example 5 per cent in the first year, 10 percent in the second year, 15 per cent in the 3rd year), it will be appropriate to use the weighted average method for finding out the average rate of gross profit.

2. Average clause. In order to discourage under-insurance, usually the "average clause" is inserted in all contracts of fire insurance. The object of inserting such a clause is to limit the liability of the insurance company to that proportion of the actual amount of loss which the insured amount bears to the actual value of the property. For example, stock worth Rs 40,000 is insured only for Rs 30,000 and if the loss amounts to Rs 18,000, the claim admitted by the insurance company will be as follows:

$$\frac{\text{Amount of loss} \times \text{Amount of policy}}{\text{Actual value of stock}}$$

$$\frac{18,000 \times 30,000}{40,000} = \text{Rs} 13,500$$

It is to be noted that the average clause comes into play only if it is proved that loss sustained by the insured is less than the sum insured. When the loss is more than the sum insured, the insured can recover the whole amount inspite of the average clause.

Illustration 5.1 A fire occurred in the premises of Agni on 25th August, 1997 where a large part of the stock was destroyed. Salvage was Rs 15,000. Agni gives you the following information for the period January 1, 1997 to August 25, 1997:

(a) Purchases Rs 85,000.
(b) Sales Rs 90,000.
(c) Goods costing Rs 5,000 were taken by Agni for personal use.
(d) Cost price of stock on January 1, 1997 was Rs 40,000.
   Over the past few years, Agni has been selling goods at a consistent gross profit margin of $33\frac{1}{3}\%$. The Insurance Policy was for Rs 50,000. It included an average clause.

Agni asks you to prepare a Statement of Claim to be made on the insurance company.

(C.A. Inter. Nov. 1997)

Solution:

STATEMENT OF CLAIM

	Rs
Closing Stock on 25th August, 1997 (as per Memorandum Trading Account)	60,000
Less: Salvage	15,000
Loss	45,000

		Rs
Application of Average Clause:		
Value of Stock on hand		60,000
Amount of Policy		50,000
Admissible Claim: $\dfrac{50,000}{60,000} \times 45,000$		37,500

Working Notes:

Memorandum Trading A/c of Mr. X
for the period ending 25.8.1997

Particulars		Rs	Particulars	Rs
To Stock (Opening)		40,000	By Sales	90,000
To Purchases	85,000		By Closing Stock	
			(Balancing amount)	60,000
Less: Drawing	5,000	80,000		
To Gross Profit @ 33.1/3%				
of sales		30,000		
		1,50,000		1,50,000

Illustration 9.2   On 30th June, 1996, accidental fire destroyed a major part of the stocks in the godown of Jay Associates. Stocks costing Rs 30,000 could be salvaged but not their stores ledgers. A fire insurance policy was in force under which the sum insured was Rs 3,50,000. From available records, the following information was retrieved:

(i) Total of sales invoices during the period April – June amounted to Rs 30,20,000. An analysis showed that goods of value Rs 3,00,000 had been returned by the customers before the date of the fire.

(ii) Opening stock on 1.4.96 was Rs 2,20,000 including stock of value of Rs 20,000 being lower of cost and net value subsequently realised.

(iii) Purchases between 1.4.96 and 30.6.96 were Rs 21,00,000.

(iv) Normal gross profit rate was 33 1/3% on sales.

(v) Salvage value of stock after fire was Rs 2,000.

(vi) A sum of Rs 30,000 was incurred by way of fire fighting expenses on the day of the fire. Prepare a statement showing the insurance claim recoverable.

(C.A. Inter Nov. 1996)

Solution:

STATEMENT OF CLAIM

Particulars	Rs
Stock on date of fire	5,00,000
Less: Stock salvaged	30,000
	4,70,000
Add: Fire Fighting Expenses *	30,000
Total Loss	5,00,000

Memorandum Trading Account

$$\text{Claim} = \frac{\text{Account of Policy}}{\text{Stock on date of fire}} \times \text{Total Loss}$$

$$= \frac{Rs\,3,50,000}{Rs\,5,00,000} \times Rs\,5,00,000 = Rs\,3,50,000$$

(i) Fire fighting expenses have been incurred for the purpose of salvaging the goods from the fire. Hence the same have been added to determine the total loss.

(ii) In case fire fighting expenses are not added, the actual loss would be Rs 4,70,000 (i.e., 5,00,000–30,000) and the claim would be Rs 3,29,900 as computed below:

$$\frac{3,50,000}{5,00,000} \times 4,70,000 = Rs\,3,29,000$$

Working Notes:

Jay Associates
MEMORANDUM TRADING ACCOUNT
1.4.96 to 30.6.96

Particulars		Dr. Amount Rs	Particulars		Cr. Amount Rs
To Opening Stock	2,20,000		By Sales	30,20,000	
Less: Abnormal Item	20,000	2,00,000	Less: Abnormal Item	20,000	
To Purchases		21,00,000		30,00,000	
To Gross Profit (33 1/3%)		9,00,000	Less: Returns	3,00,000	27,00,000
			By Closing Stock (Bal.fig.)		5,00,000
		32,00,000			32,00,000

Illustration 5.3 A fire occurred on 15th September, 1994 in the premises of X Co. Ltd. From the following figures, calculate the amount of claim to be lodged with the insurance company for loss of stock:

	Rs
Stock at cost as on 1st January, 1993	20,000
Stock at cost as on 1st January, 1994	30,000
Purchase-1993	40,000
Purchases from 1st January, 1994 to 15th Sept., 1994	88,000
Sales-1993	60,000
Sales from 1st January, 1994 to 15th Sept., 1994	1,05,000

During the current year, cost of purchase has risen by 10% above year's level. Selling prices have gone up by 5%.

Salvage value of stock after fire was Rs 2,000   (C.A. Inter. N.S. November 1974)

Solution:

TRADING ACCOUNT
for the year ending 31st December, 1993

Particulars	Rs	Particulars	Rs
To Opening Stock	20,000	By Sales	60,000
To Purchases	40,000	By Closing Stock	30,000
To Gross Profit (50% on sales)	30,000		
	90,000		90,000

Memorandum Trading Account
from 1st Jan., 1994 to 15th Sept., 1994

Particulars	Actuals Rs	At Last Year's Rates* Rs	Particulars	Actuals Rs	At Last Year's Rates* Rs
To Opening Stock	30,000	30,000	By Sales	1,05,000	1,00,000
To Purchases	88,000	80,000	By Closing Stock	66,000	60,000
To Gross Profit	53,000	50,000			
	1,71,000	1,60,000		1,71,000	1,60,000

* Last year's rates have been given only for information sake.

Amount of claim   The amount of claim shall be the equal to the value of the closing stock at current rates *less* amount of salvage, i.e. Rs 66,000 – Rs 2,000 = Rs 64,000.

Working Notes:
   (1) Gross Profit from 1st January to 15th September, 1994 has been first calculated at last year's rate, i.e. 50% on sales of Rs 1,00,000.
   (2) Closing Stock at last year's rate is the balancing figure, taking gross profit at Rs 50,000.
   (3) Closing Stock at current rates on FIFO basis shall be 10% higher than previous year's rate. It comes to Rs 66,000.

Illustration 5.4   On 1st April, 1990, the stock of Sri Vyas was destroyed by fire but sufficient records were saved from which the following particulars were ascertained:

Stock at Cost—1st January,1989	Rs 73,500
Stock at Cost—31st December, 1989	79,600
Purchases — 31st December, 1989	3,98,000
Sales — 31st December, 1989	4,87,000
Purchases — 1.1.90 to 30.3.90	1,62,000
Sales — 1.1.90 to 30.3.90	2,31,200

In valuing the stock for the Balance Sheet at 31st December, 1989 Rs 2,300 had been written off for certain stock which was a poor selling line, it having cost Rs 6,900. A portion of these goods were sold in March 1990 at a loss of Rs 250 on original cost of Rs 3,450. The remainder of this stock was now estimated to be worth its original cost. Subject to the above exception, gross profit had remained at a uniform rate throughout the year.

The value of stock salvaged was Rs 5,800. The policy was for Rs 50,000 and was subject to the average clause adapted. Show the amount of the claim for loss by fire.

   (*C.A.Inter. New Scheme, May, 1981,Nov. 1985, Nov. 1989 adapted; CS Inter, Dec. 1989*)

Solution:

STATEMENT OF CLAIM FOR LOSS OF STOCK BY FIRE

Cost of normal items [Working note (ii)]	Rs 54,600
Cost of abnormal items—one-half of original cost Rs 6,900	3,450
	58,050
Less: Value of Stock salvaged	5,800
Lost Stock	52,250

Amount of claim after application of Average Clause:

$$\frac{\text{Loss of stock} \times \text{Amount of Policy}}{\text{Value of stock on the date of fire}} = \frac{52,250}{58,050} \times 50,000 = \text{Rs } 45,004 \text{ or say, Rs } 45,000$$

Working Notes:
(i)

TRADING & PROFIT & LOSS ACCOUNT
for the year ending 31st December, 1989

	Rs			Rs
To Opening Stock	73,500	By Sales		4,87,000
To Purchases	3,98,000	By Closing Stock at Cost:		
To Gross Profit		Normal Items	75,000	
(4,87,000 × 20/100)	97,400	Abnormal Items	6,900	81,900
	5,68,900			5,68,900

(ii)

MEMORANDUM TRADING & PROFIT & LOSS ACCOUNT
for the period ending 31st March, 1990

Particulars	Normal items Rs	Abnormal items Rs	Particulars	Normal items Rs	Abnormal items Rs
To Opening Stock	75,000	6,900	By Sales	2,28,000	3,200
To Purchases	1,62,000	–	By Loss on Sales		250
To Gross Profit		–	By Closing Stock		
(20% of sales)	45,600		(Balancing figure)	54,600	3,450
	2,82,600	6,900		2,82,600	6,900

Illustration 5.5 Koustuth Fair Price Shop suffered loss of stock due to fire on August 20, 1997. From the following particulars, calculated claim to be made by the shop:

(1) Stock on December 31, 1995 (including stock purchased during
the year at Rs 8,000 valued at Rs 4,000 because of poor selling price) — 1,00,000

(2) Wages paid—1996 (including wages paid for the construction of
a showroom for which workers of the factory worked, Rs 2000.
Manufacturing wages Rs 1,500 were — 30,000

(3) Freight inwards—1996 — 5,000

(4) Purchases—1996 (including purchases of furniture of Rs 1,500
wrongly passed through invoice book) — 1,20,000

(5) Sales—1996 (including sale of 1/4th of the stock at Rs 1,000
which had a poor selling line and was value at Rs 4,000 on
December 31, 1995) — 2,46,000

(6) Stock on December 31, 1996 (including remaining stock which
had a poor selling line at the same value) — 42,000

(7) Purchases upto August 20, 1997 — 1,42,800

(8) Sales upto August 20, 1997 (including sale of 1/3rd remaining
stock which had a poor selling line at Rs 800) — 1,42,900

The remaining stock which had a poor selling line was considered at 80% of the original cost for the purpose of claim. The salvage was Rs 47,400. The shop had taken the policy of Rs 40,000. There was an average clause in the policy. *(C.S. Inter. N.S June 1978)*

Solution:

STATEMENT OF NORMAL GROSS PROFIT FOR 1996

Particulars	Rs	Rs
Sales (excluding poor line sale of Rs 1,000)		2,45,000
Less: Cost of goods sold (other than of poor line)		
Opening Stock (excluding of poor line)	96,000	
Purchases (excluding of furniture of Rs 1,500)	1,18,500	
Wages (paid Rs 30,000 plus outstanding Rs 1,500 less for		
showroom construction Rs 2,000	29,500	
Freight	5,000	
	2,49,000	
Less: Closing stock (excluding Rs 3,000 of poor line)	39,000	2,10,000
Gross Profit (G.P.)		35,000

$$\text{G.P. Ratio to sales}: \frac{35,000}{2,45,000} = \frac{1}{7}$$

STATEMENT OF UNSOLD STOCK
on August 20, 1997 (Date of Fire)

Particulars	Rs	Rs
Stock as at 1 January, 1997 (excluding of poor line)	39,000	
Add: Purchases to date of fire	1,42,800	
Cost of goods available for sale (excluding of poor line)		1,81,800
Less: Cost of sales (on normal selling line) upto fire date:		
Sales (excluding Rs 800 of poor line)	1,42,100	
Less: 1/7 being gross profit	20,300	1,21,800
Stock of normal selling line at fire date:		60,000
Add: Admissible value of poor line stock (80% of the original cost		
of Rs 4,000 remaining unsold upto date of fire)		3,200
		63,200
Less: Salvage		47,400
Stock lost by fire		15,800

Amount of claim after application to average clause

$$\frac{\text{Lost Stock} \times \text{policy Amount}}{\text{Stock at Fire Date}} = \text{Rs } 15,800 \times \frac{40,000}{63,200} = \text{Rs } 10,000$$

LOSS OF PROFITS OR CONSEQUENTIAL LOSS

Fire results not only in loss of property but also of profits to the business on account of its dislocation. Such a loss can be got covered by taking a loss of profits policy.

Amount of Policy

Considerable care should be exercised in determining the amount for which a loss of profit policy should be taken. The policy should be adequate to cover the likely amount of loss which the insured may suffer on account of dislocation of the business. The policy specifies both the period as well as amount it covers. While determining the amount of policy the insured should take into account not only the amount of net profit he earns but also the amount of standing or fixed charges which have been charged against the revenue for determining the amount of net profit. Of course, he may not get such incomes covered by the insurance policy which will not be affected by dislocation of his business on account of fire, e.g. income from investments, rent from the property let out, etc.

Illustration 5.6 A company has decided to arrange for a loss of profit insurance. You are asked to compute the sum for insurance from the following figures for the last financial year. It is anticipated that the current financial year turnover will increase by 10% and that all standing charges will remain unchanged.

PROFIT AND LOSS ACCOUNT

Particulars	Amount Rs	Particulars	Amount Rs
Variable Expenses	2,10,000	Sales	3,00,000
Fixed Expenses:		Interest on Investment	5,000
Wages of skilled employees — Adm. staff	30,000		
Depreciation	10,000		
Insurance premium	1,000		
Audit fee	400		
Directors' fees	400		
Travelling expenses	4,000		
Postage and telephones	300		
Trade subscriptions	100		
Rent, rates and taxes	3,000		
Net Profit	45,800		
	3,05,000		3,05,000

Solution:

AMOUNT OF POLICY

Particulars	Rs	Rs
Trading Profit:		
Sales	3,30,000	
Less: Variable Costs	2,31,000	99,000

The policy should be taken as Rs 99,000

Alternatively, the amount of policy can be ascertained as follows

Net Profit as shown by P. & L. Account	45,800
Add: Increase in profit on account of increase in sales	9,000
(Increase in sales – Increase in variable costs)	9,000
Fixed Expenses	49,200
	1,04,000
Less: Interest on investment (non-trading income)	5,000
Amount of policy	99,000

Computation of Claim

Loss of profit occurs because of loss of sales on account of dislocation of the business. Moreover, the insured may have to incur certain additional expenses to mitigate the amount of loss. There may also be certain savings in expenses of the business because of its being closed down for some period. All these have to be taken into account while calculating the amount of insurance claim. This has been explained below:

1. Short sales   The term short sales refers to the loss of sales on account of fire resulting in dislocation of business. This is the difference between the 'standard turnover' and the 'actual turnover' during the period of fire.

Computation of short sales requires the understanding of the following terms:

(a) *Standard turnover*   The term standard turnover refers to the turnover for the period corresponding with the indemnity period during the preceding accounting year adjusted in view of the trends noticed during the accounting year in which the fire occurred.

(b) *Indemnity period*   The term indemnity period refers to the period beginning with the occurrence of the damage, and ending not later than 12 months, thereafter during which the results of the business shall be affected in consequence of the damage. This period is selected by the insured himself. It is not necessary for the policy to cover the entire indemnity period. Of course, it is essential that, on the date of fire leading to partial or complete closure of the business activity, the policy must be in force.

Illustration 5.7   Fire occurs on 1st March, 1990 resulting in dislocation of the business activities for a period of 3 months. During the same period the sales in the last year amounted to Rs 10,000. However during the current year beginning with 1st January, 1990, the sales were showing an increasing trend of 10%. The actual sales during the period of dislocation amounted to Rs 4,000. Calculate the short sales.

Solution:

Computation of short sales:	Rs
Standard turnover (Rs 10,000 + Rs 1,000)	11,000
Less: Actual sales during the period of dislocation	4,000
Short sales	7,000

2. Rate of gross profit   The term gross profit here has got a different meaning than that of what is commonly understood. It is ascertained as follows:

$$\frac{\text{Net Profit} + \text{Insured Standing Charges}}{\text{Turnover}} \times 100$$

All the figures relating to net profit, insured standing charges, and turnover relate to the last accounting period.

In case of net loss, the rate of gross profit will be determined as follows:

$$\frac{\text{Insured Standing Charges} - \text{Net Loss}}{\text{Turnover}} \times 100$$

If all the standing charges are not insured, the amount of net loss will have to reduced as follows:

3. Loss due to short sales   The loss due to short sales is calculated by applying the rate of gross profit to short sales. For example, if the short sales are Rs 7,000 and the rate of gross profit is 20%, the loss of profit on account of short sales amounts to Rs 1,400 (*i.e.* Rs 7,000 × 20/100).

4. Increased cost of working   The insured may have to incur certain additional expenses to keep the business running during the indemnity period. Such increased working expenses will be allowed subject to a limit which is the least of the two figures resulting from the following:

(a) $\dfrac{\text{Net Profit} + \text{Insured Standing Charges}}{\text{Net Profit} + \text{All Standing Charges}} \times \text{Increased Cost of Working}$

(b) Short Sales avoided through increased cost of working × Rate of Gross profit

Illustration 5.8   Calculate from the following data the amount of permissible increased working expenses:

Short sales	Rs 10,000
Rate of gross profit	20%
Increased working expenses	Rs 1,000
Insured standing charges	Rs 5,000
Uninsured standing charges	Rs 3,000
Short sales avoided through increased cost of working	Rs 4,000
Net profit	Rs 5,000

Solution:

The amount of increased working expenses will be the least of the two limits, calculated as follows:

(i) $\dfrac{\text{Net Profit} + \text{Insured Standing Charges}}{\text{Net Profit} + \text{All Standing Charges}} \times \text{Increased Working Expenses}$

$\dfrac{5,000 + 5,000}{5,000 + 8,000} \times 1,000 = \text{Rs } 769$

(b) Short Sales avoided through increased Cost of Working × Rate of Gross Profit
$4,000 \times 20\% = \text{Rs } 800$

The increased working expenses will be allowed only to the extent of Rs. 769. Both the claim for loss of profit on account of short sales and increased working expenses should not exceed the amount calculated by applying the rate of gross profit to standard sales

Illustration 5.9

Standard sales	Rs 20,000
Rate of gross profit	20%
Actual sales	Rs. 4,000
Increased working expenses	Rs 1,000

Calculate the overall limit for loss of profit on account of short sales and increased working expenses.

Solution:

	Rs
Loss of profit due to short sales (16,000 × 20/100)	3,200
Increased working expenses	1,000
	4,200

However, the total of claim for increased working expenses and loss of profit due to short sales should not exceed Rs 4,000 (i.e. 20,000 × 20/100). This is on the logic that if the insured had not done anything, the maximum loss would have been restricted to this amount. Insurance company will, therefore, pay Rs 4,000 only.

5. Saving in expenses   Any saving in expenses will have to be deducted from the amount calculated as explained above.

6. Average clause   Finally the amount calculated will be proportionally reduced if the sum insured under the policy is less than the amount for which the policy should have been taken.

The amount for which the policy should have been taken is determined by applying the rate of gross profit to the turnover for 12 months immediately preceding the date of fire. Such turnover may have to be adjusted keeping in view the trend of sales in the accounting year in which the fire occurs.

Illustration 5.10

Short sales	Rs	20,000
Increased working expenses	Rs	1,000
Rate of gross profit		20%
Saving in expenses	Rs	200
Sales during 12 months immediately preceding the fire	Rs	1,00,000
Amount of policy	Rs	15,000

The sales are showing an increasing trend of 10% since the commencement of the accounting year.

Calculate the amount of claim to be admitted by the insurance company.

Solution:

Loss of profit due to short sales: (20,000 × 20/100)	4,000
Increased working in expenses	1,000
	5,000
Less: Saving in expenses	200
Claim for loss of profit and increased working expenses	4,800

However, the above claim will be subject to the average clause.

Amount for which the policy should have been taken: (1,10,000 × 20/100)	22,000
Amount for which the policy has been taken	15,000

Amount of claim to be admitted by the insurance company:

$$= \frac{\text{Amount of claim} \times \text{Amount of policy}}{\text{Amount for which the policy should have been taken}}$$

$$= \frac{4,800 \times 15,000}{22,000} = \text{Rs } 3,273$$

Illustration 5.11   From the following data, compute a consequential loss claim:

Financial year ends on 31st December, Turnover Rs 2,00,000

Indemnity period 6 months

Period of interruption—1st July to 31st October

Net Profit Rs 18,000

Standing charges Rs 42,000 out of which Rs 10,000 have not been insured

Sum assured Rs 50,000

Standard turnover Rs 65,000

Turnover in the period of interruption Rs 25,000 out of which Rs 6,000 was from a rented place at Rs 600 per month.

Annual turnover Rs 2,40,000

Savings in standing charges Rs 4,725 per annum

Date of fire—night of 30th June.

It was agreed between the insurer and the insured that the business trends would lead to an increase of 10% in the turnover.   (*C.A. Inter, New Scheme, May, 1979*)

Solution:

STATEMENT OF CLAIM FOR LOSS & PROFIT

	Rs
Computation of Short of Sales:	
Standard Turnover	65,000
Add: 10% increase in turnover	6,500
	71,500
Less: Sales during the dislocation period	25,000
Short Sales	46,500
Gross Profit on short sales @ 25%	11,625
Add: Increased cost of working, limited to Gross profit on Rs 6,000	
(sales resulting from increased expenses)	1,500
	13,125
Less: Saving in Expenses or Standing charges (4,725 ÷ 3)	1,575
Gross claim	11,550

Since the sum assured is less than the amount for which the policy should have been taken, the average clause shall apply.

Amount for which policy should have been taken:

25% of Rs 2,64,000 (i.e. Rs 2,40,000 + 24,000) = Rs 66,000.

$$\text{Amount of claim} = \text{Gross Claim} \times \frac{\text{Amount of policy}}{\text{Amount for which the policy should have been taken}}$$

$$= 11,550 \times \frac{50,000}{66,000} = \text{Rs } 8,750$$

Working Notes:

	Rs
1. Gross Profit Rate: Net Profit	18,000
Add: Insured Standing Charges (42,000–10,000)	32,000
Gross Profit	50,000
Turnover	2,00,000
Gross Profit Rate	25%

2. Increased cost of working: (lowest of the following):

   (i) $\text{Rent for premises} \times \dfrac{\text{Net Profit} + \text{Insured standing Charges}}{\text{Net Profit} + \text{All Standing Charges}}$

   $$= 2,400 \times \frac{50,000}{66,000} = \text{Rs } 2,000$$

   (ii) Gross Profit on additional sales: 25% of 6,000 = Rs 1,500.

3. The amount of Rs 13,125 (i.e. gross profit on short sales and increased working expenses) is within the overall limit of 20% of Rs 71,500.

Illustration 5.12   A fire occurred in the premises of a businessman on 31st January 1997, which destroyed most of the building. However, stock worth Rs 5,940 was salvaged.

The company's insurance policy covers the following:

		Rs
Stock	Rs	9,00,000
Building	Rs	12,00,000
Loss of profit (including standing charges)	Rs	3,75,000
Period of indemnity: six months		

The summarised Profit & Loss Account for the year ended 31st December 1996, is as follows:

Particulars	Rs	Rs
Turnover		30,00,000
Closing Stock		7,87,500
		37,87,500
Opening Stock	6,18,750	
Purchases	27,18,750	
Standing Charges	2,51,250	
Variable expenses	1,20,000	37,08,750
		78,750

The transactions for month of January, 1997 were as under:

	Rs
Turnover	1,50,000
Payments to Creditors	1,60,020
Trade Creditors: Balance as on 1.1.1997	2,26,000
Trade Creditors: Balance as on 31.1.1997	2,30,980

The company's business was disrupted until 30.4.1997, during which period the reduction in turnover amounted to Rs 2,70,000 as compared with the turnover of same period corresponding to the previous year.

Building was worth Rs 15,00,000 on the date of fire and three-quarter of its value was lost by fire.

You are required to submit the claim for insurance for loss of stock, loss of building, and loss of profit.

(C.A. Inter, N.S. Nov., 1980 & C.A. Final, O.S. May, 1977)

Solution:

(1) Claim for Loss of Stock

MEMORANDUM TRADING ACCOUNT
for the month ending 31st January 1997

Particulars	Rs	Particulars	Rs
To Opening stock	7,87,500	By Sales	1,50,000
To Purchases [Note (ii)]	1,65,000	By Closing stock (Balancing fig.)	8,25,000
To Gross Profit @ 15%	22,500		
	9,75,000		9,75,000

		Rs	
Closing stock as on 31st January, 1997		8,25,000	
Less: Stock Salvaged		5,940	
Claim for stock		8,19,060	

(2) Claim for Loss of profit

	Rs
Short Sales	2,70,000
Gross Profit Ratio [Note(iii)]	11%
Gross Profit on Short Sales	29,700

(3) Claim for Loss of Building

Loss of Building (3/4 of Rs 15,00,000) Rs 11,25,000. The building insured for Rs 12,00,000 only. Hence, the claim is subject to the average clause presuming that the policy contains such a clause.

$$\text{Amount of claim} = \text{Amount of Loss} \times \frac{\text{Sum Assured}}{\text{Value of the Property}}$$

$$= \text{Rs } 11,25,000 \times \frac{12,00,000}{15,00,000} = \text{Rs } 9,00,000$$

(4) Total claim (Rs 8,19,060 + Rs 29,700 + Rs 9,00,000) = 17,48,760

Working Notes:

(i) Rate of Gross Profit for the year ending 31st December, 1996:

TRADING ACCOUNT
for the year ending 31st December, 1996

Particulars	Rs	Particulars	Rs
To Opening stock	6,18,750	By Sales	30,00,000
To Purchases	27,18,750	By Closing stock	7,87,500
To Gross Profit	4,50,000		
	37,87,500		37,87,500

Rate of Gross Profit comes to 15% (i.e. Rs 4,50,000/30,00,000)

(ii)

TOTAL CREDITORS ACCOUNT

Date	Particulars	Rs	Date	Particulars	Rs
1997			1997		
Jan. 31	To Bank	1,60,020	Jan. 1	By Balance b/d	2,26,000
	To Balance c/d	2,30,980		By purchases (Balancing fig.)	1,65,000
		3,91,000			3,91,000

(iii) Calculation of Gross Profit Ratio for Loss of Profit

Sales for 1996		30,00,000
Net Profit + Insured Standing Charges:		
Net Profit	78,750	
Standing charges (assumed all insured)	2,51,250	3,30,000
Rate of Gross Profit	11%	

Illustration 5.13 The following are the details of certain fixed assets of *A* Ltd. on 1st April,

Building (Depreciation provided Rs 40,000) at cost	Rs 2,00,000
Machinery (Depreciation provided Rs 80,000) at cost	3,00,000
Furniture at cost	10,000

On December 31, 1990 a fire destroyed the entire premises including machinery. The Oriental Insurance Company admitted the following claims:

Buildings	Rs 2,10,000
Machinery	2,00,000
Furniture	6,000
Stock damaged	30,000
Stock destroyed	40,000
Loss of Profit	50,000

Depreciation on Buildings was provided at 5% p.a. and that on Machinery at 10% p a. on original cost. The amounts claimed for stock damaged and stock destroyed were Rs 50,000 and Rs 45,000 respectively. The claim admitted for loss of profits was for 5 months.

You are required to pass the necessary journal entries in the books of *A* Ltd.

Solution:

JOURNAL ENTRIES

Date	Particulars		Dr. Rs	Cr. Rs

1991 Dec. 31	Oriental Insurance Company
	    To Buildings
	    To Machinery
	    To Furniture
	    To Stock damaged
	    To Stock destroyed
	    To Profit & Loss Account
	    To Profit & Loss Suspense Account (for 1991 claim)
	    (Being claims admitted by the Insurance Co.)
		Dr.	5,36,000	2,10,000
				 2,00,000
				 6,000
				 30,000
				 40,000
				 30,000
				 20,000

	Bank Account To Oriental Insurance Company (*Being payment received from the Insurance company*)	Dr.	5,36,000	5,36,000
	Stock Damaged Account Stock Destroyed Account To Trading Account (*Being full value of stock credited to Trading Account*)	Dr. Dr.	50,000 45,000	95,000

	Profit and Loss Account
	    To Stock Damaged Account
	    To Stock Destroyed Account
	 (*Being loss on account of difference between full value of stocks and amounts admitted transferred to Profit & Loss A/c*).
		Dr.	25,000	20,000
				 5,000

	Depreciation Account
	    To Building Account
	    To Machinery Account
	 (*Being depreciation for 9 months on buildings @ 5% p.a. and on Machinery at 10% p a. on cost*).
		Dr.	30,000	7,500
				 22,500

	Building Account
	 Machinery Account
	    To Profit & Loss Account
	    To Capital Reserve
	 (*Amount recovered for building and machinery exceeds the book value less depreciation upto 31st Dec., 1990; the profit over the original cost credited to Capital Reserve*)
		Dr.
		 Dr.
			57,500
			 2,500
				50,000
				 10,000

	Profit & Loss Account To Furniture Account (*Being loss suffered on furniture since the amount recovered is less than the book value*)	Dr.	4,000	4,000

KEY TERMS

☐ **Average clause:** It is the clause which limits the liability of the insurer to that proportion of actual loss which the insured amount bears to the actual value of the asset insured.

☐ **Indemnity period:** The period beginning with the occurrence of the damage and ending not later then twelve months thereafter during which the results of the business will be affected in consequence of the damage.

☐ **Short sales:** Loss of sales because of dislocation of the business due to fire

TEST QUESTIONS

Objective type   TEST YOUR UNDERSTANDING

1. State whether each of the following statements is 'True' or 'False':

(i) The loss of profit policy covers loss of profits due to loss of sales as well as loss of standing charges due to their non-recovery.

(ii) The insertion of the Average Clause in an insurance policy results in bearing a part of the loss by the insured himself

(iii) It is not necessary to make any adjustment in the standard sales of the preceding period in the light of any change in future prospects

(iv) The term 'gross profit' in case of a loss of profit policy is different from the term 'gross profit' as used in case of a loss of stock policy.

(v) Any saving in expenses is to be deducted for determining the final claim.

[Ans. (i) True, (ii) True, (iii) False, (iv) True, (v) True]

2. Select the most appropriate answer.

(i) The main objective of the average clause is to

(a) encourage full insurance, (b) encourage under insurance, (c) discourage full insurance.

(ii) In case of average clause the loss is suffered by both the insurer and the insured

(a) in the ratio of risk covered, (b) in equal ratio, (c) only by insurer.

(iii) A plant worth Rs 40,000 has been insured for Rs 30,000, the loss on account of fire is Rs 25,000. The insurance company will bear loss of extent of

(a) Rs 30,000, (b) Rs 25,000, (c) Rs 18,750.

(iv) In case the net profit is Rs 10,000, insured standing charges Rs 5,000 and the sales Rs 1,00,000, the rate of gross profit will be (a) 10%, (b) 15%, (c) 5%.

(v) A property worth Rs 20,000 is insured for Rs 15,000. It is completely destroyed by fire. The policy contains an average clause. The loss to be born by the insurance company will be (a) Rs 15,000, (b) Rs 10,000, (c) Rs 20,000.

[Ans. (i) (a), (ii) (a), (iii) (c), (iv) b, (v) (a)]

Essay type   FOR REVIEW, DISCUSSION AND PRACTICE

1. Explain the meaning of a 'loss of profit policy'. Explain the various step you will take for ascertaining the amount of claim under a loss of profit policy.

2. Write short notes on the following:
    (a) Average Clause,
    (b) Short Sales, and
    (c) Standard Turnover.

PRACTICAL PROBLEMS

Loss of Stock

1. On 1st July 1996 a fire took place in the godown of Ramkumar which destroyed all stocks. Calculate the amount of insurance claim for stock from the following details:

Sales in 1994	Rs	2,00,000
Gross Profit on 1994	Rs	60,000
Sales in 1995	Rs	3,00,000
Gross Profit in 1995	Rs	60,000
Stock as on 1.1.1996	Rs	2,70,000
Purchases from 1.1.1996 to 30.6.1996	Rs	4,00,000
Sales from 1.1.1996 to 30.6.96	Rs	7,20,000

The following are also to be taken into consideration:

1. Stock as on 31st December, 1995 had been undervalued by 10 per cent.
2. A stock taking conducted in March 1996 had revealed that stocks costing Rs 80,000 were lying in a damaged condition. 50% of these stocks had been sold in May 1996 at 50% of cost and the balance were expected to be sold at 40 per cent of cost.

(C.A. Inter N.S., Nov., 1976, adapted)

[Ans. Claim for Loss of Stock Rs 1,46,000; Gross Profit Ratio 30%].

2. The whole stock of goods of Ram Ratan and Co. was destroyed by fire on 3rd February 1993. No stock register was maintained but the following particulars were available:

Stock at cost on 1st January 1992	*Rs* 26,580
Stock as per Balance Sheet as at 31st December, 1992	22,530
Purchases for 1992	62,310
Purchases from 1st January to 3rd February, 1993	22,410
Sales for 1992	91,500
Sales from 1st January, 1993 to 3rd February, 1993	35,400

While valuing the stock as on 31st December 1992, Rs 480 was written off out of the cost price of Rs 1,080 and this stock was sold in January 1993 for Rs 1,050. Except for this item, the ratio of gross profit was uniform throughout.

Value of stock salvaged was Rs 3,063.

The stock was fully insured against fire.

You are required to find out the amount for which claim for loss of stock should be made to the Insurer.

(C.A. Inter, O.S., May, 1973, adapted)

[Ans. Gross Profit Ratio 28%, Claim for Loss of Stock Rs 16,545].

3. The premises of Fire-proof Ltd. were destroyed by fire on 30.6.1999. The following figures were ascertained.

You are required to prepare a statement of claim in respect of loss of stock to be submitted to the insurance company.

Particulars	1996	1997	1998	1.1.1999 to 30.6.1999
	Rs	*Rs*	*Rs*	*Rs*
Opening Stock	2,000	2,200	1,180	3,402
Purchases	16,000	14,500	17,000	3,500
Sales	20,000	19,850	18,750	2,600
Carriage Inwards	500	300	500	100
Freight Outwards	600	600	300	25

In 1996, while valuing closing stock, some defective goods costing Rs 500 were valued at Rs 400. These were sold for Rs 450 in 1997.

In 1997, an item costing Rs 600 was wrongly valued at Rs 700. This was sold for Rs 550 in 1998.

In 1998, items costing Rs 1,200 were valued at Rs 1,000. 50% of these items were sold in June, 1999 for Rs 600.

Subject to this, the gross profit rate is more or less uniform. The value of salvage was Rs 800.

(C.A. Inter, N.S., Nov., 1979, adapted)

[Ans. Average Rate of Gross Profit 20%; Amount of claim Rs 4,202]

4. A trader took out a fire policy containing an average clause covering his stock for Rs 15,000. His practice was to base his selling price at cost plus 33 1/3%.

He closes his books on 30th June, every year.

On 31st March, 1998, a fire occurred at his premises and destroyed his stock. The salvaged stock was Rs 6,000. During the period of 9 months preceding the fire, his purchases amounted to Rs 61,000 and sales Rs 84,000. His stock at 1st July, 1997 was valued at Rs 20,000.

You are required to prepare a statement showing the amount of claim.

(C.S Inter June, 1990, adapted)

[Ans. Rs 10,000]

5. On 1st April, 1998, the godown of Hindustan Limited was destroyed by fire. From the books of account, the following particulars are gathered.

	Rs
Stock at cost on 1st January 1997	7,570
Stock as per Balance Sheet on 31st Dec. 1997	51,120
Purchases during 1997	2,71,350
Purchases from 1st January, 1998 to 31st March, 1998	75,000
Sales during 1997	3,51,000
Sales from 1st January, 1998 to 31st March, 1998	91,500
Value of goods salvaged	6,300

Goods of which original cost was Rs 3,600 had been valued at Rs 1,500 on 31st December, 1997. These were sold in March 1998 for Rs 2,700. Except this transaction, the rate of gross profit has remained constant.

On 31st March, 1998 goods worth Rs 15,000 had been received by the godown keeper, but had not been entered in the purchases account.

Calculate the value of goods destroyed by fire.   (C.A Inter, Nov 1988, adapted)

[Ans. Value of goods destroyed by fire Rs 71,160; Rate of Gross Profit 30%]

6. A fire occurred in the premises of Shri Romesh on 1st April, 1996, and considerable part of the stock was destroyed. The stock salvaged was Rs 1,12,000. Shri Romesh had taken a fire insurance policy for Rs 6,84,000 to cover the loss of stock by fire.

   You are required to ascertain the insurance claim due from the Insurance Company for the loss of stock by fire. The following particulars are available:

	Rs
Purchase for the year 1995	37,52,000
Sales for the year 1995	46,40,000
Purchases from 1st January, 1996 to 1st April, 1996	7,28,000
Sales from 1st January, 1996 to 1st April 1996	9,60,000
Stock on 1st January, 1995	5,76,000
Stock on 31st December, 1995	9,68,000
Wages paid during the year 1995	4,00,000
Wages paid during the 1st January, 1996 to 1st April 1996	72,000

Shri Romesh has on 1st June consigned goods worth Rs 2,00,000 which were lost in an accident. As there was no insurance the loss was borne by him in full.

Stock at end of each year for and till the end of calendar year 1994 had been valued at cost less

10%. From 1995, however, there was a change in the valuation of closing stock which was ascertained by adding 10% to cost.

(C.A. Inter, Nov., 1986)

[Ans. Gross Profit Ratio 20%, Amount of claim (after application of average clause) Rs 6,00,000]

Loss of Profits

7. A fire occurred on 1st July, 1990 in the premises of Arolite Ltd. and business was practically disorganised upto 30th November, 1990. From the books of account, the following information was extracted:

1. Actual turnover from 1st July, 1990 to 30 Nov., 1990   *Rs*   60,000
2. Turnover from 1st July, 1999 to 30 Nov., 1999   2,00,000
3. Net profit for the last financial year   90,000
4. Insured standing charges for the last financial year   60,000
5. Turnover for the last financial year   5,00,000
6. Turnover for the year ending 30th June, 1990
7. Total standing charges for the year   72,000

The company incurred additional expenses amounting to Rs 9,000 which reduced the loss in turnover. There was also a saving during the indemnity period Rs 2,486.

The company hold a "Loss of profit" policy for Rs 1,65,000 having an indemnity period for 6 months. There had been a considerable increase in trade and it had been agreed that an adjustment of 20% be made in respect of upward trend in turnover.

Compute claim under 'Loss of profit insurance'.

(C.A. Inter, New Scheme, Nov., 1981, adapted)

[Ans. Short Sales Rs 1,80,000; Rate of Gross Profit 30%. Addl. working expenses Rs 8,333. Amt. of claim Rs 49,872.50].

8. From the following information, find the claim under a loss of profit policy:

Sales in 1991	*Rs* 1,00,000
Sales in 1992	1,20,000
Sales in 1993	1,44,000
Sales in 1994	1,72,800
Net Profit in 1994	10,000
(All insured) Standing charges in 1994	7,280
Date of dislocation by fire 1.1.1995	
Period of dislocation 3 months	
Sales from 1.1.94 to 31.3.94	43,200
Sales from 1.1.95 to 31.3.95	11,840
Indemnity Period	9 month
Policy value	Rs 50,000

There was no reduction in standing charges during the dislocation period nor were there any additional costs.

(C.A. Inter, New Scheme, Nov., 1975, adapted)

[Ans. Amount of Claim Rs 4,000]

9. A fire occurred on 1st February 1997 in premises of Pioneer Ltd., a retail store and business was partially disorganised upto 30th June 1997. The company was insured under a loss of profits for Rs 1,25,000 with a six months period indemnity. For the following information, compute the amount of claim under the loss of profit policy.

	Rs
Actual turnover from 1st February to 30th June, 1997	80,000
Turnover from 1st February to 30th June, 1996	2,00,000
Turnover from 1st February, 1996 to 31st January, 1997	4,50,000
Net Profit for last financial year	70,000
Insured standing charges for last financial year	56,000
Total standing charges for last financial year	64,000
Turnover for the last financial year	4,20,000

The company incurred additional expenses amounting to Rs 6,700 which reduced the loss in turnover. There was also a saving during the indemnity period of Rs 2,450 in the insured standing charges as a result of the fire.

There has been a considerable increase in trade since the date of the last annual accounts and it has been agreed that an adjustment of 15% be made in respect of the upward trend in turnover.

(C.A Inter May, 1988)

[**Ans.** Gross Profit Ratio — 30%

Amount claimed before application of average clause — Rs 18,922.00

Amount of claim under the policy — Rs 39,390]

10. A fire occurred in the premises of Bala Shoe Co Ltd. on 1st May, 1995. The company had a loss of profit policy for Rs 1,20,000. Sales from 1st May, 1994 to 30th April, 1995 were Rs 10,00,000; the sales from 1st May 1994 to 31st August, 1994 being Rs 3,00,000. During the indemnity period which lasted for four months, sales amounted to only Rs 40,000. The company made up its accounts on 31st December. The profit and loss account for 1994 is given below:

PROFIT AND LOSS ACCOUNT
for the year 1994

Particulars	*Rs*	Particulars	*Rs*
Opening Stock	1,00,000	Sales	9,50,000
Purchases	6,00,000	Closing stock	50,000
Manufacturing expenses	67,000		
Variable selling expenses	90,500		
Fixed expenses	72,500		
Net profit	70,000		
	10,00,000		10,00,000

Comparing the sales of first four months of 1995 with those of 1994 it was found that sales were 20% higher in 1995. Ascertain the loss of profit.

(C.S Inter, June, 1989, adapted)

[**Ans.** Rs 32,000, G.P. Ratio 15%]

11. Stores Ltd which runs a shop makes up its accounts annually to 31st January. For the year ended 31st January 1994, the Profit and Loss Account was summarised as under:

		Rs 21,60,000
Sales		
Less: Cost of Sales (net after discount received)	9,38,400	
Wages	4,80,000	14,18,400
Gross Profit		7,41,600
Less: Fixed Charges (including shop assistants salary)		5,41,600
Net Profit		2,00,000

On 1st Oct 1994, a fire occurred as a result of which no trading was possible till Feb 1, 1995. On that date half the shop was reopened for business, the other half reopened on 1st April 1995. The consequential Loss Policy covered gross profit and workroom wages and accountancy charges at

Rs 5,000 or 2% of the amount of the claim before such charges, whichever is greater. The insurers agreed that:

1. Turnover increased by 15% p.a.
2. Workroom wages increases by 10% p.a.
3. The period 1st Oct. to 31st Dec. accounts for one-half of the annual turnover.
4. Fixed charges and wages occur evenly throughout the year.
5. Discounts received equal 1% of turnover.
   You are requested to compute the consequential loss claim.

(*ICWA Final, June, 1990, adapted*)

[**Ans**. Short Sales Rs 15,38,700; Amount of Claim including accountancy charges Rs 7,67,741]

12. On 31st December 1993, a fire damaged the premises of Shanker Ltd. and the business of the Company was disorganised until 31st March 1994. The company was insured under a loss of profit policy for Rs 1,95,000 with a six months' period indemnity.

    The company's accounts for the year ended 31st October, 1993 showed a turnover of Rs 5,25,000 with a net profit of Rs 60,000. The amount of standing charges covered by the insurance and debited in that year was Rs 1,50,000.

    The turnover for the twelve months ended on 31st December 1993 was Rs 5,85,000. The turnover during the period the business was dislocated amounted to Rs 60,000 while during the corresponding period in the preceding year it was Rs 1,27,500.

    A sum of Rs 15,000 was spent as additional expenses to mitigate the effect of the loss, there being however no saving in standing charges as a result of fire.

    Prepare a claim to be submitted in respect of the consequential loss policy.

    (*C.A Inter, May, 1985*)

    [**Ans**. Amount of Claim Rs 39,857, presumed that all standing charges are insured]

13. Bright Ltd. has a 'loss of profit' insurance policy of Rs 12,60,000. The period of indemnity is three months. A fire occurred on 31st March, 1999. The following information is available.
    Sales:

for the year ended 31st December, 1998	Rs 42,00,000
for the period 1st April, 1998 to 31st March, 1999	48,00,000
for the period from 1st April, 1998 to 30th June, 1998	10,80,000
for the period from 1st April, 1999 to 30th June 1999	72,000
Standing charges for 1998	9,60,000
Profit for 1998	3,00,000
Saving in standing charges because of fire	30,000
Additional expenses to reduce loss of turnover	60,000

    Assuming that no adjustment has to be made for the upward trend in turnover compute the claim to be made on the insurance company

    (*C.S. Inter, June, 1990*)

    [**Ans**. Rs 2,57,250]

14. A loss of profit policy was taken for Rs 80,000. Fire occured on 15th March, 1999. Indemnity period was for three months. Net profit for 1998 year ending on 31st December was Rs 56,000 and standing charges (all insured) amounted to Rs 49,600. Determine Insurance claims from the following details available from quarterly sales tax returns:

Sales	1996	1997	1998	1999
	Rs	Rs	Rs	Rs
From 1st January to 31st March	1,20,000	1,30,000	1,42,000	1,30,000
From 1st April to 30th June	80,000	90,000	1,00,000	40,000
From 1st July to 30th September	1,00,000	1,10,000	1,20,000	1,00,000
From 1st October to 31st December	1,36,000	1,50,000	1,66,000	1,60,000

Sales from 16.3.1998 to 31.3.1998 were Rs 28,000.

Sales from 16.3.1998 to 31.3.1999 were NIL.

Sales from 16.6.1998 to 30.6.1998 were Rs 24,000.

Sales from 16.3.1999 to 31.3.1999 were Rs 6,000   (*C.A Inter, Nov., 1990*)

[**Ans.** Short Sales Rs 80,400, Gross Profit Ratio 20%,
Average Percentage Increase in sales 10%, Amount of claim Rs 10749]

15. A fire occurred in the premises of a businessman on 30th June 1994.

From the following data, compute a consequential loss claim:

Financial year ends on 31st December

Turnover Rs 2,00,000

Indemnity period 6 months

Period of interruption—1st July to 31st October

Net Profit—Rs 18,000

Standing charges Rs 42,000 out of which Rs 10,000 have not been insured.

Sum assured—Rs 50,000

Standard turnover—Rs 65,000

Turnover in the period of interruption—Rs 25,000 out of which Rs 6,000 was from a place rented at Rs 600 a month.

Annual turnover—Rs 2,40,000

Savings in standing charges—Rs 4,725 per annum

Date of fire—30th June

It was agreed between the insurer and the insured that the business trends would lead to an increase of 10% in the turnover.   (*ICWA, Final, June, 1995*)

[**Ans.** Short sale Rs 46,500, G.P Ratio 25%, Gross claim Rs 11,550,
Net claim after application of average clause Rs 8,750]

16. Hiroo Idnoni effected a policy of insurance covering loss of profits and standing charges to the extent of Rs 46,000 (based on the previous year's profits) plus an allowance of Rs 8,000 for Profits and Standing Charges expected to accrue from increased turnover, the period of indemnity being three months. The turnover for the previous year ended 28th February was Rs 1,12,500 and for the ensuring year was estimated at Rs 1,35,000. A fire occured on 1st October.

The following relative figures have been ascertained:

Month	Sales (Previous year) Rs	Sales Budget Current year (Previous Year +20%) Rs	Actual Sales Rs
October	9,750	11,700	Nil
November	10,500	12,600	Nil
December	9,000	10,800	2,100

Upon investigation, it was found that the increased sales for the past seven months were overestimated by 50% and that the ratio of expense was consistent with such reduction.

The additional expenses of carrying on the business during partial disablement amounted to Rs 850. Prepare statement of claim against the insurance company and show workings.

(*C.S. Inter, New Scheme, Dec., 1977*)

[**Ans.** Short Sales Rs 30,075; Gross Profit 40.4%; Amount of claim Rs 12,998]

17. The premises of a company were partly detroyed by fire which took place on 1st March 1992 and as a result of which the business was disorganised from 1st March to 31st July 1992. Accounts are closed on 31st December every year. The Company is insured under a Loss of Profits policy for

Rs 7,50,000. The period of indemnity specified in the policy is 6 months. From the following informations, you are required to compute the amount of claim under the loss of Profits policy.

	Rs
Turnover for the year 1991	40,00,000
Net profits for the year 1991	2,40,000
Insured standing charges	4,80,000
Uninsured standing charges	80,000
Turnover during the period of dislocation (from 1.3.92 to 31.7.92)	8,00,000
Standard turnover for the corresponding period in the preceding year (from 1.3.91 to 31.7.91)	20,00,000
Annual turnover for the year immediately preceding the fire (from 1.3.91 to 29.2.92)	44,00,000
Increased cost working	1,50,000
Savings in insured standing charges	30,000
Reduction in turnover avoided through increase working cost	4,00,000

Owing to reasons acceptable to the insurer, the "special circumstances clause" stipulates for:
(a) Increase of turnover (standard and annual) by 10% and
(b) Increase of rate profit by 2%.

(*C.A. Inter, N.S., May, 1983; ICWA Final Dec.1983, adapted*)

[**Ans**. Gross Profit Ratio 20%; Amount of claim Rs 2,55,680]

Comprehensive Problems

18. Uttams Ltd., which runs a beauty parlour, draws its accounts annually at 31st December. A summarised Trading and Profit & Loss Account for the year ended 31st December, 1996 was as follows:

Sales		2,50,000
Less: Cost of sales (less discount) received	Rs 60,000	
Wages of workmen in parlour	40,000	1,00,000
Gross Profit		1,50,000
Less: Fixed charges		1,20,000
		30,000

On 1st Sept. 1997, a fire occurred and damaged the premises and no business was possible till 1st January, 1998, on which date one-half of shop was reopened for business and the other half was reopened two months later.

The consequential loss policy covered the following:
(i)   The gross profit, including discount received (i.e. sales less variable charges).
(ii) The parlour workers wages.
(iii) Fixed expenses Rs 3,000 or 2% of the amount of the claim before charging such expenses, whichever is higher.

The following points were also discussed and settled with the insurers:
(a) Increase in sales was 10% per annum.
(b) Parlour workers wages increased by 10% per annum.
(c) The turnover during the period from 1st October to 31st December accounts for a uniform half of the annual turnover and was uniform.
(d) Fixed expenses occurred evenly throughout the year.
(e) The rate of gross profit is steady.
(f) The discount of 10% received is uniform throughout the year.
(g) The amount of cover and period of indemity are adequate.

Compute the consequential loss claim for the period during which trading was affected by fire.

[**Ans**. Rate of Gross Profit 50% Short Sales Rs 1,69,584; Amount of claim Rs 1,23,450]

19. Mr Careful has insured his business against fire insurance for loss of goods, destruction of building, loss of profit, and standing charges as under:

Stock	Rs	10 lacs
Building		5 lacs
Loss of profit and standing charges		5 lacs

Fire occurred on the 31st of January destroying the stock, damaging the building and causing business distruption for a period of three months.

From the following particulars, prepare insurance claims on the above three heads.

The following are the transactions of the previous year ended 31st December:

Opening Stock	Rs	5,75,000
Purchases		21,00,000
Sales		24,00,000
Closing Stock		7,55,000
Standing charges		3,60,000
Other expenses		1,00,000
Dividends received		20,000
Net Profit		1,40,000

During the month of January in the current year, cash purchases amounted to Rs 1,89,000 and credit purchases for the month of January in the current year Rs 31,000.

Value of goods salvaged	Rs	1.05,000
Value of the Building		10 lacs
Damage to the building		6 lacs
Fall in turnover during the period of disruption		2,00,000
Turnover for January of the current year		2,00,000

(C.A. Final, O.S., November, 1981)

[**Ans**. Claim for Loss of Stock Rs 7,10,000, Building Rs 3,00,000, Profit Rs 31,667, Total claim Rs 10,41,667].

20. Tiny Tods Ltd. suffered loss by fire in 1990. They had got the various losses insured from the New Asiatic Insurance Co. The claims made against and admitted by the insurance company were as follows:

	Claimed Rs	Admitted Rs
Loss of Profits	30,000	20,000
Stock Damaged	20,000	10,000
Stock Destroyed	25,000	20,000
Building Damaged	6,000	5,000
Fittings Destroyed	5,000	4,500
Fire Expenses	400	400

Repairs to buildings cost Rs 5,500. Fittings were replaced at a cost of Rs 4,750. Fire expenses amounted to Rs 400.

The amount claimed and admitted for loss of profits were half in respect of profits in 1990 and 1991 and half in respect of advertising expenditure equally in 1990,1991, and 1992. The expenditure had been rendered partly useless on account of fire.

Renewals of fittings (which originally cost Rs 4,000 and had not been written down) to building were completed by and paid for on 31st December, 1990. The expenses were also paid on that date. The insurance company paid the sum admitted on 1st November 1990.

You are required to pass the necessary Journal entries in the books of the company.

[**Ans**. Amount debited to Profit & Loss Account on account of loss of stock Rs 15,000. Amount credited to P & L on account of excess recovery for fittings Rs 500]

2.114

21. *S & M* Ltd. gives the following Trading and Profit & Loss Account for the year ended 31st March 1994

TRADING AND PROFIT & LOSS ACCOUNT
for the year ended 31st December, 1994

Particulars	Amount Rs	Particulars	Amount Rs
To Opening Stock	50,000	By Sales	8,00,000
To Purchases	3,00,000	By Closing Stock	70,000
To Wages (Rs 20,000 for skilled labour)	1,60,000		
To Manufacturing Exp.	1,20,000		
To Gross Profit	2,40,000		
	8,70,000		8,70,000
To Office Administrative Expenses	60,000	By Gross Profit	2,40,000
To Advertising	20,000		
To Selling Expenses (Fixed)	40,000		
To Commission on Sales	48,000		
To Carriage Outward	16,000		
To Net Profit	56,000		
	2,40,000		2,40,000

The company had taken out policies both against loss of stock and against loss of profit, the amounts being Rs 80,000 and Rs 1,72,000. Fire occurred on 1st May, 1995 and as a result of which sales were seriously affected for the period of four months. You are given the following further information:

(a) Purchases, wages and other manufacturing expenses for the first four months of 1995 were Rs 1,00,000, Rs 50,000 and Rs 36,000 respectively.

(b) Sales for the same period were Rs 2,40,000.

(c) Other sales figures were follows:

From 1st January 1994 to 30th April 1994	*Rs*	3,00,000
From 1st May 1994 to 31st August 1994		3,60,000
From 1st May 1995 to 30th August 1995		60,000

(d) Due to rise in wages, net profit during 1995 was expected to decline by 2% on sales.

(e) Additional expenses incurred during the period after fire amounted to Rs 1,40,000. The amount of the policy included Rs 1,20,000 for expenses leaving Rs 20,000 uncovered. Ascertain the claim for loss of stock and for loss of profit.

All working should form particular answers.

(*C.A. Inter, May 1981, adapted*)

[**Ans**. Amount of claim for loss of Profit Rs 57,600 (i.e. gross profit on short sales Rs 45,600 plus additional expense Rs 12,000), Amount of ciaim for loss of stock Rs 80,000, Gross Profit ratio 28%].

Chapter 6

GOODS ON SALE OR RETURN

LEARNING OBJECTIVES

After studying this chapter you should be able to:

- [ ] Understand the meaning of sending goods to customers on sale or return basis;
- [ ] Make accounting entries according to different methods in case of sending "goods on sale or return" and
- [ ] Explain the meaning of certain key terms.

INTRODUCTION

A firm may send goods to its customers "on sale or return basis". In case of such a sale, the customers are given a stipulated time within which they should either send the goods back to the seller or send their approval. In case they do not send their approval within the stipulated time or if no time is fixed within a reasonable time, it is presumed that they have agreed to buy the goods.

The following are the essential features of goods on sale or return:

(i)   The goods are sent only on approval. There is no actual sale.

(ii)   The ownership of the goods passes to the buyer only when the buyer gives his approval for the goods.

(iii) The buyer is given a stipulated time by the seller within which he should approve or dis-approve the goods. In case the buyer does not send the approval of the goods, he should return them back to the seller or inform him accordingly.

The approval of the goods is said to have been given in each of the following cases:

(a)   If the buyer informs the seller of his desire to accept the goods, or

(b)   In case the buyer does not inform the seller about his disapproving of the goods within the stipulated time; or if no time is fixed within a reasonable time; or

(c)   If the buyer deals with the goods in a manner which shows that he has accepted the goods e.g. he pledges or sells the goods.

GOODS ON SALE OR RETURN

The customers are given a stipulated time within which they should either return the goods back or send their approval. In case they do not send their approval within this stipulated time, it is presumed that they have agreed to buy the goods.

ACCOUNTING TREATMENT

The goods sent to customers on 'sale or return' basis can be recorded by the following three methods depending upon the number of such transactions:

1. **When transactions are only casual**   In case "goods on sale or return" basis are sent casually to customers, the following procedure may be followed:

   (a) When goods are sent on approval, it may be recorded as an actual sale. The Journal entry will be:

Customer's A/c	Dr.
To Sales A/c	

   (b) On return of goods by the customer:

Sales A/c	Dr.
To Customer's A/c	

   (c) In case the customer sends his approval for the goods, no further entry will be passed in the books.

   (d) Goods not approved by the customers which have been either returned by them to the firm or lying with them will be included in the firm's stock.

   (e). In case, at the end of the accounting year, certain customers have not yet sent their approval and the return period has not yet expired, two entries will be necessary —

      (i) for cancelling the sales as recorded earlier and

      (ii) for inclusion of the goods in the stock of the firm by debiting the stock with the Customers A/c and crediting the Trading A/c.

   Alternatively, no entry may be passed in respect of such goods. In case the goods are returned next year, it may be recorded as a sales return.

2. **When number of transactions is more**   In case the number of transactions or sale or return is considerable, a separate "Sale or Return Day Book" may be maintained by the firm as a memorandum record. The book is in the following form:

SALE OR RETURN DAY BOOK

Goods sent on approval (1)			Goods approved (2)			Goods returned (3)			Balance (4)	
Date	Particulars	Rs	Date	Particulars	Rs	Date	Particulars	Rs	Particulars	Rs

The recording of transactions may be done in the following way:

  (i) *When goods are sold on approval.*   The details in respect of such goods are entered in the first column of the book only as a memorandum record.

  (ii) *When goods are approved.*   The details are entered in the second column of the book. The personal accounts are debited as and when goods are approved. The sales account is credited with the total amount at the end of the month.

  (iii) *When goods are returned.*   The details are recorded in the third column. However, no entry is made for such return of goods since no entry was made at the time when such goods were sent for approval.

(*iv*) *Balance of stock.* The balance of the goods lying with the customers ascertained and recorded in the 4th column. At the end of the accounting year stock with the customers A/c is debited and Trading Account is credited with the value of such goods.

3. **When there is a general practice to sell goods on "sale or return basis".** In case the firm deals in goods in respect of which there is a general practice to sell goods on "Sale or Return Basis", the following books or accounts are kept:

(*i*) *Sale or return day book.* The book is on the pattern of sales book. As soon as the goods are sold on "sale or return" basis, they are recorded in this book.

(*ii*) *Sold and returned day book.* The book records the goods retained and goods returned by customers out of the goods sent on sale or return. It has separate columns for "goods sold" and "goods returned".

(*iii*) *Sale or return ledger.* The book contains separate accounts of each of the customers to whom goods have been sent on sale or return basis and a Sale or Return Account for total goods sent on sale or return. This ledger may also be termed as a "Kacha Ledger".

(*iv*) *Main ledger.* This is the real ledger of the business. It contains all real, nominal, and personal accounts.

ACCOUNTING ENTRIES

(*i*) *On sale of goods on 'sale or return' basis:*

   (a) The sales are recorded in the Sale or Return Book.

   (b) In the Sale of Return Ledger, the customers accounts are debited with respective amount of goods sent on sale or return. The Sale or Return Account is credited with the total goods sent on 'sale or return' during a particular period.

(*ii*) *On return of goods by the customers.* In Sale or Return Ledger, the respective personal accounts are credited and the Sale or Return Account is debited.

(*iii*) *On approval of goods by the customers.* The following entries are passed.

   (a) To Customer A/c (in Main Ledger)   Dr.
        Customer A/c (in Sale or Return Ledger)

   (b) Sale or Return A/c (in Sale or Return Ledger)   Dr.
        To Sales A/c (in Main Ledger)

(*iv*) *For stock with the customers.* The balance in the Sale or Return Account in the sale or return ledger represents the value of the goods still lying with the customers for their approval. The balance of this account should tally with the total of the balance of the various personal accounts in the sale or return ledger. This stock with the customers is brought into accounts at cost by means of the following journal entry:

Stock with Customers A/c   Dr.
    To Trading Account

Illustration 6.1 Messrs. Awaaz Electronics supplied goods on "Sale or Return" basis, the particulars of which are as under:

Date of Despatch	Party's Name	Amount Rs	Date	Other Particulars
10.3.1990	ABC Co.	2,600	14.3.1990	Returned
15.3.1990	XYZ Co.	3,400	17.3.1990	Retained
20.3.1990	PQR Co.	1,900	25.3.1990	Goods worth Rs 800 returned
27.3.1990	XYZ Co.	2,200		No intimation till 31.3.1990
28.3.1990	PQR Co.	1,700		No intimation till 31.3.1990

The books of Awaaz Electronics are closed on the 31st day of March, each year.

Exhibit the entries as they would appear in the books of Awaaz Electronics, viz., the "Goods sent on Sale or Return Day Book", "Goods Sold and Return Day Book" and show how the "Total Goods on Sale or Return Account" would appear.

Solution:

M/S. AWAAZ ELECTRONICS
GOODS SENT ON SALE OR RETURN DAY BOOK

Date	To Whom Sent	L.F.	Amount
1990 March, 10	M/s ABC Co. Ltd.	—	2,600
" 15	M/s XYZ Co. Ltd.	—	3,400
" 20	M/s PQR Co. Ltd.	—	1,900
" 27	M/s XYZ Co. Ltd.	—	2,200
" 28	M/s PQR Co. Ltd.	—	1,700
			11,800

GOODS SOLD AND RETURNED DAY BOOK

Date	Particulars	Returned Rs	Sold Rs
1990 March, 14	M/s ABC Co. Ltd.	2,600	—
March, 15	M/s XYZ Co. Ltd.	—	3,400
March, 25	M/s PQR Co. Ltd.	800	1,100
		3,400	4,500

SALE OR RETURN LEDGER
ABC & CO.

1990	Particulars	Rs	1990	Particulars	Rs
Mar. 10	To Sale or Return A/c	2,600	Mar. 14	By Sale or Return A/c	2,600
		2,600			2,600

XYZ & CO.

1990	Particulars	Rs	1990	Particulars	Rs
Mar. 15	To Sale or Return A/c	3,400	Mar. 17	By XYZ & Co. (In Main Ledger)	3,400
Mar. 27	To Sale or Return A/c	2,200	Mar. 31	By Balance c/d	2,200
		5,600			5,600

PQR & CO.

1990	Particulars	Rs	1990	Particulars	Rs
Mar. 20	To Sale or Return A/c	1,900	Mar. 25	By Sale or Return A/c	800
Mar. 28	To Sale or Return A/c	1,700	Mar. 25	By PQR & Co.	
				(In Main Ledger)	1,100
			Mar. 31	By Balance c/d	1,700
		3,600			3,600

SALE OR RETURN ACCOUNT

1990	Particulars	Rs	1990	Particulars	Rs
Mar. 14	To ABC & Co.	2,600	Mar. 31	By Sundries	11,800
Mar. 25	To PQR & Co.	800			
Mar. 31	To Sales A/c				
	(In Main Ledger)	4,500			
Mar. 31	To Balance c/d	3,900			
		11,800			11,800

MAIN LEDGER
XYZ & CO.

1990	Particulars	Rs	1990	Particulars	Rs
Mar. 17	To XYZ & Co.				
	(Sale or Return Ledger)	3,400	Mar. 31	By Balance c/d.	3,400
		3,400			3,400

PQR & CO.

1990	Particulars	Rs	1990	Particulars	Rs
Mar. 25	To PQR & Co.				
	(In Sale or Return Ledger)	1,100	Mar. 31	By Balance c/d.	1,100
		1,100			1,100

SALES ACCOUNT

1990	Particulars	Rs	1990	Particulars	Rs
Mar. 31	To Balance c/d	4,500	Mar. 3	By Sale or Return A/c (In Sale or Return Ledger)	4,500
		4,500			4,500

KEY TERMS

☐ **Goods on sale or return basis:** It is a method of sale where the customers are given a stipulated time within which they should either return the goods sent to them for approval or send their approval. The goods are presumed to have been sold either on receipt of approval or not returning the goods even after the expiry of the stipulated time.

☐ **Kacha Ledger:** A ledger containing a separate account for each of the customers to whom goods have been sent on sale or return basis and a Sale or Return Account for total goods sent on sale or return.

TEST QUESTIONS

Objective type | TEST YOUR UNDERSTANDING |

1. State whether each of the following statement is 'True' or 'False'.

   (*i*)   In case of goods sent on sale or return basis, the buyer has a right to return the goods any time he likes.

   (*ii*) Sale or Return Day Book may be maintained as a memorandum record.

   (*iii*) The risk as to damage to the goods is that of the buyer as soon as the goods are sold on sale or return basis.

   (*iv*) Sold and Returned Day Book and Sale or Return Day Book have synonymous functions.

   (*v*)   Sale or Return Account in the Sale or Return Ledger represents the value of goods still lying with the customers for approval.

   [**Ans.** (i) False (ii) True (iii) False (iv) False (v) True]

Essay type | FOR REVIEW, DISCUSSION AND PRACTICE |

1. Define the term goods on sale or return basis. Explain the different methods used for recording transactions relating to goods on sale or return basis.

2. Write short notes on —

   (*i*)   Sale or Return Day Book;

   (*ii*) Sale or Return Ledger;

   (*iii*) Sold and Returned Day Book.

PRACTICAL PROBLEMS

1. Suneel Bros. Sent out goods on sale as follows:

   March, 10: X300; March, 13: Return Rs. 100. Rest retained

   March, 20: Y200; March, 22: All retained

   March, 30: Z1, 500; March, 31: No intimation

   Show how these transactions will appear when books are kept on double entry system. Give journal entries and ledger accounts.

   [**Ans.** Balance in Sale or Return Account Rs 1,500].

2. A firm sends goods on sale or return basis, to customers' having the choice of returning the goods within a month. During April, 1998, the following are the details of the goods sent:

1998	Customer	Value	Proforma Invoice No.
		Rs.	
April 2	A	10,000	004
4	B	18,000	007
16	C	25,000	023
20	D	8,000	032
24	E	21,000	041
28	F	30,000	049

Within the stipulated time, A and C returned the goods while B, D and E signified that they have accepted the goods. Show the following accounts in the books of the firm:

Sale on Approval Account and Customers for Sale on Approval Account as on 15th May, 1992.

[**Ans.** Balance: Sale on Approval A/c Rs. 30,000 (Cr.).,
Customers for Sale on Approval A/c Rs 30,000 (Dr.)]

SECTION III

PARTNERSHIP ACCOUNTS

Chapter 1

FUNDAMENTALS

LEARNING OBJECTIVES

After studying this chapter you should be able to:

☐ understand the meaning of partnership;

☐ enumerate the essential characteristics of partnership;

☐ appreciate the importance of partnership deed;

☐ state the rights and duties of partners;

☐ get familiarise with the basic accounting problems concerning partnership firms; and

☐ explain the meaning of certain key terms.

MEANING OF PARTNERSHIP

Partnership form of business organisation came into existence on account of limitations of sole proprietary concerns. The major limitations of sole proprietary concerns are those of shortage of funds, uncertainty about existence, unlimited personal liability etc. In case of a partnership business two or more persons join hands together to do a business. Thus, the risk, funds, responsibility all are shared. The Indian Partnership Act, 1932 is applicable to contracts of Partnership. According to Section 4 of the said Act partnership is "the relation between persons who have agreed to share the profits of a business carried on by all or any of them acting for all". Persons who have entered into partnership with one another are called individually 'partners' and collectively a 'firm' and the name under which the business is carried on is called the 'firm's name'.

The term 'firm' is merely a commercial notion. Law does not invest the firm with legal personality apart from its partners except for the purposes of assessment of income-tax. A 'firm' cannot become a member of another partnership firm though its partners can join any other firm as partners.

ESSENTIAL CHARACTERISTICS OF PARTNERSHIP

A partnership business must satisfy all the following essential elements. They must exist together. Absence of any one of them may cut the roots of partnership.

1. **There must be an association of two or more persons.** A person cannot become a partner with himself. Reduction in the number of partners to one shall bring about compulsory dissolution of the firm. The term 'person' does not include 'firm' (since it does not have a separate legal existence) and as such only the partners of the firms can enter into

partnership provided the combined strength of partners does not exceed the statutory limit. The number of members in a partnership firm should not exceed 10 if it carrying on a banking business, or 20 if it is engaged in any other business. An association or a partnership firm having members more than this statutory limit must be registered as a joint stock company, under the Companies Act or formed in pursuance of some other Indian law, otherwise it shall become an illegal association.[1]

2. **There must be an agreement entered into by all persons concerned.** The relation of partnership arises from contract and not from status or by operation of law. Partners must enter into an agreement voluntarily to form a partnership. The agreement may be express or implied. It may be for a fixed period or for a particular venture or at will, *i.e.,* for an uncertain duration. Co-owners of a property or heirs of a sole proprietor who has died will not *ipso facto* become partners in the business, unless there is an agreement between them to carry on business as partners.

Partners must enter into the contract with a motive to earn and distribute amongst themselves profits of the business. Agreement to share losses is not essential. Agreement to share profits also implies an agreement to share losses.

3. **Business must be carried on by all or any of the persons concerned acting for all.** Partners in a firms act in both the capacities of an agent as well as principal. Active partners act as agents and conduct the business for all the partners under an implied authority to do so by the latter. Partners are mutual agents for each other and principals for themselves. A partner has an authority to bind his co-partners by his acts done in the ordinary course of the business of the firm. Partner's liability is not limited to his share in the business but it extends to his personal assets too.

PARTNERSHIP DEED

Partnership is created by an agreement. It is not necessary that the agreement should be in writing. It may be oral but to avoid future disputes it is always better to have it in writing. The document in writing containing the important terms of partnership as agreed by the partners between themselves is called the *Deed of Partnership*. It should be properly drafted and stamped according to the provisions of The Stamp Act.

Contents of the deed.

The deed usually contains the following information:
1. Name of the firm.
2. Names of partners.
3. Nature and place of the business of the firm.
4. Date of commencement of partnership.
5. Duration of the firm.
6. Capital employed or to be employed by different partners.
7. Rules regarding operation of bank accounts.
8. Ratios in which profits and losses are to be shared.
9. How the business is to be managed?
10. Rules to be followed in case of admission, retirement, expulsion etc., of a partner.
11. Salaries etc., if payable to partners.

---

[1] Section 11 of the Companies Act, 1956.

12. Interest on partners' capitals, loans, drawings etc. to be allowed or charged.
13. Settlement of accounts on the dissolution of the firm.
14. Arbitrations clause.

It is better if the deed is very elaborate and clear about all questions which may arise in the course of partnership. In the absence of any agreement the rights and duties of partners will be those which have been given in the Partnership Act.

Provisions affecting accounting treatment

The partnership deed is usually very elaborate. It covers all matters affecting the partnership business. However, *in the absence of any provision to the contrary in the partnership deed/agreement*, the following provisions govern the accounting treatment of certain items:

1. **Right to share profits:** Partners are entitled to share equally in the profits earned and to contribute equally to losses incurred.

2. **Interest on capital:** No interest is payable on the capitals contributed by them. Similarly no interest is to be charged on drawings. However, where partnership agreement provides for payment of interest on capital, such interest is payable out of profits of the business unless otherwise provided.

3. **Interest on advances:** A partner who makes an advance of money to the firm beyond the amount of his capital for the purpose of business, is entitled to get interest thereon at the rate of 6% p.a.

4. **Right to share subsequent profits after retirement:** Where any member of a firm has died or otherwise ceased to be a partner and the surviving or continuing partners carry on the business of the firm with the property of the firm without any final settlement of accounts as between them, the outgoing partner or his estate is entitled, at the option of himself or his representatives to such share of the profits made since he ceased to be a partner as may be attributable to the use of his share of the property of the firm or to interest at the rate of six per cent per annum on the amount of his share in the property of the firm.

5. **No remuneration for firm's work:** A partner is required to attend diligently to his duties in conducting the business of the firm. He has no right to receive remuneration or salary for taking part in the conduct of the business.

FINAL ACCOUNTS

The method of preparing final accounts for the partnership firm is not different from the one followed for preparation of final accounts of a sole proprietary concern. Some of the important points to be taken care of while preparing the final accounts are as follows:

1. Capital Accounts

There will be a separate capital account for each partner. For example, if A, B and C are three partners in a partnership firm, there will be three capital accounts, one each of A, B and C. The capital accounts may be maintained either on fixed or fluctuating capital system. This has been explained in detail later in the chapter.

2. Profit and Loss Appropriation Account

A separate Profit & Loss Appropriation Account may be prepared to show the distribution of profits among different partners. The amount of profit to be distributed is arrived at after making following adjustments:

3.6

(a) **Interest on capital**

Interest will be allowed to each partner on the capital contributed by him. While computing such interest, due care must be taken of the capital introduced or withdrawn by a partner during course of an accounting year. The accounting entries for such interest on capital will be as follows:

(i) Interest on Capital A/c   Dr.
    To Partners' Capital Accounts (individually)

(ii) Profit & Loss Appropriation A/c   Dr.
    To Interest on Capital A/c

Alternatively, only one entry may be passed in place of the above two entries, as follows:

(iii) Profit & Loss Appropriation A/c   Dr.
    To Partners' Capital Accounts (individually)

Illustration 1.1. A, B & C are partners in a firm. Their capital accounts as on 1.1.1988 were Rs 1,00,000, Rs 50,000 and Rs 30,000 respectively. They are sharing profits and losses equally. Interest on capital is allowed at 12% p.a. On 1.7.1988, the partners decided that their capital should be Rs 50,000 each. The necessary adjustment in the capitals are to be made by introducing or withdrawing cash. Profit for the year ended on 31.12.1988 before charging interest on capital amounts to Rs 50,000. You are required to prepare a Profit & Loss Appropriation Account showing the distribution of profit among the partners.

Solution:

PROFIT AND LOSS APPROPRIATION ACCOUNT
for the year ending 31.12.1988

Particulars		Rs		Particulars	Rs
To Interest on Capital:				By Profit for the year	50,000
	A	9,000			
	B	6,000			
	C	4,800	19,800		
To Net Profit transferred to Capital					
Accounts:					
	A	10,067			
	B	10,067			
	C	10,066	30,200		
		50,000			50,000

Working Note:

COMPUTATION OF INTEREST ON CAPITAL

				Rs	Rs
A	$\frac{1,00,000 \times 12 \times 6}{100 \times 12}$		=	6,000	
	$\frac{50,000 \times 12 \times 1}{100 \times 2}$		=	3,000	9,000
B	$\frac{50,000 \times 12}{100}$				6,000
C	$\frac{30,000 \times 12 \times 6}{100 \times 12}$		=	1,800	
	$\frac{50,000 \times 12 \times 6}{100 \times 12}$		=	3,000	4,800

Interest on capital is allowed to partners on the capital balances standing to their credit in the beginning of the accounting year. Of course, as explained above, suitable adjustments are made for the capital introduced or withdrawn by a partner during the course of the accounting year. In case, in an examination question, information regarding capitals of partners in the beginning of the accounting year has not been given, such capitals will have to be found out by making suitable adjustments and interest will have to be charged accordingly. The following illustration clarifies this point:

Illustration 1.2. A & B are partners in a partnership business sharing profits and losses in the ratio of 3:2. They are entitled to interest on capital @ 10% p.a. Balance Sheet at the end of 31.12.1988 of the firm was as follows:

BALANCE SHEET

Liabilities	Amount Rs	Assets	Amount Rs
Capital Accounts:		Sundry Assets	40,000
A	20,000	Drawings of A	5,000
B	15,000		
Profit & Loss			
Appropriation Account	10,000		
	45,000		45,000

During the year, A withdrew Rs 5,000 while B withdrew Rs 3,000. Profits for the year 1988 before charging interest on capital amounted to Rs 15,000. You are required to calculate interest on capital due to partners, prepare a Profit & Loss Appropriation A/c, Capital Accounts of Partners and revised balance sheet of the firm, presuming that no adjustments for interest on capital have so far been made.

Solution:

In order to calculate interest on capital, it will be necessary to compute the capitals of the partners in the beginning of the year. In the balance sheet, capitals of the partners at the end of the accounting year have been given. The drawings made by A have not been adjusted/deducted out of his capital since they are appearing in the balance sheet of the firm. Similarly, a part of the profit made in the year i.e., Rs 5,000 (i.e., 15,000 – 10,000) has already been credited to the partners in the ration of 3:2. In order to compute the capitals of the partners at the beginning, it will be necessary to make adjustments for the above items as given below:

Particulars	Rs
A's Capital as on 31.12.88	20,000
Less: Profit credited during the year	3,000
Capital as on 1.1.1988	17,000
Interest on Capital @ 10% p.a.	1,700
B's Capital on 31.12.88	15,000
Add: Drawings made during the year	3,000
	18,000
Less: Profit credited during the year	2,000
Capital as on 1.1.1988	16,000
Interest on Capital @ 10% p.a.	1,600

PROFIT AND LOSS APPROPRIATION ACCOUNT
for they year ending 31st December, 1988

Particulars		Rs	Particulars	Rs
To Interest on Capital			By Profit during the year	15,000
A		1,700		
B		1,600		
To Net Profit transferred to				
Partners' Capital A/cs				
A	7,020			
B	4,680	11,700		
		15,000		15,000

CAPITAL ACCOUNTS
for 1988

Particulars	A Rs	B Rs	Particulars	A Rs	B Rs
To Drawings	5,000	3,000	By Balance b/d	17,000	16,000
To Balance c/d	20,720	19,280	By Interest on Capital	1,700	1,600
			By Share of Profit	7,020	4,680
	25,720	22,280		25,720	22,280

REVISED BALANCE SHEET OF THE FIRM
As on 31.12.88

Liabilities	Amount Rs	Assets	Amount Rs
Capital Accounts:		Sundry Assets	40,000
A	20,720		
B	19,280		
	40,000		40,000

(b) Interest on drawings

The partnership agreement may provide for charging of interest on drawings *i.e.*, the money withdrawn by the partners for their personal use out of the firm. All such interest is computed on the basis of the period for which the money remained outstanding from the partners during the course of the accounting year.

The accounting entries for the interest on drawings will be as follows:

(*i*)   Partners' Capital Accounts (individually)   Dr.
         To Interest on Drawings A/c

(*ii*) Interest on Drawings A/c   Dr.
         To Profit & Loss Appropriation A/c

Alternatively, a single entry may be passed in place of the above two entries as follows:

(*iii*) Partners' Capital Accounts (individually)   Dr.
         To Profit & Loss Appropriation A/c

Computation of interest on drawings

(*i*) **When drawings are of uneven amounts and/or made at uneven time intervals:**
It will be convenient in such a case to calculate the interest on drawings according to the product method as illustrated below.

Illustration 1.3. A, B & C are three partners in a partnership firm since 1.1.1988. They are sharing profits and losses equally. According to the partnership agreement, interest on drawings is to be charged at the rate of 10% p.a. Drawings made by the partners during the year 1988 are as follows:

Date	A (Rs)	B (Rs)	C (Rs)
January 1	5,000	3,000	2,000
April 1	3,000	2,000	3,000
September 1	5,000	4,000	2,000
December 1	2,000	1,000	1,000

The profits for the year amount to Rs 30,000. You are required to compute the interest on drawings recoverable from the partners and prepare the Profit & Loss Appropriation Account showing the distribution of profits among the partners.

Solution:

COMPUTATION OF INTEREST ON DRAWINGS

A			B			C		
Amount (1)	Period (2)	Product (3)	Amount (1)	Period (2)	Product (3)	Amount (1)	Period (2)	Product (3)
		(1×2)			(1×2)			(1×2)
5,000	12	60,000	3,000	12	36,000	2,000	12	24,000
3,000	9	27,000	2,000	9	18,000	3,000	9	27,000
5,000	4	20,000	4,000	4	16,000	2,000	4	8,000
2,000	1	2,000	1,000	1	1,000	1,000	1	1,000
		1,09,000			71,000			60,000

Amount of Interest (On the total product of one month):

A $\dfrac{1,90,000 \times 10 \times 1}{100 \times 12} = 908$

B $\dfrac{71,000 \times 10 \times 1}{100 \times 12} = 592$

C $\dfrac{60,000 \times 10 \times 1}{100 \times 12} = 500$

PROFIT AND LOSS APPROPRIATION ACCOUNT
for the year ending 31st December, 1988

Particulars		Rs	Particulars		Rs
To Net Profit transferred to Capital			By Profit for the year		30,000
Accounts (individually)			By Interest on Drawings		
A	10,667		A	908	
B	10,667		B	592	
C	10,666	32,000	C	500	2,000
		32,000			32,000

(*ii*) When Drawings are of even amounts and made at equal time intervals:

In case drawings are of even amounts and have been made at equal time intervals during the course of the year, the interest on drawings may be calculated on the basis of the following simple rules:

(*a*) In case it is presumed that money for drawings was withdrawn on a date middle of each month, interest should be charged for the six months on the full amount of drawings.

(*b*) In case it is presumed that money was withdrawn on the 1st day of each month, interest should be charged for 6 ½ months on the full amount of drawings.

(*c*) In case it is presumed that money was withdrawn at the end of each month, interest should be charged for 5 ½ months on the full amount of drawings.

It is to be noted that in each of the above cases, the total amount of interest, if calculated by the product method, will be the same as above.

In the absence of any instruction in the question, it will the appropriate to work out the interest on the basis of presumption (*a*) above.

Illustration 1.4. *A & B* are partners in a business. During the course of 1988, *A* withdrew Rs 12,000 while *B* withdrew Rs 6,000 out of the business for personal use. Interest on drawings to be charged at 10% p.a. You are required to calculate the amount of interest on drawings making such presumptions as you deem necessary.

Solution:

Since the question does not mention the dates of each amount of drawings by each partner, it may be presumed that drawings were made by each partner evenly during the course of the accounting year. The interest on drawings may, therefore, be calculated according to any of the following three presumptions:

(*i*) Drawings were made in the middle of each month.

(*ii*) Drawings were made on the first of each month.

(*iii*) Drawings were made on the last date of the month.

The interest on drawings in each case will be as follows:

(*i*) *When drawings were made in the middle of each month*

A			B		
Amt. of Drawings (Rs)	Period (Months)	Product	Amt. of Drawings (Rs)	Period (Months)	Product
1	2	3 (1 × 2)	1	2	3 (1 × 2)
1,000	11.5	11,500	500	11.5	5,750
1,000	10.5	10,500	500	10.5	5,250
1,000	9.5	9,500	500	9.5	4,750
1,000	8.5	8,500	500	8.5	4,250
1,000	7.5	7,500	500	7.5	3,750
1,000	6.5	6,500	500	6.5	3,250
1,000	5.5	5,500	500	5.5	2,750
1,000	4.5	4,500	500	4.5	2,250
1,000	3.5	3,500	500	3.5	1,750
1,000	2.5	2,500	500	2.5	1,250
1,000	1.5	1,500	500	1.5	750
1,000	0.5	500	500	0.5	250
		72,000			36,000

Interest on drawings (On total product for one month)

$$A \quad \frac{72,000 \times 1}{12} \times \frac{10}{100} = \text{Rs } 600 \qquad B \quad \frac{36,000 \times 1}{12} \times \frac{10}{100} = \text{Rs } 300$$

Alternatively, the interest on drawings may be calculated on the basis of the average of the first and the last periods for which the drawings remained outstanding i.e., $\frac{11.5 + 0.5}{2} = 6$ months as shown below:

$$A \quad \frac{12,000 \times 10 \times 6}{100 \times 12} = \text{Rs } 600 \qquad B \quad \frac{6,000 \times 10 \times 6}{100 \times 12} = \text{Rs } 300$$

(ii) *When drawings were made on the first day of each month*

The interest on such drawings can be calculated either by the product method or by taking the average of period for which the first and the last instalments of drawings remained outstanding.

The first instalment of drawings remained outstanding for 12 months while the last instalment of drawings remained outstanding for one month. The interest total drawings may, therefore, be charged for 6 ½ months i.e., $\left(\frac{12+1}{2}\right)$.

The amount of interest will, therefore, be calculated as follows:

Interest on Drawings of A $\qquad \frac{12,000 \times 13 \times 10}{2 \times 12 \times 100} = \text{Rs } 650$

Interest on Drawings of B $\qquad \frac{6,000 \times 13 \times 10}{2 \times 12 \times 100} = \text{Rs } 325$

The amount of interest on drawings will also be the same as given above, if calculated according to the product method.

(iii) *When drawings were made on the last date of each month*

Interest on such drawings can also be calculated either according to the product method or by taking the average of the periods for which the first instalment and the last instalment of drawings remained outstanding. In this case, the interest on total drawings would be charged for 5 ½ months i.e., $\left(\frac{11+0}{2}\right)$.

The amount of interest on drawings will, therefore, be calculated as follows:

Interest on drawings of A $\qquad \frac{12,000 \times 11 \times 10}{2 \times 12 \times 100} = \text{Rs } 550$

Interest on drawings of B $\qquad \frac{6,000 \times 11 \times 10}{12 \times 2 \times 100} = \text{Rs } 275$

Tutorial Note: In the illustration given above, the students may calculate interest on drawings by taking any one of the three presumptions, given above.

(c) **Salaries to partners**

Partnership agreement may provide for payment of salaries to partners who are taking active part in the management of the firm. Accounting entry for such salaries will be as follows:

(i) Salaries to Partners' A/c $\qquad\qquad\qquad$ Dr.

$\qquad$ To Partners' Capital Accounts (individually)

(*ii*) Profit & Loss Appropriation A/c Dr.
    To Salaries to Partners A/c

Alternatively, a single entry may be passed in place of two entries, as follows:

Profit & Loss Appropriation A/c Dr.
    To Partners' Capital A/cs (individually)

(*d*) Distribution of profits

As stated in the preceding pages, in the absence of any agreement to the contrary, the profits and losses are shared equally by the partners. The share in profit or loss does not usually depend upon the capital of a partner in the firm. However, the partners may agree to share the profits and losses in the ratio of their capitals. In such an event, no problem will arise if the capitals of the partners remain fixed throughout the accounting year. However, in case of frequent withdrawals and introduction of capitals during the course of the accounting year, it will be appropriate to calculate the weighted average ratio keeping in view the time when the additional capital was introduced or withdrawn from the business. This will be clear with the following illustration.

The accounting entry for distribution of profits amongst the partners will be as follows:

Profit & Loss Appropriation A/c . Dr.
    To Partners' Capital A/cs (individually)

Illustration 1.5. A and B started a business on 1.1.1988 with capitals of Rs 40,000 and Rs 20,000 respectively. They agreed to share the profits and losses in the ratio of their capitals. The profits for the year 1988 amounted to Rs 20,000. Following are the details regarding additional capital introduced or capital withdrawn by the partners during the year 1985:

	Capital Introduced		Capital Withdrawn	
	A	B	A	B
1.4.88		5,000	10,000	
1.6.88	4,000			8,000
1.11.88	5,000			3,000

Solution:

COMPUTATION OF TOTAL CAPITAL EMPLOYED BY A FOR ONE MONTH

Capital	Months for which capital remained in the business	Product
40,000	3	1,20,000
30,000	2	60,000
34,000	5	1,40,000
39,000	2	78,000
		3,98,000

COMPUTATION OF TOTAL CAPITAL EMPLOYED BY B FOR ONE MONTH

Capital	Months for which capital remained in the business	Product
20,000	3	60,000
25,000	2	50,000

Contd....

Capital	Months for which capital remained in the business	Product
17,000	5	85,000
14,000	2	28,000
		2,23,000

On the basis of capitals, profits are to be shared in a ratio of 398 : 223.

The profit of Rs 20,000 will, therefore, be shared as follows:

			Rs
A	$\dfrac{20,000 \times 398}{621}$	=	12,818
B	$\dfrac{20,000 \times 223}{621}$	=	7,182
			20,000

3. Guarantee of profit to a partner

The partnership agreement may provide for a guaranteed amount as profit to a partner (or partners). In such a case, the term of guaranteed profit will be significant only in those years, when the guaranteed amount of profit is more than the share or profit which the partner (or partners) concerned would have got otherwise in the absence of any guarantee. In such an event, the partner (or partners) to whom guarantee has been given will get the guaranteed share of profit while the others will have to share the remaining profits (or bear the losses) as per the terms of the partnership agreement. This can be understood with the help of the following illustration.

Illustration 1.6. A, B and C are partners in a firm sharing profits in the ratio of 2:2:1. According to the terms of the partnership agreement, C has to get a minimum of Rs 6,000 irrespective of the profits of the firm. Any excess payable to C on account of such guarantee shall be borne by A. Prepare the profit and loss appropriation account showing the distribution of profits among the partners in case the profits for the year 1988 are (a) Rs 25,000 and (b) Rs 40,000.

Solution:

(a) *In case the profit are Rs 25,000:*

In this case, C's guaranteed share is Rs 6,000 while he would have got Rs 5,000 in the absence of any such guarantee. The excess of the guaranteed amount over his normal share of profit will have to be borne by A as per the terms of partnership agreement. B's share will remain unaffected on account of this guarantee. In other words, B's share of profit will remain Rs 10,000 (*i.e.*, 25,000 × 2/5). The Profit and Loss Appropriation Account can now be prepared as follows:

PROFIT AND LOSS APPROPRIATION ACCOUNT
for the year ending 31st December, 1988

Particulars		Rs	Particulars	Rs
To Profit transferred to			By Net Profit for the year	25,000
Capital Accounts				
A 2/5	10,000			
Less: Given to C	1,000	9,000		
B 2/5		10,000		
C 1/5	5,000			
Add: Received from A	1,000	6,000		
		25,000		25,000

(b) In case the profits are Rs 40,000:

In this case, C is getting Rs 8,000 (*i.e.*, 40,000 × 1/5) as his share of profits. The amount is more than his guaranteed share. Hence, he will get Rs 8,000 and A will not have to make any sacrifice. The Profit and Loss Appropriation Account can now be prepared as follows:

PROFIT AND LOSS APPROPRIATION ACCOUNT
for the year ending 31st December, 1988

Particulars	Rs	Particulars	Rs
To Profit transferred to Partners' Capital A/cs		By Net Profit for the year	40,000
A	16,000		
B	16,000		
C	8,000		
	40,000		40,000

Illustration 1.7. Mehra and Ratnam are in partnership with capitals of Rs 28,000 and Rs 14,000 respectively sharing profits and losses as 2:1. Interest on capital @ 5% per annum and salary of Rs 2,800 per annum to Ratnam are allowable.

Due to ill health, Mehra ceased to take active part in the business with effect from 1 January, 1992 and the following terms were agreed upon:

(1) That the Manager, Jahar, shall be taken as a partner with a capital of Rs 5,000, he being entitled to a salary of Rs 5,250, per annum, the excess over Rs 2,800 (the salary received by him as Manager) to be borne by Mehra personally,

(2) That Ratnam shall get a salary of Rs 3,500 per annum,

(3) That Jahar shall be entitled to one-tenth share of profits and losses after charging interest on capitals and partners' salaries,

(4) That interest on capital shall be allowed @ 5% per annum.

The net profit for the year ended 31 December 1992 was Rs 22,400 before charging interest on capital and partners' salaries.

You are required to show the division of the profits for the year 1992 between the partners.

Solution:

Books of Mehra & Ratnam
PROFIT & LOSS APPROPRIATION ACCOUNT
for the year ending 31st December, 1992

Particulars	Rs		Particulars	Rs
To Ratnam's salary		3,500	By Net Profit b/d	22,400
To Jahar's salary		5,250		
To Interest on capitals:				
Mehra	1,400			
Ratnam	700			
Jahar	250	2,350		
To Capital Accounts:				
Net Profit:				
Mehara (Balance)		6,045		
Ratnam [³⁄₁₀ of 13,750 profit after interest and salaries				

Contd....

Particulars	Rs	Particulars	Rs
(taking Jahar's Salary to be Rs 2,800)]	4,125		
Jahar 1/10 of Rs 11,300, profit after interest and partners' salaries	1,130		
	22,400		22,400

The comprehensive illustration given in the following pages clarify further items peculiar to partnership final accounts as explained in the preceding pages.

Illustration 1.8. Following is the Trial Balance for the year ending 31st December, 1988 of M/s Maheshwari Brothers.

Particulars	Dr. Rs	Cr. Rs
Purchases and Sales	50,000	1,00,000
Opening Stock	30,000	
Wages	10,000	
Salaries	10,000	
Plant	20,000	
Furniture	10,000	
Printing & Stationery	5,000	
Debtors & Creditors	40,000	60,000
Cash	20,000	
Drawings:		
Sunil	10,000	
Sharad	5,000	
Capital:		
Sunil		30,000
Sharad		20,000
	2,10,000	2,10,000

The following adjustments are to be taken into account:
(i) Wages Outstanding Rs 5,000.
(ii) Plant is to be depreciated at 10% and Furniture at 5%.
(iii) A provision for doubtful debt is to be created @ 5% on debtors.
(iv) Interest on capital is to be allowed at 5% p.a. while on drawings it is to be charged at 6% p.a.
(v) Sunil and Sharad, each is to be allowed salary @ Rs 200 p.m.
(vi) Profits & losses are to be shared equally.
(vii) Closing stock on 31st December, 1988 is valued at Rs 30,000.

You are required to prepare the Trading and Profit and Loss Account of the business for the year ending on 31st Dec., 1988 and the Balance Sheet as on that date.

Solution:

TRADING AND PROFIT AND LOSS ACCOUNT
for the year ending 31st December, 1988

Particulars	Rs	Particulars	Rs
To Opening Stock	30,000	By Sales	1,00,000
To Purchases	50,000	By Closing Stock	30,000

Contd....

Particulars		Rs	Particulars	Rs
To Wages	10,000			
Add: Outstanding	5,000	15,000		
To Gross Profit c/d		35,000		
		1,30,000		1,30,000
To Salaries		10,000	By Gross Profit b/d	35,000
To Printing and Stationery		5,000		
To Depreciation				
Plant	2,000			
Furniture	500	2,500		
To Provision for doubtful debts		2,000		
To Profit for the year		15,500		
		35,000		35,000

PROFIT AND LOSS APPROPRIATION ACCOUNT
for the year ending 31st December, 1988

Particulars		Rs	Particulars		Rs
To Interest on capital:			By Profit for the year		15,500
Sunil	1,500		By Interest on drawings		
Sharad	1,000	2,500	Sunil	300	
			Sharad	150	450
To Net Profit					
Sunil	6,725				
Sharad	6,725	13,450			
		15,950			15,950

BALANCE SHEET
as on 31st December, 1988

Liabilities		Amount Rs	Assets		Amount Rs
Outstanding Wages		5,000	Cash		20,000
Creditors		60,000	Debtors	40,000	
Capital:			Less: Provision for		
Sunil	30,000		bad debts	2,000	38,000
Add: Profit	6,725		Closing Stock		30,000
Interest on capital	1,500		Furniture	10,000	
	38,225		Less: Depreciation	500	9,500
Less: Drawings 10,000			Plant	20,000	
Interest on			Less: Depreciation	2,000	18,000
Drawings 300	10,300	27,925			
Sharad	20,000				
Add: Profit	6,725				
Interest on Capital	1,000				
	27,725				
Less: Drawings 5,000					
Interest on					
Drawings 150	5,150	22,575			
		1,15,500			1,15,500

Illustration 1.9. Leo was carrying on business as a wholesale businessman. He closes his accounts by 31st March every year. Libra was his manager on a monthly salary of Rs 1,500 till 30.9.1987 and from 1.10.1987 it was agreed that he will be admitted as a partner with ⅓ share in the profits and losses without any salary. The books of the firm yielded the following Trial Balance at the end of the year on 31.3.1988:

Particulars	Dr. Rs	Cr. Rs
Leo's Capital A/c		35,000
Leo's Drawing A/c	18,000	
Furniture & Fittings	9,000	
Motor Car	15,000	
Stock (1.4.1987)	30,000	
Debtors	14,000	
Bank Balance	15,000	
Cash in Hand	900	
Purchases (1,00,000 till 30.9.1988)	2,10,000	
Sales		3,30,000
Creditors		7,700
Salaries	15,000	
Selling Expenses	33,000	
Audit Fees	2,400	
Rent	6,400	
Rent Advance	4,000	
	3,72,700	3,72,700

The following additional information is available:

(i) Furniture and fittings are to be depreciated at 10% and Motor Car at 20%.

(ii) Rent which was Rs 500 p.m. till 30.11.1987 was increased to Rs 600 p.m. from 1.12.1987.

(iii) Sales during the first six months of the year were Rs 1,10,000. Stock on 30.9.1987 was Rs 50,000 and on 31.3.1988 was Rs 20,000.

You are requested to prepare the Trading and Profit and Loss Account in columnar form showing the shares of the partners and the Balance Sheet of the firm as at 31.3.1988.

Solution:

Leo and Libra

TRADING AND PROFIT & LOSS ACCOUNT
for the year ending March 31, 1988

Particulars	Upto Sept. 30,,1987 Amt. Rs	Oct. 1 to March 31, 1988 Amt. Rs	Particulars	Upto Sept. 30, 1987 Amt. Rs	Oct. 1 to March 31, 1988 Amt. Rs
To Opening Stock	30,000	50,000	By Sales	1,10,000	2,20,000
To Purchases	1,00,000	1,10,000	By Closing Stock	50,000	20,000
To Gross Profit c/d	30,000	80,000			
	1,60,000	2,40,000		1,60,000	2,40,000

Contd....

Particulars	Upto Sept. 30,,1987	Oct. 1 to March 31, 1988	Particulars	Upto Sept. 30, 1987	Oct. 1 to March 31, 1988
To Salaries:			By Gross Profit b/d	30,000	80,000
Manager's Salary	9,000	—			
Others	3,000	3,000			
To Selling Expenses	11,000	22,000			
To Audit Fees	1,200	1,200			
To Rent	3,400	3,400			
To Depreciation:					
Furniture etc.	450	450			
Motor car	1,500	1,500			
To Net Profit:					
Leo's Capital A/c	850	32,300			
Libra's Capital A/c	—	16,150			
	30,000	80,000		30,000	80,000

BALANCE SHEET OF LEO & LIBRA
as on March 31st, 1988

Liabilities	Rs	Amount Rs	Assets	Rs	Amount Rs
Creditors		7,700	Cash in hand		900
Capitals:			Bank Balance		15,000
Leo	35,000		Debtors		14,000
Add: Share of			Rent Advance		4,000
Net Profit	33,150		Stock		20,000
	68,150		Furniture and Fittings	9,000	
Less: Drawings	18,000	50,150	Less: Depreciation	900	8,100
Libra		16,150	Motor Car	15,000	
			Less: Depreciation	3,000	12,000
		74,000			74,000

Notes:

(i) Selling expenses have been apportioned in the ratio of sales.

(ii) Rent: Rs 3,000 @ Rs 500 p.m. for the first six months and the balance pertains to the last six months.

(iii) Other expenses have been apportioned on the basis of time.

ADJUSTMENTS AFTER CLOSING ACCOUNTS

Sometimes after closing the partnership accounts for a particular period, it is found that certain matters were left out by mistake or have been wrongly entered. For example, interest on capital has not been allowed at all, while as per agreement it was to be allowed at 10% per annum on the opening balance or interest on capital has been allowed at 12% in place of 10% while interest on drawings has been charged at 10% in place of 12%.. In such an event adjustments will have to be made in the partners' capital accounts directly or through a Profit & Loss Adjustment Account.

Illustration 1.10. A, B and C are three partners in a business having capitals of Rs 30,000, Rs 20,000 and Rs 10,000 respectively. After closing their books of accounts for the year 1988, they find that interest on capital @ 10% p.a. on the opening balance in the capital accounts has not been allowed. Partners share profits and losses equally. You are required to pass the necessary adjustment entry in the beginning of the next year.

Solution:

In order to make the necessary adjustment entry, it will be necessary to find out the amount should have been credited to partners and which has been wrongly credited. The total interest of Rs 6,000 should have been credited to the partners. Since no interest has been allowed to the partners, the figure of profit for 1989 has been inflated by Rs 6,000 which has gone equally to the partners.

Partners	Amount which should have been credited Rs	Amount which has been credited Rs	Amount to be credited or debited now
A	3,000	2,000	Cr. 1,000
B	2,000	2,000	–
C	1,000	2,000	Dr. 1,000

The journal entry should therefore be:

C's Capital A/c	Dr.	1,000
To A's Capital A/c		1,000

Illustration 1.11. Below is given the Profit and Loss Account (Appropriation Section) of Ramu Kalu & Co. for the year ending 31 December, 1989 as prepared by the accountant.

PROFIT AND LOSS APPROPRIATION ACCOUNT

Particulars		Amount Rs	Particulars		Amount Rs
To Interest on Capital:			By Net Profit		50,000
Ramu 6% on	50,000	3,000	By Interest on drawings		
Kalu 6% on	30,000	1,800	Ramu at 5% on	12,000	600
To Salary:			Kalu at 5% on	10,000	500
Ramu		3,600			
To Balance of Profit:					
Ramu		25,620			
Kalu		17,080			
		51,100			51,000

After passing the entries, it was later on discovered that:

(i) Interest on capital was to be allowed at 5% and interest on drawings to be charged at 6%.

(ii) Ramu was not to be allowed any partnership salary but Kalu was to be allowed instead at Rs 200 per month which was not drawn by him during the year.

(iii) The profit or loss was to be shared by the partners in the ratio of their capital accounts.

(iv) A partnership loan stood in the books in the name of Ramu at Rs 10,000.

You are required to pass the necessary adjustment entry for rectifying the matters.

Solution:

PROFIT AND LOSS APPROPRIATION ACCOUNT
(as corrected)

Particulars		Amount Rs	Particulars		Amount Rs
To Interest on Capital			By Net Profit		50,000
Ramu 5% on Rs	50,000	2,500	By Interest on Drawings:		
Kalu 5% on Rs	30,000	1,000	Ramu 6% on Rs	12,000	360
To Salary: Kalu		2,400	(for 6 month)		
To Interest on Loan:			Kalu 6% on Rs	10,000	300
Ramu 6% on	10,000	600	(for six months)		
To Balance of Net Profit:					
Ramu		27,287.50			
Kalu		16,372.50			
		50,660.00			50,660

*Presuming that drawings were made evenly during the year and in the middle of each month.

STATEMENT OF ADJUSTMENT

	Amts. as entered		Amts as should have been entered		Adjustment Dr./Cr.
	Dr.	Cr.	Dr.	Cr.	
Ramu:					
Int. on Capital		3,000		2,500	
Salary		2,600			
Share of Profit		25,620		37,287.50	
Int. on loan		—		600.00	
Int. on drawings	600		360		
	600	32,220	360	30,387.50	
Net		31,620		30,027.50	Dr 1,592.50
Kalu:		—			
Salary				2,400	
Int on Capital		1,800		1,500	
Share of Profit		17,080		16,372.50	
Int. on Drawings	500		300		
	500	18,880	300	20,272.50	
Net		18,380		19,972.50	Cr 1,592.50

Adjustment entry will be:

		Rs	Rs
Ramu's Capital A/c	Dr.	1,592.50	
To Kalu's Capital A/c			1,592.50

FIXED AND FLUCTUATING CAPITALS

Partners capital accounts can be maintained either on 'fixed capital system' or 'fluctuating capital system'.

In case of a fixed capital system, there are two accounts for each partner:

(i) Partner's Capital Account.

(ii) Partner's Current Account.

The partner's capital account is credited with the original amount of capital introduced by the partner into the business. It is to be credited subsequently with extra capital introduced by the partner or debited with the amount of capital permanently withdrawn by the partner. No other adjustments are made in this account.

The partner's current account is maintained for making all entries relating to interest, share of profit, drawings, etc. The balance in this account will go on fluctuating but the balance of the capital account will remain fixed. That is why the system is termed as "fixed capital system".

In case of fluctuating capital system there is only one account for each partner. This account is termed as his "Capital Account". All entries relating to introduction of fresh capital, drawings, interest. profit etc. are made in this account. The balance in the capital account, therefore, goes on fluctuating. The system is, therefore, called as 'fluctuating capital system'.

Illustration 1.12. A and B started a partnership business on 1, January 1989 with capitals of Rs 15,000 and Rs 10,000 respectively. On 30th June 1989, A introduced a further capital of Rs 5,000. Drawings during the year amounted to Rs 3,000 and Rs 2,000 respectively for A and B. Interest on capital is to be allowed at 5% p.a. No interest is to be charged on drawings. B is to be allowed a salary of Rs 500 p.m. The profit for the year before charging salary and interest amounted to Rs 20,000.

You are required to prepare the accounts of the partners presuming:

(i) Capitals to be fixed, and

(ii) Capitals to be fluctuating.

Solution:

PROFIT & LOSS APPROPRIATION ACCOUNT
for the year ending 31 December, 1989

Particulars	Amt. Rs	Particulars	Amt. Rs
To Interest on Capital:		By Net profit for the year	20,000.00
A (Rs 750+Rs 125)	815.00		
B	500.00		
To Salary:			
B	6,000.00		
To Net Profit:			
A	6,312.50		
B	6,312.50		
	20,000.00		20,000.00

When Capitals are Fixed:

Dr. CAPITAL ACCOUNTS Cr.

Date	Particulars	A Rs	B Rs	Date	Particulars	A Rs	B Rs
Dec. 31	To Balance c/d	20,000	10,000	Jan. 1	By Cash	15,000	10,000
				June 30	By Cash	5,000	—
		20,000	10,000			20,000	10,000

CURRENT ACCOUNTS

Date	Particulars	A Rs	B Rs	Date	Particulars	A Rs	B Rs
Dec. 31	To Drawings To Balance c/d	3,000.00 4,187.50	10,812.50		By Interest By Salary By Net Profit	875.00 6,312.50	500.00 6,000.00 6,312.50
		7,187.50	12,812.50			7,187.50	12,812.50

When Capitals are Fluctuating

CAPITAL ACCOUNTS

Date	Particulars	A Rs	B Rs	Date	Particulars	A Rs	B Rs
31 Dec.	To Drawings To Balance c/d	3,000.00 24,437.50	2,000.00 20,812.50	1 Jan. 30 June 31 Dec.	By Cash By Cash By Interest By Salary By Net Profit	15,000.00 5,000.00 875.00 — 6,437.50	10,000.00 500.00 6,000.00 6,812.50
		27,437.50	22,812.50			27,437.50	22,812.50

GOODWILL

It is generally observed that a firm, which has been in existence for a number of years, is in a position to earn a higher amount of profits year after year in comparison to a new firm in spite of all other things (such as investment, location, quality of goods etc.,) remaining the same. This is because over a period of time a firm establishes its reputation on account of which not only the old customers continue to patronise the firm but they also bring new customers. This result in enabling an old established firm to earn excess profits as compared to a new firm. Goodwill has, therefore, been defined as "The present value of firm's anticipated excess earnings". The term "excess earnings" is an indicator of this fact that goodwill is there when a business is earning over and above the normal earnings made by other similar firms in the same business or industry. Prof. Dicksee has, therefore, also observed, "when a man pays for goodwill, he pays for something which places him in the position of being able to earn more money than he would be able to by his own unaided efforts".

Factors affecting the value of goodwill. Value of goodwill depends upon the capacity of the business to earn excess profits. Thus, all such factors which help in increasing the profitability of the business, will also affect the value of the goodwill. These factors are:

(i) **Location.** A favourable location of the business helps to a great extent in attracting customers. It increases profitability and thus also the value of goodwill.

(ii) **Time.** A business older in age will have more goodwill since it is better known to the customers.

(iii) **Nature of business.** A business dealing in goods of a monopolistic type or goods having a stable demand will have a higher value of goodwill as compared to a business which does not have these characteristics. Thus, more risky is the business, the less will be the value of its goodwill.

(iv) **Capital required.** A business requiring less capital will have many buyers and hence its value of goodwill be high as compared to a business requiring higher amount of capital.

(*v*) **Types of customers.** The value of goodwill depends upon the extent to which the old customers will continue to give patronage to the new owner. Depending upon their attachment, customers can be categorised as cats, dogs and rates. Cats have more attachment with the house than the persons. In case a business has more of such customers (this is particularly true when the products are sold by their trade names), the value of goodwill be quite high. Dogs are loyal to the persons. Hence, if a business has more of such customers (that is particularly true in case of professional services such as of a doctor or a lawyer) the value of goodwill will not be much. Rats have no such attachment and therefore this factor may be ignored while valuing goodwill in case business has customers which are more or less of a floating type.

(*vi*) **Reputation of management.** A business managed by persons of high integrity and efficiency will have higher profitability and thus will have more value for its goodwill.

Nature of goodwill. Goodwill is an intangible asset but not a fictitious one. However, in case of concerns suffering losses, if goodwill is shown as an asset, it will be of a fictitious type.

Need for valuing goodwill. The need for valuation of goodwill in case of a partnership firm arises in the following circumstances:

(*i*) Admission of partner

(*ii*) Retirement or death of a partner

(*iii*) Change in the profit sharing ratio of partners

(*iv*) Amalgamation of a partnership firm with another firm

(*v*) Sale of partnership business.

Treatment of goodwill in each of the above cases has been dealt with at proper places.

Methods of Valuation

Following are the different methods for valuation of goodwill:

1. **Average profits method.** In case of this method the value of goodwill depends on two factors:

(*i*) *Average expected profits.* These are calculated on the basis of past performance of the business adjusted in the light of future possibilities.

(*ii*) *Number of years.* This denotes the average period which a new businessman would take in bringing the business to a stage where it will be in a position to give the average profit as indicated in point (*i*) above.

Illustration 1.13. Ram purchased Shyam's business with effect from 1st January, 1989.

The profits disclosed by Shyam's business for the last three years were as follows:

1986   Rs 40,000 (including an abnormal gain of Rs 5,000)
1987   Rs 50,000 (after charging an abnormal loss of Rs 10,000)
1988   Rs 45,000 (excluding Rs 5,000 as insurance premium on firm's property—now to be insured)

Calculated the value of firm's goodwill on the basis of 2 years' purchase of the average profits for the last three years.

Solution:

AVERAGE MAINTAINABLE PROFITS

	Rs
Profit for 1986 (Rs 40,000—Rs 5,000)	35,000
Profit for 1987 (Rs 50,000 + 10,000)	60,000
Profit for 1988 (Rs 45,000—Rs 5,000)	40,000
Total profit for three years	1,35,000

$$\text{Average Profit} = \frac{1,35,000}{3} = \text{Rs } 45,000$$

Goodwill at 2 years' purchase of the average profits = 45,000 × 2 = Rs 90,000.

2. **Super profits method.** The term 'super profit' refers to the 'excess profit' made by a concern over 'normal profit'. The valuation of goodwill in such a case depends on the following factors:

   (a) *Average capital employed in the business.* This is the average of the capital employed in the beginning and the capital employed at the end of accounting period. The capital employed is calculated as follows:

	Rs
Assets (other than goodwill, preliminary expenses or fictitious assets) (say)	1,50,000
Less: Liabilities due to outsiders (such as creditors, bills payable,	
outstanding expenses etc. (say)	50,000
Capital employed	1,00,000

   (b) *Normal profit.* The normal profit is calculated on the basis of normal rate of return earned by similar business applied to average capital employed in the business.

   Average capital employed × Normal rate of return.

For example if the average capital employed in the business is Rs 1,00,000 and the normal rate of profit is 10%, the normal profit would amount to Rs 10,000.

   (c) *Average expected profit.* This is calculated on the basis of past profit adjusted in the light of future expectation.

For example if the average profits of the business for the last three years have been Rs 15,000 and it is expected that they will further go up by 10% on account of exploring new markets, the average expected profit would amount to Rs 16,500 (*i.e.* Rs 15,000 + Rs 1,500).

   (d) *Super profit.* The difference between the average expected profit and normal profit is the amount of super profit. In the present case it would amount to Rs 6,500 (*i.e.* Rs 16,500–Rs 10,000).

   (e) *Number of years.* The amount of super profit so calculated will be multiplied by the number of years for which the super profit is expected to continue. For example, if it estimated that the super profit will continue to the new buyer of the business for two years, the amount of goodwill be Rs 13,000 (*i.e.* 6,500 × 2).

Illustration 1.14. From the following particulars calculate the value of goodwill on the basis of 3 years' purchase of super profits of the business.

(*i*) Capital employed		Rs 50,000
(*ii*) Trading Profits:		
	1989 Profit	Rs 12,300
	1990 Profit	Rs 15,000

Contd....

1991 Loss	Rs 2,000
1992 Profit	Rs 21,000

(*iii*) Normal Rate to Return 20%

(*iv*) Remuneration for alternative employment to the proprietor if not engaged in the business Rs 5,000.

Solution:

(*i*) **Average expected profit.** The year 1991 seems to be an abnormal year. The business in all other years is giving profits except 1991. Hence, this year this should be ignored for calculating average expected profits.

Year	Profit
1989	12,300
1990	15,000
1992	21,000
Total Profits	48,300

Average Expected Profit $= \dfrac{48,300}{3} = 16,100$

Less: Remuneration for alternative employment 5,000

Expected Profit 11,100

(*ii*) **Normal Profit:**

$$50,000 \times \frac{20}{100} = \text{Rs } 10,000$$

(*iii*) **Super Profit**

Average Expected Profit—Normal Profit

= Rs 11,100 – Rs 10,000

= Rs 1,100

(*iv*) **Goodwill at 3 years' purchase**

Rs 1,100 × 3 = Rs 3,300

3 **Capitalisation of profits method.** The capitalisation of profit method values goodwill at the excess of capital that should have been employed for earning the average profit over the capital which has been actually employed.

Illustration 1.15. On the basis of data given in Illustration 1.14 calculate the value of goodwill according to capitalisation of profits method.

Solution:

Average Profit of Rs 11,100

Capitalised value of Profit @ 20%

$$= \frac{11,100 \times 100}{20} = \text{Rs } 55,500$$

Capital actually employed	= Rs 50,000	
Value of goodwill	= Rs 55,500 – Rs 50,000	
	= Rs 5,500	

JOINT LIFE POLICY

A partnership firm may decide to take a joint life insurance policy on the lives of all partners. The firm pays the premium and the amount of policy is payable to the firm in the event of death of any partner or on the maturity of policy, whichever is earlier. The objective of taking such a policy is to minimise the financial hardship to the firm in the event of payment of a large sum to the legal representative of a deceased partner. The accounting treatment for the premium paid and the joint life policy may be on any of the following basis:

(i) **The premium paid may be taken as a revenue expenditure.** In such a case the accounting entries will be as follows:

(a) On payment of premium

Joint Life Policy Insurance Premium A/c	Dr.
To Bank	

(b) On charging from P & L A/c

P. & L. Account	Dr.
To Joint Life Policy Insurance Premium A/c	

(c) On maturity of the policy

Insurance Company/Bank A/c	Dr.
To Partners' Capital Accounts (individually)	

(including the account of the legal representative of a deceased partner.)

Illustration 1.16. A, B and C are partner in a business sharing profits and losses in the ratio of 3:2:1. The firm has taken a joint life insurance policy on the lives of partners for a joint life with effect from 1, January 1986. The annual premium is Rs 2,000. On 31, December 1988, C dies and the full money is received from the Life Insurance Corporation. The firm has charged the premium to Profit & Loss Account each year on 31, December. You are required to make the necessary journal entries.

Solution:

JOURNAL

Date	Particulars		Dr. Amount Rs	Cr. Amount Rs
1986 1 Jan.	Insurance Premium A/c To Bank (Being payment of premium on joint life policy)	Dr.	2,000	2,000
31 Dec.	P. & L. A/c To Insurance Premium A/c (Premium written off)	Dr.	2,000	2,000
1987 1 Jan.	Insurance Premium A/c To Bank (Being payment of premium on joint life policy)	Dr.	2,000	2,000
31 Dec.	P. & L. A/c To Insurance Premium A/c (Being premium written off)	Dr.	2,000	2,000
1988 1 Jan.	Insurance Premium A/c To Bank (Being payment of premium on joint life policy)	Dr.	2,000	2,000

Contd....

Date	Particulars		Dr. Amount Rs	Cr. Amount Rs
	P. & L. A/c	Dr.	2,000	
	To Insurance Premium A/c			2,000
	(Being premium written off)			
	Bank A/c	Dr.	30,000	
	To A's Capital A/c			15,000
	To B's Capital A/c			10,000
	To C's Capital A/c			5,000
	(Being receipt of policy money from the Corporation)			

(*ii*) **The premium paid may be taken as a capital expenditure.** In such a case a 'Joint Life Insurance Policy A/c' is opened in the books. The amount of premium paid is debited to this account. The surrender value of the policy is credited to the account as balance to be carried forward to the next period. The difference of the two sides is written off from the Profit & Loss Account. On maturity of the policy, the amount realised is credited to the joint life policy account and the final balance distributed among the partners.

Illustration 1.17. With the data given in Illustration 1.16 prepare the Joint Life Policy Account, if the surrender value of policy is as follows:

At the end of 1986	Nil
At the end of 1987	Rs 500
At the end of 1988	Rs 2,000

Solution:

JOINT LIFE POLICY ACCOUNT

Date	Particulars	Rs	Date	Particulars	Rs
1986					
1 Jan.	To Bank	2,000	31 Dec.	By P. & L. A/c	2,000
			31 Dec.	By Balance c/d	Nil
		2,000			2,000
1987					
1 Jan.	To Bank	2,000	31 Dec.	By P. & L A/c	1,500
			31 Dec.	By Balance c/d	500
		2,000			2,000
1988					
1 Jan.	To Balance b/d	500	31 Dec.	By Bank	30,000
1 Jan.	To Bank	2,000			
31 Dec.	To A's Capital A/c	13,750			
	To B's Capital A/c	9,167			
	To C's Capital A/c	4,583			
		30,000			30,000

(*iii*) **Creation of joint life policy reserve account.** In case of this method Profit and Loss Appropriation Account is charged and Joint life Policy Reserve account is credited with the full amount of premium paid. The Joint Life Policy Account is debited with the amount of premium paid and credited with the surrender value of the policy as being the balance to be carried forward to the next period. The balance in the Joint Policy Account is written off from the Joint Life Policy Reserve Account. Thus, there is a balance in the "Joint Life Policy Reserve Account" equivalent to the balance in the "Joint Life Policy Account" The method can be well understood with the help of the following illustration.

Illustration 1.18. A B and C are partners in the business sharing profits and losses in ratio of 2:2:1. The firm has taken a joint life insurance policy for a sum of Rs 30,000 with effect from 1 January, 1986. The annual premium is Rs 2,000. The surrender value of the policy at the end of 1986, 1987 and 1988 are nil, 1,000 and 2,000 respectively.

On 15 June 1989, C dies and the firm gets the full money of the policy on 30th June.

You are required to pass necessary Journal entries and prepare the Joint Life Policy Account and Joint Life Policy Reserve Account in the books of the firm.

Solution:

JOURNAL

Date	Particulars		Dr. Rs	Cr. Rs
1986 1 Jan.	Joint Life Policy A/c To Bank (Being premium paid)	Dr.	2,000	2,000
31 Dec.	P. & L Appropriation A/c To Joint Life Policy Reserve A/c (Being the amount of premium charged from P & L Appropriation A/c)	Dr.	2,000	2,000
31 Dec.	Joint Life Policy Reserve A/c To Joint Life Policy A/c (Being the amount written off)	Dr.	2,000	2,000
1987 1 Jan.	Joint Life Policy A/c To Bank (Being premium paid)	Dr.	2,000	2,000
31 Dec.	P & L Appropriation A/c To Joint Life Policy Reserve A/c (Being amount of premium charged to P & L App. A/c)	Dr.	2,000	2,000
31 Dec.	Joint Life Policy Reserve A/c To Joint Life Policy A/c (Being amount written off)	Dr.	1,000	1,000
1988 1 Jan.	Joint Life Policy A/c To Bank (Being premium paid)	Dr.	2,000	2,000
31 Dec.	P & L Appropriate A/c To Joint Life Policy Reserve A/c (Being amount of premium charged to P & L App. A/c)	Dr.	2,000	2,000
31 Dec.	Joint Life Policy Reserve A/c To Joint Life Policy A/c (Being amount written off)	Dr.	1,000	1,000
1989 1 Jan.	Joint Life Policy A/c To Bank (Being the amount of premium paid)	Dr.	2,000	2,000

Contd....

Date	Particulars		Dr. Rs	Cr. Rs
15 June	Joint Life Policy A/c	Dr.	2,000	
	To Joint Life Policy A/c			2,000
	(Being amount transferred)			
	Bank	Dr.	30,000	
	To Joint Life Policy A/c			30,000
	(Being amount recovered from Life Insurance Corporation on death of C)			
	Joint Life Policy A/c	Dr.	28,000	
	To A's Capital A/c			11,200
	To B's Capital A/c			11,200
	To C's Capital A/c			5,600
	(Being the net profit on policy distribution among partners)			

Note. Since the Joint Life Policy has matured before the end of the accounting year, no entry has been passed for transferring premium paid from P & L Appropriation Account to Joint Life Policy Reserve Account in 1989.

JOINT LIFE POLICY ACCOUNT

Date	Particulars		Rs	Particulars	Rs
1986	To Bank		2,000	By Joint Life Policy Reserve A/c	2,000
			2,000		2,000
1987	To Bank		2,000	By Joint Life Policy Reserve A/c	1,000
				By Balance c/d	1,000
			2,000		2,000
1988	To Balance b/d		1,000	By Joint Life Policy Reserve A/c	1,000
	To Bank		2,000	By Balance c/d	2,000
			3,000		3,000
1989	To Balance b/d		2,000	By Joint Life Policy Reserve A/c	2,000
	To Bank		2,000	By Bank	30,000
	To A's Capital A/c	11,200			
	To B's Capital A/c	11,200			
	To C's Executor A/c	5,600	28,000		
			32,000		32,000

JOINT LIFE POLICY RESERVE ACCOUNT

Date	Particulars	Rs	Particulars	Rs
1986	To Joint Life Policy A/c	2,000	By P & L Appropriation A/c	2,000
		2,000		2,000
1987	To Joint Life Policy A/c	1,000	By P & L Appropriation A/c	2,000
	To Balance c/d	1,000		
		2,000		2,000

Contd....

Date	Particulars	Rs	Particulars	Rs
1988	To Joint Life Policy A/c	1,000	By Balance b/d	1,000
	To Balance c/d	2,000	By P & L Appropriate A/c	2,000
		3,000		3,000
1989	To Joint Life Policy A/c	2,000	By Balance b/d	2,000
		2,000		2,000

Note. In the Illustration given above the balance of Rs 2,000 standing credit to the Joint Life Policy Reserve Account has been transferred to Joint Life Policy Account at the end of the accounting period. The amount may alternatively by transferred directly to the Partners Capital Accounts in their profit sharing ratio.

CHANGE IN PROFIT SHARING RATIO

In the event of change in the profit sharing ratio among the partners, adjustments for goodwill, distribution of reserve etc. will be required. A partner who is gaining on account of such change should compensate the partner who is losing on account of such change. Consider the following illustration.

Illustration 1.19. *A* and *B* are sharing profits in the ratio of 3:2. The following is their Balance Sheet on 31 December, 1988.

Liabilities		Rs	Assets	Rs
Creditors		10,000	Buildings	20,000
Capital :	A	15,000	Plant	10,000
	B	10,000	Cash	5,000
		35,000		35,000

The goodwill of the firm has been valued at Rs 10,000 and the buildings at Rs 25,000 on 31st December, 1988.

The partners decide to share profits equally with effect from 1 January, 1989. You are required to pass the adjustment entry or entries necessary on account of such change in the share of profits.

Solution:

There are two alternatives:

(*i*) Crediting the partners with the increase in the value of the assets in the old ratio and then writing off such increase in the new ratio.

(*ii*) Passing a net entry with the amount of profit or loss.

First Alternative

JOURNAL

Date	Particulars		Dr. Rs	Cr. Rs
	Goodwill A/c	Dr.	10,000	
	Building A/c	Dr.	5,000	
	To A's Capital A/c			9,000
	To B's Capital A/c			6,000
	(Being the amount of goodwill and appreciation in the value of buildings credited to partners in the old ratio)			

Contd....

Date	Particulars		Dr. Rs	Cr. Rs
	A's Capital A/c	Dr.	7,500	
	B's Capital A/c	Dr.	7,500	
	To Goodwill A/c			10,000
	To Building A/c			5,000
	(Being the goodwill and appreciation in the value of building written off in the new ratio)			

Second Alternative

On account of change in the profit sharing ratio A's loss has been 1/10 while B's gain has been 1/10. Thus, A should be compensated by Rs 1,500 (*i.e.*, 1/10 of Rs 15,000) by B. The Journal entry therefore should be:

Particulars		Rs	Rs
B's Capital A/c	Dr.	1,500	
To A's Capital A/c			1,500
(Being adjustment required on account of goodwill and revaluation of buildings)			

KEY TERMS

☐ **Goodwill:** An intangible asset arising from business connections, trade name or reputation of an enterprise.

☐ **Partnership:** The relation between persons who agreed to share the profits of business carried on by all and any of them acting for all.

☐ **Partnership Deed:** A document in writing containing the important terms of partnership as agreed by the partners between themselves.

TEST QUESTIONS

Objective type   TEST YOUR UNDERSTANDING

1. State whether each of the following statements is '*True*' or '*False*'.
   (a) A partnership firm enjoys a separate legal personality apart from its partners.
   (b) Every partner has a right to be consulted in all matters affecting the business of partnership.
   (c) Current Accounts are maintained in case of Fluctuating Capital System.
   (d) In the absence of any contract to the contrary partners are required to share profits and losses equally.
   (e) Partners are mutual agents for each other.

   [**Ans.** (a) False; (b) True; (c) False; (d) True; (e) True].

2. Select the most appropriate answer:
   (a) An ordinary partnership firm can have
      (i) not more than 20 partners.
      (ii) not more than 50 partners.
      (iii) any number of partners
   (b) A banking partnership firm can have

(i) not more than 50 partners.
(ii) not more than 10 partners.
(iii) not more than 5 partners.
(c) In the absence of any provisions in the partnership agreement partners can
  (i) charge interest at 6% p.a.
  (ii) charge interest at 12% p.a.
  (iii) no interest
    on loans given by them to the partnership firm.
(d) In the absence of any provision in the partnership agreement, profits and losses are shared by partners.
  (i) in the ratio of their capitals.
  (ii) equally.
  (iii) in the ratio of loans given by them to the partnership firm.
(e) The value of the goodwill of the business will be the highest if the majority of the customers of the firm are of the nature of
  (i) cats.
  (ii) dogs.
  (iii) rats.

[Ans. (a) (i), (b) (ii), (c) (i), (d) (ii), (e) (i)]

Essay type | FOR REVIEW, DISCUSSION AND PRACTICE |

1. Define partnership, Explain its salient features.
2. Explain the meaning of a "Partnership Deed". State the rights and duties of partners in the absence of a partnership deed.
3. (a) What is goodwill? How is it valued?
   (b) Differentiate between fixed and fluctuating capital systems.
4. How the arrangement regarding "joint life policy" on the lives of the partners is recorded in the accounts of a partnership firm.
5. State the rule applicable to each of the following cases in the absence of a partnership agreement :
   (a) Salaries to partners;
   (b) Interest on a loan given by a partner to the firm;
   (c) Interest on capital;
   (d) Sharing profit and losses;
   (e) Interest on drawings.

PRACTICAL PROBLEMS

Final Accounts

1. Ramjee was the sole proprietor of a trading firm till 30 June. On 1 July, 1985 he admitted his major son Balajee into partnership for a 1/5th share in profit and interest on capital. The following Profit and Loss Account was extracted from the books of the business for the year 1985:

Particulars	Amount Rs	Particulars	Amount Rs
To Rent	2,400	By Gross Profit	2,00,000
To Depreciation	3,600		
To Advertisement	6,000		
To Salaries	6,000		
To Administration Expense	60,000		

Contd....

Particulars	Amount Rs	Particulars	Amount Rs
To Packing and Forwarding	12,000		
To Interest on Capital	12,000		
To Net Profit	98,000		
	2,00,000		2,00,000

It is ascertained that sales for 6 months ending 30th June, 1985 were Rs 2,40,000. Due to the admission of the new partner on 1st July, the average sales thereafter increased by 50%. The administration and other similar expenses remained uniform throughout the year. Consequently expenses which are likely to vary with turnover may be apportioned on the basis of the turnover in the respective half years while other expenses may be apportioned on time basis.

You are required to prepare the Profit and Loss Account in columnar fashion showing the profit prior to admission of the new partner and the profits distributable between the partners.

[Ans. Profit upto 30 Jan. 1985 Rs 36,800; Profit from 1 July, 1985 to 31 Dec. Rs 61,200]

2. On 1 January 1987, John and Robert commenced business as partners with an initial capital of Rs 20,000 and Rs 30,000 in their respective accounts. The partnership deed provided *inter-alia*, that:

(i) Profits/Losses shall be shared in the ratio of 2:3 as between John and Robert;

(ii) Partners shall be entitled to interest on capital at the commencement of each year at 6% p.a; and

(iii) Interest on drawings shall be charged at 8% p.a.

During the year ended 31 December, 1987, the firm made a profit of Rs 19,280 before adjustment of interest on capital and drawings. The partners withdrew during the year Rs 3,000 each at the end of every quarter commencing from 31 March, 1987.

You are required to open a Profit and Loss Adjustment Account and show the entries for interest and distribution of profit.

Show also the Capital Accounts of partners for the year.

[Ans. Net profit to John Rs 6,800; Robert Rs 10,200 Balance in Capital Accounts: John Rs 15,640; Robert Rs 29,640]

3. Abraham, Basu and Chatterjee carry on business in partnership with Head Office at Delhi and branches at Bombay and Calcutta. Under their agreement Basu and Chatterjee (respectively managing Bombay and Calcutta Branches) are entitled to a fixed annual salary of Rs 5,000 and to a commission equal to 30% of the Profit respective branches after deducting therefrom the aforesaid salary amount and an equivalent to 10% of the average net assets (excluding cash) employed in the branch. Interest @ 5% on capital is to be charged. Further if the total share of Chatterjee is to be less than Rs 30,000 (for which purpose the salary, interest commission and the share of profit are to be aggregated), the shortfall is to be borne equally by Abraham and Basu. The profit sharing ratio is 5:3:2 From the following information show the allocation amongst the partners.

S. No.	Particulars	Dr. Amount Rs	Cr. Amount Rs
1.	Capital and Drawings:		
	Abraham	30,000	2,00,000
	Basu	17,500	80,000
	Chatterjee	14,000	60,000
2.	Assets (excluding cash) and Liabilities as on 31 October 1988		
	Delhi	2,35,900	21,400
	Bombay	93,800	12,200
	Calcutta	71,100	8,500

Contd....

S. No.	Particulars	Dr. Amount Rs	Cr. Amount Rs
3.	Profit for the year to 31 October, 1987 (without making any appropriations for the partners)		
	Delhi		63,350
	Bombay		31,900
	Calcutta		27,600

It is ascertained that the net assets (excluding cash) of the Bombay and Calcutta branches have registered an increase of Rs 5,200 and Rs 3,200 respectively, as compared to November 1, 1986.

[Ans. Commission Basu Rs 5,700, Chatterjee Rs 4,920, Profit Abraham Rs 42,598, Basu Rs 25,552, Chatterjee Rs 17,080]

4. Weakheart and Longhead are in partnership sharing profits and losses in the ratio of 3:2. They decided to admit Coramin, their Manager, as a partner with effect from 10 April 1988, giving one-fourth share of profits.

C ramin, while a manager, was in receipt of salary and of Rs 13,500 per annum and 10 per cent of the net profits after charging such salary and commission.

In terms of the partnership deed, any excess amount, which Coramin will be entitled to receive as a partner over the amount which would have been due to him if he continued to be the manager, would have to be personally borne by Weakheart out of his share of profit.

Profit for the year ended 31 March, 1989 amounted to Rs 1,12,500.

You are required to show the division of profit among partners for the year ended 31st March, 1989.

[Ans. Share of Coramin Rs 28,125, Weakheart Rs 48,375, Longhead Rs 36,000]

Adjustment of Closed Partnership Accounts

5. A and B are equal partners. The capitals are Rs 8,000 and Rs 16,000 respectively. After the accounts for the year are prepared, it is discovered that interest at 5% p.a. as provided in the partnership agreement has not been credited to the capital accounts before distribution of profits. It is decided to make an adjustment entry at the beginning of the next year.

Give the necessary Journal entry along with narration.

[Ans. A to be debited by Rs 200 and B to be credited by Rs 200]

6. Mohan, Vijay and Anil are partners, the balances on their capital accounts, being Rs 30,000, Rs 25,000 and Rs 20,000 respectively. In arriving at these figures, the profits for the year ended December 31, 1982 Rs 24,000 has already been credited to partners in the proportion in which they shared profits. Their drawings were Rs 5,000 (Mohan), Rs 4,000 (Vijay) and Rs 3,000 (Anil) in 1982. Subsequently, the following omissions were noticed and it was decided to bring them into account.

(i) Interest on capital at 10% per annum.

(ii) Interest on drawings Mohan Rs 250, Vijay Rs 200 and Anil Rs 150.

Make the necessary correction through Profit and Loss Adjustment account and through a Journal entry.

[Ans. Debit Anil by Rs 550 and Credit Mohan by Rs 550]

7. The summarised capital accounts of M/s Kay & Kay appear as under:

Date	Kamal Rs	Kumar Rs	Keerti Rs	Date	Kamal Rs	Kumar Rs	Keerti Rs
31 Dec. 1986				1 January 1986			
To Drawings	12,000	12,000	12,000	By Balance b/d	20,000	30,000	40,000
To Balance c/d	23,000	33,000	43,000	By Profit for 1986	15,000	15,000	15,000
	35,000	45,000	55,000		35,000	45,000	55,000

On 1 January 1987, it is agreed that the following would be effective retrospectively from 1 January, 1986

(*i*) Kamal shall be entitled to salary of Rs 750 p.m.

(*ii*) Interest shall be allowed on partners' capital accounts at 5% p.a. on the opening balances.

(*iii*) Keerti's share of profit exclusive of interest on his capital shall not fall below Rs 15,000 the deficit if any, being contributed by Kamal out of his share.

You are required to show the entries in the capital accounts on 1 January, 1987 to give the effect to the above arrangements.

(C.A. Entrance, Nov., 1977, adapted)

[Ans. (Dr.) Kumar by Rs 3,000 and (Cr.) Kamal by Rs 1,000 and (Cr.) Keerti
by Rs 2,000]

8. Weak, Able and Lazy are in partnership sharing profits and losses in the ratio of 2:1:1. It is agreed that interest on capital will be allowed @ 5 per cent per annum and interest on drawings will be charged @ 4 per cent per annum. (No interest will be charged/allowed on current accounts).

The following are the particulars of the Capital, Current and Drawings Accounts of the partners:

Particulars	Weak Rs	Able Rs	Lazy Rs
Capitals (1 January, 1990)	75,000	40,000	30,000
Current Accounts (1 January, 1990)	10,000	5,000	5,000 (Dr.)
Drawings	15,000	10,000	10,000
Interest on Drawings (1990)	500	190	350

The draft accounts for 1990 showed a net profit of Rs 60,000 before taking into account interest on capital and drawings and subject to following rectification of errors:

(*a*) Life Insurance Premium of Weak amounting to Rs 750 paid by the firm on 31 December, 1990 has been charged to Miscellaneous Expenditure A/c.

(*b*) Repairs of machinery amounting to Rs 10,000 has been debited to Plant Account and depreciation thereon charged @ 20 per cent.

(*c*) Travelling expenses of Rs 3,000 of Able for a pleasure trip to U.K. paid by the firm on 30 June 1990 has been debited to Travelling Expenses A/c.

You are required to prepare the Profit and Loss Appropriation Account for the year ended 31 December 1990 and the partners' current accounts for the year.

[Ans. Share of Profit: Weak Rs 24,800, Able Rs 12,400, Lazy Rs 12,400;
Current Account Balances: Weak Rs 22,300 (Cr.); Able Rs 6,150 (Cr.). Lazy
Rs 1,450 (Dr.)]

Goodwill

10. Calculate the value of goodwill, on the basis of 3 years' purchase the annual average super profits, from the following information:

	Rs
Average Capital employed	50,000
Normal Rate of Return	10%
Average Profits	7,000

[Ans. Rs 6,000]

11. Calculate the value of goodwill with the information given in the above question if the average profits of Rs 7,000 are capitalised at 10%.

[Ans. Rs 20,000]

12. Calculate the amount of goodwill in the following case:

Three years' purchase of the last four years' average profits. The profits and losses for the last four years are:

	Rs
I year	5,000
II year	8,000
III year	3,000 (Loss)
IV year	6,000

[Ans. Rs 12,000]

13. Calculate the amount of Goodwill in the following cases;

(*i*) Three years' purchase of the last five years' average profits. The profits for the last five years' are:

		Rs
I year	...	4,800
II year	...	7,200
III year	...	10,000
IV year	...	3,000
V year	...	5,000

(*ii*) The average Net Profits expected in the future by *ABC* Firm are Rs 36,000 per year. The average capital employed in the business by the Firm is 2,00,000. The rate of interest expected from capital invested in this class of business is 10%. The remuneration of the partners is estimated to be Rs 6,000 per annum. Find out the value of goodwill on the basis of two years' purchase of super profits.

[Ans. (*i*) Rs 18,000; (*ii*) Rs 20,000]

Fixed and Fluctuating Capital Accounts

14. *X* and *Y* are partners sharing profits in proportion of 7/10ths and 3/10th with capitals of Rs 15,000 and 10,000 respectively. 5% interest was agreed to be calculated on the capital of each partner and *Y* is to be allowed an annual salary of Rs 2,400 which has not been withdrawn. During the year 1987 *X* withdrew Rs 1,200 and *Y* Rs 2,000 in anticipation of profits.

The profits for the year prior to calculation of interest on capital but after charging *Y*'s salary amounted to Rs 8,000. A provision of 7 1/2% on this amount is to be made in respect of commission to the manager. Show the partners' accounts: (*a*) where capitals are fluctuating; (*b*) where the capitals are fixed and; (*c*) the Profit & Loss account showing the allocation of profits.

[Ans. (*a*) Capitals fluctuating: Balances: *X*'s Capital A/c Rs 18,855 *Y*'s Capital A/c Rs 12,745.

(*b*) Capital fixed: *X*'s Capital A/c Rs 15,000
Y's Capital A/c Rs 10,000
X's Current A/c Rs 3,855
Y's Current A/c Rs 2,745

(*c*) *X*'s share of profit Rs 4,305; *Y*'s share of profit Rs 1,845]

15. *A*, *B* and *C* are in partnership with respective fixed capitals of Rs 40,000, Rs 30,000 and Rs 20,000. *B* and *C* are entitled to annual salaries of Rs 2,000 and Rs 1,500 respectively payable before division of profits. Interest on capital is allowed at 5% per annum, but no interest is charged on drawings.

Of the first 12,000 divisible profits in the year, *A* is entitled to 50%, *B* to 30% and *C* to 20%. Annual profits in excess of Rs 12,000 are divisible equally.

The profits for the year ended 31 December, 1986 were Rs 20,100 after debiting partners' salaries but before charging interest on capital.

The partners' drawings for the year were. *A* Rs 8,000 *B* Rs 7,500, *C* Rs 4,000.

The balances on the partners current accounts on 1 January 1986 were: A Rs 3,000 (Cr.), B Rs 500 (Cr.), C Rs 1,000 (Dr.).

Prepare the partners current accounts for the year 1986.

[Ans. Current account balances: A Rs 4,200; B Rs 1,300; C Rs 1,100]

Joint Life Policy

16. A, B and C sharing profits and losses in the ratio of 5:3:2 took out a Joint Life Policy for Rs 20,000 paying an annual premium of Rs 800 starting from January 1, 1981. The surrender value of the policy was as follows:

1981-Nil;   1982-Rs 200;   1983-Rs 500;
1984-Rs 900;   1985-Rs 1,200.

On 1st November 1985 A died and the Insurance Company paid Rs 20,000 on December 1, 1985. Write up the joint policy account assuming that surrender value is treated as an asset.

[Ans. Profit on Joint Life Policy Rs 18,300]

17. A, B and C were partners sharing profits and losses in the ratio of 3:2:1. In order to meet the financial requirements in case of death of a partner the firm took a joint life policy for Rs 12,000 on 1 January 1980 paying an annual premium of Rs 1,000. The firm closes its books on 31 December each year, and the policy was shown at its surrender value each year. Such values at 31 December each year were as follows: 1980 Rs Nil, 1981 Rs 240, 1982 Rs 540, 1983 Rs 800. B died on 30 September, 1984 and the policy money was received on 18 November, 1984.

You are required to show the Joint Life Policy Account in the books of the firm from 1 January 1980 to 31 December 1984.

[Ans. A, B's executors and C will be credited by Rs 5,100, 3,400 and 1,700 respectively]

18. X and Y sharing profits in the ratio of 3:2 took out a joint life policy on 1 January, 1980 for Rs 20,000 for 20 years. Annual premium is Rs 1,000 which is paid by the firm in four equal instalments of Rs 250 each on 1 January, 1 April, 1 July and 1 October every year.

The surrender value were 1980: Nil, 1981: Rs 200, 1982: Rs 550, 1983: Rs 970.

Y died on 8 March 1982 and due claim was received on 30th April. Show Life Policy Account and Life Policy Reserve Account.

[Ans. X gets Rs 11,400 and Y's executors get Rs 7,600]
[Hint. Insurance premium will be charged for the full year in 1982].

Change in Profit sharing ratio

19. A and B are sharing profits and losses of a business equally. They decide to change the profit sharing ratio to 3:2. The value of firm's goodwill (for which no account appears in the books) on this date is Rs 5,000. General Reserve is appearing in the books at Rs 4,000.

You are required to pass the necessary adjustment journal entry.

[Ans. Debit A by Rs 900 and Credit B by Rs 900)

20. X, Y and Z were partner sharing profits and losses in the ratio of 4:3:2 Goodwill does not appear in the books but it is worth Rs 36,000.

The partners decide to share future profits in equal proportions. Give a journal entry to record the above change. Also indicate the individual partner's gain or loss due to change in the ratio. Show your working clearly.

[Ans. Debit Z by Rs 4,000 and Credit X by Rs 4,000]

21. The following is the Balance Sheet of M/s X, Y and Z sharing profits in the ratio of 2:2:1 as on 31st December, 1988:

Liabilities	Amount Rs	Assets	Amount Rs
Creditors	10,000	Goodwill	10,000
Bills Payable	5,000	Plant	20,000

Contd....

Liabilities	Amount Rs	Assets	Amount Rs
Capitals:		Buildings	10,000
X	20,000	Stock	10,000
Y	10,000	Debtors	3,000
Z	5,000	Cash	1,000
General Reserve	4,000		
	54,000		54,000

The partners decide to share the profits equally with effect from 1st January, 1989. The goodwill was valued at Rs 15,000. However, it was decided to continue the Goodwill at its present value and leave the General Reserve undisturbed.

You are required to make the necessary journal entry.

[Ans. *Debit Z* by Rs 1,200 and *Credit X* and *Y* with Rs 600 each]

Chapter 2

RECONSTITUTION OF PARTNERSHIP FIRM–I
(Admission)

LEARNING OBJECTIVES

After studying this chapter you should be able to:

- ☐ explain the meaning of reconstitution of a partnership firm;
- ☐ identify the accounting problems arising on admission of a partner;
- ☐ appreciate the need for making different accounting adjustments on admission of a partner;
- ☐ make appropriate accounting entries for different accounting adjustments; and
- ☐ explain the meaning of certain key terms.

Any change in the relations of the partners will result in the reconstitution of a partnership firm. The firm is, therefore, said to be reconstituted when there is admission, retirement or death of a partner or where a partnership firm gets amalgamated with another partnership firm. In the present chapter, the accounting entries relating to admission of a partner are being explained. The accounting entries relating to retirement or death of a partner and amalgamation of a partnership firm with another firm are being explained in the next chapter.

ADMISSION OF PARTNER

Section 31 of the Partnership Act deals with the statutory provision regarding admission of a new partner. These provisions are summarised below:

- (*i*) A new partner cannot be admitted without the consent of all the partners unless otherwise agreed upon.
- (*ii*) A new partner admitted to an existing firm, is not liable to any debts of the firm incurred, before he comes in as a partner. The new partner cannot be held responsible for the acts of the old partners unless it is proved that:
- (*a*) the reconstituted firm has assumed the liability to pay the debt; and
- (*b*) that the creditor concerned has agreed to accept the reconstituted firm as his debtor and to discharge the old firm from liability.

However, a minor admitted to the benefits of partnership, who, if he elects to become a partner in the firm after attaining majority, shall become personally liable for all the acts of the firm done since he was admitted to the benefits of partnership.

A newly admitted partner shall be liable only for the debts incurred or transactions entered into by the firm subsequent to his becoming a partner.

ACCOUNTING PROBLEMS

The accounting problems on admission of a new partner can be put as follows:

(i) Adjustment in the profit sharing ratio.

(ii) Adjustment for goodwill.

(iii) Adjustment for revaluation of assets and liabilities.

(iv) Adjustment for reserves and other accumulated profits.

(v) Adjustment for capital.

Each of the above problems are being discussed in the following pages.

Adjustment in the Profit Sharing Ratio

A newly admitted partner will be entitled to share the profits or bear the losses with the other partners. Hence the profit sharing ratio of the partners will change. There can be two situations.

1. The new partner may be given a certain proportion of the total profit or required to bear a certain proportion of the total loss and the old partners continue to share the balance of profit or bear the balance of loss in the old ratio in between themselves.

Illustration 2.1. A and B are partners in a business sharing profits and losses in the ratio of 3:2. They admit a new partner C with 1/5 share in the profits. Calculate the new profit sharing ratio of the partners.

Solution:

C's share is 1/5 of the total profit. Thus, for A and B remaining profit is only 4/5 (i.e. $1 - 1/5$).

A and B continue to share profits in old ratio.

The shares of the two partners will therefore be:

$A \quad \frac{4}{5} \times \frac{3}{5} = \frac{12}{25}$ $\qquad$ $B \quad \frac{4}{5} \times \frac{2}{5} = \frac{8}{25}$

Thus the new profit sharing ratio is

	A		B		C
	$\frac{12}{25}$	:	$\frac{8}{25}$	:	$\frac{1}{5}$
or	12	:	8	:	5

Illustration 2.2. A and B sharing profits in the ratio of 3:2. They admit C with ⅕ share in the profits, which he gets equally from A and B. Calculate the new profit sharing ratio.

Solution:

C's share is $1/5$ of total profits. He gets it equally from A and B i.e. $\dfrac{1}{5} \times \dfrac{1}{2} = \dfrac{1}{10}$ from A and $\dfrac{1}{5} \times \dfrac{1}{2} = \dfrac{1}{10}$ from B.

A's share of profit will therefore be:

$$\frac{3}{5} - \frac{1}{10} = \frac{6-1}{10} = \frac{5}{10}$$

B's share of profit will therefore be:

$$\frac{2}{5} - \frac{1}{10} = \frac{4-1}{10} = \frac{3}{10}$$

Thus, the new profit sharing ratio is:

	A	:	B	:	C
	$\dfrac{5}{10}$	:	$\dfrac{3}{10}$	:	$\dfrac{1}{5}$
or	5	:	3	:	2

Illustration 2.3. A and B are partners sharing profits in the ratio of 7.3. A surrenders 1/7th of his share and B surrenders 1/3rd of his share in favour of C, the new partner. What is the new ratio and what is the sacrificing ratio?

Solution:

Old Profit sharing ratio

$$A : B$$
$$7 : 3$$

Surrender by A: $\quad 7/10 \times 1/7 = 7/70$
Surrender by B: $\quad 3/10 \times 1/3 = 3/30$

New Ratio:

$$A : 7/10 - 7/70 = \frac{49-7}{70} = 42/70 = 6/10$$

$$B : 3/10 - 3/30 = \frac{9-3}{30} = 6/30 = 1/5$$

$$C : 7/70 + 3/30 = 1/10 + 1/10 = 2/10$$

New Ratio:

$A : 6/10, B : 1/5, C : 2/10$

Or	12	:	4	:	4
Or	3	:	1	:	1

Adjustment for Goodwill

Since the new partner gets a share in the profits of the firm, he should compensate the old partners for sharing the earning of the firm on account of the reputation or goodwill earned by the partnership firm so far.

The problem of goodwill on admission of a new partner can be dealt in two different ways:

1. When the goodwill account already appears in the books.
2. When the goodwill account is not appearing in the books at the time of admission of a partner.

If the goodwill account is already appearing in the books. There can be three situations:

(i) The goodwill account is appearing at a proper value. In such an event no adjustment will be required for goodwill.

Illustration 2.4. A and B are sharing profits in the ratio 3 : 2. They admit a new partner C with 1/5 share in the profits. At the time of admission of C, goodwill is appearing in the firm's books at Rs 10,000 and it is agreed by all partners (including C) that it is properly valued. Should C pay anything for goodwill?

Solution:

Since goodwill is already appearing in the books, it shows that the old partners have already got credit to their capital accounts with the value of goodwill. Moreover, it is properly valued and hence C will not be required to pay anything for goodwill nor any further adjustment will be required.

(ii) The goodwill account is to be revalued. In such an event entry will be made only with the difference. The amount of over or under-valued goodwill is debited or credited to the old partners in the old ratio and credited or debited to goodwill account.

Illustration 2.5. With the information given in Illustration 2.4, pass the necessary journal entry if the goodwill is agreed to be valued at Rs 15,000 on C's admission.

Solution:

Goodwill A/c	Dr.	5,000	
To A's Capital A/c			3,000
To B's Capital A/c			2,000
(Being value of goodwill raised by Rs 5,000)			

(iii) Sometimes adjustment may have to be made for undisclosed goodwill. This happens when goodwill account is already appearing in the books but the new partner is required to bring premium for sharing future profits of the firm. In such an event the goodwill brought in by the new partner will be utilised as basis for revaluation of goodwill.

Illustration 2.6. A and B are partners sharing profits in the ratio of 3:2. Goodwill appears in the books at Rs 4,000. C is admitted as a partner and pays Rs 1,000 as premium for 1/5 share of the profits of the firm. Journalise the above transaction presuming that the profit sharing ratio between A and B remains unchanged.

Solution:

The question can be solved by taking any of the following two presumptions:

(i) Goodwill account is not to be disturbed.

(ii) Goodwill account is to be disturbed.

Where goodwill account is not to be disturbed

As C is acquiring 1/5 share of goodwill for Rs 1,000 the whole goodwill is Rs 5,000, of which Rs 4,000 already appears in the books. Hence, the value of undisclosed goodwill is Rs 1,000 and C's share, thereof is Rs 200. This amount should be debited to his capital account and credited to A and B in the ratio in which they sacrifice on account of admission of C. The amount of Rs 1,000 brought in by C, should then be credited to his capital account. C's account thus gets a credit of Rs 800. The journal entries will be:

Particulars		Dr. Amount Rs	Cr. Amount Rs
C's Capital A/c	Dr.	200	
To A's Capital A/c			120
To B's Capital A/c			80
(Being premium charged to C for 1/5 share of the undisclosed goodwill)			
Bank A/c	Dr.	1,000	
To C's Capital A/c			1,000
(Being payment by C of the premium for 1/5 share of the goodwill)			

In case, on dissolution of the firm the goodwill realises Rs 5,000, C will get Rs 200 (*i.e.* 1/5 of Rs 1,000) out of the profit on account of sale of goodwill.

Thus, he is compensated for Rs 200 with which he was charged on his admission.

When goodwill account is to be disturbed

There could be two alternatives:

(*a*) The increase or decrease in the value of the goodwill be debited or credited to old partners capital accounts in the old ratio. The entire premium brought in by the new partner may be credited to his capital account.

The following journal entries will be passed in such a case on basis of information given in the Illustration 2.6.

Particulars		Dr. Amount Rs	Cr. Amount Rs
Goodwill a/c	Dr.	1,000	
To A's Capital A/c			600
To B's Capital A/c			400
(Being goodwill revalued)			
Bank A/c	Dr.	1,000	
To C's Capital A/c			1,000
(Premium brought in by C credited to his capital account)			

Thus, C has not paid anything to A and B for goodwill because goodwill has now been revalued on his admission and A and B have got due credit for it.

(*b*) The old goodwill may be written off and charged to old partners in the old ratio. Cash brought in by C should be credited to the old partners in their sacrificing ratio. Goodwill account is then raised at the new value and credit is given to all the partners in their new ratio. The journal entries will be as follows:

Particulars		Dr. Amount Rs	Cr. Amount Rs
A's Capital A/c	Dr.	2,400	
B's Capital A/c	Dr.	1,600	
To Goodwill A/c			4,000
(Being goodwill account written off)			
Bank	Dr.	1,000	
To A's Capital A/c			600
To B's Capital A/c			400
(Cash brought in by C for goodwill being credited to A and B)			

Contd....

Particulars		Dr. Amount Rs	Cr. Amount Rs
Goodwill A/c	Dr.	5,000	
To A's Capital A/c			2,400
To B's Capital A/c			1,600
To C's Capital A/c			1,000
(Goodwill account raised)			

The net affect of these entries is the same as given in case of alternative (*a*), discussed above.

When the goodwill account is not appearing in the books. There can be several alternatives.

(*i*) The new partner may bring cash for his share of goodwill. The amount so brought in by the new partner will be credited to the old partners in the ratio in which they sacrifice on admission of the new partner.

Illustration 2.7. *A* and *B* are sharing profits equally. They admit a new partner *C* with 1/5 share in profits. The new profit sharing ratio being 2 : 2 : 1. The value of firm's goodwill is Rs 10,000. *C* brings his share of goodwill in cash. Pass the necessary journal entry.

Solution:

A and *B* were sharing profits in the ratio of 1/2 and 1/2.

Under the new agreement *A* gets 2/5 and *B* gets 2/5.

Thus, sacrifice made by *A* and *B* is equal:

$$A \qquad \frac{1}{2} - \frac{2}{5} = \frac{5-4}{10} = \frac{1}{10}$$

$$B \qquad \frac{1}{2} - \frac{2}{5} = \frac{5-4}{10} = \frac{1}{10}$$

The amount of goodwill Rs 2,000 (*i.e.* $10,000 \times \frac{1}{5}$) will, therefore, be shared by *A* and *B* equally, The journal entry will be:

Particulars		Dr. Amount Rs	Cr. Amount Rs
Bank A/c	Dr.	2,000	
To A's Capital A/c			1,000
To B's Capital A/c			1,000
(Being goodwill brought in by C)			

Alternatively, the amount brought in cash for goodwill by the new partner be credited to the goodwill account. It may then be transferred to old partners' capital accounts in the sacrificing ratio. However, the method is not preferable to one discussed above.

The journal entries in such a case would be:

Particulars		Dr. Amount Rs	Cr. Amount Rs
Bank A/c	Dr.	2,000	
To Goodwill A/c			2,000
(Being amount of goodwill brought in by the new partner)			
Goodwill A/c	Dr.	2,000	
To A's Capital A/c			1,000
To B's Capital A/c			1,000
(Goodwill distributed among the old partners)			

Another alternative could be to credit the new partner's capital account with the cash brought in by him for capital and goodwill. A goodwill account is raised in the books with full value and the amount is credited to the old partners in the old profit sharing ratio. The goodwill account is then written off to all partners in the new profit sharing ratio.

Illustration 2.8. A and B are two partners sharing profits in the ratio of 3 : 2. They admit a new partner C. The new ratio being 2 : 2 : 1 for A, B and C respectively. C brings Rs 10,000 as capital and Rs 5,000 as goodwill. Pass the necessary journal entries.

Solution:

JOURNAL

Particulars		Dr. Amount Rs	Cr. Amount Rs
Bank A/c	Dr.	15,000	
To C's Capital A/c			15,000
(Being the amount of goodwill and capital brought in by C)			
Goodwill A/c	Dr.	25,000	
To A's Capital A/c			15,000
To B's Capital A/c			10,000
(Being goodwill account raised)			
A's Capital A/c	Dr.	10,000	
B's Capital A/c	Dr.	10,000	
C's Capital A/c	Dr.	5,000	
To Goodwill			25,000
(Being goodwill account written off)			

The amount brought in by new partner for goodwill may be either wholly or partly withdrawn by the old partners. For example, if in the Illustration 2.7 A and B withdraw in cash 50% of the amount of goodwill brought in by C, the accounting entry will be:

Particulars		Dr. Amount	Cr. Amount
A's Capital A/c	Dr.	500	
B's Capital A/c	Dr.	500	
To Bank			1,000
(Being 50% goodwill brought in cash withdrawn)			

(*ii*) A goodwill account may be raised in the books. In such an event the new partner will not bring any cash for his share of goodwill. The goodwill so raised will be credited to the old partners in their old profit sharing ratio.

Illustration 2.9. A and B are sharing profits in a business in ratio of 3:2. They admit C as a partner. The new ratio being 2 : 2 : 1 for A, B and C respectively. The value of the firm's goodwill is estimated at Rs 15,000. C is not in a position to bring any cash for his share of goodwill. Pass a suitable journal entry for adjustment of goodwill in the partners' capital accounts.

Solution:

Particulars		Dr. Amount	Cr. Amount
Goodwill A/c	Dr.	15,000	
To A's Capital A/c			9,000
To B's Capital A/c			6,000
(Being goodwill account raised)			

(*iii*) The new partners may not like to continue with the goodwill account in the firm's books. In such an event the goodwill account which was raised on admission of a partner, will be written off among all the partners in the new profit sharing ratio.

Illustration 2.10. With the information given in Illustration 2.9 state the journal entries to be passed when the partners first decide to raise the goodwill account and subsequently decide to write it off.

Solution:

JOURNAL

Particulars		Dr. Amount Rs	Cr. Amount Rs
Goodwill A/c	Dr.	15,000	
To A's Capital A/c			9,000
To B's Capital A/c			6,000
(Being goodwill account raised)			
A's Capital A/c	Dr.	6,000	
B's Capital A/c	Dr.	6,000	
C's Capital A/c	Dr.	3,000	
To Goodwill A/c			15,000
(Being goodwill account written off)			

(*iv*) The partners may desire to make adjustment for goodwill without raising the goodwill account at all. In such an event the following entry may be passed on the basis of data given in Illustration 2.9.

Particulars		Dr. Amount Rs	Cr. Amount Rs
C's Capital A/c	Dr.	3,000	
To A's Capital A/c			3,000

C has been debited because he gets 1/5 share in the profits and the entire sacrifice has been made by *A*.

(*v*) The new partner may be in a position to pay cash only for a part of his share of goodwill. In such an event the amount received as premium will be credited to the old partners in their sacrificing ratio and for the balance of his share, a goodwill account will be raised in the firm's books.

Illustration 2.11. *X*, *Y* and *Z* were partners sharing profits and losses as to *X* one-half: *Y* one- third and *Z* one-sixth. As from 1 January 1988, they agreed to admit *A* into partnership for a one-sixth share in profits and losses, which he acquired equally from *X* and *Y*, and he agreed to bring in Rs 20,000 for his capital and Rs 10,000 as premium for goodwill. *A* paid in his capital money but in respect of premium for goodwill he could bring in only Rs 5,000 and in regard to the unpaid amount he agreed to the raising of goodwill account in the books of the new firm as would be appropriate in the circumstances.

You are requested to:

(*i*) give the Journal entries to carry out the above arrangements, and

(*ii*) work out the new profit sharing ratio of the partners.

(C.A. Entrance, May, 1978, adapted)

Solution:

(*i*)   JOURNAL ENTRIES IN RECONSTITUTED PARTNERSHIP FIRM'S BOOKS
(as on 1 January, 1988)

Particulars		Dr. Amount Rs	Cr. Amount Rs
Cash	Dr.	25,000	
To A's Capital A/c			25,000
(Introduction of Rs 25,000 by incoming member A into the firm)			
A's Capital	Dr.	5,000	
To X's Capital			2,500
To Y's Capital			2,500
(Payment for goodwill credited in the sacrificing ratio to old partners)			
Goodwill	Dr.	30,000	
To X's Capital			15,000
To Y's Capital			10,000
To Z's Capital			5,000
(Raising of 50% of goodwill)			

(*iii*) New profit sharing ratio of partners X, Y, Z & A,

$$X = 3/2 - 1/12 = 5/12$$
$$Y = 1/3 - 1/12 = 3/12$$
$$Z = 1/6 - 0 \quad = 2/12$$
$$A = 1/6 \qquad\quad = 2/12$$

or X, Y, Z & A's new profit sharing ratio is 5 : 3 : 2 : 2 respectively.

Goodwill to be inferred. Sometimes the value of goodwill has to be inferred on the basis of total capital of the firm.

Illustration 2.12. A and B are equal partners in a partnership firm with capitals of Rs 14,000 each. They admit a new partner C in the firm with 1/4 share in the profits of the firm. C is to bring Rs 12,000 as his capital. No Goodwill account, at present, appears in the books of the firm. Pass the necessary journal entry for Goodwill in the books of the firm.

Solution:

Since C is required to bring Rs 12,000 as capital for 1/4 share in the profits of the firm, the total capital of the firm would be taken as Rs 48,000. The total capitals of the partners (including C) now stands at Rs 40,000. It means Rs 8,000 is hidden goodwill which should be credited to old partners in their old profit sharing ratio. The following journal entry would therefore be passed in the books of the firm:

Particulars		Dr. Amount Rs	Cr. Amount Rs
Goodwill A/c	Dr.	8,000	
To A's Capital A/c			4,000
To B's Capital A/c			4,000
(Being goodwill inferred on admission of C)			

Adjustment for Revaluation of Assets and Liabilities

The assets and liabilities may have to be revalued on admission of a partner so that the profit or loss on account of improper valuation of the assets or liabilities is shared or borne only by the old partners. The adjustment can be done in two ways:

When assets and liabilities have to appear in the books at the revised values.

In such a case a Profit and Loss Adjustment Account or Revaluation Account is opened in the books. The following entries are to be passed.

   (*i*) For increase in the value of an asset or decrease in the value of a liability:

      Asset/Liability A/c   Dr.
         To P. & L. Adjustment A/c

   (*ii*) For decrease in the value of an asset or increase in the value of a liability.

      P. & L. Adjustment A/c   Dr.
         To Asset/Liability A/c

   (*iii*) The profit on revaluation will be transferred to old partners' capital accounts in the old profit sharing ratio.

      P. & L. Adjustment A/c   Dr.
         To Old Partners Capital A/cs. (Individually)

In the event of loss, the entry will be reversed.

When assets and liabilities have to appear at old values in the books

A Memorandum Profit and Loss Adjustment Account will be opened in the books. The increase in the value of assets or decrease in the value of liabilities will be credited to this account. The decrease in the value of assets or increase in the value of liabilities will be debited to this account. However only two entries will be passed:

   (*i*) For credited in the profit on revaluation to old partners' accounts:

      Memorandum P. & L. Adjustment A/c   Dr.
         To Old Partners' Capital Accounts (in old ratio)

In case of loss the entry will be reversed.

   (*ii*) For writing off the profit on revaluation to all partners' capital accounts (including the new partner):

      Partners' Capital Accounts (in the new ratio)   Dr.
         To Memorandum P. & L. Adjustments A/c

In case of loss the entry will be reversed.

Illustration 2.13. Following is the Balance Sheet of Messrs *A* and *B* who are sharing profits in the ratio of 3:2.

BALANCE SHEET
as on 31 December, 1988

Liabilities	Amount Rs	Assets	Amount Rs
Sundry Creditors	10,000	Cash	5,000
Capitals:		Sundry Debtors	10,000
A	20,000	Buildings	20,000
B	10,000	Plant	5,000
	40,000		40,000

C is admitted as a partner with effect from 1 January, 1989. The new profit sharing ratio being 2 : 2 : 1. The following information has been given to you:

   (*i*) *C* will bring Rs 10,000 as capital.

   (*ii*) The value of the firm's goodwill is Rs 5,000.

(iii) An amount of Rs 2,000 owing to D for purchase of goods has been omitted from the list of sundry creditors.

(iv) Building is to be revaluted at Rs 30,000 and Plant at Rs 7,000.

You are required to pass the necessary Journal entries and prepare the Balance Sheet of the new firm when:

(a) assets and liabilities have to be shown in the books at the revised values.

(b) assets and liabilities have to continue in the books at the old values.

Solution:

(a) **When new values have to be recorded in the books.**

JOURNAL

Particulars		Dr. Amount Rs	Cr. Amount Rs
Cash A/c	Dr.	10,000	
To C's Capital A/c			10,000
(Being capital brought in by C)			
Goodwill A/c	Dr.	5,000	
To A's Capital A/c			3,000
To B's Capital A/c			2,000
(Goodwill A/c raised on C's admission)			
P. & L. Adjustment A/c	Dr.	2,000	
To Sundry Creditors			2,000
(A liability omitted now recorded)			
Plant A/c	Dr.	2,000	
Building A/c	Dr.	10,000	
To P. & L. Adjustment A/c			12,000
(Increase in the value of assets recorded)			
P. & L. Adjustment A/c	Dr.	10,000	
To A's Capital A/c			6,000
To B's Capital A/c			4,000
(Profit on revaluation credited to partners)			

BALANCE SHEET
as on 1 January, 1989

Liabilities	Amount Rs	Assets	Amount Rs
Sundry Creditors	12,000	Cash	15,000
Capital:		Sundry Debtors	10,000
A	29,000	Plant	7,000
B	16,000	Buildings	30,000
C	10,000	Goodwill	5,000
	67,000		67,000

Working Notes:

P. & L. ADJUSTMENT ACCOUNT

Particulars	Amount Rs	Particulars	Amount Rs
To Sundry Creditors	2,000	By Plant A/c	2,000
To Profit:		By Building A/c	10,000

Contd....

Particulars	Amount Rs	Particulars	Amount Rs
A's Capital A/c	6,000		
B's Capital A/c	4,000		
	12,000		12,000

PARTNERS' CAPITAL ACCOUNTS

Particulars	A Rs	B Rs	C Rs	Particulars	A Rs	B Rs	C Rs
To Balance c/d	29,000	16,000	10,000	By Balance b/d	20,000	10,000	—
				By Goodwill	3,000	2,000	—
				By P. & L. Adjustment A/c	6,000	4,000	—
				By Cash			10,000
	29,000	16,000	10,000		29,000	16,000	10,000

(b) When new values have not to be recorded in the books

Particulars	Dr. Amount Rs	Cr. Amount Rs
Cash A/c Dr.	10,000	
To C's Capital A/c		10,000
(Being capital brought in by C)		
Goodwill A/c Dr.	5,000	
To A's Capital A/c		3,000
To B's Capital A/c		2,000
(Goodwill A/c raised on C's admission		
A's Capital A/c Dr.	2,000	
B's Capital A/c Dr.	2,000	
C's Capital A/c	1,000	
To Goodwill A/c		5,000
(Goodwill account written off)		
Memorandum P. & L. Adj. A/c Dr.	10,000	
To A's Capital A/c		6,000
To B's Capital A/c		4,000
(Being profit on revaluation credited to partners capital accounts)		
A's Capital A/c Dr.	4,000	
B's Capital A/c Dr.	4,000	
C's Capital A/c Dr.	2,000	
To Memorandum P. & L. Adj A/c		10,000
(Being profit on revaluation written off)		

PARTNERS' CAPITAL ACCOUNTS

Particulars	A Rs	B Rs	C Rs	Particulars	A Rs	B Rs	C Rs
To Goodwill A/c	2,000	2,000	1,000	By Balance b/d	20,000	10,000	—
To Memorandum P.				By Goodwill	3,000	3,000	—

Contd....

Particulars	A Rs	B Rs	C Rs	Particulars	A Rs	B Rs	C Rs
& L. Adjustment A/c	4,000	4,000	2,000	By Memorandum P.	6,000	6,000	
To Balance c/d	23,000	10,000	7,000	& L. Adjustment A/c			
				By Cash			10,000
	29,000	16,000	10,000		29,000	16,000	10,000

BALANCE SHEET
as on 1 January, 1989

Liabilities	Amount Rs	Assets	Amount Rs
Sundry Creditors	10,000	Cash	15,000
Capital:		Sundry Debtors	10,000
A	23,000	Plant	5,000
B	10,000	Buildings	20,000
C	7,000		
	50,000		50,000

Working Notes:

MEMORANDUM P. & L. ADJUSTMENT ACCOUNT

Particulars	Amount Rs	Particulars	Amount Rs
To Sundry Creditors	2,000	By Plant A/c	2,000
To Profit:		By Building A/c	10,000
A's Capital A/c	6,000		
B's Capital A/c	4,000		
	12,000		12,000
To Reversal of entry (increase in the value of assets)	12,000	By Reversal of entry (increase in the value of liabilities)	2,000
		By A's Capital A/c	4,000
		By B's Capital A/c	4,000
		By C's Capital A/c	2,000
	12,000		12,000

Adjustments for Reserves and other Accumulated Profits

The amount standing to the credit of Reserves, representing accumulated profits or balance in the Profit & Loss Account should be distributed among the old partners in the old profit sharing ratio. The accounting entry will be:

P. & L. Account (if profit)	Dr.
General Reverse	Dr.
To Old Partners' Capital Accounts (in the old ratio)	

In case it is desired to leave the Reserves and P. & L. Account undisturbed, one more entry reversing the amount credited may be passed:

All Partners' Capital Accounts	Dr.
(in the new ratio)	
To P. & L. A/c	
To General Reserve	

In place of passing two entries only one entry may be passed crediting or debiting the partners with the net amount.

Illustration 2.14. *A* and *B* are partners in a business sharing profits and losses in the ratio of 3:2. They admit a new partner *C* with ⅕ share in the profits. The following amounts represented undistributed profits among the partners on the date of admission of *C*:

		Rs
(i)	P. & L. A/c balance	5,000
(ii)	General Reserve	10,000

You are required to pass the necessary Journal entries when:

(i) Old P. & L. A/c and General Reserve balances are not to appear in the New Firm's books:

(ii) Old P. & L. A/c and General Reserve balances are to appear in the New Firm's books.

Solution:

(i)

JOURNAL ENTRIES

Particulars		Dr. Amount Rs	Cr. Amount Rs
P. & L. A/c	Dr.	5,000	
General Reserve	Dr.	10,000	
To A's Capital A/c			9,000
To B's Capital A/c			6,000
(Being the amount of P. & L. A/c and General Reserve distributed among the partners)			

(ii)

JOURNAL ENTRIES

Particulars		Amount	Amount
P. & L. A/c	Dr.	5,000	
General Reserve	Dr.	10,000	
To A's Capital A/c			9,000
To B's Capital A/c			6,000
(Being the amount credited to old partners on account of P. & L. A/c balance and General Reserve)			
A's Capital A/c	Dr.	7,200	
B's Capital A/c	Dr.	4,800	
C's Capital A/c	Dr.	3,000	
To P & L. A/c			5,000
To General Reserve			10,000
(The amount credited to partners written off)			

OR

In place of passing the two entries one entry may be passed. The new partner may be debited with the share in the P. & L. A/c and General Reserve balances and the old partners be credited in the ratio in which they lose.

Particulars		Dr. Amount Rs	Cr. Amount Rs
C's Capital A/c	Dr.	3,000	
To A's Capital A/c			1,800
To B's Capital A/c			1,200
(Being adjmnt. for accumulated profit on admission of C)			

Adjustment for Capital

Adjustment for capital may be on any of the following two patterns:

1. The new partner may be required to bring proportionate capital on the basis of capitals of the old partners remaining after adjustments.

Illustration 2.15. A and B are partners in a business sharing profits and losses equally. Their original capitals were Rs 15,000 and Rs 10,000 respectively. The admit a new partner C with 1/5 share in the profits. The revaluation of assets and liabilities show a Profit of Rs 5,000. Goodwill has been valued at Rs 10,000. C is required to bring proportionate capital. Show how much capital C should bring?

Solution:

Particulars	A Rs	B Rs
Original Capital	15,000	10,000
Profit on Revaluation	2,500	2,500
Goodwill	5,000	5,000
	22,500	17,500

The total capital of A and B together is Rs 22,500 + Rs 17,500 = Rs 40,000. This is their capital for 4/5 share in the profits. Thus, the total capital of the firm should be 40,000 × 5/4 = Rs 50,000. C should therefore bring Rs 10,000 (*i.e.* 1/5 of Rs 50,000) as capital.

In case it is desired that capitals of the partners should be in their profit sharing ratio, the capitals of A and B may have also to be adjusted without affecting the total capital of the firm. In the present case the capitals of A and B should be Rs 20,000 each. This means A should be paid Rs 2,500 being excess capital and B should bring Rs 2,500 as additional capital.

2. The new partner may bring a fixed amount by way of capital and the capitals of other partners may have to be adjusted on the basis of capital brought in by the new partner. The excess of or deficit in capital may be paid off or brought in by the partners concerned or be transferred to their current accounts.

Illustration 2.16. A and B sharing profit in the ratio of 3 : 2 have capitals of Rs 40,000 and Rs 25,000 respectively. They admit a new partner C. The new profit sharing ratio of A, B and C is 2 : 2 : 1 respectively. C is required to bring Rs 15,000 as capital. The loss on revaluation of assets and liabilities is Rs 5,000. It is agreed that capitals of partners should be in the new profit sharing ratio. Any excess or deficit amount should be transferred to their current accounts. Pass suitable adjusting entries.

Solution:

Particulars	A Rs	B Rs
Original Capitals	40,000	25,000
Less: Loss on revaluation	3,000	2,000
	37,000	23,000
Capitals should be	30,000	30,000
	+7,000	−7,000

The journal entries would be as follows:

Particulars		Dr. Amount Rs	Cr. Amount Rs
A's Capital A/c	Dr.	7,000	
To A's Current A/c			7,000
(Being excess capital transferred to current account)			
B's Current A/c	Dr.	7,000	
To B's Capital a/c			7,000
(Being deficit in capital transferred to current account)			

It should be noted that it is not necessary that the new partner brings his entire share of capital in cash only. He may also bring other assets of his business in place of or in addition to cash. Such assets brought will form his capital.

Illustration 2.17. P and Q are partners sharing profits and losses in the ratio of 2:1. They admit R for 1/4 share. No goodwill appears in the books but it is valued at Rs 20,000. R brings the following towards Capital and Goodwill.

	Rs		Rs
Cash	2,000	Goodwill	3,000
Debtors	5,000	Creditors	2,000
Stock	4,000		

Give Journal entries at the time of R's admission.

Solution:

JOURNAL ENTRIES

Particulars		Dr. Amount Rs	Cr. Amount Rs
Goodwill A/c	Dr.	20,000	
To P's Capital A/c			13,334
To Q's Capital A/c			6,666
(Being Goodwill account raised on R's admission			
Cash A/c	Dr.	2,000	
Debtors A/c	Dr.	5,000	
Stock A/c	Dr.	4,000	
Goodwill A/c	Dr.	3,000	
To Creditors A/c			2,000
To R's Capital A/c			12,000
(Being net assets brought in by R)			

3. In case the new partner is not in a position to bring his required share of capital, a Capital Purchase Account (or Loan Account) may be raised in the books for the "short amount." This account may be written off in future against the new partner's share of profit.

Illustration 2.18. B and D are equal partners, each having a capital of Rs 18,000. Since the firm is in desperate need of cash they admit G to a one-third share in the capital and the profits of the firm upon his investment of only Rs 12,000 in cash.

Give journal entry to record the admission of G and also show your calculations.

Solution:

G should have brought Rs 18,000 as capital for 1/3 share in the profits of the firm. Since he is bringing only Rs 12,000, a Capital Purchase Account may be raised by Rs 6,000. The journal entry will be as follows.

Particulars		Dr. Amount Rs	Cr. Amount Rs
Bank A/c	Dr.	12,000	
G's Capital Purchase A/c	Dr.	6,000	
To G's Capital A/c			18,000
(For Cash brought in by G and raising a Capital Purchase Account for short capital)			

Alternatively, it could also be presumed that G is bringing Rs 6,000 goodwill attached to his business. The journal entry in such case will be as follows:

Particulars		Dr. Amount Rs	Cr. Amount Rs
Bank A/c	Dr.	12,000	
Goodwill A/c	Dr.	6,000	
To G's Capital			18,000

However, the first alternative is better.

Distinction between Contribution and Purchase of Share

An incoming partner may contribute to the assets of the firm or he may purchase his share from one or more existing partners of the firm. In case the incoming partner contributed to the assets of the firm, the capital of the incoming partner is in addition to other partners' capital and therefore there will be increase in the total resources or the assets of the firm. However, if the incoming partner purchases his share from one or more existing partners of the firm, the total assets of the firm will not change. The amount brought in by the incoming partner will be paid to the existing partner or partners from whom he has purchased his share.

Illustration 2.19. X and Y are partners in a business sharing profit and losses in the ratio of 3:2. Their Balance-Sheet as on 31st Dec. 1988 is as follows:

BALANCE SHEET OF X & Y
as on 31.12.1988

Liabilities		Amount Rs	Assets	Amount Rs
Capitals: X	20,000		Sundry Assets	20,000
Capitals: Y	10,000	30,000	Goodwill	10,000
		30,000		30,000

They decide to admit Z as partner w.e.f. 1st January 1989. You are required to prepare the balance sheet of the new firm in each of the following cases:

(i) Z is given 1/5th share in the profits of the firm and he is to contribute proportionate capital for the purpose.

(ii) Z buys 1/5th share of the profits of the firm from X.

Solution:

(i) Z is getting 1/5th share in the profits of the firm, hence, the share of X and Y together will be 4/5th (i.e., 1 – 1/5). The total capital of X and Y amounts to Rs 30,000. On this basis, the total capital of the firm will be Rs 37,500 (i.e., 30,000 × 5/4). Hence, Z should contribute Rs 7,500 (i.e., 37,500 × 1/5) as capital. The new profit sharing ratio of X, Y and Z in the firm will be 12 : 8 : 5 respectively.

The Balance Sheet of the new firm will now appear as follows:

BALANCE SHEET OF X, Y AND Z
as on 1.1.1989

Liabilities		Amount Rs	Assets	Amount Rs
Capital Accounts:			Sundry Assets	20,000
X	20,000		Cash	7,500
Y	10,000		Goodwill	10,000
Z	7,500	37,500		
		37,500		37,500

(ii) In case Z buys 1/5th share of the profits of the firm from X, the total capital of the firm will remain unaffected. This means Z will have to pay Rs 6,000 (i.e., 1/5th of Rs 30,000) to X. The new profit sharing ratio between X, Y and Z will be 2 : 2 : 1, respectively. In other words Y's share of profit in the new firm remains unaffected on account of admission of Z. The Balance Sheet of the new firm will be as under:

BALANCE SHEET OF X, Y AND Z
as on 1.1.1989

Liabilities		Amount Rs	Assets	Amount Rs
Capital Accounts:			Sundry Assets	24,000
X (20,000 - 6,000)		14,000	Goodwill	6,000
Y		10,000		
Z		6,000		
		30,000		30,000

Illustration 2.20. M/s. A, B and C with respective capitals of Rs 30,000, Rs 20,000 and Rs 10,000 are sharing profits in the ratio of 3 : 2 : 1. They agreed to admit Mr. D as a partner for 1/6th share on the terms that he brings in Rs 20,000 as capital and Rs 10,000 as premium for goodwill and that Mr. C would retain his original share.

Mr. D paid in his capital money but in respect of premium he could bring in only Rs 5,000 and therefore he agreed to the raising of goodwill account in the books of the firm as would be appropriate in the circumstances.

You are required to: (1) give the Journal Entries to carry out the above arrangement; (2) construct the capital accounts of the partners; and (3) work out the new profit sharing ratio of the partners.

Solution:

JOURNAL ENTRIES

Particulars		Dr. Amount Rs	Cr. Amount Rs
1. Bank Account	Dr.	25,000	
To D's Capital A/c			20,000
To A's Capital A/c			3,000
To B's Capital A/c			2,000
(Being the cash brought in by D towards his share of capital and goodwill. The amount of goodwill credited to A and B in their sacrificing ratio i.e. 3 : 2)			

Contd....

	Particulars		Dr. Amount Rs	Cr. Amount Rs
2.	Goodwill A/c	Dr.	30,000	
	To A's Capital			15,000
	To B's Capital			10,000
	To C's Capital			5,000
	(Being goodwill raised in the books of account to the extent or Rs 30,000 and credited to old partners accounts)			

CAPITAL ACCOUNTS OF PARTNERS

Particulars	A Rs	B Rs	C Rs	D Rs	Particulars	A Rs	B Rs	C Rs	D Rs
To Balance c/d	40,000	32,000	15,000	20,000	By Balance b/d	30,000	20,000	10,000	—
					By Bank	3,000	2,000	—	20,000
					By Goodwill	15,000	10,000	5,000	—
	48,000	32,000	15,000	20,000		48,000	32,000	15,000	20,000

Working Notes:

COMPUTATION OF NEW PROFIT SHARING RATIO

	A		B		C		D
Old Ratio	3/6	:	2/6	:	1/6	:	

D gets 1/6 : 3/5 from A i.e. 1/6 × 3/5 = 3/30

2/5 from B i.e., 1/6 × 2/5 = 2/30

New Profit Sharing Ratio:	(3/6 – 3/30)	:	(2/6 – 2/30)	:	1/6	:	1/6
Or	12/30	:	8/30	:	5/30	:	5/30
Or	12	:	8	:	5	:	5

Illustration 2.21. The Balance Sheet of Sridhar and Ghanshyam as on 31st December, 1987 is set out below. They share profits and losses in ratio of 2:1 :

Liabilities	Amount Rs	Assets	Amount Rs
Sridhar's Capital	60,000	Freehold Property	20,000
Ghanshyam's Capital	30,000	Furniture	6,000
General Reserve	24,000	Stock	12,000
Creditors	16,000	Debtors	80,000
		Cash	12,000
	1,30,000		1,30,000

They agree to admit Prem into the firm subject to the following terms and conditions:

(a) Prem will bring in Rs 21,000 of which Rs 9,000 will be treated as his share of Goodwill to be retained in the business.

(b) 50% of the General Reserve is to remain as a Provision for Bad and Doubtful Debts.

(c) Depreciation is to be provided on Furniture at the rate of 5%.

(d) Stock is to be revalued at Rs 10,500.

Draft the Journal entries giving effect to the aforesaid arrangements (including cash transactions) and prepare the opening Balance Sheet of the new partnership.

(C.A. Entrance, Nov., 1988)

3.58

Solution:

BOOKS OF SRIDHAR AND GHANSHYAM

	Particulars		Dr. Amount Rs	Cr. Amount Rs
(i)	Bank A/c	Dr.	21,000	
	To Prem's Capital A/c			12,000
	To Sridhar's Capital A/c			6,000
	To Ghanshyam's Capital A/c			3,000
	(Being amount brought in by Mr. Prem on admission as partner for capital Rs 30,000 and goodwill Rs 9,000. Goodwill credited to existing partners in sacrificing ratio)			
(ii)	Profit & Loss Adjustment A/c	Dr.	1,800	
	To Furniture A/c			300
	To Stock A/c			1,500
	(Being amount written off Furniture @ 5% and Stock Rs 1,500 before admission of Mr. Prem)			
(iii)	Sridhar's Capital A/c	Dr.	1,200	
	Ghanshayam's Capital A/c	Dr.	600	
	To Profit & Loss Adjustment A/c			1,800
	(Being loss on revaluation of assets debited to existing partners)			
(iv)	General Reserve	Dr.	24,000	
	To Provision for Bad & Doubtful Debts			12,000
	To Sridhar's Capital A/c			8,000
	To Ghanshyam's Capital A/c			4,000
	(Being 50% of General Reserve transferred to Provision for Bad and Doubtful debts and the balance credited to old partners)			

Ms. Sridhar, Ghanshyam And Prem
BALANCE SHEET
as on 1st January, 1988

Liabilities	Amount Rs	Assets		Amount Rs
Capital Accounts:		Freehold Property		20,000
Shridhar's Capital	72,800	Furniture		5,700
Ghanshyam's Capital	36,400	Stock in Trade		10,500
Prem's Capital	12,000	Sundry Debtors	80,000	
Sundry Creditors	16,000	Less: Provision for bad		
		& doubtful debts	12,000	68,000
		Cash at Bank (12,000 + 21,000)		33,000
	1,37,200			7,37,200

Working Note:

CAPITAL ACCOUNTS OF PARTNERS

Particulars	Sridhar Rs	Ghanshyam Rs
Opening Balance	60,000	30,000
Add: Goodwill	6,000	3,000

Contd....

Particulars	Sridhar Rs	Ghanshyam Rs
Add: Reserve	8,000	4,000
	74,000	37,000
Less: Loss on Revaluation	1,200	600
	72,800	36,400

Illustration 2.22. The following is the Balance Sheet of P and S trading as P & S Co. on 31 December 1984, profits being divided 3/5 to P and 2/5 to S.

Liabilities	Amount Rs	Assets	Amount Rs
P's Capital Account	7,000	Debtors	4,400
S's Capital Account	4,000	Buildings	3,000
Sundry Creditors	3,000	Plant	5,000
		Bank	1,600
	14,000		14,000

They agree to admit a new partner B on 1 January, 1985 and the following arrangements are made:

(a) Goodwill to be created amounting to Rs 3,500, to be credited to P and S in the same proportions as they divide profits.

(b) The Buildings and Plant are independently valued at Rs 3,500 and Rs 6,000 respectively, the increased valued to be similarly credited to P and S.

(c) B to bring Rs 4,000 cash as his Capital.

(d) All partners to be credited with 5% interest per annum on Capital and to be charged 5% interest on Drawings, which amount to Rs 200 a month, drawn by each partner at the end of each month.

(e) Profits to be divided in the proportion P 5, S 3 and B 2. The profit to 30 June, 1985 before allowing interest was Rs 15,000.

Prepare the Firm's Balance Sheet and Partners' Capital Accounts as on 30 June, 1985.

Solution:

PROFIT AND LOSS ADJUSTMENT ACCOUNT

Particulars		Amount Rs	Particulars	Amount Rs
To Profit transferred to:			By Buildings	500
P's Capital A/c	900		By Plant	1,000
S's Capital A/c	600	1,500		
		1,500		1,500

BANK ACCOUNT

Date	Particulars	Amount Rs	Date	Particulars		Amount Rs
1985			1985			
1 Jan.	To Balance b/d	1,600	30 June	By Drawings:		
1985	To B's Capital A/c	4,000		P	1,200	
30 June	To Profit earned			S	1,200	
	(presuming all in cash)	15,000		B	1,200	3,600
				By Balance c/d		17,000
		20,600				20,600

PROFIT AND LOSS APPROPRIATION ACCOUNT

Particulars		Amount Rs	Particulars		Amount Rs
To Interest on Capital:			By Net profit		15,000.00
P	250		By Interest on Drawings		
S	150		P	12.50	
B	100	500.00	S	12.50	
The Profit transferred to			B	12.50	37.50
P's Capital A/c		7,268.75			
S's Capital A/c		4,361.25			
B's Capital A/c		2,907.50			
		15,037.50			15,037.50

P's CAPITAL ACCOUNT

Date	Particulars	Amount Rs	Date	Particulars	Amount Rs
1985			1985		
1 Jan.	To Balance c/d	10,000.00	1 Jan.	By Balance b/d	7,000.00
			1 Jan.	By P. & L. Adjustment A/c	900.00
			1 Jan.	By Goodwill	2,100.00
		10,000.00			10,000.00
1985			1985		
30 June	To Drawings	1,200.00	1 Jan.	By Balance b/d	10,000.00
30 June	To Interest on Drawings	12.50	30 June	By Interest on Capital	250.00
30 June	To Balance c/d	16,306.25	30 June	By P. & L. App. A/c	7,268.75
		17,518.75			17,518.75

S's CAPITAL ACCOUNT

Date	Particulars	Amount Rs	Date	Particulars	Amount Rs
1985			1985		
1 Jan.	To Balance c/d	6,000.00	1 Jan.	By Balance b/d	4,000.00
			1 Jan.	By P. & L. Adj. A/c	600.00
			1 Jan.	By Goodwill	1,400.00
		6,000.00			6,000.00
30 June	To Drawings	1,200.00	1 Jan.	By Balance b/d	6,000.00
30 June	To Interest on Drawings	12.50	30 June	By Interest on Capital	150.00
30 June	To Balance c/d	9,298.75	30 June	By P. & L. App. A/c	4,361.25
		10,511.25			10,511.25

B's CAPITAL ACCOUNT

Date	Particulars	Amount Rs	Date	Particulars	Amount Rs
June 30	To Drawings	1,200.00	Jan. 1	By Bank	4,000.00
June 30	To Interest on Drawings	12.50	June 30	By Interest on Capital	100.00
June 30	To Balance c/d	5,795.00	June 30	By P. & L. A/c	2,907.50
		7,007.50			7,007.50

BALANCE SHEET
As on 30th June, 1985

Liabilities		Amount Rs	Assets	Amount Rs
Sundry Creditors		3,000.00	Bank	17,000.00
Capital Accounts:			Debtors	4,400.00
P	16,306.25		Plant	6,000.00
S	9,298.75		Buildings	3,500.00
B	5,795.00	31,400.00	Goodwill	3,500.00
		34,400.00		34,400.00

Note: Interest on Drawings has been calculated as given below:

Particulars	Amount Rs	Months	Product
Drawings on 31 January	200	5	1,000
Drawings on 28 February	200	4	800
Drawings on 31 March	200	3	600
Drawings on 30 April	200	2	400
Drawings on 31 May	200	1	200
Drawings on 30 June	200	0	0
	1,200		3,000

$$\text{Interest} = \frac{3,000 \times 5}{12 \times 100} = \frac{25}{2} \qquad = \text{Rs } 12.50$$

Illustration 2.23. *P, Q* and *R* were in partnership sharing profits and losses in the ratio of 6 : 3 : 1. They decided to take *S* into partnership with effect from 1 April, 1988 on the following terms and conditions:

(*i*) *S* is to bring in his proportionate share of goodwill in cash. Goodwill is not to be brought into the books but necessary adjustments are to be made in the old partners' capital accounts.

(*ii*) Goodwill to be valued at 60% of the average annual profits of the previous three or four years whichever is the higher.

(*iii*) The average profits for the purpose of goodwill for the past years were:

	Rs
Year ended 31 March, 1988	48,000
Year ended 31 March, 1987	30,300
Year ended 31 March, 1986	31,200
Year ended 31 March, 1985	42,200

(*iv*) The new profit sharing ratio between *P, Q, R* and *S* will be 3 : 3 : 3 : 1

(*v*) *S* should bring in Rs 20,000 as capital.

(*vi*) The new partner is to receive an annual salary of Rs 12,000 in addition to his share of profit. *R* personally guaranteed that the aggregate of salary and share of profit of the new partner shall not be less than Rs 25,000 per annum.

The draft accounts for the year ended 31 March, 1989 showed a profit of Rs 1,32,800 before taking into account the salary of *S*.

Show the Journal entries (including cash entries) passed at the time of admission of the partner and also the distribution of the net profit for the year ended 31st March, 1989 between the partners.

Solution:

JOURNAL OF P, Q, R & S.

	Particulars		Dr. Amount Rs	Cr. Amount Rs
1.	Cash Account	Dr.	2,275.50	
	B's Capital A/c	Dr.	4,551.00	
	To P's Capital A/c			6,826.50
	(Amount paid in by S and debited to R, for credit to P in respect of adjustment for goodwill on admission of S accompanied by change in the profit sharing ratio.)			
2.	Cash Account	Dr.	20,000.00	
	To S's Capital Account			20,000.00
	(Amount paid in by S as his capital on his joining the firm)			

Distribution of Profit earned in 1988–1989

PROFIT & LOSS APPROPRIATION ACCOUNT

Particulars		Amount Rs	Particulars	Amount Rs
To Salary to S		12,000	By Net Profit b/d	1,32,800
To Profit transfd. to Capital A/cs:				
P (3/10)		36,240		
Q (3/10)		36,240		
R (3/10)	36,240			
Less due to S	920	35,320		
S (1/10)	12,080			
Add to make ap				
minimum debited to R	920	13,000		
		1,32,800		1,32,800

Working Notes:

(1) Valuation of Goodwill

	Profit for 4 years	Profit for 3 years
1984–85	42,200	—
1985–86	31,200	31,200
1986–87	30,300	30,300
1987–88	48,000	48,000
Total	1,51,700	1,09,500
Average	37,925	36,500
60% of the average (4 years' basis since this amount is higher)	22,755	

(2) Adjustment for Goodwill

Partners	Raised Rs	Written off Rs	Net Rs
P	13,653.00 (6/10)	6,826.50 (3/10)	6,826.50 (Cr.)
Q	6,826.50 (3/10)	6,826.50 (3/10)	4,551.00 (Dr.)
R	2,275.50 (1/10)	2,275.50 (1/10)	2,275.50 (Dr.)
	22,755.50	22,755.50	

Alternatively, the amount of goodwill to be credited to P's Capital account can be ascertained as follows:

Sacrifice by P on admission of S:

Old Ratio – New Ratio

$Or \quad \dfrac{6}{10} - \dfrac{3}{10} = \dfrac{3}{10}$

Gain to S $\quad = 1/10)$

Gain to R : New Ratio – Old Ratio

$Or \quad \dfrac{3}{10} - \dfrac{3}{10} = \dfrac{2}{10}$

The total value of Goodwill is Rs 22,755

S should pay Rs 2,275.50 $\left(i.e. \ \dfrac{1}{10} \times 22,755 \right)$

R should pay Rs 4,551.00 $\left(i.e. \ \dfrac{2}{10} \times 22,755 \right)$

KEY TERMS

☐ **Memorandum Revaluation Account:** This is also known as Memorandum Profit & Loss Adjustment Account. It is similar to revaluation account except that it is only a memorandum record of increase or decrease in the values of assets and liabilities on reconstitution of a partnership firm. The assets and liabilities continue to appear at their old values in the balance sheet and entry is passed only with the net profit or loss made or suffered by the partners on reconstitution of the firm.

☐ **Revaluation Account:** This is also known as Profit & Loss Adjustment account. The account records any increase or decrease in the values of assets and liabilities as agreed by the partners on reconstitution of a partnership firm. The balance of the account represents profit or loss made on revaluation to be shared by the partners.

☐ **Sacrificing Ratio:** The term is used generally in case of admission of a partner. It is the ratio in which the existing partners lose on admission of a new partner.

TEST QUESTIONS

Objective type

1. State whether each of the following statements is 'True' or 'False':
   - (a) In case the newly admitted partner pays cash for his share of goodwill, it will be credited to the old partners in their sacrificing ratio.
   - (b) In case Memorandum Revaluation account is opened, the assets and liabilities appear in the New Balance Sheet at their revised values.
   - (c) All accumulated profits and reserves are to be transferred to the Profit and Loss Adjustment Account on admission of a new partner.
   - (d) When Goodwill account is raised on admission of a partner the amount is credited to the old partners in their old profit sharing ratio.
   - (e) When goodwill account is appearing in the books at a proper value, the new partner has to pay proportionate amount by way of goodwill to the old partners.

   [Ans. (a) True; (b) False; (c) False; (d) True; (e) False.].

2. Select the most appropriate answer:
   - (i) General Reserve at the time of admission of a new partner is transferred to:
     - (a) Profit and Loss Adjustment Account
     - (b) Partners' Capital Accounts
     - (c) Neither of the two.
   - (ii) Depreciation Fund at the time of admission of a new partner is transferred to:
     - (a) Revaluation Account
     - (b) Partners Capital Accounts
     - (c) Neither of the two.
   - (iii) A and B are sharing profits in the ratio of 3 : 2. They admit a new partner C with 1/5 share in profits of the firm. The new profit sharing ratio between the partners will be: (a) 12 : 8 : 5 (b) 8 :12 : 5 (c) 2 : 2 : 1.
   - (iv) P and Q are partners sharing profits in the ratio of 3:2. They admit a new partner R with 1/5 share in the profits which he takes equally from P and Q. The new profit sharing ratio between the partners will be: (a) 2 : 2 : 1 (b) 5 : 3 : 2 (c) 8 : 12 : 5.
   - (v) A and B are partners in a business sharing profits in the ratio of 5 : 3. They admit C as a partner with 1/4 share in the profits which he acquires 3/4 from A 1/4 from B. He pays Rs 4,000 for his share of goodwill. A and B will be credited by:
     - (a) Rs 2,500 and Rs 1,500 respectively
     - (b) Rs 3,000 and Rs 1,000 respectively
     - (c) Rs 2,000 each.
   - (vi) X and Y are partners sharing profits in the ratio of 3 : 1. They admit Z as a partner who pays Rs 4,000 as Goodwill. The new profit ratio being 2 : 1 : 1 among X, Y and Z respectively. The amount of goodwill will be credited to :
     - (a) X and Y as Rs 3,000 and Rs 1,000 respectively.
     - (b) X only
     - (c) Y only.

   [Ans. (i) (b); (ii) (c); (iii) (a); (iv) (b); (v) (b); (vi) (b)].

Essay type

1. Why assets and liabilities are revalued on admission of a partner? Give imaginary entries covering such revaluation.
2. What could be the several alternatives regarding adjustment for goodwill in the event of admission of a partner?

3. State the ratio and the Journal entry for the following adjustments in the event of admission of a partner:
   (a) When goodwill account is raised.
   (b) When goodwill account is written off.
   (c) When the new partner brings cash for his share of goodwill.
   (d) When there is profit or loss on revaluation of assets.

   Ans. (a) old, (b) new, (c) sacrificing, (d) old].

4. What is 'Goodwill'?
   Explain the following methods of calculating goodwill of a partnership firm:
   (i) Purchase of a certain number of years' average profit method.
   (ii) Super-Profits method.

5. If there is a change in the profit sharing ratio of the existing partners, is it necessary to revalue the assets and liabilities ? Give reasons for your answer.

6. Distinguish between Revaluation Account and Memorandum Revaluation Account.

7. Explain the accounting treatment of 'Goodwill' when at the time of admission, the new partner can not bring his share of goodwill in cash.

PRACTICAL PROBLEMS

General Problems

1. Suneel and Sharad are partners in a business sharing profits and losses in the ratio of 7/10 and 3/10. They admit Sidharth as partner. Suneel sacrificed 1/7 of his share and Sharad sacrificed 1/3 of his share in favour of Sidharth. Calculate the new profit sharing ratio.

   [Ans. New ratio 3 : 1 : 1].

2. A and B are partners in a business sharing profits in the ratio of 3 : 2. They admit C as a partner with 1/5 share in the profits. The new profit sharing ratio is 2 : 2 : 1. The value of the firm's goodwill (for which no account appears in the books) is valued at Rs 15,000. Pass journal entries for each of the following cases:
   (i) Partners decide to raise the goodwill account with full value.
   (ii) Partners raise the goodwill account and subsequently write it off.
   (iii) C brings his share of goodwill in cash and the same is retained in the firm.
   (iv) C brings his share of goodwill in cash and the same is withdrawn by the partners.

3. A & B are partners sharing profits in the ratio of 3 : 2. They admit C into the firm for 3/7th profit which he takes (2/7th from A and 1/7 from B) and brings Rs 3,000 as premium out of his share of Rs 3,600. Goodwill appears in the books at Rs 5,000 but the new firm decides that goodwill should appear in the books at the value of Rs 1,750. Give journal entries to record the above arrangement.

   [Ans. Credit cash brought in by C to his capital account. Increase goodwill account to its full value i.e. Rs 8,400 and credit old partners, write off Rs 6,650 in the new ratio among all partners to maintain Goodwill at Rs 1,750].

4. X and Y are partners in a business sharing profits and losses in the ratio of 3 : 2. They admit Z into partnership. The new profit sharing ratio being X 2, Y 2 and Z 1. On the date of Z's admission, it is decided to revalue the assets and liabilities as follows:

   Building, Plant and Stock to be increased by Rs 5,000, Rs 3,000 and Rs 2,000 respectively. A provision for bad debts to be created by Rs 1,000 and sundry creditors to be increased by Rs 1,000.

   Partners desire that necessary adjustments should be made without in any way affecting the values of assets and liabilities in the books.

   You are required to pass necessary journal entries and prepare a Memorandum Profit and Loss Adjustment Account.

   [Ans. Profit on Revaluation Rs 8,000].

5. Alok and Pulok are carrying on a partnership business sharing profits and losses in the ratio of 3 : 2. They admit Chhandok into partnership on the basis of his buying 1/5th of Alok's share and 1/6th of Pulok's. After two years, Alok and Pulok permit Chhandok to purchase a further 1/10 of their remaining shares. How much did Chhandok pay each of the others on each occasion for goodwill assuming that the goodwill of the firm was Rs 15,000 on the first occasion and Rs 20,000 on the second ? What is the ultimate share of each partner in the business ?

[**Ans.** On admission Chhandok pays Rs 1,800 to Alok and Rs 1,000 to Pulok. Subsequently he pays them respectively Rs 960 and Rs 667. Ultimate ratio: Alok 324/750, Pulok 225/750 and Chhandok 201/750].

6. Oberoi and Taj were in partnership sharing profits and losses in the ratio of 3 : 2. They close their accounts annually to 30 June every year.

On 1st July 1983. Ashok was taken as a partner from which date the profits were agreed to be shared as Oberoi 5, Taj 3 and Ashok 2. Taj retired on 1 September, 1983, and the remaining partners agreed to share profits as Oberoi 7 and Ashok 3.

The goodwill of the firm was agreed to be valued at 2 years' purchase of the average of the last three years' trading result which were:

1st year	...	Profit Rs 20,000
2nd year	...	Loss Rs 10,500
3rd year	...	Profit Rs 22,000

It was agreed that goodwill shall be adjusted between the partners on each occasion of change in the constitution of the firm without however recording the value thereof, but making adjustments through their respective Capital Accounts only.

You are required to show the relevant entries in the Partners' Capital Accounts for adjusting the value goodwill on both the occasions.

[**Ans.** *July 1: Dr.* Ashok by Rs 4,200, *Cr.* Oberoi Rs 2,100 and Taj by Rs 2,100
Sept. 1: *Dr.* Oberoi Rs 4,200, *Dr.* Ashok Rs 2,100, *Cr.* Taj Rs 6,300].

Comprehensive Problems

7. Mr. X and Mr.Y are partners sharing profits in the ratio of 3:1. Their Balance Sheet as at 31st March, 1989 was as follows:

Liabilities	Amount Rs	Assets	Amount Rs
Sundry Creditors	40,000	Cash at Bank	25,000
Capital A/cs:		Sundry Debtors	9,000
Mr. X 30,000		Stock	20,000
Mr. Y 10,000	40,000	Furniture	6,000
		Premises	20,000
	80,000		80,000

They decide to admit Mr. Z into partnership on the following terms:

(i) Goodwill of Rs 30,000 be created.

(ii) Depreciate Furniture by 10%.

(iii) Stock has to be valued at Rs 18,000.

(iv) Provision for doubtful debts at 10% be created on Sundry Debtors.

(v) Premises have to be valued higher by 25%.

(vi) Mr. Z shall bring Rs 10,000 for 1/4th shares of profits.

Pass Journal Entries and also show the Revaluation Account, Capital Accounts of Partners and Balance Sheet after admission of Mr. Z.

(C.A. Entrance, Nov., 1989)

[**Ans.** Revaluation Profit Rs 1,500; Balance Sheet total - Rs 1,21,500].

8. Soor and Tulsi share profits in the proportion of three-fourths and one-fourth. The Balance Sheet of the firm on 31 December 1987 was as under:

Liabilities	Amount Rs	Assets	Amount Rs
Sundry Creditors	4,150	Cash at Bank	2,250
Capital Accounts:		B/R	300
Soor	3,000	Book Debts	1,600
Tulsi	1,600	Stock	2,000
		Furniture	100
		Buildings	2,500
	8,750		8,750

On 1 January, 1988 Keshav was admitted into partnership on the following terms :

(i) Keshav pays Rs 1,000 as capital and Rs 500 as goodwill for 1/5 share. Half of the amount of goodwill is to be withdrawn by Soor and Tulsi.

(ii) Stock and Furniture be reduced by 10% and 5%. Provision for Doubtful Debts be created on Book Debts and B/R.

(iii) Value of Buildings be increased by 20%.

(iv) A liability to the extent of Rs 100 be created in respect of a claim for damages against the firm.

(v) An items of Rs 65 included in Sundry Creditors is not likely to be claimed.

[**Ans.** Profit on Revaluation Rs 160, and Total of Balance Sheet Rs 10,195].

9. The Balance Sheet of Appu and Pappu as on 31st December, 1989 is set out below. They share profits and losses in the ratio of 2:1.

Liabilities	Amount Rs	Assets	Amount Rs
Appu's Capital	40,000	Freehold Property	20,000
Pappu's Capital	30,000	Furniture	6,000
General Reserve	24,000	Stock	12,000
Creditors	16,000	Debtors	60,000
		Cash	12,000
	1,10,000		1,10,000

They agreed to admit Kappu into the firm subject to the following terms and conditions:

(a) Kappu will bring in Rs 21,000 of which Rs 9,000 will be treated as his share of goodwill to be retained in the business.

(b) He will be entitled to one-fourth share of profits.

(c) 50% of the General Reserve is to remain as a Provision for Bad and Doubtful Debts.

(d) Depreciation is to be provided on Furniture @ 5%.

(e) Stock is to be revalued at Rs 10,500.

Give Journal entries to give effect to these arrangements and construct the Balance of the new firm.

(*B.Com. Pass, Delhi, 1984*)

[**Ans.** Loss on revaluation Rs 1,800; Capitals in the new firm; Appu Rs 52,800; Pappu Rs 36,400; Kappu Rs 12,000; Balance Sheet Total Rs 1,17,200].

10. A and B are partners in a firm sharing profits and losses as 5 : 3. The position of the firm as on 31st March, 1984 was as follows:

Liabilities	Amount Rs		Assets	Amount Rs
Capital Accounts			Plant and Machinery	40,000
A 30,000			Stock	30,000
B 20,000		50,000	Sundry Debtors	20,000
Sundry Creditors		15,000	Bills Receivable	10,000
Bank Overdraft		42,500	Cash at Bank	7,500
		1,07,500		1,07,500

C now joins them on condition that he will share 3/4 th of the future profits, the balance of profits being shared by A and B as 5 : 3. He introduces Rs 40,000 by way of capital and further Rs 4,000 by way of premium for goodwill. He also provides loans to the firm to pay off bank overdraft. A and B agree to depreciate Plant by 10% and to raise a Provision against Sundry Debtors @ 5%.

You are asked to journalise the entries in the books of the firm and show the resultant Balance Sheet. How will the partners share the future profits ?

(B.Com. Pass, Delhi, 1985)

[**Ans.** Loss on revaluation Rs 5,000; Capital Accounts Balances in new firm: A Rs 29,375; B Rs 19,625; C Rs 40,000; Balance Sheet Total Rs 1,46,500].

11. The following is the Balance Sheet of A and B as on 31.12.1985,. who share profits and losses equally:

Liabilities	Amount Rs		Assets	Amount Rs
Capitals: A	15,000		Machinery	50,000
B	15,000		Stock	15,000
Creditors	15,000		Debtors	10,000
Current Accounts			Bills Receivable	5,000
A	20,000		Cash/Bank	5,000
B	20,000			
	85,000			85,000

They admit C as an equal partner on 1.1.1986. Goodwill is valued at Rs 30,000. Stock to be valued at Rs 25,000; Machinery at Rs 60,000. C is to bring in Rs 15,000 as his capital and the necessary cash towards his share of goodwill. Goodwill account will not remain the books.

Show necessary Journal entries and also the balance Sheet after admission of C.

(C.A. Entrance, May, 1986)

[**Ans.** Revaluation Profit Rs 50,000, Closing Balances of Capital Accounts (1986) of A: Rs 30,000, B: Rs 30,000 and C: Rs 15,000]

12. Mr. Giridhar and Mr. Gopal are partners in a firm sharing profits and losses as 5:3. The position of the firm as on 31st March, 1987 is as follows:

Liabilities	Amount Rs		Assets	Amount Rs
Capital Accounts:			Plant and Machinery	40,000
Mr. Giridhar	30,000		Stock	30,000
Mr. Gopal	20,000	50,000	Sundry Debtors	20,000
Sundry Creditors		15,000	Bill Receivable	10,000
Bank Loan		42,500	Cash at Bank	7,500
		1,07,500		1,07,500

Mr. Ghanshyam now joins them on condition that he will share 3/4 of future profit, the balance being shared by the old partners in the old ratio. He introduces Rs 40,000 by way of capital in cash and pay off the Bank Loan, such amount being credited to Ghanshyam's Loan Account.

He also pays Rs 4,000 by way of premium for goodwill of the business and this amount is to remain in the business. The partners agree to depreciate Plant and Machineries by 10% and raise a Reserve against Sundry Debtors at 5%.

You are asked (*i*) to journalise the entries in the books of the firm and show the resultant Balance Sheet, and (*ii*) to ascertain the new profit sharing ratio.

(C.A. Entrance, May, 1987)

[Ans. (*i*) Revaluation loss Rs 5,000; Total of Balance Sheet Rs 1,46,500,
(*ii*) New Ratio 5 : 3 : 24].

13. *K* and *L* are partners sharing profits and losses in the ratio of 5:3. Their Balance Sheet as at 30th June, 1987 is as follows:

Liabilities		Amount Rs	Assets		Amount Rs
Creditors		30,000	Furniture		40,000
Reserve		14,000	Patents		10,000
Capital Account			Debtors	44,000	
K	40,000		*Less*: Reserve for		
L	50,000	90,000	Bad Debts	5,000	39,000
			Stock		20,000
			Cash in Hand		25,000
		1,34,000			1,34,000

On 1st July, 1987 they take *M* into partnership. *M* brings Rs 25,000 as his capital but cannot bring Rs 3,600 as his share of goodwill. The new profit sharing ratio of *K*, *L* and *M* is 2 : 4 : 1. Patent is written off from the books and a Reserve for Bad debt is created at 5%. Reserve appears in the books of the firm at its original figure.

Show the necessary Journal entries to carry out the above transactions and prepare a Balance Sheet of the new firm as at 1 July, 1987.

(I.C.W.A. Inter, Dec., 1987)

[Ans. Loss on Revaluation Rs 7,200; Balance Sheet Total Rs 1,77,000].

14. Mr *X* and Mr. *Y* are partners sharing profits in the ratio of 3 : 1. Their Balance Sheet as at 31st March, 1989 was as follows:

Liabilities		Amount Rs	Assets	Amount Rs
Sundry Creditors		40,000	Cash at Bank	25,000
Capital Accounts			Sundry Debtors	9,000
Mr. X	30,000		Stock	20,000
Mr. Y	10,000	40,000	Furniture	6,000
			Premises	20,000
		80,000		80,000

They decide to admit Mr *Z* into partnership on the following terms:

(*i*) Goodwill of Rs 30,000 be created.
(*ii*) Depreciate Furniture by 10%.
(*iii*) Stock has to be valued at Rs 18,000.
(*iv*) Provision of doubtful debts at 10% to be created on debtors
(*v*) Premises have to be valued higher by 25%.
(*vi*) Mr. *Z* shall bring Rs 10,000 for 1/4th shares of profits.

Pass Journal Entries and also show the Revaluation Account, Capital Accounts of the partners and Balance Sheet after admission of Mr. *Z*.

(C.A. Entrance, Nov., 1989)

[Ans. Revaluation Profit Rs 1,500; Balance Sheet Total Rs 1,21,500].

15. M/s Dalal, Banerji and Malick is a firm sharing profit and losses in the ratio of 2:2:1. Their Balance Sheet as on 31 March, 1987 is as given below:

Liabilities		Amount Rs	Assets	Amount Rs
Sundry Creditors		12,850	Land and Buildings	25,000
Outstanding Liabilities		1,500	Furniture	6,500
General Reserve		6,500	Stock of Goods	11,750
Capital Accounts:			Sundry Debtors	5,500
Mr. Dalal	12,000		Cash on hand	140
Mr. Banerji	12,000		Cash at Bank	960
Mr. Malick	5,000	29,000		
		49,850		49,850

The partners have agreed to take Mr Mistri as a partner with effect from 1 April 1987 on the following terms:

1. Mr. Mistri shall bring Rs 5,000 towards has capital.
2. The value of stock should be increased by Rs 2,500.
3. Reserve for bad and doubtful debts should be provided at 10% of the debtors.
4. The furniture should be depreciated by 10%.
5. The value of the land and buildings should be enhanced by 20%.
6. The value of the goodwill be fixed at Rs 15,000.
7. General reserve will be transferred to the Partners' Capital Accounts.
'. The new profit sharing ratio shall be:

Mr. Dalal	5/15	Mr. Malick	3/15
Mr. Banerji	5/15	Mr. Mistri	2/15

9. The goodwill account shall be written back to the partners' accounts in accordance with the new profit sharing proportion. The outstanding liabilities include Rs 1,000 due to Mr. Sen which has been paid by Mr. Dalal. Necessary entries were not made in the books.

Prepare (i) Revaluation Account, (ii) the Capital Accounts of the partners, and (iii) the Balance Sheet of the firm as newly constituted (Journal entries are not required).

[**Ans.** Revaluation Profit Rs 6,300 Capital Accounts Balances: Dalal Rs 19,120, Banerjee Rs 18,120, Malick Rs 7,560 Mistri Rs 3,000, B/S Total Rs 61,150].

[**Hint.** Goodwill Account is to be raised and written off]

16. John and Dickson are partners sharing profits and losses in the ratio of 3 : 2. Their Balance Sheet as at 31 August, 1986 was as follows:

Liabilities		Amount Rs	Assets	Amount Rs
Creditors		8,000	Goodwill	15,000
General Reserve		6,000	Land & Buildings	75,000
Capital Accounts:			Investments	20,000
John	60,000		Debtors	30,000
Dickson	72,000	1,32,000	Cash	6,000
		1,46,000		1,46,000

They agreed to admit Parkson as a partner with effect from 1 September, 1986 on the following terms:

(i) The new profit sharing ratio will be 2:1:1.

(ii) The following amounts of the revaluation have been agreed upon:

		Rs
(a)	Goodwill	24,000
(b)	Land and Buildings	85,000

Contd....

(c)	Investments	15,000
(d)	Creditors	9,000

(*iii*) The revalued amount of goodwill shall be written off in the old partners' capital accounts.

(*iv*) Parkson shall bring in Rs 40,000 in all as his capital and his proportionate share of revalued amount of goodwill of the firm.

Show the journal entries, prepare the capital accounts of the partners and also draw the Balance Sheet of the new firm.

[**Ans.** Revaluation Profit Rs 13,000 Capitals John Rs 59,400, Dickson Rs 73,600, Parkson Rs 34,000, Balance Sheet Total Rs 1,76,000].

17. A and B are partners in a firm sharing profits and losses in 3:2. Their Balance Sheet as on 31 December, 1990 stood as follows:

Liabilities	Amount Rs	Assets		Amount Rs
Sundry Creditors	20,000	Goodwill		12,000
Capitals Accounts		Cash in hand		15,000
A Rs 12,000		Sundry Debtors	Rs 21,000	
B Rs 30,000	42,000	*Less:* Reserve for		
		Bad debts	1,000	20,000
		Stock-in-trade		10,750
		Furniture & Fittings		250
		P. & L. A/c		4,000
	62,000			62,000

On 1st January, 1991 they admit C as a partner on the following terms:

(*a*) The new profit sharing ratio of A, B and C becomes 5 : 3 : 2.

(*b*) Agreed value of Goodwill is Rs 20,000 and C brings the necessary premium for Goodwill in cash, half of which is retained in the business. Book value of Goodwill should remain undisturbed.

(*c*) The Reserve for Bad Debts is to be raised to 10% of Sundry Debtors.

(*d*) Stock-in-trade is to be revalued at Rs 12,000 but the effect is not to be shown in the books.

(*e*) Fixtures and Fittings are to be reduced to Rs 150.

(*f*) C should bring further sum in cash in order to make his capital equal to 1/5th of the combined adjusted capital of A and B.

Show the necessary journal entries and the Capital Accounts of the Partners and also prepare the Balance Sheet of the new firm as on 1 January, 1991.

(I.C.W.A. Inter, June, 1981, adapted)

[**Ans.** Capital Accounts Balances 1.1.1991 A Rs 9,405; B Rs 28,445; C Rs 7,570; Balance Sheet Total Rs 65,420].

18. Marigold and Rose were in partnership sharing profits and losses as to two thirds and one-third. As from 1 October, 1989 they agreed to take Jasmine as a new partner. The new partner will have one-sixth share, the old partners agreeing to share equally as between them in the firm. Jasmine brings in Rs 50,000 as capital and Rs 4,000 as his share of goodwill to be retained in the firm.

The following is the Balance Sheet of the old firm as on 30 September, 1989.

Liabilities	Amount Rs	Assets	Amount Rs
Capital Accounts:		Cash	7,000
Marigold	62,500	Stock	50,000
Rose	37,500	Debtors	30,000

Contd....

Liabilities	Amount Rs	Assets	Amount Rs
Creditors	50,000	Plant	25,000
		Investments	38,000
	1,50,000		1,50,000

The following revaluation is agreed upon:

	Rs
Stock	55,000
Plant	20,000
Investments	35,000

Debtors: subject to reserve for bad debts of 5%.

It is further agreed that Marigold alone is to be charged with any loss arising from the above. The profit for the year ended 30th September, 1990 was Rs 1,20,000 and the drawings of the partners were:

	Rs
Marigold	40,000
Rose	40,000
Jasmine	10,000

You are required to journalise the opening adjustments and draw up the Balance Sheet as on 30 September, 1990 making such assumptions as may be necessary.

[**Ans.** Capitals: Marigold Rs 74,000; Rose 45,500; Jasmine Rs 60,000; Balance Sheet Total: Rs 2,29,500].

[**Hint.** Presume profit realised during the year wholly in cash].

19. A, B and C are partners in a firm of accountants, who maintain accounts on the cash basis sharing profits and losses in the ratio 2:3:1. Their Balance Sheet as on 31 March, 1986 on which date D is admitted as a partner is as follows:

Liabilities	Amount Rs	Assets	Amount Rs
B's Capital	35,000	Furniture	10,000
C's Capital	22,000	Motor Car	20,000
		Cash at Bank	18,000
		A's Capital	9,000
	57,000		57,000

D is given 1/4th share in the profits and losses in the firm and the profit and loss sharing ratio as between the other partners remains as before. The following adjustments are to be made prior to D's admission:

(a) The Motor Car is taken over by B at a value of Rs 25,000.

(b) The furniture is revalued at 18,000.

(c) Goodwill account is raised in the books at Rs 50,000. It is agreed among A, B and C that C is interested in goodwill only upto a value of Rs 30,000.

(d) Fees billed but not realised Rs 11,600, are brought into account.

(e) Expenses incurred but not paid Rs 3,000 are provided for.

D brings in Rs 20,000 in cash as his capital contribution. He is also to be credited with Rs 20,000 for having agreed to amalgamate his separate practice as Chartered Accountant with this firm.

Pass necessary journal entries and prepare the Balance Sheet of the firm after *D's* admission.

(C.A. Inter NS, Nov., 1976, adapted)

[**Ans.** Balance Sheet Total Rs 1,37,000, Capitals *A* Rs 16,000; *B* Rs 47,500; *C* Rs 30,500; and *D* Rs 40,000].

[**Hint.** On raising of goodwill account by Rs 50,000, credit amount upto Rs 30,000 to *A*, *B* and *C*, and credit excess, *i.e.* Rs 20,000 only to *A* & *B* in their mutual ratio].

20. On 1 January 1991, Abraham and Bhagwanji who were in partnership sharing 7/12 and 5/12 respectively, take in Cooverji giving him 1/6 share. Abraham and Bhagwanji were to share future profits in the ratio of 13/24 and 7/24.

    Over and above his capital, Cooverji brings in Rs 96,000 as his goodwill for the 1/6 share. The cash brought in by Cooverji as his capital and his goodwill is credited to one separate account in his personal name. On 31st December, 1991, the Trial Balance of the firm stood as follows:

Particulars	Amount Rs	Particulars	Amount Rs
Machinery	6,00,000	Abraham's Capital	3,36,000
Furniture	40,000	Bhagwanji's Capital	2,40,000
Stock	1,20,000	Cooverji's Personal Account	2,24,000
Debtors	2,00,000	Creditors	48,000
Abraham's Drawings	32,000	Current Year's Profit	2,32,000
Bhagwanji's Drawings	52,000		
Cooverji's Drawings	8,000		
Cash in hand	28,000		
	10,80,000		10,80,000

Interest on drawings is to be ignored but interest on capital accounts is to be allowed at 5% per annum after the necessary adjustments therein consequent on Cooverjis' admission. Prepare the Balance Sheet of the firm as on December 31, 1991.

[**Ans.** Capital Accounts Balances: Abraham Rs 4,50,000; Bhagwanji, Rs 3,31,600 and Cooverji, Rs 1,58,400; Balance Sheet Total, Rs 9,88,000].

Chapter 3

RECONSTITUTION OF PARTNERSHIP FIRM–II
(Retirement, Death and Amalgamation)

LEARNING OBJECTIVES

After studying this chapter you should be able to:

- ☐ state the circumstances under which a partner may retire from the firm;

- ☐ identify the accounting problems on retirement or death of a partner;

- ☐ compute amount payable to a retiring partner or to the legal representative of a deceased partner;

- ☐ state the rights of an outgoing partner;

- ☐ make appropriate accounting entries in case of amalgamation of partnership firms; and

- ☐ explain the meaning of certain key terms.

RETIREMENT OF PARTNER

Section 32 of the Partnership Act deals with the statutory provisions relating to retirement of a partner from partnership firm. These provisions are summarised below:

(*i*) A partner may retire from the firm:

    (*a*) in accordance with an express agreement; or

    (*b*) with consent of all other partners; or

    (*c*) where the partnership is at will, [1] by giving a notice in writing to all the other partners of his intention to retire.

(*ii*) A retiring partner may carry on business competing with that of the firm and may advertise such business. But he has no right to:

    (*a*) use the name of the firm,

    (*b*) represent himself as carrying on the business of the firm, or

---

[1] A partnership which is neither for a fixed period nor for a specific purpose. It can be dissolved by any partner by giving a notice in writing to the other partners.

(c) solicit the custom of the old customers of the firm except when he obtains these rights by an agreement with the other partners of the firm.

(iii) A retiring partner will not be liable for liabilities incurred by the firm after his retirement. However, he must give a public notice to that effect. Such a public notice is not necessary in case of a sleeping or dormant partner.[1]

(iv) Retirement of a partner by death or insolvency also does not require any public notice.

Accounting Problems

The accounting problems in the event of retirement of a partner can be put as follows:

(i) Adjustment for Goodwill.

(ii) Revaluation of assets and liabilities.

(iii) Adjustment regarding Reserves and other undistributed profits.

(iv) Adjustments regarding profit sharing ratios.

(v) Payment to the retiring partner.

1. **Goodwill.** The retiring partner will be entitled to his share of goodwill in the firm. The problem of goodwill can be dealt in the following two different ways:

(a) *Where goodwill account is already appearing in the books*:

(i) In such a case if goodwill is properly valued, no further adjustment will be needed. The amount has already been credited to all the partners including the retiring partner.

(ii) In case goodwill is not properly valued, an adjustment entry will be required only for the difference. For example A, B and C are three partners sharing profits and losses in the ratio of 2 : 2 : 1. The goodwill is appearing in the books at Rs 10,000. C retires and on the date of his retirement, the goodwill is valued at Rs 15,000. The following Journal entry will be passed for Rs 5,000.

Goodwill A/c	Dr.	5,000	
To A's Capital A/c			2,000
To B's Capital A/c			2,000
To C's Capital A/c			1,000

(Being adjustment for goodwill on retirement of C)

(b) *Where goodwill account is not appearing in the books*:

There could be several alternatives:

(i) Goodwill account may be raised in the books.

Goodwill A/c	Dr.
To Old Partners' Capital A/cs	

(The amount of goodwill credited to old partners including the retiring partner in their old profit sharing ratio)

(ii) In case continuing partners decide not to continue with the goodwill account, it may be written off.

Continuing Partners Capital A/cs	Dr.
To Goodwill A/c	

(Goodwill written off to the continuing partners A/cs (*i.e.* new partners) in the new ratio).

---

[1] A sleeping or a dormant partner is one who does not actively participate in the activities of the firm.

(iii) Entry may be made only with the share of goodwill of the retiring partner.

Goodwill A/c   Dr.
(only with the share of the retiring partner).
     To Retiring Partner's Capital A/c

(iv) The share of goodwill of the retiring partner may be adjusted in the accounts of the continuing partners without raising a goodwill account.

Continuing Partners' Capital A/cs   Dr.
(in the ratio in which they gain on retirement)
     To Retiring Partner's Capital A/c

Illustration 3.1. *A, B* and *C* are partners in business sharing profits and losses in the ratio of 2 : 2 : 1. *C* retires from the firm and on this date the value of firm's goodwill (for which no account appears in the books) was determined at Rs 10,000.

You are required to pass suitable Journal entries for each of the following cases.

(i) When goodwill account is to be raised in the books.

(ii) When the goodwill account raised is subsequently written off.

(iii) When only *C*'s share is to be recorded.

(iv) When *C*'s share it to be adjusted into accounts of *A* and *B* without raising a Goodwill account in the firm's book.

Solution:

JOURNAL

	Particulars		Dr. Amount Rs	Cr. Amount Rs
(i)	Goodwill A/c	Dr.	10,000	
	To *A*'s Capital A/c			4,000
	To *B*'s Capital A/c			4,000
	To *C*'s Capital A/c			2,000
	(Goodwill account raised in the books)			
(ii) (a)	Goodwill A/c	Dr.	10,000	
	To *A*'s Capital A/c			4,000
	To *B*'s Capital A/c			4,000
	To *C*'s Capital A/c			2,000
	(Being goodwill account raised)			
(b)	*A*'s Capital A/c	Dr.	5,000	
	B's Capital A/c	Dr.	5,000	
	To Goodwill A/c			10,000
	(Being goodwill raised now written off in the new profit sharing ration)			
(iii)	Goodwill A/c	Dr.	2,000	
	To *C*'s Capital A/c			2,000
	(Being share of goodwill recorded)			
(iv)	*A*'s Capital A/c	Dr.	1,000	
	B's Capital A/c	Dr.	1,000	
	To *C*'s Capital A/c			2,000
	(*A* and *B* debited with *C*'s share of goodwill in the ratio of their gain on *C*'s retirement)			

2. **Revaluation of assets and liabilities.** A Profit and Loss Adjustment account will be opened in the books and profit or loss on revaluation will be credited or debited to all the partners (including the retiring partner) in the old ratio. The assets and liabilities will appear at the revised values in the new balance sheet after retirement.

In case it is desired that assets and liabilities should continue to appear at the old values, the entries for profit or loss on revaluation will be done through Memorandum Profit and Loss Adjustment Account as explained in the previous pages in "Admission of a Partner".

Illustration 3.2. A, B and C are sharing profits in a business in the ratio of 3:2:1. Their Balance Sheet on 31 December 1988 was a under.

Liabilities	Rs	Assets	Rs
Sundry Creditors	10,000	Cash	5,000
Loan from D	20,000	Debtors	10,000
Capitals A	20,000	Stock	20,000
B	20,000	Plant	50,000
C	15,000		
	85,000		85,000

C retires on this date. The following arrangement is agreed upon:

(i) The value of the Firm's goodwill is Rs 15,000. C's share of the same is to be adjusted in the accounts of A and B.

(ii) The assets are revalued as follows:

Stock	25,000
Plant	52,000

(iii) A provision for bad debts is to be created on debtors @ 10% of debtors.

(iv) The amount due to C is to be transferred to a loan account in his name.

You are required to prepare the Profit and Loss Adjustment Account, Capital Accounts of the Partners and the Balance Sheet of the business:

(a) When assets are to be shown at new values in the books.

(b) When assets are to be shown at old values.

Solution:

(a) *When assets are to be shown at new values.*

P. & L. ADJUSTMENT ACCOUNT

Particulars	Rs	Particulars	Rs
To Provision bad debts	1,000	By Stock	5,000
To Profit:		By Plant	2,000
A's Capital A/c	3,000		
B's Capital A/c	2,000		
C's Capital A/c	1,000		
	7,000		7,000

CAPITAL ACCOUNTS

Particulars	A Rs	B Rs	C Rs	Particulars	A Rs	B Rs	C Rs
To C's Capital A/c (Goodwill)	1,500	1,000		By Balance b/d	20,000	20,000	15,000
				By P. & L. Adj. A/c	3,000	2,000	1,000

Contd....

Particulars	A Rs	B Rs	C Rs	Particulars	A Rs	B Rs	C Rs
To Balance c/d	21,500	21,000		By A's Cap. A/c			
To C's Loan A/c			18,500	(Goodwill)			1,500
				By B's Cap. A/c			
				(Goodwill)			1,000
	23,000	22,000	18,500		23,000	22,000	18,500

BALANCE SHEET
as on 1st January, 1989

Liabilities	Rs	Assets		Rs
Sundry Creditors	10,000	Cash		5,000
Loan from D	20,000	Debtors	10,000	
Loan from C	18,500	Less: Provision	1,000	9,000
Capitals:				
A	21,500	Stock		25,000
B	21,000	Plant		52,000
	91,000			91,000

(b) *When assets are to be shown at old values.*

MEMORANDUM P. & L. ADJUSTMENT ACCOUNT

Particulars	Rs	Particulars	Rs
To Provision for bad debts	1,000	By Stock	5,000
To Profit:		By Plant	2,000
A's Capital A/c	3,000		
B's Capital A/c	2,000		
C's Capital A/c	1,000		
	7,000		7,000
To Reversal of entry (increase in	7,000	By Reversal of entry (decrease in	
the value of assets)		the value of assets)	1,000
		By A's Capital A/c	3,600
		By B's Capital A/c	2,400
	7,000		7,000

PARTNER'S CAPITAL ACCOUNTS

Particulars	A Rs	B Rs	C Rs	Particulars	A Rs	B Rs	C Rs
To C's Capital A/c	1,500	1,000		By Balance b/d	20,000	20,000	15,000
To Memorandum				By Memorandum			
P. & L. Adj. A/c	3,600	2,400	—	P. & L. Adj. A/c	3,000	2,000	1,000
To C's Loan A/c	—	—	18,500	By A's Capital A/c			
				(Goodwill)	—	—	1,500
To Balance c/d	17,900	18,600	—	By B's Capital A/c			
				(Goodwill)	—	—	1,000
	23,000	22,000	18,500		23,000	22,000	18,500

BALANCE SHEET
as on 1st January, 1989

Liabilities	Rs	Assets	Rs
Sundry Creditors	10,000	Cash	5,000
Loan from D	20,000	Debtors	10,000
Loan from C	18,500	Stock	20,000
Capitals:		Plant	50,000
A	17,900		
B	18,600		
	85,000		85,000

Reserves and other Undistributed Profits

The amount standing as reserves or undistributed profits in the books of the firm will be distributed among all the partners in their old profit sharing ratio.

The journal entry will be:

Reserves or P. & L. A/c   Dr.
     To Partners' Capital A/cs.

In case it is desired that only retiring partner should be credited with his share in reserves or distributed profit, the following journal entry will be passed:

Reserves or P. & L. A/c   Dr.
     To Retiring Partner's Capital A/c
         (only with his share)

The balance of Reserves or undistributed profits will continue to appear in the Balance Sheet after such retirement.

In case it is desired that the retiring partner should be given the benefit of Reserves or undistributed profits without in any way disturbing the Reserves or undistributed profits, the following journal entry will be passed:

Continuing Partners' Capital A/cs   Dr.
     (in the ratio they gain)
     To Retiring Partner's Capital A/c
         (only with his share)

Illustration 3.3. A, B and C are partners in a business sharing profits and losses in the ratio of 2 : 2 : 1. C retires from the business. The General Reserve stands at Rs 5,000 on the date of C's retirement. A and B agree to share the future profits in the ratio of 3 : 2 respectively.

You are required to pass the necessary journal entry for distribution of General Reserve if

(a) The General Reserve is not allowed to be kept in the books.

(b) The General Reserve is kept only at an amount remaining after giving C his share.

(c) The General Reserve is allowed to be kept at the full value.

Solution:

	Particulars		Dr. Amount Rs	Cr. Amount Rs
(a)	General Reserve A/c	Dr.	5,000	
	To A's Capital A/c			2,000
	To B's Capital A/c			2,000
	To C's Capital A/c			1,000
	(General Reserve distributed among the partners)			
(b)	General Reserve	Dr.	1,000	
	To C's Capital A/c			1,000
	(C's share in General Reserve credited to his account)			
(c)	A's Capital A/c	Dr.	1,000	
	To C's Capital A/c			1,000
	(A's debited with C's share of General Reserve since he alone stands to gain on account of C's retirement).			

Profit Sharing Ratio

In the absence of any other agreement between the partners, the continuing partners will continue to share the profits or losses in between themselves in the same ratio in which they were sharing before retirement of a partner.

For example if A, B and C were sharing profits in the ratio of 3 : 2 : 1 respectively and C retires, the profit sharing ratio between A and B would continue to be 3 : 2.

In other words it can be said that the share of the retiring partner will be shared by the continuing partners in their old profit sharing ratio. The ratio in which they share the retiring partner's share is termed as their "*gaining ratio*".

In the above example, the share of retiring partner is 1/6. This shall go to A and B in the ratio of ⅗ to A and ⅖ to B which means:

$$A\text{'s share} = \frac{3}{6} + \frac{1}{6} \times \frac{3}{5}$$

$$= \frac{3}{6} + \frac{3}{30} = \frac{15+3}{30} = \frac{18}{30}$$

$$B\text{'s share} = \frac{2}{6} + \frac{1}{6} \times \frac{2}{5}$$

$$= \frac{2}{6} + \frac{2}{30} = \frac{10+2}{30} = \frac{12}{30}$$

or   the ratio comes to 3 : 2.

The continuing partners may agree to share, the share of the retiring partner in an agreed ratio. For example, if in the above example, C's share of ⅙ is shared by A and B equally, the new profit sharing ratio will be:

$$A \qquad \frac{3}{6} + \frac{1}{12} = \frac{6+1}{12} = \frac{7}{12}$$

$$B \qquad \frac{2}{6} + \frac{1}{12} = \frac{4+1}{12} = \frac{5}{12}$$

Thus, the new profit sharing ratio of A and B will be 7 : 5 respectively.

Illustration 3.4. A, B and C were partners sharing profits and losses in the ratio of 3/6, 2/6 and 1/6.

Calculate the new and gaining ratios in each of the following cases:

(*a*) A retires; (*b*) B retires; or (*c*) C retires.

Solution:

New Ratios:

(*i*) **When A retires.** B and C will continue to share the profits in the old ratio *i.e.*, 2/6 and 1/6 or 2 : 1.

(*ii*) **When B retires.** A and C will continue to share the profits in the old ratio *i.e.*, 3/6 and 1/6 or 3 : 1.

(*iii*) **When C retires.** A and B will continue to share the profits in the old ratio *i.e.*, 3/6 and 2/6 or 3 : 2.

Gaining Ratios:

In each of the above cases, since nothing contrary has been given, the gaining ratio will be the same as old profit sharing ratio *i.e.*, (*i*) 2 : 1 (*ii*) 3 : 1 and (*iii*) 3 : 2. This can be verified as follows:

Gaining Ratio = New Ratio − Old Ratio

When A retires

For B $\qquad = \dfrac{2}{3} - \dfrac{2}{6} = \dfrac{4-2}{6} = \dfrac{2}{6}$

For C $\qquad = \dfrac{1}{3} - \dfrac{1}{6} = \dfrac{2-1}{6} = \dfrac{1}{6}$

Gaining Ratio $\qquad = \dfrac{2}{6} : \dfrac{1}{6}$ or 2 : 1

When B retires

For A $\qquad = \dfrac{3}{4} - \dfrac{3}{6} = \dfrac{18-12}{24} = \dfrac{6}{24}$

For C $\qquad = \dfrac{1}{4} - \dfrac{1}{6} = \dfrac{6-4}{24} = \dfrac{2}{24}$

Gaining Ratio $\qquad \dfrac{6}{24} : \dfrac{2}{24}$ or 3 : 1

When C retires

For A $\qquad = \dfrac{3}{5} - \dfrac{3}{6} = \dfrac{18-15}{30} = \dfrac{3}{30}$

For B $\qquad = \dfrac{2}{5} - \dfrac{2}{6} = \dfrac{12-10}{30} = \dfrac{2}{30}$

Gaining Ratio $\qquad = \dfrac{3}{30} : \dfrac{2}{30}$ or 3 : 2.

Illustration 3.5. A, B and C are partners in a business, sharing profits in the ratio of 2 : 2 : 1. A retires and he sells his share in the business for a sum of Rs 6,000, Rs 4,800 is paid by B and Rs 1,200 by C. The profit for the year after A's retirement amounts to Rs 10,000.

You are required to give the necessary Journal entries.

Solution:

JOURNAL

Particulars		Dr. Amount Rs	Cr. Amount Rs
Bank A/c	Dr.	6,000	
To B's Capital A/c			4,800
To C's Capital A/c			1,200
(Being cash brought by B & C to pay off A on his retirement)			

Contd....

Particulars		Dr. Amount Rs	Cr. Amount Rs
A's Capital A/c	Dr.	6,000	
To Bank			6,000
(Being amount paid to A on his retirement)			
Profit and Loss Appropriation A/c	Dr.	10,000	
To B's Capital A/c			7,200
To C's Capital A/c			2,800
(Being the amount of profit distributed among partners)			

Working Notes:

The new profit sharing ratio has been calculated as under:

$$B \text{ pays Rs } 4,800$$
$$C \text{ pays Rs } 1,200$$

This means B has bought ⅘ of A's share and C has bought ⅕.

B's share would therefore be:

$$\frac{2}{5} + \frac{2}{5} \times \frac{4}{5} = \frac{2}{5} + \frac{8}{25}$$

$$= \frac{10 + 8}{25} = \frac{18}{25}$$

C's share would therefore be:

$$\frac{1}{5} + \frac{2}{5} \times \frac{1}{5} = \frac{1}{5} + \frac{2}{25}$$

$$\frac{5 + 2}{25} = \frac{7}{25}$$

Thus, the new ratio would be:

$$\frac{18}{25} : \frac{7}{25} = \text{ or } 18 : 7$$

Payment

The amount due to the retiring partner will be paid as per terms of the partnership agreement or as otherwise mutually agreed. When the amount payable to the retiring partner is determined, it will be transferred to his loan account. The Journal entry will be:

Retiring Partner's Capital A/c   Dr.
     To Retiring Partner's Loan A/c

In case the continuing partners agree to bring cash to pay off the retiring partner, the entries will be

Bank   Dr.
     To Continuing Partners' Capital A/cs
(For cash brought in by the partners in the agreed ratio to pay off the retiring partner)
Retiring Partner's Capital A/c   Dr.
     To Bank
(For cash paid to the retiring partner)

In case the continuing partners decide to pay the retiring partner in their individual capacity in their profit sharing ratio, the entry will be:

Retiring Partner's Capital Loan A/c   Dr.
     To Continuing Partners' Capital A/cs

Payment in Instalments

The amount due to the retiring partner may be agreed to be paid in equal instalments together with interest at the agreed rate.

In such a case there may be two situations:

- (i) Equal instalments may only be regarding 'principal' amount. Interest on outstanding balance is paid in addition to the instalment amount (*See* Illustration: 3.6).

- (ii) Equal instalment may be both as regards interest as well as principal. In such a case the amount of instalment is calculated with the help of Annuity Table (*See* Illustration 3.8).

Illustration 3.6. The total amount due to the retiring partner *A* is Rs 12,000. It is to be paid in ten equal annual instalments with interest at 10% p.a. The first instalment to be paid after the expiry of one year after from the date of retirement. Prepare *A*'s loan account for the first three years.

Solution:

A'S LOAN ACCOUNT

Particulars	Rs	Particulars	Rs
1st Year			
To Bank	2,400	By *A*'s Capital A/c	12,000
(Principal 1,200 + Interest 1,200)		By Interest	1,200
To Balance c/d	10,800		
	13,200		13,200
2nd Year			
To Bank (1,200 + 1,080)	2,280	By Balance b/d	10,800
To Balance c/d	9,600	By Interest	1,080
	11,880		11,880
3rd Year			
To Bank (1,200 + 960)	2,160	By Balance b/d	9,600
To Balance c/d	8,400	By Interest	960
	10,560		10,560

Illustration 3.7. Nut, Bolt and Screw are partners sharing profits and losses in the ratio of 4 : 2 : 1. On 1st January, 1983, Screw retires. On that date, the capital accounts of the partners showed credit balances of Nut Rs 12,000, Bolt Rs 10,000 and Screw Rs 9,000. It was provided in the Partnership Deed that in case of retirement, the retiring partner should be entitled to a share of the goodwill of the firm to be calculated at two years' purchase of the average profits of the last three years, and that the payment of the capital and share of goodwill to the retiring partner shall be made by annual instalment of Rs 4,000 each, for the first two years and the balance in the last year, interest being calculated at 10% on the unpaid balances.

The Profit for the years 1980, 1981 and 1982 were Rs 8,600, Rs 7,600 and Rs 4,800 respectively.

The first instalment was paid on 31st December, 1983.

Show Screw's Loan Account until the payment of the whole amount due to him was made.

(C.A. Entrance, Nov., 1986)

Solution:

SCREW'S CAPITAL ACCOUNT

Date	Particulars	Rs	Date	Particulars	Rs
1983			1983		
Jan. 1	To transfer to Screw's Loan A/c	11,000	Jan. 1	By Balance b/d	9,000
				By Goodwill A/c	2,000
		11,000			11,000

SCREW'S LOAN ACCOUNT

Date	Particulars	Rs	Date	Particulars	Rs
1983			1983		
Dec. 31	To Bank	4,000	Jan. 1	By Transfer from Screw's Capital A/c	11,000
	To Balance c/d	8,100	Dec. 31	By Interest @ 10% (11,000 × 10/100)	1,100
		12,100			12,100
			1984		
Dec. 31	To Bank	4,000	Jan. 1	By Balance b/d	8,100
	To Balance c/d	4,910	Dec. 31	By Interest @ 10% (8,100 × 10/100)	810
		8,910			8,910
			1985		
Dec. 31	To Bank	5,401	Jan. 1	By Balance b/d	4,910
			Dec. 31	By Interest (4,910 × 10/100)	491
		5,401			5,401

Working Note:

Computation of Goodwill:

Profits for the three years were:

	Rs
1980	8,600
1981	7,600
1982	4,800
Total Profits for three years	21,000

Average Profit = 21,000/3 = Rs 7,000.
Value of Goodwill = Rs 7,000 × 2 = Rs 14,000
Screw's Share of Goodwill = 14,000 × 1/7 = Rs 2,000.

Illustration 3.8. A, B and C were carrying on business in partnership sharing profit and losses in the ratio of 3 : 2 : 1 respectively. On 31st December, 1987 Balance Sheet of the firm stood as follows:

Liabilities	Rs		Assets	Rs
Sundry Creditors		13,590	Cash	5,900
Capital Accounts:			Debtors	8,000
A	15,000		Stock	11,690
B	10,000		Buildings	23,000
C	10,000	35,000		
		48,590		48,590

B retired on the above mentioned date on the following terms:

(*i*) Buildings be appreciated by Rs 7,000.

(*ii*) Provision for bad debts be made @ 5% on Debtors.

(*iii*) Goodwill of the firm be valued at Rs 9,000 and adjustment in this respect be made without raising a Goodwill Account.

(*iv*) Rs 5,000 be paid to *B* immediately and the balance due to him be treated as a loan carrying interest @ 6% per annum. Such loan is to be paid in three equal annual instalments including interest.

Pass Journal entries to record above mentioned transactions and show the Balance Sheet of the firm as it would appear immediately after *B*'s retirement. Prepare also *B*'s Loan Account till it is finally closed.

Solution:

JOURNAL

Particulars		Dr. Amount Rs	Cr. Amount Rs
Buildings A/c	Dr.	7,000	
To P. & L. Adjustment A/c			7,000
(Being appreciation in the value of buildings)			
P. & L. Adjustment A/c	Dr.	400	
To Provision for Bad Debts			400
(Being provision for bad debts created on debtors)			
Profit and Loss Adjustment A/c	Dr.	6,600	
To A's Capital A/c			3,300
To B's Capital A/c			2,200
To C's Capital A/c			1,100
(Being profit on revaluation credited to old partners)			
A's Capital A/c	Dr.	2,250	
C's Capital A/c	Dr.	750	
To B's Capital A/c			3,000
(Being B's share of goodwill adjusted)			
B's Capital A/c	Dr.	5,000	
To Bank A/c			5,000
(Being the amount paid to B on retirement)			
B's Capital A/c	Dr.	10,200	
To B's Loan A/c			10,200
(Balance of amount due to B transferred to his loan account on his retirement)			

BALANCE SHEET
as on 1 January, 1988

Liabilities		Rs	Assets		Rs
Sundry Creditors		13,590	Cash		900
B's Loan A/c		10,200	Debtors	8,000	
Capital Accounts:			*Less:* Prov. for bad debts	400	7,600
A	16,050		Stock		11,690
C	10,350	26,400	Buildings	23,000	
			Add: Appreciation	7,000	30,000
		50,190			50,190

B'S LOAN ACCOUNT

Particulars	Rs	Particulars	Rs
1988			
To Bank	3,816	By Balance b/d	10,200
To Balance c/d	6,996	By Interest	612
	10,812		10,812
1989			
To Bank	3,816	By Balance b/d	6,996
To Balance c/d	3,600	By Interest	420
	7,416		7416
1990			
To Bank	3,816	By Balance b/d	3,600
		By Interest	216
	3,816		3,816

Working Notes:

(*i*) The old profit sharing ratio was *A, B, C,* $\frac{3}{6}$: $\frac{2}{6}$: $\frac{1}{6}$.

B has retired. The ratio between *A* & *B* would therefore be 3:1 or $\frac{3}{4}$: $\frac{1}{4}$.

(*ii*) The amount payable to *B* for goodwill will be charged to *A* and *C* in the ratio in which they gain on account of *C*'s retirement *i.e.*, 3:1, calculated as follows:

Gain for *A* $\qquad \frac{3}{4} - \frac{3}{5} = \frac{15-12}{20} = \frac{3}{20}$

Gain for *C* $\qquad \frac{1}{4} - \frac{1}{5} = \frac{5-4}{20} = \frac{1}{20}$

(*iii*) According to Annuity Table Re .37410981 must be paid every year to repay rupee one with 6% interest in three years. The annual instalment for payment of Rs 10,200 comes to $10,200 \times .37410981 = $ Rs 3,816.

Illustration 3.9. Ajoy, Bijoy and Sanjoy were partners sharing profits and losses in the ratio of 5:3:2 respectively. They had taken out a joint life policy of the face value of Rs 2,00,000. On 31st December, 1988, its surrender value was Rs 40,000. On this date the Balance Sheet of the firm stood as follows:

Liabilities	Rs	Assets	Rs
Sundry Creditors	53,000	Fixed Assets	2,50,000
Expenses Outstanding	7,000	Stock	1,10,000
Reserve	30,000	Book Debts	90,000
Capitals:		Cash at Bank	20,000
Ajoy	2,00,000		
Bijoy	1,00,000		
Sanjoy	80,000	3,80,000	
	4,70,000		4,70,000

On that date Bijoy decided to retire and for that purpose:

(*a*) Goodwill was valued at Rs 1,50,000.

(*b*) Fixed assets were valued at Rs 3,00,000.

(*c*) Stock was considered as worth Rs 10,000.

Bijoy was to be paid in cash brought in by Ajoy and Sanjoy in such a way so as to make their capitals proportionate to their new profit sharing ratio which was to be 3 : 2 respectively. Goodwill was to be passed through books without raising a Goodwill Account; the joint life policy was also not to appear in the Balance Sheet. Prepare the capital accounts and the resultant Balance Sheet.

Solution:

JOURNAL

Particulars		Dr. Amount Rs	Cr. Amount Rs
Ajoy's Capital A/c	Dr.	19,000	
Sanjoy's Capital A/c	Dr.	38,000	
To Bijoy's Capital A/c			57,000
(Being Bijoy's share in unrecorded assets namely Goodwill Rs 1,50,000 and Joint Life Policy Rs 40,000 at its surrender value, adjusted into the capital accounts of the continuing partners in their gaining ratio)			
Fixed Assets A/c	Dr.	50,000	
To P. & L. Adjustment A/c			50,000
(Being increase in the value of fixed assets)			
P. & L. Adjustment A/c	Dr.	1,00,000	
To Stock			1,00,000
(Being decrease in the value of stock)			
Ajoy's Capital A/c	Dr.	25,000	
Bijoy's Capital A/c	Dr.	15,000	
Sanjoy Capital A/c	Dr.	10,000	
To P. & L. Adjustment A/c			50,000
(Being loss on revaluation of assets)			
Reserve A/c	Dr.	30,000	
To Ajoy's Capital A/c			15,000
To Bijoy's Capital A/c			9,000
To Sanjoy's Capital A/c			6,000
(Being reserve distributed)			
Bank A/c	Dr.	1,51,000	
To Ajoy's Capital A/c			45,000
To Sanjoy's Capital A/c			1,06,000
(Being cash brought in by Ajoy and Sanjoy)			
Bijoy's Capital A/c	Dr.	1,51,000	
To Bank A/c			1,51,000
(Being Bijoy's Capital balance paid to him)			

AJOY'S CAPITAL ACCOUNT

Particulars	Rs	Particulars	Rs
To Bijoy's Capital A/c	19,000	By Balance b/d	2,00,000
To P. & L. Adj. A/c	25,000	By Reserves A/c	15,000
To Balance c/d	2,16,000	By Cash A/c	45,000
	2,60,000		2,60,000

SANJOY'S CAPITAL ACCOUNT

Particulars	Rs	Particulars	Rs
To Bijoy's Capital A/c	38,000	By Balance b/d	80,000
To P. & L. Adj. A/c	10,000	By Reserve A/c	6,000
To Balance c/d	1,44,000	By Bank A/c	1,06,000
	1,92,000		1,92,000

BIJOY'S CAPITAL ACCOUNT

Particulars	Rs	Particulars	Rs
To P. & L. Adj. A/c	15,000	By Balance b/d	1,00,000
To Bank	1,51,000	By Reserve A/c	9,000
		By Ajoy's Cap. A/c	19,000
		By Sanjoy's Cap. A/c	38,000
	1,66,000		1,66,000

BALANCE SHEET
(after Bijoy's Retirement)

Liabilities	Rs	Assets	Rs
Sundry Creditors	53,000	Fixed Assets	3,00,000
Exp. outstanding	7,000	Stock	10,000
Capitals:		Book Debts	90,000
Ajoy	2,16,000	Cash at Bank	20,000
Sanjoy	1,44,000		
	4,20,000		4,20,000

Working Notes:

1. Gaining Ratio is calculated as under :

Ajoy's Gain = His New Share − His Old Share

i.e.,
$$\frac{3}{5} - \frac{5}{10} = \frac{6-5}{10} = \frac{1}{10}$$

Sanjoy's Gain = His New Share − His Old Share

i.e.,
$$\frac{2}{5} - \frac{2}{10} = \frac{4-2}{10} = \frac{2}{10}$$

∴ Gaining Ratio = 1 : 2

2. Cash to be brought in by partners:

	Rs
Amount needed to pay Bijoy	1,51,000
Capital of Ajoy before bringing cash	1,71,000
Capital of Sanjoy before bringing cash	38,000
Total Capital	3,60,000

In the new firm capitals of Ajoy and Sanjoy should be in the ratio of 3:2.

	Rs
Ajoy's Capital	2,16,000
Sanjoy's Capital	1,44,000
Hence, Ajoy brings in Rs 2,16,000 − 1,71,000 =	45,000
Sanjoy brings in Rs 1,44,000 − Rs 38,000 =	1,06,000

Illustration 3.10. Paras, Rajesh and Moti are partners in a firm. They shared profits and losses in the ratio of 3 : 2 : 1. On 1st April, Rajesh retired and on that date the Balance Sheet of the firm was as under:

Liabilities	Rs	Assets	Rs
Capital A/cs:		Land and Buildings	2,50,000
Paras	3,40,000	Plant and Machinery	3,00,000
Rajesh	2,20,000	Investments	50,000
Moti	1,90,000	Stock	1,80,000
Sundry Creditors	1,60,000	Bills Receivable	20,000
Bills Payable	50,000	Sundry Debtors	1,00,000
		Cash at Bank	60,000
	9,60,000		9,60,000

(1) Paras and Moti decided to share future profits and losses in the ratio of ⅝ and ⅜ respectively.

(2) The Goodwill of the firm was valued at two years' purchase based on the average of last three years' profits. The profits of the last years were as under:

		Rs
1989–90	Profit	2,48,000
1988–89	Loss	36,000
1987–88	Profit	1,48,000

It was decided that Rajesh's share of Goodwill be adjusted in the Capital Accounts of Paras and Moti. (No Goodwill A/c is to be raised in the books of the firm).

(3) Stock and Land and Buildings are to be depreciated by 10% and Plant & Machinery to be increased by 10%.

(4) 5% is to be provided for Doubtful Debts on Sundry Debtors and Provision is to be made for Rs 12,000 for Outstanding Legal expenses.

(5) The amount due to Shri Rajesh was transferred to his Loan Account.

Pass the necessary journal entries for the above adjustments. Prepare Profit and Loss Adjustment Account, Partners' Capital Accounts and Balance Sheet of the Firm after the retirement of Rajesh.   *(C.A. Entrance, Nov., 1991)*

Solution:

JOURNAL ENTRIES

Date	Particulars		Dr. Amount Rs	Cr. Amount Rs
1991				
	Paras's Capital A/c	Dr.	30,000	
	Moti's Capital A/c	Dr.	50,000	
	To Rajesh's Capital A/c			80,000
	(Being adjustment for Rajesh's share of goodwill [See W. Note])			
	Profit and Loss Adjustment A/c	Dr.	60,000	
	To Stock			18,000
	To Land and Buildings			25,000
	To Provision for Doubtful Debts			5,000
	To Outstanding Legal Expenses A/c			12,000
	(Being losses on revaluation)			

Contd....

Date	Particulars		Dr. Amount Rs	Cr. Amount Rs
	Plant and Machinery A/c	Dr.	30,000	
	To Profit & Loss Adjustment A/c			30,000
	(Being increase in the value of Plant and Machinery)			
	Paras's Capital A/c	Dr.	15,000	
	Rajesh's Capital A/c	Dr.	10,000	
	Moti's Capital A/c	Dr.	5,000	
	To Profit & Loss Adjustment A/c			30,000
	(Being Loss transferred to Capital A/cs.)			

PROFIT AND LOSS ADJUSTMENT ACCOUNT

Date	Particulars	Rs	Date	Particulars	Rs
1991			1991		
	To Stock	18,000		By Plant & Machinery	30,000
	To Land & Buildings	25,000		By Loss transferred	
	To Provision for Bad			to Capital A/cs:	
	& Doubtful Debts	5,000		Paras	15,000
	To Outstanding Legal			Rajesh	10,000
	Expenses	12,000		Moti	5,000
		60,000			60,000

PARTNERS' CAPITAL ACCOUNTS

Particulars	Paras	Rajesh	Moti	Particulars	Paras	Rajesh	Moti
To Rajesh				By Balance b/d	3,40,000	2,20,000	1,90,000
Cap. A/c	30,000	—	50,000	By Paras's			
To P & L Adj.	15,000	10,000	5,000	Cap. A/c	—	30,000	—
To Rajesh's				By Moti's Cap.			
Loan A/c	—	2,90,000	—	A/c	—	50,000	—
To Balance c/d	2,95,000	—	1,35,000				
	3,40,000	3,00,000	1,90,000		3,40,000	3,00,000	1,90,000

BALANCE SHEET OF M/S. PARAS AND MOTI
as on 1.4.1991

Liabilities	Rs	Assets		Rs
Capital Accounts:		Land & Buildings		2,25,000
Paras	2,95,000	(2,50,000 – 25,000)		
Moti	1,35,000	Plant & Machinery		3,30,000
Rajesh Loan Account	2,90,000	(3,00,000 + 30,000)		
Sundry Creditors	1,60,000	Investments		50,000
Bills Payable	50,000	Stock (1,80,000 – 18,000)		1,62,000
Outstanding Legal Expenses	12,000	Bills Receivable		20,000
		Sundry Debtors	1,00,000	
		Less: Provision for		
		Doubtful Debts	5,000	95,000
		Cash at Bank		60,000
	9,42,000			9,42,000

Working Notes:

Valuation of Goodwill

Average of the last 3 years' Profits : $\dfrac{\text{Rs } 2,48,000 - \text{Rs } 36,000 + \text{Rs } 1,48,000}{3}$

$$= \dfrac{\text{Rs } 3,60,000}{3} = \text{Rs } 1,20,000$$

Goodwill at two years' purchase = Rs $1,20,000 \times 2 = $ Rs $2,40,000$

∴ Rajesh Share of goodwill $\dfrac{2}{6} \times$ Rs $2,40,000 = $ Rs $80,000$

This is to be borne by Paras and Moti in the ratio of gain.

Gain of Paras $= \dfrac{5}{8} - \dfrac{3}{6} = \dfrac{6}{48}$ Gain of Moti $= \dfrac{3}{8} - \dfrac{1}{6} = \dfrac{10}{48}$

Ratio of Gain $= 3 : 5$

Goodwill to be borne by Paras and Moti:

$$\text{Paras} = \dfrac{3}{8} \times 80,000 = \text{Rs } 30,000$$

$$\text{Moti} = \dfrac{5}{8} \times 80,000 = \text{Rs } 50,000$$

DEATH OF PARTNER

According to Section 35 of the Partnership Act, a partnership firm may not be dissolved on the death of a partner.

Where under a contract between the partners the firm is not dissolved by the death of a partner, the estate of the deceased partner is not liable for any act done or liability incurred after his death. No public notice is required for this purpose.

In the event of death of a partner, the legal representatives of the deceased partner will be entitled to get from the firm, amounts due on account of following:

(*i*) Capital standing to the credit of the deceased partner on the date of his death.

(*ii*) Share of goodwill.

(*iii*) Profit on revaluation of assets and liabilities as reduced by any loss on any such revaluation.

(*iv*) Share out of the proceeds of a joint life insurance policy.

In case the firm has taken insurance policies severally on the life of each partner, the deceased's partner's executor's will be entitled to get not only a share out of the proceeds of the policy on his life but also a share out of the surrender values of the policies on the lives of other partners. However, the latter part will be applicable only when the entire premium paid on these policies has been charged to Profit & Loss Account and the policies are not appearing in the books of account.

For example, a Firm has taken life policies on the lives of all partners severally for A Rs 10,000, B Rs 5,000 and C Rs 5,000. A dies. The premium paid has been charged to Profit & Loss Account each year. The surrender values of the policies of B and C are Rs 2,000 each. The partners share profits and losses in the ratio of 2:2:1.

In this case, A's executors will be entitled to:

	Rs
(*a*) Share out of the proceeds of life insurance policy on the life of A *i.e.* 10,000 × 2/5	4,000

(b) Share out of the surrender values
of the life insurance policies on
lives of B and C i.e. 4,000 × 2/5   1,600
                         5,600

(v) Share out of the reserves or other undistributed profits.

(vi) Share in the profits of the firm earned by the firm from the date of beginning of the year to the date of his death.

(vii) Interest on capital from the beginning of the year to the date of his death.

The deceased partner's capital account will be charged with his share of the following amounts:

(i) Drawings and interest thereon from the beginning of the accounting year to the date of his death.

(ii) Loss on revaluation of assets and liabilities.

(iii) Loss in the business from the beginning of the accounting year till the date of his death.

Ascertainment of the deceased partner's share in the profit of the firm. The actual share of the deceased partner in the profit of the firm till the date of death can be calculated only by preparing the final accounts up to that date. However, it may not be very convenient. The profit may, therefore, be calculated according to any of the following methods:

1. **Time basis.** The profit for the year can be divided between two periods:

(i) beginning of the accounting year to the date of death of the partner.

(ii) from the date of death of partner till the end of the accounting year.

The deceased partner's share can now be ascertained out of the profit ascertained for the period (i) stated above.

Illustration 3.11. A. B and C are partners in a business sharing profits in the ratio of 2 : 2 : 1. C dies on 1st April 1988. The profit for the accounting year ending on 31st December, 1988 amounts to Rs 16,000. Calculate the share of the deceased partner in profits of the firm.

Solution:

Profit for the year is Rs 16,000

Profit from 1st January to 1st April, 1988 i.e. for 3 months.

$$16,000 \times 1/4 = \text{Rs } 4,000$$

C's share will be $4,000 \times 1/5 = \text{Rs } 800$.

2. **Sales basis.** The deceased partner's share in profits up to the date of his death can be determined on the basis of sales.

Illustration 3.12. A, B and C are sharing profits in the ratio of 2 : 2 : 1. C dies on 1 April, 1988. Sales for the year 1988 amount to Rs 3,00,000 out of which sales of Rs 1,00,000 amounted between the period from 1 January, 1988 to 1 April, 1988. The profit for the year amounted to Rs 30,000.

Calculate the deceased partner's share in the profits of the firm.

Solution:

The profit up to the death on the basis of turnover:

$$30,000 \times \frac{1,00,000}{3,00,000}$$
$$= \text{Rs } 10,000.$$

C's share will be:

$$10,000 \times 1/5 = \text{Rs } 2,000.$$

In both cases the share of the deceased partner can also be ascertained on the basis of firm's past performance instead of actual figures for the current year.

Rights of an Outgoing Partner

An outgoing partner may carry on a business competing with that of the firm in the absence of any contract to the contrary.

Section 37 of the Partnership Act further provides that where any partner of a firm has died or otherwise ceased to be a partner, and the surviving or continuing partners carry on the business with the property of the firm without finally settling the accounts of the outgoing partner, such partner or his legal representative, in the absence of any contract to the contrary can claim at his option;

(*i*) Such share of the profits after his leaving the firm as may be attributable to the use of his share of property of the firm, or

(*ii*) Interest at the rate of 6% per annum on the amount of his share in the property of the firm.

It may be further noted that the outgoing partner is not bound to make election until the share of the profit that would be payable to him has been ascertained. In case the subsequent business shows a loss or the subsequent profit is less than the interest that will be due to him, he may claim interest on his share in the property of the firm.

Illustration 3.13. *A*, *B* and *C* are partners in a business sharing profits and losses equally. *C* dies on 31 December, 1982. The capitals of the partners after all necessary adjustments stood at Rs 40,000, Rs 60,000 and Rs 1,00,000 respectively. *A* and *B* continued to carry on the business for three months without settling the accounts of the Executors of *C*. The profit made during this period amounted to Rs 18,000. State which of the two options available under Section 37 of the Partnership Act should be execised by the Executors.

Solution:

(*i*) *Share in the profit of the Partnership Firm*:

Profit made during three months Rs 18,000
C's Executors' share: $18,000 \times 1,00,000/2,00,000 = \text{Rs } 9,000$

(*ii*) *Interest at 6% p.a.*

$$1,00,000 \times 6/100 \times 3/12 = \text{Rs } 1,500$$

Since, the amount payable to the Executors under option (*i*) is more as compared to the amount payable under option (*ii*), they should exercise option (*i*).

Illustration 3.14. The following figures were extracted from the accounts books of Vimal & Co., a partnership firm having partners Mr. Anil and Mr. Bimal who were sharing profits and losses in equal ratio as on 31st March, 1987:

Particulars	Dr. Amount Rs	Cr. Amount Rs
Mr. Anil's Capital Account		46,000
Mr. Bimal's Capital Account		26,000
Mr. Anil's Drawings Account	9,000	
Mr. Bimal's Drawings Account	7,000	
Gross Profit		33,600

Contd....

Particulars	Dr. Amount Rs	Cr. Amount Rs
Salaries	15,000	
Rent, Rates and Taxes	4,000	
Other Overheads	4,000	
Discount received		400
Fixed Assets	65,000	
Current Assets	2,000	
	1,06,000	1,06,000

The partnership deed provides that:

(i) Interest at 5% per annum is to be allowed on capitals, but no interest is to be charged on drawings (from 1.1.1987 to 31.3.1987).

(ii) On the death of a partner the surviving partner shall pay out the interest of the deceased partner.

(iii) The deceased partner shall be entitled to his share of Goodwill of the firm calculated at two and half years' purchase of the average profits of the preceding three years profit prior to the date of death of a partner.

(iv) Assets are to be taken at their Book value on the date of death.

Mr. Anil died on 31st March, 1987.

The profits of the preceding three years ending on 31.12.1984, 31.12.1985 and 31.12.1986 respectively were Rs 30,000, Rs 25,000, and Rs 35,000. The accounts were closed on 31st December each year.

Prepare the Profit & Loss Account and the account to be produced to the executors of Mr. Anil showing the amount due to his estate.   (C.A. Entrance, Nov., 1987)

Solution:

Vimal & Co.
PROFIT & LOSS ACCOUNT
for the year ended 31st March, 1987

Particulars		Rs	Particulars	Rs
To Salaries		15,000	By Gross Profit b/d	33,600
To Rent, Rates and Taxes		4,600	By Discount Received	400
To Other overheads		4,000		
To Net Profit		11,000		
		34,000		34,000
			By Net Profit	11,000
To Interest on Capital:				
Mr. Anil's Capital A/c	575			
Mr. Bimal's Capital A/c	325	900		
To Anil's Capital A/c 1/2	5,050			
To Bimal Capital A/c 1/2	5,050	10,100		
		11,000		11,000

MR. ANIL'S EXECUTORS ACCOUNT

Particulars	Rs	Particulars	Rs
To Drawings	9,000	By Mr. Anil's Capital A/c	46,000
To Balance c/d	80,125	By Interest on Capital	575
		By Share of Profit	5,050

Contd....

Particulars	Rs	Particulars	Rs
		By Share of Goodwill (WN-1)	37,500
	89,125		89,125

Working Note:

Mr. Anil's Share of Goodwill:

Year	Profit Rs
1984	30,000
1985	25,000
1986	35,000
Total Profit for three years ...	90,000

Average Profit = 90,000/3 = Rs 30,000

Goodwill = 2 1/2 years' purchase of the average profits of three years.

Goodwill = 5/2 × 30,000 = Rs 75,000

Mr. Anil's share of goodwill = 75,000 × 1/2 = Rs 37,500.

Illustration 3.15. A and B were partners. The partnership deed provided *inter alia*, that:

(a) The accounts be made up to 31 December each year.

(b) The profits be divided as follows: A ½, B ⅓ and Reserves ⅙.

(c) In the event of death of a partner, his representative be entitled to:

    (i) the capital to his credit at the date of death;

    (ii) his proportion of profits to date of death based on the average profits of the last three completed years;

    (iii) by way of goodwill his proportion of the total profits for the three preceding completed years.

On 31 December, 1985 the ledger balances were:

	Dr.	Cr.
A's Capital		90,000
B's Capital		60,000
Reserve		30,000
Creditors		30,000
Bills Receivable	20,000	
Investments	50,000	
Cash	1,40,000	
	2,10,000	2,10,000

The profits for the last three years were 1983 Rs 42,000, 1984 Rs 39,000 and 1985 Rs 45,000. B died on 1st May, 1986. Show the necessary accounts.

Solution:

B's CAPITAL ACCOUNT

Particulars	Rs	Particulars	Rs
To Balance taken B's Executor's Account	1,28,000	By Balance b/d	60,000
		By Reserve (30,000 × 2/5)	12,000
		By Share of Goodwill	50,400
		By Share of Profit	5,600
	1,28,000		1,28,000

B's EXECUTOR'S ACCOUNT

Particulars	Rs	Particulars	Rs
To Balance c/d	1,28,00	By B's Capital A/c	1,28,000
	1,28,000		1,28,000

Working Notes:

1. The effective ratio between A and B is ½ : ⅓ or 3 : 2.
2. B's share of Goodwill:

	Rs
Profits for 1983	42,000
1984	39,000
1985	45,000
	1,26,000

B's Share = 1,26,000 × 2/5 = Rs 50,400.

3. B's Share of Profit:

Average profit for the last three years $= \dfrac{Rs\ 1,26,000}{3} = Rs\ 42,000$

B's Share $= 42,000 \times \dfrac{2}{5} \times \dfrac{4}{12} = Rs\ 5,600.$

Illustration 3.16. The partnership agreement of a firm consisting of three partners A, B and C (who share profits one-half, one-quarter and one-quarter and whose fixed capitals are Rs 10,000, Rs 6,000 and Rs 4,000 respectively) provides as follows:

(a) That partners be allowed interest at 10 per cent per annum on their fixed capitals, but no interest be allowed on undrawn profits or charged on drawings.

(b) That, upon the death of a partner, the goodwill of the firm be valued at two years' purchase of the average net profits (after charging interest on capital) for the three years to 31st December preceding the death of a partner.

(c) That an insurance policy of Rs 10,000 each to be taken in individual names of each partner, the premium to be charged against the profits of the firm.

(d) That, upon the death of a partner, he be credited with his shares of the profits, interest on capital, etc. calculated on 31st December following his death.

(e) That the share of the partnership policy and goodwill be credited to a deceased partner as on 31st December following his death.

(f) That the partnership books be closed annually on 31st December.

A died on 30th September 1983, the amount standing to the credit his current account on 31st December 1982 was Rs 450 and from the date to the date of death he had drawn Rs 3,000 from the business.

An unrecorded liability of Rs 2,000 was discovered on 30th September 1983. It was decided to record it and be immediately paid off.

The trading results of the firm (before charging interest on capital) has been as follows: 1980 Profit Rs 9,640; 1981 Profit Rs 6,720; 1982 loss Rs 640; 1983 Profit Rs 3,670.

Assuming the surrender value of the policy to be 20 per cent of the sum assured, you are required to prepare an account showing the amount due to A's legal representative as on 31st December, 1983.

(C.A. Entrance, Dec., 1984)

Solution:

A's CAPITAL ACCOUNT

Date	Particulars	Rs	Date	Particulars	Rs
1983			1983		
Sept. 30	To Current A/c		Jan. 1	By Balance b/d	10,000
	(3,000 − 450)	2,550	Dec. 31	By Profit & Loss A/c:	
Dec. 31	To Profit & Loss			Interest on Capital	1,000
	Adjustment A/c	1,000		Share of Profit	835
	(unrecorded liability)			By Goodwill	3,240
Dec. 31	To Balance transferred to			By Insurance Policies A/c	7,000
	A's Executors A/c	18,525			
		22,075			22,075

Working Notes:

(i) Valuation of Goodwill:

Year	Profit before Interest on fixed capital	Interest	Profit after interest
	Rs	Rs	Rs
1980	9,640	2,000	7,640
1981	6,720	2,000	4,720
1982	−640	2,000	−2,640
	15,720	6,000	9,720

	Rs
Average Net Profits (9,720/3)	3,240
Goodwill at two year's purchase of average net profits	6,480
Share of A in Goodwill	3,240

(ii) Profit on Joint life policy:

	Rs
A's policy	10,000
B & C's policy @ 20%	4,000
	14,000
Share of A	7,000

(iii) Share in Profit for 1983

	Rs
Profit for the year	3,670
Less: Interest on Capitals	2,000
	1,670
A's share in Profit (½)	835

(iv) As unrecorded liability of Rs 2,000 has been charged to capital accounts through Profit & Loss Adjustment Account. No further adjustment in current year's profit is required.

(v) In the absence of precise information, profits for 1980, 1981 & 1982 have not been adjusted (for valuing goodwill) for unrecorded liability.

AMALGAMATION OF PARTNERSHIP FIRMS

Two partnership firms may merge with one another and form a new partnership firm. For example, there are two partnership firms of A & B and C & D. They may merge and form a new partnership firm of A, B, C & D.

Such a merger is termed as "amalgamation of partnership firms". The accounting entries will be as follows.

In the Books of the Old Firms

1. **For goodwill.** The value of goodwill will be ascertained in case of each firm and the amount will be credited to their respective partners' capital accounts in their respective books.

Goodwill A/c	Dr.
To Partners' Capital Accounts	
(in old profit sharing ratio)	

2. **Reserves and other undistributed profits.** They will be credited to the partners of each of the firms in their respective books.

Reserves	Dr.
P. & L. A/c	Dr.
To Partners' Capital A/cs	
(in old profit sharing ratio)	
In case of losses the entry will be reversed.	

3. **Revaluation of assets and liabilities.** A Profit and Loss Adjustment Account will be opened in each firm's books. The profit or loss will be credited or debited to their partners capital accounts in the old profit sharing ratio.

   (*i*) Assets/Liabilities   Dr.
        To P. & L. Adjustment A/c
   (For increase in the value of assets or decrease in the value of liabilities).

   (*ii*) P. & L. Adjustment A/c.   Dr.
        To Assets/Liabilities A/c
   (For decrease in the value of assets or increase in the value of liabilities).

   (*iii*) P. & L. Adjustment A/c   Dr.
        To Partners' Capital A/cs
   (For distribution of Profits)
       In case of loss the entry will be reversed.

4. **For an asset taken over by a partner**

Partner's Capital A/c	Dr.
To Asset A/c	
(at the value taken over)	

5. **For a liability taken over by a partner.**

Liability A/c	Dr.
To Partner's Capital A/c	
(at the value taken over)	

6. **For assets and liabilities taken over by the New Firm.**

New Firm	Dr.
Liabilities taken over	Dr.
To Assets taken over	

7. Assets/liabilities not taken over by the new firm will be either sold away or paid off and any profit or loss on such selling or payment will be transferred to Partner's Capital Accounts in their profit and loss sharing ratio. In case they are not disposed of, they will be transferred to partners' capital accounts in the ratio of their capitals.

8. Partners' capital accounts will be closed by transferring them to the new firm's account.

Partners' Capital accounts		Dr.
To New Firm		

In the books of the New Firm

1. For assets and liabilities taken over

Assets taken over		Dr.
To Liabilities taken over		
To Partners' Capital A/cs.		

2. For any further contribution towards capitals by the partners

Bank A/c		Dr.
To Partners' Capital A/cs		

3. For any Capital withdrawn by the partners

Partners' Capital A/cs		Dr.
To Bank A/c.		

Illustration 3.17. *A* and *B*, who were partners, and *C* and *D* who were partners, decided to amalgamate as on 1 January, 1987 under the name Bharat Trading Company. Their Balance Sheets were as follows on 31 December, 1986.

A AND B

Liabilities	Rs	Assets	Rs
Creditors	10,000	Buildings	18,000
Reserve	20,000	Stock	30,000
Capitals:		Debtors	12,000
A	30,000	Investment	20,000
B	20,000		
	80,000		80,000

C AND D

Liabilities	Rs	Assets	Rs
Bank Loan	8,000	Goodwill	10,000
Creditors	20,000	Stock	26,000
Capitals:		Debtors	24,000
C	15,000		
D	15,000		
	60,000		60,000

A, B shared profits in proportion to their capitals; while *C* and *D* shared profits equally. The terms of amalgamation were:

(i) *A, B, C* and *D* to be partners in the new firm and to share profits and losses in the same ratio as their capitals in the new firm after all adjustments had been made.

(*ii*) The buildings owned by *A* and *B* to be taken over by the new firm at a valuation of Rs 23,000. However, the new firm does not take over their investments.

(*iii*) The goodwill appearing in the Balance Sheet of *C* and *D* was worthless.

(*iv*) After the above adjustments have been made *C* and *D* each to bring in Rs 5,000 as additional capitals.

On the assumption that the above transactions were duly completed on 1st January, 1987 show the journal entries necessary to close the books of the old firms and open the books of the new firm and prepare its Balance Sheet.

Solution:

Books of *A* and *B*
JOURNAL

Particulars		Dr. Amount Rs	Cr. Amount Rs
Building A/c	Dr.	5,000	
To P. & L. Adj. A/c			5,000
(Being building revalued)			
Reserve	Dr.	20,000	
P. & L. Adj. A/c	Dr.	5,000	
To *A*'s Capital A/c			15,000
To *B*'s Capital A/c			10,000
(Profit on revaluation and reserve distributed)			
Bharat Trading Company	Dr.	65,000	
To Building			23,000
To Stock			30,000
To Debtors			12,000
(Assets taken over)			
Creditors	Dr.	10,000	
To Bharat Trading Co.			10,000
(Creditors taken over)			
A's Capital A/c	Dr.	12,000	
B's Capital A/c	Dr.	8,000	
To Investments			20,000
(Investments not taken over transferred to capital accounts in the ratio of capitals)			
A's Capital A/c	Dr.	33,000	
B's Capital A/c	Dr	22,000	
(Capital accounts balances transferred)			55,000

Books of *C* and *D*
JOURNAL

Particulars		Dr. Amount Rs	Cr. Amount Rs
P. & L. Adjustment A/c	Dr.	10,000	
To Goodwill			10,000
(Being Goodwill considered worthless)			
C's Capital A/c	Dr.	5,000	
D's Capital A/c	Dr.	5,000	
To P. & L. Adj. A/c			10,000
(Loss on Revaluation written off)			

Contd....

Particulars		Dr. Amount Rs	Cr. Amount Rs
Bharat Trading Co.	Dr.	50,000	
To Stock			26,000
To Debtors			24,000
(Being assets taken over)			
Bank Loan	Dr.	8,000	
Creditors	Dr.	22,000	
To Bharat Trading Co.			30,000
(Being liabilities taken over)			
C's Capital A/c	Dr.	10,000	
D's Capital A/c	Dr.	10,000	
To Bharat Trading Co.			20,000
(Being balances in the capital accounts transferred)			

Books of Bharat Trading Co.

JOURNAL

Particulars		Dr. Amount Rs	Cr. Amount Rs
Buildings	Dr.	23,000	
Stock	Dr.	30,000	
Debtors	Dr.	12,000	
To Creditors			10,000
To A's Capital A/c			33,000
To B's Capital A/c			22,000
(Being business taken over from A and B)			
Stock	Dr.	26,000	
Debtors	Dr.	24,000	
To Creditors			22,000
To Bank Loan			8,000
To C's Capital A/c			10,000
To D's Capital A/c			10,000
(Being business taken over from C and D)			
Bank A/c	Dr.	10,000	
To C's Capital A/c			5,000
To D's Capital A/c			5,000
(Being additional Capital brought in by C and D)			

BALANCE SHEET
as on 1st January, 1987

Liabilities	Rs	Assets	Rs
Creditors	32,000	Bank	10,000
Bank Loan	8,000	Debtors	36,000
Capitals:		Stock	56,000
A	33,000	Buildings	23,000
B	22,000		
C	15,000		
D	15,000		
	1,25,000		1,25,000

KEY TERMS

☐ **Gaining Ratio:** The term is generally used in case of retirement or death of a partner. It is the ratio in which the continuing partners gain on retirement or death of a partner.

☐ **Amalgamation:** It refers to the merger of two or more partnership firms to form a new partnership firm.

TEST QUESTIONS

Objective type | TEST YOUR UNDERSTANDING

1. State whether each of the following statements is 'True' or 'False':
   (a) A dormant partner has to give public notice of his retirement.
   (b) The amount due to the retiring partner is transferred to his loan account in case it is not paid immediately.
   (c) The amount due to the retiring partner on account of goodwill is debited to the continuing partners in their gaining ratio.
   (d) In the event of death of a partner the amount realised on account of a joint life insurance policy is credited only to the deceased partner's executors account.
   (e) The retiring partner may claim a share in the profits of the firm even after his retirement if his accounts are not settled.
   (f) The assets and liabilities not taken over by the new firm on amalgamation of two or more partnership firms, are transferred to partners' capital accounts in their profit sharing ratio.

   [Ans. (a) False; (b) True; (c) True; (d) False; (e) True; (f) False]

2. Select the most appropriate answer:
   (i) A, B and C are partners sharing profits in the ratio of 2:2:1. C retired. The new profit-sharing ratio between A and B will be:
      (a) 2:1.
      (b) 1:1.
      (c) 3:2.
   (ii) P, Q and R are sharing profits equally. P retires. The goodwill is appearing in the books at Rs 3,000. It is valued at Rs 6,000. P will be credited with:
      (a) Rs 2,000.
      (b) Rs 1,000.
      (c) Rs 3,000.
   (iii) In the event of death of a partner, the accumulated profits and losses are shared by the partners:
      (a) old profit sharing ratio.
      (b) new profit sharing ratio.
      (c) capital ratio.
   (iv) In the event of amalgamation of partnership firms, the goodwill of each business is credited to the partners of the respective firms in:
      (a) old profit sharing ratio.
      (b) new profit sharing ratio.
      (c) capital ratio.

   [Ans. (i) (b); (ii) (b); (iii) (a); (iv) (a)]

Essay type | FOR REVIEW, DISCUSSION AND PRACTICE |

1. How can a partner retire from a partnership firm? Is a retiring partner liable for liabilities incurred by the partnership firm after his retirement?
2. State the rights of an outgoing partner in case the continuing partners do not settle his accounts and continue to carry on business.
3. State the journal entries that are to be passed in the event of amalgamation in the books of (*i*) the firms to be amalgamated and (*ii*) New firm.

PRACTICAL PROBLEMS

Retirement of a Partner

1. Ram, Shyam and Rahim are partners sharing profits in the ratio of 4:3:2. Shyam retires and the goodwill is valued at Rs 21,600. No goodwill appears as yet in the books of the firm. Assuming that Ram and Rahim will share profits in the future in the ratio of 5:3, pass entries for goodwill separately under the following conditions:
   (*a*) When goodwill account is raised.
   (*b*) When goodwill account is raised but written off.
   (*c*) When only Shyam's goodwill account is raised and then written off.

   (C.A. Entrance, Nov., 1979)

2. Tea, Coffee and Tobacco are in partnership sharing profits and losses in proportion of 2:2:1 respectively. It was agreed that in case of retirement or death of a partner, the value of the goodwill shall be determined at 1 1/2 year's purchase of the average profits of the last four years. Tobacco retired from the business with effect from 1st July, 1989, and the following matters came up for consideration in connection therewith:
   (*i*) Capital expenditure of Rs 3,000 incurred on 15th November, 1985 wrongly debited to purchases account is to be written back and depreciation at 10% is to be charged annually on the closing balances on reducing balance method.
   (*ii*) No adjustment was made for goods worth Rs 1,000 taken over by Tea on 28th March, 1989.
   (*iii*) The profits for the four years ended 30th June, 1986, 1987, 1988 and 1989 were Rs 12,000, Rs 15,000, Rs 14,000 and Rs 16,000 respectively.
   (*iv*) Tobacco's Capital Account stood at Rs 55,000 as on 30th June, 1989.
   You are required to draw up the capital account of Tobacco and find out the amount due to him.

   [**Ans.** P. & L. Adjustment Account Profit Rs 2,968; Value of Goodwill
   Rs 22,488, Amount due to Tobacco Rs 60,092]

   (**Hint.** Goodwill is to be valued on the basis of adjusted profits. Such profits for
   the year ended 30th June 1986, 1987, 1988 and 1989 are Rs 14,700, Rs 14,730,
   Rs 13,757, Rs 16,781 respectively.)

3. The Balance Sheet of Aloo, Baloo and Kaloo, who were sharing profits in proportions of their capitals stood as follows:

Liabilities		Rs	Assets		Rs
Sundry Creditors		6,900	Cash at Bank		5,500
Capital Accounts:			Sundry Debtors	5,000	
Aloo	20,000		*Less:* Provision	100	4,900
Baloo	15,000		Stock		8,000
Kaloo	10,000	45,000	Plant & Machinery		8,500
			Factory Buildings		25,000
		51,900			51,900

Baloo retired on the above date and the following was agreed upon:
   (*i*) that the stock be depreciated by 6%.
   (*ii*) that the provision be brought upto 5% on debtors.

(iii) that a provision of Rs 770 be made in respect of outstanding legal charges.

(iv) that the factory building be appreciated by 20%.

(v) that the goodwill of the entire firm be fixed at Rs 10,800 and Baloos' share of it be adjusted into the accounts of the continuing partners who are going to share future profits in the ratio of Aloo 5/8 and Kaloo 3/8.

(vi) that the assets and liabilities (except cash) were to appear in the Balance Sheet at their old figures.

(vii) that the entire capital of the new firm be fixed at Rs 28,000 between Aloo and Kaloo in proportions of 5:3. Actual cash be brought in or paid off, as the case may be.

You are required to prepare the Balance Sheet of the New Firm after Baloo's retirement and also Baloo's Loan Account till it is finally paid off presuming that loan is to be paid in three equal annual installments with interest at 12% p.a.

[**Ans.** Profit in P. & L. Adjustment A/c Rs 3,600; Balance due to Baloo Rs 19,800; Total of Balance Sheet Rs 54,700]

4. Dosi and Desai are in partnership as equal partners. Dosi, by agreement, retires and his son Dinesh joins the firm on the basis that he would get one third share of the profits.

The balances of the books of M/s Dosi and Desai were:

Particulars	Dr.	Cr.
Goodwill	12,000	
Bank	8,000	
Debtors	3,000	
Stock	26,000	
Creditors		6,000
Capital Account		
Dosi		23,000
Desai		20,000

Goodwill is agreed at Rs 30,000 and written up accordingly. Sufficient money is to be introduced so as to enable Dosi to be paid off and leave Rs 4,000 in bank; Desai and Dinesh are to provide such sum as to make their capitals proportionate to their share of profit. Dosi agrees to contribute from his capital half of the amount Dinesh has to provide.

Assuming the agreement was carried out, show the journal entries required and prepare the Balance Sheet of the firm of M/s Desai and Dinesh.

[**Ans.** Capitals: Desai Rs 38,000, Dinesh Rs 19,000, Balance Sheet Total Rs 63,000]

5. P, Q and R were in partnership sharing profits and losses in the ratio of 4:2:1 respectively. As per their Deed of partnership on the retirement of a partner, the partnership position shall be reviewed for the purpose of arriving at the amount to be paid to the retiring partner. The goodwill of the firm was to be taken at 2 years' purchase of the average profits of the 4 years preceding the retirement.

R retired from the firm on 31 December 1990. For the purpose of arriving at the amount to be paid to him, the following points were to be considered and the necessary entries passed in the Books of the firm:

(1) Provision for Doubtful Debts amounting to Rs 46,000 was to be made:

(2) Plant and Machineries were revalued at a figure of Rs 25,000 in excess of the book values.

(3) A sum of Rs 40,000 being expenditure of capital nature was written off as revenue expenditure in 1987. It was decided to write back this expenditure after providing depreciation at the rate of 10 per cent per annum for 3 years on the reducing balance method.

(4) The actuarial valuation of liability for gratuities to staff was determined at Rs 1,56,000. So far the actual gratuities paid were charged to revenues.

(5) *R*'s share of Income Tax liability was determined at Rs 4,200 which should be charged to him.

You are required to prepare an Account showing the amount to be credited or debited to *R* as a result of the above points, assuming that the profit of the firm (upon which goodwill was to be calculated) for 4 years preceding his retirement were:

1987	3,24,500
1988	2,78,600
1989	2,84,000
1990	1,94,500

P and *Q* agreed to share profit in the same relative proportion as before and to write back the entries made in respect of goodwill and the liability on account of Gratuities. Show also the retiring partner's Loan Account.

[Ans. Amount to be credited to *R* Rs 56,137]

6. Abraham, Birdy and Chapman were in partnership sharing profits and losses in the ratio of 5:4:3. The following is the Balance Sheet of the firm as on 31 March, 1990:

BALANCE SHEET

Liabilities	Rs	Assets	Rs
Capitals:		Goodwill	8,000
Abraham	27,186	Fixtures	1,640
Birdy	19,024	Stock	31,460
Chapman	12,234	Debtors	18,700
Creditors	8,338	Cash	6,982
	66,782		66,782

Abraham was suffering from ill-health and gave notice that he wished to retire from 1 April, 1990. An agreement was drawn up on the following basis:

(a) The Profit & Loss A/c for the year ended 31 March, 1990 showing a net profit of Rs 9,600, should be re-opened. Birdy was to be credited with Rs 800 as remuneration in consideration of the extra services rendered by him. The profit-sharing ratio was to be revised from 1 April, 1989 as 3:4:4 for sharing of profit only.

(b) Goodwill was to be valued at two years' purchase of the average profits of the preceding five years. Fixtures were revalued. A provision for doubtful debts of 2 per cent was to be made and the remaining assets were to be taken at book values.

Accordingly, Goodwill and fixtures were respectively valued at Rs 11,360 and Rs 2,196.

Birdy and Chapman agreed to continue the business, sharing profits and losses in the ratio of 4:3, to eliminate Goodwill Account, to retain fixtures at revised values and to increase the provision for doubtful debts to 6 per cent.

You are required to show the accounts of Abraham, Birdy and Chapman and the revised Balance Sheet of Birdy and Chapman. Show your workings.

[Ans. Capitals Birdy Rs 14,074, Chapman Rs 8,688, Abraham's Loan Rs 27,116, B/S Total Rs 58,216]

7. Ram and Co. is a partnership firm with the partners Mr. *A*, Mr. *B* and Mr. *C*, sharing profits and losses in the ratio of 5:3:2. The Balance Sheet of the firm as on 30th June, 1987 is as under:

Liabilities	Rs	Assets	Rs
Capitals Mr. *A*	80,000	Land Building	2,10,000
Mr. *B*	20,000	Plant and Machinery	1,30,000
Mr. *C*	30,000	Furniture and Fittings	40,000
Appropriated Profit (Reserve)	20,000	Investments	12,000

Contd....

Liabilities	Rs	Assets	Rs
Long term loan	3,000,000	Stock	1,26,000
Bank Overdraft	44,000	Debtors	1,39,000
Trade Creditors	1,63,000		
Total	6,57,000		6,57,000

It was mutually agreed that Mr. *B* will retire from partnership and in his place Mr. *D* will be admitted as a partner with effect from 1st July, 1987. For this purpose the following adjustments are to be made:

(*a*) Goodwill is to be valued at Rs 1 lakh but the same will not appear as an asset in the books of the reconstituted firm.

(*b*) Land and Buildings and Plant and Machinery are to be depreciated by 10% and 5% respectively. Investments are to be taken over by the retiring partner at Rs 15,000. Provision of 20% is to be made on debtors to cover doubtful debts.

(*c*) In the reconstituted firm, the total capital will be Rs 2 lakhs which will be contributed by Mr. *A*, Mr. *C* and Mr. *D* in their new profit sharing ratio which is 2:2:1.

(*d*) The surplus funds, if any, will be used for repaying the Bank Overdraft.

(*e*) The amount due to retiring partner shall be transferred to his loan account.

You are required to prepare:

(1) Revaluation Account, (2) Partners' Capital Accounts (3) Bank Account, and (4) Balance Sheet of the reconstituted firm as on 1 July, 1987.

(C.A. Entrance, May, 1988)

(**Ans.** Revaluation Loss Rs 52,300; Total of Balance Sheet Rs 6,88,310).

8. Singh, Pandey and Gupta are partners in a firm sharing profits and losses in the ratio of 3:2:1. The Balance Sheet of their business as at 31st March, 1988 is given below:

BALANCE SHEET
as on 31st March, 1988

Liabilities	Rs	Assets	Rs
Capital Accounts		Machineries	40,000
Singh	50,000	Furniture	20,000
Pandey	40,000	Motor Car	30,000
Gupta	30,000	Stock	25,000
General Reserve	12,000	Debtors	75,000
		Cash	2,000
	1,92,000		1,92,000

Singh retired with effect from 1 April, 1988. Goodwill of the firm was valued at Rs 24,000. On revaluation Machineries and Furniture are to be appreciated by 10%. Debtors include Rs 1,500 as bad and doubtful are to be written off. Value of stock to be reduced to Rs 23,000. Creditors include Rs 800 as no more payable.

It was decided that due effect to be given to the retiring partner's capital account with his share of goodwill without raising goodwill account. Pandey and Gupta are to share future profits in equal proportions. Amounts payable to Singh is to be treated as loan to the firm.

You are requested to prepare the Revaluation Account, Capital Accounts of the partners and the Balance Sheet of the firm after Singh's retirement.

(I.C.W.A. Inter, June, 1988)

(**Ans.** Profit on revaluation: Rs 3,300; Singh's loan: Rs 69,650, Capital Accounts Balances: Pandey Rs 41,100; Gupta Rs 24,550; Total of Balance Sheet: Rs 1,94,500).

9. The Balance Sheet of *A*, *B* and *C*, who were sharing profits and losses in proportion of their capitals *i.e.* 4:3:2, stood as follows as on 31st December, 1988:

Liabilities		Rs	Assets		Rs
Sundry Creditors		6,900	Cash at Bank		5,500
Capital Accounts:			Sundry Debtors	5,000	
A	20,000		*Less:* Provision	100	4,900
B	15,000		Stock		8,000
C	10,000	45,000	Plant and Machinery		8,500
			Factory, Land & Building		25,000
		51,900			51,900

On 31.12.1988 *B* retires and the following adjustments of the assets and liabilities have been agreed upon before the ascertainment of the amount payable by the firm to *B*:

(1) The Stock to be written off by 6%. (2) The provision for doubtful debts be brought up to 5% on Sundry Debtors. (3) The Factory, Land and Building be appreciated by 20%. (4) A provision of Rs 770 be made in respect of outstanding legal charges. (5) The Goodwill of the entire firm be fixed at Rs 10,800 and *B*'s share of the same be adjusted in the accounts of *A* and *C* who are going to share the future profits in the proportions of $\frac{5}{8}$ and $\frac{3}{8}$, respectively (no Goodwill A/c is to be raised). (6) The entire capital of the firm, as newly constituted be fixed at Rs 28,000 between *A* and *C* in the proportion of $\frac{5}{8}$ and $\frac{3}{8}$ after passing entries in the accounts for Goodwill (*i.e.* actual cash to be paid off to or be brought in by the continuing partners, as the case may be).

Pass Journal Entries to give effect to the above arrangements and prepare the Balance Sheet of *A* and *C*, transferring *B*'s share of capital and goodwill to a separate Loan Account in his name, on 1st January 1989.

(C.A. Entrance, May, 1989)

(Ans. *B*'s Loan Rs 19,000; Total of Balance Sheet—Rs 55,470).

Death of a Partner

10. Iqbal and Kapoor are in partnership sharing profits and losses in the ratio of 3 : 2. They insure their lives jointly for Rs 75,000 at an annual premium of Rs 3,400 to be debited to the business. Kapoor dies three months after the date of the last Balance Sheet. According to the partnership deed, the legal personal representative of Kapoor are entitled to the following payments:

(*a*) His capital as per the last Balance Sheet.

(*b*) Interest on above capital at 3 per cent per annum to the date of death.

(*c*) His share of profit to the date of death calculated on the basis of last year's profits.

His drawings are to bear interest at an average rate of 2 per cent on the amount irrespective of the period.

The net profits for the last three years after charging insurance premium were Rs 20,000, Rs 25,000 and Rs 30,000 respectively. Kapoor's capital as per Balance Sheet was Rs 40,000 and his drawings upto the date of death were Rs 5,000.

Draw Kapoor's Account to be rendered to his representative.

[Ans. Balance due Rs 68,200]

11. *A*, *B* and *C* were partners sharing profits and losses in the ratio of 5 : 3 : 2. On 31 December, 1988 their Balance Sheet was as follows:

Liabilities		Rs	Assets	Rs
Sundry Creditors		1,100	Goodwill	500
General Reserve		600	Leasehold Premises	2,000
Capital Accounts:			Patents	600
A	3,000		Machinery	3,000
B	2,500		Stock	1,000

Contd....

Liabilities		Rs	Assets	Rs
C	1,500	7,000	Sundry Debtors	800
			Cash at Bank	800
		8,700		8,700

C died on 1st May, 1989. It was agreed between his executors and the remaining partners that:

(a) Goodwill should be valued at 2 1/2 years purchase of four year's profits which were: 1985, Rs 1,300; 1986, Rs 1,200; 1987, Rs 1,600; and 1988, Rs 1,500.

(b) Patents be valued at Rs 800, Machinery at Rs 2,800 and Leasehold Premises at Rs 2,500 as on 31 December, 1988.

(c) Profits during 1989 should be taken to have accrued on the same scale as in 1988, for the purpose of calculating C's share.

(d) A sum of Rs 420 to be paid immediately and the remainder to be paid in four equal half-yearly instalments together with interest at 6% per annum.

Give Journal entries to be recorded on C's death and C's Executor's Account for 1989.

[Ans. Amount due to C on his death Rs 2,420]

11. Wise, Clever and Dull were trading in partnership sharing profits and losses 4:3:3 respectively. The accounts of the firm are made upto 31st December every year.

The partnership provided, *inter alia*, that:

On the death of a partner the Goodwill was to be valued at three years' purchase of average profits of the three years upto the date of death after deducting interest @ 8 per cent on capital employed and a fair remuneration of each partner. The profits are assumed to be earned evenly throughout the year.

On 30 June, 1990 Wise died and it was agreed to adjust Goodwill in the capital accounts without showing any amount of goodwill in the Balance Sheet.

It was agreed for the purpose of valuation of goodwill that the fair remuneration for work done by each partner would be Rs 15,000 per annum and that the capital employed would be Rs 1,56,000.

Clever and Dull were to continue the partnership, sharing profits and losses equally after the death of Wise.

The following were the amounts of profits of earlier years before charging interest on capital employed:

	Rs
1987	67,200
1988	75,600
1989	72,000
1990	62,400

You are required to compute the value of goodwill and show the adjustment thereof in the books of the firm.

[Ans. Value of Goodwill Rs 39,960, Credit Wise by Rs 15,984 and Debit Clever and Dull by Rs 7,992 each]

13. The following is the Balance Sheet of the firm *ABC* as on 31.12.1983. Their profits sharing ratio in 3 : 2 : 1.

Capital & Liabilities	Rs	Assets	Rs
Capital A/cs:		Fixed Assets	40,000
A	16,000	Sundry Debtors	32,000
B	12,000	Insurance Policy on Joint	
C	10,000	Life of Partners	6,000
Current A/cs:		Stock	24,000
A	4,000	Bank	9,000

Contd....

Capital & Liabilities		Rs	Assets	Rs
B		3,000	Cash	3,000
C		1,000		
Reserve		18,000		
P & L Account:				
Opening Balance	6,000			
Profit for the year	14,000	20,000		
Creditors		20,000		
Bank O/D		10,000		
		1,14,000		1,14,000

B died on 31.3.1984. His account has to be settled and paid. For the year 1984 proportionate profit of 1983 is to be taken into account. For 1983, a bad debt of Rs 2,000 has to be adjusted. Goodwill has to be calculated 3 times of the four years average profits. A policy is taken on the joint life of partners for 35,000 and the annual premium of Rs 2,000 has to be paid on February 1, every year. The profits are for 1982 Rs 16,000, 1981 Rs 20,000 and 1980 Rs 12,000. Goodwill account need not be kept in the books. Calculate the amount payable to B's heirs. Show necessary ledger accounts of all partners and other detailed calculations.

(C.A. Entrance, June, 1985)

(Ans. Amount payable to B's heirs Rs 52,000; Balances in Current Accounts A: Rs 24,250 (Cr.); C Rs 7,750 (Cr.); Capital Accounts Balances. A Rs 16,000; C Rs 10,000).

14. The following was the Balance Sheet of A, B and C who share profits in the ratio of 1:2:2 as on 31.12.1988. C died on 31st March 1989. His account has to be settled under the following terms:

BALANCE SHEET

Liabilities	Rs	Assets	Rs
Sundry Creditors	10,000	Goodwill	15,000
Capital A	10,000	Debtors	10,000
B	20,000	Machinery	20,000
C	20,000	Building	30,000
General Reserve	5,000	Stock	10,000
Investment Fluctuation Fund	3,000	Cash at Bank	5,000
Bad Debt Reserve	2,000	Investments	10,000
Bank Loan	30,000		
	1,00,000		1,00,000

Goodwill is to be calculated at the rate of 2 years' purchase on the basis of average of five years' profit or loss. Profit for Jan./March 1989 is to be calculated proportionately on the average of 3 years. The profits are 1984: Rs 3,000; 1985: Rs 7,000; 1986: Rs 10,000; 1987: Rs 14,000; 1988 Loss: Rs 12,000. During 1988 a moped costing Rs 4,000 was purchased and debited to travelling account on which depreciation is to be calculated at 25%. Other values agreed on assets are Stock Rs 12,000, Building Rs 35,000, and Machinery Rs 25,000. Investment is valued at Rs 8,000. Debtors are considered good.

Prepare New Balance Sheet of the firm, necessary Journal entries and Ledger Accounts of the Partners.

(C.A. Entrance, Dec., 1985)

(Ans. Value of Goodwill Rs 10,000; Closing Balances of Capital Accounts of partners; A: Rs 13,600; B: Rs 27,200, C's executor's account: Rs 27,700; Total Balance Sheet: Rs 1,08,500).

15. Maheswari Brothers has three partners, A, B and C who shared profits and losses in the proportion of 6 : 4 : 3. The Partnership Deed provided, amongst other things, that on the retirement or death of a partner the firm would continue in the old name and the amount due to the retiring or deceased partner would be paid by the firm in three instalments on the next three successive anniversaries of the date of retirement or death, each of the first two instalments being 40% of the amount due at the date of retirement or death. The amount due would be calculated by taking into consideration the following.

   (a) The amount of the capital at the end of the year preceding the one in which he retires or dies.

   (b) His share of profits in the year of retirement or death, the profits being calculated *pro rata* over the twelve months of the years.

   (c) His share of the goodwill of the firm, the goodwill being equivalent to two years' purchase of the average of the profits of the immediately preceding three years and of that part of the year of his retirement or death during which he continued in the firm.

   (d) His drawings to the date of retirement or death.

   A died on 1 January 1990. The book are closed on 31 March, every year. The following were the profits of the firm (after allowing 5% interest on capitals):

	Rs		Rs
1986–87	42,000	1988–89	48,000
1987–88	46,500	1989–90	52,250

Interest allowed on capitals, Rs 2,750 in 1989–90.

The capital of each partner on 31 March, 1989 was Rs 20,000. Drawings to A's death were: A Rs 6,200; B Rs 7,000; C Rs 6,150. Show the account of A for 1989–90 and the account of his executors till the amount due is fully paid. Assume that the executors exercised their rights under Section 37 of the Partnership Act.

[Ans. Amount due to A's Executors on 1 Jan. 1990 Rs 75,750, Share of profit for 1989–90 Rs 5,935]

Amalgamation of Partnership Firms

16. Following were the Balance Sheet as at December 31, 1987 of two firms M/s A & B and M/s X & Y:

Liabilities	A & B Rs	X & Y Rs	Assets	A & B Rs	X & Y Rs
Sundry Creditors	20,000	25,000	Cash at Bank	5,600	6,700
Mrs A's Loan	5,000	—	Stock	20,400	18,300
Capitals:			Sundry Debtors	15,000	20,000
A	40,000		Office Furniture	4,000	5,000
B	20,000		Premises	40,000	—
X		24,000	Investments		15,000
Y		16,000			
	85,000	65,000		85,000	65,000

The two firms decided to amalgamate their business as from 1st Jan., 1988. For this purpose it was agreed that:

   (a) Mrs A's Loan should be repaid.

   (b) Goodwill of M/s A & B be fixed at Rs 8,000 and that of X & Y at Rs 10,000.

   (c) Premises be valued at Rs 50,000.

   (d) Stock of M/s A & B be written down by Rs 4,000 and that of M/s X & Y be written up by Rs 2,000.

   (e) A provision on debtors be created in both firms at 5%.

(f) The total capital of the new firm be fixed at Rs 80,000 to be contributed in the profit-sharing ratio of A 3, B 2, X 3 and Y 2.

(g) Goodwill Account in the new firm be written off.

Close the books of two firms and open the books of the new firm giving its Balance Sheet.

[Ans. Total of Balance Sheet Rs 1,51,250]

17. Two partnership firms, carrying on business under the styles of Black and Co. and White and Co. respectively, decide to amalgamate into Grey and Co. with effect from 1 April, 1985. The respective Balance Sheets, as on 31 March 1985, are:

Black & Co.

BALANCE SHEET

as on 31st March, 1985

Liabilities	Rs	Assets	Rs
Mr B's Capital Account	19,000	Plant and Machinery	10,000
Sundry Creditors	10,000	Stock-in-trade	20,000
Bank Overdraft	15,000	Sundry Debtors	10,000
		Mr. A's Capital A/c	4,000
	44,000		44,000

A and B share profits and losses in the proportion of 1:2.

White & Co.

BALANCE SHEET

as on 31st March, 1985

Liabilities	Rs	Assets	Rs
Mr X's Capital Account	10,000	Goodwill	10,000
Mr Y's Capital Account	2,000	Stock-in-trade	5,000
Sundry Creditors	28,000	Sundry Debtors	10,000
		Cash in hand	6,000
		Cash at Bank	9,000
	40,000		40,000

X and Y share profits and losses equally.

The following further information is given:

(1) All fixed assets are to be devalued by 20%.

(2) All stock-in-trade is to be appreciated by 50%.

(3) Black and Co. owes Rs 5,000 to White and Co., as on 31 March, 1985. This debt is settled at Rs 2,000.

(4) Goodwill is to be ignored for the purpose of amalgamation.

(5) The fixed capital accounts in the new firm are to be

	Rs
Mr A	2,000
Mr B	3,000
Mr X	1,000
Mr Y	4,000

(6) Mr B takes over the bank overdraft of Black & Co. and gifts to Mr A the amount of money to be brought in by Mr A to make up his capital contribution.

(7) Mr. X is paid off in cash from White & Co. and Mr Y brings in sufficient cash to make up his required capital contribution.

Pass journal entries to colse the books of both the firms as on 31 March, 1985.

[Ans. Profit on Revaluation: Black and Co. Rs 11,000; Loss on Revaluation White & Co. Rs 10,500]

Chapter 4

DISSOLUTION OF PARTNERSHIP FIRM

LEARNING OBJECTIVES

After studying this chapter you should be able to:

☐ differentiate between dissolution of partnership and dissolution of firm;

☐ state the modes of dissolution of firm;

☐ enumerate the rules regarding settlement of accounts of a dissolved firm;

☐ make appropriate accounting entries regarding dissolution of a firm; and

☐ explain the meaning of certain key terms.

DISTINCTION BETWEEN DISSOLUTION OF PARTNERSHIP AND DISSOLUTION OF FIRM

Dissolution of partnership is different from dissolution of firm.

Dissolution of partnership. Any change in the relations of the partners is called dissolution of partnership. Thus, in all those cases were a partnership is reconstituted (as discussed in chapters 2 and 3), there is a dissolution of the partnership. For example, in case there is a partnership between X & Y, and a new partner Z is admitted, the partnership between X and Y comes to an end and a new partnership between X, Y and Z comes into existence. Hence, in dissolution of partnership, the firm continues in a reconstituted form.

Dissolution of firm. The dissolution of partnership between all the partners of a firm is called the dissolution of the firm. In the case of dissolution of a firm, the business of the firm is closed down and its affairs are wound up. The assets are realised and the liabilities are paid off.

The dissolution of a partnership may or may not result in the dissolution of a firm but the dissolution of a firm will necessarily result in the dissolution of the partnership. For example, if there are three partners A, B and C in a business and C becomes insolvent, in the absence of any contract to the contrary, the firm will stand dissolved on the insolvency of C. This will automatically result in the dissolution of partnership. However, A and B may agree to continue the business of the firm. In such a case, the firm continues though in a reconstituted form and, therefore, there is only the dissolution of the partnership.

MODES OF DISSOLUTION OF FIRM

A partnership firm may be dissolved with or without the intervention of the court.

1. Dissolution without the intervention of the court

A partnership firm may be dissolved without the intervention of the court in any of the following ways:

(a) **Dissolution by agreement.** A partnership firm comes into existence by mutual agreement and, therefore, it can also be dissolved by the mutual consent of all partners.

(b) **Compulsory dissolution.** In the following cases a partnership firm will have to be compulsorily dissolved.

    (i) by the adjudication of all the partners or of all the partners but one as *insolvent.*, or

    (ii) by the business of firm becoming *unlawful* due to the happening of any such event.

(c) **Dissolution on the happening of certain contingencies.** In the absence of any contract to the contrary, a firm will be dissolved on the happening of any of the following contingencies:

    (i) on the *expiry of the fixed period* for which the firm was constituted;

    (i) on the *completion of the adventure* or undertaking for the carrying out of which the firm was constituted;

    (iii) on the *death* of a partner; and

    (iii) on the *adjudication* of a partner as *insolvent.*

(d) **Dissolution by notice.** When a partnership is at will, the firm may be dissolved by any partner giving a notice in writing to all the other partners of his intention to dissolve the firm.

The firm will be taken to be dissolved from the date as specified in the notice, or if no date is mentioned from the date of the communication of the notice to the last of the partners.

2. Dissolution by the Court

Following are the cases when a court, on a suit by a partner, will intervene and may order for the dissolution of the firm.

(a) **Insanity.** When a partner has become of *unsound mind.* Lunacy of a partner does not of itself dissolve the partnership but it will be a ground for dissolution at the instance of other partners.

(b) **Permanent incapacity.** When a partner, other than the partner suing, has become, in any way, *permanently incapable* of performing has duties as a partner.

(c) **Misconduct.** When a partner, other than the partner suing, is guilty of *misconduct* which may prejudicially affect the carrying on of the business. It is not necessary that the conduct complained of, should be directly connected with the business *e.g.*, conviction of a partner for travelling on the railway without ticket with intention to defraud.

(d) **Breach of agreement.** When a partner, other than the partner suing, *wilfully* or *persistently commits breach of agreement* regarding the conduct of business or the management of the affairs of the firm or he conducts himself in matters relating to the business in such a manner that other partners cannot reasonably carry on business in partnership with him. Court will interfere only when the misconduct is of such a nature as will destroy the mutual confidence between the partners.

(e) **Transfer of interest.** When a partner, other than the partner suing, has *transferred* the whole of his interest in the firm to a third party or has allowed his share to be charged or sold by the court.

(f) **Loss in business.** When the business of the firm cannot be *carried on except at a loss*.

(g) **Just and equitable.** When the court considers any other ground to be *just and equitable* for the dissolution of the firm. *e.g.*, deadlock in the management, partners stop talking to each other, disappearance of the *substratum* of the business etc.

Liabilities of a Partner after Dissolution of the Firm

Partners shall continue to be liable as such to third parties for any act done by any of them which would have been an act of the firm if done before the dissolution, till they give a *public notice* of the dissolution of the firm. But a deceased or an insolvent or a dormant partner shall not be liable for acts done after he has cased to be a partner. In his case public notice of dissolution need not be given.

SETTLEMENT OF ACCOUNTS

The Partnership Act incorporates various sections (*viz.* 48 and 55) laying down the following rules for the settlement of accounts and division of profits and losses after dissolution. However, these rules may be changed by and are subject to an agreement entered into by the partners.

1. In settling the accounts of a firm after its dissolution, the goodwill shall be included in the assets and may be sold either separately or along with other property of the firm and any partner may make an agreement with the buyer that such a partner will not carry on any business similar to that of the firm for a specified period of time or within specified local limits and such an agreement is valid if the restrictions imposed are reasonable (Sec. 55).

2. Losses, including deficiencies of capital, shall be paid first out of profit, next out of capital, and lastly, if necessary by the partners individually in the proportion in which they were entitled to share profits (Sec. 48(*a*)]

Example. A and B were partners in a firm sharing profits and losses equally. A dies. The partnership accounts show that he contributed Rs 1,929 to the capital of the firm while B's contribution was only Rs 29. The assets amounted to Rs 1,400. It was held that the deficiency of Rs 558 (*i.e.*, 1,958-1,400) must be shared equally by B and the estate of A.

3. The assets of the firm, including any sums of money contributed by the partners to make up deficiencies of capital shall be applied in the following order:

(a) In paying the debts of the firm to third parties.

(b) In paying to each partner rateably, what is due to him from the firm for advances as distinguished from capital.

(c) In paying to each partner rateably what is due to him on account of capital.

(d) The residue, if any, shall be divided among the partners in the proportion in which they were entitled to share profits [Sec. 48(*b*)].

Example. *A, B* and *C* were partners in a business sharing profits and losses equally. The accounts show that their contributions to the firm's capital were Rs 10,000, Rs 5,000 and Rs 1,000 respectively. The assets of the firm after satisfying the outside liabilities are only Rs 7,000. The deficiency is, therefore, a sum of Rs 9,000. *A, B* and *C* must contribute Rs 3,000 each. This will make the assets Rs 16,000. The distribution of these assets to partners will result in a net loss of Rs 3,000 each partner. In actual practice only *C* would be required to bring a sum of Rs 2,000 in cash. Out of the assets of Rs 9,000 (Rs 7,000 + Rs 2,000) *A* and *B* will be paid Rs 7,000 and Rs 2,000 respectively.

Payment of firm's debts and of separate debts

When there are joint debts due from the partnership and also any separate debts due from any partner, firm's property must be first applied in the payment of the debt of the firm and if there is any surplus then the share of each partner in such surplus must be applied in payment of his separate debts or paid to him, if he has no debts. So also the separate property of any partner must be first applied in payment of his separate debts, and the surplus, if any, in the payment of the debts of the firm. Where partnership assets are insufficient to meet out the liabilities of the partnership, the creditors of the firm can resort to the partners' personal property outside the firm provided their personal and private creditors have already been paid out of it.

Order of payment

The assets of the firm, including any sums of money contributed by the partners to make up deficiencies of capital, shall be applied in the following order:

(*a*) In paying the debts of the firm to third parties.

(*b*) In paying to each partner rateably what is due to him from the firm for advances as distinguished from capital.

(*c*) In paying to each partner rateably what is due to him on account of capital.

(*d*) The residues if any, shall be divided among the partners in the proportion in which they were entitled to share profits.

ACCOUNTING ENTRIES

In the event of dissolution of a firm, all its assets are sold away and liabilities are paid off. A Realisation Account is opened in order to find out any profit or loss on realisation of assets and making payment of liabilities. The journal entries will be as follow:

1. *For transfer of assets:*

Realisation A/c   Dr.
    To Sundry Assets

(Each assets will be credited individually, with its books value. Cash and bank balances will not be transferred unless the business has been taken over by a new firm or company. This will close all accounts of the assets transferred.)

It is to be noted that when an asset is transferred to the Realisation Account, its corresponding provision or reserve appearing on the liabilities side of the balance sheet, will also be transferred to the Realisation Account. For example, Investments and Joint Life Insurance Policy appear on the assets side of the balance sheet while Investments Fluctuation Fund and Joint Life Insurance Policy Reserve appear on the Liabilities side of the balance sheet. The accounting entries in the event of dissolution of the firm would be as follows:

(i) Realisation A/c.   Dr.
    To Investments A/c
    To Joint Life Insurance Policy A/c

(ii) Investments Fluctuation Fund A/c   Dr.
    Joint Life Insurance Policy Reserve A/c   Dr.
    To Realisation A/c

2. *For transfer of liabilities:*

Liabilities A/c
    To Realisation A/c   Dr.

(All liabilities excluding partners' loans will be transferred at book values. Each liability should be debited individually. This will close accounts of all liabilities transferred.)

3. *For realisation of assets:*

Cash/Bank A/c   Dr.
    To Realisation A/c

4. *For payment of liabilities:*

Realisation A/c   Dr.
    To Bank/Cash A/c

5. *In case a partner takes an asset:*

Partner's Capital A/c   Dr.
    To Realisation A/c

6. *In case a partner agrees to meet a liability:*

Realisation A/c   Dr.
    To Partner's Capital A/c

7. *For expenses on realisation:*

Realisation A/c   Dr.
    To Bank/Cash A/c

8. *For profit on realisation:*

Realisation A/c   Dr.
    To Partners' Capital A/cs
    (In the profit sharing ratio.)
In case of loss the entry will be reversed.

9. *For paying off partner's loan:*

Partner's Loan A/c   Dr.
    To Bank/Cash A/c

10. *For distribution of reserves, undistributed profit etc.:*

P & L A/c   Dr.
Reserves A/c   Dr.
    To Partners' Capital A/cs

11. *For cash brought in by a partner on account of his 'account' showing a debit balance.*

Cash/Bank A/c   Dr.
    To Partner's Capital A/c

12. *The credit balance in a partner's capital account will be paid off:*

Partner's Capital A/c	Dr.
To Bank/Cash A/c	

Thus, all accounts in the firm will be closed.

When a partner is made incharge of realisation

The partners by mutual agreement may decide that one of them will be responsible for realisation of firm's assets and making payment of firm's liabilities. The partner so appointed may be given remuneration for such work. Such remuneration may be in the form of a certain percentage of the assets realised or liabilities paid or both. It may be in the form of a lump-sum also. The partner made 'incharge' of the realisation may also agree to bear all costs of realisation.

Besides the usual accounting entries, as discussed above, the following entries for remuneration etc. due to the partner 'incharge' of realisation will be made:

1. *For remuneration due:*
   Realisation Account   Dr.
       To Partner's Capital A/c
2. *For Realisation expenses incurred by the partner:*
   Realisation Account   Dr.
       To Partner's Capital A/c

In case the partner has agreed to bear all expenses on realisation in consideration of the remuneration to be received by him on realisation work, no entry will be required in the firm's books for realisation expenses incurred by the partner in-charge of realisation. However, if in such a case the firm has paid the realisation expenses on behalf of the partner incharge, the following entry will be passed in the firm's books:

Partner's Capital A/c	Dr.
To Bank/Cash A/c	

The accounts of the partners will be settled in the usual manner.

Illustration 4.1 *A, B* and *C* were three partners in a business sharing Profits & Losses in the ratio of 2:2:1. The following was their balance sheet as on 31st Dec., 1989:

Liabilities	Rs	Assets	Rs
Creditors	30,000	Bank	20,000
Capital A/cs:		Current Assets	30,000
A 40,000		Fixed Assets	70,000
B 30,000			
C 20,000	90,000		
	1,20,000		1,20,000

It was decided to dissolve the firm *w.e.f.* 31st Dec., 1989 and *C* was appointed as incharge of realisation. He was to receive 5% commission on the amounts realised from fixed and current assets. He was also to bear all expenses of realisation.

The fixed assets realised Rs 80,000 and the current assets Rs 20,000. The realisation expenses amounted to Rs 2,000 which were paid by the firm.

You are required to prepare the necessary ledger accounts and close the books of the firm.

Solution:

REALISATION ACCOUNT

Particulars	Amount Rs	Particulars		Amount Rs
To Fixed Assets	70,000	By Creditors		30,000
To Current Assets	30,000	By Bank (assets realised)		1,00,000
To Bank (Creditors)	30,000	By Realisation Loss:		
To C's Capital A/c (Comm.)	5,000	A's Capital A/c	2,000	
		B's Capital A/c	2,000	
		C's Capital A/c	1,000	5,000
	1,35,000			1,35,000

BANK ACCOUNT

Particulars	Amount Rs	Particulars	Amount Rs
To Balance b/d	20,000	By Realisation A/c	
To Realisation A/c		(Creditors)	30,000
(assets realised)	1,10,000	By C's Capital A/c	2,000
		(realisation expenses)	
		By A's Capital A/c	38,000
		By B's Capital A/c	28,000
		By C's Capital A/c	22,000
	1,20,000		1,20,000

CAPITAL ACCOUNTS OF PARTNERS

Particulars	A	B	C	Particulars	A	B	C
To Realisation A/c				By Balance b/d	40,000	30,000	20,000
(loss)	2,000	2,000	1,000	By Realisation			
To Bank				Account	–	–	5,000
(Expenses)	–	–	2,000				
To Bank A/c	38,000	28,000	22,000				
	40,000	30,000	25,000		40,000	30,000	25,000

Treatment of unrecorded assets and liabilities

In case certain assets or liabilities have not been recorded in the books of the partnership firm at all and on dissolution of the partnership firm they realise some money or some money is paid for them, the following entries will be passed:

(i) On realisation of unrecorded asset:

Bank A/c   Dr.
   To Realisation A/c

(ii) On payment of unrecorded liability:

Realisation A/c   Dr.
   To Bank A/c

(iii) In case a partner agrees to take an unrecorded asset:

Partner's Capital A/c   Dr.
   To Realisation A/c

(*iv*) In case a partner agrees to take an unrecorded liability:

Realisation A/c Dr.
   To Partner's Capital A/c

(*vi*) In case a creditor agrees to take an unrecorded asset. For example, a creditor of Rs 10,000 agrees to take an unrecorded asset of Rs 6,000 and the balance to that creditor is paid in cash. The following journal entries will be passed.

	Particulars		Dr. Amount Rs	Cr. Amount Rs
(*a*)	Creditor's A/c	Dr.	10,000	
	Realisation A/c			10,000
	(For transfer of the creditor to Realisation A/c)			
(*b*)	Realisation A/c	Dr.	4,000	
	To Bank			4,000
	(Payment to the creditor net Rs 10,000-Rs 6,000)			

Illustration 4.2. *A* and *B* who were in partnership sharing profits and losses in the proportion of 4:3 respectively, decided to dissolve the partnership firm as on 31st December, 1987. At the date of dissolution *A*'s capital was Rs 1,25,030 and *B*'s Rs 2,070; the creditors amounted to Rs 23,150 and cash at bank Rs 4,520. The remaining assets realised Rs 1,24,910 and the expenses of dissolution were Rs 1,860. Both *A* and *B* were solvent.

Prepare the Balance Sheet of the firm as on the date of dissolution and also the accounts necessary to close the books of the firm, showing the final adjustment of cash between the partners.

Solution:

BALANCE SHEET OF *A* & *B*
As on December 31, 1987

Liabilities	Amount Rs	Assets	Amount Rs
Sundry Creditors	23,150	Sundry Assets	1,45,730
Capital:		(balancing figure)	
A	1,25,030	Bank balance	4,520
B	2,070		
	1,50,250		1,50,250

REALISATION ACCOUNT

Particulars	Amount Rs	Particulars	Amount Rs
To Sundry Assets	1,45,730	By Creditors	23,150
To Bank	23,150	By Bank	1,24,910
(creditors paid)		(assets realised)	
To Cash (expenses)	1,860	By Loss transferred:	
		A's capital A/c	12,960
		B's capital A/c	9,720
	1,70,740		1,70,740

PARTNERS' CAPITAL ACCOUNTS

Particulars	A Rs	B Rs	Particulars	A Rs	B Rs
To Loss on Realisation	12,960	9,720	By Balance b/d	1,25,030	2,070
To Bank	1,20,070	—	By Bank		7,650
	1,25,030	9,720		1,25,030	9,720

BANK ACCOUNT

Particulars	Amount Rs	Particulars	Amount Rs
To Balance b/d	4,520	By Realisation A/c	23,150
To Realisation A/c	1,24,910	By Realisation A/c	1,860
To B's Capital	7,650	By A's Capital A/c	1,12,070
	1,37,080		1,37,080

Illustration 4.3. A, B and C were partners sharing profits and losses in the ratio of 2:2:1. On Jan. 1, 1987 their Balance Sheet was as follows:

Liabilities	Amount Rs		Assets	Amount Rs	
Sundry Creditors		12,000	Cash at Bank		12,200
General Reserve		5,000	Debtors	8,000	
Capital Accounts:			Less: Provision	200	7,800
A	15,000		Stock		6,000
B	12,000		Furniture		2,000
C	6,000	33,000	Buildings		22,000
		50,000			50,000

The firm was dissolved on that date. The assets realised as under:

	Rs
Debtors	7,000
Stock	5,000
Furniture	1,000
Buildings	25,000

The creditors were settled for Rs 11,000. It was found, however, that there was a liability for Rs 3,000 for damages which had to be paid. The expenses of dissolution amounted to Rs 1,000.

Give the Realisation Accounts, the Bank Account and the Capital Accounts of the partners.

Solution:

REALISATION ACCOUNT

Particulars	Amount Rs		Particulars	Amount Rs
To Sundry Assets:			By Sundry Creditors	12,000
Debtors	8,000		By Provision for Bad &	
Stock	6,000		Doubtful Debts	200
Furniture	2,000		By Bank	38,000
Building	22,000	38,000	By Loss on Realisation:	
To Bank (payment of liabilities)		14,000	A	1,120

Contd....

Particulars	Amount Rs	Particulars	Amount Rs
To Bank (expenses)	1,000	B	1,120
		C	560
	53,000		53,000

BANK ACCOUNT

Particulars	Amount Rs	Particulars	Amount Rs
To Balance b/d.	12,200	By Realisation A/c	14,000
To Realisation	38,000	By Realisation A/c	1,000
		By A's Capital A/c	15,880
		By B's Capital A/c	12,880
		By C's Capital A/c	6,440
	50,200		50,200

CAPITAL ACCOUNTS

Particulars	A Rs	B Rs	C Rs	Particulars	A Rs	B Rs	C Rs
To Loss on Realisation	1,120	1,120	560	By Balance b/d	15,000	12,000	6,000
To Bank	15,880	12,880	6,440	By General Reserve	2,000	2,000	2,000
	17,000	14,000	7,000		17,000	14,000	7,000

Illustration 4.4. The following was the Balance Sheet of Deepak and Neeru sharing profits and losses in the ratio of 3 : 2 as on 31st December 1985:

Liabilities	Amount Rs	Assets		Amount Rs
Creditors	38,000	Bank		11,500
Mrs. Deepak's Loan	10,000	Stock		6,000
Neeru's loan	15,000	Debtors	20,000	
Reserve Fund	2,500	Less Provision	1,000	19,000
Deepak's Capital	10,000	Furniture		4,000
Neeru's Capital	8,000	Plant		28,000
		Investments		10,000
		P. & L. A/c		5,000
	83,500			83,500

The firm was dissolved on 31st December, 1985 and the following was the result:

(a) Deepak took over investment at Rs 8,000 and agreed to pay off the loan of his wife.

(b) The assets realised as follows:

Stock: Rs 1,000 less; Debtors: Rs 18,500; Furniture: Rs 500 more; Plant: Rs 3,000 less.

(c) Expenses of realisation were Rs 600.

(d) Creditors were paid off less 2 1/2% discount.

Show ledger accounts to close the books of the firm.

Solution:

REALISATION ACCOUNT

Particulars		Amount Rs	Particulars	Amount Rs
To Sundry Assets:			By Sundry Creditors	38,000
Stock	6,000		By Provision for bad	
Debtors	20,000		and doubtful debts	1,000
Furniture	4,000		By Bank (assets realised)	53,000
Plant	28,000		By Deepak	8,000
Investments	10,000	68,000	By Loss on Realisation:	
To Bank (expenses)		600	Deepak	3,390
To Bank (creditors paid)		37,050	Neeru	2,260
		1,05,650		1,05,650

DEEPAK'S CAPITAL ACCOUNT

Particulars	Amount Rs	Particulars	Amount Rs
To Realisation A/c (Loss)	3,390	By Balance b/d	10,000
To Realisation A/c (Investment)	8,000	By Mrs Deepak's Loan	10,000
To P. & L. A/c	3,000	By Reserve	1,500
To Bank A/c	7,1'0		
	21,500		21,500

NEERU'S CAPITAL ACCOUNT

Particulars	Amount Rs	Particulars	Amount Rs
To Realisation A/c (Loss)	2,260	By Balance b/d	8,000
To P. & L. A/c	2,000	By Reserve	1,000
To Bank A/c	4,740		
	9,000		9,000

NEERU'S LOAN ACCOUNT

Particulars	Amount Rs	Particulars	Amount Rs
To Bank A/c	15,000	By Balance b/d	15,000
	15,000		15,000

BANK ACCOUNT

Particulars	Amount Rs	Particulars	Amount Rs
To Balance b/d	11,500	By Realisation A/c:	
To Realisation A/c	53,000	Expense	600
		Creditors.	37,050
		By Deepak's Capital A/c	7,110
		By Neeru's Capital A/c	4,740
		By Neeru's Capital A/c	15,000
	64,500		64,500

Illustration 4.5. Read, Write and Add give you the following Balance Sheet a. on Dec. 31, 1985.

Liabilities		Amount Rs	Assets		Amount Rs
Read's Loan		15,000	Plant and Machinery at cost		30,000
Capital Accounts			Fixtures and Fittings		2,000
Read	30,000		Stock		10,400
Write	10,000		Debtors	18,400	
Add	2,000	42,000	Less: Provision	400	18,000
Sundry Creditors		17,800	Joint Life Policy		15,000
Loan on Hypothecation of Stock		6,200	Patents and Trade Marks		10,000
Joint Life Policy Reverse		12,400	Cash at Bank		8,000
		93,400			93,400

The partners shared profits and losses in the ratio of Read 4/9, Write 2/9 and Add 1/3. The firm was dissolved on December 31, 1985 and you are given the following information:

(a) Add had taken a loan form Insurers for Rs 5,000 on the security of Joint Life Policy. The policy was surrendered and Insurers paid a sum of Rs 10,200 after deducting Rs 5,000 for Add's loan and Rs 300 interest thereon.

(b) One of the creditors took some of the patents whose book value was Rs 6,000 at a valuation of 4,500. The balance to that creditor was paid in cash.

(c) The firm had previously purchased some shares in a joint stock company and had written them off on finding them useless. The shares were now found to be worth Rs 3,000 and the loan creditor agreed to accepts the shares at this value.

(d) The remaining assets realised the following amounts:

	Rs
Plant and Machinery	17,000
Fixtures and Fittings	1,000
Stock	9,000
Debtors	16,500
Patents 50% of their book value	

(e) The liabilities were paid and a total discount of Rs 500 was allowed by the creditors.

(f) The expenses of Realisation amounted to Rs 2,300.

Prepare the Realisation Account, Bank Account and Partners Capital Accounts in columnar form.

Solution:

REALISATION ACCOUNT

Particulars	Amount Rs	Particulars	Amount Rs
To Plant & Machinery	30,000	By Sundry Creditors	17,800
To Fixtures & Fittings	2,000	By Loan	6,200
To Stock	10,400	By Joint Life Policy Reserve	12,400
To Debtors	18,400	By Provision for doubtful debts	400
To Joint Life Policy	15,000	By Add's Capital A/c	5,300
To Patents & Trade Marks	10,000	By Bank (Insurance Co.)	10,200
			Contd....

Particulars	Amount Rs	Particulars		Amount Rs
To Bank (payment of creditors, loan—*see working note*)	16,000	By Bank (realisation of assets):		
To Bank (expenses)	2,300	Plant & Machinery	17,000	
		Fixtures & Fittings	1,000	
		Stock	9,000	
		Debtors	16,500	
		Patents	2,000	45,000
		By Loss:		
		Read's Capital A/c		2,800
		Write's Capital A/c		1,400
		Add's Capital A/c		2,100
	1,04,100			1,04,100

CAPITAL ACCOUNTS

Particulars	Read Rs	Write Rs	Add Rs	Particulars	Read Rs	Write Rs	Add Rs
To Realisation A/c	—	—	5,300	By Balance b/d	30,000	10,000	2,000
To Realisation A/c (loss)	2,800	1,400	2,100	By Bank			5,400
To Bank	27,200	8,600	—				
	30,000	10,000	7,400		30,000	10,000	7,400

READ'S LOAN ACCOUNT

Particulars	Amount RS	Particulars	Amount Rs
To Bank	15,000	By Balance b/d	15,000
	15,000		15,000

BANK ACCOUNT

Particulars	Amount Rs	Particulars	Amount Rs
To Balance b/d	8,000	By Realisation A/c	
To Realisation A/c	10,200	(creditors and loan paid off)	16,000
To Realisation A/c	45,500	By Realisation A/c (expenses)	2,300
To Add's Capital A/c	5,400	By Read's Loan A/c	15,000
		By Read's Capital A/c	27,200
		By Write's Capital A/c	8,600
	69,100		69,100

Working Note:

The amount paid to creditors and repayment of the loan has been arrived at as follows:

			Rs
Amount due:	Sundry Creditors		17,800
	Loan on Hypothecation		6,200
		Rs	24,000
Less:	Patents taken	4,500	
	Shares taken	3,000	
	Discount allowed	500	8,000
	Amount paid		16,000

Illustration 4.6. X, Y and Z carrying on business since 1975 decided to dissolve their partnership on 30th June, 1988 when their Balance Sheet was as under:

Liabilities		Amount Rs	Assets	Amount Rs
Creditors		34,000	Cash	25,000
Capital Accounts:			Debtors	62,000
X	1,20,000		Stock	37,000
Y	90,000		Tools	8,000
Z	60,000	2,70,000	Motor Cars	12,000
			Machinery	60,000
			Freehold Building	1,00,000
Total		3,04,000	Total	3,04,000

Y and Z agreed to form a new partnership to carry on the business and it is agreed that they shall acquire from the old firm the following assets at amounts shown hereunder:

	Rs
Stock	40,000
Tools	5,000
Motor Cars	25,000
Machineries	78,000
Freehold Building	84,000
Goodwill	60,000

The partnership agreement of X, Y and Z provided that trading profits or losses shall be divided in the ratio of 3:2:1 and that capital profits or losses shall be divided in proportion of their capitals:

Debtors Realise Rs 59,000 and discount amounting to Rs 720 are secured on payments due to creditors.

Prepare the necessary accounts of X, Y and Z giving effect to these transactions and prepare the Opening Balance Sheet of Y and Z who bring the necessary cash to pay X in the ratio of 3:2.

Solution:

M/s X, Y & Z

REALISATION ACCOUNT

Particulars	Amount Rs	Particulars		Amount Rs
To Sundry Assets:		By Cash (Debtors)		59,000
Debtors	62,000	By Sundry Creditors A/c		720
Stock	37,000	(Discount)		
Tools	8,000	By Y & Z Joint Account		
Motor Cars	12,000	Stock	40,000	
Machinery	60,000	Tools	5,000	
Freehold Buildings	1,00,000	Motor Cars	25,000	
To Profit transferred to Capital A/cs:		Machinery	78,000	
X	32,000	Freehold		
Y	24,000	Buildings	84,000	
Z	16,000	72,720	Goodwill	60,000	2,92,000
	3,51,720			3,51,720

CASH ACCOUNT

Particulars	Amount Rs	Particulars	Amount Rs
To Balance b/d	25,000	By Sundry Creditors	33,280
To Realisation A/c (Debtors)	59,000	By X's Capital Account	1,52,360
To Y's Capital Account	60,984		
To Z's Capital Account	40,656		
	1,85,640		1,85,640

CAPITAL ACCOUNTS

Particulars	X Rs	Y Rs	Z Rs	Particulars	X Rs	Y Rs	Z Rs
To Cash	1,52,360			By Balance b/d	1,20,000	90,000	60,000
To Y & Z Joint				By Realisation			
Account	—	1,75,224	1,16,776	A/c (Profit)	32,360	24,240	16,120
				By Cash	—	60,984	40,656
	1,52,360	1,75,224	1,16,776		1,52,360	1,75,224	1,16,776

Y & Z JOINT ACCOUNT

Particulars	Amount Rs	Particulars	Amount Rs
To Realisation Account	2,92,000	By Y's Capital	1,75,224
		By Z's Capital	1,16,776
	2,92,000		2,92,000

M/s Y & Z

BALANCE SHEET
as on July 1, 1988

Liabilities	Amount Rs	Assets	Amount Rs
Y's Capital	1,75,224	Goodwill	60,000
X's Capital	1,16,776	Freehold Buildings	84,000
		Machineries	78,000
		Motors	25,000
		Tools	5,000
		Stock	40,000
	2,92,000		2,92,000

Working Notes:

(1) Ascertainment of Capital Profit:

Assets	Book Value Rs	Value at which taken over Rs
Motors	12,000	25,000
Tools	8,000	5,000
Machinery	60,000	78,000
Freehold Buildings	1,00,000	84,000
Goodwill	—	60,000
	1,80,000	2,52,000

Capital Profit Rs 72,000 (*i.e.* Rs 2,52,000-1,80,000)

This is divided in the ratio of Capitals:

(2) Ascertainment of Trading Profit:

Asset/Liability	Book Value Rs	Value Rs
Stock-in-trade	37,000	40,000
Sundry Debtors	62,000	59,000
Discount on Creditors	—	720
	99,000	99,720

Trading Profit is Rs 720, credited in the ratio of 3 : 2 : 1.

(3) Division of Profit:

	Capital Profit + Trading Profit	Total
A	32,000 + 360	– 32,360
B	24,000 + 240	– 24,240
C	16,000 + 120	– 16,120

INSOLVENCY OF PARTNERS

A partner may owe some money to a partnership firm. This money should be paid by him to the firm. However, in case he becomes insolvent, he may not be in a position to pay the amount owed by him to the firm in full. The amount not so paid is a loss to the firm. This loss has to be borne by the solvent partners on the basis of the following rules based on the decision given in the case of *Garner vs. Murray*:

(1) The solvent partners should bring in cash their share of loss on realisation.

(2) The loss on account of insolvency of partner should then be borne by the solvent partners in the ratio of their capitals after bringing in cash such loss on realisation.

In other words, according to *Garner vs. Murray*, the loss on account of insolvency of a partner should be borne by the solvent partners in the ratio of their capitals standing in the balance sheet, just before the dissolution of the partnership firm. In this connection, the following points should be noted:

(1) The term capital here mean the real capitals of the partners and not capitals as may be standing in the books of the partnership firm in the names of different partners. This distinction is particularly important when the partners are maintaining their capital accounts on fluctuating capital system. The true capitals in case of this system will be ascertained after making all adjustments regarding reserves, drawings unrecorded assets on the date of the balance sheet, just before dissolution of the partnership firm.

(2) In case a partner, though solvent has a debit balance in his capital account, just before the dissolution of the partnership firm, such a partner will not be required to bear the loss on account of insolvency of a partner.

Illustration 4.7. The following is the balance sheet of a firm as on 31st December 1991, when *D* has become insolvent:

BALANCE SHEET
as on 31 December, 1991

Liabilities	Amount Rs	Assets	Amount Rs
Sundry Creditors	10,000	Sundry Assets	50,000
General Reserve	10,000	C's Capital A/c	10,000

Contd....

Liabilities	Amount Rs	Assets	Amount Rs
A's Capital A/c	30,000	D's Capital A/c	10,000
B's Capital A/c	20,000		
	70,000		70,000

The assets realised Rs 40,000. Creditors are paid in full. Partners share profits and losses equally. You are required to close the books of the firm applying *Garner vs. Murray* rule.

Solution:

REALISATION ACCOUNT

Particulars	Amount Rs	Particulars		Amount Rs
To Sundry Assets	50,000	By Sundry creditors		10,000
To Bank	10,000	By Bank		40,000
		By Loss on realisation:		
		A's Capital A/c	2,500	
		B's Capital A/c	2,500	
		C's Capital A/c	2,500	
		D's Capital A/c	2,500	10,000
	60,000			60,000

BANK ACCOUNT

Particulars	Amount Rs	Particulars	Amount Rs
To Realisation A/c	40,000	By A's Capital A/c	26,000
To A's Capital A/c	2,500	By B's Capital A/c	18,410
To B's Capital A/c	2,500	By Sundry Creditors	10,000
To C's Capital A/c	2,500		
To C's Capital A/c	7,500		
	55,000		55,000

CAPITAL ACCOUNTS

Particulars	A Rs	B Rs	C Rs	D Rs	Particulars	A Rs	B Rs	C Rs	D Rs
To Balance b/d			10,000	10,000	By Balance b/d	30,000	20,000		
To Realis. A/c	2,500	2,500	2,500	2,500	By General				
To D's Cap. A/c	5,910	4,090			Reserve	2,500	2,500	2,500	2,500
To Bank	26,590	18,410			By Bank (Loss on Realisation)				
						2,500	2,500	2,500	2,500
					By A's Cap. A/c				5,910
					By B's Cap. A/c				4,090
					By Bank			7,500	
	35,000	25,000	12,500	12,500		35,000	25,000	12,500	12,500

Working Notes:

The deficiency of D will have to be borne by partners A and B. C will not have to bear the deficiency because he had a debit balance in his capital account. The ratio has been ascertained as follows:

Particulars	A	B
Capitals	30,000	20,000
Add: Reserve	2,500	2,500
Realisation loss brought in cash	2,500	2,500
	35,000	25,000
Less: Loss on Realisation	2,500	2,500
Real capitals (in which deficiency of D has to be shared)	32,500	22,500
Share of D's deficiency (Rs 10,000)	5,910	4,090

Tutorial Notes

(i) While attempting an examination problem, the solvent partners may not be required to bring the loss on realisation in cash. The deficiency of the insolvent partner may be distributed among the solvent partners in the ratio of their capitals standing in the balance sheet just before dissolution of the partnership firm. However, where an examination problem specifies that the rule in *Garner vs. Murray* is to be applied, the solvent partners should be required to bring the loss on realisation in cash.

(ii) In the above illustration if the partners had been following fixed capital system (i.e. when separate current accounts are maintained) the deficiency of the insolvent partner D would have been borne by the solvent partners A and B in the ratio of their fixed capital i.e. 3 : 2.

In Case of Insolvency of All Partners

In case all partners become insolvent, the loss on account of insolvency of the partners will have to be borne by the creditors. The creditors may be transferred to the Realisation Account. The amount available may be paid to them through the Realisation Account. Any balance remaining unpaid to them represents their sacrifice on account of insolvency of partners.

Illustration 4.8. Ram and Shyam were in equal partnership. Their Balance Sheet stood as under on 31 December, 1991 when the firm was dissolved.

Liabilities	Amount Rs	Assets	Amount Rs
Creditors	3,200	Machinery and Plant	1,200
Ram's Capital	400	Furniture	300
		Debtors	500
		Stock	400
		Cash	180
		Shyam's Drawings	1,020
	3,600		3,600

The assets realised as under:

	Rs		Rs
Machinery	600	Debtors	400
Furniture	100	Stock	300

The expenses of realisation amounted to Rs 140. Ram's private estate is not sufficient even to pay his private debts, whereas in Shyam's private estate there is a surplus of Rs 140 only.

Give accounts to close the books of the firm.

Solution:

REALISATION ACCOUNT

Particulars	Amount Rs	Particulars	Amount Rs
To Machinery & Plant	1,200	By Creditors	3,200
To Furniture	300	By Cash (assets realised)	1,400
To Debtors	500		
To Stock	400		
To Cash (expenses)	140		
To Cash (creditors paid)	1,580		
To Profit on Realisation:			
Ram's Capital A/c	240		
Shyam's Capital A/c	240		
	4,600		4,600

CASH ACCOUNT

Particulars	Amount Rs	Particulars	Amount Rs
To Balance b/d	180	By Realisation account	140
To Realisation A/c	1,400	By Creditors	1,580
To Shyam	140		
	1,720		1,720

CAPITAL ACCOUNTS

Particulars	Ram Rs	Shyam Rs	Particulars	Ram Rs	Shyam Rs
To Balance b/d		1,020	By Balance b/d	400	
To Shyam's Capital A/c	640		By Cash	—	140
			By Realisation A/c	240	240
			By Ram's Capital A/c	—	640
	640	1,020		640	1,020

Alternatively, the creditors may not be transferred to the Realisation Account. In case this is done, any balance remaining unpaid to the creditors will be transferred to a "Deficiency Account". Similarly, the amounts not paid by the partners will also be transferred to the deficiency amount.

The books of accounts will be closed as follows in case the alternative method is followed:

REALISATION ACCOUNT

Particulars	Amount Rs	Particulars	Amount Rs
To Machinery & Plant	1,200	By Cash (assets realised)	1,400
To Furniture	300	By Loss on Realisation:	
To Debtors	500	Ram's Capital A/c	570
To Stock	400	Shyam's Capital A/c	570
To Cash (expenses)	140		
	2,540		2,540

CASH ACCOUNT

Particulars	Amount Rs	Particulars	Amount Rs
To Balance b/d	180	By Realisation Account	140
To Shyam's Capital A/c	140	By Creditors A/c	1,580
To Realisation A/c	1,400		
	1,720		1,720

CREDITORS ACCOUNT

Particulars	Amount Rs	Particulars	Amount Rs
To Cash	1,580	By Balance b/d	3,200
To Deficiency Account	1,620		
	3,200		3,200

CAPITAL ACCOUNTS

Particulars	Ram Rs	Shyam Rs	Particulars	Ram Rs	Shyam Rs
To Balance b/d		1,020	By Balance b/d	400	
To Realisation A/c	570	570	By Cash		140
			By Deficiency Account	170	1,450
	570	1,590		570	1,590

DEFICIENCY ACCOUNT

Particulars	Amount Rs	Particulars	Amount Rs
To Ram's Capital A/c	170	By Creditors A/c	1,620
To Shyam's Capital A/c	1,450		
	1,620		1,620

KEY TERMS

☐ **Dissolution of Partnership:** It implies change in the relations of partners. In other words there is dissolution of partnership whenever a partnership is reconstituted viz., admission, retirement, death or insolvancy of a partner. In dissolution of partnership the firm continues to carry on its business in a reconstituted form.

☐ **Dissolution of Firm:** It is dissolution of partnership among all the partners of a firm. In such an event the business of the firm is closed down and its affairs are wound up.

☐ **Garner Versus Murray Rule:** The rule provides that loss on account of insolvancy of a partner should be borne by the solvent partners in the ratio of capitals standing in the Balance Sheet just before the dissolution of the firm. The rule is applicable in the absence of any contract to the contrary amongst the partners.

TEST QUESTIONS

Objective type | TEST YOUR UNDERSTANDING |

1. State whether each of the following statement is 'True' or 'False':
    (a) Dissolution of a firm automatically results in dissolution of a partnership.
    (b) Only firm's assets can be used for payment of firm's liabilities.
    (c) Loss on realisation is transferred to partners' capital account in their capital ratio.
    (d) Any amount realised from the sale of an unrecorded asset is credited to the Realisation Account.
    (e) Partner's wife loan is treated at par with other liabilities of the partnership firm.
    (f) Partner's loan is transferred to the Realisation account with liabilities of the firm.
    (g) A partnership firm will get dissolved if all partners except one are declared insolvent.
    (h) In case of insolvency of a partner, his deficiency is borne by the solvent partners in their profit sharing ratio.

    [Ans. (a) True; (b) False; (c) False; (d) True; (e) True; (f) False; (g) True; (h) False].

2. Select the most appropriate answer:
    (i) In the event of dissolution of a partnership firm, the provision for doubtful debts is transferred to:
        (a) Realisation Account
        (b) Partners' Capital Accounts
        (c) Sundry Debtors Account.
    (ii) Unrecorded liability when paid on dissolution of a firm is debited to:
        (a) Realisation Account
        (b) Partners' Capital Accounts
        (c) Liability Account.
    (iii) In the event of dissolution of firm, the partners assets are first used for payment of the
        (a) personal liabilities
        (b) firm's liabilities
        (c) none of the two.
    (iv) In the absence of any contract to the contrary, capital profit on dissolution of a partnership firm is credited to the partners:
        (a) in Capital Ratio
        (b) in Profit Sharing Ratio
        (c) equally.

    [Ans. (i) (a); (ii) (a); (iii) (a); (iv) (b)].

Essay type | FOR REVIEW, DISCUSSION AND PRACTICE |

1. Differentiate between dissolution of partnership and dissolution of firm. State the circumstances under which a partnership firm may be dissolved.
2. When does the implied authority of a partner to bind the firm terminate in the event of dissolution of a partnership firm?
3. State the rules regarding:
    (a) payment of firm's debts and separate debts;
    (b) the order of distribution of firm's assets;
    in the event of dissolution of a partnership firm.

PRACTICAL PROBLEMS

Simple Dissolution

1. The partnership between A and B was dissolved on December 31, 1985. On that date the respective credits to the capitals were A Rs 1,70,000 and B Rs 30,000. Rs 20,000 were owed by B to the firm; Rs 1,00,000 were owed by the firm to A and Rs 2,00,000 were due to the trade creditors. Profits and Losses were shared in the proportion of 2/3 to A and 1/3 to B.

   The assets represented by the above stated net liabilities realised Rs 4,50,000 exclusive of Rs 20,000 owed by B. The liabilities were settled at book figures. Prepare the Realisation Account, Cash Account and Capital Accounts showing the distribution to the partners.

   [Ans. Loss on Realisation Rs 30,000. A gets Rs 1,50,000].

2. X, Y and Z commenced business on 1st January, 1988 with capitals of Rs 1,00,000, Rs 80,000 and Rs 60,000 respectively. Profits and loses were shared in the ratio of 4:3:3. Capitals carried interest at 5% p.a. During 1988 and 1989 they made profits of Rs 40,000 and Rs 50,000 (before allowing interest on capitals). Drawings of each partner were Rs 10,000 per year.

   On 31 December, 1989 the firm was dissolved. Creditors on that date were Rs 24,000. The assets realised Rs 2,60,000 net. Give the necessary accounts to close the books of the firm.

   [Ans. Assets at the time of dissolution were of Rs 2,94,000; Loss on Realisation Rs 34,000; X gets Rs 1,02,910; Y Rs 77,570 and Z Rs 55,520].

3. Kaju, Mutter and Kishmish were sharing profits in the ratio of 3:2:1 in a partnership business. Their Balance Sheet as on 31 December, 1988 was as follows:

Liabilities	Amount Rs	Assets		Amount Rs
Sundry Creditors	1,54,000	Cash at bank		35,000
Bills Payable	36,000	Stock		1,98,000
Kaju's Loan A/c	1,00,000	Debtors	1,50,000	
Capitals Accounts:		Less: Provision	10,000	1,40,000
Kaju	2,00,000	Joint Life Policy		40,000
Mutter	1,60,000	Plant & Machinery		4,37,000
Kishmish	80,000			
Reserve Fund	1,20,000			
	8,50,000			8,50,000

   The firm was dissolved on 1 January, 1989. Joint life policy was taken over by Kaju at Rs 50,000. Stock realised Rs 1,80,000. Debtors realised Rs 1,45,000. Plant and Machinery was sold for Rs 3,60,000. Liabilities were paid in full. In addition one bill for Rs 7,000 under discount was dishonoured and had to be taken up by the firm.

   Give journal entries and the necessary ledger accounts to close the books of the firm.

   [Ans. Loss on Realisation Rs 87,000; Kaju gets Rs 1,66,500; Mutter gets Rs 1,71,000; and Kishmish gets Rs 85,500].

4. The following is the Balance Sheet of Suneel and Sharad on 31 December, 1988.

Liabilities	Amount Rs	Assets		Amount Rs
Creditors	3,00,000	Cash in hand		5,000
Bills Payable	80,000	Cash at bank		80,000
Mrs Suneel's Loan	50,000	Investments		1,00,000
Mrs Sharad's Loan	1,00,000	Stock		50,000
Reserve Fund	1,00,000	Debtors	2,00,000	
Investment Fluctuation Fund	10,000	Less: Provision of		
Suneel's Capital	1,00,000	Bad Debts	20,000	1,80,000

Contd

Liabilities	Amount Rs	Assets	Amount Rs
Sharad's Capital	1,00,000	Plant & Fittings	2,00,000
		Buildings	1,50,000
		Goodwill	40,000
		Profit & Loss Account	35,000
	8,40,000		8,40,000

The firm was dissolved on 31 December, 1988 and the following was the position:

(a) Suneel promised to pay of Mrs. Suneel's loan and took away stock at Rs 40,000.

(b) Sharad took away half of the investments at a discount of 10 per cent.

(c) Debtors were realised at Rs 1,90,000.

(d) Creditors and Bills Payable were paid at discount of Rs 1,500 and 400 respectively

(e) Other assets realised as follows:

	Rs
Plant	2,50,000
Buildings	4,00,000
Goodwill	60,000
Investments (balance)	45,000

(f) There was an old typewriter which had been written off completely from the books, it is now estimated to realise Rs 3,000. It was taken away by Sharad at the estimated price.

(g) Realisation expenses amounted to Rs 10,000.

Make journal entries and prepare various ledger accounts.

[Ans. Profit on Realisation Rs 3,14,900; Suneel gets Rs 2,99,950 and Sharad gets Rs 2,41,950]

5. Apple and Orange are equal partners. They decided to dissolve the partnership on 31 December, 1991 when their Balance Sheet was as follows:

BALANCE SHEET
as at 31 December, 1991

Liabilities	Rs	Assets	Rs
Creditors	1,200	Premises	30,000
Capitals:		Plant	9,600
Apple	24,000	Debtors	2,880
Orange	24,00	Stock	3,480
		Cash at Bank	3,240
	49,200		49,200

Apple is to take over the business and pay Rs 6,000 for goodwill, which had not been previously valued. He is also to take over the premises and stock at book values and plant at Rs 9,000.

During the period upto 30 April, 1992 he collects Rs 2,400 from the firm's debtors and pays the liabilities getting Rs 120 for cash discount. He also pays for the cost of dissolution agreement amounting to Rs 240.

You are required to prepare the Realisation Account, Cash Account and the Partners' Capital Accounts showing the amount Apple pays to Orange, assuming that settlement was made on 30 April, 1992.

(C.A. Inter OS, May, 1972, adapted)

[Ans. Realisation Profit Rs 4,800; Apple brings Rs 22,080; Orange is paid Rs 26,400]

6. A, B and C were in partnership sharing profits and losses in the ratio 3 : 2 : 1. They decided to dissolve the partnership on 31 December, 1987, when the partnership assets and liabilities were as under:

Liabilities		Amount Rs	Assets	Amount Rs
Capital Accounts:			Goodwill	45,630
A	42,000		Plant & Machinery	60,750
B	22,500		Furniture	6,465
C	12,000	76,500	Stock	23,670
Loan: Mrs. A		15,000	Book Debts	53,400
Sundry Creditors		56,700	Joint Life Policy	26,550
Bank Overdraft		60,645	Accrued Agency Commission	14,055
Life Policy Fund		26,550	Cash at Bank	4,875
		2,35,395		2,35,395

The following particulars are pertinent:

(1) The Life Policy was surrendered for Rs 23,250.

(2) A took over goodwill and plant and machinery for Rs 90,000.

(3) A also agreed to discharge Bank-Overdraft and loan from Mrs. A.

(4) Furniture and stock were divided equally between A and B at an agreed valuation of Rs 36,000.

(5) Book Debts were assigned to firm's creditors in full satisfaction of their claim.

(6) The agency commission was received in time.

(7) A Bill Receivable discounted was returned dishonoured and subsequently proved valueless Rs 3,075 (including Rs 50 noting charges).

(8) A paid the expenses of dissolution Rs 1,800.

(9) C agreed to receive Rs 15,000 in full satisfaction of his rights, title and interest in the firm.

You are required to show the accounts relating to final dissolution of the firm.

(C.A. Final O.S., November, 1978, adapted)

[**Ans.** Realisation Profit Rs 8,160. Amounts paid A Rs 16,341, B Rs 7,764, C Rs 15,000]

7. The following is the Balance Sheet of Sudhir and Romesh as on 31 December, 1989:

Liabilities		Amount Rs	Assets		Amount Rs
Sundry Creditors		76,000	Cash at Bank		23,000
Loan from Lata wife of Sudhir		20,000	Stock in Trade		12,000
Loan from Romesh		30,000	Sundry Debtors	40,000	
Reserve Fund		10,000	Less: Provision	2,000	38,000
Capitals:			Furniture		8,000
Sudhir		20,000	Plant		56,000
Romesh		16,000	Investments		20,000
			Profits & Loss A/c		15,000
		1,72,000			1,72,000

The firm was dissolved on 31 December, 1989 and following was the result:

(i) Sudhir took over investment at an agreed value of Rs 16,000 and agreed to pay off the Loan to Lata wife of Sudhir.

(ii) The assets realised as under:

		Rs
(a)	Stock	10,000
(b)	Debtors	37,000
(c)	Furniture	9,000
(d)	Plant	50,000
	The expenses were	2,200

(iii) The sundry creditors were paid off *less* 2 ½% discount. Sudhir and Romesh shared Profits & Losses in the ratio of 3 : 2. Show Realisation Account, Bank Accounts and Partners' Capital Accounts.

(I.C.W.A. Inter, June, 1980, adapted).

[Ans. Realisation Loss Rs 12,300, Sudhir gets Rs 13,620 and Romesh gets Rs 9,080]

Insolvency

8. The following is the Balance Sheet of a firm as on 31 December 1990, where capitals of the partners are fixed:

Liabilities	Amount Rs	Assets	Amount Rs
Creditors	1,02,400	Bank	5,500
Loans:		Debtors	96,060
P	30,000	Stock	64,000
Q	12,000	Machinery	28,600
Current Accounts:		Land	84,000
P	21,200	R's Current Account	9,940
Q	2,500		
Capital Accounts			
P	60,000		
Q	40,000		
R	20,000		
	2,88,100		2,88,100

Owing to heavy losses in the past two years, it was decided to close the business. The assets with the exception of bank balance realised Rs 2,26,880. The firm has to pay Rs 1,500 for an outstanding bill not recorded in the books: R becomes insolvent and Rs 1,000 is realised from his estate.

Prepare necessary accounts to close the books of the firm.

(B.Com. Pass, Delhi, 1981, adapted)

[Ans. Realisation Rs 47,280; P gets Rs 62,620, Q gets Rs 24,860]

9. P, Q, R and S are partners sharing profits and losses in the ratio of 4 : 3 : 2 : 1. Their position statement was follows:

Liabilities	Amount Rs	Assets	Amount Rs
Bank Loan	20,000	Cash	1,500
Creditors	40,000	Buildings	44,000
P's Capital	30,000	Stock	60,000
Q's Capital	20,000	R's Capital	3,500
		S's Capital	1,000
	1,10,000		1,10,000

The firm is dissolved. All assets realised Rs 82,000. All outside liabilities are paid Rs 58,500 in full satisfaction. Outstanding creditors are also paid Rs 500. The expenses of dissolution are Rs 600. *S* becomes insolvent and *R* paid only Rs 3,000.

Prepare ledger accounts to close the books of the firm.

(B.Com. Pass, Delhi, 1987)

[Ans. Realisation loss Rs 21,600; *R*'s deficiency Rs 4,820; *S*'s deficiency Rs 3,160; Final payments to *P* Rs 16,572; *Q* Rs 10,328]

10. *A, B* and *C* were carrying on business in partnership sharing profits and losses in the ratio of 3 : 2 : 1. They decided to dissolve the firm on 31.12.1987, on which their balance sheet stood as follows:

Liabilities		Amount Rs	Assets	Amount Rs
Creditors		94,000	Land and Buildings	1,14,000
A's Loan A/c		20,000	Stock	1,00,000
Capital Accounts			Debtors	1,00,000
A	1,80,000		Cash	6,000
B	20,000		Profit and Loss	3,000
C	20,000	2,20,000	*B*'s Current Account	4,000
			C's Current Account	10,000
		3,37,000		3,37,000

Land and Buildings were sold for Rs 80,000, Stock and Debtors realised Rs 60,000 and Rs 84,000 respectively. The Goodwill was sold for Rs 1,200. The expenses of realisation amounted to Rs 2,400. *C* is insolvent and a final dividend of 50 paise in a rupee is received from his estate in full settlement.

Prepare the necessary accounts closing the books of the firm applying the ruling given in *Garner Vs Murray*.

[Ans. Realisation loss Rs 91,200; *C*'s deficiency Rs 2,850 borne by *A*-Rs 2,565 and *B*-Rs 285].

11. *X, Y* and *Z* are partners sharing profits and losses in the ratio of 3 : 2 : 3. Their Balance Sheet on the date of dissolution was as follows:

BALANCE SHEET

Liabilities	Amount Rs	Assets	Amount Rs
Creditors	3,40,000	Cash	25,000
X's Capital	2,60,000	Debtors	3,00,000
Z's Capital	1,55,000	Stock	2,31,000
		Land and Buildings	1,50,000
		Y's Capital	49,000
	7,55,000		7,55,000

The assets realised Rs 2,61,000. The creditors were paid Rs 2,55,000 in full settlement. Expenses of dissolution were Rs 2,000. *Y* became insolvent and 50% was received from his private estate.

Prepare necessary ledger accounts to close the books of the firm in accordance with the decision in *Garner Vs Murray* case.

(B.Com. Pass, Delhi, 1990)

[Ans. Realisation Loss Rs 3,37,000; *Y*'s deficiency total Rs 66,625 shared by *X* Rs 41,741 and *Z* Rs 24,884]

12. The following was the Balance Sheet of *P, Q* and *R* on 31 March 1988.

Liabilities	Amount Rs	Assets	Amount Rs
P's Capital	25,000	Freehold Property	10,000
R's Capital	15,000	Furniture	5,000
P's Current Account	1,000	Stock-in-trade	23,100
R's Current Account	500	Debtors	30,000
Sundry Creditors	30,000	Cash	2,500
Loan on mortgage of freehold property	4,000	Q's Current Account	4,900
	75,500		75,500

The partners shared profits and losses in the proportion of 6 : 3 : 5. It was decided to dissolve the partnership as on the date of the Balance Sheet.

The assets realised as under:

	Rs
Freehold Property	6,000
Furniture	2,000
Stock-in-trade	15,000
Debtors	20,000

The expenses on realisation amounted to Rs 2,000. The sundry creditors agreed to take 75 p. in the rupee in full satisfaction. It was ascertained that Q has become insolvent. A dividend of 50 p in the rupee was received from the Court Receiver.

Write up the Realisation Account, Bank Account, Capital and Current Accounts of the partners. Indicate the basis adopted for distributing the deficiency in the capital accounts.

(I.C.W.A. Final, June, 1979, adapted)

[Ans. Realisation Loss Rs 19,600; P gets Rs 15,325 and R gets Rs 7,135.].

13. A, B, C and D were partner sharing profits and losses in the Ratio of 3:3:2:2 respectively. The following is their Balance Sheet as at 31 December, 1988:

Liabilities	Amount Rs		Assets		Amount Rs
Creditors		31,000	Cash in hand		4,000
A's Loan		20,000	Debtors	32,000	
Capital Accounts:			Less: Provision for		
A	40,000		doubtful debts	1,000	31,000
B	30,000	70,000	Stock		20,000
			Furniture		8,000
			Car		14,000
			Capital Accounts:		
			C	12,000	
			D	32,000	44,000
		1,21,000			1,21,000

It was decided to dissolve the firm with effect from 31 December 1988, and B was appointed to liquidate the assets and pay the creditors. He was entitled to receive 5% commission on the amounts finally paid to other partners towards capitals. He was to bear the expenses of realisation which amounted to Rs 500.

The assets realised Rs 54,000 excluding cash on hand. Creditors were paid in full. In addition a sum of Rs 5,000 was also paid to staff on retrenchment in full settlement of their claim:

D was insolvent and the partners accepted Rs 7,400 from his estate in settlement.

Applying the rule in the leading case of *Garner vs Murray* prepare the necessary ledger accounts and close the books of the firm.

[Ans. Realisation Loss Rs 24,000, Final Payment to A Rs 22,438, B Rs 18,162, C brings Rs 16,800 (including realisation loss)].

14. Hope, Faith Wisdom and Courage had been carrying on business in partnership sharing profits and losses in the ratio of 3 : 2 : 1 : 1.

They decided to dissolve the partnership on the basis of the following Balance Sheet as on 30 April, 1992.

Liabilities		Amount Rs	Assets		Amount Rs
Capital Account:			Premises		60,000
Hope	50,000		Furniture		20,000
Faith	30,000	80,000	Stock		50,000
			Debtors		20,000
General Reserve		28,000	Cash		4,000
Capital Reserve		7,000	Capital Overdrawn		
Sundry Creditors		10,000	Wisdom	5,000	
Mortgage Loan		40,000	Courage	6,000	11,000
		1,65,000			1,65,000

(1) The assets were realised as under:

	Rs
Debtors	12,000
Stock	30,000
Furniture	8,000
Premises	45,000

(2) Expenses of dissolution amounted to Rs 2,000.

(3) Further creditors of Rs 6,000 had to be met.

(4) General Reserve unlike Capital Reserve was built up by appropriation of profits.

You are required to draw up the Realisation Account, Partners' Capital Accounts and the Cash Account assuming that Wisdom became insolvent and nothing was realised from his private estate. Apply the principles laid down in *Garner vs. Murray.*

(C.A. Final OS, May, 1975, adapted)

[Ans. Realisation Loss Rs 63,300; Final payment to Hope Rs 59,428, Faith Rs 36,572, Courage brings Rs 1,000]

Suggested Answers

CA FOUNDATION EXAMINATION
MAY 1997
Fundamentals Of Accounting

Q.1 (Final Accounts). From the following particulars prepare trading and profit and loss account of Mr. *R* for the year ended 31.3.1997 and a balance sheet as on 31.3.1997 :

	Dr. Rs.	Cr. Rs.
Building	5,00,000	
Machineries	2,00,000	
Furniture	1,00,000	
Cash at Bank	90,000	
Cash on hand	10,000	
18% p.a. loan obtained by Mr. *R* on 1.6.1996 on mortgage of his building		3,00,000
R's Capital		5,20,000
Sundry Debtors/Sundry Creditors	5,00,000	4,00,000
Stock on 1.4.1996	1,20,000	
Purchases/Sales	25,00,000	32,20,000
Sales Returns/Purchases Returns	1,20,000	1,00,000
Rent	60,000	
Establishment Expenses	1,80,000	
Electricity Charges	15,000	
Telephone Charges	10,000	
Commission on Sales	30,000	
Insurance Premium	10,000	
Bad Debts	20,000	
Bills Receivable	75,000	
	45,40,000	45,40,000

You are required to provide for depreciation on buildings at 5% p.a.; on machineries at 25% p.a.; on furniture at 10% p.a. Provision for bad and doubtful debts is to be made at 5% on sundry debtors. Mr. *R*'s manager is entitled to a commission of 10% on the net profit after charging his commission. Closing stock was not taken on 31.3.1997 but only on 7.4.1997. Following transactions had taken place during the period from 1.4.1997 to 7th April, 1997 :

Sales Rs. 2,50,000, Purchases 1,50,000, Stock on 7th April, 1997 was Rs. 1,80,000 and the Rate of Gross Profit on Sales was 20%.

Insurance premium mentioned in the trial balance was in respect of building and machineries. Interest on mortgage loan to be provided up to 31.3.1997.   *(20 Marks)*

Solution :

Mr *R*
TRADING AND PROFIT AND LOSS ACCOUNT
For the year ended 31st March, 1997

Particulars		Rs.	Particulars		Rs.
To Opening Stock		1,20,000	By Sales	32,20,000	
To Purchases	25,00,000		*Less :* Returns	1,20,000	31,00,000
Less : Returns	1,00,000	24,00,000			
To Gross Profit c/d		8,10,000	By Closing Stock (*WN* 1)		2,30,000
		33,30,000			33,30,000
To Rent		60,000	By Gross Profit b/d		8,10,000
To Establishment Expenses		1,80,000			
To electricity Charges		15,000			
To Telephone Charges		10,000			
To Commission on Sales		30,000			
To Insurance Premium		10,000			
To Bad Debts		20,000			
To Provision for Doubtful Debts		25,000			
(5,00,000 × 5/100)					
To Interest on Loan		45,000			
(3,00,000 × 18/100 × 10/12)					
To Depreciation (*WN* 2)		85,000			
To Manager's Commission (*WN* 3)		30,000			
To Net Profit		3,00,000			
		8,10,000			8,10,000

Mr. *R*
BALANCE SHEET AT 31ST MARCH, 1997

Liabilities		Rs.	Assets		Rs.
Capital Account :			Building	5,00,000	
Opening Balance	5,20,000		*Less :* Depreciation	25,000	4,75,000
Add : Profit	3,00,000		Machineries	2,00,000	
		8,20,000	*Less :* Depreciation	50,000	1,50,000
18% Mortgage Loan		3,00,000	Furniture	1,00,000	
Interest accrued on Loan		45,000	*Less :* Depreciation	10,000	90,000
Sundry Creditors		4,00,000	Closing Stock		2,30,000
Commission due to			Sundry Debtors	5,00,000	
R's Manager		30,000	*Less :* Provision for		
			Bad & Doubtful		
			Debts	25,000	4,75,000

(Contd.)

Liabilities	Rs.	Assets	Rs.
		Bills Receivable	75,000
		Cash at Bank	90,000
		Cash on Hand	10,000
	15,95,000		15,95,000

Working Notes :

Rs.

1. *Computation of value of Closing Stock*

Stock as on 7th April 1997			1,80,000
Add : Cost of sales during the intervening period			
Sales made between 1.4.1997 and 7.4.1997	2,50,000		
Less : Gross Profit @ 20% on Sales	50,000		
			2,00,000
			3,80,000
Less : Purchases during the intervening period			1,50,000
Value of Stock as on 31.3.1997			2,30,000

2. Depreciation :

Buildings	(5,00,000 × 5/100)	25,000
Machineries	(2,00,000 × 25/100)	50,000
Furniture	(1,00,000 × 10/100)	10,000
		85,000

3. Manager's Commission

Profit before charging commission	3,30,000
Commission (3,30,000 × 10/110)	30,000

Q.2 (Partnership - Retirement). On 31st March, 1997 the Balance Sheet of M/s Ram, Hari & Mohan sharing profits and losses in the ratio of 2 : 3 : 2, stood as follows :

Liabilities	Rs.	Rs.	Assets	Rs.
Capital Accounts :			Land and Buildings	10,00,000
Ram	10,00,000		Machinery	17,00,000
Hari	15,00,000		Closing Stock	5,00,000
Mohan	10,00,000	35,00,000	Sundry Debtors	6,00,000
Sundry Creditors		5,00,000	Cash and Bank Balances	2,00,000
		40,00,000		40,00,000

On 31st March, 1997 Hari desired to retire from the firm and the remaining partners decided to carry on. It was agreed to revalue the Assets and Liabilities on that date on the following basis:

1. Land & Building be appreciated by 30%.

2. Machinery be depreciated by 20%.

3. Closing Stock to be valued at Rs. 4,50,000.

4. Provision for bad debts be made at 5%.

5. Old credit balances of Sundry Creditors Rs. 50,000 be written back.

6. Joint Life Policy of the partners surrendered and cash obtained Rs. 3,50,000.

7. Goodwill of the entire firm be valued at Rs. 6,30,000 and Hari's share of the Goodwill be adjusted in the accounts of Ram and Mohan who share the future profits and losses in the ratio of 3 : 2. No Goodwill Account being raised.

8. The total capital of the firm is to be the same as before retirement. Individual capital be in their profit sharing ratio.

9. Amount due to Hari is to be settled on the following basis :

   50% on retirement and the balance 50% within one year.

Prepare Revaluation Account, Capital Accounts of Partners, Cash Account and Balance Sheet as on 1.4.1997 of M/s Ram & Mohan. *(15 Marks)*

Solution :

Dr.   REVALUATION ACCOUNT   Cr.

Particulars	Rs.	Particulars		Rs.
To Machinery A/c	3,40,000	By Land and Buildings A/c		3,00,000
To Closing Stock A/c	50,000	By Sundry Creditors A/c		50,000
To Provision for		By Loan to Partners' Capital A/cs :		
Bad Debts A/c	30,000	Ram	20,000	
		Hari	30,000	
		Mohan	20,000	70,000
	4,20,000			4,20,000

Dr.   PARTNERS' CAPITAL ACCOUNTS   Cr.

Particulars	Ram Rs.	Hari Rs.	Mohan Rs.	Particulars	Ram Rs.	Hari Rs.	Mohan Rs.
To Hari's Capital (A/c - (Goodwill)	1,98,000	—	72,000	By Balance b/d	10,00,000	15,00,000	10,00,000
To Revaluation A/c	20,000	30,000	20,000	By Joint Life Policy A/c	1,00,000	1,50,000	1,00,000
To Cash and Bank A/c	—	9,45,000	—	By Ram's Capital A/c (Goodwill)	—	1,98,000	—
To Hari's Loan A/c	—	9,45,000	—	By Mohan's Capital A/c (Goodwill)	—	72,000	—
To Balance c/d	21,00,000	—	14,00,000	By Cash/Bank A/c (Balancing figure)	12,18,000	—	3,92,000
	23,18,000	19,20,000	14,92,000		23,18,000	19,20,000	14,92,000

Dr.   CASH/BANK ACCOUNT   Cr.

Particulars	Rs.	Particulars	Rs.
To Balance b/d	2,00,000	By Hari's Capital A/c	9,45,000
To Joint Life Policy A/c	3,50,000	By Balance c/d	12,15,000
To Ram's Capital A/c	12,18,000		
To Mohan's Capital A/c	3,92,000		
	21,60,000		21,60,000

M/s Ram & Mohan
BALANCE SHEET AS ON 1ST APRIL, 1997

Liabilities		Rs.	Assets		Rs.
Capital Accounts			Land and Buildings		13,00,000
Ram	21,00,000		Machinery		13,60,000
Mohan	14,00,000	35,00,000	Closing Stock		4,50,000
			Sundry Debtors	6,00,000	
Sundry Creditors		4,50,000	Less : Provision for		
Hari's Loan Account		9,45,000	Bad Debts	30,000	5,70,000
			Cash and Bank Balances		12,15,000
		48,95,000			48,95,000

Working Notes :

1. Computation of Gaining Ratio   Rs.
   Ram $3/5 - 2/7 = 11/35$
   Mohan $2/5 - 2/7 = 4/35$
2. Adjustment for Goodwill
   Total Goodwill of the Firm   6,30,000
   Hari's Share $(6,30,000 \times 3/7)$ 2,70,000
   Hari's Share of goodwill is to be borne by Ram and Mohan
   in their gaining ratio (i.e. 11 : 4)
   Ram $= 2,70,000 \times 11/15$ 1,98,000
   Mohan $= 2,70,000 \times 4/15$ 72,000

Q.3 (Bank Reconciliation Statement). Following are the entries recorded in the Bank Column of the Cash Book of Mr. X for the month ending on 31.3.1997 :

CASH BOOK (BANK COLUMN)

Date	Particulars	Rs.	Date	Particulars	Rs.
15.3.97	To Cash	36,000	1.3.97	By Balance b/d	40,000
20.3.97	To Roy	24,000	4.3.97	By John	2,000
22.3.97	To Kapoor	10,000	6.3.97	By Krishnan	400
31.3.97	To Balance c/d	7,640	15.3.97	By Kailash	240
			20.3.97	By Joshi	35,000
		77,640			77,640
				By Balance b/d	7,640

On 31.3.1997 Mr. X received the Bank Statement. On perusal of the statement Mr. X ascertained the following information :

(i) Cheques deposited but not credited by the bank Rs. 10,000.

(ii) Interest on securities collected by the bank but not received in cash book Rs. 1,080.

(iii) Credit transfer not recorded in the cash book Rs. 200.

(iv) Dividend collected by the bank directly but not recorded in the cash book Rs. 1,000.

(v) Cheques issued but not presented for payment Rs. 37,400.

(vi) Interest debited by the bank but not recorded in the cash book Rs. 1,000.

(vii)   Bank charges not recorded in the cash book Rs. 340.

From the above information you are asked to prepare a Bank Reconciliation Statement to ascertain the balance as per Bank Statement.   *(15 Marks)*

Solution :

BANK RECONCILIATION STATEMENT
As on 31st March, 1997

Particulars	+ Rs.	− Rs.
Overdraft as per Cash Book		7,640
Less : Cheques deposited but not credited by the bank		10,000
Interest debited by the bank but not recorded in the cash book		1,000
Bank Charges not recorded in the cash book		340
Add : Interest on securities collected by the bank but not		
recorded in cash book	1,080	
Credit transfer not recorded in the cash book	200	
Dividend collected by the bank directly but not recorded		
in the cash book	1,000	
Cheques issued but not presented for payment	37,400	
	39,680	18,980
Balance as per Bank Statement (Cr.)	20,700	20,700

Q.4 (a) (Negotiable Instruments). On 1st January, 1997, *A* sells goods for Rs. 10,000 to *B* and draws a bill at three months for the amount. *B* accepts it and returns it to *A*. On 1st March, 1997, *B* retires his acceptance under rebate of 12% per annum. Record these transactions in the journals of *A* and *B*.   *(6 Marks)*

Solution :

Books of A
JOURNAL ENTRIES

Date	Particulars		Debit Rs.	Credit Rs.
1997 Jan. 1	*B* To Sales Account (Being the goods sold to *B* on credit)	Dr.	10,000	10,000
	Bills Receivable Account To *B* (Being the acceptance of bill received)	Dr.	10,000	10,000
Mar. 1	Bank Account Rebate on Bills Discounted Account To Bills Receivable Account (Being retirement of bill by *B* one month before maturity, the rebate being given to him at 12% p.a.)	Dr. Dr.	9,900 100	10,000

Books of B
JOURNAL ENTRIES

Date	Particulars		Rs.	Rs.
Jan. 1	Purchases Account To A (Being the goods purchased from A on credit)	Dr.	10,000	10,000
	A To Bills Payable Account (Being the acceptance of bill given to A)	Dr.	10,000	10,000
Mar. 1	Bills Payable Account To Bank Account To Rebate on Bills Discounted Account (Being the bill discharged under rebate @ 12% p.a.)	Dr.	10,000	9,900 100

Working Note :

1. Computation of Rebate :

$$10,000 \times \frac{12}{100} \times \frac{12}{100} = \text{Rs. } 100$$

Q.4 (b) (Depreciation Accounting). A purchased on 1st January, 1993 certain machinery for Rs. 1,94,000 and spent Rs. 6,000 on its erection. On 1st July, 1993 additional machinery costing Rs. 1,00,000 was purchased. On 1st July, 1995 the machinery purchased on 1st January, 1993 having become absolute was auctioned for Rs. 1,00,000 and on the same date a new machinery was purchased at a cost of Rs. 1,50,000. Depreciation was provided for annually on 31st December at the rate of 10% per annum on the original cost of the machinery. No depreciation need be provided when a machinery is sold or auctioned, for that part of the year in which sale or auction took place. But for the above, depreciation shall be provided on time basis. In 1996 however, A changed this method of providing depreciation and adopted the method of writing off 15% p.a. on the written down value on the balance as appeared in machinery account on 1.1.1996.

Show the machinery account for the calendar years 1993 to 1996.

Solution :

Dr.   **MACHINERY ACCOUNT**   Cr.

1993	Particulars	Rs.	1993	Particulars	Rs.
Jan. 1	To Bank A/c (Purchase price) To Bank A/c (Cost of erection)	1,94,000 6,000	Dec. 31	By Depreciation A/c By Balance c/d	25,000 2,75,000
July 1	To Bank A/c (Purchase price)	1,00,000			
		3,00,000			3,00,000
1994			1994		
Jan. 1	To Balance b/d	2,75,000	Dec. 31	Depreciation A/c By Balance c/d	30,000 2,45,000
		2,75,000			2,75,000

(Contd.)

1993	Particulars	Rs.	1993	Particulars	Rs.
1995			1995		
Jan. 1	To Balance b/d	2,45,000	July 1	By Bank A/c (Sale)	1,00,000
July 1	To Bank A/c	1,50,000	Dec. 31	By Profit and Loss A/c (loss on sale of machinery)	60,000
				By Depreciation A/c	17,500
				By Balance c/d	2,17,500
		3,95,000			3,95,000
1996			1996		
Jan. 1	To Balance b/d	2,17,500	Dec. 31	By Depreciation A/c (15% on 2,17,500)	32,625
				By Balance c/d	1,84,875
		2,17,500			2,17,500

Working Notes :

1. *Computation of Depreciation*
   (10% per annum on the original cost)

	Machinery *I* [Date of Purchase : 1st Jan., 1993	Machinery *II* 1st July, 1993	Machinery *III* 1st July, 1995]
	Rs.	Rs.	Rs.
1993	20,000	5,000	
	$2,00,000 \times 10/100$	$1,00,000 \times 10/100 \times 6/12$	
	= 20,000	= 10,000	
1994			—
1995	20,000	10,000	= 7,500 $1,50,000 \times 6/12 \times 10/100$

2. Loss on Sale of Machinery

	Rs.
Original Cost (including erection charges)	2,00,000
Less : Total Depreciation (on Machinery *I*)	40,000
WDV on the date of sale	1,60,000
Less : Sale proceeds	1,00,000
Loss on sale of machinery	60,000

Alternate to Q.4 (Consignment Accounts). X of Calcutta on 15th January, 1997 sent to Y of Bombay a consignment of 250 televisions costing Rs. 10,000 each. Expenses of Rs. 7,000 were met by the consignor. Y of Bombay spent Rs. 4,500 for clearance on 30th January, 1997 and the selling expenses were Rs. 500 per television as and when the sale made by Y.

Y sold, on 4th March, 1997, 150 televisions at Rs. 14,000 per television and again on 10th April, 1997, 75 televisions at Rs. 14,400.

Mr. Y was entitled to a commission of Rs. 500 per television sold plus one-fourth of the amount by which the gross sale proceeds *less* total commission there on exceeded a sum calculated at the rate of Rs. 12,500 per television sold. Y sent the account sale and the amount due to X on 30th April, 1997 by bank demand draft.

You are required to show the consignment account and Y's account in the books of X.

(15 Marks)

Solution :

Dr.   CONSIGNMENT ACCOUNT   Cr.

Date 1997	Particulars	Rs.	Date 1997	Particulars	Rs.
Jan. 15	To Goods sent on Consignment A/c	25,00,000	March 4	By Y (Sales)	21,00,000
Jan. 15	To Bank A/c	7,000	April 10	By Y (Sales)	10,80,000
Jan. 30	To Y (Clearance expenses)	4,500	April 30	By Consignment Stock A/c	2,51,150
March 4	To Y (Selling expenses)	75,000			
April 10	To Y (Selling expenses)	37,500			
April 30	To Y (Commission)	1,63,500			
	To Profit transferred to Profit and Loss A/c	6,43,650			
		34,31,150			34,31,150

Dr.   Y BOMBAY   Cr.

Date 1997	Particulars	Rs.	Date 1997	Particulars	Rs.
March 4	To Consignment A/c	21,00,000	Jan. 30	By Consignment A/c (Clearance Expenses)	4,500
April 10	To Consignment A/c	10,80,000	March 4	By Consignment A/c (Selling Expenses)	75,000
			April 10	By Consignment A/c (Selling Expenses)	37,500
			April 30	By Consignment A/c (Commission)	1,63,500
				By Bank A/c	28,99,500
		31,80,000			31,80,000

Working Notes :

1. Computation of Commission

Let total commission be x

$$x = 225 \times 500 + \frac{1}{4}[(21,00,000 + 10,80,000 - x - (12,500 \times 225)]$$

$$x = 1,12,500 + \frac{1}{4}\ [31,80,000 - x - 28,12,500]$$

$$x = 1,12,500 + 91,875 - \frac{x}{4}$$

$$\frac{5x}{4} = 2,04,375$$

$$x = 1,63,500$$

Total Commission   Rs. 1,63,500

2. *Computation of Closing Stock.*

	Rs.
25 Televisions @ Rs. 10,000	2,50,000
Add : Proportionate Expenses of the Consignor (7,000 × 25/250)	700
Add : Proportionate Clearance expenses paid by the consignee (4,500 × 25/250)	450
	2,51,150

Q.5 (Basic Concepts). State with reasons whether the following statements are True or False:

(1) The gain from sale of capital assets need not be added to revenue to ascertain the net profit of a business.

(2) Discount account should be balanced in the cash book.

(3) The expressions-depreciation is to be charged at 10% and 10% p.a. on furniture and fittings carry the same meaning.

(4) Error of principle involves an incorrect allocation of expenditure or receipt between capital and revenue.

(5) Interest charged by the bank will be deducted when the overdraft as per pass book is the starting point for preparing the bank reconciliation statement to arrive at the balance as per cash book at the end.

(6) No cancellation entry is required when a bill is renewed.

(7) Under the self-balancing system the general ledger adjustment account is always opened in the general ledger.

(8) If the consignee is not authorised to get the *del credere* commission, then he is liable for all losses on account of non-recovery of debts.

(9) A joint venture business has a definite life.

(10) If there appears a sports fund, the expenses incurred on sports activities will be taken to income and expenditure account. *(20 Marks)*

Solution :

(1) **True.** In order to ascertain the net profit from the business only revenue incomes and expenses are considered. Moreover, gain from the sale of capital asset is an item which is not from normal operations of the business.

(2) **False.** The discount account is not balanced in the cash book. The totals of debits and credits in the discount column, maintained in the Cash Book, are taken separately to the Discount Account in the ledger.

(3) **False.** The depreciation at 10% means depreciation has to be charged for the full period for which the accounts are made irrespective of the fact whether the asset was purchased during the course of the accounting period. However, depreciation at 10% per annum means depreciation has to be charged for the actual period the asset has been with the business.

(4) **True.** An error of principle is committed when a proper distinction is not made between a capital and revenue item.

(5) **True.** Interest charged by the bank is deducted from the overdraft shown by the bank pass book which has been taken as the starting point since this amount must not have been entered in the cash book. Hence, the balance as per cash book (overdraft) should be less than what has been shown as per the bank pass book.

(6) **False.** In case a bill is renewed, cancellation entry is required for the old bill.

(7) **False.** Under the self balancing system, the general ledger adjustment account is kept in the sales ledger as well as in the purchases ledger.

(8) **False.** The consignee is to bear loss for non-recovery of dues only when he gets special commission known as *del credere* commission for the purpose.

(9) **True.** A joint venture is for a particular adventure or business. It automatically comes to an end on the completion of that business or venture.

(10) **False.** In case a sports fund is maintained, all expenses and incomes relating to sports should be taken to that fund and not to the income and expenditure account.

Q.6 (Miscellaneous). Distinguish between any three of the following :

(1) Commission and Discount.

(2) Trial Balance and Balance Sheet.

(3) Fixed Capital and Fluctuating Capital.

(4) Capital Expenditure and Revenue Expenditure.

(5 × 4 = 20 Marks)

Solution :

(1) *Commission and Discount*

Commission may be termed as a remuneration payable to an employee for his services to the firm or to the agent for purchasing or selling goods, collection of debtors on behalf of the firm etc. The commission is computed as a percentage of the amount involved. The commission earned is considered as an income while commission allowed is considered as an expense for the business.

Following are examples of persons to whom commission may be allowed :-

(1) Selling or buying agents.

(2) Brokers and bankers.

(3) Property dealers for helping in renting out or purchases or sale of properties.

(4) Import-export agent in foreign trade.

Discount is a rebate allowed out of the sum due on account of any of the following events:-

(1) Settlement of debt before due date. It is termed as cash discount.

(2) Discount given to wholesellers or bulk buyers on the list price. This is termed as trade discount. Discount is also allowed on goods to the customers for purchasing of goods in excess of a certain quantity. It is termed as quantity discount.

Trade discount and quantity discount are not disclosed in the books. They are deducted from the list price of the goods in the invoice itself.

(3) Discount allowed on issue of shares and debentures.

(4) Discount charged by a bank on discounting of negotiable instruments.

(2) *Trial Balance and Balance Sheet*

The following are the points of distinction between a Trial Balance and a Balance Sheet:-

1. *Objective :* A trial balance is a statement prepared on a particular date to check primarily the arithmetical accuracy of books of account, while a balance sheet is prepared to disclose the financial position of a business on a particular date.

2. *Content :* A trial balance contains balances of ledger accounts, while a balance sheet contains all the balances relating to those ledger accounts which are either assets or liabilities of the business.

3. *Periodicity :* A trial balance may be prepared on a daily, weekly, monthly, quarterly or yearly basis, while a balance sheet is prepared only at the.end of the year. However, some time a half-yearly balance sheet is also prepared.

4. *Preparation :* A trial balance precedes a balance sheet, while a balance sheet succeeds a trial balance.

(3) *Fixed Capital and Fluctuating Capital*

Please refer to page 3.20 of the book.

(4) *Capital Expenditure and Revenue Expenditure*

Please refer to page 1.158 of the book.

CA FOUNDATION EXAMINATION
NOVEMBER 1997
Fundamentals Of Accounting

Q.1 (Non-profit Organisations). From the following Receipts and Payments Account of Mumbai Club, prepare Income and Expenditure A/c for the year ended 31.12.1996 and its Balance Sheet as on that date :

Receipts	Rs.	Payments	Rs.
Cash in Hand	4,000	Salary	2,000
Cash at Bank	10,000	Repair Expenses	500
Donations	5,000	Purchase of Furniture	6,000
Subscriptions	12,000	Misc. Expenses	500
Entrance Fees	1,000	Purchase of Investments	6,000
Interest on Investments	100	Insurance Premium	200
Interest Received from Bank	400	Billiard Table	8,000
Sale of Old Newspaper	150	Paper, Ink, etc.	150
Sale of Drama Tickets	1,050	Drama Expenses	500
		Cash in Hand (Closing)	2,650
		Cash at Bank (Closing)	7,200
	33,700		33,700

Information :

(1) Subscriptions in arrear for 1996 Rs. 900 and subscriptions in advance for 1997 Rs. 350.

(2) Insurance premium Outstanding Rs. 40.

(3) Misc. Expenses Prepaid Rs. 90.

(4) 50% of donation is to be capitalised.

(5) Entrance Fees are to be treated as revenue income.

(6) 8% interest has accrued on investment for five months.

(7) Billiard Table costing Rs. 30,000 was purchased during the last year and Rs. 22,000 were paid for it.   *(20 Marks)*

Solution :

Mumbai Club
INCOME AND EXPENDITURE ACCOUNT
For the year ended 31st December, 1996

Expenditure		Rs.	Income		Rs.
To Salary		2,000	By Donations	5,000	
To Repair Expenses		500	*Less :* 50% Capitalised	2,500	
To Misc. Expenses	500				2,500
Less : Prepaid	90	410			
To Insurance Premium	200		By Subscriptions	12,000	
Add : Outstanding	40	240	*Add :* Outstanding	900	
				12,900	
To Paper, Ink, etc.		150	Less : Advance for 97	350	
To Drama Expenses		500			12,550
To Surplus - Excess of			By Entrance Fees		1,000
Income over Expenditure		14,150	By Interest on Investment	100	
			Add : Accrued Interest	200	300
			$(6,000 \times 8/100 \times 5/12)$		
			By Interest received from Bank		400
			By Sale of Old Newspapers		150
			By Sale of Drama tickets		1,050
		17,950			17,950

Mumbai Club
BALANCE SHEET AS ON 31ST DECEMBER, 1996

Liabilities		Rs.	Assets	Rs.
Capital Fund			Billiard Table	30,000
Opening Balance	36,000		Furniture	6,000
Add : Surplus	14,150		Investments	6,000
Capitalised Donations	2,500	52,650	Interest Accrued	200
Outstanding Insurance Premium		40	Prepaid Expenses	90
Subscriptions Received in advance		350	Subscriptions Receivable	900
			Cash in Hand	2,650
			Cash at Bank	7,200
		53,040		53,040

Working Note :

Mumbai Club
BALANCE SHEET AS ON 31ST DECEMBER, 1995

Liabilities	Rs.	Assets	Rs.
Capital Fund	36,000	Billiard Table	30,000
(Balancing Figure)		Cash in Hand	4,000
Creditors for Billiard Table	8,000	Cash at Bank	10,000
	44,000		44,000

Note : In the absence of information, no depreciation has been charged on Billiard Table.

Q.2 (Partnership-Admission). *A, B* and *C* were in partnership, sharing profits and losses as to *A* one-half, *B* one-third and *C* one-sixth. As from 1st January, 1996 they admitted *D* into partnership on the following terms :

D to have a one-sixth share which he purchased entirely from *A* paying *A* Rs. 8,000 for that share of Goodwill. Of this amount, *A* had withdrawn Rs. 6,000 and put the balance in the firm as additional capital . As a condition to admission of *D* as a partner *D* also brought Rs. 5,000 capital into the firm. It was further agreed that the investments should be valued at its market value of Rs. 3,600 and plant be valued at Rs. 5,800.

The Balance Sheet of the old firm on 31.12.1995 was as follows :

Cash at Bank Rs. 8,000; Debtors Rs. 12,000; Stock Rs. 10,000; Investments at cost Rs. 6,000; Furniture Rs. 2,000; Plant Rs. 7,000; Creditors Rs. 21,000; Capital : *A* Rs. 12,000; *B* Rs. 8,000 and *C* Rs. 4,000.

The profits for the year 1996 were Rs. 12,000 and the drawings were : *A* Rs. 6,000, *B* Rs. 6,000, *C* Rs. 3,000 and *D* Rs. 3,000.

You are required to journalise the opening adjustments, prepare the opening Balance Sheet of the new firm as on 1st January, 1996 and given the capital account of each partner as on 31st December, 1996. *(15 Marks)*

Solution :

Journal Entries

Particulars		Dr. Rs.	Cr. Rs.
Bank A/c	Dr.	8,000	
To *A's* Capital A/c			8,000
(Being amount paid by *D* for share of goodwill purchased from *A*)			
A's Capital A/c	Dr.	6,000	
To Bank A/c			6,000
(Being amount withdrawn by *A*)			
Bank A/c	Dr.	5,000	
To *D's* Capital A/c			5,000
(Being capital brought in by *D*)			
Revaluation A/c	Dr.	3,600	
To Investments A/c			2,400
To Plant A/c			1,200
(Being revaluation of investments and plant recorded)			
A's Capital A/c	Dr.	1,800	
B's Capital A/c	Dr.	1,200	
C's Capital A/c	Dr.	600	
To Revaluation A/c			3,600
(Being loss on revaluation transferred to old partners in 3:2:1 ratio)			

BALANCE SHEET OF A, B, C & D (NEW FIRM)
As on 1st January, 1996

Liabilities	Rs.	Assets	Rs.
Capital Accounts :		Plant	5,800
A	12,200	Furniture	2,000
B	6,800	Investments	3,600
C	3,400	Stock	10,000
D	5,000	Debtors	12,000
Creditors	21,000	Cash at Bank	15,000
	48,400		48,400

Dr.   A'S CAPITAL ACCOUNT   **Cr.**

1996	Particulars	Rs.	1996	Particulars	Rs.
Dec. 31	To Drawings	6,000	Jan. 1	By Balance b/d	12,200
	To Balance c/d	10,200	Dec. 31	By Profit	4,000
		16,200			16,200

Dr.   B'S CAPITAL ACCOUNT   **Cr.**

1996	Particulars	Rs.	1996	Particulars	Rs.
Dec. 31	To Drawings	6,000	Jan. 1	By Balance b/d	6,800
	To Balance c/d	4,800	Dec. 31	By Profit	4,000
		10,800			10,800

Dr.   C'S CAPITAL ACCOUNT   **Cr.**

1996	Particulars	Rs.	1996	Particulars	Rs.
Dec. 31	To Drawings	3,000	Jan. 1	By Balance b/d	3,400
	To Balance c/d	2,400	Dec. 31	By Profit	2,000
		5,400			5,400

Dr.   D'S CAPITAL ACCOUNT   **Cr.**

1996	Particulars	Rs.	1996	Particulars	Rs.
Dec. 31	To Drawings	3,000	Jan. 1	By Bank	5,000
	To Balance c/d	4,000	Dec. 31	By Profit	2,000
		7,000			7,000

Working Notes :

(1) BALANCE SHEET OF A, B & C (OLD FIRM)
As on 31st December, 1995

Liabilities		Rs.	Assets	Rs.
Capital Accounts			Plant	7,000
A	12,000		Furniture	2,000
B	8,000		Investments	6,000
C	4,000	24,000	Stock	10,000
Creditors		21,000	Debtors	12,000
			Cash at Bank	8,000
		45,000		45,000

(2) Computation of New Profit Sharing Ratio :

	Old Ratio	New Ratio
A	$\dfrac{3}{6}$	$\dfrac{3}{6} - \dfrac{1}{6} = \dfrac{2}{6}$
B	$\dfrac{2}{6}$	$\dfrac{2}{6}$
C	$\dfrac{1}{6}$	$\dfrac{1}{6}$
D		$\dfrac{1}{6}$

Q.3 (Joint Venture). A and B decided to work a joint venture fore the sale of electric motors. On 21st May, 1996, A purchased 200 electric motors at Rs. 1,750 each and dispatched 150 motors to B incurring Rs. 10,000 as freight and insurance charges. Ten electric motors were damaged in transit. On 1st February, 1997, Rs. 5,000 was received by A from the insurance company in full settlement of his claim. On 15th March, 1997, A sold 50 electric motors at Rs. 2,250 each. He received Rs. 1,50,000 from B on 1st April, 1997.

On 25th May, 1996 B took delivery of electric motors and incurred the following expenses :

Clearing charges Rs. 1,700; Repair charges for motors damaged in transit Rs. 3,000, Godown rent Rs. 6,000. He sold the electric motors as below :

1.2.1997	10 damaged motors at Rs. 1,700 each
1.2.1997	40 motors at Rs. 2,000 each
15.3.1997	20 motors at Rs. 3,150 each
1.4.1997	80 motors at Rs. 2,500 each

It is agreed that they are entitled to commission at 10% on the respective sales effected by them and that the profits and losses shall be shared by A and B in the ratio of 2 : 1

B remits to A the balance of money due on 30th April, 1997.

Prepare : (i) Joint Venture Account in the books of A and (ii) Memorandum joint Venture Account.

Solution :

Books of A

Dr.   **JOINT VENTURE ACCOUNT WITH B**   Cr.

1996	Particulars	Rs.	1997	Particulars	Rs.
May 21	To Bank (Purchases)	3,50,000	Feb. 1	By Bank	
	To Bank (Expenses)	10,000		(Insurance claim)	5,000
1997			Mar. 15	Bank (Sale	
Mar. 15	To Commission	11,250		of 50 motors)	1,12,500
Apr. 30	To Profit taken to	39,700	Apr. 1	By Bank (B)	1,50,000
	Profit & Loss Account		Apr. 30	By Bank (B)	1,43,450
		4,10,950			4,10,950

MEMORANDUM JOINT VENTURE ACCOUNT

Particulars		Rs.	Particulars	Rs.
To A			By A	
Cost of Motors		3,50,000	(Insurance Claim)	5,000
Freight and Insurance		10,000	By A (Sales proceeds)	1,12,500
To B			By B (Sales)	3,60,000
Clearing charges		1,700		
Repairs		3,000		
Godown Rent		6,000		
To A (Commission)		11,250		
To B (commission)		36,000		
To Net Profit taken to P & L A/c				
A	39,700			
B	19,850	59,550		
		4,77,500		4,77,500

Q.4 (a) (Rectification of Errors). Briefly explain 'Suspense Account' appearing in a Trial balance. *(5 Marks)*

(For answer please refer to page 1.244 of the book.)

Q.4 (b) (Self Balancing). From the following particulars prepare Customers Control Account in General Ledger :

	Rs.
Opening Balance in Customers Ledger : (Dr.)	2,35,000
Opening Balance in Customers Ledger : (Cr.)	3,500
Goods Sold During the Year	7,65,000
Returns Inwards	15,000
Cash/Cheques Received	5,90,000
Bills Received	1,10,000
Discount Allowed	9,000
Cheque Received Dishonoured	5,000
Bills Received Dishonoured	7,000
Bad Debts	9,000

A debit of Rs. 1,500 is to be transferred from Customers Ledger to Suppliers Ledger. Similarly a credit entry of Rs. 1,600 is to be transferred from Suppliers Ledger to Customers Ledger. Closing credit balance in Customers Ledger is Rs. 3,000. *(10 marks)*

Solution :

General Ledger

Dr.   CUSTOMERS CONTROL ACCOUNT   Cr.

Particulars	Rs.	Particulars	Rs.
To Balance b/d	2,35,000	By Balance b/d	3,500
To General Ledger		By General Ledger Control A/c :	
Control A/c :		Bank/Cash	5,90,000
Sales	7,65,000	Returns Inwards	15,000
Bank (Cheque dishonoured)	5,000	Bill Receivable	1,10,000
Bills Receivable (dishonoured)	7,000	Discount	9,000
To Balance c/d	3,000	Transfer (1,500 + 1,600)	3,100
		By Balance c/d	2,75,400
		(Balancing figure)	
	10,15,000		10,15,000

Q.5 (a) (Account Current). What is an Account Current ? Explain Briefly. *(5 Marks)*

(For answer please refer to page 2.53 of the book)

Q.5 (b) (Average Due Date). Calculate Average Due Date from the following information:

Date of the bill	Term	Amount Rs.
August 10, 1996	3 Months	6,000
October 23, 1996	60 Days	5,000
December 4,1996	2 Months	4,000
January 14, 1997	60 Days	2,000
March 8, 1997	2 Months	3,000

(10 Marks)

Solution :

COMPUTATION OF AVERAGE DUE DATE

Date of Bill	Term	Due Date	No. of Days from the Basic date (10th August)	Amount Rs.	Product Rs.
Aug. 10, 1996	3 Months	Nov. 13, 1996	95	6,000	5,70,000
Oct. 23, 1996	60 Days	Dec. 24, 1996	136	5,000	6,80,000
Dec. 04, 1996	2 Months	Feb. 07, 1997	181	4,000	7,24,000
Jan. 14, 1997	60 Days	Mar. 18, 1997	220	2,000	4,40,000
Mar. 08, 1997	2 Months	May 11, 1997	274	3,000	8,22,000
				20,000	32,36,000

$$\text{Average Due Date} \quad = \quad \text{Basic date} + \frac{\text{Total of Products}}{\text{Total of Amounts}}$$

$$= \quad \text{10th August} + \frac{32,36,000}{20,000} \quad = \quad \text{10th August} + 161.8$$

$$= \text{162 days (approx.) after}$$
$$\text{10th August, 1996}$$
$$\text{i.e. 19th January, 1997.}$$

Note : The due date of the second bill dated 23rd October, 1996 is 25th December, 1996. However, 25th December is a public holiday hence, the preceeding day i.e., 24th December has been taken as the due date of the bill.

Q.5 (Basic Concepts). State with reasons whether the following statements are True or False:

   (1)   An expenditure intended to benefit the current period is a revenue expenditure.

   (2)   The Trial Balance ensures the arithmetical accuracy of the books.

   (3)   The relationship between the consignor and the consignee is that of Principal and Agent.

   (4)   Depreciation cannot be provided incase of loss, in a financial year.

   (5)   Profit and loss account shows the financial position of the concern.

   (6)   Bank Reconciliation statement is prepared to arrive at the bank balance.

   (7)   Sale of office furniture should be credited to sales account.

   (8)   Receipts and payments account is a summary of all capital receipts and payments.

   (9)   The proprietor of a shop feels that he has made a loss due to closing stock being zero.

  (10) Expenditure which results in acquisition of a permanent asset of enduring benefit to the business is a capital expenditure.   *(20 marks)*

Solution :

   (1)   **True.** An expenditure is taken to be a revenue expenditure if its benefit does not extend beyond the current accounting period.

   (2)   **True.** One of the objectives of the trial balance is to check the arithmetical accuracy of the books of account.

   (3)   **True.** The relationship between he consignor and the consignee is that of principal and agent since the consignee agrees to sell goods on behalf of and at the risk of the consignor.

   (4)   **False.** Depreciation is charged against profits and hence it is to be provided whether there is a profit or a loss.

   (5)   **False.** The profit and loss account shows a profit or a loss made or incurred by a business during a period. The financial position is shown by the balance sheet.

   (6)   **False.** Bank reconciliation statement is prepared to reconcile the balance shown by the bank pass book with the balance as shown by the cash book. This helps in identifying the causes of difference between the two and errors, if any.

   (7)   **False.** Sales account should be credited only when the sale of goods and not with the sale of capital assets.

   (8)   **False.** Receipts and payments account is a summary of all receipts and payments whether of capital or revenue nature.

(9) **False.** Profit or loss made or incurred by a business is ascertained by comparing sales with the cost of sales. The closing stock does not determine the operational profit of a business.

(10) **True.** Capital expenditure is an expenditure incurred for acquisition of an asset to give a long-term advantage to the business.

Q.6. Distinguish between any three of the following :

(a) Real Account and Nominal Account.

(b) Partnership and Joint Venture.

(c) Consignment and Sale.

(d) Bill of Exchange and Promissory Note.

(4 × 5 = 20 Marks)

Solution :

(a) *Real Account and Nominal Account*

For answer please refer to page 1.32 of the book.

(b) *Partnership and Joint Venture*

For answer please refer to page 2.32 of the book.

(c) *Consignment and Sale :* The following are the points of distinction between consignment and sale.

1. *Parties :* In a consignment transaction are termed as consignor and consignee while in the concerned parties the case of a sale the concerned parties are known as seller and buyer.

2. *Transfer of Ownership :* In the case of a consignment, the property in goods does not pass from the consignor to the consignee while in the case of a sale of goods, the property in goods passes from the seller to the buyer. Thus, the consignment is a transfer of mere possession of goods while the sale is a transaction involving transfer of ownership of goods.

3. *Transfer of risk :* In the case of a consignment, the consignee acts as agent of the consignor. Hence, all risks relating to destruction or damage of goods etc. are to be borne by the consignor. While in the case of a sale the buyer having bought the goods becomes buyer of the goods and, therefore, has to bear all risks.

(d) *Bill of Exchange and Promissory Note*

(1) *Number of parties :* There are three parties in the case of a bill of exchange - drawer, drawee and payee. One person may, however, assume any of the two capacities out of the three. But in the case of promissory note, there are only two parties - maker and payee.

In the case of a promissory note maker cannot be the payee but in the case of a bill of exchange drawer and payee or drawer and drawee may be one and the same person. Where in a bill of exchange, the drawer and drawee are the same person, the holder may treat instrument at his option, either as a bill of exchange or as a promissory note.

(2) *Promise and Order :* A promissory note contains a promise and an undertaking and not an order to pay. A bill must at least imply that the drawer has a right to ask the drawee to pay, though however politely it may be worded.

(3) *Acceptance :* A bill payable after sight requires acceptance of the drawee before it is presented for payment while a pronote does not.

(4) *Nature of liability :* The liability of the maker of a note is primary and absolute but that of a drawer of a bill of exchange is secondary and conditional since he can be held liable only on the default of the acceptor in payment of the money due and provided the fact of dishonour has been notified to him.

(5) *Maker's position :* In a promissory note maker stands in an immediate relationship with the payee, whereas in a bill of exchange, the maker (i.e. drawer) stands in immediate relationship with the acceptor and not the payee.

The position of a maker of a promissory note also differs from the position of an acceptor of a bill of exchange. Maker himself being the originator of a promissory note, cannot make it condition, while the acceptor can accept the bill conditionally because his contract is only supplementary, being superimposed on that of the drawer.

CA FOUNDATION EXAMINATION
MAY 1998
Fundamentals Of Accounting

Q.1 (Final Accounts). From the following balances and information, prepare Trading and Profit and Loss Account of Mr. *X* for the year ended 31st March, 1998 and a Balance Sheet as on that date :

	Dr. Rs.	Cr. Rs.
X's Capital Account	—	10,000
Plant and Machinery	3,600	—
Depreciation on Plant and Machinery	400	—
Repairs to Plant	520	—
Wages	5,400	—
Salaries	2,100	—
Income-tax of Mr. X	100	—
Cash in Hand and at Bank	400	—
Land and Building	14,900	—
Depreciation on Building	500	—
Purchases	25000	—
Purchases Return	—	300
Sales	—	49,800
Bank Overdraft	—	760
Accrued Income	300	—
Salaries Outstanding	—	400
Bills Receivable	3,000	—
Provision for Bad Debts	—	1,000
Bills Payable	—	1,600
Bad Debts	200	—
Discount on Purchases	—	708
Debtors	7,000	—
Creditors	—	6,252
Opening Stock	7,400	—
	70,820	70,820

Information :

(i) Stock on 31st March, 1998 was Rs. 6,000.

(ii) Write off Rs. 600 for Bad Debt and maintain a provision for Bad Debts at 5% on Debtors.

(iii) Goods costing Rs. 1,000 were sent to customer for Rs. 1,200 on 30th March, 1998 on sale or return basis. This was recorded as actual sales.

(iv) Rs. 240 paid as rent of the office were debited to Landlord account and were included in the list of debtors.

(v) General manager is to be given commission at 10% of net profit after charging the commission of the works manager and his own.

(vi) Works manager is to be given commission at 12% of net profit before charging the commission of General Manager and his own. *(20 Marks)*

Solution :

Mr. X
TRADING AND PROFIT AND LOSS ACCOUNT
For the year ended 31st March, 1998

Particulars		Rs.	Particulars		Rs.
To Opening Stock		7,400	By Sales	49,800	
To Purchases	25,000		*Less :* Sale on		
Less : Returns	300		approval basis	1,200	48,600
Discount on Purchases	708	23,992			
To Wages		5,400			
To Gross Profit c/d		18,808	By Closing Stock	6,000	
			Add : Stock with		
			Customers (at cost)	1,000	7,000
		55,600			55,600
To Repairs to Plant		520	By Gross Profit b/d		18,808
To Salaries		2,100			
To Rent		240			
To Bad Debts	200				
Add : Addl. Bad Debts	600				
New Provision	248				
	1,048				
Less : Old Provision	1,000	48			
To Depreciation :					
Plant & Machinery	400				
Building	500	900			
To Commission to					
Works Manager (WN 3)		1,800			
To Commission to					
General Manager (WN 4)		1,200			
To Net Profit (transferred					
to Capital A/c)		12,000			
		18,808			18,808

Mr. X
BALANCE SHEET AS ON 31ST MARCH, 1998

Liabilities		Amount Rs.	Assets		Amount Rs.
Capital Account	10,000		Land and Building		14,900
Less : Income Tax	100		Plant and Machinery		3,600
	9,900		Stock in Hand	6,000	
Add : Net Profit	12,000	21,900	Add : Stock with Customer	1,000	7,000
Bank Overdraft		760	Debtors (WN 1)	4,960	
Bills Payable		1,600	Less : Provision for		
Sundry Creditors		6,252	Bad Debts	248	4,712
Salaries Outstanding		400	Bills Receivable		3,000
Outstanding Commission			Accrued Income		300
Works Manager	1,800		Cash in Hand and at Bank		400
General Manager	1,200	3,000			
		33,912			33,912

Working Notes :

(1) Computation of Debtors :

	Rs.	Rs.
Debtors as per Trial balance		7,000
Less : Debtors on account of goods sold on approval basis	1,200	
Landlord Account wrongly considered as debtor	240	1,440
		5,560
Less : Bad Debts written off		600
		4,960

(2) New Provision for Bad Debts Required :
5% on Debtors Rs. 4,960 = Rs. 248

(3) Computation of Commission payable to Works Manager :
12% of Rs. 15,000 = Rs. 1,800

(4) Computation of Commission payable to General Manager :

$$\frac{10}{110} \times Rs. \ (15,000 - 1,800) = Rs. \ 1,200$$

Q.2 (Partnership-Retirement). A, B and C were in partnership sharing profits in the proportions of 5 : 4 : 3. The Balance Sheet of the firm as on 31st March, 1998 was as under :

Liabilities		Rs.	Assets	Rs.
Capital Accounts :	A	1,35,930	Goodwill	40,000
	B	95,120	Fixtures	8,200
	C	61,170	Stock	1,57,300
Sundry Creditors		41,690	Sundry Debtors	93,500
			Cash	34,910
		3,33,910		3,33,910

A had been suffering from ill-health and gave notice that he wished to retire. An agreement was, therefore, entered into as on 31st March, 1998, the terms of which were as follows :

(i) The Profit and Loss Account for the year ended 31st March, 1998 which showed a net profit of Rs. 48,000 was to be re-opened. *B* was to be credited with Rs. 4,000 as bonus, in consideration of the extra work which had devolved upon him during the year. The profit-sharing ratio was to be revised as from 1st April, 1997 to 3 : 4 : 4.

(ii) Goodwill was to be valued at two years' purchase of the average profits of the preceding five years. The Fixtures were to be valued by an independent valuer. A provision of 2% was to be made for doubtful debts and the remaining assets were to be taken at their book values.

The valuations arising out of the above agreement were Goodwill Rs. 56,800 and Fixtures Rs. 10,980.

B and *C* agreed, as between themselves, to continue the business, sharing profits in the ratio of 3 : 2 and decided to eliminate Goodwill from the Balance Sheet, to retain the Fixtures on the books at the revised value, and to increase the provision for doubtful debts to 6%.

You are required to submit the journal entries necessary to give effect to the above arrangements and to draw up the capital accounts of the partners after carrying out all adjusting entries as stated above. *(15 Marks)*

Solution :

JOURNAL ENTRIES

Particulars		Dr. Rs.	Cr. Rs.
A's Capital Account	Dr.	20,000	
B's Capital Account	Dr.	16,000	
C's Capital Account	Dr.	12,000	
To Profit and Loss Adjustment Account			48,000
(Being profit written back for making adjustments)			
Profit and Loss Adjustment Account	Dr.	4,000	
To *B's* Capital Account			4,000
(Being bonus credited to *B's* Capital Account)			
Profit & Loss Adjustment Account	Dr.	44,000	
To *A's* Capital Account			12,000
To *B's* Capital Account			16,000
To *C's* Capital Account			16,000
(Being distribution of profits in the new ratio of 3 : 4 : 4)			
Goodwill Account	Dr.	16,800	
Fixtures Account	Dr.	2,780	
To Provision for Bad Debts Account			1,870
To *A's* Capital Account			4,830
To *B's* Capital Account			6,440

(Contd.)

Particulars		Dr. Rs.	Cr. Rs.
To C's Capital Account (Being revaluation of assets on A's retirement)			6,440
A's Capital Account To A's Loan Account (Being transfer of A's Capital Account to his Loan Account)	Dr.	1,32,760	1,32,760
B's Capital Account C's Capital Account To Goodwill Account To Provision for Bad Debts Account (Being writing off goodwill and increasing provision for bad debts)	Dr. Dr.	36,324 24,216	56,800 3,740

Dr.   PARTNERS' CAPITAL ACCOUNT   Cr.

Particulars	A Rs.	B Rs.	C Rs.	Particulars	A Rs.	B Rs.	C Rs.
To Profit & Loss Adjustment A/c	20,000	16,000	12,000	By Balance b/d	1,35,930	95,120	61,170
To A's Loan A/c	1,32,760	—	—	By Profit and Loss Adjustment A/c	—	4,000	—
To Goodwill A/c and Provision For Bad Debts A/c	—	36,324	24,216	By Profit and Loss Adjustment A/c	12,000	16,000	16,000
To Balance c/d	—	69,236	47,394	By Goodwill A/c and Fixtures A/c	4,830	6,440	6,440
	1,52,760	1,21560	83,610		1,52,760	1,21,560	83,610

Q.3 (a) Inventory Valuation. From the following information, ascertain the value of stock as on 31.3.1997 :

	Rs.
Value of Stock on 1.4.1996	70,000
Purchases during the period from 1.4.1996 to 31.3.1997	3,46,000
Manufacturing Expenses during the above period	70,000
Sales during the same period	5,22,000

At the time of valuing stock on 31.3.1996, a sum of Rs. 6,000 was written off a particular item which was originally purchased for Rs. 20,000 and was sold for Rs. 16,000. But for the above transaction the gross profit earned during the year was 25% on cost. *(10 Marks)*

Solution :

The value of stock on 31.3.1997 can be found out by preparing a Memorandum Trading Account.

MEMORANDUM TRADING ACCOUNT
For the year ending on 31.3.1997

Particulars	Rs.	Particulars	Rs.
To Opening Stock	76,000	Py Sales	5,22,00C
(70,000 + 6,000)		By *P&L* (Loss on sale of	
To Purchases	3,46,000	Abrormal Stock)	4,000
To Manufacturing Expenses	70,000	By Closing Stock	67,200
To Gross Profit			
(5,06,000 × 25/125)	1,01,200		
	5,93,200		5,93,200

Alternatively the value of stock on 31.3.197 can also be found out by the following statement:

STATEMENT OF VALUATION OF STOCK AS ON 31ST MARCH, 1997

		Rs.
Value of Stock on 1st April, 1996		70,000
Add : Purchases during the period		
From 1.4.1996 to 31.3.1997		3,46,000
Add : Manufacturing Expenses during		
the above period		70,000
		4,86,000
Less : Cost of sales during the period		
Sales	5,22,000	
Less : Gross Profit (See *WN*)	1,03,200	
		4,18,800
Value of Stock as on 31.3.1997		67,200

Working Note :

	Rs.
Computation of Gross Profit :	
Gross Profit on Normal Sales	1,01,200

$$\left[\frac{20}{100} \times (5,22,000 - 16,000) \right]$$

Gross Profit on an Abnormal Item	2,000
[16,000 − (20,000 − 6,000)]	
	1,03,200

Q.3 (b) Write a short note on "Depletion Method" of providing depreciation.

For answer please refer to page 1.286 of the book

Alternate to Q 3 (Consignment). *D* of Delhi appointed *A* of Agra as its selling agent on the following terms :

(a) Goods to be sold at invoice price or over.

(b) A to be entitled to a commission of 7.5% on the invoice price and 20% of any surplus price realised.

(c) The principals to draw on the agent of 30 days bill for 80% of the invoice price.

On 1st February, 1998, one thousand cycles were consigned to A, each cycle costing Rs. 640 including freight and invoiced at Rs. 800.

Before 31st March, 1998 (when the principal's books are closed) A met his acceptance on the due date; sold off 820 cycles at an average price of Rs. 930 per cycle, the sale expenses being Rs. 12,500; and remitted the amount due by means of Bank Draft.

Twenty of the unsold cycles were shop-soiled and were to be valued at a depreciation of 50%.

Show by means of ledger accounts how these transactions would be recorded in the books of A, and find out the value of closing stock with A at which value D will account for the balance stock. *(15 Marks)*

Solution :

Dr.			D			Cr.
1998	Particulars	Rs.	1998	Particulars		Rs.
Feb. 1	To Bills Payable A/c (80% of Rs. 8,00,000)	6,40,000	Mar. 31	By Cash/Bank A/c (820 × 930)		7,62,600
Mar. 31	To Cash A/c (Expenses)	12,500				
	To Commission A/c	70,520				
	To Bank A/c	39,580				
		7,62,600				7,62,600

Dr.		BILLS PAYABLE ACCOUNT			Cr.
1998	Particulars	Rs.	1998	Particulars	Rs.
Mar. 4	To Cash/Bank A/c	6,40,000	Feb. 1	By D	6,40,000
		6,40,000			6,40,000

VALUE OF CLOSING STOCK WITH A

	Rs.
160 cycles at Rs. 640 (cost price including freight)	1,02,400
20 cycles (shop-soiled) at 50% of the cost i.e. at Rs. 320 each	6,400
Value of Closing stock with A (at cost)	1,08,800

Working Note :

Computation of Commission

	Rs.
7.5% on the invoice price amount (820 × Rs. 800) Rs. 6,56,000	49,200
20% on the surplus price amount (820 × Rs. 120) Rs. 1,06,600	21,320
	70,520

Q.4 (Rectification Errors). A book-keeper finds the difference in the Trial Balance amounting to Rs. 1,000 and puts it in the Suspense Account.

Later on he detects following errors.

1. Purchased goods from Ravi Rs. 15,000 but entered into Sales Book.
2. Received one bill for Rs. 2,50,000 from Arun but recorded in Bills Payable Book.

3. An item of Rs. 3,500 relating to prepaid rent account was omitted to be brought forward.

4. An item of Rs. 2,000 in respect of purchase returns, had been wrongly entered in the purchase book.

5. Rs. 25,000 paid to Hari against our acceptance were debited to Harish Account.

6. Bills received from Janaki for repairs done to radio Rs. 2,500 and radio supplied for Rs. 45,000 were entered in the Purchase Book as Rs. 46,000.

Give rectifying journal entries with full narration and prepare Suspense Account.

(15 Marks)

Solution :

RECTIFYING JOURNAL ENTRIES

S.No.	Particulars		Debit Rs.	Credit Rs.
1.	Purchases A/c	Dr.	15,000	
	Sales A/c	Dr.	15,000	
	To Ravi A/c			30,000
	(Being rectification of error due to purchases being wrongly entered in the Sales Book)			
2.	Bills Receivable A/c	Dr.	25,000	
	Bills Payable A/c	Dr.	25,000	
	To Arun			50,000
	(Being the rectification of the wrong recording in Bills Payable Book in place of Bills Receivable Book)			
3.	Prepaid Rent A/c	Dr.	3,500	
	To Suspense A/c			3,500
	(Being prepaid rent account was omitted to be brought forward, the error rectified)			
4.	Suspense A/c	Dr.	4,000	
	To Purchases A/c			2,000
	To Purchase Returns A/c			2,000
	(Being purchase returns wrongly entered in the Purchase Book, the error now rectified)			
5.	Bills Payable A/c	Dr.	25,000	
	To Harish			25,000
	(Being the rectification of wrong debit to Harish in place of Bills Payable Account)			
6.	Repairs A/c	Dr.	2,500	
	Radio A/c	Dr.	45,000	
	To Purchases A/c			46,000
	To Suspense A/c			1,500
	(Being the recording of amount of repairs and cost of radio purchased in the Purchases Book, the error now rectified)			

Suspense Account

Dr.				Cr.
Particulars	Rs.	Particlars		Rs.
To Balance b/d	1,000	By Prepaid Rent A/c		3,500
To Purchases A/c	2,000	By Repairs and Radio A/c		1,500
To Purchase Returns A/c	2,000			
	5,000			5,000

Q.5 (Basic Concepts). State with reasons whether the following statements are True or False:

(1) The provision for discount on debtors is calculated after deducting the provision for doubtful debts from Debtors.

(2) Freight and Cartage expenses paid on purchases of goods is added to the amount of purchase.

(3) Goodwill is a current asset.

(4) Loss of stock is said to be normal loss when such loss is not due to inherent characteristics of the commodities.

(5) A tallied Trial Balance will not reveal compensating errors and errors on account of wrong balancing.

(6) Wages paid to workers to produce a tool to be captively consumed is capital expenditure.

(7) Accrual concept implies accounting on cash basis.

(8) The relationship between the consignor and the consignee is that of a Principal and Agent.

(9) Error of Principle involves an incorrect allocation of expenditure or receipt between capital and revenue.

(10) No cancellation entry is required when a bill is renewed. *(20 Marks)*

Solution :

(1) **True.** The provision for discount on debtors is deducted from debtors to compute the amount of good debtors who may make prompt payment for earning discount.

(2) **True.** Any expenditure incurred in bringing purchase of goods to the godown and making them fit for sale is taken as cost of purchases.

(3) **False.** The goodwill is an intangible asset and falls in the category of a fixed asset.

(4) **False.** The loss due to inherent characteristics is taken as a normal loss. The loss caused by theft, fire, etc. is an abnormal loss.

(5) **Partly True and partly false.** A tallied trial balance does not disclose the loss due to compensating errors. A trial balance will not tally if the errors are on account of wrong balancing. However, this statement proved to be true in case wrong balancing is fully compensated by mutual errors.

(6) **True.** Wages paid to workers for creation of an asset for long-term use in the business is a capital expenditure.

(7) **False.** Accrual concept involves consideration of all incomes and expenses whether paid in cash or not. They should have become due only.

(8) **True.** The relationship between the consignor and the consignee is that of principal and agent since the consignee agrees to sale goods on behalf of and at the risk of the consignor.

(9) **True.** An error of principle is committed when a proper distinction is not made between a capital and revenue item.

(10) **False.** In case a bill is renewed, cancellation entry is required for the old bill.

Q. 6 (Miscellaneous). Briefly explain the difference between any three of the following:

(a)	Contingent Liability and Other Liabilities.	*(5 Marks)*
(b)	Capital Receipts and Revenue Receipts.	*(5 Marks)*
(c)	Commission and Discount.	*(5 Marks)*
(d)	Trial Balance and Balance Sheet.	*(5 Marks)*

Solution :

(a) *Contingent Liability and Other Liabilities*

Liability has been defined as "the financial obligation of an enterprise other than owners' funds."[1]

While contingent liability is "an obligation relating to an existing condition or situation which may arise in future depending upon the occurrence non-occurrence of one or more uncertain future events."[2] Thus, a liability indicates a definite obligation on the part of the business while a contingent liability may or may not arise depending upon the contingency concerned.

A liability is shown in the balance sheet while a contingent liability is shown outside the balance sheet. A contingent liability would become a liability only on the happening or non-happening of the even on which it is depending.

(b) *Capital Receipts and Revenue Receipts*

For answer please refer to page 1.161 of the book.

(c) For answer please refer to Q 6 (1) of May, 1997 examination

(d) For answer please refer to Q 6 (2) of May 1997 examination.

1, 2 Terminology adopted, ICAI.

CA FOUNDATION EXAMINATION
NOVEMBER 1998
Fundamentals Of Accounting

Q.1 (Non-profit making Organisations). The following informations were obtained from the books of Delhi Club as on 31.3.1998. at the end of the first year of the Club. You are required to prepare Receipts and Payments Account, Income and Expenditure Account for the year ended 31.3.1998 and a Balance Sheet as at 31.3. 1998 on mercantile basis :

(*i*)   Donations received for Building and Library Room   Rs. 2,00,000.

(*ii*) Other revenue income and actual receipts :

	Revenue Income Rs.	Actual Receipts Rs.
Entrance Fees	17,000	17,000
Subscription	20,000	19,000
Locker Rents	600	600
Sundry Income	1,600	1,060
Refreshment Account	—	16,000

(*iii*) Other revenue expenditure and actual payments :

	Revenue Expenditure Rs.	Actual Payments Rs.
Land (cost Rs. 10,000)	—	10,000
Furniture (cost Rs. 1,46,000)	—	1,30,000
Salaries	5,000	4,800
Maintenance of Playgrounds	2,000	1,000
Rent	8,000	8,000
Refreshment Account	—	8,000

Donations to the extent of Rs. 25,000 were utilised for the purchase of Library Books, balance was still unutilised. In order to keep it safe, 9% Govt. Bonds of Rs. 1,60,000 were purchased on 31.3.1998. Remaining amount was put in the Bank on 31.3.1998 under the term deposit. Depreciation at 10% p.a. was to be provided for the whole year on Furniture and Library Books.   *(20 marks)*

Solution :

Delhi Club
RECEIPTS AND PAYMENTS ACCOUNT
For the year ended 31st March, 1998

Receipts	Rs.	Payments	Rs.
To Donations for Building		By Land	10,000
and Library Room	2,00,000	By Furniture	1,30,000
To Entrance Fees	17,000	By Salaries	4,800
To Subscription	19,000	By Maintenance of Playgrounds	1,000
To Locker Rents	600	By Rent	8,000
To Sundry Income	1,060	By Refreshment Account	8,000
To Refreshment Account	16,000	By Library Books	25,000
To Balance c/d :		By 9% Govt. Bonds	1,60,000
(Overdraft)	1,08,140	By Bank Term Deposit	15,000
	3,61,800		3,61,800

Delhi Club
INCOME AND EXPENDITURE ACCOUNT
For the year ended 31st March, 1998

Expenditure		Rs.	Income		Rs.
To Salaries	4,800		By Entrance Fees*		17,000
Add : Outstanding	200	5,000	By Subscription	19,000	
To Maintenance of			Add : Outstanding	1,000	20,000
Playgrounds	1,000				
Add : Outstanding	1,000	2,000	By Locker Rents		600
To Rent		8,000	By Sundry Income	1,060	
To Depreciation :			Add : Outstanding	540	1,600
Furniture	14,600				
Library Books	2,500	17,100	By Refreshment Account		8,000
			(16,000 − 8,000)		
To Surplus - Excess of					
Income over Expenditure		15,100			
		47,200			47,200

Delhi Club
BALANCE SHEET AS ON 31ST MARCH, 1998

Liabilities	Rs.	Assets		Rs.
Capital Fund (Surplus from				
Income & Expenditure A/c	15,100	Land		10,000
Building & Library		Furniture	1,46,000	
Room Fund	2,00,000	Less : Depreciation	14,600	1,31,400
Creditors for Furniture	16,000	Library Books	25,000	
Creditors for Expenses :		Less : Depreciation	2,500	22,500

(Contd..)

Liabilities		Rs.	Assets	Rs.
Salaries Outstanding	200		9% Govt. Bonds	1,60,000
Maintenance of			Bank Term Deposit	15,000
Playgrounds	1,000	1,200	Subscription Receivable	1,000
Bank Overdraft		1,08,140	Sundry Income Receivable	540
		3,40,440		3,40,440

Q.2 (Partnership - Admission). A and B partners of X & Co. sharing profits and losses in 3 : 2 ratio between themselves. On 31st March, 1998, the Balance Sheet of the firm was as follows :

BALANCE SHEET OF X & CO. AS AT 31.3.1998

Liabilities		Rs.	Assets	Rs.
Capital Accounts :			Plant and Machinery	20,000
A	37,000		Furniture and Fitting	5,000
B	28,000	65,000	Stock	15,000
			Sundry Debtors	20,000
Sundry Creditors		5,000	Cash on Hand	10,000
		70,000		70,000

X agrees to join the business on the following conditions as and from 1.4.1998 :

(a) He will introduce Rs. 25,000 as his capital and pay Rs. 15,000 to the partners as premium for Goodwill for 1/3rd share of the future profits of the firm.

(b) A revaluation of assets of the firm will be made by reducing the value of Plant and Machinery to Rs. 15,000, Stock by 10%, Furniture and Fitting by Rs. 1,000 and by making a provision of bad and doubtful debts at Rs. 750 on sundry debtors.

You are asked to prepare Profit and Loss adjustment Account, Capital accounts of partners including the incoming partner X, Balance Sheet of the firm after admission of X and also find out the new profit sharing ratio assuming the relative ratio of the old partners will be in equal proportion after admission. *(15 Marks)*

Solution :

Dr.   PROFIT AND LOSS ADJUSTMENT ACCOUNT   Cr.

Particulars	Rs.	Particulars		Rs.
To Plant and Machinery A/c	5,000	By Partners' Capital Accounts :		
To Stock A/c	1,500	- Loss on revaluation		
To Furniture and Fitting A/c	1,000	A (3/5)	Rs. 4,950	
To Provision for Bad and		B (2/5)	Rs. 3,300	8,250
Doubtful Debts	750			
	8,250			8,250

| Dr. | | | | PARTNERS' CAPITAL ACCOUNTS | | | | Cr. |

Particulars	A Rs.	B Rs.	X Rs.	Particulars	A Rs.	B Rs.	X Rs.
To Profit & Loss Adjustment A/c	4,950	3,300		By Balance b/d	37,000	28,000	
To A's & B's				By Cash A/c			40,000
Capital A/cs			15,000	By X's Capital A/c [WN 2]	12,000	3,000	
To Balance c/d	44,050	27,700	25,000				
	49,000	31,000	40,000		49,000	31,000	40,000

A, B and X
BALANCE SHEET AS ON 1ST APRIL, 1998

Liabilities		Rs.	Assets		Rs.
Capital Accounts :			Plant and Machinery		15,000
A	44,050		Furniture and Fitting		4,000
B	27,700		Stock		13,500
X	25,000	96,750	Sundry Debtors	20,000	
			Less : Provision for Bad		
Sundry Creditors		5,000	and Doubtful Debts	750	19,250
			Cash on Hand		50,000
		1,01,750			1,01,750

Working Notes :

(1) *COMPUTATION OF NEW PROFIT SHARING RATIO :*

X the new partner, will be entitled to 1/3rd share of the future profits of the firm. A and B would share the remaining 2/3rd share in equal proportion i.e, 1 : 1

$$A : \frac{2}{3} \times \frac{1}{2} = \frac{1}{3}$$

$$B : \frac{2}{3} \times \frac{1}{2} = \frac{1}{3}$$

$$X : \frac{1}{3}$$

A, B and X would share profits and losses in equal ratio.

(2) Adjustment of Goodwill :

X pays Rs. 15,000 as premium for goodwill for 1/3rd share of the future profits. Hence, total value of goodwill is Rs. 15,000 x 3 i.e. Rs. 45,000.

Computation of Sacrificing ratio :

$$A : \frac{3}{5} - \frac{1}{3} = \frac{4}{15}$$

$$B : \frac{2}{5} - \frac{1}{3} = \frac{1}{15}$$

Hence, Sacrificing Ratio between A & B is 4 : 1

X's share of goodwill can be adjusted through existing partners' capital accounts in the sacrificing ratio* :

Rs.

$A : Rs. 15,000 \times \dfrac{4}{5} =$ 12,000

$B : Rs. 15,000 \times \dfrac{1}{5} =$ 3,000

15,000

Note : * Alternatively, full value of goodwill may be raised and credited to existing partners' capital accounts in old profit sharing ratio, then the amount written off by debiting all partners' capital accounts in new profit sharing ratio.

Q.3 (Consignment Accounts). Mr. *Y* consigned 800 packets of toothpaste, each packet containing 100 toothpastes. Cost price of each packet was Rs. 900. Mr. *Y* spent Rs. 100 per packet as cartage, freight, insurance and forwarding charges. One packet was lost on the way and Mr. *Y* lodged claim with the insurance company and could get Rs. 570 as claim on average basis. Consignee took delivery of the rest of the packets and spent Rs. 39,950 as other non-recurring expenses and Rs. 22,500 as recurring expenses. He sold 740 packets at the rate of Rs. 12 per toothpaste. He was entitled to 2% commission on sales plus 1% del-credere commission.

You are required to prepare Consignment Account. Calculate the cost of stock at the end, abnormal loss and profit or loss on consignment. *(15 Marks)*

Solution :

Dr.	CONSIGNMENT ACCOUNT			Cr.
Particulars		Rs.	**Particulars**	Rs.
To Good sent on Consignment A/c (800 × Rs. 900)		7,20,000	By Consignee's A/c (Sales : 740 × 100 × Rs. 12)	8,88,000
To Cash A/c (Expenses : 800 × Rs. 100)		80, 000	By Cash A/c (Insurance Claim)	570
To Consignee's A/c :			By Profit and Loss A/c (Abnormal Loss)	430
Recurring Expenses	22,500		By Consignment Stock A/c	61,950
Non-recurring Expenses	39,950			
Commission @ 2% on Rs. 8,88,000	17,760			
Del-credere Commission @ 1% on Rs. 8,88,000	8,880	89,090		
To Profit and Loss A/c (Profit on consignment)		61,860		
		9,50,950		9,50,950

Working Notes :

			Rs.
1.	Abnormal Loss		
	Cost of packet lost during transit		900
	Add : Expenses incurred by *Y*		100
			1,000
	Less : insurance claim received		570
	Actual Loss		430
2.	Value of Closing Stock :		
	59 Packets* @ Rs. 900		53,100
	Add : Expenses incurred by *Y* (59 × Rs. 100)		5,900
	Add : Proportionate (non-recurring) expenses incurred by the consignee		

$$\left(\frac{59}{799} \times \text{Rs. } 39,950\right)$$ 2,950

61,950

* Closing Stock

Packets consigned		800
Less : Packet lost in transit		1
		799
Less : Packets sold		740
Balance of Packets in stock		59

Q.4 (a) (Self Balancing). The following transactions have been extracted from the books of M.. X. You are required to prepare the Sales Ledger Adjustment Account as on 31.3.1998:

	Rs.
Debtors balance on 1.3.1998	50,000
Transactions during the period were :	
Sales (including cash sales of Rs. 20,000)	1,28,000
Cash received from Debtors	90,000
Discount allowed to Debtors	500
Acceptances received from Debtors	8,000
Returns from Debtors	6,000
Bills receivable dishonoured	1,500
Bad Debts written off (after deducting bad debts recovered Rs. 1,000	4,000
Sundry charges debited to customers	600
Transfers to bought ledger	300

(8 Marks)

Solution :

General Ledger

Dr.   SALES LEDGER ADJUSTMENT ACCOUNT   Cr.

Particulars	Rs.	Particulars	Rs.
To Balance b/d	50,000	By General Ledger	
To General Ledger		Adjustment A/c :	
Adjustment A/c :		Cash	90,000
Sales (Credit W.N.1)	1,08,000	Discount	500
Bills Receivable		Bills Receivable	8,000
Dishonoured	1,500	Returns Inwards	6,000
Sundry Charges	600	Bad Debts (WN 2)	5,000
		Transfers	300
		By Balance c/d	50,300
	1,60,100		1,60,100

Working Notes :

		Rs.
(i)	Credit Sales	1,28,000
	Less : Cash Sales	20,000
		1,08,000
(ii)	Bad Debts	
	Bad Debts written off (after deducting bad debts recovered)	4,000
	Add : Bad Debts recovered	1,000
		5,000

Q. 4 (b) (Average Due Date). Mr. Green and Mr. Red had the following mutual dealings and desire to settle their account on the average due date :

	Rs.
Purchases by Green from Red :	
6th January, 1998	6,000
2nd February, 1998	2,800
31st March, 1998	2,000
Sales by Green to Red :	
6th January, 1998	6,600
9th March 1998	2,400
20th March, 1998	500

You are asked to ascertain the average due date.   *(7 Marks)*

Solution :

COMPUTATION OF AVERAGE DUE DATE

Due Date	Amount Rs.	No. of days from the basic date, (6th Jan')	Product
(1)	(2)	(3)	(4)
1998			
For Green's Payments			
6th January	6,000	0	0
2nd February	2,800	27	75,600

Due Date (1)	Amount Rs. (2)	No. of days from the basic date, (6th Jan') (3)	Product (4)
31st March	2,000	84	1,68,000
Total	10,800		2,43,600
For Red's Payments			
6th January	6,600	0	0
9th March	2,400	62	1,48,800
20th March	500	73	36,500
Total	9,500		1,85,300

Excess of Green's Product over Red's Product
= Rs. 2,43,600 − Rs. 1,85,300
= Rs. 58,300

Balance due to Red
= Rs. 10,800 − Rs. 9,500
= Rs. 1,300

Number of days from the basic date to the date of settlement is $\dfrac{58,300}{1,300}$ = 45 days (approx.)

Thus, the date of settlement of the balance amount is 45 days after 6th January, i.e., on 20th February.

On 20th February, 1998, Green should pay Red Rs. 1,300 to clear the account.

Q.5. Discuss briefly the relationship of Accounting with :

(i) Economics.

(ii) Statistics.

(iii) Mathematics.

(iv) Law.

(v) Management.

(3 × 5 = 15 Marks)

Solution :

For answer to (i), (ii), (iii) and (iv), please refer to page 1.8 of the book.

(v) *Accounting and Management*

Management involves optimum utilisation of resources *i.e.* men, materials machine and money. The functions of management are planning, organising, directing, controlling, communicating, etc. Accounting provides information to the management for all the above functions. As a matter of fact, these days a new branch of accounting popularly known as Management Accounting has come into existence. Management Accounting is accounting for the management i.e. accounting which helps the management performance of its functions - particularly decision making. Management Accountant is a member of the top management team. He collects information, sorts its out between relevant and irrelevant information and submits relevant information to be management at regular intervals. Hence, accounting and management are closely related.

CA FOUNDATION EXAMINATION
MAY 1999
Fundamentals Of Accounting

Q.1 (Final Accounts). From the following trial balance and information, prepare Trading and Profit and Loss Account of Mr. Rishabh for the year ended 31st March, 1999 and a Balance Sheet as on that date:

Particulars	Dr. Rs.	Cr. Rs.
Capital	—	1,00,000
Drawings	12,000	—
Land and Buildings	90,000	—
Plant and Machinery	20,000	—
Furniture	5,000	—
Sales	—	1,40,000
Returns Outward	—	4,000
Debtors	18,400	—
Loan from Gajanand on 1.7.98 @ 6% p.a.	—	30,000
Purchases	80,000	—
Returns Inward	5,000	—
Carriage	10,000	—
Sundry Expenses	600	—
Printing and Stationery	500	—
Insurance Expenses	1,000	—
Provision for Bad and Doubtful Debts	—	1,000
Provision for Discount on Debtors	—	380
Bad Debts	400	—
Profit of Textile Deptt.	—	10,000
Stock of General Goods on 1.4.98	21,300	—
Salaries and Wages	18,500	—
Creditors	—	12,000
Trade Expenses	800	—
Stock of Textile Goods on 31.3.99	8,000	—
Cash at Bank	4,600	—
Cash in Hand	1,280	—
	2,97,380	2,97,380

Information:

(*i*)   Stock of General goods on 31.3.99 valued at Rs. 27,300.

(*ii*)   Fire occurred on 23rd March, 1999 and Rs. 10,000 worth of general goods were destroyed. The Insurance Company accepted claim for Rs. 6,000 only and paid the claim money on 10th April, 1999.

(*iii*) Bad Debts amounting to Rs. 400 are to be written off. Provision for Bad and Doubtful debts is to be made at 5% and for discount at 2% on debtors. Make a provision of 2% on creditors for discount.

(*iv*) Received Rs. 6,000 worth of goods on 27th March, 1999 but the invoice of purchase was not recorded in Purchases Book.

(*v*)   Rishabh took away goods worth Rs. 2,000 for personal use but no record was made thereof.

(*vi*) Charge depreciation at 2% on Land and Buildings, 20% on Plant and Machinery, and 5% on Furniture.

(*vii*) Insurance prepaid amounts to Rs. 200.   **(20 Marks)**

Solution :

Trading and Profit and Loss Account of Mr. Rishabh
for the year ended 31st March, 1999

Dr.   Cr.

Particulars		Rs.	Particulars		Rs.
To Opening Stock		21,300	By Sales	1,40,000	
To Purchases (*WN* 1)	84,000		*Less :* Returns		
Less : Returns			Inward	5,000	1,35,000
Outward	4,000	80,000	By P & L A/c		10,000
To Carriage		10,000	(Loss by Fire)		
To Gross Profit		61,000	By Closing Stock		27,300
		1,72,300			1,72,300
To Sundry Expenses		600	By Gross Profit		61,000
To Printing and Stationery		500	By Provision for Discount on		
To Insurance Expenses	1,000		Debtors (Excess provision		
Less : Prepaid	200	800	= 380 − 342)		38
To Salaries and Wages		18,500	By Provision for Discount		360
To Trade Expenses		800	on Creditors		
To Trading A/c (Loss by Fire)		4,000	By Profit of Textile Deptt.		10,000
To Interest on Loan (*WN* 5)		1,350			
To Bad Debts	400				
Add : Additional					
Bad Debts	400				
Add : New Provision for					
Bad and Doubtful					
Debts	900				
	1,700				
Less : Old Provision	1,000	700			

(Contd..)

Particulars		Rs.	Particulars	Rs.
To Depreciation (WN 6)				
Land and Buildings	1,800			
Plant and Machinery	4,000			
Furniture	250	6,050		
To Net Profit		38,098		
(transferred to capital account)				
		71,398		71,398

BALANCE SHEET
As on 31st March, 1999

Liabilities		Amount Rs.	Assets		Amount Rs.
Capital Account	1,00,000		Land and Buildings	90,000	
Add : Net Profit	38,098		Less : Depreciation	1,800	88,200
	1,38,098		Plant and Machinery	20,000	
Less : Drawings (WN 7)	14,000	1,24,098	Less : Depreciation	4,000	16,000
Loan from Gajanand		30,000	Furniture	5,000	
Interest Accrued		1,350	Less : Depreciation	250	4,750
Creditors (WN 3)	18,000		Stock :		
Less : Provision			General Goods	27,300	
for Discount	360	17,640	Textile Goods	8,000	35,300
			Debtors	18,400	
			Less : Addl. Bad Debts	400	
				18,000	
			Less : Provision for Bad and Doubtful Debts	900	
				17,100	
			Less : Provision for Discount	342	16,758
			Insurance Claim Receivable		6,000
			Prepaid Insurance		200
			Cash at Bank		4,600
			Cash in hand		1,280
		1,73,088			1,73,088

Working Notes :

	Rs.
(1) Purchases	80,000
Add : Unrecorded goods (Invoice omitted)	6,000
	86,000
Less : Drawings	2,000
	84,000

		Rs.
(2)	Debtors (as per Trial Balance)	18,400
	Less : Additional Bad Debts	400
		18,000
	Less : New Provision for Bad and Doubtful Debts (5% of Rs. 18,000)	900
		17,100
	Less : New Provision for Discount on Debtors (2% of Rs. 17,100)	342
		16,758
(3)	Creditors (given)	12,000
	Add : For unrecorded purchases	6,000
		18,000

Provision for discount on creditors (2%) = 18,000 × 2/100 = Rs. 360

(4)	Loss by fire	10,000
	Less : Insurance claim (accepted)	6,000
	Balance of loss charged to Profit and Loss Account	4,000

(5) Interest on Loan from Gajanand from 1.7.98 to 31.3.99, i.e., for 9 months

$$\text{Rs. } 30,000 \times \frac{6}{100} \times \frac{9}{12} = \text{Rs. } 1,350$$

(6) Depreciation

Land and Buildings	$90,000 \times \dfrac{2}{100}$		1,800
Plant and Machinery	$20,000 \times \dfrac{20}{100}$		4,000
Furniture	$5,000 \times \dfrac{5}{100}$		250
			6,050

(7)	Drawings as per Trial Balance	12,000
	Add : Drawings of Goods	2,000
	Total Drawings	14,000

Q.2 (Partnership - Dissolution). Ram and Hanuman are partners in a firm. They share profits and losses in the ratio of 1 : 2. On 1st April, 1999, they decided to dissolve the partnership and on that date the Balance Sheet of the firm was as under:

Ram and Hanuman
BALANCE SHEET AS ON 1ST APRIL, 1999

Liabilities	Rs.	Assets		Rs.
Sundry Creditors	50,000	Cash at Bank		10,000
General Reserve	60,000	Sundry Debtors	Rs. 50,000	
Hanuman's Loan	30,000	Less : Provision for		
Capital Accounts :		Doubtful Debts	Rs. 2,000	48,000

Liabilities	Rs.	Assets	Rs.
Ram	1,50,000	Stock	1,02,000
Hanuman	1,00,000	Furniture	30,000
		Machinery and Plant	80,000
		Land Building	1,20,000
	3,90,000		3,90,000

The sales of firm's properties realised Rs. 1,00,000 from stock, Rs. 34,000 from furniture and Rs. 1,00,000 from Land and Building. Rs. 45,000 were collected from Debtors and Creditors were paid off at a discount of Rs. 1,000.

Machinery and plant are taken over by Ram at their book value. The expenses of realisation amounted to Rs. 4,000.

Pass Journal Entries to close the books of the firm and prepare necessary ledger accounts. *(15 Marks)*

Solution :

Books of M/s Ram and Hanuman
JOURNAL ENTRIES

Particulars		Dr. Rs.	Cr. Rs.
Realisation Account	Dr.	3,82,000	
To Sundry Debtors Account			50,000
To Stock Account			1,02,000
To Furniture Account			30,000
To Machinery and Plant Account			80,000
To Land and Building Account			1,20,000
(Being transfer of assets to realisation account)			
Sundry Creditors Account	Dr.	50,000	
Provision for Doubtful Debts Account	Dr.	2,000	
To Realisation Account			52,000
(Being transfer of sundry creditors and provision for doubtful debts to realisation account)			
Bank Account	Dr.	2,79,000	
To Realisation Account			2,79,000
(Being realisation in cash on account of sale of furniture, land and building, stock and debtors)			
Ram's Capital Account	Dr.	80,000	
To Realisation Account			80,000
(Being taking over of machinery and plant by Ram at book value)			
Realisation Account	Dr.	4,000	
To Bank Account			4,000
(Being expenses of realisation paid)			

(Contd.)

Particulars		Dr. Rs.	Cr. Rs.
Realisation Account	Dr.	49,000	
To Bank Account			49,000
(Being sundry creditors paid off)			
Ram's Capital Account	Dr.	8,000	
Hanuman's Capital Account	Dr.	16,000	
To Realisation Account			24,000
(Being realisation loss transferred to capital accounts of partners)			
Hanuman's Loan Account	Dr.	30,000	
To Bank Account			30,000
(Being the Hanuman's Loan paid off)			
General Reserve Account	Dr.	60,000	
To Ram's Capital Account			20,000
To Hanuman's Capital Account			40,000
(Being transfer of general reserve to partners' capital accounts)			
Ram's Capital Account	Dr.	82,000	
Hanuman's Capital Account	Dr.	1,24,000	
To Bank Account			2,06,000
(Being payment of partners' capital accounts)			

Ledger Accounts

Dr.   REALISATION ACCOUNT   Cr.

Particulars	Rs.	Particulars		Rs.
To Sundry Debtors	50,000	By Sundry Creditors		50,000
To Stock	1,02,000	By Provision for Doubtful Debts		2,000
To Furniture	30,000	By Bank :		
To Machinery and Plant	80,000	Stock	1,00,000	
To Land and Building	1,20,000	Furniture	34,000	
To Bank (Expenses)	4,000	Land and Building	1,00,000	
To Bank (Sundry Creditors)	49,000	Debtors	45,000	2,79,000
		By Ram's Capital Account		80,000
		(Machinery and Plant		
		taken over)		
		By Loss transferred to		
		Capital Accounts :		
		Ram	8,000	
		Hanuman	16,000	24,000
	4,35,000			4,35,000

Dr.			CAPITAL ACCOUNTS OF PARTNERS			Cr.
Particulars	Ram	Hanuman	Particulars	Ram	Hanuman	
	Rs.	Rs.		Rs.	Rs.	
To Realisation Account (Machinery and Plant taken over)	80,000	—	By Balance b/d	1,50,000	1,00,000	
			By General Reserve	20,000	40,000	
To Realisation Account (Loss)	8,000	16,000				
To Bank Account	82,000	1,24,000				
	1,70,000	1,40,000		1,70,000	1,40,000	

Dr.		BANK ACCOUNT		Cr.
Particulars	Rs.	Particulars	Rs.	
To Balance b/d	10,000	By Realisation Account (Sundry Creditors)	49,000	
To Realisation Account (Sale of assets)	2,79,000	By Realisation Account (Expenses)	4,000	
		By Hanuman's Loan Account	30,000	
		By Ram's Capital Account	82,000	
		By Hanuman's Capital Account	1,24,000	
	2,89,000		2,89,000	

Q.3 (Self Balancing). Prepare the General Ledger Adjustment Accounts as will appear in the Debtors' and Creditors' Ledger, from the information given below :

Balances on 1.4.98	Dr. Rs.	Cr. Rs.
Debtors' Ledger	47,200	240
Creditors' Ledger	280	26,300
Transactions for the year ended 31.3.99		
Total Sales		1,20,000
Cash Sales		8,100
Total Purchases		89,500
Credit Purchases		67,000
Creditors paid off (in Full Settlement of Rs. 40,000)		39,500
Received from Debtors (in Full Settlement of Rs. 59,000)		58,200
Returns from Debtors		2,600
Returns to Creditors		1,800
Bills Accepted for Creditors		5,500
Bills Payable Matured		8,000
Bills Accepted by Customers		20,100
Bills Receivables Dishonoured		1,500
Bills Receivables Discounted		5,000
Bills Receivables Endorsed to Creditors		4,000
Endorsed Bills Dishonoured		1,000
Bad-debts Written off (after Deducting Bad-debts Recovered Rs. 300)		2,200
Provision for Doubtful Debts		550

Transfer from Debtors' Ledger to Creditors' Ledger		1,100
Transfer from Creditors' Ledger to Debtors' Ledger		1,900
Balances on 31.3.99		
Debtors' Ledger (Cr.)		380
Creditors' Ledger (Dr.)		420

(15 Marks)

Solution :

In Debtors' Ledger
Dr.   GENERAL LEDGER ADJUSTMENT ACCOUNT   Cr.

Dr.   Cr.

Date	Particulars		Rs.	Date	Particulars		Rs.
1.4.98	To Balance b/d		240	1.4.98	By Balance b/d		47,200
	To Debtors' Ledger				By Debtors' Ledger		
	Adjustment Account :				Adjustment Account :		
	Bank	58,200			Sales (credit)	1,12,000	
	Discount	800			Bills Receivable		
	Returns	2,600			dishonoured	1,500	
	Bills Receivable	20,100			Endorsed Bills		
	Bad Debts				Receivable		
	written off	2,500	84,200		dishonoured	1,000	1,14,500
	To Debtors' Ledger						
	Adjustment Account :			31.3.99	By Balance c/d		380
	Transfer from						
	Debtors' Ledger to						
	Creditors' Ledger	1,100					
	Transfer from						
	Creditors' Ledger to						
	Debtors' Ledger	1,900	3,000				
31.3.99	To Balance c/d		74,640				
	(Balancing figure)						
			1,62,080				1,62,080

In Creditors' Ledger
GENERAL LEDGER ADJUSTMENT ACCOUNT

Date	Particulars		Rs.	Date	Particulars		Rs.
1.4.98	To Balance b/d		26,300	1.4.98	By Balance b/d		280
	To Creditors' Ledger				By Creditors' Ledger		
	Adjustment Account :				Adjustment Account :		
	Purchases	67,000			Bank	39,500	
	Endorsed Bills				Discount Received	500	
	Receivable				Returns	1,800	
	dishonoured	1,000	68,000		Bills Payable	5,500	
31.3.99	To Balance c/d		420		Bills Receivable		
					endorsed	4,000	51,300
					By Creditors' Ledger		
					Adjustment Account :		
					Transfer from Debtors'		
					Ledger to Creditors'		
					Ledger		1,100

(Contd..)

Date	Particulars	Rs.	Date	Particulars		Rs.
			31.3.99	Transfer from Creditors' Ledger to Debtors' Ledger	1,900	3,000
				By Balance c/d (Balancing Figure)		40,140
		94,720				94,720

Note : No entries are to be made for the following transactions since they do not affect General Ledger Adjustment Accounts :

(i)   Cash Sales

(ii)   Bills Payable Matured

(iii) Bills Receivable Discounted

(iv) Bad Debts Recovered

(v)   Provision for Doubtful Debts.

Q.4 (Negotiable Instruments). Shubham draws on Rajendra a bill for Rs. 45,000 on 1st June, 1998 for 3 months. Rajendra accepts the bill and sends it to Shubham who gets it discounted for Rs. 44,100. Shubham immediately remits Rs. 14,700 to Rajendra. On the due date Shubham, being unable to remit the amount due, accepts a bill for Rs. 63,000 for three months which is discounted by Rajendra for Rs. 61,650. Rajendra sends Rs. 11,100 to Shubham. On the due date Shubham becomes insolvent, his estate paying forty paise in the rupee. Give Journal Entries in the books of Shubham and Rajendra. *(15 Marks)*

Solution :

Books of Shubham
JOURNAL ENTRIES

Date	Particulars		Dr. Rs.	Cr. Rs.
1998 June 1	Bills Receivable Account To Rajendra (Being acceptance received from Rajendra for mutual accommodation)	Dr.	45,000	45,000
June 1	Bank Account Discount Account To Bills Receivable Account (Being discounting of Bill for Rs. 44,100)	Dr. Dr.	44,100 900	45,000
June 1	Rajendra To Bank Account To Discount Account (Being remittance of one-third of proceeds to Rajendra)	Dr.	15,000	14,700 300
Sept. 4	Rajendra To Bills Payable A/c (Being acceptance given to Rajendra, due to inability to remit the amount due to him)	Dr.	63,000	63,000

(Contd..)

Date	Particulars		Dr. Rs.	Cr. Rs.
Sept. 4	Bank Account	Dr.	11,100	
	Discount Account	Dr.	900	
	To Rajendra			12,000
	(Being receipt of amount from Rajendra and discount amount credited to him)			
Dec. 7	Bills Payable Account	Dr.	63,000	
	To Rajendra			63,000
	(Being dishonour of acceptance to Rajendra because of insolvency)			
Dec. 7	Rajendra	Dr.	42,000	
	To Bank Account			16,800
	To Deficiency Account			25,200
	(Being amount paid (40%) and balance credited to Deficiency Account due to inability to pay)			

Books of Rajendra
JOURNAL ENTRIES

Date	Particulars		Dr. Rs.	Cr. Rs.
1998 June 1	Shubham	Dr.	45,000	
	To Bills Payable Account			45,000
	(Being acceptance given for the bill)			
June 1	Bank Account	Dr.	14,700	
	Discount Account	Dr.	300	
	To Shubham			15,000
	(Being one-third of the proceeds of bill after discounting, received from Shubham)			
Sept. 4	Bills Receivable Account	Dr.	63,000	
	To Shubham			63,000
	(Being acceptance received from Shubham to cover the amount due from him)			
Sept. 4	Bank Account	Dr.	61,650	
	Discount Account	Dr.	1,350	
	To Bills Receivable Account			63,000
	Being discounted Shubham's acceptance for Rs. 61,650)			
Sept. 4	Bills Payable Account	Dr.	45,000	
	To Bank Account			45,000
	(Being meeting of own acceptance due on this date)			

Date	Particulars		Dr. Rs.	Cr. Rs.
Sept. 4	Shubham	Dr.	12,000	
	To Bank Account			11,100
	To Discount Account			900
	(Being remittance of amount to Shubham, after discounting the bill)			
Dec. 7	Shubham	Dr.	63,000	
	To Bank Account			63,000
	(Being dishonoured of Shubham's acceptance because of his insolvency)			
Dec. 7	Bank Account	Dr.	16,800	
	Bad Debts Account	Dr.	25,200	
	To Shubham			42,000
	(Being amount received and debts written off in respect of amount due from Shubham)			

Working Note :

Computation of discount to be borne by Shubham :

Rs. 15,000 has been paid to Rajendra out of the bill of Rs. 45,000. Hence, Rs. 45,000 − Rs. 15,000 = Rs. 30,000 are due to Rajendra. Moreover, Rs. 11,100 are further received from Rajendra. Hence, 30,000 + 11,100 = Rs. 41,100 are shared by Shubham, out of total proceeds Rs. 61,650. Shubham will have to bear discount in this proportion.

$$\text{Discount to be shared/borne by Shubham} = \frac{41,100}{61,650} \times (63,000 - 61,650)$$

$$= \frac{41,100}{61,650} \times 1,350 = \text{Rs. } 900$$

Q.5 (Miscellaneous). State with reasons whether the following statements are true or false:

(*i*) Average due date is the median average of several due dates for payments.

(*ii*) Goodwill is in the nature of Personal Account.

(*iii*) The balance in the Petty Cash Book represents amount spent.

(*iv*) Nominal accounts are balanced in the end of the accounting year.

(*v*) If the amount is posted in the wrong account or it is written on the wrong side of an account, it is called error of omission.

(*vi*) If payment is made on the average due date it results in loss of interest to the creditor.

(*vii*) Expenses incurred on white-washing of factory building done after every six months is Revenue expenditure.

(*viii*) In the calculation of average due date only the due date of the first transaction must be taken as the base date.

(*ix*) Higher depreciation will not affect cash profit of the business.

(*x*) Amount spent for replacement of worn out part of a machine is Capital Expenditure.

(20 Marks)

Solution :

(i) **False.** Average due date is the mean or equated date which one payment may be made in lieu of several payments.

(ii) **False.** Goodwill is an intangible asset. It is an item of Real Account.

(iii) **False.** The balance in the Petty Cash Book represents the amount unspent lying with the Petty Cashier at the end of the period.

(iv) **False.** Nominal accounts are not balanced at the end of the accounting year. The balances in the respective nominal accounts are transferred to the Profit and Loss Account.

(v) **False.** Posting in the wrong account or wrong amount on the wrong side is an error of commission.

(vi) **False.** Payment on the average due date results in loss to neither party.

(vii) **True.** Expenses on white-washing of factory building is a normal maintenance expenditure and hence it is revenue expenditure.

(viii) **False.** Due date of any transaction can be taken as base date. Of course, it is preferable to take the due date of the first transaction as the base date.

(ix) **True.** Depreciation is not a cash expenditure of the business. Hence, it will not affect the cash profits of the business. Of course, a higher depreciation may indirectly increase the cash from operations because of lower tax liability.

(x) **False.** Amounts spent for replacement of a worn-out part is an ordinary maintenance expenditure. Hence, it is a revenue expenditure.

Q.6 Write short notes on any three of the following :

(*i*) Fundamental Accounting Assumptions.

(*ii*) Double Entry System.

(*iii*) Receipts and Expenditure Account.

(*iv*) Adjusted Selling Price Method of Valuation of Stock.

(4 × 5 = 20 Marks)

Solution :

(i) *Fundamental Accounting Assumptions :* Please refer to Accounting concepts on page 1.17 of the book.

(ii) *Double Entry System :* Please refer to page 1.24 of the book.

(iii) *Receipts and Expenditure Account :* Please refer to page 1.380 of the book.

(iv) *Adjusted Selling Price Method of Valuation of Stock :* This is also termed as Retail Inventory Method. It is widely used in businesses where the inventory comprises items, individual costs of which are not readily ascertainable. The historical cost of inventory is estimated by calculating it in the first instance at the selling price and then deducting an amount equal to the estimated gross margin of profit on such stocks. The calculation of the estimated gross margin of profit may be made for individual items or groups of items or by departments, as may be appropriate to the circumstances. This method is also used by some manufacturing concerns for valuing the inventory of finished products held against forward sale contracts.

CA FOUNDATION EXAMINATION
NOVEMBER 1999
Fundamentals Of Accounting

Q. 1 (Accounts of Non-Profit Organisations). Mahaveer Sports Club gives the following Receipts and Payments Account for the year ended March 31, 1998:

RECEIPTS AND PAYMENTS ACCOUNT

Receipts	Rs.	Payment	Rs.
To Opening Cash and		By Salaries	15,000
Bank Balances	5,200	By Rent and Taxes	5,400
To Subscriptions	34,800	By Electricity Charges	600
To Donations	10,000	By Sports Goods	2,000
To Interest on Investments	1,200	By Library Books	10,000
To Sundry Receipts	300	By Newspapers and Periodicals	1,080
		By Miscellaneous Expenses	5,400
		By Closing Cash and Bank Balances	12,020
	51,500		51,500

Liabilities	As on 31.3.97 Rs.	As on 31.3.98 Rs.
Outstanding Expenses:		
Salaries	1,000	2,000
Newspapers and Periodicals	400	500
Rent and Taxes	600	600
Electricity Charges	800	1,000
Library Books	10,000	
Sports Goods	8,000	
Furniture and Fixtures	10,000	
Subscription Receivable	5,000	12,000
Investment – Government Securities	50,000	
Accrued Interest	600	600

Provide Depreciation on:

Furniture and Fixtures	@ 10% p.a.
Sports Goods	@ 20% p.a.
Library Books	@ 10% p.a.

You are required to prepare Club's opening Balance Sheet as on 1.4.97, Income and Expenditure Account for the year ended on 31.3.98 and Balance Sheet as on that date.

(20 Marks)

Solution:

Mahaveer Sports Club
BALANCE SHEET AS ON 1ST APRIL, 1997

Liabilities	Rs.	Rs.	Assets	Rs.	Rs.
Capital fund		86,000	Library Books		10,000
(Balancing Figure)			Sports Goods		8,000
Outstanding			Furniture and Fixtures		10,000
Expenses:			Subscriptions Receivable		5,000
Salaries	1,000		Investment – Govt. Securities		50,000
Newspapers and Periodicals	400		Accured Interest		600
Electricity Charges	800		Cash and Bank Balances		5,200
Rent and Taxes	600	2,800			
		88,800			88,800

Mahaveer Sports Club
INCOME AND EXPENDITURE ACCOUNT
For the year ended on 31st March, 1998

Expenditure	Rs.	Income	Rs.
To Salaries	16,000	By Subscriptions (WN 1)	41,800
To Electricity Charges	800	By Interest on Investments (WN 2)	1,200
To Rent and Taxes	5,400	By Sundry Receipts	300
To Newspapers and Periodicals	1,180	By Donation	10,000
To Misc. Expenses	5,400		
To Depreciation on Fixed assets (WN 4)	5,000		
To Excess of Income over expenditure (transferred to capital Fund)	9,520		
	43,300		43,300

Mahaveer Sports Club
BALANCE SHEET
as on 31st March, 1998

Liabilities	Rs.	Rs.	Assets	Rs.	Rs.
Capital Fund			Fixed Assets (WN 4):		
Opening balance	86,000		Furniture and Fixtures	9,000	
Add: Excess of Income			Sports Goods	8,000	
over Expenditure	19,520	1,05,520	Library Books Investment –	18,000	35,000
Outstanding Expenses			Govt. Securities		50,000
Salaries (W.N.3):	2000		Accrued Interest		600
Newspapers and Periodicals	500		Subscriptions Receivable		12,000
Electricity Charges	1000		Cash and Bank Balances		12,020
Rent and Taxes	600	4,100			
		1,09,620			1,09,620

Working Notes:

Subscriptions for the year ended 31st March, 1998:

	Rs.
Subscriptions received during the year	34,800
Add: Subscriptions receivable on 31.3.98	12,000
	46,800
Less: subscriptions receivable on 31.3.97	5,000
	41,800

Interest on Investments for the year ended 31st March, 1998:

	Rs.
Interest received during the year	1,200
Add: Accrued Interest on 31.3.98	600
	1,800
Less: Accrued Interest on 31.3.97	600
	1,200

Expenses for the year ended 31st March, 1998:

Expenses	Salaries Rs.	Electricity Charges Rs.	Rent and Taxes Rs.	Newspapers and Periodicals Rs.
Paid during the year	15,000	600	5,400	1,080
Add: Outstanding (as on 31.3.98)	2,000	1,000	600	500
	17,000	1,600	6,000	1,580
Less: Outstanding (as on 31.3.97)	1,000	800	600	400
Expenses for the year	16,000	800	5,400	1,180

Depreciation on Fixed Assets:

Assets	Book Value (31.3.97) Rs.	Additions during the year Rs.	Total Rs.	Rate of Depreciation p.a.	Depreciation Rs.	W.D.V. as on 31.3.98 Rs.
Furniture and fixtures	10,000	—	10,000	10%	1,000	9,000
Sports Goods	8,000	2,000	10,000	20%	2,000	8,000
Library Books	10,000	10,000	20,000	10%	2,000	18,000
Total					5,000	35,000

Notes:

1. Donations could have been also capitalised
2. It has been assumed that the fixed assets were acquired at the beginning of the year. Depreciation has therefore been charged for the full year.

Q.2 (Partnership). K, L and M are partners sharing Profits and Losses in the ratio 5 : 3 : 2 Due to illness, L wanted to retire from the firm on 31.3.99 and admit his son N in his place.

BALANCE SHEET OF K, L AND M AS ON 31.3.99

Liabilities		Rs.	Assets	Rs.
Capital:			Goodwill	30,000
K	40,000		Furnitures	20,000
L	60,000		Sundry Debtors	50,000
M	30,000	1,30,000	Stock in Trade	50,000
Reserve		50,000	Cash and Bank Balances	50,000
Sundry Creditors		20,000		
		2,00,000		2,00,000

On retirement of 'L' assets were revalued:

Goodwill Rs. 50,000, Furniture Rs. 10,000, Stock in Trade Rs. 30,000.

50% of the amount due to 'L' was paid off in cash and the balance was retained in the firm as capital of N.

On admission of the new partner, goodwill has been written off.

M is paid off his extra balance to make capital proportionate.

Pass necessary Journal Entries and prepare Balance Sheet of M/s K, M, N as on 1.4.99.

Show necessary workings.   (15 Marks)

Solution:

JOURNAL ENTRIES

Date	Particulars		Dr. Rs.	Cr. Rs.
31.3.99	Goodwill A/c	Dr.	20,000	
	To Profit and Loss Adjustment A/c			20,000
	(Being revaluation of goodwill on L's retirement)			
	Profit and Loss Adjustment A/c	Dr.	30,000	
	To Furniture A/c			10,000
	To Stock in Trade A/c			20,000
	(Being recording of revaluation of furniture and stock in trade)			
	K's Capital A/c	Dr.	5,000	
	L's Capital A/c	Dr.	3,000	
	M's Capital A/c	Dr.	2,000	
	To Profit and Loss Adjustment A/c			10,000
	(Being revaluation loss transferred to capital accounts of K, L and M in the ratio of 5:3:2)			
	Reserve A/c	Dr.	50,000	
	To K' Capital A/c			25,000
	To L's Capital A/c			15,000
	To M's Capital A/c			10,000
	(Being reserve transferred to capital accounts of K, L and M)			

(Cont.)

Date	Particulars		Dr. Rs.	Cr. Rs.
	L's Capital A/c	Dr.	72,000	
	To Cash / Bank A/c			36,000
	To N's Capital A/c			36,000
	(Being 50% of the amount due to L was paid off in cash and the balance was retained in the firm as capital of N)			
	K's Capital A/c	Dr.	25,000	
	M's Capital A/c	Dr.	10,000	
	N's Capital A/c	Dr.	15,000	
	To Goodwill A/c			50,000
	(Being goodwill written off, as agreed after retirement of L and admission of N in the new profit sharing ratio)			
	M's Capital A/c	Dr.	14,000	
	To Bank/Cash A/c			14,000
	(Being amount paid to M to make his capital proportionate)			

M/s K, M, N
BALANCE SHEET AS ON 1ST APRIL, 1999

Liabilities		Rs.	Assets	Rs.
Capital Accounts			Furniture	10,000
K	35,000		Sundry Debtors	50,000
M	14,000		Stock in Trade	30,000
N	21,000	70,000		
Sundry Creditors		20,000		
		90,000		90,000

Working Note:

PARTNERS' CAPITAL ACCOUNTS

Dr.   Cr.

	K Rs.	L Rs.	M Rs.	N Rs.		K Rs.	L Rs.	M Rs.	N Rs.
To Profit & Loss Adjustment A/c	5,000	3,000	2,000	–	By Balance b/d	40,000	60,000	30,000	–
					By Reserve	25,000	15,000	10,000	–
To Bank/ Cash A/c	–	36,000	–	–	By L's Capital A/c	–	–	–	36,000
To N's Capital A/c	–	36,000	–	–					
To Goodwill A/c	25,000	–	10,000	15,000					
To Bank/Cash A/c (Balancing figure)	–	–	14,000	–					
To Balance b/d	35,000	–	14,000	21,000					
	65,000	75,000	40,000	36,000		65,000	75,000	40,000	36,000
					By Balance b/d	35,000		14,000	21,000

Q. 3 (Joint Venture).   Arun and Balu entered into a Joint Venture to purchase, recondition and sell second-hand cars. Arun purchased 100 cars during the period 1.1.99 to 30.6.99 at the following prices and paid for the same:

20 cars	@ Rs. 15,000 each
40 cars	@ Rs. 25,000 each
40 cars	@ Rs. 55,000 each

Balu during the same period reconditioned the cars by spending the following amounts:

	Rs.
Spare Parts used	1,80,000
Painting	2,00,000
Air-conditioning- 10 cars	3,00,000
Testing Charges	20,000
Insurance	60,000
Labour Charges	10,40,000

Arun and Balu sold the cars, the details of which are as under:

	Sold by	
	Arun	Balu
A.C. Cars	5	4
Non-A.C. Cars	35	46

A.C. cars were sold at Rs. 1,75,000 each. Non-A.C. cars were sold:
Arun 35 cars @ Rs. 1.25 lakhs each
Balu 35 cars @ Rs. 1.10 lakhs each
       11 cars @ Rs. 0.80 lakhs each

During testing, one non-A.C. car met with an accident and the Insurance Company paid the actual cost as claim amount. Prepare the Memorandum Joint-venture Account and Account of Balu in the Books of Arun.   (15 Marks)

Solution:

MEMORANDUM JOINT VENTURE ACCOUNT

Dr.   Cr.

Rs. '000	Rs. '000		Rs. '000	Rs. '000	
To Arun (Cost of			By Sales:		
Cars purchased)		3500	Arun		5250
To Balu (Reconditioning			Balu		5430
charges):			By Insurance Claim		50
Spare parts	180		By Closing Stock:		
Painting	200		A.C. Car	80	
Air conditioning	300		Non-A.C. Cars	400	480
Testing charges	20		(8 Rs.50,000)		
Insurace	60				
Labour charges	1040	1800			
To Net Profit on Venture:					
Arun	2955				
Balu	2955	5910			
		11210			11210

Books of Arun
BALU'S ACCOUNT

	Rs. '000		Rs. '000
To Joint Venture with Balu A/c (Sales)	5430	By Joint Venture with Balu A/c (Reconditioning charges)	1800
		By Joint Venture with Balu A/c (Share of Profit)	2955
		By Balance c/d	675
	5430		5430

JOINT VENTURE WITH BALU ACCOUNT

	Rs. '000		Rs. '000
To Bank A/c (Cost of cars purchased)	3500	By Bank A/c (Sale proceeds)	5250
To Balu's A/c (Reconditioning charges)	1800	By Balu/s A/c (Sale proceeds)	5430
		By Insurance claim	50
To Net profit transferred to - Profit & Loss A/c 2955		By Closing Stock	480
Balu's A/c 2955	5910		
	11210		11210

2. Purchases

20 cars × Rs. 15,000 + 40 cars × Rs. 25,000 + 40 cars × Rs. 55,000 = Rs. 35,00,000

3. Sales

	A.C. Cars	Non-A.C. Cars	
Arun	5 × Rs. 1,75,000 + 35 × Rs. 1,25,000		= Rs. 52,50,000
Balu	4 × Rs. 1,75,000 +	$\begin{bmatrix} 35 \times Rs.1,10,000 \\ 11 \times Rs.80,000 \end{bmatrix}$	= Rs. 54,30,000

4. Cost per A.C. and Non-A.C. car

	Rs.
Purchase price of cars	35,00,000
Add: Reconditioning Charges (except air conditioning)	15,00,000
Total Cost other than A.C.	50,00,000
Total No. of cars	100
Cost per Non-A.C. Car	50,000
Cost of 10 A.C.s	3,00,000
Cost per A.C.	30,000
Cost per A.C. car (Rs. 50,000 + Rs. 30,000)	80,000

Insurance claim settled for the actual cost of one non-A.C. car i.e., Rs. 50,000

Q. 4(a) (Depreciation Accounting). Hanuman Enterprises purchased on 1.4.95 certain machinery for Rs. 72,800 and paid Rs. 2,200 on its installation. On 1.10.95 another machinery for Rs. 25,000 was acquired. On 1.4.96, the first machinery was sold at Rs. 50,000 and on the same date a fresh machinery was purchased at a cost of Rs. 45,000.

Depreciation was annually provided on 31st March at 10% p.a. on written down value.

On 1.4.97, however, the firm decided to change the method of providing depreciation and adopted the method of providing depreciation @ 10% p.a. on the original cost, with retrospective effect.

Ascertain the value of machinery as on 31.3.98.

(7 Marks)

Solution:

(a) The value of machinery as on 31.3.98 can be ascertained by preparing Machinery Account from 1st April, 1995 to 31st March 1998 as shown below:

Hanuman Enterprises

MACHINERY ACCOUNT

Dr.   Cr.

Date	Particulars	Rs.	Date	Particulars	Rs.
1.4.95	To Bank A/c (Cost of new machinery)	72,800	31.3.96	By Depreciation A/c (Rs. 7,500 + Rs. 1,250)	8,750
	To Bank A/c (Installation Charges)	2,200		By Balanced c/d (Rs. 67,500 + Rs. 23,750)	91,250
1.10.95	To Bank A/c	25,000			
		1,00,000			1,00,000
1.4.96	To Balance b/d	91,250	1.4.96	By Bank A/c	50,000
	To Bank A/c	45,000		By Profit and Loss A/c (Loss on sale - WN 1)	17,500
			31.3.97	By Depreciation A/c (Rs. 2,375 + Rs. 4,500)	6,875
				Balanced c/d (Rs. 21,375 + Rs. 40,500)	61,875
		1,36,250			1,36,250
1.4.97	To Balance b/d	61,875	31.3.98	By Profit and Loss A.c (WN 3)	125
				By Depreciation A/c (Rs. 2,500 + Rs. 4,500)	7,000
				By Balance c/d	54,750
		61,875			61,875

Working Notes:

1. Book Value of Machines (Reducing Balance Method)

	Machine I	Machine II	Machine III
	Rs.	Rs.	Rs.
Cost	75,000	25,000	45,000
Depreciation for 1995-96	7,500	1,250	
Written down value	67,500	23,750	
Sale proceeds	50,000		
Loss on sale	17,500		
Depreciation for 1996-97		2,375	4,500
Written down value as on 31.3.97		21,375	40,500

2. Book Value of Machines (Straight Line Method)

	Machine II Rs.	Machine III Rs.
Cost	25,000	45,000
Depreciation	3,750	4,500
	(for 1-1/2 years)	(for 1 year)
Written down value on 31.3.97	21,250	40,500

3. Retrospective effect of change in depreciation method for machines II and III (1995-97)

	Rs.
Depreciation under Straight Line Method (3,750 + 4,500)	8,250
Depreciation under WDV method (1,250 + 2,375 + 4,500)	8,125
Deficiency arising from restrospective recomputation of depreciation due to change in method to be charged to Profit and Loss A/c	125

Q. 4(b) (Inventory Valuation). Navkar Ltd. was following LIFO method of valuation of stock. Due to promulgation of revised accounting standard, they want to switch over to FIFO method. From the following information:

(i) Draw up stock ledgers under FIFO and LIFO methods of valuation of stocks.

(ii) Find out the closing stock and cost of materials consumed under each of the above two methods:

Opening stock 5,000 MT @ Rs. 22 per MT Rs. 1,10,000

Purchases:

1.6.99	1,000 MT @ Rs. 30 per MT
5.6.99	2,000 MT @ Rs. 35 per MT
10.6.99	1,500 MT @ Rs. 38 per MT
15.6.99	1,500 MT @ Rs. 35 per MT
20.6.99	2,000 MT @ Rs. 32 per MT
28.6.99	2,000 MT @ Rs. 35 per MT
30.6.99	1,500 MT @ Rs. 30 per MT

Issues:

1 - 5.6.99	2,000 MT
6 - 10.6.99	3,000 MT
11 - 20.6.99	4,000 MT
21 - 25.6.99	3,000 MT
26 - 30.6.99	3,000 MT

(8 Marks)

4.64

Solution:

Navkar Ltd.
STOCK LEDGERS

(a) Under FIFO Method:

Date	Receipts			Issues			Balance		
	Units (MT)	Rate Rs.	Amount Rs.	Units (MT)	Rate Rs.	Amount Rs.	Units (MT)	Rate Rs.	Amount Rs.
Opening balance	5,000	22	1,10,000				5,000	22	1,10,000
1.6.99	1,000	30	30,000				5,000	22	1,10,000
							1,000	30	30,000
5.6.99	2,000	35	70,000	2,000	22	44,000	3,000	22	66,000
							1,000	30	30,000
							2,000	35	70,000
10.6.99	1,500	38	57,000	3,000	22	66,000	1,000	30	30,000
							2,000	35	70,000
							1,500	38	57,000
15.6.99	1,500	35	52,500				1,000	30	30,000
							2,000	35	70,000
							1,500	38	57,000
							1,500	35	52,500
20.6.99	2,000	32	64,000	1,000	30	30,000	500	38	19,000
				2,000	35	70,000	1,500	35	52,500
				1,000	38	38,000	2,000	32	64,000
25.6.99				500	38	19,000	1,000	32	32,000
				1,500	35	52,500			
				1,000	32	32,000			
28.6.99	2,000	35	70,000				1,000	32	32,000
							2,000	35	70,000
30.6.99	1,500	30	45,000	1,000	32	32,000	1,500	30	45,000
				2,000	35	70,000			
	16,500		4,98,500	15,000		4,53,500			

(b) Under LIFO method

Date	Receipts			Issues			Balance		
	Units (MT)	Rate Rs.	Amount Rs.	Units (MT)	Rate Rs.	Amount Rs.	Units (MT)	Rate Rs.	Amount Rs.
Opening Balance	5,000	22	1,10,000				5,000	22	1,10,000
1.6.99	1,000	30	30,000				5,000	22	1,10,000
							1,000	30	30,000
5.6.99	2,000	35	70,000	2,000	35	70,000	5,000	22	1,10,000
							1,000	30	30,000
10.6.99	1,500	38	57,000	1,500	38	57,000	4,500	22	99,000
				1000	30	30,000			
				500	22	11,000			
15.6.99	1,500	35	52,500				4,500	22	99,000
							1,500	35	52,500

(Cond.)

Date	Receipts			Issues			Balance		
	Units (MT)	Rate Rs.	Amount Rs.	Units (MT)	Rate Rs.	Amount Rs.	Units (MT)	Rate Rs.	Amount Rs.
20.6.99	2,000	32	64,000	2,000	32	64,000	4,000	22	88,000
				1,500	35	52,500			
				500	22	11,000			
25.6.99				3,000	22	66,000	1,000	22	22,000
28.6.99	2,000	35	70,000				1,000	22	22,000
							2,000	35	70,000
30.6.99	1,500	30	45,000	1,500	30	45,000	1,000	22	22,000
				1,500	35	52,500	500	35	17,500
	16,500		4,98,500	15,000		4,59,000			

(ii) **Value Of Closing Stock**

			Rs.
Under	FIFO Method		
	1,500 MTs @ Rs. 30		45,000
Under	LIFO Method		
	500 MTs @ Rs. 35		17,500
	1,000 MTs @ Rs. 22		22,000
			39,500

Cost of materials consumed (15,000 MTs)

Under FIFO method   Rs. 4,53,000

Under LIFO method   Rs. 4,59,000

Q. 5. State with reasons whether the following statements are True or False:

(i) Temporary shed put up at project site to house materials is a capital expenditure.

(ii) Tallying of the trial balance only proves arithmetical accuracy.

(iii) Companies can keep their accounts under cash basis.

(iv) A partnership firm stands dissolved if the business which is carried on becomes illegal.

(v) Heavy advertising to introduce a new product is capital expenditure.

(vi) Receipts and payments account highlights total income and expenditure.

(vii) Current cost gives an alternative measurement base.

(viii) Joint-venture is a very short duration of business mainly confined to single deal entered into by two or more persons jointly.

(ix) In Current Account, Red Ink Interest is treated as negative interest.

(x) Legal fees paid to acquire a property is capital expenditure.

(20 Marks)

Solution:

(i) The statement is **True**. Temporary shed put up at a project site to house materials is incidental to the main construction. The expenditure on it is a part of construction cost. Hence, it is a capital expenditure.

(ii) The Statement is **True**. Trial balance helps to establish the arithmetical accuracy of the ledger books of account. A tallied trial balance does not reveal errors of principle and compensating errors.

(iii) The Statement is **False**. It is mandatory for companies to keep their accounts under accrual basis as per the provisions of Company Law.

(iv) The Statement is **True**. A firm is compulsorily dissolved when the business becomes illegal.

(v) The Statement is **False**. The effect of heavy advertising with regard to the launching of a new product generally lasts for more than one accounting period. It does not create any property of tangible or intangible nature. Hence, the expenditure is spread over the period for which its effect would remain. This type of expenditure is a deferred revenue expenditure.

(vi) The Statement is **False**. Receipts and payments account is a classified summary of cash receipts and payments over a certain period along with the cash and bank balances at the beginning and end of the period.

(vii) The Statement is **True**. The value of an asset is usually determined on the basis of acquisition cost. Current cost is another alternative measurement basis according to which assets are carried at the amount that would be required to be paid if the same or an equivalent asset has to be acquired presently.

(viii) The Statement is **True**. Joint Venture is a very short duration business. It is generally confined to a single transaction entered into by two or more persons jointly.

(ix) The Statement is **True**. In case the due date of a bill falls after the date of closing the account, no interest is allowed. However, interest from the date of closing to such due date is written in 'Red Ink' in the appropriate side of the Account Current. This Red Ink interest is taken as negative interest.

(x) The Statement is **True**. Legal fees paid to acquire a property is part of the cost of that property. It is incurred to acquire the ownership right of the property. Hence, it is taken as a capital expenditure.

Miscellaneous

Briefly explain the differences between any three of the following:

(a) Bills of Exchange and Promissory Note.

(b) Self and Sectional Balancing System.

(c) Personal and Impersonal Accounts.

(d) Errors of Principle and Errors of Omission.   (5 marks each)

Solution:

(a) Bill of Exchange and Promissory Note:

The following are the points of the difference between a Bill of Exchange and a Promissory Note:

(1) Number of parties. There are three parties in the case of a bill of exchange - drawer, drawee and payee. One person may, however, assume any of the two capacities out of the three. But in the case of promissory not, there are only two parties - maker and payee.

In the case of a promissory note maker cannot be payee, but in the case of a bill of exchange drawer and payee or drawer and drawee may be one and the same person. Where in a bill of exchange, the drawer and drawee are the same person, the holder may treat the instrument at his option, either as a bill of exchange or as a promissory note.

(2) **"Promise" and "order".** A promissory note contains a promise and an undertaking and not an order to pay. A bill must at least imply that the drawer has a right to ask the drawee to pay, though however politely it may be worded.

(3) **Acceptance.** A bill payable after sight requires acceptance of the drawee before it is presented for payment, while a promissory note does not.

(4) **Nature of liability.** The liability of the maker of a note is primary and absolute, but that of the drawer of a bill of exchange is secondary and conditional, since he can be held liable only on the default of the acceptor in payment of the money due and provided the fact of dishonour has been notified to him.

(5) **Maker's position.** In a promissory note maker stands in an immediate relationship with the payee, whereas in a bill of exchange the maker i.e. drawer stands in an immediate relationship with the acceptor with the acceptor and not the payee.

The position of a maker of a promissory note also differs from the position of an acceptor of a bill of exchange. Maker himself being the originator of a promissory note, cannot make it conditional, while the acceptor can accept the bill conditionally because his contract is only supplementary, being superimposed on that of the drawer.

(6) **Formalities in case of dishonour.**

  (i) Notice to prior parties. In the case of dishonour of a bill either by non acceptance or non-payment, notice of dishonour must be given by the holder to all prior parties (including drawer and endorsers) while in the case of a dishonour of a promissory note no notice is necessary to the maker.

  (ii) Protest. Foreign bills must be protested for dishonour if such protest is necessary according to the law of the place where they are drawn. No protest is necessary in the case of a promissory note, whether inland or foreign.

(7) **Copies.** Foreign bills are drawn in sets, normally three copies are prepared, while only one copy of foreign promissory note is prepared.

(b) Self and Sectional Balancing System:

The following are the points of difference between a Self and Sectional Balancing System:

(1) **Meaning.** A Self Balancing System is a system where each group of ledger can be balanced while in a Sectional Balancing System only one section or a group of ledger can be balanced;

(2) **Completion of Double Entry.** In case of Self Balancing, double entry is completed for all ledgers while in of Sectional Balancing double entry is completed only in respect of General Ledger and not for Sales and Purchases Ledger.

(3) **Test of arithmetical accuracy.** In case of Self Balancing System a trial balance can be prepared for all ledgers namely, Sales Ledger, Purchases Ledger and General Ledger and hence, the accuracy of each of these ledgers can be verified independently. Whereas in case of Sectional Balancing System trial balance can be prepared only of one ledger i.e. General Ledger. The trial balance for the other two ledgers namely, Sales and Purchases Ledgers cannot be prepared. Thus, only the accuracy of General Ledger can be verified independently. The accuracy of Sales and Purchase Ledgers can be verified only by comparing their balances respectively with the Total Debtor's Account and Total Creditors' Account maintained in the General Ledger.

In case of a large concern, it is always better to maintain the accounts on a Self Balancing System as compared to Sectional Balancing System.

(c) Personal and Impersonal Accounts:

Personal Accounts. It include accounts of three types of persons.

(i) Natural persons i.e. Human beings;

(ii) Artificial persons i.e. institutions which are creation of law, e.g., limited companies, cooperative societies etc.

(iii) Representative persons i.e. accounts representing a group of persons e.g., Outstanding Salaries Account, Outstanding Rent Account etc.

The rule for journalisation of personal accounts is : "Debit the Receiver, Credit the Giver".

Impersonal Accounts. Impersonal accounts include all Real and Nominal accounts. The Real accounts may be of the following two types;

(i) Tangible Real Accounts e.g. Building, Furniture, Stock Accounts etc.

(ii) Intangible Real Accounts i.e. Patents, Goodwill Accounts etc.

In case of Real accounts the rule of journalisation is: "Debit what comes in, Credit what goes out".

Nominal Accounts are opened in the books simply to explain the nature of the transactions. The do not really exist. All expenses, losses, incomes and gains come in this category. The rule for journalisation of nominal accounts is: "Debit all expenses and losses, credit all gains and incomes".

For more details please refer to the topic "Rules Debit and Credit" in the Chapter 3 (sec.1) "Journalisation of Transactions" of the book.

(d) Errors of Principles and Errors of Omission.

For answer please refer to 'Classification of Errors' in Chapter 11 (sec.1) of the book.

CA FOUNDATION EXAMINATION
MAY 2000
Fundamentals Of Accounting

Q. 1 (Final Accounts). The following is the Trial Balance of Shri Arihant as on 31st December, 1999:

	Debit Rs.	Credit Rs.
Capital	–	14,00,000
Drawings	75,000	–
Opening Stock	80,000	–
Purchases	16,20,000	–
Freight on Purchases	15,000	–
Wages	1,10,000	–
Sales	–	25,00,000
Salaries	1,00,000	–
Travelling Expenses	23,000	–
Miscellaneous Expenses	35,000	–
Printing and Stationery	27,000	–
Advertisement Expenses	25,000	–
Postage and Telegrams	13,000	–
Discounts	7,600	14,500
Bad Debts written off (after adjusting recovery of bad debts of Rs. 6,000 written off in 1997)	14,000	–
Building	10,00,000	–
Machinery	75,000	–
Furniture	40,000	–
Debtors	1,50,000	–
Provision for Doubtful Debts	–	19,000
Creditors	–	1,60,000
Investments (12% Purchased on 1.10.99)	6,00,000	–
Bank Balance	83,900	–
	40,93,500	40,93,500

Adjustments:

   (i) Closing Stock Rs. 2,25,000.
   (ii) Goods worth Rs. 5,000 were taken for personal use, but no entry was made in the books.
   (iii) Machinery worth Rs. 35,000 purchased on 1.1.97 was wrongly written off against Profit and Loss Account. This asset is to be brought into account on 1.1.99 taking depreciation at 10% per annum on straight line basis upto 31.12.98.

(iv) Depreciate Building at 2-1/2% p.a., Machinery at 10% p.a. and Furniture at 10% p.a.

(v) Provision for Doubtful Debts should be 6% on Debtors.

(vi) The Manager is entitled to a commission of 5% of Net Profits after charging his commission.

Prepare Trading and Profit and Loss Account for the year ending 31st December, 1999 and a Balance Sheet as at that date. (20 Marks)

Solution:

SHRI ARIHANT TRADING AND PROFIT AND LOSS ACCOUNT
for the year ended 31st December, 1999

		Rs.			Rs.
To Opening stock		80,000	By Sales		25,00,000
To Purchases	16,20,000		By Closing Stock		2,25,000
Less: Goods for Personal use	5,000	16,15,000			
To Freight on purchases		15,000			
To Wages		1,10,000			
To Gross Profit c/d		9,05,000			
		27,25,000			27,25,000
To Salaries		1,00,000	By Gross Profit b/d		9,05,000
To Travelling expenses		23,000	By Discounts received		14,500
To Miscellaneous Expenses		35,000	By Bad debts recovered		6,000
To Printing and Stationery		27,000	By Interest on investments		
To Advertisement Expenses		25,000	$\left(\dfrac{12}{100}\times\dfrac{3}{12}\times 6,00,000\right)$		18,000
To Postage and Telegrams		13,000			
To Discount allowed		7,600			
To Bad debts (14,000 + 6,000)	20,000				
$\left(\dfrac{6}{100}\times 1,50,000\right)$	9,000				
	29,000				
Less: Old Provision	19,000	10,000			
To Depreciation:					
Machinery (7,500 + 3,500)	11,000				
Furniture	4,000				
Building	25,000	40,000			
To Manager's Commission					
$\left(\dfrac{5}{105}\times 6,62,900\right)$		31,567			
To Net Profit taken to B/s		6,31,333			
		9,43,500			9,43,500

BALANCE SHEET OF SHRI ARIHANT
AS AT 31ST DECEMBER, 1999

Liabilities		Rs.	Assets		Rs.	
Capital	14,00,000		Building	10,00,000		
Add: Machinery			Less: Depreciation	25,000	9,75,000	
Capitalised	28,000		Machinery	1,03,000		
	14,28,000		Less: Depreciation	11,000	92,000	
Add: Profit	6,31,333		Furniture	40,000		
	20,59,333		Less: Depreciation	4,000	36,000	
Less: Drawings	80,000		Investments		6,00,000	
(75,000 + 5,000)		19,79,333	Interest accrued		18,000	
Creditors		1,60,000	Stock		2,25,000	
Outstanding Commission		31,567	Debtors	1,50,000		
			Less: Provision for			
			Doubtful debts	9,000	1,41,000	
			Bank Balance		83,900	
		21,70,900			21,70,900	

Working Note:

1. Machinery purchased on 1.1.97 wrongly written off, to be capitalised on 1.1.99:

	Rs.
Cost of Machinery on 1.1.97	35,000
Less: Depreciation for the years 1997 and 1998	
(3,500 + 3,500)	7,000
Value of Machinery capitalised	28,000
Less: Depreciation for the current year @ 10% p.a. on final year 1999	3,500
	24,500

2. Machinery as on 31.12.1999

	Rs.
Value of Machinery (75,000 + 28,000)	1,03,000
Less: Depreciation (7,500 + 3,500)	11,000
	92,000

Q. 2 (Partnership). The following was the Balance of Om & Co. in which X, Y and Z were partner sharing profits and losses in the ratio of 1 : 2 : 2 as on 31.3.1999. Mr. Z died on 31st December, 1999. His account has to be settled under the following terms:

BALANCE SHEET OF OM & CO.
as on 31.3.1999

Liabilities		Rs.	Assets	Rs.
Sundry Creditors		20,000	Goodwill	30,000
Bank Loan		50,000	Building	1,20,000
General Reserve		30,000	Computers	80,000
Capital Accounts:			Stock	20,000
X	40,000		Sundry Debtors	20,000
Y	80,000		Cast at Bank	20,000
Z	80,000	2,00,000	Investments	10,000
		3,00,000		3,00,000

Goodwill is to be calculated at the rate of two years' purchase on the basis of average of last three years' profits and losses. The profits and losses for the three years were as detailed below:

Year ending on	Profit/Loss
	Rs.
31.3.1999	30,000
31.3.1998	20,000
31.3.1997	(10,000) Loss

Profit for the period from 1.4.1999 to 31.12.1999 shall be ascertained proportionately on the basis of average profits and losses of the preceding three years.

During the year ending on 31.3.1999 a car costing Rs. 40,000 was purchased on 1.4.1998 and debited to travelling expenses account on which depreciation is to be calculated at 20% p.a. This asset is to be brought into account at the depreciated value.

Other values of assets were agreed as follows:

Stock at Rs. 16,000; Building at Rs. 1,40,000; Computers at Rs. 50,000; Investments at Rs. 6,000. Sundry Debtors were considered good. You are asked to prepare partners' Capital Accounts and Balance Sheet of the firm Om & Co. as on 13.12.1999 assuming that other items of assets and liabilities remained the same. (15 Marks)

Solution:

PARTNERS' CAPITAL ACCOUNTS

Dr.   Cr.

	X	Y	Z		X	Y	Z
To Revaluation A/c				By Balanced b/d	40,000	80,000	80,000
(Loss)	3,600	7,200	7,200	By General Reserve	6,000	12,000	12,000
To Z's Executor's				By Goodwill	3,600	7,200	7,200
Account	-	-	1,12,000	(48,000-30,000=18,000)			
To Balance c/d	52,400	1,04,800	-	By Car Account	6,400	12,800	12,800
				By Profit and Loss			
				Suspense Account	-	-	7,200
	56,000	1,12,000	1,19,000		56,000	1,12,000	1,19,200

Om and Co.
BALANCE SHEET AS AT 31.12.1999

Liabilities	Rs.	Assets	Rs.
Sundry Creditors	20,000	Goodwill	48,000
Bank Loan	50,000	Building	1,40,000
Capital Accounts:		Car	32,000
X	52,400	Stock	16,000
Y	1,04,800	Computers	50,000
Z's Executor's Account	1,12,000	Investments	6,000
		Sundry Debtors	20,000
		Cash at Bank	20,000
		Profit and Loss Suspense Account	7,200
	3,39,200		3,39,200

Working Notes:

(1) Computation of goodwill and Z's share of profits:

(a) Adjusted profit for the year ended 31.3.1999

			Rs.
Profit (given)			30,000
Add back: Cost of Car wrongly written off		40,000	
Less: Depreciation for the year 1998-99			
(20% on Rs. 40,000)		8,000	32,000
			62,000

(b) Average of Last three years' Profit and Losses

Year ended on	Profit (Loss) Rs.
31.3.1997	(10,000)
31.3.1998	20,000
31.3.1999	62,000
	72,000

Average Profit $\left(\dfrac{72,000}{3}\right)$ = Rs. 24,000

(c) Goodwill at 2 years' purchase

Rs. $24,000 \times 2$ = Rs. 48,000

(d) Z's share of profits for the period from 1.4.1999 to 31.12.1999

Rs. $24,000 \times \dfrac{9}{12} \times \dfrac{2}{5}$ = Rs. 7,200

(2)

REVALUATION ACCOUNT

Dr.   Cr.

	Rs.			Rs.
To Stock Account	4,000	By Building Account		20,000
To Computers Account	30,000	By Loss transferred to capacity is		
To Investments Account	4,000	X	3,600	
		Y	7,200	
		Z	7,200	18,000
	38,000			38,000

Q. 3 (Self Balancing). From the following information available from the books from 1.1.2000 to 31.3.2000, you are required to draw up the Debtors ledger Adjustment Account in the General Ledger:

(a) Total sales amounted to Rs. 1,80,000 including the sale of old Zerox Machine for Rs. 4,800 (Book value Rs. 8,000). The total Cash sales were 80% less than the total Credit sales.

(b) Cash collections from debtors amounted to 70% of the aggregate of the opening debtors and Credit sales for the period. Debtors were allowed a cash discount of Rs. 20,000.

(c) Bills Receivable drawn during the three months totalled Rs. 30,000 of which bills amounting to Rs. 10,000 were endorsed in favour of suppliers. Out of the endorsed Bills, one bill for Rs. 6,000 was dishonoured for non-payment as the party became insolvent, his estate realised nothing.

(d) Cheques received from customers Rs. 8,000 were dishonoured, a sum of Rs. 2,000 was irrecoverable; Bad debts written off in the earlier years realised Rs. 11,000.

(e) Sundry debtors as on 1.1.200 stood at Rs. 50,000.   (15 Marks)

Solution:

General Ledger
DEBTORS LEDGER ADJUSTMENT ACCOUNT

Dr.   Cr.

	Rs.			Rs.
(i) 2000				
Jan. 1 To Balance b/d	50,000	Mar. 31	By General Ledger Adjustment Account: Collection – Cash and Bank (70% of Rs. 1,96,000)	1,37,200
Mar. 31 To General Ledger Adjustment Account: Sales				
$\left[\dfrac{100}{120} \times (1,80,000 - 4,800)\right]$	1,46,000		Discount	20,000
Creditors – Bill Receivable dishonoured	6,000		Bills Receivable	30,000
			Bad Debts	
Bank – Cheques dishonoured	8,000		(6,000 + 2,000)	8,000
			By Balance c/d	14,800
	2,10,000			2,10,000

Q. 4 (Negotiable Instruments).

(a) On 1st July, 1999 G drew a bill for Rs. 80,000 for 3 months on H for mutual accommodation. He accepted the bill of exchange.

G had purchased goods worth Rs. 81,000 from J on the same date. G endorsed H's acceptance to J in full settlement.

On 1st October, 1999 J purchased goods worth Rs. 90,000 from H. J endorsed the bill of exchange received from G to H and paid Rs. 9,000 in full settlement of the amount due to H.

On 1st October, 1999 H purchased goods worth Rs. 1,00,000 from G. He paid the amount due to G by cheque.

(b) (Inventory Valuation) The Profit and Loss Account of Hanuman showed a net profit of Rs. 60,000, after considering the closing stock of Rs. 37,500 on 31st March, 1999. Subsequently the following information was obtained from scrutiny of the books:

(i) Purchases for the year included Rs. 1,500 paid for new electric fittings for the shop.

(ii) Hanuman gave away goods valued at Rs. 4,000 as free samples for which no entry was made in the books of accounts.

(iii) Invoices for goods amounting to Rs. 25,000 have been entered on 27th March, 1999, but the goods were not included in stock.

(iv) In March, 1999 goods of Rs. 20,000 sold and delivered were taken in the Sales for April, 1999.

(v) Goods costing Rs. 7,500 were sent on sale or return in March, 1999 at a margin of Profit of 33-1/3% on cost. Though approval was given in April, 1999 these were taken as sales for March, 1999.

Calculate the value of stock on 31st March, 1999 and the adjusted Net Profit for the year ended on that date. (9 Marks)

Solution:

(a)

Books of H
JOURNAL ENTRIES

Date	Particulars		Dr. Rs.	Cr. Rs.
1.7.99	G's Dr. To Bills Payable Account (Being Acceptance of bill drawn by G)	Dr.	80,000	80,000
1.9.99	J's To Sales Account (Being Sales made to J)	Dr.	90,000	90,000
1.9.99	Bills Receivable Account Bank Account Discount Account To J's Account (Being our own acceptance received through J's endorsement of bill accepted in form of G for Rs. 80,000 and Rs. 9,000 in cash received in full Settlement of the amount due)	Dr. Dr. Dr.	80,000 9,000 1,000	90,000
	Bills Payable Account To Bills Receivable Account (Being own acceptance received through J's endorsement, cancelled)	Dr.	80,000	80,000
1.10.99	Purchase Account To G' (Being purchases made from G)	Dr.	1,00,000	1,00,000
	G' To Bank Account (Being amount paid to G after adjusting Rs. 80,000 for accommodation extended to him)	Dr.	20,000	20,000

(b)

PROFIT AND LOSS ADJUSTMENT ACCOUNT

Dr.   Cr

	Rs.		Rs.
To Advertisement (samples)	4,000	By Net profit	60,000
To Sales (Goods approved in April		By Electric fittings	1,500
to be taken as April sales:		By Samples	4,000
7,500 + 2,500)	10,000	By Stock (Purchases of March,	
To Adjusted Net Profit	1,04,000	not included in stock)	25,000
		By Sales (goods sold in March	
		Wrongly taken as April sales)	20,000
		By Stock (goods sent on approval	
		basis not included in stock)	7,500
	1,18,000		1,18,000

COMPUTATION OF VALUE OF STOCK ON 31ST MARCH, 1999

	Rs.
Stock on 31st March, 1999 (given)	37,500
Add: Purchases of March, 1999 not included in stock	25,000
Goods lying with customers on a approval basis	7,500
	70,000

Q. 5 (Basic concepts). State with reasons whether the following statements are True or False:

(i) Expenditure on renovation of a theatre which has increased the seating capacity by 10% is deferred revenue expenditure.

(ii) A has drawn a bill on B. B accepts the same and endorses the bill to C.

(iii) Outstanding expenditure is a nominal account.

(iv) A joint venture is a partnership under the Partnership Act.

(v) A partner who devotes more time to a business than other partners is entitled to get a salary.

(vi) A tailed trial balance means that the books if accounts have been prepared as per accepted accounting principles.

(vii) Provision for Bad debts is debited to Sundry Debtors Account.

(viii) Discount account in Cash-book should be balanced.

(ix) Travelling expenses of Rs. 80,000 paid to a technician for the installation of a new machine is debited to Profit and Loss Account.

(x) Goodwill brought in by incoming partner in cash for joining a partnership firm is taken away by the old partners in their new profit sharing ratio.

(20 marks)

Answer

(i) **False:** Expenditure on renovation of a theatre which has increased the seating capacity is capital expenditure as it has contributed to the revenue earning capacity of the business over more than one accounting period.

(ii) **False:** B cannot endorse the bill to C as he is drawee. Only A, the drawer can do so.

(iii) **False:** Outstanding expenditure represents a liability due to some person, therefore it is a personal account.

(iv) **False:** Joint venture is not a partnership since it is only a kind of temporary trading relationship between coventurers to carry out a commercial venture.

(v) **False:** No partner is entitled to a salary unless the deed of partnership specifically provides for the same.

(vi) **False:** Trial balance only checks the arithmetical accuracy of books. Errors of principles and errors of omissions will not affect the agreement of the Trial Balance.

(vii) **False:** Provision for Bad debts is debited to profit and loss account. In the balance sheet, it is shown as deduction from 'Debtors'.

(viii) **False:** Discount account in Cash-book should not be balanced. Debit total of discount column represents discount allowed and that of credit side represents discount received. These balances are transferred to Profit and Loss Account.

(ix) **False:** The expenditure is a capital expenditure since it has been incurred to put the asset in working condition.

(x) **False:** When a new partner brings in cash for goodwill, it is taken away by the old partners not in the new profit sharing ratio but in the profit sacrificing ratio.

Solution:

(1) The Statement is **False**. Expenditure on renovation of a Theatre has increased the sitting capacity and, therefore also the earning capacity of the business also for over more than one accounting period. Hence, it is a capital expenditure.

(2) The Statement is **False**. The bill can be endorsed either by the drawer or by the holder. B is the acceptor and hence he cannot endorse the bill to another person.

(3) The Statement is **False**. Outstanding expenditure represents account of a person to whom payment regarding expenditure is to be made. Hence, it is a personal account.

(4) The Statement is **False**. Joint Venture is made only for a temporary period and for a single dealing and not for a series of dealings. A partnership agreement is made for carrying out business for a long period. Hence Joint Venture is only a temporary trading relationship and not a partnership.

(5) The Statement is **False**. In the absence of any contract to the contrary a partner is not entitled to any salary for looking after the business of the firm.

(6) The Statement is **False**. The trial balance checks only the arithmetical accuracy of the books of accounts. A trial balance may tally inspite of the fact that books of accounts have not been prepared according to accepted principles.

(7) The Statement is **False**. The provision for bad debts is debited to the Profit & Loss Account. The amount of provision is deducted from Sundry Debtors in the Balance Sheet.

(8) The Statement is **False**. The Discount Account the cash book should not be balanced. Both discount allowed and discount received are separately taken to the Profit & Loss Account.

(9) The Statement is **False**. Travelling expenses incurred for installing a new machine is of capital nature and should be debited to the machine account and not to the profit & Loss Account.

(10) The Statement is **False**. Goodwill brought in by the new partner should be credited to the old partners or is taken equally by them in their profit sacrificing ratio and not in the new profit sharing ratio.

Q. 6 (Basic concepts). Briefly explain any three of the following:

(a) Periodicity Concept.

(b) Sinking Fund Method. (5 Marks)

(c) Receipts and Payments Account. (5 Marks)

(5 Marks)

(d) Causes of difference between the balance shown by the Pass-book and the Cash-book.

(5 Marks)

Solution:

(a) **Periodicity Concept.**

For answer please refer to the "Accounting Period Concept" in Chapter 2 (Section I) "Accounting Principles", of the Book.

(b) **Sinking Fund Method.**

For answer please refer to "Depreciation or Sinking Fund Method" in Chapter 13 (Section I) "Depreciation Accounting", of the Book.

(c) **Receipts & Payments Account.**

For answer please refer to "Receipts & Payments Account" in Chapter 15, (Section I) "Accounts of Non Profit Making Organisation", of the Book.

(d) **Causes of difference in the balance shown by the Pass Book and Cash Book.**

For answer please refer to "Causes of difference" in Chapter 7 (Section 1) "Bank Reconciliation Statement", of the Book.

CA FOUNDATION EXAMINATION
NOVEMBER 2000
Fundamentals Of Accounting

Q. 1 (Final Accounts). The following is the Trial Balance of K on 31st March, 2000:

	Dr. Rs.	Cr. Rs.
Capital	–	8,00,000
Drawings	60,000	–
Opening Stock	75,000	–
Purchases	15,95,000	–
Freight on Purchases	25,000	–
Wages (11 months upto 29.2.2000)	66,000	–
Sales	–	23,10,000
Salaries	1,40,000	–
Postage, Telegrams, Telephones	12,000	–
Printing and Stationery	18,000	–
Miscellaneous Expenses	30,000	–
Creditors	–	3,00,000
Investments	1,00,000	–
Discounts Received	–	15,000
Debtors	2,50,000	–
Bad Debts	15,000	–
Provision for Bad Debts	–	8,000
Building	3,00,000	–
Machinery	5,00,000	–
Furniture	40,000	–
Commission on Sales	45,000	–
Interest on Investments	–	12,000
Insurance (Year upto 31.7.2000)	24,000	–
Bank Balance	1,50,000	–
	34,45,000	34,45,000

Adjustments:

(i) Closing Stock Rs. 2,25,000.

(ii) Machinery worth Rs. 45,000 purchased on 1.10.99 was shown as Purchases. Freight paid on the Machinery was Rs. 5,000, which is included in Freight on Purchases.

(iii) Commission is payable at 2% on Sales.

(iv) Investments were sold at 10% profit, but the entire sales proceeds have been taken as Sales.

(v)   Write off Bad Debts Rs. 10,000 and create a provision for Doubtful Debts at 5% of Debtors.

(vi)   Depreciate Building by 2% p.a. and Machinery and Furniture at 10% p.a.

Prepare Trading and Profit and Loss Account for the year ending 31st March, 2000 and a Balance Sheet as on that date.   (20 Marks)

Solution:

TRADING AND PROFIT AND LOSS ACCOUNT OF K

for the year ending or 31st March, 2000

Particulars		Rs.	Particulars		Rs.
To Opening Stock		75,000	By Sales	23,10,000	
To Purchases	15,95,000		Less: Sale of		
Less: Transfer to			Investments	1,10,000	22,00,000
Machinery A/c	45,000	15,50,000	By Closing Stock		2,25,000
To Freight on Purchases	25,000				
Less: Transfer to					
Machinery A/c	5,000	20,000			
To Wages	66,000				
Add: Outstanding	6,000	72,000			
To Gross Profit c/d		7,08,000			
		24,25,000			24,25,000
To Salaries		1,40,000	By Gross Profit b/d		7,08,000
To Postage, Telegrams					
& Telephones		12,000	By Interest on investments		12,000
To Printing and Stationery		18,000	By Profit on sale of		
			Investments		10,000
To Miscellaneous Expenses		30,000	By Discounts received		15,000
To Commission on Sales	45,000				
Add: Outstanding	10,000	55,000			
To Insurance	24,000				
Less: Prepaid	8,000	16,000			
To Provision for Bad and					
Doubtful Debts:					
Bad Debts	15,000				
Add: Written off	10,000				
Add: Provision for					
Doubtful Debts					
(5% of Rs. 2,40,000)	12,000				
	37,000				
Less: Old Provision	8,000	29,000			
To Depreciation:					
Building	7,500				
Machinery					
(Rs. 50,000 + Rs. 2,500)	52,500				
Furniture	4,000	64,000			
To Net Profit		3,81,000			
		7,45,000			7,45,000

BALANCE SHEET OF K AS AT 31ST MARCH, 2000

Liabilities		Rs.	Assets		Rs.
Capital	8,00,000		Building	3,00,000	
Add: Profit	3,81,000		Less: Depreciation	7,500	
	11,81,000				2,92,500
Less: Drawings	60,000		Machinery	5,00,000	
		11,21,000	Additions	50,000	
Creditors		3,00,000		5,50,000	
Outstanding Expenses:			Less: Depreciation	52,500	
Wages	6,000				4,97,500
Commission	10,000		Furniture	40,000	
		16,000	Less: Depreciation	4,000	36,000
			Debtors	2,50,000	
			Less: Bad Debts	10,000	
				2,40,000	
			Less: Provision for		
			Doubtful Debts	12,000	2,28,000
			Prepaid Insurance		8,000
			Stock		2,25,000
			Bank Balance		1,50,000
		14,37,000			14,37,000

Q. 2 (Partnership). Hari and Ram were in partnership, sharing profits and losses equally. On 1st January, 1999, Suraj was admitted into partnership on the following terms:

Suraj is to have one-sixth share in the profits/losses, which he has got from Hari, paying him Rs. 40,000 for that share as goodwill. Out of this amount, Hari is to withdraw Rs. 30,000 and the balance amount is to remain in the firm. It was further agreed that the value of investments should be reduced to Rs. 18,000 and plant to be valued at Rs. 29,000. Creditors were to be reduced by Rs. 3,000 as one of the creditors has closed his business and gone.

Suraj is to bring in proportionate capital on his admission.

The Balance Sheet as at 31st December, 1998 was as follows:

		Rs.		Rs.
Creditors		1,05,000	Cash at Bank	40,000
Capitals:			Book Debts	60,000
Hari	60,000		Stock	50,000
Ram	60,000	1,20,000	Investments	30,000
			Furniture	10,000
			Plant	35,000
		2,25,000		2,25,000

The profits for the year ended 31st December, 1999 were Rs. 60,000 and the drawings were: Hari Rs. 15,000; Ram Rs. 22,500 and Suraj Rs. 7,500.

Journalise the entries on Suraj's admission and give the Capital Accounts and the Balance Sheet as at 31st December, 1999.

(15 marks)

Solution:

JOURNAL ENTRIES

		Rs.	Rs.
Bank Account	Dr.	40,000	
To Hari's Capital Account			40,000
(Being amount paid by Suraj credited to Hari for share of goodwill purchased from him)			
Hari's Capital Account	Dr.	30,000	
To Bank Account			30,000
(Being amount withdrawn by Hari)			
Sundry Creditors Account	Dr.	3,000	
Revaluation Account	Dr.	15,000	
To Investments Account			12,000
To Plant Account			6,000
(Being recording of revaluation of investments, plant and sundry creditors)			
Hari's Capital Account	Dr.	7,500	
Ram's Capital Account	Dr.	7,500	
To Revaluation Account			15,000
(Being transfer of loss on revaluation to old partners in equal ratio)			
Bank Account	Dr.	23,000	
To Suraj's Capital Account			23,000
(Being proportionate capital brought in by Suraj)			

PARTNERS' CAPITAL ACCOUNTS

1999		Hari Rs.	Ram Rs.	Suraj Rs.	1999		Hari Rs.	Ram Rs.	Suraj Rs.
Jan.1	To Revaluation A/c	7,500	7,500	-	Jan.1	By Balance b/d	60,000	60,000	-
	To Bank A/c	30,000	-	-		By Bank A/c (goodwill)	40,000	-	-
Dec.31	To Bank A/c (drawings)	15,000	22,500	7,500		By Bank A/c (capital)	-	-	23,000
	To Balance c/d	67,500	60,000	25,500	Dec.31	By Profit & loss A/c	20,000	30,000	10,000
		1,20,000	90,000	33,000			1,20,000	90,000	33,000

BALANCE SHEET AS AT 31ST DECEMBER, 1999

Liabilities		Rs.	Assets	Rs.
Capital Accounts:			Plant	29,000
Hari	67,500		Furniture	10,000
Ram	60,000		Investments	18,000
Suraj	25,500		Stock	50,000
		1,53,000	Book Debts	60,000
Creditors		1,02,000	Cash at Bank	88,000
		2,55,000		2,55,000

Working Notes:

(1) New Profit Sharing Ratio:

	Old Ratio	New Ratio
Hari	1/2	3/6
Ram	1/2	1/2 – 1/6 = 2/6
Suraj		1/6

(2) Amount of capital brought in by suraj:

	Rs.
Capital on 1.1.99	
Hari (1,00,000 - 30,000 - 7,500)	62,500
Ram (60,000 - 7,500)	52,500
	1,15,000

Let the total capital after admission of Suraj be Rs. x

$$\text{Rs. } 1,15,000 + \frac{1x}{6} = x$$

$$\frac{5}{6}x = \text{Rs.} 1,15,000$$

$$x = \text{Rs. } 1,15,000 \times \frac{6}{5} = \text{Rs.} 1,38,000$$

$$\text{Proportional Capital of Suraj} = \text{Rs. } 1,38,000 \times \frac{1}{6}$$

$$= \text{Rs. } 23,000$$

(3) Cash at Bank on 31st December, 1999

		Rs.
Cash at Bank on 31st December, 1998		40,000
Add:	Amount paid by Suraj for goodwill	40,000
	Amount paid by Suraj for capital	23,000
	Profits earned during the year*	60,000
		1,63,000
Less:	Drawings - Hari (30,000 + 15,000)	45,000
	Ram	22,500
	Suraj	7,500	75,000
		88,000

The amount has been computed as if profit earned during the year has all been realised as cash in bank balance.

Q. 3.   (Inventory Valuation).

(a) Physical verification of stock in a business was done on 23rd June, 2000. The value of the stock was Rs. 4,80,000. The following transactions took place between 23rd June to 30th June, 2000:

   (i)   Out of the goods sent on consignment, goods at cost worth Rs. 24,000 were unsold.

   (ii) Purchases of Rs. 40,000 were made out of which goods worth Rs. 16,000 were delivered on 5th July, 2000.

(iii) Sales were Rs. 1,36,000 which include goods worth Rs. 32,000 sent on approval. Half of these goods were returned before 30th June, 2000, but no information is available regarding the remaining goods.

(iv) Goods are sold at cost plus 25%. However goods costing Rs. 24,000 had been sold for Rs. 12,000.

Determine the value of stock on 30th June, 2000

(b) (Average due sale) E owes to F the following amounts :

(i) Rs. 5,000 due on 10th March, 1999

(ii) Rs. 18,000 due on 2nd April, 1999

(iii) Rs. 60,000 due on 30th April, 1999

(iv) Rs. 2,000 due on 10th June, 1999.

He desires to make full payment on 30th June, 1999 with interest at 10% per annum from the average due date. Find out the average due date and the amount of interest. (6 marks)

Solution:

(a)

STATEMENT OF VALUATION OF STOCK ON 30TH JUNE, 2000

		Rs.
Value of Stock as on 23rd June, 2000		4,80,000
Add: Unsold Stock out of the goods sent on consignment	24,000	
Purchases during the period from		
23rd June, 2000 to 30th June, 2000	24,000	
Goods in transit on 30th June, 2000	16,000	
Cost of goods sent on approval basis		
(80% of Rs. 16,000)	12,800	76,800
		5,56,800
Less: Cost of Sales during the period from 23rd June, 2000		
to 30th June, 2000		
Sales (Rs. 1,36,000 - Rs. 16,000)	1,20,000	
Less: Gross Profit	9,600	1,10,400
Value of Stock as on 30th June, 2000		4,46,400

Working Notes:

1. Computation of Normal Sales

Actual Sales		1,36,000
Less: Abnormal Sales	12,000	
Return of goods sent on approval	16,000	28,000
		1,08,000

2. Computation of Gross Profit:

Gross Profit on normal sales	21,600
$\dfrac{20}{100} \times$ Rs. 1,08,000	
Less: Loss on sale of particular (abnormal) goods	12,000
(Rs. 24,000 - Rs. 12,000)	
Gross Profit	9,600

(b)

COMPUTATION OF AVERAGE DUE DATE

Taking 10th March, 1999 as the base date.

Due Date 1999	Amount Rs.	No. of days from the base date i.e., 10th March	Product Rs.
10th March	5,000	0	0
2nd April	18,000	23	4,14,000
30th April	60,000	51	30,60,000
10th June	2,000	92	1,84,000
	85,000		36,58,000

$$\text{Average Due Date} = \text{Base date} + \text{days equal to } \frac{\text{Sum of products}}{\text{Sum of amounts}}$$

$$\text{10th March} + \frac{\text{Rs. } 36,58,000}{\text{Rs. } 85,000} \text{ i.e., 43 days (approx.)} = \text{22nd April, 1999}$$

Interest Amount: Interest can be calculated on Rs. 85,000 at 10% p.a. from 22nd April, 1999 to 30th June, 1999 for 69 days.

$$= \text{Rs. } 85,000 \times \frac{10}{100} \times \frac{69}{365}$$

$$= \text{Rs. } 1,607 \text{ (approx.)}$$

Q. 4 (Consignment)

(a) A of Agra sent on consignment goods valued Rs. 1,00,000 to B of Bombay on 1st March, 1999. He incurred an expenditure of Rs. 12,000 on Freight and Insurance. A's accounting year closes on 31st December. B was entitled to a commission of 5% on gross sales plus a delcredere commission of 3 per cent. B took delivery of the consignment by incurring expenses of Rs. 3,000 for goods consigned.

On 31.12.1999, B informed on phone that he had sold all the goods for Rs. 1,50,000 by incurring selling expenses of Rs. 2,000. He further informed that only Rs. 1,48,000 had been

realised and rest was considered irrecoverable, and would be sending the cheque in a day

or so for the amount due alongwith the accounts sale.

On 5.1.2000, A received the cheque for the amount due from B and incurred bank charges of Rs. 260 for collecting the cheque. The amount was credited by the Bank on 9.1.2000. Write up the Consignment account finding out the profit/loss on the consignor, recording the transactions upto the receipt and collection of the cheque. **(9 Marks)**

(b) (Capital & Revenue) State with reasons, how you would classify the following items of expenditure:

(i) Overhauling expenses of Rs. 25,000 for the engine of a motor car to get better fuel efficiency.

(ii) Inauguration expenses of Rs. 25 lakhs incurred on the opening of a new manufacturing unit in an existing business.

(iii) Compensation of Rs. 2.5 crores paid to workers, who opted for voluntary retirement.

Solution:

Books of Mr. A

CONSIGNMENT ACCOUNT

Dr.   Cr.

		Rs.		Rs.
To Goods sent on Consignment A/c		1,00,000	By B	1,50,000
To Cash A/c (Freight and Insurance)		12,000		
To B				
Clearance Expenses	3,000			
Selling Expenses	2,000			
Commission @ 5% On Rs. 1,50,000	7,500			
Delcredere Commission @ 3% On Rs. 1,50,000	4,500			
		17,000		
To Provision for Expenses (Bank charges)		260		
To Profit and Loss A/c (Profit on consignment)		20,740		
		1,50,000		1,50,000

B' ACCOUNT

	Rs.		Rs.	
To Consignment A/c	1,50,000	By Consignment A/c		
		Clearance expenses	3,000	
		Selling expenses	2,000	
		Commission	7,500	
		Delcredere Commission	4,500	17,000
		By Balance c/d		1,33,000
	1,50,000			1,50,000

BANK ACCOUNT

	Rs.			Rs.
To B's Account	1,33,000	By Bank Charges		260
		By Balance c/d		1,32,740
	1,33,000			1,33,000

PROVISION FOR EXPENSES ACCOUNT

	Rs.		Rs.
To Bank Charges	260	By Balance b/d	260

Solution:

(i) Bring the overhauling expenses have been incurred for the engine of a motor car to derive better fuel efficiency. These expenses will reduce the running the future running cost. The benefit is therefore in form of endurable long term advdantage. Hence, the expenditure should be capitalised.

(ii) Inauguration expenses incurred on the opening of a new unit may help more customers. This expenditure is in the nature of revenue expenditure as the expenditure may not generate any enduring benefit to the business for over more than one accounting period.

(iii) The amount paid to workers on account voluntary retirement is of the nature of revenue expenditure. The amount of expenditure is quite heavy hence, it may be appropriate to defer it over future years.

Q. 5 State with reasons whether the following statements are True or False:

(1) Purchase Ledger Adjustment Account under sectional balancing system is also known as Creditors Ledger Control Account.

(2) Freight paid on purchases of goods is added to the amount of purchases.

(3) Incorrect allocation of expenditure or receipt between capital and revenue is an error of commission.

(4) Wages paid for erection of new machinery are debited to Machinery Account.

(5) The relationship between the consignor and the consignee is that of Principal and Agent.

(6) The Purchase Day-Book is a part of the Ledger.

(7) Expenditure which results in acquisition of a permanent asset is a revenue expenditure.

(8) There is no difference between the written down value method and diminishing balance method of depreciation.

(9) A promissory note cannot be made payable to bearer.

(10) Bank Reconciliation Statement is not prepared to arrive at the Bank Balance.

(20 marks)

Solution:

(1) The Statement is **True**. Purchase Ledger Adjustment Account is in fact a Total Creditors Account. Hence it can also be termed as 'Creditors Ledger Control Account' under Sectional Balancing System.

(2) The Statement is **True**. The true cost of purchases include the cost of freight also. However, for accounting purposes such cost should not be included in the purchases but rather shown separately in the Trading Account.

(3) The Statement is **False**. Incorrect allocation of expenditure and receipt between capital revenue is an error of principle and not an error of commission.

(4) The Statement is **True**. Any expenditure incurred for installing a new machinery should be taken as capital expenditure and added to the Machinery Account.

(5) The Statement is **True**. The Consignee sells goods on behalf and risk of the Consignor and hence he is an agent of the Consignor.

(6) The Statement is **False**. Purchase Day Book is a book of prime entry and hence it is a part of journal and not ledger.

(7) The Statement is **False**. Any expenditure incurred in acquisition of a permanent asset is a capital expenditure and not a revenue expenditure.

(8) The Statement is **True**. The Written Down Value Method and Diminishing Balance Method are synonymous of each other.

(9) The Statement is **True**. Section 31 of the Reserve Bank of India Act does not permit making of promissory note payable to the bearer.

(10) The Statement is **True**. A bank reconciliation statement is prepared to ascertain the causes of difference between the balances as shown by the Cash Account and Pass Book. It is not prepared to arrive at the bank balance.

Q. 6 (Basic concepts). Briefly explain the difference between any three of the following:

(a) Commission and Discount.

(b) Bill of Exchange and Promissory Note.

(c) Provision and Reserve.

(d) Fixed Capital and Fluctuating Capital. (15 marks)

(a) Difference between Commission and Discount. The term 'Commission' refers to remuneration to an employee or an agent for the services performed by him regarding sales, purchases, collection or any other type of business. It is usually computed as a percentage of the amount involved. The following are a few cases where Commission is allowed:

(i) Commission is paid to selling or buying agent;

(ii) Commission is paid to brokers and bankers for services rendered;

(iii) Commission is paid to property dealers for assisting in renting out the properties or making available properties on rent or assisting in purchase or sale of properties.

(iv) Commission is paid to an Export-Import agent in foreign trade transactions. Commission earned is an income for the business while commission paid is an expense of the business.

The term 'Discount' refers to any deduction or rebate allowed by a person in the following situations:

(i) Settlement of a debt before it becomes due;

(ii) Purchasing in bulk results in discount allowed by the seller over and above the normal trade discount.

A trade discount is not shown in the books of both Sellers and Buyer. The sales and purchases are shown at net price respectively. However a cash discount is shown in the books of account as a loss.

(b) Bill of Exchange and Promissory Note.

(a) For answer please refer answer to Question 6 (a) of CA Foundation November, 1999.

(c) Provision and Reserve.

The following are the points of difference between a Provision and a Reserve.

(i) A Reserve is an appropriation of profits while a provision is a charge against profits. In other words true profits cannot be determined without making adjustments for the provisions required.

(ii) Creation of reserves increases proprietor's funds while creation of provisions decreases his funds in the business.

(iii) Provisions are created to meet some known contingency, the amount of which cannot be precisely determined. Reserves are created to meet some unknown contingency. In other words, creation of reserves strengthens the financial position of the business while creation of provision help in maintaining the existing financial position.

(d) Fixed Capital and Floating Capital.

For answer please refer to Chapter I Section III of the Book "Fixed and Floating Capitals".

CA FOUNDATION EXAMINATION
MAY 2001
Fundamentals Of Accounting

Q. 1. (Final Accounts).   Shri Patit Bansali submitted to you the following Trial Balance, which he has not been able to agree. Rewrite the Trial Balance and prepare Trading and Profit and Loss Account for the year ended 31.12.2000 and a Balance Sheet as on that date after giving effect to the undermentioned adjustments:

	Dr. Amount Rs.	Cr. Amount Rs.
Capital		16,000
Opening Stock	17,500	
Closing Stock		18,790
Drawings	3,305	
Return inward		550
Carriage inward	1,240	
Deposit with X		1,400
Return outward	840	
Carriage outward		725
Rent paid	800	
Rent outstanding	150	
Purchases	13,000	
Sundry Debtors	5,000	
Sundry Creditors		4,000
Furniture	1,500	
Sales		29,000
Wages	850	
Cash	1,370	
Goodwill	1,800	
Advertisement	950	
	48,305	70,465

Adjustments:

(1) Write off Rs. 600 as Bad Debts and make Reserve for Bad Debts on Sundry Debtors at 5%.

(2) Stock valued at Rs. 2,000 was destroyed by fire on 25th December, 2000, but Insurance Company admitted a claim for Rs. 1,500 only and paid the sum in January, 2001.

(3) Depreciate Furniture by 10%.

Solution:

SHRI PATIT BANSALI REDRAFTED TRIAL BALANCE
as on 31st December, 2000

	Dr. Amount Rs.	Cr. Amount Rs.
Capital		16,000
Opening stock	17,500	
Drawings	3,305	
Return inward	550	
Carriage inward	1,240	
Deposit with X	1,400	
Return outward		840
Carriage outward	725	
Rent paid	800	
Rent outstanding		150
Purchases	13,000	
Sundry debtors	5,000	
Sundry creditors		4,000
Furniture	1,500	
Sales		29,000
Wages	850	
Cash	1,370	
Goodwill	1,800	
Advertisement	950	
	49,990	49,990

SHRI PATIT BANSALI TRADING AND PROFIT AND LOSS ACCOUNT
for the year ended 31st December, 2000

		Amount Rs.			Amount Rs.
To Opening Stock		17,500	By Sales	29000	
To Purchases	13,000		Less: Return Inward	550	28,450
Less: Return Outward	840	12,160	By Stock lost by fire		2,000
To Wages		850	By Closing Stock		18,790
To Carriage Inward		1,240			
To Gross Profit c/d		17,490			
		49,240			49,240
To Carriage Outward		725	By Gross Profit b/d		17,490
To Rent		800			
To Advertisement		950			
To Bad debts		600			
To Reserve for Bad Debts (5% of Rs. 4,400)		220			
To Loss of stock by fire		500			
To Depreciation on Furniture (10% of Rs. 1,500)		150			
To Net Profit		13,545			
		17,490			17,490

Shri Patit Bansali

BALANCE SHEET AS AT 31ST DECEMBER, 2000

Liabilities		Rs.			Rs.
Capital	16,000		Goodwill		1,800
Add: Net Profit	13,545		Furniture	1,500	
	29,545		Less: Depreciation	150	1,350
Less: Drawings	3,305		Deposit with X		1,400
		26,240	Closing Stock		18,790
Sundry Creditors		4,000	Sundry Debtors	5,000	
			Less: Bad debts	600	
Outstanding rent		150		4,400	
			Less: Reserve for Bad debts	220	4,180
			Insurance Claim Recoverable		1,500
			Cash		1,370
		30,390			30,390

Q. 2. (Partnership). A, B and C were equal partners. Their Balance Sheet on 31.12.2000 stood as under, when the firm was dissolved.

BALANCE SHEET AS AT 31.12.2000

Liabilities	Rs.	Assets	Rs.
Sundry Creditors	32,000	Machinery	12,000
A's Capital	4,000	Furniture	3,000
B's Capital	3,000	Sundry Debtors	5,000
		Stock	4,000
		Cash at Bank	2,800
		C's Capital	12,200
	39,000		39,000

The Assets realised as under:

Machinery Rs. 6,000; Furniture Rs. 1,000; Sundry Debtors Rs. 4,000 and Stock Rs. 3,000.

The expenses of realisation came to Rs. 1,400.

A's personal properties are not sufficient to pay his personal liabilities, whereas in B's and C's private estate there is a surplus of Rs. 2,400 and Rs. 3,000 respectively.

Show Necessary Accounts closing the books of the Firm. (15 marks)

Solution:

Books of A, B and C

REALISATION ACCOUNT

Dr. Cr.

		Rs.			Rs.
To Sundry Assets:			By Bank A/c:		
Machinery	12,000		Machinery	6,000	
Furniture	3,000		Furniture	1,000	

(Cont.)

Dr.						Cr.
		Rs.				Rs.
Debtors	5,000		Debtors	4,000		
Stock	4,000	24,000	Stock	3,000		14,000
To Bank A/c: (Expenses)		1,400	By Partners'			
			(capital Accounts :			
			Realisation on)			
			A		3,800	
			B		3,800	
			C		3,800	11,400
		25,400				25,400

BANK ACCOUNT

Dr.				Cr.
	Rs.			Rs.
To Balance b/d	2,800	By Realisation A/c		1,400
To Realisation A/c	14,000	By Creditors A/c		20,800
To B's Capital A/c	2,400	(Balancing figure)		
To C's Capital A/c	3,000			
	22,200			22,200

CREDITORS ACCOUNT

Dr.		Cr.	
	Rs.		Rs.
To Bank A/c	20,800	By Balance b/d	32,000
To Deficiency A/c	11,200		
	32,000		32,000

PARTNERS CAPITAL ACCOUNTS

Dr.								Cr.
2000 Dec. 31	A Rs.	B Rs.	C Rs.	2000 Dec. 31	A Rs.	B Rs.	C Rs.	
To Balance b/d	–	–	12,200	By Balance b/d	4,000	3,000	–	
To Realisation A/c	3,800	3,800	3,800	By Bank A/c	–	2,400	3,000	
To Deficiency A/c	200	1,600		By Deficiency A/c	–	–	13,000	
	4,000	5,400	16,000		4,000	5,400	16,000	

DEFICIENCY ACCOUNT

Dr.				Cr.
2000	Rs.	2000	Rs.	
Dec. 31 To C's Capital A/c	13,000	Dec. 31	By Creditors A/c	11,200
			By A's Capital A/c	200
			By B's Capital A/c	1,600
	13,000			13,000

Q. 3 (Negotiable Instruments).

- (a) Explain a Bill of Exchange and the various parties to it. (6 marks)
- (b) Record the following transactions in the journals of Ram and Hari :

    Ram sells goods for Rs. 1,00,000 to Hari on 1st January, 2001 and on the same day draws a bill on Hari at three months for the amount. Hari accepts it and returns it to Ram, who discounts it on 4th January, 2001 with his bank at 12% per annum. The acceptance is dishonoured on due date and the bank pays Rs. 250 as noting charges. (9 marks)

Solution: For answer refer to Bill of Exchange in chapter 6 (Section I) "Negotiable Instruments" of the book.

RAM'S JOURNAL ENTRIES

(b)

2001			Rs.	Rs.
Jan. 1	Hari	Dr.	1,00,000	
	To sales Account			1,00,000
	(Being Sale of goods to Hari on credit)			
	Bills Receivable Account	Dr.	1,00,000	
	To Hari			1,00,000
	(Being bill accepted by Hari for the amount due)			
Jan. 4	Bank Account	Dr.	97,000	
	Discount Account	Dr.	3,000	
	To Bills Receivable Account			1,00,000
	(Being bill accepted by Hari discounted with the bank at 12% p.a.)			
Jan. 4	Hari	Dr.	1,00,250	
	To Bank Account			1,00,250
	(Being the amount of bill dishonoured and noting charges paid thereon, debited to Hari's account)			

HARI'S JOURNAL ENTRIES

2001			Rs.	Rs.
Jan. 1	Purchase Account	Dr.	1,00,000	
	To Ram			1,00,000
	(Being purchase of goods from Ram on credit)			
	Ram	Dr.	1,00,000	
	To Bills Payable Account			1,00,000
	(Being acceptance given on the bill drawn by Ram)			
April 4	Bills Payable Account	Dr.	1,00,000	
	Trade Expenses Account	Dr.	250	
	To Ram			1,00,250
	(Being dishounour of the bill accepted by Ram on the due date)			

Q. 4 (Rectification of Errors). (a) On 31st March, 2001, a book-keeper finds the difference in the Trial Balance and the puts it in the Suspense Account. Later on he detects the following errors:

(i) Rs.50,000 received from A was posted to the debit of his Account.

(ii) Rs. 20,000 being purchase returns were posted to the debit of Purchases Account.

(iii) Discount of Rs. 8,000 received were posted to the debit of Discount Account.

(iv) Rs. 9,060 paid for repairs of Motor Car was debited to Motor Car Account as Rs. 7060.

(v) Rs. 40,000 paid to B was debited to A's Account.

Give Journal Entries to rectify the above errors and ascertain the amount transferred to Suspense Account on 31st March, 2001 by showing the Suspense Account, assuming that the Suspense Account is balanced after the above corrections. (9 marks)

Q. 4 (Insurance Claims). (b) Mr. James submits you the following information for the year ended 31.3.2001 :

	Rs.
Stock as on 1.4.2000	1,50,500
Purchases	4,37,000
Manufacturing Expenses	85,000
Expenses on Sales	33,000
Expenses on Administration	18,000
Financial Charges	6,000
Sales	6,25,000

During the year damaged goods costing Rs. 12,000 were sold for Rs. 5,000. Barring the above transaction the Gross Profit has been @ 20% on Sales.

Compute the Net Profit of Mr. James for the year ended 31.3.2001. (6 marks)

Solution:

RECTIFICATION ENTRIES

			Dr. Rs.	Cr. Rs.
(i)	Suspense Account	Dr.	1,00,000	
	To A			1,00,000
	(Being the rectification of error for amount received from A was wrongly debited to his account)			
(ii)	Suspense Account	Dr.	40,000	
	To Purchase Account			20,000
	To Purchase Returns Account			20,000
	(Rectification of error for purchases returns being posted to the purchase account)			
(iii)	Suspense Account	Dr.	16,000	
	To Discount Account			16,000
	(Being discount received wrongly debited to discount account — error rectified)			

(Cont.)

			Dr. Rs.	Cr. Rs.
(iv)	Motor Car Repairs Account	Dr.	9,060	
	To Motor Car Account			7,060
	To Suspense Account			2,000
	(Being the motor car repair expenses Rs. 9,060 wrongly debited to motor Car account as Rs. 7,060, error now rectified)			
(v)	B'		40,000	
	To A'			40,000
	(Being amount paid to B wrongly debited to A, error rectified)			

SUSPENSE ACCOUNT

		Rs.				Rs.
To	A	1,00,000	By	Balance b/d		1,54,000
To	Purchase A/c	20,000		Difference in		
To	Purchase Returns A/c	20,000		trial balance (bal. fig.)		
To	Discount A/c	16,000	By	Motor Car Repairs A/c		2,000
		1,56,000				1,56,000

COMPUTATION OF NET PROFIT OF MR. JAMES
For the year ended 31.3.2001

	Rs.	Rs.
Gross Profit on Normal Sales $\left(\text{Rs. } 6,20,000 \times \dfrac{20}{100}\right)$		1,24,000
Less: Loss on sale of damaged goods (Rs. 12,000 – Rs. 5,000)		7,000
		1,17,000
Less: Overhead Expenses		
Administration Expenses	18,000	
Selling Expenses	33,000	
Financial charges	6,000	57,000
Net Profit		60,000

Working Notes:
COMPUTATION OF NORMAL SALES

Actual Sales	6,25,000
Less: Abnormal sales (sale of damaged goods)	5,000
Normal Sales	6,20,000

Alternatively, Trading and Profit and Loss Account for the year ended 31st March, 2001 can be prepared to compute the amount of net profit for the year.

Mr. James

TRADING AND PROFIT AND LOSS ACCOUNT

for the year ended 31st March, 2001

	Rs.		Rs.
To Opening Stock	1,50,500	By Sales	6,25,000
To Purchases	4,37,000	By Closing Stock	1,64,500
To Manufacturing Expenses	85,000	(balancing figure)	
To Gross Profit c/d	1,17,000		
(Rs. 1,24,000 - Rs. 7,000)			
	7,89,500		7,89,500
To Administration Expenses	18,000	By Gross Profit b/d	1,17,000
To Selling Expenses	33,000		
To Financial Charges	6,000		
To Net Profit	60,000		
	1,17,000		1,17,000

Q. 5. State with reasons whether the following statements are 'True' or 'False' :

(1) The debit balance in the Profit and Loss Account is surplus.

(2) Consignee has no right in the profit on goods sent on consignment.

(3) Compensating Errors do not disturb agreement of Trial Balance.

(4) Partners can share profits or losses in their capital ratio, when there is no agreement.

(5) Goodwill is a fictitious asset.

(6) If a partner retires, then other partners have a gain in their profit sharing ratio.

(7) Land is also a depreciable asset.

(8) Capital is all assets less fictitious assets.

(9) If the business carried on by a Partnership Firm becomes illegal, it stands dissolved.

(10) Cancelling old bill and drawing new bill is called renewal of Bill.   (20 marks)

Solution:

(1) The Statement is **False**. The Debit balance in the Profit & Loss A/c shows a deficit and not a surplus.

(2) The Statement is **True**. The Consignee acts only as an agent of the Consignor. Hence he is entitled only to the accrued commission and not a share in the profit on goods sent on consignment.

(3) The Statement is **True**. The compensating errors cancels out effect of each other and therefore, do not disturb the accuracy of the trial balance.

(4) The Statement is **False**. In the absence of agreement, the partners are required to share profits equally and not in the ratio of their capitals.

(5) The Statement is **False**. Goodwill is an intangible asset and not a fictitious asset. However, it will become fictitious in case it has no value.

(6) The Statement is **True**. If a partner retires, the share of the retiring partner goes to the other partners. Hence they stand to gain.

(7) The Statement is **False**. Land is not depreciable asset.

(8) The Statement is **False**. Capital is the total of all assets less fictitious assets and all external liabilities.

(9) The Statement is True. A partnership business is compulsorily dissolved in case it becomes illegal.

(10) The Statement is True. When the acceptor fails to meet the bill on maturity he may get the old bill cancelled and accept a new bill in its place.

Q. 6 (Basic Concepts). Briefly explain any three of the following

    (a) Accrual Basic of Accounting

    (b) Account Sales

    (c) Errors of Principle

    (d) Consignment liability   (15 marks)

Solution:

    (a) Accrual basis of accounting. For answer please refer to "Systems of Accounting" in Chapter 2 (Section I) "Accounting Principles", of the book.

    (b) Account Sales. For answer please refer to 'Important terms' in Chapter I, (Section II) "Consignment Accounts", of the book.

    (c) Errors of Principle. For answer please refer to 'Classification of Errors' in Chapter 2, (Section I) "Rectification of Errors", of the book.

    (d) Contingent Liability. It has been defined as "an obligation relating to an existing condition or situation which may arise in future depending on the occurrence or non occurrence of one or more uncertain future events". In other words, it is a liability which may or may not happen. The following are the examples of contingent liabilities:

       (i) Claims against the company not acknowledged as debts.

      (ii) Uncalled money on shares partly paid up.

    (iii) Arrears of fixed cumulative dividend;

    (iv) Estimated amount of contracts remaining to be executed on capital account and not provided for.

CA FOUNDATION EXAMINATION
NOVEMBER 2001
Fundamentals Of Accounting

Q. 1 (Non-Profit making Organisations). Summary of Receipts and Payments of Bombay Medical Aid Society for the year ended 31.12.2000 are as follows :

Opening Cash balance in hand Rs. 8,000, Subscription Rs. 50,000, Donation Rs. 15,000, Interest on Investments @ 9% p.a. Rs. 9,000, Payments for medicine supply Rs. 30,000, Honorarium to Doctors Rs. 10,000, Salaries Rs. 28,000, Sundry Expenses Rs. 1,000, Equipment purchase Rs. 15,000, Charity show expenses Rs. 1,500, Charity show collections Rs. 12,500.

Additional informations:

	1.1.2000	31.12.2000
Subscription due	1,500	2,200
Subscription received in advance	1,200	700
Stock of medicine	10,000	15,000
Amount due for medicine supply	9,000	13,000
Value of equipment	21,000	30,000
Value of building	50,000	48,000

You are required to prepare Receipts and Payments Account and Income and Expenditure Account for the year ended 31.12.2000 and Balance Sheet as on 31.12.2000.   (20 Marks)

Solution:

Bombay Medical Aid Society
RECEIPTS AND PAYMENTS ACCOUNT
for the year ended 31st December, 2000

Dr.   Cr.

Receipts	Rs.	Payments	Rs.
To Opening Balance	8,000	By Medicine supply	30,000
To Subscription	50,000	By Honorarium to Doctors	10,000
To Donation	15,000	By Salaries	28,000
To Interest on Investments	9,000	By Sundry Expenses	1,000
To Charity show Collections	12,500	By Purchase of Equipment	15,000
		By Charity Show Expenses	1,500
		By Closing Balance	9,000
	94,500		94,500

Bombay Medical Aid Society
INCOME AND EXPENDITURE ACCOUNT
for the year ended 31st December, 2000

Dr.   Cr.

Expenditure		Rs	Income		Rs.
To Medicine consumed		29,000	By Subscription		51,200
To Honorarium to doctors		10,000	By Donation		15,000
To Salaries		28,000	By Interest on investments		9,000
To Sundry Expenses		1,000	By Profit on Charity Show :		
To Depreciation :			Show collections	12,500	
Equipment	6,000		Show expenses	1,500	11,000
Building	2,000	8,000			
To Surplus-Excess					
of Income					
over Expenditure		10,200			
		86,200			86,200

Bombay Medical Aid Society
BALANCE SHEET AS ON 31ST DECEMBER, 2000

Liabilities	Rs.	Rs.	Assets	Rs.	Rs.
Capital Fund:			Building	50,000	
Opening Balance	1,80,300		Less: Depreciation	2,000	48,000
Add: Surplus	10,200	1,90,500	Equipment	21,000	
Subscription received in advance		700	Add: Purchase	15,000	
Amount due for medicine supply		13,000		36,000	
			Less: Depreciation	6,000	30,000
			Stock of medicine		15,000
			Investments		1,00,000
			Subscription receivable		2,200
			Cash in hand		9,000
		2,04,200			2,04,200

Working Notes:

1. Subscription for the year ended 31st December, 2000   Rs.
   Subscription received during the year   50,000

Less: Subscription receivable on 1.1.2000	1,500	
Less: Subscription received in advance on 31.12.2000	700	2,200
		47,800
Add: Subscription receivable on 31.12.2000	2,200	
Add: Subscription received in advance on 1.1.2000	1,200	3,400
		51,200

2. Purchase of Medicine

Payment for Medicine Supply	30,000
Less: Amounts due for medicine supply on 1.1.2000	9,000
	21,000
Add: Amounts due for medicine supply on 31.12.2000	13,000
	34,000

3. Medicine consumed

	Rs.
Stock of medicine on 1.1.2000	10,000
Add: Purchase of medicine during the year	34,000
	44,000
Less: Stock of medicine on 31.12.2000	15,000
	29,000

4. Depreciation on Equipment

	Rs.
Value of equipment on 1.1.2000	21,000
Add: Purchase of equipment during the year	15,000
	36,000
Less: Value of equipment on 31.12.2000	30,000
Depreciation on equipment for the year	6,000

5.

Medical Aid Society
BALANCE SHEET AS ON 31ST DECEMBER, 2000

Liabilities	Rs.	Assets	Rs.
Capital Fund (balancing figure)	1,80,300	Building	50,000
Subscription received in advance	1,200	Equipment	21,000
Amount due for medicine supply	9,000	Stock of medicine	10,000
		Investments $\left(\text{Rs. } 9,000 \times \dfrac{100}{9} \right)$	1,00,000
		Subscription receivable	1,500
		Cash in hand	8,000
	1,90,500		1,90,500

Q. 2 (Partnership). The Balance Sheet of A & B, a partnership firm, as at 31st March, 2001 is as follows:

Liabilities	Rs.	Assets	Rs.
Capital Account:		Goodwill	14,000
A 26,400		Land and Building	14,400
B 33,600	60,000	Furniture	2,200
Contingency Reserve	6,000	Stock	26,000
Sundry Creditors	9,000	Sundry Debtors	6,400
		Cash at Bank	12,000
	75,000		75,000

A & B share profits and losses as 1 : 2. They agree to admit C (who is also in business on his own) as a third partner from 1.4.2001.

The Assets are revalued as under:

Goodwill - Rs. 18,000, Land and Building Rs. 30,000, Furniture Rs. 6,000. C brings the following assets into the partnership - Goodwill Rs. 6,000, Furniture Rs. 2,800, Stock Rs. 13,600.

Profits in the new firm are to be shared equally by the three partners and the Capital Accounts are to be so adjusted as to be equal. For this purpose, additional cash should be brought in by the partner or partners concerned.

Prepare the necessary accounts and the opening Balance Sheet of new firm, showing the amount of cash, if any, which each partner, may have to provide. (15 marks)

Solution:

PROFIT AND LOSS ADJUSTMENT ACCOUNT

Dr. | | | | Cr.

	Rs.		Rs.
To Partners' Capital accounts: (Profit on revaluation)		By Goodwill	4,000
		By Land & Building	15,600
A 7,800		By Furniture	3,800
B 15,600	23,400		
	23,400		23,400

PARTNERS' CAPITAL ACCOUNTS

Dr. | | | | | | | | Cr.

	A	B	C		A	B	C
To Balance c/d	53,200	53,200	53,200	By Balance b/d	26,400	33,600	-
				By Contingency Reserve	2,000	4,000	-
				By Profit & Loss Adjustment A/c	7,800	15,600	-
				By Sundry Assets	-	-	22,400
				By Bank A/c	17,000	-	30,800
	53,200	53,200	53,200		53,200	53,200	53,200

BANK ACCOUNT

Dr. | | | | Cr.

	Rs.	Rs.	
To Balance b/d	12,000	By Balance c/d	59,800
To A's Capital A/c	17,000		
To C's Capital A/c	30,800		
	59,800		59,800

BALANCE SHEET OF NEW FIRM AS ON 1ST APRIL, 2001

Liabilities	Rs.	Rs.	Assets	Rs.
Capital Accounts:			Goodwill (18,000+6,000)	24,000
A 53,200			Land & Building	30,000
B 53,200			Furniture (6,000+2,800)	8,800
C 53,200		1,59,600	Stock (26,000+13,600)	39,600
Sundry Creditors		9,000	Sundry debtors	6,400
			Cash at Bank	59,800
		1,68,600		1,68,600

Note: The Capital accounts of partners are to be so adjusted so that they have equal capitals. Additional cash is to be brought in by the partner or partners concerned. The highest capital of the partners is to be taken as base for this purpose. In this case B's Capital is the highest. Hence A is required to bring in Rs. 17,000 (53,200 - 36,200) and C has to bring in Rs. 30,800 (53,200 - 22,400).

4.102

Q. 3 (a) (Depreciation Accounting). A firm purchased, on 1st January, 1996, certain, machinery for Rs. 19,40,000 and spend Rs. 60,000 on its erection. On 1st July in the same year additional machinery costing Rs. 10,00,000 was acquired. On 1st July, 1998 the machinery purchased on 1st January, 1996 having become obsolete was auctioned for Rs. 8,00,000 and on the same date fresh machine was purchased at a cost of Rs. 15,00,000.

Depreciation was provided for annually on 31st December at the rate of 10% per annum on the original cost of the asset. In 1999 however, the firm changed this method of providing depreciation and adopted the method of writing off 20% on the written down value.

Give the Machinery Account as it would stand at the end of each year from 1996 to 2000.

(9 Marks)

Solution:

(a)

MACHINERY ACCOUNT

Dr.   Cr.

1996		Rs.	1996		Rs.
Jan. 1	To Bank A/c (Cost of new machinery)	19,40,000	Dec. 31	By Depreciation A/c (Rs. 2,00,000+Rs. 50,000)	2,50,000
	To Bank A/c (Erection charges)	60,000	Dec. 31	By Balance c/d (Rs. 18,00,000+Rs. 9,50,000)	27,50,000
July 1	To Bank A/c (Cost of new machinery)	10,00,000			
		30,00,000			30,00,000
1997			1997		
Jan. 1	To Balance b/d	27,50,000	Dec. 31	By Depreciation A/c (Rs. 2,00,000+Rs. 1,00,000)	3,00,000
				By Balance c/d	24,50,000
		27,50,000			27,50,000
1998		Rs.	1998		Rs.
Jan. 1	To Balance b/d	24,50,000	July 1	By Bank A/c	8,00,000
July 1	To Bank A/c	15,00,000	Dec. 31	By Profit and Loss A/c (Loss on sale - W.N.)	7,00,000
				By Depreciation (Rs. 1,00,000 + Rs. 1,00,000 + Rs. 75,000)	2,75,000
				By Balance c/d (Rs. 7,50,000 + 14,25,000)	21,75,000
		39,50,000			39,50,000
1999			1999		
Jan. 1	To Balance b/d	21,75,000	Dec. 31	By Depreciation A/c (Rs. 1,50,000 + Rs. 2,85,000)	4,35,000
				By Balance c/d (Rs. 6,00,000 + Rs. 11,40,000)	17,40,000
		21,75,000			21,75,000

1996		Rs.	1996			Rs.
2000			2000			
Jan. 1	To Balance b/d	17.40.000	Dec. 31	By Depreciation A/c		3.48.000
				(Rs. 1.20.000 + Rs. 2.28.000)		
				By Balance c/d		
				(Rs. 4.80.000 + Rs. 9.12.000)		13.92.000
		17.40.000				17.40.000

Working Note:

Loss on sale on machinery purchased on 1st January, 1996 has been computed as under

Cost	20.00.000
Depreciation for 1996	2.00.000
	18.00.000
Depreciation for 1997	2.00.000
	16.00.000
Depreciation for 1998 (half year)	1.00.000
Written down value	15.00.000
Sale proceeds	8.00.000
Loss on sale	7.00.000

Q. 3(b) (Final Accounts). What is a Balance Sheet? (6 Marks)

Solution:

The 'Balance Sheet' may be defined as "a statement which sets out the assets and liabilities of a firm or an institution as at a certain date". It shows the financial position of the business. what a firm owns and owes as on a particular date. Every single transaction will make a difference to some of the assets or liabilities, and hence the balance sheet is true only at particular point of time. Balance sheet is prepared only after preparation of the profit and loss account. A balance sheet consists mainly of personal and real account balances and is generally prepared annually. However in some cases it may be prepared half-yearly or quarterly. Since capital always equals the difference between assets and liabilities and since the capital account will independently arrive at this figure. the two sides of the balance sheet must have the same totals. If it is not so. there is certainly an error somewhere.

Q. 4 (a) (Self-Balancing). The following information is extracted from the books of Shri Hari for the year ended 31st March, 2001:

	Rs.
Sales	3.80.800
Purchases	3.26.000
Return outward	14.000
Cash received from debtors	1.78.200
Bills payable accepted	1.22.000
Returns inward	17.600
Cash paid to creditors	1.86.000
Bills receivable received	1.36.000
Discount received	4.000
Bad debts written off	24.000
Reserve for discount to debtors	2.000
Discount allowed	1.800
Transfers from purchases ledger	26.600

The total of the Sales Ledger balances on 1st April 2000 was Rs. 90,600 and that of the purchases Ledger balances on the same date was Rs. 78,600.

Prepare Sales Ledger and Purchases Ledger Adjustment Accounts from the above information. (9 Marks)

Solution:

(a)

SALES LEDGER ADJUSTMENT ACCOUNT

		Rs.				Rs.
1.4.2000	To Balance b/d	90,600	1.4.2000	By General Ledger		
1.4.2000	To General Ledger			Adjustment Account:		
	Adjustment Account:					
31.3.2001	Sales	3,80,800	31.3.2001	Cash		1,78,200
				Returns Inward		17,600
				Bills Receivable		1,36,000
				Bad debts written off		24,000
				Discount allowed		1,800
				Transfer from		
				Purchases Ledger		26,600
			31.3.2001	By Balance c/d		87,200
		4,71,400				4,71,400

PURCHASE LEDGER ADJUSTMENT ACCOUNT

		Rs.				Rs.
1.4.2000	To General Ledger		1.4.2000	By Balance b/d		78,600
	djustment Account:		1.4.2000	By General Ledger		
				Adjustment Account:		
31.3.2001	Cash	1,86,000	31.3.2001	Purchases		3,26,000
	Returns outward	14,000				
	Bills payable	1,22,000				
	Discount received	4,000				
	Transfer to Sales					
	Ledger	26,600				
31.3.2001	To Balance c/d	52,000				
		4,04,600				4,04,600

Q. 4 (b) Define Accounting. (6 Marks)

Solution:

For answer please refer to "Definition and Function of Accounting" in Chapter 2 (Section 1) of the Book.

Q. 5. State with reasons whether the following statements are 'True' or 'False':

(i) Finished goods are normally valued at cost or market price, which ever is lower.

(ii) Expenditure, which results in acquisition of a permanent asset is a Revenue Expenditure.

(iii) Patent-Right is in the nature of Real Account.

(iv) Goodwill is a fictitious asset.

(v) A cancellation entry is required, when a bill is renewed.

(vi) A bill given to a creditor is called Bills Receivable

(vii) The Sales Day-book is a part of the Ledger.

(viii) Sale of office furniture should be credited to Sales Account.

(ix) The Trial Balance does not ensure the arithmetical accuracy of the books.

(x) Accrual concept implies accounting on cash basis.

(10 × 2 = 20 marks)

Solution:

(1) The Statement is **True**. According to concept of conservatism the stock of finished goods is to be valued at cost or market price whichever is less. The term "market price" here refers to net resaleable value i.e selling price less cost of completion or cost to be incurred in making the sale.

(2) The Statement is **False**. The expenditure which results in acquisition of a permanent asset is a capital expenditure and not a revenue expenditure.

(3) The Statement is **True**. Patent Right is an intangible asset. Hence it is a Real Account.

(4) The Statement is **False**. Goodwill is not a fictitious asset but an tangible asset. It will be termed as fictitious only when it has no value.

(5) The Statement is **True**. When a Bill is renewed, a cancellation entry is required for canceling the old bill.

(6) The Statement is **False**. A bill given to a Creditor is called bills payable and not bills receivable.

(7) The Statement is **False**. Sales Day Book is a part of Journal and not a part of ledger.

(8) The Statement is **False**. Sale of office furniture cannot be taken as sale of goods. Hence, it should have been credited to the office furniture account and not sales account.

(9) The Statement is **False**. Trial Balance discloses arithmetical accuracy of books of account. It is only a proof of this fact that the books of account are arithmetically accurate.

(10) The Statement is **False**. Accrual concept implies recognition of revenue and costs as and when they accrue and not as and when they are received or paid.

Q. 6. Briefly explain the difference between any three of the following :

(a) Journal and Ledger.

(b) Sales Day-book and Sales Account.

(c) Charge against Profit and Appropriation of Profit.

(d) Capital Expenditure and Revenue Expenditure. (5 marks each)

Solution:

(a) **Difference between Journal and Ledger**. The following are the points of difference between a Journal and a Ledger. (i) Journal is the book of prime entry where the transactions are recorded first of all in a chronological order while Ledger is a book in which the transactions are classified. It contains a set of accounts. (ii) The transactions are first recorded in the Journal and they are subsequently transferred from the Journal to the Ledger.

(b) **Sales Day Book and Sales Account.** Sales Day Book is a specific journal kept for recording of transactions relating to credit sale of goods. It is also a book of prime entry. While Sales Account is kept in the ledger it is a complete record of all sales made whether on cash or credit.

(c) **Charge against profit and Appropriation of profit.** The term 'Charge against profit' means deduction from revenue to arrive at the net profit or net loss while "Appropriation of profit" means distribution of net profits under various heads of accounts. In other words, true profits of business cannot be ascertained without deducting a charge against profits while an appropriation of profit should not be deducted for arriving at a true figure of profit.

CA FOUNDATION EXAMINATION
MAY 2002
Fundamentals Of Accounting

Q. 1 (Non-Profit Organisation). Smith Library Society showed the following position on 31st March, 2001:

BALANCE SHEET AS ON 31ST MARCH, 2001

Liabilities	Rs.	Assets	Rs.
Capital Fund	7,93,000	Electrical Fittings	1,50,000
Expenses Payable	7,000	Furniture	50,000
		Books	4,00,000
		Investment in Securities	1,50,000
		Cash at Bank	25,000
		Cash in hand	25,000
	8,00,000		8,00,000

The Receipt and Payment Account for the year ended on 31st March, 2002 is given below:

Receipts		Rs.	Payments		Rs.
To Balance b/f			By Electric Charges		7,200
Cash at Bank	25,000		By Postage and Stationery		5,000
Cash in hand	25,000	50,000	By Telephone Charges		5,000
To Entrance Fees		30,000	By Books Purchased		60,000
To Membership Subscription		2,00,000	By Outstanding Expenses paid		7,000
To Sale proceeds of Old papers		1,500	By Rent		88,000
To Hire of Lecture Hall		20,000	By Investment in Securities		40,000
To Interest on Securities		8,000	By Salaries		66,000
			By Balance c/f		
			Cash at Bank		20,000
			Cash in Hand		11,300
		3,09,500			3,09,500

You are required to prepare an Income and Expenditure Account for the year ended 31st March, 2002 and a Balance Sheet as at 31st March, 2002 after making the following adjustments:

(i) Membership Subscription included Rs. 10,000 received in advance.

(ii) Provide for outstanding rent Rs. 4,000 and salaries Rs. 3,000.

(iii) Books to be depreciated @ 10% including additions. Electrical Fittings and Furnitures are also to be depreciated at the same rate.

(iv) 75% of the Entrance Fees is to be capitalised.

(v) Interest on Securities is to be calculated @ 5% p.a. including purchases made on 1.10.2001 for Rs. 40,000.

Solution:

Smith Library Society
INCOME AND EXPENDITURE ACCOUNT
for the year ended 31st March, 2002

Expenditure		Rs	Income		Rs
To Electric Charges		7,200	By Entrance fees (25%		7,500
To Postage and Stationery		5,000	of Rs. 30,000)		
To Telephone Charges		5,000	By Membership subscription	2,00,000	
To Rent	88,000		Less: Received in advance	10,000	1,90,000
Add: Outstanding	4,000	92,000	By Sale proceeds of old papers		1,500
To Salaries	66,000		By Hire of lecture hall		20,000
Add: Outstanding	3,000	69,000	By Interest on securities (WN 2)	8000	
To Depreciation (WN 1)			Add: Receivable		8,500
Electrical fittings	15,000		By Deficit - Excess of		
Furniture	5,000		Expenditure over Income		16,700
Books	46,000	66,000			
		2,44,200			2,44,200

Smith Library Society
BALANCE SHEET AS ON 31ST MARCH, 2002

Liabilities	Rs.	Rs.	Assets	Rs.	Rs.
Capital fund	7,93,000		Electrical fittings	1,50,000	
Add: Entrance fees	22,500		Less: Depreciations	15,000	1,35,000
	8,15,000		Furniture	50,000	
Less: Excess of expenditure			Less: Depreciation	5,000	45,000
over Income	16,700	7,98,800	Books	4,60,000	
Outstanding expenses			Less: Depreciation	46,000	4,14,000
Rent	4,000		Investment		
Salaries	3,000	7,000	Securities	1,90,000	
Membership subscription			Accrued interest	500	1,90,500
received in advance		10,000	Cash at bank		20,000
			Cash in hand		11,300
		8,15,800			8,15,800

Working Notes:

			Rs.
1. Depreciation			
Electrical fittings	10% of Rs. 1,50,000		15,000
Furniture	10% of Rs. 50,000		5,000
Books	10% of Rs. 4,60,000		46,000
2. Interest on Securities			
Interest @ 5% p.a. on Rs. 1,50,000 for full year			7,500
Interest @ 5% p.a on Rs. 40,000 for half year			1,000
			8,500
Received			8,000
Receivable			500

Q. 2 (Partnership).

M/s X and Co. is a partnership firm with the partners. A, B and C sharing Profits and Losses in the ratio of 3 : 2 : 5. The Balance Sheet of the firm as on 30th June 2001 was as under:

X and Co.
BALANCE SHEET AS ON 30.06.2001

Liabilities	Rs.	Assets	Rs.
A's Capital A/c	1,04,000	Land	1,00,000
B's Capital A/c	76,000	Building	2,00,000
C's Capital A/c	1,40,000	Plant and Machinery	3,80,000
Long term loan	4,00,000	Investments	22,000
Bank overdraft A/c	44,000	Stock	1,16,000
Trade Creditors	1,93,000	Sundry Debtors	1,39,000
	9,57,000		9,57,000

It was mutually agreed that B will retire from Partnership and his place D will be admitted as a partner with effect from 1st July, 2001. For this purpose, the following adjustments are to be made:

(a) Goodwill of the firm is to be valued at Rs. 2 lakh due to the firm's locational advantage but the same will not appear as an asset in the books of the reconstituted firm.

(b) Building and Plant and Machinery are to be valued at 90% and 85% of the respective Balance Sheet values. Investments are to be taken over by the retiring partner at Rs. 25,000. Sundry Debtors are considered good only 90% of Balance Sheet figure. Balance to be considered Bad.

(c) In the reconstituted firm, the total Capital will be Rs. 3 lakh, which will be contributed by A, C and D in their new profit sharing ratio, which is 3 : 4 : 3.

(d) The surplus funds, if any, will be used for repaying bank overdraft.

(e) The amount due to retiring partner shall be transferred to his Loan Account. You are required to prepare (1) Revaluation Account (2) Partner's Capital Accounts (3) Bank Account and (4) Balance Sheet of the reconstituted firm as on 1st July, 2001.

(15 marks)

Solution:

(1)

REVALUATION ACCOUNT

Dr.						Cr.
2001		Rs.	2001			Rs.
July 1	To Building	20,000	July 1	By Investments (25,000 - 22,000)		3,000
	To Plant and Machinery	57,000		By Partners' Capital Accounts - Loss on revaluation		
	To Bad debts	13,900		A (3/10)	26,370	
				B (2/10)	17,580	
				C (5/10)	43,950	87,900
		90,900				90,900

(2)

PARTNERS' CAPITAL ACCOUNTS

Dr.   Cr.

	A Rs	B Rs	C Rs	D Rs		A Rs	B Rs	C Rs	D Rs
To Revaluation A/c	26.370	17.580	43.950	-	By Balance b/d	1.04.000	76.000	1.40.000	-
To B's and C's Capital A/cs				60.000	By D's Capital A/c (W. N. 1)	-	40.000	20.000	-
To Investment A/c		25.000			By Bank A/c	12.370		3.950	1.50.000
To B's Loan A/c		73.420							
To Balance c/d (W. N. 2)	90.000		1.20.000	90.000					
	1.16.370	1.16000	1.63.950	1.50.000		1.16.370	1.16.000	1.63.950	1.50.000

(3)

BANK ACCOUNT

Dr.   Cr.

	Rs		Rs
To A's Capital A/c	12.370	By Balance b/d (overdraft)	44.000
To C's Capital A/c	3.950	By Balance c/d	1.22.320
To D's Capital A/c	1.50.000		
	1.66.320		1.66.320

(4)

M/s X and Co.

BALANCE SHEET AS ON 1ST JULY. 2001

Liabilities		Rs.	Assets		Rs.
Capital Accounts:			Land		1.00.000
A	90.000		Building	2.00.000	
B	1.20.000		Less: Depreciation	20.000	1.80.000
C	90.000	3.00.000	Plant and Machinery	3.80.000	
Long-term Loan		4.00.000	Less: Depreciation	57.000	3.23.000
B's Loan Account		73.420	Stock		1.16.000
Trade Creditors		1.93.000	Debtors	1.39.000	
			Less: Bad debts	13.900	1,25.100
			Cash at Bank		1.22.320
		9.66.420			9.66.420

Working Notes:

1. Adjustment of Goodwill

   Goodwill of the firm is valued at Rs. 2 lakhs

Sacrificing ratio:

A	$3/10 - 3/10$	$= 0$
B	$2/10 - 0$	$= 2/10$
C	$5/10 - 4/10$	$= 1/10$

The sacrificing ratio of B and C is 2 : 1. A has not sacrificed any share in profits after retirement of B and admission of D in his place.

D's share of goodwill has to be adjusted through existing partners' capital accounts in the profit sacrificing ratio:

Rs.

B : Rs. $60,000 \times 2/3$ $= 40,000$

C : Rs. $60,000 \times 1/3$ $= 20,000$

60,000

2. The Capitals of the partners in the reconstituted firm can be as certained as follows.

	Rs.
Total capital of the reconstituted firm (given)	3,00,000
A (3/10)	90,000
B (4/10)	1,20,000
C (3/10)	90,000

Q. 3 (Rectification of Errors).

(a) There was an error in the Trial Balance of Mr. Steel on 31st March, 2002 and the difference in Books was carried to a Suspense Account. On going through the Books you find that:

   (i) Rs. 5,400 received from Mr. A was posted to the debit of his account.

   (ii) Rs. 1,000 being purchases return were posted to the debit of purchase Account.

   (iii) Discount received Rs. 2,000 was posted to the debit of Discount Account.

   (iv) Rs. 2,740 paid for Repairs to Motor Car was debited to Motor Car Account as Rs. 1,740.

   (v) Rs. 4,000 paid to B was debited to A's Account.

Give Journal Entries to rectify the above error and ascertain the amount transferred to Suspense Account on 31st March, 2002 by showing the Suspense Account, assuming that the Suspense Account is balanced after the above corrections.

(b) State which types of errors are not disclosed by the agreement of the Trial Balance.

(10 + 5 = 15 marks)

Solution:

Books of Mr. Steel

JOURNAL ENTRIES

Dr.				Cr.
Particulars			Amount Rs	Amount Rs
Suspense Account	Dr.		10,800	
To A's Account				10,800
(Being the amount of Rs. 5,400 received from A wrongly debited to his account error now rectified).				

Dr.   Cr.

Particulars		Amount Rs	Amount Rs
Suspense Account	Dr.	2,000	
To Purchase Account			1,000
To Purchase Return Account			1,000
(Being purchases returns wrongly debited to purchases account error now rectified).			
Suspense Account	Dr.	4,000	
To Discount Account			4,000
(Being Discount received wrongly debited to discount account, error how rectified).			
Repairs to Motor Car Account	Dr.	2,740	
To Motor Car Account			1,740
To Suspense Account			1,000
(Being expenses on Motor Car repairs Rs. 2,740 wrongly debited to motor car account as Rs. 1,740, now rectified).			
B's	Dr.	4,000	
To A			4,000
(being the amount paid to B wrongly debited in A error now rectified).			

SUSPENSE ACCOUNT

Dr.   Cr.

	Rs.		Rs.
To A	10,800	By Balance b/d	15,800
To Purchases A/c	1,000	(Difference in the beginning -balancing figure)	
To Purchase Returns A/c	1,000		
To Discount A/c	4,000	By Repairs to Motor Car A/c	1,000
	16,800		16,800

(b) Errors may remain in the books in spite of the agreement of the trial balance. These errors may be of the following types.

  (1) Errors of omission,

  (2) Errors of principle,

  (3) Compensating errors,

For more details please refer to "Types of Errors" in Chapter 11 Section 1 of the book.

Q. 4 (Joint Venture). Ram and Rahim enter into a Joint Venture to take a building contract for Rs. 24,000,000. They provide the following information regarding the expenditure incurred by them:

	Ram	Rahim
	Rs.	Rs.
Materials	6,80,000	5,00,000
Cement	1,30,000	1,70,000

Wages	-	2,70,000		
Architect's Fee	1,00,000	-		
Licence Fees	-	50,000		
Plant	-	2,00,000		

Plant was valued at Rs. 1,00,000 at the end of the contract and Rahim agreed to take it at that value. Contract amount of Rs. 24,00,000 was received by Ram. Profits or losses to be shared equally. You are asked to show:

(i) Joint Venture Account and Rahim's Account in the books of Ram; and

(ii) Joint Venture Account and Ram's account in the books of Rahim. (15 marks)

Solution:

In the books of Ram
JOINT VENTURE ACCOUNT

	Rs.	Rs.		Rs.	Rs.
To Bank A/c			By Bank A/c		24,00,000
Material	6,80,000		By Rahim (Plant)		1,00,000
Cement	1,30,000				
Architect's Fee	1,00,000	9,10,000			
To Rahim					
Material	5,00,000				
Cement	1,70,000				
Wages	2,70,000				
Licence Fees	50,000				
Plant	2,00,000	11,90,000			
To Net Profit					
transferred to:					
Rahim	2,00,000				
Profit & Loss A/c	2,00,000	4,00,000			
		25,00,000			25,00,000

RAHIM

	Rs.		Rs.
To Joint Venture A/c (Plant)	1,00,000	By Joint Venture A/c (Sundries)	11,90,000
To Balance c/d*	12,90,000	By Joint Venture A/c (Profit)	2,00,000
	13,90,000		13,90,000

In the books of Rahim
JOINT VENTURE ACCOUNT

	Rs.	Rs.		Rs.
To Ram			By Ram (Contract	
Material	6,80,000		amount)	24,00,000
Cement	1,30,000		By Plant A/c	1,00,000
Architect's Fee	1,00,000	9,10,000		
To Bank A/c				
Material	5,00,000			

		Rs.			Rs.
Cement	1.70.000				
Wages	2.70.000				
Licence Fees	50,000				
Plant	2.00.000	11.90.000			
To Net Profit transferred to:					
Ram	2.00.000				
Profit & Loss A/c	2.00.000	4.00.000			
		25.00.000			25.00.000

RAM

	Rs.		Rs.
To Joint Venture A/c	24.00.000	By Joint Venture A/c (Sundries)	9.10.000
(Contract amount)		By Joint Venture A/c (Profit)	2.00.000
		By Balance c/d*	12.90.000
	24.00.000		24.00.000

Note: *It may be taken that Rs. 12,90,000 is settled by way of payment from Ram to Rahim.

Q. 5. State with reasons whether the following statements are True or False:

(1) The relationship between the consignor and the consignor is that of a principal and agent.

(2) Error of principle involves an incorrect allocation of expenditure or receipt between capital and revenue.

(3) Discount at the time of retirement of a Bill is a gain for the drawer.

(4) Purchases Book records all credit purchases of goods.

(5) Wages paid for erection of machinery are debited to the Machinery Account.

(6) Book Reconciliation Statement is prepared to arrive at the bank balance.

(7) Under the self-balancing system the general ledger adjustment account is always opened in the general ledger.

(8) In double accounting all business transactions are recorded as having dual aspect.

(9) A joint venture business does not have a definite life.

(10) The debts written off as bad. if recovered subsequently are credited to debtor's account. (20 marks)

Solution:

(1) The Statement is **True**. The relationship between Consignor and Consignee is that of a Principal and an Agent. Consignee acts on behalf of and at the risk of the Consignor.

(2) The Statement is **True**. An error of principle is involved when appropriate distinction between capital revenue items is not made.

(3) The Statement is **False**. Discount allowed at the time of retirement of the bill is gain for the drawee and loss for the drawer.

(4) The Statement is **True**. The Purchase Book is meant for recording only credit pur-·chase of goods.

(5) The Statement is **True**. The wages paid for erection of machinery is a capital expenditure and hence, it should be debited to the Machinery Account.

(6) The Statement is **False**. Bank Reconciliation Statement is prepared to identify the causes of difference between the balance shown by the bank pass and the cash book.

(7) The Statement is **False**. The General Ledger Adjustment Account is opened (i) in the Sales Ledger and (ii) in the Purchase Ledger. A Sales Ledger Adjustment Account and a Purchase Ledger Adjustment Account are opened in the General Ledger.

(8) The Statement is **True**. Double Account is associated with double entry book keeping where every transaction has got two fold effect.

(9) The Statement is **False**. A Joint Venture account has a definite life. It automatically comes to an end on the completion of the term of the venture for which it has been formed.

(10) The Statement if **False**. Debt in the past and recovered now are credited to the Bad Debts Recovered Account and not to the Debtors Personal Account.

Q. 6. Briefly explain the differences between any three of the following:

(a) Consignment Sale and Normal Sale.

(b) Trial Balance and Balance Sheet.

(c) FIFO and Weight Average price method of Stock Valuation.

(d) Provision for depreciation under Straight Line method and under written down value method. (15 marks)

Solution:

(a) Consignment Sale and Normal Sale.

(*i*) Transfer of Property. In case of consignment sale, the property in goods remain with the Consignor till the goods are actually sold and the consignee acts only as a custodian of the goods sent to him by the consignor. Which in case of a normal sale, the ownership of the goods passes to the buyer immediately after the sale is made.

(*ii*) Transfer of Risk. In consignment sale, the risk of the goods remains with the consignor till the goods are sold while in case of normal sale, the risk passes to the buyer immediately.

(*iii*) Relationship. The relationship between the consignor and consignee is that of a principal and an agent while in a normal rule the relationship between the seller and the buyer is that of a debtor and a creditor.

(b) Trial Balance and Balance Sheet. The following are the points of difference between a Trial Balance and a Balance Sheet.

(*i*) Trial Balance is a statement of various assets and liabilities as on a particular date while the Balance Sheet is a statement of various assets and liabilities on a particular date.

    (*ii*)   Trial Balance shows arithmetical accuracy of the books of account while the Balance Sheet shows the financial position of the business as on a particular date.

    (*iii*) Trial Balance precedes a Balance Sheet i.e. it is prepared first and afterwards a Balance Sheet is prepared.

(c) FIFO and Weighted Average Price Method of Stock Evaluation. For answer please refer to 'FIFO method and Weighted Average Price Methods' in Chapter 4 (Section II) "Inventory Valuation", of the Book.

(d) Provision for Depreciation under Straight Line Method and Written Down Value Method. For answer please refer to 'Straight Line Method and Written Down Value Method' in Chapter 13 (Section I) of "Depreciation Accounting", of the book.

ICAI PROFESSIONAL EDUCATION EXAMINATION I
NOVEMBER 2002
Paper 1: Fundamentals of Accounting

Answer ALL Questions

Q. 1. (Final Accounts). From the following particulars for the year ending 31st March, 2002 of M/s *ABC* Company, prepare Trading and Profit and Loss Account and Balance Sheet on that date:

Particulars	Rs.	Particulars	Rs.
Stock 1.4.2001	23,200	Advertisement	15,950
Capital 1.4.2001	1,45,000	Apprenticeship Premium	3,480
Purchases	58,000	Bills Receivable	10,150
Sales	2,32,000	Bills Payable	7,250
Office Expenses	23,345	Sundry Debtors	58,000
Return Inward	4,350	Plant and Machinery	13,050
Interest on Loan	870	Sundry Creditors	45,820
Return Outward	1,160	Loan (Dr.), @ 10% on 1.4.2001	14,500
Drawings	8,700	Investment	8,700
Wages	20,010	Cash at Bank	10,150
Land and Building	1,59,500	Cash in Hand	725
Furniture and Fixtures	7,250	Stock 31.3.2002	20,300

Adjustment to be made for the Current Year are:
- (*i*) Interest on Capital to be allowed at 5% for the year.
- (*ii*) Interest on Drawings to be charged to him as ascertained for the year Rs. 232.
- (*iii*) Apprenticeship Premium is for three years received in advance in 1st April, 2001.
- (*iv*) Stock valued at Rs. 8,700 destroyed by fire on 25.03.2002, but the Insurance company admitted a claim of Rs. 5,800 only to be paid in the year 2003.
- (*v*) Rs. 14,500 out of Advertisement Expenses are to be carried forward.
- (*vi*) The Manager is entitled to a commission of 10% at the Net Profit calculated after charging such commission.
- (*vii*) The stock includes material worth Rs. 2,900 for which bill had not been received and therefore, not yet accounted for. **(20 Marks)**

Solution:

M/s ABC Company
TRADING AND PROFIT AND LOSS ACCOUNT
for the year ending 31st March, 2002

Particulars		Rs.	Particulars		Rs.
To Opening Stock		23,200	By Sales	2,32,00	
To Purchases	58,000		*Less*: Return Inward	4,350	2,27,650
Less: Return Outward	1,160		By Closing Stock		20,300
	56,840				
Add: Unrecorded Purchases	2,900				
	59,740				
Less: Loss of Stock by Fire	8,700	51,040			
To Wages		20,010			
To Gross Profit c/d		1,53,700			
		2,47,950			2,47,950

Contd...

To Interest on Capital			By Gross Profit b/d			1,53,700
(5% on Rs. 1,45,000)		7,250	By Interest on Drawings			232
To Loss of Stock by Fire			By Interest on Loan		870	
(Rs. 8,700 – Rs, 5,800)		2,900	Add: Accrued Interest			
To Office Expenses		23,345	(Rs. 1,450 – Rs. 870)		580	1,450
To Advertisement	15,950		By Apprenticeship			
Less: Carried Forward	14,500	1,450	Premium		3,480	
To Manager's Commission			Less: Received in Advance			
(10/110 × Rs. 1,21, 597)		11,054	(2/3 × Rs. 3,480)		2,320	1,160
To Net Profit		1,10,543				
		1,56,542				1,56,542

M/s ABC Company
BALANCE SHEET
as on 31st March, 2002

Liabilities		Amount Rs.	Assets		Amount Rs.
Capital	1,45,000		Land and Building		1,59,500
Add: Interest on Capital	7,250		Plant and Machinery		13,050
Profit	1,10,543		Furniture and Fixtures		7,250
	2,62,793		Investment		8,700
Less: Drawings	8,700		Bills Receivable		10,150
Interest on Drawings	232	2,53,861	Sundry Debtors		58,000
Sundry Creditors	45,820		Insurance Claim Receivable		5,800
Add: Unrecorded			Loan	14,500	
Purchases	2,900	48,720	Add: Accured Interest	580	15,080
Bills Payable		7,250	Advertisement (Carried Forward)		14,500
Manager's Commission Payable		11,054	Closing Stock		20,300
Apprenticeship Premium			Cash at Bank		10,150
Received in Advance		2,320	Cash in Hand		725
		3,23,205			3,23,205

Q. 2. *(a)* **(Insurance claims).** Mr. 'A' prepares accounts on 30th September each year, but on 31st December, 2001 fire destroyed the greater part of his stock. Following information was collected from his books :

	Rs.
Stock as on 1.10.2001	29,700
Purchases from 1.10.2001 to 31.12.2001	75,000
Wages from 1.10.2001 to 31.12.2001	33,000
Sales from 1.10.2001 to 31.12.2001	1,40,000

The rate of Gross Profit is $33\frac{1}{3}$% on cost. Stock to the value of Rs. 3,000 was salvaged. Insurance policy was Rs. 25,000 and claim was subjected to average clause.

Additional Informations:
   (*i*) Stock in the beginning was calculated at 10% less than cost.
   (*ii*) A plant was installed by firm's own worker. He was paid Rs. 500, which was included in wages.
   (*iii*) Purchases include the purchase of the plant for Rs. 5,000.
   You are required to calculate the claim for the loss of Stock.

(b) (*i*) **(Inventory valuation).** What are principal methods of ascertaining the cost of inventory as suggested in Accounting Standard 2 (Revised)?

(*ii*) **(Basic concepts).** What services can a Chartered Accountant provide to the Society (Give names only)?   **(7 + 8 = 15 Marks)**

Solution:

(a) COMPUTATION OF CLAIM FOR LOSS OF STOCK

	Rs.
Stock on the date of fire, *i.e.*, 31.12.2001 (Refer *WN*)	30,500
Less: Salvaged Stock	3,000
Loss of Stock	27,500

Amount of Claim after application of average clause

$$\frac{\text{Insured value}}{\text{Total cost of stock on the date of fire}} \times \text{Loss of stock}$$

$$\frac{\text{Rs.}25,000}{\text{Rs.}30,500} \times \text{Rs. }27,500 = \text{Rs. }22,541.$$

Working Note:

Memorandum Trading Account can be prepared for ascertaining stock on 31.12.2001.

MEMORANDUM TRADING ACCOUNT
for period from 1.10.2001 to 31.12.2001

Particulars		Rs.	Particulars	Rs.
To Opening Stock			By Sales	1,40,000
(Rs. 29,700 × 100/90)		33,000	By Closing Stock	
To Purchases	75,000		(balancing figure)	30,500
Less: Cost of Plant	5,000	70,000		
To Wages	33,000			
Less: Wages paid for Plant	500	32,500		
To Gross Profit		35,000		
(33¹/₃% on Cost or 25% on Sales)				
		1,70,500		1,70,500

(b)(i) **Valuation of Inventory as per AS 2 (Revised):** The specific identification method, first-in-first-out (FIFO) and the weighted average cost formula are the principal methods of ascertaining the cost of inventory as suggested in Accounting Standard 2 (Revised).

The cost of inventories of items that are not ordinarily interchangeable and goods or services produced and segregated for specific projects should be assigned by specific identification of their individual costs under the specific identification method. The cost of inventories other than those covered under specific identification method should be assigned by using the *FIFO* or weighted average cost formula. The formula used should reflect the fairest possible approximation to the cost incurred in bringing the items of inventory to their present location and condition. Techniques for the measurement of the cost inventories, such as the standard cost method or the retail method, may be used for convenience if the results approximate the actual cost. The revised standard also dispenses with the direct costing method and permits only the absorption costing method for arriving at the cost of finished goods.

(ii) **Services of a Chartered Accountant:** A Chartered Accountant with his education, training, analytical mind and experience is best qualified to provide multiple need-based services to the ever-growing society.

For services rendered by the accountants please refer to "Accountant's Services" on page 1.10 of the book.

Q. 3. (a) **(Bank Reconciliation Statement).** Prepare a Bank Reconciliation Statement from the following particulars on 31st March, 2002:

		Rs.
(i)	Debit Balance as per bank column of the Cash-book.	3,72,000
(ii)	Cheque issued to creditors, but not yet presented to the bank for payment	72,000
(iii)	Dividend received by the bank, but not entered in the Cash-book.	5,000
(iv)	Interest allowed by the Bank	1,250
(v)	Cheques deposited into bank for collection, but not collected by bank upto this data.	15,400
(vi)	Bank charges	200
(vii)	A cheque deposited into bank was dishonoured but no intimation received.	320
(viii)	Bank paid House tax on our behalf, but no information received from bank in this connection	350

(b) **(Bill of Exchange).** For the mutual accommodation of 'X' and 'Y' on 1st April, 2001, 'X' drew a four months' bill on 'Y' for Rs. 4,000. 'Y' returned the bill after acceptance on the same date. 'X' discounts the bill from his bankers @ 6% per annum and remits 50% of the proceed to 'Y'. On due date 'X' is unable to send the amounts due and therefore 'Y' draws a bill for Rs. 7,000, which is duly accepted by 'X'. 'Y' discounts the bill for Rs. 6,600 and sends Rs. 1,300 to 'X'. Before the bill is due for payment 'X' becomes insolvent. Later 25 paisa in a rupee received from his estate.
Record Journal Entries in the book of 'X'.

(c) **(Average Due Date):** 'A' lent Rs. 25,000 to 'B' on 1st January, 2000. The amount is repayable in 5 half-yearly instalments commencing from 1st January, 2001. Calculate the Average due date and interest @ 10% per annum. **(6 + 6 + 3 = 15 Marks)**

Solution:

(a)

BANK RECONCILIATION STATEMENT

as on 31st March, 2002

Particulars	Rs. (+)	Rs. (−)
Debit balance as per Cash book	3,72,000	
Add: Cheque issued but not yet presented to book for payment	72,000	
Dividend received by bank not entered in Cash book	5,000	
Interest allowed by bank	1,250	
Less: Cheques deposited into bank but not yet collected		15,400
Bank charges		200
A cheque deposited into bank was dishonoured		320
House tax paid by bank		350
	4,50,250	16,270
Credit balance as per Pass Book	4,33,980	

(b)

Books of X

JOURNAL ENTRIES

Date 2001	Particulars		Dr. Rs.	Cr. Rs.
April 1	Bills Receivable Account	Dr.	4,000	
	To Y			4,000
	(Being acceptance received from Y for mutual accommodations)			
	Bank Account	Dr.	3,920	
	Discount Account	Dr.	80	
	To Bills Receivable Account			4,000
	(Being discounted for Rs. 3,920)			

Contd...

	Y	Dr.	2,000	
	To Cash Account			1,960
	To Discount Account			40
	(Being half of proceeds remitted to Y)			
Aug. 4	Y	Dr.	7,000	
	To Bills Payable Account			7,000
	(Being acceptance given to Y, being unable to remit the due amount)			
	Bank Account	Dr.	1,300	
	Discount Account	Dr.	200	
	To Y			1,500
	(Being received from Y and discount amount credited to him)			
	Bills Payable Account	Dr.	7,000	
	To Y			7,000
	(Being acceptance to Y dishonoured because of insolvency)			
	Y	Dr.	3,500	
	To Bank Account			875
	To Deficiency Account			2,625
	(Being amount paid @ 25 paisa in a rupee and balance credited to deficiency account as Y being unable to pay)			

(c) **Computation of sum of period from the date of each transaction:**

1st payment is made after 12 months from the date of loan.
2nd payment is made after 18 months from the date of loan.
3rd payment is made after 24 months from the date of loan.
4th payment is made after 30 months from the date of loan.
5th payment is made after 36 months from the date of loan.
$$\overline{120}$$

$$\text{Average due date} = \text{Date of loan} + \frac{\text{Sum of months from 1st January, 2000 to the date of each instalment}}{\text{Number of instalments}}$$

$$= \text{1st January, 2000} + \frac{120 \text{ months}}{5}$$
$$= \text{1st January, 2000} + 24 \text{ months}$$
$$= \text{1st January, 2002}$$

$$\text{Interest} = \text{Rs. } 25,000 \times \frac{10}{100} \times 2$$
$$= \text{Rs. } 5,000$$

Q. 4. (Partnership). A and B are partners in a firm, sharing profits and Losses in the ratio 3 : 2. The Balance Sheet of A and B on 1.1.2000 was as follow :

Liabilities	Amount Rs.	Assets		Amount Rs.
Sundry Creditors	12,900	Building		26,000
Bill Payable	4,100	Furniture		5,800
Bank Overdraft	9,000	Stock-in-Trade		21,400
Capital Account :		Debtors	35,000	
A 44,000		Less: Provision	200	34,800
B 36,000	80,000	Investment		2,500
		Cash		15,500
	1,06,000			1,06,000

'C' was admitted to the firm on the above date on the following terms:

(i) He is admitted for 1/6th share in future profits and to introduce a Capital of Rs. 25,000.

(*ii*) The new profit sharing ratio of *A*, *B* and *C* will be 3 : 2 : 1 respectively.

(*iii*) '*C*' is unable to bring in cash for his share of goodwill, partners therefore, decide to raise goodwill account in the books of the firm. They further decide to calculate goodwill on the basis of '*C*' share in the profits and the capital contribution made by him to the firm.

(*iv*) Furniture is to be written down by Rs. 870 and stock to be depreciated by 5%. A provision is required for debtors @ 5% for Bad Debts. A provision would also be made for outstanding wages for Rs, 1,560. The value of Buildings having appreciated be brought upto Rs. 29,200. The value Investment is increased by Rs. 450.

(*v*) It is found that the creditors included a sum of Rs, 1,400, which is not be paid off.

Prepare the following:
(*i*) Revaluation Account.
(*ii*) Partners' Capital Accounts.
(*iii*) Balance Sheet of New Partnership firm after admission of '*C*'.   **(15 Marks)**

Solution:

(*i*)

Dr.		REVALUATION ACCOUNT		Cr.
Particulars	Rs.	Particulars		Rs.
To Furniture	870	By Building		3,200
To Stock	1,070	By Sundry Creditors		1,400
To Provision of Doubtful		By Investment		450
Debts (Rs. 1,750 – Rs. 200)	1,550			
To Outstanding Wages	1,560			
	5,050			5,050

PARTNERS' CAPITAL ACCOUNTS

Particulars	A Rs.	B Rs.	C Rs.	Particulars	A Rs.	B Rs.	C Rs.
To Balance c/d	71,000	54,000	25,000	By Balance b/d	44,000	36,000	—
				By Cash A/c	—	—	25,000
				By Goodwill A/c			
				(See Working Note)	27,000	18,000	—
	71,000	54,000	25,000		71,000	54,000	25,000

BALANCE SHEET OF NEW PARTNERS FIRM (AFTER ADMISSION OF *C*)
as on 1.12.2000

Liabilities		Rs.	Assets		Rs.
Sundry Creditors			Goodwill		45,000
(12,900 – 1,400)		11,500	Building (26,000 + 3,200)		29,200
Bills Payable		4,100	Furniture (5,800 – 870)		4,930
Bank Overdraft		9,000	Stock-in-Trade (21,400 – 1,070)		20,330
Outstanding Wages		1,560	Debtors	35,000	
Capital Accounts :			*Less*: Provisions for Bad Debts	1,750	33,250
A	71000		Investment (2,500 + 450)		2,950
B	54,000		Cash (15,500 + 25,000)		40,500
C	25,000	1,50,000			
		1,76,160			1,76,160

Working Note:

Computation of goodwill

C's contribution of Rs. 25,000 consists only 1/6th of capital.

Hence, total capital of firm should be Rs. 25,000 × 6 = Rs. 1,50,000.

However, the combined capital of *A*, *B* and *C* amounts Rs. 44,000 + 36,000 + 25,000 = Rs. 1,05,000

Thus, hidden goodwill is Rs. 45,000 (*i.e.*, Rs. 1,50,000 – Rs. 1,05,000).

Q. 5. (Basic Concepts). State with reasons whether the following Statements are True or False:

    (*i*) In Consignment Account, ownership of the goods remains with the consignor.

    (*ii*) A crossed cheque is always payable across the bank counter.

    (*iii*) Legal fees paid to acquire a building is a capital expenditure.

    (*iv*) Debit balance of profit and loss account is a real asset.

    (*v*) Depreciation is a cash expenditure like other normal expenses.

    (*vi*) Transactions and events are guided by generally accepted accounting principles subject to laws of land.

    (*vii*) In Self-balancing system, whenever a balance is transferred from an account in one ledger to that in another, only one entry is recorded through the respective ledger.

    (*viii*) The objective of taking a Joint Life Policy by the partnership firm is secure the lives of the existing partners of the firm.

    (*ix*) Under the 'Liquidity Approach' assets which are most liquid are presented at the bottom of the Balance Sheet.

    (*x*) The Sales-book is kept to record both cash and credit sales. **(10 × 2 = 20 Marks)**

Solution:

    (*i*) **True:** The ownership of goods remains with the consignor. The consignee does not become owner even though the goods are in his possession since he has been given their possession only for a special purpose.

    (*ii*) **False:** Only a bearer cheque is payable across bank counter.

    (*iii*) **True:** Legal fees paid to acquire a building is capital expenditure. It should be taken as part of the cost of building.

    (*iv*) **False:** Debit balance of Profit and Loss Account is a fictitious asset.

    (*v*) **False:** Depreciation is not a cash expenditure like other normal expenses (for example, wages, rent etc.) It therefore does not result in any cash outflow.

    (*vi*) **True:** Transactions and events are guided by generally accepted principles subject to laws of land. For example, the Companies Act has prescribed the format of financial statements of companies. All the transactions with suppliers and customers are governed by the Contract Act, the Sale of Goods Act and the Negotiable Instruments Act, etc.

    (*vii*) **False:** Whenever a balance is transferred from one account in one ledger to that in another, the entry is recorded through the journal. Moreover an additional entry is made in the control accounts for recording the corresponding effect.

    (*viii*) **False:** The objective of taking a joint life policy is to minimise the financial hardships in the event of payment of a large sum to the legal representatives of a deceased partner or to the retiring partner.

    (*ix*) **False:** In case 'liquidity approach', assets which are most liquid are presented first while under 'permanent approach' they are presented at the bottom of the balance sheet.

    (*x*) **False:** The Sales Book is a register specially kept to record credit sales of goods. Cash sales are recorded in the cash book and not in the sales book.

Q. 6. Briefly explain the difference between any **three** of the following:

    (*a*) Receipt and Payment and Income and Expenditure Account.

4.124

    (*b*) Cash Discount and Trade Discount.
    (*c*) Self-balancing and Sectional Balancing system.
    (*d*) Joint-venture and Partnership.   **(5 × 3 = 15 Marks)**

Solution:

(*a*) **Receipt and Payment and Income and Expenditure Account :** For answer, please refer to page 1.354 of the book.

(*b*) **Cash Discount and Trade Discount:** For answer, please refer to page 1.74 of the book.

(*c*) **Self-balancing and Sectional Balancing System:** For answer, please refer to page 1.332 of the book.

(*d*) **Joint venture and Partnership:** For answer, please refer to page 2.32 of the book.

ICAI PROFESSIONAL EDUCATION EXAMINATION I
MAY 2003
Paper 1: Fundamentals of Accounting

Answer ALL Questions

Q. 1. (Non-profit Organisation). The Receipts and Payments account of Trustwell Club prepared on 31st March, 2003 is as follows:

RECEIPTS AND PAYMENTS ACCOUNT

Receipts		Amount Rs.	Payments	Amount Rs.
To Balance b/d		450	By Expenses (including Payment for Sports material Rs. 2,700)	6,300
To Annual Income from Subscription	Rs. 4,590		By Loss on Sale of Furniture (cost price Rs. 450)	180
Add: Outstanding of last year received this year	180		By Balance c/d	90,450
	4,770			
Less: Prepaid of last year	90	4,680		
To Other Fees		1,800		
To Donation for Building		90,000		
		96,930		96,930

Additional Information:

Trustwell club and balances as 1.4.2002:

Furniture Rs. 1,800; Investment at 5% Rs. 27,000;

Sports Material Rs. 6,660;

Balance as on 31.3.2003: Subscription Receivable Rs. 270;

Subscription received in advance Rs. 90;

Stock of sports material Rs. 1,800.

Do you agree with above Receipts and Payment account ? If not, prepare correct Receipts and Payments Account and income and Expenditure Account for the year ended on 31st March, 2003 and Balance Sheet on that date. **(20 Marks)**

Solution:

Trustwell Club
CORRECTED RECEIPTS AND PAYMENTS ACCOUNT
for the year ended 31st March, 2003

Receipts		Amounts Rs.	Payments	Amount Rs.
To Balance b/d		450	By Expenses (Rs. 6,300 – Rs. 2,700)	3,600
To Subscription Annual Income	Rs. 4,590		By Sports Material	2,700
Less: Receivable as on 31.3.2003	270		By Balance c/d (Cash in Hand and at Bank)	90,720
Add: Advance Received for the year 2003-2004	90			
Add: Receivable as on 31.3.2002	180			
Less: Advance received as on 31.3.2002	90	4,500		

Contd...

4.126

	Amount Rs.		Amount Rs.
To Other Fees	1,800		
To Donation for Building	90,000		
To Sale of Furniture	270		
	97,020		97,020

Trustwell Club
INCOME AND EXPENDITURE ACCOUNT
for the year ended 31st March, 2003

Expenditure		Amount Rs.	Income	Amount Rs.
To Sundry Expenses		3,600	By Subscriptions	4,590
To Sports Material			By Other Fees	1,800
Balance as on 1.4.2002	6.660		By Interest on Investment	1,350
Add: Purchases	2,700		(5% on Rs, 27,000)	
Less: Balance as on			By Excess of Expenditure over	
31.3.2003	1,800	7,560	Income	3,600
To Loss on Sale of				
Furniture		180		
		11,340		11,340

Trustwell Club
BALANCE SHEET
as on 31st March, 2003

Liabilities		Amount Rs.	Assets		Amount Rs.
Capital Fund	36,000		Furniture	1,800	
Less: Excess of Expenditure			*Less*: Sold	450	1,350
over Income	3,600	32,400	5% Investment		27,000
Building Fund		90,000	Interest Accrued on Investment		1,350
Subscription Received in Advance		90	Sports Material		1,800
			Subscription Receivable		270
			Cash in Hand and at Bank		90,720
		1,22,490			1,22,490

Working Note:

Trustwell Club
BALANCE SHEET
as on 1st April, 2002

Liabilities	Amount Rs.	Assets	Amount Rs.
Subscription received in advance	90	Furniture	1,800
Capital Fund	36,000	Investment	27,000
(Balancing Figure)		Sports Material	6,660
		Subscription Receivable	180
		Cash in Hand and at Bank	450
	36,090		36,090

Q. 2. (*a*) **(Consignments Accounts).** '*X*' of Delhi purchased 10,000 pieces of Sarees @ Rs. 100 per Saree. Out of these Sarees, 6,000 were sent on consignment to '*Y*' of Agra at a selling price of Rs. 120 per Saree. The Consignor paid Rs. 3,000 for packing and freight.

'*Y*' sold 5,000 Sarees at Rs. 125 per Saree and incurred Rs. 1,000 for selling expenses and remitted Rs. 5,00,000 to Delhi on account. They are entitled to a commission of 5% on total sales plus a further 20% commission on any surplus price realised over Rs. 120 per Saree.

3,000 Sarees were sold in Delhi at Rs. 110 per Saree. Owing to fall in market price, the value of stock of Sarees in hand is to be reduced by 10%.

Prepare the consignment Account in the books of 'X' and their account in the books of the agent 'Y' of Agra.

(b) **(Accounting Principles):** What are the Fundamental Assumptions as stated in Accounting Standard – 1 (AS-1), on 'Disclosure of Accounting Policies'.

(12 + 3 = 15 Marks)

Solution:

(a)

Books of X

Dr.   CONSIGNMENT ACCOUNT   Cr.

Particulars		Amount Rs.	Particulars	Amount Rs.
To Goods sent on Consignment A/c			By Y Sales	
(6,000 × Rs 120)		7,20,000	(5,000 × Rs. 125)	6,25,000
To Bank A/c (Expenses)		3,000	By Goods sent on Consignment	
To Y – Selling Expenses	1,000		A/c (Loading)	
Commission (WN 1)	36,250	37,250	(6,000 × Rs. 20)	1,20,000
To Stock Reserve (WN 3)		18,000	By Stock on Consignment	
To Net Profit		75,200	(WN 2)	1,08,450
		8,53,450		8,53,450

Books of 'Y' of Agra
X's ACCOUNT

Particulars	Rs.	Particulars	Rs.
To Bank A/c (Expenses)	1,000	By Bank A/c (Sales)	6,25,000
To Commission	36,250		
To Bank A/c (Remittance)	5,00,000		
To Balanced c/d	87,750		
	6,25,000		6,25,000

Working Notes:

Rs.

1. Commission Payable
   5% on Rs. 6,25,000   31,250
   20% on Rs. (6,25,000 – 6,00,000 = 25,000)   5,000
        36,250

2. Valuation of Closing Stock on Consignment
   1,000 Sarees × Rs. 120   1,20,000
   Add: Proportionate Expenses Rs. $3,000 \times \dfrac{1,000}{6,000} =$ 500
        1,20,500
   Less: 10%   12,050
   Value of Closing Stock   1,08,450

3. Loading of Closing (Stock Reserve)
   1,000 Sarees × Rs 20   20,000
   Less: 10%   2,000
        18,000

(b) **Fundamental Accounting Assumptions:** Fundamental accounting assumptions underlie the preparation and presentation of financial statements. They are usually not specifically stated because their acceptance and use are assumed. Disclosure is necessary if they are not followed. The Institute of Chartered Accountants of India issued Accounting Standard (AS-1). 'Disclosure of Accounting Policies' according to which the following have been generally accepted as fundamental accounting assumptions:

(*i*) *Going Concern :* The enterprise is normally viewed as a going concern, *i.e.*, as continuing operations for the foreseeable future. It is assumed that the enterprise has neither the intention nor the necessity of liquidation or of curtailing materially the scale of the operations.

(*ii*) *Consistency :* It is assumed that accounting policies are consistent from one period to another.

(*iii*) *Accrual :* Revenues and costs are accured, *i.e.*, recognised as they are earned of incurred (and not as money is received or paid) and recorded in the financial statements of the periods to which they relate.

Q. 3. (*a*) **(Goods on Sale or Return).** '*X*' supplied goods on sale or return basis to customers, the particulars of which are as under:

Date of Despatch	Party's Name	Amount	Remarks
10.12.2002	ABC & Co.	10,000	No information till 31.12.2002
12.12.2002	DEF & Co.	15,000	Returned on 16.12.2002
15.12.2002	GHI & Co.	12,000	Goods worth Rs, 2,000 Returned on 20.12.2002
20.12.2002	DEF & Co	16,000	Goods Retained on 24.12.2002
25.12.2002	ABC & Co.	11,000	Good Retained on 28.12.2002
30.12.2002	GHI & Co.	13,000	No information till 31.12.2002

Goods are to be returned within 15 days from the date of despatch, failing which it will be treated as Sales. The books of '*X*' are closed on the 31st December, 2002.

Prepare the following account in the book of '*X*'.

(*i*) Goods on Sales or Return, Sold and Returned Day Books.

(*ii*) Goods on Sales or Return Total Account.

(*b*) **(Valuation of Inventory).** A trader prepared his accounts on 31st March, each year. Due to some unavoidable reasons, no stock taking could be possible till 15th April, 2002 on which date the total cost of goods in his godown came to Rs. 50,000. The following facts were established between 31st March and 15th April, 2002.

(*i*) Sales Rs. 41,000 (including cash Sales Rs. 10,000)

(*ii*) Purchases Rs, 5,034 (including cash purchases Rs. 1,990)

(*iii*) Sales Return Rs. 1,000.

(*iv*) On 15th March, goods of the sale value of Rs. 10,000 were sent on sale or return basis to a customer, the period of approval being four weeks. He returned 40% of the goods on 10th April, approving the rest; the customer was billed on 16th April.

(*v*) The trader has also received goods costing Rs. 8,000 in March, for sale on consignment basis, 20% of the goods had been sold by 31st March, and another 50% by the 15th April. These sales are not included in above sales.

Goods are sold by the trader at a profit of 20% on sales.

You are required to ascertain the value of Inventory as on 31st March, 2002.

(6 + 9 = 15 Marks)

Solution:

(a) (i)   **Books of 'X'**
GOODS ON SALES OR RETURN BOOK

Date	Party to whom goods were sent	L.F	Amount Rs.
2002			
Dec. 10	M/s ABC & Co.		10,000
Dec. 12	M/s DEF & Co.		15,000
Dec. 15	M/s GHI & Co.		12,000
Dec. 20	M/s DEF & Co.		16,000
Dec. 25	M/s ABC & Co.		11,000
Dec. 30	M/s GHI & Co.		13,000
			77,000

GOODS SOLD AND RETURNED DAY BOOK

Date	Party to whom goods were sent	Sold Rs.	Returned Rs.
Dec. 25	M/s ABC & Co.	10,000	—
Dec. 16	M/s DEF & Co.	—	15,000
Dec. 20	M/s GHI & Co.	10,000	2,000
Dec. 24	M/s DEF & Co.	16,000	—
Dec. 28	M/s ABC & Co.	11,000	—
		47,000	17,000

(ii)   GOODS ON SALES OR RETURN TOTAL ACCOUNT

Date	Particulars	Amount Rs.	Date	Particulars	Amount Rs.
2002			2002		
Dec. 31	To DEF & Co.	15,000	Dec. 31	By Sundries	77,000
	To GHI & Co.	2,000			
	To Sales	47,000			
	To Balanced c/d	13,000			
		77,000			77,000

(b)   STATEMENT OF VALUATION OF STOCK
as on 31st March, 2002

Particulars	Rs.	Rs.
Value of stock on 15th April, 2002		50,000
Add: Cost of sales during the period from 31st March , 2002 to 15th April, 2002		
Sales (Rs. 41,000 – Rs 1,000)	40,000	
Less: Gross Profit (20% of Rs. 40,000)	8,000	32,000
Cost of goods sent on approval basis (80% of Rs. 6,000)		4,800
		86,800
Less: Purchases during the period from 31st March, 2002 to 15th April, 2002	5,034	
Unsold stock out of goods received on consignment basis (30% of Rs. 8,000)	2,400	7,434
		79,366

Q 4. (a) **(Partnership Accounts).** Explain the rule of 'Garner Vs. Murray'.

(b) **(Depreciation Accounting).** Green Channel Co. purchased a second-hand machine on 1st January, 1999 for Rs. 1,60,000. Overhauling and erection charges amounted to Rs. 40,000.

Another machine was purchased for Rs. 80,000 on 1st July, 1999.

On 1st July, 2001, the machine installed on 1st January, 1999 was sold for Rs. 1,00,000. On the same date another machine was purchased for Rs. 30,000 and was installed on 30th September, 2001.

Under the existing practice the company provide depreciation @ 10% p.a. on original cost. However, from the year 2002 it decided to adopt *WDV* method and to charge depreciation @ 15% p.a. This change was to be made with retrospective effect.

Prepare Machinery Account in the book of Green Channel Co. for the year 1999 to 2002.

(12 + 3 = 15 Marks)

Solution:

(a) For answer pleas refer page 3.127 of the book.

(b)

Books of Green Channel Co.

Dr.   MACHINERY ACCOUNT   Cr.

Date	Particulars	Rs.	Date	Particulars	Rs.
1.1.1999	To Bank A/c	1,60,000	31.12.1999	By Depreciation A/c (Rs, 20,000 + Rs. 4,000)	24,000
	To Bank A/c (Erection charges)	40,000	31.12.1999	By Balance c/d (Rs. 1,80,000 + Rs. 76,000)	2,56,000
1.7.1999	To Bank A/c	80,000			
		2,80,000			2,80,000
1.1.2000	To Balance b/d	2,56,000	31.12.2000	By Depreciation A/c (Rs. 20,000 + Rs. 8,000)	28,000
			31.12.2000	By Balance c/d (Rs, 1,60,000 + Rs. 68,000)	2,28,000
		2,56,000			2,56,000
1.1.2001	To Balance b/d	2,28,000	1.7.2001	By Bank A/c	1,00,000
30.9.2001	To Bank A/c	30,000		By Profit and Loss A/c (Loss on Sale – *WN* 1)	50,000
			31.12.2001	By Depreciation A/c (Rs. 10,000 + Rs. 8,000 + Rs. 750)	18,750
				By Balance c/d (Rs. 60,000 + Rs. 29,250)	89,250
		2,58,000			2,58,000
1.1.2002	To Balance b/d	89,250	31.12.2002	By Profit and Loss A/c (*WN* 3)	6,910
				By Depreciation A/c (Rs. 8,019.75 + 4,331.25)	12,351
				By Balance c/d (Rs. 45,445.25 + Rs. 24,543.75)	69,989
		89,250			89,250

Working Notes:

1. Book Value of Machines (as per straight line method)

	Machine I Rs.	Machine II Rs.	Machine III Rs.
Cost	2,00,000	80,000	30,000
Depreciation for 1999	20,000	4,000	
Written down values as on 31.12.1999	1,80,000	76,000	
Depreciation for 2000	20,000	8,000	
Written down values as on 31.12.2000	1,60,000	68,000	
Depreciation for 2001	10,000	8,000	750
Written down values as on 31.12.2001	1,50,000	60,000	29,250
Sale proceeds	1,00,000		
Loss on sale	50,000		

2. Depreciation of Machines (as per written down value method)

	Machine II Rs.	Machine III Rs.
Cost	80,000	30,000
Depreciation		
1999	6,000	
2000	11,100	
2001	9,435	1,125
Total Depreciation for 1999-2001	26,535	1,125

3. Effect of change in depreciation method with retrospective effects for machines *II* and *III* (1999-2001)

	Rs.
Depreciation under written down value method (Rs. 26,535 + Rs. 1,125)	27,660
Depreciation under straight line method (Rs. 20,000 + Rs. 750)	20,750
Deficiency arising from retrospective recomputation of depreciation to be charged to Profit and Loss A/c	6,910

Q. 5. (Basic Concepts). State with reasons with the following Statements are True and False:

(i) Accounting can be viewed as an information systems which has its input processing method and output.

(ii) The value of human resources is generally shown as assets in the Balance Sheet.

(iii) Revenues are matched with expenses in accordance with the matching principle.

(iv) The financial statement must disclose all the relevant and reliable information in accordance with the Full Disclosure Principle.

(v) The debit notes issued are used to prepare Sales Return Book.

(vi) In Account Current, Red Ink Interest is treated as negative interest.

(vii) A Joint Venture is a partnership under the Partnership Act.

(viii) A tallied trial balance means that the books of accounts have been prepared as per accepts accounting principles.

(ix) Equity + $LTL - CL = FA + CA$.

(x) If the balance as per Cash Book and Pass Book are the same, there is no need to prepare Bank Reconciliation Statement. **(10 × 2 = 20 Marks)**

Solution:

(i) **True:** Accounting is the process of identifying measuring and communicating information to permit informed judgement and decisions. It covers the preparation of financial statements and communication of information to the users of accounts.

(*ii*) **False:** The value of human resources cannot be measured in monetary terms. Hence it will not be shown in the balance sheet as per money measurement concept.

(*iii*) **False:** Both accrual and periodicity concepts are accrued revenues are matched with accrued expenses of a definite accounting period.

Alternatively, this statement may be considered true since matching concept requires matching revenues with expenses, in general.

(*iv*) **True:** The financial statement must disclose all the relevant and reliable information in accordance with the Full Disclosure Principle.

(*v*) **False:** The debit notes issued are used to prepare Purchase Return Book.

(*vi*) **True:** In case the due date of a bill falls, after the date of closing the account no interest is allowed for that. However, interest from the date of closing to such due date is written in 'Red Ink' in the appropriate side of Account Current. This Red Ink Interest is treated as negative interest.

(*vii*) **False:** Joint Venture is a very short duration mainly confined to a single deal entered into by two or more persons jointly. A joint venture is not partnership.

(*viii*) **False:** Trial balance only checks the arithmetical accuracy of the books. Errors of principle and errors of commission will not affect the agreement of the trial balance.

(*ix*) **False:** The basic accounting equation is given by
Equity $+ LTL = FA + CA - CL$

(*x*) **False:** A Bank reconciliation statement is prepared to find out the causes of difference in individual items of cash book and pass book even if the balances as per cash book and balance pass book are the same.

Q. 6. Briefly explain any three of the following :
(*a*) Cash and Mercantile system.
(*b*) Realisation and Revaluation Accounts in Partnership.
(*c*) Noting charges.
(*d*) Joint Venture Account.
(*e*) Average clause

(5 × 3 = 15 Marks)

Solution:

(*a*) **Cash and Mercantile System :** For answer, please refer to "Systems of Accounting" on page 1.31 of the book.

(*b*) **Realisation and Revaluation Account in Partnership:** Realisation account is opened in the event of dissolution of a partnership firm for closing the books of the firm. All assets and liabilities except cash and bank balances, partners' capital/current account balance and profit and loss and reserves are closed by transferring them to realisation account. All subsequent transactions are then passed through only realisation account. Revaluation Account is opened in the books of a partnership firm whenever there is a change in the constitution of partnership firm.

Both in case of realisation account and revaluation account, the profit or loss of realisation and revaluation is transferred to the partners' capital accounts in their profit-sharing ratio.

(*c*) **Noting Charges :** For answer, please refer to "Dishonour of a Bill of Exchange" on page 1.108 of the book.

(*d*) **Joint Venture Account :** Joint venture account is a nominal account. It is prepared by the co-venturers engaged in the joint venture. The joint venture account is prepared with the objective of ascertaining the profit of loss made in a joint venture business. The account is debited with the cost of goods purchased and the expenses incurred for carrying out the joint venture. It is credited with the sale proceeds of the goods and the closing stock at the end of the venture. The profit or loss shown by the joint venture is shared by the co-venturers in the agreed ratio.

(*e*) **Average Clause :** For answer, please refer to page 2.91 of the book.

ICAI PROFESSIONAL EDUCATION EXAMINATION I
NOVEMBER 2003
Paper 1: Fundamentals of Accounting

Answers ALL Questions

Q. 1. (Final Accounts). The following is the Trial of Mr. '*A*' as on 31st March, 2003. You are required to prepare the Trading and Profits and Loss Account for the year ended 31st March, 2003 and Balance Sheet as on that date after making the necessary adjustments:

	Rs.	Rs.
Stock 1.4.2002	5,50,000	—
Purchases and Sales	19,25,000	29,35,000
Wages and Salaries	1,25,000	—
Discount	—	2,000
Carriage Inward	40,000	—
Bills Receivable and Bills Payable	2,25,000	1,85,000
Insurance	35,000	—
Debtors and Creditors	15,00,000	9,32,500
Consignor's Balance (1.4.2002)	—	4,00,000
Capital	—	8,95,000
Commission	40,000	—
Cash sent to Consignor	8,00,000	—
Interest	35,000	—
Trade Expenses	34,500	—
Furniture (1.4.2002)	60,000	—
Consignment Sales	—	6,40,000
Cash in hand and at Bank	4,22,500	—
Rent and Taxes	1,27,500	—
Sales of Furniture (31.3.2003)	—	10,000
Charges Paid against Consignment	80,000	—
	59,99,500	59,99,500

Adjustments:

(*i*) Stock on 31st March, 2003 was valued at Rs. 8,00,000 (including stock of stationery Rs. 800).

(*ii*) Bills receivable include a dishonoured bill of Rs. 8,000.

(*iii*) Trade expenses include payment for stationery of Rs. 22,500.

(*iv*) Stock in the beginning stock of stationery Rs. 1,800.

(*v*) Furniture sold was appearing in the Balance Sheet on 31st March, 2002 at Rs. 13,000.

(*vi*) Creditors at the end include creditors for stationary Rs. 3,000 for credit purchases.

(*vii*) Commission receivable on sale of consignment is Rs. 40,000.

(*viii*) Stationary of Rs. 2,000 was consumed by Mr. '*A*'.

(*ix*) Make provisions for bad doubtful debts at 5% on debtors.

(*x*) Depreciate furniture at 10% p.a. **(20 Marks)**

Solution:

Mr. *A*'s TRADING AND PROFIT AND LOSS ACCOUNT
for the year ended 31st March, 2003

Particulars		Amount Rs.	Particulars		Amount Rs.
To Opening Stock	5,50,000		By Sales		29,35,000
Less : Stock of			By Closing Stock	8,00,000	
Stationery	1,800	5,48,200	Less: Stock of		
To Purchases	19,25,000		Stationery	800	7,99,200
Less : Stationery	3,000	19,22,000			
To Wages and Salaries		1.25,000			
To Carriage Inward		40,000			
To Gross Profit c/d		10,99,000			
		37,34,200			37,34,200
To Insurance		35,000	By Gross Profit b/d		10,99,000
To Commission		40,000	By Discount		2,000
To Interest		35,000	By Commission from		
To Rent and Taxes		1,27,500	Consignment Business		40,000
To Trade Expenses	34,500				
Less : Stationary	22,500	12,000			
To Stationary Consumed		24,500			
To Provision for Doubtful Debts		75,400			
To Loss on sale of Furniture		1,700			
To Depreciation on Furniture		6,000			
To Net Profit Transferred to					
Capital Account		7,83,900			
		11,41,000			11,41,000

Mr. *A*'s BALANCE SHEET
as on 31st March, 2003

Liabilities		Amount Rs.	Assets		Amount Rs.
Capital	8,95,000		Furniture	60,000	
Add : Net Profit of			Less: Furniture sold (WDV)	11,700	
Current Year	7,83,900			48,300	
	16,78,900		Less: Depreciation	6,000	42,300
Less : Drawings	2,000	16,76,900	Debtors	15,00,000	
Consignor's Balance		1,20,000	Add: Bill Receivable		
Creditors for Goods		9,29,500	Dishonoured	8,000	
Creditors for Stationery		3,000	Less: Provision for Bad		
Bills Payable		1,85,000	& Doubtful Debts	75,400	14,32,600
			Bill Receivable	2,25,000	
			Less: Receivable Dishonoured	8,000	2,17,000
			Closing Stock		7,99,200
			Stock Stationery		800
			Cash in Hand and at Bank		4,22,500
		29,14,400			29,14,400

Working Notes: (*i*)   CONSIGNOR'S ACCOUNT

Particulars	Rs.	Particulars	Rs.
To Cash	8,00,000	By Balance b/d	4,00,000
To Charges	80,000	By Consignment Sales	6,40,000
To Commission	40,000		
To Balance c/d	1,20,000		
	10,40,000		10,40,000

(*ii*) **Furniture:** Loss on sale of furniture:

Cost 31.3.2002	Rs.	13,000	
Depreciation 10%	Rs.	1,300	
		11,700	WDV (A)
Sold 31.3.2003	Rs.	10,000	(B)
Loss on sale of furniture	Rs.	1,700	(A) – (B)

(*iii*)

STATIONERY ACCOUNT

Particulars	Rs.	Particulars	Rs.
To Balance b/d	1,8000	By Drawing	2,000
To Cash (Purchases)	22,500	By Profit and Loss A/c	
To Creditors A/c (Purchases)	3,000	(balancing figure for	
		stationery consumed)	24,500
		By Balance c/d	800
	27,300		27,300

Q. 2. (*a*) **(Insurance Claim).** On account of a fire on 15 June, 2002 in the business house of a company, the working remained disturbed upto 15 Dec., 2002 as a result of which, it was not possible to affect any sales. The company had taken out an insurance policy with an average clause against consequential losses for Rs. 1,40,000 and a period of 7 months has been agreed upon as indemnity period. An increase of 25% was marked in the current year's sales as compared to last year. The company incurred an additional expenditure of Rs. 12,000 to make sales possible and made a saving of Rs. 2,000 in the insured standing charges.

Ascertain the claim under the consequential loss policy keeping the following additional information in view:

	Rs.
Actual Sales form 15 June, 2002 to 15 Dec., 2002	70,000
Sales form 15 June, 2001 to 15 Dec., 2001	2,40,000
Net Profit for last financial year	80,000
Insured Standing Charges for the last financial year	70,000
Total Standing Charges for the last financial year	1,20,000
Turnover for the last financial year	6,00,000
Turnover for one year : 16 June 2001 to 15 June, 2002	5,60,000

(*b*) **(Bank Reconciliation Statement).** On 31st March, 2003 the Pass-book of a trader showed a Credit Balance on Rs. 1,565, but the passbook balance was different for the following reasons from the Cash Book Balance:

(*i*) Cheques issued to 'X' for Rs. 600 and to 'Y' Rs. 384 were not yet presented for payment.

(*ii*) Bank charged Rs. 35 for Bank charges and 'Z' directly deposited Rs. 816 into the Bank account, which were not entered in the Cash Book.

(*iii*) Two cheques one from 'A' for Rs. 515 and another from 'B' for Rs. 1,250 were collected in the first week of April, 2003 although they were banked on 25.03.2003.

(*iv*) Interest allowed by Bank Rs. 45.

Prepare Bank Reconciliation Statements as on 31st March, 2003.

(9 + 6 = 15 Marks)

Solution:

(a) (1) Computation of Short Sales:

	Rs.
Sales for the period 15.6.2001 to 15.12.2001	2,40,000
Add : 25% increase in sales	60,000
Estimated Sales in current period	3,00,000
Less: Actual sales from 15.6.2002 to 15.12.2002	70,000
Short Sales	2,30,000

(2) Computation of Gross Profit Ratio:

$$\text{Gross Profit} = \frac{\text{Net Profit} + \text{Insured Standing Charges}}{\text{Turnover}} \times 100$$

$$= \frac{\text{Rs. } 80,000 + \text{Rs. } 70,000}{\text{Rs. } 6,00,000} \times 100 = \frac{\text{Rs. } 1,50,000}{\text{Rs. } 6,00,000} \times 100 = 25\%$$

(3) Calculation of Loss of Profit:

Rs. 2,30,000 × 25% = Rs. 57,500

(4) Calculation of Claim for increased cost of working:

Least of the following :

(*i*) Actual expenses = Rs. 12,000

(*ii*) $\text{Expenditure} \times \dfrac{\text{Net Profit} + \text{Insured Standing Charges}}{\text{Net Profit} + \text{Total Standing Charges}}$

$$= \text{Rs. } 12,000 \times \frac{\text{Rs. } 80,000 + \text{Rs. } 70,000}{\text{Rs. } 80,000 + \text{Rs. } 1,20,000} = \text{Rs. } 9,000$$

(*iii*) Gross profit on sales generated due to additional expenses

= Rs. 70,000 × 25%

= Rs. 17,500

Rs. 9,000 being the least, shall be the increased cost of working.

(5) Computation of Total Loss of Profit:

	Rs.
Loss of Profit	57,500
Add: Increased cost of working	9,000
	66,500
Less: Saving in standing charges	2,000
	64,500

(6) Computation of Insurable amount:

Adjusted sales × G.P. Ratio

	Rs.
Turnover from 16.06.2001 to 15.06.2002	5,60,000
Add: 25% increase	1,40,000
Adjusted Sales	7,00,000

Insurance amount = Rs. 7,00,000 × 25% = Rs. 1,75,000

(7) Computation claim for consequential loss profit application of average clause:

$$\text{Total Claim} = \frac{\text{Insured Amount}}{\text{Insurable Amount}} \times \text{Total Loss of Profit}$$

$$\text{Total Claim} = \frac{\text{Rs. } 1,40,000}{\text{Rs. } 1,75,000} \times 64,500 = \text{Rs. } 51,600$$

(b)   **BANK RECONCILIATION STATEMENT**

as on 31st March, 2003

Particulars		Rs.	Rs. (+)	Rs. (−)
Credit Balance as per Bank Pass Book			1,565	
Add: Cheques deposited into bank but not				
yet collected	A:	515		
	B:	1,250	1,765	
Bank charges debited by bank			35	
Less: Cheques issued but not				
yet presented for payment	X:	600		
	Y:	384		984
Direct deposit of cash in bank by Z.				816
Interest allowed by bank				45
			3,365	1,845
Debit Balance as per Cash Book			1,520	

EITHER

Q. 3. (a) (Rectification of Errors). The Trial Balance of *ABC* Ltd. as on Dec. 31, 2002 did not agree. The difference was put to a Suspense Account. During the next trading period, the following errors were discovered:

    (*i*) The total of the Sales-book of one page Rs. 6,531 was carried forward to the next page as Rs. 6,351.

    (*ii*) Goods returned by a customer for Rs. 1,200 but entered in Purchases Return Book.

    (*iii*) Personal Car Expenses amounting to Rs. 250 were debited to Trade Expenses.

    (*iv*) Sales Return Book was undercast by Rs. 2,750.

    (*v*) Rs. 50 discount allowed by a supplier, was wrongly posted to debit side of Discount Account.

    (*vi*) An item of purchases of Rs. 151 was entered in Purchases Book as Rs. 15 and posted to Supplier's as Rs. 51.

You are required to give journal entries to rectify the errors through Profit and Loss Adjustment Account in a way so as to show the Current year's profit or loss correctly.

OR

Q. 3. (a) (Joint Venture). '*D*' of Delhi and '*B*' of Mumbai entered into Joint Venture to purchase and sell old machines. '*D*' to make the purchases and '*B*' to make the sales. It was decided to share profit and loss in proportion of 2 : 3 respectively. '*B*' remitted Rs. 40,000 to '*D*' towards the Joint Venture. '*D*' purchased old machines worth Rs. 45,000 and paid 2% purchase commission, Rs. 12,000 for its repairs and Rs. 600 for other Sundry expenses. He despatched the machines to Mumbai.

'*B*' took delivery of the machine paying Rs. 2,400 for freight and Rs. 6,000 for octroi. He sold some of machines for Rs. 85,000 and kept the remaining machines for himself at an agreed value of Rs. 7,200. His other expenses were Godown rent Rs. 500 and Advertisement Rs. 1,700. Final settlement was made on Joint Venture.

Prepare Memorandum Joint Venture Account and also Joint Venture with *D*'s Account in the book of '*B*' and Joint Venture with '*B*' Account in the books of '*D*'.

Q. 3. (b) (Self Balancing). From the following, prepare Sales Ledger Adjustment Account in the General Ledger:

4.138

On 1.4.2002 Balance in Sales Ledger (Dr.) Rs. 1,41,880
(Cr.) Rs. 2,240

On 31.3.2003   Rs.
Total Sales   7,68,000
Cash Sales   40,000
Sales Return   10,000
Cash received from customers   6,24,000
Discount allowed   11,200
Cash paid to supplier   4,80,000
Transfer from sales to bought ledger   20,800
Discount received   7,200
B/R received   40,000
Reserve for doubtful debts   9,160
Cash paid to Customer   1,840
Bill received dishonoured   6,000
Sales Ledger Balance (Dr.)   1,83,200
Sales Ledger Balance (Cr.)   13,720

(7 + 8 = 15 Marks)

Solution:
First Alternative

(a)   **Books of ABC Ltd.**
                      JOURNAL ENTRIES

Date 2001	Particulars	Dr. Rs.	Cr. Rs.
(i)	Suspense Account Dr. To Profit and Loss Adjustment Account (Being total of sales book of one page Rs. 6,531 carried forward wrongly as Rs. 6,351 error, now rectified.)	180	180
(ii)	Profit and Loss Adjustment Account Dr. To Customer's Account (Being goods returned by a customer, wrongly entered in Purchase Return Book last, error now rectified.	2,400	2,400
(iii)	Drawings Account Dr. To Profit and Loss Adjustment Account (Being personal car expenses wrongly debited to trade expenses last year, error now rectified.)	250	250
(iv)	Profit and Loss Adjustment Account Dr. To Suspense Account (Being sales return book under case last year, error now rectified.)	2,750	2,750
(v)	Suspense Account Dr. To Profit and Loss Adjustment Account (Being discount received Rs. 50 wrongly debited to discount account, error, now rectified.)	100	100

(vi)	Profit and Loss Adjustment Account Dr.
	   To Supplier's Account
	   To Suspense Account
	 (Being purchases account short debited by Rs. 136 and supplier account short credited by Rs. 100, error now rectified.)
		136	100
			 36

Second Alternative:

(a)

Dr.   MEMORANDUM JOINT VENTURE ACCOUNT   Cr.

Particulars		Rs.	Particulars	Rs.
To Purchases (D)		45,000	By Sales (B)	85,000
To Expenses			By Stock (B)	7,200
D	13,500			
B	5,200	18,700		
To Division of Profit				
D	11,400			
B	17,100	28,500		
		92,200		92,200

Books of 'D'

Dr.   JOINT VENTURE WITH 'B' ACCOUNT   Cr.

Particulars	Rs.	Particulars	Rs.
To Bank A/c (Purchases)	45,000	By Bank A/c	40,000
To Bank A/c (Repairs and Others)	13,500	(Received from B)	
To Profit and Loss A/c		By Bank A/c	29,900
(Share or profit)	11,400	(Final settlement)	
	69,900		69,900

Books of 'B'

Dr.   JOINT VENTURE WITH 'D' ACCOUNT   Cr.

Particulars	Rs.	Particulars	Rs.
To Bank (Remittance)	40,000	By Bank (Sales)	85,000
To Bank Expenses	3,000	By Purchases (Stock)	7,200
To Bank Expenses	2,200		
To Profit and Loss A/c	17,100		
(Share of profit)			
To Bank A/c	29,900		
(Final settlement)			
	92,200		92,200

(b)   **General Ledger**

SALES LEDGER ADJUSTMENT ACCOUNT

Dr.   Cr.

Date	Particulars		Rs.	Date	Particulars		Rs.
01.04.2002	To Balance b/d		1,41,880	01.04.2002	By Balance b/d		2,240
31.03.2003	To General Ledger			31.03.2003	By General Ledger		
	Adjustment				Adjustment A/c		
	A/c in Sales Ledger:				in Sales Ledger:		
	Credit Sales	7,28,000			Cash	6,24,000	
	Cash Paid	1,840			Discount allowed	11,200	
	Bills				Transfers	20,800	
	Receivable				Bills Receivable	40,000	
	Dishonoured	6,000	7,35,840		Sales Return	10,000	7,06,000
	To Balance c/d		13,720		By Balance c/d		1,83,200
			8,91,440				8,91,440

Q. 4. (Partnership Accounts). A, B, C and D were partners sharing profit and losses in the ratio of 3 : 3 : 2 : 2. Following was the Balance Sheet as on 31st March, 2003:

4.140

Liabilities		Amount Rs.	Assets		Amount Rs.
Sundry Creditors		15,500	Sundry Debtors	16,000	
A's Loan		10,000	Less: Provision for		
			Bad debts	500	15,500
Capital Accounts :			Stock-in-Trade		10,000
A	20,000		Cash Bank		2,000
B	15,000	35,000	Furniture and Fixtures		4,000
			Trade Mark		7,000
			Capital Account :		
			C	16,000	
			D	6,000	22,000
		60,500			60,500

On 31st March, 2003, the partnership firm was dissolved and B, was appointed to realise the assets and pay off the liabilities. He was entitled to receive 5% commission on the amount finally paid to other partners as capital. He was to bear the expenses of realisation.

The assets realised were as follows : Sundry Debtors Rs. 11,000; Stock Rs. 8,000; Furniture and Fixture Rs. 1,000; Trade Mark Rs. 4,000; Creditors were paid off in full; in addition a contingent liability of bills receivable discounted, materialised to the extent of Rs. 2,500. Also there was a joint life insurance policy for Rs. 30,000. This was surrendered for Rs. 3,000. Expenses of realisation amounted to Rs. 500. 'C' was insolvent, but Rs. 3,700 were recovered from his estate.

You are required to show the following account in the book of partnership firm :
(i) Realisation Account
(ii) Cash Account
(iii) Partners' Capital Accounts. **(15 Marks)**

Solution:

(i)
REALISATION ACCOUNT
Dr.   as on 31.3.2003   Cr.

Date	Particulars		Rs.	Date	Particulars		Rs.
2003 March 31	To Sundry Assets:			2003 March 31	By Provision for Bad & Doubtful Debts		500
	Furniture & Fixture	4,000			By Sundry Creditors		15,500
	Trade Mark	7,000			By Cash:		
	Debtors	16,000			Furniture & Fixtures	1,000	
	Stock-in-trade	10,000	37,000		Trade Marks	4,000	
	To Cash (Creditors)		15,500		Debtors	11,000	
	To Cash (liability for bills discounted)		2,500		Stock-in-trade	8,000	
					Surrender Value of Joint Life Policy	3,000	27,000
					By Partners' Capital Accounts: (loss on realisation)		
					A	3,600	
					B	3,600	
					C	2,400	
					D	2,400	12,000
			55,000				55,000

(ii)

Dr.				CASH ACCOUNT			Cr.
Date	Particulars	Rs.		Date	Particulars		Rs.
2003				2003			
March 31	To Balance b/d	2,000		March 31	By Realisation A/c		15,500
	To Realisation A/c	27,000			By Realisation A/c		2,500
	To C's Capital A/c	3,700			By A's Loan A/c		10,000
	To D's Capital A/c	8,400			By A's Capital A/c		7,619
					By B's Capital A/c		5,481
		41,100					41,100

(iii)

Dr.						PARTNERS' CAPITAL ACCOUNTS					Cr.
Date	Particulars	A Rs.	B Rs.	C Rs.	D Rs.	Date	Particulars	A Rs.	B Rs.	C Rs.	D Rs.
2003						2003					
March	To Balance b/d	—	—	16,000	6,000	March	By Balance b/d	20,000	15,000	—	—
	To Realisation						By Cash A/c	—	—	3,700	8,400
	A/c (Loss)	3,600	3,600	2,400	2,400		By A's Capital A/c	—	—	8,400	—
	To C's Capital A/c	—	—				By A's Capital A/c	—	—	6,300	—
	(Loss of Capital						By A's Capital A/c	—	381	—	—
	written off)	8,400	6,300				(Commission)				
	To B's Capital A/c	381	—	—	—						
	(Commission)										
	To Cash A/c	7,619	5,481	—	—						
		20,000	15,381	18,400	8,400			20,000	15,381	18,400	8,400

Working Note:

1. There was a debit balance of Rs. 8,400 in D's Capital Account 'D' is a solvent partner, hence he must bring cash for balance capital.

2. 'C' is insolvent therefore he is not able to bring cash. The deficiency in his account is borne by 'A' and 'B' in the ratio of 4 : 3 (capital ratio).
    Deficiency in C's Account = Rs. 16,000 + Rs. 2,400 – Rs. 3,700 = Rs. 14,700

$$\text{Borne by } A = \frac{4}{7} \times \text{Rs. } 14,700 = \text{Rs. } 8,400$$

$$\text{Borne by } B = \frac{3}{7} \times \text{Rs. } 14,700 = \text{Rs. } 6,300$$

3. 'B' is entitled to get 5% commission on the amount finally paid to partner 'A' only. The calculation is as follows : Rs. 20,000 – Rs. 3,600 – Rs. 8,400 = Rs. 8,000 × 5/105 = Rs. 381.

4. Mr. A's Loan is paid off in cash.

Q. 5. (Basic Concepts). Explain whether the following statements are True or False:

(i) Accounting involves communication.

(ii) The economic life of an enterprise is artificially split into periodic intervals in accordance with the going concern assumption.

(iii) If a cheque received is further endorsed, it must be entered on both sides of the Cash Book.

(iv) The return of goods by a customer should be debited to Return Outward Account.

(v) The balance of an account is always known by the side which is shorter.

(vi) Depreciation is a process of allocation of the cost of fixed assets.

(vii) Inventory by-product should be valued at net realisable value where cost of by-product can be separately determined.

(*viii*) The party to whom goods are sent is called 'consignee'.

(*ix*) In the calculation of average due date, only the due date of the first transaction must be taken as the base date.

(*x*) Closing entries are recorded in Journal Proper. **(2 × 10 = 20 Marks)**

Solution:

(*i*) **True:** Accounting is the process of identifying, measuring and **communicating** economic information to permit judgements and decisions by the users of accounts. Accounting thus involves communication.

(*ii*) **False:** The economic life of an enterprise is artificially split into periodic intervals in accordance with the accounting period concept. While the going concern concepts assumes that an enterprise will continue in operation for an indefinite period of time.

(*iii*) **True:** When a cheque received is further endorsed, it must be entered on both sides of the cash book. The cash book is debited when the cheques is received and it is credited when it is endorsed in favour another person.

(*iv*) **False :** The return of goods by a customer is a Sales Return transaction. Hence, it should be debited to Returns Inward or Sales Return Account.

(*v*) **False:** The balance of an account is the difference between the total of debits and total of credits appearing in the account. If the debit side total is higher, it shall be a debit balance and if the credit side total is higher, it shall be a credit balance.

(*vi*) **True:** Depreciation is a measure of the wearing out, consumption or other loss of values of depreciable assets arising from use, effluxion of time or obsolescence. Depreciation is allocated so as to charge a fair proportion of the depreciable amount in each accounting period during the expected useful life of the asset.

(*vii*) **False:** Inventory of by-products, the cost of which cannot be separately determined, should be valued at net realisable value.

(*viii*) **True:** In consignment accounts, the party which sends the goods is called the consignor, while the party to whom goods are sent is called the consignee.

(*ix*) **False:** While calculating the average due date, any transaction date may be taken as the base date.

(*x*) **True:** All the closing entries are recorded in the journal proper.

Q. 6. Briefly explain any **three** of the following :

(*a*) What is the objective of 'Accounting Standards' ? State the advantage of setting Accounting Standards.

(*b*) What is meant by Accounting Policies ? Give four example of Accounting Policies.

(*c*) Receipts and Expenditure Account for Professional Firms.

(*d*) Retirement of bills of exchange.

(*e*) Over-riding Commission. **(5 × 3 = 15 Marks)**

Solution:

(*a*) **Objectives of Accounting Standards :** The Institute of Chartered Accountants of India (ICAI) consisted on 21 April, 1977, the Accounting Standards Board (ASB) for formulating the Accounting Standards to be established by the Council of ICAI. The basic objective of establishing the accounting standards is to harmonize diverse accounting policies and practices in use in India in order to ensure that financial statements are in accordance with the Generally Accepted Accounting Principles (GAAP). While formulating the accounting standards, the ASB gives due consideration to the International Accounting Standards and tries to integrate them to the extent possible. It also takes into account the applicable laws, customs usage and the business environment prevailing in India.

Advantages of Setting Accounting Standards: The following are the advantages of establishing accounting standards :

1. They ensure uniformity, comparability and qualitative improvement in the preparation and presentation of financial statements.
2. They facilitate both inter-firm and intra-firm comparisons.
3. They ensure disclosures as required by Statutes.
4. They make the financial statements globally acceptable, particularly, in view of the globalisation of trade and commerce.

(b) **Accounting Policies :** For answer, please refer to page 1.28 of the book.

(c) **Receipts and Expenditure Account :** For answer, please refer to page 1.388 of the book.

(d) **Retirement of Bills of Exchange :** For answer, please refer to page 1.106 of the book.

(e) **Over-riding Commission :** This commission is allowed in case of Consignment. This commission is allowed by Consignor to Consignee over and above the normal commission in case the sales by the consignee exceed a specified amount. This additional commission is allowed with the following objectives:

(i) To provide additional incentive to the consignee for ensuring that the goods are sold by the consignee at the highest possible price.

(ii) To provide incentive to the consignee for supervising the performance of other agents in particular area or locality.

The over-riding commission is normally calculated on total sales made by the consignee.

ICAI PROFESSIONAL EDUCATION EXAMINATION I
MAY 2004
Paper 1: Fundamentals of Accounting

Answer ALL Questions
Working notes should form part of the answer.

Q. 1. (Final Accounts). Mr. Neel had prepared the following Trial Balance from his Ledger as on 31st March, 2004.

	Dr. (Rs.)	Cr. (Rs.)
Stock as on 1st April, 2003	5,00,000	
Purchases and Returns	31,00,000	45,000
Sales and Return	55,000	41,50,000
Cash in Hand	2,50,000	
Cash at Bank	5,00,000	
Trade's Capital		22,59,200
Rates and Taxes	50,000	
Drawings	45,000	
Salaries	95,000	
Postage and Telegram	1,05,000	
Insurance	90,000	
Salesman Commission	78,000	
Printing and Stationery	95,500	
Advertisement	1,70,000	
Furniture and Fittings	5,50,000	
Motor Car	48,000	
Discounts	50,000	75,000
General Expenses	65,700	
Carriage Inward	10,000	
Carriage Outward	22,000	
Wages	50,000	
Sundry Debtors/Creditors	10,00,000	4,00,000
Total	69,29,200	69,29,200

You are required to prepare Trading and Profit & Loss Account for the year ended on 31st March, 2004 and Balance Sheet as on that date after making the necessary adjustments.

You are provided with the following information:
(i) Closing Stock as on 31st March, 2004 Rs, 1,45,000.
(ii) Neel had withdrawn goods worth Rs. 50,000 during the year.
(iii) Purchases include Purchase of furniture worth Rs. 1,00,000.
(iv) Debtors include Rs. 50,000 bad debts.
(v) Sales include goods worth Rs. 1,50,000 sent out to NN & Co. on approval and remained unsold as on 31st March, 2004. The cost of the goods was Rs. 1,00,000.
(vi) Provision for Bad debts is to be created at 5% of Sundry Debtors.
(vii) Depreciate Furniture and Fittings by 10% and Motor Car by 20%.
(viii) The salesman is entitled to a commission of 10% on total sales. **(20 Marks)**

Solution:

Mr. Neel
TRADING AND PROFIT AND LOSS ACCOUNT
for the year ending 31st March, 2004

Particulars		Amount Rs.	Particulars		Amount Rs.
To Opening Stock		5,00,000	By Sales	41,50,000	
To Purchases	31,00,000		Less: Returns	55,000	
Less: Returns	45,000			40,95,000	
	30,55,000		Less: Goods Sent on		
Less: For Personal			Approval	1,50,000	39,45,000
Use	50,000		By Closing Stock	1,45,000	
	30,05,000		Add: Cost of Goods		
Less: Purchase of			Sent on Approval	1,00,000	2,45,000
Furniture	1,00,000	29,05,000			
To Carriage Inward		10,000			
To Wages		50,000			
To Gross Profit c/d		7,25,000			
		41,90,000			41,90,000
To Rates and Taxes		50,000	By Gross Profit b/d		7,25,000
To Salaries		95,000	By Discounts Received		75,000
To Postage and Telegram		1,05,000	By Net Loss Transferred		5,02,300
To Salesman's			to Balance sheet		
Commission	78,000				
Add: Outstanding	3,16,500	3,94,500			
To Insurance		90,000			
To Advertisement		1,70,000			
To Printing and					
Stationery		95,500			
To Bad Debts		50,000			
To Provision for					
Doubtful Debts		40,000			
(5% of Rs. 8,00,000)					
To Discounts allowed		50,000			
To General Expenses		65,700			
To Carriage Outward		22,000			
To Depreciation:					
Furniture and Fittings	65,000				
Motor Car	9,600	74,600			
		13,02,300			13,02,300

BALANCE SHEET OF Mr. NEEL
as on 31st March, 2004

Liabilities		Amount Rs.	Assets		Amount Rs.
Capital	22,59,200		Furniture & Fittings	5,50,000	
Less: Net Loss	5,02,300		Addition	1,00,000	
	17,56,900			6,50,000	
Less: Drawings			Less: Depreciation	65,000	5,85,000
(45,000 + 50,000)	95,000	16,61,900	Motor Car	48,000	
Sundry Creditors		4,00,000	Less: Depreciation	9,600	38,400
Outstanding Salesman's Commission		3,16,500	Sundry Debtors	10,00,000	
			Less: Sales on Approval	1,50,000	
				8,50,000	

Contd....

		Less: Bad Debts	50,000	
		Provision for		
		Doubtful Debits	40,000	7,60,000
		Cash in Hand		2,50,000
		Cash at Bank		5,00,000
		Closing Stock	1,45,000	
		Add: Cost of Goods		
		Sent on Approval	1,00,000	?,45,000
	23,78,400			23,78,400

Q. 2. (a) (Valuation of Inventory). From the following information ascertain the value of stock as on 31st March, 2004 and also the profit for the year:

	Rs.
Stock as on 1.4.2003	14,250
Purchases	76,250
Manufacturing Expenses	15,000
Selling Expenses	6,050
Administrative Expenses	3,000
Financial Charges	2,150
Sales	1,24,500

At the time of valuing stock as on 31st March, 2003, a sum of Rs. 1,750 was written off on a particular item, which was originally purchased for Rs. 50,000 and was sold during the year at Rs. 4,500. Barring the transaction relating to this item, the gross profit earned during the year was 20 percent on sales.

Q. 2. (b) (Consignment Accounts). Mr. Anand consigned 800 packets of soaps, each packet containing 100 soaps. Cost price of each packet was Rs. 900. Mr. Anand spent Rs. 100 per packet as cartage, freight, insurance and forwarding charges. One packet was lost on the way and Mr. Anand lodged claim with the insurance company and could get Rs. 570 as claim on average basis. Consignee took delivery of the rest of the packets and spent Rs. 39,950 as other non-recurring expenses and Rs. 22,500 as recurring expenses. He sold 740 packets at the rate of Rs. 12 per soap. He was entitled to 2% commission on sales plus 1% del-credere commission.

You are required to prepare Consignment Account. Calculate the cost of stock at the end, Abnormal loss and Profit-Loss on consignment. **(5 + 10 = 15 Marks)**

Solution:

2. (a)(i) STATEMENT OF VALUATION OF STOCK
as on 31st March, 2004

	Rs.	Rs.
Stock as on 31st March, 2003	14,250	
Less: Book value of abnormal stock (Rs. 5,000 – 1,750)	3,250	11,000
Add: Purchases		76,250
Manufacturing Expenses		15,000
		1,02,250
Less: Cost of Sales:		
Sales as per books	1,24,500	
Less: Sale of Abnormal Item	4,500	
	1,20,000	
Less: Gross Profit @ 20%	24,000	96,000
Stock as on 31st March, 2004		6,250

(ii)

STATEMENT SHOWING PROFIT FOR THE YEAR

	Rs.	Rs.
Gross Profit on Normal Sales		24,000
Add: Profit on Abnormal Item:		
Sales Values	4,500	
Less: Book Value on 31st March, 2003	3,250	1,250
		25,250
Less: Overhead Expenses:		
Selling Expenses	6,050	
Administrative Expenses	3,000	
Financial Charges	2,150	11,200
Net Profit		14,050

(b)

Dr.   CONSIGNMENT ACCOUNT   Cr.

Particulars	Amount Rs.	Particulars	Amount Rs.
To Goods Sent on Consignment A/c (800 × Rs. 900)	7,20,000	By Consignee's A/c: Sales (740 × 100 × Rs. 12)	8,88,000
To Cash A/c: Expenses (800 × Rs. 100)	80,000	By Profit & Loss A/c (Abnormal Loss)	430
To Consignee's A/c:		By Cash A/c (Insurance Claim)	570
Recurring Expenses	22,500	By Consignment Stock A/c	61,950
Non-recurring Expenses	39,950		
Ordinary Commission (0.01 × Rs. 8,88,000)	17,760		
Del-credere Commission (0.01 × Rs. 8,88,000)	8,880		
To Profit and Loss A/c (Profit on Consignment)	61,860		
	9,50,950		9,50,950

Working Notes:

1. Computation of Cost of Stock at the end:

	Rs.
59 Packets (WN 2) @ Rs. 900	53,100
Add: Expenses incurred by Mr. Anand (59 × Rs. 100)	5,900
Add: Proportionate (non-recurring) Expenses incurred by the consignee	2,950
$\left(\dfrac{59}{799} \times Rs.\,39,950\right)$	61,950

2. Computation of Stock at end:

Packets consigned	800
Less: Packet lost in transit	1
	799
Less: Packets sold	740
Packets at end	59

3. Loss on account of Abnormal loss:

	Rs.
Cost of packet lost during transit	900
Add: Expenses incurred by Mr. Anand	100
	1,000
Less: Insurance claim received	570
Loss	430

Q. 3. (*a*) **(Bank Reconciliation Statement).** Prepare a Bank Reconciliation Statement as on 30th September, 2003 from the following particulars:

	Rs.
Bank balance as per the Pass-book	10,000
Cheque deposited into the bank, but no entry was passed in the Cash-book	500
Cheque received, but not sent to bank	1,200
Credit side of the bank column cast short	200
Insurance Premium paid directly by the bank under the standing advice	600
Bank charges entered twice in the Cash-book	20
Cheque issued, but not presented to the bank for payment	500
Cheque received entered twice in the Cash-book	1,000
Bills discounted not recorded in the Cash-book	5,000

(*b*) What are the Fundamental Accounting Assumptions? Discuss briefly.   **(9 + 6 = 15 Marks)**

Solution :

(*a*)   BANK RECONCILIATION STATEMENT
                     as on 30th September, 2003

Particulars	Rs. (+)	Rs. (−)
Bank Balance as per Pass Book	10,000	
Add: (*i*) Cheque received but not sent to the bank	1,200	
(*ii*) Credit side of the bank column cast short	200	
(*iii*) Insurance Premium paid directly not recorded in the cash book	600	
(*iv*) Cheque received entered twice in the cash book	1,000	
(*v*) Bills dishonoured not recorded in the cash book	5,000	
Less : (*i*) Cheque deposited into the bank but no entry was passed in the cash book		500
(*ii*) Bank charges recorded twice in the cash book		20
(*iii*) Cheque issued but not presented to the bank		500
	18,000	1,020
Bank Balance as per Cash book	16,980	

(*b*) **Fundamental accounting assumptions:** For answer please refer to page 1.22 of the book and also answer to 2(*b*) of PEE-I May 2003 Examination.

Q. 4. (Partnership Accounts): The Balance Sheet of *X* & *Y*, a partnership firm, as at 31st March, 2004 is as follows:

Liabilities		Amount Rs.	Assets	Amount Rs.
Capital Account:			Goodwill	14,000
X	26,400		Land and Building	14,400
Y	33,600	60,000	Furniture	2,200
General Reserve		6,000	Stock	26,000
Sundry Creditors		9,000	Sundry Debtors	6,400
			Cash at Bank	12,000
		75,000		75,000

X & *Y* share profits and losses as 1 : 2. They agree to admit *Z* (who is also in business of his own) as a third partner from 1.4.2004.

The assets are revalued as under:

Goodwill Rs. 18,000, Land and Building Rs. 30,000, Furniture Rs. 6,000. *Z* brings the following assets into the partnership: Goodwill Rs. 6,000, Furniture Rs. 2,800, Stock Rs. 13,600.

Profit in the new firm are to shared equally by three partners and the Capital Accounts are to be so adjusted as to be equal. For this purpose, additional cash should be brought in by the partner or partners concerned.

Prepare the necessary accounts and the opening Balance Sheet of new firm, showing the amounts of cash, if any, which each partner may have to provide. **(15 Marks)**

Solution:

Dr.   PROFIT AND LOSS ADJUSTMENT ACCOUNT   *Cr.*

Particulars		Rs.	Particulars	Rs.
To Partners' Capital Accounts:			By Goodwill	4,000
(Profit on revaluation)			By Land and Building	15,600
X	7,800		By Furniture	3,800
Y	15,600	23,400		
		23,400		23,400

Dr.   PARTNERS' CAPITAL ACCOUNTS   *Cr.*

Particulars	X Rs.	Y Rs.	Z Rs.	Particulars	X Rs.	Y Rs.	Z Rs.
To Balance c/d	53,200	53,200	53,200	By Balance b/d	26,400	33,600	—
				By General Reserve	2,000	4,000	—
				By Profit & Loss			
				Adjustment A/c	7,800	15,600	—
				By Sundry Assets	—	—	22,400
				By Bank A/c	17,000	—	30,800
	53,200	53,200	53,200		53,200	53,200	53,200

Dr.   BANK ACCOUNT   *Cr.*

Particulars	Rs.	Particulars	Rs.
To Balance b/d	12,000	By Balance c/d	59,800
To X's Capital A/c	17,000		
To Z's Capital A/c	30,800		
	59,800		59,800

BALANCE SHEET OF NEW FIRM
as on 1st April, 2004

Liabilities		Amount Rs.	Assets	Amount Rs.
Capital Accounts:			Goodwill (18,000 + 6,000)	24,000
X	53,200		Land & Building	30,000
Y	53,200		Furniture (6,000 + 2,800)	8,800
Z	53,200	1,59,600	Stock (26,000 + 13,600)	39,600
Sundry Creditors		9,000	Sundry Debtors	6,400
			Cash at Bank	59,800
		1,68,600		1,68,600

Note: Capital accounts of partners are to be so adjusted as to be equal. This requires additional cash to be brought in by the partner or partners concerned. For this purpose, highest capital of the partner is to be taken as the base. In this case Y's capital is the highest, accordingly X is required to bring in Rs. 17,000 (*i.e.*, Rs. 53,200 – 36,200) and Z has to bring in Rs. 30,800 (*i.e.*, 53,200 – 22,400).

Q. 5. (Basic Concepts). State with reasons whether the following statements are True or False:

    (i) Accrual concept implies accounting on cash basis.

    (ii) The Trial Balance does not ensure the arithmetical accuracy of the books.

    (iii) Sale of office furniture should be credited to Sales account.

    (iv) The Sales Day-book is a part of the Ledger.

    (v) A bill given to a creditor is called Bills Receivable.

    (vi) A cancellation entry is required, when a bill is renewed.

    (vii) Goodwill is a fictitious asset.

    (viii) Patent-Right is in the nature of Real Account.

    (ix) Damaged inventory should be valued at cost or market price, whichever is lower.

    (x) Depreciable amount refers to the difference between historical cost and the market values of an asset. **(20 Marks)**

Solution:

    (i) **False:** Accrual concept implies accounting on 'due' or 'accural' basis. Accrual basis of accounting involves recognition of revenues and costs as they accrue irrespective of actual cash receipts or payments.

    (ii) **False:** Trial Balance helps to establish the arithmetical accuracy of ledger balances. However, a tallied trial balance will not reveal errors of principle and compensation errors.

    (iii) **False:** Sale of office furniture should be credited to furniture account since it is a capital receipt.

    (iv) **False:** Sales Day-Book is a book of prime entry. It is therefore a part of the journal.

    (v) **False:** A bill given to a creditor is called bill payable as the debtor commits to pay by giving a bill to creditor.

    (vi) **True:** When a bill is renewed, entries are passed for cancellation of the old bill and for recording of the new bill.

    (vii) **False:** Goodwill is an intangible asset but not fictitious.

    (viii) **True:** Patent-right is an intangible asset. It is therefore a real account.

    (ix) **False:** Damaged inventory should be valued at Net Realisable Value.

    (x) **False:** Depreciable amount refers to historical cost *less* salvage value.

Q. 6. Write short notes on any three of the following:

    (i) Del-credere commission.

    (ii) Red-Ink Interest.

    (iii) Deferred Revenue Expenditure.

    (iv) Self-balancing Ledgers.

    (v) Garner Vs. Murray Rule. **(5 Marks each)**

Solution:

    (i) **Del-credere Commission :** In case of consignment transaction a consignee may agree to meet any loss which the consignor might suffer by reason of bad debts. In other words, the consignee ensures the consignor that there will be no loss on account of credit sales.

    For this service, the consignor is paid an extra commission and this commission is termed as Del-credere Commission.

    (ii) **Red-ink Interest:** For answer, please refer to page 2.55 of the book.

    (iii) **Deferred Revenue Expenditure:** For answer, please refer to page 1.167 of the book.

    (iv) **Self-balancing Ledgers:** For answer, please refer to page 1.332 of the book.

    (v) **Garner Vs. Murray Rule:** For answer, please refer to page 3.129 of the book.

Appendix. l'

Present Value of Re 1

(This table is used for determining the amount which can be deposited to get rupee one at a certain rate of interest after certain period)

Years	5%	6%	8%	10%	12%	14%	15%	16%	18%	20%	22%	24%	25%	28%	30%
1	0.952	0.943	0.926	0.909	0.893	0.877	0.870	0.862	0.847	0.833	0.820	0.806	0.800	0.781	0.769
2	0.907	0.890	0.857	0.826	0.797	0.769	0.756	0.743	0.718	0.694	0.672	0.650	0.640	0.610	0.592
3	0.864	0.840	0.794	0.751	0.712	0.675	0.658	0.641	0.609	0.579	0.551	0.524	0.512	0.477	0.450
4	0.823	0.792	0.735	0.683	0.686	0.592	0.572	0.552	0.516	0.482	0.451	0.423	0.410	0.373	0.350
5	0.784	0.747	0.681	0.621	0.567	0.519	0.497	0.476	0.437	0.402	0.370	0.341	0.328	0.291	0.269
6	0.746	0.705	0.630	0.564	0.507	0.456	0.432	0.410	0.370	0.335	0.303	0.275	0.262	0.227	0.207
7	0.711	0.665	0.583	0.513	0.452	0.400	0.376	0.354	0.314	0.279	0.249	0.222	0.210	0.170	0.159
8	0.677	0.627	0.540	0.467	0.404	0.351	0.307	0.305	0.266	0.233	0.204	0.179	0.118	0.139	0.123
9	0.645	0.592	0.500	0.424	0.361	0.308	0.284	0.263	0.225	0.193	0.167	0.144	0.134	0.108	0.094
10	0.614	0.558	0.463	0.386	0.322	0.270	0.247	0.227	0.191	0.162	0.137	0.116	0.107	0.085	0.073
11	0.385	0.527	0.429	0.350	0.287	0.237	0.215	0.195	0.162	0.135	0.112	0.094	0.087	0.066	0.056
12	0.557	0.497	0.397	0.319	0.257	0.208	0.187	0.168	0.137	0.112	0.092	0.076	0.069	0.032	0.043
13	0.530	0.469	0.368	0.290	0.229	0.182	0.163	0.145	0.116	0.093	0.075	0.061	0.055	0.040	0.033
14	0.505	0.442	0.340	0.263	0.205	0.160	0.141	0.125	0.099	0.078	0.062	0.049	0.044	0.032	0.025
15	0.481	0.417	0.315	0.239	0.183	0.140	0.123	0.108	0.084	0.065	0.051	0.040	0.035	0.025	0.020
16	0.458	0.394	0.292	0.218	0.163	0.123	0.107	0.093	0.071	0.054	0.042	0.032	0.028	0.019	0.015
17	0.436	0.371	0.270	0.198	0.146	0.108	0.093	0.080	0.060	0.045	0.034	0.026	0.023	0.015	0.012
18	0.416	0.350	0.250	0.180	0.130	0.095	0.081	0.069	0.051	0.038	0.028	0.021	0.018	0.012	0.009
19	0.396	0.331	0.232	0.164	0.116	0.083	0.070	0.060	0.043	0.031	0.023	0.017	0.014	0.009	0.007
20	0.377	0.312	0.215	0.149	0.104	0.073	0.061	0.051	0.037	0.026	0.019	0.014	0.012	0.007	0.005

Appendix 2

Present Value of Re 1 Received Annually for N Years

(This table is used for determining the present value of an annuity of rupee one at a certain rate of interest for a certain period)

Years	5%	6%	8%	10%	12%	14%	15%	16%	18%	20%	22%	24%	25%	28%	30%
1	0.952	0.943	0.926	0.909	0.893	0.877	0.870	0.862	0.847	0.833	0.820	0.806	0.800	0.781	0.769
2	1.859	1.833	1.783	1.736	1.690	1.647	1.646	1.605	1.566	1.528	1.492	1.457	1.440	1.392	1.361
3	2.723	2.676	2.577	2.487	2.402	2.322	2.283	2.246	2.174	2.106	2.042	1.981	1.952	1.868	1.816
4	3.546	3.465	3.312	3.170	3.037	2.914	2.855	2.798	2.690	2.589	2.494	2.404	2.362	2.241	2.166
5	4.330	4.212	3.993	3.791	3.605	3.433	3.352	3.274	3.127	2.991	2.864	2.745	2.689	2.532	2.346
6	5.076	4.917	4.623	4.335	4.111	3.889	3.784	3.685	3.498	3.326	3.167	3.020	2.951	2.759	2.643
7	5.786	5.582	5.206	4.868	4.564	4.288	4.160	4.039	3.812	3.605	3.416	3.242	3.161	2.937	2.802
8	6.463	6.210	5.747	5.335	4.968	4.639	4.487	4.344	4.078	3.837	3.619	3.421	3.329	3.076	2.925
9	7.105	6.802	6.247	5.759	5.328	4.946	4.772	4.607	4.303	4.031	3.786	3.566	3.463	3.184	3.019
10	7.722	7.360	6.710	6.145	5.650	5.216	5.019	4.833	4.494	4.192	3.923	3.682	3.571	3.269	3.092
11	8.306	7.887	7.139	6.495	5.937	5.453	5.234	5.029	4.656	4.327	4.035	3.776	3.656	3.335	3.147
12	8.863	8.384	7.536	6.814	6.194	5.660	5.421	5.197	4.793	4.439	4.127	3.851	3.725	3.387	3.190
13	9.394	8.853	7.904	7.103	6.424	5.842	5.583	5.342	4.910	4.533	4.203	3.912	3.780	3.427	3.223
14	9.895	9.295	8.244	7.367	6.628	6.002	5.724	5.468	5.008	4.611	4.265	3.962	3.824	3.459	3.249
15	10.380	9.712	8.559	7.606	6.811	6.142	5.847	5.575	5.092	4.675	4.315	4.001	3.859	3.483	3.268
16	10.838	10.106	8.851	7.824	6.974	6.265	5.954	5.669	5.162	4.730	4.357	4.033	3.887	3.503	3.283
17	11.274	10.477	9.122	8.022	7.120	6.373	6.047	5.749	5.222	4.775	4.391	4.059	3.910	3.518	3.295
18	11.690	10.828	9.372	8.201	7.250	6.457	6.128	5.818	5.273	4.812	4.419	4.080	3.928	3.529	3.304
19	12.085	11.158	9.614	8.365	7.366	6.550	6.198	5.877	5.316	4.844	4.442	4.097	3.942	3.539	3.311
20	12.462	11.470	9.818	8.514	7.469	6.623	6.259	5.929	5.353	4.870	4.460	4.110	3.954	3.546	3.316

Appendix 3

Periodic deposit which will amount to Re 1

This table is also called Sinking Fund Table and is used for determining the amount of deposit which if made annually will produce rupee one at a certain rate of interest after a certain period

riods	2½%	3%	3½%	4%	5%	6%
1	1.00000000	1.00000000	1.00000000	1.00000000	1.00000000	1.00000000
2	.49382716	.49261084	.49140049	.49019608	.48780488	.48543689
3	.32513717	.32353036	.32193418	.32034854	.31720856	.31410981
4	.24081788	.23902705	.23725114	.23549005	.23201183	.22859149
5	.19024686	.18835457	.18648137	.18462711	.18097480	.17739640
6	.15654997	.15459750	.15266821	.15076190	.14701747	.14336263
7	.13249543	.13050635	.12854449	.12660961	.12281982	.11913502
8	.11446735	.11245639	.11047665	.10852783	.10472181	.10103594
9	.10045683	.09843386	.09644601	.09449299	.09069008	.08702224
10	.08925876	.08723051	.08524137	.08329094	.07950458	.07586796
11	.08010596	.07807745	.07609197	.07414904	.07038889	.06679294
12	.07248713	.07046209	.06848395	.06655217	.06282541	.05927703
13	.06604827	.06402954	.06206157	.06014373	.05645577	.05296011
14	.06053652	.05852634	.05657073	.05466897	.05102397	.04758490
15	.05570646	.05376658	.05182507	.04994110	.04634229	.04296276
16	.05159809	.04961085	.04768483	.04582000	.04226991	.03895214
17	.04792777	.04595253	.04404313	.04219852	.03869914	.03544480
18	.04467008	.04270870	.04081684	.03899333	.03554622	.03235654
19	.04171062	.03981388	.03794033	.03613861	.03274501	.02962086
20	.03914713	.03721571	.03536108	.03358175	.03024259	.02718456
21	.03678733	.03487178	.03303659	.03128011	.02799611	.02500455
22	.03464661	.03274739	.03093207	.02919881	.02597051	.02304557
23	.03269638	.03081390	.02901880	.02730906	.02413682	.02127848
24	.03091282	.02904742	.02727283	.02558683	.02247090	.01967901
25	.02927592	.02742787	.02567404	.02401196	.02095246	.01822672
26	.02776875	.02593829	.02420540	.02256738	.01956432	.01690435
27	.02637687	.02456421	.02285241	.02123854	.01829186	.01569717
28	.02508793	.02329323	.02160265	.02001298	.01712253	.01459255
29	.02389127	.02211467	.02044538	.01887993	.01604551	.01357961
30	.02277764	.02101926	.01937133	.01783010	.01505144	.01264891
31	.02173900	.01999893	.01837240	.01685535	.01413212	.01179222
32	.02076831	.01904662	.01744150	.01594859	.01528042	.01100234
33	.01985938	.01815612	.01657242	.01510357	.01249004	.01027294
34	.01900675	.01732196	.01575966	.01431477	.01175545	.00959843
35	.01820558	.01653929	.01499835	.01357732	.01107171	.00897386
36	.01745158	.01580370	.01428416	.01288688	.01043446	.00839483
37	.01674090	.01511162	.01361325	.01223957	.00983979	.00785743
38	.01607012	.01445934	.01298214	.01163192	.00928423	.00735812
39	.01543615	.01384385	.01238775	.01106083	.00876462	.00689377
40	.01483623	.01326238	.01182728	.01052349	.00827816	.00646154
41	.01426786	.01271241	.01129822	.01001738	.00782229	.00605886
42	.01372876	.01219167	.01079828	.00954020	.00739472	.00568342
43	.01311668	.01169811	.01032539	.00908989	.00699333	.00533312
44	.01273037	.01122985	.00987768	.00866454	.00661625	.00500606
45	.01226751	.01078518	.00945343	.00826246	.00626173	.00470050
46	.01182676	.01036254	.00905108	.00788205	.00592820	.00441485
47	.01140669	.00996051	.00866919	.00752189	.00561421	.00414768
48	.01100599	.00957777	.00830646	.00718065	.00531843	.00389765
49	.01062348	.00921314	.00796167	.00685712	.00503965	.00366356
50	.01025806	.00886550	.00763371	.00655020	.00477674	.00344429

Appendix 4

Periodic payment required to amortize Re 1 and interest

This table is used for determining the amount which will write off rupee one together with interest at a certain rate of interest over a certain period

Periods	2½%	3%	3½%	4%	5%	6%
1	1.02500000	1.03000000	1.03500000	1.04000000	1.05000000	1.06000000
2	.51882716	.52261084	.52640049	.53019608	.53780488	.54543689
3	.35013717	.35353036	.35693418	.36034854	.36720856	.37410981
4	.26581788	.26902705	.27225114	.27549005	.28201183	.28859149
5	.21524686	.21835457	.22148137	.22462711	.23097480	.23739640
6	.18154997	.18459750	.18766821	.19076190	.19701747	.20336263
7	.15749541	.16050635	.16354449	.16660963	.17281982	.17913502
8	.13946735	.14245639	.14547665	.14852783	.15472181	.16103594
9	.12545689	.12843386	.13144601	.13449299	.14069008	.14702224
10	.11425876	.11723051	.12024137	.12329094	.12950458	.13586796
11	.10510596	.10807745	.11109197	.11414904	.12038889	.12679294
12	.09748713	.10046209	.10348395	.10655217	.11282541	.11927703
13	.09104827	.09402954	.09706157	.10014373	.10645577	.11296011
14	.08553653	.08852634	.09157073	.09466897	.10102397	.10758491
15	.08076646	.08376653	.08682507	.08994110	.09634229	.10296276
16	.07659899	.07961085	.08268483	.08582000	.09226991	.09895214
17	.07292777	.07595253	.07904313	.08219852	.08869914	.09544480
18	.06967008	.07270870	.07581684	.07899333	.08554612	.09235654
19	.06676062	.06981388	.07294033	.07613862	.08274501	.08962086
20	.06414713	.06721571	.07036108	.07358175	.08024259	.08718456
21	.06179733	.06487178	.06803659	.07128011	.07799611	.08500455
22	.05964661	.06274739	.06593207	.06919881	.07597051	.08304557
23	.05769638	.06081390	.06401880	.06733906	.07413632	.08127848
24	.05591282	.05904742	.06227283	.06558683	.07247000	.07967901
25	.05427592	.05742787	.06067404	.06401196	.07095246	.07822672
26	.05276875	.05593829	.05920540	.06256738	.06956432	.07690435
27	.05137687	.05456421	.05785241	.06123854	.06829186	.07569717
28	.05008793	.05329323	.05660265	.06001298	.06712253	.07459255
29	.04889127	.05211467	.05544538	.05887993	.06604551	.07357961
30	.04777764	.05101926	.05437133	.05783010	.06505144	.07264891
31	.04673900	.04999893	.05337240	.05685535	.06413212	.07179222
32	.04576831	.04904662	.05244150	.05594859	.06328042	.07100234
33	.04485938	.04815612	.05157242	.05510357	.06249004	.07027294
34	.04400675	.04732196	.05075966	.05431477	.06175545	.06959843
35	.04320558	.04653929	.04999835	.05357732	.06107171	.06897386
36	.04245158	.04580379	.04928416	.05208688	.06043446	.06839483
37	.04174090	.04511162	.04861325	.05223957	.05983979	.06785743
38	.04107012	.04445934	.04798214	.05163192	.05928423	.06735812
39	.04043615	.04384385	.04738775	.05106083	.05876462	.06689377
40	.03983623	.04326238	.04682728	.05052349	.05827816	.06646154
41	.03926786	.04271241	.04629822	.05001738	.05782229	.06605886
42	.03872876	.04219167	.04579828	.04954020	.05739471	.06568342
43	.03821688	.04169811	.04532539	.04908989	.05699333	.06533312
44	.03773037	.04122985	.04487768	.04866454	.05661625	.06500606
45	.03726752	.04078518	.04445343	.04826246	.05626173	.06470050
46	.03682676	.04036254	.04405108	.04788205	.05592820	.06441485
47	.03640669	.03996051	.04366919	.04752189	.05561421	.06414768
48	.03600599	.03957777	.04330646	.04718065	.05531843	.06389765
49	.03562348	.03921314	.04296167	.04685712	.05503965	.06366356
50	.03525806	.03886550	.04263371	.04655020	.05477674	.06344429